JEE MAIN & ADVANCED TEST SERIES

40+ Tests

PHYSICS

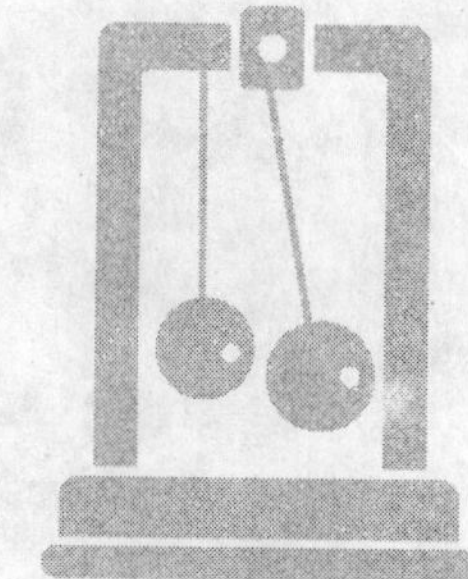

JEE MAIN & ADVANCED TEST SERIES

40+ Tests

PHYSICS

Author
Prateek Arora
B.Tech from IIT, Delhi

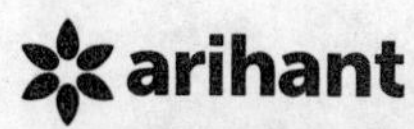

ARIHANT PRAKASHAN (SERIES), MEERUT

ARIHANT PRAKASHAN (SERIES), MEERUT

卐 **ADMINISTRATIVE & PRODUCTION OFFICES**

Regd. Office
'Ramchhaya' 4577/15, Agarwal Road, Darya Ganj, New Delhi -110002
Tele: 011- 47630600, 43518550

Head Office
Kalindi, TP Nagar, Meerut (UP) - 250002, Tel: 0121-7156203, 7156204

卐 **SALES & SUPPORT OFFICES**

Agra, Ahmedabad, Bengaluru, Bareilly, Chennai, Delhi, Guwahati, Hyderabad, Jaipur, Jhansi, Kolkata, Lucknow, Nagpur & Pune.

卐 **ISBN** 978-93-27194-13-5

卐 **PRICE** ₹ 375.00

PO No. : TXT-59-T051818-2-23

Published By Arihant Publications (India) Ltd.

For further information about the books published by Arihant, log on to www.arihantbooks.com or e-mail at info@arihantbooks.com

Follow us on   

Contents

Syllabus

JEE MAIN

SECTION- A

UNIT 1 Physics and Measurement

Physics, technology and society, SI units, Fundamental and derived units. Least count, accuracy and precision of measuring instruments, Errors in measurement, Significant figures. Dimensions of Physical quantities, dimensional analysis and its applications.

UNIT 2 Kinematics

Frame of reference. Motion in a straight line: Position-time graph, speed and velocity. Uniform and non-uniform motion, average speed and instantaneous velocity.

Uniformly accelerated motion, velocity-time, position time graphs, relations for uniformly accelerated motion.

Scalars and Vectors, Vector addition and Subtraction, Zero Vector, Scalar and Vector products, Unit Vector, Resolution of a Vector. Relative Velocity, Motion in a plane, Projectile Motion, Uniform Circular Motion.

UNIT 3 Laws of Motion

Force and Inertia, Newton's First Law of motion; Momentum, Newton's Second Law of motion; Impulse; Newton's Third Law of motion. Law of conservation of linear momentum and its applications, Equilibrium of concurrent forces.

Static and Kinetic friction, laws of friction, rolling friction.

Dynamics of uniform circular motion: Centripetal force and its applications.

UNIT 4 Work, Energy and Power

Work done by a constant force and a variable force; kinetic and potential energies, work-energy theorem, power.

Potential energy of a spring, conservation of mechanical energy, conservative and nonconservative forces; Elastic and inelastic collisions in one and two dimensions.

UNIT 5 Rotational Motion

Centre of mass of a two-particle system, Centre of mass of a rigid body; Basic concepts of rotational motion; moment of a force, torque, angular momentum, conservation of angular momentum and its applications; moment of inertia, radius of gyration. Values of moments of inertia for simple geometrical objects, parallel and perpendicular axes theorems and their applications.

Rigid body rotation, equations of rotational motion.

UNIT 6 Gravitation

The universal law of gravitation.

Acceleration due to gravity and its variation with altitude and depth.

Kepler's laws of planetary motion.

Gravitational potential energy; gravitational potential.

Escape velocity. Orbital velocity of a satellite.

Geo-stationary satellites.

UNIT 7 Properties of Solids & Liquids

Elastic behaviour, Stress-strain relationship, Hooke's. Law, Young's modulus, bulk modulus, modulus of rigidity.

Pressure due to a fluid column; Pascal's law and its applications.

Viscosity, Stokes' law, terminal velocity, streamline and turbulent flow, Reynolds number. Bernoulli's principle and its applications.

Surface energy and surface tension, angle of contact, application of surface tension - drops, bubbles and capillary rise.

Heat, temperature, thermal expansion; specific heat capacity, calorimetry; change of state, latent heat.

Heat transfer-conduction, convection and radiation, Newton's law of cooling.

UNIT 8 Thermodynamics

Thermal equilibrium, zeroth law of thermo-dynamics, concept of temperature. Heat, work and internal energy. First law of thermodynamics.

Second law of thermodynamics: reversible and irreversible processes. Camot engine and its efficiency.

UNIT 9 Kinetic Theory of Gases

Equation of state of a perfect gas, work done on compressing a gas.

Kinetic theory of gases - assumptions, concept of pressure. Kinetic energy and temperature: rms speed of gas molecules; Degrees of freedom, Law of equipartition of energy, applications to specific heat capacities of gases; Mean free path, Avogadro's number.

UNIT 10 Oscillations And Waves

Periodic motion - period, frequency, displacement as a function of time. Periodic functions. Simple harmonic motion (S.H.M.) and its equation; phase; oscillations of a spring - restoring force and force constant; energy in S.H.M. - kinetic and potential energies; Simple pendulum - derivation of expression for its time period; Free, forced and damped oscillations, resonance.

Wave motion Longitudinal and transverse waves, speed of a wave. Displacement relation for a progressive wave. Principle of superposition of waves, reflection of waves, Standing waves in strings and organ pipes, fundamental mode and harmonics, Beats, Doppler effect in sound.

UNIT 11 Electrostatics

Electric charges Conservation of charge, Coulomb's law-forces between two point charges, forces between multiple charges; superposition principle and continuous charge distribution.

Electric field Electric field due to a point charge, Electric field lines, Electric dipole, Electric field due to a dipole, Torque on a dipole in a uniform electric field.

Electric flux, Gauss's law and its applications to find field due to infinitely long, uniformly charged straight wire, uniformly charged infinite plane sheet and uniformly charged thin spherical shell.

Electric potential and its calculation for a point charge, electric dipole and system of charges; Equipotential surfaces, Electrical potential energy of a system of two point charges in an electrostatic field.

Conductors and insulators, Dielectrics and electric polarization, capacitor, combination of capacitors in series and in parallel, capacitance of a parallel plate capacitor with and without dielectric medium between the plates, Energy stored in a capacitor.

UNIT 12 Current Electricity

Electric current, Drift velocity, Ohm's law, Electrical resistance, Resistances of different materials, V-I characteristics of Ohmic and nonohmic conductors, Electrical energy and power, Electrical resistivity, Colour code for resistors; Series and parallel combinations of resistors; Temperature dependence of resistance.

Electric Cell and its Internal resistance, potential difference and emf of a cell, combination of cells in series and in parallel.

Kirchhoff's laws and their applications. Wheatstone bridge, Metre bridge.

Potentiometer - principle and its applications.

UNIT 13 Magnetic Effects of Current and Magnetism

Biot-Savart law and its application to current carrying circular loop. Ampere's law and its applications to infinitely long current carrying straight wire and solenoid. Force on a moving charge in uniform magnetic and electric fields Cyclotron.

Force on a current-carrying conductor in a uniform magnetic field. Force between two parallel current-carrying conductors-definition of ampere. Torque experienced by a current loop in uniform magnetic field, Moving coil galvanometer, its current sensitivity and conversion to ammeter and voltmeter.

Current loop as a magnetic dipole and its magnetic dipole moment. Bar magnet as an equivalent solenoid, magnetic field lines; Earth's magnetic field and magnetic elements. Para, dia and ferro-magnetic substances

Magnetic susceptibility and permeability, Hysteresis, Electromagnets and permanent magnets.

UNIT 14 Electromagnetic Induction and Alternating Currents

Electromagnetic induction; Faraday's law, induced emf and current; Lenz's Law, Eddy currents. Self and mutual inductance.

Alternating currents, peak and rms value of alternating current/ voltage; reactance and impedance; LCR series circuit, resonance; Quality factor, power in AC circuits, wattless current. AC generator and transformer.

UNIT 15 Electromagnetic Waves

Electromagnetic waves and their characteristics. Transverse nature of electromagnetic waves.

Electromagnetic spectrum (radio waves, microwaves, infrared, visible, ultraviolet, X-rays, gamma rays). Applications of e.m. waves.

UNIT 16 Optics

Reflection and refraction of light at plane and spherical surfaces, mirror formula, Total internal reflection and its applications, Deviation and Dispersion of light by a prism, Lens Formula, Magnification, Power of a Lens, Combination of thin lenses in contact, Microscope and Astronomical Telescope (reflecting and refracting) and their magnifying powers.

Wave optics wave front and Huygens' principle, Laws of reflection and refraction using Huygen's principle. Interference, Young's double slit experiment and expression for fringe width, coherent sources and sustained interference of light. Diffraction due to a single slit, width of central maximum. Resolving power of microscopes and astronomical telescopes, Polarisation, plane polarized light; Brewster's law, uses of plane polarized light and Polaroids.

UNIT 17 Dual Nature of Matter and Radiation

Dual nature of radiation. Photoelectric effect, Hertz and Lenard's observations; Einstein's photoelectric equation; particle nature of light. Matter waves-wave nature of particle, de Broglie relation. Davisson-Germer experiment.

UNIT 18 Atoms and Nuclei

Alpha-particle scattering experiment; Rutherford's model of atom; Bohr model, energy levels, hydrogen spectrum.

Composition and size of nucleus, atomic masses, isotopes, isobars; isotones. Radioactivity-alpha, beta and gamma particles/rays and their properties; radioactive decay law. Mass-energy relation, mass defect; binding energy per nucleon and its variation with mass number, nuclear fission and fusion.

UNIT 19 Electronic Devices

Semiconductors; semiconductor diode: I-V characteristics in forward and reverse bias; diode as a rectifier; I-V characteristics of LED, photodiode, solar cell, and Zener diode; Zener diode as a voltage regulator. Junction transistor, transistor action, characteristics of a transistor transistor as an amplifier (common emitter configuration) and oscillator. Logic gates (OR, AND, NOT, NAND & NOR). Transistor as a switch.

UNIT 20 Communication Systems

Propagation of electromagnetic waves in the atmosphere; Sky and space wave propagation, Need for modulation, Amplitude and Frequency Modulation, Bandwidth of signals, Bandwidth of Transmission medium, Basic Elements of a Communication System (Block Diagram only)

SECTION- B

UNIT 21 Experimental Skills

Familiarity with the basic approach and observations of the experiments and activities

1. Vernier callipers - its use to measure internal and external diameter and depth of a vessel.
2. Screw gauge - its use to determine thickness/diameter of thin sheet/wire.
3. Simple Pendulum - dissipation of energy by plotting a graph between square of amplitude and time.
4. Metre Scale - mass of a given object by principle of moments.
5. Young's modulus of elasticity of the material of a metallic wire.
6. Surface tension of water by capillary rise and effect of detergents.
7. Coefficient of Viscosity of a given viscous liquid by measuring terminal velocity of a given spherical body.
8. Plotting a cooling curve for the relationship between the temperature of a hot body and time.
9. Speed of sound in air at room temperature using a resonance tube.
10. Specific heat capacity of a given (i) solid and (ii) liquid by method of mixtures.
11. Resistivity of the material of a given wire using metre bridge.
12. Resistance of a given wire using Ohm's law.
13. Potentiometer
    (i) Comparison of emf of two primary cells.
    (ii) Internal resistance of a cell.
14. Resistance and figure of merit of a galvanometer by half deflection method.
15. Focal length of
    (i) Convex mirror
    (ii) Concave mirror
    (iii) Convex lens
16. Using parallax method. Plot of angle of deviation vs angle of incidence for a triangular prism.
17. Refractive index of a glass slab using a travelling microscope.
18. Characteristic curves of a p-n junction diode in forward and reverse bias.
19. Characteristic curves of a Zener diode and finding reverse break down voltage.
20. Characteristic curves of a transistor and finding current gain and voltage gain.
21. Identification of Diode, LED, Transistor, IC, Resistor, Capacitor from mixed collection of such items.
22. Using multimeter to
    (i) Identify base of a transistor.
    (ii) Distinguish between npn and pnp type transistor.
    (iii) See the unidirectional flow of current in case of a diode and an LED.
    (iv) Check the correctness or otherwise of a given electronic component (diode, transistor or IC).

JEE ADVANCED

General

General Units and dimensions, dimensional analysis; least count, significant figures; Methods of measurement and error analysis for physical quantities pertaining to the following experiments: Experiments based on using Vernier calipers and screw gauge (micrometer), Determination of gusing simple pendulum, Young's modulus - elasticity of the material Surface tension of water by capillary rise and effect of detergents. Specific heat of a liquid using calorimeter, focal length of a concave mirror and a convex lens using u-v method, Speed of sound using resonance column, Verification of Ohm's law using voltmeter and ammeter, and specific resistance of the material of a wire using meter bridge and post office box.

Mechanics

Kinematics in one and two dimensions (Cartesian coordinates only), projectiles; Uniform circular motion; Relative velocity.

Newton's laws of motion; Inertial and uniformly accelerated frames of reference; Static and dynamic friction; Kinetic and potential energy; Work and power; Conservation of linear momentum and mechanical energy.

Systems of particles; Centre of mass and its motion; Impulse; Elastic and inelastic collisions.

Rigid body, moment of inertia, parallel and perpendicular axes theorems, moment of inertia of uniform bodies with simple geometrical shapes; Angular momentum; Torque; Conservation of angular momentum; Dynamics of rigid bodies with fixed axis of rotation; Rolling without slipping of rings, cylinders and spheres; Equilibrium of rigid bodies; Collision of point masses with rigid bodies. Forced and damped oscillation (in one dimension), resonance.

Linear and angular simple harmonic motions.

Hooke's law, Young's modulus.

Law of gravitation; Gravitational potential and field; Acceleration due to gravity; Kepler's law, Geostationary orbits, Motion of planets and satellites in circular orbits; Escape velocity. Pressure in a fluid; Pascal's law;Buoyancy; Surface energy and surface tension, angle of contact, drops, bubbles and capillary rise. Viscosity (Poiseuille's equation excluded), Modulus of rigidity and bulk modulus in mechanics. Stoke's law; Terminal velocity, Streamline flow, equation of continuity, Bernoulli's theorem and its applications. Wave motion (plane waves only), longitudinal and transverse waves, superposition of waves; Progressive and stationary waves; Vibration of strings and air columns; Resonance; Beats; Speed of sound in gases; Doppler effect (in sound)

Thermal Physics

Thermal expansion of solids, liquids and gases; Calorimetry, latent heat; Heat conduction in one dimension; Elementary concepts of convection and radiation; Newton's law of cooling; Ideal gas laws; Specific heats (Cv and Cp for monoatomic and diatomic gases); Isothermal and adiabatic processes, bulk modulus of gases; Equivalence of heat and work; First law of thermodynamics and its applications (only for ideal gases); Second law of thermodynamics, reversible and irreversible processes, Carnot engine and its efficiency; Blackbody radiation: absorptive and emissive powers; Kirchhoff's law; Wien's displacement law, Stefan's law.

Electricity and Magnestism

Coulomb's law; Electric field and potential; Electrical potential energy of a system of point charges and of electrical dipoles in a uniform electrostatic field; Electric field lines; Flux of electric field; Gauss's law and its application in simple cases, such as, to find field due to infinitely long straight wire, uniformly charged infinite plane sheet and uniformly charged thin spherical shell. Capacitance; Parallel plate capacitor with and without dielectrics; Capacitors in series and parallel; Energy stored in a capacitor.

Electric current; Ohm's law; Series and parallel arrangements of resistances and cells; Kirchhoff's laws and simple applications; Heating effect of current. Biot–Savart's law and Ampere's law; Magnetic field near a current-carrying straight wire, along the axis of a circular coil and inside a long straight solenoid; Force on a moving charge and on a current-carrying wire in a uniform magnetic field. Magnetic moment of a current loop; Effect of a uniform magnetic field on a current loop; Moving coil galvanometer, voltmeter, ammeter and their conversions.

Electromagnetic induction: Faraday's law, Lenz's law; Self and mutual inductance; RC, LR, LC and LCR(in series) circuits with DC and AC sources.

Electromagnetic Waves

Electromagnetic waves and their characteristics. Electromagnetic spectrum (radio waves, microwaves, infrared, visible, ultraviolet, x-rays, gamma rays) including elementary facts about their uses.

Optics

Rectilinear propagation of light; Reflection and refraction at plane and spherical surfaces; Total internal reflection; Deviation and dispersion of light by a prism; Thin lenses; Combinations of mirrors and thin lenses; Magnification.

Wave nature of light: Huygen's principle, interference limited to Young's double slit experiment. Diffraction due to a single slit. Polarization of light, plane polarized light; Brewster's law, Polaroids.

Modern Physics

Atomic nucleus; α, β and γ-radiations; Law of radioactive decay; Decay constant; Half-life and mean life; Binding energy and its calculation; Fission and fusion processes; Energy calculation in these processes.

Photoelectric effect; Bohr's theory of hydrogen-like atoms; Characteristic and continuous X-rays, Moseley's law; de Broglie wavelength of matter waves.

JEE MAIN & ADVANCED

The Qualifiers

One Test for each Unit of JEE Physics

To ensure good score in JEE, You must be sure of the good understanding of each unit of JEE Syllabus. You must complete these tests with atleast 75% score, then only move to the next section.

QUALIFIER **01**

Physics & Measurement and Experimental Skills

Section I Objective Type Questions

1. Area of a triangular plate is $3.24\,m^2$. Area of 9 such plates considering the rules of significant figures is

(a) $29\ m^2$ (b) $29.1\ cm^2$ (c) $29.2\ cm^2$ (d) $29.16\ m^2$

2. For the four sets of three measured physical quantities as given below, which of the following options is correct?

(i) $A_1 = 24.46, B_1 = 0.0724, C_1 = 256.2$
(ii) $A_2 = 24.44, B_2 = 16.082, C_2 = 240.2$
(iii) $A_3 = 25.2, B_3 = 19.2812, C_3 = 236.183$
(iv) $A_4 = 25, B_4 = 236.191, C_4 = 19.6$

(a) $A_1 + B_1 + C_1 < A_3 + B_3 + C_3 < A_2 + B_2 + C_2 < A_4 + B_4 + C_4$
(b) $A_4 + B_4 + C_4 < A_1 + B_1 + C_1 = A_2 + B_2 + C_2 = A_3 + B_3 + C_3$
(c) $A_4 + B_4 + C_4 < A_1 + B_1 + C_1 = A_3 + B_3 + C_3 < A_2 + B_2 + C_2$
(d) $A_1 + B_1 + C_1 = A_2 + B_2 + C_2 = A_3 + B_3 + C_3 < A_4 + B_4 + C_4$

3. Two resistors R_1 and R_2 have resistances measured equal to $a \pm \Delta a$ and $b \pm \Delta b$, respectively. Maximum possible error in computation for equivalent resistance (R_{PQ}) of parallel combination of R_1 and R_2 shown is

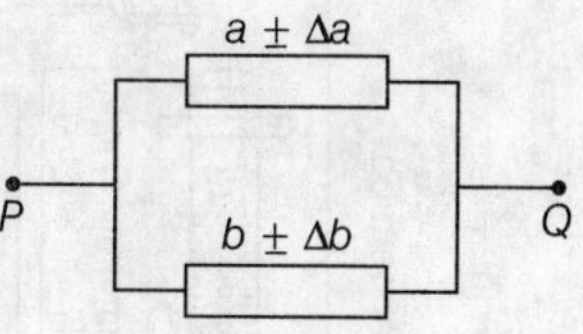

(a) $\left(\frac{ab}{a+b}\right)^2\left(\frac{\Delta a}{a}+\frac{\Delta b}{b}\right)$ (b) $\left(\frac{ab}{a+b}\right)^2\left(\frac{\Delta a}{a^2}+\frac{\Delta b}{b^2}\right)$

(c) $\frac{ab}{a+b}\left(\frac{\Delta a}{a}+\frac{\Delta b}{b}\right)$ (d) $\left(\frac{ab}{a+b}\right)^2\left(\frac{\Delta a}{a^2}+\frac{\Delta b}{b^2}\right)^{1/2}$

4. In experimental set-up shown here, the voltmeter and ammeter read 20.0 V and 2.00 A, respectively. If length of the wire (resistance) used is measured to be 10.0 cm using a scale of least count 0.2 cm while diameter of the wire is measured to be 2.50 mm, then maximum permissible percentage error in computation of resistivity is

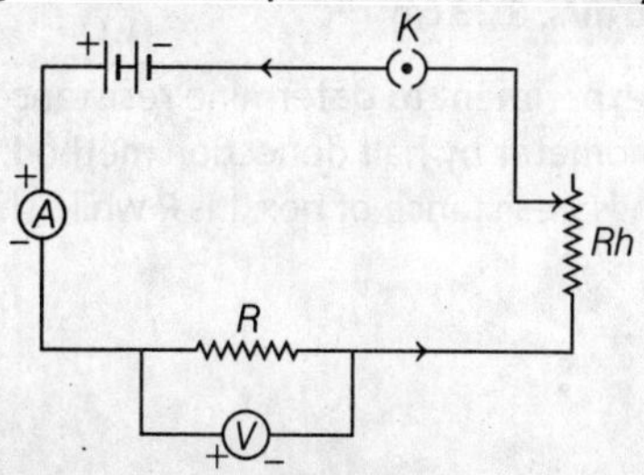

(a) 3.5 (b) 3.8
(c) 4.1 (d) 4.4

5. Potential energy of a gas particle is given as function of its position x and gas temperature T hypothetically as

$$U = cx + a^2 b e^{-\frac{bx^2}{kT}} + d \sin\frac{x}{f}$$

Here, a, b, c, d, f are constants and k is Boltzmann's constant. Which of the following relation is not a dimensionless combination?

(a) $\frac{bx^2}{U}$ (b) $\frac{cf}{d}$

(c) $\frac{a^2 b}{d}$ (d) $\frac{fd}{U}$

6. A boomerang of mass m, surface area A and radius of curvature of the lower surface r (C being corresponding centre of curvature) is moving with speed v through air of density ρ. Which of the following can possibly represent resistive force on the boomerang?

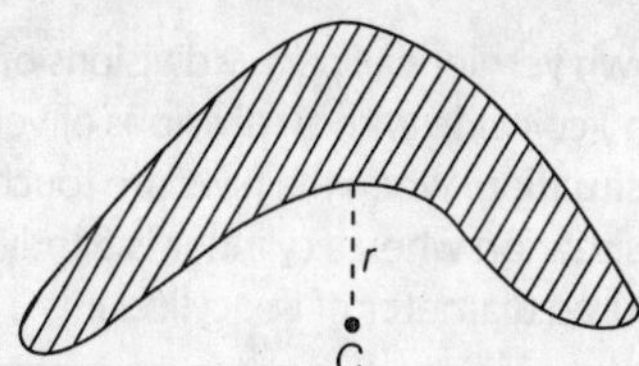

(a) $2\rho Av^2 \log\frac{\rho Ar}{\pi m}$ (b) $2\rho Av^2 \log\frac{\rho A}{\pi mr}$

(c) $\frac{2\rho Av}{r^2}\log\frac{\rho Ar}{\pi m}$ (d) $\frac{2\rho Av}{r^2}\log\frac{\rho A}{\pi mr}$

7. Eötvös or Bond number is a dimensionless number used to describe shape of bubbles rising through a surrounding fluid. It depends on acceleration due to gravity g, density of fluid ρ, surface tension S and a characteristic length l. The bond number could possibly be

(a) $\frac{\rho g l^2}{S}$ (b) $\frac{\rho l^2}{gS}$

(c) $\frac{\rho S}{l^2 g}$ (d) $\frac{\rho}{gSl^2}$

8. Planck system of units comprises of a set of units of measurement defined in terms of four universal physical constants namely c (speed of light in vacuum), G (universal gravitational constant), h (reduced Planck's constant) and k (Boltzmann constant). In this system, temperature called Planck's temperature possibly has the expression

(a) $\sqrt{\frac{hG}{kc^3}}$ (b) $\sqrt{\frac{hc^5}{k^2G}}$ (c) $\sqrt{\frac{hc}{Gk}}$ (d) $\sqrt{\frac{hc^8}{G^5k^3}}$

9. In an experiment to determine g on a planet using pendulum, time taken for 25 oscillations is measured by using a watch of least count 1 s. Average values of time comes out to be 40 s and length of the pendulum is measured using a meter scale of least count 1 mm to be 50.0 cm. Determine percentage error in determination of g on the planet's surface.

(a) 5.2 (b) 4.8 (c) 7 (d) zero

10. Current I in a diode varies with applied voltage V as per the law $I = e^{2V} - 1$

Here, I is in mA while V is in volts.

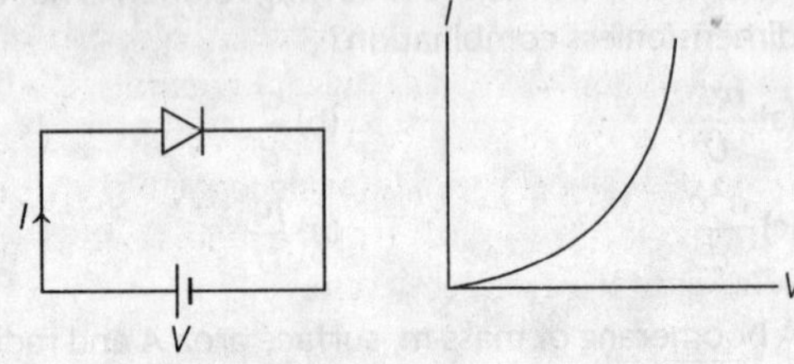

If error in measurement of voltage V is $\pm$ 0.02 V, while the corresponding current is 3 mA, percentage error in measurement of current is

(a) 5.33 (b) 4.87 (c) 7.24 (d) zero

11. For the shown vernier callipers, 9 divisions of main scale (1 mm each) coincide with 10 divisions of vernier scale. If Fig.1 shows the situation, when the jaws are touching, while Fig.2 shows the situation when a cylinder is tightly held between the jaws, measured diameter of the cylinder is

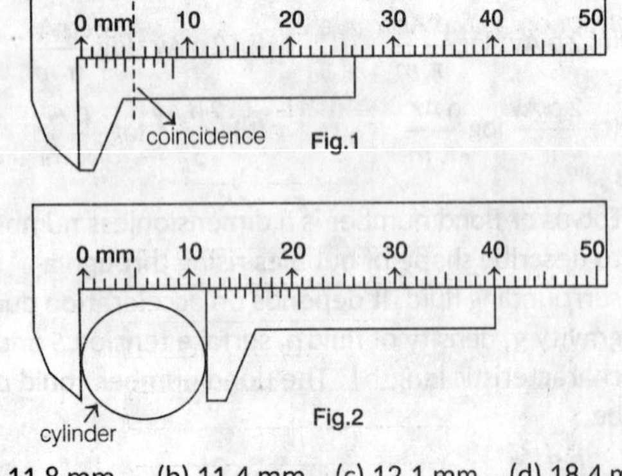

Fig.1

Fig.2

(a) 11.8 mm (b) 11.4 mm (c) 12.1 mm (d) 18.4 mm

12. In an experiment to measure surface tension of liquid shown below, it can be calculated by using the formula

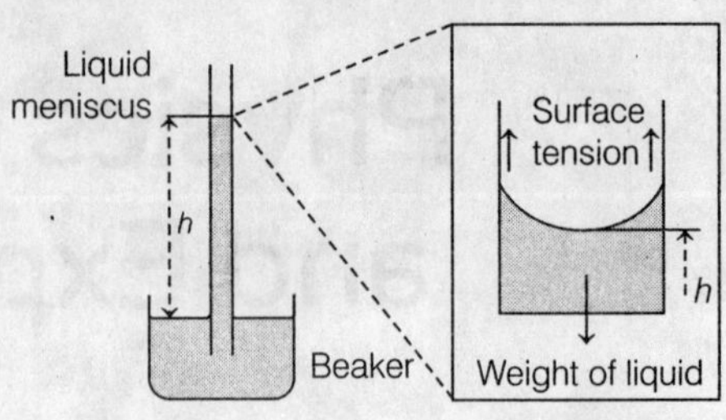

(a) $T = \frac{(h+r)\rho rg}{2\cos\theta}$ (b) $T = \frac{(3h+r)\rho rg}{6\cos\theta}$

(c) $T = \frac{(h+3r)\rho rg}{2\cos\theta}$ (d) $T = \frac{(h-r)\rho rg}{6\cos\theta}$

(Here, T is surface tension, h is height of ascent, r is capillary radius, θ is angle of contact, ρ is density of liquid and g is acceleration due to gravity.)

13. In resonance air column experiment, lengths of the air column corresponding to first and second resonance are measured to be $L_1 = 23$ cm and $L_2 = 73$ cm respectively, using a tuning fork of frequency 330 Hz. Speed of sound in air and radius of the resonance tube respectively are

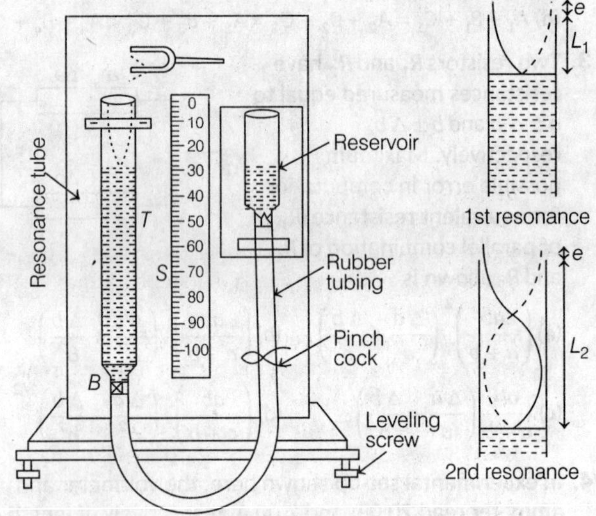

(a) 330 m/s, 6.67 cm
(b) 330 m/s, 3.33 cm
(c) 310 m/s, 6.67 cm
(d) 310 m/s, 3.33 cm

14. In an experiment to determine resistance of galvanometer by half deflection method, in one set of readings, resistance of box 1 is R while shunt resistance

(resistance box 2) is $S = \frac{R}{3}$. Resistance of the galvanometer, from the given information is

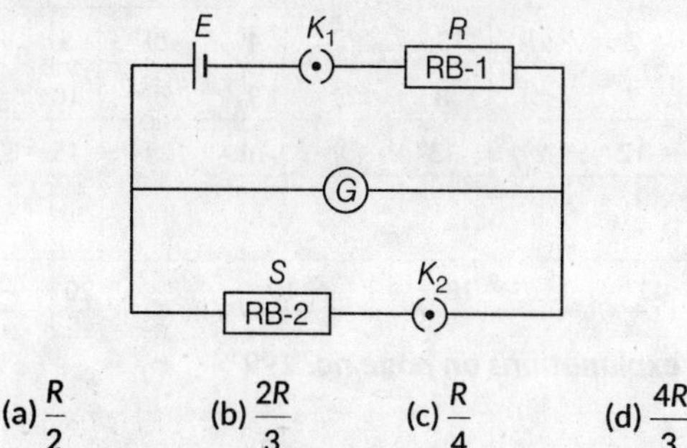

(a) $\frac{R}{2}$ (b) $\frac{2R}{3}$ (c) $\frac{R}{4}$ (d) $\frac{4R}{3}$

15. Which of the following will not be observed when a multimeter (operating in resistance measuring mode) probes connected across a component, are just reversed?

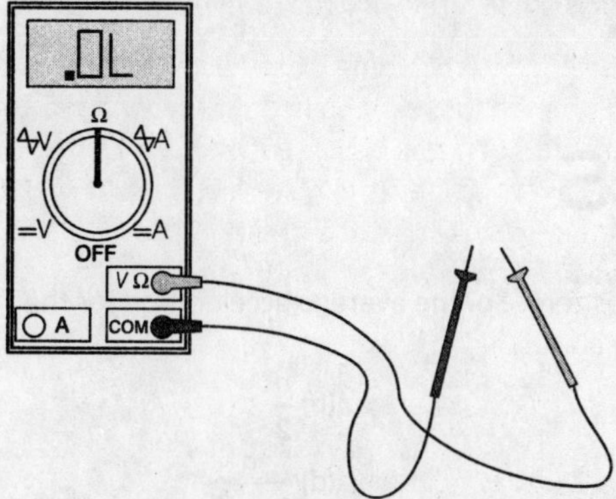

(a) Multimeter shows no deflection in both cases, i.e. before and after reversing the probes if the chosen component is metal wire.
(b) Multimeter shows an equal deflection in both cases, i.e. before and after reversing the probes, if the chosen component is resistor.
(c) Multimeter shows no deflection in both cases, i.e., before and after reversing the probes, if the chosen component is capacitor.
(d) Multimeter shows a deflection, accompanied by a splash of light out of connected component in one direction and no deflection on reversing the probes, if the chosen component is LED.

Section II *Numerical Value Questions*

16. To measure diameter of a wire, a screw gauge is used. The main scale division is of 1 mm. In a complete rotation, the screw advances by 1 mm and the circular scale has 100 divisions. The reading of screw gauge is as shown in figure. If there is no error in mass measurement but error in length measurement is 1%, then find maximum possible error in density.

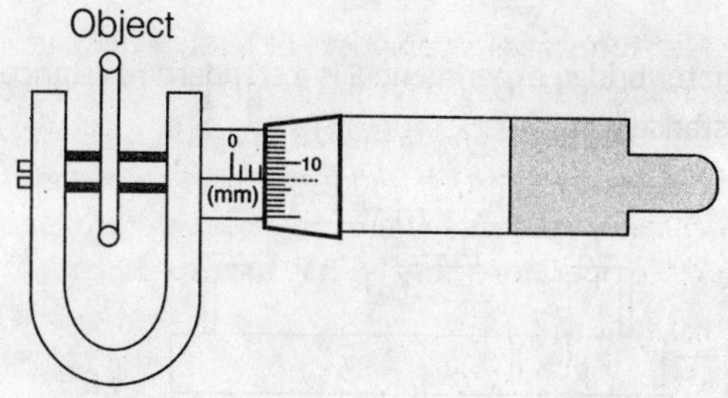

17. In an experiment to determine Young's modulus of a wire using Searle's method, extension in the wire is measured to be 1.6 mm when the wire is loaded with mass of 2.0 kg. Also, diameter of the wire is measured to be 0.5 mm with uncertainty of ± 0.01 cm. If Young's modulus of the wire is computed to be 2×10^{11} N/m^2, uncertainty in computation of Young's modulus is $x \times 10^y$ N/m^2. Find $x + y$. Assume that, length of wire and acceleration due to gravity are known exactly $(1 < x < 10)$.

18. 8 vernier divisions of a specially designed vernier calliper coincides with 6 main scale divisions (1 mm each) as shown. When jaws of the callipers are in contact, zero of the main scale lies between zero and 1st division of vernier scale while 4th vernier scale division exactly coincides with one of the main scale divisions. When a cylinder is grabbed tightly between jaws of the calliper, zero of the vernier lies between 4th and 5th divisions of the main scale while 6th division of the vernier scale coincides with one of the main scale divisions. Find diameter of the cylinder in mm.

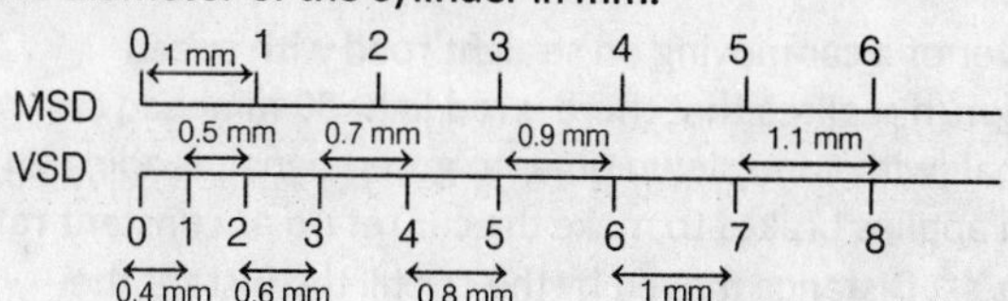

19. In the given circuit of potentiometer potential difference E across AB(10 m length) is larger than E_1 and E_2 as well. For key K_1 (closed), the jockey is adjusted to touch the wire at point J_1, so that there is no deflection in the galvanometer. Now, the first battery (E_1) is replaced by second battery (E_2) for working by making K_1 open and K_2 closed. The galvanometer gives, then null deflection at J_2. The value of $\frac{E_1}{E_2}$ is $\frac{a}{75}$, where $a =$ ....

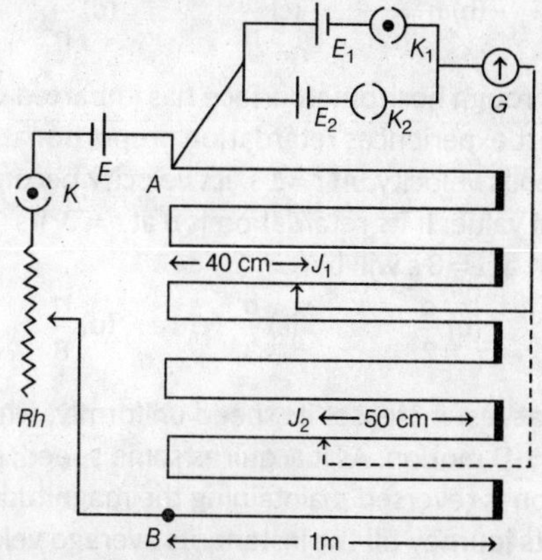

20. In a meter bridge experiment, S is a standard resistance, R is a resistance wire.

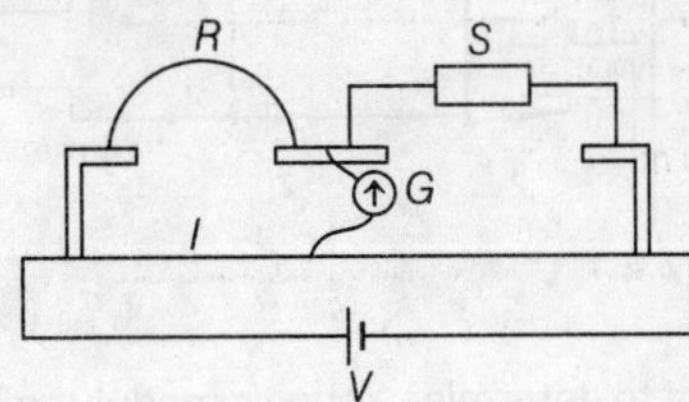

It is found that balancing length, l is 25 cm. If R is replaced by a wire of half length and half diameter as that of R of same material, then the balancing distance l' (in cm) will be ....

Answers

Section I

1	(d)	2	(d)	3	(b)	4	(b)	5	(d)
6	(a)	7	(a)	8	(b)	9	(a)	10	(a)
11	(c)	12	(b)	13	(b)	14	(a)	15	(c)

Section II

16	1.65	17	13.05	18	4.3	19	36	20	40

See detailed explanations on page no. 199

QUALIFIER 02

Kinematics

Section I *Objective Type Questions*

1. Driver of a car moving on straight road with speed 36 km/h realises that there is red light 30 m ahead on signal (with countdown timer to green signal, reading 34 s) and applies brakes to make the car retard at constant rate 2 m/s^2. Distance moved by the car till the instant the countdown timer reads 28 s is

(a) 25 m (b) 24 m (c) 20 m (d) 180 m

2. A ball thrown vertically upward takes time T to reach maximum height while it takes time nT to reach the ground from the maximum height. Ratio of distance moved by the ball during 1st second of descent to that during last second of its ascent is (assume drag is constant)

(a) $\sqrt{n}$ (b) n^2 (c) $\frac{1}{n}$ (d) $\frac{1}{n^2}$

3. A block on rough horizontal surface has imparted velocity v_0 at $t = 0$. It experiences retardation proportional to its instantaneous velocity. At $t = 1$ s, its velocity becomes half of its initial value. If its retardation is a at $t = 0$, its retardation at $t = 3$ s will be

(a) a (b) $\frac{a}{2}$ (c) $\frac{a}{3}$ (d) $\frac{a}{8}$

4. A particle at rest increases its speed uniformly, while moving in 1-D motion. As it acquires some speed, its acceleration is reversed maintaining the magnitude. Consider its journey till the instant, its average velocity becomes zero. So, the average acceleration for the journey is

(a) zero (b) $\frac{a}{2}$

(c) $\frac{a}{\sqrt{2}}$ (d) $\frac{a}{1+\sqrt{2}}$

5. Position-time graph for a particle moving on X-axis is as shown. Choose the **incorrect** statement from the following options.

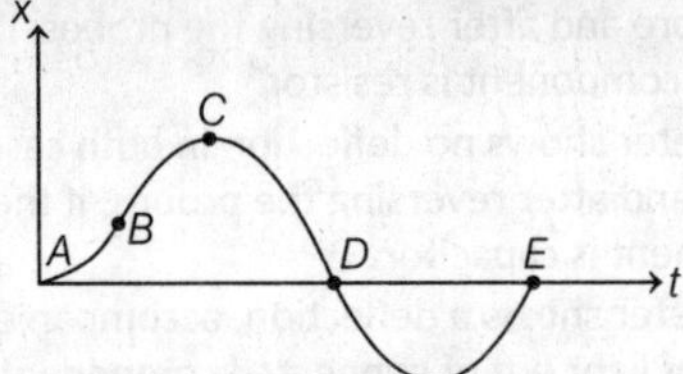

(a) Particle is retarding in its motion from B to C.
(b) Acceleration is in same direction as velocity during some instants during motion between D to E.
(b) Average velocity of the particle for motion from A to D is same as that for A to E.
(d) Motion must be non-uniformly accelerated between B and D.

6. Suppose acceleration due to gravity was directly proportional to mass of object. If Galileo had dropped two solid spheres of same uniform material having 4 percent difference in their surface areas during one of his experiments, he would have observed that smaller sphere would (ignore the effect of air resistance on motion of spheres)

(a) take 2 per cent more time to reach ground
(b) take 3 times the time taken by larger sphere to reach ground
(c) take same time as that taken by larger sphere
(d) take 0.97 times the time taken by larger sphere to reach ground

7. Acceleration time graph for a particle moving in positive x-direction is as shown. Speed of the particle is maximum at t equal to

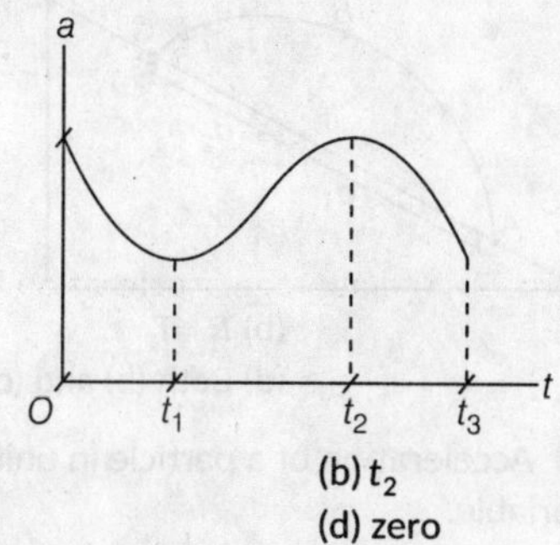

(a) t_1 (b) t_2
(c) t_3 (d) zero

8. Rain appears to be falling with a speed 5 m/s at angle 53° with the vertical to Shruti when she is at rest. Now, Shruti begins to speed up uniformly and rain appears to rotate by 8° to her during 1st second of her motion. So, at what further time will the rain again appear to be falling at 53° with vertical to her?
(a) 5 (b) 6
(c) 7 (d) 8

9. Three particles named P, Q and R initially on vertices of an equilateral triangle (of side L) start moving with constant speed v, such that P is chasing Q, Q is chasing R and R is chasing P. Time taken by P, till the instantaneous separation between the particles reduces to half of the initial separation, is
(a) $\frac{L}{2v}$ (b) $\frac{L}{3v}$ (c) $\frac{L}{4v}$ (d) $\frac{L}{v}$

10. Sachin(S), Virat (V) and Rohit (R) start swimming with same speed of 5m/s (w.r.t. river flowing with 4 m/s) from a river bank, stroking in different directions, as shown in figure. Sachin reaches the other bank on directly opposite point and stays there. Others start walking with constant speeds in upstream direction immediately after all have reached the other bank. Ratio of speeds of Virat to that of Rohit to reach Sachin simultaneously is (given that width of the river is 60 m)

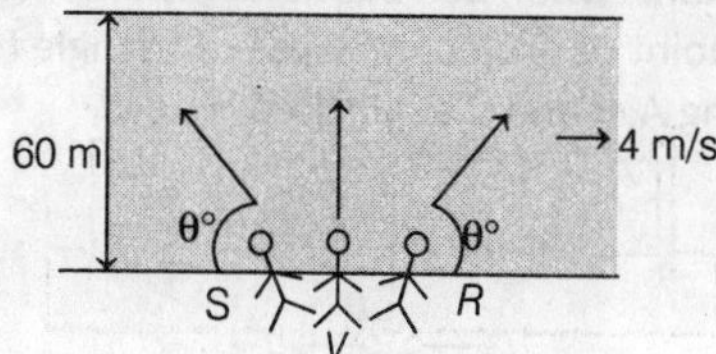

(a) 11 : 30 (b) 3 : 10
(c) 4 : 11 (d) 1 : 1

11. Dhoni riding in an ascending hot air balloon (moving vertically up and speeding at rate 5 m/s^2) throws a ball downwards with a speed of 5 m/s with respect to his balloon, at the instant shown . At a later instant, velocity of the ball relative to Dhoni is 35 m/s and Salman's vertically descending balloon (speeding down at the rate 5m/s^2) crosses past Dhoni with 15 m/s as observed by Dhoni. Taking g =10 m/s^2 , vertical separation H between the persons at the instant shown is

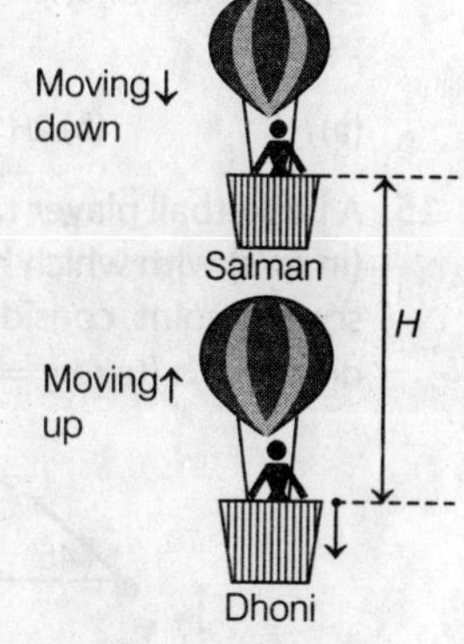

(a) 20 m
(b) 30 m
(c) 40 m
(d) Indeterminate due to insufficient information

12. A cannon fires two shells with same speed, one at the angle 53° with horizontal while the other at 53° with vertical, in the same vertical plane. If the time interval (in s) between the firings resulting in collision of the shells is 6 s, find speed of firing (in m/s). Consider acceleration of shells due to gravity only equal to 10 m/s^2.
(a) 100 (b) 125 (c) 150 (d) 175

13. A fighter plane has to fly along AB (directed NE) followed by BC (directed SE) with speed v w.r.t air as shown to avoid getting hit by missile. Wind is blowing in SE direction with speed $u = \frac{v}{2}$. It takes T seconds to reach from A to B. So, the time taken by it to move equal distance BC is

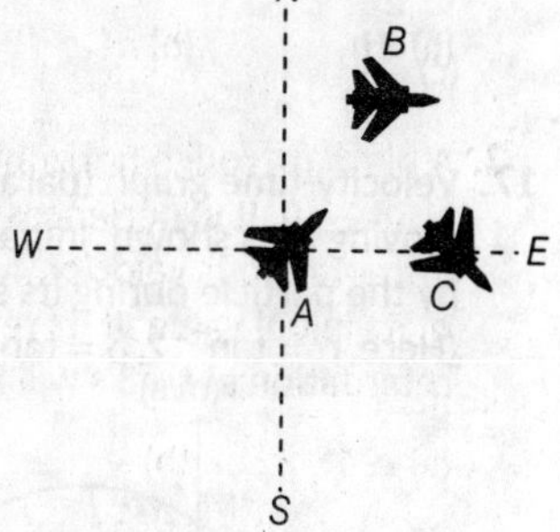

(a) $2T$ (b) $\frac{T}{\sqrt{3}}$
(c) T (d) $\frac{T}{\sqrt{2}}$

14. Three small balls A, B, C are projected from a high tower with same speed in different directions as shown in figure. At the instant, when ball B is at its maximum height H w.r.t. its point of projection, area of triangle formed by considering A, B and C as vertices is

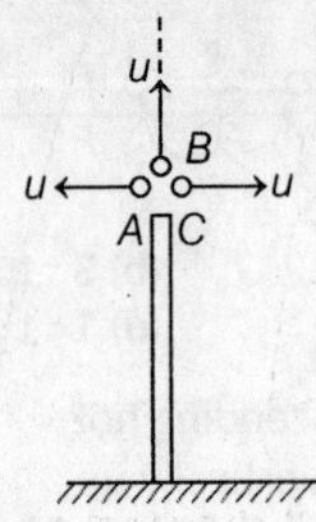

(a) H^2 (b) $2H^2$ (c) $4H^2$ (d) $8H^2$

15. A basketball player takes a shot to basket as shown. Speed (in m/s) with which he should throw the basketball to score a point, considering the information shown in the diagram, is (take $g = 10\ \text{m/s}^2$)

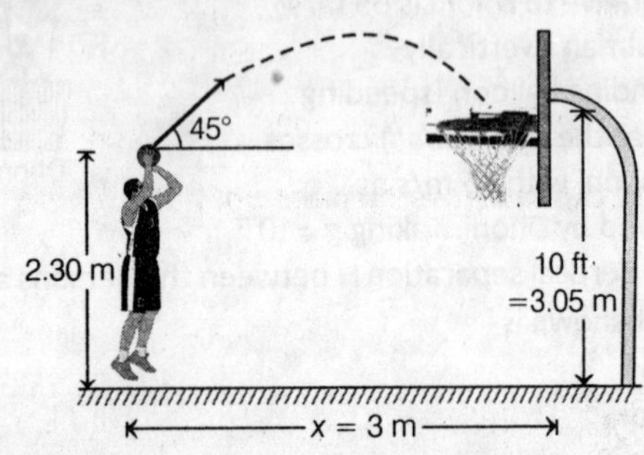

(a) $\sqrt{10}$ (b) $2\sqrt{10}$
(c) $3\sqrt{10}$ (d) $4\sqrt{10}$

16. Top point A of a building AB of height H has angle of elevation 45° with respect to a point C on the ground. A ball is dropped from top of the building, while another ball is projected simultaneously from C towards top of the building with speed $\sqrt{2gH}$. The balls collide in mid-air at a height

(a) $\frac{H}{2}$ (b) $\frac{H}{3}$
(c) $\frac{3H}{4}$ (d) $\frac{2H}{3}$

17. Velocity-time graph (parabola) for a particle initially moving is as shown. Initial and maximum speeds acquired by the particle during its shown motion respectively are (Here, $\alpha = \tan^{-1} 2, \beta = \tan^{-1} 4$)

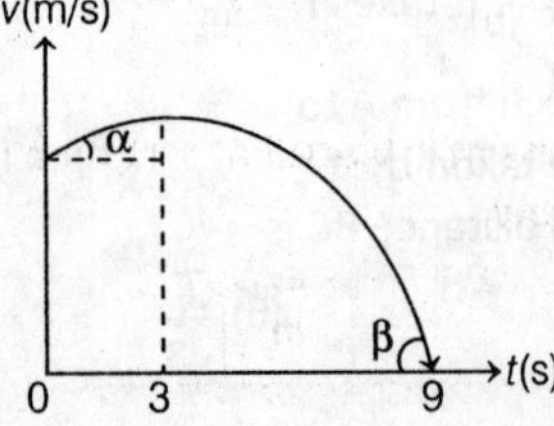

(a) 8 m/s, 12 m/s
(b) 2 m/s, 3 m/s
(c) 9 m/s,12 m/s
(d) Indeterminate due to lack of information, 12m/s

18. A bullet is fired targeting a bird perching on a tower. The bird just manages to escape the bullet and begins to fly horizontally. If the bullet still hits the bird, ratio of times of flight of the bullet to that of the bird till the instant of hitting is [given that height of tower is (3/4)th of the maximum height acquired by the bullet]

(a) 1 : 1 (b) 3 : 2 (c) 3 : 4 (d) $\sqrt{3} : 1$

19. A particle is projected on an incline from point A as shown. B is the instant of maximum separation from the incline. The particle strikes the incline normally at C as shown in figure. Time of flight from A to B is T_1, while from B to C is T_2. Displacement along incline from A to B is d_1, while from B to C is d_2. Choose the most appropriate option (diagram may not be depicting the actual geometrical situation)

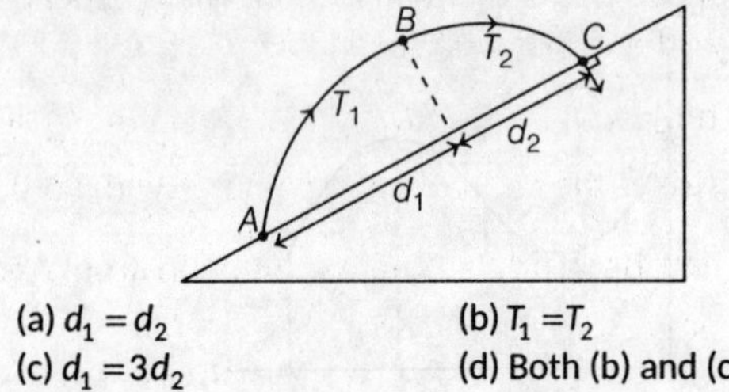

(a) $d_1 = d_2$ (b) $T_1 = T_2$
(c) $d_1 = 3d_2$ (d) Both (b) and (c)

20. **Statement I** Acceleration of a particle in uniform circular motion is variable.

Statement II Velocity of a particle in uniform circular motion is variable.

(a) Statement I is false, statement II is true.
(b) Statement I is true, statement II is true, statement II is correct explanation for statement I.
(c) Statement I is true, statement II is true, statement II is not a correct explanation for statement I.
(d) Statement I is true, statement II is false.

Section II *Numerical Value Questions*

21. A parachutist jumping from a high rise building switches ON a propeller 4 s after falling freely from a certain height. After the propeller is switched ON, the parachutist retards at a rate numerically equals to its instantaneous speed. If parachutist reaches the ground with zero speed, find height of the building (in m).

22. A particle moves in XY-plane according to the equations $x = 3t$ and $y = 3t(1-t)$, here x, y and t are X coordinate in m, Y coordinate in m and time in s respectively. Find the time (in s), when the angle between the direction of velocity and acceleration of particle becomes 30°.

23. A ball projected perpendicularly (with speed u) from an incline at P strikes an adjacent shown incline at Q (with speed v) perpendicular to the incline. Find $\frac{v}{u}$.

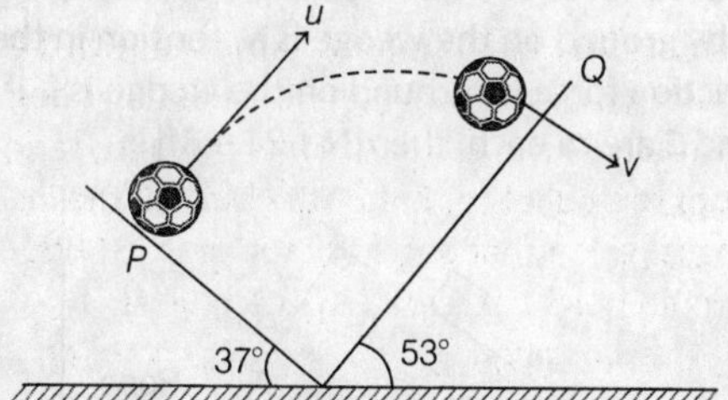

24. A novice swimmer in danger of drowning in a river is being carried downstream by a current that flows uniformly. Realising this, his friend calls the rescue SOS services. The swimmer is 1.8 km from shore and 2.4 km downstream of a helipad at shore when the rescue helicopter sets out. The helicopter flying at its maximum constant velocity of 80 m/s (in river's frame), reaches the swimmer in x s. Find x. River speed is 16 m/s while air is blowing perpendicular from the other shore with speed 12 m/s.

25. A ball is projected from a tower as shown in the figure. If the ball strikes the ground making angle $\frac{\pi}{x}$ with vertical at D. Also, horizontal displacement for motion from A to C is y times the horizontal displacement from C to D. Taking $g = 10\text{ m/s}^2$, find $x + y$.

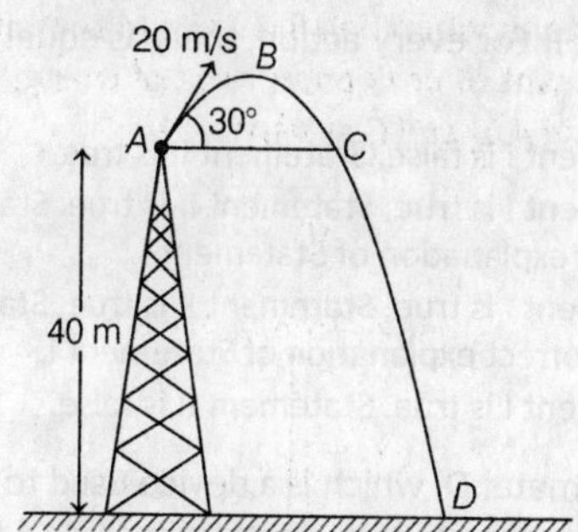

Answers

Section I

1	(a)	2	(b)	3	(d)	4	(d)	5	(d)
6	(d)	7	(c)	8	(c)	9	(b)	10	(b)
11	(b)	12	(c)	13	(b)	14	(c)	15	(b)
16	(a)	17	(c)	18	(b)	19	(c)	20	(c)

Section II

21	120	22	1.36	23	0.75	24	50	25	7

See detailed explanations on page no. 201

QUALIFIER 03

Laws of Motion

Section I Objective Type Questions

1. A rod AB is moving with its ends A and B in contact with a parabolic surface $y = x^2$ as shown in figure. At the instant shown, coordinates of A and B are given. Find ratio of speed of ends A to that of B. (Take, $\sqrt{5} = 2.2$)

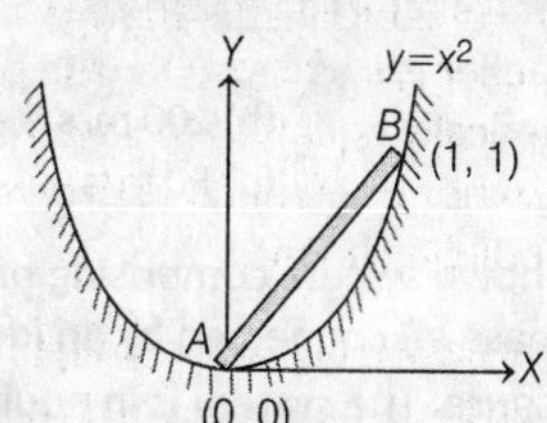

(a) 0.92 (b) 1.12
(c) 1.32 (d) 1.52

2. A ball is suspended using a thread and a spring as shown. Acceleration of the ball just after cutting the spring is a_1, while it is a_2 just after cutting the string. $\frac{a_1}{a_2}$ is equal to

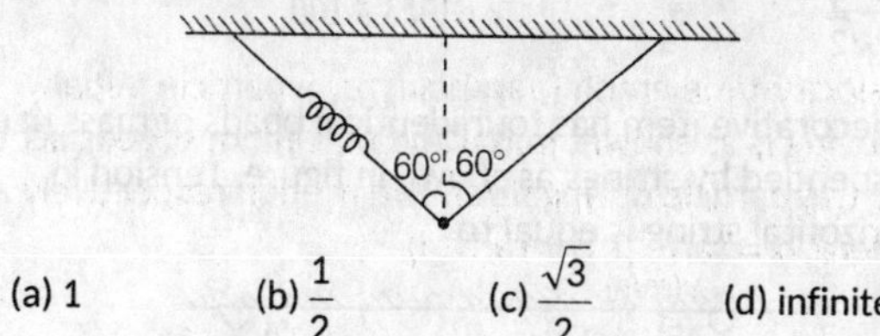

(a) 1 (b) $\frac{1}{2}$ (c) $\frac{\sqrt{3}}{2}$ (d) infinite

3. A block of mass m is placed at rest on a fixed horizontal surface as shown

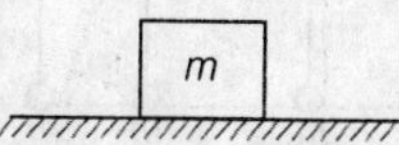

Statement I Normal reaction by surface on the block is equal and opposite to its weight *mg*.

Statement II For every action, there is equal but opposite reaction.

(a) Statement I is false, Statement II is true.
(b) Statement I is true, Statement II is true, Statement II is correct explanation of Statement I.
(c) Statement I is true, Statement II is true, Statement II is not a correct explanation of Statement I.
(d) Statement I is true, Statement II is false.

4. A dynamometer *D*, which is a device used to measure force, is attached to two blocks of masses 6 kg and 4 kg. Forces of 20 N and 10 N are applied on the blocks as shown in the figure. The reading of the dynamometer (light) is

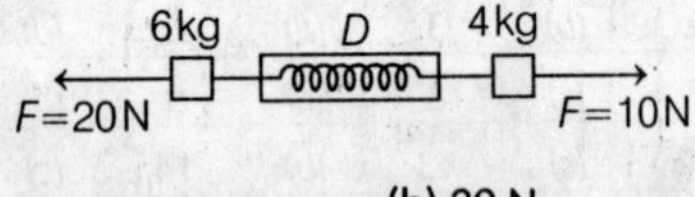

(a) 10 N (b) 20 N
(c) 6 N (d) 14 N

5. A rope *PQ* on a smooth surface is being pulled by a constant force *F* as shown in figure. If linear mass density of the rope increases from λ_0 to $2\lambda_0$ linearly as we move from end $P(x=0)$ towards end $Q(x=L)$, tension at mid-point of the rope is

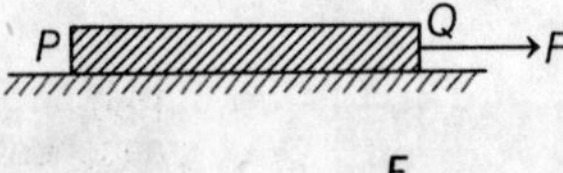

(a) F (b) $\frac{F}{2}$
(c) $\frac{2F}{3}$ (d) $\frac{5F}{12}$

6. A cubical block of mass *m* is pushed by force $F(=mg)$ horizontally on a smooth surface as shown in figure. Contact force by shaded half of the block *A* on the other half *B* is

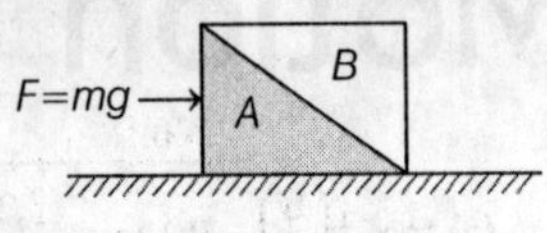

(a) mg (b) $\frac{mg}{2}$
(c) $\frac{mg}{\sqrt{2}}$ (d) $\sqrt{2}\,mg$

7. A decorative item has four identical beads of mass *m* each suspended by strings as shown in figure. Tension in horizontal string is equal to

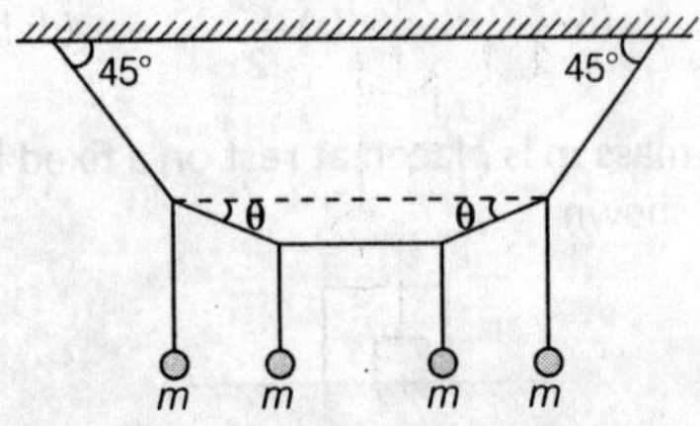

(a) 0 (b) mg
(c) $2mg$ (d) a value dependent on θ

8. Blocks *A* and *B* are released in the positions shown on two smooth surfaces of a double incline *C*. Normal contact force by ground on the wedge is **N**, tension in the rope is **T** and friction force by ground on the wedge is **f**. If masses of *A*, *B* and *C* are *m* each, then $|\mathbf{N}+2\mathbf{T}-3\mathbf{f}|$ is

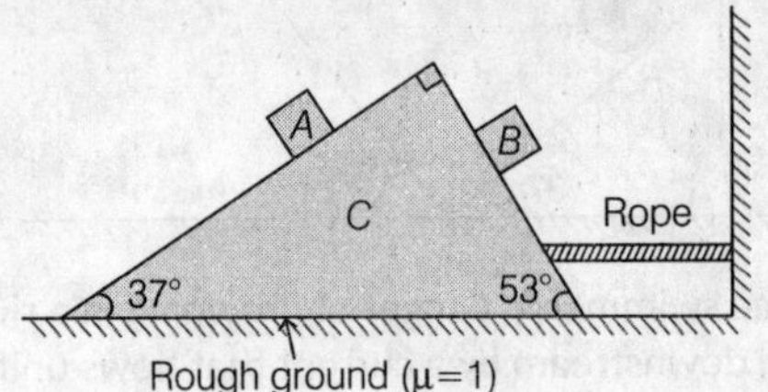

(a) $\frac{24}{25}mg$ (b) $\frac{49}{25}mg$ (c) $2mg$ (d) $3mg$

9. Wedge shown in the figure, has velocity given by the law $\mathbf{v}=kt^2\hat{\mathbf{i}}$. Here, *t* is time and *k* is a positive constant. Tension in the string, at the instant the block leaves contact with the wedge, is (Mass of the block = *m*)

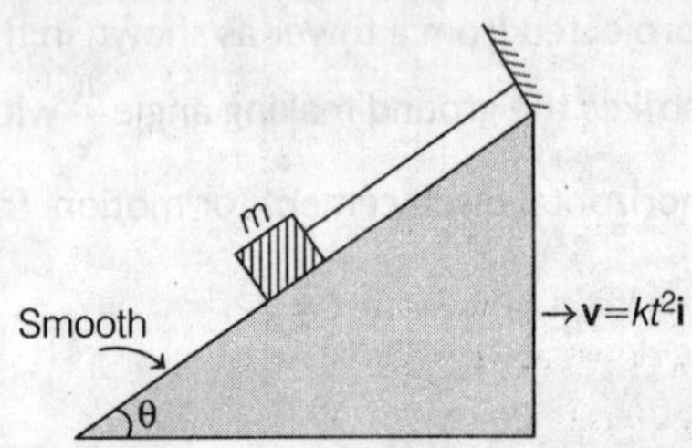

(a) $mg\sin\theta$ (b) $mg\cos\theta$ (c) $mg\sec\theta$ (d) $mg\,\text{cosec}\,\theta$

10. In the arrangement shown, vertical force of 10*t* newton acts on the pulley. Here, *t* is time in s. Velocity of the pulley, at the instant when 10 kg block just lifts from the ground, is (Take, $g=10\text{ m/s}^2$)

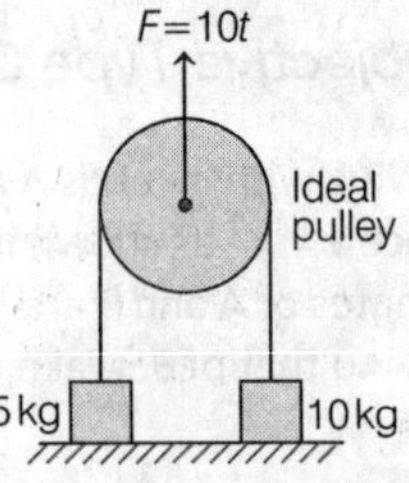

(a) 100 m/s (b) 200 m/s
(c) 25 m/s (d) 50 m/s

11. Consider the shown system comprising of blocks *A* and *B* (each having mass *m*) connected by an ideal string as shown in the figure. The system is in equilibrium under influence of an external horizontal force *F* (equal to $\frac{3mg}{4}$) acting on block *B*. The force *F* is now withdrawn. If acceleration of block *A* just after withdrawing *F* is *a*, then acceleration of *B* is

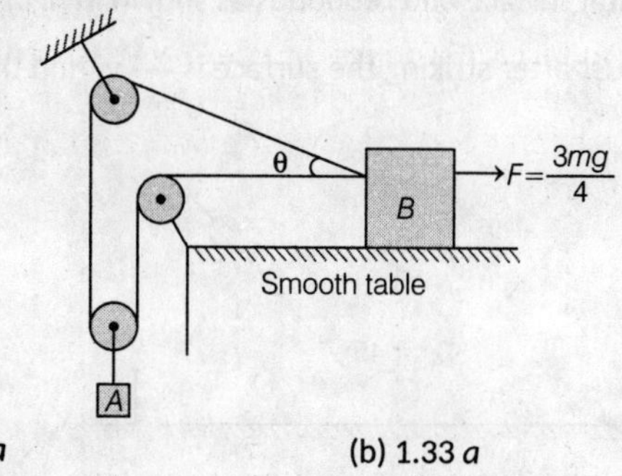

(a) *a* (b) 1.33 *a*
(c) 2*a* (d) $\frac{a}{\sqrt{2}}$

12. The man in shown arrangement climbs up the ladder such that the block (100 kg) is in limiting equilibrium with tendency to slide down. The man is (Take, $g = 10\ m/s^2$)

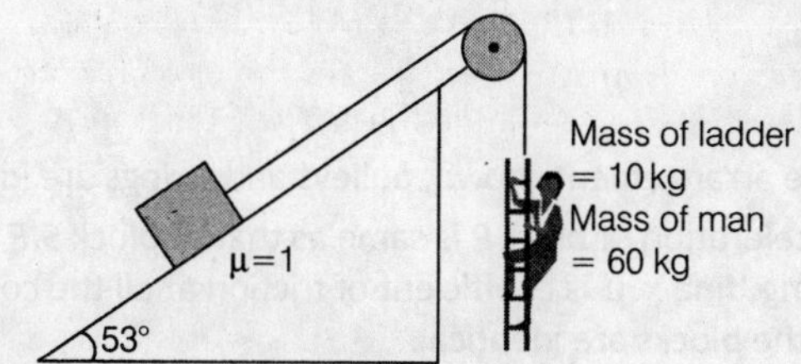

(a) speeding up at rate (35/3) m/s^2
(b) slowing down at rate (25/3) m/s^2
(c) moving uniformly
(d) speeding up at rate (35/3) m/s^2 or speeding down at rate (25 / 3) m/s^2

13.

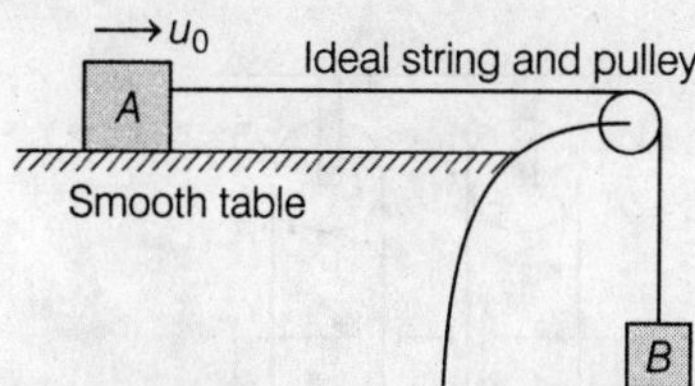

Consider the arrangement of two identical blocks *A* and *B* shown. While block *B* is released from rest, block *A* is imparted a velocity u_0 as shown. Assuming that *A* does not strike the pulley, common speed of the blocks just after the string taut is

(a) $\frac{u_0}{2}$ (b) $\frac{2u_0}{3}$
(c) $\frac{3u_0}{2}$ (d) $2u_0$

14. Masses of cubical blocks *A*,*B*,*C* and *L*-shaped block *D* are equal in the system shown. On releasing the system in position shown, blocks *A* and *B* are observed to move without slipping with respect to *D*. Assuming coefficient of friction between *A* and *D* is same as that between *B* and *D* and is equal to μ, then the minimum value of μ is

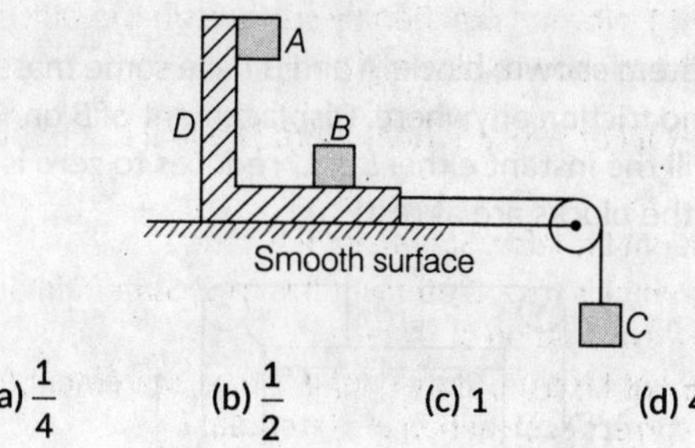

(a) $\frac{1}{4}$ (b) $\frac{1}{2}$ (c) 1 (d) 4

15. The arrangement shown here is in equilibrium. Strings and spring are ideal. If the string connecting the blocks on table is now cut, for which of the following relation between masses of the blocks, accelerations of blocks on the table are in ratio 1 : 2 just after cutting the string?

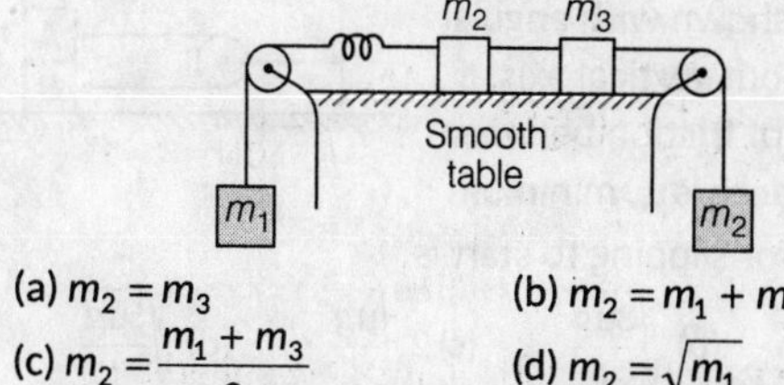

(a) $m_2 = m_3$ (b) $m_2 = m_1 + m_3$
(c) $m_2 = \frac{m_1 + m_3}{3}$ (d) $m_2 = \sqrt{m_1}$

16. The shown system of blocks *A* and *B* of respective masses *m* and 4*m* is in limiting equilibrium on a fixed wedge as shown in figure. If coefficient of friction at all contacts is $\frac{2}{3}$, then θ is

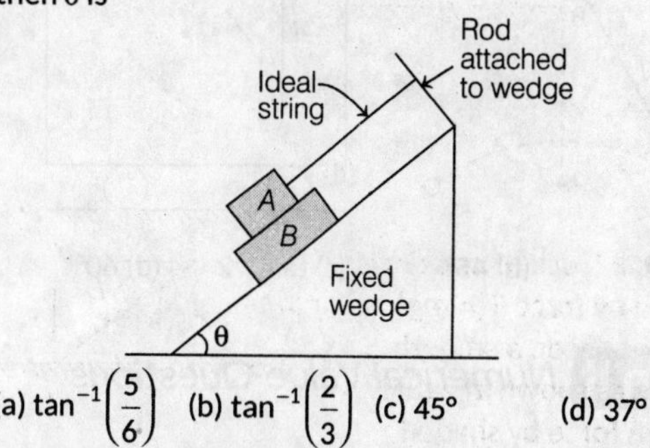

(a) $\tan^{-1}\left(\frac{5}{6}\right)$ (b) $\tan^{-1}\left(\frac{2}{3}\right)$ (c) 45° (d) 37°

17. Consider the arrangement shown with infinite ideal pulleys and infinite blocks connected to ideal strings. If the arrangement is released to move under influence of gravity, force by the clamp on the fixed pulley is

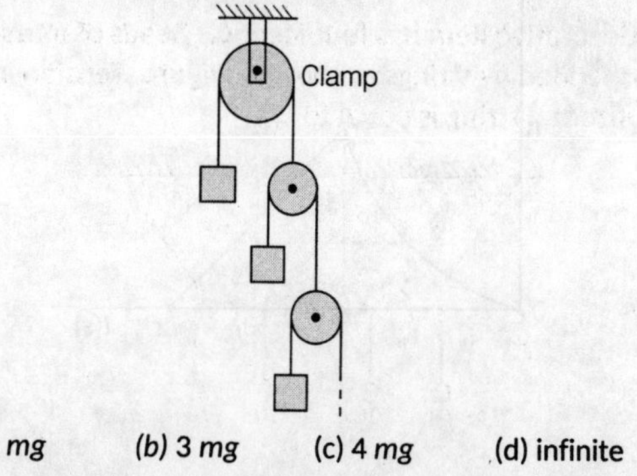

(a) 2 *mg* (b) 3 *mg* (c) 4 *mg* (d) infinite

18. In the system shown, blocks A and B have same mass and there is no friction anywhere. Displacement of B on ground till the instant either L or L' reduces to zero is (initially the blocks are at rest)

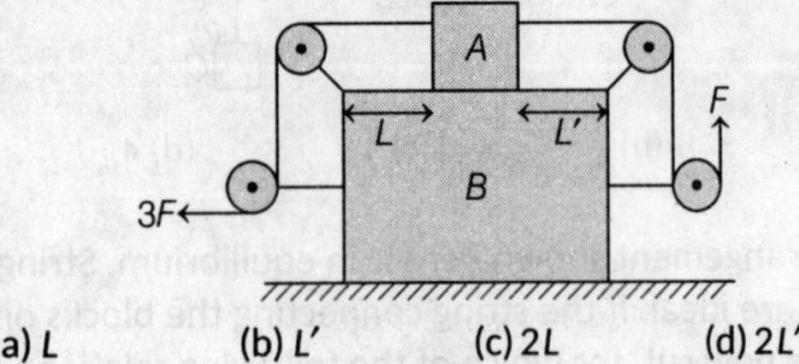

(a) L (b) L' (c) $2L$ (d) $2L'$

19. The arrangement of two blocks of masses m and $2m$ is rotated as shown with angular speed ω about vertical axis. If coefficient of friction between all the surfaces is μ, minimum value of ω for slipping to start is

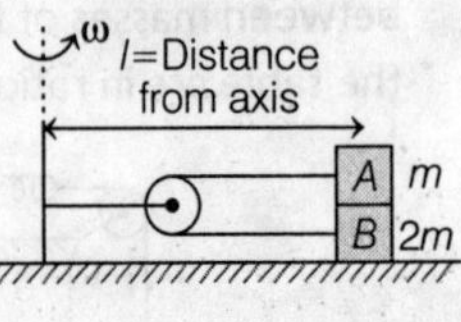

(a) $\sqrt{\frac{2\mu g}{l}}$ (b) $\sqrt{\frac{3\mu g}{l}}$ (c) $2\sqrt{\frac{\mu g}{l}}$ (d) $\sqrt{\frac{5\mu g}{l}}$

20. For what value of θ, time periods of the two conical pendulums of length l each are equal?

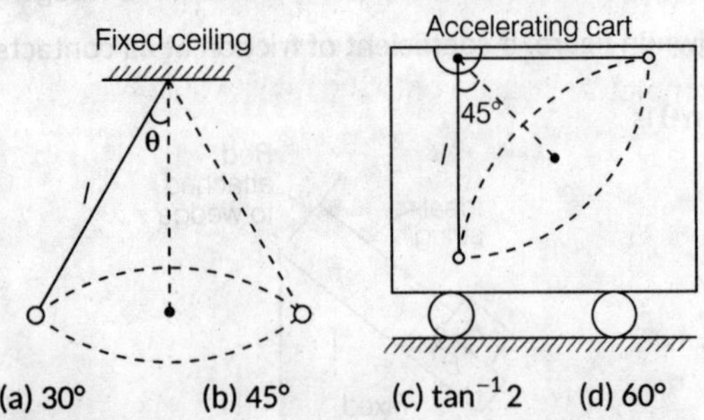

(a) 30° (b) 45° (c) $\tan^{-1} 2$ (d) 60°

Section II *Numerical Value Questions*

21. For a particle, momentum varies with time as shown. If magnitude of force is same at time instants $t = t_1$ and $t = t_2$, average force on the particle (in N) between $t = 0$ and $t = t_1$, is ....

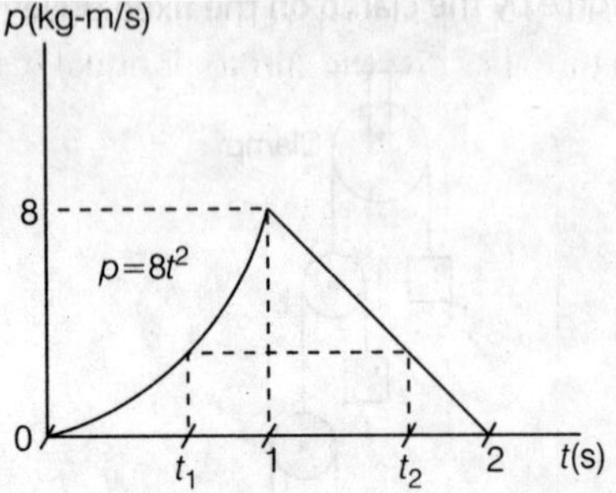

22. A ball moving with velocity $v\mathbf{i} - v\mathbf{j}$ strikes a rough horizontal surface and rebounds as shown in figure. If speed just after striking the surface is $\frac{\sqrt{2}}{x}v$, find the value of x.

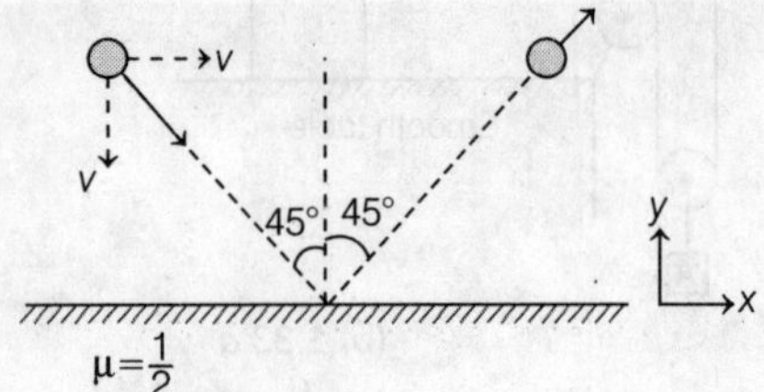

23.

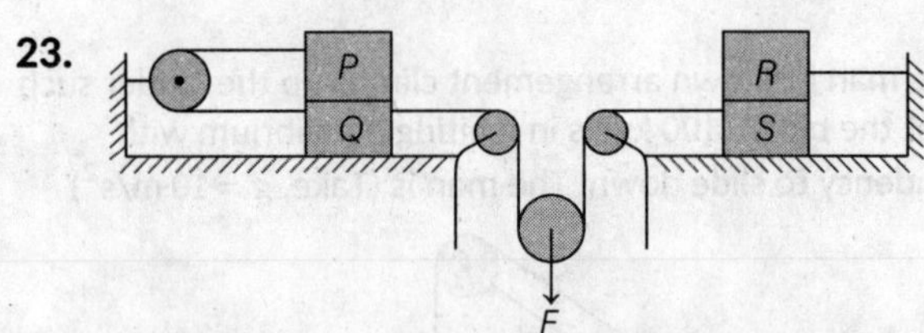

In the arrangement shown, pulleys and strings are ideal. If acceleration of block P is same as that of block S, F is $x^2 \mu mg$, find x. μ is coefficient of friction at all the contacts and the blocks are identical.

24. A man in a lift is pulling ropes in the arrangement making the lift move up uniformly with constant velocity as shown in figure. Mass of the man is twice that of the lift. If readings of spring balance and weighing machine are x and y, find $\frac{x}{y}$.

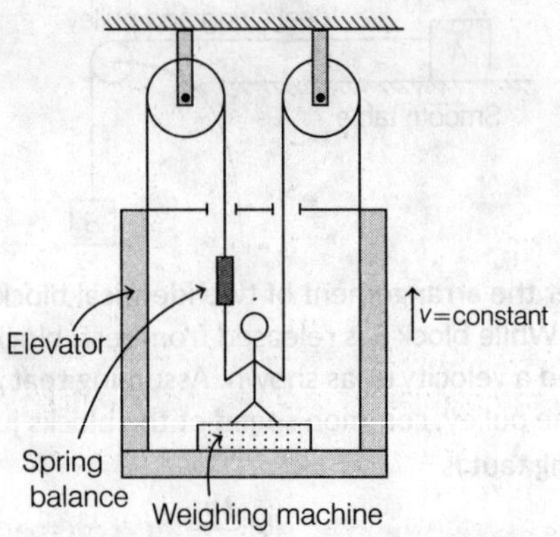

25. Two particles of masses m and M are attached to end B of a freely hanging rod AB with support of ideal strings of lengths l and L respectively as shown. Fourth power of angular speed (in rad^4/s^4) of the rod, so that it remains vertical, is $\frac{100}{x}$.

Find the value of x. Given that, $m = 2$ kg, $M = \sqrt{2}$ kg, $l = 2$ m, $L = 1$ m and $g = 10$ m/s^2.

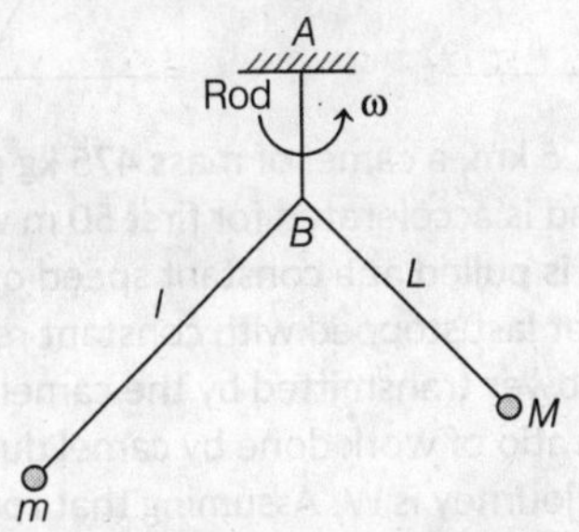

Answers

Section I

1	(c)	2	(c)	3	(c)	4	(d)	5	(d)
6	(c)	7	(c)	8	(c)	9	(d)	10	(c)
11	(b)	12	(b)	13	(c)	14	(d)	15	(a)
16	(c)	17	(b)	18	(a)	19	(d)	20	(d)

Section II

21	4	22	3	23	2	24	1.5	25	7

See detailed explanations on page no. 206

QUALIFIER **04**

Work, Energy and Power

Section I Objective Type Questions

1. A man applying a force F upon a stretched spring is stationary in a compartment moving with constant speed v. The work done by friction acting on man during time t, with respect to ground, is

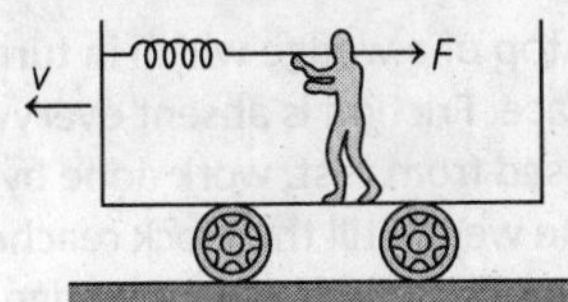

(a) Fvt
(b) $-Fvt$
(c) 0
(d) Indeterminate as spring constant is unknown

2. Motion of a particle of mass m in a plane is described by the non-orthogonal set of coordinates (p, q) given by $K = \frac{1}{2} m(\dot{p}^2 + \dot{q}^2 + 2\dot{p}\dot{q}\cos\theta)$ where $\dot{p}$ and $\dot{q}$ are inclined at an angle θ with respect to each other. If momentum of the particle is increased by 100 percent, the quantity K (Note that dot above p and q signifies their time derivatives)

(a) increases by 300 percent
(b) becomes thrice
(c) decreases by 300 percent
(d) becomes (1/4) th

3. A uniform chain on smooth horizontal table is held at rest such that half of it overhangs the table. It is now slowly dragged on the table by a person. Work done in doing so is W. If the instantaneous force applied to drag the chain is four times in magnitude, kinetic energy of the chain as it is completely dragged onto the table would be

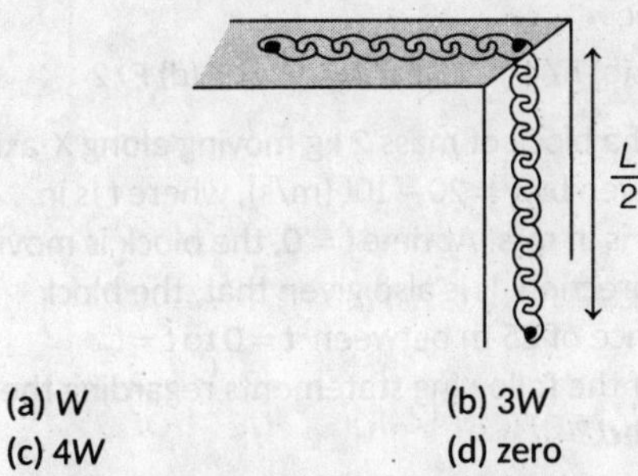

(a) W
(b) $3W$
(c) $4W$
(d) zero

4. A block is moved slowly along a parabolic surface (given by $x = y^2$ from point A to B) as shown in figure. If heat dissipated due to friction is equal to increase in potential energy of the block, sum of y-coordinates of the points A and B is equal to (given that coefficient of friction between the block and the surface is equal to μ)

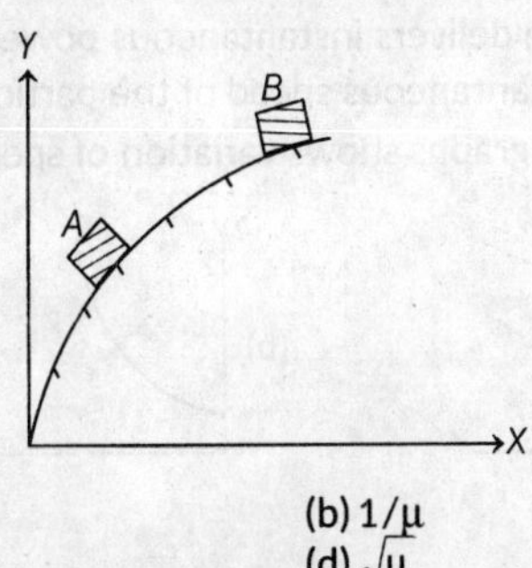

(a) μ
(b) $1/\mu$
(c) $\mu + 1$
(d) $\sqrt{\mu}$

5. The system shown has two blocks of mass $m_1 = m$ and $m_2 = 2m$ connected by an ideal spring. Initially, the system is at rest on a rough horizontal surface (having coefficient of friction μ) and the spring is in its natural length. Now the left block is imparted a velocity u towards right as shown. Maximum possible value of u^2 for which the block of mass m_2 never moves is

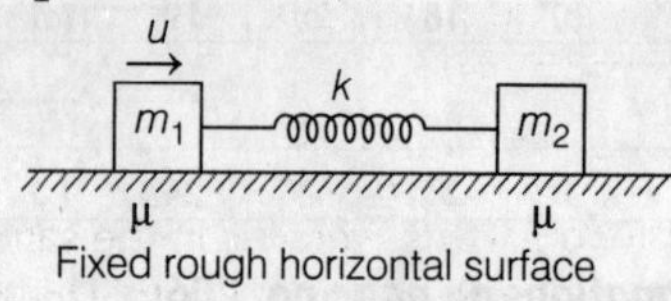

(a) $\frac{m\mu^2g^2}{k}$ (b) $\frac{2m\mu^2g^2}{k}$

(c) $\frac{4m\mu^2g^2}{k}$ (d) $\frac{8m\mu^2g^2}{k}$

6. A body moves along a straight line and the variation of its kinetic energy with time is linear as depicted in the figure below.

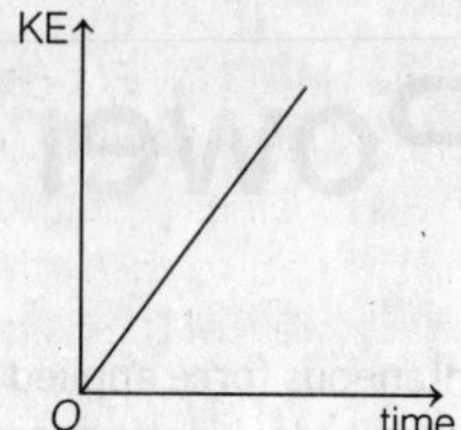

Force acting on the body at $t = 1$ s is F. Magnitude of force at $t = 4$ s will be

(a) F (b) $F/4$ (c) $4F$ (d) $F/2$

7. The velocity of a block of mass 2 kg moving along X-axis at any time t is given by $v = 20 - 10t$ (m/s), where t is in seconds and v is in m/s. At time $t = 0$, the block is moving in positive x-direction. It is also given that, the block covers a distance of 25 m between $t = 0$ to $t = t_1$. Then, which of the following statements regarding the block is **incorrect**?

(a) At $t = 3$ s, net force on the block is 20 N.

(b) The power due to net force on block at $t = 3$s is 200 W.

(c) The kinetic energy of block at $t = 2$ s is zero.

(d) The work done by net force on the block in time $t = 0$ to t_1 is -200 J.

8. A particle of unit mass is moving on a straight path with some speed at $t = 0$. Now a force starts acting on the particle which delivers instantaneous power equal to square of instantaneous speed of the particle. Which of the following graphs shows variation of speed with time?

(a) 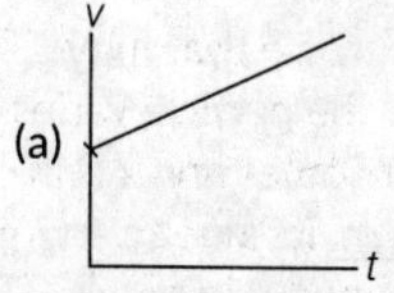

(b) 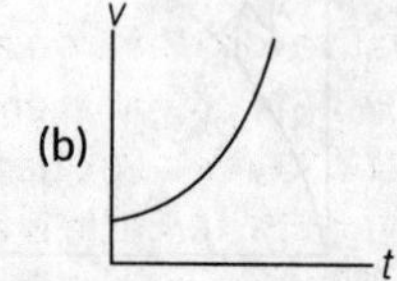

(c) 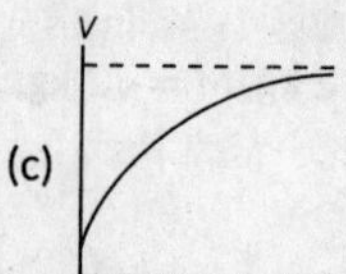

(d) 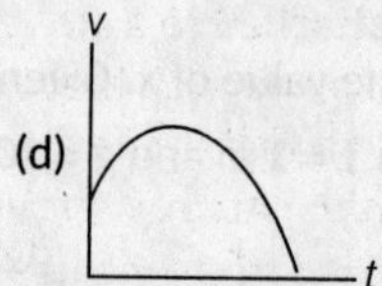

9. In a trip of 1.6 km, a camel of mass 475 kg pulls a load of 1000 kg. Load is accelerated for first 50 m with constant rate, then it is pulled at a constant speed of 5 m/s for 1.5 km and at last stopped with constant retardation. Maximum power transmitted by the camel to the load is P watt and ratio of work done by camel during first and last 50 m of journey is W. Assuming that ropes used for pulling load are almost horizontal, choose the correct values.

(Take, coefficient of friction between load and ground = 0.1 and acceleration due to gravity $g = 10$ m/s^2)

(a) $P = 6250, W = 1$ (b) $P = 1250, W = 1.67$

(c) $P = 6250, W = 1.67$ (d) $P = 1250, W = 1$

10. In the arrangement shown in figure, a block of mass m is released from rest when the spring is in its natural length. The pulley is perfectly smooth and have same mass m. Value of m is chosen such that M just leaves contact with the ground. Maximum force by rod on the pulley during subsequent motion is

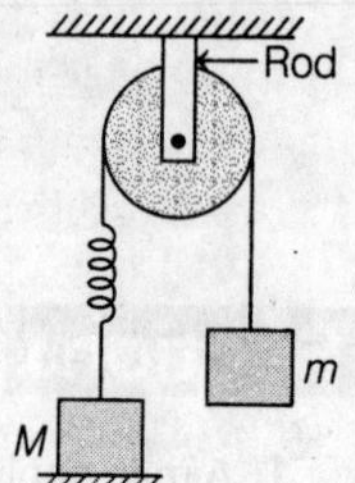

(a) $2(2M + m)g$ (b) $(M + 2m)g$

(c) $2(M + m)g$ (d) $(2M + m)g$

11. A block lies on top of a wedge which in turn lies on a horizontal surface. Friction is absent everywhere. If the system is released from rest, work done by normal reactions on the wedge till the block reaches bottom of the wedge is (here h is the height of wedge)

(a) zero

(b) mgh

(c) less than mgh

(d) greater than mgh but lesser than $(m + M)gh$

12. In the set-up shown in the figure the block of mass 1 kg is initially compressed against spring (of spring constant 110N/m) such that the spring has length 4m. When block is not attached to the spring, natural length of the spring is 6m. The block is now released and is observed to climb up the smooth incline of length 8m. Maximum height of the block from the ground is (Take, $g = 10$ m/s^2)

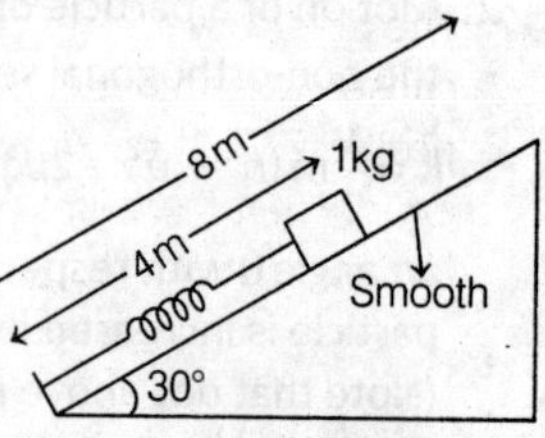

(a) 5 m (b) 7 m (c) 9 m (d) 11 m

13. A ball attached to a string fixed to ceiling oscillates in a vertical plane such that its acceleration in the extreme position is half of the acceleration at lowest position in magnitude. Area swept by the string (of length L) as the ball moved from one extreme to the other is KL^2. The value of K is

(a) π (b) $\pi/2$ (c) $\cot^{-1} 2$ (d) $2\cot^{-1} 2$

14. The arrangement is dropped from rest with spring relaxed at the instant shown. The lower block collides with the ground and does not rebound. Minimum value of h for which the lower block may be lifted off the ground is

(Given that masses of the upper and the lower blocks are m and $2m$ respectively and stiffness constant of the spring is k)

(a) mg/k (b) $2mg/k$ (c) $3mg/k$ (d) $4mg/k$

15. A block of mass m is hanging from a vertical spring of spring constant k. A bullet of same mass m moving upward with velocity v strikes the hanging block and is embedded in it. If v is chosen such that the spring just attains its natural length during subsequent motion, energy loss due to collision is

(a) $\dfrac{m^2g^2}{2k}$ (b) $\dfrac{2m^2g^2}{3k}$ (c) $\dfrac{3mg^2}{2k}$ (d) $\dfrac{3m^2g^2}{2k}$

16. A bungee jumper of mass m has a bungee cord of length l, that is initially folded back on itself, attached to his feet as shown in the figure. Initially when he jumps, he is in free fall for the length of the bungee l. After that distance, the bungee starts to stretch and obeys Hooke's law. If it is given that stiffness constant of the bungee is mg/l, maximum speed acquired by the jumper during the fall is

(a) $\sqrt{2gl}$ (b) $\sqrt{3gl}$

(c) $\sqrt{4gl}$ (d) $\sqrt{5gl}$

17. The potential energy of a particle experiencing conservative force is represented as function of its position x in the following graph. As shown, the potential energy first increases parabolically and then decreases linearly with x.

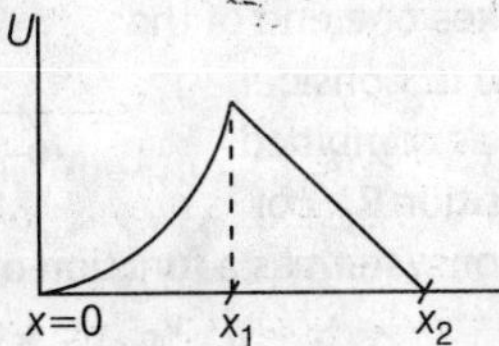

Conservative force acting on the system as a function of x may be represented by

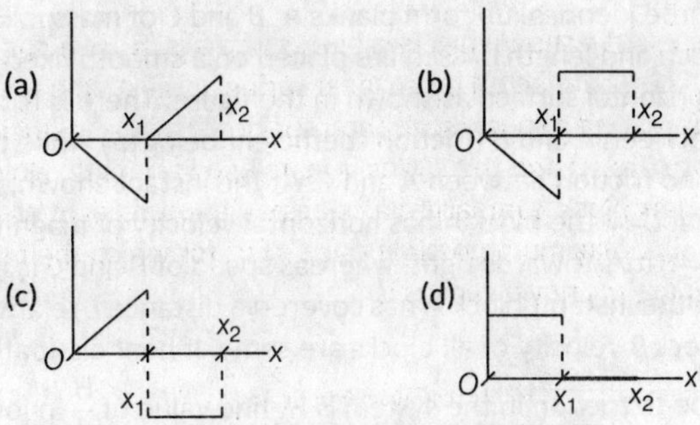

18. **Statement I** Two particles moving in the same direction do not lose all their energy in completely inelastic collision.

Statement II Principle of conservation of momentum holds true for all kinds of free collisions.

(a) Both statement I and statement II are true.
(b) Only statement I is true but II is false.
(c) Only statement II is true but I is false.
(d) Both statement I and statement II are false.

19. A ball A moving with kinetic energy K collides with another ball B at rest. After the collision, the two balls move with same speeds such that their directions of motion makes an angle of 60° with respect to each other as shown. Kinetic energy of the system of the balls after the collision is

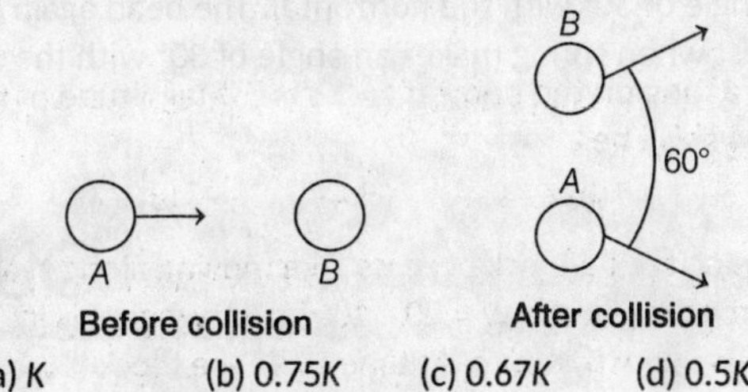

(a) K (b) $0.75K$ (c) $0.67K$ (d) $0.5K$

20. Two massless strings of same length hang from the ceiling very near to each other as shown in the figure. Two balls A and B of masses m and $3m$ are attached to the string. The ball A is released from rest at a height h as shown in the figure. Given that the collision between the balls has coefficient of restitution 1/3, maximum height attained by ball B after collision is

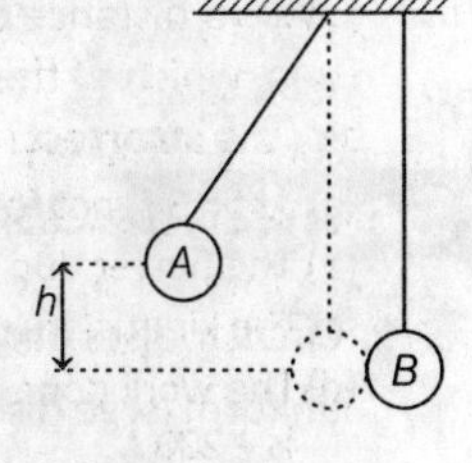

(a) h (b) $h/2$ (c) $h/3$ (d) $h/9$

Section II *Numerical Value Questions*

21. A conservative force acts on a 1 kg particle that moves along X-axis. The potential energy of the particle varies with x as $U = 30 + (x-3)^2$, here U is in joules and x is in metres. When the particle is at $x = 6$ m, its kinetic energy K is 7J, find the difference of maximum and minimum possible values of x that can be taken by the particle.

22. Three identical uniform planks A, B and C of mass $m = 1$ kg each and length $L = 2$ m are placed on a smooth fixed horizontal surface as shown in the figure. There is friction between A and B (friction coefficient being μ) while there is no friction between A and C. At the instant shown, that is at $t = 0$ the block A has horizontal velocity of magnitude $v = 6$ m/s towards right, whereas speed of B and C is zero. At the instant, block A has covered a distance L relative to block B velocity of all blocks are same. If heat dissipated due to friction in the system is H, find value of $\frac{H}{\mu}$ in joule.

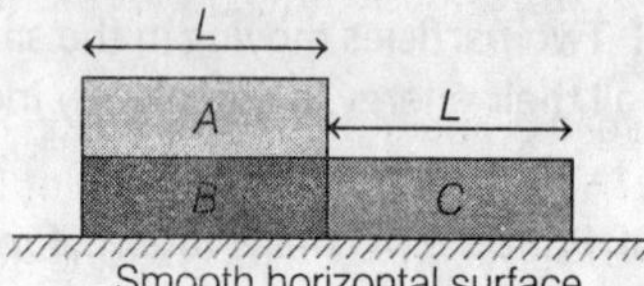

23. A rod AB is fixed between a vertical wall and a horizontal surface. A smooth bead of mass $(\sqrt{3} - 1)$ kg constrained to move along the rod is released in the position shown in the figure, for which the spring is vertical and relaxed. The natural length of the spring is $(2 + 2\sqrt{3})$ m. Rod makes an angle of 30° with the horizontal. The bead again comes to rest when spring makes an angle of 30° with the vertical. Determine spring constant (in N/m). (Take, $g = 10 \text{ ms}^{-2}$)

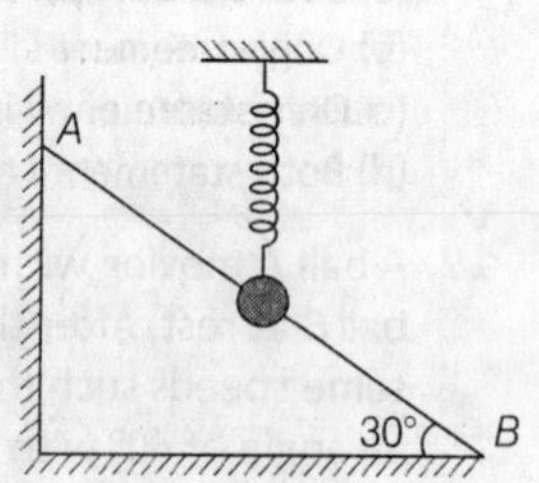

24. Power supplied by a force acting on a particle (initially at origin and at rest) moving along X-axis is constant. As x of the particle increases from $x = 1$ to $x = 8$, its kinetic energy becomes n times. Find n.

25. A smooth ball is dropped on to a smooth hemisphere (of same mass) placed on smooth horizontal surface. The ball collides elastically with the hemisphere at a point and is observed to move horizontally after collision. Consider a vertical line passing through centre of the sphere. If angular position of the point of collision with respect to the line is $\theta = \cot^{-1}\sqrt{x}$, find x.

Answers

Section I

1	(b)	2	(a)	3	(b)	4	(b)	5	(d)
6	(d)	7	(d)	8	(b)	9	(c)	10	(d)
11	(c)	12	(c)	13	(b)	14	(d)	15	(d)
16	(b)	17	(b)	18	(a)	19	(c)	20	(d)

Section II

21	8	22	10	23	2.5	24	4	25	2

See detailed explanations on page no. 210

QUALIFIER 05

Rotational Motion

Section I *Objective Type Questions*

1. Circular discs of radius r, $\sqrt{2}r$ and $2r$ are taken out of a uniform large disc as shown.

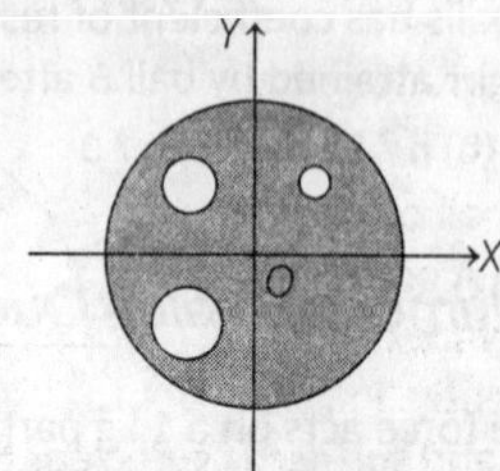

If respective position vectors of centres of the discs are **a**, **b** and **c**, which of the following relations is to be correct for centre of mass of the remaining disc to be at centre O (origin) of the original disc?

(a) $\mathbf{a} + \sqrt{2}\mathbf{b} + 2\mathbf{c} = 0$ (b) $\mathbf{a} + \sqrt{2}\mathbf{b} = 2\mathbf{c}$

(c) $\mathbf{a} + 2\mathbf{b} + 4\mathbf{c} = 0$ (d) $\mathbf{a} + 2\mathbf{b} = 4\mathbf{c}$

2. A uniform rod of length L and mass M rests on horizontal frictionless table. A particle of equal mass M is moving along the X-axis at a speed v_0. At time $t = 0$, the particle strikes one end of the rod and sticks to it. Consider (particle + rod) as combined system. The position $\mathbf{R}_{CM}$ of centre of mass of system as a function of time is

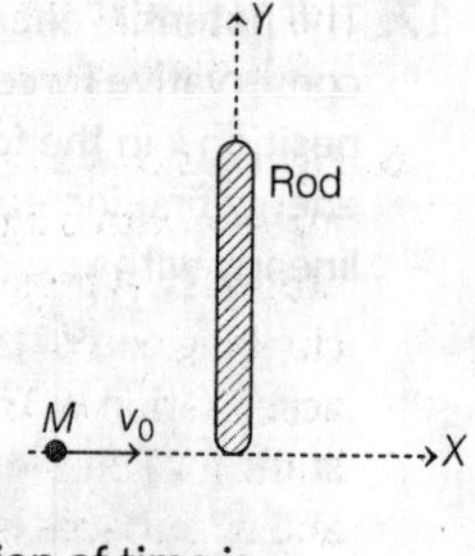

(a) $\frac{v_0}{2}t\,\hat{\mathbf{i}} + \frac{L}{4}\hat{\mathbf{j}}$ (b) $\frac{v_0}{2}t\,\hat{\mathbf{i}} + \frac{L}{2}\hat{\mathbf{j}}$

(c) $v_0 t\,\hat{\mathbf{i}} + \frac{L}{2}\hat{\mathbf{j}}$ (d) $v_0 t\,\hat{\mathbf{i}} + \frac{L}{4}\hat{\mathbf{j}}$

3. Two beads each of mass m are fixed on a light rigid rod of length $2l$ which is free to rotate in a horizontal plane. The bead on the far end is given some velocity v as shown in the figure. If K_{CM} represents the kinetic energy of the centre of mass of the system and K_R represents the rotational kinetic energy of the system, then what is the value of $\frac{K_{CM}}{K_R}$?

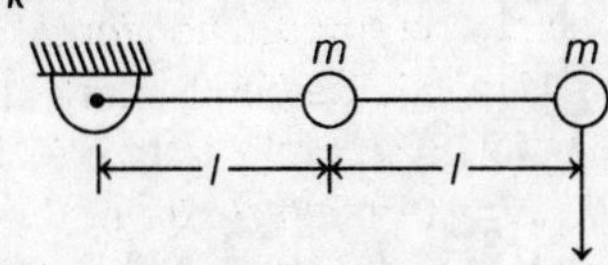

(a) 1.1 (b) 0.9
(c) 2 (d) 0.5

4. A uniform hollow sphere of radius R is melted and casted into a hollow cylinder of same radius R and length L.

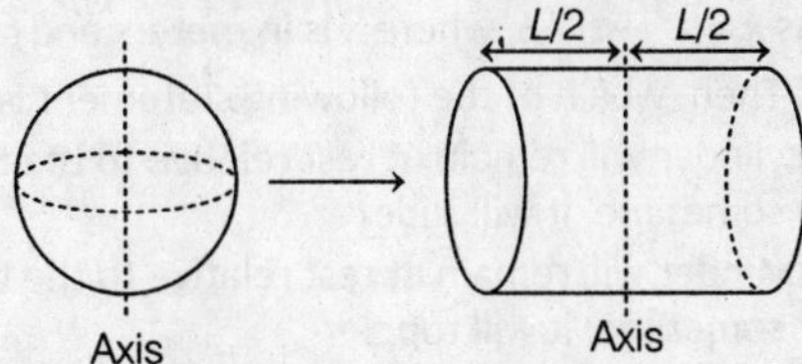

If moment of inertia of the two bodies are equal about the shown axes, radius of gyration of the cylinder about the shown axis is

(a) $\sqrt{\frac{2}{3}}L$ (b) $\frac{L}{\sqrt{3}}$
(c) L (d) $\frac{L}{2\sqrt{3}}$

5. A particle falls freely near the surface of the earth. Consider a fixed point O (not vertically below the particle) on the ground. Choose the **incorrect** alternative for motion of the particle before hitting the ground.

(a) Angular momentum of the particle about O is increasing.
(b) The angular velocity of the particle about O is increasing.
(c) The moment of inertia of the particle about O is decreasing.
(d) Torque of the gravitational force on the particle about O is decreasing.

6. Figure shows a uniform cylinder of mass m with a light rope wrapped around it. A person of mass $m/4$ is climbing end of the rope with acceleration a. The coefficient of static friction between the cylinder and all surfaces is 0.5. Maximum value of a with which a person can climb the rope without causing the cylinder to rotate is

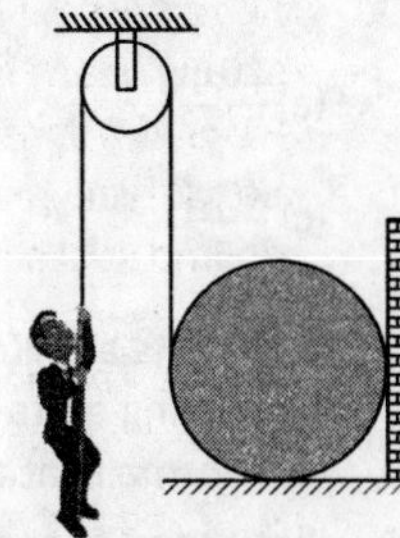

(a) g (b) $0.7g$ (c) $0.5g$ (d) $0.3g$

7. A spool of mass M and radius $2R$ lies on an inclined plane as shown in figure. A light thread is wound around the connecting tube of the spool and its free end carries a weight of mass m. The value of m, so that system is in equilibrium is

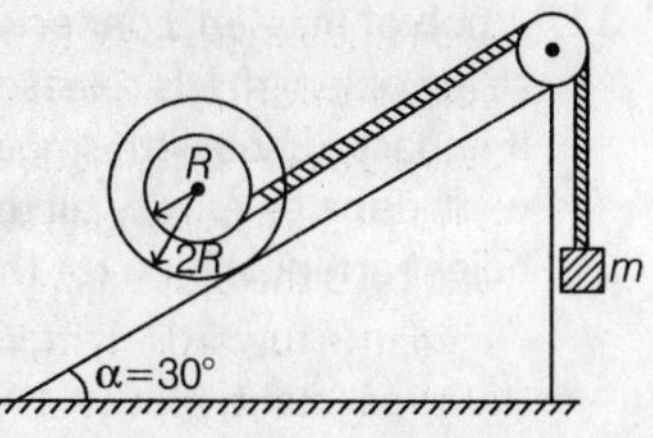

(a) M (b) $2M$ (c) $0.5M$ (d) $\frac{\sqrt{3}}{2}M$

8. A uniform solid cylinder of mass $m = 1$ kg, radius $R = 3$ m and length $l = 2$ m is on a rough surface. It is pulled by a constant horizontal force $F = 12$ N acting at top of the cylinder on one end as shown in the figure. The cylinder rolls without slipping. Acceleration of centre of mass of the sphere (in m/s^2) and net torque of friction (in N-m) about centre of mass respectively are

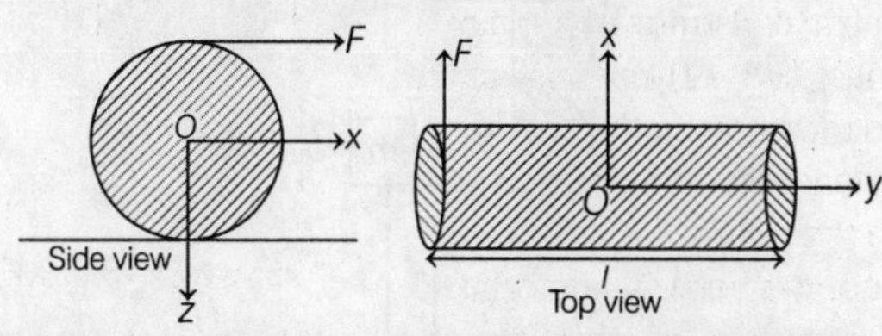

(a) $16\hat{i}, 12\hat{j} + 12\hat{k}$ (b) $8\hat{i}, 12\hat{j} - 12\hat{k}$
(c) $16\hat{i}, 12\hat{j} - 12\hat{k}$ (d) $8\hat{i}, 12\hat{j} + 12\hat{k}$

9.

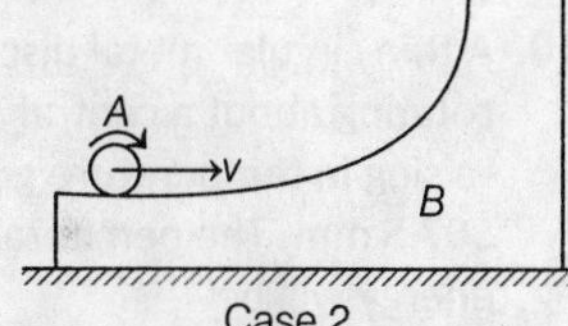

In the case 1 shown, a ring A is rolling without sliding with a velocity v on the horizontal surface of the body B (of same mass as A). All surfaces are smooth. B has no initial velocity. Maximum height reached by A on B is h. If there was sufficient friction between A and B to prevent slipping while the ground is still smooth (case 2), maximum height reached by A on B would be

(a) h (b) $2h$ (c) $3h$ (d) $4h$

10. Consider the arrangement shown in figure.

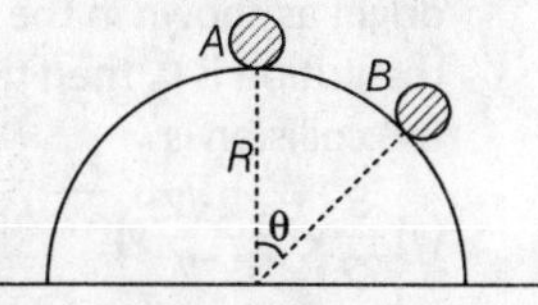

A small solid ball of mass m initially at top A of a fixed cylindrical surface of radius R is pushed gently. Friction between ball and surface is sufficient to prevent slipping. Kinetic energy of the ball at point B, where it leaves contact with the cylindrical surface, is

(a) $\frac{7mgR}{17}$ (b) $\frac{10mgR}{17}$ (c) $\frac{13mgR}{17}$ (d) $\frac{mgR}{3}$

11. A bob of mass m, connected to the end of an inextensible string of length l, is released from position shown in figure. If impact of bob with smooth floor is perfectly inelastic, work done by gravity till the bob acquires maximum height after collision for the first time is

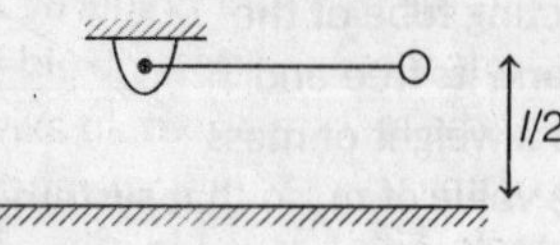

(a) $\frac{mgl}{4}$ (b) $\frac{3\,mgl}{8}$ (c) $\frac{15\,mgl}{32}$ (d) zero

12. A block of mass m is attached to one end of a light string which is wrapped on a disc of mass $2m$ and radius R. The total length of the slack portion of the string is l. The block is released from rest. The velocity of the block just after the string becomes taut is

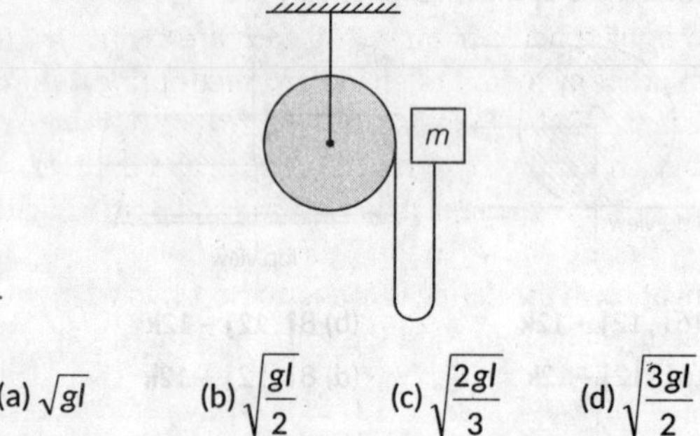

(a) $\sqrt{gl}$ (b) $\sqrt{\frac{gl}{2}}$ (c) $\sqrt{\frac{2gl}{3}}$ (d) $\sqrt{\frac{3gl}{2}}$

13. A thin circular metal disc of the radius 500 mm is set rotating about a central axis normal to its plane. Upon raising in temperature gradually, the radius increases to 507.5 mm. The percentage change in the rotational kinetic energy will be

(a) 1.5% (b) −1.5%
(c) 3% (d) −3%

14. A small smooth disc of mass m and radius r moving with an initial velocity v along the positive X-axis collided with a big disc of mass $2m$ and radius $2r$ which was initially at rest with its centre at origin as shown in the figure. If the coefficient of restitution is 0, then the velocity of the larger disc after the collision is

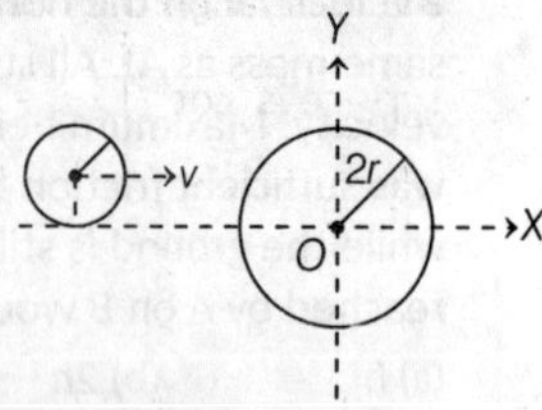

(a) $\frac{8}{27}v\hat{i}-\frac{2\sqrt{2}}{27}v\hat{j}$ (b) $\frac{8}{27}v\hat{i}-\frac{\sqrt{2}}{27}v\hat{j}$

(c) $\frac{v}{3}\hat{i}$ (d) $\frac{2\sqrt{2}}{27}v\hat{i}-\frac{8}{27}v\hat{j}$

15. A solid cylindrical roller of mass m is moving without slipping in contact with two planks as shown. If velocities of the two masses in the arrangement are as shown, kinetic energy of the roller is

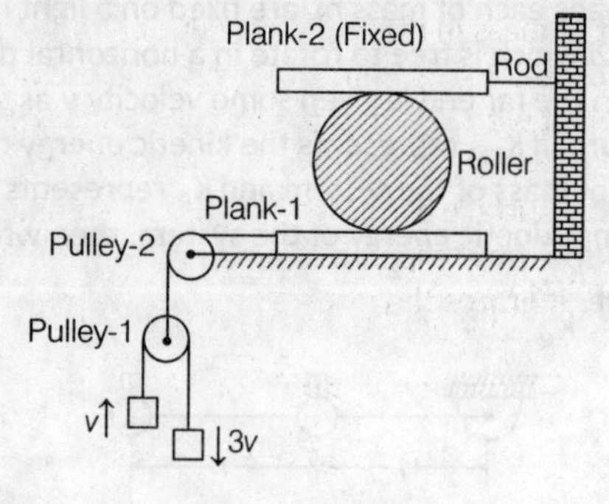

(a) $\frac{3}{8}mv^2$ (b) $\frac{3}{16}mv^2$ (c) $\frac{3}{4}mv^2$ (d) zero

16. A solid cylinder of diameter 1m and height 4m is placed on a truck. The coefficient of friction between truck and cylinder is $\mu = 0.4$.

The truck is moving such that its displacement (x) varies with time (t) as $x = (t^3 + t)/6$, where x is in meters and t is in seconds. Then, which of the following statement is correct?

(a) The cylinder will remain at rest relative to the truck and after sometime, it will slide.

(b) The cylinder will remain at rest relative to the truck and after sometime, it will topple.

(c) The cylinder start sliding and after sometime, it will topple.

(d) The cylinder will neither slide nor topple relative to the truck.

17. A rod of mass m is held between 4 discs each of mass $M = 0.4m$, as shown. Vertical reaction on any of the discs by the support, immediately after the rod has been released from rest, is (Assume that the normal forces exerted on the discs are sufficient to prevent any slipping and the discs are attached to the fixed supports on wall)

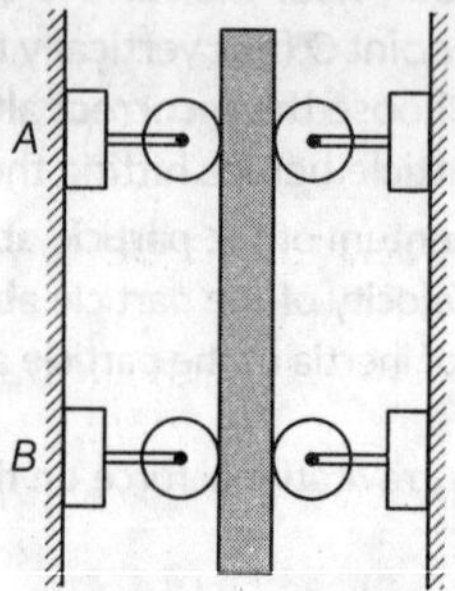

(a) $\frac{10mg}{9}$ (b) $\frac{23mg}{45}$

(c) $\frac{2mg}{5}$ (d) $\frac{mg}{9}$

18. A ball hits a uniform vertical rod AB of length l held at rest by holding at its upper end A by a man. The ball hits the rod normally at C.

If the man experiences no jerk at its hand, distance AC is equal to

(a) $\frac{l}{2}$ (b) $\frac{l}{3}$ (c) $\frac{l}{6}$ (d) $\frac{2l}{3}$

19. A bullet of mass m moving with velocity v_0 just grazes (bullet ceases to slip immediately slip on the disc during the contact with the disc) the top of a uniform circular disc of mass $M = 8m/3$ and radius R resting on a rough horizontal surface as shown in figure. Assuming that the disc rolls without slipping, find the velocity of the bullet just after it grazes the disc.

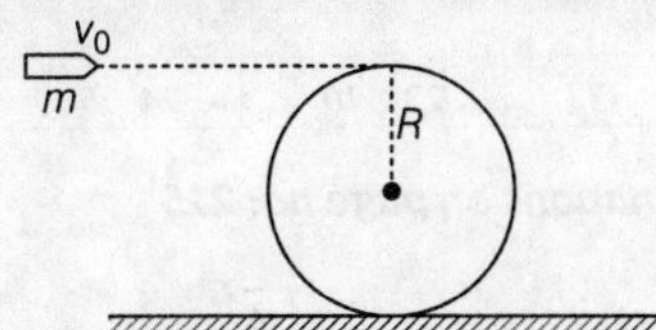

(a) $\frac{v_0}{2}$ (b) $\frac{v_0}{4}$

(c) $\frac{3v_0}{8}$ (d) $\frac{v_0}{8}$

20. A thin hollow spherical shell of mass m and radius r is set into pure rolling on a rough horizontal surface with its centre of mass having velocity v initially as shown. Work done by the upper hemispherical portion (shaded in the figure shown) on the lower hemispherical portion, as the sphere displaces by πr, is

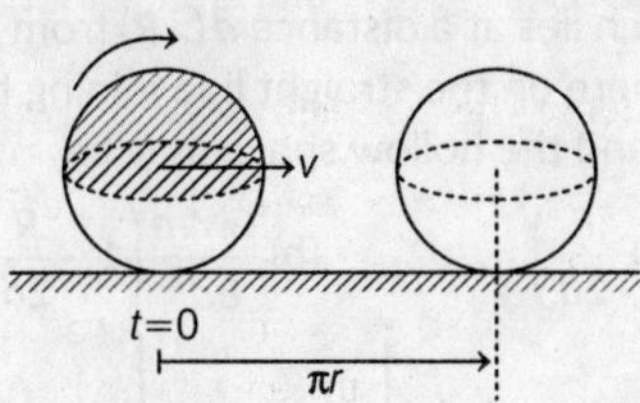

(a) $\frac{1}{2}mv^2 + \frac{mgr}{2}$ (b) $\frac{1}{2}mv^2 + mgr$

(c) $\frac{1}{3}mv^2 + mgr$ (d) $\frac{1}{3}mv^2 - mgr$

Section II *Numerical Value Questions*

21. A hemispherical cavity of radius R is created in a solid sphere of radius $2R$ as shown in the figure. The y-coordinate of the centre of mass of the remaining sphere is $-\frac{R}{x}$. Find the value of x.

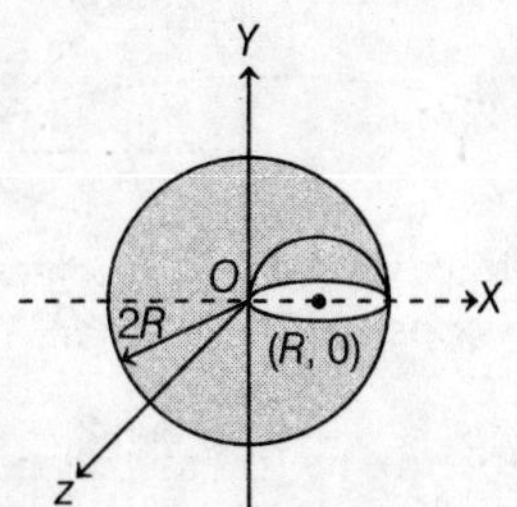

22. Three solid spheres each of mass m and diameter d are stuck together such that the lines connecting the centres form an equilateral triangle of side length d. $\frac{I_0}{I_A}$ is $\frac{n}{23}$, where I_0 is the moment of inertia of the system about an axis passing through the centroid and I_A is the moment of inertia of the system about an axis passing through the centre of any sphere and perpendicular to the plane of the triangle. Find the value of n.

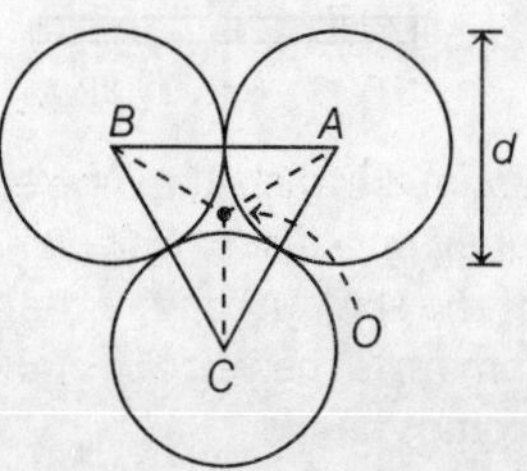

23. Two small spheres of mass 2 kg each are connected to each other by means of an undeformed spring of force constant 175 N/m and natural length 1 m. The system is placed on a smooth horizontal surface and the two spheres are given velocities v_0 along and perpendicular to the spring, as shown in the figure. The maximum elongation in the spring is found to be 1 m during the subsequent motion. Find the value of v_0 in m/s.

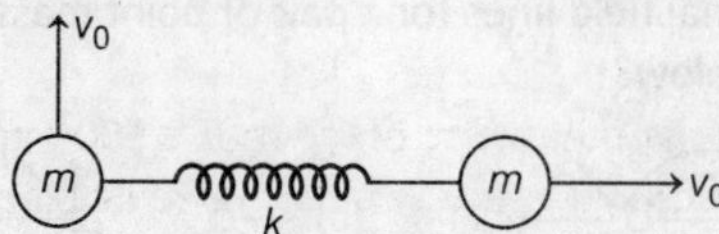

24. A thin uniform equilateral plate rests in a vertical plane with one of its vertex A on a rough horizontal floor and another vertex B on a smooth vertical wall. If the coefficient of friction between plate and floor is μ, then the least angle θ its base AB can make with the horizontal surface is $\cot^{-1}\left[x\mu + \frac{1}{\sqrt{y}}\right]$. Find $x + y$

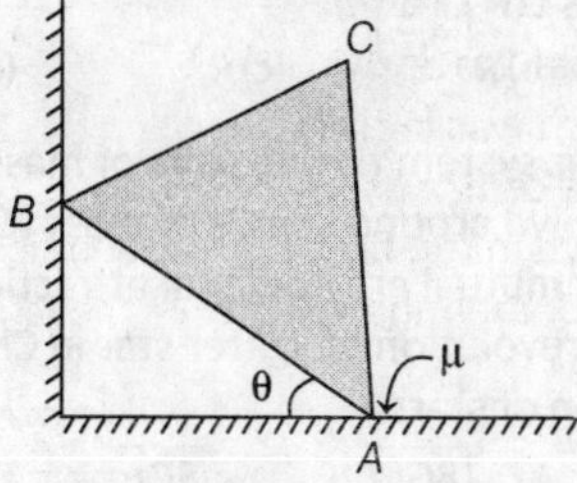

25. The toy-top (initially at rest) shown in the figure, has a moment of inertia 4×10^{-4} kg-m^2 and it is free to rotate about the stationary axis AA'. The string wrapped around the peg of the toytop is pulled outwards without letting it slip and simultaneously maintaining a constant tension of 5.625 N. If ω is the angular speed (in rad s^{-1}) of the top after 80 cm of string has been pulled off the peg, then mark your answer as $\frac{\omega}{10}$.

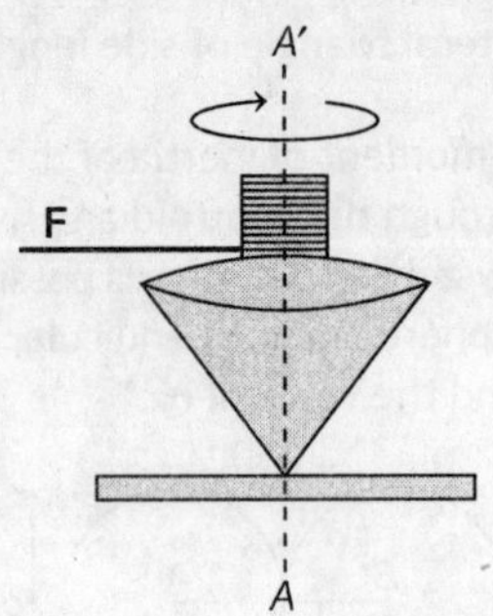

Answers

Section I

1 *(c)*	2 *(a)*	3 *(b)*	4 *(b)*	5 *(d)*
6 *(c)*	7 *(a)*	8 *(c)*	9 *(c)*	10 *(a)*
11 *(c)*	12 *(b)*	13 *(d)*	14 *(a)*	15 *(b)*
16 *(b)*	17 *(b)*	18 *(d)*	19 *(a)*	20 *(a)*

Section II

21 *40*	22 *13*	23 *10*	24 *5*	25 *15*

See detailed explanations on page no. 215

QUALIFIER 06

Gravitation

Section I *Objective Type Questions*

1. Which of the following diagrams correctly represents the gravitational field lines for a pair of point masses shown in options below?

(a) 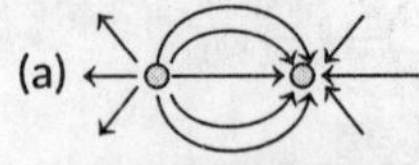 (b) 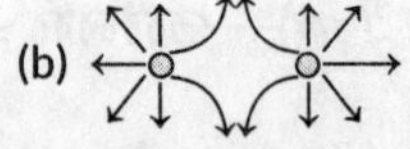

(c)  (d)

2. Suppose the gravitational force varies inversely as the *n*th power of distance, then the time period of a planet in circular orbit of radius *R* around the sun will be proportional to

(a) $R^{\left(\frac{n+1}{2}\right)}$ (b) $R^{\left(\frac{n-1}{2}\right)}$ (c) R^n (d) $R^{\left(\frac{n-2}{2}\right)}$

3. In a binary star system having stars of mass *m* and 8*m*, the two stars revolve around centre of mass (CM) of the system under mutual gravitational attraction. Angular frequency of revolution of lighter star in CM frame is (r = separation of stars)

(a) $\sqrt{\frac{Gm}{r^3}}$ (b) $\sqrt{\frac{8Gm}{r^3}}$ (c) $\sqrt{\frac{9Gm}{r^3}}$ (d) $\sqrt{\frac{8Gm}{9r^3}}$

4. A spherical hollow space is made in a lead sphere of radius *R* such that its surface touches the outside surface of the lead sphere and passes through the centre. The mass of the lead sphere before hollowing was *M*. The force of attraction that this sphere would exert on a particle of mass *m* which lies at a distance $d\,(>R)$ from the centre of the lead sphere on the straight line joining the centres of the sphere and the hollow space may be

(a) $\frac{GMm}{d^2}\left(1+\frac{R}{2d}\right)^2$ (b) $\frac{GMm}{8d^2}\left(1-\frac{R}{2d}\right)^2$

(c) $\frac{GMm}{d^2}\left[1+\frac{1}{8\left(1+\frac{R}{2d}\right)}\right]$ (d) $\frac{GMm}{d^2}\left[1-\frac{1}{8\left(1-\frac{R}{2d}\right)^2}\right]$

5. In an imaginary situation, consider earth to be moving in a circular orbit of radius *R* (equal to astronomical unit) under influence of two suns (having masses same as that of sun in our solar system) distant 2*R* from earth. Time period of earth in this imaginary situation is equal to (T = actual earth period)

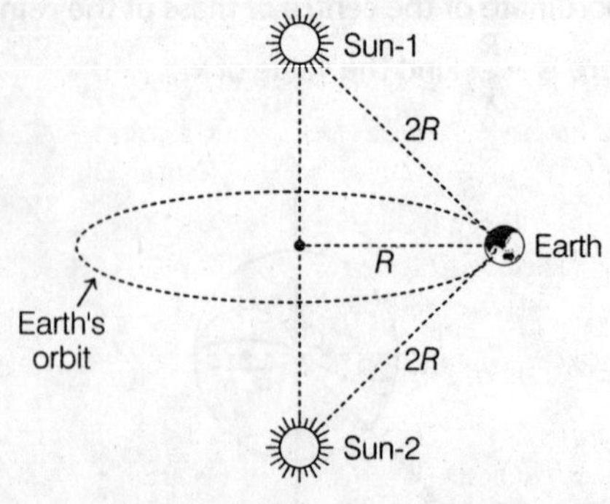

(a) T (b) $2T$ (c) $\sqrt{2}T$ (d) $4T$

6. If the radius of the earth were to shrink by 1% while its mass remaining same, the acceleration due to gravity on the earth's surface would

(a) decrease by 2% (b) remain unchanged
(c) increase by 2% (d) become zero

7. A body of mass m hanging from a spring stretches it to a spring of potential energy E at earth's surface. Potential energy to which the spring is stretched, if the arrangement is at height R above earth's surface, is

(a) $\frac{E}{2}$ (b) $\frac{E}{4}$ (c) $\frac{E}{16}$ (d) E

8. The shown planet is made up of two materials of density σ (for $0 \le r \le R$) and ρ (for $R < r \le R'$). Given that $3\sigma = 7\rho$, the value of $\frac{R'}{R}$ for acceleration due to gravity to be exactly equal at the surface of the planet and interface of the two materials may be

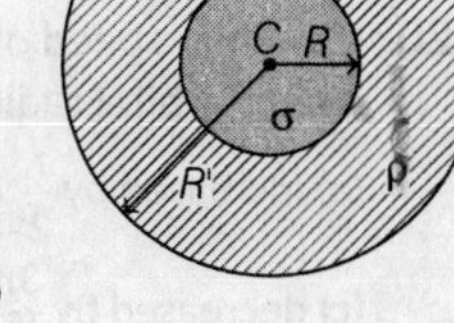

(a) 2 (b) 3
(c) 4 (d) 5

9. A pan balance in a room has a light rod AB pivoted at its centre O. The two light identical pans are connected to ends A and B by light strings of lengths l and $2l$, respectively.

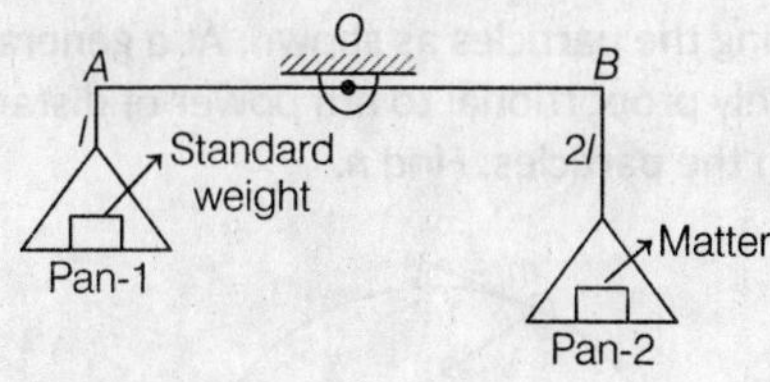

Matter to be weighed (actual mass m) is placed in pan-2 as shown. Error in measurement of mass is (Take, R = radius of earth and g = acceleration due to gravity at earth's surface)

(a) $\frac{2ml}{R}$ (b) $\frac{ml}{R}$ (c) $\frac{2mR}{l}$ (d) $\frac{mR}{l}$

10. A particle is released at the end A of a small tube AB of length h along a thin diametrical tunnel inside earth. Time taken by the particle to reach end B is t. Approximate time for the particle to reach centre C of the earth is

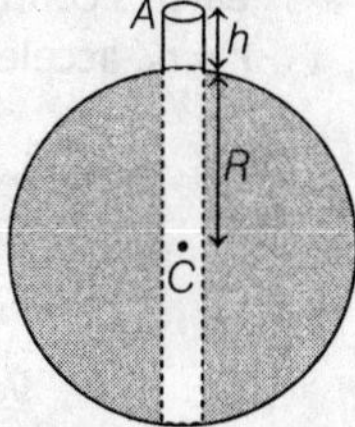

(R = radius of earth)

(a) $\pi\sqrt{\frac{R}{h}}t$ (b) $\pi\sqrt{\frac{R}{8h}}t$

(c) $\frac{\pi}{2\sqrt{2}}\sqrt{\frac{h}{R}}t$ (d) $\frac{tR}{h}$

11. If gravitational field due to shown uniform hemispherical shell at point P is I, then the magnitude of gravitational field at Q is (Mass of hemispherical shell is M and radius is R)

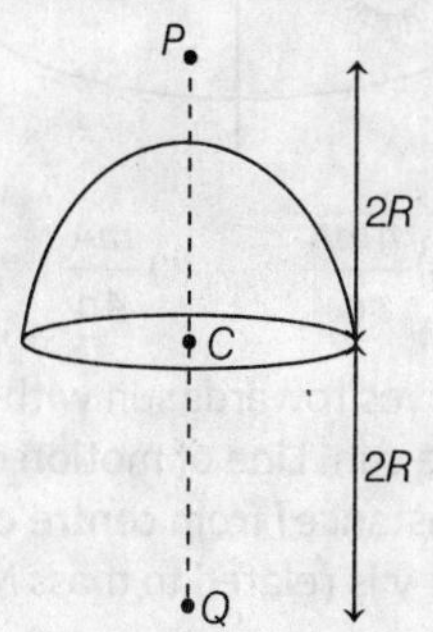

(a) $\frac{GM}{2R^2} - I$ (b) $\frac{GM}{2R^2} + I$ (c) $\frac{GM}{4R} - I$ (d) $2I - \frac{GM}{2R^2}$

12. Gravitational potential at centre O of the shell is (Given that, $\theta = \tan^{-1}\frac{1}{2}$)

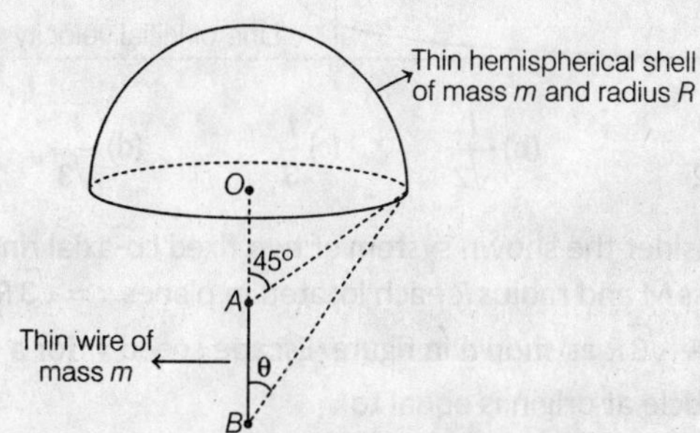

(a) $-\frac{Gm}{R}\ln 2$ (b) $-\frac{Gm}{R}(1 + \ln 2)$

(c) $-\frac{Gm}{R}\left(\frac{1 + \ln 4}{2}\right)$ (d) $-\frac{Gm}{R^2}(1 + \ln 2)$

13. The potential energy of gravitational interaction of a point mass m and a thin uniform rod of mass M and length l, if they are located along a straight line with nearer end of the rod at distance a from the point mass is

(a) $U = \frac{GMm}{a}\log_e\left(\frac{a+l}{a}\right)$ (b) $U = GMm\left(\frac{1}{a} - \frac{1}{a+l}\right)$

(c) $U = -\frac{GMm}{l}\log_e\left(\frac{a+l}{a}\right)$ (d) $U = -\frac{GMm}{a}$

14. If Newton's law of gravitation was not an inverse square law, which of the following Kepler's laws of planetary motion would still be valid?

(a) First law or Law of orbits (b) Second law or Law of areas
(c) Third law or Law of periods (d) None of these

15. A planet of mass m moves around the sun in an elliptical orbit of eccentricity $e = \frac{\sqrt{3}}{2}$ and semi-major axis a. If areal speed of the planet at position P is A, its momentum in position Q is

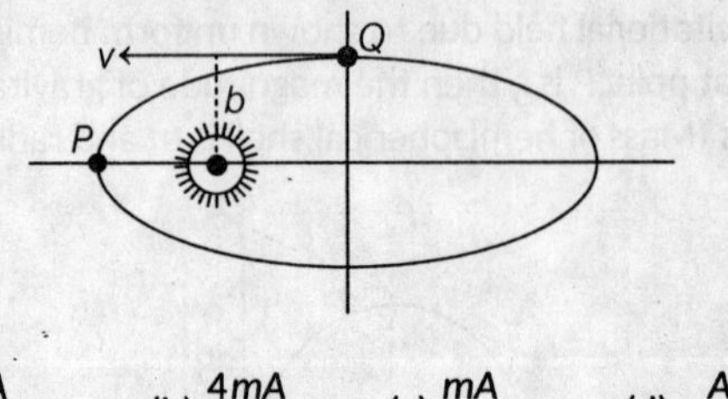

(a) $\frac{mA}{2}$ (b) $\frac{4mA}{a}$ (c) $\frac{mA}{4a}$ (d) $\frac{A}{4ma}$

16. A comet at P moves towards sun with velocity v, when it is very far from the sun. Line of motion of the comet is at a perpendicular distance l from centre of the sun at position P. It is given that v is related to mass M of sun as $v^2 = \frac{\sqrt{3}GM}{l}$. Minimum separation at Q, between the comet and the sun, is

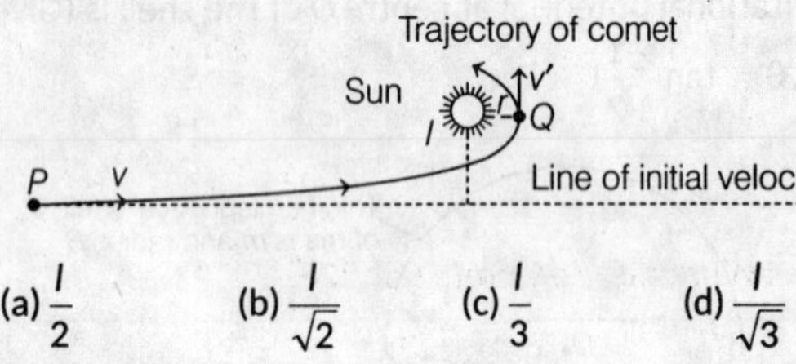

(a) $\frac{l}{2}$ (b) $\frac{l}{\sqrt{2}}$ (c) $\frac{l}{3}$ (d) $\frac{l}{\sqrt{3}}$

17. Consider the shown system of two fixed co-axial rings of mass M and radius R each located in planes $x = \sqrt{3}R$ and $x = -\sqrt{3}R$ as shown in figure. Escape speed v for a particle at origin is equal to

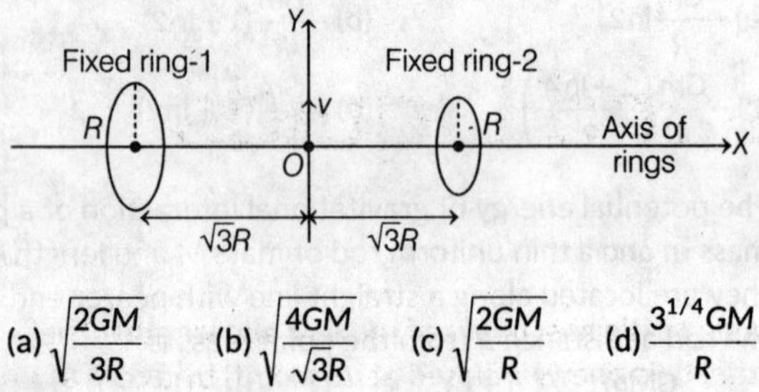

(a) $\sqrt{\frac{2GM}{3R}}$ (b) $\sqrt{\frac{4GM}{\sqrt{3}R}}$ (c) $\sqrt{\frac{2GM}{R}}$ (d) $\sqrt{\frac{3^{1/4}GM}{R}}$

18. A satellite is moving around the earth in a circular orbit and in this orbit magnitude of its acceleration is a_1. Now, a rocket is fired in the direction of motion of satellite from the satellite due to which its speed instantaneously becomes half of initial, just after the rocket is fired and acceleration of satellite has magnitude a_2. Then the ratio $\frac{a_1}{a_2}$ is (Assume there is no external force other than the gravitational force of earth before and after the firing of rocket from the satellite)

(a) 1 (b) 2 (c) 0.5 (d) 0.25

19. A satellite is orbiting around the earth in a circular orbit with orbital speed half of escape speed at earth's surface. If it is suddenly stopped in position P, it strikes earth's surface at Q with kinetic energy K. If instead it is provided energy, such that its energy is increased by K in position S it escapes to point T very far from earth's surface. Kinetic energy of the satellite at T is

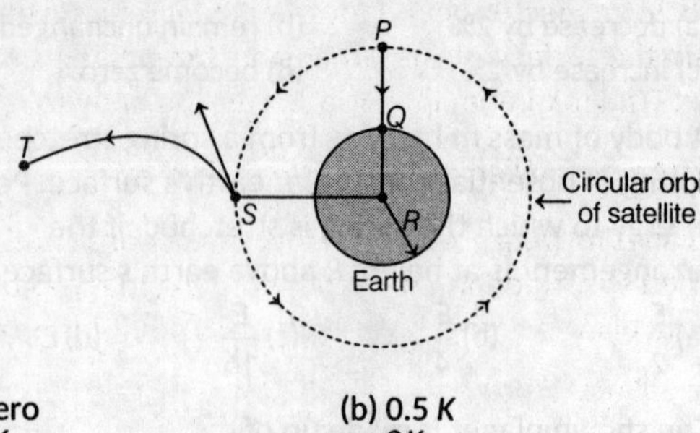

(a) zero (b) 0.5 K
(c) $\frac{K}{\sqrt{2}}$ (d) $\frac{2K}{3}$

20. If angular speed of earth becomes 8 times in a natural event, orbital radius r of a geo-stationary planet has to be

(a) increased by $\frac{r}{2}$ (b) decreased by $\frac{r}{2}$
(c) decreased by $\frac{3r}{4}$ (d) increased by $\frac{r}{4}$

Section II *Numerical Value Questions*

21. A particle of mass m is moving on a circle under influence of gravity of another fixed particle of mass M as shown. Assume that, gravitational force F between the particles may not follow inverse square law but is directed along line joining the particles as shown. At a general point P, F is inversely proportional to nth power of distance r between the particles. Find n.

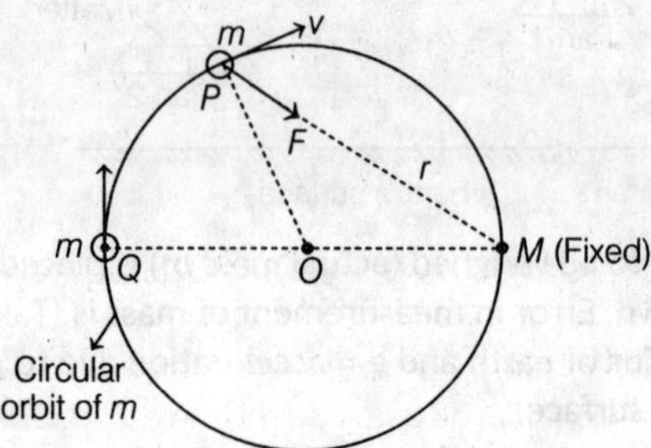

22. Acceleration due to gravity varies with distance r from earth's centre as shown by the graph here. For $r = r_1$ and $r = r_2$, accelerations due to gravity are equal as shown.

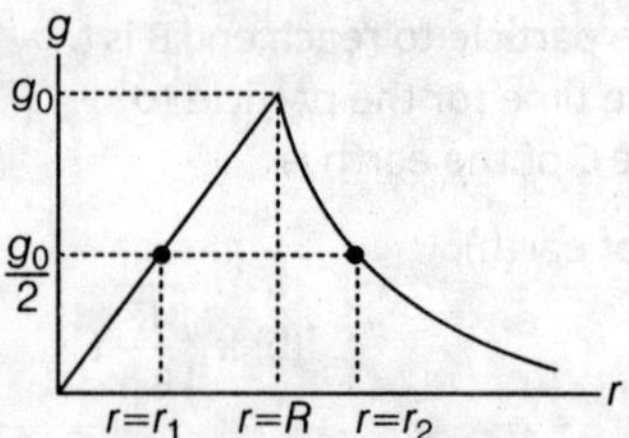

If $r_2 + r_1 = xR$, find x. Here, R is radius of earth. (Take, $\sqrt{2} = 1.41$)

23. Distance between the centres of two stars is $10a$. The masses of these stars are M and $16M$ and their radii are a and $2a$, respectively. A body of mass m is fired straight from the surface of the larger star towards the smaller star. The minimum initial speed for the body to reach the surface of smaller star is $\frac{3}{2}\sqrt{\frac{kGM}{a}}$. Find k.

24. A planet moving around sun in a circular orbit with time period T is suddenly stopped. Assuming that orbital radius of the planet is far greater than solar radius, time taken by the planet to strike sun is $\frac{T}{2^x}$. Find x.

25. In a solar system having three planets, $\log R$ is plotted against $\log T$. Here, R and T represent circular orbit radius in metre and time period of revolution in seconds, respectively. The graph is as shown with y-intercept equal to 7. Mass of sun in this system is $a \times 10^b$ kg, find $\frac{b}{a}$.

(Here, $1 \le a \le 10$)

(Take, $\pi^2 = 10$ and $G = \frac{20}{3} \times 10^{-11}$ Nm^2 kg^{-2})

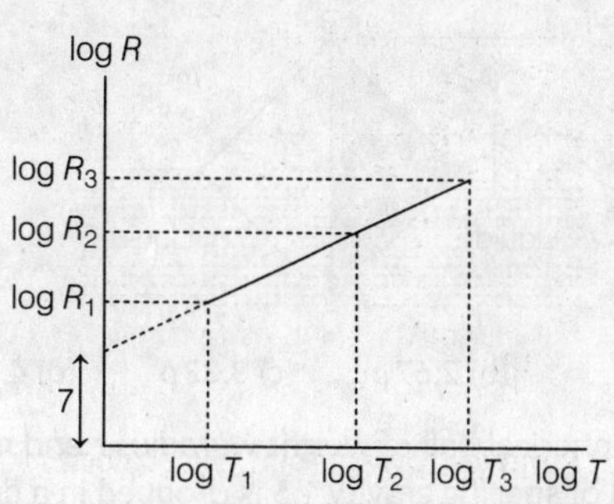

Answers

Section I

1 (c)	2 (a)	3 (c)	4 (d)	5 (b)
6 (c)	7 (c)	8 (a)	9 (a)	10 (b)
11 (a)	12 (b)	13 (c)	14 (b)	15 (b)
16 (d)	17 (c)	18 (a)	19 (b)	20 (c)

Section II

21 5	22 1.91	23 5	24 2.5	25 5.33

See detailed explanations on page no. 220

QUALIFIER 07

Properties of Solids and Liquids

Section I *Objective Type Questions*

1. In the arrangement shown, pulleys are ideal and strings are light. Masses of blocks A, B and C are $12m$, $3m$ and $6m$, respectively. If l, Y, A represent length, Young's modulus and cross-sectional area of string connecting A and moving pulley, then extension produced in the string is

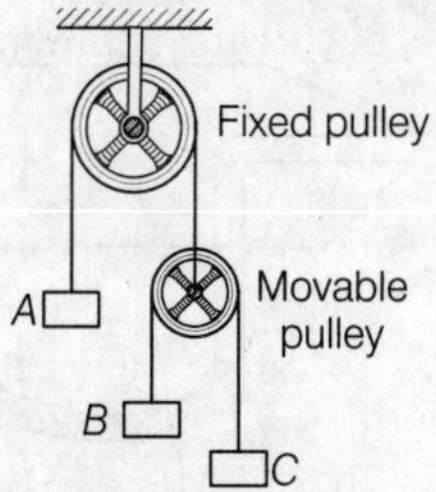

(a) $\frac{3mgl}{AY}$ (b) $\frac{48mgl}{5AY}$ (c) $\frac{4mgl}{AY}$ (d) $\frac{36mgl}{7AY}$

2. A wine bottle has mouth of radius r and length l. The bottle, being new, is closed at its mouth by a cork of radius $r + d$, where $d << r$. If compressibility of the cork's material is k, coefficient of friction between the bottle and the cork is μ, minimum pulling force needed to pull the cork out is

(a) $4\pi\mu dlK$ (b) $\frac{4\pi\mu dl}{K}$

(c) $\frac{\pi\mu dl}{4K}$ (d) $\frac{\mu dl}{K}$

3. A square plate $ABCD$ is constructed by welding together two right angled geometrically identical plates DAB and BCD of densities ρ and 2ρ, respectively. The plate is hinged at point A and can rotate in vertical plane about horizontal axis through O. If the plate is in equilibrium in the position shown such that its half ACD is immersed in a liquid, then density of the liquid is

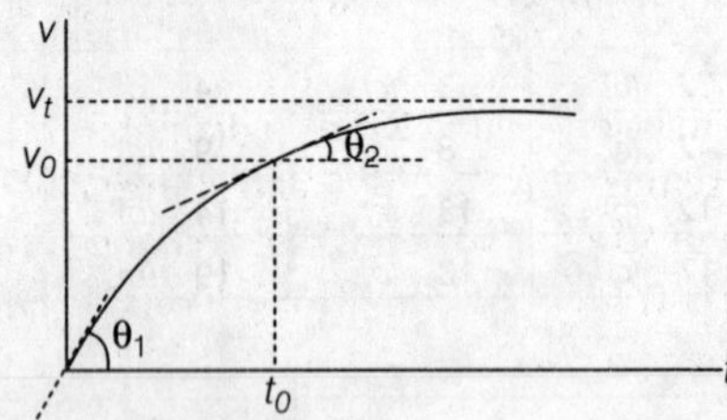

(a) 1.5 ρ (b) 2.67 ρ (c) 3.33 ρ (d) 4.5 ρ

4. A solid spherical ball of weight w, radius r and made of material of specific gravity 1.5 is dropped in a deep lake at $t = 0$. Variation of velocity of ball as function of time t is shown in graph here.

As, shown in the graph, tangents at $t = 0$ and $t = t_0$ make $\theta_1 = \tan^{-1} x$ and $\theta_2 = \tan^{-1}\frac{x}{4}$ with time axis, respectively. Also, velocity of ball at $t = t_0$ is v_0. η (coefficient of viscosity of water) is equal to

(a) $\frac{w}{18\pi r v_0}$ (b) $\frac{w}{24\pi r v_0}$ (c) $\frac{w}{6\pi r v_t}$ (d) $\frac{w}{24\pi r v_t}$

5. A liquid of density ρ is flowing in a horizontal tube of cross-sectional area a with speed v as shown. Force by bend on the liquid is

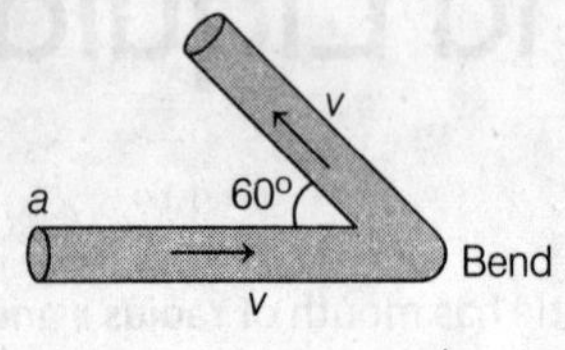

(a) zero (b) $\rho a v^2$ (c) $\sqrt{3}\rho a v^2$ (d) $\frac{\rho a v^2}{2}$

6. A circular disc of radius r is placed in contact with a thin layer (of thickness t) of highly viscous liquid of coefficient of viscosity η spread on horizontal ground. The disc is to be rotated with constant angular frequency ω, about vertical axis passing through centre of the disc. Torque required for the same is

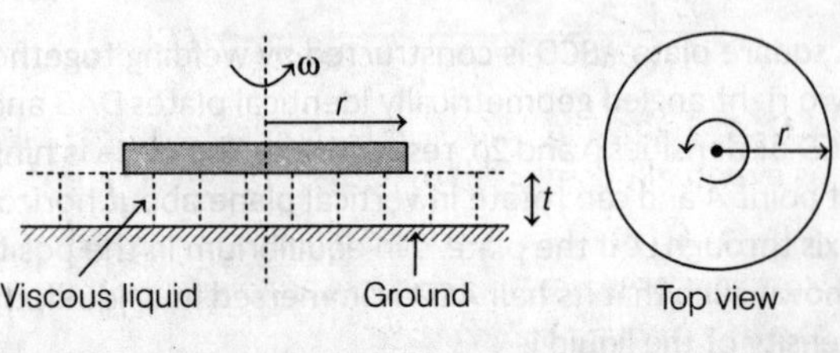

(a) $\frac{\pi\eta\omega r^4}{2t}$ (b) $\frac{\pi\eta\omega r^2}{t}$ (c) $\frac{\eta\omega r^4}{\pi t}$ (d) $\frac{\pi\eta\omega t^4}{2r}$

7. Velocity distribution of Newtonian fluid between two wide parallel plates is given by $v = v_0\left(1 - \frac{y^2}{l^2}\right)$ for $-l \le y \le l$

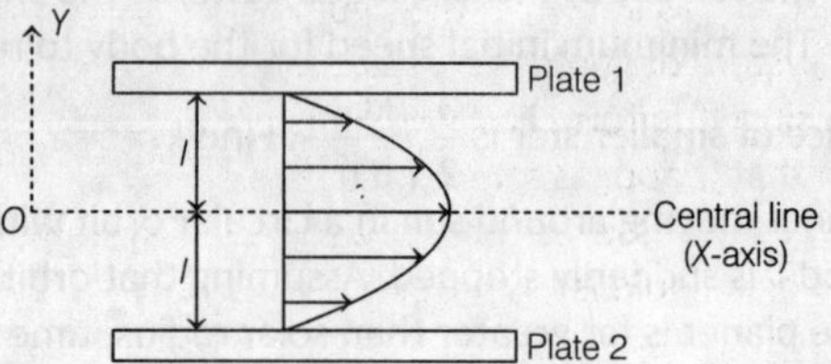

If volume flow rate per unit width between plates is Q and coefficient of viscosity of fluid is η, shear stress at $y = \frac{l}{2}$ is

(a) $\frac{\eta Q}{2l^2}$ (b) $\frac{3\eta Q v_0}{4l^2}$ (c) $\frac{\eta Q v_0}{l^2}$ (d) $\frac{3\eta Q}{4l^2}$

8. Water is gushing out of a pipe of radius $\frac{5}{\pi}$ cm at rate 100 L min^{-1}. Given that density of water is 1000 kg/m^3 and coefficient of viscosity of water is 1 mPa-s. Reynold's number for the flow is

(a) 6.67×10^4 (b) 3.33×10^4 (c) 4×10^8 (d) 2×10^8

9. A closed tube of length $3r$ filled with water is rotating with constant angular speed ω as shown, about axis XY as shown in figure. Difference in readings P_1 and P_2 of manometers A and B is (Take, ρ = density of water)

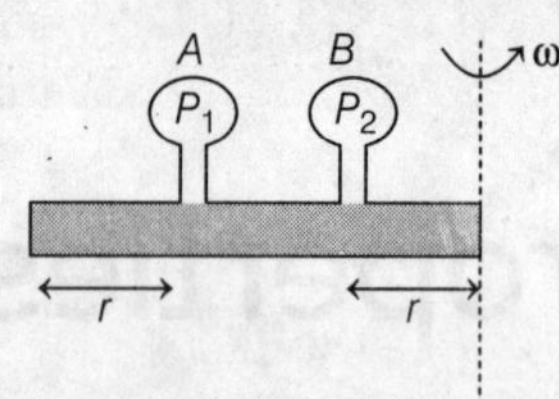

(a) $\rho\omega^2 r^2$ (b) $1.5\rho\omega^2 r^2$ (c) $3\rho\omega^2 r^2$ (d) zero

10. Difference in heights of mercury while the pitot tube shown is placed in path of wind is H. Assuming that air at inlet P of the tube is brought to rest while air speed just outside of B is unchanged, wind speed v is approximately equal to (ρ = density of mercury, σ = density of air and g = acceleration due to gravity, ρ >> σ)

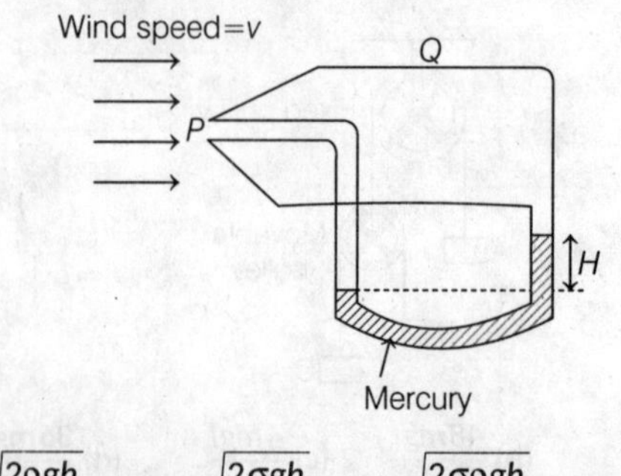

(a) $\sqrt{\frac{2\rho g h}{\sigma}}$ (b) $\sqrt{\frac{2\sigma g h}{\rho}}$ (c) $\sqrt{\frac{2\sigma\rho g h}{(\sigma + \rho)}}$ (d) $\sqrt{2gh}$

11. A tall rectangular vessel contains equal volumes (each having height H) of a series of infinite immiscible liquids of respective densities $\rho, \frac{\rho}{2}, \frac{\rho}{4}$ and so on (as shown in the figure). If this system of liquids is to be replaced by a single uniform liquid of density ρ such that it applies same force on side wall of the vessel as that applied by the system, height of the single liquid is (atmosphere is absent)

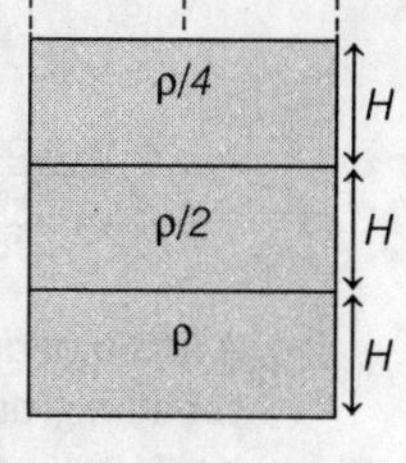

(a) $2H$ (b) $3H$
(c) $6H$ (d) infinite

12. A tank of height H filled upto top with an ideal liquid is mounted on a platform of height $\frac{H}{2}$. It is emptied through a small orifice at its bottom starting at $t = 0$ as shown. It takes time T to completely empty the tank. Liquid stream strikes the ground at point A at $t = 0$ while it strikes the ground at point B at $t = \frac{T}{2}$. $CA - CB$ is equal to (Here, C is bottom point of stand of the platform)

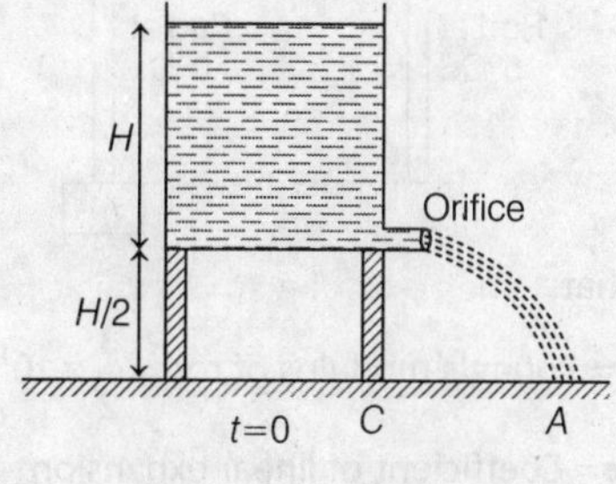

(a) H (b) $\frac{H}{\sqrt{2}}$ (c) $\sqrt{2}H$ (d) $\frac{H}{4}$

13. A thin soap bubble of radius r and thickness t collapses into a drop. This drop is now divided into 8 identical droplets by some mechanism as shown.

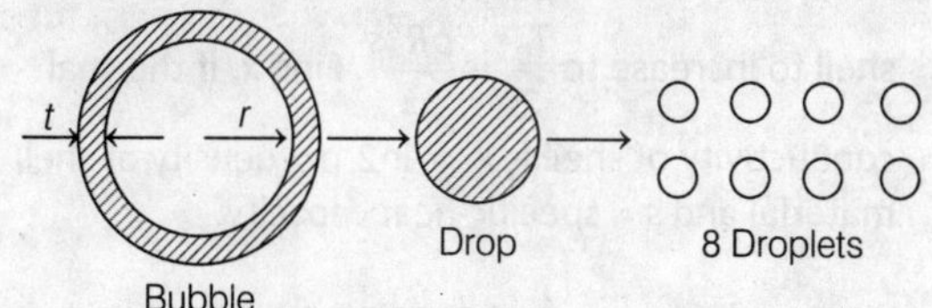

Excess pressure inside the drop formed on collapse of bubble is x times that inside the bubble while energy spent to break the drop in droplets is y times surface energy of the drop. Choose the correct pair of x and y.

(a) $x = \frac{1}{2}, y = 2$ (b) $x = \left(\frac{r}{2t}\right)^{\frac{1}{3}}, y = 1$

(c) $x = \left(\frac{r}{24t}\right)^{\frac{1}{3}}, y = 1$ (d) $x = \frac{1}{2}, y = \left(\frac{r}{2t}\right)^{\frac{1}{3}}$

14. A drop of mass m and density ρ is trapped between two glass plates separated by d. Force needed to separate the plates, to pull them apart is F (as shown). The same liquid is filled in a tank in which a capillary of radius d is in contact with the liquid surface (as shown). Length of the liquid rising in the capillary is (consider angle of contact $= 0°$)

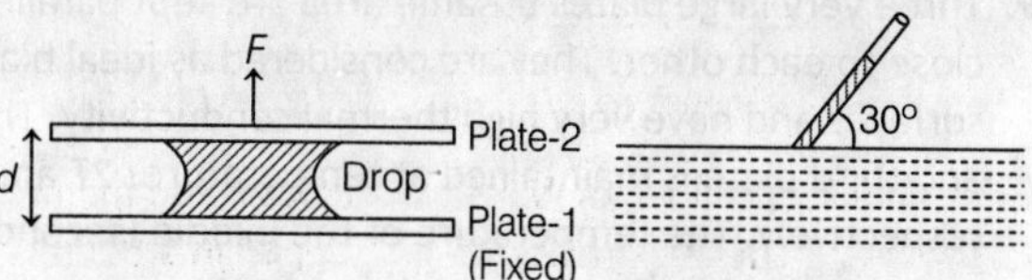

(a) $\frac{2Fd}{mg}$ (b) $\frac{Fd}{mg}$ (c) $\frac{Fd}{2mg}$ (d) d

15. A wire 3 m in length and 1 mm in diameter at 30°C is kept in a low temperature $-170°$ C and is stretched by hanging a weight of 10 kg at one end, so the change in length of the wire is ($Y = 2 \times 10^{11}$ Nm^{-2}, $g = 10$ ms^{-2} and $\alpha = 1.2 \times 10^{-5}$ °C^{-1})

(a) -5.2 mm (b) -2.5 mm (c) -52 mm (d) -25 mm

16. A vertical column whose density is 50 g cm^{-3} at 50°C balances another column of same liquid whose density is 60 g cm^{-3} at 100°C. The coefficient of cubical expansion of the liquid is

(a) 0.009/°C (b) -0.005/°C
(c) 0.001/°C (d) -0.015/°C

17. Calculate the heat required to convert 3 kg of ice at -12°C kept in a calorimeter to steam at 100°C at atmospheric pressure. Given specific heat capacity of ice is 2100 J kg^{-1} K^{-1}, specific heat capacity of water is 4186 J kg^{-1} K^{-1}, latent heat of fusion of ice is 3.35×10^5 J kg^{-1} and latent heat of steam is 2.256×10^6 J kg^{-1}.

(a) 8×10^4 J (b) 9.1×10^6 J
(c) 4×10^3 J (d) 7×10^6 J

18. p-T phase diagram for CO_2 gas is given. Which of these are correct according to p-T graph?

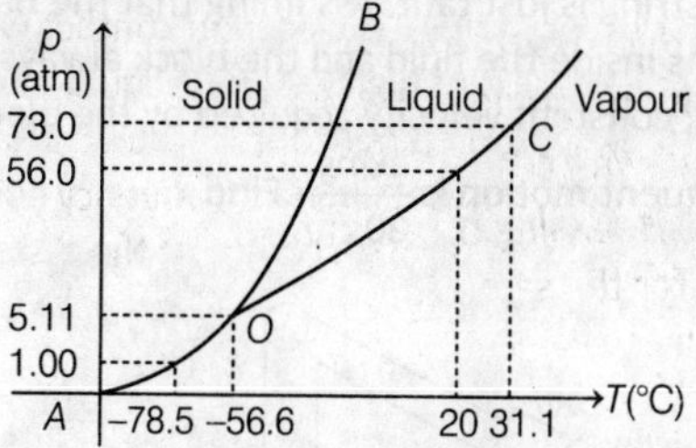

I. CO_2 at 1 atm and $-60°$ C is compressed isothermally, it is eventually converted to liquid form.

II. When CO_2 at 4 atm is cooled from room temperature at constant pressure, it is condensed to solid without passing through liquid phase.

III. CO_2 at 10 atm and $-65°C$ is heated, it turns to liquid then into vapour.

IV. CO_2 is compressed at 70°C isothermally, it becomes liquid and then solid.

(a) Both I and II (b) Both II and III
(c) Both III and IV (d) All of these

19. Three very large plates of same area are kept parallel and close to each other. They are considered as ideal black surfaces and have very high thermal conductivity. The first and third plate is maintained at temperatures $2T$ and $3T$, respectively. The temperature of the middle (second) plate under steady state condition is

(a) $\left(\frac{65}{2}\right)^{1/4} T$ (b) $\left(\frac{97}{4}\right)^{1/4} T$
(c) $\left(\frac{97}{2}\right)^{1/4} T$ (d) $(97)^{1/4} T$

20. A copper ball of radius r is surrounded by air having temperature slightly lesser than the ball. Rate of cooling of the ball is proportional to

(a) r (b) r^{-1}
(c) r^2 (d) r^{-2}

Section II Numerical Value Questions

21. A cylinder with movable piston contains air at pressure p and a soap bubble of surface tension T and radius r. The piston is slowly pushed into the cylinder thereby reducing volume of bubble to (1/8)th. Increment in pressure of air surrounding the bubble in this process is $xp + \frac{yT}{r}$. Find $\frac{y}{x}$. (Assuming temperature constant)

22. Consider the arrangement shown here, block of mass $5m$ is connected to a small spherical solid ball of mass m, radius r and density ρ by an ideal string passing over an ideal pulley. Coefficient of friction between the inclined plane and the block is 0.02. The ball is in a liquid of density $\frac{\rho}{2}$ and coefficient of viscosity η. The block is released, when string is just taut. Assuming that the ball always remains inside the fluid and the block always on the incline, constant velocity acquired by the block during subsequent motion is $\frac{xmg}{30\pi\eta r}$. Find x.

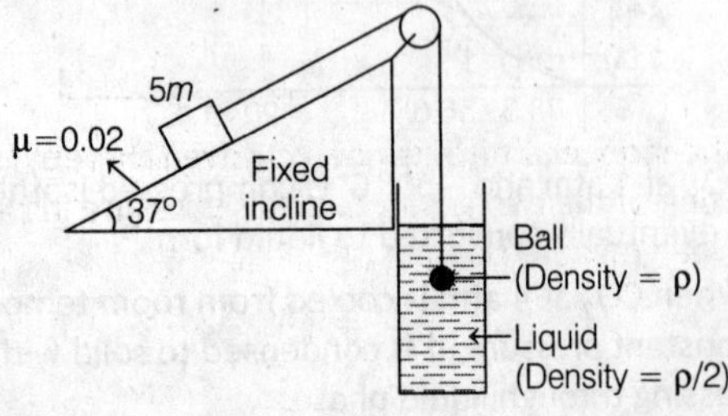

23.

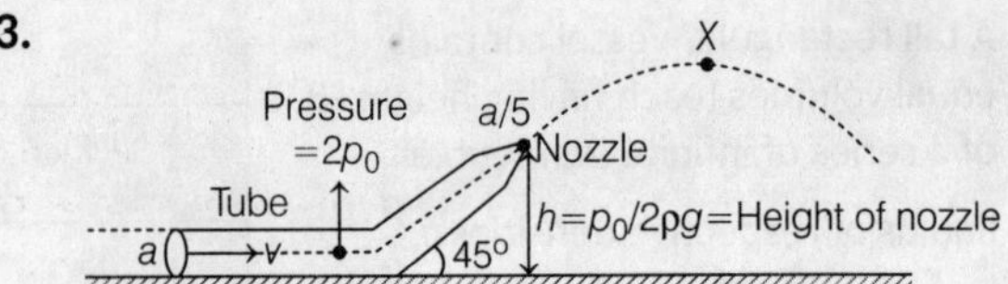

A liquid of density ρ maintained at flow velocity v in a thin tube on ground as shown having its one end with nozzle bent at 45° with horizontal. Considering cross-sectional area of nozzle (1/5)th of the cross-section area a of tube, maximum height (at X) w.r.t. ground attained by liquid particles is $\frac{\alpha h}{\beta}$. Find $\alpha - \beta$, if α and β are least possible positive integers. (p_0 = Atmospheric pressure)

24. A thin rod of negligible mass and cross-sectional area A(8 mm^2) suspended vertically has length l (1 m) at T_1(5°C). The rod is cooled to T_2 (0°C), but prevented from contracting by attaching a mass of m kg at its bottom end. Elastic potential energy stored in the rod at 0°C is U millijoule. Find $m + U$.

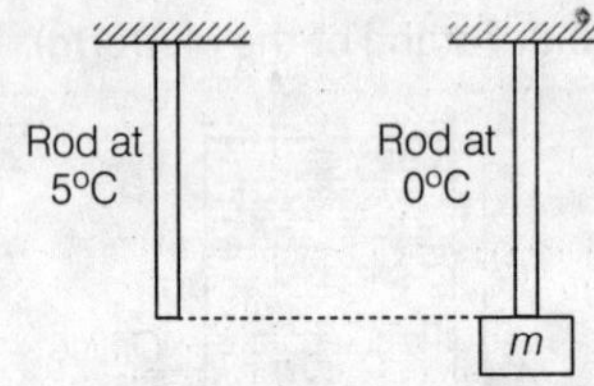

Given that,

$$Y = \text{Young's modulus of rod} = \frac{3}{2} \times 10^{11}\ \text{Nm}^{-2}$$

$$\alpha = \text{Coefficient of linear expansion} = 2 \times 10^{-5}\ \text{per K}$$

$$g = 10\ \text{m/s}^2$$

25. A thick conducting shell of inner radius R and outer radius $2R$ is surrounded by air at constant temperature $T_0 > 0°C$. Time taken for temperature of water (at 0°C) inside the shell to increase to $\frac{T_0}{2}$ is $\frac{\rho R^2 s}{x}$. Find x, if thermal conductivity of shell is $k = \ln 2$, ρ = density of shell material and s = specific heat capacity.

Answers

Section I

1 (b)	2 (b)	3 (c)	4 (b)	5 (c)
6 (a)	7 (d)	8 (a)	9 (b)	10 (a)
11 (c)	12 (b)	13 (c)	14 (a)	15 (a)
16 (b)	17 (b)	18 (b)	19 (c)	20 (b)

Section II

21 3.42	22 12.1	23 25	24 18	25 6

See detailed explanations on page no. 224

QUALIFIER 8

Thermodynamics & Kinetic Theory of Gases

Section I Objective Type Questions

1. In the given figure, the area of the frictionless piston is A and it is being held in equilibrium by an external force. Now, the external force is slowly removed and heat is supplied to the gas due to which the piston displaces by $\frac{L}{2}$, where L is the natural length of the springs. The final pressure of the gas will be

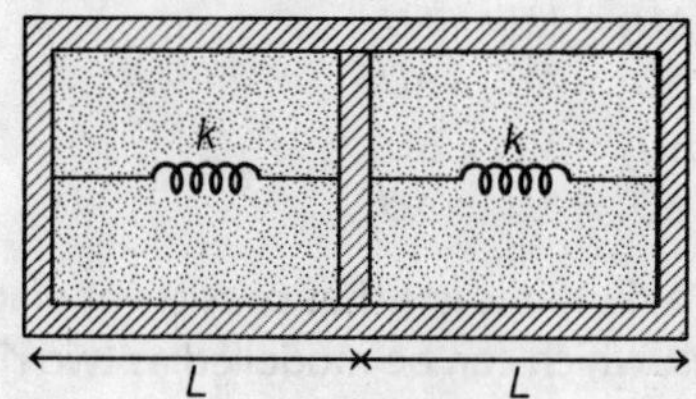

(a) $\frac{L}{2k}$ (b) $\frac{A}{2L}$

(c) $\frac{kL}{A}$ (d) $\frac{2kL}{A}$

2. Consider a ring shaped tube which contains same masses of two different ideal gases-1 and 2 as shown below.

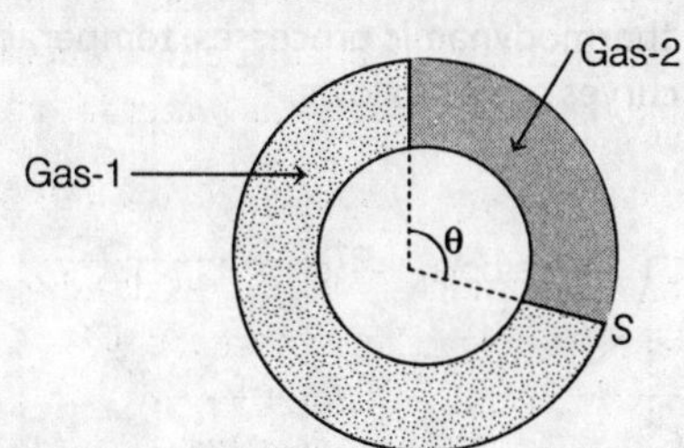

The gases are separated by a fixed partition and a movable conducting stopper S, which can move freely without friction inside the ring. So, the value of θ is (Take, relative molar mass of Gas-1, $M_1 = 32$ and for Gas-2, $M_2 = 28$)

(a) 60° (b) 72°

(c) 192° (d) 38°

3. Considering the specifications given in the diagram here, constant velocity (v) with which block moves down is

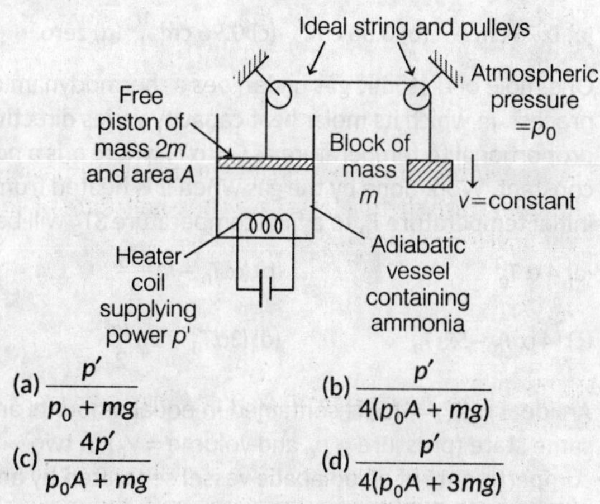

(a) $\frac{p'}{p_0 + mg}$ (b) $\frac{p'}{4(p_0A + mg)}$

(c) $\frac{4p'}{p_0A + mg}$ (d) $\frac{p'}{4(p_0A + 3mg)}$

4. An adiabatic rigid evacuated flask is sealed at its opening by a cork. The flask is fixed in large chamber filled with an ideal gas (adiabatic exponent $= \gamma$). The cork is suddenly removed making the gas suddenly fill the flask. If volume of the chamber is extremely large compared to the flask, temperature of gas inside the flask just after thermodynamic equilibrium is attained in the flask is (Here, T = thermodynamic temperature of the surrounding gas before the cork is opened)

(a) T (b) γT

(c) $\frac{T}{\gamma - 1}$ (d) $\frac{\gamma T}{\gamma - 1}$

5. In the arrangement here, a thin tube connects two adiabatic vessels containing helium (pressure $= p_0$, volume $= V_0$) and oxygen (pressure $= 2p_0$, volume $= 2V_0$).

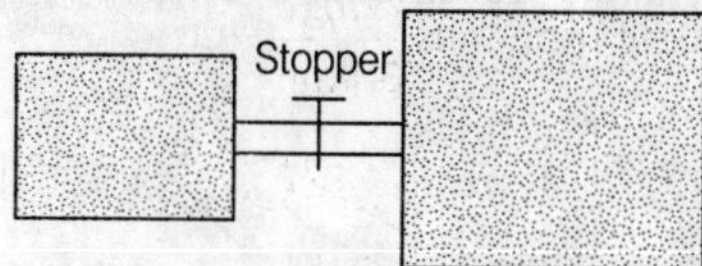

If the stopper shown is now removed thereby allowing mixing of the two gases, final gas pressure in the helium oxygen mixture created is

(a) $\frac{3}{2}p_0$ (b) $\frac{23}{24}p_0$ (c) $\frac{23}{13}p_0$ (d) $\frac{5}{2}p_0$

6. A vertical conducting tube contains $l_1 = 66.42$ cm length of oxygen trapped by 10 cm of mercury as shown. The tube is now tilted gradually such that length of oxygen column changes to l_2 and l_3 at the two instants shown. $l_3 - l_2$ (in cm) is equal to (atmospheric pressure is equivalent to 76 cm of mercury)

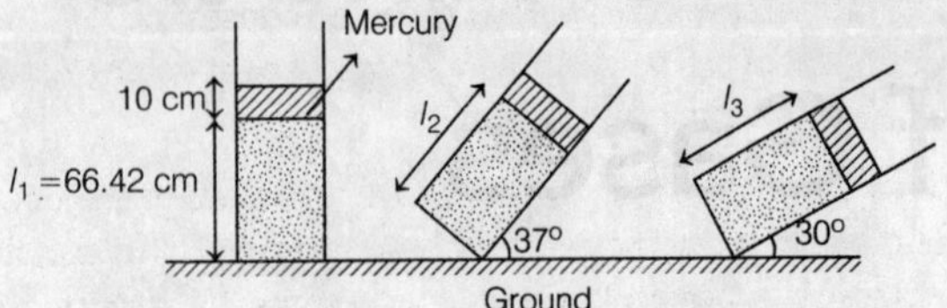

(a) 0.76 cm (b) 0.86 cm (c) 0.96 cm (d) zero

7. One mole of diatomic gas undergoes a thermodynamic process, in which its molar heat capacity varies directly proportional to temperature as $C = \alpha T$, where α is a positive constant. Work done by the gas when it is heated from initial temperature T_0 to a final temperature $3T_0$ will be

(a) $4\alpha T_0^2$ (b) $(\alpha T_0 - R)\frac{3T_0}{2}$

(c) $(4\alpha T_0 - 5R)T_0$ (d) $(3\alpha T_0 - 5R)\frac{T_0}{2}$

8. An ideal gas ($\gamma = 1.5$) is contained in equal amounts and in same state (pressure $= p_0$ and volume $= V_0$) in two compartments of an adiabatic vessel separated by an adiabatic frictionless separator.

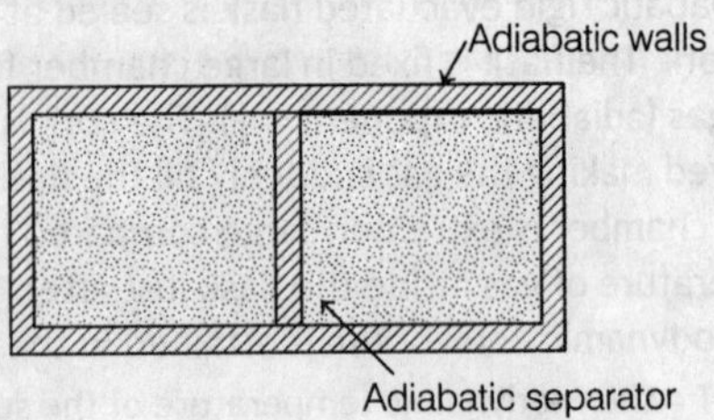

The separator is now sliding slowly towards right such that pressure in right compartment becomes 8 times that in left compartment. Ratio of internal energies of gas in left compartment to that in right compartment is

(a) 1 (b) 0.5 (c) 2 (d) 1.5

9. Two ideal gas samples are undergoing separate thermodynamic processes as shown.

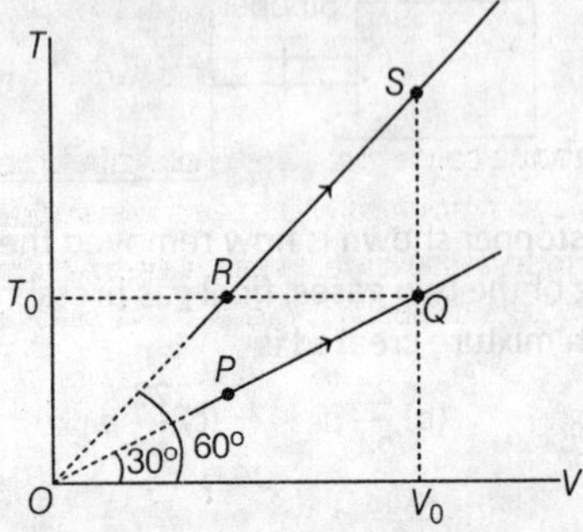

Coefficients of cubical expansion of the gases in states P, Q, R and S are $\gamma_P, \gamma_Q, \gamma_R$ and γ_S, respectively. The ratios of $\frac{\gamma_R}{\gamma_Q}$ and $\frac{\gamma_S}{\gamma_Q}$ are

(a) 1, 3 (b) 3, 1

(c) $1, \frac{1}{3}$ (d) $\frac{1}{3}, 1$

10. Three of the four processes shown here are isobaric expansion, adiabatic expansion and isothermal expansion undergone by nitrogen while one of the four processes is adiabatic expansion of argon. If internal energy changes (in magnitude) in the four processes are $\Delta U_1, \Delta U_2, \Delta U_3$ and ΔU_4 respectively, which of these is correct relation?

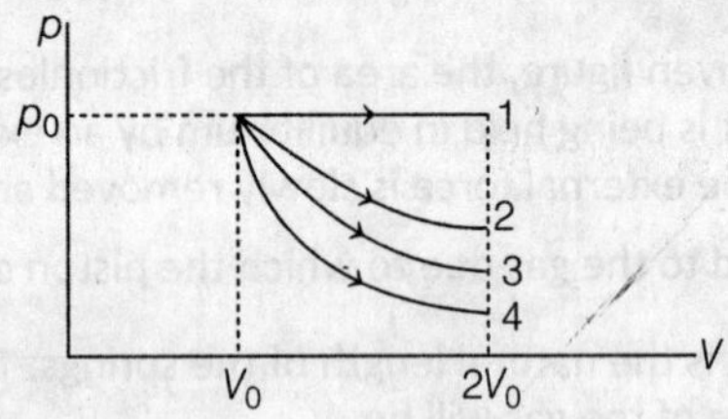

(a) $\Delta U_1 = \Delta U_2 = \Delta U_3 = \Delta U_4$
(b) $\Delta U_1 > \Delta U_3 > \Delta U_4 > \Delta U_2$
(c) $\Delta U_1 > \Delta U_2 > \Delta U_3 > \Delta U_4$
(d) $\Delta U_1 > \Delta U_3 = \Delta U_4 > \Delta U_2$

11. Consider a diatomic gas that consists of diatomic molecules, which can be modelled as two rigid balls connected with a spring. These balls can vibrate with respect to the centre of mass of the system (spring + balls).

If the gas performs 10 J of work under isobaric condition, then the heat given to the gas (in J) is

(a) 260 (b) 890
(c) 100 (d) 35

12. For two thermodynamic processes, temperature *versus* volume curves are as follows.

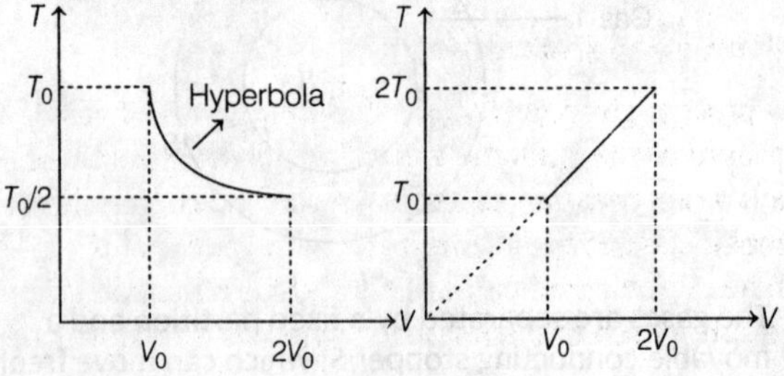

Now, study the following statements and choose which statements are correct?

Statement I Ratio of the work done in the first process to that in the second process is 2 : 1.

Statement II First process is isentropic in nature.

(a) I only (b) II only
(c) Both I and II (d) Neither I nor II

13. A gas undergoes a cyclic process *ABCA* as shown by *p-V* diagram here.

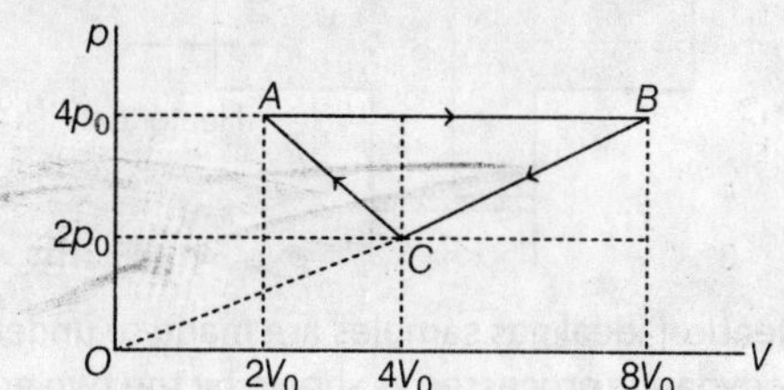

Which of the following is correct *T-V* indicator diagram, representing the same process?

(a) 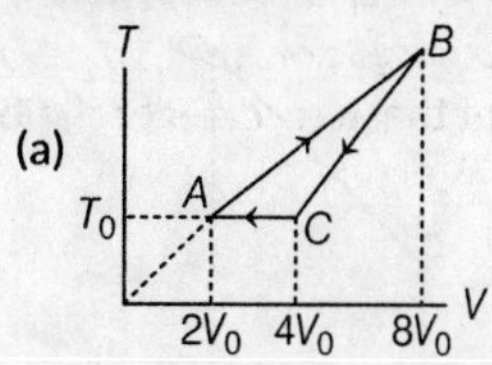
(b) 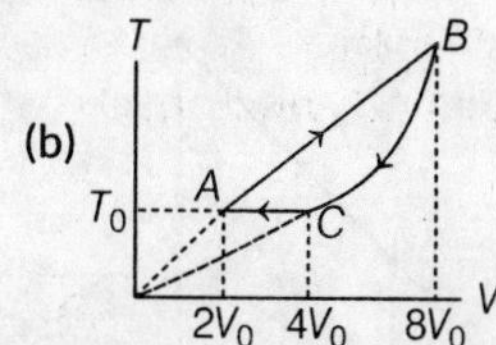
(c) 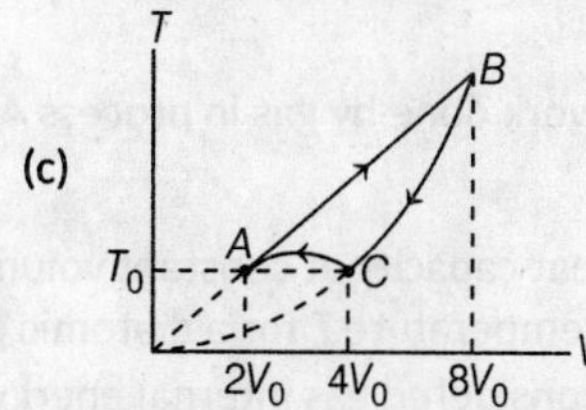
(d) 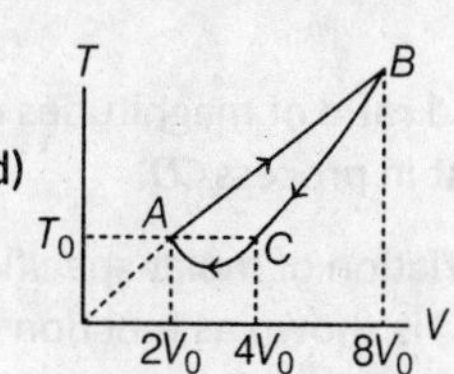

(Here, T_0 = temperature in state *A*)

14. Certain amount of methane undergoes a cyclic process *ABCA* as shown in *y-x* indicator diagram.

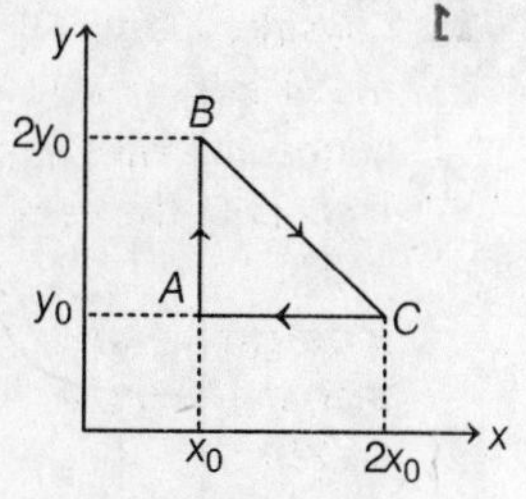

If *y* and *x* represent pressure and volume respectively, efficiency of the cycle is η. For *y* and *x* corresponding to thermodynamic temperature and entropy, efficiency of the cycle would be

(a) η (b) 3η (c) $\frac{\eta}{3}$ (d) γη

(Here, γ = adiabatic exponent)

15. A process given by pV^x = constant in terms of gas pressure *p* and volume *V* is called polytropic process. Here, *x* is a real constant called polytropic index. Variation of molar specific heat capacity (*C*) with variation of *x* is shown here. Some coordinates *p*, *q*, *r* and *s* are marked in the graph. Which of the following depends on nature of gas?

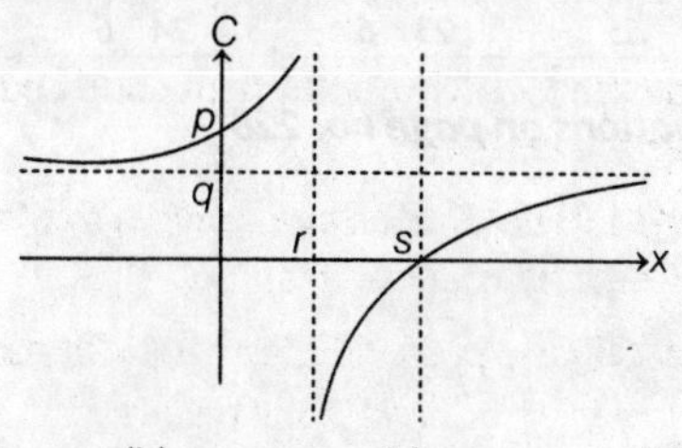

(a) $p - q$ (b) $p - qs$ (c) r (d) $ps - r$

16. Which of the following statement is incorrect?

(a) If initial volume in a thermodynamic process is same as final volume, work done by gas may not be zero.
(b) If a bicycle tyre bursts, its temperature drops.
(c) On keeping room heater switched ON for sometime, internal energy of ambient air in the room increases (atmospheric pressure is assumed constant).
(d) 100% of the heat input in a cycle of heat engine cannot be converted into work.

17. Two Carnot engines C_1 and C_2 are arranged in series as shown. In the arrangement, heat given by C_1 to common reservoir is used by C_2 to produce work.

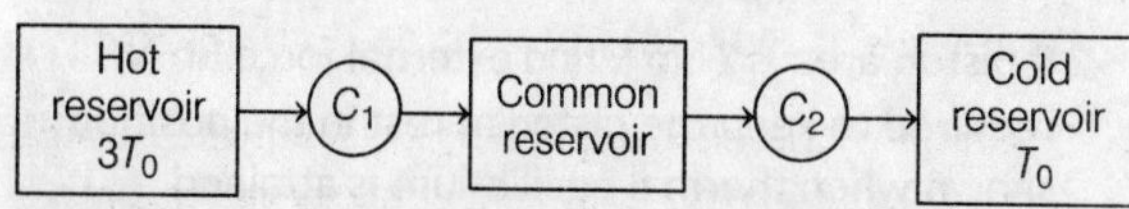

If both the engines produce equal amounts of work, temperature of the common reservoir is

(a) $2T_0$ (b) $\sqrt{3}T_0$ (c) $\frac{3T_0}{4}$ (d) $\frac{3T_0}{2}$

18. An ideal argon sample is suddenly compressed resulting in doubling rms speed of gas molecules. Average time between successive molecular collisions will

(a) be doubled (b) get halved
(c) remain same (d) become one-sixteenth

19. Suppose in a gas sample *dN* denotes number of gas molecules having speeds between *v* and $v + dv$. Then, $\frac{dN}{dv}$ *versus v* graph for the sample is called velocity distribution graph. Such a graph for a hypothetical gas sample is parabolic as shown with v_0 as maximum molecular speed.

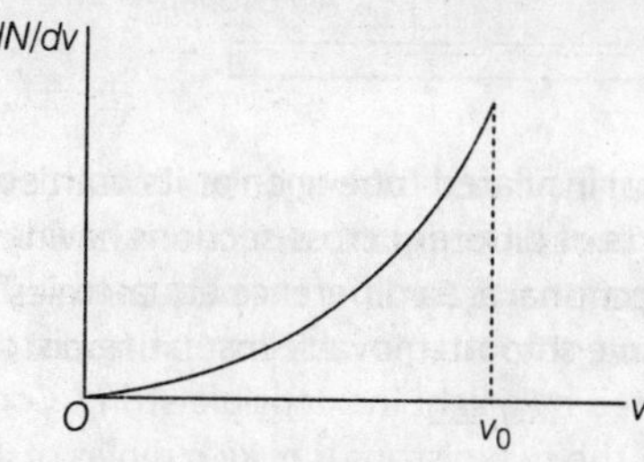

If slope of graph at *O* is zero, mean square speed of the sample is

(a) v_0^2 (b) $0.8\,v_0^2$
(c) $0.6\,v_0^2$ (d) $0.4\,v_0^2$

20. An adiabatic container having certain amount of ideal diatomic gas moving with speed *v* is suddenly stopped. If gas temperature remains unchanged in the process but the gas molecules dissociate, initial molar mass of the gas is

(a) $\frac{RT}{v^2}$ (b) $\frac{RT}{2v^2}$
(c) $\frac{2RT}{v^2}$ (d) $\frac{RT}{\sqrt{2}v^2}$

Section II Numerical Value Questions

21. An insulated vessel of volume $2\,m^3$ is divided into two equal parts by a conducting free piston as shown. Each part contains monoatomic gas having initial state as shown in diagram.

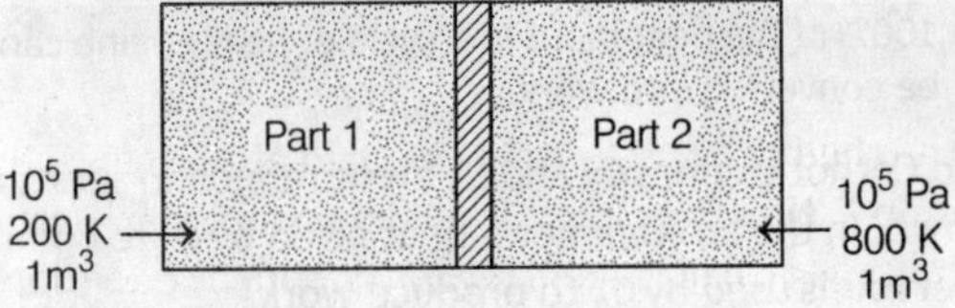

If piston area is $2\,cm^2$, find external force (in N) required to keep the piston at rest in the position shown when thermal equilibrium is attained.

22. An ideal monoatomic gas is confined in a cylinder which is attached to a massless piston of cross-section $4\times 10^{-3} m^2$. Initially, the gas is at 100 K and occupies a volume of $1.2\times 10^{-3} m^3$ and the spring is in releaxed position. If the gas is now slowly heated by an external source, the piston moves out slowly by 0.2 m. The final temperature (in 10^2 K) of the gas will be ....

(Neglect the friction between piston and the cylinder and take, $1\text{ atm} = 1\times 10^5 N/m^2$)

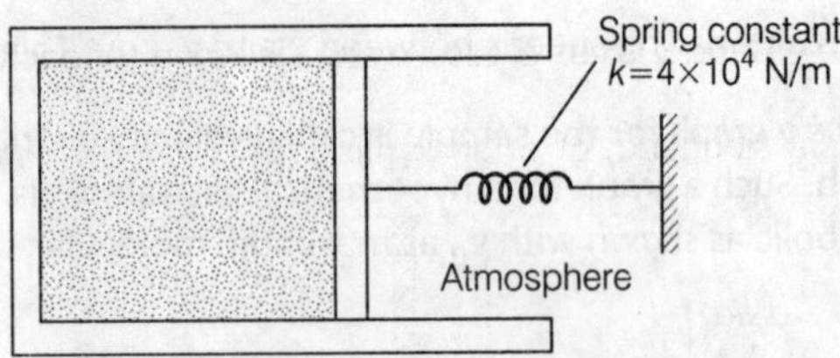

23. A vertical insulated tube open at its both ends has two parts of different cross-sections having cross-sectional area difference equal to A. The two parts have smooth movable insulating pistons connected by a light inextensible string. Combined mass of the two pistons is m kg.n moles of an ideal contained in this tube is slowly heated by a heater making the pistons displace upward by distance d. Find increase in gas temperature in kelvin. Given that, $m = 10$ kg, $g = 10\,m/s^2$, $A = 30\,cm^2$, $n = 3$, $d = 40$ cm, atmospheric pressure, $p_0 = 10^5$Pa, $R = \frac{25}{3}$ J/mol K.

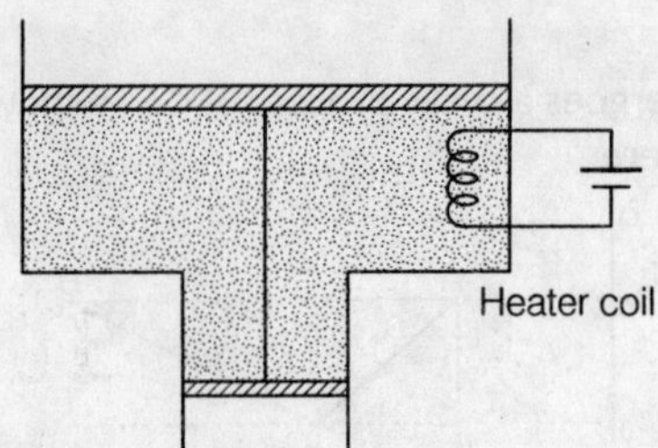

24. Two identical ideal gas samples are made to undergo two thermodynamic processes as shown by the two graphs here from same initial state. U, ρ, v and V represent internal energy, density, average molecular speed and gas volume, respectively.

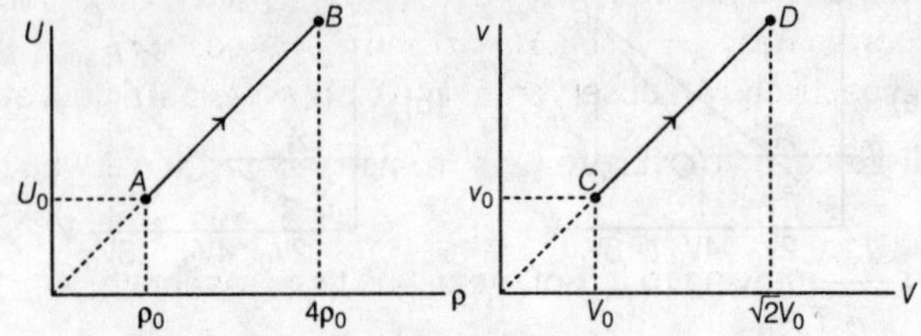

Find ratio of magnitudes of work done by gas in process AB to that in process CD.

25. Variation of molar specific heat capacity at constant volume (C_V) is shown as function of temperature T for a diatomic gas. If for a certain amount of the considered gas internal energy in state C is 14 times the sum of internal energies in states A and B, find x.

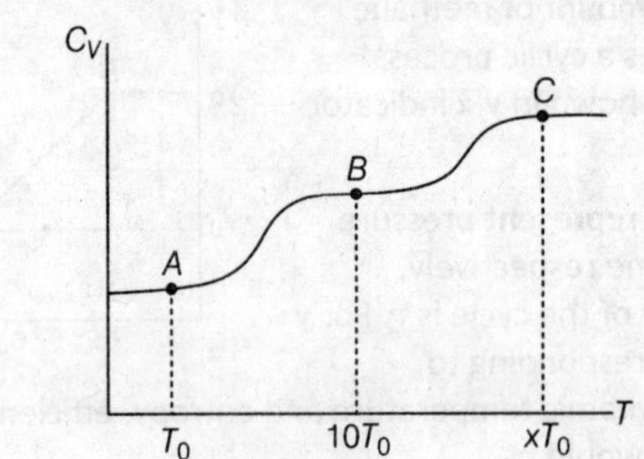

Answers

Section I

1 (c)	2 (c)	3 (b)	4 (b)	5 (c)
6 (b)	7 (c)	8 (b)	9 (c)	10 (b)
11 (d)	12 (d)	13 (c)	14 (b)	15 (d)
16 (c)	17 (a)	18 (d)	19 (c)	20 (a)

Section II

21 24	22 35	23 6.4	24 6	25 106

See detailed explanations on page no. 228

QUALIFIER 09

Oscillations and Waves

Section I *Objective Type Questions*

1. Two particles A and B executing linear SHM, have position coordinates $x_A = A\sin(\omega t + \alpha)$ and $x_B = A\cos(\omega t + \beta)$, respectively. An observer (at $t = 0$) observes particle A at a distance $\frac{A}{\sqrt{2}}$ moving to right from mean position O while B at $\frac{\sqrt{3}A}{2}$ moving to left of mean position O as shown in figure. Least possible value of $(\alpha + \beta)$ is

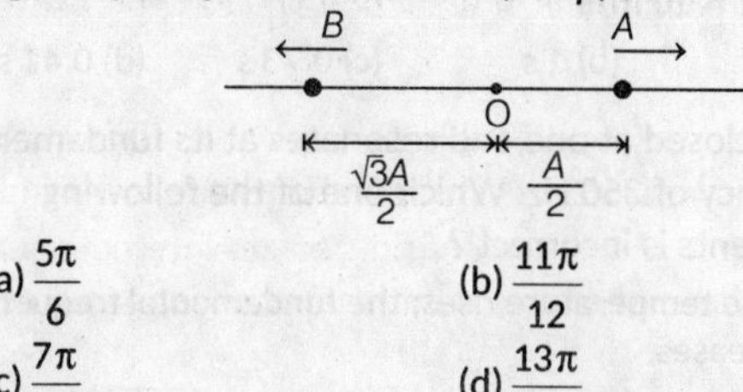

(a) $\frac{5\pi}{6}$ (b) $\frac{11\pi}{12}$
(c) $\frac{7\pi}{12}$ (d) $\frac{13\pi}{12}$

2. Time period of oscillation of ball of mass m_1 in arrangement-1, if the ball is slightly displaced along the length of spring attached to it and released is T_1. Time period of oscillation of another ball of mass m_2 in arrangement-2, if the ball is slightly displaced along the vertical spring and released is T_2. If the springs are identical and the space is gravity free, choose the correct relation, if $T_1 = T_2$.

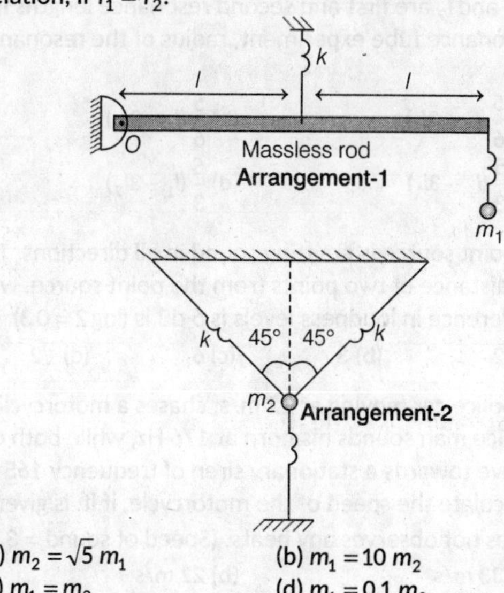

(a) $m_2 = \sqrt{5}\, m_1$ (b) $m_1 = 10\, m_2$
(c) $m_1 = m_2$ (d) $m_1 = 0.1\, m_2$

3. A stretched string of length l clamped at both ends has tension T. Now, the string is pulled as shown by vertical distance $y(<<l)$ at its centre. Considering the tension to remain unchanged by small transverse displacement, energy of oscillation of the string can be expressed as

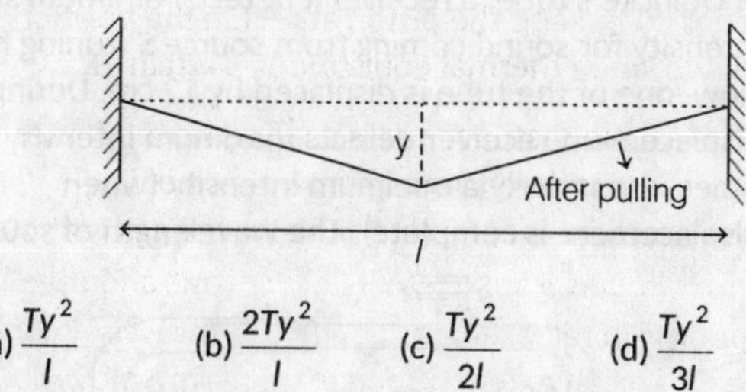

(a) $\frac{Ty^2}{l}$ (b) $\frac{2Ty^2}{l}$ (c) $\frac{Ty^2}{2l}$ (d) $\frac{Ty^2}{3l}$

4. A non-conducting piston of mass m and area A divides a non-conducting closed cylinder into two parts as shown in figure. Piston is connected to right wall of cylinder by a spring of spring constant k. Right part is evacuated while the left part is filled with a gas of adiabatic exponent $\alpha = \frac{kl}{pA}$. Here, p is gas pressure and l is length of each part.

Angular frequency of small oscillations is

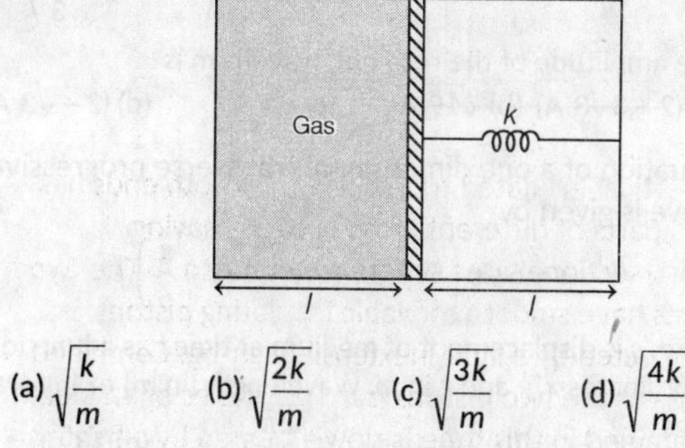

(a) $\sqrt{\frac{k}{m}}$ (b) $\sqrt{\frac{2k}{m}}$ (c) $\sqrt{\frac{3k}{m}}$ (d) $\sqrt{\frac{4k}{m}}$

5. For the rigid rod shown in diagram, density varies according to $\rho = 1 + x$ with distance x from left end. If amplitude of vibrator performing SHM is A, amplitude of point at a distance $x = 1$ is

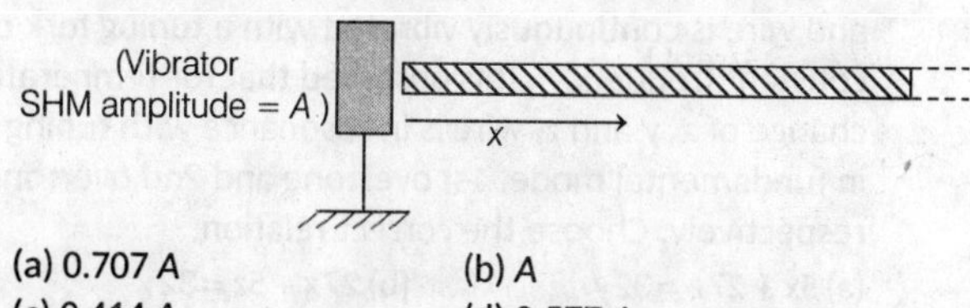

(a) 0.707 A (b) A
(c) 0.414 A (d) 0.577 A

6. A pendulum is constructed as a thin walled sphere of radius r filled with water and suspended from a point from a light rigid rod. Distance between point and centre of sphere is $\sqrt{40}r$. First, the pendulum is slightly displaced and released making it oscillate. Secondly, the water is somehow frozen and again the pendulum undergoes small oscillations. Percentage change in oscillation time period with respect to the time period in first case is

(a) 0.5 percent increase (b) 0.5 percent decrease
(c) 0.25 percent increase (d) 0.25 percent decrease

7. Under similar conditions of temperature and pressure, in which of the following gases the velocity of sound will be least?

(a) H_2 (b) N_2 (c) He (d) CO_2

8. In Quincke's tube, a receiver R detects minimum sound intensity for sound coming from source S (tuning fork). Now, one of the tube is displaced by 12 cm. During displacement receiver detects maximum intensity 12 times, then finally a minimum intensity (when displacement is complete). The wavelength of sound is

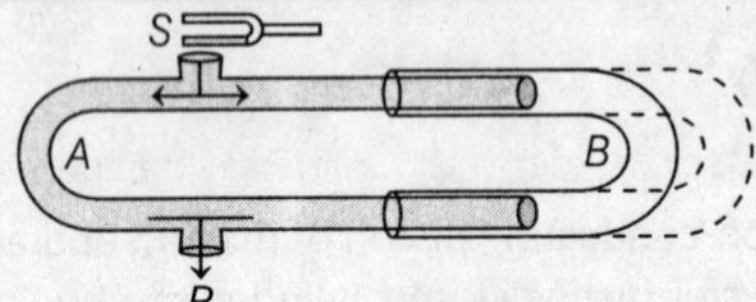

(a) 12 cm (b) 2 cm (c) 11 cm (d) (12/11) cm

9. Three waveforms travelling along a straight line have the forms

$$2A\sin\left(kx-\omega t+\frac{\pi}{3}\right),\ \sqrt{3}A\cos\left(kx-\omega t-\frac{\pi}{3}\right),$$
$$2\sqrt{3}A\cos\left(kx-\omega t+\frac{\pi}{3}\right)$$

The amplitude of the resulting waveform is

(a) $(2+3\sqrt{3}\ A)$ (b) $\sqrt{19}\ A$ (c) $\sqrt{7}\ A$ (d) $(2-\sqrt{3}\ A)\ A$

10. Equation of a one dimensional transverse progressive wave is given by

$$s=6\sin\left(5t-3x+4y-12z+\frac{\pi}{6}\right)$$

Here, s is displacement of medium at time t as a function of coordinates x, y and z in m. Wavelength (in m) of the wave is

(a) $\frac{\pi}{5}$ (b) $\frac{2\pi}{13}$ (c) $\frac{2\pi}{11}$ (d) 13

11. A wire is fixed at both the ends between two rigid supports which have separation equal to its natural length. Now, surrounding temperature is slowly decreased and wire is continuously vibrated with a tuning fork of constant frequency. It is observed that for temperature change of x, y and z, wire is in resonance with tuning fork in fundamental mode, 1st overtone and 2nd overtone, respectively. Choose the correct relation.

(a) $5x+27z=32y$ (b) $27x+5z=32y$
(c) $5z+27y=32x$ (d) $32x+27z=5y$

12. A taut string of length L, fixed at its both ends, is vibrating in its 1st overtone. Consider two elements of the string of same small length at positions $x_1=0.29\ L$ and x_2 from one end. If K_1 and K_2 are their respective maximum kinetic energies, then $K_1>K_2$ for x_2 equal to

(a) 0.25 L (b) 0.28 L (c) 0.69 L (d) 0.77 L

13. An end of a long horizontal string is oscillated up and down harmonically by a bar attached to it, thereby generating a sinusoidal wave of amplitude 1 cm. The motion is continuous and is repeated regularly $60/\pi$ times per second. If the string has linear density 90 g/m and is kept under a tension of 900 N, maximum power transmitted along the string is closest to

(a) 12 W (b) 13 W (c) 14 W (d) 7 W

14. A heavy but uniform rope of length $L=10$ m is suspended from a ceiling. A ball near ceiling is dropped t time after the bottom end is given a jerk creating wave pulse. If the ball meets the pulse at mid-point of the rope, t equals (Take, $g=10\ \text{m/s}^2$)

(a) 2 s (b) 1 s (c) 0.73 s (d) 0.41 s

15. A pipe closed at one end resonates at its fundamental frequency of 350 Hz. Which one of the following statements is incorrect ?

(a) If the temperature rises, the fundamental frequency increases.
(b) The second overtone is of frequency 1750 Hz.
(c) An open pipe with the same fundamental frequency has twice the length.
(d) If the pressure rises, the fundamental frequency increases.

16. Length of a sonometer wire is L. It is divided into three segments having fundamental frequencies in the ratio 1 : 2 : 3. Length of the largest segment will be

(a) $L/6$ (b) $6L/11$ (c) $L/2$ (d) $3L/11$

17. If l_1 and l_2 are first and second resonance lengths in resonance tube experiment, radius of the resonance tube is

(a) $\frac{5}{6}(l_2-3l_1)$ (b) $\frac{5}{6}(l_1-3l_2)$
(c) $\frac{5}{3}(l_2-3l_1)$ (d) $\frac{5}{3}(l_1-3l_2)$

18. A point source is emitting sound in all directions. The ratio of distance of two points from the point source, where the difference in loudness levels is 6 dB is ($\log 2=0.3$)

(a) 2 (b) 3 (c) 6 (d) $\sqrt{2}$

19. A police car moving at 22 m/s, chases a motorcyclist. The police man sounds his horn at 176 Hz, while both of them move towards a stationary siren of frequency 165 Hz. Calculate the speed of the motorcycle, if it is given that he does not observes any beats. (Speed of sound = 330 m/s)

(a) 33 m/s (b) 22 m/s
(c) Zero (d) 11 m/s

20. A person riding on a source S of sound (frequency 30 Hz) moves in a medium (in which velocity of sound is 310 m/s) with speed 10 m/s as towards an open liquid reservoir (in which velocity of sound is 1240 m/s). A detector D in the reservoir moves towards the free surface of the reservoir (along vertical line joining S and D) at a speed 20m/s. Beat frequency observed by person and frequency (in Hz) received by detector respectively are

(a) 1, 31.5 (b) 2, 31.5 (c) 1, 30 (d) 2, 30

Section II *Numerical Value Questions*

21. A block of mass m is suspended at rest from a string of elastic constant $\frac{mg}{l}$. The block is imparted a velocity $\sqrt{2gl}$ downwards. Time period of the resulting oscillation is $x\sqrt{\frac{l}{g}}$. Find x.

22. A solid cylinder of mass m and radius R is placed on a plank of same mass m attached to two springs of force constants k each on both sides as shown. Surface between plank and ground is smooth while that between cylinder and plank is sufficiently rough to prevent slipping. Assuming no slipping between cylinder and plank, time period of oscillations for slight displacement of system from equilibrium is $2\pi\sqrt{\frac{m}{xk}}$. Find the value of x.

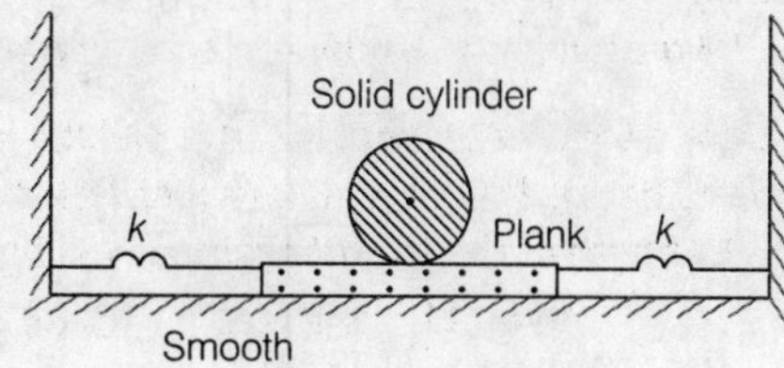

23. A rod (Fig. 1) suspended at its centre by a vertical string is performing SHM as torsional pendulum in horizontal plane.

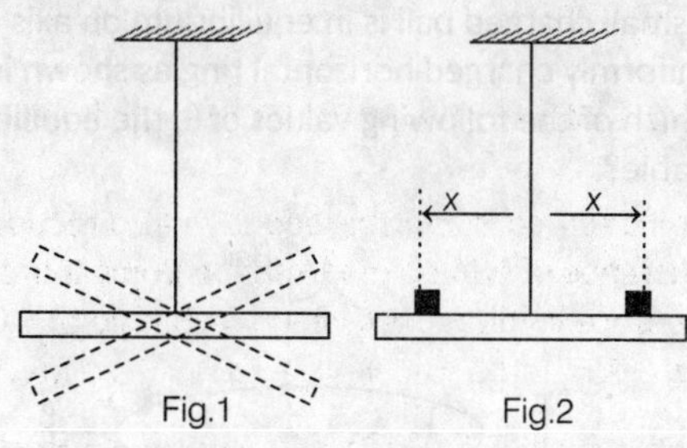

If two particles (each having mass equal to mass of rod are stuck to the rod symmetrically w.r.t. centre, at a distance x from centre (as shown in Fig. 2) such that time period of oscillation doubles, find $\frac{l}{x}$. Here, l is length of rod.

24. Consider the arrangement shown. A uniform wire (linear mass density 0.2 g/m) vibrating in its fundamental mode is in resonance with air column in a resonance tube vibrating in 1st overtone. Given that speed of sound in air is 400 m/s and $g = 10$ m/s^2, find m (in kg).

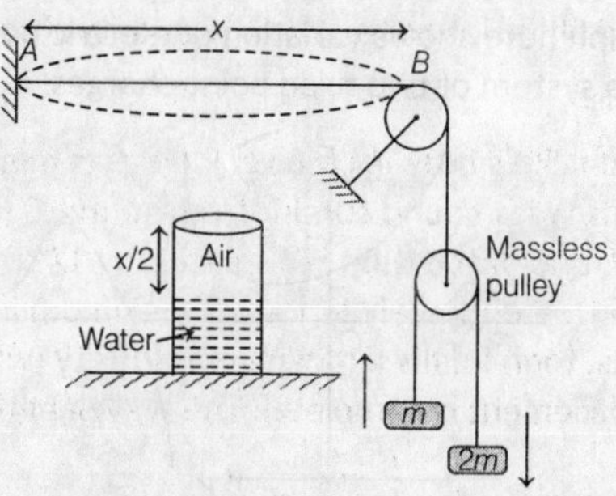

25. Consider two identical coherent line sources of sound S_1 and S_2 separated by a distance 8 m. A detector is moved along a circle (radius 6 m) with centre at S_2. Find greatest integral value of ratio of resultant intensity of sound at B to intensity at A due to S_2 only, if wavelength of sound is 2 m.

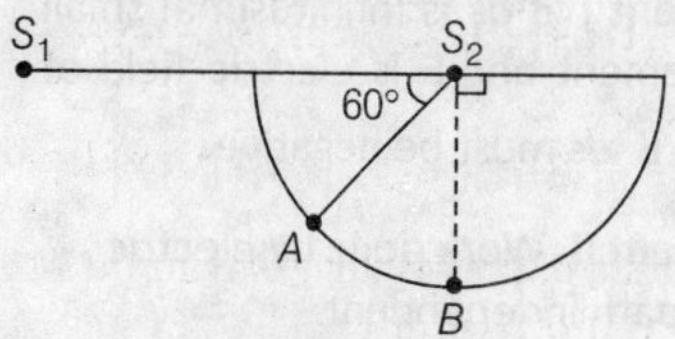

Answers

Section I

1 (d)	2 (d)	3 (b)	4 (b)	5 (a)
6 (a)	7 (d)	8 (b)	9 (c)	10 (b)
11 (a)	12 (c)	13 (b)	14 (d)	15 (d)
16 (b)	17 (a)	18 (a)	19 (b)	20 (b)

Section II

21 6.71	22 1.5	23. 2.82	24 10.8	25 3

See detailed explanations on page no. 233

QUALIFIER 10

Electrostatics

Section I Objective Type Questions

1. Graph here shows variation of electric field on X-axis due to a system of two fixed point charges. $x_2 - x_1$ is equal to

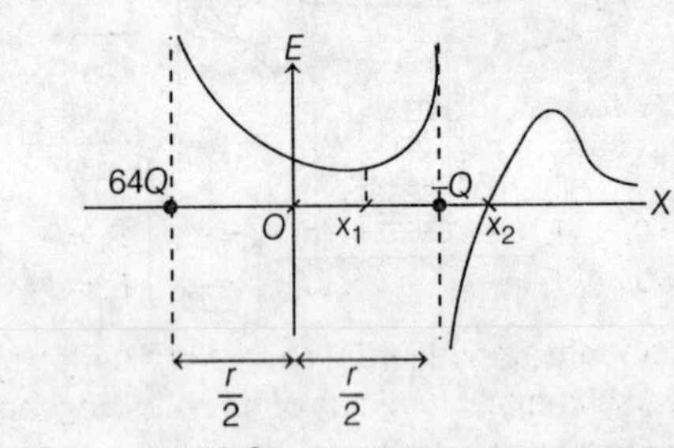

(a) $\frac{12r}{35}$ (b) $\frac{2r}{35}$ (c) $\frac{r}{2}$ (d) $\frac{37r}{35}$

2. The figure here shows an arbitrary path connecting points A and B in an electric field of a uniformly charged finite straight wire.

Statement I If ds is infinitesimal small displacement and $\mathbf{E}$ is electric field of wire, $\int_A^B \mathbf{E} \cdot d\mathbf{s}$ must be negative.

Statement II Work done by electric field is path independent.

(a) Statement-I is true, Statement-II is true; Statement-II is a correct explanation of Statement-I.
(b) Statement-I is true, Statement-II is true; Statement-II is not a correct explanation for Statement-I.
(c) Statement-I is true, Statement-II is false.
(d) Statement-I is false, Statement-II is true.

3. A straight long uniformly charged wire of charged density λ has a circular arc portion AB (of angular thickness 74° and radius R) having a point charge q placed at arc centre. The wire is supported at A and B by identical strings. Tension in either string, if the wire is in equilibrium, is

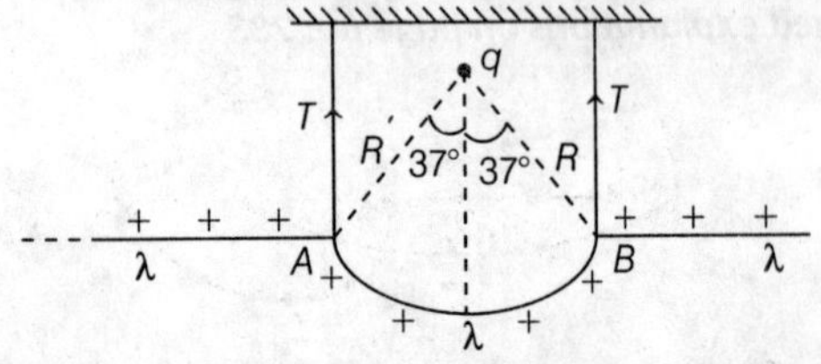

(a) $\frac{2.2\,k\lambda q}{R}$ (b) $\frac{2\,k\lambda q}{R}$ (c) $\frac{1.2\,k\lambda q}{R}$ (d) $\frac{1.1\,k\lambda q}{R}$

4. Figure here shows point P on an imaginary circle (having zero potential at all points) centered at C, in a region with two fixed point charges. If electric field $\mathbf{E}$ at P is $E_x\hat{\mathbf{i}} + E_y\hat{\mathbf{j}}$, $\frac{E_x}{E_y}$ is equal to

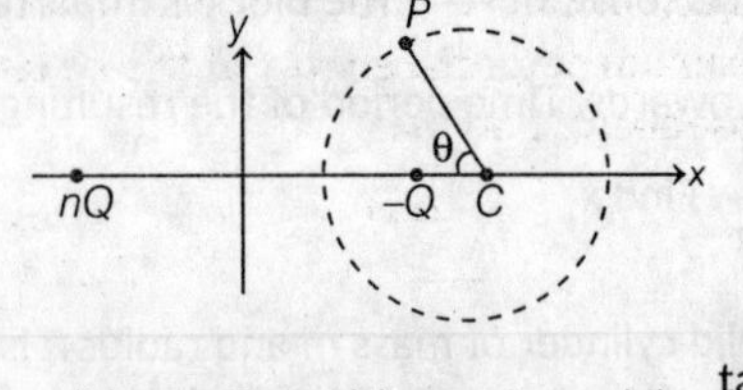

(a) $\cot\theta$ (b) $n\cot\theta$ (c) $-\cot\theta$ (d) $-\frac{\tan\theta}{n+1}$

5. A point charge is located a distance d from infinite neutral conducting plane. Surface charge density at P is proportional to

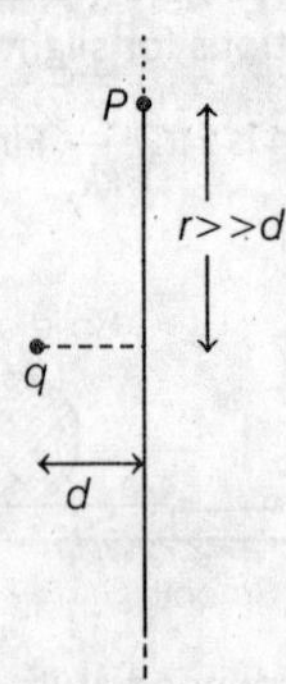

(a) r^2 (b) r^{-2} (c) r^3 (d) r^{-3}

6. A small charged ball is in equilibrium on axis of a fixed uniformly charged horizontal ring as shown in figure. For which of the following values of θ, the equilibrium is stable?

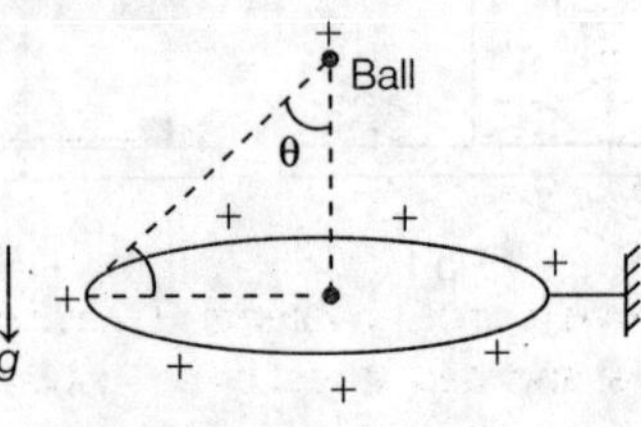

(a) $\tan^{-1} 2$ (b) $\tan^{-1}\sqrt{2}$ (c) 60° (d) 45°

7. A short electric dipole can be moved freely inside a uniformly charged solid sphere. Assuming its motion from position A to B radially, electric force on it

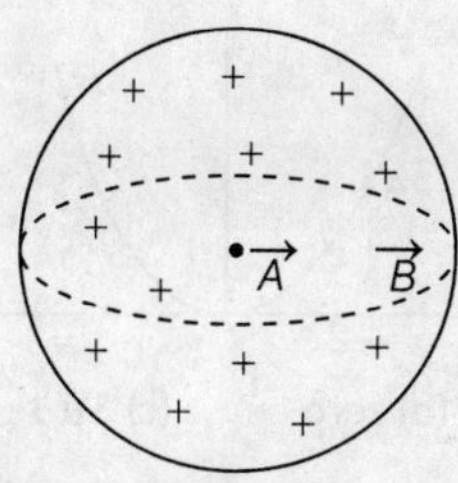

(a) decreases
(b) increases
(c) may increase or decrease depending on distances of A and B from centre.
(d) remains unchanged

8. Two identical charged blocks initially at large distance are at rest on a smooth surface. If one of the blocks is projected towards the other with kinetic energy K, maximum potential energy of the system during subsequent motion is

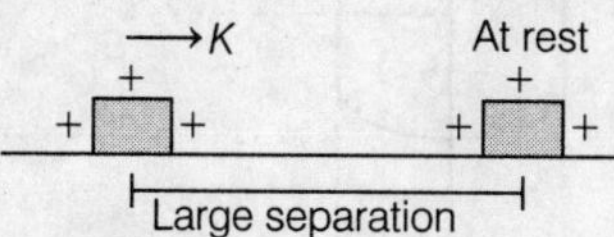

(a) K (b) $\frac{K}{2}$ (c) $\frac{K}{4}$ (d) $\frac{3K}{4}$

9. Volumetric charge density in region between $x = -a$ to $x = +a$ varies with x as shown by graph here. Which of these represents correct variation of electric field with x?

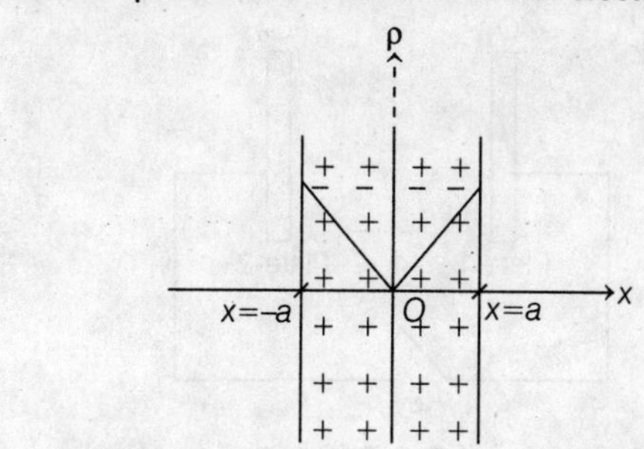

(a) 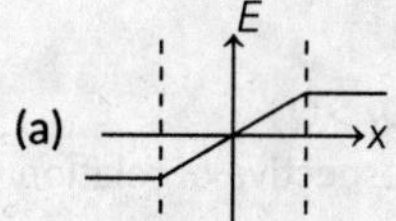
(b) 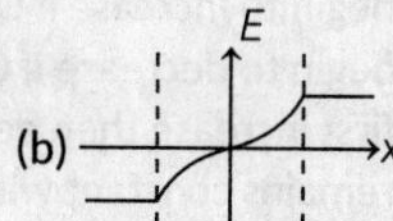
(c) 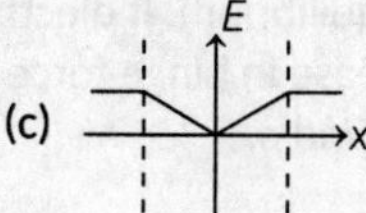
(d) 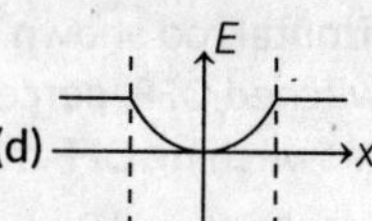

10. Figure shows a small charged ball (having charge q) suspended at rest by an insulating thread. A feeble horizontal field $E << \frac{mg}{q}$ is switched ON making ball ascend. Field is turned OFF when ball is at highest point. Time taken by ball to reach back of its initial position is

(a) equal to time of ascent
(b) greater than time of ascent
(c) half of time of ascent
(d) more than half of time of ascent

11. Force by larger hemisphere on the smaller is $F_x\hat{\mathbf{i}} + F_y\hat{\mathbf{j}}$. Choose the correct possibility, regarding the values of F_x and F_y if centres of hemispheres coincide (charging is uniform).

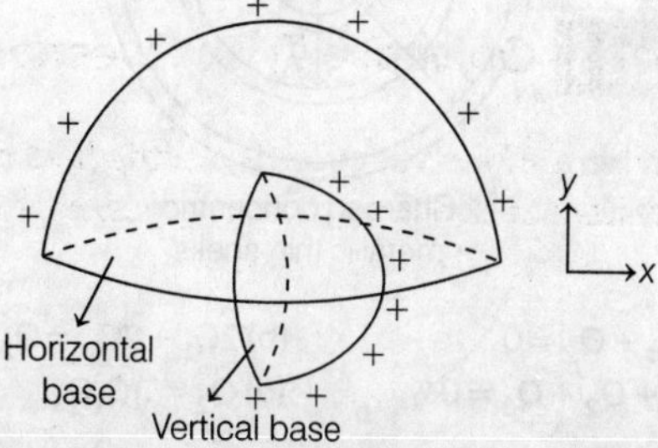

(a) $F_x = 0$, $F_y = +$ (b) $F_x = +$, $F_y = -$
(c) $F_x = 0$, $F_y = -$ (d) $F_x = -$, $F_y = -$

12. A thin smooth groove ABC is carved in a uniform positively charged solid cube along one of its body diagonals, as shown. An electron of charge $-e$ and mass m is released at end A of the groove. If potential at centre B of the cube is V, speed of electron as it reaches B is

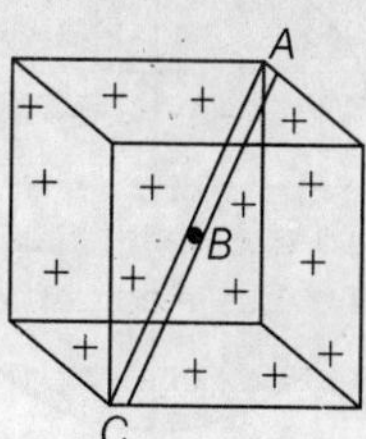

(a) $\sqrt{\frac{2eV}{m}}$ (b) $\sqrt{\frac{eV}{2m}}$
(c) $\sqrt{\frac{eV}{m}}$ (d) $2\sqrt{\frac{eV}{m}}$

13. Figure shows a uniformly charged hemispherical shell with horizontal base centred at origin O. A point charge $-q$ is moved in plane of its base as shown. Work done against electrostatic force in the process is
($AO = \frac{R}{2}$, $OB = \frac{R}{3}$, BDC = semi-circular arc of radius $\frac{2R}{3}$)

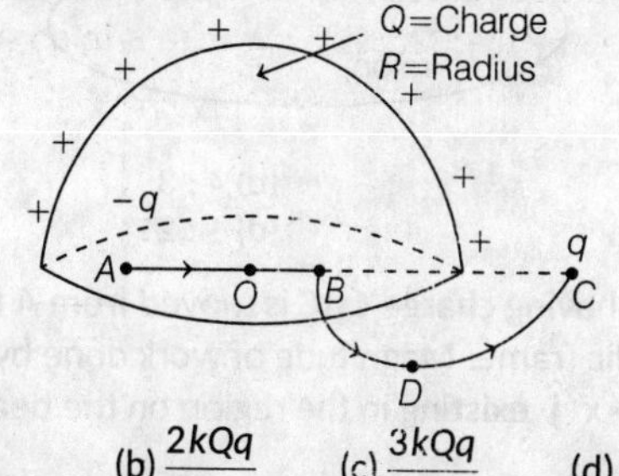

(a) $\frac{kQq}{R}$ (b) $\frac{2kQq}{R}$ (c) $\frac{3kQq}{5R}$ (d) $\frac{2kQq}{5R}$

14. If no heat is dissipated after key is closed, shown in figure then the correct relation between the charges Q_1, Q_2 and Q_3 will be

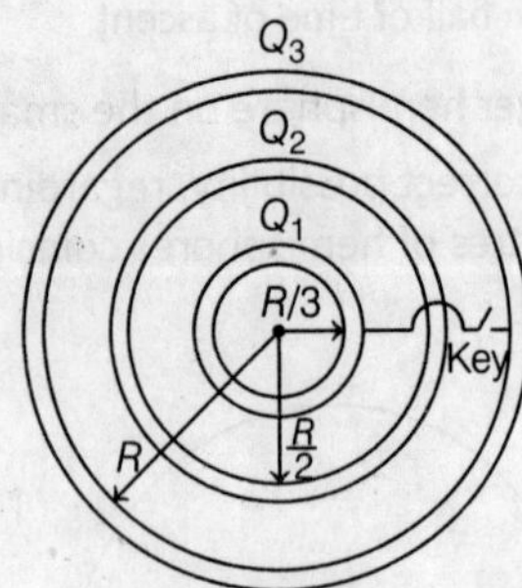

Charged concentric metallic thin shells

(a) $2Q_1 + Q_2 = 0$ (b) $2Q_1 + 2Q_3 = Q_2$
(c) $Q_1 + Q_2 + Q_3 = 0$ (d) $Q_2 = \sqrt{Q_1 Q_3}$

15. A short electric dipole, of dipole moment **p** along horizontal diameter of a neutral solid metal ball, is placed just near its surface. Electric potential due to induced charge on the ball's surface at a point P on vertical diameter distant $\sqrt[3]{2}\,R$ from the dipole is (R = Radius of the metal ball)

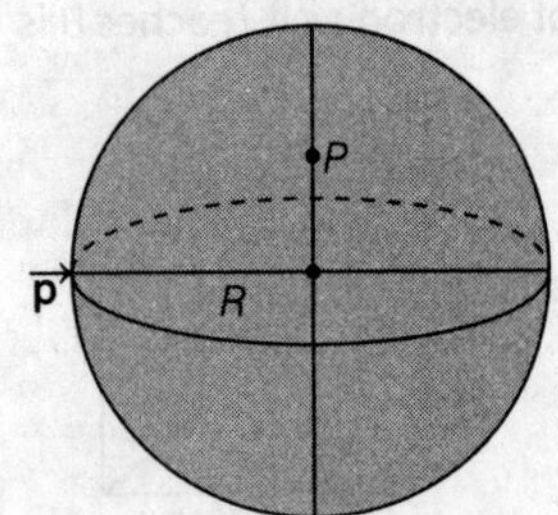

(a) $\frac{kp}{R^2}$ (b) zero
(c) $\frac{kp}{2R^2}$ (d) $\frac{\sqrt{5}kp}{R^2}$

16. In a hypothetical hydrogen atom, electron orbits around a fixed proton in an elliptical orbit of eccentricity 0.5, as shown in figure. Ratio of electrostatic potential energy to kinetic energy of electron when it is closest to proton is

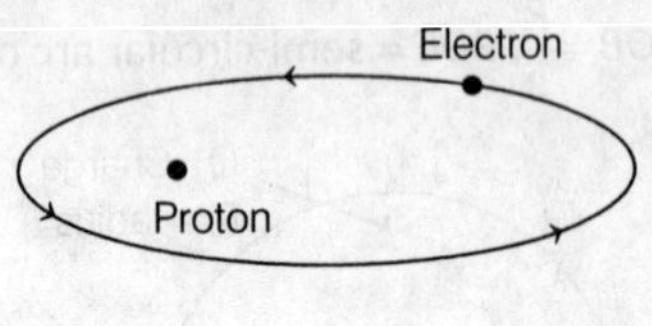

(a) 1 : 1 (b) 4 : 3
(c) 2 : 1 (d) 1 : 2

17. A bead having charge 1 μC is moved from A to B along a parabolic frame. Magnitude of work done by electric field $-2xy\hat{\mathbf{i}} - x^2\hat{\mathbf{j}}$ existing in the region on the bead is

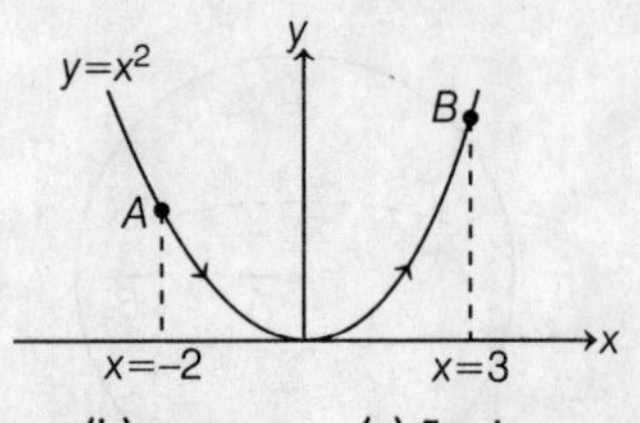

(a) 65 μJ (b) zero (c) 5 μ J (d) 1 μJ

18. If work done in moving a proton against electric field from A to B is same as work done in moving a positron against field from B to C in vicinity of long uniform solid cylinder, choose the correct relation between radial distances of A, B and C.

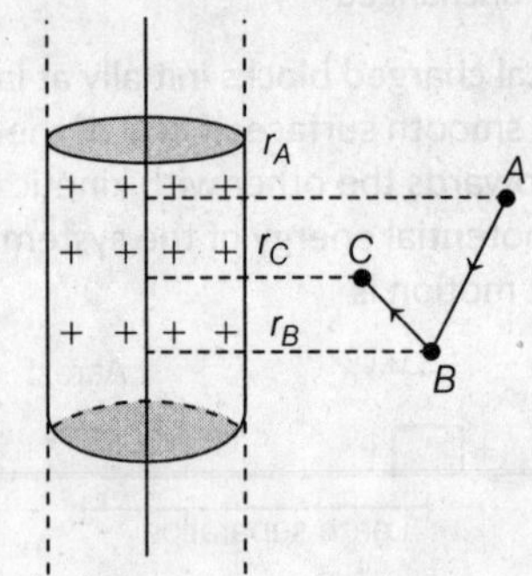

(a) $r_B = \frac{r_A + r_C}{2}$ (b) $r_B = \sqrt{r_A r_C}$ (c) $2r_B = r_A - r_C$ (d) $r_B = 2(r_A - r_C)$

19. Figure shows two charged large parallel metal plates carrying charges Q_1 and Q_2 connected by a wire (key open). If key is closed, then charge on left surface of plate-1 will

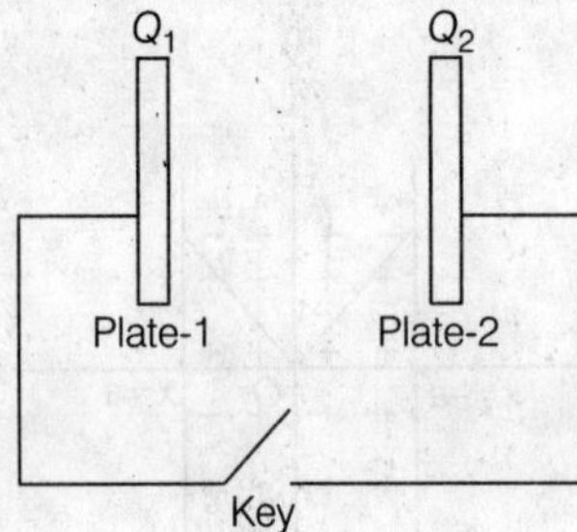

(a) begin to increase if $Q_1 > Q_2$
(b) begin to decrease if $Q_1 < Q_2$
(c) first increase then decrease if $Q_1 > Q_2$
(d) remains constant with time irrespective of relation between Q_1 and Q_2

20. Horizontal rod shown here is in equilibrium. If electric field is switched OFF, percentage decrease in hinge force just after switching OFF the field is p. Find p.

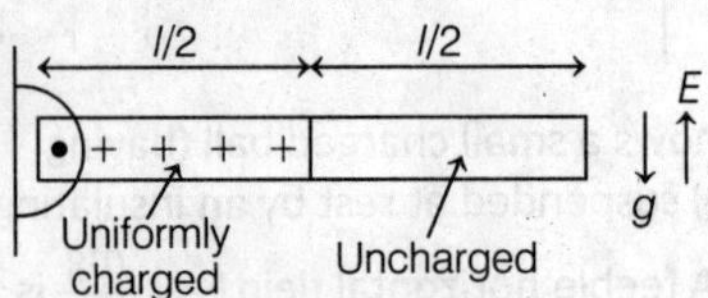

Here, E = Uniform electric field and g = Uniform gravitational field.

(a) 0 (b) 7.56 (c) 75 (d) 11.28

Section II *Numerical Value Questions*

21. Consider a thin uniformly charged spherical shell of radius R and surface charge density σ. Electrostatic force on the shaded portion of upper hemisphere is $\frac{x\sigma^2R^2}{\varepsilon_0}$ for $\theta = \sin^{-1}\sqrt{\frac{3}{\pi}}$. Find x.

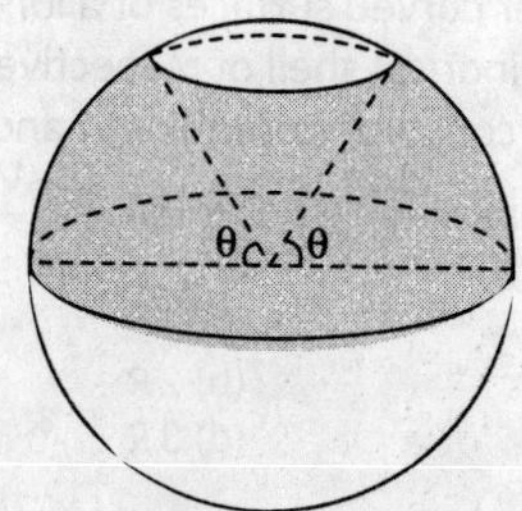

22. A block of mass m and charge q is suspended by an ideal insulating spring of spring constant k from a large ceiling having surface charge density $\sigma = \frac{4\varepsilon_0 mg}{q}$. The block, initially held at rest with spring relaxed, is released. If $g = 10\ \text{m/s}^2$, $m = 1$ kg and $k = 100$ N/m, find maximum speed (in m/s) acquired by the block during subsequent motion.

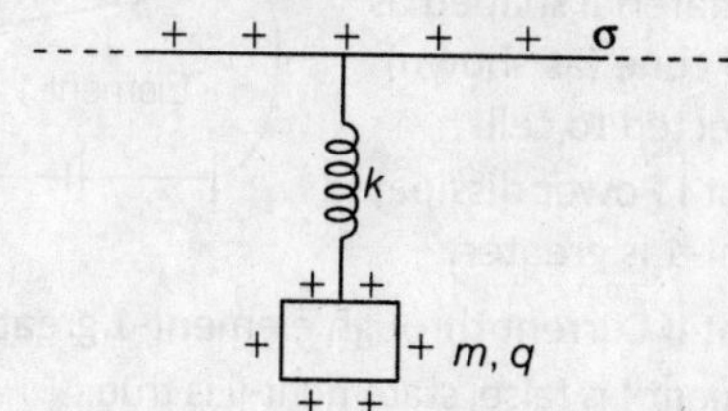

23. A dipole clock has an arrangement of 12 dipoles as shown. If net electric field at centre of the clock is along hour hand at the instant shown, find $\frac{p'}{p}$. (Take, $\sqrt{3} = 1.73$)

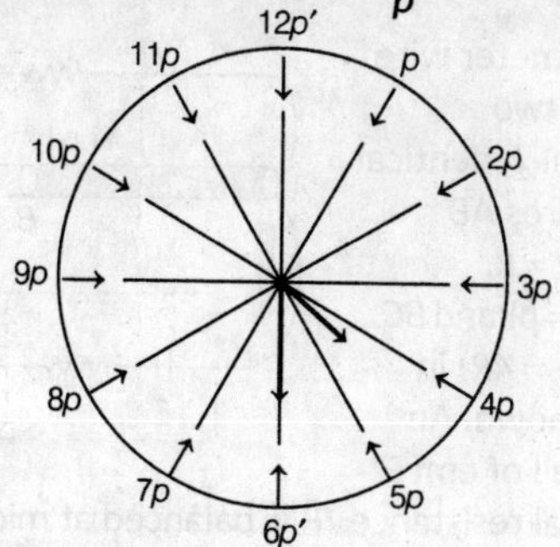

24. Consider the shown section at a perpendicular distance $\frac{R}{\sqrt{2}}$ from centre of the shown uniform solid sphere. Electric flux through the section is $\frac{Q}{x\,\varepsilon_0}$. Find x. (Take, $\sqrt{2} = 1.41$)

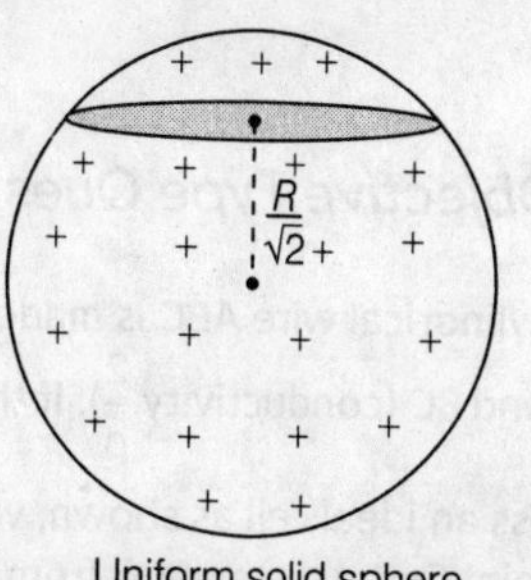

Uniform solid sphere
(Total charge = Q, Radius = R)

25. Figure here shows a system of three identical charged balls suspended in equilibrium from a common point by three identical insulating threads. Electrostatic potential energy of the system is U if each ball carries charge q. If charge on each ball was $8q$ instead of q potential energy of the system would be kU. Find k. (Assuming that separation between balls is very small compared to length of each string)

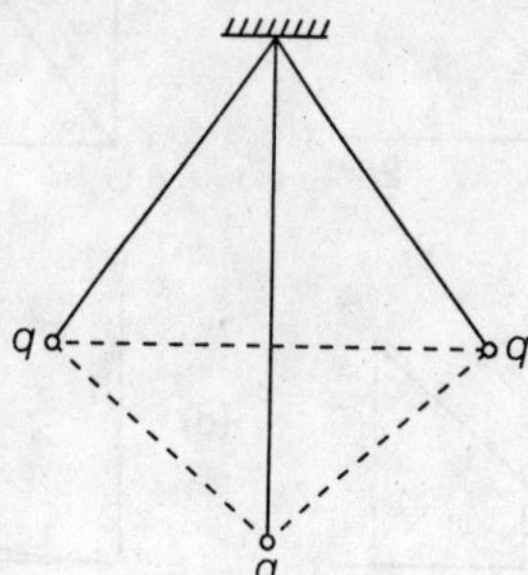

Answers

Section I

1 (a)	2 (b)	3 (d)	4 (c)	5 (d)
6 (d)	7 (d)	8 (b)	9 (b)	10 (d)
11 (c)	12 (c)	13 (d)	14 (a)	15 (c)
16 (b)	17 (a)	18 (b)	19 (d)	20 (c)

Section II

21 1.5	22 3	23 3.73	24 11.28	25 16

See detailed explanations on page no. 239

QUALIFIER 11

Current Electricity

Section I Objective Type Questions

1. A composite cylindrical wire ABC is made of wires AB (resistivity ρ) and BC (conductivity $\frac{2}{\rho}$). If the wire is arranged across an ideal cell as shown, variation of potential at point D at a distance x from end A may be represented by

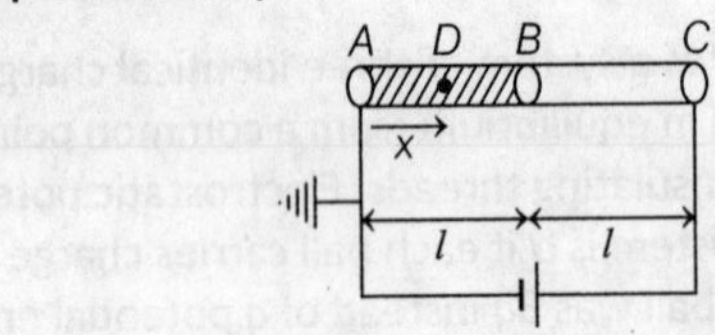

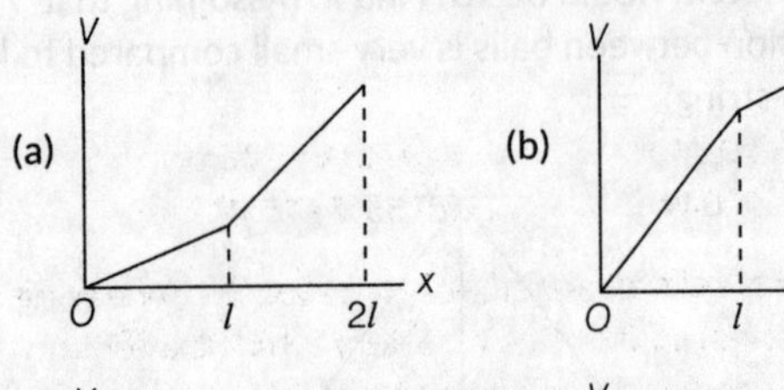

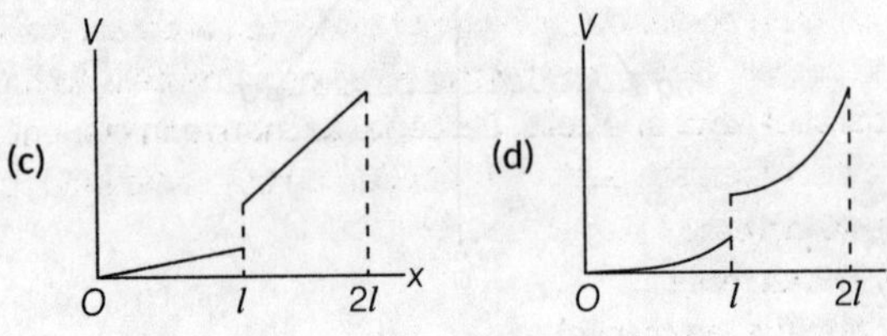

2. Average speed of electron due to random thermal motion and average drift speed of electron in a conductor may respectively be around

(a) 10^6 m/s, 10^{-3} m/s (b) 10^{-3} m/s, 10^{-6} m/s
(c) 10^{-3} m/s, 10^6 m/s (d) 10^{-6} m/s, 10^3 m/s

3. Figure shows a composite wire ABC in which cross-section radius of wire AB (resistivity ρ) increases linearly from r at end A to $3r$ at end B while resistivity of wire BC increases linearly from ρ at B, as we move towards C. If electric fields at mid-points of AB and BC are same, resistivity at end C is

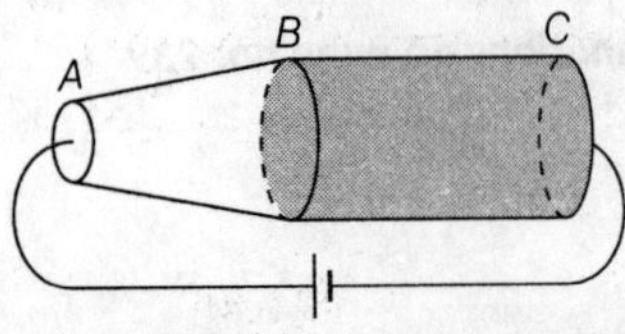

(a) 1.5ρ (b) 2.5ρ (c) 3.5ρ (d) 2.25ρ

4. Inner and outer curved surfaces of a long uniform thick conducting cylindrical shell of respective radii R and $4R$ are maintained at constant potentials V_1 and V_2, respectively. Distance of point having potential $\frac{V_1+V_2}{2}$ from axis of the cylinder is

(a) $1.5R$ (b) $2R$
(c) $2.5R$ (d) $3R$

5. Standard resistance coils are made using metal alloys as their

(a) thermal conductivity is high
(b) thermal resistivity is high
(c) thermal coefficient of resistivity is negative
(d) resistance depends weakly on temperature

6. Consider two elements of same thickness in a solid conductor made up of uniform material shaped as truncated cone (as shown) and connected to cell.

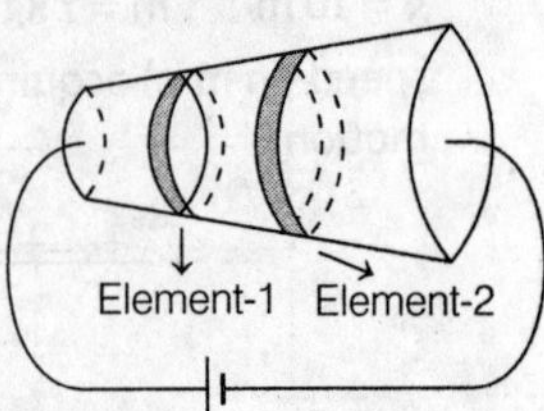

Statement I Power dissipated in element-1 is greater.

Statement II Current through element-1 greater.

(a) Statement-I is false, statement-II is true.
(b) Statement-I is true, statement -II is true, statement-II is correct explanation of statement-I.
(c) Statement-I is true, statement-II is true, statement-II is not correct explanation for statement-I.
(d) Statement-I is true, statement-II is false.

7. A potentiometer wire is made of two geometrically identical uniform wires AB (resistance $= R$, resistivity $= \rho$) and BC (resistance $= 4R$) in series as shown. An external cell of emf E and internal resistance $7R$ is balanced at mid-point of BC at D. Excess charge accumulated on interface of AB and BC is

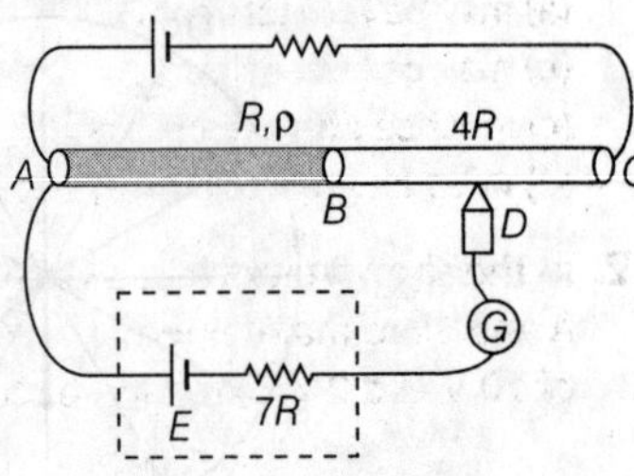

(a) $\frac{\varepsilon_0 E\rho}{R}$ (b) $\frac{\varepsilon_0 E\rho}{3R}$
(c) $\frac{3\varepsilon_0 E\rho}{R}$ (d) zero

8. N identical bulbs of resistance R each are connected in parallel to a cell. For $N = 5$, 6 and 7 collective powers consumed by bulbs are a, b and c respectively, such that $a < b > c$. Which of these may be resistance of cell?

(a) $\frac{5R}{35}$ (b) $\frac{6R}{35}$ (c) $\frac{7R}{35}$ (d) $\frac{8R}{35}$

9. Bands A, B, C and D of two identical resistors in parallel are grey, red, black and gold, respectively. Effective resistance of the combination between P and Q is

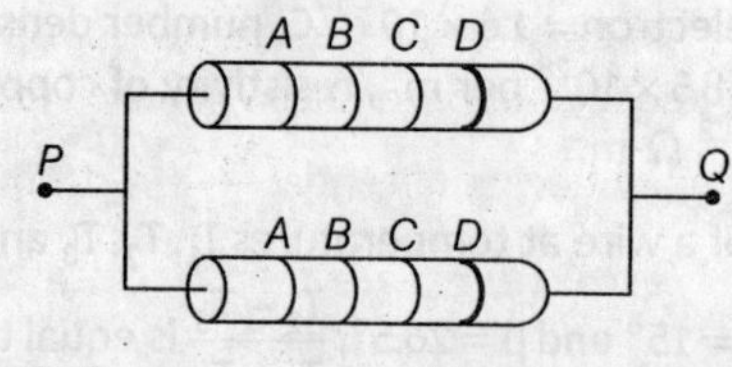

(a) $41 \pm 5\%\ \Omega$ (b) $41 \pm 2.5\%\ \Omega$
(c) $82 \pm 5\%\ \Omega$ (d) $82 \pm 2.5\%\ k\Omega$

10. Value of r for the external circuit to dissipate maximum power

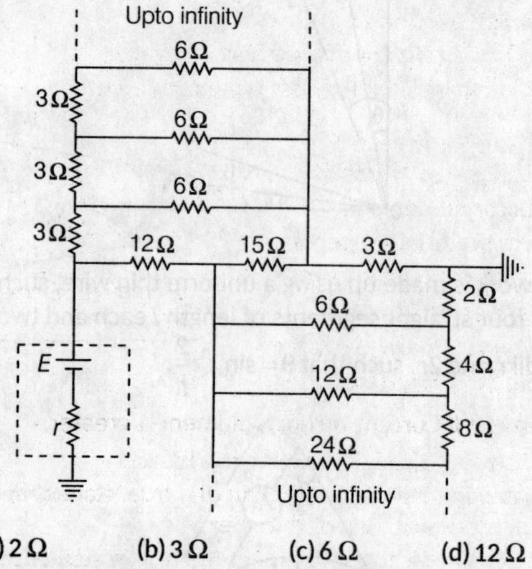

(a) 2 Ω (b) 3 Ω (c) 6 Ω (d) 12 Ω

11. Equivalent emf of two non-ideal cells of emfs E_1 and E_2 in parallel ($E_1 < E_2$)

(a) may be greater than E_2
(b) may be lesser than E_1
(c) must be average of E_1 and E_2
(d) must be greater than E_1 but lesser than E_2

12. In the shown branch of a circuit with identical cells, points A and B are maintained at constant respective potentials of 10 V and 2 V. Direction of current in resistor R

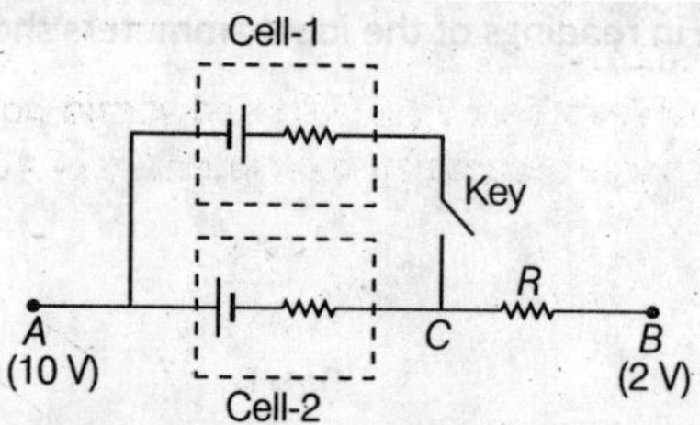

(a) must be from C to B, if key is open
(b) may be from B to C, if key is closed
(c) may be from B to C, if key is open
(d) must change, if key is closed from initial open state

13. Two cells of emf E each have internal resistances r and $3r$. Series combination of these cells is connected across an external resistance $2r$. Potential difference across the cell of internal resistance $3r$

(a) may be zero or E
(b) must be zero
(c) must be between zero and E
(d) may be greater than E

14. In the circuit shown, bulb-1 (resistance R) consumes same power on closing key-1 as that consumed by bulb-2 on closing key-2. If rating of bulb-1 is 220 V - 100 W, possible rating of bulb-2 is

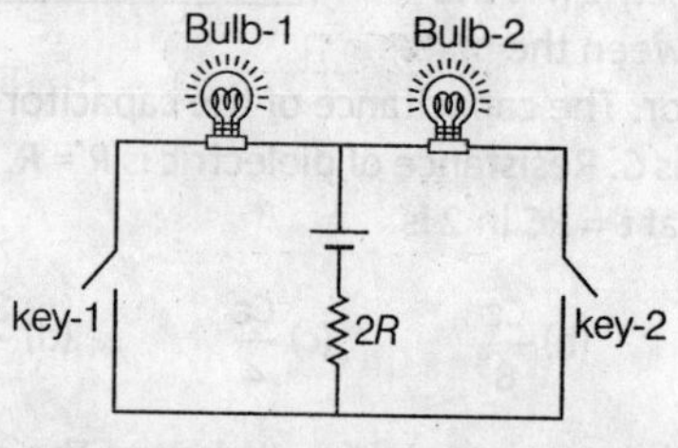

(a) 220 V - 50 W (b) 440 V - 100 W
(c) 110 V - 200 W (d) 55 V - 25 W

15. 12 identical cells arranged in 4 rows (each row having 3 cells in series) constitutes a battery which exhibits maximum power output when connected across a load. The battery is now re-structured using same cells to have 3 parallel rows of 4 cells. Percentage change in current drawn, when the battery is applied across same load, is

(a) 4% increase
(b) 4% decrease
(c) zero (i.e. no change)
(d) indeterminate due to insufficient information

16. Current I enters in shown network of twelve resistors at A and leaves at B, the current I' in 10 Ω resistor is (resistance of all resistors in Ohm are shown in the diagram)

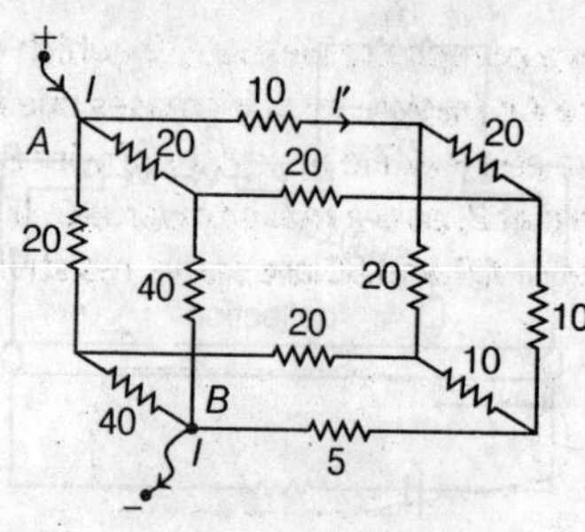

(a) $0.3I$ (b) $0.4I$
(c) $0.5I$ (d) $0.6I$

17. Readings of voltmeter and ammeter and their respective resistances are as shown in figure.

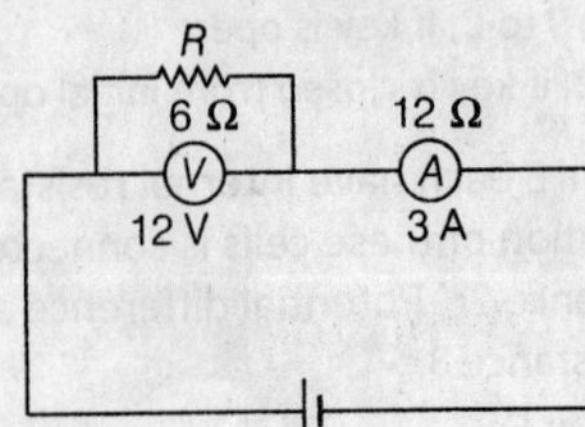

If positions of the meters are interchanged, voltmeter will read

(a) 12 V (b) 24 V (c) 36 V (d) 48 V

18. In the circuit diagram a capacitor which is initially uncharged is connected to an ideal cell of emf ε through a resistor R. A leaky dielectric fills the space between the plates of capacitor. The capacitance of the capacitor with dielectric is C. Resistance of dielectric is $R' = R$. Charge on capacitor at $t = RC \ln 2$ is

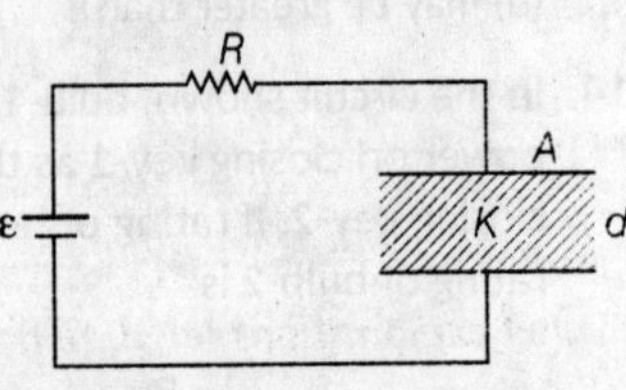

(a) $\frac{C\varepsilon}{2}$ (b) $\frac{C\varepsilon}{8}$ (c) $\frac{C\varepsilon}{4}$ (d) $\frac{3C\varepsilon}{8}$

19. Consider the steady state circuit shown. The charge q on the capacitor and sum of currents through 1 Ω and 3 Ω resistor, respectively are

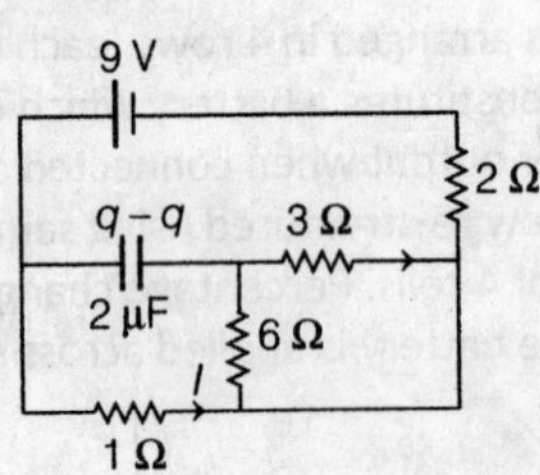

(a) 6 μC, 2 A (b) 18 μC, 2 A (c) 6 μC, 3 A (d) 18 μC, 3 A

20. As shown in the figure of meter bridge circuit, R_1 and R_2 have thermal coefficients of resistances as α_1 and α_2, respectively. On increasing the temperature of all resistors by same amount, balancing length l will change only when

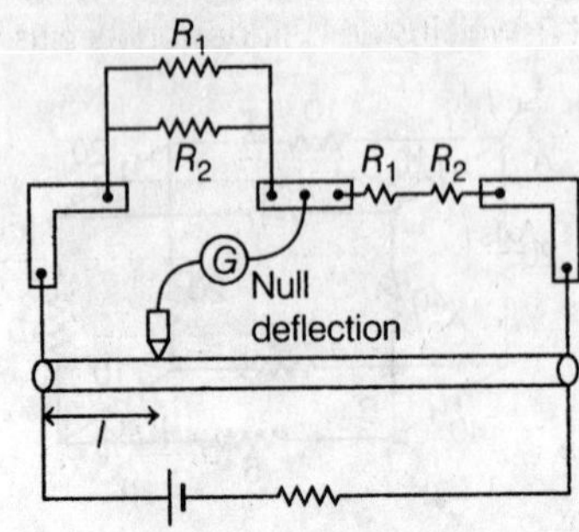

(a) $R_1 = 3R_2$ and $\alpha_1 = \alpha_2$
(b) $R_1 = R_2$ and $\alpha_1 = 4\alpha_2$
(c) $R_1 = R_2$ and $\alpha_1 = \alpha_2$
(d) $R_1 = 3R_2$ and $\alpha_1 = 4\alpha_2$

Section II *Numerical Value Questions*

21. Mean free time between collisions of electrons in copper at room temperature is of the order 10^{-x}. Find x, given that at room temperature mass of electron $= 9.11 \times 10^{-31}$ kg, charge on electron $= 1.6 \times 10^{-19}$C, number density of electrons $= 8.5 \times 10^{28}$ per m^3, resistivity of copper $= 1.72 \times 10^{-8}$ Ω-m.

22. V-I graphs of a wire at temperatures T_1, T_2, T_3 and T_4 are as shown. If $\theta = 15°$ and $\beta = 26.5°$, $\frac{T_2 - T_3}{T_1 - T_4}$ is equal to $\frac{3}{\sqrt{x}}$, find x.

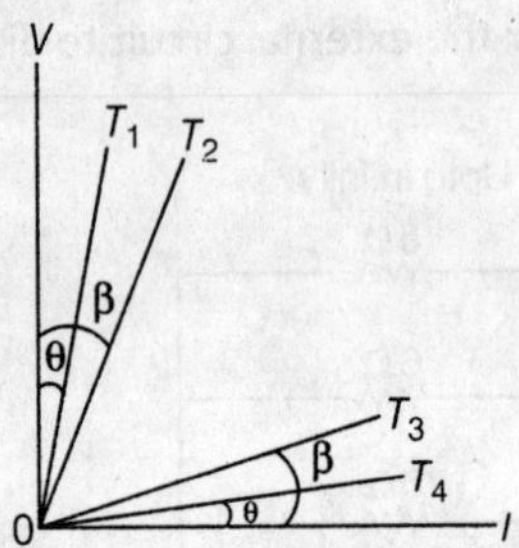

23. A network is made up using a uniform thin wire, such that it has four straight segments of length l each and two rings of radii r and $2r$, such that $\theta = \sin^{-1}\frac{2}{\pi}$.

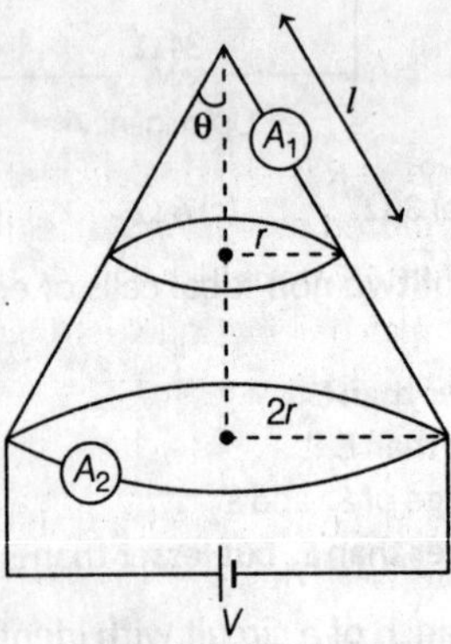

Resistance of each of the straight segments is R. Difference in readings of the ideal ammeters shown is $\frac{V}{xR}$.

Find x.

24. Power consumed by the shown circuit is independent of number of sections in the circuit. What is reading of the ideal ammeter in branch *AB* in amperes?

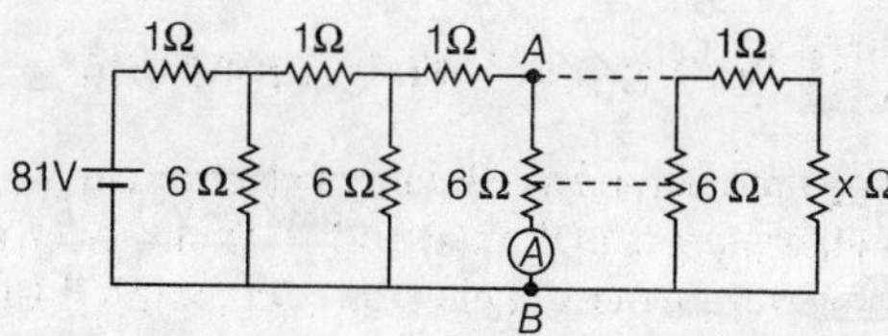

25. The figure shows *RC* circuit with a parallel plate capacitor. Before switching ON the circuit, plate *A* of the capacitor has a charge $-Q_0$ while plate *B* has no net charge. Now, at $t = 0$, the circuit is switched ON. Time at which net charge on plate *A* becomes zero is $RC \ln x$. Find *x*, if $Q_0 = CE$.

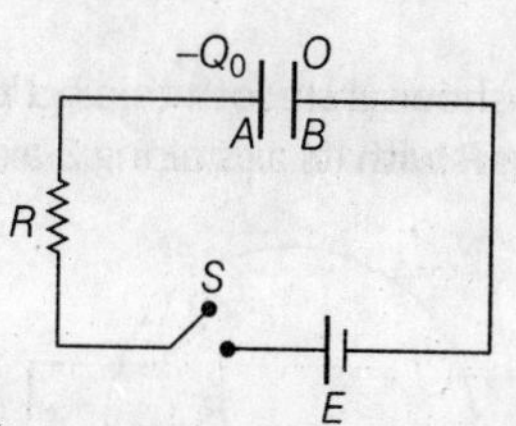

Answers

Section I

1 (b)	2 (a)	3 (c)	4 (b)	5 (d)
6 (d)	7 (a)	8 (b)	9 (a)	10 (c)
11 (d)	12 (c)	13 (a)	14 (b)	15 (b)
16 (b)	17 (b)	18 (d)	19 (c)	20 (d)

Section II

21 14	22 48	23 8	24 4	25 3

See detailed explanations on page no. 242

QUALIFIER 12

Magnetic Effects of Current and Magnetism

Section I *Objective Type Questions*

1. A cylinder of radius *R* is carrying current parallel to its axis uniformly distributed over its cross-section. Magnetic field at point *P*, distant 2*R* from its axis is *B*. Another point *Q*, inside cylinder also has same field. Magnetic field at mid-point of line joining *P* and *Q* is

(a) 1.2 *B* (b) 1.4 *B* (c) 1.6 *B* (d) 1.8 *B*

2. Current density in a thick cylindrical shell of inner radius *R* and outer radius 2*R* varies with distance *r* from axis as $J = \frac{k}{r}$, here *k* is a constant. Which of the following gives correct variation of $\oint \mathbf{B} \cdot d\mathbf{l}$ over an imaginary Amperian loop of radius *r* as function of *r*?

(a) 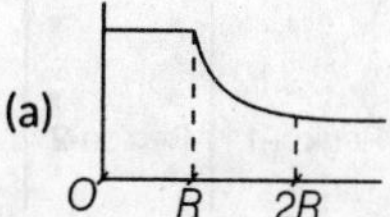

(b) 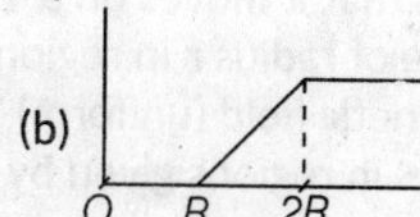

(c) 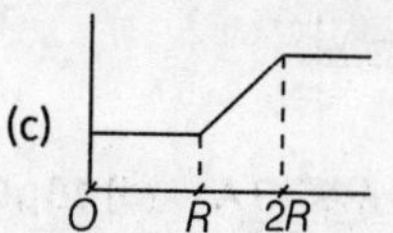

(d) 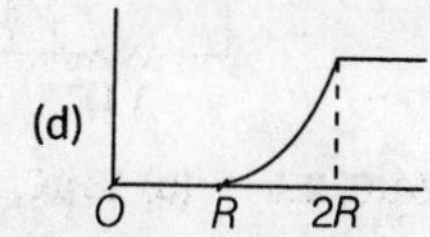

3. A thin long uniformly charged hollow cylinder is rotating about its axis with angular speed ω. If *R* represents radius of cylinder and *Q* is charge per unit length, magnetic field at point *P* well inside cylinder on its axis is

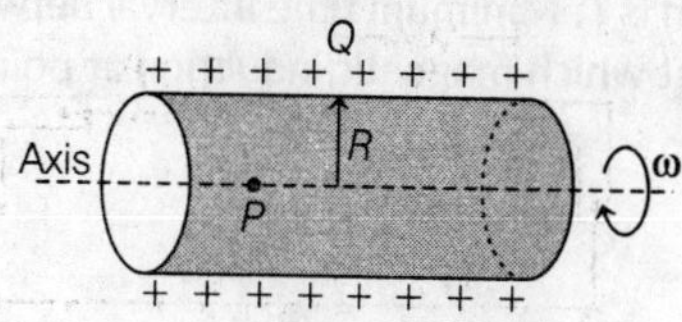

(a) $\mu_0 Q\omega$ (b) $\frac{\mu_0 Q}{\omega}$

(c) $\frac{\mu_0 Q\omega}{2\pi}$ (d) zero

4. The figure here shows a smooth thin hollow cylindrical surface of radius R with its axis along Z-axis.

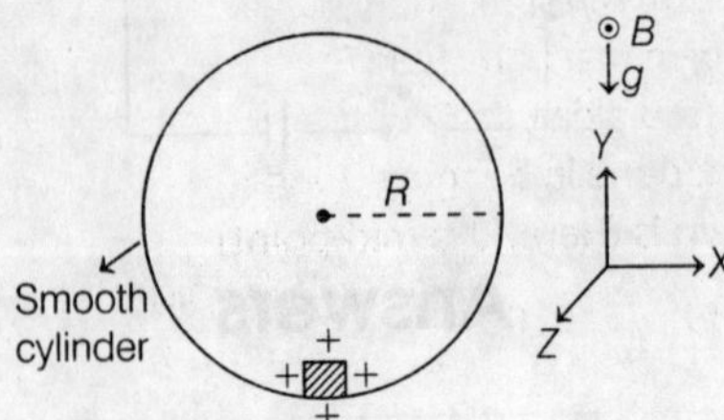

The region has uniform magnetic field $B\hat{k}$ and uniform gravitational field $-g\hat{j}$. A block of mass m and carrying charge q is imparted velocity $\frac{2mg}{qB}\hat{i}$. Minimum contact force applied by the block on the cylinder during subsequent motion is (Given that, $B=\frac{mg}{q\sqrt{2gR}}$)

(a) 2.6 mg (b) 3 mg
(c) 4.4 mg (d) zero

5. An infinite uniform horizontal sheet of current in XZ-plane carries current per unit width λ in positive x-direction. A particle P having charge q and mass m is moving with constant velocity $v\hat{i}$ at a perpendicular distance d below the sheet. If gravity disappears suddenly, radius of path followed by the particle is

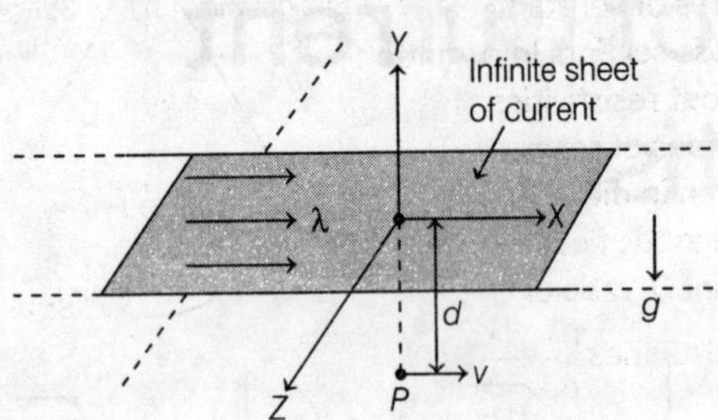

(a) $\frac{4m^2g}{q\mu_0^2\lambda^2}$ (b) $\frac{m^2g}{4q\mu_0^2\lambda^2}$
(c) $\frac{4m^2g}{q^2\mu_0^2\lambda^2}$ (d) $\frac{m^2g}{4q^2\mu_0^2\lambda^2}$

6. A positron is moving with constant speed on a circle of radius R in XY-plane centred at origin. Its time period of revolution is T. Minimum time interval between the instants at which magnetic induction at point $P(0, 2R, 0)$ is zero is

(a) $\frac{T}{6}$ (b) $\frac{T}{4}$
(c) $\frac{T}{3}$ (d) T

7. A charged particle (of charge q and mass m) is released at origin O in a region having uniform electric field (E) and magnetic field (B) as shown. The particle follows the path shown to $P(x, y)$. Speed of the particle at P is

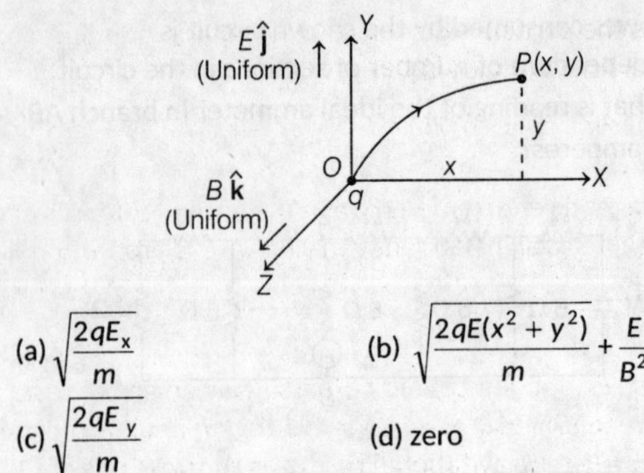

(a) $\sqrt{\frac{2qEx}{m}}$ (b) $\sqrt{\frac{2qE(x^2+y^2)}{m}+\frac{E}{B^2}}$
(c) $\sqrt{\frac{2qEy}{m}}$ (d) zero

8. A proton is projected with velocity $\mathbf{v}=v\hat{\mathbf{j}}$ in a region with uniform magnetic field $\mathbf{B}=B\hat{\mathbf{i}}$ at $t=0$. As the proton returns to its projection point for the first time at $t=T$, the uniform electric field $\mathbf{E}=E\hat{\mathbf{i}}$ is switched ON in the region. If average velocity in the time interval between $t=T$ and $t=2T$ is v, average velocity between $t=2T$ and $t=3T$ is

(a) v (b) 2 v (c) 3v (d) 4v

9. A vertical wire PQ of length l (hinged at P) carrying current I is attached to a thread QR at its end Q. Magnetic field in the region is uniform and is equal to B directed perpendicular inwards. Reaction at hinge, just after cutting the thread, is

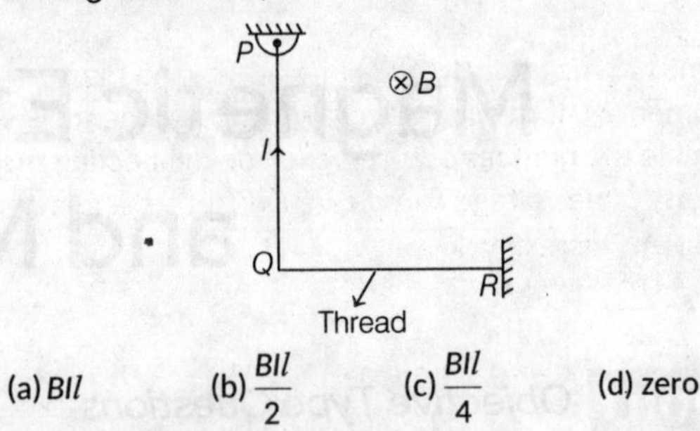

(a) BIl (b) $\frac{BIl}{2}$ (c) $\frac{BIl}{4}$ (d) zero

10. A uniformly charged infinite wire (charge density λ) carries current I along its length. A charge q moves with constant velocity v parallel to the wire. $\frac{v}{c^2}$ is equal to (Here, c is speed of light in vacuum)

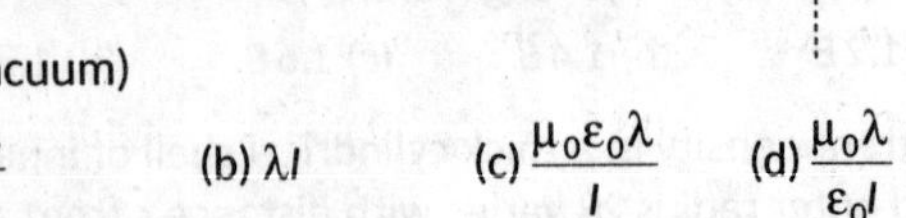

(a) $\frac{\lambda}{I}$ (b) λI (c) $\frac{\mu_0\varepsilon_0\lambda}{I}$ (d) $\frac{\mu_0\lambda}{\varepsilon_0 I}$

11. A charged particle of mass m and charge $+q$ enters a region of magnetic field moving with velocity $v\hat{i}$ such that it moves on a circle of radius r in region-1. Magnetic field (uniform) exists in regions given by

$\mathbf{B}=-B\hat{\mathbf{k}}$ $(0<x<d)$

$\mathbf{B}=B\hat{\mathbf{k}}$ $(d<x<2d)$

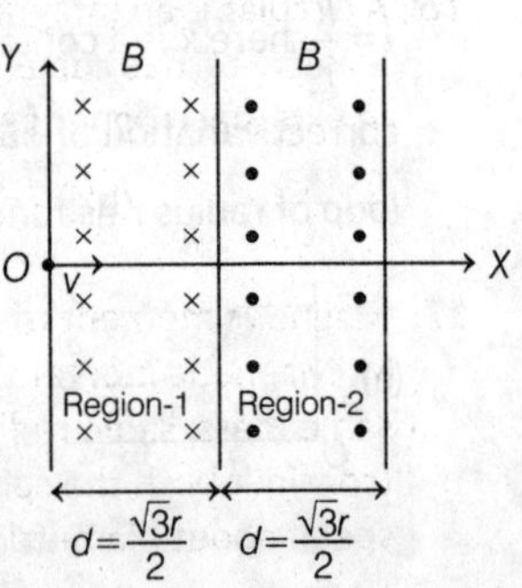

As the particle exits region-2, angular momentum of the particle, w.r.t. O, is

(a) mvr (b) $2mvr$ (c) $\frac{mvr}{2}$ (d) zero

12. Magnetic energy density at a distance r from axis of an infinite straight current carrying wire is proportional to

(a) r (b) $\frac{1}{r}$ (c) r^2 (d) $\frac{1}{r^2}$

13. A solid wooden cuboid of mass m is hanging at rest from threads P and Q at its ends in a region of uniform magnetic field B and gravitational field g as shown. Consider the dimensions in figure, current I in shown loop wound on the cuboid is

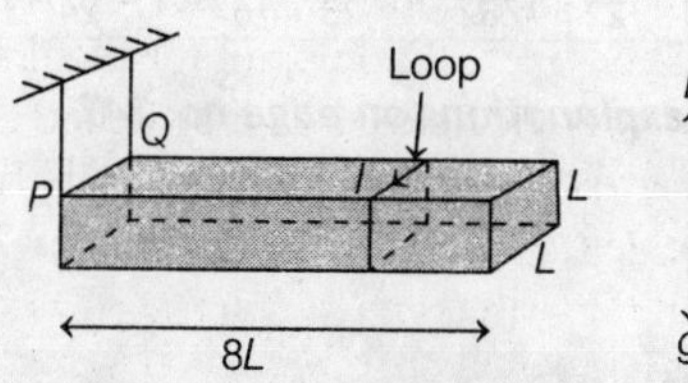

(a) $\frac{4mg}{BL}$ (b) $\frac{mg}{BL}$

(c) $\frac{mg}{4BL}$ (d) Indeterminate

14. A planar current carrying circular coil with N number of turns has magnetic field B at its centre and magnetic moment M. If the coil is redrawn into another coil with double the number of turns, then on connecting the coil across same voltage source, field at centre and magnetic moment respectively are

(a) $4B, \frac{M}{2}$ (b) $4B, 4M$

(c) $\frac{B}{2}, 4M$ (d) $2B, \frac{M}{2}$

15. Magnetic field due to a fixed current carrying straight wire at P is B with respect to a stationary observer. Now, the observer begins to move parallel to current with velocity $\frac{v}{4}$. Here, v is drift velocity of electrons. Magnetic field at same point P (w.r.t. observer) is

(a) B (b) $\frac{B}{4}$ (c) $\frac{3B}{4}$ (d) $\frac{5B}{4}$

16. A circular loop (magnetic moment M) made up of wire of length L carries current I. If the loop is in stable equilibrium in external magnetic field B, tension in the loop is

(a) $\frac{BM}{L}$ (b) $\frac{2BM}{L}$ (c) $\frac{BM}{IL}$ (d) $\frac{2BM}{IL}$

17. Magnetic moment of a uniformly charged solid sphere is M. Magnetic moment of a conducting solid sphere of same mass, same radius and carrying same charge is (consider both the sphere are rotating with same angular speed about diametrical axis).

(a) M (b) $1.67\ M$ (c) $0.6\ M$ (d) Infinite

18. A bar magnet PR (P being south pole) of magnetic moment M is placed in uniform magnetic field B directed along its length. Work done in bending it as shown is (Here, Q is mid-point)

(a) MB (b) $\frac{MB}{2}$ (c) $\frac{3MB}{2}$ (d) $\frac{3MB}{4}$

19. Apparent inclinations of magnetic field of earth measured by orienting dip circle in two mutually perpendicular vertical planes are 45° and $\cot^{-1}\sqrt{2}$. True dip at the location of measurements is

(a) 30° (b) $\cot^{-1}\sqrt{5}$ (c) 60° (d) $\tan^{-1}\sqrt{2}$

20. If a diamagnetic material is brought near one pole of a bar magnet, it is

(a) attracted feebly
(b) repelled feebly
(c) attracted if the pole is north
(d) attracted if the pole is south

Section II *Numerical Value Questions*

21. Current enters P and exits R in a loop $PQRS$ made of wires of constant cross-section. Information about resistivities and shapes of segments is given in diagram. If net magnetic field is zero at point O, ratio of resistivities $\frac{\rho_2}{\rho_1}$ is $\frac{x}{y}$. If x and y are minimum possible positive integers, find $x + y$.

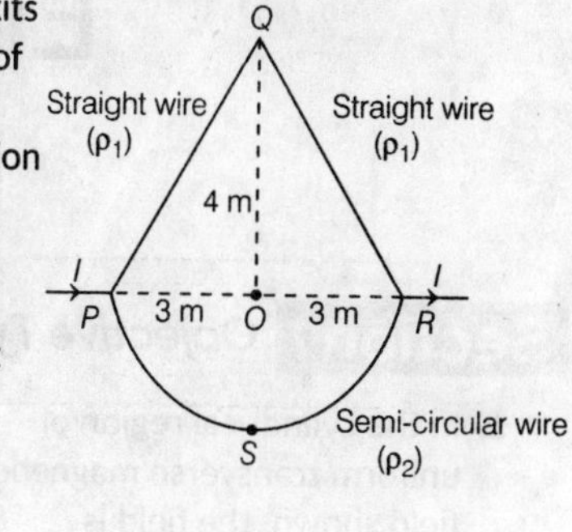

22. A charged block having specific charge 1 C/kg is released at rest on an smooth long incline in a region with uniform magnetic field. Find time (in s) at which the block leaves contact with the incline.

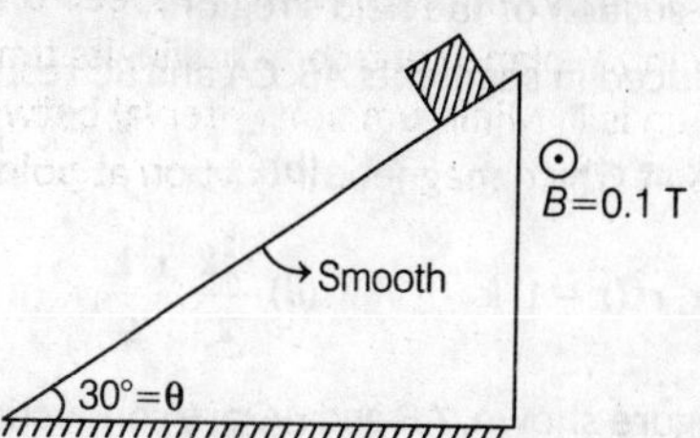

23. On slightly disturbing (vertically) wire PQ in equilibrium in Fig. 1, oscillates with time period T. On slightly disturbing the same wire in another arrangement in Fig. 2, it oscillates with time period T'. Find square of $\frac{T'}{T}$.

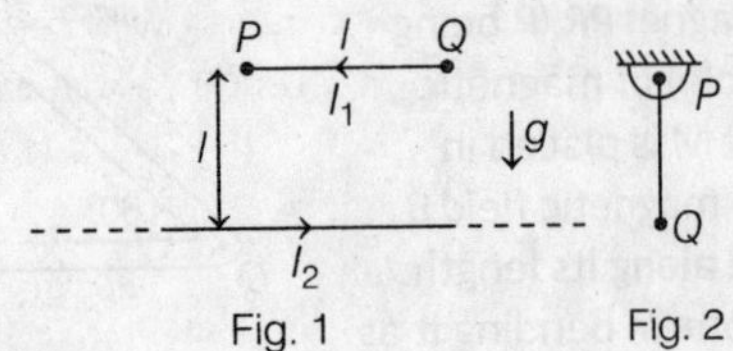

Fig. 1 Fig. 2

24. Four identical charges are fixed on periphery of a non-conducting ring (of radius R) rotating with angular speed ω about O. Force on any one of the charges due to magnetic interaction with the other three is $\frac{\mu_0 q^2 \omega^2}{\pi}\left(\frac{2\sqrt{2}+1}{x}\right)$. Find x.

25. Two short bar magnets are placed co-axially. If separation between the magnets is doubled, fractional decrease in magnetic force between the magnets is $\frac{x}{2}$. Find x.

Answers

Section I

1 (c)	2 (b)	3 (c)	4 (c)	5 (c)
6 (c)	7 (c)	8 (c)	9 (c)	10 (a)
11 (a)	12 (d)	13 (a)	14 (a)	15 (a)
16 (b)	17 (b)	18 (d)	19 (a)	20 (b)

Section II

21 41	22 17.32	23 0.67	24 16	25 1.87

See detailed explanations on page no. 247

QUALIFIER 13

Electromagnetic Induction & Alternating Current

Section I Objective Type Questions

1. In the cylindrical region of uniform transverse magnetic field shown, the field is increasing at constant rate k. A conducting loop ABC, shaped as a quarter circle of radius $2r$, has its plane perpendicular to the field. Side AB of the loop has its centre at point O which is centre of cross-section of the field's region.

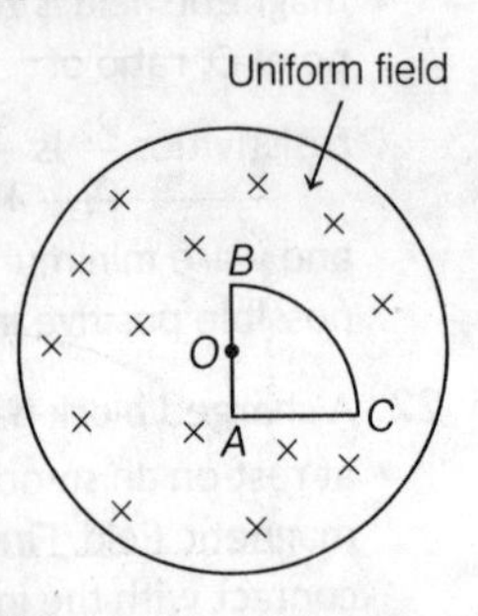

Emf induced in segments AB, CA and BC respectively are

(a) $0, r^2k, \pi r^2 k$
(b) $\frac{\pi r^2 k}{3}, \frac{\pi r^2 k}{3}, \frac{\pi r^2 k}{3}$
(c) $0, r^2 k, r^2(\pi - 1) k$
(d) $\frac{r^2 k}{2}, \frac{r^2 k}{2}, r^2(\pi - 1) k$

2. In the figure shown, AB and AC are conducting surfaces. A conducting wire PQ always in contact with the surfaces is moved by moving end Q with constant speed v along surface AC. The magnetic field B in the region is uniform and directed perpendicularly inwards. At the instant when no current is flowing in the loop PAQ, α is equal to

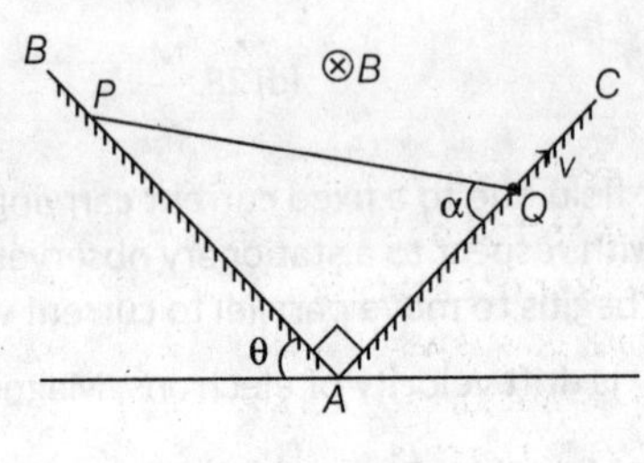

(a) θ
(b) $90° - \theta$
(c) $45°$
(d) $0°$ (approximately)

3. A long solenoid of radius R carries a time (t) dependent current $I(t) = I_0 t(1-t)$. A ring of radius $2R$ is placed coaxially near its middle. During the time interval $0 \le t \le 1$, the induced current (I_R) and the induced emf (V_R) in the ring change as

(a) direction of I_R remains unchanged and V_R is maximum at $t = 0.5$ s
(b) at $t = 0.25$ s, direction of I_R reverses and V_R is maximum
(c) direction of I_R remains unchanged and V_R is zero at $t = 0.25$ s
(d) at $t = 0.5$ s, direction of I_R reverses and V_R is zero

4. A very small circular loop of radius a is initially (at $t = 0$) coplanar and concentric with a much larger fixed circular loop of radius b. A constant current I flows in the larger loop. The smaller loop is rotated with a constant angular speed ω about the common diameter. The emf induced in the smaller loop as a function of time t is

(a) $\frac{\pi a^2 \mu_0 I}{2b} \omega \cos\omega t$
(b) $\frac{\pi a^2 \mu_0 I}{2b} \omega \sin\omega^2 t^2$
(c) $\frac{\pi a^2 \mu_0 I}{2b} \omega \sin\omega t$
(d) $\frac{\pi a^2 \mu_0 I}{2b} \omega \sin^2 \omega t$

5.

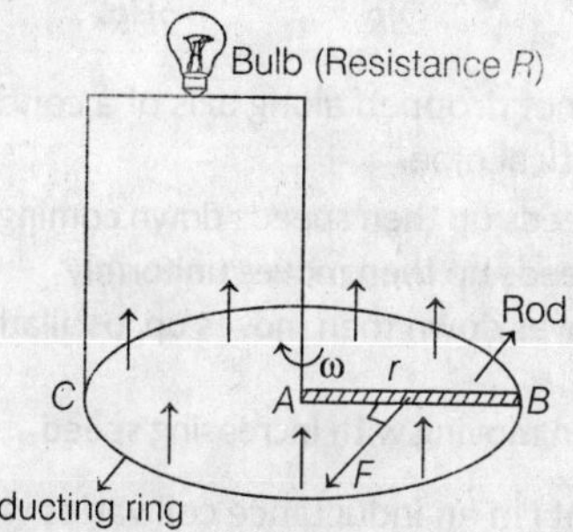

Figure here depicts a conducting rod AB pivoted at end A and free to move in horizontal plane about vertical axis through A in vertical magnetic field B. End B of the rod is in contact with a conducting ring of negligible resistance. One end of a bulb of resistance R is joined to point A and another end to the point C of the ring. A horizontal force of magnitude F (constant) acts at the centre of the rod perpendicular to the length of the rod making it to rotate with constant angular speed ω. Power delivered by the force F to the rod is $\frac{\omega^p r^q B^s}{tR}$. Value of $\sqrt{p \cdot q \cdot s \cdot t}$ is equal to

(a) 8
(b) 4
(c) $4\sqrt{2}$
(d) 1

6. Two long vertical parallel smooth rails are connected by a resistance R and capacitor of capacitance C at the two ends as shown in figure. A connector of mass m and length l in contact with the rails is released in the position shown. The arrangement is in a vertical plane perpendicular to magnetic meridian. If magnetic field of earth and angle of dip are B and θ respectively, steady state charge on the capacitor is

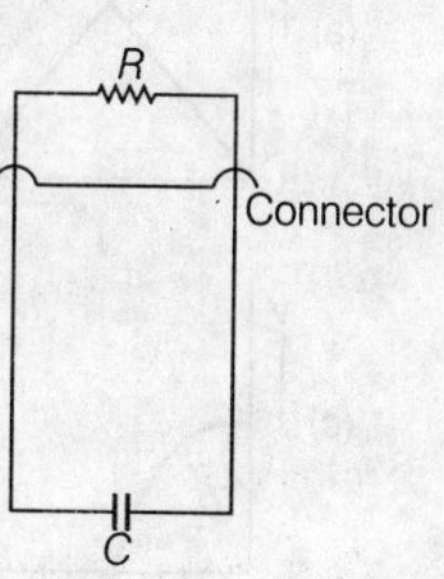

(a) $\frac{mgRC}{Bl\cos\theta}$
(b) $\frac{mgRC}{B^2 l^2 \cos^2\theta}$
(c) $\frac{mgRC}{Bl\sin\theta}$
(d) $\frac{mgRC}{B^2 l^2 \sin^2\theta}$

7. Segments of the shown arrangements are made up of uniform conducting wire. Magnetic field, which is perpendicularly inwards to the plane of arrangements, is uniform. If it is uniformly increasing with time, then which of the induced currents is correctly shown in direction?

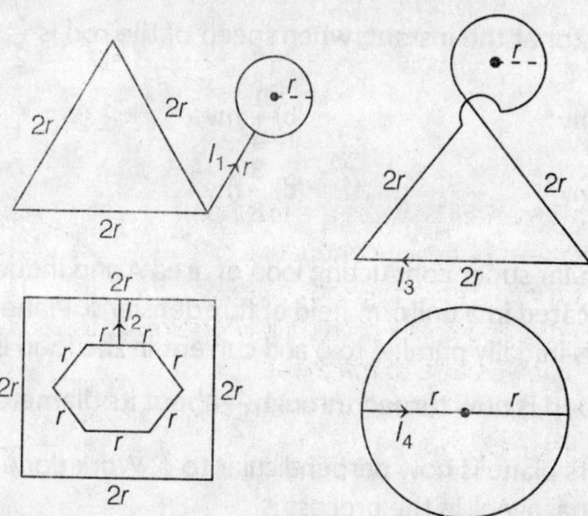

(The figures may not be upto the scale. The segments shown are triangular, straight, circular, square and hexagonal)

(a) I_1
(b) I_2
(c) I_3
(d) I_4

8. Iron cored coil in the Fig. 1 shown has been connected across the cell for a long time. If the core is now abruptly removed at $t = 0$, current I in the modified circuit shown in Fig. 2 is best represented as function of time t by

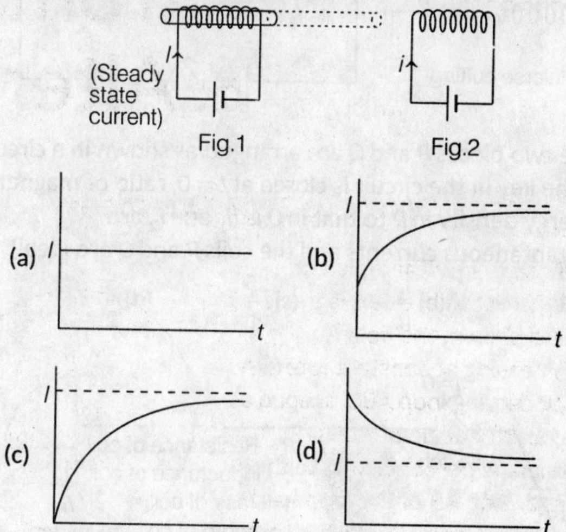

9. A gravity free space containing uniform magnetic field B is as shown.

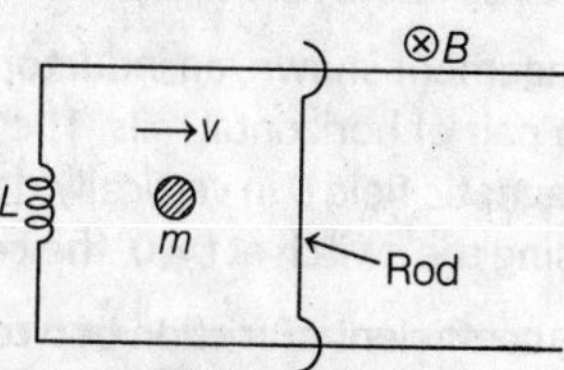

An arrangement of parallel rails is joined at one side by an ideal inductor of inductance L. A rod of mass m is resting on these rails in the diagram shown. A ball of mass m moving with speed v collides perpendicularly at the

centre of the rod elastically. There is no friction and resistance anywhere. Magnetic energy stored in the inductor at the instant, when speed of the rod is $\frac{v}{2}$, is

(a) $\frac{1}{2}mv^2$ (b) $\frac{1}{4}mv^2$

(c) $\frac{3}{4}mv^2$ (d) $\frac{3}{8}mv^2$

10. A circular super conducting loop of area A and inductance L is located in a uniform field of flux density ϕ. Plane of the loop is initially parallel to ϕ and current in the loop is zero. The loop is now turned through $\frac{\pi}{2}$ about its diameter such that its plane is now perpendicular to ϕ. Work done by external agent in the process is

(a) $\frac{\phi A}{2L}$ (b) $\frac{\phi^2 A^2}{2L}$ (c) $\frac{\phi A}{L}$ (d) zero

11. A uniform coil of inductance L is cut into two pieces in ratio 2 : 5 by length as shown.

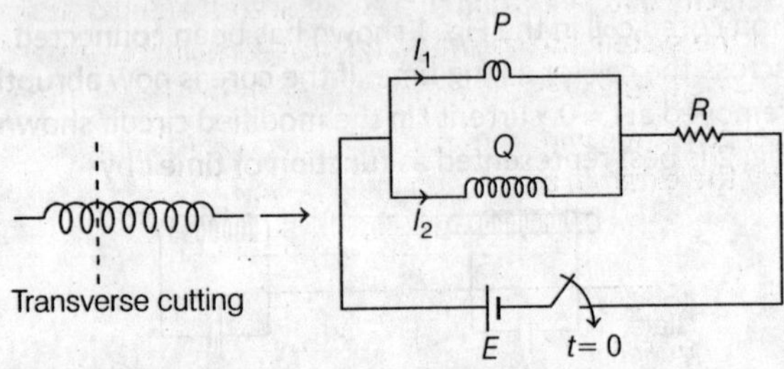

The two pieces P and Q are arranged as shown in a circuit. If the key in the circuit is closed at $t = 0$, ratio of magnetic energy density in P to that in Q is (I_1 and I_2 are instantaneous currents and the coils P and Q are ideal)

(a) 1 (b) $\frac{I_1}{I_2}$ (c) $\frac{25}{4}$ (d) $\frac{5}{2}$

12.

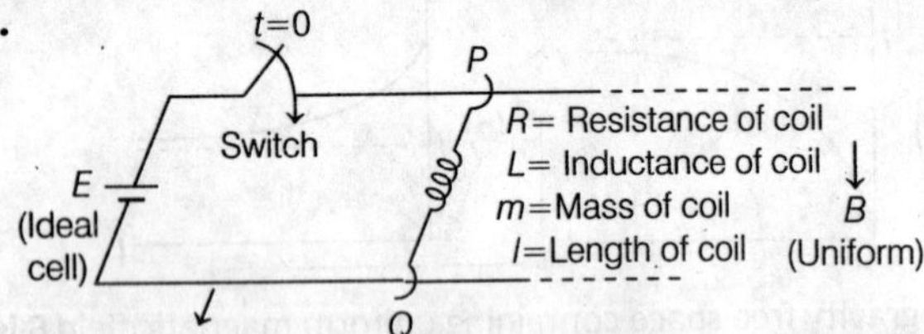

In the arrangement shown, an inductor coil PQ is placed at rest on a pair of horizontal rails. The region has a uniform magnetic field B in vertically downward direction. If after closing the switch at $t = 0$, the coil begins to slide at $t = \frac{L}{R}\ln 2$, coefficient of friction between coil and rails is

(a) $\frac{BEl}{2\,mgR}$ (b) $\frac{2BEl}{mgR}$

(c) $\frac{BEl}{mgR}(1 - e^{-1})$ (d) $\frac{BEle}{mgR}$

13. Figure here shows a system of coplanar regular hexagonal loop of side l and a small ring of radius $r(<<l)$ having its centre coinciding with centre of hexagon. Current I in the ring is changing with time t as $I = I_0 t$, here I_0 is constant. If resistance of hexagonal loop is R, power dissipated in one of the sides of the loop is

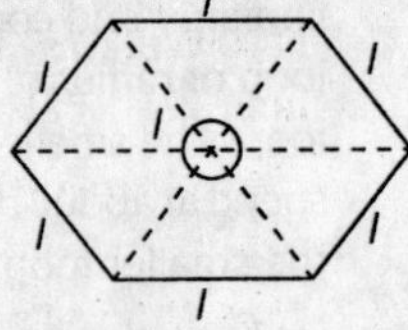

(a) $\frac{3\mu_0 I_0 r^2}{lR}$ (b) $\frac{\mu_0 I_0 r^2}{2lR}$ (c) $\frac{\mu_0^2 I_0^2 r^4}{2l^2 R}$ (d) $\frac{3\mu_0^2 I_0^2 r^4}{l^2 R}$

14. A bar magnet dropped along axis of a conducting large hollow vertical pipe

(a) first speeds up then speeds down coming to rest

(b) first speeds up then moves uniformly

(c) first moves down then moves up, oscillating during the motion

(d) keeps on moving with increasing speed

15. The current I in an inductance coil varies with time according to the graph given in the figure.

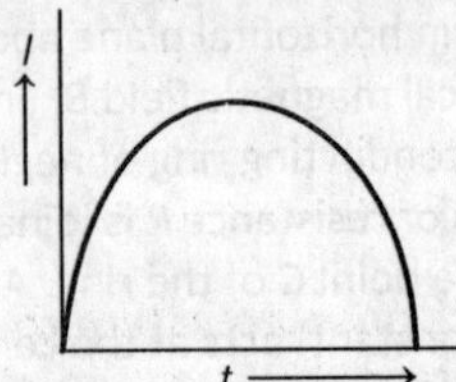

Which one of the following graphs may possibly give the variation of voltage with time across the inductor?

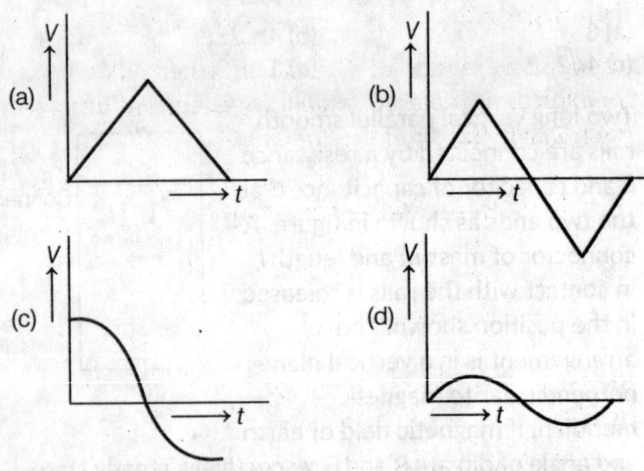

16. A series R-C circuit is connected to AC voltage source. Consider two cases : (A) when C is without a dielectric medium and (B) when C is filled with dielectric of constant 4. The current I_R through the resistor and voltage V_C across the capacitor are compared in the two cases. Which of the following is true?

(a) $I_R^A > I_R^B$ (b) $I_R^A < I_R^B$

(c) $V_C^A = V_C^B$ (d) $V_C^A < V_C^B$

17. In the circuit shown, the key is initially open. If the key is now closed for long time, power consumed by bulb-1 (100 W-220 V) is double the power being consumed by bulb-2.

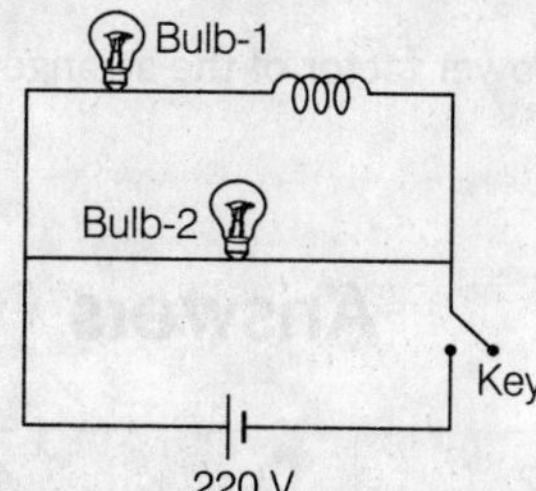

The key is now opened. Just after the key is opened, total power consumed by both the bulbs together is

(a) zero (b) 150 W
(c) 300 W (d) 100 W

18. In the shown circuit, specifications of various elements are $L = \frac{1}{\pi}$ H, $C = \frac{50}{\pi}$ μF, $R = 100\ \Omega$, $V = 400\sqrt{2}\sin(100\pi t)$.

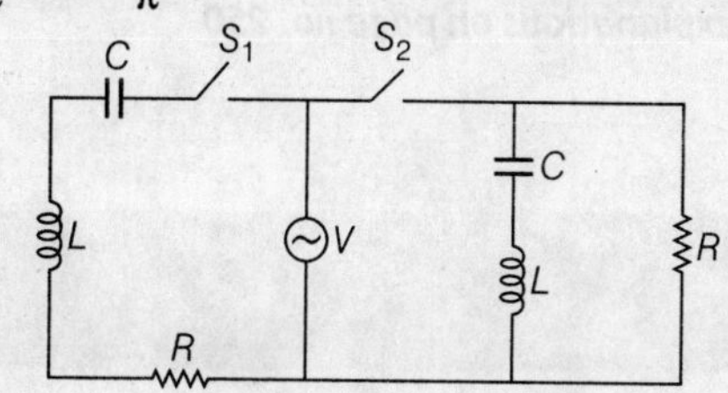

If only S_1 is closed, rms current through the AC source is I_1, while phase difference between applied voltage and current is ϕ_1. On closing S_2 only, corresponding values are I_2 and ϕ_2. Choose the correct option.

(a) $I_1 = I_2, \phi_1 = \phi_2$ (b) $I_2 = 2I_1, \phi_1 = \phi_2$
(c) $I_1 = I_2, \phi_2 = 2\phi_1$ (d) $I_2 = 2I_1, \phi_2 = 2\phi_1$

19. In the shown series *L-C-R* AC circuit when either capacitor or inductor is replaced by plain wire, current becomes half. Quality factor of the circuit is

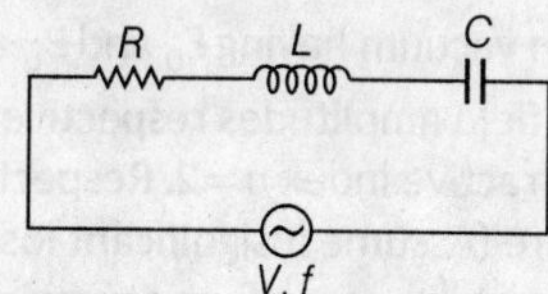

(a) 1 (b) 2
(c) $\sqrt{3}$ (d) 4

20. A transformer consisting of 300 turns in the primary and 150 turns in the secondary gives output power of 2.2 kW. If the current in the secondary coil is 10 A, then the input voltage and current in the primary coil are

(a) 440 V and 5 A (b) 220 V and 20 A
(c) 220 V and 10 A (d) 440 V and 20 A

Section II *Numerical Value Questions*

21. Consider the figure shown. A rectangular loop of sides *a* and *b* is located near an infinite wire carrying current *I*.

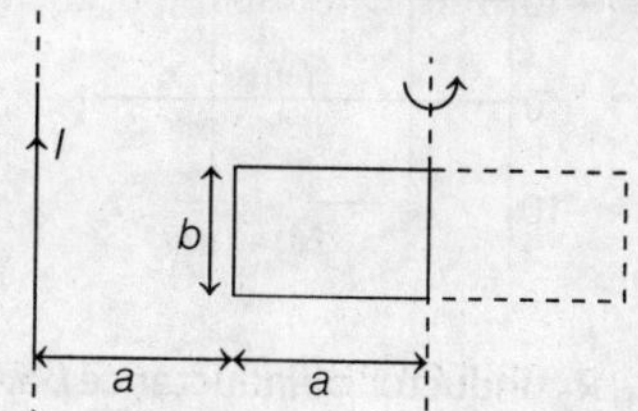

Charge that flows through the loop as it is turned by 180° about the edge shown is *q*, if current in straight wire is $I = I_0$ (constant). But if the loop is fixed in the position shown and current is varied according to the equation $I = I_0 e^{-t}$, *t* is time in seconds, initial current in the loop is *c*. Find $\frac{q}{c}$, if $\frac{\ln 3}{\ln 2} = 1.57$.

22. In the set-up shown, a conducting rod of zero resistance is pulled on a pair of horizontal U-shaped rails with constant velocity of 0.1 m/s. Initial position of rod and dimensions of the system are shown. A uniform vertical magnetic field $B = 4t$ T pervades the region shown. If resistance per unit length of rail wire is $r = 0.8\ \Omega$/m, find force *F* applied (in N) by the external agent/person at $t = 2$ s.

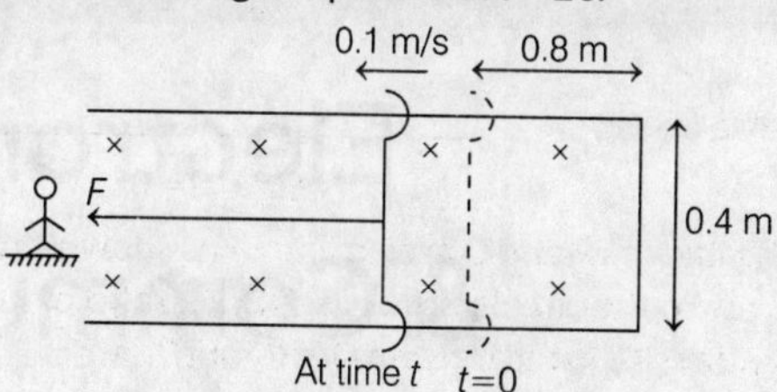

23. A non-conducting ring of mass *m*, radius 2*R* and uniform linear charge density σ is at rest in a gravity free space in *YZ*-plane with centre at origin as shown.

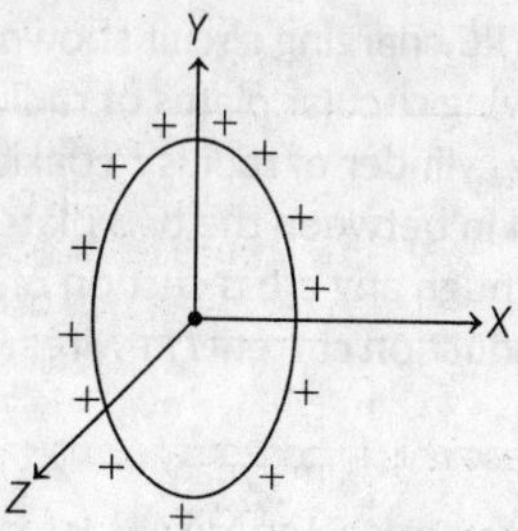

A uniform magnetic field $B\hat{i}$ is switched ON in the region $y^2 + z^2 = R^2$

As a result of sudden switching ON of magnetic field, the ring begins to rotate instantly about *X*-axis with angular speed $\frac{\sigma RB}{nm}$. Find *n*. $\left(\text{Take, } \pi = \frac{22}{7}\right)$

24. Find rms voltage (in V) of the waveform shown in volt.

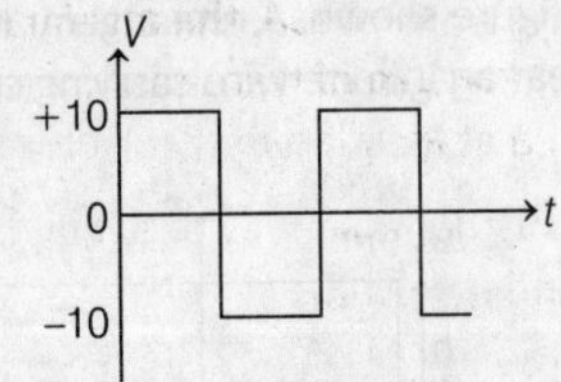

25. Resistors R_1, R_2, inductor of inductance L and capacitor of capacitance C are arranged in following three manners.

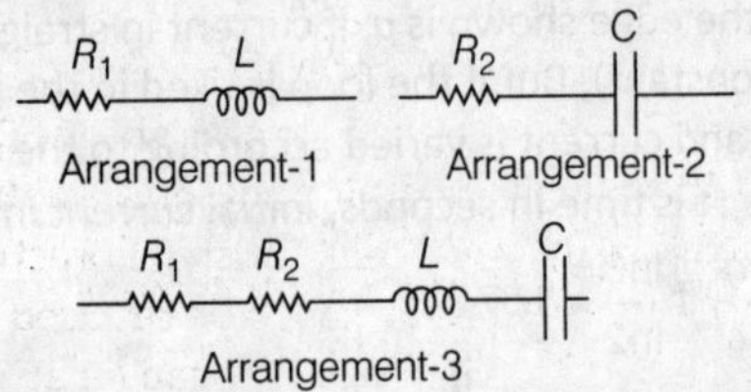

Power factor of arrangement-1 is 0.6 while that of arrangement-3 is 1 (corresponding to resonance). If AC source applied across the three arrangements is same and $R_2 = 8R_1$, power factor of the arrangement-2 is $\sqrt{\dfrac{x^2}{x^2+1}}$.

Find x.

Answers

Section I

1 (c)	2 (c)	3 (d)	4 (c)	5 (a)
6 (a)	7 (c)	8 (d)	9 (d)	10 (b)
11 (c)	12 (a)	13 (c)	14 (b)	15 (c)
16 (b)	17 (c)	18 (b)	19 (c)	20 (a)

Section II

21 1.57	22 3.2	23 0.63	24 10	25 6

See detailed explanations on page no. 250

QUALIFIER 14

Electromagnetic Waves & Communication Systems

Section I *Objective Type Questions*

1. Consider the *RC* charging circuit shown, with parallel plate capacitor having circular plates of radius $2r$. Also, consider an imaginary cylinder of radius r coaxial with the system of plates and in between the two plates. Displacement current I' through any cross-section of the cylinder in terms of conduction current I in wires, is

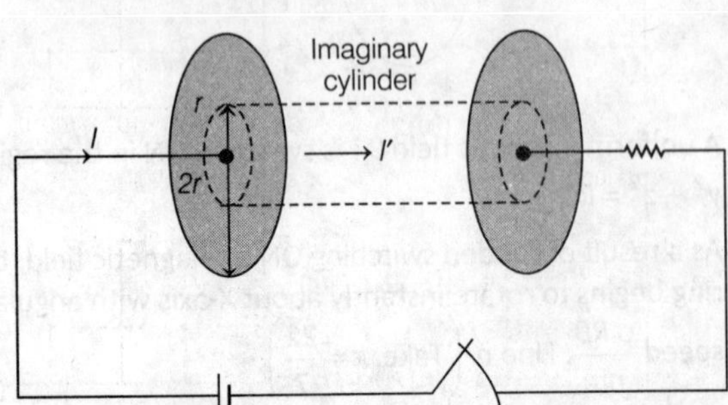

(a) I (b) $\dfrac{I}{2}$ (c) $\dfrac{I}{4}$ (d) $\dfrac{3I}{4}$

2. An EM wave in vacuum having E_0 and B_0 as electric field and magnetic field amplitudes respectively, enters a medium of refractive index $n = 2$. Respective amplitudes in the medium are (Assume insignificant loss and relative magnetic permeability of medium approximately equal to 1)

(a) $\dfrac{E_0}{\sqrt{2}}, \dfrac{B_0}{\sqrt{2}}$ (b) $\dfrac{E_0}{\sqrt{2}}, \sqrt{2}\,B_0$

(c) $\sqrt{2}\,E_0, \sqrt{2}\,B_0$ (d) $\sqrt{2}\,E_0, \dfrac{B_0}{\sqrt{2}}$

3. In a plane EM wave, directions of electric and magnetic fields are represented by $\sqrt{3}\,\hat{i} + \hat{j}$ and $\hat{k}$, respectively. Unit vector in direction of propagation of wave is

(a) $\dfrac{\hat{i} + \sqrt{3}\,\hat{j}}{2}$ (b) $\dfrac{\hat{i} - \sqrt{3}\,\hat{j}}{2}$ (c) $\dfrac{\sqrt{3}\,\hat{i} + \hat{j}}{4}$ (d) $\dfrac{\sqrt{3}\,\hat{i} - \hat{j}}{2}$

4. Poynting vector of an electromagnetic wave may be represented as (**E** = electric field, **B** = magnetic field, **c** = wave velocity, ε_0 = permittivity of free space, μ_0 = permeability of free space)

(a) $\mu_0 \mathbf{B} \times (\mathbf{c} \times \mathbf{B})$ (b) $\mu_0 (\mathbf{c} \times \mathbf{B}) \times \mathbf{B}$

(c) $\varepsilon_0 \mathbf{E} \times (\mathbf{c} \times \mathbf{E})$ (d) $\varepsilon_0 (\mathbf{c} \times \mathbf{E}) \times \mathbf{E}$

5. The electric field in a plane electromagnetic wave is given by $\mathbf{E} = \frac{1}{\sqrt{8.85}} \cos\left[\left(\frac{0.75 \times 10^3}{m}\right)x - \left(1.5 \times 10^{11} \frac{\text{rad}}{s} \times t\right)\right] \frac{\text{V}}{\text{m}} \hat{\mathbf{j}}$

This wave falls normally on a perfectly reflecting surface have an area of 72 cm^2. Radiation pressure (pascal) exerted by the EM wave on the surface during a 2 min exposure is

(a) 10^{-8} (b) 10^{-10}

(c) 10^{-12} (d) 10^{-14}

6. Electric field wave amplitude at a distance r from a point source/bulb of power P emitting EM wave with efficiency η is

(a) $\sqrt{\frac{\eta P}{2 \pi \varepsilon_0 c r^2}}$ (b) $\sqrt{\frac{2 \pi \eta P}{\varepsilon_0 c r^2}}$

(c) $\sqrt{\frac{2 \pi \varepsilon_0 c r^2}{\eta P}}$ (d) $\sqrt{\frac{\varepsilon_0 c r^2}{2 \pi \eta P}}$

7. Match List-I (Electromagnetic wave type) with List-II (Its association/application) and select the correct option from the choices given below the lists.

	List-I		List-II
A.	Infrared waves	1.	To treat muscular strain
B.	Radiowaves	2.	For broadcasting
C.	X-rays	3.	To detect fracture of bones
D.	Ultraviolet rays	4.	Absorbed by the ozone layer of the atmosphere

(a) A-4 B-3 C-2 D-1 (b) A-1 B-2 C-4 D-3

(c) A-3 B-2 C-1 D-4 (d) A-1 B-2 C-3 D-4

8. Two antennas having heights in the ratio 4 : 9 are separated by distance d as shown below. If the shorter one is receiving antenna, the minimum possible height of the transmitting antenna in terms of radius of curvature R of earth is

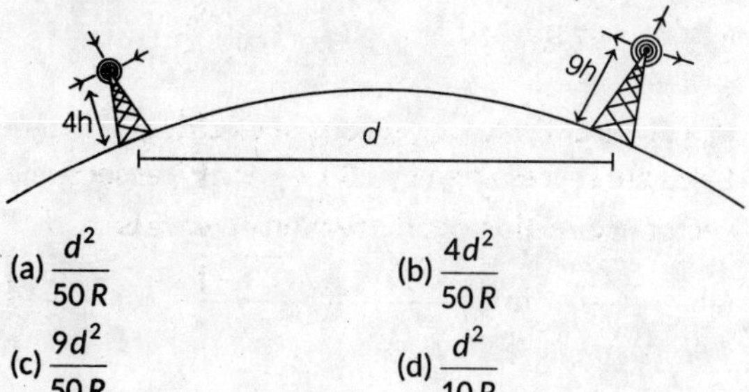

(a) $\frac{d^2}{50 R}$ (b) $\frac{4d^2}{50 R}$

(c) $\frac{9d^2}{50 R}$ (d) $\frac{d^2}{10 R}$

9. A signal of power P is transmitted in a cable. While the signal is getting transmitted, the attenuation, it suffers in decibel per unit length of transmission cable is constant. If power received at location of receiver is P', then power P_m at cable's section mid-way between locations of transmitter and receiver is

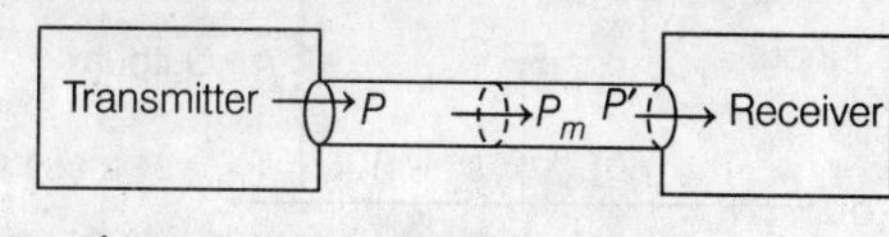

(a) $\frac{P + P'}{2}$ (b) $P + P'$

(c) $P - P'$ (d) $\sqrt{PP'}$

10. A TV transmission antenna is at a height of 80 m above earth's surface while receiving antenna is at height of 20 m above earth's surface. If for some practical reason, receiving antenna's height has to be reduced to zero, percentage decrease in range that can be achieved by the pair of antennas is

(a) 20% (b) 33.33%

(c) 50% (d) 66.67%

11. A carrier wave is modulated by infinite number of sine waves having individual modulation indices $\frac{1}{4}, \frac{1}{4\sqrt{2}}, \frac{1}{8}, \frac{1}{8\sqrt{2}}$ and so on. Modulation index of the AM wave is

(a) $\frac{1}{2}$ (b) $\frac{1}{2\sqrt{2}}$

(c) $\frac{\sqrt{2}}{4(\sqrt{2}-1)}$ (d) $\frac{\sqrt{2}+1}{4}$

12. An AM wave is represented by the equation

$V = (a + 4 \sin 10^4 \pi t) \sin\left(10^7 \pi t + \frac{\pi}{4}\right)$

Here, a is constant. If modulation index of the wave is 0.5, which of the following correctly represents frequency spectrum of the given AM wave?

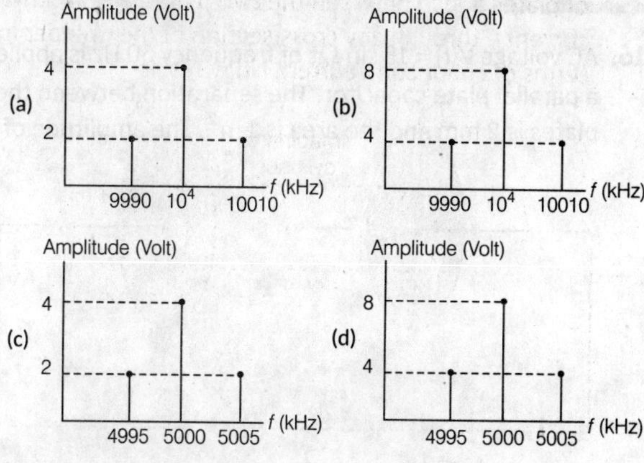

13. R and C in the envelope detector circuit shown are $0.5\,k\Omega$ and $2\,\mu F$, respectively. The detector will be most suitable for detection of carrier wave having frequency

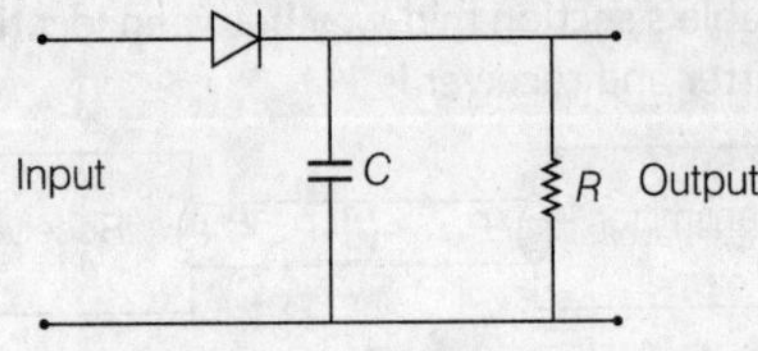

(a) 0.2 kHz (b) 0.8 kHz (c) 1.6 kHz (d) 16 kHz

14. On a certain day, electromagnetic signals of frequency greater than 6 MHz are not reflected back to earth by F_1 layer of ionosphere. Maximum electron density of the F_1 layer of ionosphere on that day is

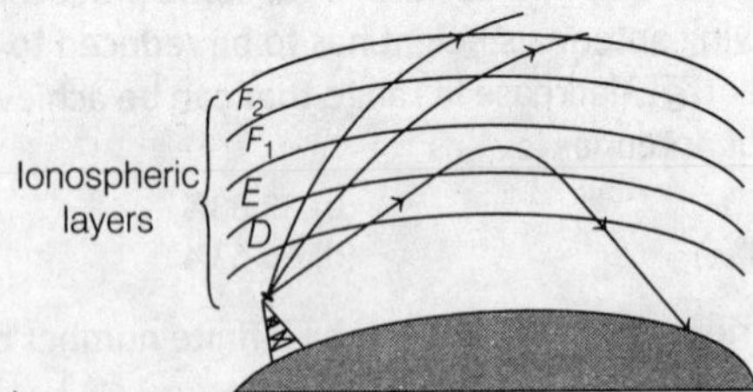

D-part of stratosphere (65 to 75 km height)
E-part of stratosphere (100 km height)
F_1-part of mesosphere (170 to 190 km height)
F_2-part of thermosphere (250 to 400 km height)

(a) $4.4 \times 10^{11}\ m^{-3}$ (b) $9\sqrt{6} \times 10^{3}\ m^{-3}$
(c) $0.16 \times 10^{-6}\ m^{-3}$ (d) $3.6 \times 10^{13}\ m^{-3}$

15. If the sum of heights of transmitting and receiving antennas in the line of sight of communication is fixed at 40 m, then the maximum range (in km) of LOS communication is (Take, radius of earth $R = 6400$ km)

(a) 16 (b) 32 (c) 64 (d) 128

Section II *Numerical Value Questions*

16. AC voltage $V(t) = 18 \sin \Omega t$ of frequency 50 Hz is applied to a parallel plate capacitor. The separation between the plates is 2 mm and the area is $1\,m^2$. The amplitude of the oscillating displacement current (in μA) for the applied AC voltage is .... [Take, $\varepsilon_0 = 8.85 \times 10^{-12}$ F/m]

17. The magnetic field vector of an electromagnetic wave is given by $B = B_0 \dfrac{\hat{i} + \hat{j}}{\sqrt{2}} \cos(kz - \omega t)$; where $\hat{\mathbf{i}}, \hat{\mathbf{j}}$ represents unit vector along X and Y-axes, respectively. At $t = 0$ s, two electric charges q_1 of 6π coulomb and q_2 of 2π coulomb located at $\left(0, 0, \dfrac{\pi}{k}\right)$ and $\left(0, 0 \dfrac{3\pi}{k}\right)$ respectively, have the same velocity of $0.25\, c\, \hat{\mathbf{i}}$, (where, c is the velocity of light). The ratio of the magnetic forces acting on charge q_1 to q_2 is ....

18. The electric fields of two plane electromagnetic plane waves in vacuum are given by

$$\mathbf{E}_1 = E_0 \hat{\mathbf{j}} \cos(\omega t - kx) \text{ and } \mathbf{E}_2 = E_0 \hat{\mathbf{k}} \cos(\omega t - ky)$$

At $t = 0$, a particle of charge q is at origin moving with a velocity $\mathbf{v} = 0.8c\hat{\mathbf{j}}$ (c is the speed of light in vacuum). The instantaneous force experienced by the particle is $E_0 q(A\hat{\mathbf{i}} + \hat{\mathbf{j}} + B\hat{\mathbf{k}})$ N. Find the value of A / B.

19. In an *FM* system a 8 kHz signal modulates 102.6 MHz, so that frequency deviation is 52 kHz. Find Carrier Swing (CS) of the wave.

20. A telephonic communication service is working at carrier frequency of 10 GHz. Only 10% of it is utilised for transmission. The telephonic channels that can be transmitted simultaneously, if each channel requires a bandwidth of 5 kHz is $x \times 10^5$. Find the value of x.

Answers

Section I

1 (c)	2 (b)	3 (b)	4 (c)	5 (c)
6 (a)	7 (d)	8 (c)	9 (d)	10 (b)
11 (b)	12 (d)	13 (d)	14 (a)	15 (b)

Section II

16 25	17 3	18 4	19 6.5	20 2

See detailed explanations on page no. 255

QUALIFIER 15

Optics

Section I Objective Type Questions

1. A small bulb is placed at the bottom of a tank containing water to a depth of 80 cm. What is the area of the surface of water through which light from the bulb can emerge out? Refractive index of water is 1.33. (Consider the bulb to be a point source).

(a) 4.6 m^2 (b) 3.2 m (c) 5.6 m^2 (d) 2.6 m^2

2. For the system shown in the figure, a luminous point object O is moving with velocity u on axis of a converging mirror moving along axis with velocity $2u$. The object is separated from the mirror by a slab of glass (refractive index equal to 1.5 and moving with speed $3u$). The image formed by the concave mirror

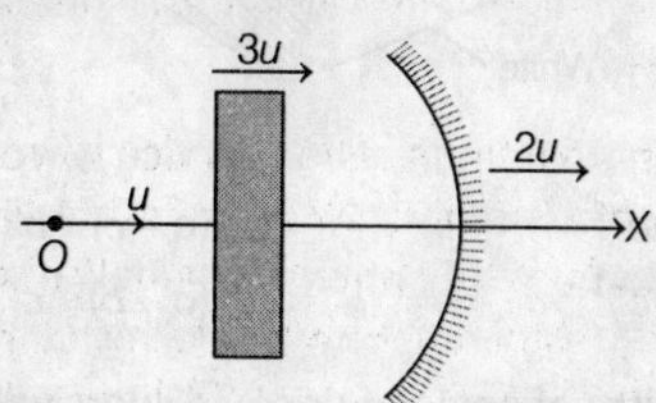

(a) will have speed greater than the speed of the object
(b) may have speed greater than the speed of the object
(c) may have speed greater than the speed of the mirror
(d) moves towards the mirror

3. In the arrangement shown, object is kept at position A, lying at the principal axis of lens as well as mirror. Final images of the object is formed at object itself. Focal lengths of converging mirror and converging lens respectively are

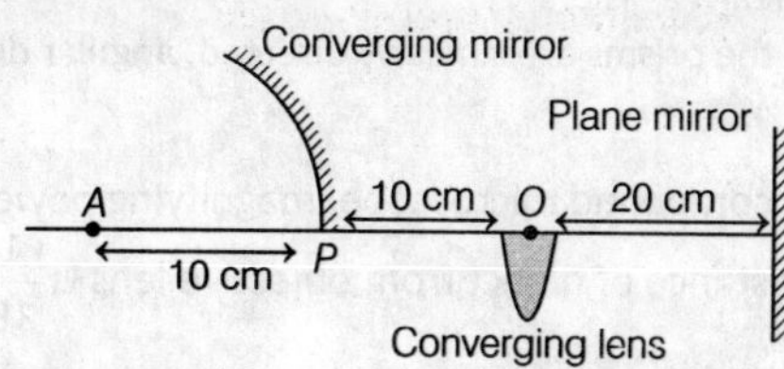

(a) 5 cm, 20 cm (b) 20 cm, 5 cm
(c) 10 cm, 10 cm (d) 20 cm, 20 cm

4. In the arrangement shown, the equiconvex lens forms image of the shown object O at 60 cm on the other side before it was cut. Also, all the optical elements are thin.

For which of the following values of x, final image will be formed at infinity? Radii of curvature and refractive indices are shown.

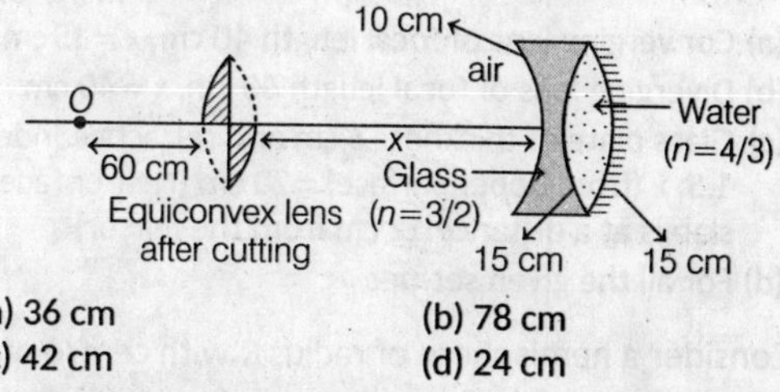

(a) 36 cm (b) 78 cm
(c) 42 cm (d) 24 cm

5. If an object is placed at $A(OA > f$, where f is the focal length of the lens) the image is found to be formed at B. A perpendicular is erected at O and a point C is chosen on it such that the angle $\angle BCA$ is a right angle. If the object is moving with velocity v_o as shown along axis of the lens, velocity of image is

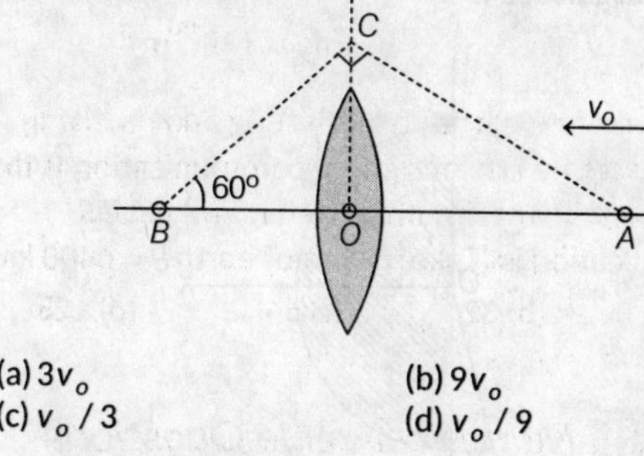

(a) $3v_o$ (b) $9v_o$
(c) $v_o/3$ (d) $v_o/9$

6. A body of elliptical cross-section is made up of material of refractive index n_2. The body is surrounded by a liquid of refractive index n_1. The figure here shows a cross-section of this body. If any ray parallel to major axis of the cross-section passes through focus of the cross-section (as shown), then the eccentricity of the elliptical cross-section is

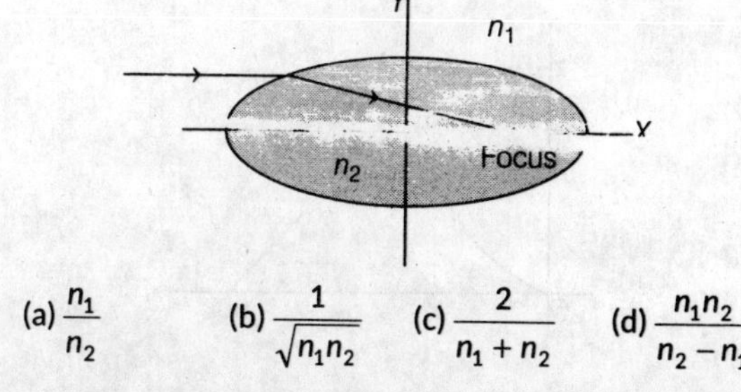

(a) $\dfrac{n_1}{n_2}$ (b) $\dfrac{1}{\sqrt{n_1n_2}}$ (c) $\dfrac{2}{n_1+n_2}$ (d) $\dfrac{n_1n_2}{n_2-n_1}$

7. In the arrangement shown here, for which of the following choice of optical element (coaxial with the mirror) and object distance x from the element, object image coincidence takes place?

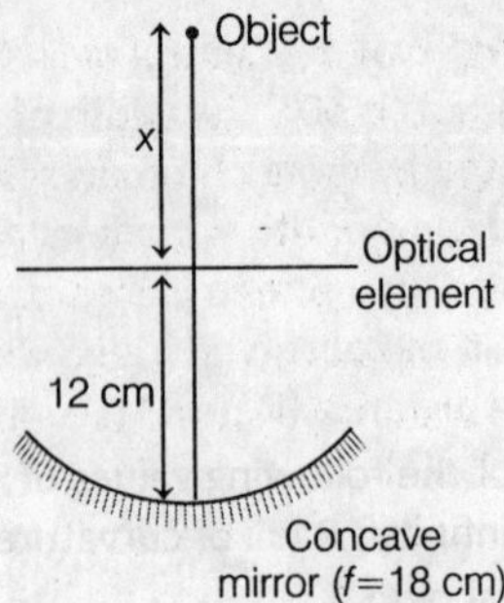

(a) Converging lens of focal length 40 cm, $x = 15$ cm
(b) Diverging lens of focal length 60 cm, $x = 40$ cm
(c) Glass plate of thickness 6 cm and refractive index equal to 1.5, x (from upper surface) = 20 cm (Nearer face of the slab is at a distance 12 cm from the mirror)
(d) For all the given set-ups

8. Consider a hemisphere of radius R with centre of curvature at origin O, as shown. Refractive index of material of the hemisphere varies as $\mu = \frac{2R}{2R - x}$, where x is x-coordinate of material point. A ray travelling in air is grazingly incident at O, as shown in figure. y-coordinate of the point where the ray comes out of the spherical surface is

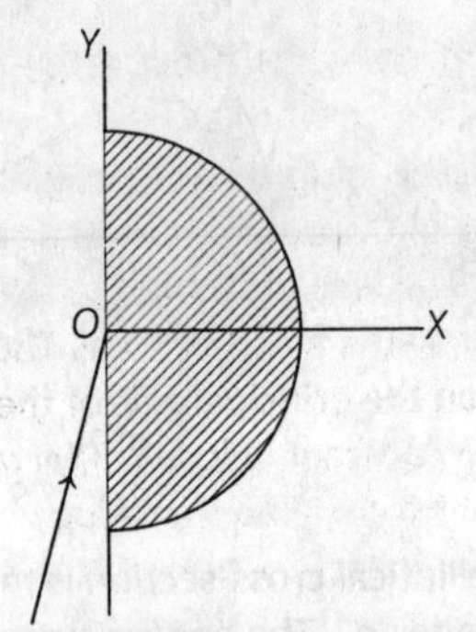

(a) $0.52\,R$ (b) $0.79\,R$ (c) $0.97\,R$ (d) $0.25\,R$

9. Light is incident from glass to air. The variation of the angle of deviation δ with the angle of incidence i for $0 < i < 90°$ is shown. The refractive index of glass is $\frac{2}{\sqrt{3}}$.

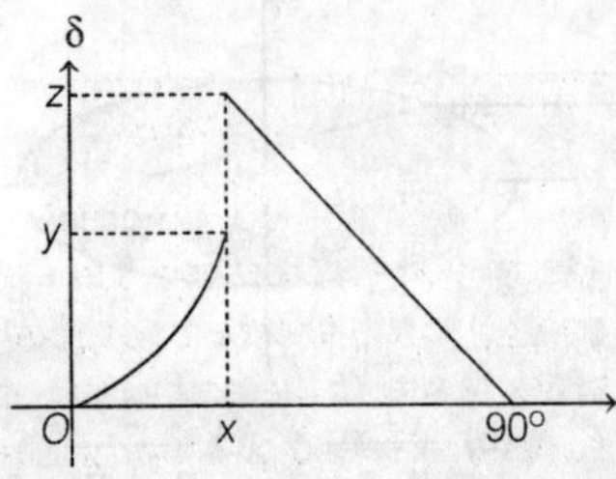

Choose the correct set of values in degrees.
(a) $x = 60°, y = 45°, z = 60°$
(b) $x = 60°, y = 30°, z = 90°$
(c) $x = 60°, y = 30°, z = 120°$
(d) $x = 60°, y = 30°, z = 60°$

10. A point source of power 6 W is placed 2 m below the free surface of liquid with refractive index equal to $\frac{3}{\sqrt{8}}$. Rate of transfer of energy from liquid surface to air, ignoring any reflection or absorption or scattering of light energy, is
(a) 1 W (b) 2 W
(c) 3 W (d) 4 W

11. Components of white light are deviated by different amounts by a convex lens as shown. The optical power of the convex lens for violet, yellow and red rays are a, b and c, respectively. Dispersive power of the material of the lens is (V and R respresent violet and red components of white respectively)

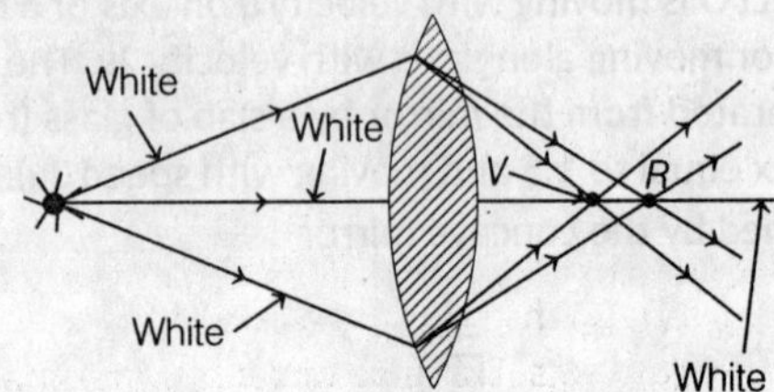

(a) $(a - c)b^{-1}$ (b) $(a - c)^{-1}b$
(c) $(a - b)c^{-1}$ (d) $(a - b)^{-1}c$

12. A thin prism of angle of prism, dispersive power and mean refractive index equal to $A = 5.0°$, $\omega = 0.07$ and $\mu_y = 1.30$ respectively is combined with another thin prism having angle of prism dispersive power and mean refractive index equal to A', $\omega' = 0.08$ and $\mu'_y = 1.50$ respectively. The combination produces no deviation in the mean ray. Choose the **incorrect** statement.
(a) Angle of the second prism is 3°.
(b) Net angular dispersion produced by the combination when a beam of white light passes through it is 0.015°.
(c) If the prisms are similarly directed, the deviation in the mean ray is 3°.
(d) If the prisms are similarly directed, angular dispersion is 0.4°.

13. For a compound microscope, magnifying power is 190 and the distance of object from objective lens is $\frac{1}{3.8}$ cm. The focal length of objective lens is $\frac{1}{4}$ cm. What is the magnification of eyepiece?
(a) 10 (b) 9
(c) 100 (d) 200

14. A ray of light is incident on a parallel glass-slab at the point *A* and it undergoes partial reflection and refraction as shown in the figure. At each reflection, 25% of the incident energy is reflected and the rest is transmitted. Assuming that the rays *AB* and *A′B′* undergo destructive interference, resultant intensity is I_0, if the incidence angle *i* is now changed such that the two rays interfere constructively, resultant intensity would increase by

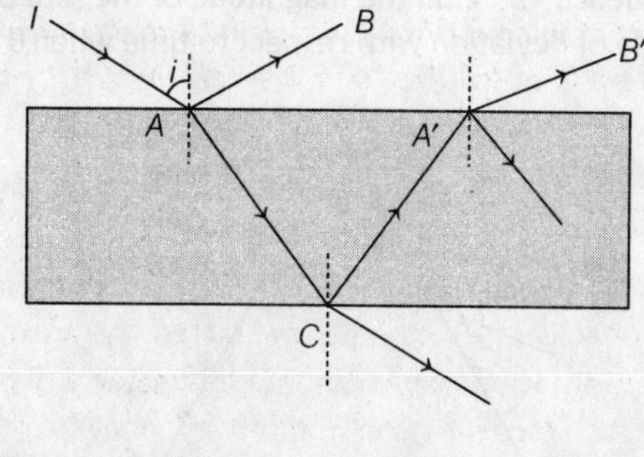

(a) $48I_0$ (b) $6I_0$ (c) $3I_0$ (d) I_0

15. The figure shows a standard YDSE setup with a parallel beam incident normally on plane of slits. The two slits are covered by a wedge shape film of refractive index $\mu = 1.5$ as shown. The thickness of film varies linearly from *t* to 3*t* from one end to the other as shown in the figure. The distance between the two slits is *d*. A large screen is at a distance *D* from slits. Distance of central maxima from point *O* (centre of the screen) will be

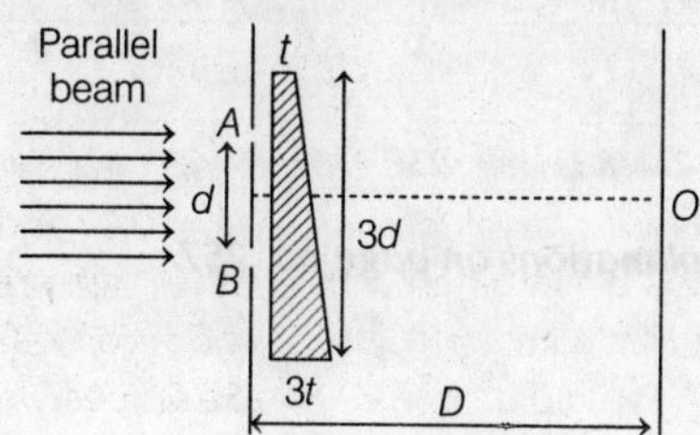

(a) $\frac{tD}{3d}$ (b) $\frac{2tD}{3d}$

(c) $\frac{tD}{d}$ (d) $\frac{4tD}{3d}$

16. Consider a Young's double slit experiment as shown in figure.

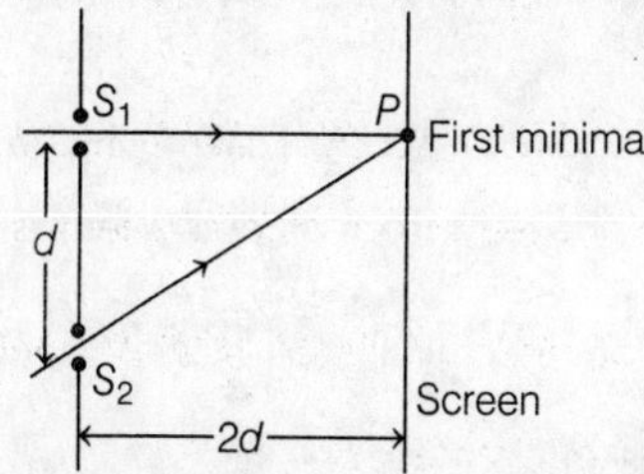

What should be the slit separation *d* in terms of wavelength λ such that the first minima occurs directly in front of the slit S_1?

(a) $\frac{\lambda}{2(5+\sqrt{2})}$ (b) $\frac{\lambda}{(5-\sqrt{2})}$

(c) $\frac{\lambda}{2(\sqrt{5}-2)}$ (d) $\frac{\lambda}{(\sqrt{5}+2)}$

17. The angular width of the central maximum in a single slit diffraction pattern is 60°. The width of the slit is 1 μm. The slit is illuminated by monochromatic plane waves. If another slit of same width is made near it, Young's fringes can be observed on a screen placed at a distance 50 cm from the slits. If the observed fringe width is 1 cm, what is slit separation distance (in μm)? (i.e. distance between the centres of each slit)

(a) 10 (b) 15 (c) 20 (d) 25

18. Assuming human pupil to have a radius of 0.25 cm and a comfortable viewing distance of 25 cm, the minimum separation between two objects that human eye can resolve at 750 nm wavelength is

(a) 1 μm (b) 45 μm (c) 90 μm (d) 300 μm

19. A telescope is used to resolve two stars separated by 4.6×10^{-6} rad. If the wavelength of light is 5460 Å, what should be the aperture of the objective of the telescope?

(a) 0.0448 m (b) 0.1448 m (c) 1.1448 m (d) 0.011 m

20. Two Nicol prisms are first crossed and then one of them is rotated through 60°. The percentage of incident unpolarised light transmitted is

(a) 1.25 (b) 25.0 (c) 37.5 (d) 50

Section II *Numerical Value Questions*

21. In the given figure, a observer *O* looking at a fish *F* (in water of $\mu = 4/3$) through a converging lens of focal length 90 cm. The lens is allowed to fall freely from a height 62.0 cm with its axis vertical. The fish and the observer are on the principal axis of the lens. The fish moves up with constant velocity 100 cm/s. Initially it was at a depth of 44.0 cm. Find the velocity (in m/s) with which the fish appears to move to the observer at $t = 0.2$ s, if he suddenly begins to move downwards with velocity 2.5 m/s. (Take, $g = 10$ m/s^2)

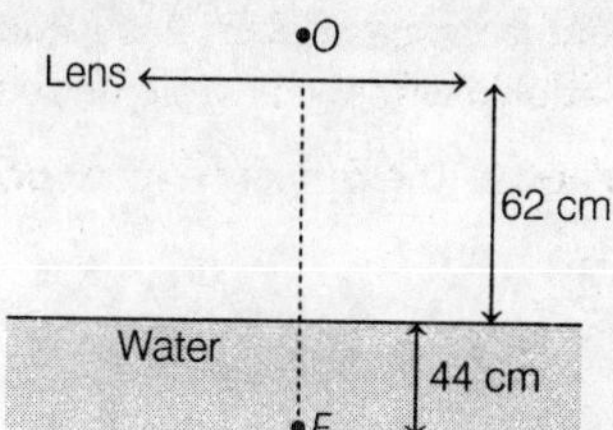

22. A boy starting from point *P* crosses a 8 km wide lagoon and reaches point *Q* in the shortest possible time by the path shown in the figure. If the boy swims at a speed of 3 km/hr and walks at a speed of 4 km/hr, then find his time of journey (in h).

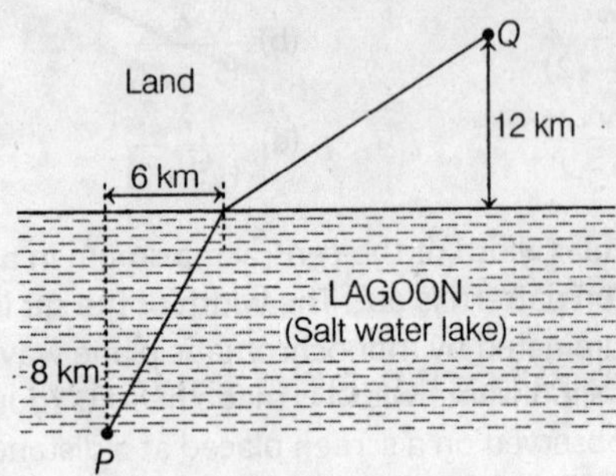

23. A light ray parallel to the principal axis is incident (as shown in the figure) on a plano-convex lens with radius of curvature of its curved part equal to 10 cm. Assuming that the refractive index of the material of the lens is 4/3 and medium on both sides of the lens is air, find the distance x of the point (in cm) from the curved surface of lens where this ray meets the principal axis

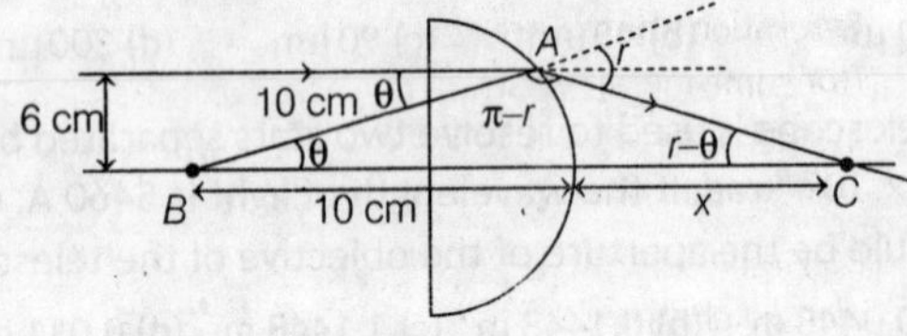

24. In Young's double slit experiment, the length of band AB is 1 mm. The fringe width is 0.021 mm. Find the number of fringes.

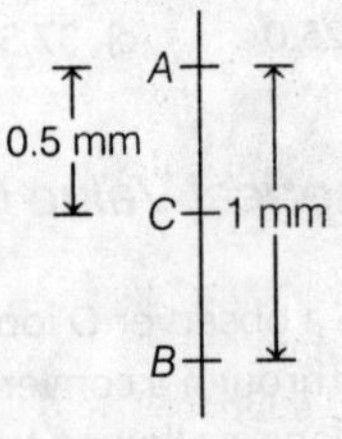

25. Consider a refracting medium of refractive index $\sqrt{2}$ kept in air and surrounded by two non-parallel surfaces, such that one surface is fixed and another surface is being rotated with constant angular velocity $\omega = 3$ rad/s about point A in clockwise direction as shown in figure. Assume that refractive media bounded by non-parallel surfaces always remains isotropic and refractive index always remains constant. A light ray falls on fixed surface at angle of incidence 45°. Find the magnitude of the rate of change of angle of deviation with respect to time when $\theta = 60°$ in rad/s.

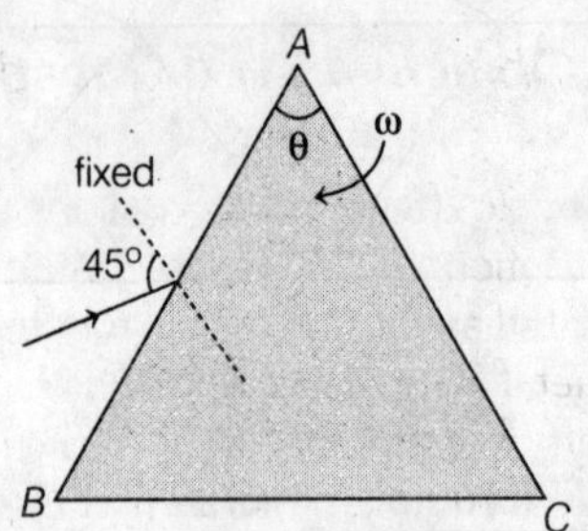

Answers

Section I

1 (d)	2 (a)	3 (a)	4 (b)	5 (d)
6 (a)	7 (d)	8 (c)	9 (d)	10 (b)
11 (a)	12 (d)	13 (a)	14 (a)	15 (a)
16 (c)	17 (d)	18 (b)	19 (b)	20 (c)

Section II

21 25.25	22 8.33	23 18.57	24 49	25 2.19

See detailed explanations on page no. 257

QUALIFIER 16

Modern Physics

(Dual Nature of Matter and Radiation & Atoms and Nuclei)

Section I Objective Type Questions

1. In a photoelectric effect set up, a point source of light of power P emits mono-energetic photons of energy E. The source is located at a distance of r from the centre of a stationary metallic sphere of work function ϕ and of radius $R << r$. The efficiency of photoelectrons emission is one for every η incident photons. Assume that the sphere is isolated and initially neutral, and that photoelectrons are instantly swept away after emission. If the emission stops after time t, then ϕ is lesser than E by amount (k = Coulomb's constant, e = electronic charge)

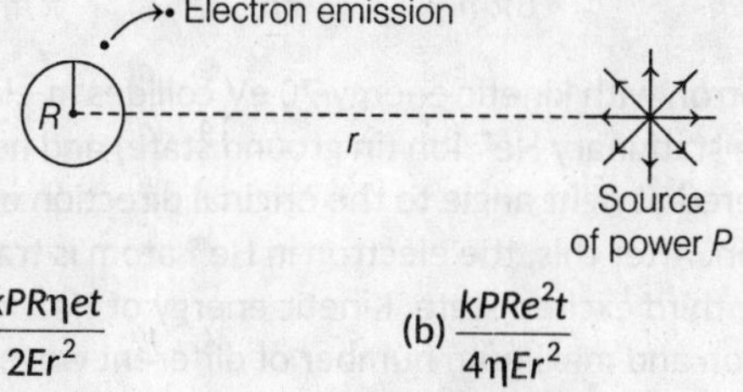

(a) $\frac{kPR\eta et}{2Er^2}$ (b) $\frac{kPRe^2t}{4\eta Er^2}$

(c) $\frac{kPR\eta e^2t}{4Er^2}$ (d) $\frac{kPRe^2t}{2\eta Er^2}$

2. Photoelectric effect experiments are performed using three different metal plates p, q and r having work functions ϕ_p, ϕ_q and ϕ_r, respectively. A light beam containing wavelengths of λ, 2λ and 3λ with equal intensities illuminates each of the plates. I-V graph for the experiment for the metal plates are as shown. Choose the incorrect alternative.

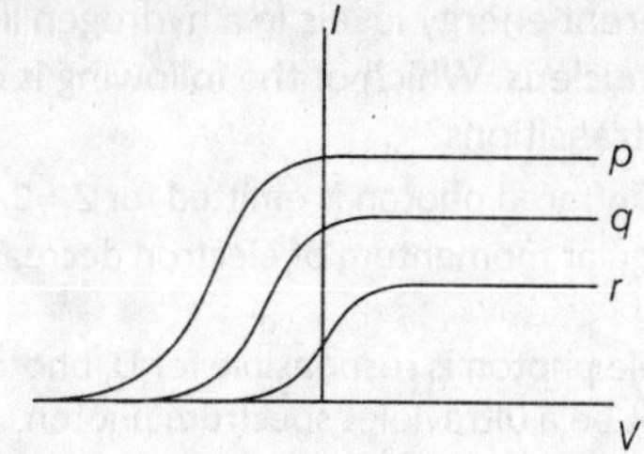

(a) $\phi_p < \phi_q < \phi_r$

(b) Stopping potential is least for r.

(c) Beam of wavelength λ is able to eject electrons from all the three metals.

(d) Photon of beam of wavelength 3λ is not able to eject electrons from metal p.

3.

	List-I		List-II
A.	Saturation photocurrent (for some metal) *versus* intensity of radiation is represented by	1.	
B.	Maximum kinetic energy of ejected photoelectrons *versus* frequency for electrodes of different work function is represented by	2.	
C.	Photocurrent *versus* applied voltage for different intensity of radiation (for same metal) is represented by	3.	
D.	Photocurrent *versus* applied voltage at constant intensity of radiation for electrodes of different work function	4.	

Choose the most appropriate match for a photoelectric cell experiment from the options given below.

(a) A-2 B-4 C-1 D-3 (b) A-2 B-1 C-4 D-3

(c) A-3 B-4 C-1 D-2 (d) A-4 B-2 C-1 D-3

4. A gas sample of unielectron ions having atomic number Z de-excites from $Z + 4 \rightarrow Z$.

The photons thus emitted are incident on a photocathode of photoelectric cell. Photoelectrons emitted by the photocathode are observed to be having matter wavelength greater than or equal to $\frac{5\sqrt{3}}{2}$ Å. If the photocathodic material is aluminium having work function equal to 2.2 eV, the gas sample is composed of

(a) H atoms (b) He^+ ions (c) Li^{2+} ions (d) Be^{3+} ions

5. Potential energy of electron in a hypothetical atom is given by $U = kr^2$, here k is a constant and r is orbital radius. Assuming Bohr model of quantization of angular momentum, area A enclosed by nth allowed orbit when plotted against n gives which of the following graphs?

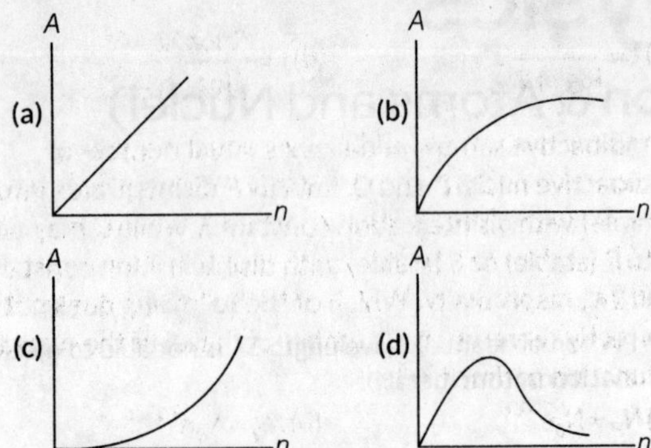

6. Positronium consists of an electron and a positron (antiparticle of electron) revolving about the system's centre of mass. Separation between electron and positron in positronium's first excited state, in terms of Bohr's radius r_0, is

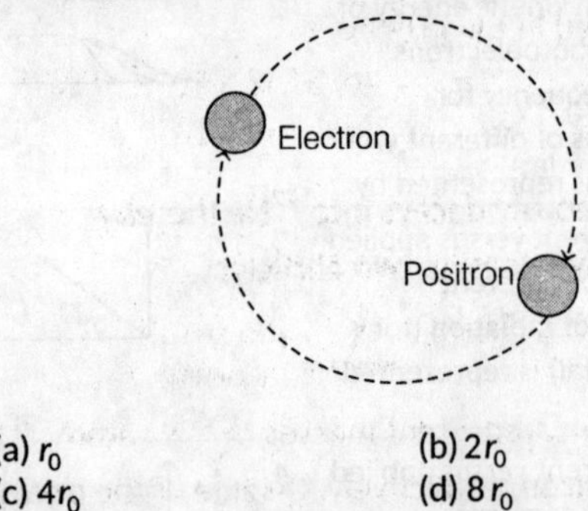

(a) r_0 (b) $2r_0$
(c) $4r_0$ (d) $8\,r_0$

7. Radius of ${}^{X}_{32}\text{Ge}$ (germanium) nuclide is measured to be twice the radius of ${}^{9}_{4}\text{Be}$. Number of neutrons in Ge are

(a) 38 (b) 40
(c) 42 (d) 44

8. The energy associated with the first orbit in the hydrogen atom is -2.18×10^{-18} J. What is the energy associated and the radius of Bohr's fifth orbit for hydrogen atom?

(a) 2.18×10^{-18} J, 1.32 nm
(b) -8.72×10^{-20} J, 1.32 nm
(c) -2.18×10^{-18} J, 0.53 nm
(d) 8.72×10^{-20} J, 0.53 nm

9. Difference between wavelengths (in pm) of first lines of the Lyman series for the two isotopes of hydrogen shown here is close to

(a) 11 (b) 22
(c) 33 (d) 44

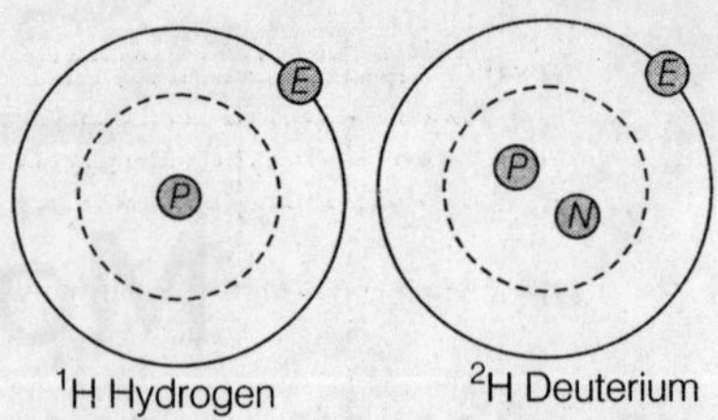

10. An electron of mass m in the ground state of hydrogen atoms is revolving in a circular orbit of radius R. The atom is placed in a uniform magnetic induction B, such that the magnetic moment μ of the atom makes 5 times the angle with B as that made by the angular momentum **L** of the electron with the external magnetic induction **B**. Torque experienced by the orbiting electron is

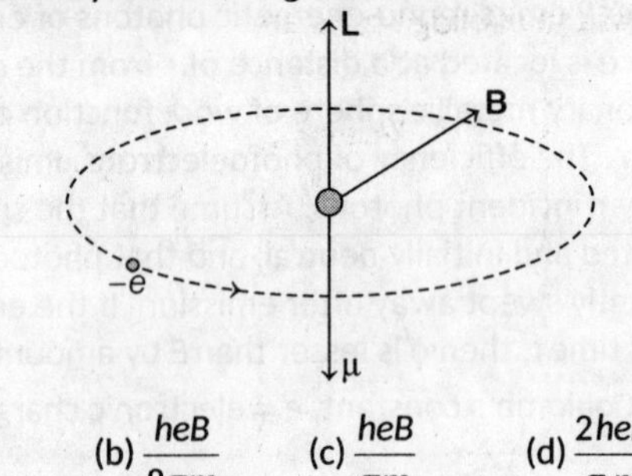

(a) $\dfrac{heB}{4\pi m}$ (b) $\dfrac{heB}{8\pi m}$ (c) $\dfrac{heB}{\pi m}$ (d) $\dfrac{2heB}{\pi m}$

11. A neutron with kinetic energy 70 eV collides in-elastically with a stationary He^+ ion (in ground state) and neutron is scattered at right angle to the original direction of its motion. After this, the electron in He^+ atom is transferred to the third excited state. Kinetic energy of He^+ ion after collision and maximum number of different wavelength that may be emitted during de-excitation of He^+ ion are respectively,

(a) 17.8 eV, 6 (b) 1.2 eV, 6 (c) 17.8 eV, 3 (d) 1.2 eV, 3

12. If wavelength of series limit of Balmer series is λ_0 in H spectrum, wavelength of 6th line of Paschen series in Li^{2+} is

(a) $\dfrac{9\lambda_0}{32}$ (b) $\dfrac{32\lambda_0}{9}$ (c) $\dfrac{9\lambda_0}{2}$ (d) $\dfrac{2\lambda_0}{9}$

13. Consider the shown possible transitions of electrons across different energy levels in a hydrogen like atom of Z protons in nucleus. Which of the following is correct for the shown transitions?

(a) In A, an infrared photon is emitted for $Z = 3$.
(b) In B, angular momentum of electron decreases by 300% for $Z = 8$.
(c) If a visible photon is responsible for D, photon emitted in C cannot be a ultraviolet spectrum photon.
(d) Photon emitted in C has less than double the wavelength of photon absorbed in D.

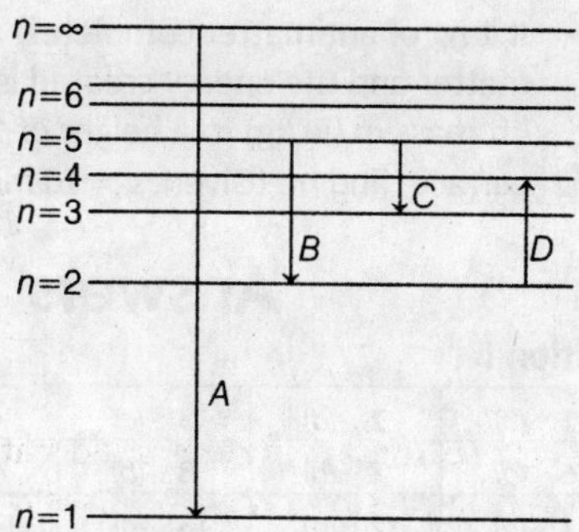

14. The figure here shows intensity *versus* wavelength for a sample of *X*-rays emitted by coolidge tube. The two series labelled *X*-series and *Y*-series are one of the *K*-series and *L*-series. Wavelength of L_α *X*-rays and accelerating voltage across the coolidge tube are

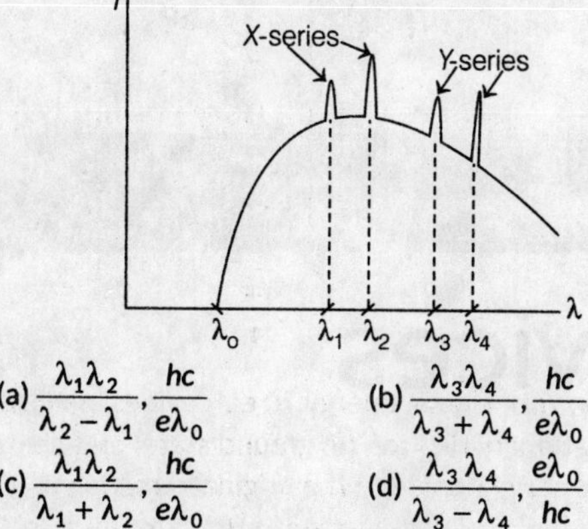

(a) $\frac{\lambda_1\lambda_2}{\lambda_2-\lambda_1}, \frac{hc}{e\lambda_0}$ (b) $\frac{\lambda_3\lambda_4}{\lambda_3+\lambda_4}, \frac{hc}{e\lambda_0}$

(c) $\frac{\lambda_1\lambda_2}{\lambda_1+\lambda_2}, \frac{hc}{e\lambda_0}$ (d) $\frac{\lambda_3\lambda_4}{\lambda_3-\lambda_4}, \frac{e\lambda_0}{hc}$

15. Assume that the de-Broglie wave associated with an electron can form a standing wave between the atoms arranged in a one-dimensional array with nodes at each of the atomic sites. It is found that one such standing wave is formed if the distance *d* between the atoms of the array is 1.2 Å. A similar standing wave is again formed if *d* is increased to 1.5 Å but not for any intermediate value of *d*. Least value of *d* in Å is equal to

(a) 1.2 (b) 0.6 (c) 0.3 (d) 0.1

16. For series decay shown here, activity of *X* and *Y* at $t=0$ are equal to A_0 each.

$$\underset{\text{(Unstable)}}{X} \xrightarrow{\lambda_X=\lambda} \underset{\text{(Unstable)}}{Y} \xrightarrow{\lambda_Y=2\lambda} \underset{\text{(Stable)}}{Z}$$

It is given that number of nuclei of *X* and *Y* are related as

$\lambda_Y N_Y = \lambda_X (N_X + N_Y) + Ce^{-\lambda_Y t}$

Here *C* is an unknown constant.

N_Y as function of time *t* is given by

(a) $\frac{A_0}{\lambda}(e^{-\lambda t}-e^{-2\lambda t})$ (b) $\frac{A_0}{2\lambda}(2e^{-\lambda t}-e^{-2\lambda t})$

(c) $\frac{A_0}{\lambda}(e^{-\lambda t}-2e^{-2\lambda t})$ (d) $\frac{A_0}{2\lambda}(e^{-\lambda t}-e^{-2\lambda t})$

17. A radioactive nucleus *A* with a half-life *T*, decays into a nucleus *B*. At $t=0$, there is no nucleus *B*. After sometime *t*, the ratio of the number of *B* to that of *A* is 0.3. Then, *t* is given by

(a) $t=T\frac{\log_e 1.3}{\log_e 2}$ (b) $t=T\log_e 1.3$

(c) $t=\frac{T}{\log_e 1.3}$ (d) $t=\frac{T\log_e 2}{2\log_e 1.3}$

18. A radioactive sample initially has equal number of radioactive nuclei *P* and *Q*. Initially *P* disintegrates into *R* (stable) with disintegration constant λ while *Q* may decay into *R* (stable) or *S* (stable) with disintegration constants λ and 2λ, respectively. Which of the following does not correctly represent the number of nuclei of the nuclides as a function of time *t* ?

(a) $N_P=N_0e^{-\lambda t}$ (b) $N_Q=N_0e^{-3\lambda t}$

(c) $N_R=N_0\left(\frac{4}{3}-e^{-\lambda t}-\frac{e^{-3\lambda t}}{3}\right)$ (d) $N_s=\frac{N_0}{3}(1-e^{-3\lambda t})$

19. Binding energy per nucleon of Helium and deuterium nuclei are 7 MeV and 1.1 MeV, respectively. When two deuterium nuclei undergo fusion to form helium nucleus, energy released in the process is

(a) 23.6 J (b) 37.76×10^{-13} MeV

(c) 23.6 eV (d) 37.76×10^{-13} J

20. ^{22}Na spontaneously decays into ^{22}Ne thereby simultaneously releasing two particles

$$^{22}\text{Na} \longrightarrow {}^{22}\text{Ne} + \underset{\text{(unknown)}}{X} + \underset{\text{(neutrino)}}{\nu}$$

If m_1, m_2 and m_e represent masses of ^{22}Na atom, ^{22}Ne atom and electron respectively, *Q*-value of the decay is

(a) $(m_1-m_2)c^2$ (b) $(m_2-m_1)c^2$

(c) $(m_1-m_2-2m_e)c^2$ (d) $(m_1-m_2-m_e)c^2$

Section II *Numerical Value Questions*

21. The surface of a metal is illuminated alternately with photons of energies $E_1=4$ eV and $E_2=2.5$ eV, respectively. The ratio of maximum speeds of the photoelectrons emitted in the two cases is 2. The work function of the metal (in eV) is ......

22. Average life time of a hydrogen atom excited to $n=2$ state is 10^{-8} s. The number of revolutions made by the electrons on the average before it jumps to ground state is close to 8×10^x. Find *x*.

23. Using Moseley's law with $b=1$ the frequency of the K_α *X*-rays of *La* ($Z=57$) is $m\times10^n$ Hz. If the frequency of the K_α *X*-rays of Cu ($Z=29$) is known to be 1.88×10^{18} Hz, find greatest integral value of $n-m$.

24. Mass spectrometric analysis of potassium (^{40}K) and argon (^{40}Ar) atoms in a rock sample shows that ratio of number of stable ^{40}Ar atoms to the number of radioactive ^{40}K atoms is 7. If all the argon atoms were produced by the decay of K atoms, find age of the rock sample in billion years. Given that half life of ^{40}K is 1.25 $\times 10^9$ years.

25. In the process of pair annihilation, matter particles interact with anti-matter particles and annihilate each other resulting in mass getting completely converted into energy, as shown.

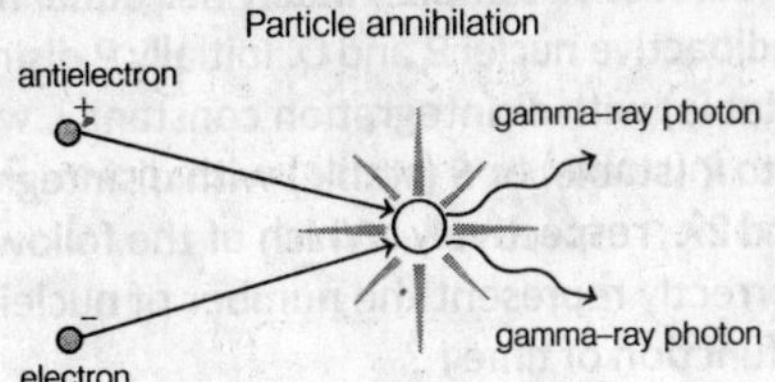

If 1 ng of antimatter completely annihilates 1 ng of matter and the energy created is just sufficient to lift mass m (in kg) to a height of 1 km above earth's surface, find m. (Given, $g = 10 \text{ m/s}^2$)

Answers

Section I

1 (b)	2 (d)	3 (c)	4 (d)	5 (a)
6 (d)	7 (b)	8 (b)	9 (c)	10 (b)
11 (a)	12 (a)	13 (c)	14 (a)	15 (c)
16 (b)	17 (a)	18 (d)	19 (d)	20 (c)

Section II

21 2	22 6	23 10	24 3.75	25 18

See detailed explanations on page no. 262

QUALIFIER 17

Electronic Devices

Section I *Objective Type Questions*

1. Which of the following may be energy level diagram of a *p*-type semiconductor at temperature $T > 0$ K? VB and CB represent valence band and conduction band respectively

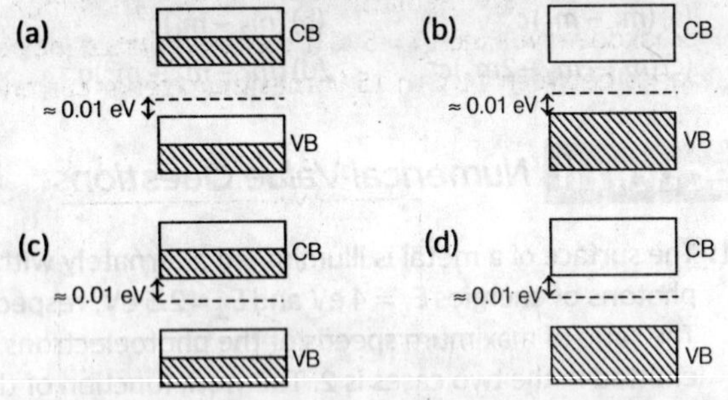

2. If voltage across a diode is slightly increased from V to V + dV as shown in the I-V characteristic of diode, corresponding change in current (dI) for very large forward voltage is (E_g = energy gap, T = thermodynamic temperature, i_s = saturation current, e = electronic charge, k = Boltzmann constant, ideality factor = 2)

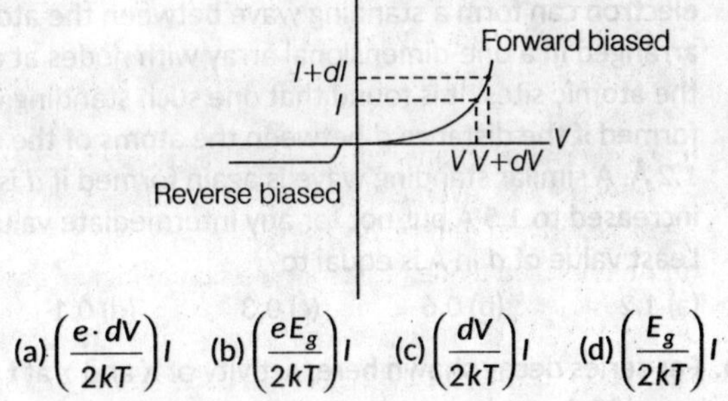

(a) $\left(\frac{e \cdot dV}{2kT}\right) I$ (b) $\left(\frac{eE_g}{2kT}\right) I$ (c) $\left(\frac{dV}{2kT}\right) I$ (d) $\left(\frac{E_g}{2kT}\right) I$

3. An intrinsic Si crystal is doped by 2 ppm concentration of phosphorus. Number density of holes (in m^{-3}) in the extrinsic sample created is [Given that number density (in m^{-3}) of atoms and intrinsic charge carriers in pure Si are 5×10^{28} and 1.6×10^{16}, respectively]

(a) 5×10^{22} (b) 2.56×10^{9}
(c) 1.6×10^{9} (d) 0.512×10^{-11}

4. The figure here shows an arrangement of three diodes

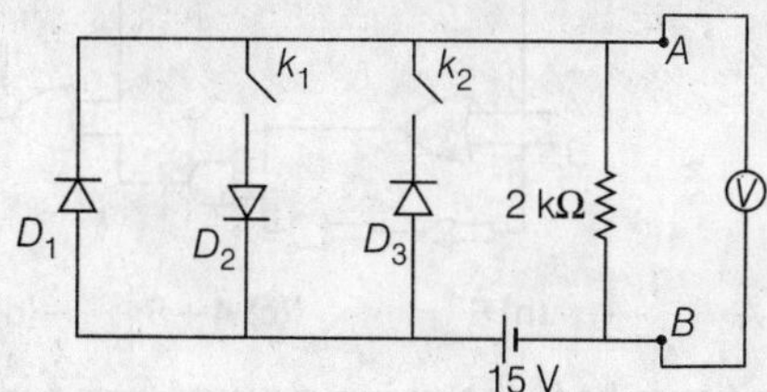

D_1 (which becomes conducting at 0.7 V) D_2 (which becomes conducting at 0.3 V) and D_3 (which becomes conducting at 0.5 V). On closing key k_1 only, voltmeter reads V_1 while on closing key k_2 only, voltmeter reads $V_2 \cdot |V_1 - V_2|$ is equal to

(a) zero (b) 0.2 V (c) 0.4 V (d) 0.7 V

5. Consider a germanium rod of length 6 mm and cross-sectional area 2 mm^2. For germanium, at a specific temperature, number density of intrinsic charge carriers $n_i = 2.5 \times 10^{19}\ \text{m}^{-3}$, electron mobility $\mu_e = 0.4\ \text{m}^2/\text{V-s}$ and hole mobility $\mu_h = 0.2\ \text{m}^2/\text{V-s}$. Resistance of the rod at this temperature is

(a) 1.25 MΩ (b) 2.5 kΩ
(c) 1.25 kΩ (d) 2.5 MΩ

6. Consider an intrinsic semiconductor with energy gap E_g at temperature T. Its specific conductance, on doubling its temperature, increases by a factor given by
(k = Boltzmann constant)

(a) $e^{\frac{E_g}{kT}}$ (b) $e^{\frac{E_g}{2kT}}$ (c) $e^{\frac{E_g}{3kT}}$ (d) $e^{\frac{E_g}{4kT}}$

7. Choose the incorrect statement.

(a) On applying forward biasing to a p-n junction diode, potential barrier is lowered.
(b) Dynamic resistance of a diode in reverse saturation state is infinite.
(c) Dominant mechanism for motion of charge carriers in forward and reverse bias of a p-n junction diode are diffusion and drift respectively.
(d) An unbiased diode has its p-type side at higher potential.

8. On decreasing temperature of both aluminium and silicon from room temperature to 200 K, resistivity of aluminium and silicon respectively

(a) decrease and decrease (b) increase and increase
(c) decrease and increase (d) increase and decrease

9. In accordance with the solar irradiance curve shown here, which of the following pair of materials are the preferred materials for fabricating solar cells?

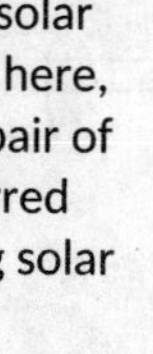

(a) Cds and Si
(b) CdSe and Ge
(c) CdS and GaAs
(d) GaAs and Si

10. The photodiode shown is fabricated from a semiconductor with bandgap 2 eV. The ammeter shown in the circuit works for incident wavelength λ lesser than

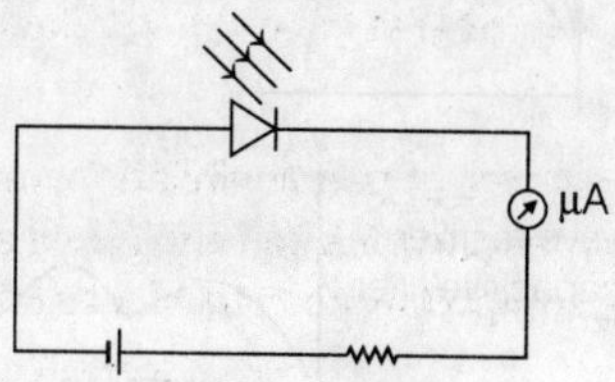

(a) 3100 Å (b) 620 nm (c) 1240 pm (d) 2480 μm

11. For sinusoidal AC input between points P and Q, output is obtained between A and B.

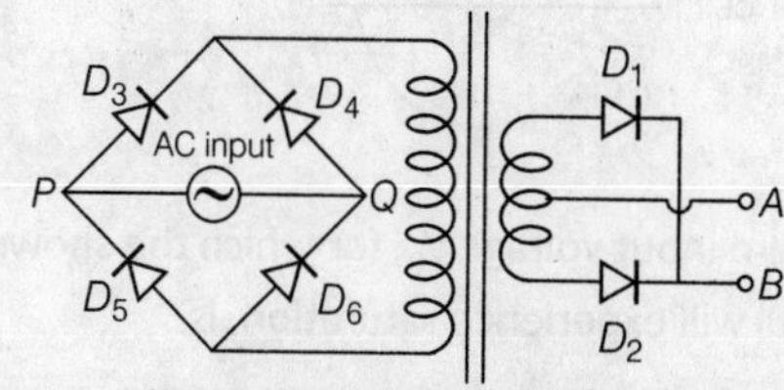

Which of the following may represent output waveform obtained?

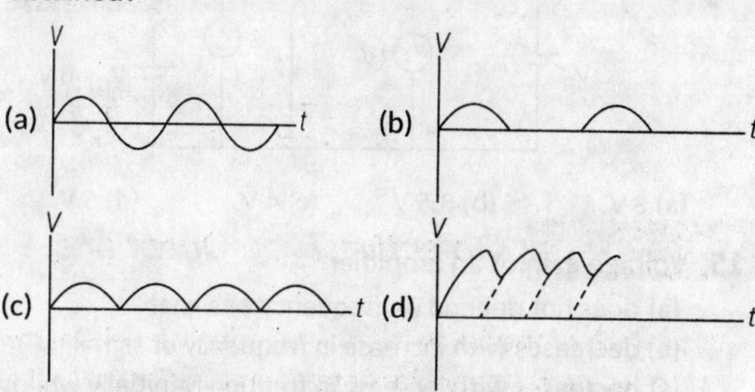

12. In the DC voltage regulator circuit shown, the zener breakdown voltage $V_Z = 5$ V. If the unregulated input varies between 11 V to 15 V, maximum zener current (in mA) is

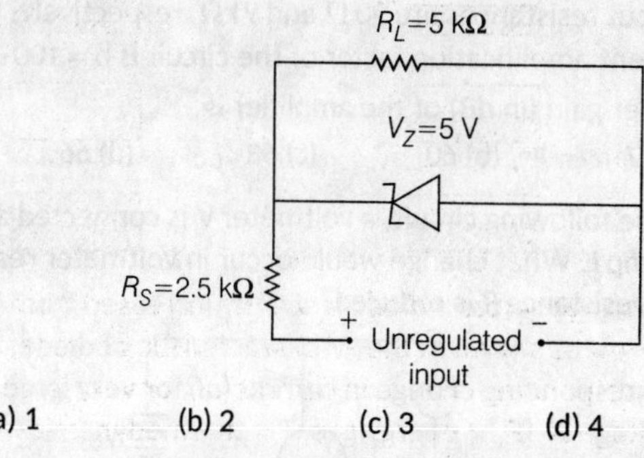

(a) 1 (b) 2 (c) 3 (d) 4

13. Which of the following characteristic or related curve and device match is incorrect?

(a) Zener diode :

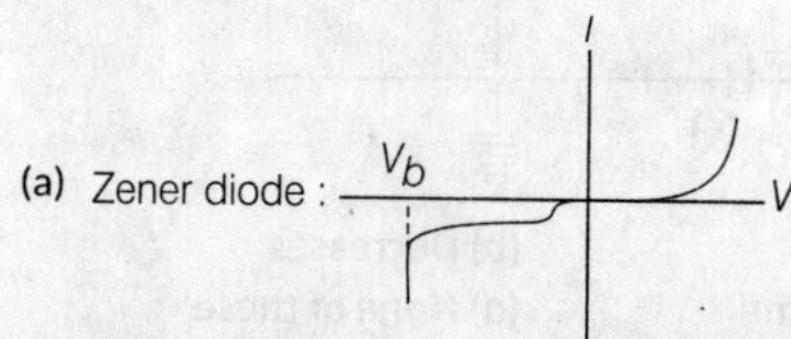

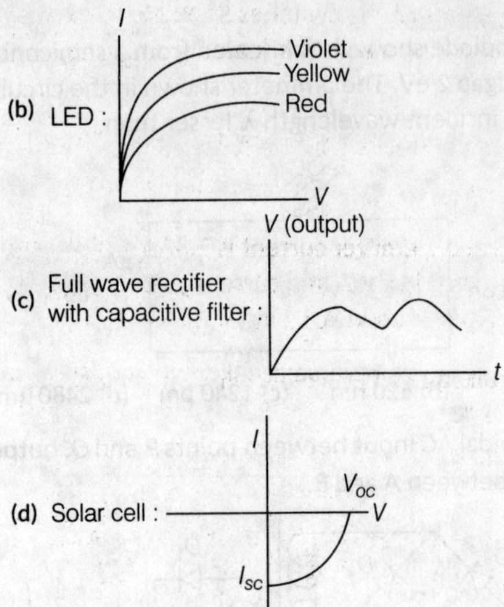

14. Minimum input voltage V_B, for which the shown transistor ($\beta = 150$) will experience saturation, is

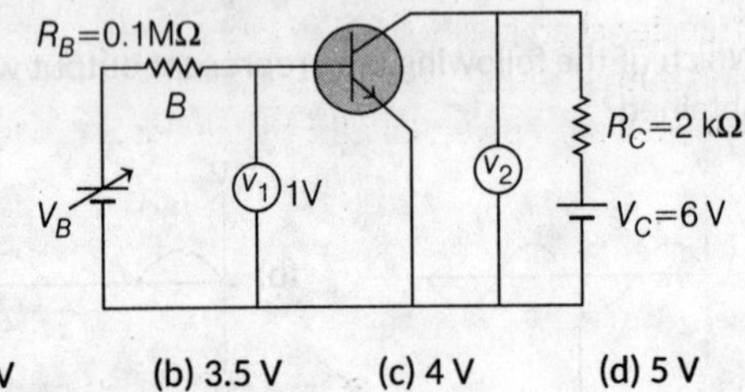

(a) 3 V (b) 3.5 V (c) 4 V (d) 5 V

15. Voltage gain of an amplifier

(a) does not depend on frequency of signal
(b) decreases with increase in frequency of signal
(c) decreases with increase in frequency initially while increases later
(d) remains constant with increase in frequency initially while decreases later

16. In a transistor amplifier in CE configuration, input and output resistances are 90 Ω and 9 kΩ, respectively. If current amplification factor of the circuit is $\beta = 100\sqrt{2}$, power gain (in dB) of the amplifier is

(a) 57 (b) 60 (c) 63 (d) 66

17. In the following circuit, a voltmeter V is connected across a lamp L. What change would occur in voltmeter reading if the resistance R is reduced?

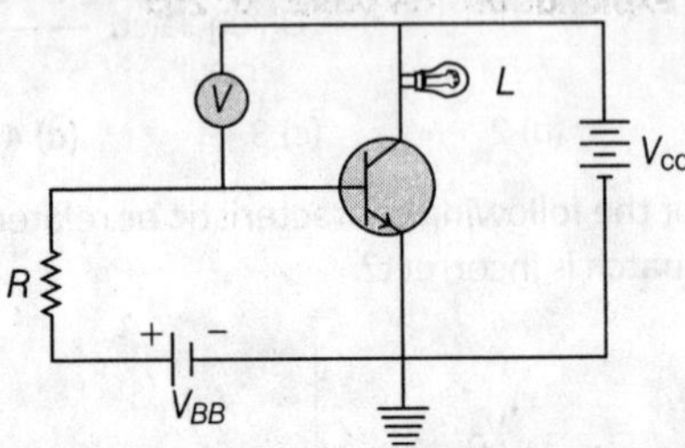

(a) Increases (b) Decreases
(c) Remains same (d) None of these

18. Output Y of the shown combination of logic gates is

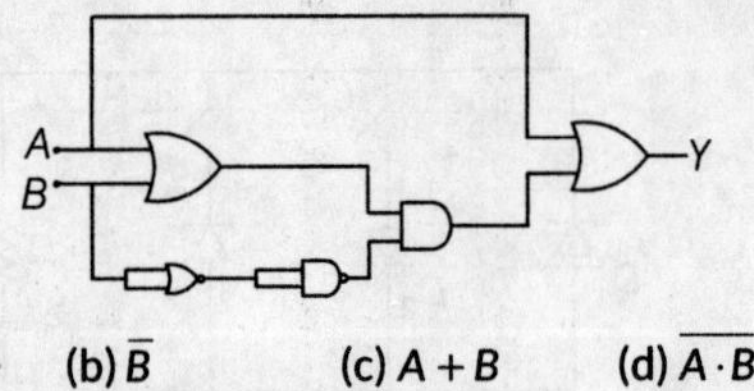

(a) A (b) $\overline{B}$ (c) $A + B$ (d) $\overline{A \cdot B}$

19. The figure here shows input waveforms applied at inputs A and B of the arrangement of gates.

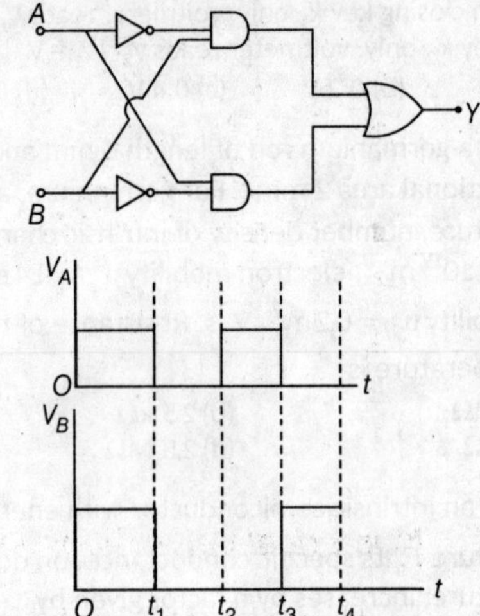

Which of the following is waveform obtained at output Y?

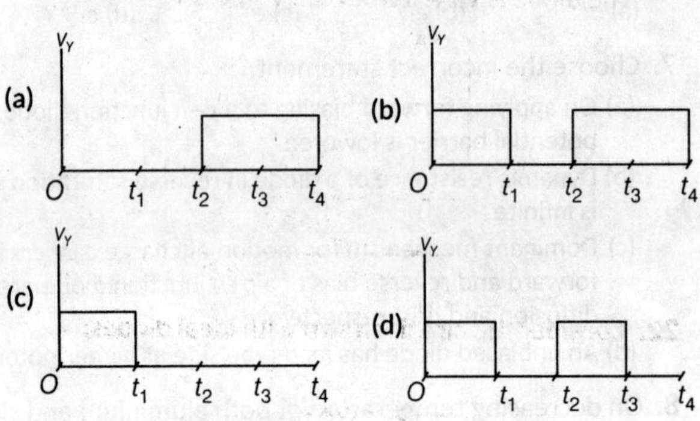

20. Truth table for the given arrangement of gates with A and B as input and Y as output is

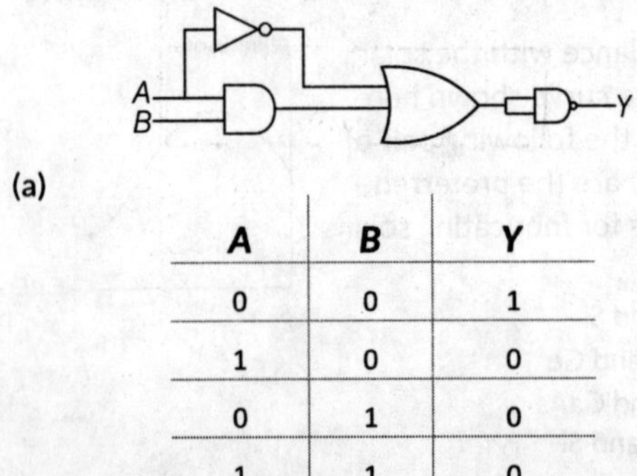

(a)

A	B	Y
0	0	1
1	0	0
0	1	0
1	1	0

(b)

A	B	Y
0	0	0
1	0	0
0	1	1
1	1	0

(c)

A	B	Y
0	0	0
1	0	1
0	1	0
1	1	0

(d)

A	B	Y
0	0	0
1	0	0
0	1	0
1	1	1

Section II *Numerical Value Questions*

21. The figure here shows forward biasing characteristics for a diode. Find resistance (in Ω) of the diode as voltage across the diode is varied from 0.7 V to 0.8 V.

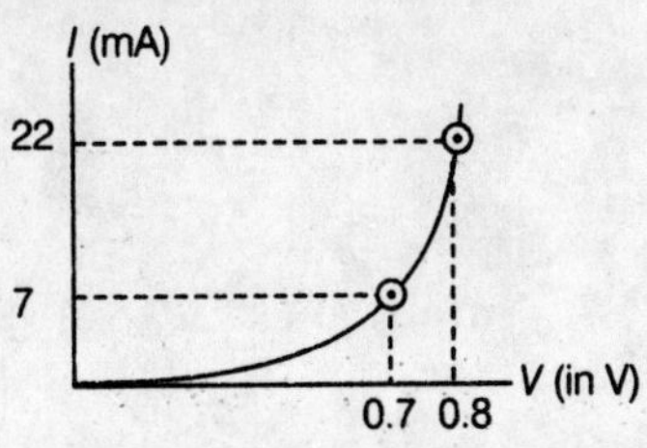

22. Consider the circuit shown with ideal diodes.

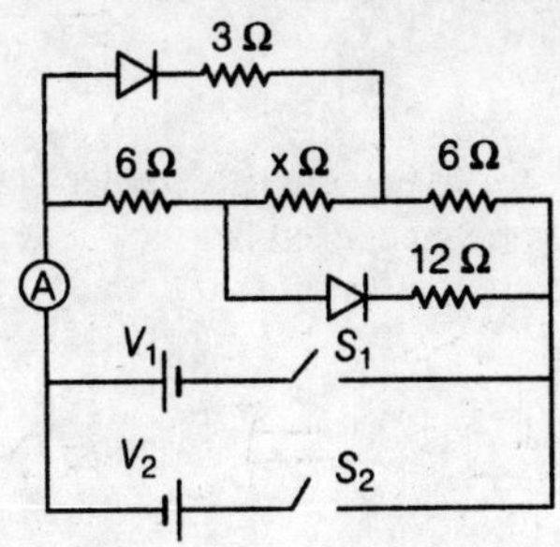

On closing either of the switches S_1 and S_2, meter gives same reading. Find value of x (unknown resistance in Ω) if $3V_1 = V_2$.

23. For a transistor amplifier in CB configuration current amplification factor is $\alpha = \frac{60}{61}$. While using the transistor in CE configuration, emitter current is 7.32 mA. Corresponding collector current in x mA and current amplification factor for the CE configuration is β. Find $x + \beta$.

24. In the circuit shown reverse breakdown voltage of zener diode is 4.2 V.

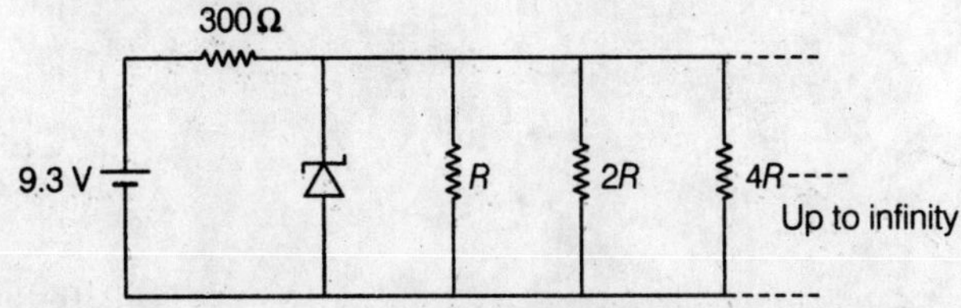

Find current (in mA) through the diode if $R = 1400\ \Omega$.

25. Transfer characteristic curve of a transistor having input and output resistances 85 Ω and 85 kΩ respectively is shown here. Power gain for the circuit is $P \times 10^6$. Find P.

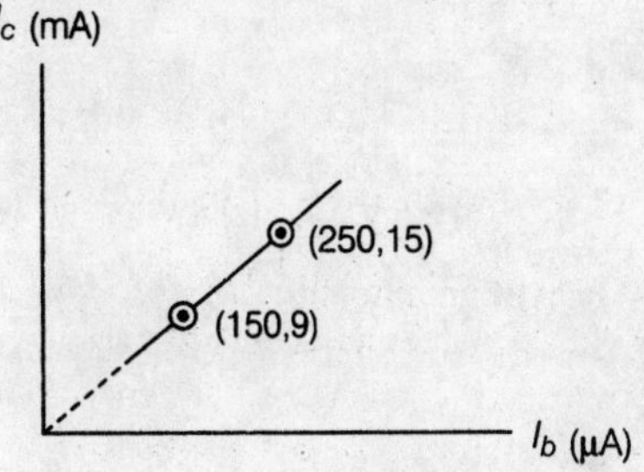

Answers

Section I

1 *(a)*	2 *(a)*	3 *(b)*	4 *(b)*	5 *(c)*
6 *(d)*	7 *(d)*	8 *(c)*	9 *(d)*	10 *(b)*
11 *(c)*	12 *(c)*	13 *(b)*	14 *(a)*	15 *(d)*
16 *(c)*	17 *(a)*	18 *(c)*	19 *(a)*	20 *(c)*

Section II

21 *6.67*	22 *6*	23 *67.2*	24 *11*	25 3.6

See detailed explanations on page no. 265

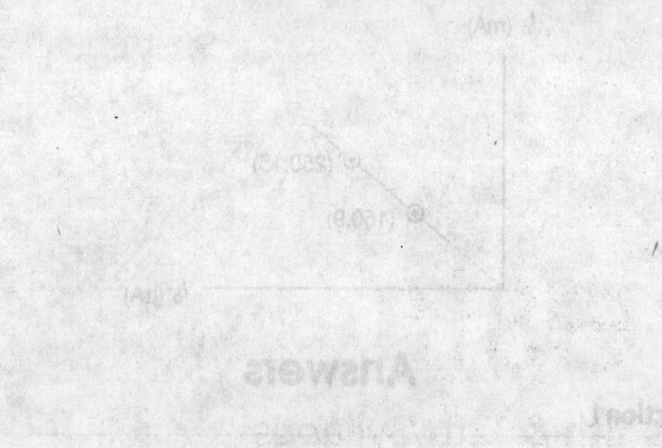

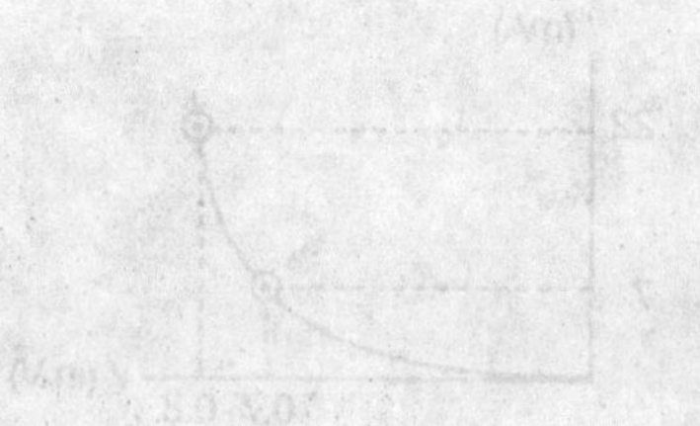

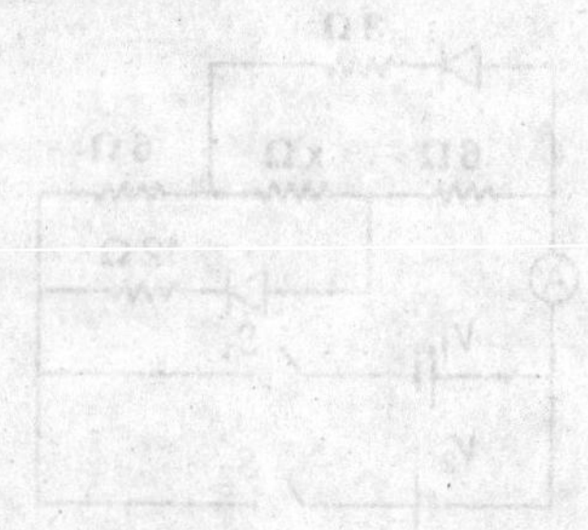

JEE MAIN & ADVANCED

Part Tests

Based on Complete Class 11th & 12th Syllabus

This section will check your overall understanding of complete syllabus of class 11 & 12, respectively.

Part Test 01

(Based on Complete Class 11 Syllabus)

JEE MAIN

Physics

Instructions

1. This question paper contains of 30 Questions of Physics, divided into two Sections : **Section I** Objective Type Questions and **Section II** Numerical Value Questions.
2. Section I contains 20 Objective questions and all Questions are compulsory (Marking Scheme : Correct + 4, Incorrect –1) .
3. Section II contains 10 Numerical value questions out of which only 5 questions are to be attempted (Marking Scheme : Correct + 4, Incorrect 0) .

Section I *Objective Type Questions*

1. A particle at an altitude $3R$ from earth's surface, at Q is projected as shown. If the particle follows the trajectory shown grazing the earth's surface at point P, speed of projection v_Q in terms of escape speed v_e at location P is

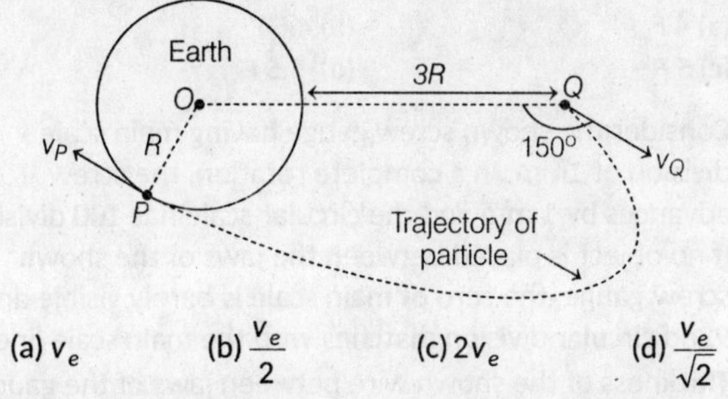

(a) v_e (b) $\frac{v_e}{2}$ (c) $2v_e$ (d) $\frac{v_e}{\sqrt{2}}$

2. Figure shows a clamped metal string of length 30 cm and linear mass density 0.1 kg/m which is taut at a tension of 40 N. A small rider (piece of paper) is placed on string at point P as shown. An external vibrating tuning fork is brought near this string and oscillations of rider are carefully observed. At which of the following frequencies of tuning fork, rider will not vibrate at all ?

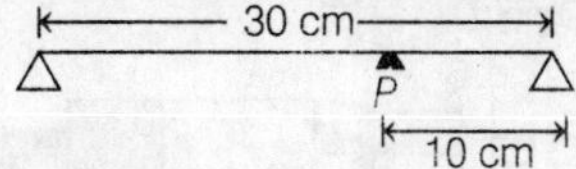

(a) (100/3) Hz (b) (200/3) Hz (c) 50 Hz (d) 300 Hz

3. A light balloon filled with gas of density ρ is tied to a long vertical light string of length l attached to ground as shown in figure.

The string attached to balloon is now slightly displaced (by 2°) from position A to position B and released. Given that density of air is 3ρ, then minimum time taken by the balloon to come to rest instantly is close to

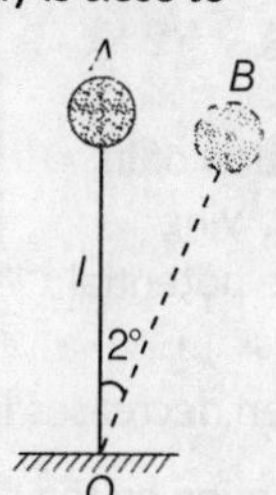

(a) $\pi\sqrt{\frac{l}{4g}}$ (b) $\pi\sqrt{\frac{l}{2g}}$ (c) $\pi\sqrt{\frac{2l}{g}}$ (d) $\frac{\ }{4g}$

4. Loudness of sound 2 m from a point loudspeaker is 10 dB. Loudness at distance of 1 m from the speaker is ($\log_{10} 2 = 0.3$)

(a) 4 dB (b) 16 dB
(c) 60 dB (d) 120 dB

5. A sphere P rolling without slipping on a smooth horizontal surface collides elastically with an identical sphere Q at rest as shown.

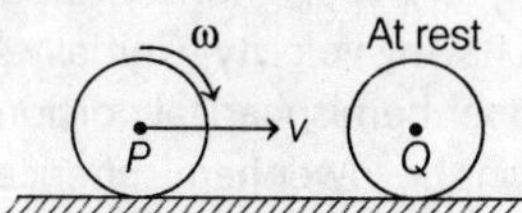

Radius of curvature of path of top point of sphere P is R_1 just before collision while it is R_2 just after collision. $\frac{R_1}{R_2}$ is

(a) 2 (b) 4
(c) 3 (d) 6

6. A block on rough horizontal surface is imparted velocity v_0 at $t = 0$. It experiences retardation proportional to its instantaneous velocity. At $t = 1$ s, its velocity becomes half of its initial value. If its retardation is a at $t = 0$, its retardation at $t = 3$ s will be

(a) a (b) $\frac{a}{2}$ (c) $\frac{a}{3}$ (d) $\frac{a}{8}$

7. A cuboidal box of mass 3 kg is kept on a rough horizontal surface ($\mu = 0.2$). A block of mass 2 kg is connected to the box by a spring of spring constant π^2 N/m. There is no friction between the block and the box and spring is initially relaxed. Now, an external horizontal force of $F = 16$ N is applied on the box as shown. Acceleration of the box and the block respectively are (Take, $g = 10$ m/s^2)

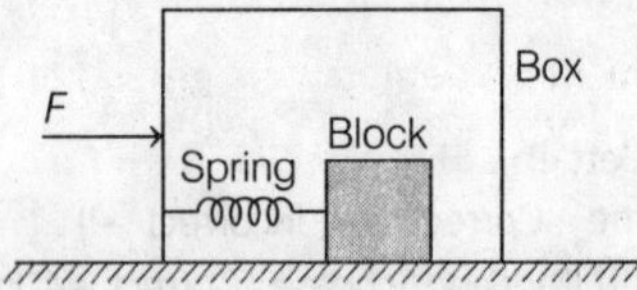

(a) 2 m/s^2, 2 m/s^2 (b) 2 m/s^2, zero
(c) zero, 2 m/s^2 (d) 1.2 m/s^2, 1.2 m/s^2

8. The potential energy of a particle experiencing conservative force is represented as function of its position x in the following graph. As shown, the potential energy first increases parabolically and then decreases linearly with x.

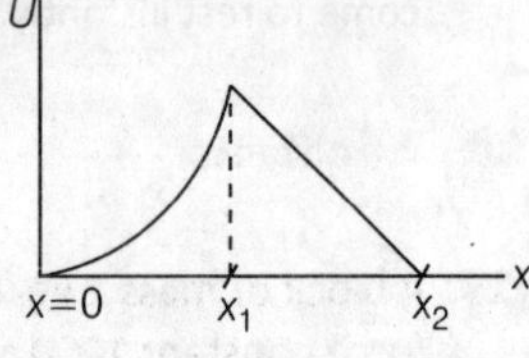

Conservative force acting on the system as a function of x may be represented by

(a) 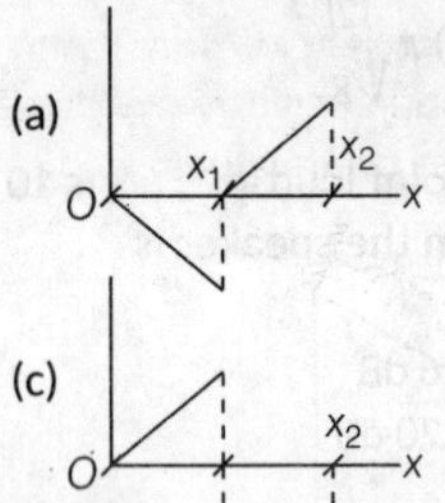

(b) 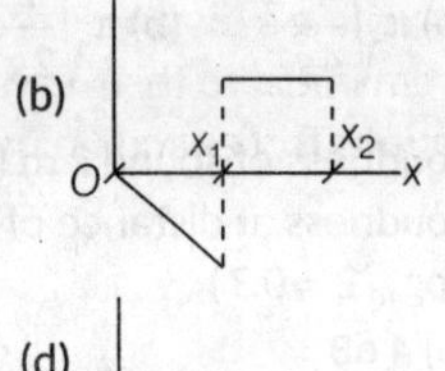

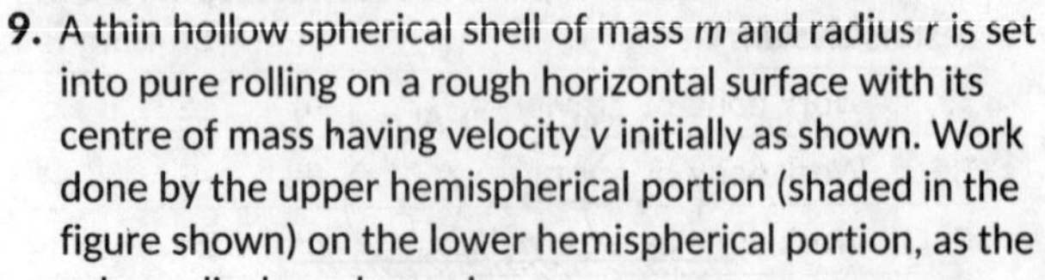

9. A thin hollow spherical shell of mass m and radius r is set into pure rolling on a rough horizontal surface with its centre of mass having velocity v initially as shown. Work done by the upper hemispherical portion (shaded in the figure shown) on the lower hemispherical portion, as the sphere displaces by πr, is

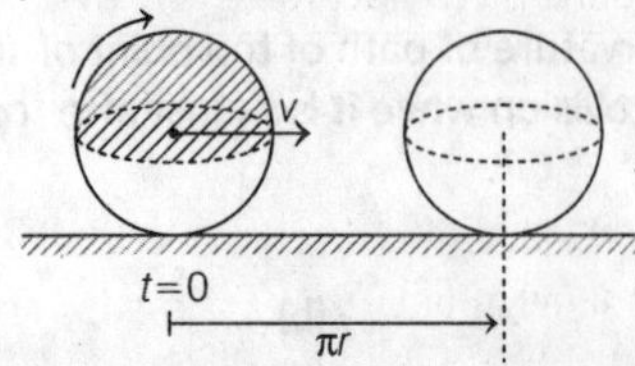

(a) $\frac{1}{2}mv^2 + \frac{mgr}{2}$ (b) $\frac{1}{2}mv^2 + mgr$
(c) $\frac{1}{3}mv^2 + mgr$ (d) $\frac{1}{3}mv^2 - mgr$

10. Suppose in a gas sample dN denotes number of gas molecules having speeds between v and $v + dv$, then $\frac{dN}{dv}$ *versus* v graph for the sample is called velocity distribution graph. Such a graph for a hypothetical gas sample is parabolic as shown with v_0 as maximum molecular speed.

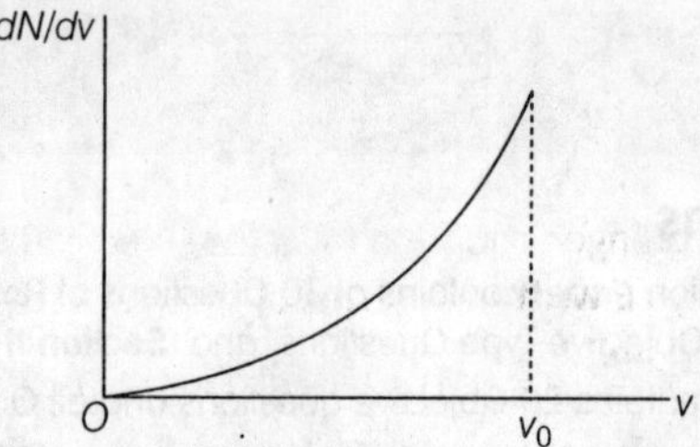

If slope of graph at O is zero, mean square speed of the sample is

(a) v_0^2 (b) $0.8\,v_0^2$ (c) $0.6\,v_0^2$ (d) $0.4\,v_0^2$

11. When a train approaches a stationary observer, the apparent frequency of the whistle is $3F$ and when the same train recedes away from the observer, the apparent frequency is $6F$. Then, the apparent frequency observed by a passenger sitting in the train is

(a) 4 F (b) 4.5 F
(c) 5 F (d) 5.5 F

12. Consider the shown screw gauge having main scale division of 1mm. In a complete rotation, the screw advances by 1 mm and the circular scale has 100 divisions. If no object is placed between the jaws of the shown screw gauge, the zero of main scale is barely visible and 92nd circular division matches with the main scale line. Thickness of the shown wire between jaws of the gauge is

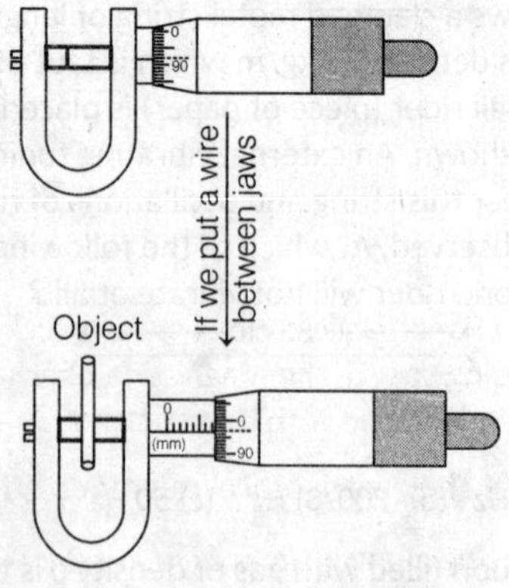

(a) 7.80 mm (b) 7.90 mm
(c) 8.05 mm (d)8.07mm

13. Figure shows a parabolic graph between T and $\frac{1}{V}$ (T = temperature, V = volume) for a mixture of a gases undergoing an adiabatic process. The square of ratio of rms velocity of molecules and speed of sound in the mixture of gases at the same temperature is

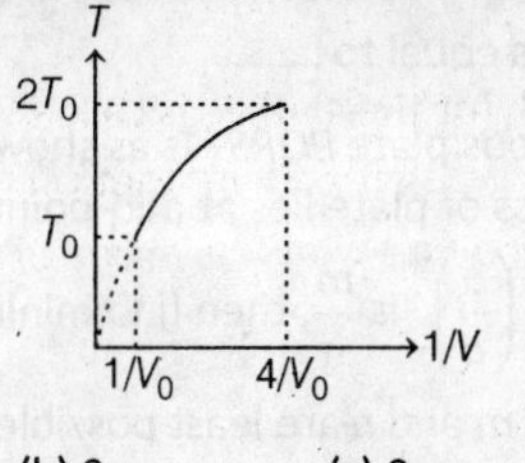

(a) 1 (b) 2 (c) 3 (d)4

14. The Schrodinger equation for a free electron of mass m and energy E written in terms of the wave function ψ is $\frac{d^2\psi}{dx^2} + \frac{8\pi^2 mE}{h^2}\psi = 0$. The dimensions of the coefficient of ψ in the second term must be

(a) $[M^1L^1]$ (b) $[L^2]$ (c) $[L^{-2}]$ (d) $[M^1L^{-1}T^1]$

15. The air column in an open organ pipe vibrating in 5th overtone is in unison with a tuning fork. If (1/3)rd length of the organ pipe is removed, then the remaining portion will be in unison with same tuning fork while vibrating in

(a) 2nd overtone (b) 3rd overtone
(c) 4th overtone (d) 5th overtone

16. Two masses A and B of 10 kg and 5 kg respectively are connected with a string passing over a frictionless pulley fixed at the corner of a table as shown. The coefficient of static friction of A with table is 0.25. The minimum mass of C that may be placed on A to prevent it from moving is

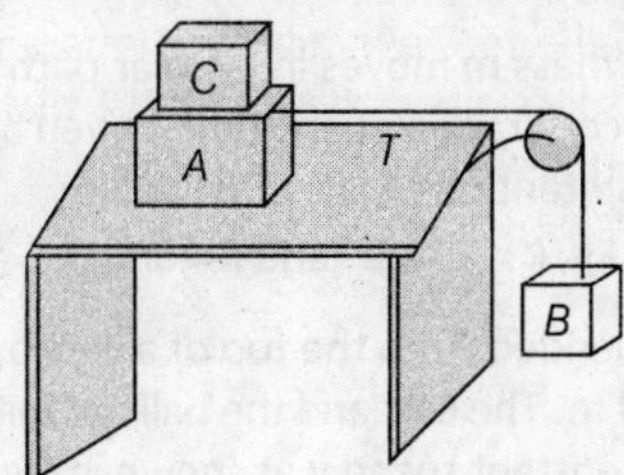

(a) 15 kg (b) 10 kg (c)5 kg (d) 12 kg

17. Statement I For a particle moving along a circular path with increasing speed, the magnitude of acceleration of particle may decrease with time.

Statement II The centripetal acceleration of a particle of mass m moving along a circle of radius R is $\frac{v^2}{R}$, where v is speed of the particle.

(a) Statement I is True, Statement II is True; Statement II is a correct explanation for Statement I.
(b) Statement I is True, Statement II is True; Statement II is not a correct explanation for Statement I.
(c) Statement I is True, Statement II is False.
(d) Statement I is False, Statement II is True.

18. A penguin of mass m stands at the right edge of a sled of mass $3m$ and length l. The sled lies on frictionless ice. The penguin starts moving towards left, reaches the left end and jumps with a velocity u and at an angle θ relative to ground. Neglecting the height of the sled, choose the incorrect statement.

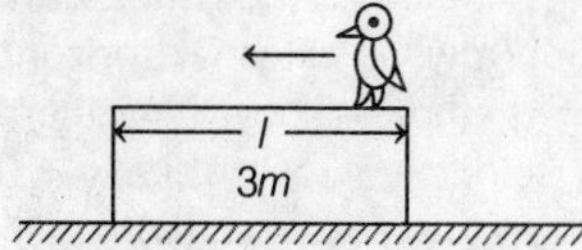

(a) Displacement of the sled w.r.t. ground till the penguin reaches left end of the sled is $\frac{l}{4}$.
(b) Displacement of the penguin w.r.t. ground till the penguin reaches left end of the sled is l.
(c) Displacement of centre of mass of the sled + penguin system w.r.t. ground till the penguin reaches left end of the sled is zero.
(d) After jumping, the penguin falls on the ground at a distance $\frac{4}{3}\frac{u^2 \sin 2\theta}{g}$ from the left end of the sled.

19. A block of mass 2 kg (connected to a massless spring of force constant 1000 N/m as shown in figure) is released from rest on a smooth inclined plane of inclination 30° and initially, the spring is in its natural length. An external variable contact force also acts on the block down the inclined plane. Block comes to rest for a moment after travelling a distance of 20 cm along the inclined plane. From initial to this moment, Column I gives work done by various forces and Column II gives their values.

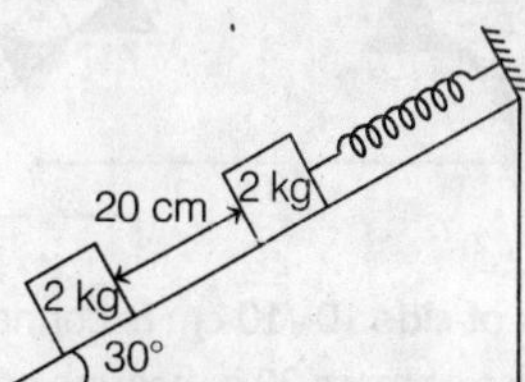

	Column I		Column II
A.	Work done by gravity	(i)	18 J
B.	Work done by spring	(ii)	−2 J
C.	Work done by external force	(iii)	2 J
D.	Work done by contact force	(iv)	−20 J

Choose the most appropriate match from the options given below.

(a) A-(ii) B-(iv) C-(i) d-(iii)
(b) A-(ii) B-(i) C-(iv) d-(iii)
(c) A-(iii) B-(iv) C-(i) d-(ii)
(d) A-(iv) B-(ii) C-(i) d-(iii)

20. Four students measure the height of a tower. Each student uses a different method and each measures the height many different times. The data for each are plotted below. The measurement with highest accuracy is

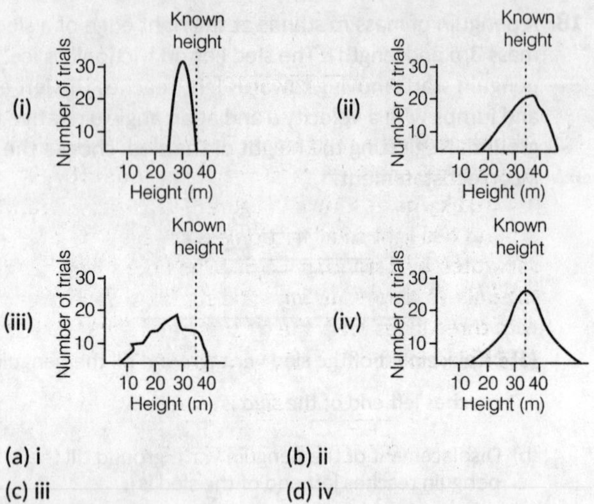

(a) i (b) ii
(c) iii (d) iv

Section II *Numerical Value Questions*

21. Distance between the centres of two stars is $10a$. The masses of these stars are M and $16M$ and their radii are a and $2a$, respectively. A body of mass m is fired straight from the surface of the larger star towards the smaller star. The minimum initial kinetic energy for the body to reach the surface of smaller star is $\frac{45GMm}{ka}$. Find the value of k.

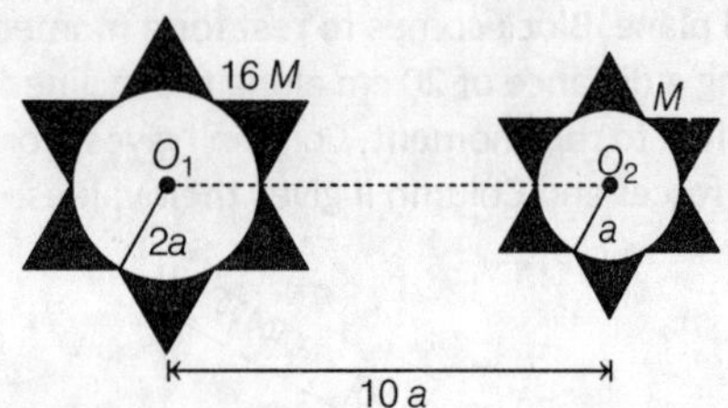

22. A cubical block of side $10\sqrt{10}$ cm is connected to a smooth and uniform disc of mass 20 g through an ideal string as shown in figure. The block is placed on a thin liquid layer of thickness 0.2 mm. Centre of the disc moves downward with constant speed of 2 cm/s after the system is released. If coefficient of viscosity of liquid is $\frac{x}{1000}$ Pa-s, then find the value of x. (Take, $g = 10\text{ m/s}^2$)

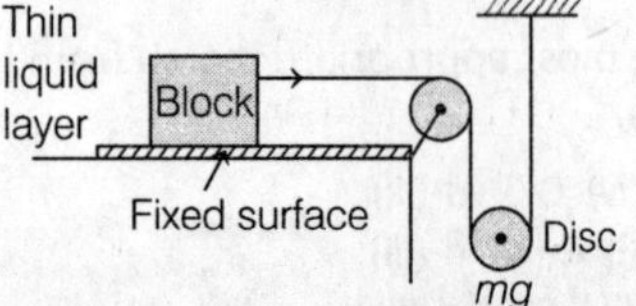

23. A horizontal oriented copper rod of length, $l = \frac{2\sqrt{2}}{3\pi}$ m is rotated about vertical axis passing through its middle. Breaking strength of copper is $\sigma = 2.5 \times 10^8$ Pa and density of copper is $\rho = 9 \times 10^3\text{ kg/m}^3$. Rotation frequency measured in (s^{-1}) at which the rod ruptures is given by $25\,n$, here n is equal to ....

24. A homogeneous plate $PQRST$ is as shown in figure. The centre of mass of plate lies at mid-point A of segment QT. If the ratio of $\left(\frac{b}{a}\right)^2$ is $\frac{m}{n}$, then find minimum value of $m + n$, where m and n are least possible integers ($PQ = PT = b$; $QR = RS = ST = a$).

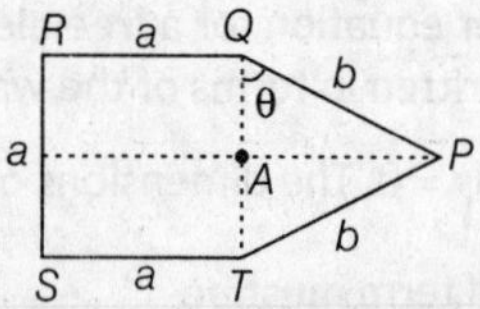

25. Figure represents a Carnot engine that works between temperatures, $T_1 = 400$ K and $T_2 = 150$ K and drives a Carnot refrigerator that works between temperature $T_3 = 325$ K and $T_4 = 225$ K. If $Q_3 = XQ_1$, find the value of X.

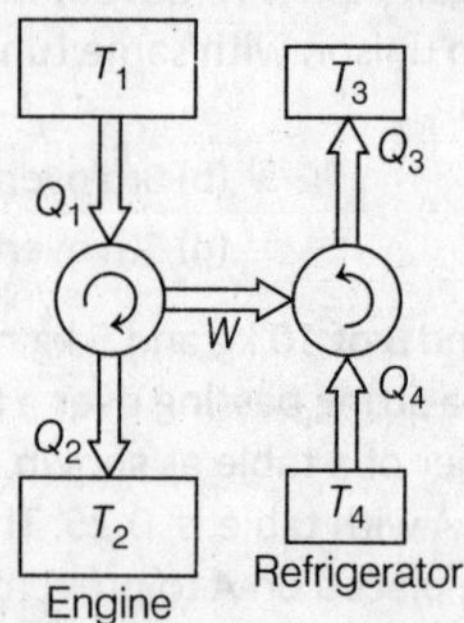

26. A particle of mass m moves in circular path of radius r with centripetal acceleration at any time t given as $a_c = kt$, then power of resultant force is ...... W.
(Take, $m = 2$ kg, $k = 1\text{ m/s}^3$ and $r = 3$m)

27. A ball is suspended from the top of a cart by a light string of length 1.0 m. The cart and the ball are initially moving to the right at constant speed v as shown in Fig. 1. The cart comes to the rest after colliding and sticking to a fixed bumper as shown in Fig. 2. The suspended ball swings through a maximum angle 60°. Square of the initial speed v is ...... m^2/s^2.
(Take, $g = 10\text{ m/s}^2$)

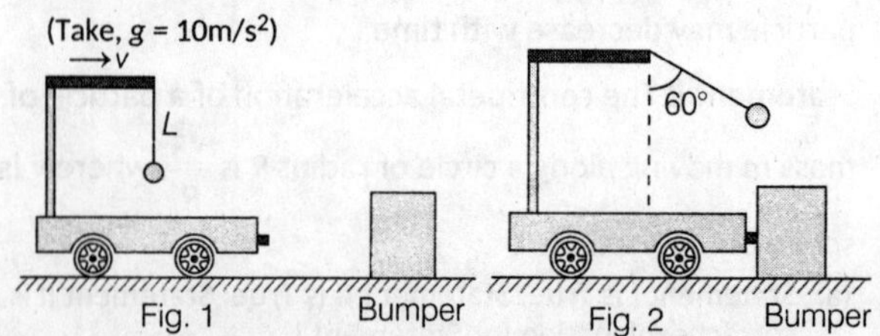

28. The vertical water tank shown has uniform cross section, is closed at the top and initial level of water is 4.5 m from bottom. The empty space of length L contains air at atmospheric pressure (10^5Pa), that can be considered as an ideal gas. When the valve at the bottom is opened, the level of water decreases by 0.5 m when the flow of water ceases though valve remains opened. Neglecting any variation in temperature during the process, find initial length of empty space L in m.

(Take, $g = 10 \text{ m/s}^2$ and density of water $= 1000 \text{ kg/m}^3$)

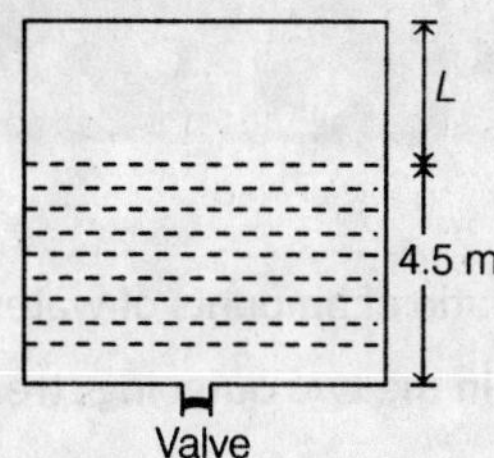

29. A rod of length 1 m and coefficient of linear expansion $\alpha = 10^{-4}$ per degree is placed symmetrically between fixed walls separated by 1001 mm. The Young's modulus of the rod is 10^{11} N/m^2. If the temperature is increased by 20°C, then the stress developed in the rod is 10^x (in N/m^2). Find the value of x.

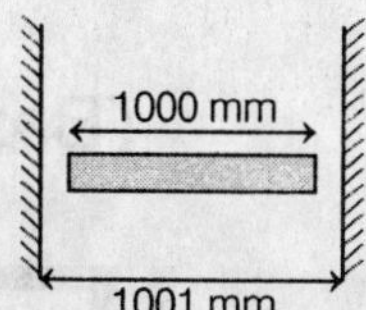

30. An object of mass M kg hangs in equilibrium from a string with a total length of $L = 16$ m and linear density of $\mu = 0.01$ kg/m, as shown in figure. The string is wrapped around two light small frictionless pulleys that are separated by distance $d = 6$ m. When the string between the pulleys vibrates to form the standing wave pattern with three loops on it, the frequency of vibration is 25 Hz. Find the value of M. (Take, $g = 10 \text{ m/s}^2$)

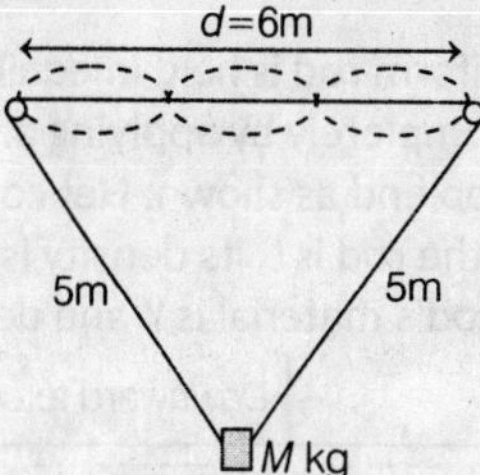

Answers

1 (b)	2 (d)	3 (b)	4 (b)	5 (b)	6 (d)	7 (b)	8 (b)	9 (a)	10 (c)
11 (a)	12 (c)	13 (b)	14 (c)	15 (b)	16 (b)	17 (b)	18 (b)	19 (c)	20 (a)
21 (8)	22 (5)	23 (10)	24 (17)	25 (2.03)	26 (3)	27 (10)	28 (0.75)	29 (8)	30 (16)

See detailed explanations on page no. 268

Part Test 02

(Based on Complete Class 11 Syllabus)

JEE Advanced

Physics

Section I *Only one correct option*

1. A vertical uniform rod is held in equilibrium after immersing completely by applying a vertically downward force at its top end as shown. Net compression in the rod is (length of the rod is L, its density is ρ and Young's modulus of rod's material is Y and density of fluid is 2ρ)

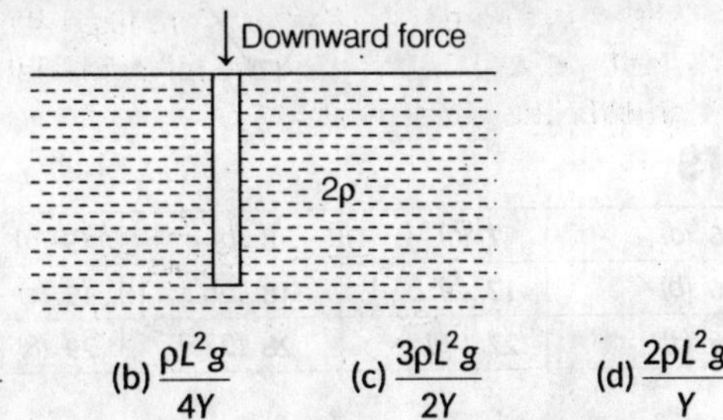

(a) $\frac{\rho L^2 g}{2Y}$ (b) $\frac{\rho L^2 g}{4Y}$ (c) $\frac{3\rho L^2 g}{2Y}$ (d) $\frac{2\rho L^2 g}{Y}$

2. Sand is transported to the construction site using a conveyor belt. The length of the belt is l, the angle with respect to the horizontal is α, the belt is driven by the lower pulley with radius R, powered externally. The sand is put onto the belt at a constant rate μ (kg/s). The minimal required torque needed to transport the sand is (The coefficient of friction is large enough for the sand grains to stop moving immediately after hitting the belt, take the initial velocity of the sand grains to be zero)

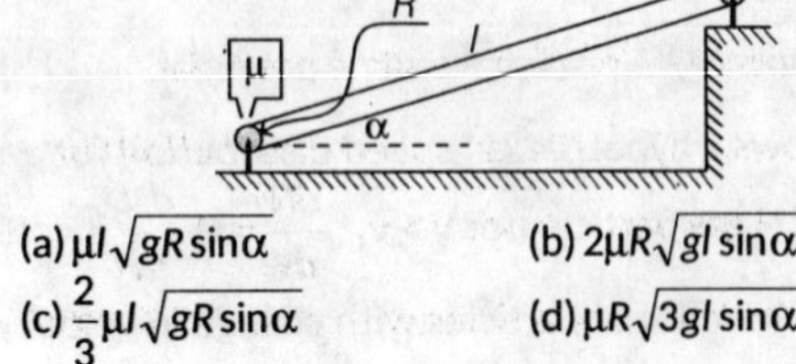

(a) $\mu l\sqrt{gR\sin\alpha}$ (b) $2\mu R\sqrt{gl\sin\alpha}$

(c) $\frac{2}{3}\mu l\sqrt{gR\sin\alpha}$ (d) $\mu R\sqrt{3gl\sin\alpha}$

3. A stream of water falls against a trough's bottom with velocity v and splits into smaller streams going to the left and to the right. The incoming stream is inclined at an angle 2α to the trough (and the resultant streams) are as shown. The ratio of amounts of water carried per unit time, i.e. $\frac{\mu_1}{\mu_2}$ in the two outgoing streams is

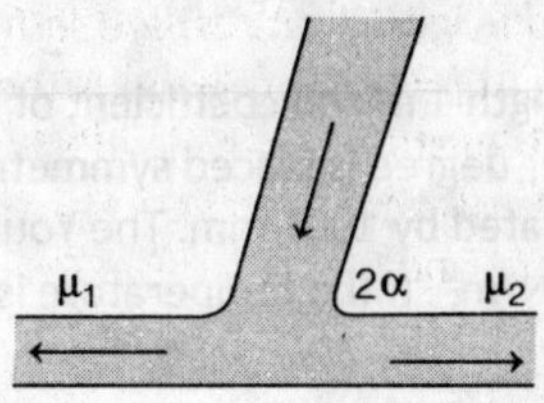

(a) $\cot\alpha\cdot\cos\alpha$ (b) $\cot^2\alpha$

(c) $\frac{\operatorname{cosec}^2\alpha}{\tan\alpha}$ (d) $\sin^3\alpha$

4. A sound source emits two sinusoidal sound waves, both of wavelength λ, along paths A and B as shown in figure. The sound travelling along path B is reflected from four surfaces as shown and then merges at point Q, producing minimum intensity at that point. The minimum value of d in terms of λ is

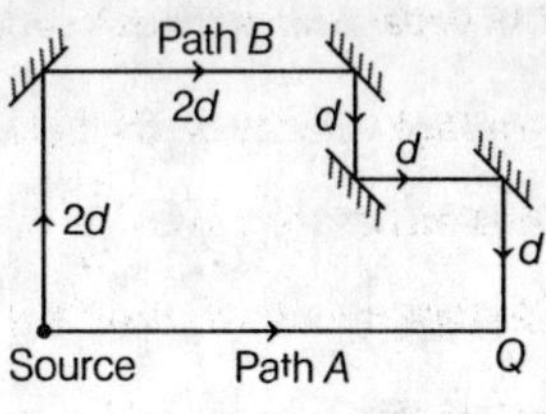

(a) λ (b) $\frac{\lambda}{2}$

(c) $\frac{\lambda}{4}$ (d) $\frac{\lambda}{8}$

Section II *More than one correct options*

5. A system of two identical blocks (each of mass m) connected by a relaxed spring of stiffness constant k is placed at rest on a smooth horizontal surface. A rotating ball of mass m is released from height h on to the left block. If the ball collides elastically with block and coefficient of friction between the block and the ball is 1, choose the correct alternative(s).

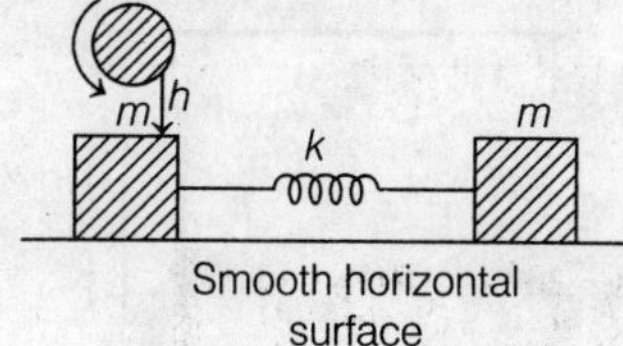

(a) Velocity of the left block just after collision is $\sqrt{2gh}$.
(b) Velocity of the left block just after collision is $2\sqrt{2gh}$.
(c) Maximum compression in the spring during subsequent motion is $\sqrt{\frac{mgh}{k}}$.
(d) Time taken for maximum compression considering time of collision as $t=0$ is $\frac{\pi}{2}\sqrt{\frac{m}{2k}}$.

6. A cat and a dog initially at rest are shown as points C and D respectively. At $t=0$, the dog sights the cat and begins to chase it with constant speed v, while the cat starts running on X-axis with constant speed u. At a later general instant, the cat and the dog are shown by C' and D' respectively.

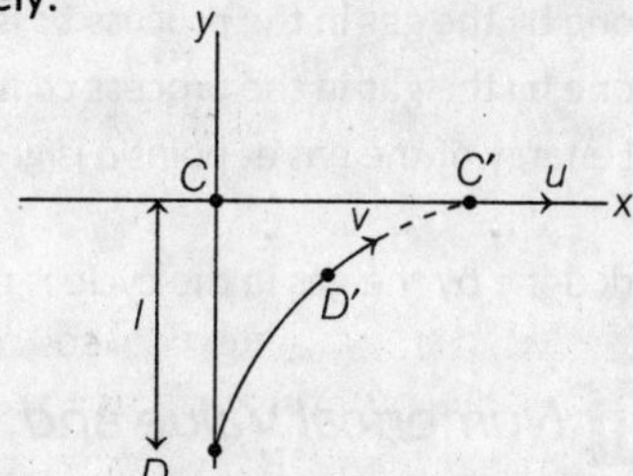

(a) If $v=2u$, dog catches cat in time $\frac{2l}{3u}$.
(b) If $v=u$, final separation between cat and dog is $\frac{l}{2}$.
(c) If $v=2u$, average velocity of dog between $t=0$ and the instant, dog catches the cat is $\frac{\sqrt{13}}{2}u$.
(d) If $v=2u$, distance moved by dog till it catches cat is $4l$.

7. A uniform rod AB of mass m and length l is free to rotate in vertical plane about horizontal axis passing through A and oriented perpendicular to the plane of paper. The rod is given a gentle push in the position shown. Consider subsequent motion of the rod till its centre C reaches bottommost point (as the rod turns by 180°).

(a) Final kinetic energy of portion CB is $\frac{mgl}{2}$.
(b) Final kinetic energy of AC is $\frac{mgl}{8}$.
(c) Work done by portion AC on CB is $-\frac{7mgl}{8}$.
(d) Work done by portion CB on AC is $-\frac{mgl}{8}$.

8. Fig. 1 shows a uniform string of length l attached to ceiling of an elevator accelerating up with acceleration $3g$. Time taken by a wave pulse generated at bottom end of string to reach top is equal to t. Fig. 2 shows a simple pendulum of same length l released making small angle 2θ with vertical in position A. The figure also shows two positions B and C of the string as it oscillates. Time period of oscillation of the pendulum is equal to T.

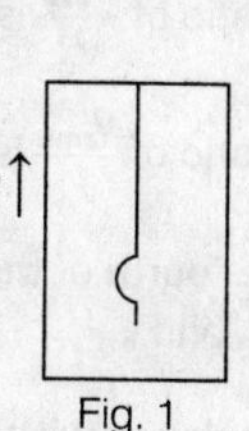

Fig. 1

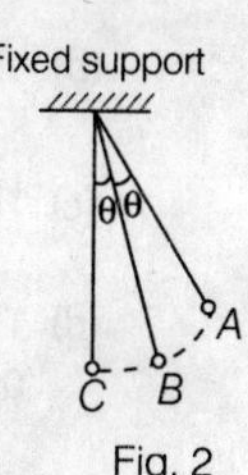

Fig. 2

(a) $T=2\pi t$
(b) Acceleration of wave pulse is $2g$.
(c) Speed of wave pulse (w.r.t. string) as it crosses mid-point of string is average of wave speed at bottom end and that at top.
(d) Pendulum is between positions A and B at time t after it is released.

9. Consider two uniform hollow spheres each of mass M (as shown in figure.), their centres are fixed at $C_1(-3R, 0, 0)$ and $C_2(+3R, 0, 0)$. Which of the following option(s) is/are true for the given system?

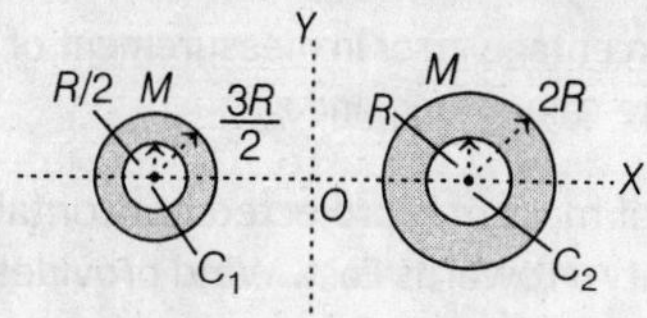

(a) Work done by gravitational force in moving a mass m from C_1 to C_2 is zero.
(b) If a particle of mass m placed at origin is slightly displace along Y-axis and released, then it will perform SHM with frequency $\frac{1}{2\pi}\sqrt{\frac{2GM}{27R^3}}$.
(c) If a particle is moving on a path $y^2+z^2=16R^2$ under the effect of gravitational force only, then its time period is $10\pi\sqrt{\frac{5R^3}{2GM}}$.
(d) All points on YZ-plane have same potential.

10. Graph shows a hypothetical speed distribution for a sample of N gas particle (for $v>v_0$; $\frac{dN}{dv}=0$, $\frac{dN}{dv}$ is rate of change of number of particles with change in velocity).

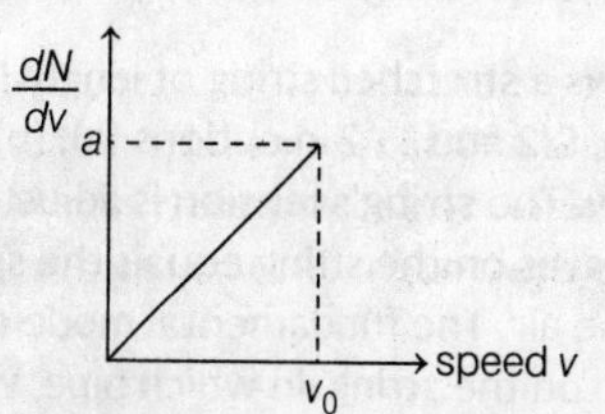

(a) The value of av_0 is $2N$

(b) The ratio of $\frac{v_{avg}}{v_0}$ is equal to $\frac{2}{3}$.

(c) The ratio of $\frac{v_{rms}}{v_0}$ is equal to $\frac{1}{\sqrt{2}}$.

(d) Three-fourth of the total particles have a speed between $0.5\,v_0$ and v_0

11. A beam balance with light rod is used to determine the unknown mass M. The rod is hinged from O. Two standard masses A(10 kg) and B(1 kg), which can slide on the rod are set at distances x_1 and x_2 from O to balance the rod in horizontal position and they are measured with maximum permissible error 0.1 cm.

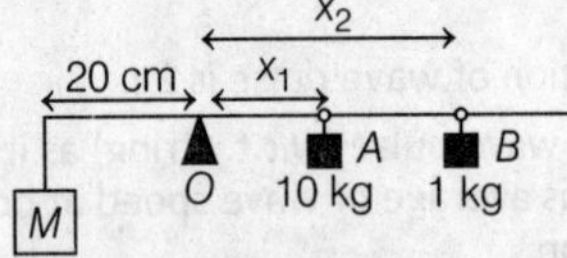

Choose the correct option(s).

(a) The maximum permissible error in M depends on absolute values of x_1 and x_2

(b) If $x_1 = 5.0$ cm and $x_2 = 10.0$ cm, then the maximum permissible error in M is 0.055 kg

(c) If $x_1 = 10.0$ cm and $x_2 = 20.0$ cm, then percentage error in measurement of M is approximately 0.9%

(d) The percentage error in measurement of M depends on absolute values of x_1 and x_2

12. A particle of mass m is projected horizontally from a tower with velocity u towards East. Wind provides constant horizontal acceleration $\frac{g}{2}$ towards West. If particle strikes the ground vertically, then

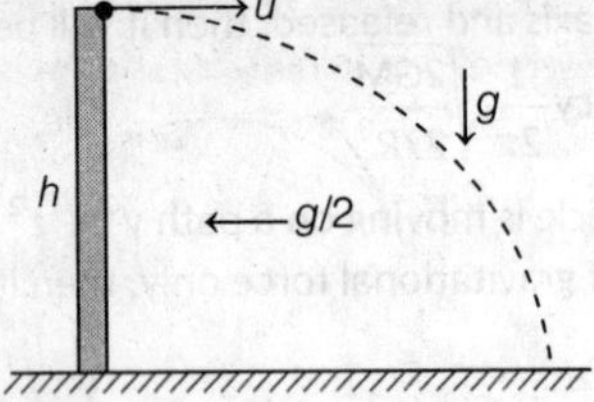

(a) height of tower is $\frac{2u^2}{g}$

(b) speed with which particle strikes ground is $2u$

(c) work done by wind force $\frac{1}{2}mu^2$

(d) particle strikes the ground after time $t = 2u / g$

13. Figure shows a stretched string of length L and pipes of length L, $2L$, $L/2$ and $L/2$ in options (a), (b), (c) and (d), respectively. The string's tension is adjusted such that the speed of waves on the string equals the speed of sound waves in the air. The fundamental mode of oscillation is then set-up on the string. In which pipe, will the air column can be in resonance with the sound produced by the string?

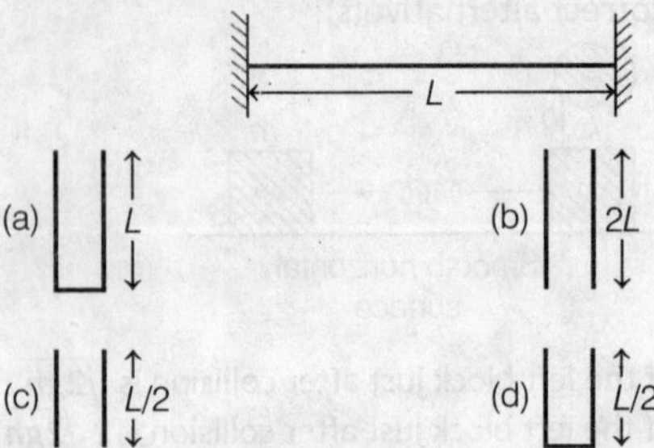

14. An ideal gas undergoes a cyclic process *abcda* shown by pressure-density curve. Choose the correct option(s).

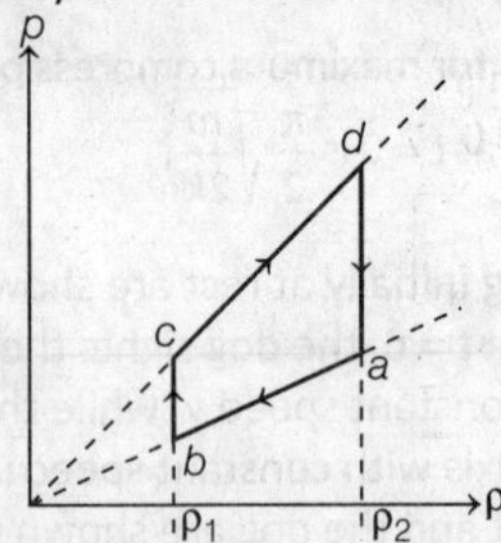

(a) Work done by the gas in the process *bc* is zero.

(b) Work done by the gas in the process *cd* is negative.

(c) Internal energy of the gas at point *a* is greater than at state *c*.

(d) Net work done by the gas in the cycle is negative.

Section III *Numerical Value and Non-negative Integer Type*

15. A capillary tube (with inner cross-section shaped as regular hexagon of a side l) is dipped vertically in a liquid of density ρ and surface tension T, which wets the surface of capillary tube with angle of contact θ. Approximate height, neglecting effect of surface tension at the corners of the tube, to which liquid will rise in the tube is $\frac{\sqrt{x}\,T\cos\theta}{\rho l g}$. Find the value of x.

16. A space object has the shape of a sphere of radius R. Heat sources ensuring the heat evolution at a constant rate are distributed uniformly over its volume . The amount of heat liberated by a unit surface area is proportional to the fourth power of thermodynamic temperature. If radius of the object becomes 16 times, the surface temperature of the object becomes n times. Find the value of n.

17. A vertical hollow cylinder is fixed on the ground. A uniform rod can be balanced partly in and partly out of the cylinder with the lower end of the rod resting against the vertical wall of the cylinder, as shown in the figure. The angle made by rod with the vertical in equilibrium is θ. Maximum and minimum possible value of θ are 53° and

37°, respectively. Coefficient of friction between rod and cylinder is $\mu = \tan\left[\frac{1}{2}\tan^{-1}\left(\frac{37}{28n}\right)\right]$. Find the value of n.

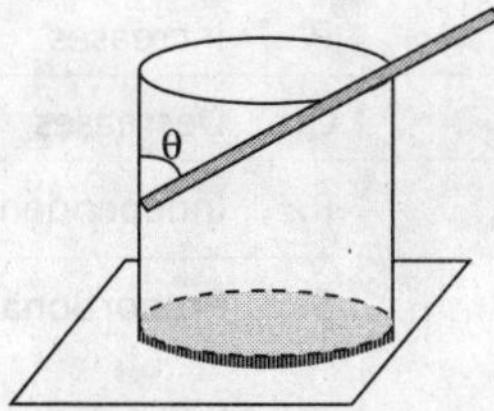

18. A gas sample undergoes a reversible isothermal expansion. Figure gives the change ΔS in entropy of the gas *versus* the final volume V_f of gas. The scale of the vertical axis is set by $\Delta S_0 = 128$ J/K. Find the approximate moles in the sample. (Take, $\log_{10}3 = 0.477$)

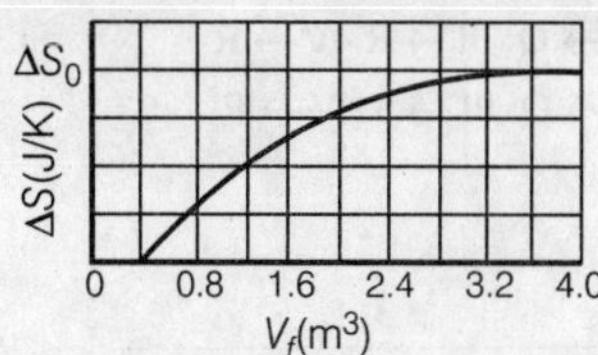

19. Figure shows a tube structure in which a sound signal is sent from one end and is received at the other end. The semi-circular part has a radius of 10.0 cm. The frequency of the sound source can be varied from 4 to 7 kHz. Frequency (in kHz) at which the ear perceives maximum intensity is .... (Take, the speed of sound in air = 342 m/s)

20. Three blocks are arranged as shown in figure. All the strings are massless and inextensible. All pulleys are frictionless and massless. Coefficient of friction between surfaces and blocks are 0.5. If the blocks were initially at rest, then the magnitude of tension in the string attached to 2 kg block (in N) is T while magnitude of contact force by the surface on 1.2 kg is R. Find $\frac{R}{T}$ in N. (Take, $\tan 37° = \frac{3}{4}$ and $g = 10$ m/s^2)

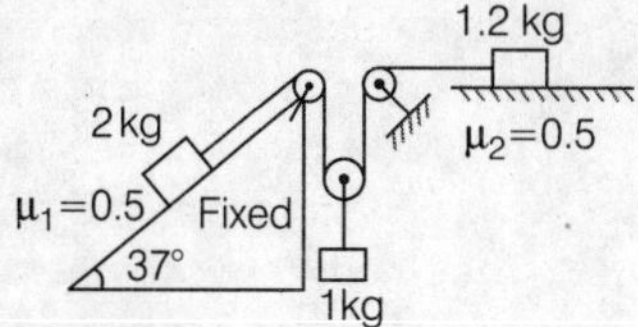

Section IV *Numerical Value Stem Questions*

Stem 1 for (Q. 21 and Q 22)

A hot air balloon consists of a large bag, called an envelope, with a basket suspended underneath. A burner in basket is used to heat air inside the envelope through an opening.

The hot air inside the envelope is less dense than the surrounding (cooler) air, this heated air generates lift by the way of buoyant force. Consider a hot air balloon (open to atmosphere) with volume $V_B = 1.1\,\text{m}^3$. The mass of the balloon, whose volume is to be neglected in comparison to V_B is $m = 0.187$ kg. The balloon shall be started, where the external air temperature is $\theta_1 = 20°$ C and the normal external air pressure is $p_0 = 1.013 \times 10^5$ Pa. Under these conditions, the density of air is $\rho_1 = 1.2$ kg/m^3.

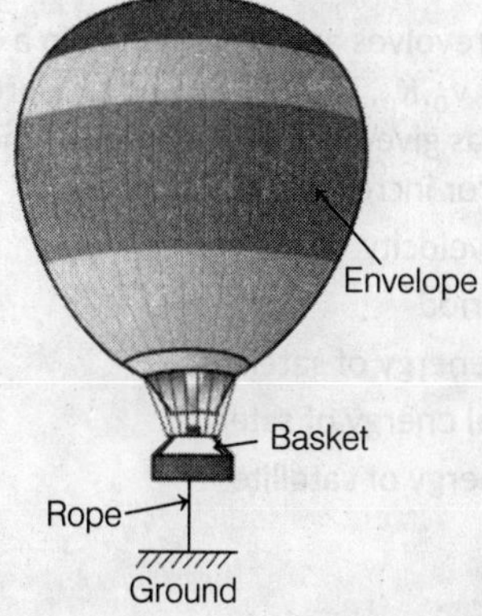

21. Temperature θ_2 to which air inside the balloon must be warmed to make the balloon just float is .... °C.

22. The balloon is fastened to the ground by a rope and the internal air is heated to steady-state temperature of $\theta_3 = 110°$C. Tension in the rope is .... N.

Stem 2 for (Q. 23 and Q. 24)

A wheel with radius R is situated at height R from the ground and is rotating at angular velocity $\omega = \sqrt{\frac{g}{R}}$. At some point A, a drop of water separates from the wheel and reaches the ground at point B situated directly below the wheel's axle (see the figure).

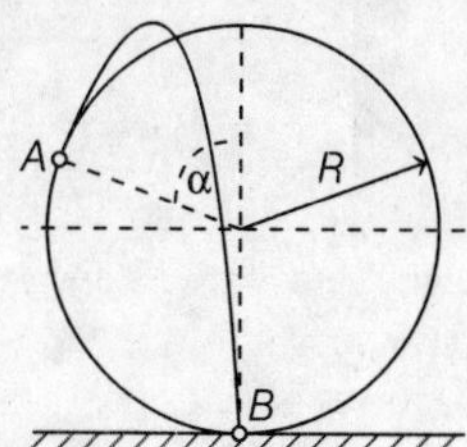

23. Falling time of the drop is ... ω^{-1}.

24. α is equal to $\tan^{-1} x$. Here, x is ..... .

Stem 3 for (Q. 25 and Q. 26)

A glass tube has three different cross-sectional areas with the values indicated in the figure. A piston at the left end of the tube exerts pressure, so that the mercury within the tube flows out of the right end with a speed of 8.0 m/s. Three points within the tube are labelled A, B and C. Point C is open to atmosphere. The atmospheric pressure is 1.01×10^5 N/m^2 and the density of mercury is 1.36×10^4 kg/m^3. (Take, $g = 10\,\text{m/s}^2$)

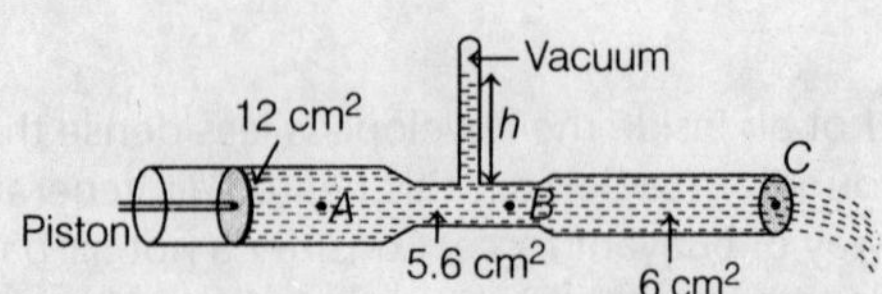

25. The pressure at point A is equal to ...... × 10^5 Pa.

26. The height h of mercury in the manometer is .... m.

Section V *Matching List Question*

27. A satellite revolves around a planet, in a certain orbit of radius r_0. If $v_0, K_0, T_0, P_0, E_0, B_0$ and L_0 represent physical quantities as given below, then match the entries of List-I and List-II for increasing radius of orbit.

v_0-Orbital velocity

T_0-Time period

K_0-Kinetic energy of satellite

P_0-Potential energy of satellite

E_0-Total energy of satellite

B_0-Binding energy of satellite

L_0-Angular momentum of satellite about the centre of planet

	List-I		List-II
I.	$v_0 K_0$	P.	Increases
II.	$B_0 L_0$	Q.	Decreases
III.	$P_0 E_0 L_0^4$	R.	Independent of r
IV.	$\frac{T_0}{L_0^3}$	S.	Proportional to $-r^{3/2}$
		T.	First increases then decreases

Which one of the following options is correct?

(a) I → S II → T III → R IV → P

(b) I → Q II → Q III → R IV → P

(c) I → S II → Q III → R IV → R

(d) I → P II → Q III → S IV → R

Answers

1 *(c)*	2 *(b)*	3 *(b)*	4 *(d)*	5 *(b,d)*	6 *(a,b,c)*	7 *(b,d)*	8 *(a,d)*	9 *(b,c)*	10 *(a,b,c,d)*
11 *(b,c,d)*	12 *(a,b,d)*	13 *(b,d)*	14 *(a,b,d)*	15 *(5.33)*	16 *(2)*	17 *(3)*	18 *(7)*	19 *(6)*	20 *(2.6)*
21 *(68.38)*	22 *(1.21)*	23 *(2.82)*	24 *(2.82)*	25 *(4.27)*	26 *(0.27)*	27 *(c)*			

See detailed explanations on page no. 272

Part Test 03

(Based on Complete Class 12 Syllabus)

JEE MAIN

Physics

Section I Objective Type Questions

1. A small uniformly charged sphere has electric field intensity $\mathbf{E} = 54\hat{i} + 72\hat{j}$ N/C and potential 900 V at P (11, 10) m. Dielectric strength of air is 3×10^6 V/m. Choose the most appropriate correct option.

(a) Charge of the sphere is 1 μC.

(b) Coordinates of centre of the sphere are (5, 2).

(c) Minimum possible radius of the sphere is $\sqrt{30}$ cm.

(d) All of the above

2. A point charge q can be placed at three different positions named A (just outside), B (apex) and C (just inside) on axis of the shown imaginary cone. Flux (magnitude) through lateral surface of the cone for A, B and C, respectively are

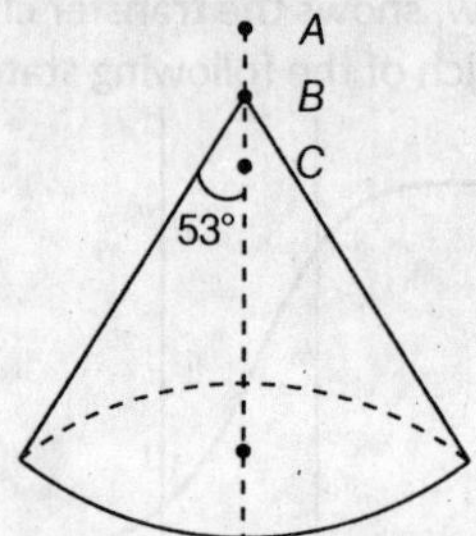

(a) $0, \frac{q}{10\varepsilon_0}, \frac{9q}{10\varepsilon_0}$ (b) $\frac{q}{5\varepsilon_0}, 0, \frac{q}{5\varepsilon_0}$

(c) $\frac{q}{5\varepsilon_0}, 0, \frac{4q}{5\varepsilon_0}$ (d) $\frac{4q}{5\varepsilon_0}, \frac{q}{5\varepsilon_0}, \frac{q}{5\varepsilon_0}$

3. In the circuit shown, AB is a uniform wire of resistance 6 Ω. With battery connected between C and D, length of AD for which current drawn from the battery is minimum will be

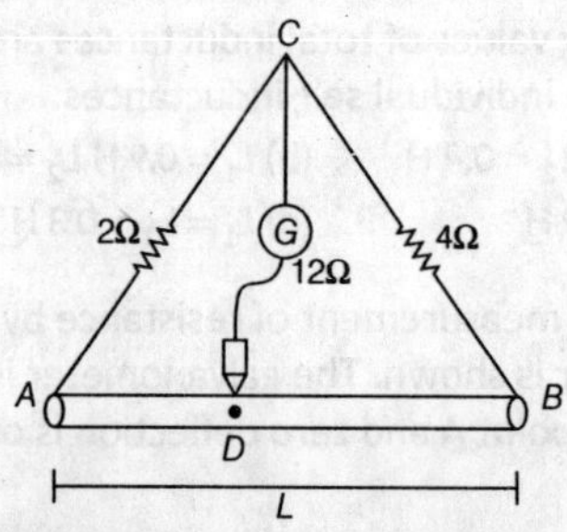

(a) $\frac{L}{2}$ (b) $\frac{L}{3}$

(c) $\frac{2L}{3}$ (d) $\frac{3L}{4}$

4. Charged particles having various velocities are sent through slit S_1. They enter in a velocity filter, where uniform magnetic field of 0.1 T and uniform electric field 100 V/m exists, which are perpendicular to each other. Only a few particles emerge from the thin slit S_2, which is exactly in front of S_1. Now, they enter in a region where only uniform magnetic field of 0.1 T pointing inwards exists and electric field is absent. If the particles strike the photographic plate at a distance of 0.42 mm from slit S_2, the particle should be

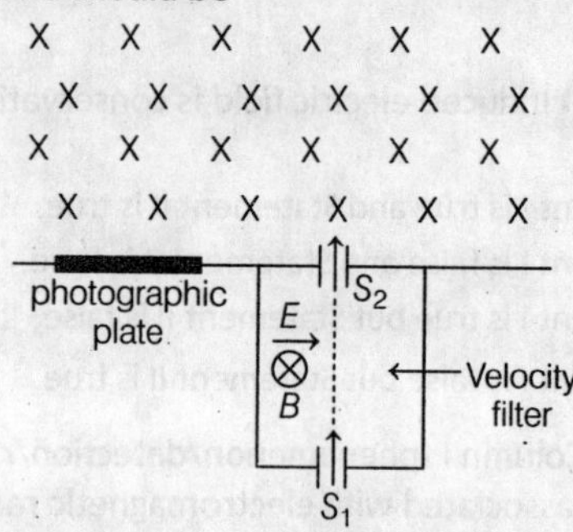

(a) α-particle (b) proton

(c) Lithium ion (Li^+) (d) Sodium ion (Na^+)

5. A telescope with objective of focal length 60 cm and eyepiece of focal length 5 cm focused on a far distance object such that the rays entering objective converge in focal plane of eyepiece. If object subtends as angle 1° on objective, then angular width of the image is

(a) 62° (b) 48° (c) 24° (d) 12°

6. Choose the correct statement for the shown circuit of logic gates.

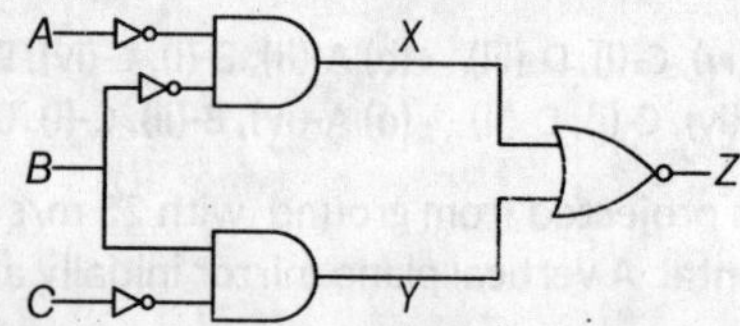

(a) For $A = 1$, $B = 1$, $C = 0$ final output $Z = 1$
(b) For $A = 0$, $B = 0$, $C = 0$ final output $Z = 1$
(c) For $A = 0$, $B = 0$, $C = 0$ final output $Z = 0$
(d) If NOR gate is replaced by OR gate, then final output of the circuit becomes $Z = 0$ for the input $A = 0$, $B = 0$ and $C = 0$.

7. A parallel plate capacitor with circular plates of radius R at short separation is filled completely with a dielectric slab of variable dielectric constant $K = k_0 r^n$, where k_0 is a positive constant and r is axial distance from axis, then equivalent dielectric constant of medium of capacitor is proportional to

(a) R^n (b) R^0
(c) R^{n+2} (d) R^{n-2}

8. There exists a uniform time varying magnetic field in cylindrical region of radius R as shown in figure.

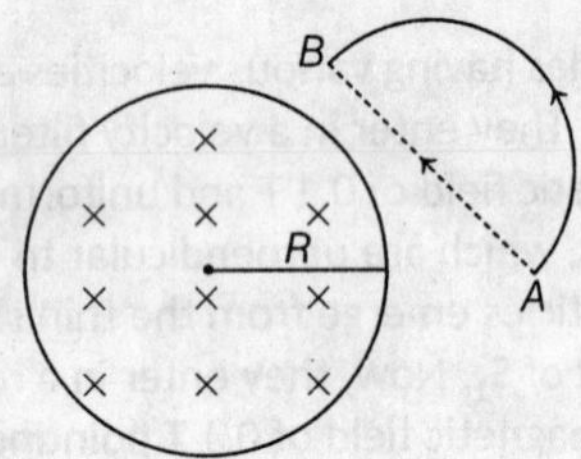

Statement I Work done by induced electric field in moving point charge from A to B is different for the two paths shown.

Statement II Induced electric field is conservative in nature.

(a) Statement I is true and Statement II is true.
(b) Statement I is false and Statement II is false.
(c) Statement I is true but Statement II is false.
(d) Statement I is false but Statement II is true.

9. Match the Column I (phenomenon/detection/range/ application associated with electromagnetic radiation) with Column II (Part of electromagnetic spectrum) and select the correct code from the choices given below the column.

	Column I		Column II
A.	Point contact diodes	(i)	UV-Rays
B.	1nm to 10^{-3}nm	(ii)	IR
C.	Laser assisted in situ keratomileusis	(iii)	Microwaves
D.	Crop growth detection using satellite	(iv)	X-ray

(a) A-(ii), B-(iv), C-(i), D-(iii) (b) A-(ii), B-(i), C-(iv), D-(iii)
(c) A-(iii), B-(iv), C-(i), D-(ii) (d) A-(iv), B-(ii), C-(i), D-(iii)

10. A particle is projected from ground with 25 m/s at 37° with horizontal. A vertical plane mirror initially at a distance 30 m from point of projection is moving away from point of projection with 10 m/s. The relative separation (in m) between particle and its image in plane mirror at t equal to 2 s will be

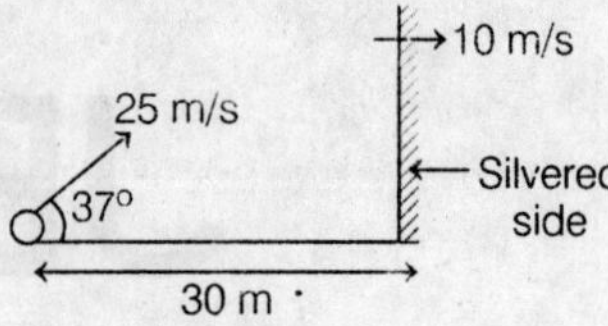

(a) 10 m (b) 20 m (c) 30 m (d) 40 m

11. An H-atom moving with speed v makes a head -on collision with another H-atom at rest. Both the atoms are in the ground state. The minimum value of velocity v for which one of the atoms may excite is

(a) 6.25×10^4 ms^{-1} (b) 8×10^4 ms^{-1}
(c) 13. 6 eV (d) 10. 2 eV

12. A uniformly charged ring of radius R is rotated about its axis with constant linear velocity v of each of its particles. The ratio of electric field to magnetic field at a point P on the axis of the ring distant $x = R$ from centre of ring is (c is speed of light).

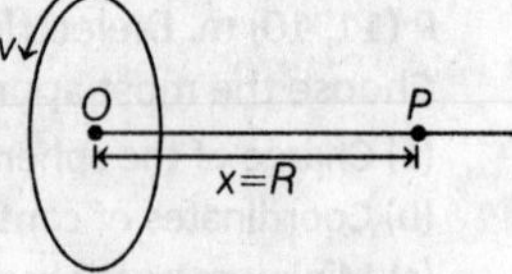

(a) $\frac{c^2}{v}$ (b) $\frac{v^2}{c}$ (c) $\frac{c}{v}$ (d) $\frac{v}{c}$

13. Figure given below, shows the transfer characteristics of a *CE* transistor. Which of the following statement is false?

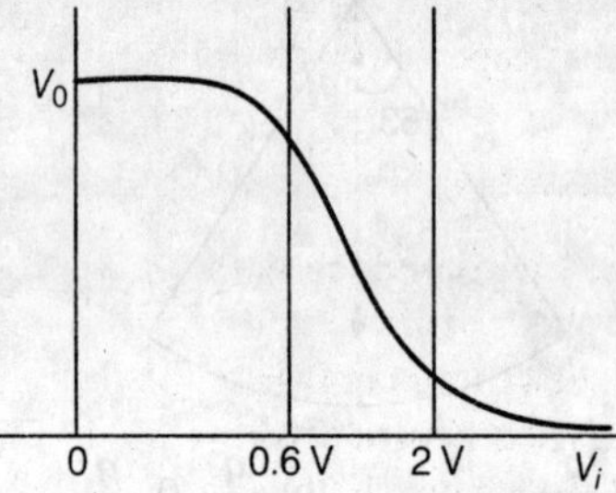

(a) At $V_i = 0.4$ V, transistor is in active state
(b) At $V_i = 1$V, it can be used as an amplifier
(c) At $V_i = 0.5$ V, it can be used as a switch turned OFF
(d) At $V_i = 2.5$ V, it can be used as switch turned ON

14. Two coils with a coupling coefficient of 0.5 between them, are connected in series, so as to magnetise first in the same direction and secondary in opposite direction. The corresponding values of total inductances are 1.9 H and 0.7 H. Find the individual self-inductances.

(a) $L_1 = 0.9$ H, $L_2 = 0.4$ H (b) $L_1 = 0.9$ H, $L_2 = 0.3$ H
(c) $L_2 = L_2 = 0.9$ H (d) $L_1 = L_2 = 0.3$ H

15. Circuit for the measurement of resistance by potentiometer is shown. The galvanometer is first connected at point A and zero deflection is observed at length $PJ = 10$ cm. In second case it is connected at point C and zero deflection is observed at a length 30 cm from P, R/X is equal to

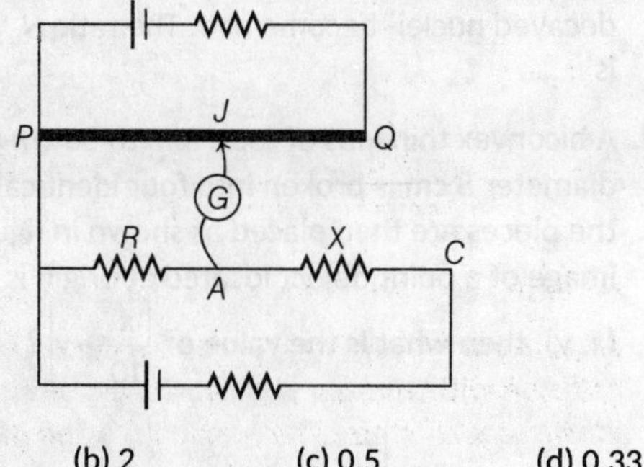

(a) 1 (b) 2 (c) 0.5 (d) 0.33

16. In the given AC circuit, if source voltage is $V = 200\sqrt{2}\sin(100\pi t)$, power delivered by source will have a power factor of

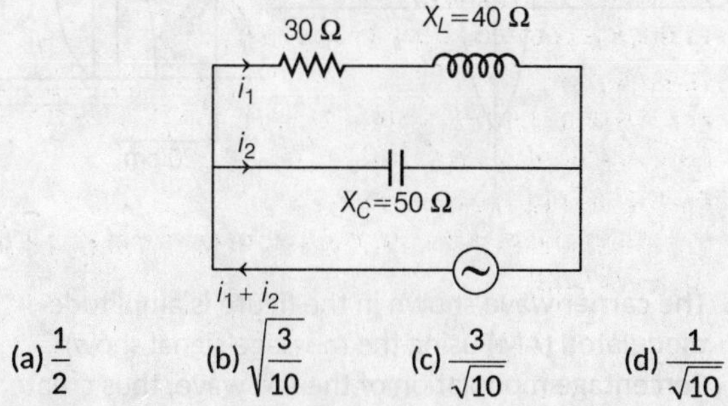

(a) $\frac{1}{2}$ (b) $\sqrt{\frac{3}{10}}$ (c) $\frac{3}{\sqrt{10}}$ (d) $\frac{1}{\sqrt{10}}$

17. A paramagnetic material is kept in a magnetic field. The field is increased till the magnetisation becomes constant. If the temperature is now decreased, the magnetisation

(a) will increase (b) decreases
(c) remains constant (d) may increase of decrease

18. Figure shows two conducting thin concentric shells of radii r and $3r$. The outer shell carries charge q and inner shell is neutral. The amount of charge which flows from inner shell to the earth after the key K is closed, is equal to

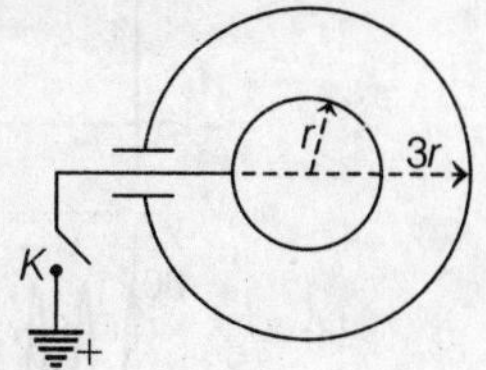

(a) q (b) $0.5\,q$ (c) $0.33\,q$ (d) $0.25q$

19. Statement I For the situation shown in the figure two monochromatic identical coherent light sources produce interference pattern on the screen. The intensity of minima nearest to S_1 is not exactly zero.

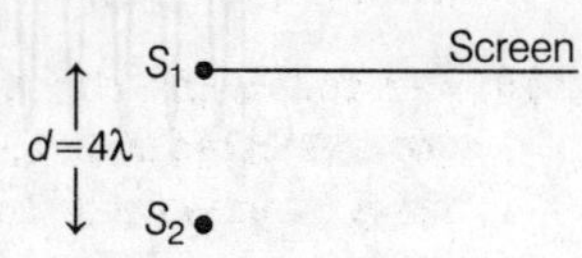

Statement II Minimum intensity is zero when interfering waves have same intensity at the location of superposition.

(a) Statement I is true, Statement II is true and Statement II is a correct explanation for Statement I.
(b) Statement I is true, Statement II is true but statement II is not the correct explanation for Statement I.
(c) Statement I is true but Statement II is false.
(d) Statement I is false but Statement II is true.

20. The switch shown in figure closes when $\Delta V_C > \frac{2V}{3}$ and opens when $\Delta V_C = \frac{V}{3}$. The voltmeter reading is plotted against time. Time period of the waveform, thus obtained, will be

(a) $(R_1 + R_2)C\ ln2$ (b) $R_2C\ ln2$
(c) $(R_1 + 2R_2)C\ln 2$ (d) Infinite

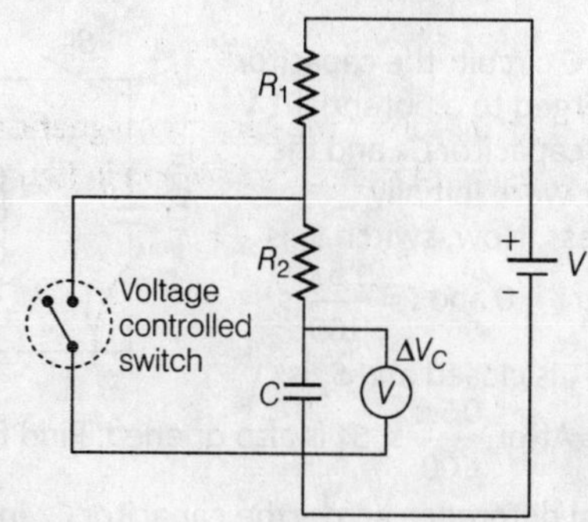

Section II Numerical Value Questions

21. A current I is flowing longitudinally and uniformly in a thick cylindrical long shell of inner radius R and outer radius $3R$. Magnetic field inside cylinder at a distance $r = 2R$ from axis of cylinder is $\frac{\mu_0 I}{x\pi R}$. Find x.

22. The ratio of acceleration of the electron in singly ionized helium atom and hydrogen atom according to Bohr's model (both in ground state) is $x:1$. When a metallic surface is illuminated with monochromatic light of wavelength λ, the stopping potential is V. When the same surface is illuminated with light of wavelength $(x-5)\lambda$, the stopping potential is $V/5$. Work function of the metallic surface is $hc/y\lambda$. Find x/y.

23. Number of nuclei of radioactive sample A to that of B is depicted as function of time t in the graphs shown here. Find the ratio of number of nuclei of B to that of A at $t = 2t_0$.

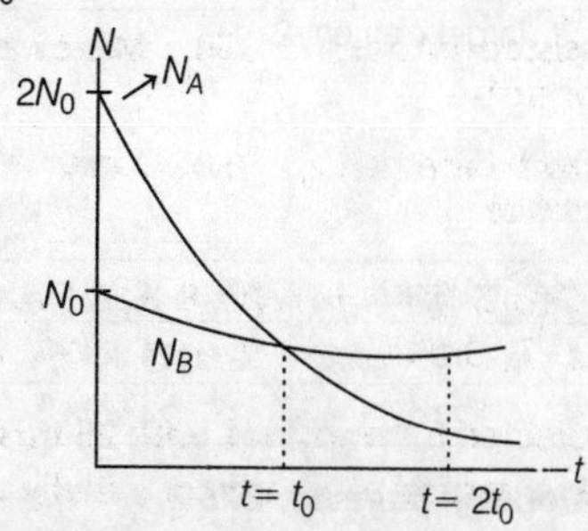

24. Light of wavelength 600 nm is incident upon a single slit with width 4×10^{-4} m. The figure shows the pattern observed on a screen positioned 2 m from the slits. Determine the distance s (in mm).

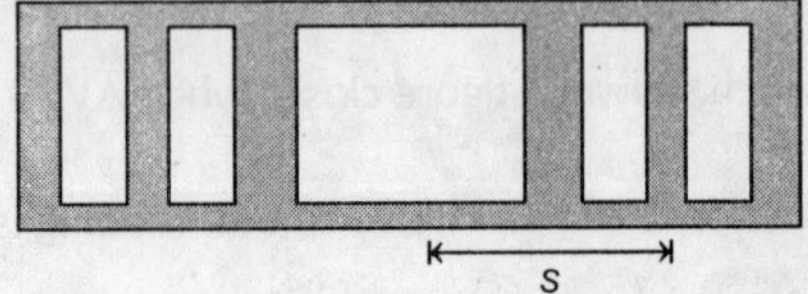

25. The value of apparent angles of dip at two places measured in two mutually perpendicular planes are 30° and 45°. The true angle of dip at the place is $\cot^{-1} \delta$. Here, δ is ....

26. In the L-C circuit, the capacitor C_1 is charged to a potential 1 V and the capacitor C_2 and the inductor were initially energyless. Now, switch S_1 is closed at $t = 0$ and $t = \frac{1.5\pi}{100}$ s, switch S_2 is closed and S_1 is opened. After $\frac{0.5\pi}{100}$ s, S_2 is also opened. Find final potential difference across the capacitor C_2 in volt.

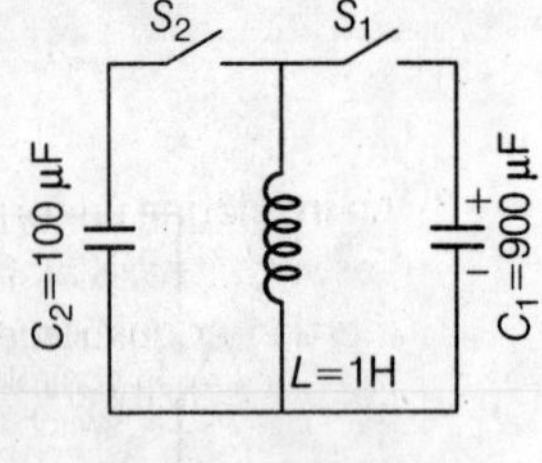

27. Intensity *versus* wavelength of X-rays graphs are given for two different elements. If number of protons in an atom of target element-1 is 37, then find the number of protons in an atom of target element-2.

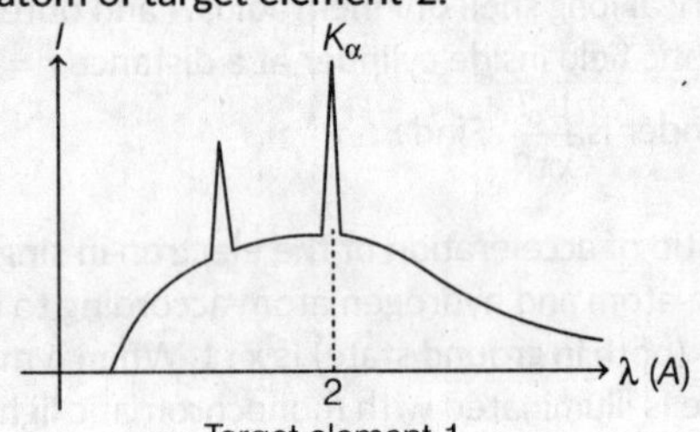

Target element-1

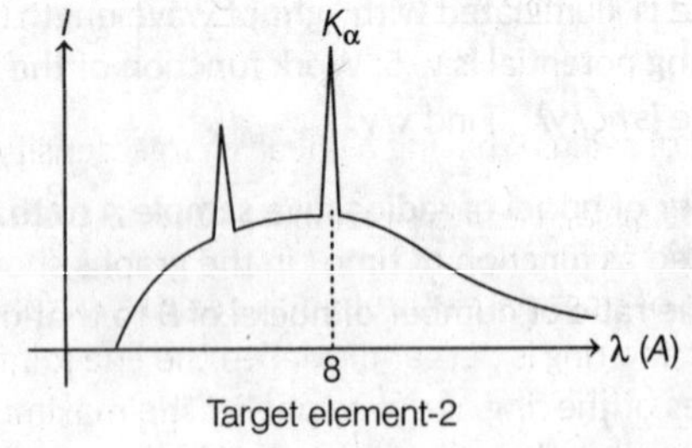

Target element-2

28. A sample contains number of stable nuclei equal to N_s and number of unstable nuclei equal to N_u. After a time T the activity of the sample decreases to one-third of the initial activity, while the total number of nuclei (excluding decayed nuclei) become half. The ratio N_u / N_s initially is ....

29. A biconvex thin lens of focal length 30 cm and aperture diameter 8 cm is broken into four identical pieces. Two of the pieces are then placed as shown in figure. If the final image of a point object located at origin is formed at point (x, y), then what is the value of $\left|\frac{x}{10} + y\right|$?

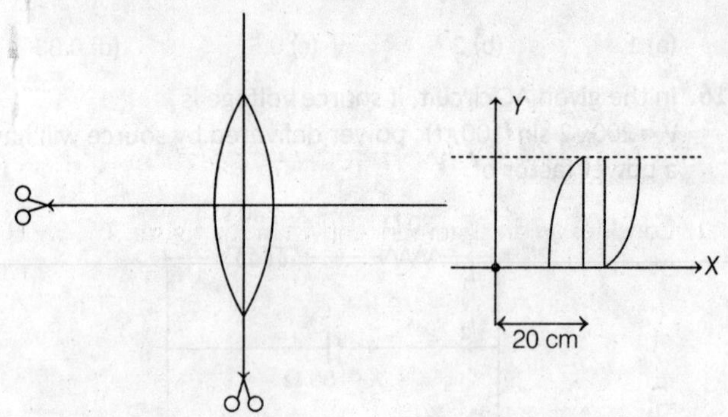

30. The carrier wave shown in the figure is amplitude modulated (AM) using the message signal shown. Percentage modulation of the AM wave, thus created is ...... (consider the given quantities in SI system)

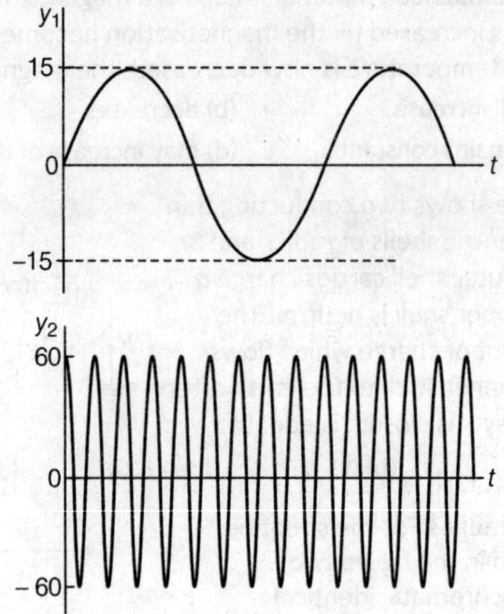

Answers

1 *(d)*	2 *(c)*	3 *(c)*	4 *(a)*	5 *(d)*	6 *(c)*	7 *(a)*	8 *(b)*	9 *(c)*	10 *(b)*
11 *(a)*	12 *(a)*	13 *(a)*	14 *(a)*	15 *(c)*	16 *(c)*	17 *(c)*	18 *(c)*	19 *(a)*	20 *(c)*
21 *(10.67)*	22 *(1.33)*	23 *(2)*	24 *(6)*	25 *(2)*	26 *(3)*	27 *(19)*	28 *(3)*	29 *(8)*	30 *(25)*

See detailed explanations on page no. 276

Part Test 04

(Based on Complete Class 12 Syllabus)

JEE Advanced

Physics

Section I Only one correct option

1. Consider an arrangement shown in the figure. The width of the slit is 1.6 cm. The convex lens placed in contact with the slit transmits 80% of the light incident on it. The radius of the sphere (placed at focus of lens) is 8 mm and the efficiency of photoelectric emission of the sphere is 10^{-4}. The power of the source is 3.2 W and the energy of the photons of the radiation emitted by the source is 5 eV. The photoelectric current (in nA) from the sphere is

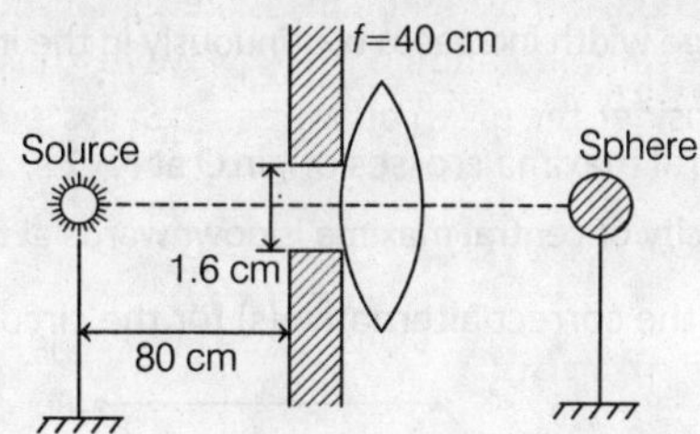

(a) 0.56 (b) 1.28 (c) 2.09 (d) 3.52

2. At time, $t = 0$, a charge q_0 is given to a capacitor C_1 (where, $C_1 = 400\,\mu F$) forming an L-C circuit with inductor L ($L = 100$ H). At $t = \frac{\pi}{10}$ s, the connection with the capacitor C_1 is broken and another capacitor C_2 is joined with the inductor. At time t, the energy stored in capacitor C_2 is 9% of the total energy available. If $C_2 = 100\,\mu F$, t (in s) is close to

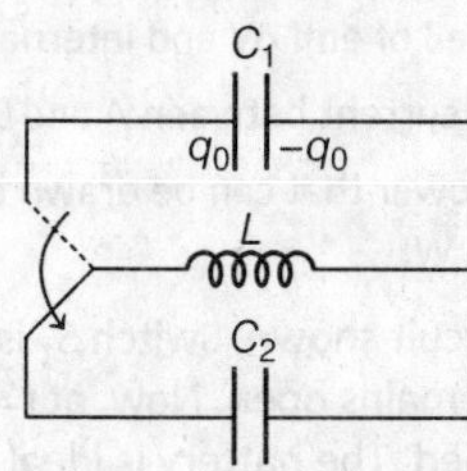

(a) $\frac{\pi}{10}$ (b) $\frac{\pi}{100}$ (c) $\frac{11\pi}{100}$ (d) $\frac{21\pi}{100}$

3. An insulating uniformly charged cylindrical shell of radius a lies with its axis along the Z-axis. The shell's moment of inertia per unit length about the Z-axis and the surface charge density are I and σ respectively. The cylinder is placed in an external uniform magnetic field $B_{ex}\hat{z}$ and is initially at rest. Starting at $t = 0$, the external magnetic field is slowly reduced to zero. What is the final angular velocity ω of the cylinder?

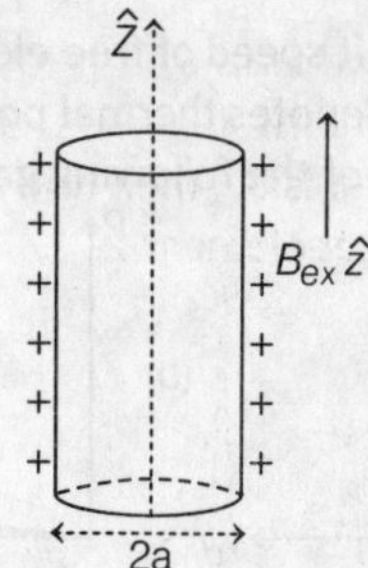

(a) $\frac{\sigma\pi a^3}{I}\left(1+\frac{\mu_0\sigma^2 a^3\pi}{I}\right)^{-1} B_{ex}$ (b) $\frac{\sigma\pi a^3}{I}\left(1+\frac{\mu_0\sigma^2 a^4\pi}{I}\right)^{-1} B_{ex}$

(c) $\frac{\sigma\pi a^3}{2I}\left(1+\frac{\mu_0\sigma^2 a^4\pi}{I}\right)^{-2} B_{ex}$ (d) $\frac{\sigma\pi a^3}{I}\left(1+\frac{I}{\mu_0\sigma^2 a^4\pi}\right)^{-1} B_{ex}$

4. A ring of radius R having a linear charge density λ move towards a solid imaginary sphere of radius $\frac{R}{2}$, so, that the centre of ring passes through the centre of sphere. The axis of the ring is perpendicular to the line joining the centres of the ring and the sphere. The maximum flux through the sphere in this process is

(a) $\frac{\pi R}{\varepsilon_0}$ (b) $\frac{\lambda R}{2\varepsilon_0}$ (c) $\frac{\lambda\pi R}{4\varepsilon_0}$ (d) $\frac{\lambda\pi R}{3\varepsilon_0}$

Section II *More than one correct options*

5. A conducting loop made of thin, light thread has a soap film inside and outside it. Length of thread is l, total resistance is R and initially area surrounded by it is $A_i = \frac{l^2}{8\pi}$. It is kept in a uniform magnetic field B in ⊗ direction and then a small puncture is made in inner film.

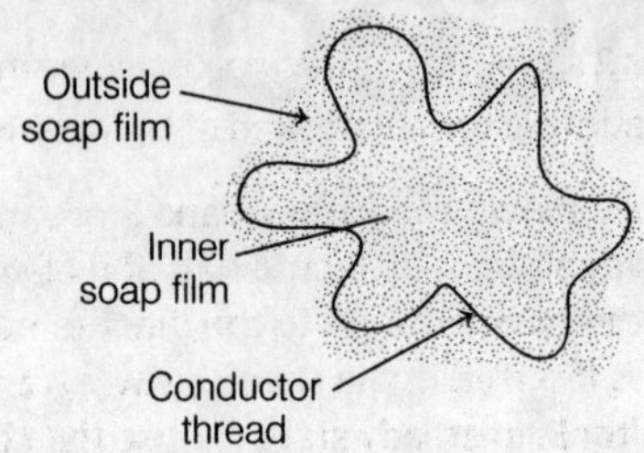

(a) Current is continuously induced in the loop.
(b) Current is induced in the loop for some time and then it will be zero.
(c) Induced current will be anti-clockwise as seen from above.
(d) Total charge flown through the loop will be $\frac{Bl^2}{8\pi R}$

6. If E denotes electric field in uniform conductor, v_d corresponding drift speed of free electrons, i current through it and P denotes thermal power generated in the conductor, which of the following graphs is/are correct?

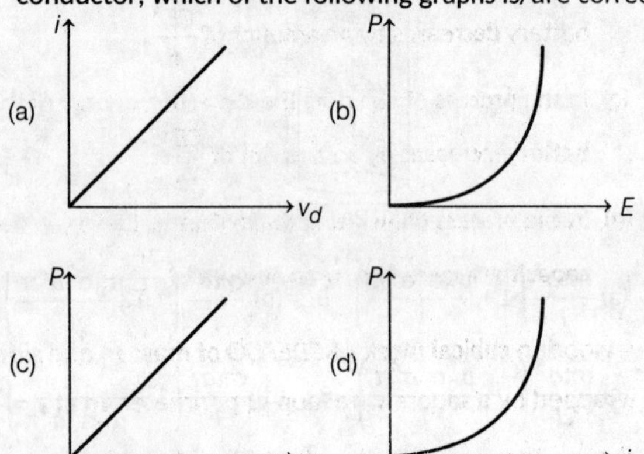

7. A uniform ring of mass 8 kg and radius 1 m initially at rest in X-Y plane is constrained to rotate about diameter along Y-axis. A uniform field $\mathbf{E} = \cos\theta\hat{\mathbf{i}} + \sin\theta\hat{\mathbf{k}}$ N/C is switched ON in the region. Left and right halves of the ring carry charges q_1 and q_2 respectively.

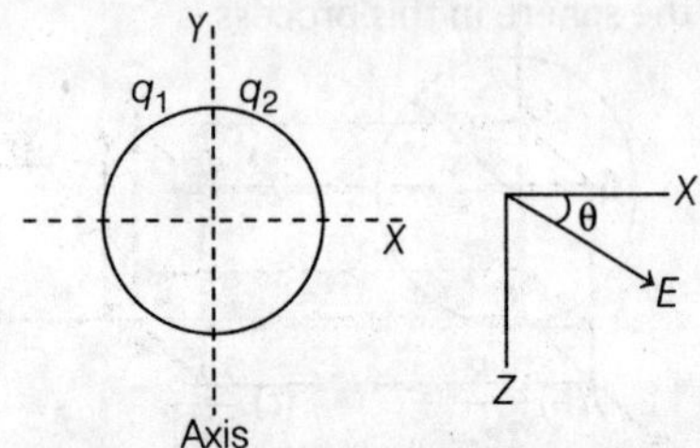

Choose correct alternative(s).

(a) For $q_1 = -q_2 = \pi C, \theta = 90°$, maximum kinetic energy acquired by the ring during subsequent motion is 4 J.
(b) For $q_1 = -2q_2 = 2\pi C, \theta = 90°$, maximum kinetic energy acquired by the ring during subsequent motion is 6J.
(c) For $q_1 = -q_2 = \pi C, \theta = 45°$, the ring executes SHM with angular amplitude 45°.
(d) For $q_1 = -q_2 = \pi C, \theta \approx 0°$, time taken by ring to come to rest for the first time is 2π s.

8. In YDSE set up a slab of refractive index $n_1 = 2$ is placed in front of one of the slits shown. Also, space between slits and screen is filled with a liquid having refractive index n_2 varying with time t (in s) given by,

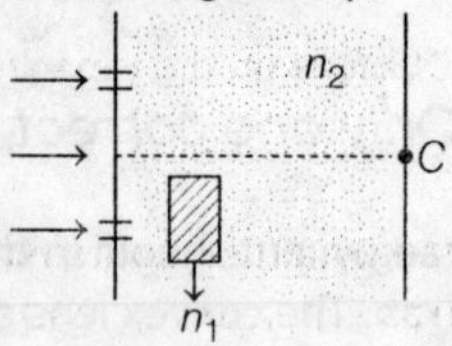

$$n_2 = 4 - t \quad 0 \le t \le 2.5$$
$$= 1.5 \quad t > 2.5$$

For the fringe pattern obtained, which of the following is/are correct?

(a) Fringe width is constant.
(b) Fringe width increases continuously in the interval $0 \le t \le 2.5$.
(c) Central maxima crosses origin O at $t = 2$ s.
(d) Velocity of central maxima is downwards at $t = 1$ s.

9. Choose the correct alternative(s) for the circuit shown.

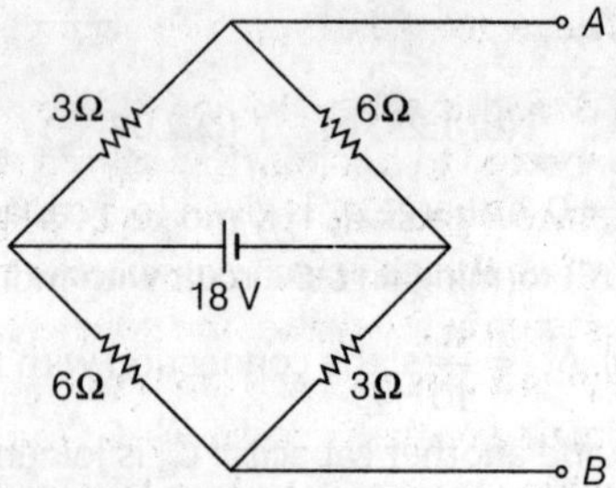

(a) A is at higher potential.
(b) Between A and B, the circuit can be replaced by an equivalent cell of emf 6V and internal resistance 4 Ω.
(c) Short circuit current between A and B is 2A.
(d) Maximum power that can be drawn between points A and B is 2.25 W.

10. Consider the circuit shown. Switch S_1 is closed for a long time while S_2 remains open. Now, at $t = 0$, S_2 is closed while S_1 is opened. The battery is ideal and connecting wires are resistanceless. If the capacitor C is initially uncharged then select correct statement(s).

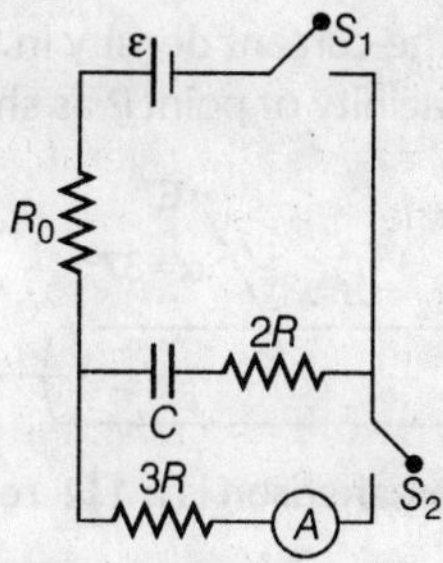

(a) At time $t = 0$, reading of ammeter is $\frac{\varepsilon}{5R}$.

(b) At time $t = 0$, reading of ammeter is zero.

(c) Heat developed till time $t = 5RC \ln 2$, in resistance $3R$, is $\frac{9}{40} C\varepsilon^2$.

(d) For time $t > 0$ charge on the capacitor follows the equation $C\varepsilon e^{-\frac{t}{5RC}}$

11. X-rays are emitted by a tube containing the element Niobium ($Z = 41$) as anti-cathode and the K_α X-rays are allowed to be incident on an unknown gas containing hydrogen like ions. It is found that the X-rays cause the emission of photoelectrons with an energy of 2.7 keV from these ions. The

(a) minimum voltage at which the X-ray tube should be operated so that the momentum of the emitted photoelectrons is doubled, is 24.4 keV

(b) approximate value of Z for the target of the anti-cathode after the momentum has been doubled, is 50

(c) approximate value of the atomic number of the atoms of the gas, is 32

(d) ionization in the gas caused by X-rays, if the intensity of X-rays is 100 mW/m^2 and 1% of the X-rays cause ionization, is 100 per m^3 per second

12. A charged dielectric sphere having charge q and negligible mass is connected to a conducting square shaped loop of total resistance R and side l by means of a light and non-conducting thread, which passes over two fixed pulleys as shown in the figure. The sphere carries a charge q and is kept in a constant and uniform electric field of strength E acting vertically downwards. The mass of the loop is m, where $mg < qE$. The loop is kept in a uniform and constant horizontal magnetic field of induction B perpendicular to the plane of the loop and localized in a finite space in and around the square loop. The system is released from rest at $t = 0$

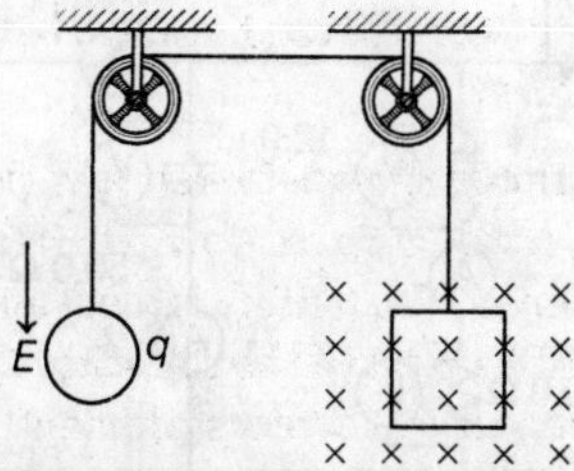

Take, $g = 10 \text{ m/s}^2$, $\frac{qE}{m} = 20 \text{ m/s}^2$ and $B^2l^2 / mR = 2\text{N-s/m}^2$

(a) Initial acceleration of the loop is 10 m/s^2

(b) The loop moves with constant velocity

(c) If after 2 s, one side of the loop emerges from the magnetic field speed of the loop as function of time till it completely comes out of the field is $v = 5[1 + 3e^{-(2t-4)}]$ m/s

(d) If after 2 s, one side of the loop emerges from the magnetic field terminal speed of the loop is 4 m/s

13. In the figure shown capacitors A and B of capacitance C are in steady state. A dielectric slab of dielectric constant $K = 2$ and dimensions equal to the inner dimensions of the capacitor is inserted in the space between the plates of the capacitor B. In steady state choose the correct options.

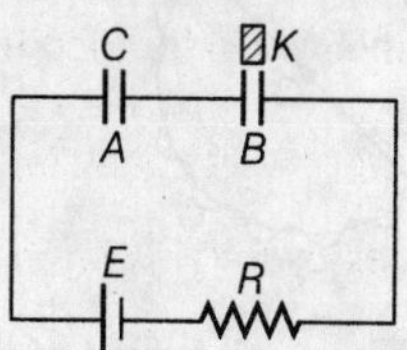

(a) Charge on each capacitor will increase by $\frac{CE}{6}$.

(b) In the process of inserting the dielectric, energy of the battery decreases by an amount of $\frac{CE^2}{6}$.

(c) In the process of inserting the dielectric, energy of the battery increases by an amount of $\frac{CE^2}{6}$.

(d) In the process of inserting the dielectric, energy in the capacitor A increases by an amount of $\frac{7CE^2}{72}$.

14. A wooden cubical block $ABCDEFGO$ of mass m and side a is wrapped by a square wire loop of perimeter $4a$ at $z = \frac{a}{2}$ as shown. The current in the wire I. The whole system is placed on frictionless horizontal surface in a uniform magnetic field $\mathbf{B} = B_0\hat{\mathbf{j}}$ in this situation. Line of action of normal force between horizontal surface and block passes through a point at a distance x from centre. Select the correct statement(s).

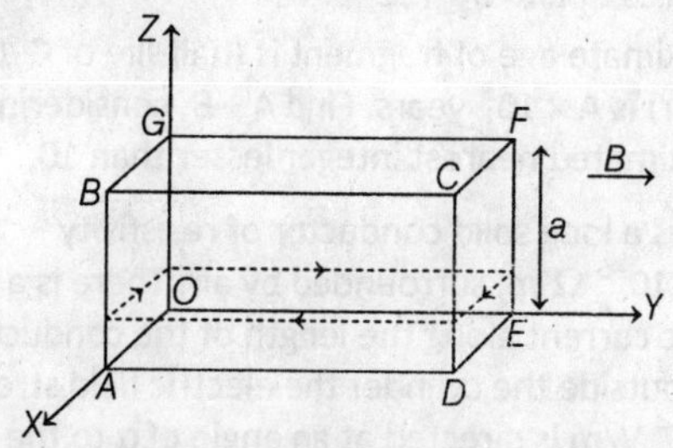

(a) The block must not topple, if $I < \frac{mg}{aB_0}$.

(b) The block must not topple, if $I < \frac{mg}{2aB_0}$.

(c) $x = \frac{a}{4}$, if $I = \frac{mg}{2aB_0}$.

(d) $x = \frac{a}{4}$, if $I = \frac{mg}{4aB_0}$.

Section III *Numerical Value and Non-negative Integer Type*

15. Consider the shown figure.

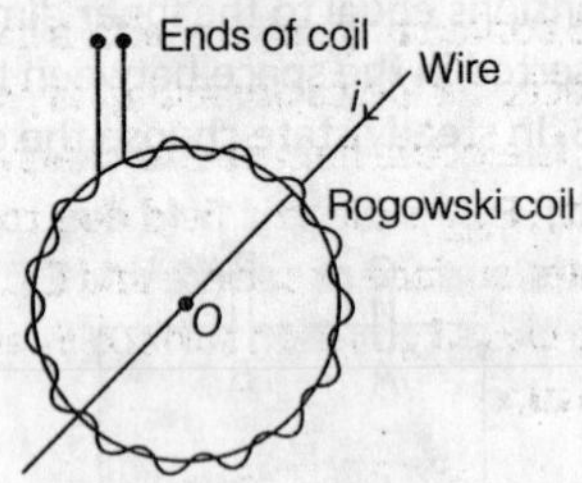

Number of turns per unit length of the coil, area of each loop in the coil, resistance of the coil, are n, S and R respectively. Current flowing through the wire crossing the plane of the coil is i. A ballistic galvanometer is connected across the ends of the coil and the current is switched off, charge that flows through the coil is measured to be Q. $\frac{\mu_0 nsi}{QR}$ is equal to........

16. A fossil fragment found in a cave believed to have been inhabited by early humans contains 0.29 times as much C-14 as an equal amount of carbon in the atmosphere, when the organism died.

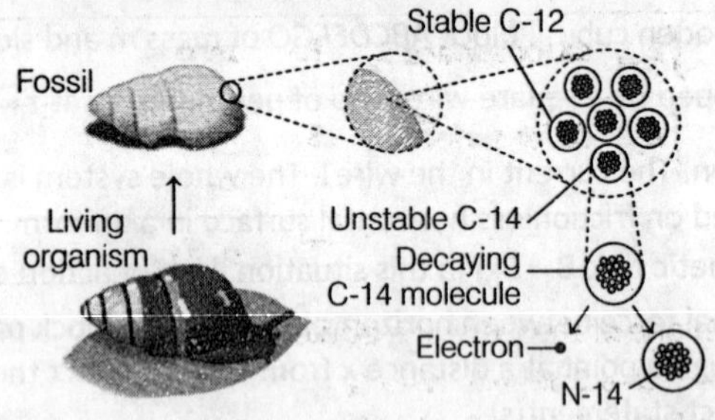

Approximate age of fragment is (half-life of C-14 is 5730 yr) is $A \times 10^B$ years. Find $A + B$, considering A is approximated nearest integer lesser than 10.

17. There is a long solid conductor of resistivity $\rho = 1 \times 10^{-5}$ Ω-m, surrounded by air. There is a steady electric current along the length of the conductor. At point P just outside the cylinder the electric field strength $E = 10^{-4}$ V/m is directed at an angle of α to the normal to the surface. Find the current density in (A/m^2) in the conductor in the vicinity of point P as shown in figure.

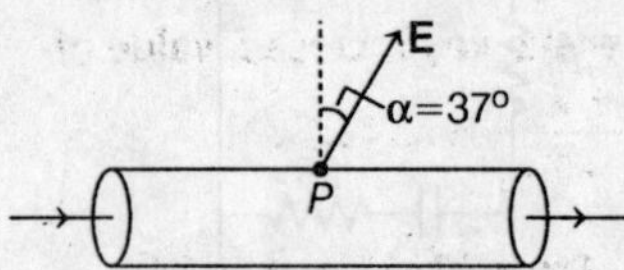

18. Each edge of an icosahedron is a 1Ω resistor. Find x if the effective resistance between two adjacent vertices is $\frac{x}{10}$ Ω. (An icosahedron consists of 20 equilateral triangles. It has 12 vertices and 30 edges with 5 edges meeting at each vertex.)

19. A hemispherical cavity of radius R is carved out from a sphere ($\mu = 1.5$) of radius $2R$ such that principal axis of cavity coincides with that of sphere. One side of sphere is silvered as shown in figure. Find the value of x (in cm) for which the image of an object at O is formed at O itself. (Take, $R = 4$ cm and $\sqrt{145} \approx 12$)

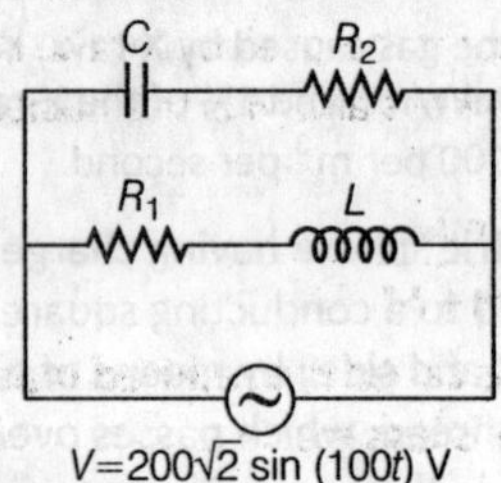

20. In the shown circuit, $R_1 = 10\Omega$, $L = \frac{\sqrt{3}}{10}$ H, $R_2 = 20\,\Omega$, $C = \frac{\sqrt{3}}{2}$ mF and t is time in seconds. Then, at the instant current through R_1 is $10\sqrt{2}$ A, find the current through resistor R_2 in amperes.

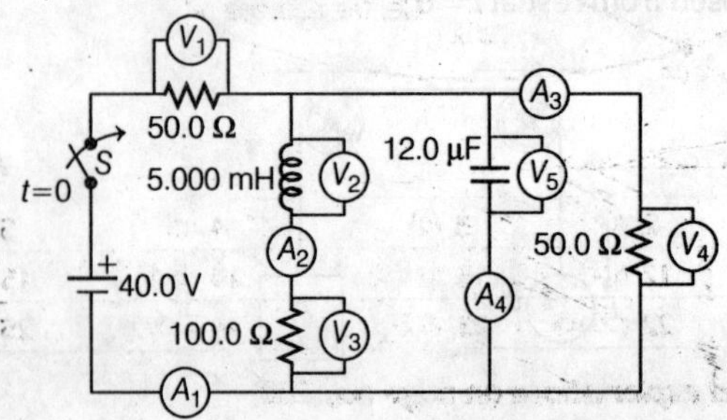

Section IV *Numerical Value Stem Questions*

Stem 1 for (Q. 21 and Q. 22)

In the circuit shown here, switch S is closed at time $t = 0$ with no charge initially on the capacitor. Respective instrumental readings are marked in the figure.

21. Value of $\dfrac{V_1+V_2+V_3+V_4+V_5}{A_1+A_2+A_3+A_4}$ is ...Ω just after the key is closed.

22. Long time after the key is closed, value of $\dfrac{V_1+V_2-V_3+V_4}{2A_1-A_2-A_3+7A_4}$ is .... Ω.

Stem (Q. 23 and Q. 24)

Figure here shows an interferometer known as Fresnel's biprism. The magnitude of the prism angle is extremely small. It is given that, $a = 0.200$ m, $A = 3.50$ mrad and $n = 1.50$.

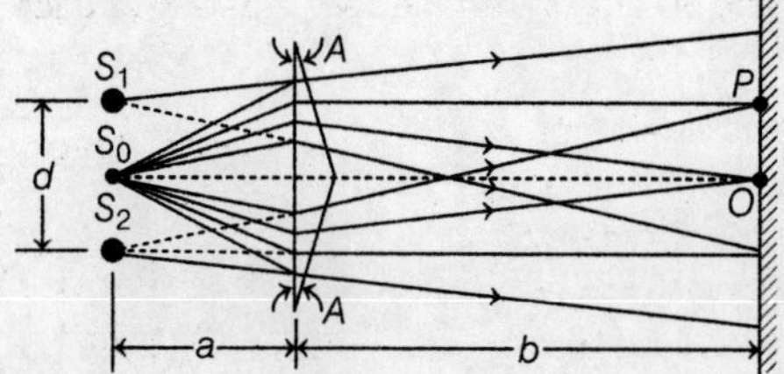

23. If S_0 is a very narrow source slit, the separation of the two virtual coherent sources is .... mm.

24. Spacing of the fringes of green light with wavelength 500 nm on a screen 2.00 m from the biprism is ... mm.

Stem for (Q. 25 and Q. 26)

Usually we have been assuming that the hydrogen nucleus (a proton) remains stationary while the orbital electron revolves around it. What must actually happen, of course, is that both nucleus and electron revolve around their common centre of mass, as shown in the figure. A system of this kind is equivalent to a single particle of mass m' that revolves around the position of the heavier particle. If m is the electron mass and M is the nuclear mass, then m' is given by

$$m' = \frac{mM}{m+M}$$

The quantity m' is called the reduced mass of the electron because its value is less than m.

To take into account the motion of the nucleus in the hydrogen atom, then all we need to do is replace the electron with a particle of mass m'.

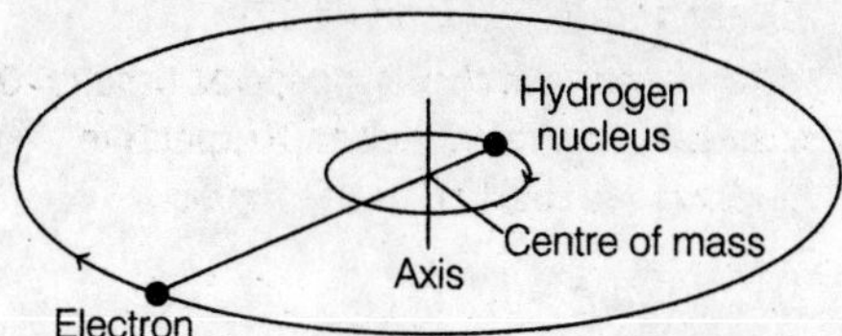

25. A positronium atom is a system that consists of a positron and an electron binding that orbit each other. If binding energy of hydrogen atom is considered to be 13.6 eV, binding energy (in eV) of the positronium atom in 1st excited state is .... eV.

26. For muonic hydrogen, a muon (having mass 207 times the mass of electron) orbits around proton (having mass 1836 times the mass of electron). Approximated orbital radius in ground state for such system is $A \times 10^{-B}$ in m. Here, A is integer lesser than 10. Find $\frac{B}{A}$.

Section V *Matching List Question*

27. Figure shows a conducting sphere with a cavity. A point charge q_1 is placed inside cavity and q_2 is placed outside the sphere. $\mathbf{E}_{in}$ is electric field due to charge induced on surface of cavity, $\mathbf{E}_{out}$ is electric field due to charge induced on outer surface of sphere and $\mathbf{E}_{net}$ is net field at any point. Two closed gaussian surface S_1 and S_2 are also drawn in the figure.

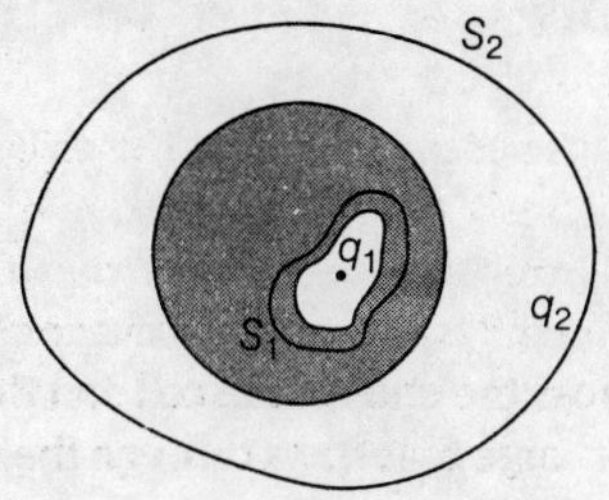

	List-I		List-II
I.	$\int \mathbf{E}_{in} \cdot \mathbf{da}$ for surface S_1	P.	$\frac{-q_1}{\varepsilon_0}$
II.	$\int \mathbf{E}_{out} \cdot \mathbf{da}$ for surface S_2	Q.	$\frac{q_1+q_2}{\varepsilon_0}$
III.	$\int \mathbf{E}_{net} \cdot \mathbf{da}$ for surface S_1	R.	zero
IV.	$\int \mathbf{E}_{net} \cdot \mathbf{da}$ for surface S_2	S.	$\frac{q_1}{\varepsilon_0}$
		T.	q_2/ε_0

Which one of the following options is correct?

(a) I → T II → S III → R IV → Q
(b) I → P II → S III → T IV → R
(c) I → P II → P III → T IV → Q
(d) I → P II → S III → R IV → Q

Answers

1 (b)	2 (c)	3 (b)	4 (d)	5 (b,c,d)	6 (a,b,d)	7 (a,b)	8 (b,c,d)	9 (a,b,d)	10 (a,c,d)
11 (a,b,c)	12 (a,c)	13 (a,b,d)	14 (b,d)	15 (1)	16 (5)	17 (6)	18 (2.67)	19 (3)	20 (0)
21 (25.00)	22 (50.00)	23 (0.7)	24 (1.57)	25 (1.7)	26 (4.33)	27 (d)			

See detailed explanations on page no. 280

The Knockouts

10 Full Syllabus Mock Tests for JEE Main & 5 for JEE Advanced

Mock Tests given here will help you to be acquainted with Pattern & Level of JEE Main & JEE Advanced. Practicing these tests in systematic manner will ensure your good score in the Exam.

Knockout 01

JEE Main

Physics

Instructions

1. This question paper contains 30 Questions of Physics, divided into two Sections : **Section I** Objective Type Questions and **Section II** Numerical Value Questions.
2. Section I contains 20 Objective questions and all Questions are compulsory (Marking Scheme : Correct + 4, Incorrect –1).
3. Section II contains 10 Numerical value questions out of which only 5 questions are to be attempted (Marking Scheme : Correct + 4, Incorrect 0).

Section I *Objective Type Questions*

1. A ball is projected from ground with kinetic energy K at angle θ with vertical. Gravitational potential energy of the ball w.r.t. ground, when it is at highest point, is

(a) K (b) $K\cos^2\theta$ (c) $K\sin^2\theta$ (d) zero

2. In the arrangement shown below, the acceleration (in m/s^2) of block with respect to pulley is (Take, $g = 10\ m/s^2$)

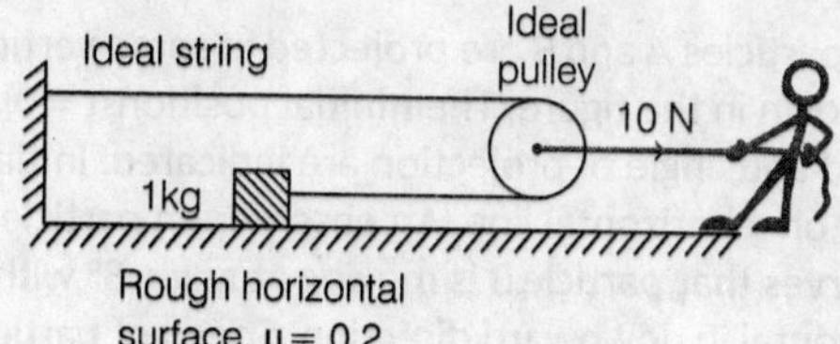

(a) 1.5 (b) 2 (c) 2.5 (d) 3

3. The magnitude of average acceleration of a particle executing SHM (with amplitude A and angular frequency ω) during its motion from mean position to extreme position is

(a) $A\omega^2$ (b) $\frac{\pi A\omega^2}{2}$ (c) $\frac{2A\omega^2}{\pi}$ (d) zero

4. Current flowing between points A and C is

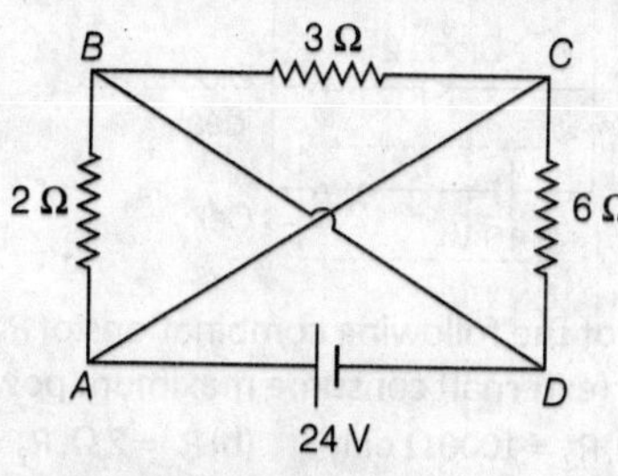

(a) zero (b) 4 A (c) 8 A (d) 12 A

5. Probability of decay of a nucleus in a radioactive sample during one mean life is

(a) 37% (b) 50% (c) 63% (d) 100%

6. An ideal gas is undergoing a thermodynamic process given by $T^3V^2 =$ constant, where T and V are thermodynamic temperature and gas volume, respectively. Which amongst the following statement(s) is(are) correct?

(a) Bulk modulus of the gas is $\frac{5}{3}p$

(b) Equation of the state is $pV^{3/5} =$ constant

(c) Bulk modulus of the gas is $\frac{3}{2}p$

(d) Both (a) and (b)

7. Average electric energy density at a point in space through which electromagnetic wave is propagating, is (where, $E_0 =$ amplitude of electric field,
$B_0 =$ amplitude of magnetic field,
$\mu_0 =$ magnetic permeability
and $\varepsilon_0 =$ electric permittivity of free space)

(a) $\frac{1}{2}\varepsilon_0 E_0^2$ (b) $\frac{1}{8}\varepsilon_0 E_0^2 + \frac{B_0^2}{8\mu_0}$

(c) $\frac{1}{4}\varepsilon_0 E_0^2 + \frac{B_0^2}{4\mu_0}$ (d) zero

8. Assuming mass of earth to be constant if density of earth's material increases by 3%, the range of a telecommunication tower on earth's surface will

(a) increase by 2% (b) decrease by 2%
(c) increase by 0.5% (d) decrease by 0.5%

9. Two thin soap bubbles (containing air) of areas A and $2A$ respectively, coalesce in isothermal condition in vacuum. Surface area of the resulting bubble is

(a) $2.5\ A$ (b) $3\ A$ (c) $\sqrt{3}\ A$ (d) $\sqrt{2}\ A$

10. A short dipole (of dipole moment p) and a point charge q are placed at equal distances $OA = OB = 2R$ from centre O of a neutral conducting metal ball of radius R.

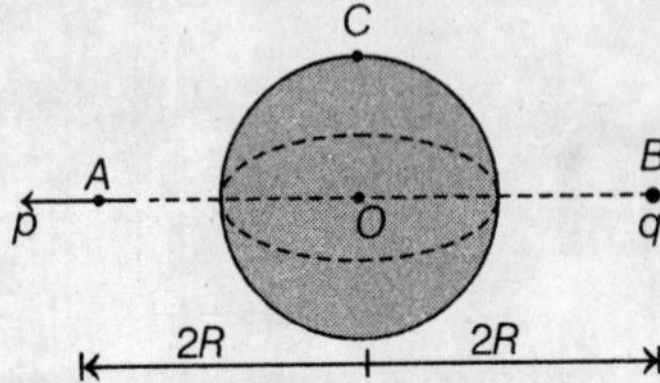

If potential at top point C of the ball is zero, electric field due to induced charges at centre O of the ball, is

(a) Zero (b) $\frac{3Kq}{4R^2}$

(c) $\frac{3Kp}{8R^3}$ (d) Both (b) and (c)

11. In the system shown, initially springs are in natural length. On applying a variable force F on block towards right, elongation in spring S_1 is x_1. If block moves slowly and floor is smooth, then

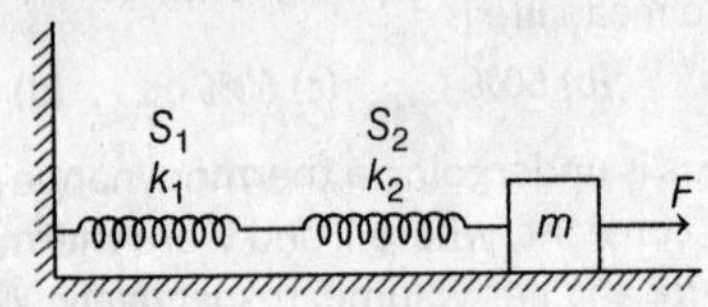

	List I		List II
A.	Work done by S_2 on block	(i)	$\frac{1}{2}\frac{k_1(k_1+k_2)x_1^2}{k_2}$
B.	Work done by S_2 on S_1	(ii)	$-\frac{1}{2}\frac{k_1(k_1+k_2)x_1^2}{k_2}$
C.	Work done by F on block	(iii)	$\frac{1}{2}k_1x_1^2$
D.	Work done by S_1 on wall	(iv)	zero

Choose the most appropriate answer from the options given below

(a) A-(i), B-(iii), C-(ii), D-(iv)
(b) A-(ii), B-(iii), C-(i), D-(iv)
(c) A-(iii), B-(ii), C(i), D-(iv)
(d) A-(ii), B-(iii), C-(iv), D-(i)

12. Average translational kinetic energy of a molecule of mass m in an ideal gas sample is equal to

(a) $\frac{1}{2}mv_{rms}^2$ (b) $\frac{1}{2}mv_{mp}^2$ (c) $\frac{1}{2}mv_{av}^2$ (d) $\frac{f}{2}kT$

(where, v_{rms} = root mean square speed, v_{mp} = most probable speed, v_{av} = average speed, f = degrees of freedom and k = Boltzmann's constant)

13. The figure here shows a compound microscope in strained eye arrangement. The focal length of the objective and eyepiece of the microscope are 2 cm and 5 cm respectively and the distance between them is 20 cm. Magnifying power of the microscope is closest to

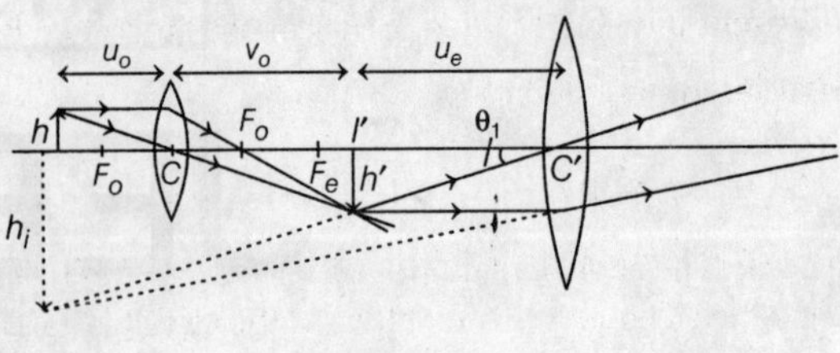

(a) 50 (b) 40 (c) 20 (d) 10

14. A bar magnet is suspended at its centre in equilibrium in a uniform magnetic field. Slight disturbance leads to oscillation of the magnet with time period T. If the magnet is cut into two pieces along its length and one of the pieces is suspended at centre in the same magnetic field, time period of oscillation on slight disturbance is

(a) T (b) $2T$ (c) $\frac{T}{2}$ (d) $\frac{T}{4}$

15. If frequency of incident light in a photoelectric cell is doubled, then stopping potential increases by

(a) 50% (b) 100%
(c) more than 100%
(d) any amount depending on work function of metal

16. Force on a rain drop of mass m falling with (1/4)th of the terminal speed is (neglect buoyancy)

(a) $\frac{mg}{4}$ (b) $\frac{3mg}{4}$ (c) mg (d) zero

17. Two particles A and B are projected in same vertical plane as shown in the figure. Their initial position ($t = 0$), initial speed and angle of projection are indicated. Initially A and B are on a horizontal line. An observer on particle A observes that particle B is moving at angle 8° with horizontal in downward direction. Speed of particle B is

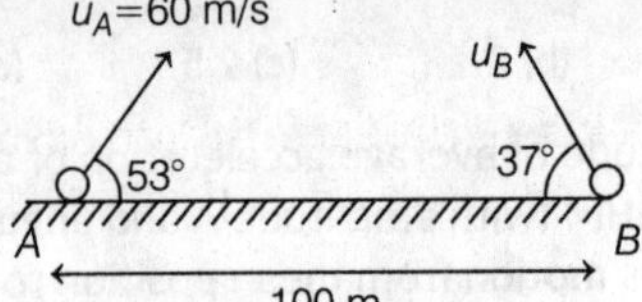

(a) 80 m/s (b) 60m/s (c) 75 m/s (d) 40 m/s

18. A circuit with two ideal diodes is as shown below.

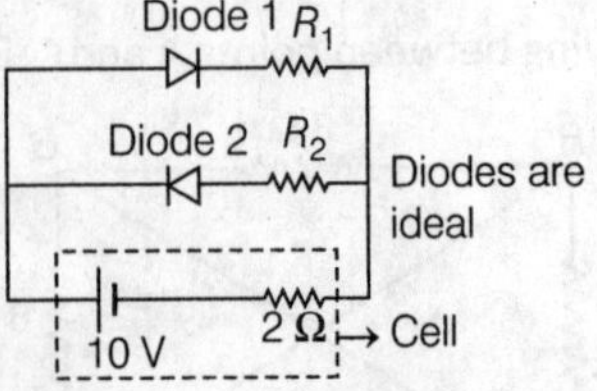

For which of the following combinations of R_1 and R_2 will the circuit (external) consume maximum power?

(a) $R_1 = 2\Omega, R_2 = 1000\Omega$ only (b) $R_1 = 2\Omega, R_2 = 0.1\Omega$ only
(c) $R_1 = 1000\Omega, R_2 = 1000\Omega$ only (d) For both (a) and (b)

19. A charged particle enters a region of a uniform magnetic field making 45° with direction of field. If P and R represent pitch and radius of helical path followed by particle, then $\frac{P}{R}$ equals to

(a) π (b) 2π (c) 1 (d) $\sqrt{\pi^2+1}$

20. In a series L-C-R AC circuit, frequency of source is half of the resonance frequency. The nature of the circuit is essentially

(a) capacitive (b) inductive
(c) resistive
(d) capacitive, inductive or resistive depending on the values of resistance

Section II *Numerical Value Questions*

21. Wavelength of first line of Lyman series is λ_1 while wavelength of series limit of Brackett series is λ_2. Find the ratio of $\frac{\lambda_2}{\lambda_1}$.

22. Wavelengths corresponding to maximum spectral emissive powers in radiations emitted by spherical black bodies A and B are λ and 1.01λ, respectively. If radius of sphere A is twice that of B, find ratio of power emitted by A to that emitted by B. Use binomial approximation, i.e. $(1+x)^n \approx 1+nx$, if $x << 1$.

23. Tension in a string vibrating in unison with a 100 Hz tuning fork is increased by 4 percent. Number of beats observed by doing so is N. Find the value of N.

24. Dimensional formula of Planck's length $\sqrt{\frac{hG}{c^3}}$ is $[M^xL^yT^z]$. Find $(x+y+z)$, where h = Reduced Planck's constant, G = universal gravitational constant, c = speed of light in vacuum.

25. Find value of mass m (in kg) in the arrangement shown for it to remain at rest. Pulleys and strings are ideal.

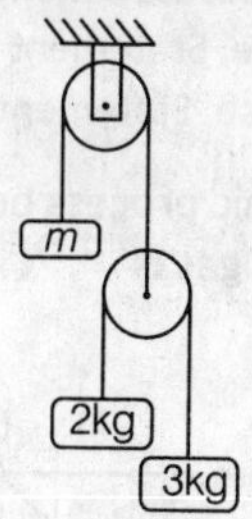

26. For the YDSE set up shown, 2000th maxima is formed at point P of screen.

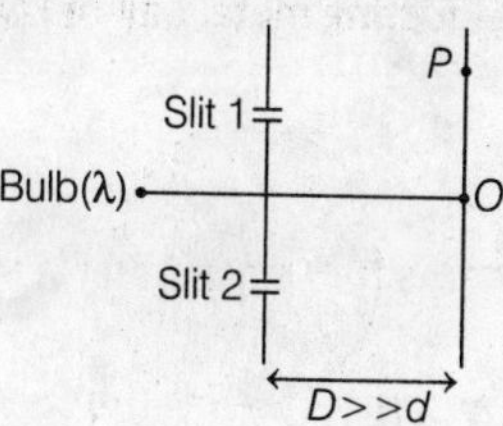

Find distance of point P (in metre) from centre O of the screen using following informations

where, d = slit separation = 2 mm

D = distance between slits and screen = 1 m

λ = wavelength of light used = 5000 Å

27. A solid sphere is released on an incline of inclination 37° with horizontal. If friction on incline is sufficient to prevent slipping, kinetic energy of the sphere as its centre descends by h is $x\ mgh$. Find x, if m is mass of the sphere.

28. At what time (in s) after the key is closed, if $i_2 = 2i_1$ is in the circuit shown?

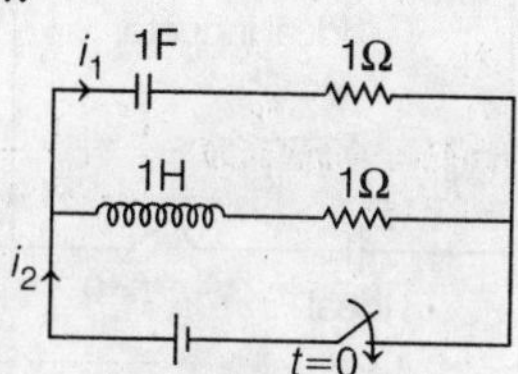

29. At what height above earth's surface (in km), acceleration due to gravity is same as 15 km below earth's surface?

30. A rod of mass m and length l is hanging at rest vertically by a hinge support at its upper end. A bullet of mass m moving with speed v hits lower end of the rod and sticks to it. The velocity of mid-point of the rod just after the collision is $\frac{v}{x}$. Find the value of x.

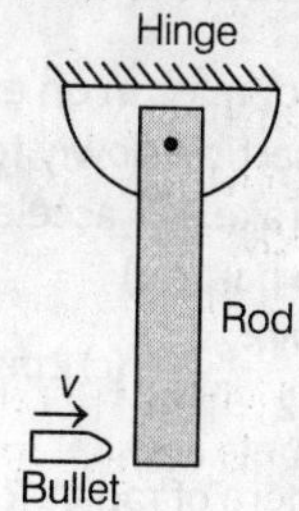

Answers

1 (b)	2 (a)	3 (c)	4 (d)	5 (c)	6 (a)	7 (b)	8 (d)	9 (b)	10 (d)
11 (b)	12 (a)	13 (b)	14 (a)	15 (c)	16 (b)	17 (b)	18 (d)	19 (b)	20 (a)
21 12	22 4.16	23 2	24 1	25 4.8	26 0.58	27 1	28 0.69	29 7.5	30 2.67

See detailed explanations on page no. 284

Knockout 02

JEE Main

Physics

Instructions See knockout 01

Section I Objective Type Questions

1. Key in the circuit shown is closed at $t = 0$. Which of the following correctly represents variation of magnetic energy stored by inductor as function of time?

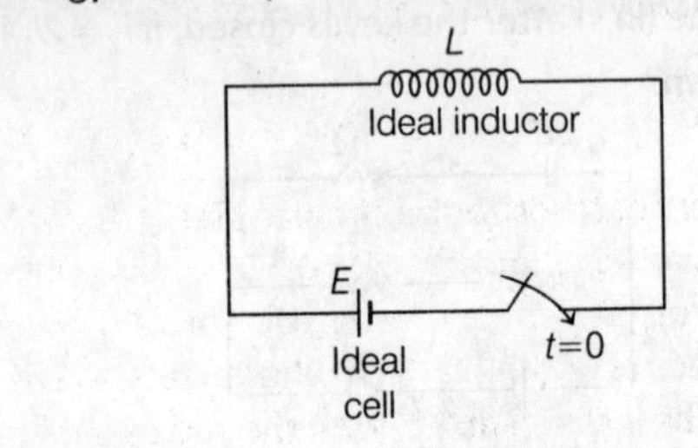

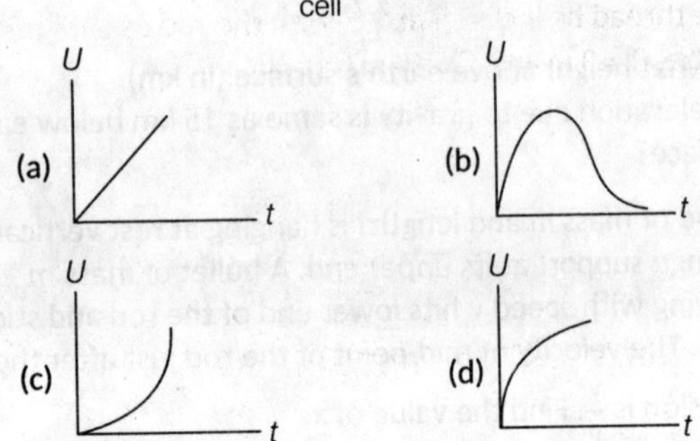

2. Consider a particle of mass m on earth's surface. Work done in lifting the particle slowly to an altitude equal to earth's radius R is (Take, g = acceleration due to gravity at final position of the particle)

(a) mgR (b) $\frac{mgR}{2}$ (c) $2mgR$ (d) $4mgR$

3. Consider a hemisphere of radius R with centre of curvature at origin O, as shown in figure. Refractive index of material of the hemisphere varies as $\mu = \frac{2R}{2R - x}$, where x is x-coordinate of material point. A ray travelling in air in XY-plane is grazingly incident at O, as shown in figure.

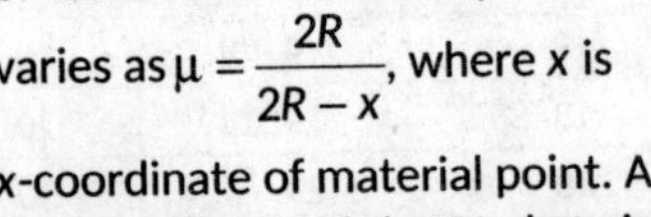

Trajectory followed by ray as it travels inside the hemisphere is

(a) circular (b) elliptical
(c) parabolic (d) hyperbolic

4. A light rod AB of length l has a particle of mass m attached to its end B while it is hinged at end A. If the rod is maintained horizontal by attaching a light vertical string at point C such that $BC = \frac{l}{3}$, reaction at hinge is

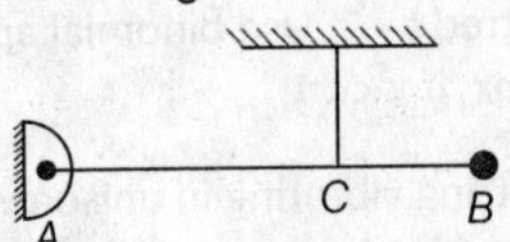

(a) mg upwards (b) mg downwards
(c) $\frac{mg}{2}$ upwards (d) $\frac{mg}{2}$ downwards

5. On increasing temperature of an ideal gas sample, for Maxwell speed distribution curve

Statement 1 Area under the curve does not change.

Statement 2 Peak in the curve displaces leftwards.

(a) Statement 1 is True, Statement 2 is True
(b) Statement 1 is False, Statement 2 is False
(c) Statement 1 is True, Statement 2 is False
(d) Statement 1 is False, Statement 2 is True

6. In the thermodynamic process between points A and B, heat supplied to the gas is

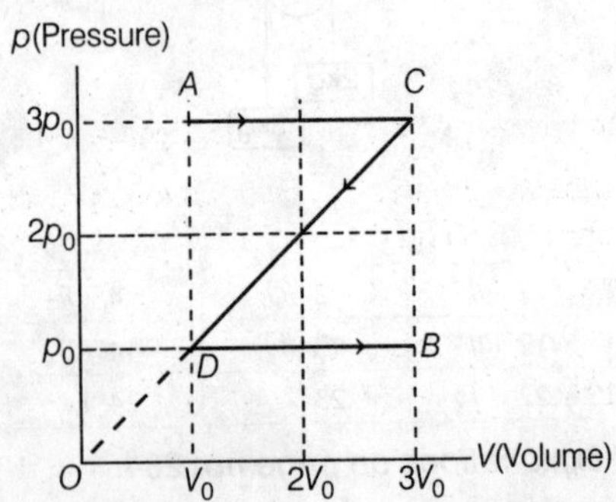

(a) $2p_0V_0$
(b) $4p_0V_0$
(c) $6p_0V_0$
(d) Indeterminate as name of gas is not given

7. If temperature of a paramagnetic substance is increased from 27°C to 327°C, its magnetic susceptibility
(a) is doubled
(b) is halved
(c) remains unchanged
(d) becomes $\frac{27}{327}$ times

8. For which of the following inputs, the gate shown here gives output $Y = 1$?

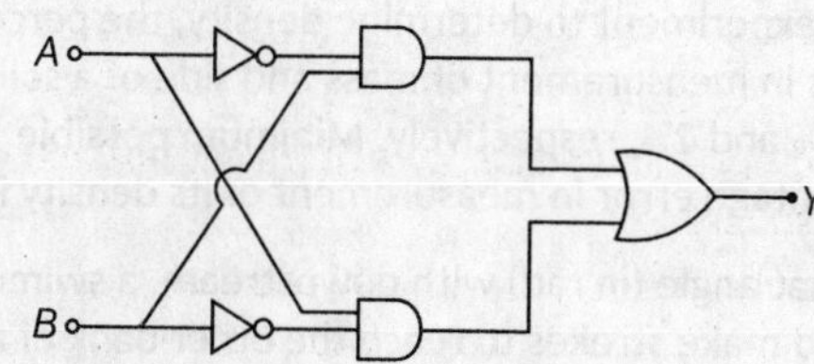

(a) $A = 0, B = 0$
(b) $A = 1, B = 1$
(c) Only for $A = 1, B = 0$
(d) For $A = 1, B = 0$ and $A = 0, B = 1$

9. In a radioactive decay process, *A* decays to *B*. Two graphs of number of nuclei of *A* and *B versus* time are given with time instants t_1 and t_2 shown. $t_2 - t_1$ equals

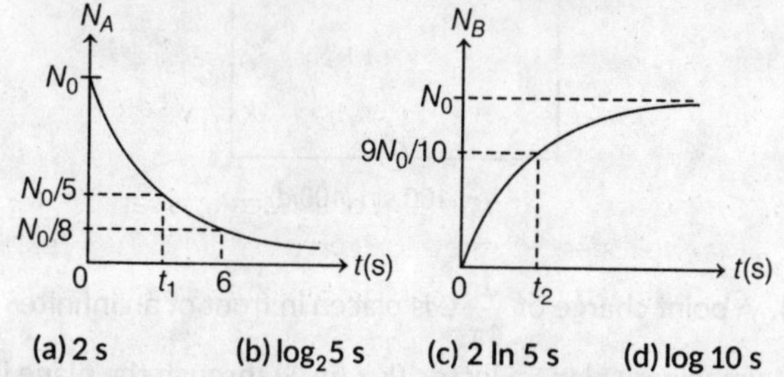

(a) 2 s (b) $\log_2 5$ s (c) 2 ln 5 s (d) log 10 s

10. A bomb projected at 45° with horizontal has kinetic energy *K*. It explodes into two identical pieces at its highest point. If one of the pieces is instantly at rest just after explosion, energy released in the explosion must atleast be
(a) *K* (b) $\frac{K}{2}$
(c) 2*K* (d) zero

11. Wavelengths of K_α and K_β X-ray photons emitting from an X-ray tube are λ_1 and λ_2, respectively. Wavelength of L_α X-ray photon will be
(a) $\frac{\lambda_1\lambda_2}{\lambda_1 - \lambda_2}$ (b) $\lambda_1 - \lambda_2$
(c) $\frac{\lambda_1\lambda_2}{\lambda_1 + \lambda_2}$ (d) $\sqrt{\lambda_1\lambda_2}$

12. A block attached to a spring is oscillating on smooth surface with amplitude *A* and time period *T*. If another identical block is placed gently on it is while it is crossing the mean position, amplitude and time period of the subsequent oscillation respectively are (Assume that slipping between the blocks stops instantly after they come in contact)

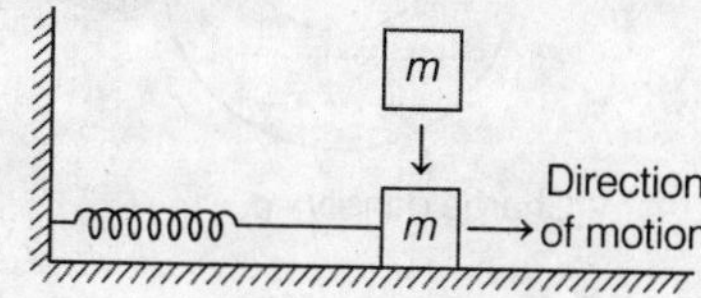

(a) $\frac{A}{\sqrt{2}}, \frac{T}{\sqrt{2}}$ (b) $\frac{A}{\sqrt{2}}, \sqrt{2}T$
(c) $\sqrt{2}A, \frac{T}{\sqrt{2}}$ (d) $\sqrt{2}A, \sqrt{2}T$

13. Difference in lengths of two rods (of lengths l_1 and l_2 with respective thermal coefficients of linear expansion α_1 and α_2) does not change with increase in temperature. Using this information, choose the correct relation.
(a) $l_1\alpha_1 = l_2\alpha_2$ (b) $l_1\alpha_2 = l_2\alpha_1$
(c) $l_1^2\alpha_1 = l_2^2\alpha_2$ (d) $l_1\alpha_1^2 = l_2\alpha_2^2$

14. On periphery of a horizontal circular platform of radius *R*, a rod is mounted as shown in figure. A ball is attached to top of the rod by a string of length *R*. For what value of angular speed ω of the platform about vertical axis, will the thread be inclined at 37° with the rod as shown? (Take, $R = 3$ m and $g = 10$ m/s^2)

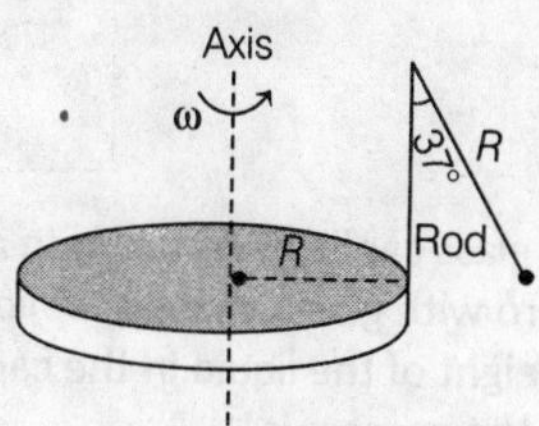

(a) 1 rad/s (b) 1.5 rad/s
(c) 0.75 rad/s (d) 1.25 rad/s

15. S_1 and S_2 are two coherent sources of radiations separated by distance 100.25λ, where λ is the wavelength of radiation. S_1 leads S_2 in phase by $\frac{\pi}{2}$. *A* and *B* are two points on the line joining S_1 and S_2 as shown in figure. The ratio of amplitudes of component waves from sources S_1 and S_2 at *A* and *B* are in ratio 1 : 2. The ratio of intensity at *A* to that of *B* is

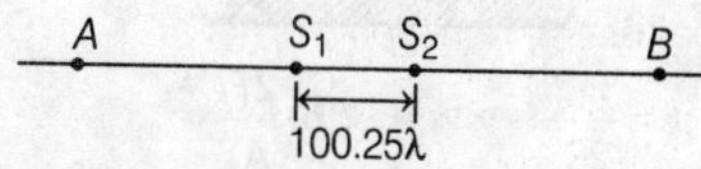

(a) 1 (b) 0 (c) 9 (d) $\frac{1}{9}$

16. A sphere of diameter d is removed from a uniform non-conducting sphere of charge density ρ and radius R thereby creating a cavity as shown.

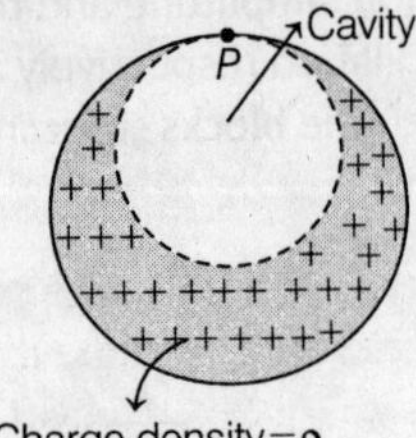

An electron (of charge $-e$ and mass m) is released at top point P of this cavity. Time after which the electron strikes the surface of the cavity is (Take, $d = R$)

(a) $\sqrt{\frac{12\,\varepsilon_0 m}{\rho e}}$

(b) $\frac{1}{2}\sqrt{\frac{\rho e}{3\varepsilon_0 m}}$

(c) $\sqrt{\frac{2\varepsilon_0 m}{\rho e}}$

(d) $\sqrt{\frac{\varepsilon_0 m}{2\rho e}}$

17. Magnetic moment of a Bohr's atom of atomic number Z, corresponding to Nth excited state, is proportional to

(a) N

(b) $N+1$

(c) $\frac{N}{Z}$

(d) $\frac{(N+1)^2}{Z}$

18. On dipping a glass capillary vertically in a liquid (of angle of contact zero with glass), mass m of liquid rises in the capillary. If height of the liquid in the capillary is h, heat dissipated in the process is

(a) mgh

(b) $\frac{mgh}{2}$

(c) $2mgh$

(d) Indeterminate as we require value of surface tension of the liquid

19. A solid cylindrical rod of cross-sectional area A, length l and Young's modulus Y is experiencing longitudinal forces as shown. Extension in the rod is equal to

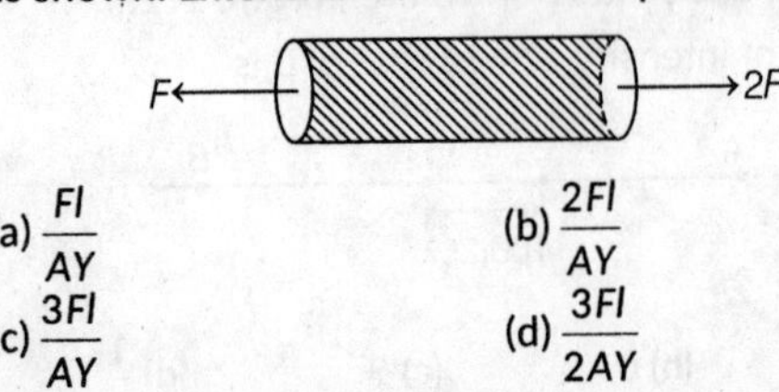

(a) $\frac{Fl}{AY}$

(b) $\frac{2Fl}{AY}$

(c) $\frac{3Fl}{AY}$

(d) $\frac{3Fl}{2AY}$

20. Sinusoidal carrier voltage of frequency 1.5 MHz and amplitude 50 V is amplitude modulated by sinusoidal voltage of frequency 10 kHz producing 50% modulation. The lower and upper side band frequencies (in kHz) are

(a) 1490, 1510

(b) 1510, 1490

(c) $\frac{1}{1490}, \frac{1}{1510}$

(d) $\frac{1}{1510}, \frac{1}{1490}$

Section II *Numerical Value Questions*

21. In an experiment to determine density, the percentage errors in measurement of mass and side of a solid cube are 1% and 2%, respectively. Minimum possible percentage error in measurement of its density is ....

22. At what angle (in rad) with downstream, a swimmer should make strokes to reach the other bank of a river on directly opposite point? (Speed of swimmer with respect to river = 6 m/s, speed of river stream = 3 m/s and take $\pi = 3.14$)

23. Wattless component of current (in A) for the circuit shown here is $(\sqrt{2})^x$. Find x.

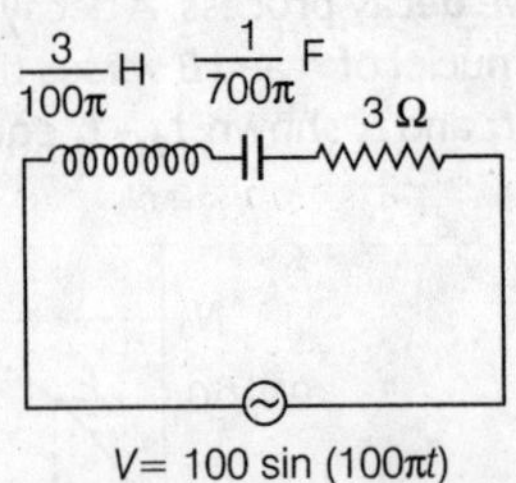

24. A point charge of $\frac{1}{4\pi}$ C is placed in front of an infinite imaginary plane. Electric flux (in G) through the plane is $a \times 10^b$. Find $a + b$ $(1 < a < 10)$.

25. Three geometrically identical rods of thermal conductivities K, $2K$ and $3K$ as shown in the figure have their ends maintained at temperatures marked. If thermal current in the rods are assumed to be H_1, H_2 and H_3, find $\frac{H_1 + H_2}{H_3}$.

600°C 300°C

H_2

H_1 $2K$

K

H_3 $3K$

500°C

26. A metal rod PQ of length l is rotating with angular speed ω about point R as shown. Magnitude of potential difference between ends P and Q is $\frac{B\omega l^2}{x}$. If B is transverse uniform magnetic field in the region, find x.

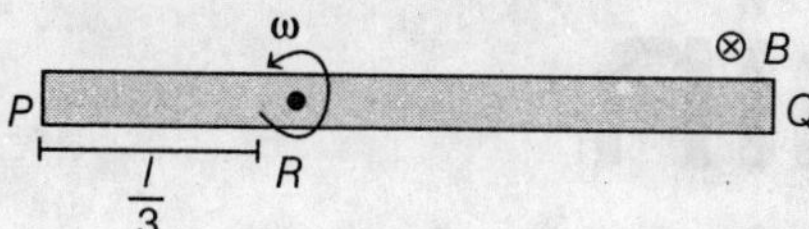

27. Consider the following relation between unknown quantities p, q, r, s and physical quantities L (inductance), R (resistance), μ_0 (magnetic permeability), ε_0(electrical permittivity), E(energy) and k(Boltzmann's constant).

$$p = qe^{\frac{rk}{sE}} + rk \cdot \sin\left(\frac{\mu_0 \varepsilon_0 L}{Rs}\right)$$

Dimensional formula of p from the given relation is $M^x T^y$, so find the value of $x + y$.

28. Find power dissipated by any of 6Ω resistance (in W) in the circuit shown.

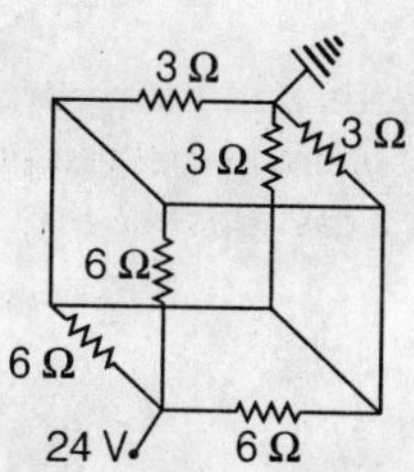

29. In the circuit shown, time at which rate of energy consumption by capacitor is same as rate of heat dissipation in resistor is xRC. Find x.

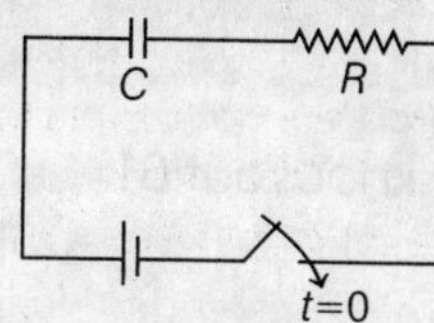

30. Resistance of a galvanometer coil is $R_g = 20\Omega$ and its maximum deflection current is $i_g = 20$ mA. The shunt resistance required to convert it into an ammeter of range $i = 4$A is $\frac{x}{199}\Omega$. Find x.

Answers

1 *(c)*	2 *(c)*	3 *(a)*	4 *(d)*	5 *(c)*	6 *(b)*	7 *(b)*	8 *(d)*	9 *(a)*	10 *(b)*
11 *(a)*	12 *(b)*	13 *(a)*	14 *(d)*	15 *(d)*	16 *(a)*	17 *(b)*	18 *(b)*	19 *(d)*	20 *(a)*
21 *5*	22 *2.09*	23 *7*	24 *13.5*	25 *3*	26 *6*	27 *2*	28 *42.67*	29 *0.69*	30 *20*

See detailed explanations on page no. 288

Knockout 03

JEE Main

Physics

Instructions See knockout 01

Section I *Objective Type Questions*

1. For an ideal gas undergoing polytropic process given by pV^x = constant, variation of molar specific heat capacity (C) with polytropic index (x) is as shown in the graph. Different relevant coordinates are marked on the two axis as p, q, r and s. Choose the **incorrect** alternative.

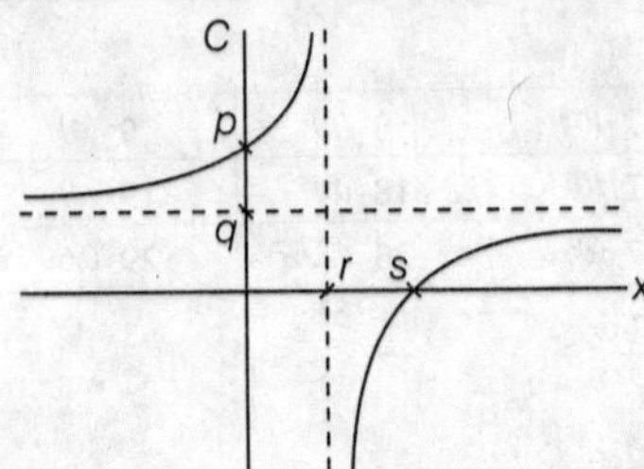

(a) $p = q / s$

(b) $pr = q \cdot s$

(c) $p - q$ does not depend on nature or atomicity of gas

(d) For helium undergoing polytropic process given by $TV^{1/2}$ = constant, temperature of gas decreases on supplying heat

2. The earth is moving around the sun in an elliptical orbit. Point A is the closest and point B is the farthest point in the orbit as shown. In comparison to the situation when the earth passes through perihelion

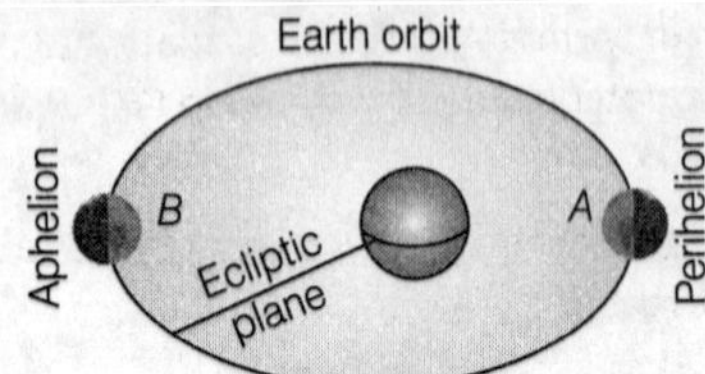

Statement 1 Gravitational potential energy of the earth-sun system is greater when the earth passes through aphelion.

Statement 2 Magnitude of angular momentum of the earth about the sun is greater when the earth passes through aphelion.

(a) Statement 1 is True, Statement 2 is False

(b) Statement 1 is False, Statement 2 is False

(c) Statement 1 is True, Statement 2 is True

(d) Statement 1 is False, Statement 2 is True

3. A bomb of mass $2m$ travelling in X-Y plane is moving with velocity $\mathbf{v}$ making 30° with X-axis in gravity free space. It explodes into two identical pieces moving with velocities $\mathbf{v}_1$ and $\mathbf{v}_2$ along X and Y axes, respectively.

(a) $\mathbf{v}_1 = \sqrt{3}\, \mathbf{v}_2$

(b) Momentum of system composed of the two pieces in reference frame of centre of mass of system is $2m\mathbf{v}$.

(c) Momentum of system composed of the two pieces in reference frame of centre of mass of system is non-zero.

(d) Minimum energy released during explosion is mv^2.

4. Time for 20 oscillations of a pendulum is measured as $t_1 = 39.6$ s, $t_2 = 39.9$ s and $t_3 = 39.5$ s. What is the least count and mean absolute error of the measurement?

(a) 0.2 s and 0.3 s respectively

(b) 0.2 s and 0.1 s respectively

(c) 0.1 s and 0.4 s respectively

(d) 0.1 s and 0.2 s respectively

5. Electromagnetic waves with wavelength

(i) λ_1 is used in satellite communication.

(ii) λ_2 is used in LASIK eye surgery.

(iii) λ_3 is used to detect leakage of oil in underground pipelines.

(iv) λ_4 is used to improve visibility in optical communication.

Then, arrange these wavelengths in ascending order of their magnitude.

(a) $\lambda_3 < \lambda_2 < \lambda_4 < \lambda_1$ (b) $\lambda_2 < \lambda_1 < \lambda_3 < \lambda_4$

(c) $\lambda_1 < \lambda_4 < \lambda_3 < \lambda_2$ (d) $\lambda_4 < \lambda_1 < \lambda_2 < \lambda_3$

6. The gas molecule of carbon monoxide (CO) and nitrogen gas at the same temperature have kinetic energies E_1 and E_2 respectively, then

(a) $E_1 = E_2$

(b) $E_1 > E_2$

(c) $E_1 < E_2$

(d) E_1 and E_2 cannot be compared

7. Figure shows a particle projected on a horizontal surface from position A with velocity u at angle θ with horizontal. C and E are highest point and landing point, respectively.

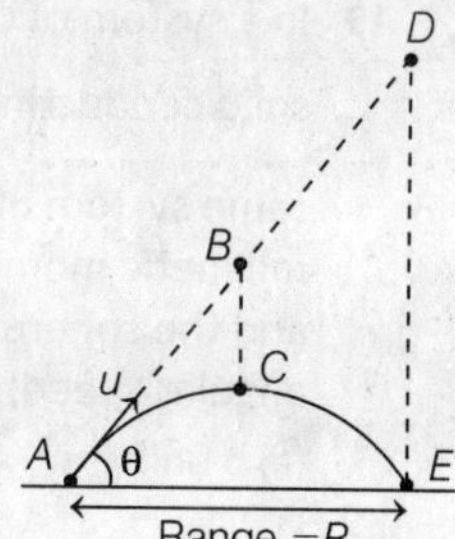

Choose the correct alternative.

(a) For $\theta = 45°$, $BC = R$

(b) For $\theta = \tan^{-1} 1/4, BC = R$

(c) For $DE = 4BC$, θ must be $\tan^{-1} 4$

(d) For $\theta = \tan^{-1} \frac{\sqrt{5}}{2}$, $DE = 4BC$

8. Choose the **incorrect** alternative.

(a) For a particle moving with uniform acceleration, path may be curved.

(b) If acceleration of a particle is given by $\mathbf{a} = \mathbf{k} \times \mathbf{v}$, path followed by particle may be helical. ($\mathbf{k}$ = constant, $\mathbf{v}$ = velocity)

(c) Acceleration of a particle is constant in a uniform circular motion.

(d) If in damped oscillation, amplitude reduces to half in 2s, it reduces to $\frac{1}{2\sqrt{2}}$ times the initial value in further 1s.

9. In the circuit shown in figure, the current gain $\beta = 100$ for an *n-p-n* transistor. The bias resistance R_B, so that $V_{CE} = 5$ V is ($V_{BE} << 10$ V)

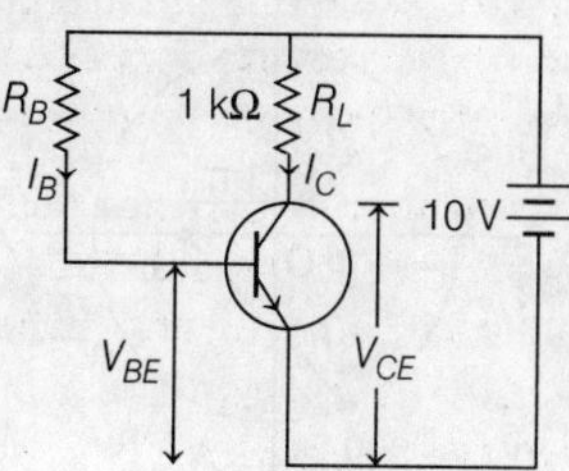

(a) $2 \times 10^3\ \Omega$ (b) $10^5\ \Omega$
(c) $2 \times 10^5\ \Omega$ (d) $5 \times 10^5\ \Omega$

10. If units of mass, length and time are doubled, then in this new system, which of the following will not have same magnitude ?

(a) Gravitational constant
(b) Gravitational force
(c) Power of gravitational force
(d) Gravitational energy

11. In AM, the total modulation index should not exceed one or else

(a) the system will fail (b) distortion will result
(c) amplifier will be damaged (d) amplification reduces

12. In a hypothetical Bohr's atom, interaction potential energy between electron and proton is given by $U = -\frac{k}{r^3}$. Here k is a constant and r is separation between electron and proton. If v, E and r stands for orbital speed, total energy of atom and radius respectively, which of the following quantities is proportional to principal quantum number?

(a) r (b) E (c) $\frac{v^2 \cdot r}{\sqrt{E}}$ (d) v / r

13. The figure shows a large conducting plane with a point charge q placed in front of it. As per electrostatics, charge induced on conducting plane can be thought of to be equivalent to an image (equal but opposite) charge on the other side at same perpendicular distance. Also shown is a point P on the conducting plane at distant r from $+q$.

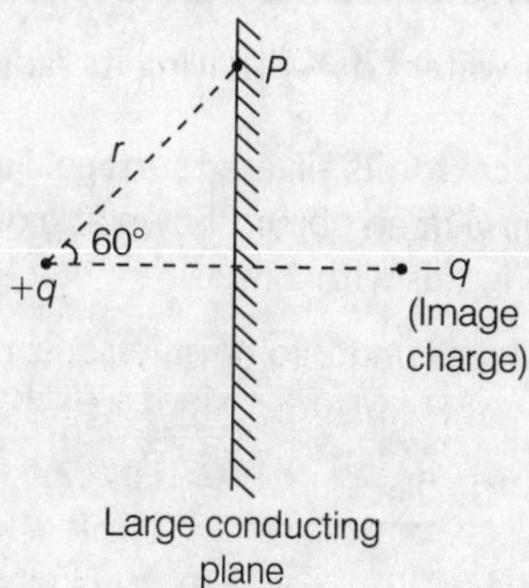

Choose the correct option.

(a) Force between point charge and conducting plane $= F = \frac{kq^2}{2r^2}$

(b) $F = \frac{kq^2}{4r^2}$

(c) Electric field at $P = \frac{2kq}{r^2}$

(d) Electric field at $P = \frac{kq}{r^2}$

14. A rod AB of cross-sectional area A, length l and Young's modulus Y experiences forces as shown. If C is mid-point of rod, choose the incorrect option.

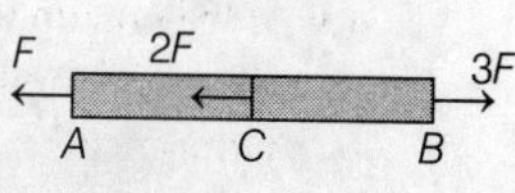

(a) Extension in rod is $\frac{2Fl}{AY}$.

(b) Stress in portion CB is thrice of that in AC.

(c) Strain in portion AC is twice of that in CB.

(d) Elastic potential energy stored in CB is 9 times of that in AC.

15. *i-t* graph for a discharging *R-C* circuit is as shown. Choose the **incorrect** alternative.

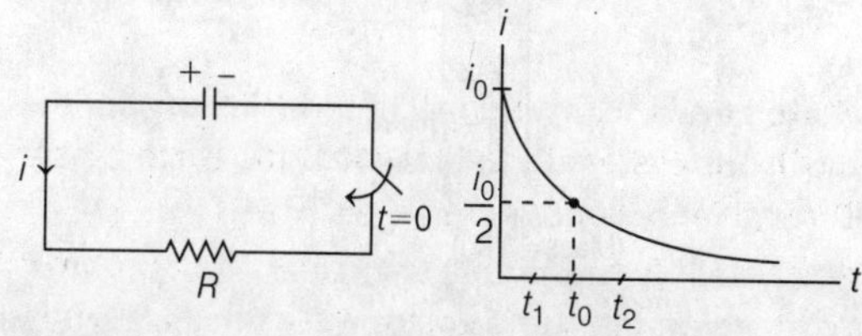

(a) Initial potential difference across capacitor plates is i_0R_0.
(b) Capacitance of capacitor is $\frac{t_0}{R\ln 2}$.
(c) t_1 can possibly be equal to time constant of the circuit.
(d) Heat dissipated in resistor between $t=0$ and $t=t_0$ is three times the heat dissipated between $t=t_0$ and $t=\infty$.

16. The arrangement shown consists of a coaxial system of adjacent concave and convex lenses with convex lens silvered on right surface. Concave lens made of glass $\left(n=\frac{3}{2}\right)$ has radii of curvature equal to 10 cm and 15 cm for left and right surfaces, respectively. Convex lens is made up of water $\left(n=\frac{4}{3}\right)$ having its radius of curvature equal to 15 cm for its silvered surface. Find velocity of image (in m/s) of an object shown at a distance of 27 cm moving along axis with 2 m/s.

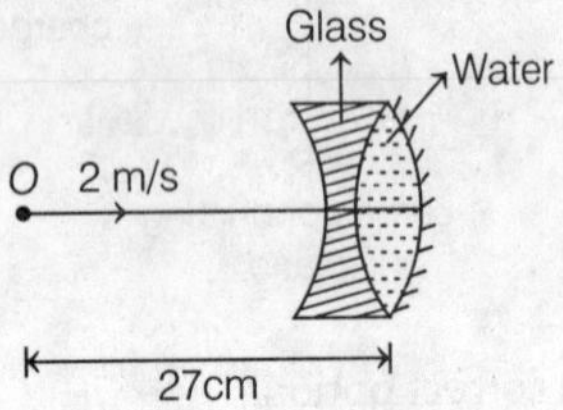

(a) 8 m/s (b) – 8 m/s (c) 4 m/s (d) – 4 m/s

17. The figure here shows two very thin long rods *PQ* and *RS* in contact inclined at 60° w.r.t. each other. If the rods move parallel to themselves with speed 3 m/s each, find speed (in m/s) of their contact point *O*.

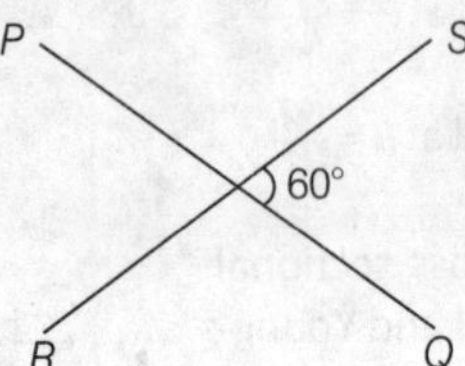

(a) 5 m/s (b) 8 m/s (c) 6 m/s (d) 6.4 m/s

18. In the arrangement shown, strings and pulleys are ideal. The ball is set on same horizontal level as the lower end of the rod and is then released. Time taken by the ball (in s) to reach upper end of the rod is
(Take, $g=10\ \text{m/s}^2$)

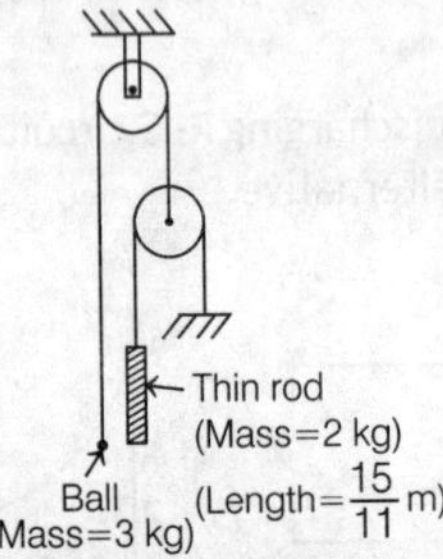

(a) 1s (b) 2s (c) 3s (d) 5s

19. In a system of units, ratio of charge to mass of a uniform solid conducting sphere is 6 unit. The value of $\frac{M}{L}$ in the same system of units is (here *M* and *L* stands for sphere's magnetic moment and angular momentum respectively and the sphere is rotating about a diameter with uniform angular speed).

(a) 6 unit (b) 8 unit (c) 3 unit (d) 5 unit

20. A radioactive isotope decays by β^+ emission. If m_1, m_2 and m_3 represent masses of parent atom, daughter atom and electron respectively, energy liberated during emission is given by $Q=(m_1-m_2-km_3)c^2$. Then value of $(k+1)$ is

(a) 1 (b) 3.0 (c) 3.7 (d) 5.5

Section II *Numerical Value Questions*

21. A bead of mass 1 kg is constrained to move on a smooth ring under the influence of a force *F* directed towards the shown fixed point *A* (distant 1 m from centre *O* of the ring of radius 2m) in plane of the ring. If $F=\frac{3}{r^2}$ N, find minimum speed (in m/s) of bead when it is nearest to *A*, so as to make it execute complete revolution on the ring. Note that *r* is instantaneous separation between bead and point *A*.

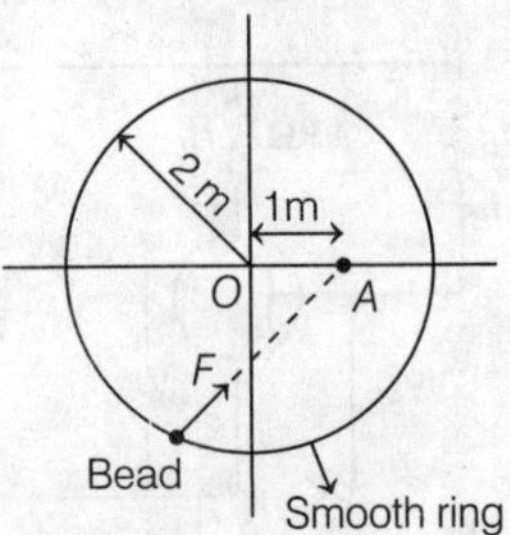

22. In the arrangement shown, *S* is a source of radiowaves of wavelength λ. Consider interference of direct and reflected waves reaching *P*. If $l=\lambda=\frac{2}{\sqrt{21}}$ m, find minimum non-zero value of *d* (in m) for destructive interference.

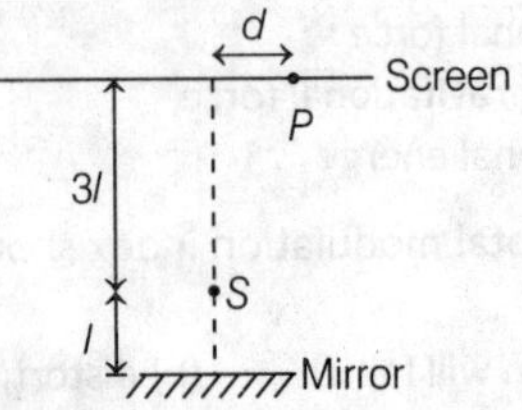

23. A rod of length *l* in the arrangement shown can slide on pair of frictionless horizontal rails in a region of uniform transverse magnetic field *B*. Starting from rest, at $t=0$, the rod is made to move with constant velocity *v* by applying a rightward force *F*.

Find F (in N) at $t = 2$ s. Given that $B = 2$T, $l = 1$m, $v = 2$ m/s, $R = 2\Omega$, $L = 8$ H

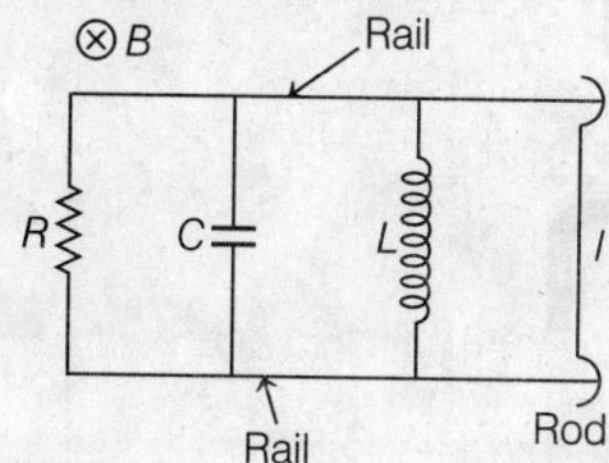

24. A simple pendulum is released in a position with string making 60° with vertical. If tensions in extreme and mean positions are T_1 and T_2 respectively, find $\frac{T_2}{T_1}$.

25. Detected frequency of sound escaping from the shown closed organ pipe, vibrating in first overtone equals fundamental frequency of vibration of air column in the organ pipe. If v and u represent speed of detector and speed of sound in air respectively, $\frac{v}{u} = \frac{a}{b}$. If a and b are least possible positive integers, find $(a+b)^2$.

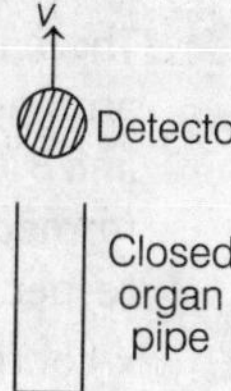

26. A water clock is designed as a vessel with its shape given by $y = kx^n$ having small orifice at its bottom. The time is calculated according to level of water in the vessel. If the time scale is uniform, find n.

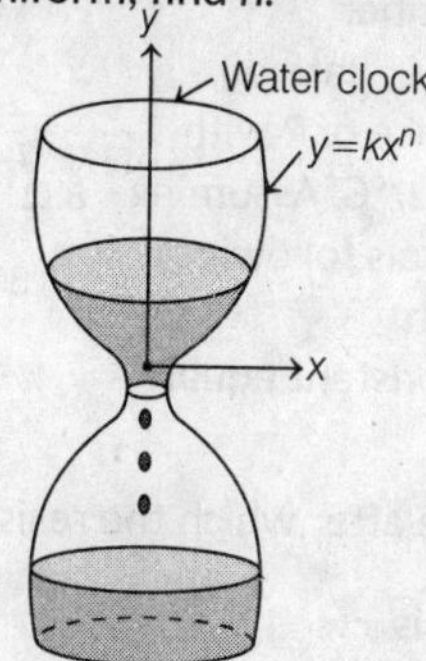

27. A horizontal wooden rod of cross-sectional radius R is suspended by a string in equilibrium in a region of uniform upward magnetic field B. Air of density ρ strikes half of the right part of the rod with speed v and instantly comes to rest. Find current I (in A) in the coil having four turns wound on the rod.

Given that $\frac{\rho v^2 L^2}{4\pi RB} = 4$ A

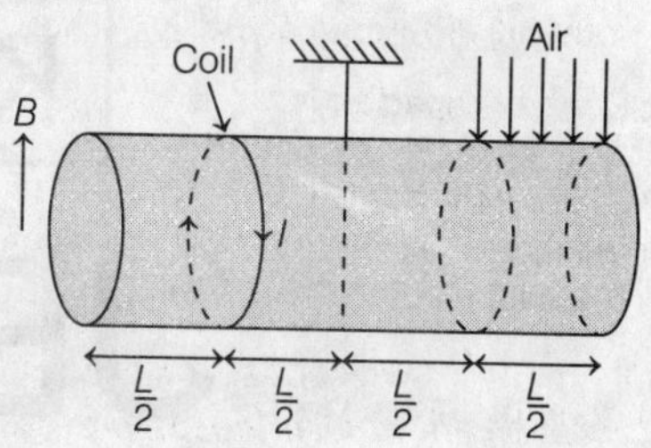

28. If power factor of the circuit shown is unity, find reciprocal of power factor of the box, if ammeter reads 40 A.

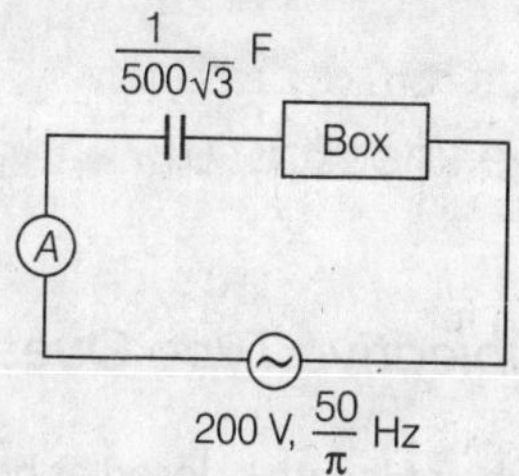

29. A metal ball of work function $\phi = 2$ eV is irradiated by a radiation of wavelength 3100Å. Consider two electrons emitted by the ball moving along X and Y axes having kinetic energies K and $K - 1.5$ eV respectively, here K is maximum kinetic energy of an emitted photoelectron. If de-Broglie wavelength of electron moving along X-axis is λ, de-Broglie of electron moving along Y-axis in centre of mass frame of the system is $\frac{4\lambda}{x}$. Find x.

(Take, $hc = 12400$ eV-Å)

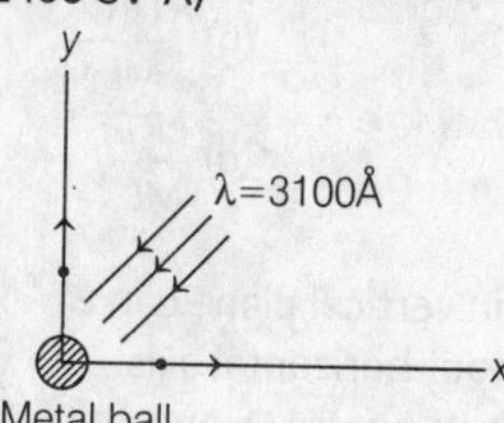

30. A block released at A on the surface shown slides down finally stopping at shown point B. If coefficient of friction between block and surface is $\frac{2}{x}$, find x.

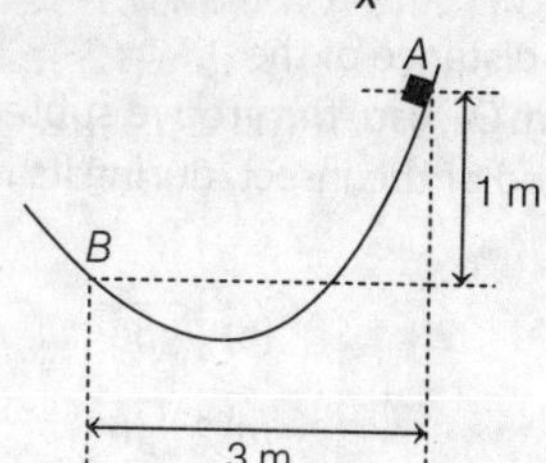

Answers

1 (a)	2 (a)	3 (d)	4 (d)	5 (a)	6 (a)	7 (c)	8 (c)	9 (c)	10 (d)
11 (b)	12 (c)	13 (d)	14 (c)	15 (c)	16 (b)	17 (c)	18 (a)	19 (d)	20 (b)
21 2	22 3	23 6	24 4	25 25	26 4	27 3	28 2	29 2.24	30 6

See detailed explanations on page no. 292

Knockout 04

JEE Main

Physics

Instructions See knockout 01

Section I Objective Type Questions

1. A horizontal tube of length L closed at both ends contains an ideal gas (of molar mass M) at thermodynamic temperature T. The tube is accelerated along its length with acceleration a such that pressure at one end is double that at the other end. The value of acceleration is

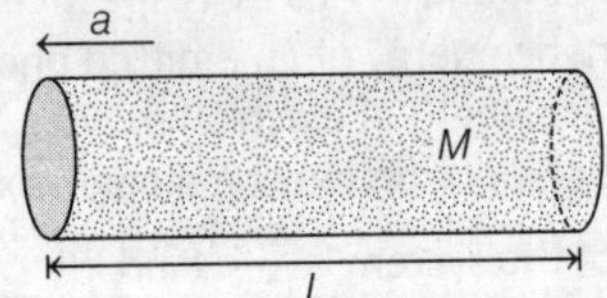

(a) $\frac{RT}{ML}$ (b) $\frac{RT\ln 2}{ML}$

(c) $\frac{RT}{\ln 2\, ML}$ (d) $\frac{eRT}{ML}$

2. A uniform disc in vertical plane can rotate freely about horizontal axis passing through its centre O. An insect is moving in a horizontal groove PQ such that the disc keeps at rest. Initially, the insect was at rest at end P of the groove.

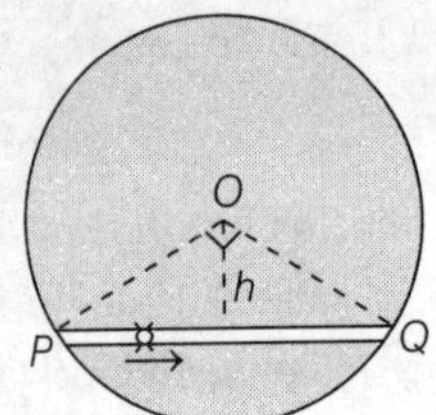

Perpendicular distance of the groove is h from O. Also, the groove subtends 90° at O. Maximum speed of the insect, during its motion along the groove, is

(a) $\sqrt{\frac{gh}{2}}$ (b) $\sqrt{gh}$

(c) $\sqrt{2gh}$ (d) $2\sqrt{gh}$

3.

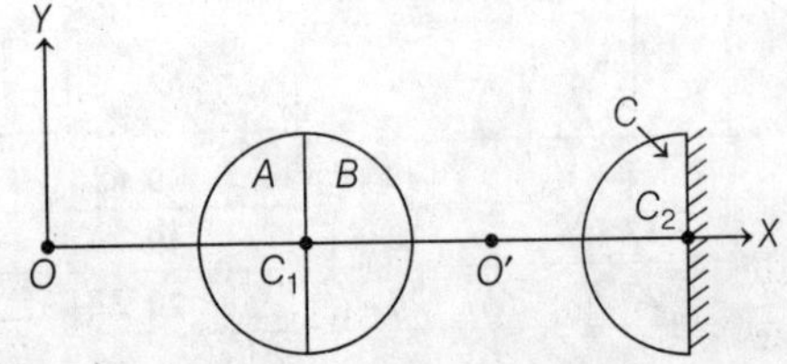

Three identical hemisphere A, B and C of radius R are arranged as shown in figure. x-coordinates of centre of A and B (C_1), centre of C (C_2), object (O), objects's image formed by system of A and B (O') are $5R$, $12R$, 0, $7R$ respectively.

x-coordinate of image of O' formed by C (silvered at one face) is

(a) 0 (b) $7R$

(c) $10R$ (d) Indeterminate

4. Consider the circuit shown. Resistance R, initially at 50°C and having resistance 15Ω, is kept inside a chamber maintained at 20°C. Rate of change of resistance of R with temperature is 1Ω/°C. Assuming that resistance cools following Newton's law with proportionality constant equal to $\frac{\ln\frac{9}{4}}{100}$ per s, time after which the resistance R consumes maximum power is

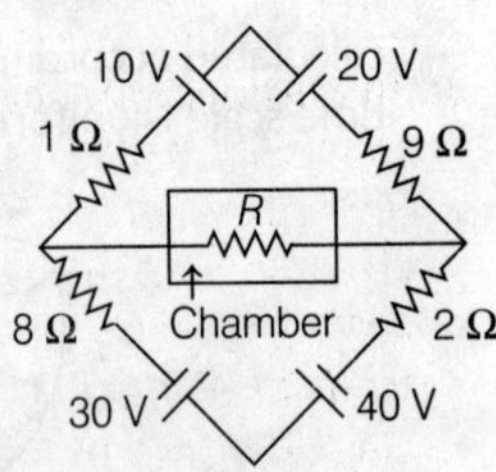

(a) 25 s (b) 50 s (c) 75 s (d) 100 s

5. The figure here shows a movable block of mass $2m$ having a cylindrical smooth cavity of radius R placed on a smooth horizontal surface. A very small ball of mass m is moving with vertical velocity $v = \sqrt{2gR}$ (relative to the block) on the cavity's surface at a specific instant. Acceleration of the block, at the same instant, is

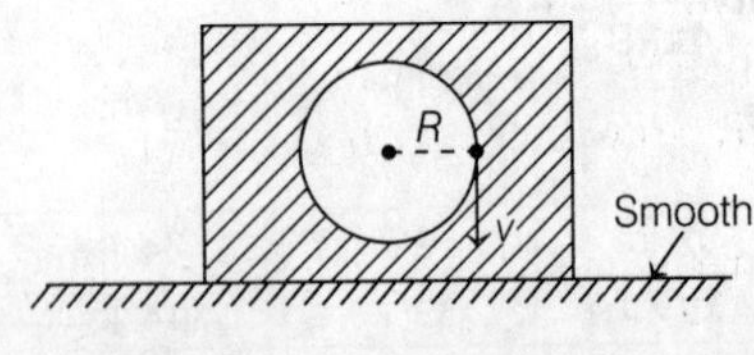

(a) g (b) $\frac{2g}{3}$ (c) $\frac{g}{3}$ (d) zero

6. A planet of mass m is revolving around Sun such that its minimum and maximum distances from the Sun are r and $4r$, respectively. Angular momentum of the planet w.r.t. centre of the Sun, in the position A shown, is (speed of the planet in position B is v)

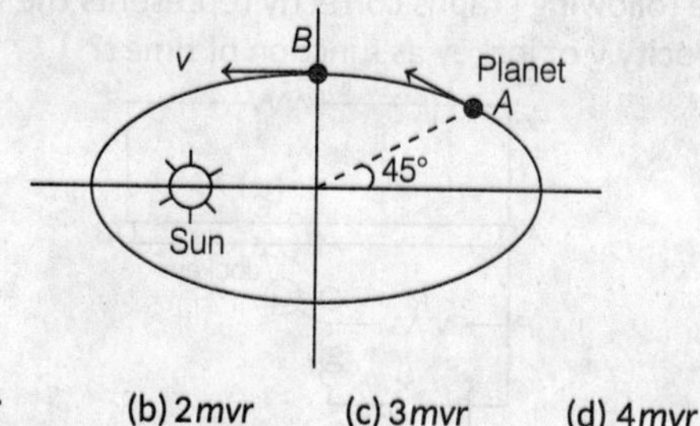

(a) mvr (b) $2mvr$ (c) $3mvr$ (d) $4mvr$

7. Ratio of magnetic flux density at A in Arrangement-1 to that at B in Arrangement-2 is

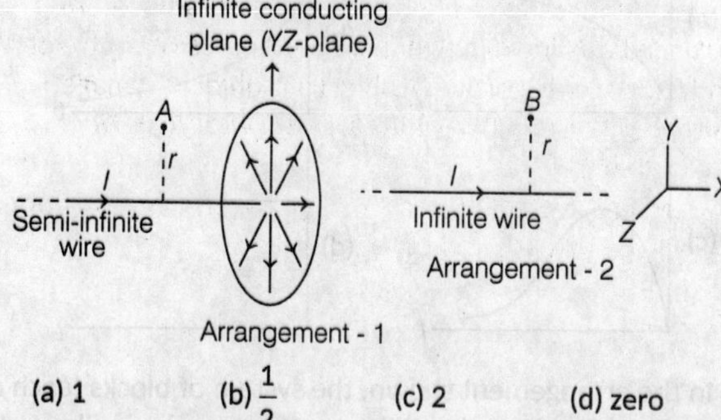

(a) 1 (b) $\frac{1}{2}$ (c) 2 (d) zero

8. The figure here shows a fixed rectangular conducting frame $ABCD$ of sides l and $2l$ in a region of transverse uniform magnetic field B_0. Two straight conducting sliders EF and GH are moving with respective speeds v and $3v$ as shown in figure. Initially, EF and GH are located very near to sides AB and AD respectively. Intersection contact of the sliders is represented by T. Emf induced in the loop $ETHD$ when it is a square, is

(a) $2B_0vl$ (b) $1.5\,B_0vl$ (c) B_0vl (d) $0.5\,B_0vl$

9. A ball is projected horizontally from top of a 80 m deep well with velocity 10 m/s, then particle will fall on the bottom at a distance of (all the collisions with the wall are elastic)

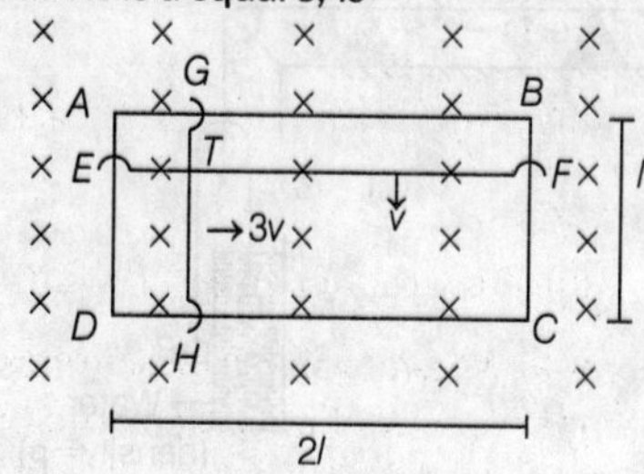

(a) 5 m from A
(b) 2 m from B
(c) 3 m from A
(d) 5 m from B

10. An ideal fluid is filled upto h in a tank of very large cross-section and having a narrow horizontal tube XYZ attached to its bottom as shown.
Cross-sectional area of the tube between X and Y is $\sqrt{2}$ times the cross-section between Y and Z. Gauge pressure of fluid between points X and Y is (ρ = density of fluid)

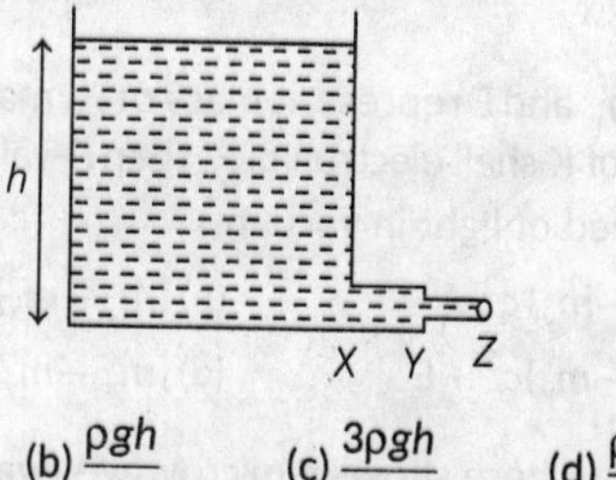

(a) ρgh (b) $\frac{\rho gh}{2}$ (c) $\frac{3\rho gh}{4}$ (d) $\frac{\rho gh}{4}$

11. Statement 1 On collision of two molecules in an ideal gas sample, kinetic energy of both molecules can't decrease.
Statement 2 Average velocity of gas molecules in an ideal gas sample is zero.
(a) Statement 1 is False, Statement 2 is False
(b) Statement 1 is True, Statement 2 is True
(c) Statement 1 is True, Statement 2 is False
(d) Statement 1 is False, Statement 2 is True

12. Photocathode of a photoelectric cell emits photoelectrons of minimum de-Broglie wavelengths λ and $2\sqrt{2}\,\lambda$, when illuminated by EM waves of wavelengths 3100 Å and 6200 Å, respectively. Taking hc = 12400 eV-Å, work function of photocathode (in eV) is equal to (approximately)
(a) 1.2 (b) 1.5
(c) 1.7 (d) 2.1

13. The arrangement of gates shown here is equivalent to

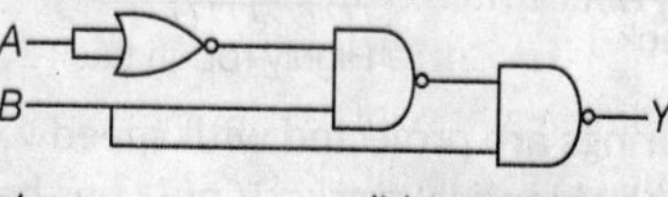

(a) NOR gate (b) NAND gate
(c) OR gate (d) AND gate

14. In the arrangement shown, the capacitors are made of square plates of edge l. Minimum kinetic energy with which the electron should be projected at point A, so that it does not collide with plate of capacitor is (Symbols have usual meaning and the space is gravity free)

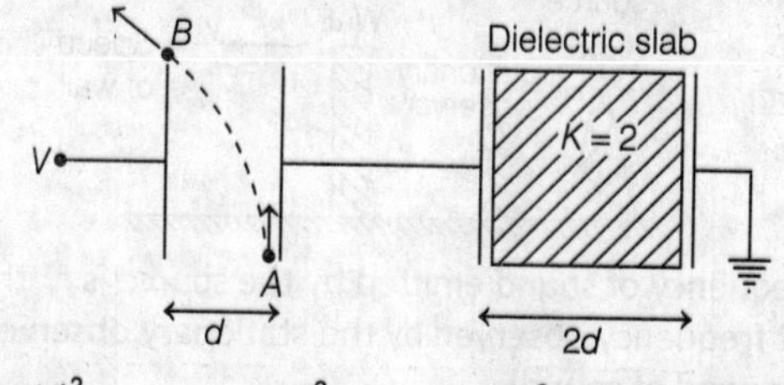

(a) $\frac{eVl^2}{4d^2}$ (b) $\frac{eVl^2}{6d^2}$ (c) $\frac{eVl^2}{8d^2}$ (d) $\frac{eVl^2}{10d^2}$

15. The figure here shows electron capture by radio nuclide X transforming itself into stable nuclide Y

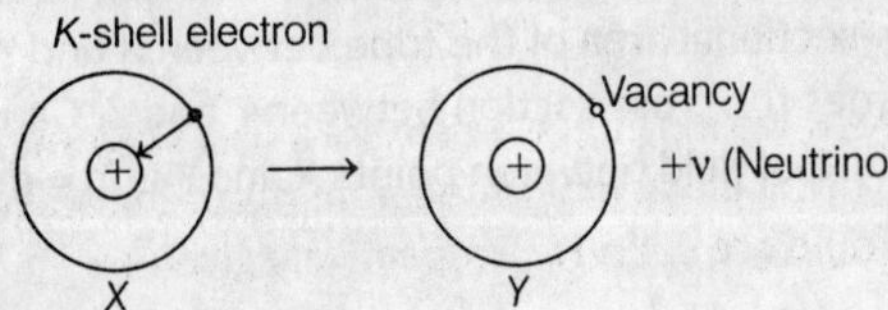

If m_x, m_y and E represent mass of X, mass of Y and binding energy of K-shell electron of X, then Q-value of the process is (c = speed of light in vacuum)

(a) $(m_x - m_y)c^2$
(b) $(m_y - m_x)c^2$
(c) $(m_x - m_y)c^2 + E$
(d) $(m_x - m_y)c^2 - E$

16. The figure here shows a microwave (wavelength $= \lambda$) transmitter mounted on a tower of height H with respect to water level in a lake of width D. For what height H' of the receiver tower on the opposite bank of the lake the receiver detects signal of maximum intensity?

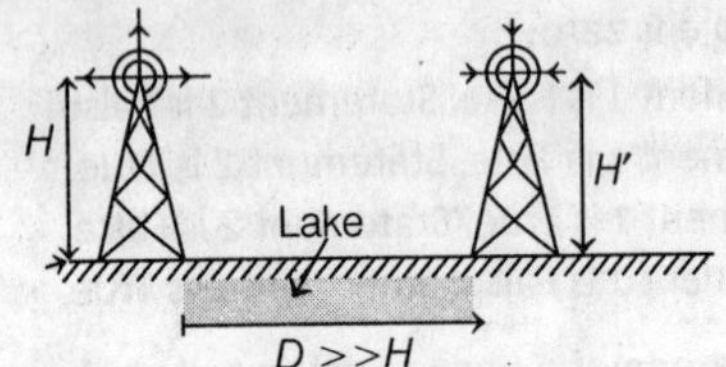

(a) $\frac{3\lambda D}{2H}$
(b) $\frac{3\lambda D}{4H}$
(c) $\frac{5\lambda D}{8H}$
(d) $\frac{\lambda D}{2H}$

17.

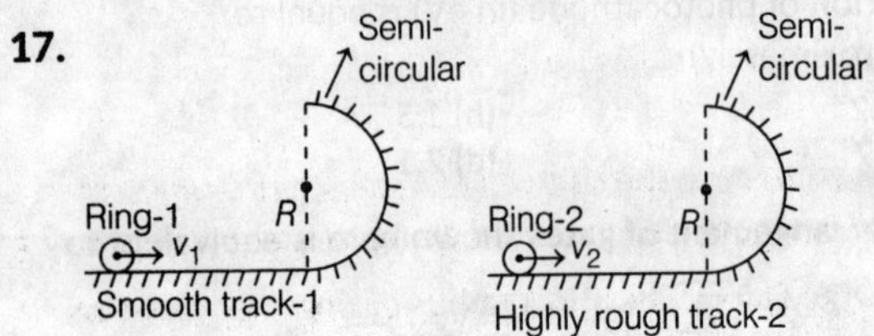

Two small rings are projected with speed v_1 and v_2 on two geometrically identical tracks. Ring-2 has been set into pure rolling. If v_1 and v_2 are just sufficient to reach top of the tracks, then $\frac{v_1}{v_2}$ is equal to

(a) 1
(b) $\sqrt{\frac{5}{3}}$
(c) $\sqrt{2}$
(d) $\frac{1}{\sqrt{2}}$

18.

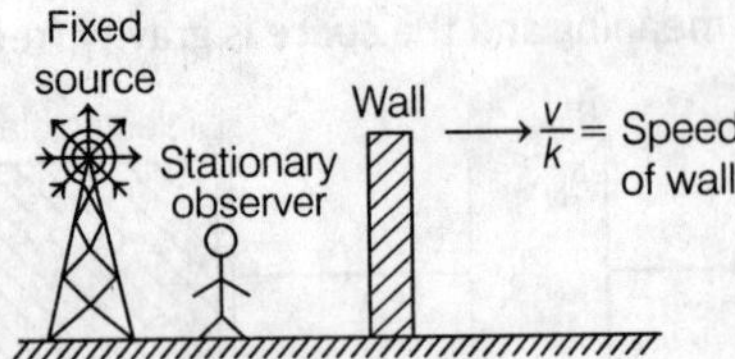

If frequency of sound emitted by the source is f, then beat frequency observed by the stationary observer is (v = speed of sound)

(a) $\frac{f}{k}$
(b) $\frac{f}{k+1}$
(c) $\frac{2f}{k+1}$
(d) $\frac{2kf}{k+1}$

19. In the arrangement shown, ends P and Q of resistor in L-R circuit established at $t = 0$ are connected to end A and point C (*via* jockey). The jockey is being moved such that the galvanometer always shows null deflection. Which of the following graphs correctly represents the variation of velocity v of jockey as function of time t?

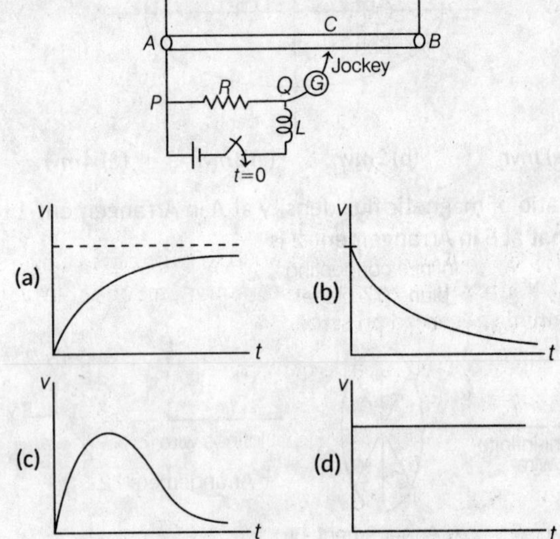

20. In the arrangement shown, the system of blocks (each of mass m) is released and the sonometer wire is vibrated using a tuning fork of frequency f. Given that μ is linear mass density of the sonometer wire and specific gravity of material of blocks (solid) is 2, separation between bridges for formation of standing wave shown in the wire is (Assume that, block A remains completely immersed in water and pulleys and strings are ideal)

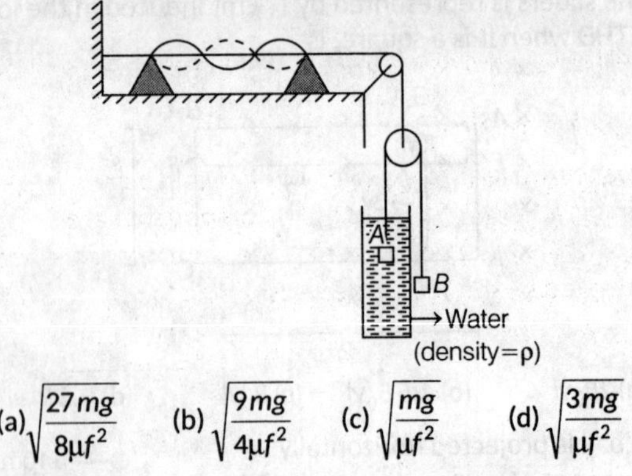

(a) $\sqrt{\frac{27mg}{8\mu f^2}}$
(b) $\sqrt{\frac{9mg}{4\mu f^2}}$
(c) $\sqrt{\frac{mg}{\mu f^2}}$
(d) $\sqrt{\frac{3mg}{\mu f^2}}$

Section II *Numerical Value Questions*

21. A uniform ring of mass m, cross-sectional radius r, radius R ($>> r$) and Young's modulus Y is rotated with angular speed ω about axis passing through its centre and perpendicular to its plane. Elastic potential energy stored in the wire is $\frac{m^a \omega^b R^c}{dr^e Y}$. Considering $\pi = \sqrt{10}$, find $a + b + c + d + e$.

22. Consider a metal ring as shown in Fig.1 with points P and Q maintained at constant temperatures. If the minor arc segment between P and Q is replaced by a straight segment as shown in Fig.2 such that heat current flowing between P and Q doubles, ratio of thermal conductivity of the straight segment to that removed is $\frac{x\sqrt{2}}{\pi}$. Find the value of x.

Assume cross-section of segments to be constant.

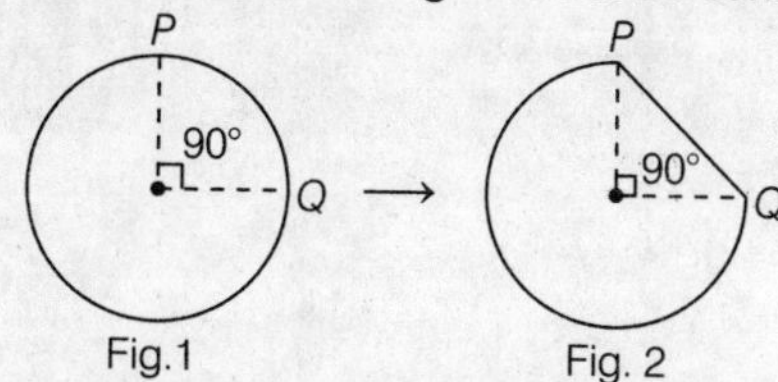

Fig.1 Fig. 2

23. Orange light (wavelength $= 6000$ Å) illuminates single slit of width $30\,\mu$m. Find the maximum number of diffraction minima observed on screen.

24. A small charged particle of mass m and carrying charge q is projected in a region of transverse magnetic field B as shown in figure, from point P of a smooth surface named Surface-1.

If distance between P and Q (intersection point of smooth Surface-2 with boundary of magnetic field in the plane) is just greater than $\frac{2mv}{qB}$, then time after which velocity of the particle becomes parallel to the initial velocity for the first time is $\frac{m}{qB}\left[x + \frac{yv}{v'}\right]$. Find $x + y$. (Given that v' is speed after collision at Surface-1 and coefficient of restitution is $\frac{9}{16}$ at both surfaces).

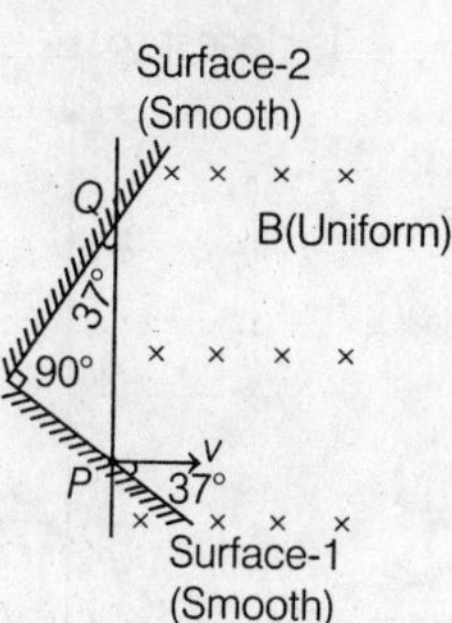

25. Respective resistance of components in a series L-C-R circuit as shown in Fig.1. If the components are rearranged as in Fig. 2, across the same source, current supplied by the source decreases by a factor of $\sqrt{x}$. Find the value of x.

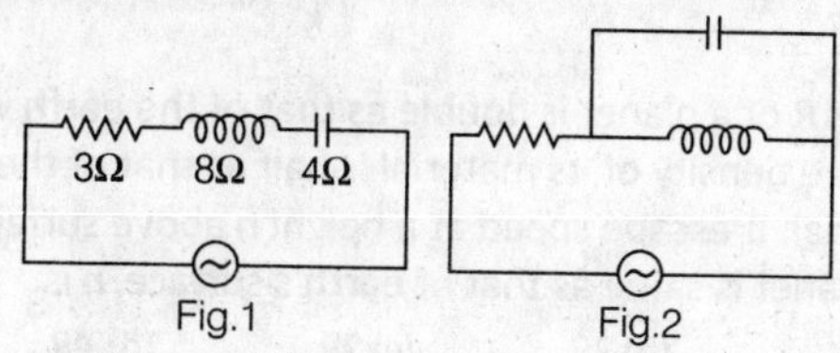

Fig.1 Fig.2

26. A force which is varying with time t as $\mathbf{F} = (3t\hat{\mathbf{i}} + 5\hat{\mathbf{j}})$ N acts on a body whose position varies with time t as $\mathbf{s} = (2t^2\hat{\mathbf{i}} - 5\hat{\mathbf{j}})$, where t is in seconds. Find the work done (in J) by this force in initial 2 s.

27. An EM wave moving in air enters a non-magnetic liquid normally. If electric field components of the wave in air and liquid are $\mathbf{E}_1$ and $\mathbf{E}_2$ respectively given by

$$\mathbf{E}_1 = a\sin(\omega t - kx)\mathbf{j},\quad \mathbf{E}_2 = b\sin\left(\frac{\omega' t}{2} - \frac{6\pi x}{\lambda}\right)\hat{\mathbf{j}}$$

where, a, b, ω, ω', k are constants and λ is wavelength of the wave in vacuum. If C represents dielectric constant of the liquid, then find $C - \frac{\omega}{\omega'}$.

28. If percentage errors in measurement of length of pendulum and time period of pendulum in an experiment to measure g are 1% and 2% respectively, find maximum possible percentage error in measurement of g.

29. A system of two blocks of masses 1 kg and 2 kg are pulled by forces 3N and 10 N respectively as shown in figure. Spring connecting the blocks has spring constant 100 N/m and is initially relaxed. Initially velocities of the blocks of masses 1 kg and 2 kg are 7 m/s and 8 m/s, respectively. Find momentum of the system (in kg-m/s) in CM frame after 2s.

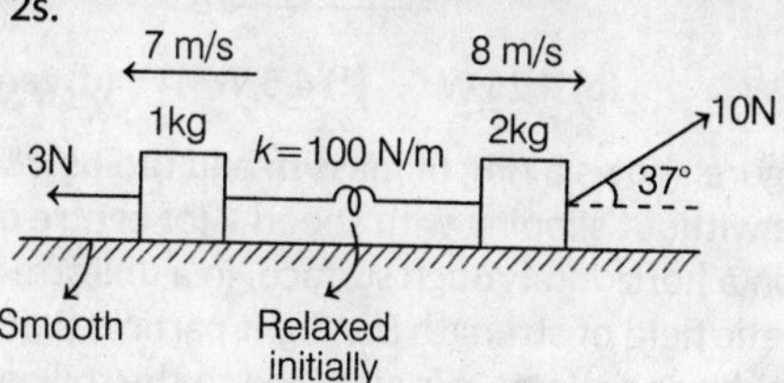

30. The system here shows two identical short dipoles of dipole moment p each placed along axis of a uniform ring of charge $Q = \frac{p}{R}$, where R is radius of ring. Net force on Dipole-2 is $\frac{p^2}{x\pi\varepsilon_0 R^4}$. Find the value of x.

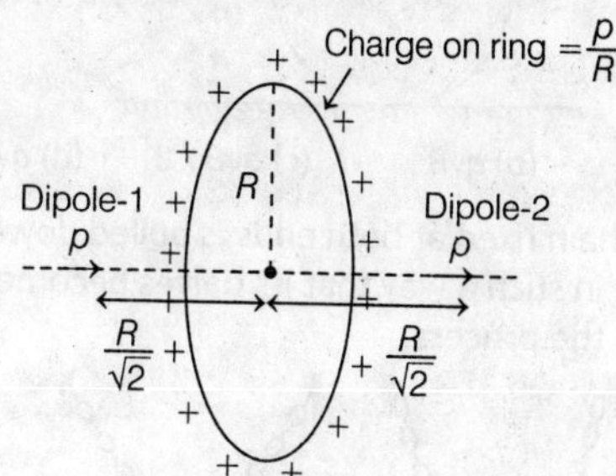

Answers

1 *(b)*	2 *(b)*	3 *(c)*	4 *(b)*	5 *(b)*	6 *(b)*	7 *(a)*	8 *(b)*	9 *(d)*	10 *(b)*
11 *(b)*	12 *(c)*	13 *(b)*	14 *(c)*	15 *(d)*	16 *(b)*	17 *(b)*	18 *(c)*	19 *(b)*	20 *(a)*
21 *51*	22 *4.67*	23 *100*	24 *5.14*	25 *2.92*	26 *32*	27 *8.5*	28 *5*	29 *0*	30 *2.67*

See detailed explanations on page no. 294

Knockout 05

JEE Main

Physics

Instructions See knockout 01

Section I *Objective Type Questions*

1. Maximum power that can be drawn between points *A* and *B* of the circuit shown is

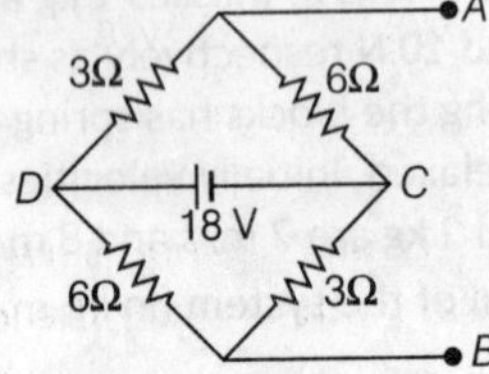

(a) 72 W (b) 2.25 W (c) 4.5 W (d) zero

2. The figure shows a ring of mass *m* and radius *R* set into rolling without slipping with speed v (of centre of mass) at $t = 0$ on a horizontal rough surface, in a uniform transverse magnetic field of strength *B*. A light particle (initially at top of ring) having charge *q* is attached to the rolling ring. Friction acting on the ring at time $t = \frac{\pi R}{2v}$ is (assuming that friction is sufficient to prevent slipping)

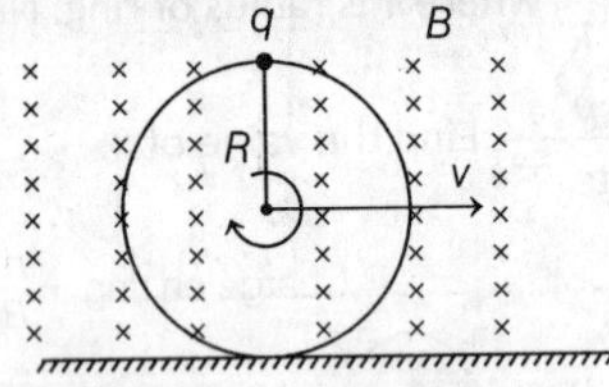

(a) zero (b) qvB (c) $qvB/2$ (d) $qvB/\sqrt{2}$

3. A heavy chain fixed at both ends is pulled down at its mid-point in such a way that its halves become straight as shown. In the process,

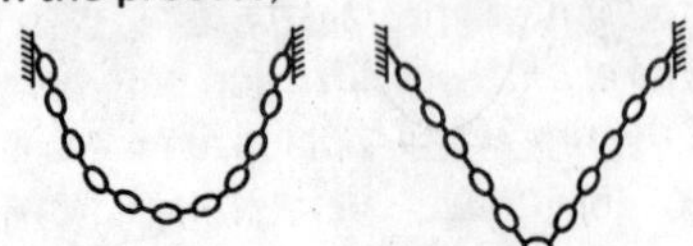

(a) centre of mass of the chain descends
(b) centre of mass of the chain ascends
(c) centre of mass of the chain remains stationary
(d) centre of mass may ascend or descend depending on exact initial shape of chain

4. One mole of an ideal gas undergoes a thermodynamic cyclic process with isochoric, isothermal and isentropic processes as its three steps. Degree of freedom of the gas is closest to

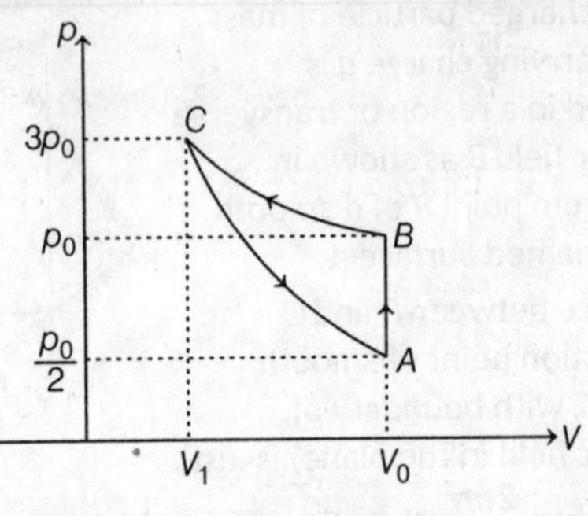

(a) π (b) 3 (c) ln9 (d) *e*

5. A particle of mass *m* moving with speed v_0 collides elastically with a smooth stationary pan of mass *M* ($M = 2m$) attached to a vertical spring of spring constant *k* as shown in figure. Maximum compression of the spring is

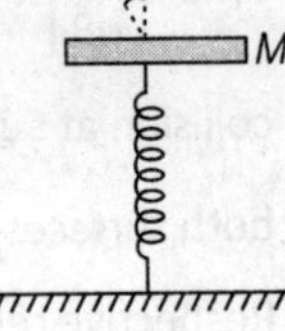

(a) $\sqrt{\frac{2m}{k}}\frac{v_0}{3}$ (b) $\sqrt{\frac{m}{k}}\frac{v_0}{3}$

(c) $\sqrt{\frac{2m}{k}}v_0$ (d) $\sqrt{\frac{m}{k}}v_0$

6. Radius *R* of a planet is double as that of the earth while average density of its material is half as that of the earth's material. If escape speed at a height *h* above surface of the planet is same as that at earth's surface, *h* is

(a) *R* (b) 2*R* (c) 3*R* (d) 4*R*

7. An ideal choke coil and a condenser (initially uncharged and having capacity *C*) are connected in series across a cell of emf *E* at $t = 0$. Maximum charge acquired by the condenser at a later instant is

(a) *CE* (b) 2 *CE* (c) 3 *CE* (d) 4 *CE*

8. In the figure shown, a child floats at rest on water surface with ears in air while, a diver is swimming upwards with constant velocity v in water. A cawing crow moves down with constant velocity v (same as that of the diver) making sound of frequency f. Product of apparent wavelength of crow's sound observed by the child with the apparent frequency observed by the diver is (the velocity of sound in air is $5v$ and that in water is $20v$.)

(a) $5.25\ v$ (b) $4.2\ v$ (c) v (d) $0.95\ v$

9. A small ball of mass m and charge q is placed at the centre of a uniformly charged sphere of radius R and charge Q. A narrow smooth groove is made in the sphere from surface to centre as shown in figure. The sphere is made to rotate about a diameter perpendicular to the groove at a constant angular speed ω. Speed w.r.t. ground with which the ball slides out from the groove is (Given that $\frac{KQq}{R} = m\omega^2R^2$)

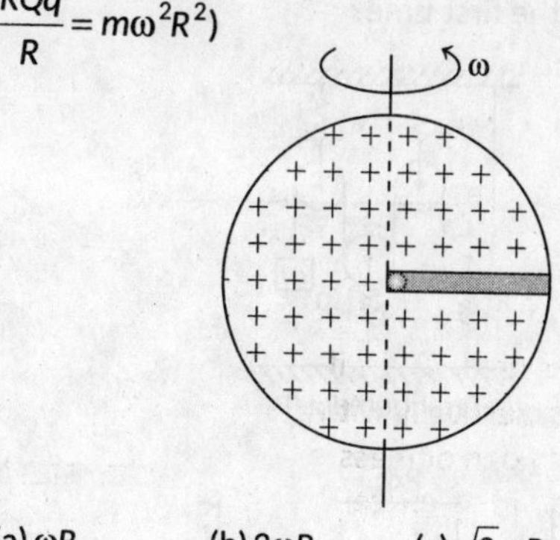

(a) ωR (b) $2\omega R$ (c) $\sqrt{2}\,\omega R$ (d) $\sqrt{3}\,\omega R$

10. Two identical particles moving at right angles have de-Broglie wavelengths λ each in ground's frame. de-Broglie wavelength of one of the particles in centre of mass frame is

(a) λ (b) $\sqrt{2}\,\lambda$ (c) $\frac{\lambda}{\sqrt{2}}$ (d) ∞

11. Percentage modulation for the AM wave shown here is

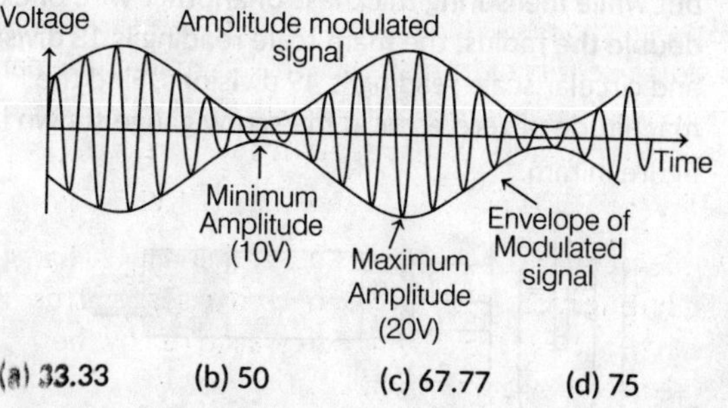

(a) 33.33 (b) 50 (c) 67.77 (d) 75

12. An inductor of inductance $(10/\pi)$ mH, a capacitor of capacitance $(2/\pi)$ mF and a resistor of resistance $3\,\Omega$ are connected in series with an AC voltage source (50 Hz) as shown in the figure. Applied voltage (of AC source)

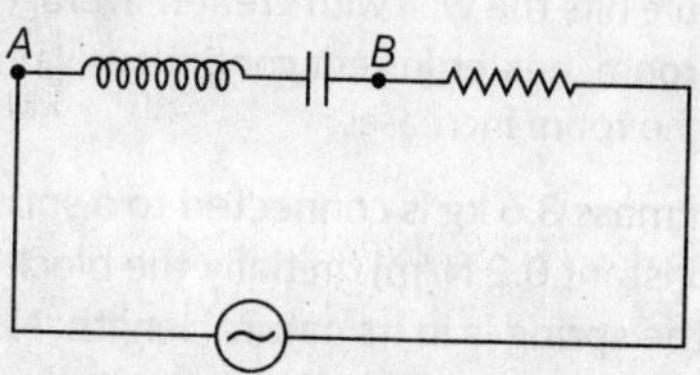

(a) leads potential difference between points A and B by 37°
(b) leads potential difference between points A and B by 53°
(c) lags potential difference between points A and B by 37°
(d) lags potential difference between points A and B by 53°

13. A uniform solid sphere of volume V and specific gravity 8 has a concentric spherical cavity of volume V', such that the sphere just sinks in water. V' equals

(a) $V/2$ (b) $V/8$ (c) $7V/8$ (d) $V/7$

14. In a YDSE, slits are separated by 0.5 mm, and the screen is placed 150 cm away. A bichromatic light consisting of two wavelengths, 650 nm and 520 nm, is used to obtain interference fringes on the screen. The least distance from the common central maximum to the point where the dark fringes due to both the wavelengths coincide is

(a) 15.6 mm
(b) 1.56 mm
(c) 7.8 mm
(d) dark fringes due to the two wavelengths don't coincide at any point of the screen

15. Find the ratio of current I supplied by the cell to current I_1 in the Zener diode as shown in given figure.

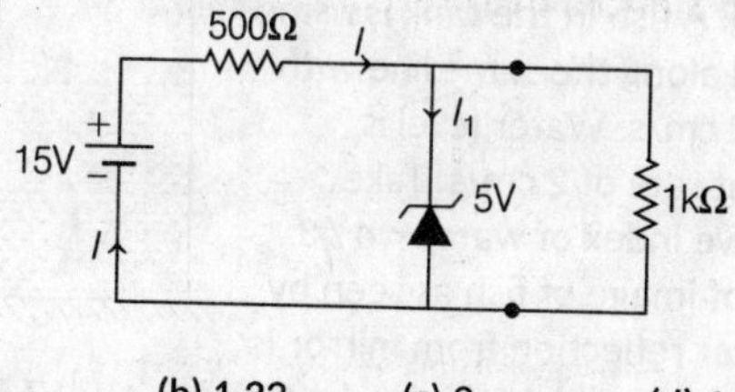

(a) 4 (b) 1.33 (c) 3 (d) 1

16. A non-conducting ring of radius R and mass m having charge q uniformly distributed over its circumference is placed on a rough horizontal table surface. A vertical time varying uniform magnetic field $B = 2t^2$ is switched ON at time $t = 0$. The coefficient of friction between the ring and the table, if the ring starts slipping at $t = 4$ s, is

(a) $8qR/mg$ (b) qR/mg (c) $2qR/mg$ (d) $qR/8mg$

17. Choose the **incorrect** statement.

(a) When an ideal gas is compressed isothermally then its pressure increases because its number of collisions per unit area with walls of container increases.

(b) In a mixture of nitrogen and helium kept at room temperature, as compared to a helium molecule nitrogen molecule hits the wall with smaller average speed.

(c) In a mixture of nitrogen and helium kept at room temperature, as compared to a helium molecule nitrogen molecule hits the wall with greater average kinetic energy.

(d) If in a room, heater in kept continuously on, internal energy of air the room increases.

18. A block of mass 3.6 kg is connected to a spring (spring constant 0.2 N/m). Initially the block is at rest and the spring is in its natural length. Now the system is released in uniform gravitational field ($g = 10\ m/s^2$) as shown and a variable force F is applied on the upper end of the spring such that the downward acceleration of the block is given as $a = 10 - t$. The point of application of force instantly come to rest for the first time at t equal to

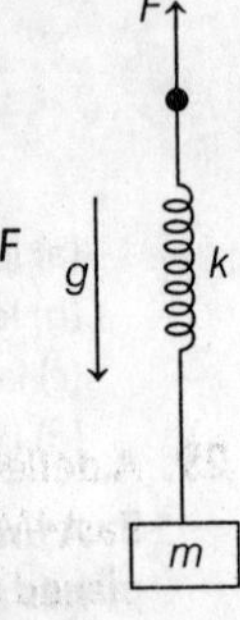

(a) 2s (b) 8s (c) 14s (d) 18s

19. In a radioactive reactor, radionuclide X are being injected at a rate of r atoms/s which decay to a stable daughter nuclide Y according to equation, $X \rightarrow Y + E$.

The energy released (E) in each decay process is transformed to electricity and used to light up a bulb. If the process starts at $t = 0$, then (At $t = 0$ the number of radionuclide $X = 0$)

(a) brightness of bulb increases with time in the beginning and then becomes constant

(b) brightness of bulb decreases with time in the beginning and then becomes constant

(c) brightness first increases then decreases later

(d) brightness first decreases then increases later

20. A bird in air is diving vertically downward over a tank with speed 5 cm/s while base of tank is silvered. A fish in the tank is rising upward along the same line with speed 2 cm/s. Water level is falling at rate of 2 cm/s. Take refractive index of water = 4 / 3. Speed of image of fish as seen by bird after reflection from mirror is

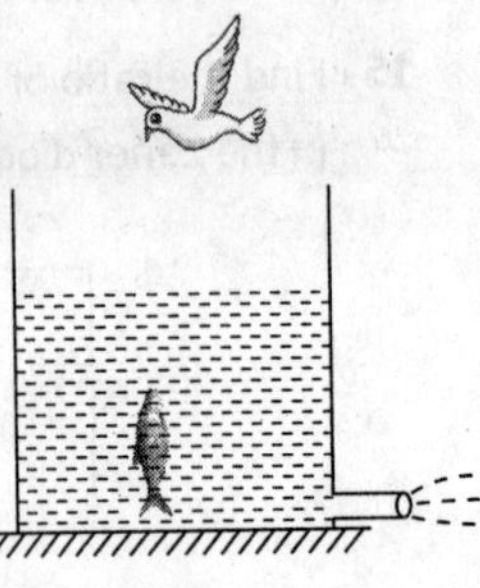

(a) 3 cm/s (b) 4.5 cm/s (c) 6 cm/s (d) 7.5 cm/s

Section II *Numerical Value Questions*

21. Two uniform rods of same lengths and equal masses are placed in contact on a smooth horizontal surface. Linear coefficient of thermal expansion of one of the rods is double that of the other.

Temperature of the system is now increased. Find the ratio of expansion of the rod with lesser thermal coefficient of expansion to shift in the junction.

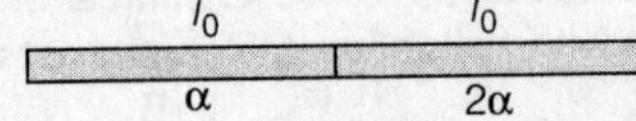

22. Two particles A and B moving with same speed along two different lines, inclined at angle 60°, are heading towards intersection P. Considering their initial positions shown in the figure, find minimum separation (in m) between them during their motion. (Take $\sqrt{3} = 1.73$)

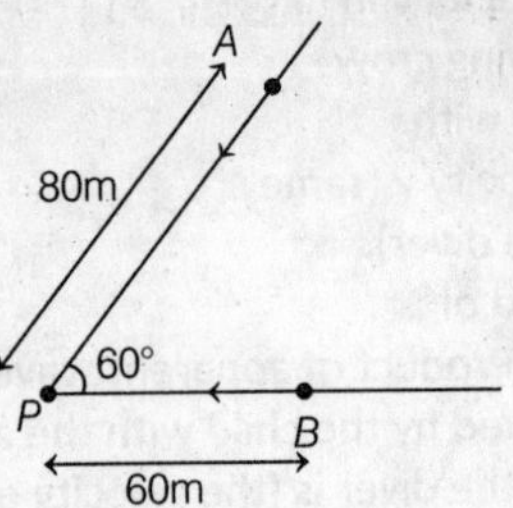

23. In the Arrangement-1, the block is pulled slightly downwards making it oscillate. In Arrangement-2, the block is displaced from shown equilibrium position by amount $2x_0$ leftwards and released at the instant of release of the block in Arrangement-1. The block collides with the wall elastically during subsequent motion. If blocks and springs in the two arrangements are identical, after how many oscillations of block in Arrangement-1 will the blocks be simultaneously at the initial positions of release for the first time?

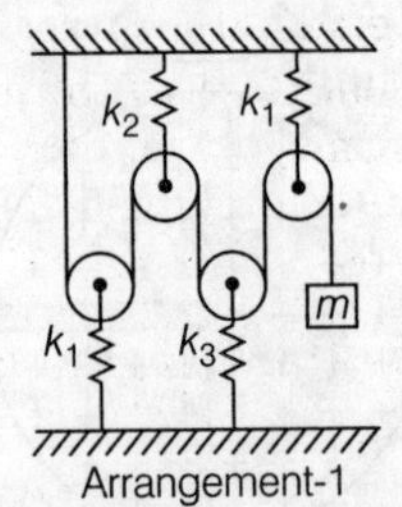

Arrangement-1

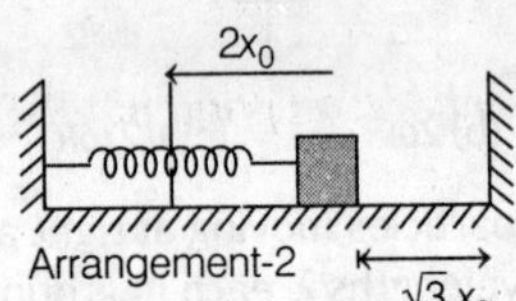

Arrangement-2

24. The pitch of a screw gauge is 0.5 mm while number of divisions on circular scale is 50. While measuring thickness of a wire using the screw gauge, the main scale reading and circular scale readings are as shown but while measuring thickness of another wire of exactly double the radius, the main scale reading is 13 divisions and circular scale reading is 49 divisions. Find the magnitude of zero error in the screw gauge shown in figure in mm.

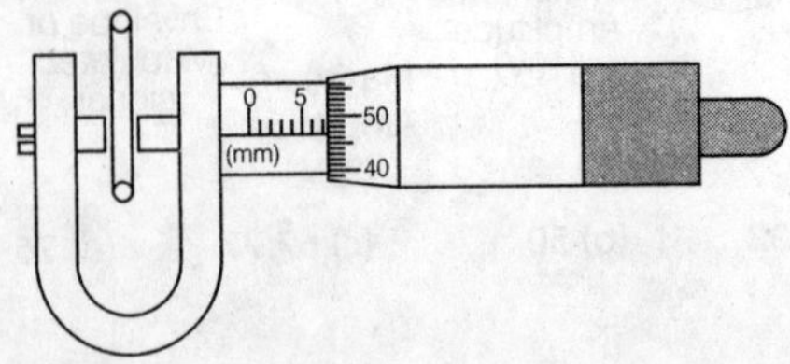

25. A particle ($m = 1$ kg) slides down a frictionless track (*AOC*) starting from rest at a point *A* (height 2 m). After reaching *C*, the particle continues to move freely in air as a projectile. When it reaches its highest point *P* (height 1 m), the kinetic energy of the particle (in J) is (Figure drawn is schematic and not to scale; take $g = 10\ ms^{-2}$) ....

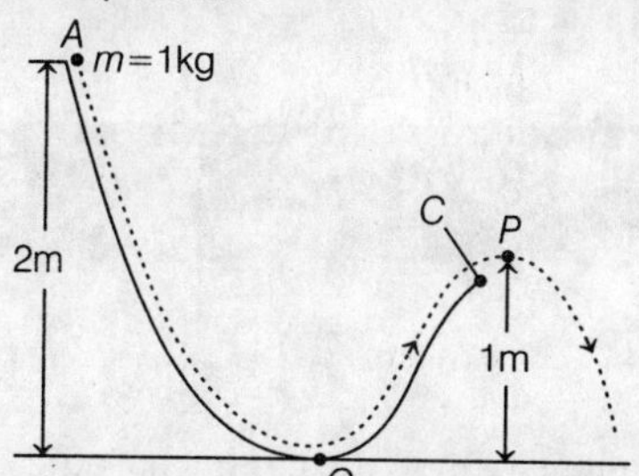

26. A spherical and a cubical body of same material and same surface area are placed in same evacuated chamber after heating to same temperature. The ratio of initial rates of cooling of sphere to that of cube in space is *x* while the ratio of buoyancy experienced by cube to that experienced by sphere if completely immersed in water is *y*. Find $x \cdot y$.

27. A particle moving with constant acceleration on a straight line covers 20 m in 7th second and 24 m in 9th second. Distance travelled by particle in 10th second is .... m.

28. Internal radius of a 10 cm long tapered capillary tube varies uniformly from 0.5 mm to 0.25 mm from one end to the other. Height of ascent is 4 cm if the larger radius end just touches the surface of water. Considering angle of contact to be zero, find surface tension in N/Km.

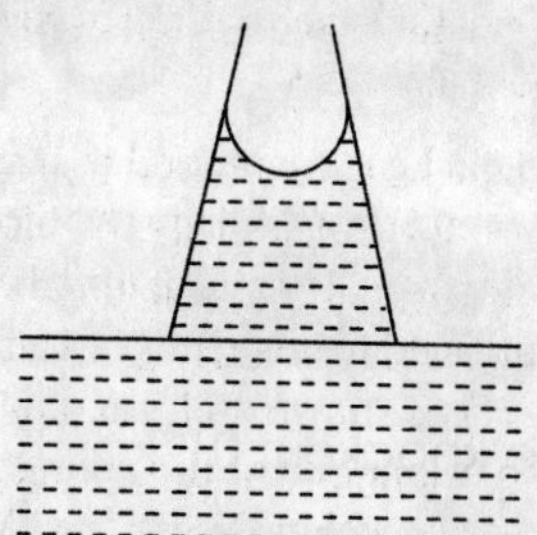

29. A deflection magnetometer is placed with its arm along the East-West direction ($\tan A$ position) and a short bar magnet is placed symmetrically along its axis at some distance with its South pole pointing towards East. In this position the needle of the magnetometer shows a deflection of 30°. If we double the distance of the bar magnet, then the deflection will be $\tan^{-1}\frac{x}{8}$. Find *x*.

30. In a system of units, units of mass, length, temperature and time are 28.8 kg, 2 cm, 32K and 1 minute respectively. Unit of thermal coefficient of conductivity in this new system is $a \times 10^{-9}$ times that in SI system. Find *a*

Answers

1 (b)	2 (b)	3 (b)	4 (a)	5 (a)	6 (a)	7 (b)	8 (a)	9 (d)	10 (b)
11 (a)	12 (a)	13 (c)	14 (d)	15 (b)	16 (a)	17 (d)	18 (a)	19 (a)	20 (a)
21 4	22 17.32	23 5	24 1.45	25 10	26 0.52	27 26	28 80	29 0.57	30 83.33

See detailed explanations on page no. 299

Knockout 06

JEE Main

Physics

Instructions See knockout 01

Section I *Objective Type Questions*

1. **Consider the shown network of identical resistors and capacitors C_1, C_2 and C_3 having capacitances 4C, 2C and 3C respectively. Ratio of energies stored by C_1, C_2 and C_3 in steady state is**

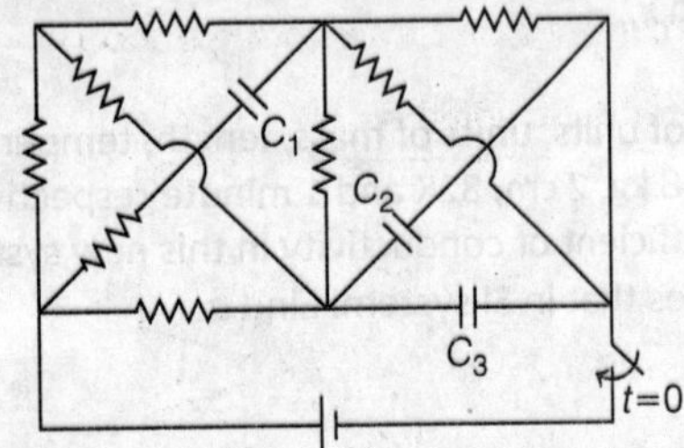

(a) 2:3:4 (b) 2:4:3 (c) 3:2:4 (d) 4:2:3

2. **A thin biconvex lens of focal length f is oscillating with small angular amplitude θ. Distance moved by convergence point of the parallel beam shown, during one complete oscillation of the lens is**

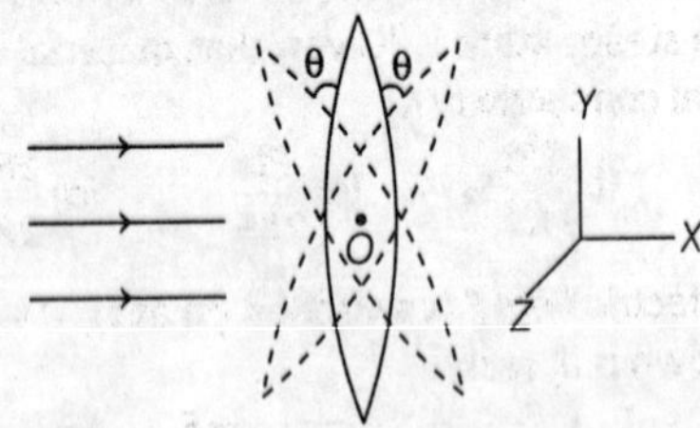

(a) $2f(1-\cos\theta)$ (b) $\frac{4f(1-\cos\theta)}{\cos\theta}$

(c) $2f(1-\sec^2\theta)$ (d) $4f\theta$

3. **Assume an extra electron revolving around nucleus in a hydrogen atom in ground state always located diametrically opposite to the other electron. Orbital radius of such an electron is**

(r_0 = Bohr's radius of hydrogen atom $= \frac{\varepsilon_0 h^2}{\pi m e^2}$)

(a) r_0 (b) $\frac{4}{3}r_0$ (c) $\frac{3}{2}r_0$ (d) $2r_0$

4. **Considering the figure, minimum possible speed of the ball (attached to a light thread attached to a peg attached to the cart) while executing looping with respect to the cart is**

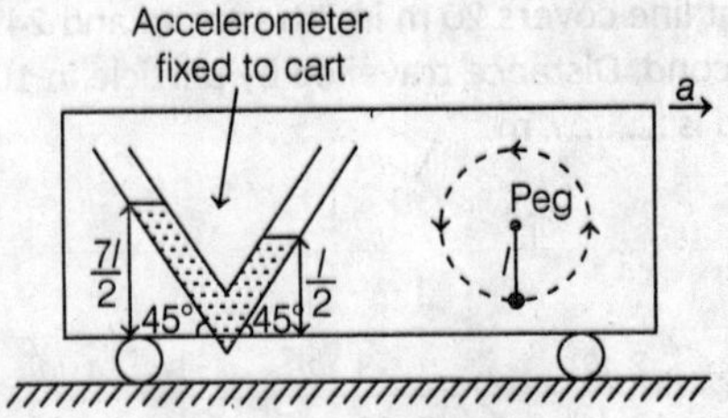

(a) $\sqrt{5gl}$ (b) $\frac{\sqrt{5gl}}{2}$

(c) $\frac{5}{2}\sqrt{gl}$ (d) $\sqrt{2gl}$

5. **Consider the shown infinite ladder circuit composed of identical ideal inductors each having inductance L and capacitors each having capacitance C. If the circuit is behaving as purely inductive irrespective of value of C, equivalent inductance of the circuit is**

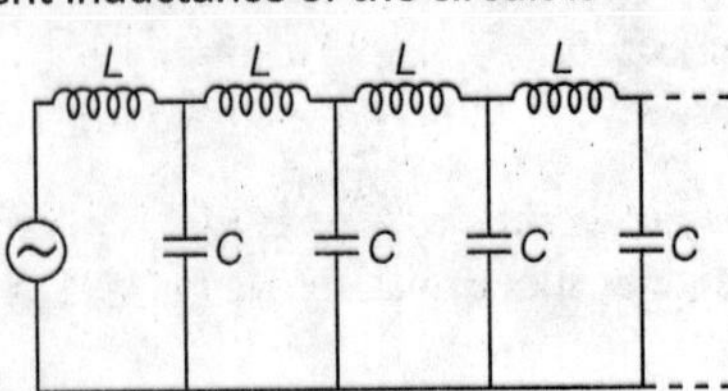

(a) $\frac{L}{2}$ (b) $(\sqrt{2}+1)L$

(c) $(\sqrt{2}-1)L$ (d) L

6. C-11 decays to B-11 by β^+decay with Q-value of 0.96 MeV. β^+particles produced in the decay combine with free electrons in the atmosphere and annihilate each other.

If 1.25 μg of C-11 is present in the sample initially ($t = 0$), then energy (in MeV) produced during two half lives starting at $t = 0$, is approximately

(a) 10^{15} (b) 10^{16} (c) 10^{17} (d) 10^{18}

7. Statement 1 Work done by a force in closed path is zero as displacement of particle in a closed path is zero

Statement 2 Internal energy of gas sample may become more than doubled on doubling thermodynamic temperature

(a) Statement-1 is False, Statement-2 is False
(b) Statement-1 is False, Statement-2 is True
(c) Statement-1 is True, Statement-2 is False
(d) Statement-1 is True, Statement-2 is True

8. A plank AB on a fixed long incline of inclination 30° is being pulled up the incline such that axis C of the small solid cylinder (of radius R) remains at rest with respect to ground. If no slipping takes place between the plank and the cylinder, angle rotated by the cylinder before the cylinder falls off its surface is (Initially the cylinder is stationary at end B of the plank which is also at rest and length of the plank is l.)

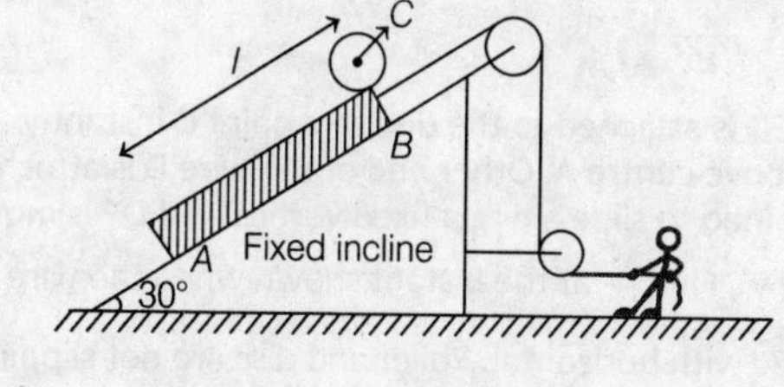

(a) $\frac{l}{R}$ (b) $\frac{2l}{R}$ (c) $\frac{l}{2R}$ (d) zero

9. Electromagnetic power P radiated by a neutron star spinning with angular speed ω is given by the relation

$$P = k\omega^a \mu_0^b m^c v^d$$

Here, k (dimensionless), a, b, c and d are constants. μ_0 is magnetic permeability of free space, m is magnetic moment of star, v is speed of light in vacuum. Choose the correct relation out of the relations given below

(a) $a + b = c + d$ (b) $a - b = c + d$
(c) $a + b = c - d$ (d) $a - b = c - d$

10. A string shaped as circular loop of radius r is rotating with constant angular speed ω as shown in Fig. 1. A point on string is disturbed at $t = 0$ thereby creating two wave pulses. Angular speed of wave pulse-2 w.r.t. wave pulse-1 at a later instant shown in Fig. 2 is

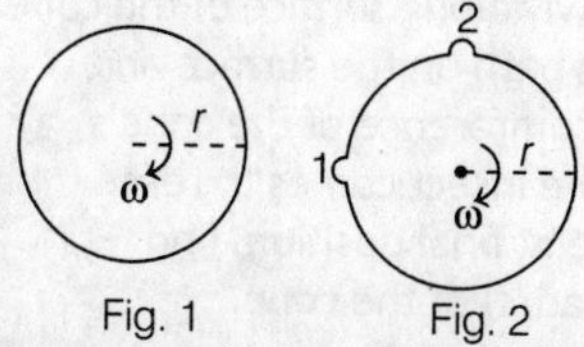

(a) ω (b) 2ω (c) 4ω (d) zero

11. Ammeter in the meter bridge has been constructed by using a shunt S across a galvanometer (identical to the galvanometers in the shown circuit) doubling its range of current. If the ammeter is further shunted by another shunt S, shift in balance point is

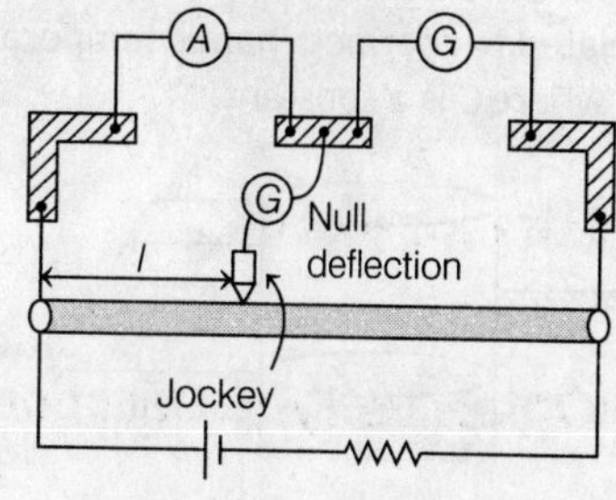

(a) $\frac{l}{4}$ (b) $\frac{l}{3}$ (c) $\frac{2l}{3}$ (d) $\frac{3l}{4}$

12. Consider the transistor circuit shown. If voltmeter V_1 reads 0.7 V and current gain for CB configuration is $\frac{100}{101}$, reading of voltmeter V_2 (in volts) is

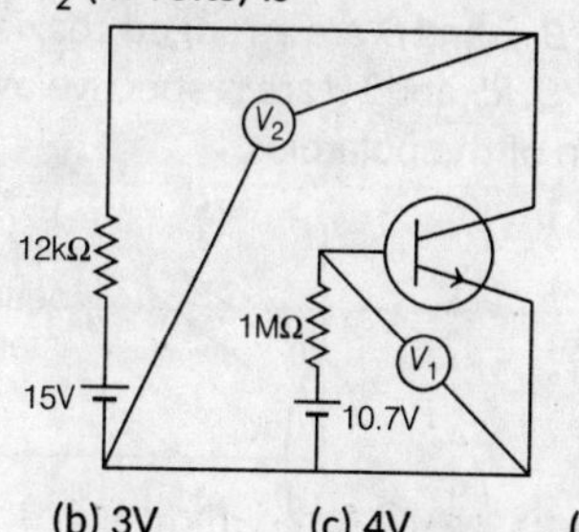

(a) zero (b) 3V (c) 4V (d) 12V

13. A point source of power P is placed at centre of a very thin spherical shell of total surface area S and thickness t. Temperature difference between its inner and outer surfaces in steady state is (Given that material of the shell has thermal conductivity K)

(a) $\frac{Pt}{KS}$ (b) $\frac{2Pt}{KS}$ (c) $\frac{Pt}{2KS}$ (d) $\frac{3Pt}{2KS}$

14. A uniform electric field E is switched on at $t = 0$ when the system shown is at rest.

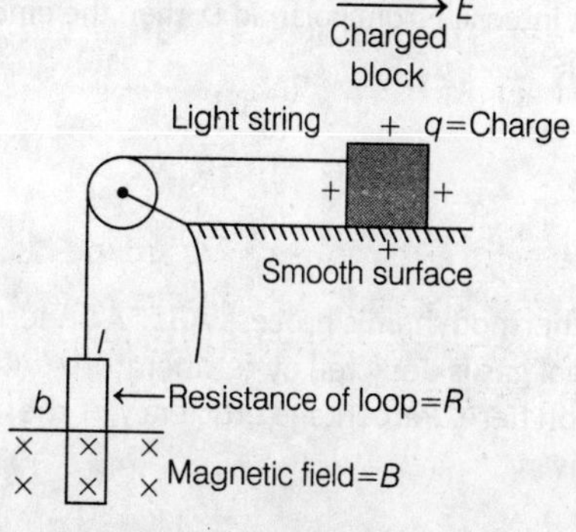

Power dissipated in the loop assuming it acquires steady state is (neglect gravity)

(a) $\frac{q^2E^2R}{Blb}$ (b) $\frac{q^2E^2R}{B^2l^2}$ (c) $\frac{qER}{B^2l^2}$ (d) $\frac{qER}{Blb}$

15. The figure shows a person dropping a stone at $t=0$ in a well with water surface at depth h. If temperature profile (not up to scale) of air in the well is as shown, find time after which the person hears the sound created. Given that speed of sound in air v is related to thermodynamic temperature T as $v=C\sqrt{T}$, where C is a constant.

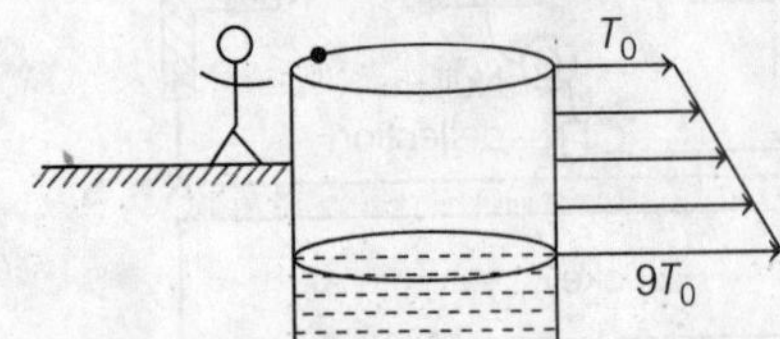

(a) $\sqrt{\frac{2h}{g}}+\frac{h}{2C\sqrt{T_0}}$ (b) $\sqrt{\frac{2h}{g}}+\frac{h}{C\sqrt{5T_0}}$

(c) $\sqrt{\frac{h}{g}}+\frac{h}{2C\sqrt{T_0}}$ (d) $\sqrt{\frac{h}{g}}+\frac{h}{C\sqrt{5T_0}}$

16. Consider the figure shown. Identical circular polaroids A, B, C and D are arranged coaxially about Z-axis. NO, PQ, RS and TU are respective axis of transmission of the polaroids.

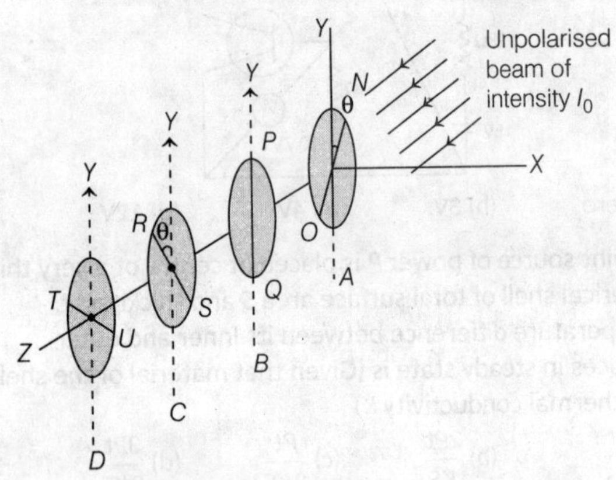

An unpolarised beam of intensity I_0 is incident on polaroid A. Polaroids B and D are crossed. If angle θ made by RS and NO with Y-axis is chosen to maximise emergent intensity from polaroid D, then the emergent intensity is

(a) $\frac{I_0}{27}$ (b) $\frac{2I_0}{27}$

(c) $\frac{I_0}{9}$ (d) $\frac{4I_0}{27}$

17. A cyclic thermodynamic process $ABCDA$ undergone by an ideal gas is depicted by temperature entropy (T-S) graph here. Percentage efficiency of the process is

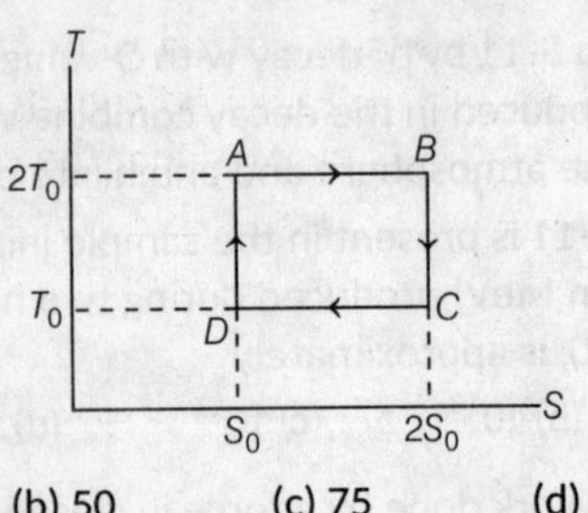

(a) 25 (b) 50 (c) 75 (d) 100

18. A solid cylinder of radius R is carrying current along its axis such that current density is directly proportional to distance r from its axis. The value of r for which magnetic flux density is same as that at a distance R from surface of the cylinder outside the cylinder is

(a) $\frac{R}{2}$ (b) $\frac{R}{\sqrt{2}}$ (c) $\frac{R}{3}$ (d) $\frac{R}{\sqrt{3}}$

19. Consider the arrangement shown. End A of rod AB is attached to centre of a disc of radius $2R$, while the rod is placed on a roller of radius R rolling with speed v as shown.

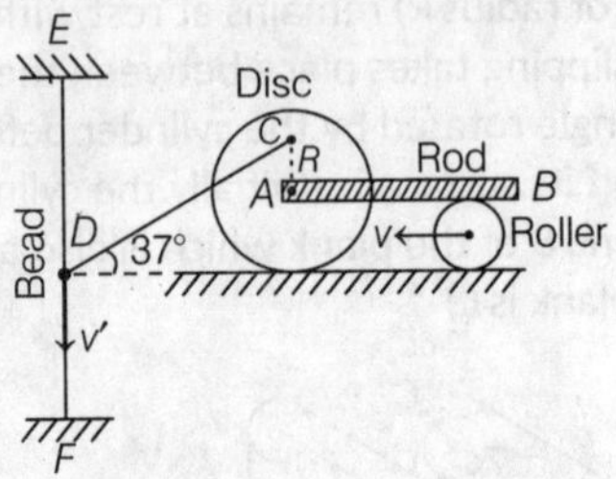

A rigid wire CD is attached to the disc to a point C instantly vertically R above centre A. Other end of the wire D is attached to a bead constrained to slide along a fixed vertical rod DF is moving with velocity v'. Find $\frac{v'}{v}$ at the instant shown when the wire is inclined at 37° with horizontal. Roller and disc are not slipping w.r.t. contact surfaces.

(a) 1 (b) 2 (c) $\sqrt{3}$ (d) 4

20. Electrons in an electron microscope are accelerated across potential difference V. Resolving power of the microscope is proportional to

(a) $\sqrt{V}$ (b) $V^{\frac{1}{2}}$ (c) V^2 (d) $V^{\frac{3}{2}}$

Section II Numerical Value Questions

21. A uniform solid cone is rotating freely about its axis with angular speed $\omega_0=\frac{13}{4}$ rad/s with an insect of same mass as that of the cone very near to the apex at its surface. The insect now begins to crawl slowly along surface of the cone following a straight path on the surface and finally reaching circumference of the cone's base as shown. If the insect comes to rest relative to the cone at final position, find angular speed (in rad/s) of the cone.

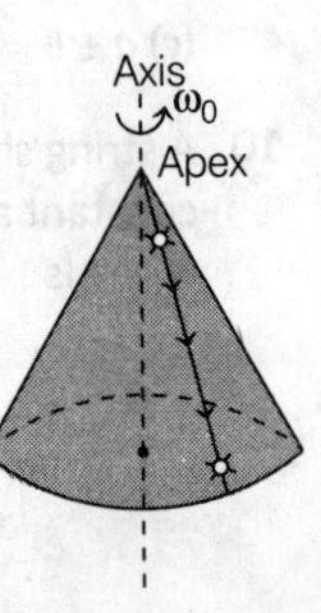

22. Calculate the approximate integral value of electric field amplitude (in V/m) in the radiation coming from a 100 W bulb at a distance of 3 m. Assume that the efficiency of the bulb is 2.5% and it is a point source.

23.

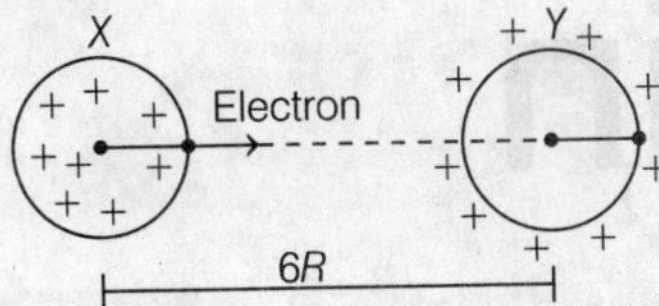

The figure here shows a system of two fixed spheres of charge namely X and Y. X is a uniform solid sphere of radius R and carrying charge Q while Y is a thin spherical shell of radius R and carrying charge $4Q$. Centres of the two spheres are separated by $6R$. An electron (having charge $-e$) is projected with minimum speed from surface of sphere X along the line joining centres of the spheres to make the electron reach surface of Y. Kinetic energy of electron just before it hits surface of Y is $\frac{xkQe}{R}$. Find x if $k = \frac{1}{4\pi\varepsilon_0}$.

24. The figure here shows a bead of mass $m = 1$ kg attached to a relaxed spring of length 80 cm and spring constant $k = 100$ N/m. The bead is constrained to slide on a smooth long vertical rod in a gravity free space. A particle of mass 1 kg moving with $v = 20$ m/s at 45° with horizontal strikes the bead and sticks to it. Find maximum displacement of bead (in cm) w.r.t. initial position.

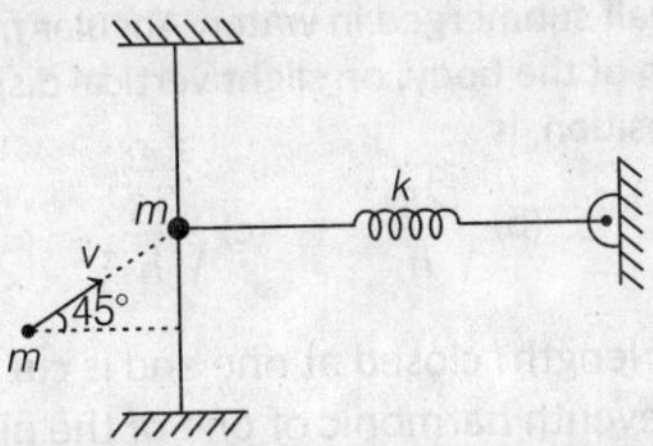

25. A vibration magnetometer has two identical bar magnets placed over each other such that they are mutually perpendicular and bisect each other. Time period of the combination is $\sqrt[4]{32}$ s. If one of the magnet is removed, find time period of the remaining magnet in second.

26. An amplitude modulated wave is given by V in volts $= (10 + 8\cos 1.57 \times 10^8 t)\cos 3.14 \times 10^{10} t$. If ratio of maximum amplitude to minimum amplitude of the wave is a while bandwidth of the signal is b MHz. Find $a + b$ if t is in seconds.

27. Find speed of image (in mm/s) of the object moving on axis of the mirror as shown. (Given that $\sqrt{7} = 2.64$)

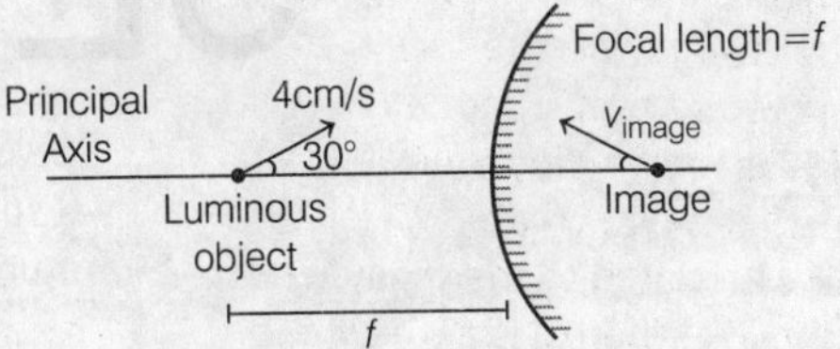

28. A planet of mass M and radius R has acceleration due to gravity g at height R above its surface. Energy needed to completely disassemble the planet against the gravitational pull amongst its constituent particles is $xMgR$. Find x.

29. A 0.1 L flask of glass contains some mercury. Determine the volume of air (in cc) in the flask if its volume remains constant at different temperatures. Given that coefficient of superficial expansion of glass is $\beta_F = 18 \times 10^{-6}$ per °C while coefficient of cubical expansion of mercury is $\gamma_M = 1.8 \times 10^{-4}$ per °C.

30. Find the thickness (in mm) of the wire. The main scale division is of 1 mm. In a complete rotation, the screw advances by 1 mm and the circular scale has 100 divisions.

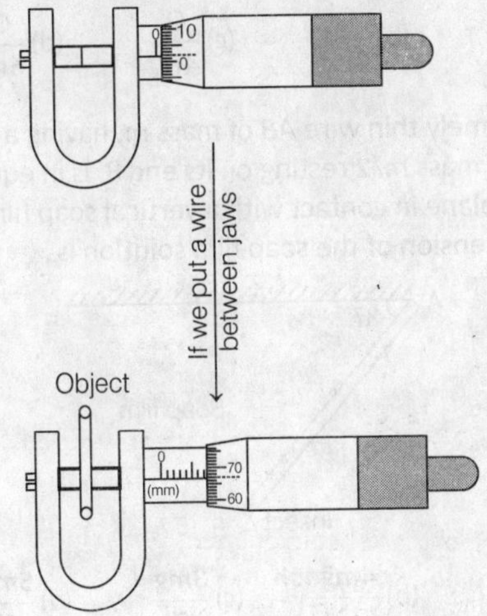

Answers

1 *(d)*	2 *(b)*	3 *(b)*	4 *(b)*	5 *(a)*	6 *(c)*	7 *(b)*	8 *(a)*	9 *(c)*	10 *(a)*
11 *(a)*	12 *(b)*	13 *(b)*	14 *(b)*	15 *(a)*	16 *(b)*	17 *(b)*	18 *(b)*	19 *(d)*	20 *(a)*
21 *0.75*	22 *4*	23 *2.7*	24 *60*	25 *2*	26 *59*	27 *13.2*	28 *2.4*	29 *85*	30 *7.65*

See detailed explanations on page no. 304

Knockout 07

JEE Main

Physics

Instructions See knockout 01

Section I Objective Type Questions

1. The figure here shows a semi-infinite uniformly charged wire with charge density λ along axis of an imaginary cone such that its end coincides with centre O of its base. A point charge Q is placed at apex of the cone. If electric flux through the base is zero, electric flux through the curved surface is

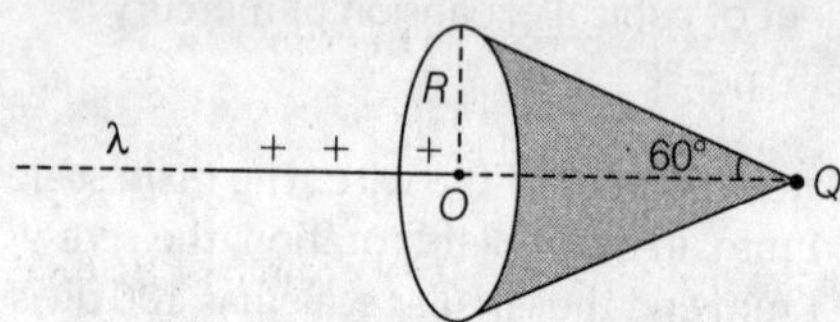

(a) $\frac{Q}{2\varepsilon_0}$ (b) $\frac{Q}{3\varepsilon_0}$ (c) $\frac{Q}{4\varepsilon_0}$ (d) $\frac{Q}{6\varepsilon_0}$

2. An extremely thin wire AB of mass m, having a very small insect of mass $m/2$ resting on its end B, is in equilibrium in vertical plane in contact with a vertical soap film as shown. Surface tension of the soap film solution is

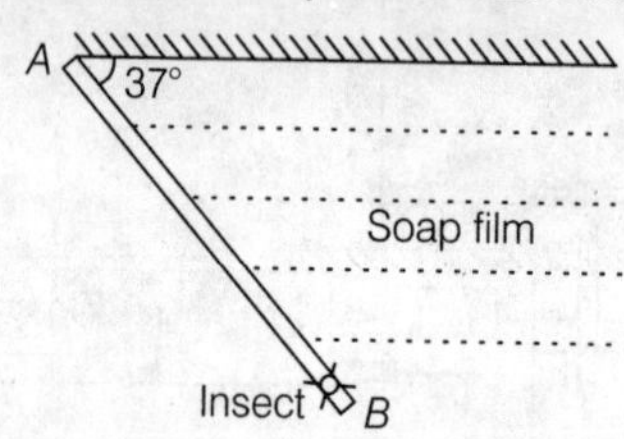

(a) $\frac{mg}{l}$ (b) $\frac{4mg}{5l}$ (c) $\frac{3mg}{5l}$ (d) $\frac{5mg}{3l}$

3. A wheel has eight equally spaced very thin spokes of length l. The wheel is rotating about axis OO' as shown with angular speed ω. It is desired to pass an arrow of length same as length of one spoke without hitting any spoke. Minimum velocity of the arrow, parallel to axis of the wheel, is

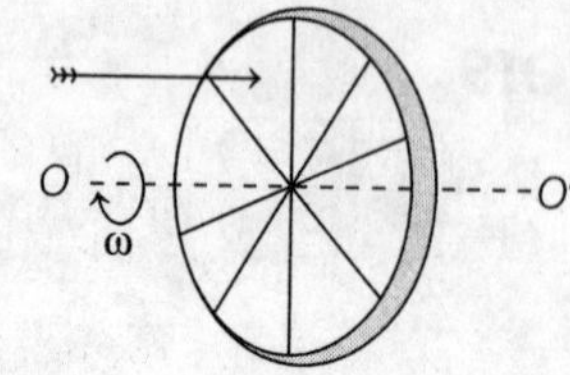

(a) $\frac{\omega l}{\pi}$ (b) $\frac{2\omega l}{\pi}$ (c) $\frac{\omega l}{4\pi}$ (d) $\frac{4\omega l}{\pi}$

4. The figure here shows a composite solid body

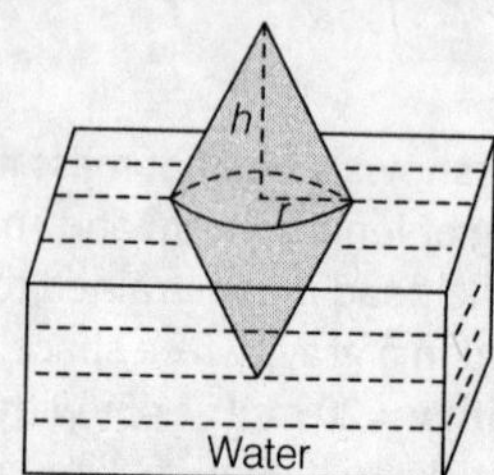

(made up by joining two identical cones of height h) floating half submerged in water. Angular frequency of oscillation of the body, on slight vertical displacement from shown position, is

(a) $\sqrt{\frac{g}{h}}$ (b) $\sqrt{\frac{2g}{h}}$ (c) $\sqrt{\frac{3g}{h}}$ (d) $2\sqrt{\frac{g}{h}}$

5. A tube of length l closed at one end is cut into equal halves. Seventh harmonic of one of the pieces is in unison with sixth overtone of the other. Radius of the tube, as per Rayleigh's suggestion, is nearest to

(a) $0.04\,l$ (b) $0.06\,l$ (c) $0.07\,l$ (d) $0.1\,l$

6. The figure shows sectional view of a parallel plate capacitor with semi-circular plates of area A and plate separation d. A semi-circularly sectioned dielectric slab completely filling the space with plates can rotate about axis perpendicular to the system and passing through O.

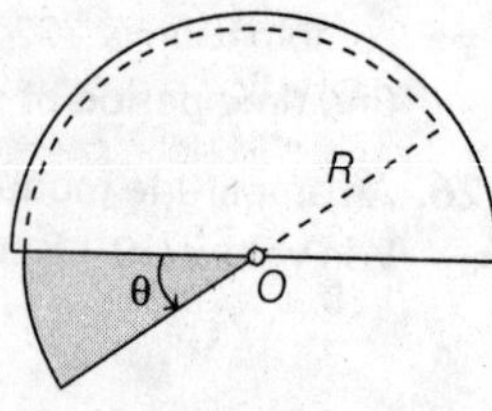

Torque required to slowly rotate the slab about O is (Given that potential difference across the capacitor is constant equal to V and dielectric constant of the slab is $K = 4\pi + 1$)

(a) $\frac{\varepsilon_0 AV^2}{d}$ (b) $\frac{2\varepsilon_0 AV^2}{d}$ (c) $\frac{3\varepsilon_0 AV^2}{d}$ (d) $\frac{4\varepsilon_0 AV^2}{d}$

7. Probability of survival of a nucleus of a radioactive sample between $t = t$ and $t = t + dt$ is

(a) λdt (b) $1 - \lambda \cdot dt$ (c) $\frac{1}{2}$ (d) Not defined

8.

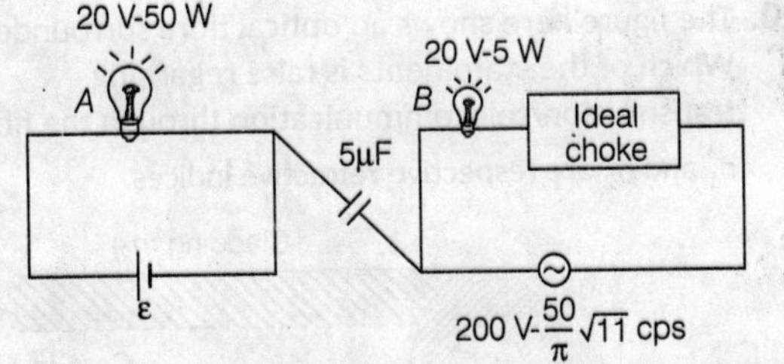

The two bulbs A and B in the circuit are consuming one-fourth power of design specification and same power as specified, respectively. Emf ε of the ideal DC source and inductance of the ideal choke respectively are

(a) 10 V, 2.4 H (b) 10 V, 80 H (c) 5 V, 2.4 H (d) 5 V, 80 H

9. The figure here shows a particle of mass m restricted to move along a linear nanobox (a box AB of length l of the order of nanometer).

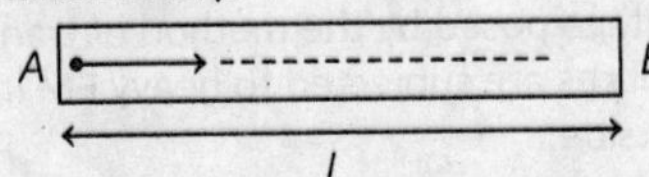

If allowed energies of the particle correspond to formation of standing matter wave with nodes at ends, difference in values of energy of particle corresponding to first and second excited state is (h = Planck's constant)

(a) $\frac{h^2}{8ml^2}$ (b) $\frac{3h^2}{8ml^2}$ (c) $\frac{5h^2}{8ml^2}$ (d) $\frac{h^2}{4ml^2}$

10.

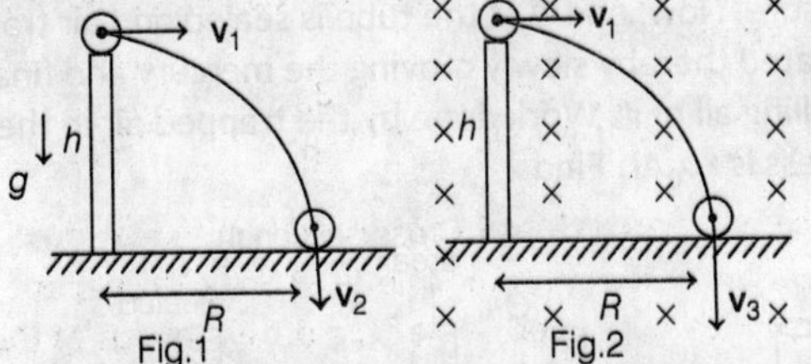

A charged particle projected from same height h has velocities as shown in figures. Fig. 1 and Fig. 2 correspond to motion in a uniform gravitational and uniform inward magnetic field. Specific charge on the particle, if horizontal ranges in both cases are equal, is ($\mathbf{v}_3 \perp \mathbf{v}_1$)

(a) $\frac{g}{B}\sqrt{\frac{|\mathbf{v}_3|}{|\mathbf{v}_1 - \mathbf{v}_2|}}$ (b) $\frac{g}{B}\frac{|\mathbf{v}_3|^2}{|\mathbf{v}_1 - \mathbf{v}_2|}$

(c) $\frac{g}{B|\mathbf{v}_2 - \mathbf{v}_1|}$ (d) $\frac{g|\mathbf{v}_3|}{B|\mathbf{v}_2 - \mathbf{v}_1|^2}$

11. Contribution in current flowing through a semiconductor rod due to electrons is $\frac{3}{4}$th of the total current. If drift speed of electrons is $\frac{11}{4}$ times that of holes at this temperature, ratio of concentration of holes to that of electron is

(a) 11 : 12 (b) 12 : 11 (c) 3 : 11 (d) 11 : 4

12. In the arrangement shown here end of a horizontal taut string is oscillated vertically sinusoidally creating a transverse wave of wavelength λ. Also, it is given that if the string (length l) is fixed at both ends, its minimum natural frequency is f. Minimum value of square root of amplitude A of the oscillator, for which an insect sitting on the string experiences weightlessness momentarily, is (Take, $g = \pi^2$)

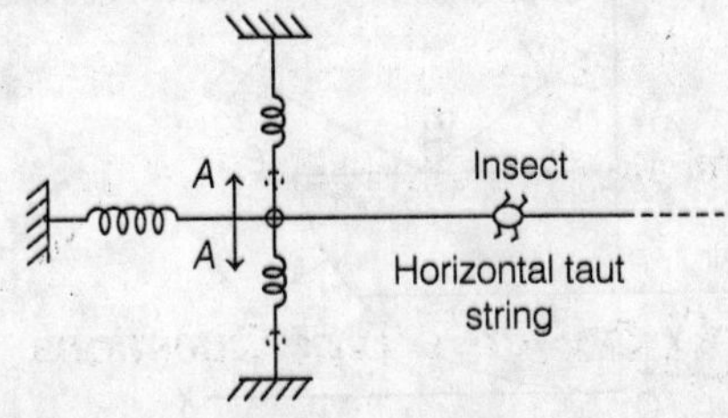

(a) $\frac{\lambda}{fl}$ (b) $\frac{\lambda^2}{2fl}$ (c) $\frac{\lambda}{4fl}$ (d) $\frac{2\lambda^2}{fl}$

13. A ring of radius $8R$ and mass $m_1 = 900$ kg has a particle of mass $m_2 = 100$ kg at a distance $6R$ from its centre on its axis. Both the ring and the particle are released from rest and move under mutual gravitational attraction. Speed of the particle as it crosses centre of the ring is

(a) $\sqrt{\frac{G}{R}}$ (b) $\sqrt{\frac{G}{2R}}$ (c) $\sqrt{\frac{2G}{R}}$ (d) $\sqrt{\frac{5G}{9R}}$

14. Fig. 1 shows a hollow cone of height double of its base radius placed on surface of a trolley accelerating horizontally. If there is sufficient friction to prevent slipping of the cone, minimum acceleration of the trolley, for which the cone topples, is $g \tan\theta$. If θ is also the minimum inclination angle for which a solid cone placed on a highly rough incline begins to topple, height of the solid cone in terms of its base radius R is

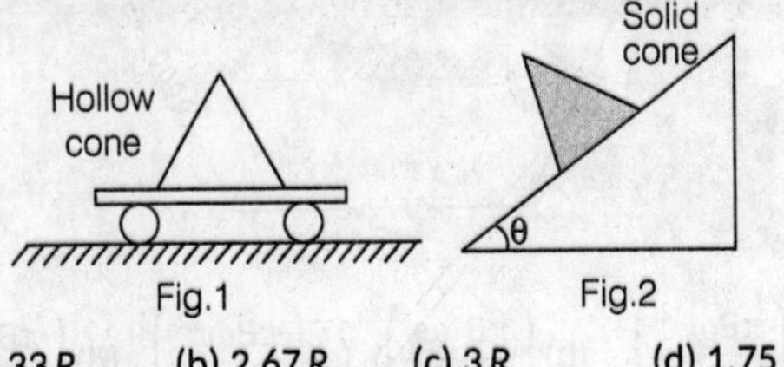

(a) 2.33 R (b) 2.67 R (c) 3 R (d) 1.75 R

15. Figure here shows cross-section of a cubical block of side L. The block is acted upon by two force couples distributed over its surface. Normal stress at the plane XX' passing through two parallel face diagonals and perpendicular to the cross-section shown is $\frac{F}{L^2}$. F is equal to

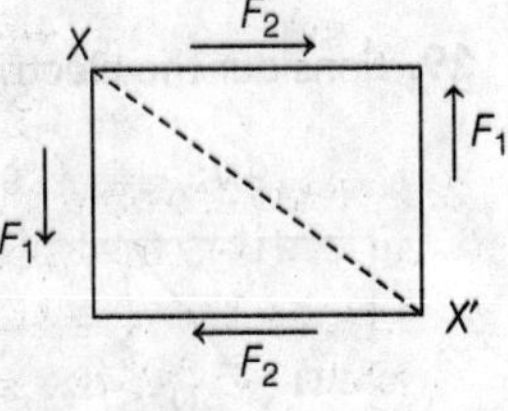

(a) $\sqrt{F_1F_2}$ (b) $F_1 + F_2$ (c) $\frac{F_1 + F_2}{2}$ (d) $\left(\frac{1}{F_1} + \frac{1}{F_2}\right)^{-1}$

16. A medium bound by the surfaces $y = y_0$, $y = x^2$ and Y-Z plane as shown is surrounded by air. An unpolarised beam incident on its interface AB with air at angle of incidence $\alpha = \tan^{-1}\frac{5}{3}$ is completely plane polarised on reflection. Another ray moving parallel to X-axis incident at interface OA at P will emerge in air from surface OB for minimum value of y equal to

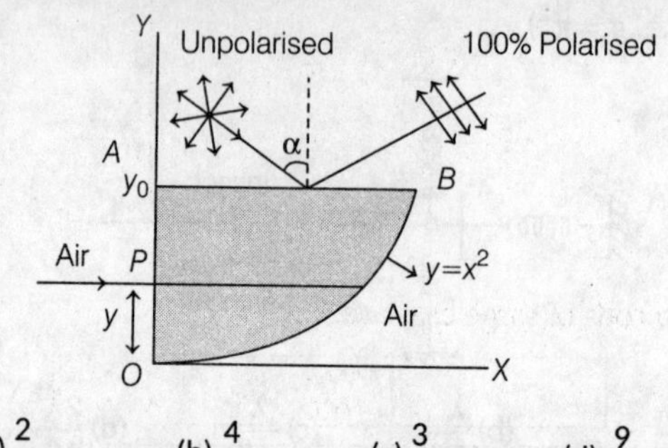

(a) $\frac{2}{3}$ (b) $\frac{4}{9}$ (c) $\frac{3}{5}$ (d) $\frac{9}{25}$

17. Hitomi satellite recently observed the Lymann alpha emission line of hydrogen like iron ion (atomic number equal to 26) from the Perseus galaxy cluster. Wavelength of the line is closest to (Take $R^{-1} = 912$ Å)

(a) 2 Å (b) 10 Å (c) 50 Å (d) 100 Å

18. A wire shaped as semi-circle of radius r is being rotated with constant angular speed ω by an external agent about axis PQ. Here ω is resonant angular frequency of the shown L-C-R circuit, in contact with the ends of the ring. If a uniform transverse magnetic field B exists in the region, maximum power delivered by the external agent is

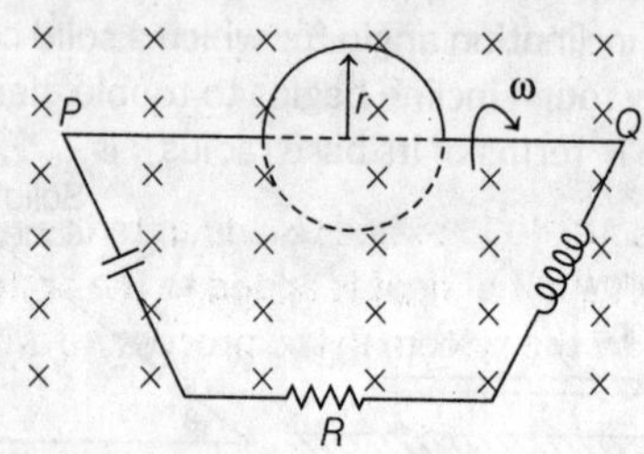

(a) $\left(\frac{\pi B\omega r^2}{2\sqrt{R}}\right)^2$ (b) $\left(\frac{\pi B^2\omega r}{2\sqrt{R}}\right)^2$ (c) $\left(\frac{\pi B\omega r^2}{\sqrt{2R}}\right)^2$ (d) $\left(\frac{\pi B^2\omega r}{\sqrt{2R}}\right)^2$

19. Consider the electrical circuit shown.

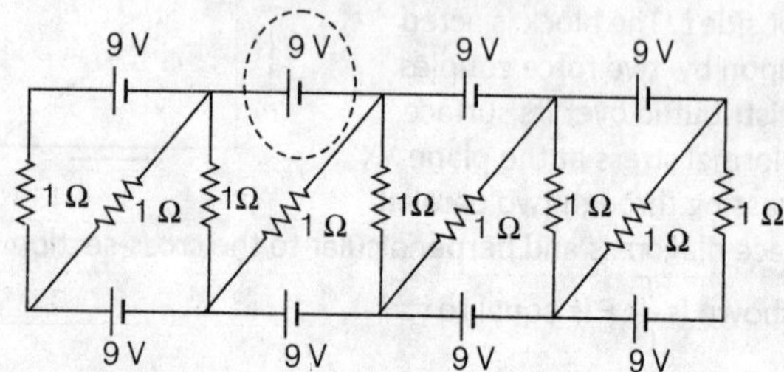

Power delivered by the cell enclosed in boundary to the circuit is

(a) 9 W (b) 18 W
(c) 27 W (d) zero

20. The figure here shows an optical fibre surrounded by air. Which of the statements is false regarding transmission/telecommunication through the fibre? n_1 and n_2 are respective refractive indices.

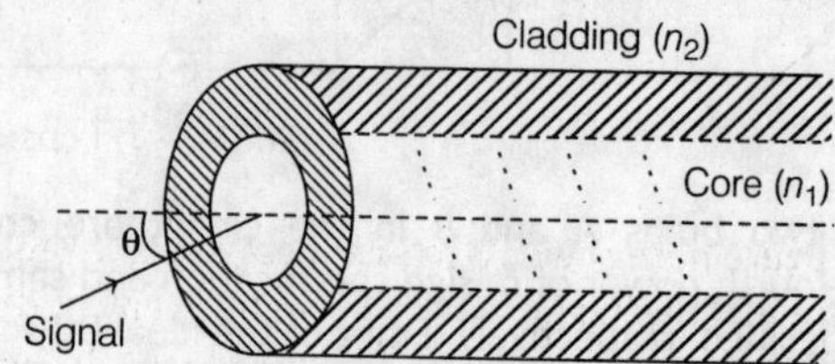

(a) Maximum acceptance angle θ for transmission of the signal is $\sin^{-1}\sqrt{n_1^2 - n_2^2}$

(b) Transmission signal has frequency range close to 10^8 to 10^9 MHz

(c) Disadvantage posed by the method of transmission is that optical fibres are subjected to heavy EM interference from outside.

(d) Advantage posed by the method of transmission is that transmission losses are extremely low.

Section II *Numerical Value Questions*

21. Mercury is filled in a U-tube PQ such that pressure in horizontal part of the tube is $2p_0$, where p_0 is atmospheric pressure. Now, end Q of the tube is sealed and air trapped is heated thereby slowly moving the mercury and finally expelling all of it. Work done by the trapped air in the process is xp_0AL. Find x

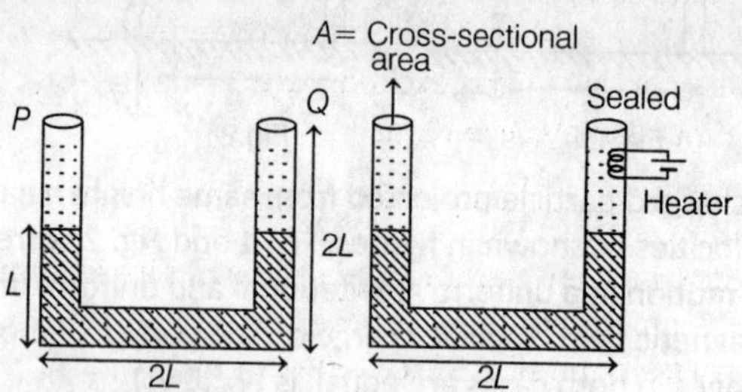

22. A ball of mass 100g strikes a stationary wedge of mass 0.4 kg while moving horizontally as shown. If velocity of the wedge just after its collision with the ball is 2 m/s and there is no friction anywhere, find impulse imparted by the ball to the wedge in N-s.

5 m/s

At rest

30°

23. Least count of main scale of a screw gauge is 0.5 mm. Find minimum number of divisions on its circular scale required to measure 10 μm diameter of a cylindrical wire.

24.

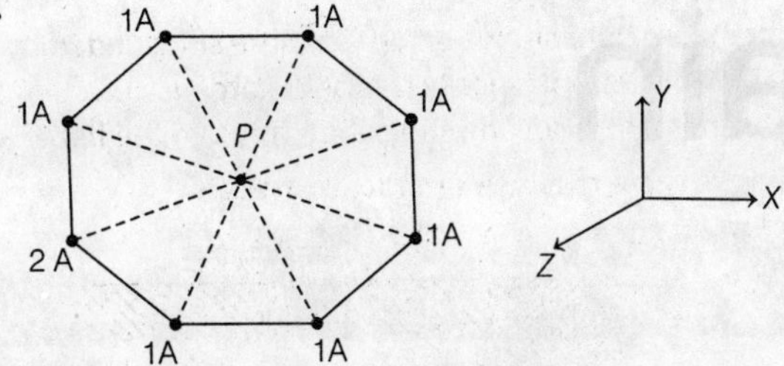

The figure here shows a regular octagon in X-Y plane with centre at P having distance $r = 4$ m from any of the vertices. Each vertex has an infinite wire each carrying current equal to 1 A in positive z-direction except one vertex having wire carrying current of 2 A in negative z-direction. Magnetic field at point P due to the given arrangement is $x \times 10^{-7}$ T. Find x.

25. Find reading of voltmeter (in V) in the circuit shown if base current is 8 μA.

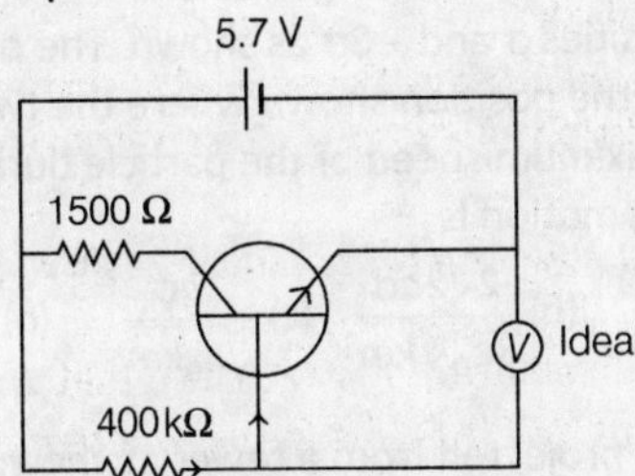

26. Electric field of an EM wave is given by $E = E_0 (1 + \cos \omega_1 t) \cos \omega_2 t$. The radiation is incident on a photosensitive cathode in a photoelectric cell. Maximum kinetic energy of the photoelectrons is observed to be equal to binding energy of He^+ in first excited state. Find work function of the metal in eV. Given that $\omega_1 = 5 \times 10^{15}\ s^{-1}$,

$\omega_2 = 2 \times 10^{16}\ s^{-1}$ and $h = 2\pi \times 6.6 \times 10^{-16}$ eV-s

27. Light is incident normally on a plane of slits separated by $d = 2$ mm. Interference is observed on a screen $D = 10$ m away from the slits. Space between plane of slits and screen is completely filled with a liquid of refractive index $n = 1.4$. A thin vacuum film of thickness $t = 0.2\,\mu$m is created in front of slit S_1. Maximum wavelength (λ) in vacuum for which a maxima is observed at point P exactly in front of slit S_1 is $x \times 10^{-7}$m.

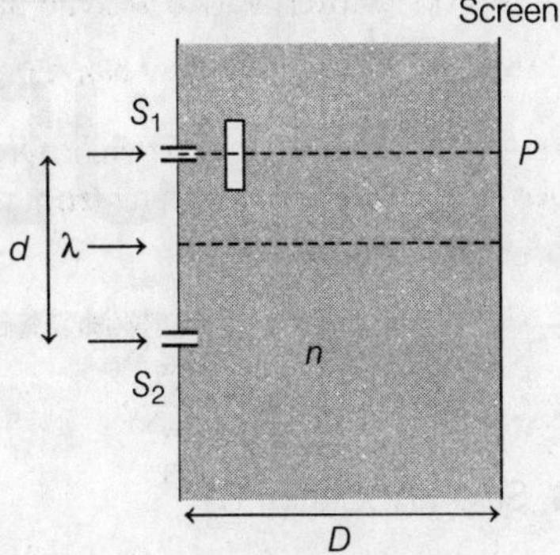

28. Two rods of same cross-section

are joined as shown. Respective lengths, thermal conductivities and temperatures of ends are shown in the figure. Find temperature of interface of the rods in °C.

29. Figure below shows two paths that may be taken by a gas to go from a state A to a state C.

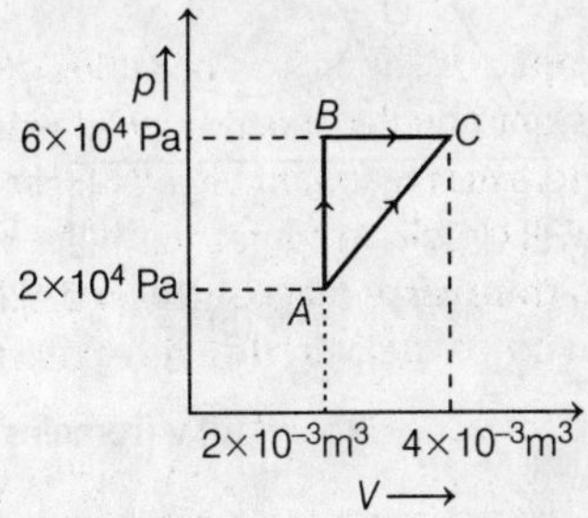

In process AB, 400 J of heat is added to the system and in process BC, 100 J of heat is added to the system. The heat absorbed by the system in the process AC will be $10x$ J. x is ......

30. Angular speed of a diatomic molecule of length l having atoms of masses $m_1 = 3m$ and $m_2 = 6m$ in second excited state is $\frac{h}{x\pi ml^2}$. Find x.

Answers

1 (c)	2 (b)	3 (d)	4 (c)	5 (c)	6 (b)	7 (b)	8 (a)	9 (c)	10 (c)
11 (a)	12 (c)	13 (b)	14 (b)	15 (c)	16 (b)	17 (a)	18 (a)	19 (c)	20 (c)
21 12	22 1.6	23 50	24 1.5	25 2.5	26 2.9	27 3.6	28 9.5	29 46	30 1.33

See detailed explanations on page no. 310

Knockout 08

JEE Main

Physics

Instructions See knockout 01

Section I *Objective Type Questions*

1. A smooth ring of mass m is placed on a table at rest. An insect of mass same as that of the ring is moving along the table with constant velocity v such that its line of motion is tangential to the ring. If the insect chooses to stick to the ring while grazing it, velocity of the insect instantly changes to

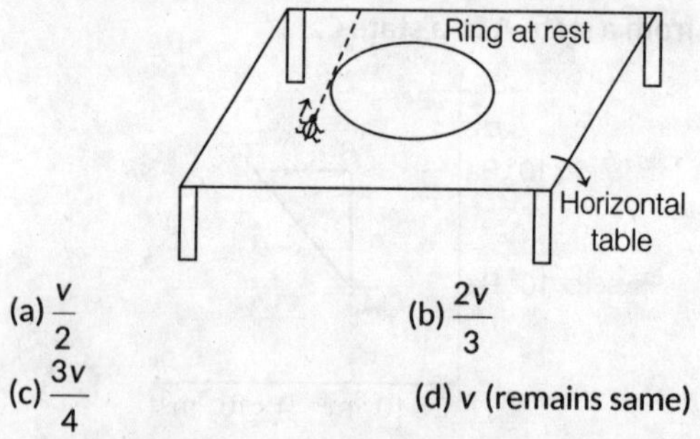

(a) $\frac{v}{2}$ (b) $\frac{2v}{3}$

(c) $\frac{3v}{4}$ (d) v (remains same)

2. A ray moving in a medium is incident on interface of the medium with air as shown in Fig. 1. Deviation δ suffered by the ray is plotted as function of i in Fig. 2.

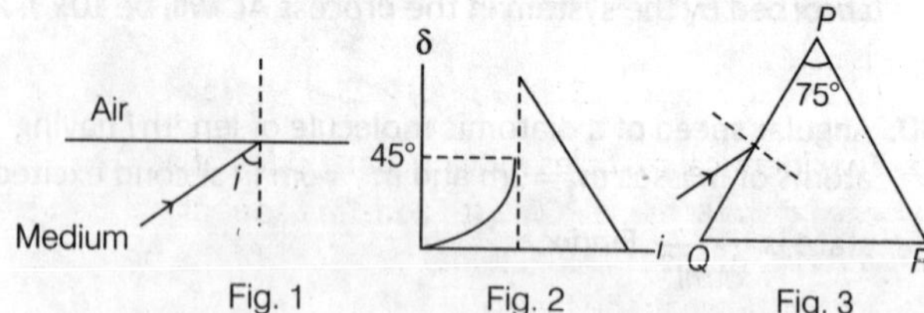

Fig. 1 Fig. 2 Fig. 3

A prism PQR made of the same medium has light incident on one of its face (PQ) as shown. Maximum possible deviation that can be suffered by the ray, if it emerges from face PR, is

(a) 45° (b) 60° (c) 90° (d) 75°

3. A metal ring of radius R is rotated about axis perpendicular to its plane and passing through its centre. Fractional increase (assuming small) in radius is proportional to

(a) R (b) R^2 (c) R^3 (d) R^4

4. In a gravity free space, a particle of mass m and charge q is connected to two springs of lengths in the ratio 1 : 2 obtained by cutting a spring of spring constant k in two pieces. Other ends of the two springs are attached to two infinite non-conducting sheets of charge densities σ and -3σ as shown. The particle is released in the position shown where the two springs are relaxed. Maximum speed of the particle during subsequent motion is

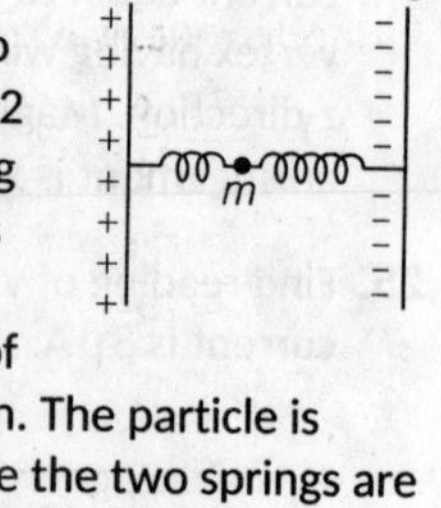

(a) $\frac{3q\sigma}{k\varepsilon_0}\sqrt{\frac{k}{m}}$ (b) $\frac{2\sqrt{2}q\sigma}{3\varepsilon_0\sqrt{km}}$ (c) $\frac{3q\sigma}{\sqrt{\varepsilon_0 km}}$ (d) $\frac{\sqrt{8}q\sigma}{3\sqrt{\varepsilon_0 km}}$

5. A particle is projected from a tower as shown in figure.

Statement - 1 Power delivered by gravity during flight is maximum when the particle is just about to strike the ground.

Statement - 2 Tangential acceleration of the particle is constant during flight.

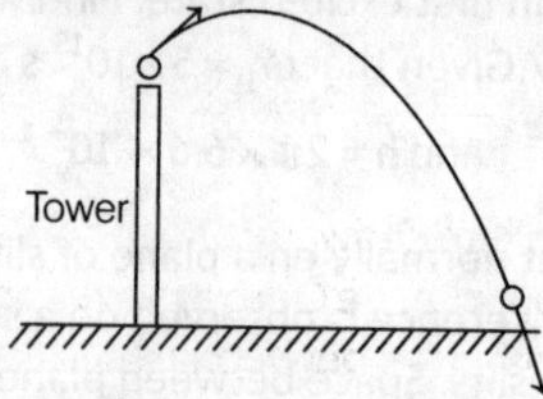

(a) Statement-1 is True, Statement-2 is False

(b) Statement-1 is True, Statement-2 is True

(c) Statement-1 is False, Statement-2 is False

(d) Statement-1 is False, Statement-2 is True

6. In the arrangement shown in figure, block A, block B and wedge C have same mass. All the surfaces are smooth and the string and the pulley are ideal. If on releasing

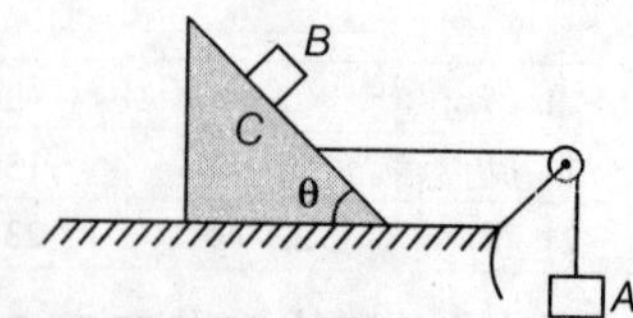

the system in position shown, block B does not slip with respect to wedge C, inclination θ of the wedge is

(a) $\sin^{-1}\frac{1}{3}$ (b) $\cos^{-1}\frac{1}{3}$ (c) $\tan^{-1}3$ (d) $\cot^{-1}3$

7. A wire of natural length l is clamped between two walls separated by l. On decreasing temperature of wire by ΔT_1 and ΔT_2, the wire vibrates as shown by using a vibrator.

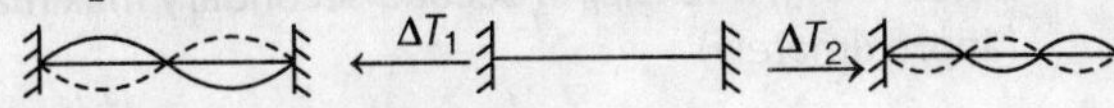

Ratio of ΔT_1 to ΔT_2 is equal to

(a) 3 : 2 (b) 2 : 3 (c) 4 : 9 (d) 9 : 4

8. Which of the following is dimensionless? Here, L = Inductance, I = Current, H = Height, E = Electric field, B = Magnetic field, ε_0 = Electrical permittivity μ_0 = Magnetic permeability, c = Speed of light in vacuum and ρ = Resistivity.

(a) $\frac{L^2I^4\mu_0 c}{H^6E^2B^2\varepsilon_0}$ (b) $\frac{L^2I^4\mu_0^2c^2}{H^4\rho^2E^2B^2\varepsilon_0^2}$

(c) $\frac{L^2I^4\mu_0}{H^4\rho^2E^2B^2\varepsilon_0^3c^2}$ (d) $\frac{L^3I^4\mu_0c^2}{H^4\rho^2E^2B^3\varepsilon_0^4}$

9. A radioactive sample with initial (at $t = 0$) number of nuclei N_0 is disintegrating into stable nuclei with half life T. In a lab, the same radioactive material is being produced at constant rate R. Variation of number of nuclei in the two processes is shown as function of time in the graph below. R is equal to

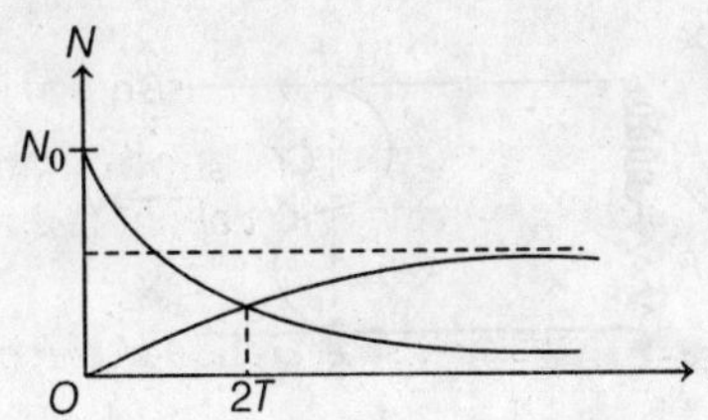

(a) $\frac{\ln 2^{\frac{1}{3}}\cdot N_0}{T}$ (b) $\frac{\ln\sqrt{2}\cdot N_0}{T}$ (c) $\frac{\ln 2\cdot N_0}{T}$ (d) $\frac{\ln 4\cdot N_0}{T}$

10. Consider the system shown in Fig. 1. Two identical capacitors of capacitance C are in series across a cell of emf E. Now, separation between plates of one of the capacitors is doubled while a dielectric of dielectric constant $k = 2$ is introduced, which completely fills the space between plates of the other capacitor as shown in Fig. 2.

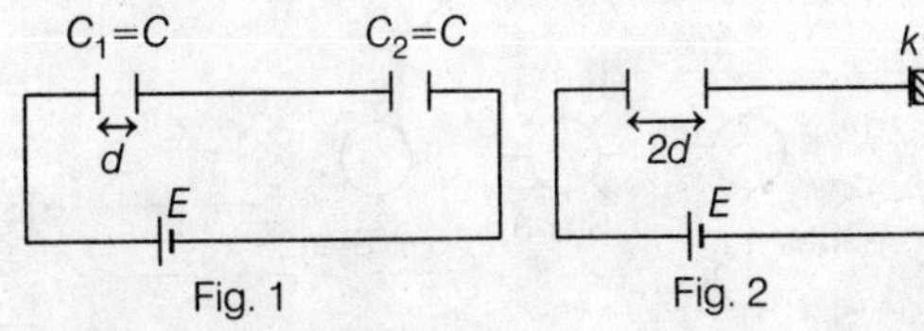

Magnitude of work done by the cell in the process is

(a) $\frac{CE^2}{2}$ (b) $\frac{CE^2}{5}$ (c) $\frac{CE^2}{10}$ (d) Zero

11. A steady current i flows through a cylindrical wire of cross-sectional area A, length l and conductivity σ. Steady state temperature of the wire is independent of

(a) A (b) l (c) σ (d) i

12. Variation of heat supplied Q with gas volume V is as shown for an isothermal process.

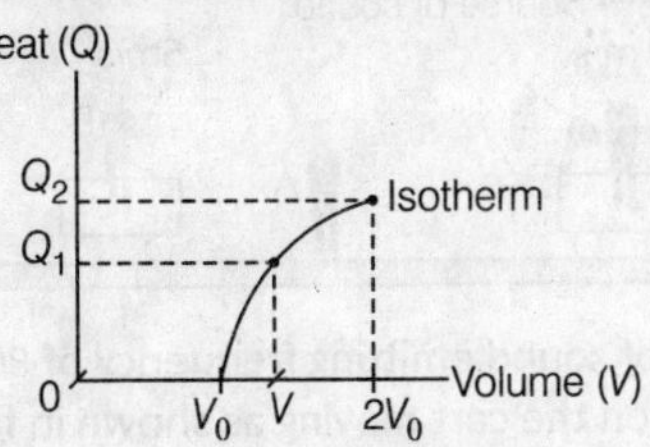

If $Q_2 = 2Q_1$, V as labelled in the indicator diagram is closest to

(a) $1.2\,V_0$ (b) $1.3\,V_0$ (c) $1.4\,V_0$ (d) $1.5\,V_0$

13. A circular disc of radius R is being rotated with constant angular speed ω. The lower surface of the disc is in contact with a layer of viscous liquid of thickness d and coefficient of viscosity η spread on a fixed surface. Torque required to maintain constant angular speed is equal to

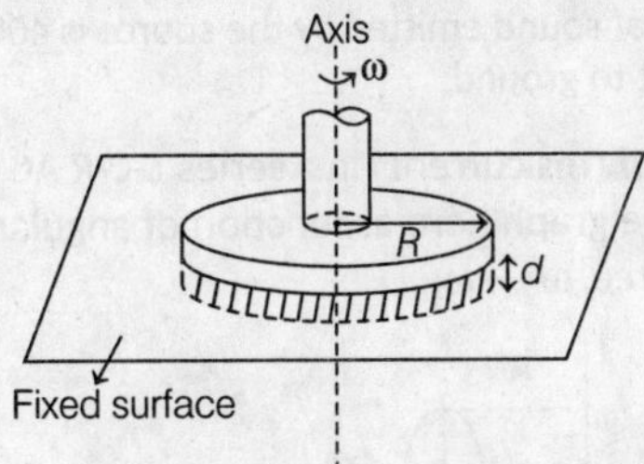

(a) $\frac{\pi\eta\omega R^4}{d}$ (b) $\frac{\pi\eta\omega R^4}{2d}$ (c) $\frac{\pi\omega R^4}{8\eta d}$ (d) $\frac{\pi\omega R^4}{16\eta d}$

14. If height of receiver and transmitter tower are both equal to H, range is R. To achieve same range with a transmitter tower of height $\frac{H}{4}$, receiver tower should have height

(a) $2H$ (b) $1.5H$ (c) $2.25H$ (d) $4H$

15. Two identical particles moving along sides of an equilateral triangle PQR with constant speeds collide at vertex Q of the triangle. Initial positions of the particles are as shown in the figure.

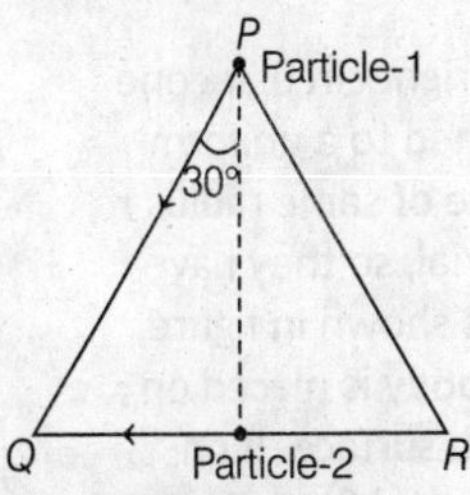

Higher of the de-Broglie wavelengths associated with the particles is λ. If the particles collide perfectly inelastically, de-Broglie wavelength of the composite body formed on collision is

(a) $\frac{\lambda}{\sqrt{7}}$ (b) $\frac{2}{\sqrt{7}}\lambda$ (c) $\sqrt{7}\lambda$ (d) $\frac{\sqrt{7}\lambda}{2}$

16. The figure here shows three men named Ajinkya (A), Bhuvneshwar (B) and Cheteshwar (C).

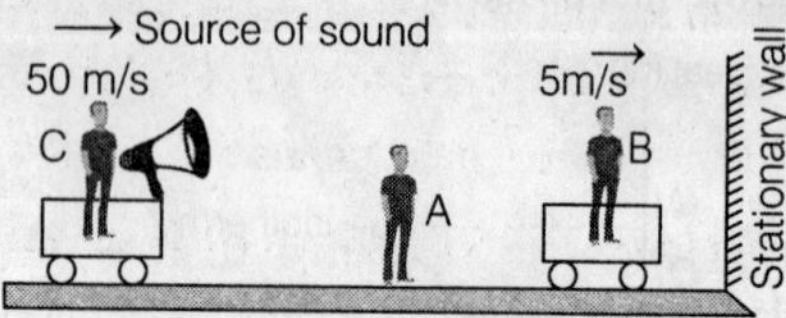

A source of sound emitting frequency of 300 Hz is mounted on the cart moving as shown in figure on which Cheteshwar is standing, while Ajinkya is standing at rest on the ground. Bhuvneshwar is also located on a cart moving as shown. Choose the **incorrect** statement for the situation shown considering speed of sound in air equal to 350 m/s.

(a) Ajinkya observes no beats.
(b) Bhuvneshwar observes ten beats in every second.
(c) Wavelength of reflected sound as observed by Cheteshwar is 1 m.
(d) Speed of sound emitted by the source is 400 m/s with respect to ground.

17. Variation of rms current I in a series L-C-R AC circuit is given in the graph here as function of angular frequency ω of the source. $\omega_2 - \omega_1$

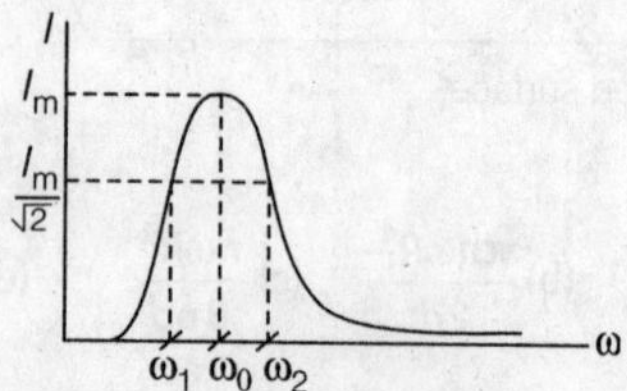

(a) does not change if ω_0 is increased
(b) may increase if ω_0 is decreased
(c) must increase if ω_0 is increased
(d) must decrease if ω_0 is increased

18. A Zener diode undergoes breakdown for electric field of 1.2 MV/m at the depletion region of p-n junction. If width of depletion region is 2 μm, reverse biased potential for breakdown to occur is

(a) zero (b) 2.4 V (c) 0.6 V (d) 2.4×10^{-6} V

19. A uniform solid right circular cone of radius r is joined to a uniform solid hemisphere of same radius r and same material, so they have common face as shown in figure. The composite body is placed on perfectly smooth surface. If on applying a horizontal force F on apex of cone, centre of base of cone C accelerates with $\frac{F}{m}$ (m is mass of the composite body), semi vertex angle θ of the cone is

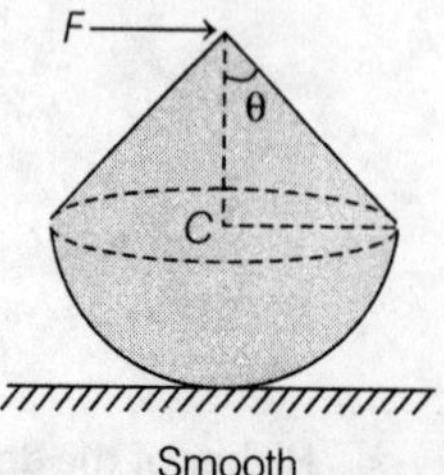

(a) 30° (b) $\tan^{-1}\frac{3}{8}$
(c) 45° (d) 60°

20. If intensity of central maxima in Fraunhoffer's diffraction pattern is I_0, intensity of second secondary maxima is (approximately)

(a) I_0 (b) $\frac{I_0}{4}$
(c) $\frac{I_0}{22}$ (d) $\frac{I_0}{61}$

Section II *Numerical Value Questions*

21. A metal wire PQS of negligible resistance is composed of two semicircular segments each of radius r. The wire is in contact with a pair of smooth resistanceless rails having its ends connected by a series combination of inductor and resistor as shown in figure. The region has a uniform transverse magnetic field B. PQS is being moved with constant speed v. Current in inductor is zero at $t = 0$. Rate of consumption of energy by inductor is maximum at $t = \frac{aL}{R}$ and is equal to $\frac{bE^2}{R}$. If a and b are constants and $E = Bvr$, find $a + b$.

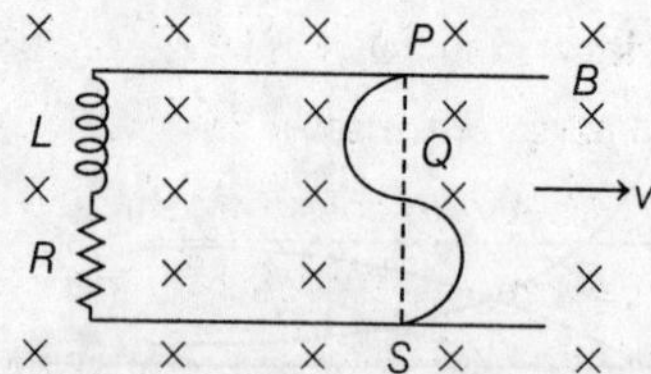

22. In a tertiary star system comprising of three identical stars having mass same as that of Sun and nearer stars having separation of one astronomical unit, two stars revolve about a central star (as shown). If time period of revolution of Earth around Sun is T, time period of revolution of both stars around the central star is $\frac{2T}{\sqrt{x}}$. Find x.

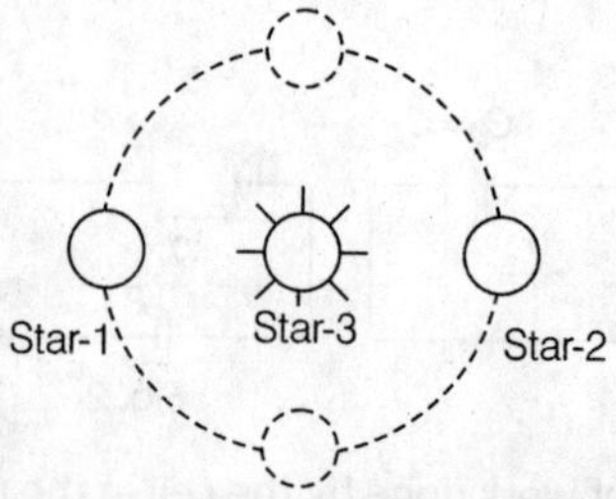

23. Consider the figure shown. The disc is rolling without slipping with velocity of CM equal to $\sqrt{3}$ m/s. A rod PQ is connected with the disc at point Q, instantly mid-way between centre and top of the disc. End P of the rod is attached to small ring constrained to slide along a vertical rod. At the instant shown, find velocity of the ring in m/s.

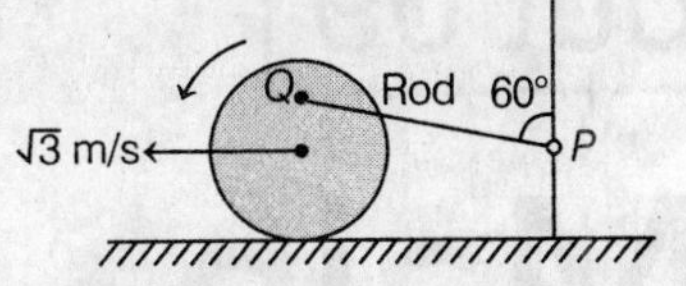

24. If two soap bubbles of total surface areas 2 cm^2 and 6 cm^2 combine isothermally in vacuum to form a bigger bubble having surface energy same as that of a square film of same soap solution, find side of square film in cm.

25.

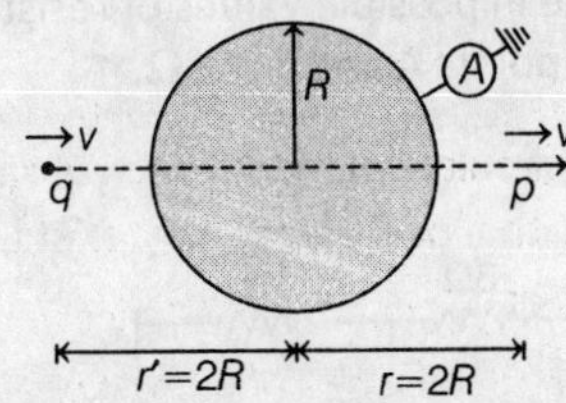

A grounded metal ball of radius R has a point change q and dipole of dipole moment p near it, both at a distance of $2R$ as shown. If both point charge and dipole start moving with velocity v as shown, find current (in A) registered by the ammeter. (Take $q = 1$ C, $p = 5$ C-m, $R = 0.5$ m, $v = 2$ m/s)

26. Three particles A (neutral, mass $= m$), B(charge $= q$, mass $= m$) and C (charge $= q$, mass $= 2m$) are projected from surface of a planet with uniformly charged surface. If ranges of A and B are R and $\frac{R}{2}$ respectively, find x if range of C is $\frac{2R}{x}$ (All are projected with same speed at same angle)

27. Average electric energy density of an EM wave with electric field amplitude E_0 is given by $\frac{x\,\varepsilon_0 E_0^2}{4}$. What is value of x?

28. A thin layer of sand on floor is piled to make a cone of maximum possible height. If coefficient of friction between sand particles is $\mu = \sqrt{3}$, find maximum height (in m) of the cone if base radius of the cone is $\sqrt{3}$ m.

29. Find momentum of a system of three particles moving in X-Y plane as shown in CM frame.

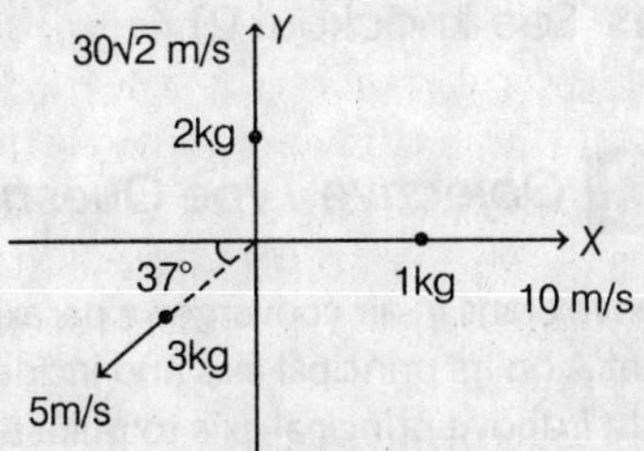

30. Ranges from small holes P (circular) and Q (square) of radius r and side l respectively are same. Find ratio of volume flow rates from the circular hole to the square hole given that

$$\frac{r}{l} = \frac{1}{2^{\frac{1}{4}}}$$

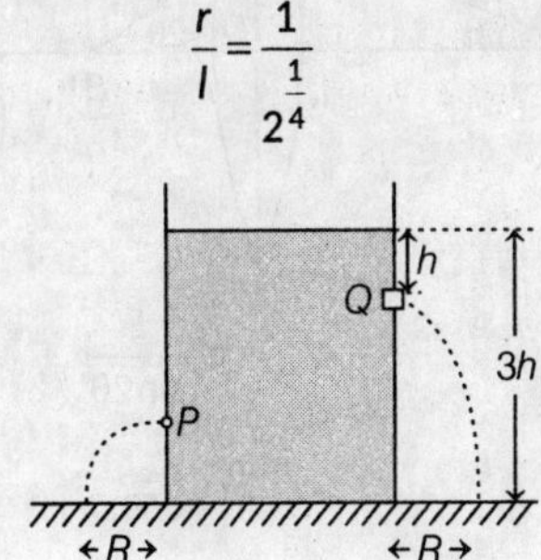

Answers

1 (b)	2 (b)	3 (b)	4 (b)	5 (a)	6 (d)	7 (d)	8 (c)	9 (a)	10 (c)
11 (b)	12 (c)	13 (b)	14 (c)	15 (a)	16 (d)	17 (b)	18 (b)	19 (a)	20 (d)
21 4.69	22 5	23 4.5	24 2	25 11	26 3	27 1	28 3	29 0	30 3.14

See detailed explanations on page no. 315

Knockout 09

JEE Main

Physics

Instructions See knockout 01

Section I Objective Type Questions

1. A thin convex lens in air converges a paraxial ray coming from point A on its principal axis and incident at point C on it at height L above principal axis to point B on the axis as shown in figure. Focal length of the lens in terms of angles made by the ray with the axis is

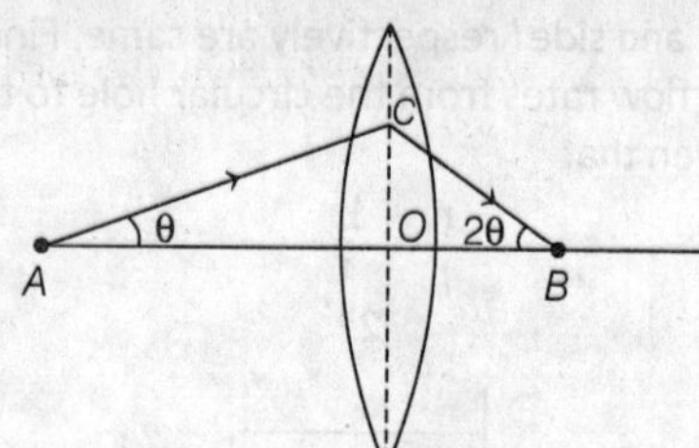

(a) $\frac{L}{\theta}$ (b) $\frac{L}{\sin 2\theta}$
(c) $\frac{L}{3\theta}$ (d) $\frac{L}{\sqrt{5\theta}}$

2. If SI unit of mass, length and time are tripled, which of the following quantities will have its unit unaltered?
(a) Mechanical power
(b) Universal gravitational constant
(c) Reynold's number
(d) All the three quantities

3. A uniformly charged horizontal ring is rotating about its vertical axis such that each particle of the ring is moving with linear speed equal to pc. Here, p is a constant and c is speed of light in vacuum. Which of the following is correct relation between electric field E and magnetic field B at shown axial point P?

P
45°

(a) $Ep = Bc$ (b) $Ec = Bp$
(c) $Ec^2 = Bp$ (d) $Ep^2 = Bc$

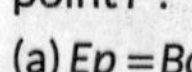

4. Difference in possible values of resistance of the circuit between points A and B is x Ω.

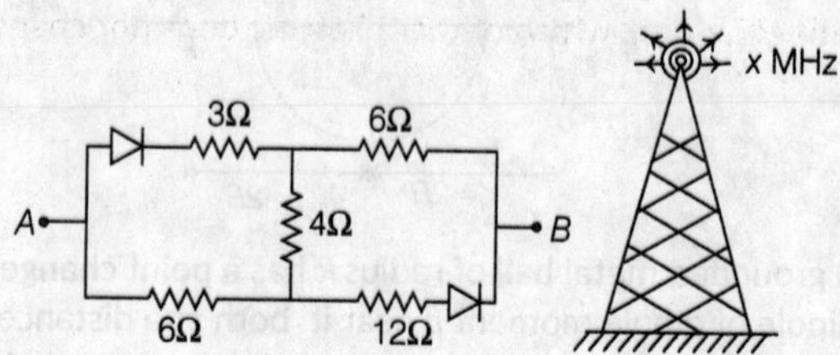

Minimum length of antenna required to transmit a radio signal of frequency x MHz is
(a) 30 m (b) 15 m (c) 7.5 m (d) 5 m

5. A sphere is projected with momentum p in a gravity free space in a medium having coefficient of viscosity $\eta = \frac{1}{2\pi}$. Distance moved by the sphere before it stops is
(a) $\frac{p}{r}$ (b) $\frac{3p}{5r}$ (c) $\frac{p}{3r}$ (d) infinite

6. A light balloon filled with gas of density ρ is tied to a long vertical light string of length l attached to ground as shown in figure.

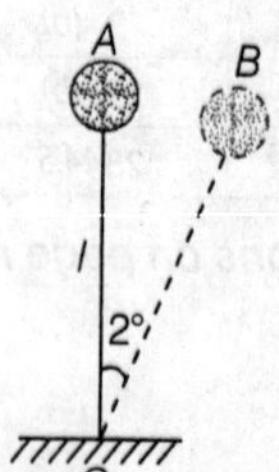

The string attached to balloon is now slightly displaced (by 2°) from position A to position B and released. Given that density of air is 3ρ, then time taken by the balloon to return to position A is close to
(a) $\pi\sqrt{\frac{l}{4g}}$ (b) $\pi\sqrt{\frac{l}{8g}}$ (c) $\pi\sqrt{\frac{2l}{g}}$ (d) $\frac{\pi}{2}\sqrt{\frac{l}{4g}}$

7. The figure shows a simple pendulum of length $5l$ held at rest in position A shown. A peg P is fixed at a depth $4l$ directly below the pendulum's support point O. θ in position A is such that the bob is just able to execute vertical looping about the peg after it is released at A and it reaches position B. Acceleration of the bob just after release is

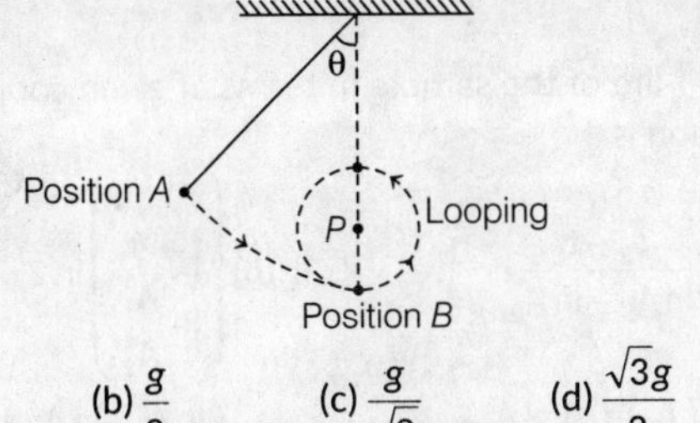

(a) zero (b) $\frac{g}{2}$ (c) $\frac{g}{\sqrt{2}}$ (d) $\frac{\sqrt{3}g}{2}$

8. The figure here shows a circular metal ring of radius r with a cut/gap of dimension d. Thickness of the ring is t. On heating the ring, which of the following does not change?

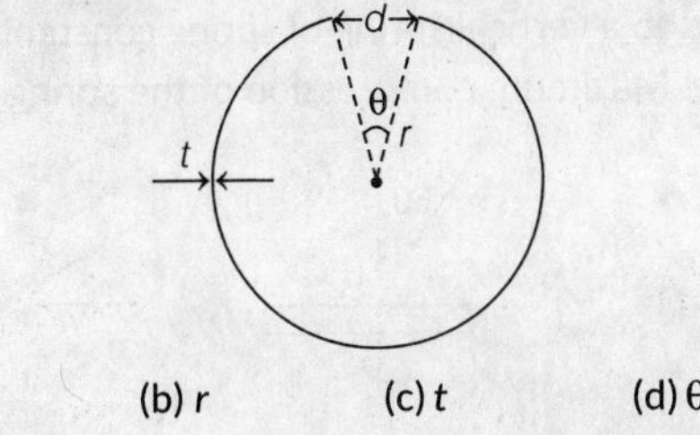

(a) d (b) r (c) t (d) θ

9. In a set up with two coherent sound sources S_1 and S_2 of respective powers P_1 and P_2, intensity observed at point P is 3 times the intensity of S_1. If speed of sound in air is 336 m/s and frequency of sound emitted by the two sources is 112 Hz, $\frac{P_1}{P_2}$ is equal to

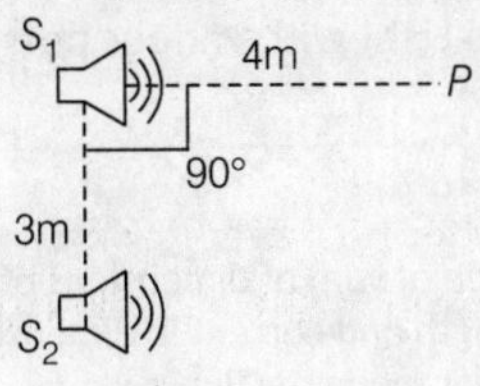

(a) $\frac{4}{5}$ (b) $\frac{5}{4}$ (c) $\frac{16}{25}$ (d) $\frac{4}{25}$

10. Consider the circuit shown

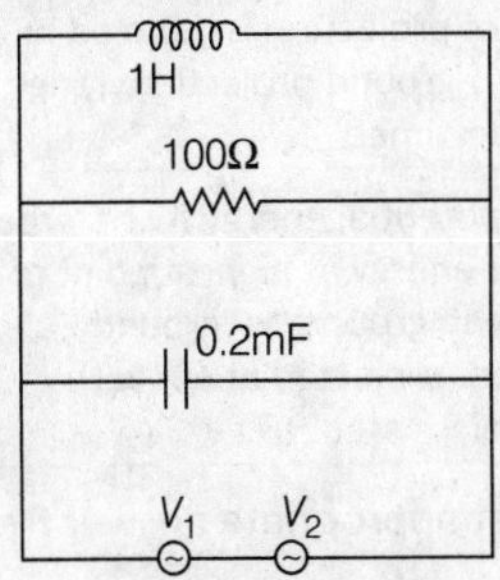

Current supplied by the combination of AC sources as function of time is (Given that $V_1 = 100 \sin \omega t$ volt, $V_2 = 100 \cos \omega t$ volt and $\omega = 100$ rad/s)

(a) $2 \sin \omega t$ (b) $2 \cos \omega t$

(c) $2\sqrt{2} \sin\left(\omega t + \frac{\pi}{4}\right)$ (d) $2\sqrt{2} \cos\left(\omega t + \frac{\pi}{4}\right)$

11. If air in a YDSE set-up is pumped out creating vacuum, fringe width

(a) will increase

(b) will decrease

(c) will remain unchanged

(d) may increase or decrease depending on wavelength of the source

12. To what approximate radius would earth (mass $\approx 6 \times 10^{24}$ kg) have to be compressed for it to become a black hole?

(a) 1 cm (b) 1 mm

(c) 1 μm (d) 1 pm

13. Two thin discs of mass $2m$, radius R and mass m, radius $2R$ are welded co-axially together forming a composite body as shown in figure. Two threads wound on the periphery of the two discs are pulled by equal and opposite force (F each) as shown in figure.

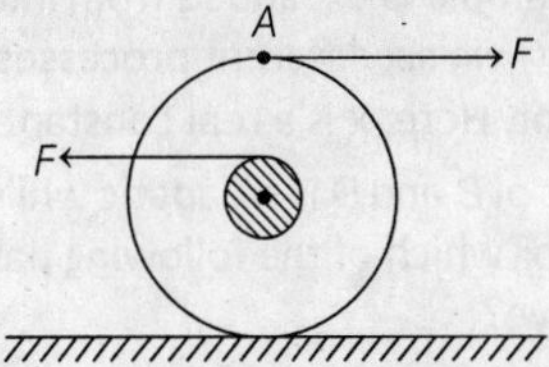

Assuming that friction is sufficient to prevent any slipping, initial acceleration of top point A of the body is (the body is initially at rest)

(a) $\frac{F}{3m}$ (b) $\frac{2F}{3m}$

(c) $\frac{4F}{15m}$ (d) $\frac{2F}{15m}$

14. Radius r of a circular ring placed in uniform transverse magnetic field is changing with time t as shown in the graph here.

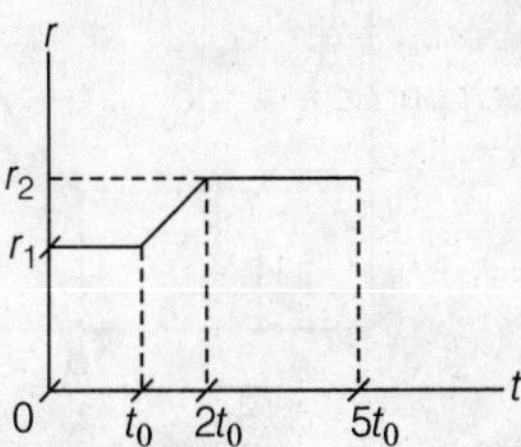

Which of the following graphs represents variation of induced emf ε as function of time t ?

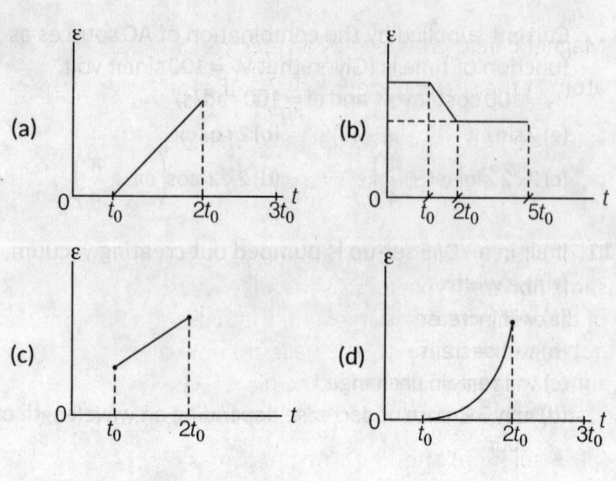

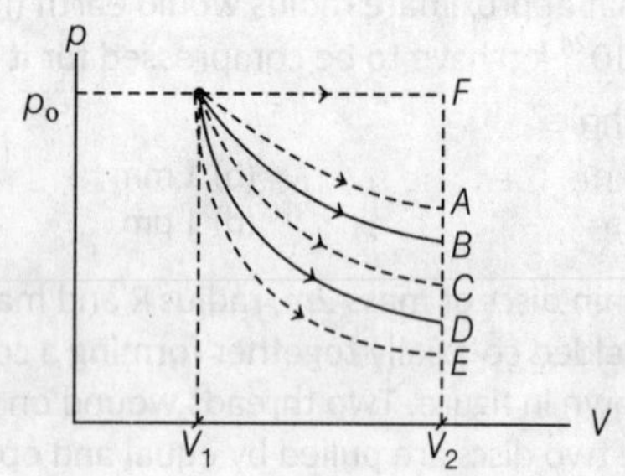

15.

An ideal gas sample is expanded from initial volume V_1 to final volume V_2 *via* six different processes/paths given by pV^x = constant. Here, x is a real constant. One of the processes out of B and D is adiabatic while the other is isothermal. For which of the following paths molar specific heat is negative?

(a) A (b) C
(c) E (d) F

16. A uniform rod of length l is hinged at a point O distant x from centre of mass of the rod as shown in figure. Initially the rod is hanging in equilibrium. On slight angular displacement, it oscillates with time period T, which depends on x as shown by the empirical curve here. A given time period T_0 is possible for two values of x; $a = \frac{l}{4}$ and b. b is equal to

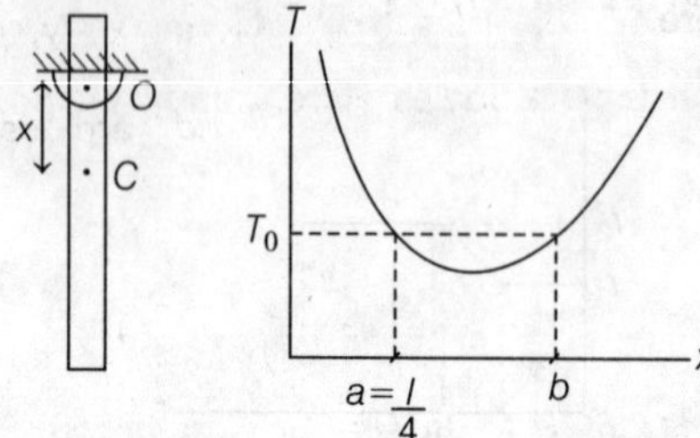

(a) $\frac{l}{3}$ (b) $\frac{l}{2}$ (c) $\frac{5l}{8}$ (d) $\frac{2l}{3}$

17. Graph here shows ln of activity of a radioactive material as function of time t

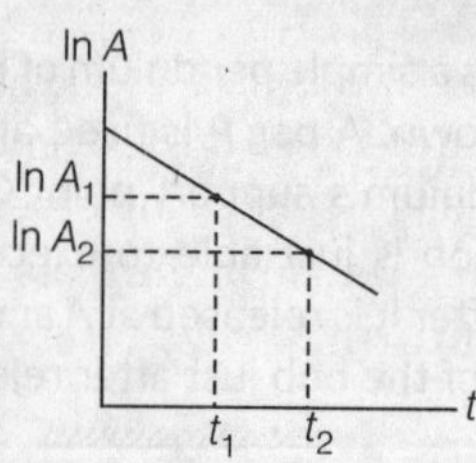

Half-life of the sample in terms of given coordinates of the graph is

(a) $\frac{t_2 - t_1}{\ln A_1 - \ln A_2}$ (b) $\left(\frac{t_2 - t_1}{\ln \frac{A_1}{A_2}}\right) \ln 2$

(c) $\left(\frac{t_2 - t_1}{\ln 2}\right) \ln \frac{A_1}{A_2}$ (d) $\left(\frac{\ln A_1 - \ln A_2}{t_2 - t_1}\right) \cdot \frac{1}{\ln 2}$

18. A particle of mass m moving with speed u collides elastically with a smooth stationary pan of mass $(M = 2m)$ attached to a vertical spring of spring constant k as shown in figure. Maximum compression of the spring is

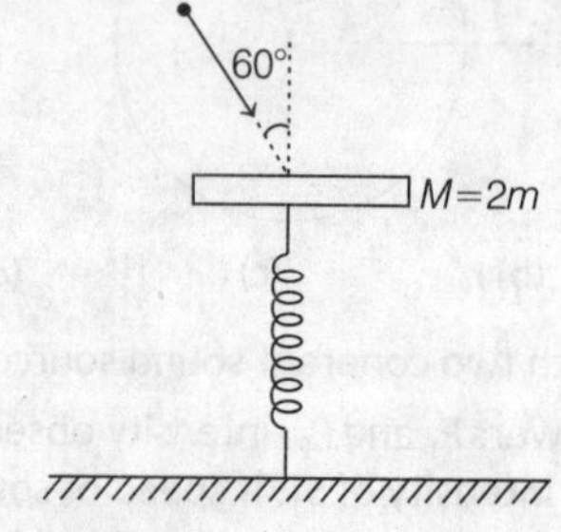

(a) $\sqrt{\frac{2m}{k}}\frac{v_0}{3}$ (b) $\sqrt{\frac{m}{k}}\frac{v_0}{3}$ (c) $\sqrt{\frac{2m}{k}}v_0$ (d) $\sqrt{\frac{m}{k}}v_0$

19. Match entries in List I with various possible values of x given in List II

	List I		List II
A.	Magnitude of sum of dimensions of mass, length and current in dimensional formula for magnetic flux is x	(i)	$x = 1$
B.	Work done by gravity becomes x times if path length is doubled, keeping initial and final points same	(ii)	$x = 2$
C.	If speed of projection is doubled in ground-to-ground projection, range becomes x times	(iii)	$x = 3$
D.	Ratio of potential energy (w.r.t. ground) to kinetic energy at highest point of a projectile in ground-to- ground projection, projected at 60° with horizontal	(iv)	$x = 4$

Choose the most appropriate answer from the options given below:

(a) A-(ii) B-(iv) C-(i) D-(iii) (b) A-(ii) B-(i) C-(iv) D-(iii)
(c) A-(iii) B-(iv) C-(i) D-(ii) (d) A-(iv) B-(ii) C-(i) D-(iii)

20. When the energy of the incident radiation is increased by 20%, the kinetic energy of the photoelectrons emitted from a metal surface increases from 0.5 eV to 0.8 eV. The work function of the metal is

(a) 0.65 eV (b) 1.0 eV (c) 1.3 eV (d) 1.5 eV

Section II *Numerical Value Questions*

21. A rectangle shaped double edged blade of negligible weight floats on a liquid of surface tension $T = \frac{1}{140}$ N/m. Its internal and external perimeters are 60 cm and 80 cm, respectively. Find minimum force (in mN) required to lift the blade from the liquid's surface.

22. A triangular surface PQR has vertices given by $P(2\text{m}, 0, 0)$, $Q(0, 1\text{m}, 0)$ and $R(0, 0, 1\text{m})$. Find electric flux (in V-m) crossing the surface PQR, if electric field in the region is $\hat{i} + 2\hat{j} + 3\hat{k}$ N/C.

23. Force applied F on the system shown here is the maximum force such that sliding does not occur between the blocks P and Q. If respective masses and friction coefficients are shown in the figure, acceleration of block P is $x\mu g$. Find x.

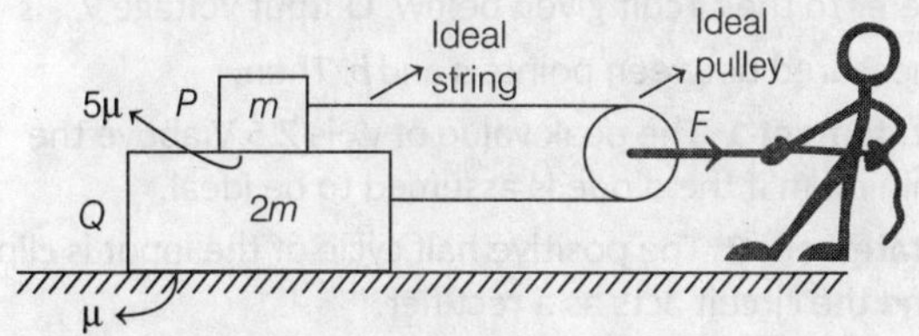

24. In circuit shown in the steady state capacitors are geometrically identical. C_1 is air cored, C_2 is half filled with dielectric of dielectric constant $K = 3$ while C_3 is completely filled with same dielectric. Ratio of charges stored by C_1, C_2 and C_3 is $2 : x : y$. Find $y - x$.

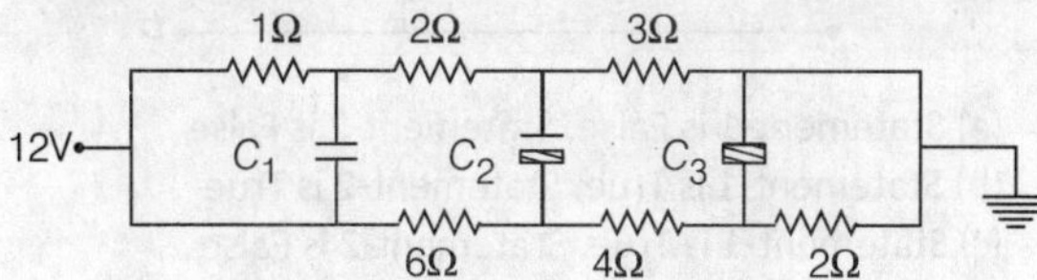

25. Magnetic field produced by an electron in 1st orbit of a Bohr's atom at the site of nucleus is $\frac{\mu_0 eh}{xmr^y}$. If e is electronic charge, m is electronic mass, r is orbital radius, h is planck's constant, μ_0 is magnetic permeability of free space, find $\frac{x}{y}$. [Take, $\pi^2 \approx 10$]

26. Two balls connected by a string of length $5l$ are initially in same horizontal plane above two heavy metal plates P and Q of different materials at height h. Initially, the distance between the balls is $3l$. The balls are now released simultaneously. Both strike the plates with coefficient of restitution 0.8 and 0.6 for ball-1 and ball-2 respectively. Time (after collision) after the string becomes taut is $\frac{xl}{\sqrt{ygh}}$. Find $\frac{x}{y}$.

27. If average speed of gas-1 molecules in a vessel is equal to rms speed of gas-2 molecules in another vessel at same temperature, then find the ratio of molecular mass of gas-2 to the molecular mass of gas-1.

28. 20 divisions on a vernier scale coincides with 19 divisions of main scale. If least count of the instrument is 0.05 mm, find the length of one Main Scale Division (MSD) in mm.

29. The shown conducting loop $PQRS$ of side l and resistance r is located in a region of transverse magnetic field **B** given by $\mathbf{B} = (x + y)t \cdot \hat{\mathbf{k}}$.

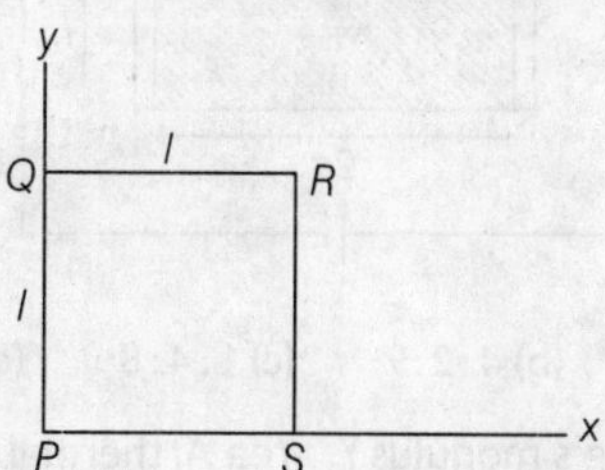

Considering $l = 3$m and $r = 9\,\Omega$, find induced current (in A) in the loop at $t = 8$s.

30. A small planet is orbiting in a circular orbit of radius r around sun of radius R. t and T represent surface temperatures of planet and sun respectively. If $\left(\frac{t}{T}\right)^x = \frac{R}{yr}$, find $x + y$, considering planet and sun as black bodies. Here, x and y are positive integers.

Answers

1 *(c)*	2 *(d)*	3 *(a)*	4 *(c)*	5 *(c)*	6 *(b)*	7 *(d)*	8 *(d)*	9 *(d)*	10 *(b)*
11 *(a)*	12 *(a)*	13 *(c)*	14 *(c)*	15 *(b)*	16 *(a)*	17 *(b)*	18 *(a)*	19 *(b)*	20 *(b)*
21 *10*	22 *5.5*	23 *7*	24 *6*	25 *26.67*	26 *10*	27 *1.17*	28 *1*	29 *3*	30 *4*

See detailed explanations on page no. 319

Knockout 10

JEE Main

Physics

Instructions See knockout 01

Section I Objective Type Questions

1. Consider the arrangement shown in figure. Energy densities in air, dielectric slab of dielectric constant 2 and slab of dielectric constant 4 are U_1, U_2 and U_3 respectively. $U_1 : U_2 : U_3$ is equal to

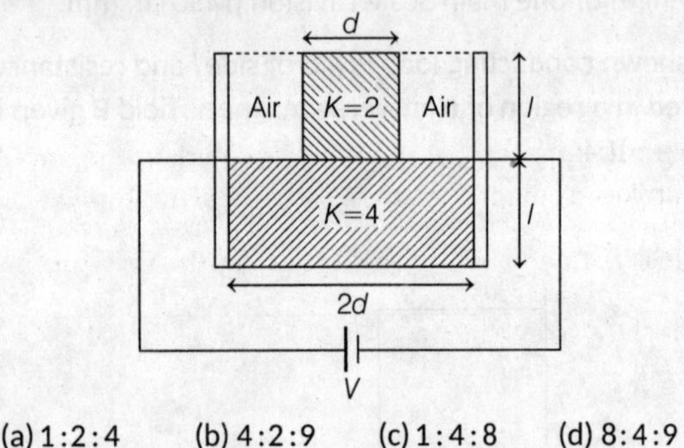

(a) 1 : 2 : 4 (b) 4 : 2 : 9 (c) 1 : 4 : 8 (d) 8 : 4 : 9

2. Rod-1 (Young's modulus Y, area A, thermal coefficient of linear expansion α, length l) and Rod-2 (area $\frac{A}{2}$, thermal coefficient of linear expansion $\frac{\alpha}{2}$, length l) are arranged as shown, in figure. On increasing temperature of system in Fig. 1, the block (heavy) does not move. If the block in Fig. 2 is slightly displaced, time period of oscillation of the block is

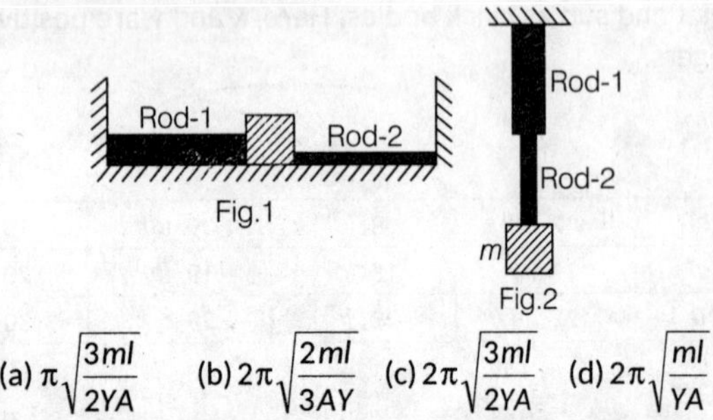

(a) $\pi\sqrt{\frac{3ml}{2YA}}$ (b) $2\pi\sqrt{\frac{2ml}{3AY}}$ (c) $2\pi\sqrt{\frac{3ml}{2YA}}$ (d) $2\pi\sqrt{\frac{ml}{YA}}$

3. A point source illuminating a photocathode in photoelectric cell is replaced by another point source of same power but half the frequency placed at half the distance. Photocurrent in the cell (assume quantum efficiency is constant)

(a) becomes twice

(b) becomes zero or eight fold

(c) becomes $\frac{1}{4}$th

(d) becomes 4 times

4. Refer to the circuit given below. Output voltage V_o, is measured between points a and b. Then,

Statement 1 The peak value of V_0 is 2.5 V above the minimum if the diode is assumed to be ideal.

Statement 2 The positive half cycle of the input is clipped and the circuit acts as a rectifier.

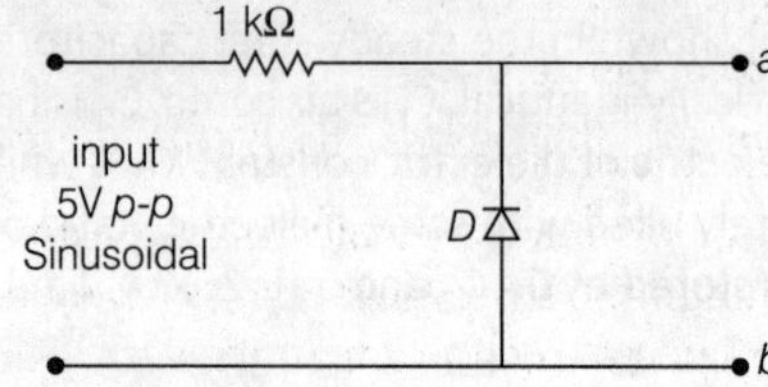

(a) Statement-1 is False, Statement-2 is False

(b) Statement-1 is True, Statement-2 is True

(c) Statement-1 is True, Statement-2 is False

(d) Statement-1 is False, Statement-2 is True

5. A composite wire PQR made up of two identical semi-circular rings of mass m and radius r each is hinged at end P. PQR is carrying current i and is located in gravity free space having uniform magnetic field B perpendicular to its plane as shown in figure. End R is connected to a string keeping PQR at rest. If the string is cut, angular acceleration of PQR just after cutting the string is

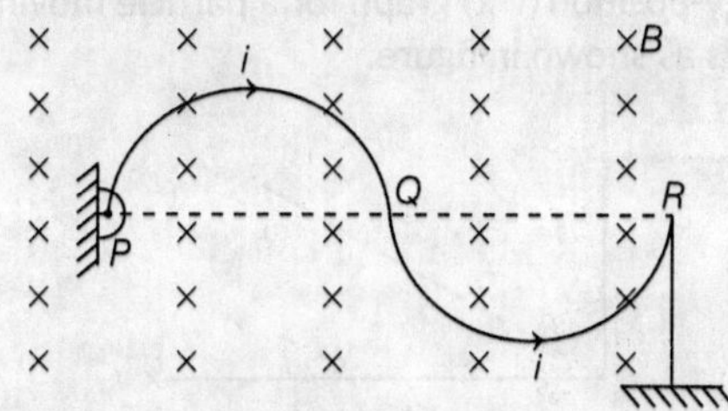

(a) $\frac{Bi}{m}$ (b) $\frac{2Bi}{3m}$ (c) $\frac{3Bi}{4m}$ (d) zero

6. A small planet is orbiting around sun of radius R in orbit of radius r. If surface temperature of sun is T, surface temperature of the planet is

(a) $\sqrt{\frac{R}{r}}T$ (b) $\sqrt{\frac{R}{2r}}T$ (c) $\sqrt[4]{\frac{R}{2r}}T$ (d) $\sqrt[4]{\frac{R}{r}}T$

7. Gravitational field in a region of space is given by $2yz\hat{\mathbf{k}} + (z^2 - y^2)\hat{\mathbf{j}}$ N/kg. Work done in slowly taking a 3 kg mass from origin to (1, 2, 3) is

(a) – 46 J (b) 8 J (c) – 54 J (d) zero

8.

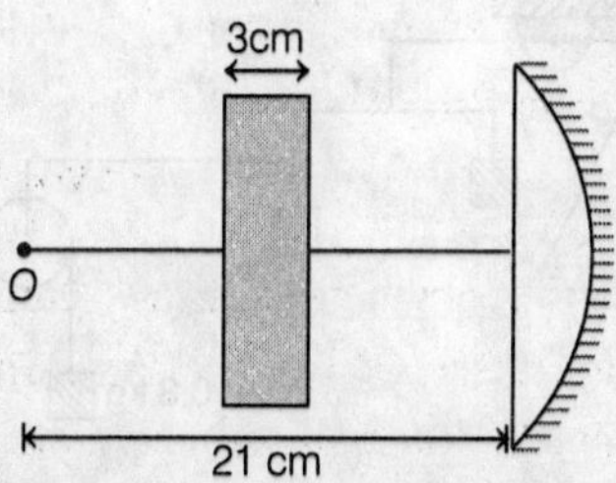

Both slab (thickness = 1 cm) and silvered thin lens have refractive index of 1.5. An object O is placed at a distance of 21 cm from the lens as shown in figure. Radius of curvature of the curved/polished lens surface for object image coincidence is

(a) 20 cm (b) 30 cm (c) 40 cm (d) 60 cm

9. A string of linear mass density λ and length l is clamped at both ends. If the string is vibrating in 1st overtone with tension T and maximum amplitude A, oscillation energy of the string is

(a) $\frac{T\pi^2A^2}{2l}$ (b) $\frac{2T\pi A^2}{l}$ (c) $\frac{T\pi^2A^2}{l}$ (d) $\frac{TA^2}{\pi l}$

10. A ball of material of specific gravity 3 is projected in water with speed equal to twice the terminal speed v in vertically upward direction as shown in figure. Acceleration of the ball just after projection is

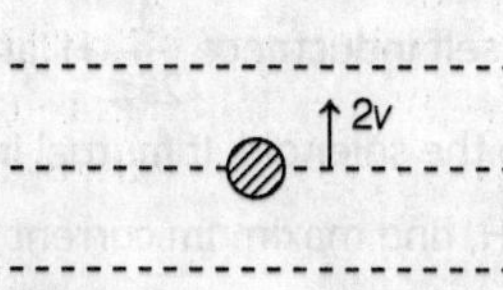

(a) g (b) $2g$ (c) $3g$ (d) zero

11. An impulse is applied at the end (normal to the rod) of a uniform rod of mass m and length l placed on a smooth horizontal table. If kinetic energy acquired by the rod is K, the impulse is given by

(a) $\sqrt{mK}$ (b) $\sqrt{2mK}$ (c) $\sqrt{\frac{mK}{2}}$ (d) $\frac{\sqrt{mK}}{2}$

12. Figure here shows an incline of inclination 45°. Few small particles arranged on X-axis, are released simultaneously from rest at $t = 0$. At $t = \frac{1}{\sqrt{5}}$ s, all the particles are observed on a parabola $y = \sqrt{2}x^2$. If coefficient of friction depends on x-coordinate of point of the incline, μ is given by (Take, $g = 10$ m/s^2 and assume $\mu > 0$)

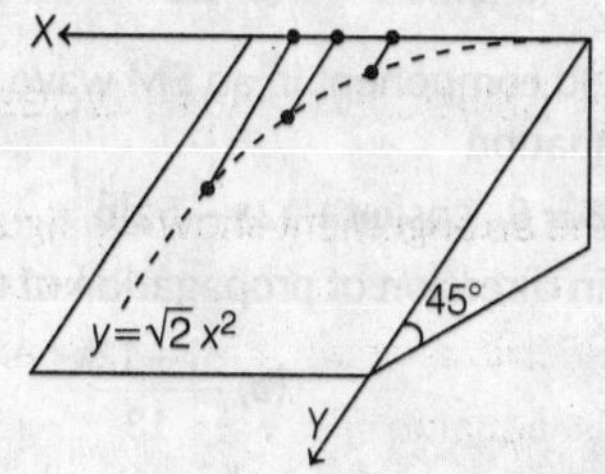

(a) $\mu = 1 - 2x^2$ (b) $\mu = \sqrt{1 + 2x^2}$

(c) $\mu = 2x^2$ (d) $\mu = 1 - x^2$

13. Consider the figure shown. A ball moving horizontally strikes a smooth parabolic surface given by $y = x^2$ at point $P(x, y)$. Coefficient of restitution for the collision is $\frac{1}{2}$. If the ball moves vertically after collision, y is equal to

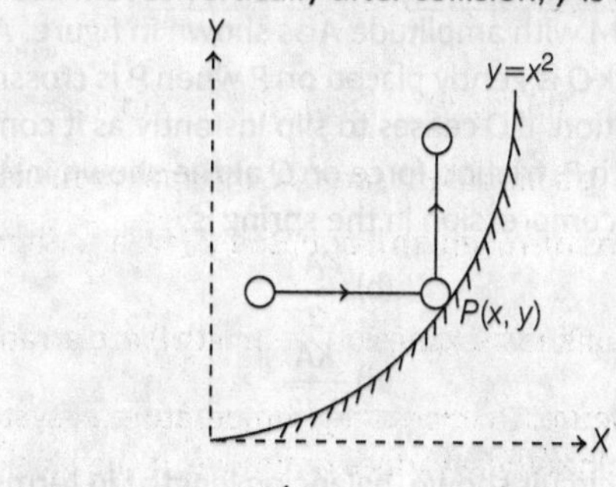

(a) 1 (b) $\frac{1}{2}$ (c) $\frac{1}{\sqrt{2}}$ (d) $\sqrt{2}$

14.

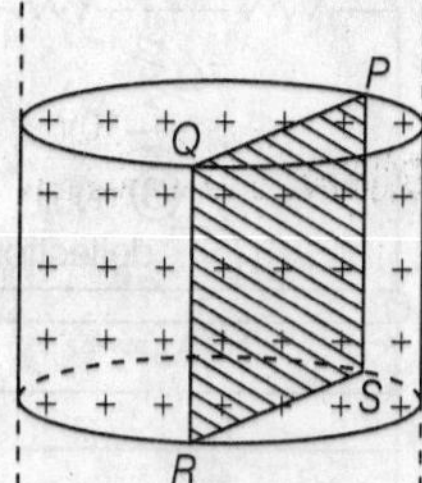

The figure here shows a uniform infinite charged solid cylinder of radius $5R$. Also shown is an imaginary square surface

PQRS of side $8R$, having its sides *QR* and *SP* along its curved surface while sides *PQ* and *RS* along its cross-sections perpendicular to its axis. If minimum electric field on surface *PQRS* is E_0, electric flux through the surface is (A = surface area of *PQRS*)

(a) E_0A (b) $2E_0A$

(c) $\frac{E_0A}{2}$ (d) zero

15. An air column in open organ pipe resonates in fundamental mode due to a tuning fork. Length and radius of the pipe are measured to be $l = 95.2 \pm 0.1$ cm and $r = 4.00 \pm 0.05$ cm respectively. If speed of sound in air is known with certainty, maximum percentage error in measurement of frequency of tuning fork is

(a) 0.08 (b) 0.16 (c) 1.6 (d) 3.2

16. Magnetic field component in an EM wave is given by the following equation

$$\mathbf{B} = B_0 \cos[\omega t + 12x - 5z]\hat{\mathbf{n}}$$

Unit vector in direction of propagation of the wave is

(a) $\frac{12\hat{\mathbf{i}} - 5\hat{\mathbf{k}}}{13}$ (b) $\frac{5\hat{\mathbf{i}} - 12\hat{\mathbf{k}}}{13}$

(c) $\frac{5\hat{\mathbf{k}} - 12\hat{\mathbf{i}}}{13}$ (d) $12\hat{\mathbf{k}} - 5\hat{\mathbf{i}}$

17.

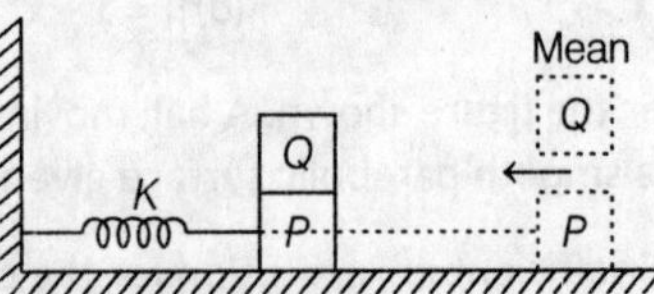

A block connected to spring of spring constant K is executing SHM with amplitude A as shown in figure. An identical block Q is gently placed on P when P is crossing its mean position. If Q ceases to slip instantly as it comes in contact with P, friction force on Q at the shown instant of maximum compression in the spring is

(a) KA (b) $\frac{KA}{\sqrt{2}}$

(c) $\frac{KA}{2}$ (d) $\frac{KA}{2\sqrt{2}}$

18. Consider the circuit shown, balancing length l in terms of length L of uniform wire AB is

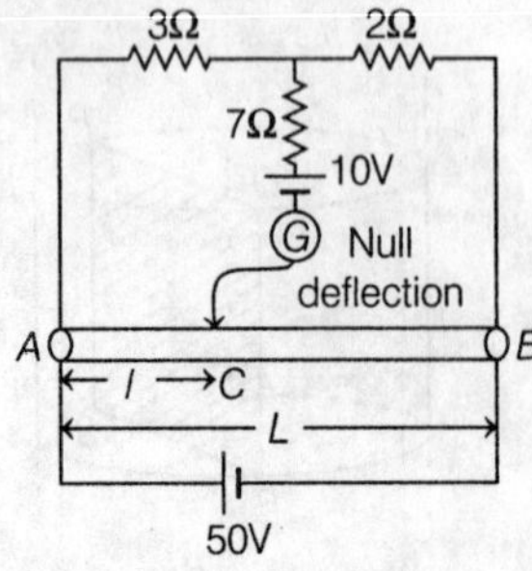

(a) $0.2\,L$ (b) $0.4\,L$

(c) $0.6\,L$ (d) $0.8\,L$

19. Velocity-position (v-x) graph for a particle moving on X-axis is as shown in figure.

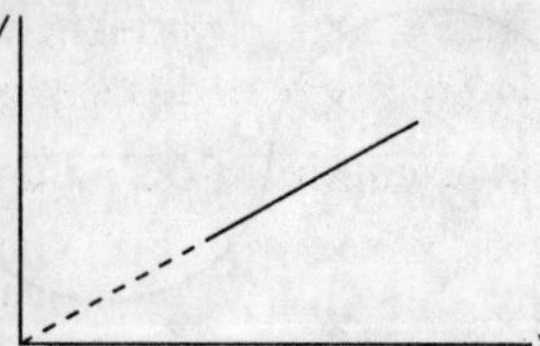

If v is equal to $2v_0$ at time t equal to t_0, average acceleration of the particle between $t = t_0$ and $t = 2t_0$ is (v_0 = initial velocity)

(a) $\frac{v_0}{t_0}$ (b) $\frac{2v_0}{t_0}$ (c) $\frac{3v_0}{t_0}$ (d) $\frac{4v_0}{t_0}$

20. Numerical Aperture (NA) of lens of a microscope is 1.2. Light of wavelength 400 nm is being employed to observe the target point objects. Minimum separation between two point objects, for them to be observed resolved, is close to

(a) 0.1 μm (b) 0.2 μm (c) 0.3 μm (d) 0.4 μm

Section II *Numerical Value Questions*

21.

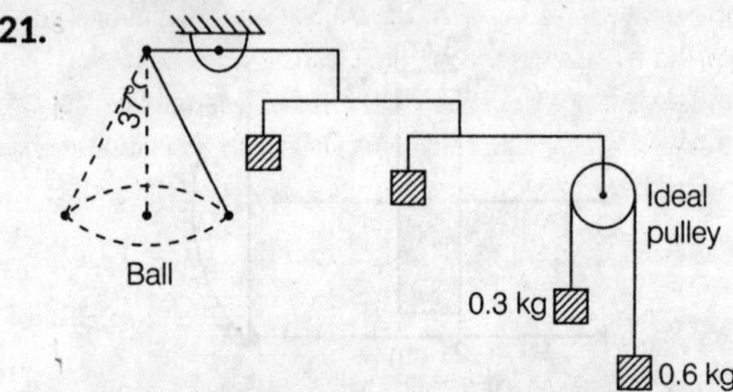

In the arrangement shown here the three rods are light and horizontal (in equilibrium). The strings are ideal. If suspension points of all the rods are such that (1/3)rd of the rod is to the left of the suspension point, find mass of the ball (in kg) executing uniform circular motion in horizontal plane.

22. For an AM wave, maximum amplitude is 9 V, modulation index is 0.8, bandwidth is 20 kHz and central frequency is 1 MHz. If lower side band frequency of the wave is f MHz and minimum amplitude is A V, find nearest integer to $f + A$.

23. A solenoid coil of self inductance $\frac{1}{25\pi}$ H and resistance 3Ω is connected across an AC source of voltage $V = 5\sin(100\pi t)$ volts. A ring of self inductance $\frac{1}{25\pi}$ H and resistance 2Ω is fixed coaxial to the solenoid. If mutual inductance of the system is $\frac{1}{50\pi}$ H, find maximum current induced in the ring (in A).

24. S_1 and S_2 are coherent sources in the arrangements shown here emitting light of wavelength λ. If number of bright fringes in Arrangement-1 is n_1 while number of bright fringes in Arrangement-2 is n_2, find $\frac{n_1}{n_2}$.

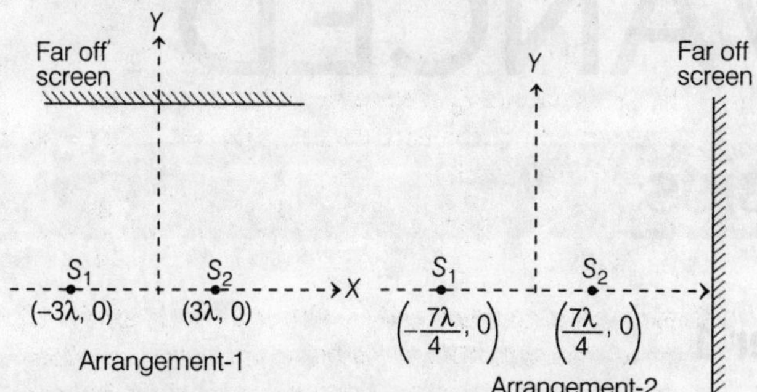

25. An ideal CO_2 sample is undergoing process given by ρ^2U^3 = constant. Here, ρ is density and U is internal energy. If universal gas constant is equal to 8.31 J/mol-K, find molar specific heat (in J/mol-K) in the given process.

26. A cylinder of radius 1.6 m placed on a horizontal surface surrounded by water on one side while by a liquid of relative density 1.69 on the other side. Respective heights are as shown in the figure. Find h (in m) for the cylinder to be in equilibrium if atmospheric pressure is negligible.

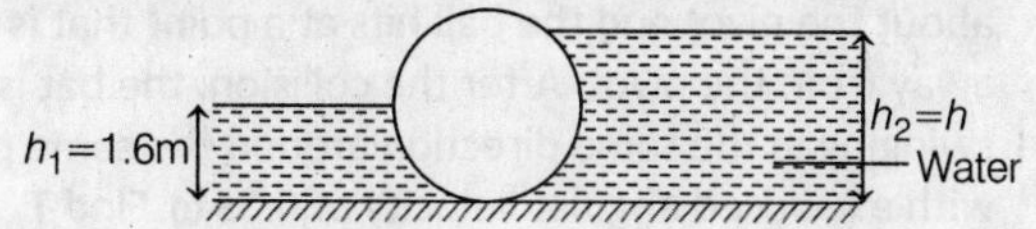

27. Determine difference of loudness (in dB) of sound observed by two persons at perpendicular distances 3m and 6m, respectively from a long line source.

28. Ratio of nuclear radius of ^{56}Fe to that of $^{14}_{7}N$ is $x^{\frac{2}{1+x}}$. Find x.

29. A horizontal wire AB of mass m in contact with a V-shaped smooth vertical frame, is supported at rest by a soap film. Springs of spring constant K and natural length l are relaxed. If the wire AB is slightly disturbed, time period of oscillation of the wire is $\pi\sqrt{\frac{xl}{g}}$. Find x. Given that $K = \frac{mg}{l}$

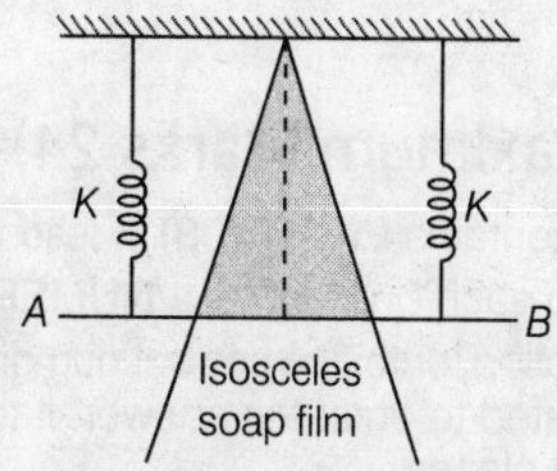

30. Find work done (in J) by spring (relaxed at the instant shown) on the wall till the instant of maximum compression.

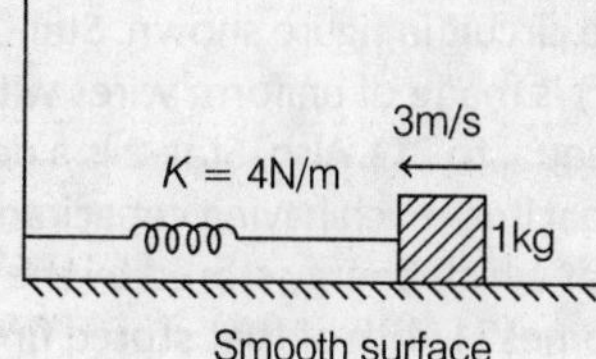

Answers

1 *(b)*	2 *(c)*	3 *(b)*	4 *(b)*	5 *(b)*	6 *(b)*	7 *(a)*	8 *(b)*	9 *(c)*	10 *(b)*
11 *(c)*	12 *(a)*	13 *(b)*	14 *(a)*	15 *(b)*	16 *(c)*	17 *(d)*	18 *(d)*	19 *(c)*	20 *(b)*
21 *14.40*	22 *2*	23 *1*	24 *3.67*	25 *33.24*	26 *2.08*	27 *3.01*	28 *2*	29 *1.33*	30 *0*

See detailed explanations on page no. 323

Knockout 11

JEE ADVANCED

Physics

Paper 1

Section I (Maximum Marks 24)

- This section contains **EIGHT (08)** questions.
- The answer to each question is a **NUMERICAL VALUE.**
- For each question, enter the correct numerical value of the answer using the mouse and the on-screen virtual numeric keypad in the place designated to enter the answer. If the numerical value has more than two decimal places, **truncate/round-off** the value to **TWO** decimal places.
- Answer to each question will be evaluated according to the following marking scheme :
  Full Marks : +3 **ONLY** if the correct numerical value is entered;
  Zero Marks : 0 In all other cases.

1. Consider the circuit in figure shown. Star-1 (a regular five pointed star) is made of uniform wires with resistance of a section *AB* equal to 2 Ω. Also, Star-2 is a network of identical capacitors each having capacitance 3.5 μF. Find time (in μs) at which energy stored by the capacitor system becomes (1/4)th of that stored finally by the arrangement. (Given that sin 18° ~ 1/3)

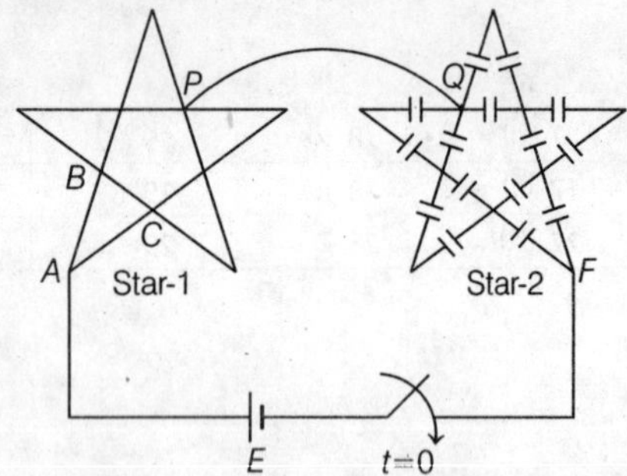

2. A baseball of mass 0.15 kg is initially travelling horizontally at 50 m/s. It is struck by a bat, after which the baseball is still travelling horizontally but in exactly the opposite direction from its initial motion at a speed of 40 m/s. Consider the collision of the bat and the ball. Assume that before the collision, the bat points are moving in a horizontal circle at an angular velocity of ω rad/s and period *T*s. Assume that the player holding the bat exerts no torque. The bat has a moment of inertia of 0.30 kg-m^2 about the pivot and the ball hits at a point that is 80 cm away from the pivot. After the collision, the bat is still swinging in the same direction around the same pivot but with a reduced angular velocity of 0.35 ω. Find *T* (in s).

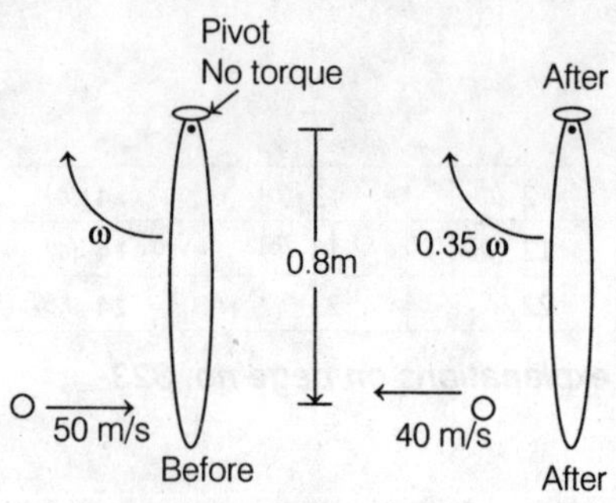

3. A beaker is filled with water as shown. The bottom surface of the beaker is a concave mirror of large radius of curvature and small aperture. The height of water is $h = 40$ cm. It is found that when an object is placed 4 cm above the water surface, the image coincides with the object. Now the water level *h* is reduced to zero (there will still be water left in the concave part of the mirror). What is the new height of the object (in m) above the new water surface, so that the image again coincides with the object ? (Refractive index of water = 4/3)

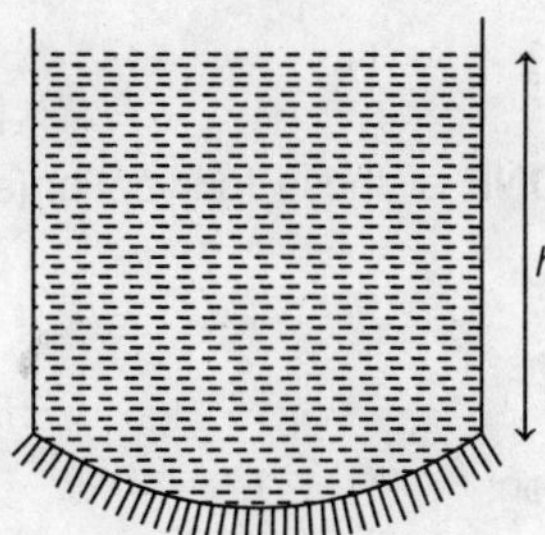

4. The average lifetime of the first excited level of a hydrogen atom is 10^{-8} s. In the Bohr's model, how many million orbits does an electron having potential energy -6.8eV complete before returning to the ground level? Time period of revolution of electron in 1st orbit $= 1.53\times 10^{-16}$ s.

5. Three resistances are measured in Ω:

$R_1 = 3\,\Omega \pm 1\%$, $R_2 = 6\,\Omega \pm 2\%$, $R_3 = 2\,\Omega \pm 1\%$

Determine maximum percentage error in parallel combination of these resistances.

6. Nuclear magnetic resonance with protons (H nuclei) is basis of Magnetic Resonance Imaging (MRI). Nuclear magnetic resonance uses flipping of nuclear spin to determine structure of chemical compounds. Suppose proton acts like magnetic dipole whose component along the applied field is $M = 1.41\times 10^{-26}$ J/T. The applied magnetic field is $B = 1.5$ T. What should be the frequency (in MHz) of radiations to be used in MRI device to flip the spin? (Take, Planck's constant $= 6.63\times 10^{-34}$ J-s)

7. A subsonic aircraft is flying in a vertical circle of radius R with constant speed v. Speed of sound in medium is v_w. Detector which can detect position of plane as well as frequency of sound emitted by plane lies vertically below the centre O of circular path at distance $2R$ from the centre.

Whenever detector detects maximum frequency, it also detects that plane is nearest to detector. Find mach number of the plane.

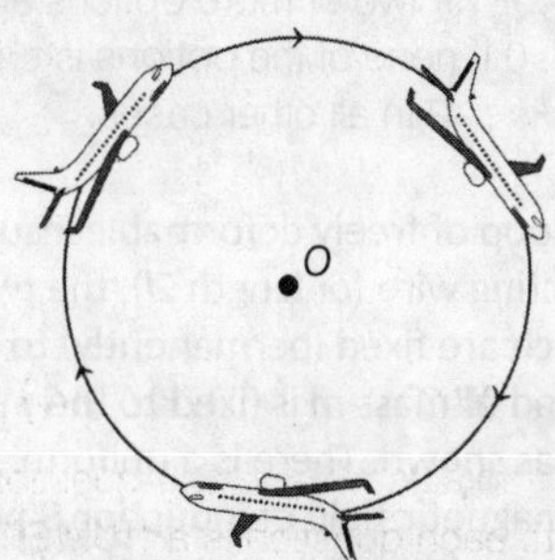

8. A guitar string of cross-sectional area $A = 0.1\text{ mm}^2$ and having $F = 100$ N tension is tuned to a fundamental frequency of 245Hz when its temperature is 20°C. Continuous playing can make the temperature of the string rise, changing its vibration frequency. Find the magnitude of change in frequency (in Hz), if the temperature of the string rises to 30°C. The steel has Young's modulus $Y = 2\times 10^{11}\text{ N/m}^2$ and coefficient of linear expansion $\alpha = 1.2\times 10^{-5}$ per °C.

Section II (Maximum Marks 24)

- This section contains **SIX (06)** questions.
- Each question has **FOUR** options (a), (b), (c) and (d). **ONE OR MORE THAN ONE** of these four option(s) is (are) correct answer(s).
- For each question, choose the option(s) corresponding to (all) the corret answer(s).
- Answer to each question will be evaluated according to the following marking scheme:
  Full Marks : +4 **ONLY** if (all) the correct option(s) is (are) chosen:
  Partial Marks : +3 If all the four options are correct but **ONLY** three options are chosen;
  Partial Marks : +2 If three or more options are correct but **ONLY** two options are chosen, both of which are correct;
  Partial Marks : +1 If two or more options are correct but **ONLY** one option is chosen and it is a correct option;
  Zero Marks : 0 If none of the options is chosen (i.e. the question is unanswered);
  Negative Marks : –2 In all other cases.

9. Consider a loop of freely deformable insulated light conducting wire (of length $2l$), the two ends of which are fixed (permanently) to the ceiling. A load of mass m is fixed to the middle of the wire as shown. There is a uniform horizontal magnetic field of induction B present in the region and free fall acceleration is g. A current i is passed through the wire.

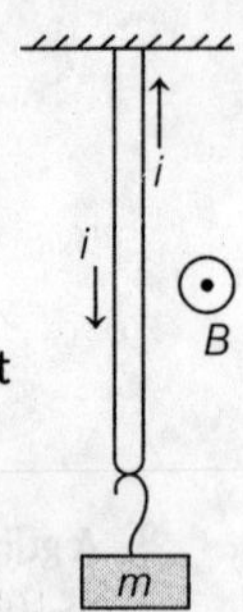

Neglecting the field induced by the wires, choose the correct alternative(s).

(a) The left and right parts of wire will take shape of circular arc.

(b) The left and right parts of wire will take shape of parabolic arc.

(c) The maximum height by which the load can be lifted is $l\left(1-\frac{3}{\pi}\right)$.

(d) To lift the load by $l\left(1-\frac{3}{\pi}\right)$, the current in wire should be $\frac{mg\,\pi}{3\sqrt{2}\,lB}$.

10. A light cylindrical vessel of a very large cross-sectional area 1000 cm^2 is containing two immiscible liquids of density $\rho_1 = 600$ kg/m^3 and $\rho_2 = 1200$ kg/m^3 as shown in figure.

A small hole having cross-sectional area 5 cm^2 is made in right side vertical wall. For the given situation, mark the correct statement (s). (Take, g = 10 m/s^2)

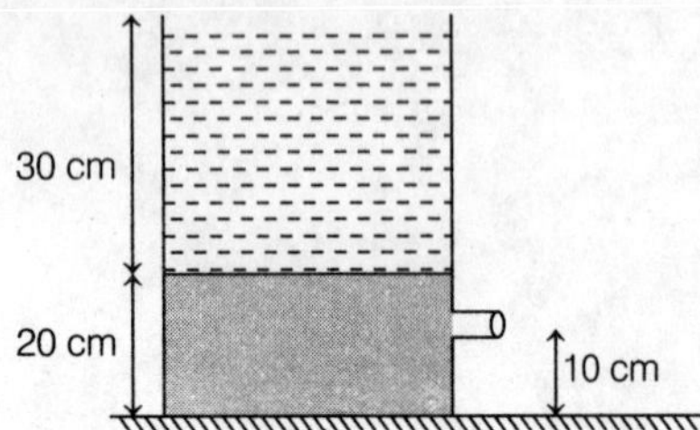

(a) If the surface is smooth, then a rightward force of magnitude 4 N is to be applied on vessel to maintain its equilibrium.

(b) If the surface is smooth, then a rightward force of magnitude 3N is to be applied on vessel to maintain its equilibrium.

(c) If the surface is rough ($\mu = 0.04$), then minimum force (horizontal) needed to be applied on the vessel to maintain equilibrium is zero.

(d) If the surface is rough ($\mu = 0.04$), then the maximum force (horizontal) needed to be applied on the vessel to maintain equilibrium is 19.8 N.

11. A bar of mass m is held as shown between 4 uniform discs, each of mass m' and radius $R = 75$ mm.

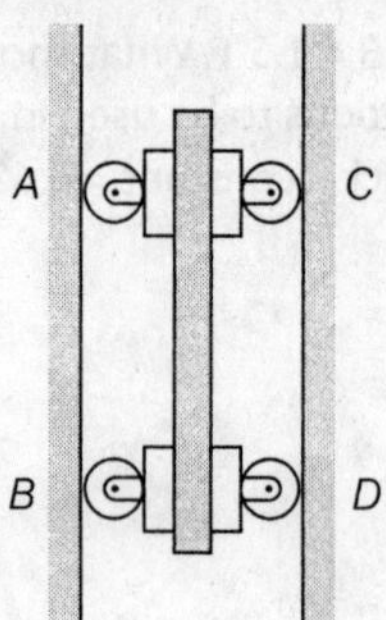

The bar has been released from rest, knowing that the normal forces exerted on the discs by vertical walls are sufficient to prevent any slipping. Assuming attachments are massless and fixed to the bar (Acceleration due to gravity is g)

(a) If $m = 5$kg and $m' = 2$kg, then acceleration of the bar is $13g/17$.

(b) If the mass m' of the discs is negligible, then acceleration of the bar is $g/2$.

(c) If the mass m of the bar is negligible, then acceleration of the bar is $2g/3$.

(d) If the mass m of the bar is negligible, then acceleration of the bar is g.

12. Consider the figure which shows roughly how the force F between two adjacent atoms in a solid varies with inter-atomic separation r. Which of the following statements are correct?

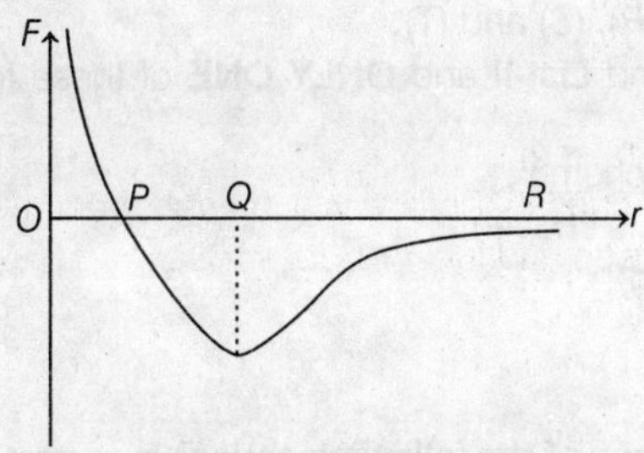

(a) OQ is the equilibrium separation.
(b) Hooke's law is obeyed near P.
(c) The potential energy of the atoms is the gradient of the graph at all points.
(d) The energy to separate the atoms completely is obtained from the magnitude of the area enclosed below the axis of r.

13. A bead is connected with a fixed disc's periphery of radius R by an inextensible massless string of length $l = \frac{\pi R}{2}$ in a smooth horizontal plane. If the bead is pushed with a velocity v_0 perpendicular to the string, the bead moves in a horizontal curve and consequently collapses on the disc after a time t. Then,

(a) work done by the string on the bead is mv_0^2
(b) time taken by bead to strike the disc is $t = \frac{l^2}{2Rv_0}$
(c) average speed of the bead during its motion before it strikes the disc is v_0
(d) kinetic energy of the bead increases gradually

14. Consider a hemisphere of radius R with centre of curvature at origin O, as shown in figure. Refractive index of material of the hemisphere varies as $\mu = \frac{2R}{2R - x}$, where x is x-coordinate of material point. A ray travelling in air in XY-plane is grazingly incident at O, as shown. Choose the correct option(s).

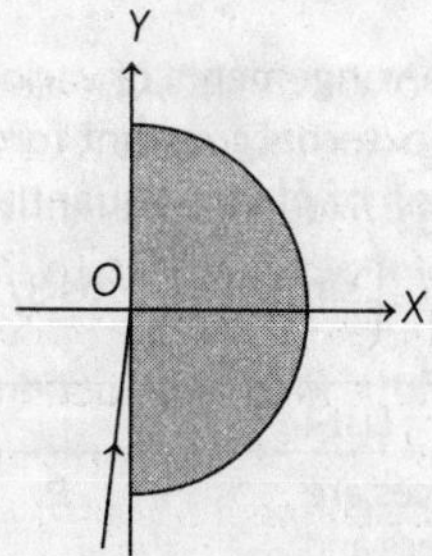

(a) Trajectory followed by ray as it travels inside the hemisphere is circular.
(b) y-coordinate of the point of hemisphere where the ray comes out of the hemisphere lies between 0.5 R and 0.75 R.
(c) Deviation suffered by the ray just before it comes out of the hemispherical surface lies between 0° and 30°.
(d) Deviation suffered by the ray just before it comes out of the hemispherical surface lies between 30° and 45°.

Section III (Maximum Marks 12)

- This section contains **FOUR (04)** Matching List Sets.
- Each set has **ONE** Multiple Choice Question.
- Each set has **TWO** lists : **List-I** and **List-II**.
- **List-I** has **Four** entries (I), (II), (III) and (IV) and **List-II** has **Five** entries (P), (Q), (R), (S) and (T).
- **FOUR** options are given in each Multiple Choice Question based on **List-I** and **List-II** and **ONLY ONE** of these four options satisfies the condition asked in the Multiple Choice Question.
- Answer to each question will be evaluated according to the following marking scheme :
  Full Marks : +3 **ONLY** if the option corresponding to the correct combination is chosen;
  Zero Marks : 0 If none of the options is chosen (i.e. the question is unanswered);
  Negative Marks : –1 In all other cases.

15. In List-I, some arrangements of various objects are given. F represents the external constant force. In List-II, the possible variation of physical quantities are given. Match List-I with List-II. $\left(\sin 37° = \frac{3}{5}, \cos 37° = \frac{4}{5}\right)$

	List-I		List-II
I.	All surfaces are frictionless and $F = mg \sin\theta \cos\theta$ 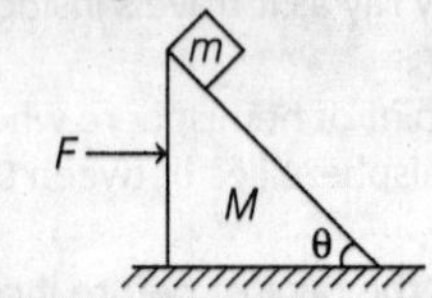 (figure: block m on wedge M, angle θ, force F)	P.	The centre of mass of the system accelerates in horizontal direction.
II.	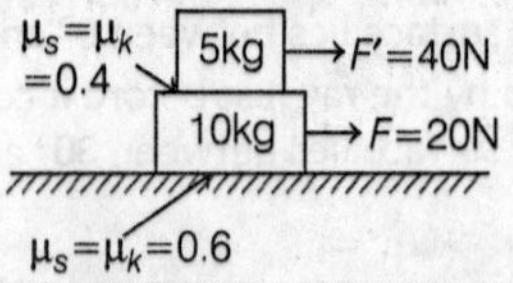 $\mu_s = \mu_k = 0.4$ between 5kg and 10kg blocks, $F' = 40$N on 5kg, $F = 20$N on 10kg; $\mu_s = \mu_k = 0.6$ with ground	Q.	The centre of mass of the system accelerates in vertical direction
III.	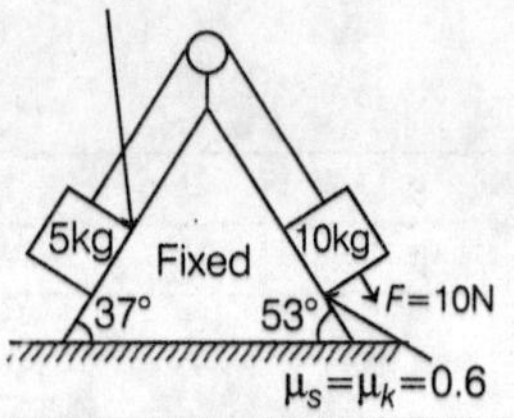 $\mu_s = \mu_k = 0.6$; 5kg and 10kg blocks on fixed wedge (37°, 53°) connected over pulley, $F = 10$N; $\mu_s = \mu_k = 0.6$	R.	The object on which F is applied remains in translatory equilibrium
IV.	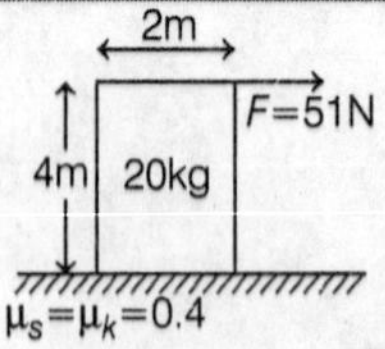 Box 2m × 4m, 20kg, $F = 51$N; $\mu_s = \mu_k = 0.4$. The box has uniform mass distribution	S.	Kinetic energy of the system increases
		T.	The friction force acting at all contact surfaces is equal to the corresponding limiting value of static friction.

Which one of the following options is correct?

(a) I → R; II → S; III → T; IV → Q
(b) I → P; II → Q; III → R; IV → S
(c) I → Q; II → R; III → S; IV → T
(d) I → R; II → R; III → T; IV → T

16. In List- II, a stretched string or an organ pipe is given. In case of strings, the tension in the string is 108.9 N and mass per unit length of string is 1 g/m. Speed of sound in air is 330 m/s. Neglect end corrections. The frequencies of resonance are given in List-I. Match situation in List-II with the possible resonance frequencies given in List-I.

	List-I		List-II
I.	300 Hz	P.	String fixed at both ends 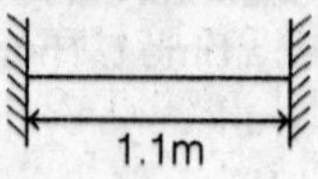 (1.1m)
II.	375 Hz	Q.	String fixed at one end and free at other end 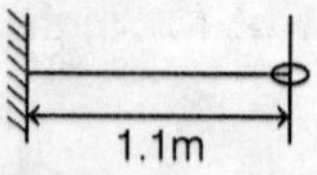 (1.1m)
III.	600 Hz	R.	Open organ pipe 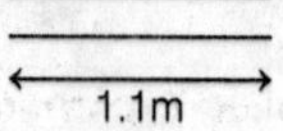 (1.1m)
IV.	675 Hz	S.	Organ pipe closed at both ends 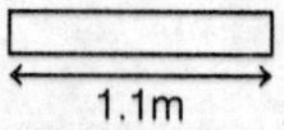 (1.1m)
		T.	Organ pipe closed at one end 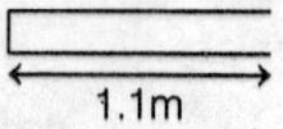 (1.1m)

Which one of the following options is correct?

(a) I → Q; II → P; III → S; IV → T
(b) I → P; II → R; III → Q; IV → T
(c) I → P; II → Q; III → R; IV → T
(d) I → P; II → Q; III → R; IV → S

17. For a Bohr atom, List-I gives some physical quantities related to electrons and List-II gives their dependence on other quantities. Match appropriately:

	List-I		List-II
I.	Angular momentum	P.	Inversely proportional to principal quantum number
II.	Reciprocal of speed	Q.	Depends on atomic number of nucleus
III.	Potential energy	R.	Increases as electron moves to higher orbits
IV.	Square root of distance from nucleus	S.	Remains same, whether orbit is elliptical or circular throughout the motion
		T.	Depends directly on principal quantum number

Which one of the following options is correct?

(a) I → S; II → Q; III → R; IV → T
(b) I → P; II → S; III → R; IV → T
(c) I → T; II → R; III → P; IV → S
(d) 1 → Q; II → P; III → T; IV → R

18. A monochromatic parallel beam of light of wavelength λ is incident normally on the plane containing slits S_1 and S_2. The slits are of unequal width such that intensity only due to one slit on screen is four times that only due to the other slit. The screen is placed along *Y*-axis as shown. The distance between slits is *d* and that between screen and slit is *D* (>> *d*). Match the statements in List-I with results in List-II.

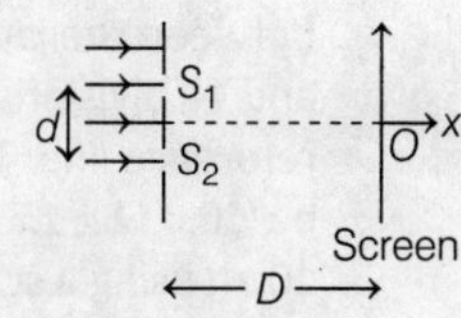

	List-I		List-II
I.	The distance between two points on screen having equal intensities, such that intensity at those points is $\frac{1}{9}$th of maximum intensity.	P.	$\frac{D\lambda}{3d}$
II.	The distance between two points on screen having equal intensities, such that intensity at those points is $\frac{3}{9}$th of maximum intensity.	Q.	$\frac{D\lambda}{d}$
III.	The distance between two points on screen having equal intensities, such that intensity at those points is $\frac{5}{9}$th of maximum intensity.	R.	$\frac{2D\lambda}{d}$
IV.	The distance between two points on screen having equal intensities, such that intensity at those points is $\frac{7}{9}$th of maximum intensity.	S.	$\frac{3D\lambda}{d}$
		T.	$\frac{2D\lambda}{3d}$

Which one of the following options is correct?

(a) I → Q; II → S; III → P; IV → T
(b) I → Q; II → S; III → R; IV → T
(c) I → T; II → P; III → T; IV → R
(d) I → P; II → Q; III → R; IV → S

Answers

1 *(4.16)*	2 *(0.11)*	3 *(0.34)*	4 *(8.19)*	5 *(1.16)*	6 *(63.80)*	7 *(0.60)*	8 *(2.94)*	9 *(a,d)*	10. *(b,c,d)*
11 *(a,c)*	12 *(b)*	13 *(b,c)*	14 *(a,c)*	15 *(a)*	16 *(c)*	17 *(a)*	18 *(b)*		

See detailed explanations on page no. 328

Paper 2

Section I (Maximum Marks 24)

- This section contains **EIGHT (08)** questions.
- The answer to each quetion is a **SINGLE DIGIT INTEGER ranging from 0 to 9, BOTH INCLUSIVE.**
- For each question, enter the correct integer corresponding to the answer using the mouse and the on-screen virtual numeric keypad in the place designated to enter the answer.
- Answer to each question will be evaluated according to the following marking scheme:
  Full Marks : +3 if **ONLY** the correct integer is entered;
  Zero Marks : 0 If the question is unanswered;
  Negative Marks : –1 In all other cases.

1. The figure here shows a system of light wheels with radius R attached to a heavy axle. The system rolls along a horizontal surface which suddenly turns into a slope with angle α. For what minimum value of $6 \cos\alpha$, the wheels move without lifting off, i.e. touch the surface at all times?

Mass of the wheels can be neglected. The axle is parallel to the boundary between horizontal and sloped surfaces and has velocity, $v = \sqrt{0.5\, gR}$

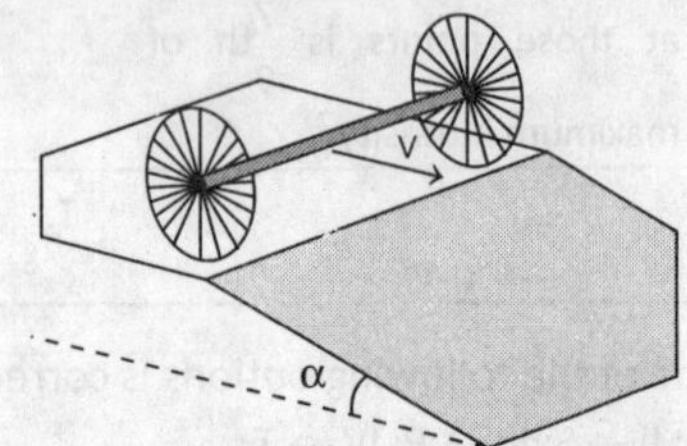

2. A capacitor is filled with three dielectrics as shown in the figure. The value of dielectric constants K_1, K_2 and K_3 are 2, 4 and 6 respectively. If the ratio of surface charge density on left half to the right half of plate of capacitor to the simplest integer is $\alpha : \beta$, then determine $\alpha + \beta$.

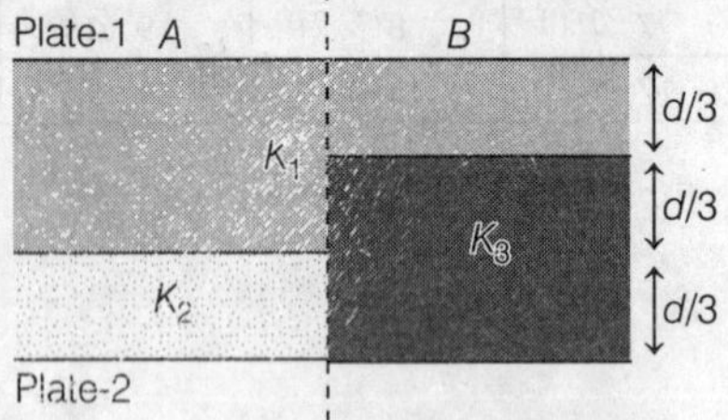

3. Consider a so-called Maxwell's bridge used for measuring the inductance L and the ohmic resistance R of an inductor coil. To achieve that other parameters are adjusted, so that the voltmeter reading will be zero. Assuming that such a state has been achieved for $R_1 = 1\Omega$, $R_2 = 2\Omega$, $R_C = 3\,\Omega$ and $C = 2\,\mu F$, find time constant (in μs) of the inductor coil when connected across a DC source.

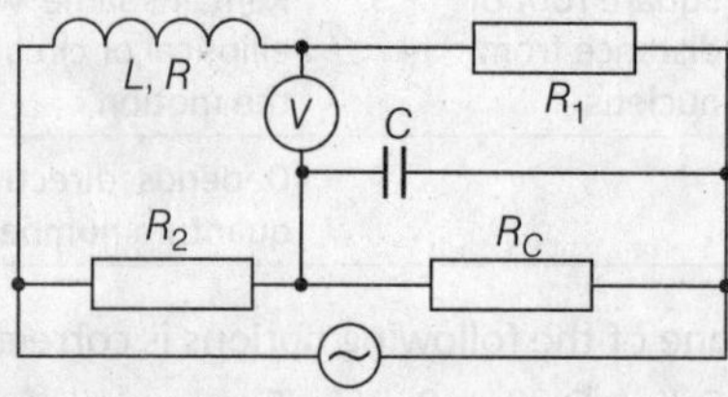

4. To measure the diameter of a wire, a screw gauge is used. In a complete rotation, spindle of the screw gauge advances by 0.5 mm and its circular scale has 50 divisions. The main scale is graduated to 0.5 mm. If the wire is put between the jaws, 8 main scale divisions are clearly visible and 10 divisions of circular scale coincide with the reference line. The resistance of the wire is measured to be $(10.0\,\Omega \pm 1.5\%)$. Length of the wire is measured to be 10cm using a scale of least count 1mm. Determine maximum percentage error in determination of its resistivity.

5. Consider a wire octahedron as shown in the figure with the number near to each edge showing the resistance of the corresponding wire in ohms. Find the reading of the ammeter (in A) between points P and Q, if all the ammeters are ideal.

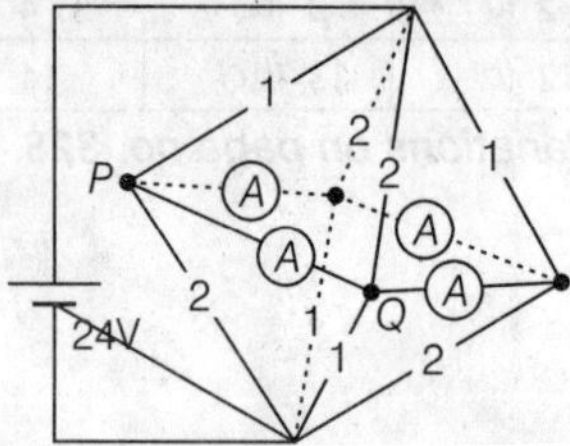

6. The potential energy of an electron moving with kinetic energy $2a$ in a potential field is given by

$$U(x) = \begin{cases} a & \text{for } 0 \le x \le 1 \quad \text{Region - 1} \\ 0 & \text{for } x > 1 \quad \text{Region - 2} \end{cases}$$

λ_1 and λ_2 are the de-Broglie wavelengths of the particle in Region-1 and Region-2 respectively. Find square of $\dfrac{\lambda_1}{\lambda_2}$.

7. A radionuclide with disintegration constant λ is produced in a reactor at a constant rate $\alpha (= 2\lambda)$ nuclei per second. At $t = 0$, there are no nuclei present in the reactor. During each decay energy E_0 is released, 20% of this energy is utilised in increasing the temperature of water. The increase in temperature of m mass of water in time $t = T_{1/2}$, if specific heat of water is s is $193nK$. Assume that, there is no loss of energy through water surface. (Given, $E_0 = 100$ times the energy required to raise the temperature of mass m of water from 0°C to 100°C). Find the value of n.

8. A container filled with air under pressure p_0 contains a soap bubble of radius R. The air pressure has been reduced to half isothermally and the new radius of the bubble becomes $\frac{5R}{4}$. If the surface tension of the soap water solution is S, p_0 is found to be $\frac{12\,nS}{R}$. Find n.

Section II (Maximum Marks 24)

- This section contains **SIX (06)** questions.
- Each question has **FOUR** options (a), (b), (c) and (d). **ONE OR MORE THAN ONE** of these four option(s) is (are) correct answer(s).
- For each question, choose the option(s) corresponding to (all) the correct answer(s).
- Answer to each question will be evaluated according to the following marking scheme:
  Full Marks : +4 **ONLY** if (all) the correct option(s) is (are) chosen:
  Partial Marks : +3 If all the four options are correct but **ONLY** three options are chosen;
  Partial Marks : +2 If three or more options are correct but **ONLY** two options are chosen, both of which are correct;
  Partial Marks : +1 If two or more options are correct but **ONLY** one option is chosen and it is a correct option;
  Zero Marks : 0 If unanswered;
  Negative Marks : –2 In all other cases.

9. The figure here shows a solid, homogeneous ball of radius R. The ball is released from height h above ground while it is spinning about a horizontal axis through its centre.

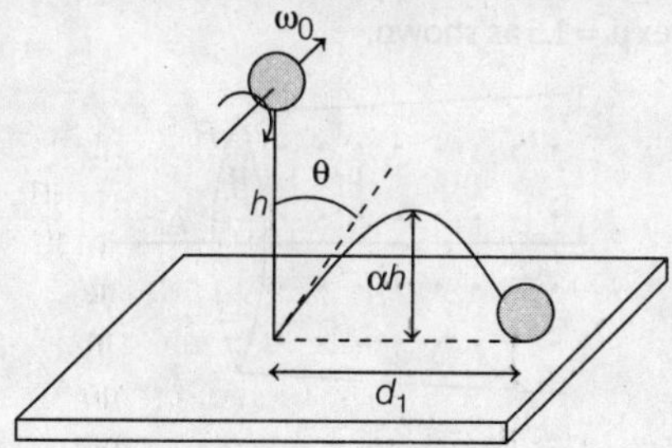

When released, the ball falls under gravity and rebounds at angle θ with vertical to a new height such that its lowest point is now αh above the floor. If $c = \sqrt{\alpha}$, choose the correct option(s).

(a) The rising and falling time of ball after it rebounds is $2c\sqrt{\frac{2h}{g}}$.

(b) $\tan\theta = \mu_k \frac{(1+c)}{c}$, here μ_k is coefficient of kinetic friction between ball and floor.

(c) Distance $d_1 = 4\mu_k(1+c)\,ch$

(d) Minimum angular velocity for the situation described is $\frac{7\mu_k(1+c)\sqrt{2gh}}{R}$.

10. Consider the experimental set-up of verification of photoelectric effect shown in the figure. The voltage across the electrodes is measured with the help of an ideal voltmeter and which can be varied by moving jockey J on the potentiometer wire. The battery used in potentiometer circuit is of 20 V and its internal resistance is 2 Ω. The resistance of 100 cm long potentiometer wire is 8 Ω.

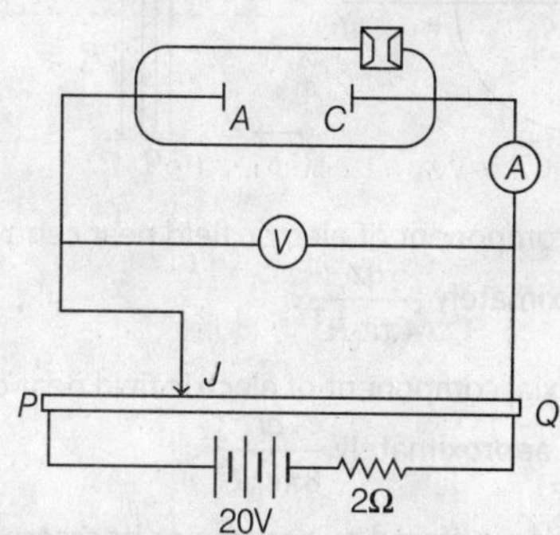

The photocurrent is measured with the help of an ideal ammeter. Two plates of potassium oxide of area 50 cm^2 at separation 0.5 mm are used in the vacuum tube. Photocurrent in the circuit is very small, so we can treat potentiometer circuit an independent circuit. Using the information in the table here, choose correct alternative(s).

Light	1 Violet	2 Blue	3 Green	4 Yellow	5 Orange	6 Red
λ (in Å)	4000-4500	4500-5000	5000-5500	5500-6000	6000-6500	6500-7000

(a) The number of electrons appearing on the surface of the cathode plate, when the jockey is connected at the end P of the potentiometer wire is $n = 8.85 \times 10^9$, even if no radiation falls on the cathode.

(b) It is found that on incidence of a light (power 4×10^{-6} W), current remains almost unchanged (20 μA) even when the jockey is moved from the end P to the middle point of the potentiometer wire. Assuming all the incident photons eject electron, the light is orange.

(c) Red may or may not eject photoelectrons but violet must eject them.

(d) When orange light falls on the anode plate, the ammeter reading remains zero till jockey is moved from the end P to the middle point of the wire PQ. Thereafter the deflection is recorded in the ammeter. Average of minimum and maximum kinetic energies of the emitted electron is 6 eV.

11. Consider the ring shown here with its axis in z-direction. The ring charge is neutral most of the time, but its charge becomes q when electrons are closer than a distance $d/2$ ($d << R$) from the plane of the ring. Assume that charging and discharging processes are instantaneous and the electric field "fills the space" instantaneously as well. Positrons of mass m and speed v approaching the ring parallel to its axis at a distance $r << R$ are focussed at point F as shown. This arrangement can be referred to as electrostatic lens.

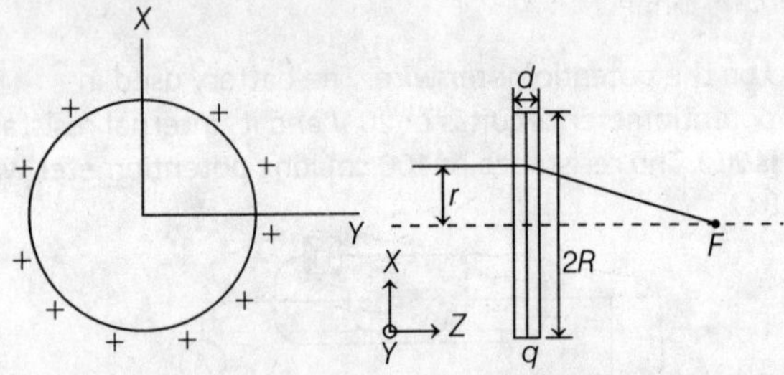

(a) Axial component of electric field near centre of the ring is approximately $\dfrac{qz}{4\pi\varepsilon_0 R^3}$.

(b) Non-axial component of electric field near centre of the ring is approximately $\dfrac{qr}{8\pi\varepsilon_0 R^3}$.

(c) Deviation suffered by positron as its crosses the lens is $\dfrac{eqrd}{8\pi\varepsilon_0 mR^3 v^3}$.

(d) Focal length f of this lens is $\dfrac{8\pi\varepsilon_0 mv^2 R^3}{qed}$.

12. A small block of mass m is fixed at upper end of a massless vertical spring of spring constant $k = \dfrac{4mg}{L}$ and natural length 10 L.

The lower end of spring is free and is at a height L from fixed horizontal floor as shown. The spring is initially unstressed and the spring-block system is released from rest in the shown position.

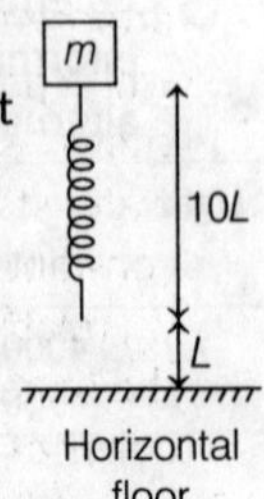

(a) At the instant speed of block is maximum, the magnitude of force exerted by spring on the block is mg.

(b) As the block is coming down, the maximum speed attained by the block is $\dfrac{3}{2}\sqrt{gL}$.

(c) Till the block reaches its lowest position for the first time, the time duration for which the spring remains compressed is $\dfrac{\pi}{4}\sqrt{\dfrac{L}{g}} + \sqrt{\dfrac{L}{4g}} \sin^{-1}\dfrac{1}{3}$.

(d) At the instant of maximum speed, force exerted by ground on spring is 1.5 mg.

13. An object O (real) is placed at focus of an equi-biconvex lens surrounded by air. The refractive index of lens is $\mu = 1.5$ and the radius of curvature of either surface of lens is R. For which of the following cases, final image is virtual and smaller in comparison to the situation before the change was made?

(a) If the refractive index of the lens is doubled, i.e. made 2μ

(b) If the radius of curvature of lens is doubled, i.e. made $2R$.

(c) If a glass slab of refractive index $\mu = 1.5$ is introduced between the object and lens as shown.

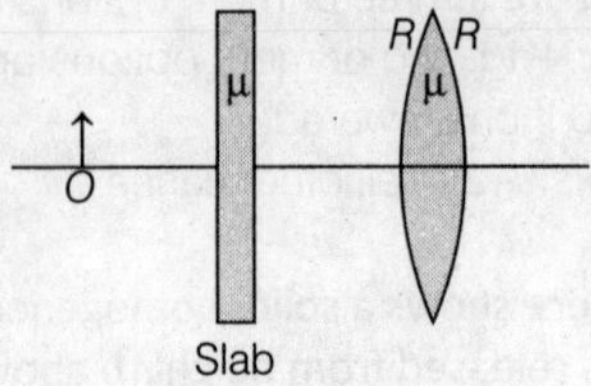

(d) If the left side of lens is filled with a medium of refractive index $\mu = 1.5$ as shown.

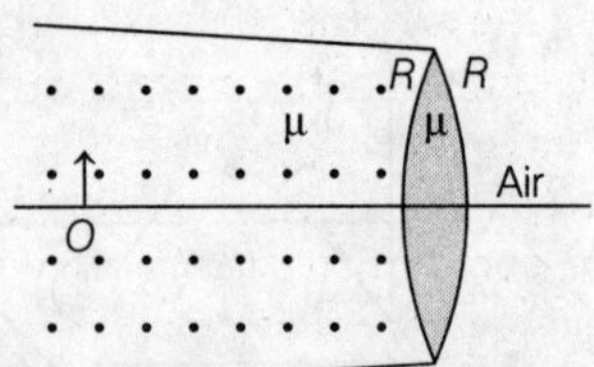

14. A thin superconducting ring is held above a vertical long solenoid, as shown in the figure, having the same axis. The cylindrically symmetric magnetic field around the ring can be described approximately in terms of the vertical and radial components of the magnetic field vector as $B_z = B_0(1 - \alpha z)$ and $B_r = B_0 \beta r$.

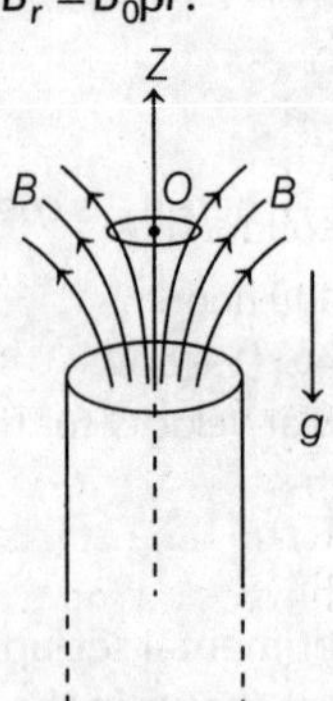

where B_r, α and β are positive constants and z and r are vertical and radial position coordinates, respectively. Initially plane of the ring is horizontal and the ring has no current flowing in it. When released, it starts to move downwards with its axis still in vertical direction. In the given diagram, point O is on the axis and slightly above the solenoid having vertical and radial position coordinates as (0, 0). Ring has mass m, radius r_0 and self-inductance L. Assume, the acceleration due to gravity as g.

(a) The current in the ring is $\frac{1}{L}B_0\alpha\pi r_0^2 z$.

(b) The force (magnitude) acting on the ring is $\frac{2B_0^2\alpha\beta\pi^2 r_0^4 z}{L}$.

(c) Vertical coordinate z for equilibrium position of the ring is $-\frac{mgL}{2B_0^2\alpha\beta\pi^2 r_0^4}$.

(d) The time period of ring's motion is $\frac{1}{B_0 r_0^2}\sqrt{\frac{2mL}{\alpha\beta}}$.

Section III (Maximum Marks 12)

- This section contains **FOUR (04)** questions.
- Each set has **FOUR** options (a), (b), (c) and (d). **ONLY ONE** of these four options is the correct answer.
- For each question, choose the option corresponding to the correct answer.
- Answer to each question will be evaluated according to the following marking scheme:
  Full Marks : +3 If **ONLY** the correct option is chosen;
  Zero Marks : 0 If none of the options is chosen (i.e. the question is unanswered);
  Negative Marks : –1 In all other cases.

15. In a liquid rocket engine, burning products (degree of freedom = 5) are formed inside the combustion chamber at a high pressure and temperature and expand adiabatically while leaving the chamber through the nozzle, upto the exit from the nozzle. As a result, a major part of the heat energy is converted into kinetic energy of the exhaust gases at the exit of the nozzle. The temperature of the exhaust gases inside the combustion chamber is T_0 at the exit, the cross-sectional area of the nozzle is S, temperature of the exhaust gases is T_1 and pressure is p_1. If the effect of atmospheric pressure on the thrust can be neglected and the kinetic energy of the gases inside the combustion chamber is negligible, thrust force F, assuming that $T_0 >> T_1$, is

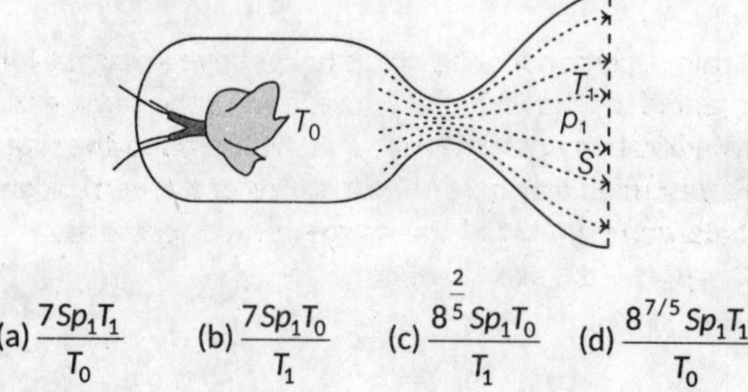

(a) $\frac{7Sp_1T_1}{T_0}$ (b) $\frac{7Sp_1T_0}{T_1}$ (c) $\frac{8^{\frac{2}{5}}Sp_1T_0}{T_1}$ (d) $\frac{8^{7/5}Sp_1T_1}{T_0}$

16. Two long, straight conducting wires having linear mass density λ are suspended from insulating cords, so that they are horizontal, parallel to each other and a distance d apart. A charged capacitor (capacitance C and having charge Q_0) is now connected to the system as shown in figure. Assume that, the time constant for the capacitor to discharge is negligible compared to the time it takes for any appreciable displacement in the position of the wires to occur. Height h each wire will rise as a result of the circuit connection is

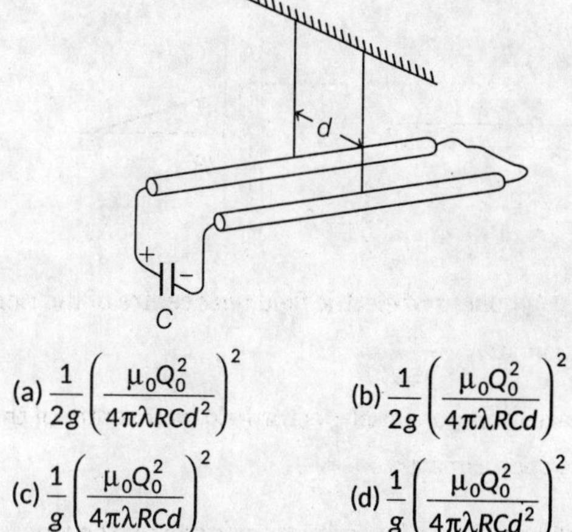

(a) $\frac{1}{2g}\left(\frac{\mu_0 Q_0^2}{4\pi\lambda RCd^2}\right)^2$ (b) $\frac{1}{2g}\left(\frac{\mu_0 Q_0^2}{4\pi\lambda RCd}\right)^2$

(c) $\frac{1}{g}\left(\frac{\mu_0 Q_0^2}{4\pi\lambda RCd}\right)^2$ (d) $\frac{1}{g}\left(\frac{\mu_0 Q_0^2}{4\pi\lambda RCd^2}\right)^2$

17. A block of mass M and a cylindrical tank which contains water having small hole at bottom, which is closed initially (total mass of cylinder + water is also M) are attached at two ends of an ideal string which passes over an ideal pulley as shown. At $t = 0$, hole is opened such that water starts coming out of the hole with a constant rate μ kg/s and constant velocity v_e, relative to the cylinder. Then, choose the correct option. (Magnitude of v_e is such that string does not get slack)

(a) Magnitude of acceleration of the block at any time t is $\dfrac{\mu(v_e + gt)}{(2M - \mu t)}$.

(b) Magnitude of acceleration of the block at any time t is $\dfrac{\mu(v_e - gt)}{(2M - \mu t)}$.

(c) Magnitude of acceleration of the block at any time t is $\dfrac{\mu g t}{2M}$.

(d) Magnitude of acceleration of the block at any time t is μg.

18. A screen, two mirrors and a source of monochromatic light are positioned as shown in figure. Due to a shade, only reflected light from the source can reach the screen. There will be a striped interference pattern on the screen, the distance between the strips is d. Express the wavelength of the light λ in terms of d and the distance a (see figure). Assume that, $a >> d$

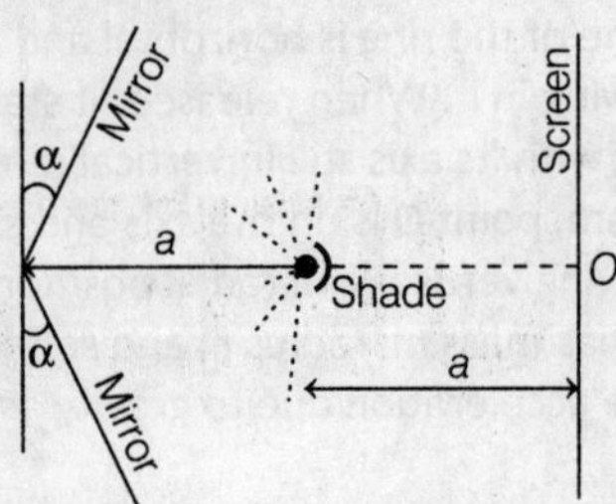

(a) $\dfrac{2d \sin 2\alpha}{\sqrt{2\cos^2 \alpha + 1}}$ (b) $\dfrac{2d \sin 2\alpha}{\sqrt{8\cos^2 \alpha + 3}}$

(c) $\dfrac{2d \sin 2\alpha}{\sqrt{8\cos^2 \alpha + 1}}$ (d) $\dfrac{2d \cos 2\alpha}{\sqrt{8\sin^2 \alpha + 3}}$

Answers

1 (5)	2 (5)	3 (6)	4 (3)	5 (3)	6 (2)	7 (4)	8 (8)	9 (a,b,c)	10. (a,b,c)
11 (a, b,c,d)	12 (a,b,c)	13 (b,c,d)	14 (a,c,d)	15 (b)	16 (b)	17 (a)	18 (c)		

See detailed explanations on page no. 332

Knockout 12

JEE ADVANCED

Physics

Paper 1

Section I *Numerical Value Type*

Instructions *See knockout 11*

1. A vessel of negligible water equivalent has some water at 0°C. One end of a rod of thermal conductivity 80 cal/s-m-K, length 20 cm and square cross-section of side 10 cm is in contact with the water while the other end is in contact with a reservoir at –100° C. It is observed that whole water freezes in 10 s. Now if a tank with constant height of water maintained in it is adding water (0°C) to the vessel as shown in figure, find time delay (in s) in complete freezing. (Take, $g = 10\ m/s^2$)

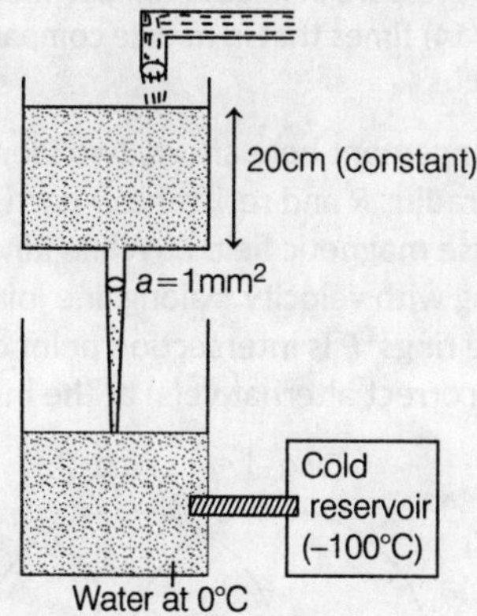

2. 40 resistors each having resistance $1\,\Omega$ are arranged as shown in the figure. Find power dissipated (in W) in the resistor cage thus formed.

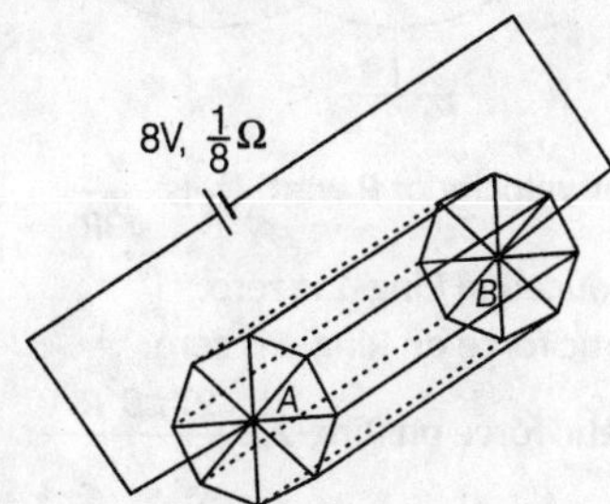

3. A vertical chain of mass m and length $l = \dfrac{\pi R}{2}$ is pulled slowly by a man on a surface having quarter circular section of radius R. Find minimum work done against gravity (in J) by the man in the process. [Take, $m = 0.1$kg, $R = 4\pi$m, $g = 9.8\ m/s^2$, $\pi^2 = 10$]

4. In a YDSE setup, distance between slits is 1mm and that between plane of slits and screen is 1.5 m. Angle between principal axis of lens and perpendicular bisector of S_1 and S_2 is 45°. A point source S is placed at a distance of 20 cm on axis of a lens and the aperture of lens is much larger than distance between slits. Assuming only reflected light is incident from plane mirror (M) on the slits, find distance (in m) of central maxima from centre O of the screen, if focal length of the lens is 20cm.

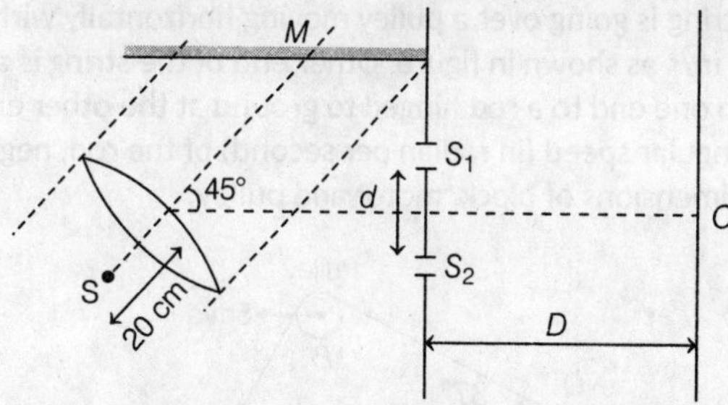

5. Three identical square metal plates of side 1 m are arranged parallel to each other as shown. A positively charged particle (of specific charge 1 C/kg) is projected in y-direction near plate-2 at point P shown, with velocity $100\ \hat{j}$ m/s. It finally reaches a symmetric point Q with $-100\ \hat{j}$ m/s. A uniform magnetic field $1\ \hat{k}$ T is present in the region $y > 1$m. Neglecting gravity, air resistance and edge effect determine charge (in μC) on the middle plate.

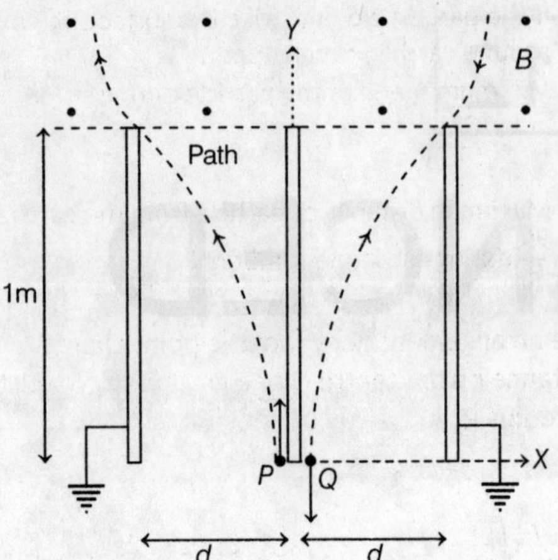

6. A light plate of area $10\ m^2$ is moved with constant velocity, $v = 40$ m/s against dust powder particles moving with constant velocity, $u = 10$ m/s by connecting to a system of two blocks *via* ideal string-pulley arrangement as shown in figure.

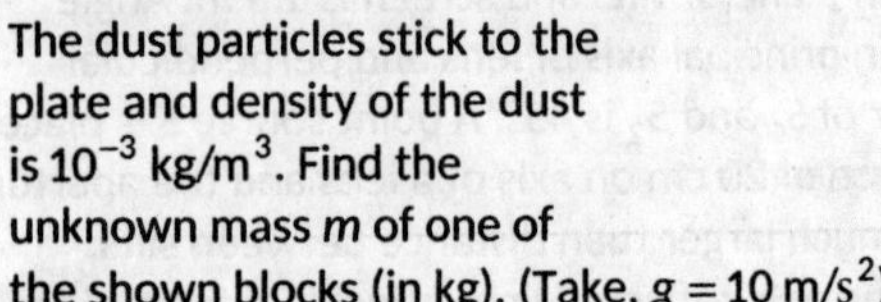

The dust particles stick to the plate and density of the dust is $10^{-3}\ kg/m^3$. Find the unknown mass m of one of the shown blocks (in kg). (Take, $g = 10\ m/s^2$)

7. A motor is installed on a block moving on horizontal surface with speed 10 m/s as shown. The motor is winding an inelastic string on its shaft at constant rate of 2m/s. The string is going over a pulley moving horizontally with 5 m/s as shown in figure. Other end of the string is attached to one end to a rod hinged to ground at the other end. Find angular speed (in radian per second) of the rod, neglecting dimensions of block, motor and pulley.

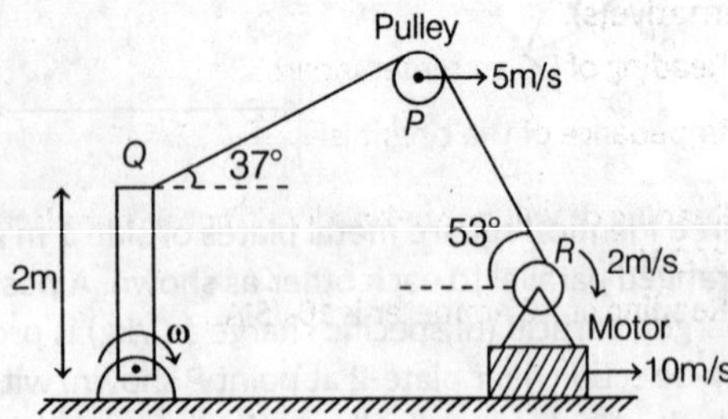

8. Intensity observed on interference of two coherent waves is given by $I = (20\pi \sin^2 \theta)\ W/m^2$. For $\theta = 30°$, intensity is $I = (5\pi \pm 0.02)\ W/m^2$. Percentage error in θ is x. Find value of 100x. (Take, $\pi^2 \approx 10$ and $\sqrt{3} = 1.73$)

Section II *One or more than one correct options*

Instructions *See knockout 11*

9. Consider the arrangement shown. The vessels contain equimolar mixture of argon and oxygen in all chambers having same thermodynamic state as shown in figure. The vessels are identical except a small difference that there is a small hole in one of the pistons in left vessel. Heat is being slowly supplied to the gases such that final volume of rightmost chamber of both the vessels is $\frac{4V_0}{9}$.

Choose the correct alternative(s).

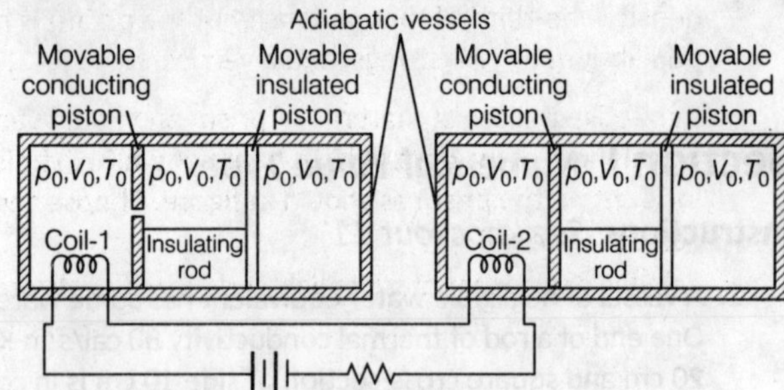

(a) Final temperature of gas in contact with coil-1 is $\frac{21}{4}T_0$.

(b) Heat supplied by coil-2 is $18p_0V_0$.

(c) Work done on the gas in rightmost compartment is p_0V_0.

(d) Final pressure in middle compartment of the left vessel is (9/14) times that in middle compartment of right vessel.

10. The arrangement here shows two identical conducting rings of radius R and resistance r each in a region of transverse magnetic field B. While Ring-1 is fixed, Ring-2 is moving with velocity v along line joining centres C_1 and C_2 of the rings. P is intersection point of the two rings. Choose correct alternative(s) at the instant shown.

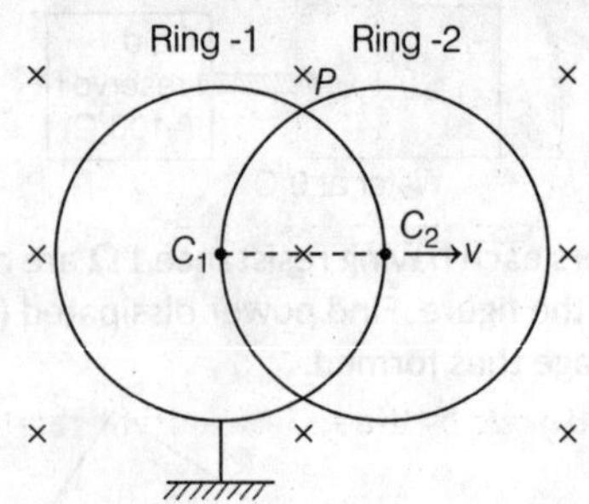

(a) Angular velocity of P w.r.t. C_1 is $\frac{v}{\sqrt{3}R}$.

(b) Emf induced in Ring-1 is zero.

(c) Magnetic force on Ring-1 is zero.

(d) Magnetic force on Ring-2 is $\frac{27\pi B^2R^2v}{4r}$.

11. Consider the figure shown.

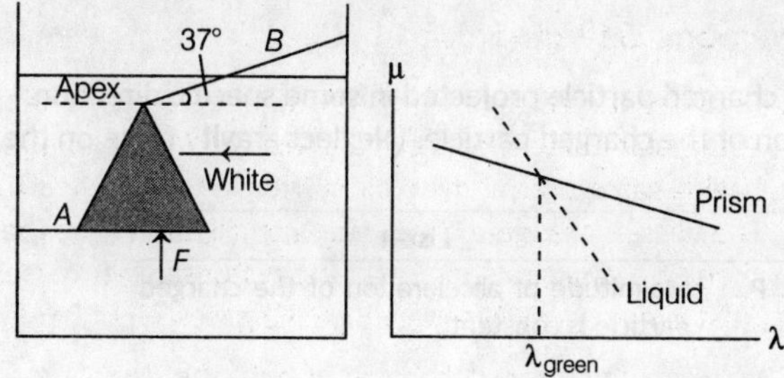

An equilateral prism of mass m immersed in a liquid (of density one-third of that of density of the prism) is held in equilibrium by two strings and a vertical force F. Refractive indices of material of prism and liquid vary with wavelength of incident light. A beam of white light is incident on the prism as shown in figure. Choose the correct option(s).

(a) Blue component of white light is deviated clockwise.

(b) Green component of white light emerges parallel to the base.

(c) Tension in the string A is lesser than $\frac{8mg}{9}$.

(d) If the liquid surface touches the apex of the prism, force by liquid on inclined surface of the prism is $\frac{2mg}{3}$.

12. Consider the figure shown. At point P, a particle projected tangentially is made to collide elastically with an inclined surface making angle θ with earth's surface. On collision, the particle enters a smooth tunnel. Moving along the tunnel, it enters another symmetrical tunnel after it exits this tunnel following the shown trajectory. Choose the correct alternative(s).

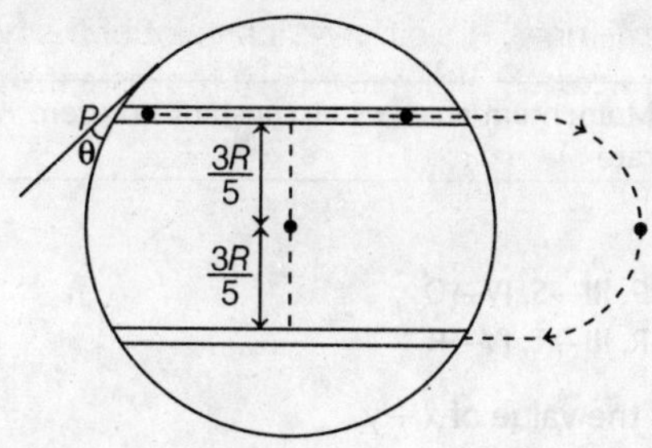

(a) Angle θ made by the surface at P with earth's surface is 53°.

(b) If the particle did not strike the surface, it would orbit around earth in circular path.

(c) Minimum speed of the particle during subsequent motion is $\frac{1}{3}\sqrt{\frac{GM}{R}}$.

(d) Maximum distance of particle from the earth's centre is $\frac{9R}{5}$ during subsequent motion.

13. The arrangement here shows a point charge q at a distance r from centre O of a grounded conducting sphere of radius R.

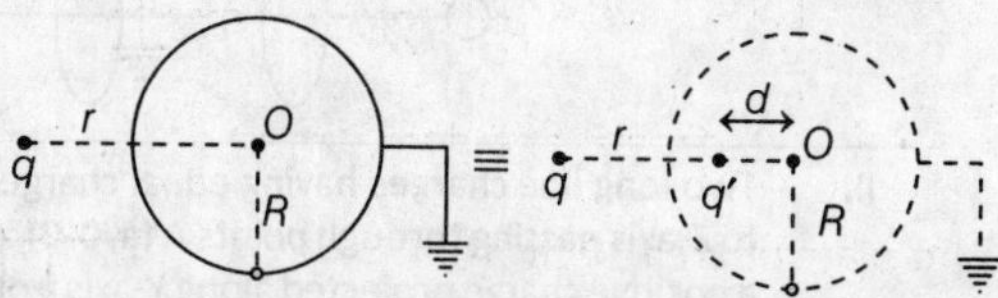

As per method of images in electrostatics, induced charge can be replaced by an equivalent charge called the image charge q' placed at a distance d from centre of the grounded sphere as shown in figure. This charge is such that potential at the location of the metal sphere is zero. Choose the correct alternative(s).

(a) $q' = -\frac{R}{r}q$ (b) $q' = -\frac{r}{R}q$ (c) $d = \frac{R^2}{r}$ (d) $d = \frac{R^3}{r^2}$

14.

DC Ammeter (Ideal) AC Voltmeter-2 (Ideal)

4Ω 3Ω 6Ω 8Ω 10Ω 10Ω 10Ω

AC Voltmeter-1 (Ideal) AC Ammeter (Ideal)

100 V

Consider the AC circuit shown and choose the correct alternative(s).

(a) Reading of DC ammeter is zero.

(b) Impedance of the circuit is $\frac{100}{\sqrt{1040}}\,\Omega$.

(c) Reading of Voltmeter-2 and Voltmeter-1 are both equal to 100 V.

(d) Reading of AC ammeter is $10\sqrt{5}$ A.

Section III Matching List Type

Instructions *See knockout 11*

15. The figures in List-I show some charge and current distributions with a charged particle projected in some specific direction. List-II gives certain conditions which may exist in the subsequent motion of the charged particle. (Neglect gravity force on the charged particle)

	List-I		List-II
I.	A positive charge projected along the axis of two co-axial current carrying loops, carrying currents in opposite directions as shown	P.	Magnitude of acceleration of the charged particle is constant
II.	Two long line charges having equal charge density λ parallel to Z-axis passing through points $A(a, 0, 0)$ and $B(-a, 0, 0)$ and a positive charge projected along Y-axis from point $C(0, 2a, 0)$	Q.	Kinetic energy of the charged particle is constant
III.	A positive charge is projected from an inside point on the axis of a long solenoid at some angle θ with axis as shown. Charge does not hit the solenoid	R.	Angular momentum of the charged particle about the point of projection is constant
IV.	A positive charge projected from a point in between two large parallel oppositely charged horizontal plates at some angle θ with horizontal as shown. Charge does not hit the plate.	S.	Path of the charged particle is straight
		T.	Momentum changes at constant non-zero rate

Which one of the following options is correct?

(a) I→R, II→P, III→Q, IV→S
(b) I→T, II→P, III→S, IV→Q
(c) I→Q, II→R, III→P, IV→P
(d) I→S, II→R, III→T, IV→R

16. List-I shows systems for which two numbers x and y are defined. List-II shows the value of $x + y$.

	List-I		List-II
I.	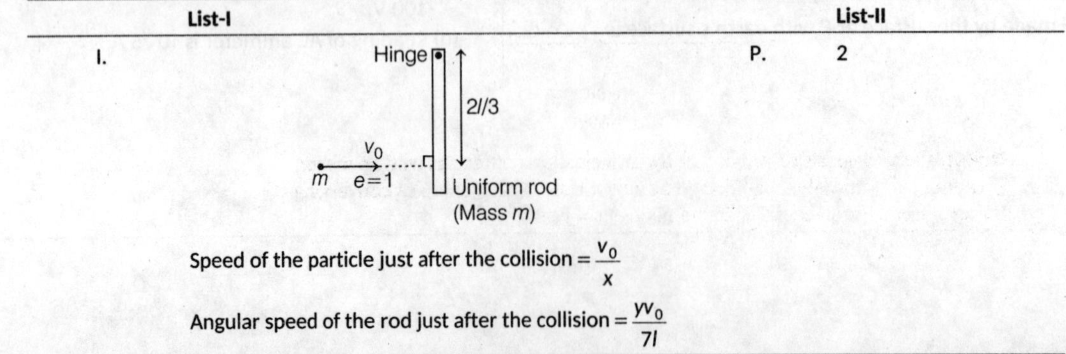	P.	2

Speed of the particle just after the collision $= \frac{v_0}{x}$

Angular speed of the rod just after the collision $= \frac{yv_0}{7l}$

List-I	List-II
II. 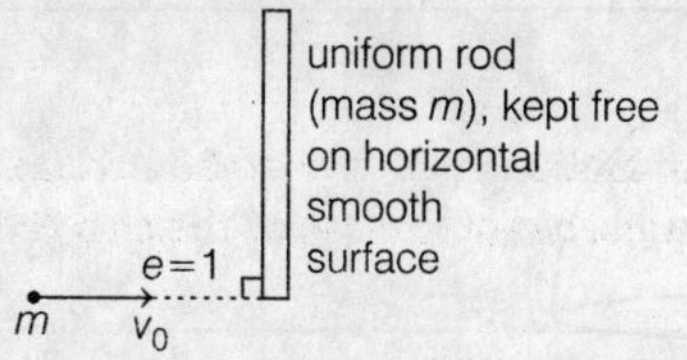 uniform rod (mass m), kept free on horizontal smooth surface; $e=1$; m, v_0 Speed of the CM of rod just after collision $= \frac{xv_0}{5}$ Speed of the particle just after collision $= \frac{yv_0}{5}$	Q. 5
III. 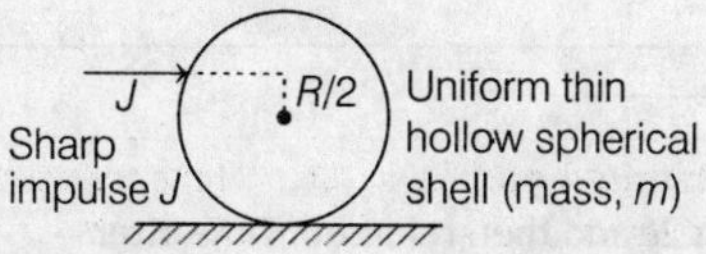 J, $R/2$, Sharp impulse J, Uniform thin hollow spherical shell (mass, m) Speed of CM of sphere after it starts pure rolling $v = \frac{xJ}{10\,m}$ Time interval after which ring starts pure rolling $= \frac{J}{y\mu mg}$	R. 7
IV. 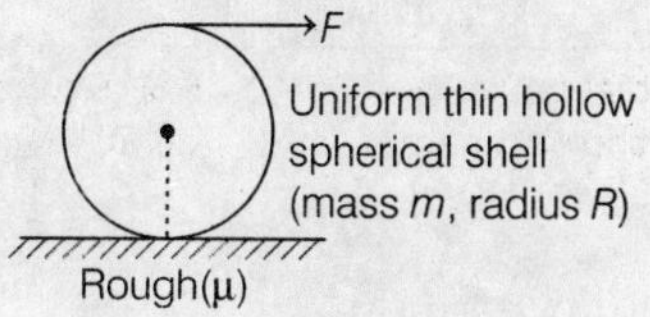 F, Uniform thin hollow spherical shell (mass m, radius R), Rough(μ) Maximum value of F for which sphere performs pure rolling $= x\,\mu mg$ If $F = 2x\,\mu mg$, angular acceleration of sphere $= \frac{27\mu g}{yR}$	S. 9
	T. 19

Which one of the following options is correct?

(a) I→P, II→Q, III→R, IV→S
(b) I→T, II→Q, III→R, IV→S
(c) I→P, II→Q, III→T, IV→R
(d) I→T, II→Q, III→T, IV→R

17. List-I shows a system for which two numbers x and y are defined, List-II shows value of $\frac{y}{x}$.

List I	List-II
I. 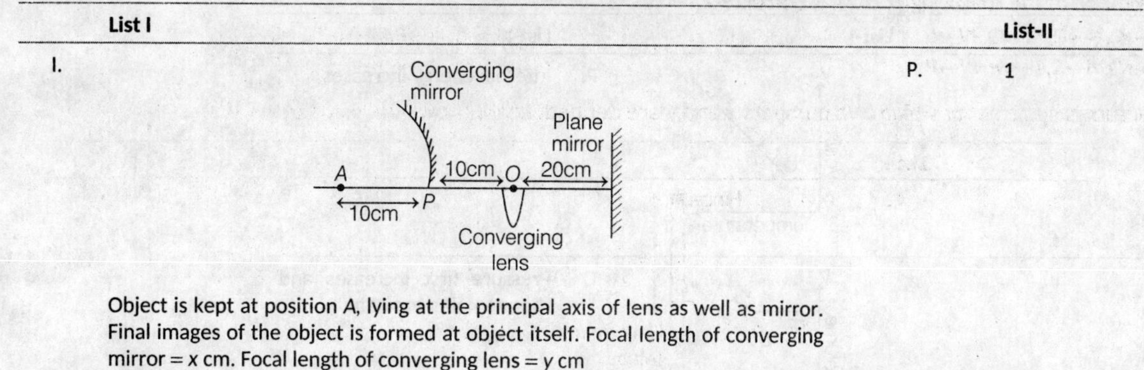 Object is kept at position A, lying at the principal axis of lens as well as mirror. Final images of the object is formed at object itself. Focal length of converging mirror $= x$ cm. Focal length of converging lens $= y$ cm	P. 1

List I	List-II
II. Hemispherical shell, having surface charge density σ (may be constant or variable). Electric field at O (if $\sigma = \sigma_0$ = constant) $= \dfrac{\sigma_0}{x\varepsilon_0}$ Electric field at O (if $\sigma = \sigma_0 \cos\theta$) $= \dfrac{\sigma_0}{y\varepsilon_0}$	Q. 1.5
III. Two identical point masses, kept at separation $2a$ and then released. Time after they collide $= \sqrt{\dfrac{\pi^2 a^3}{xGm}}$ Velocity of approach of particles when separation between them is $a = \sqrt{\dfrac{yGm}{a}}$	R. 4
IV. Uniformly charged long cylinder, charge density ρ, having long cylindrical cavity inside its. Electric field at the axis of long cylinder $= \dfrac{x\rho R}{4\varepsilon_0}$ Electric field at the axis of cavity $= \dfrac{2\rho R}{y\varepsilon_0}$ (R = Radius of cylinder)	S. 8
	T. 10.5

Which one of the following options is correct?

(a) I→P, II→Q, III→S, IV→R
(b) I→R, II→Q, III→P, IV→S
(c) I→S, II→Q, III→P, IV→T
(d) I→T, II→S, III→P, IV→Q

18. In each situation of List-I, a process $A \to B \to C$ is given for an ideal gas.

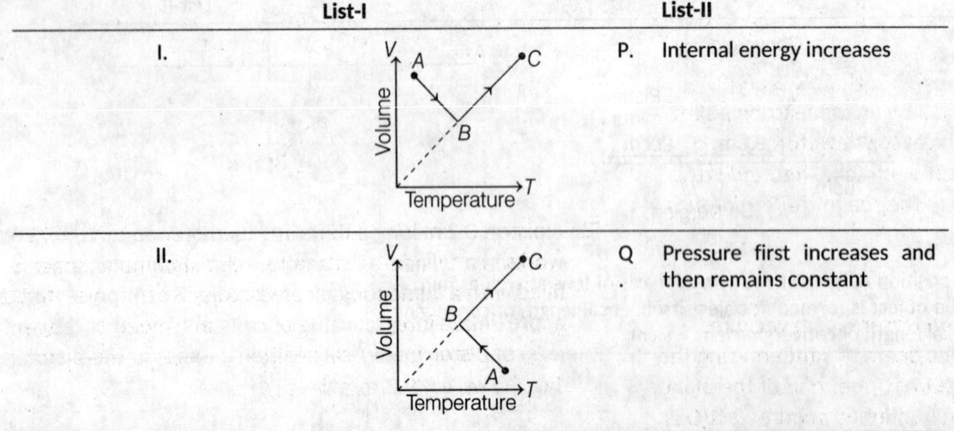

List-I	List-II
I. (Volume–Temperature graph, $A \to B \to C$)	P. Internal energy increases
II. (Volume–Temperature graph, $A \to B \to C$)	Q Pressure first increases and then remains constant

List-I	List-II
III. (graph)	R. Temperature first decreases and then increases
IV. (graph)	S. Pressure first decreases and then remains constant
	T. Internal energy decreases

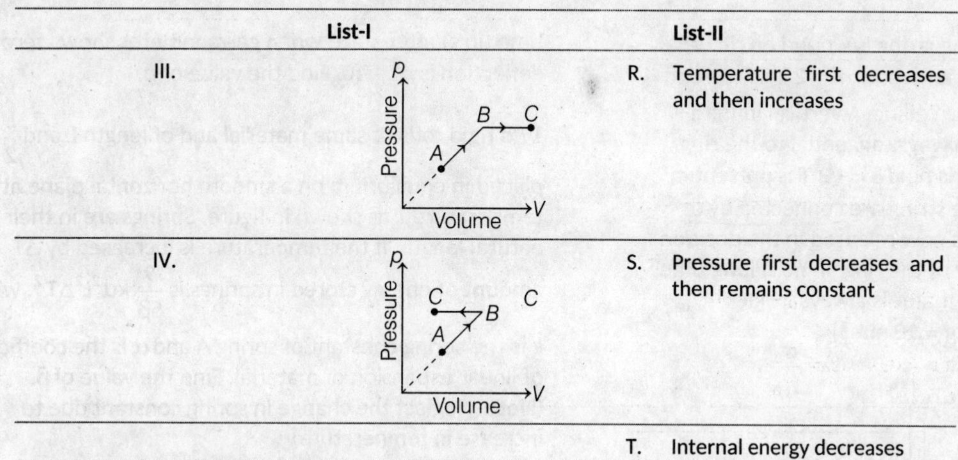

Which one of the following options is correct?

(a) I→P, II→Q, III→R, IV→T
(b) I→P, II→R, III→S, IV→Q
(c) I→Q, II→R, III→P, IV→T
(d) I→P, II→R, III→P, IV→Q

Answers

1 (6.67)	2 (96)	3 (17.64)	4 (1.50)	5 (17.70)	6 (0.79)	7 (5.62)	8 (6.92)	9 (b,c,d)	10. (a,b)
11 (a,b,c)	12 (b,c,d)	13 (a,c)	14 (a,b,c,d)	15 (c)	16 (d)	17 (b)	18 (d)		

See detailed explanations on page no. 336

Paper 2

Section I *Single Digit Integer Type*

Instructions *See knockout 11*

1.

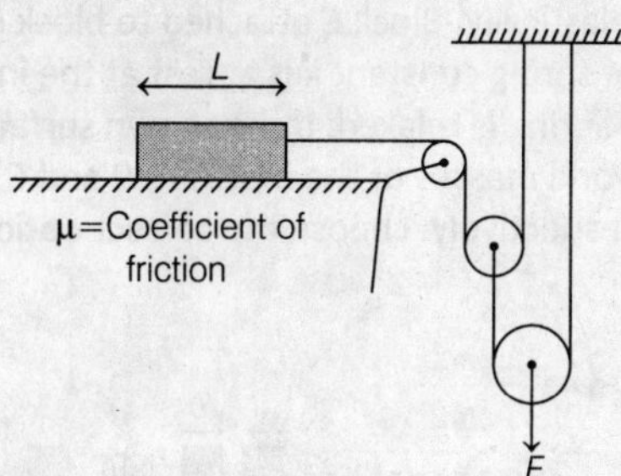

A rod of mass m, length L, cross-sectional area S and Young's modulus Y is being pulled by an ideal-string pulley arrangement by applying a vertical constant force F as shown. Coefficient of friction between table and rod is μ. Elastic potential energy stored in the rod in the situation is $\frac{(F - a \cdot \mu\, mg)^2 L}{(b^2 - 4)AY}$. Find $\frac{b}{2+a}$.

2. Consider the thin plano-convex lens shown, in vacuum. Wavelength of a monochromatic beam of light entering the lens reduces from 6000 Å to 4000Å. Upper half of the plane surface of the lens is polished. A luminous point object O is moving with speed $\frac{12}{17}$ cm/s along the axis of the lens as shown in figure. Find velocity of image-1 (I_1) relative to image-2 (I_2) in cm/s at the instant, the object is at a distance $3R$ from optical centre of the lens. R is radius of curvature of the curved surface of the lens.

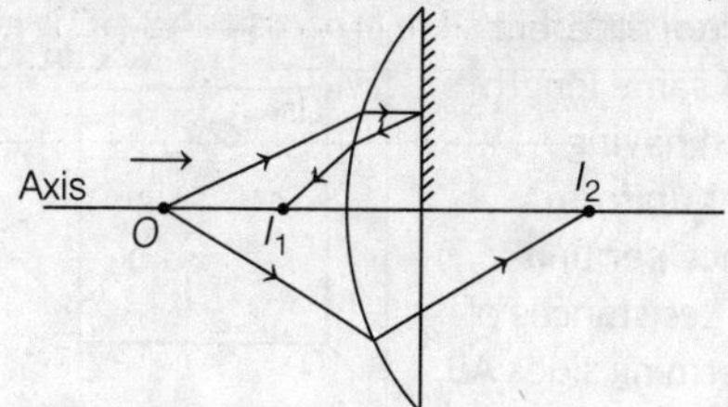

3. A piston 0.2 m long and having diameter equal to 0.796 m works in a cylinder of diameter 0.8m. If annular space is filled with a lubricating oil of viscosity 5 centipoise, find the approximate integral value of constant speed of descent (in m/s) of piston in vertical position, if mass of the piston is 1kg. (Take, $g = 9.8\ \text{m/s}^2$)

4. A light inextensible conducting string is wound on rim of a metal ring of radius $r = \sqrt{5}$ m and mass $m = 2$ kg. Free end of the string is attached to the ceiling. A vertical infinite smooth conducting plane is always tangential to the ring. A uniform transverse magnetic field $B = \sqrt{2}$ T is present in the region. The plane and the string are connected by a resistance $R = 4\ \Omega$. The ring is now released in the position shown in figure. Find velocity of the ring (in m/s) long time after it is released, assuming that it is always inside magnetic field region. (Take, $g = 10$ m/s^2)

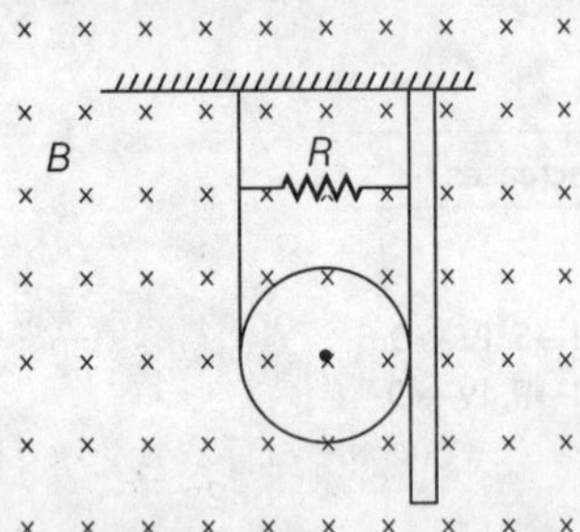

5. The figure here shows a system of two discs fixed to each other, such that their centres are along same vertical line (axis of the system). The lower disc is rotated on a smooth horizontal table. If the axis remains stationary after the system is released from rest, find $\frac{m_1}{m_2}$. Given that, radii of discs, $r_1 = 0.3$ m, $r_2 = 0.2$ m, combined moment of inertia, $I = 0.25$ kg-m^2 and $m_2 = 25$ kg.

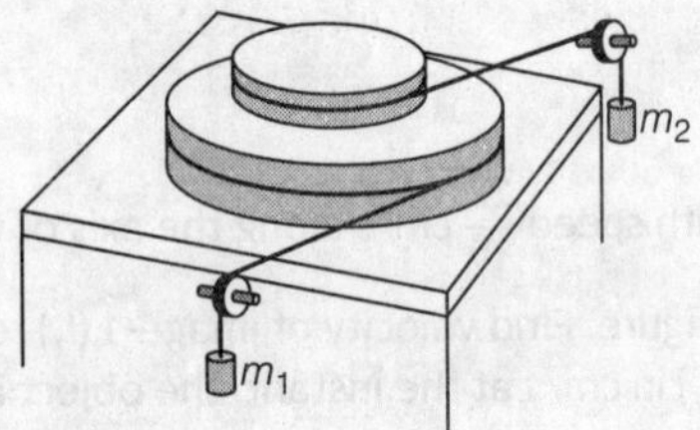

6. *ABCD* is a square frame made from different wires of same length and each having different uniform resistance per unit length. Resistances of wires forming sides *AB*, *BC*, *CD* and *DA* are 100 Ω, 400 Ω, 500 Ω and 200 Ω, respectively. An ideal cell is connected across *B* and *D*. A straight conducting wire containing a resistance and a galvanometer in series starts rotating about pivoted point *A* from initial position as shown in figure with uniform angular velocity $\omega = \frac{\pi}{360}$ rad/s. One end of the straight wire (rotating) is pivoted at *A* and other end always in sliding contact with a side of the square. The time (in s) after start, when galvanometer shows zero deflection is $n^2 + 10$. Find the value of *n*.

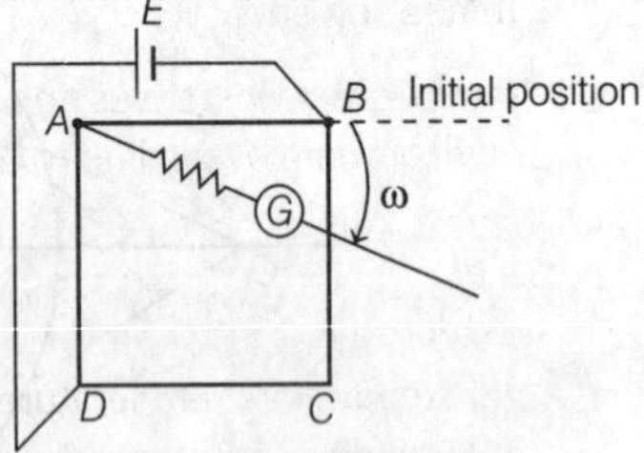

7. Two rigid rods of same material and of length *L* and $\frac{L}{2}$ are placed in equilibrium on a smooth horizontal plane at temperature *T* as shown in figure. Springs are in their natural length. If the temperature is increased by ΔT amount of energy stored in springs is $\frac{9}{5\beta} k\alpha^2 L^2 \Delta T^2$, where *k* is the spring constant of spring *A* and α is the coefficient of linear expansion of material. Find the value of β.
(**Note** Neglect the change in spring constant due to increase in temperature)

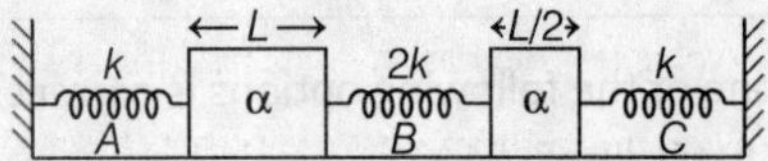

8. Polonium ($_{84}Po^{210}$) emits α-particles and is converted into lead ($_{82}Pb^{206}$). This reaction is used for producing electric power. Polonium has half-life 138.6 days. Assuming an efficiency of 10% for the thermoelectric machine, the amount of polonium required to produce 1.2×10^7 J of electric energy per day at the end of 693 days is 80*n* g. Find *n*. Masses of nuclei are $Po^{210} = 209.98264$ amu, $Pb^{206} = 205.97440$ amu, $He^4 = 4.00260$ amu, 1 amu $= 931$ MeV/c^2. Avogadro's number $= 6 \times 10^{23}$ per mol.

Section II *One or more than one correct options*

Instructions *See knockout 11*

9. Consider the figure shown. Blocks *A* and *B* are moving with equal speed *u* in opposite directions are just about to collide elastically. Block *C* attached to block *B* by an ideal spring of spring constant *k* is at rest at the instant shown and the spring is relaxed. If the shown surfaces are smooth and masses of the blocks *A*, *B* and *C* are *m*, 2*m* and *m* respectively, choose the correct option(s).

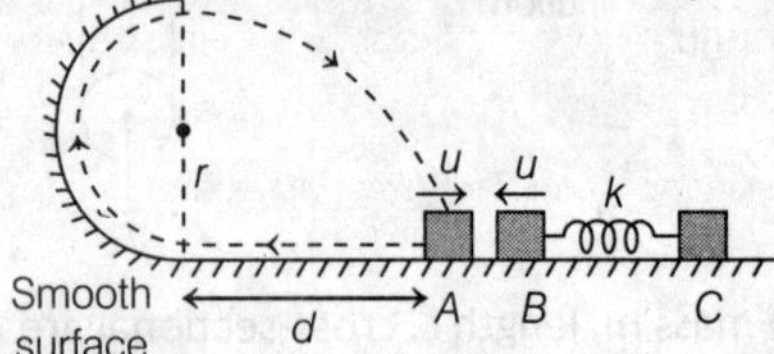

(a) Minimum value of *u*, so that block *A* can climb the semi-circular part is $u_0 = \sqrt{\frac{9gr}{5}}$.

(b) *d* for which block *A* follows the dotted path shown is equal to 2*r* (if $u = u_0$).

(c) Maximum compression in the spring during subsequent motion is $\frac{2u}{3}\sqrt{\frac{m}{k}}$.

(d) Minimum speed of *B* during subsequent motion after collision is $\frac{u}{9}$.

10. A system of two identical balls of mass m having short dipoles embedded inside are connected by an ideal spring. The system is initially at rest on a smooth surface with separation r between the balls. Considering r to be extremely large compared to natural length of the spring, choose the correct alternative(s).

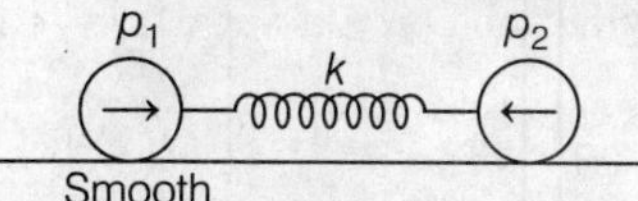

(a) Potential energy (spring + electrostatic) is close to zero.

(b) $k \approx \frac{6\,c\,p_1 p_2}{r^5}$, here $c = \frac{1}{4\pi\varepsilon_0}$.

(c) If left ball is held at rest by external means and right ball is slightly displaced, time period of resulting SHM is $2\pi\sqrt{\frac{m}{5k}}$.

(d) If the two balls are simultaneously displaced towards each other and released, time period of resulting SHM is $2\pi\sqrt{\frac{m}{5k}}$.

11. The star (Mass $= M_0$ and radius $= R_0$) shown is in equilibrium due to inward gravitational pull being balanced by outward radiation pressure.

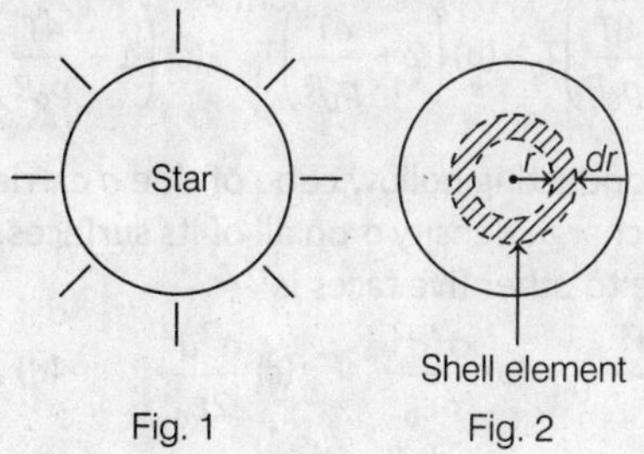

Fig. 1 Fig. 2

The figure here shows a shell element of radius r and thickness dr inside a star. If M is mass of gases inside the space bound by the shell and ρ is local density, choose the correct alternative(s).

(a) Difference in pressure across the shell is $|dp| = \frac{GM\rho}{r^2}dr$.

(b) Radiation pressure at star's centre is $\frac{6GM_0}{\pi R_0^4}$.

(c) Radiation pressure at star's centre is $\frac{3GM_0^2}{2\pi R_0^4}$.

(d) Pressure at centre of sun is nearly $5\times10^{14}\,N/m^2$, if $M_0 = 2\times10^{30}$ kg and $R_0 = 7\times10^5$ km for the sun.

12. Consider a long double tape line carrying current I as shown in Fig.1. Inductance and capacitance of the line per unit length are L_0 and C_0, respectively. Also shown is an L-C circuit in Fig. 2 having respective specifications shown in the figure.

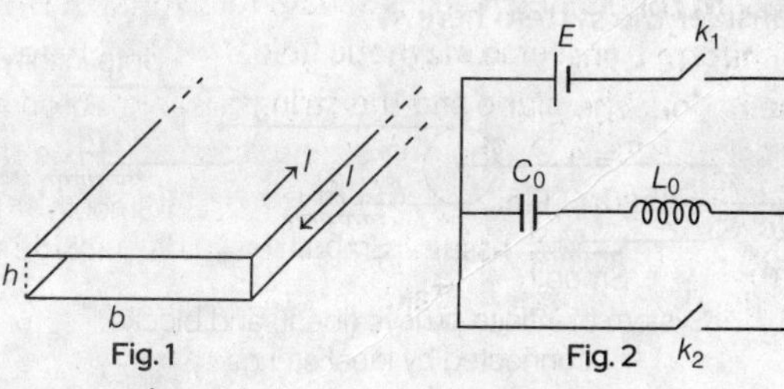

(a) $L_0 = \frac{\mu_0 h}{b}$

(b) $C_0 = \frac{\varepsilon_0 b}{h}$

(c) If capacitor in Fig.2 has some charge and k_2 is closed, charge oscillates with angular frequency numerically equal to c.

(d) With capacitor uncharged, if k_1 is closed maximum charge acquired by the capacitor is $\frac{2\varepsilon_0 bE}{h}$.

13. A coolidge tube with target ${}^{A}_{Z}X$ emits strong k_α lines for X and two weak k_α lines for impurities. Wavelengths of k_α lines are $\lambda_1, \lambda_2, \lambda_3$ for impurity-1, impurity-2 and X, respectively. If, $\lambda_3 = 4\lambda_1$ while $\lambda_2 = 4\lambda_3$, then we may conclude that,

(a) atomic number of impurity-1 is $2Z-1$

(b) atomic number of impurity-1 is $2Z+1$

(c) atomic number of impurity-2 is $0.5Z+1$

(d) atomic number of impurity-2 is $0.5(Z+1)$

14. A straight nichrome wire is initially at room temperature 20°C. It is connected to an ideal battery of 500 V. Just after switching ON, the current detected is 5 A. Due to heating effect its

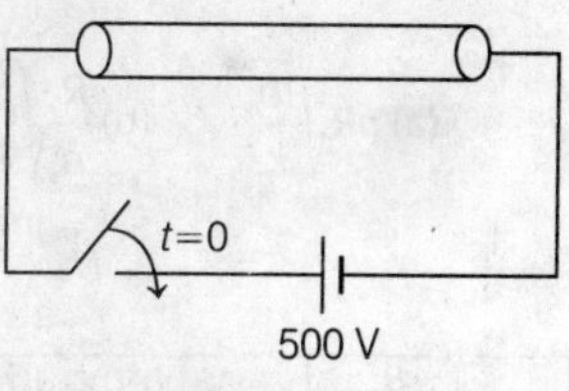

temperature increases and is also losing heat to the environment according to Newton's cooling law as $\frac{dQ_{loss}}{dt} = 45(T - 20°C)$ J/s. At steady state, the current detected is 4.5 A.

(a) Steady state temperature of the wire is 70°C.

(b) Steady state temperature of the wire is 75.5°C.

(c) Temperature coefficient of resistance of the wire is nearly $2.2\times10^{-3}/°C$.

(d) Temperature coefficient of resistance of the wire is nearly $1.57\times10^{-3}/°C$.

Section III Only one correct option

Instructions *See knockout 11*

15. Consider the system here.

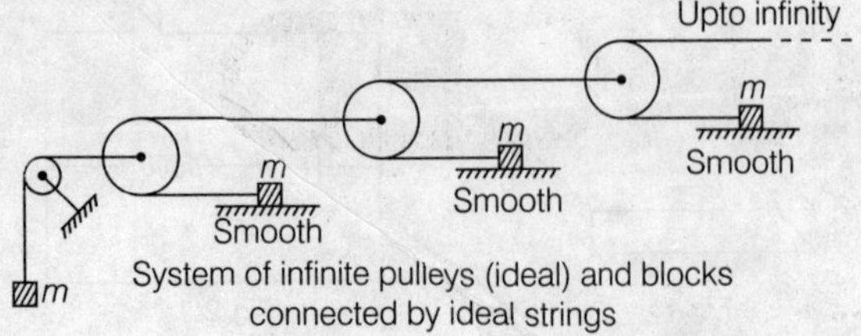

System of infinite pulleys (ideal) and blocks connected by ideal strings

Power delivered by tension to the leftmost block placed on horizontal surface, t time after the system is released from rest, is

(a) $\frac{mg^2t}{8}$ (b) $\frac{7mg^2t}{32}$ (c) $\frac{9mg^2t}{64}$ (d) $\frac{11mg^2t}{128}$

16. An extremely thin transparent sphere of radius R in vacuum contains a liquid of refractive index n. A point source of light of mass m attached to an ideal spring of spring constant k is hanging in equilibrium, located at centre of the sphere. Minimum velocity (along the spring) to be imparted to the source, so that a thin dark ring will be observed by an observer in vacuum is

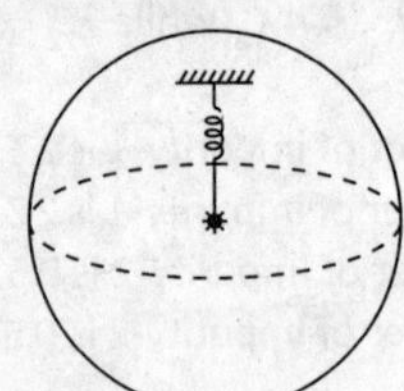

(a) $nR\sqrt{\frac{m}{k}}$ (b) $\frac{R}{n}\sqrt{\frac{m}{k}}$ (c) $nR\sqrt{\frac{k}{m}}$ (d) $\frac{R}{n}\sqrt{\frac{k}{m}}$

17.

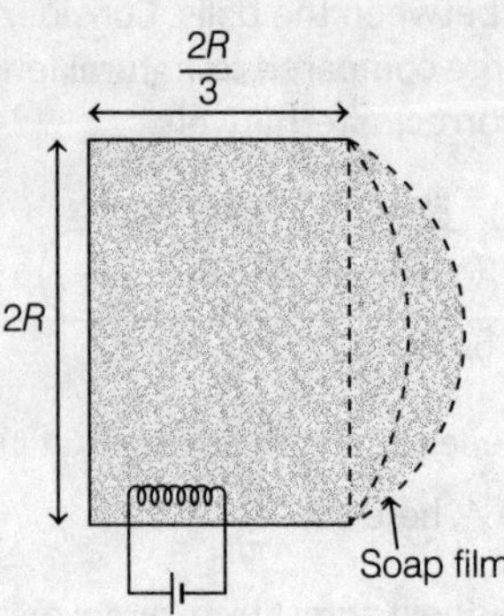

An insulated cylindrical tube of diameter $2R$ and height $\frac{2R}{3}$ has a flat soap film of surface tension T at its open end. Initially, air pressures outside as well as inside the tube are equal to p_0. Heat is now slowly supplied to the air inside the tube thereby slowly increasing inside pressure. Temperature of air inside the tube, at the instant when air pressure is maximum, is (V_0 = Initial volume of air inside the tube and T_0 = initial temperature of air inside the tube)

(a) $\left(2+\frac{8T}{p_0R}\right)T_0$ (b) $\left(2+\frac{4T}{p_0R}\right)T_0$ (c) $\left(1+\frac{4T}{p_0R}\right)T_0$ (d) $2T_0$

18. A non-conducting hollow cube of side d carries uniform surface charge density σ on all of its surfaces. Force on a face due to other five faces is

(a) $\frac{2\sigma^2d^2}{\varepsilon_0}$ (b) $\frac{\sigma^2d^2}{6\varepsilon_0}$ (c) $\frac{\sigma^2d^2}{2\varepsilon_0}$ (d) zero

Answers

1 (5)	2 (3)	3 (8)	4 (2)	5 (2)	6 (8)	7 (4)	8 (4)	9 (a,b,d)	10. (b,c)
11 (a,c,d)	12 (a,b,c,d)	13 (a,d)	14 (a,c)	15 (c)	16 (d)	17 (a)	18 (c)		

See detailed explanations on page no. 341

Knockout 13

JEE ADVANCED

Physics

Paper 1

Section I *Numerical Value Type*

Instructions *See knockout 11*

1. The arrangement (initially at rest) here shows block *A* of mass *m* placed on another block *B* of mass 2*m* connected to spool *C* (having mass *m*, inner radius *r*, outer radius 2*r* and moment of inertia about axis through CM equal to mr^2) *via* an ideal string wound over spool's periphery of radius *r*. Another ideal string is wound around outer periphery of radius 2*r*, which is pulled (from rest) by a person with force *F* horizontally. There is no friction between *B* and ground while coefficient of friction between blocks is $\mu = 0.5$. The spool is observed to execute rolling without slipping.

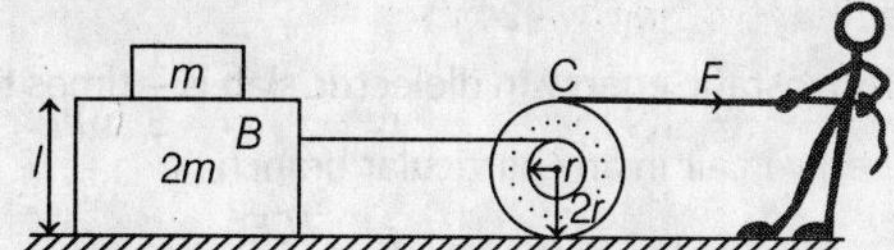

For $F = \frac{55}{24} mg$, tension in the string connecting *B* and *C* is *x mg*. Find the value of *x*.

2. 3 moles of oxygen is undergoing a cyclic process *ABCDA* as shown by pressure-temperature indicator diagram here. The diagram is not upto scale. It is known that *AB* and *CD* are adiabatic steps and volume in state *A* is 32 times that in state *B*. Determine fractional efficiency of the cycle. (Take, $R = \frac{25}{3}$ J/mol-K)

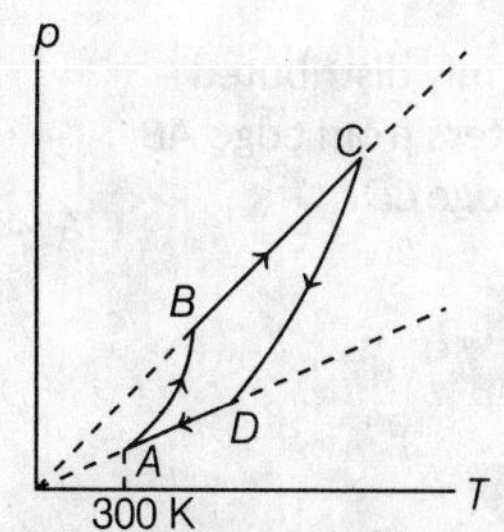

3. In the arrangement shown, a concave mirror of mass $m = 0.1$ kg and radius of curvature $R = 2$ m attached to spring of spring constant $k = 10^3$ N/m is released with spring relaxed. A bee is fluttering at rest at a distance $d =$ 50 cm from the mirror as shown. Amplitude of oscillation of image of bee is *a* (in mm) w.r.t. the mirror while time period of oscillation is $\frac{\pi}{b}$ in seconds. Find the value of $a + b$. (Take, $g = 10$ m/s^2)

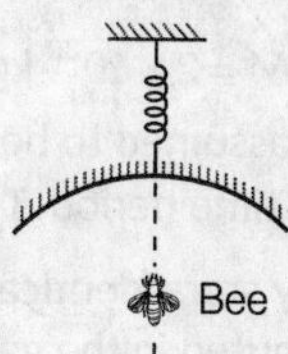

4. Consider the circuit shown. Find time (in s) at which the voltmeters (ideal) read the same.

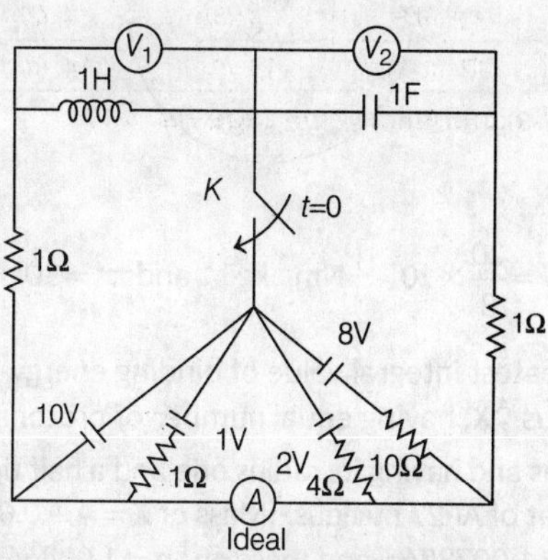

5. In a YDSE set-up, a point source *S* of white light is placed at perpendicular distance *l* from the central line such that green ($\lambda = 5000$ Å), is missing at centre O of the screen. When a monochromatic green light source is placed at

S' on the central line, central maxima is observed at O due to S'. Intensities of S and S' are equal at location of screen.

Minimum value of $l(l_1)$ is ....$\times 10^{-4}$ m.

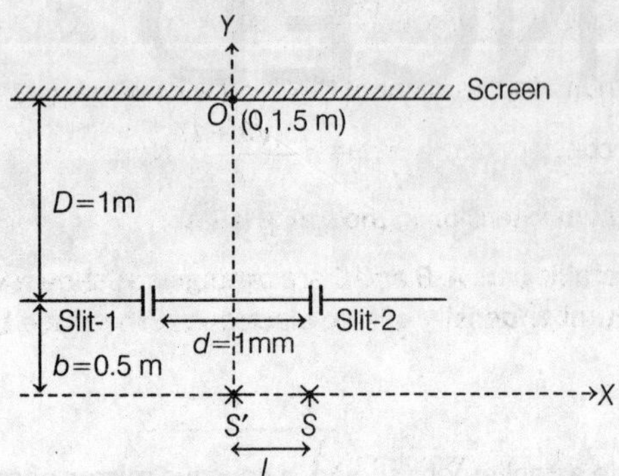

6. A photocell is operating in saturation mode having photo-current equal to 4.8mA, when a radiation of 3000Å and 1 W is incident on the photocathode. For another radiation of 1650Å and 5mW, maximum speed of photoelectrons is double of that for 3000 Å radiation. Assuming quantum efficiency of photoelectron generation per incident photon equal in both cases, find the threshold wavelength of the cell in μm.

7. A star having mass, $M = 2 \times 10^{30}$ kg is revolving on the edge of milky-way (assumed to be of spherical shape of radius 10^{20} m) with time period, $T = 10^{15}$ s.

Assuming that many stars identical to the revolving star are uniformly distributed in the galaxy, number of stars is close to $x \times 10^{y}$. Find $x + y$. $(1 < x < 10)$

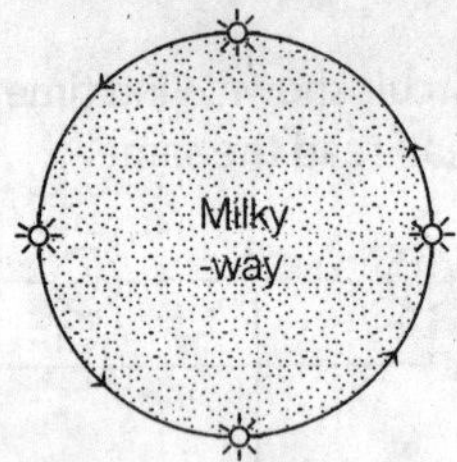

(Take, $G = \frac{20}{3} \times 10^{-11}$ Nm^2 kg^{-2} and $\pi^2 = 10$)

8. Find greatest integral value of binding energy (in MeV) of a nucleus ${}^{A}_{Z}X$, having equal number of protons and neutrons and having its radius one and a half times smaller than that of Al-27 nucleus. (Mass of X = A + 0.0053 u, mass of ${}_1H^1$ = 1.007826 u and mass of ${}^{1}_{0}n$ = 1.008665 u)

Section II *One or more than one correct options*

Instructions *See knockout 11*

9. The arrangement here has fourteen air cored capacitors each of capacitance C and plate separation d. Every branch has double the number of capacitors compared to number in the lower branch. The lowermost branch having two capacitors. The arrangement is in steady state across a cell of emf E. Now, dielectric slabs (of dielectric constant $K = 3$) having area equal to plate area and thickness equal to $\frac{3}{4}$th of the plate separation are introduced in every alternate capacitor as shown.

Choose the correct alternative(s), considering that the circuit acquires steady state again.

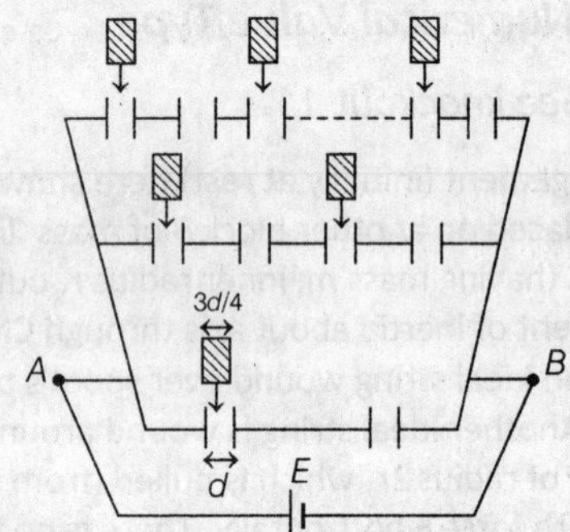

(a) Capacitance of the arrangement doubles on introduction of slabs

(b) Work done by cell is $\frac{7}{24} CE^2$

(c) Electrostatic energy in dielectric slab is $\frac{1}{5}$ times that of energy in air in any particular branch

(d) Heat dissipated in the circuit is $\frac{7CE^2}{24}$

10. A solid hemisphere of density σ and radius r lies at bottom of a tank filled with liquid of density ρ, such that flat top surface of the hemisphere is h depth below water surface. Net contact force on the hemisphere is independent of

(a) ρ (b) σ
(c) R (d) h

11. An aluminium foil is bent into the shape shown in the figure. Dimensions of the foil are as shown with $k >> 1$.

Current i uniformly distributed over width l enters from edge AB and leaves at edge CD.

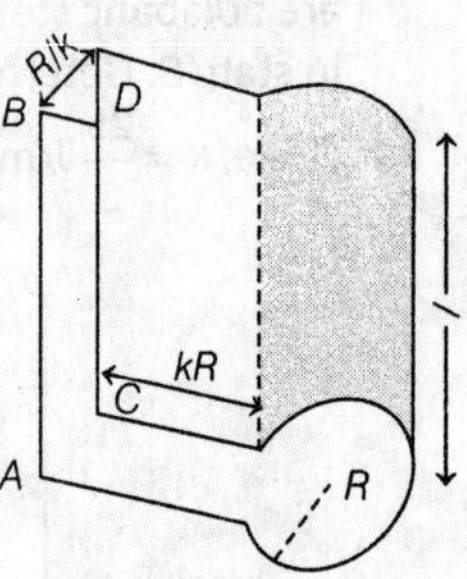

Choose the correct alternative(s).

(a) Energy stored by the arrangement is $\frac{2\mu_0 R^2(\pi+1)^2 i^2}{l}$.

(b) Magnetic flux density at centre of the cylinder is $\frac{\mu_0 i}{l}$.

(c) Ratio of energy stored in cylindrical volume and energy stored in space between the planes is π.

(d) Self-inductance of the arrangement is $\frac{\mu_0 R^2}{l}(\pi+1)$.

12. Sand is dropped vertically downward at constant rate of μ kg/s on conveyor belt, which is moving horizontally with constant speed v. Assume that, the sand particles come to rest immediately after landing on the belt. Choose the correct alternative(s).

(a) Force that must be applied on the belt to move it with constant speed is μv.

(b) Rate at which work is done by friction force on sand is $-\frac{\mu v^2}{2}$.

(c) Power delivered by external agent to the belt is μv^2.

(d) Work done by friction force on sand in time t is $-\mu v^2 t$.

13. The figure here shows a heavy box sliding freely on fixed smooth very long incline. A smooth rigid wire PQ is fixed to the box as shown. A bead R (of mass 1 kg) attached to a spring of natural length $(\sqrt{3}+1)$ m can slide freely along the wire. At the instant shown, the spring is relaxed and oriented perpendicular to the incline while the bead is at rest w.r.t. wire. During subsequent motion, the bead comes to rest w.r.t. wire when spring has rotated by 30°. Taking, $g = 10\ \text{m/s}^2$, choose the correct alternative(s).

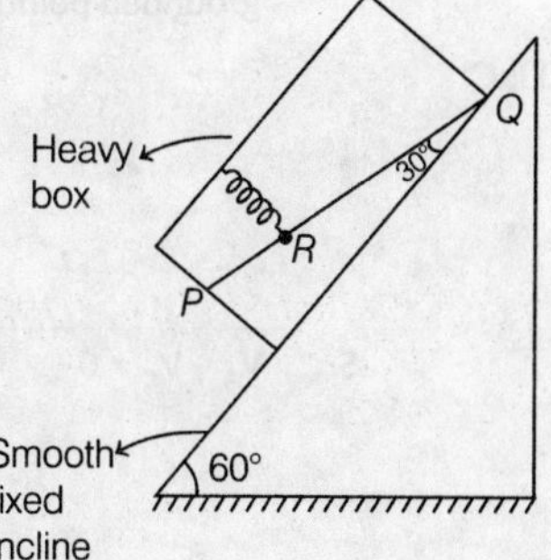

(a) Normal force on the bead by the wire when the bead is at rest again w.r.t. wire is $\frac{(5\sqrt{3}-1)}{4}$ N.

(b) Maximum displacement of the bead w.r.t wire is $(\sqrt{3}+1)$ m.

(c) Force constant of the spring is $\frac{5(\sqrt{3}+1)}{4}$ N/m.

(d) Maximum extension in the spring is 2 m.

14. Three metallic bars A, B and C are arranged as shown in the figure. Number density of free electrons in the three bars are in ratio,

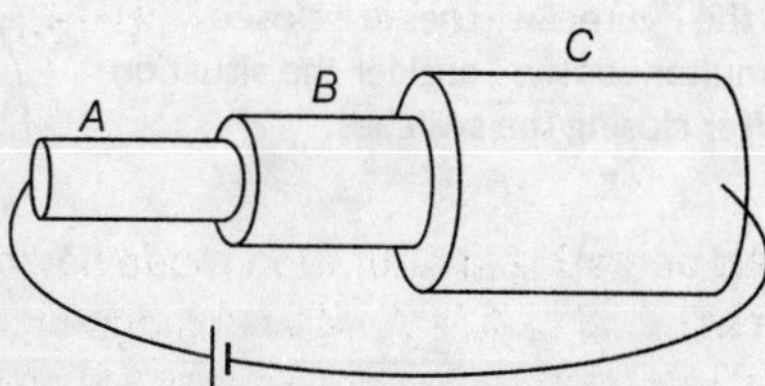

$N_A : N_B : N_C = 1:2:3$, ratio of resistivities of the bar is $\rho_A : \rho_B : \rho_C = 2:3:1$, lengths are in ratio $l_A : l_B : l_C = 2:2:3$ and radii are in the ratio $r_A : r_B : r_C = 1:2:3$ as shown.

Choose the correct alternative(s).

(a) Power dissipated in A is $4\sqrt{2}$ times the geometric mean of powers dissipated in B and C.

(b) Electric fields in the wires A, B and C are related as $32E_B^2 = 81E_A E_C$.

(c) Drift speed of electrons in the wire B is arithmetic mean of drift speeds in wire A and C.

(d) Potential differences across the wires are related as $V_A : V_B : V_C = 24:9:2$.

Section III *Matching List Type*

Instructions *See knockout 11*

15. List-I gives different arrangements. List-II gives information about the arrangements. V in List-II signifies potential.

	List-I		List-II
I.	All the conducting equi-spaced plates are identical. Initial charges are shown in the figure. Switches are closed simultaneously. Consider the situation after closing the switches (10μC, 4μC, 6μC, 8μC; plates A, B, C, D; switches S_1, S_2)	P.	$V_B - V_A = V_B - V_C$
II.	The conducting spheres are concentric. Initial charges are shown in the figure. Switches are closed simultaneously. Consider the situation after closing the switches. (30μC, 10μC, 20μC; A, B, C; R, 2R, 3R; S_1, S_2)	Q.	Net charge on any of the grounded surface is zero
III.	Initially the capacitors are charged and then connected to a battery. Consider the situation after closing the switch. (200μF, 10μF, 30V, 10μF, 200μC, 300μF, 10μF; A, B, C; S)	R.	On closing the switch, the electron flow takes place to the earth from one of the grounded point(s)
IV.	The magnetic field is present into the plane of paper and is varying with time. A uniform metallic triangular loop is considered in the region inside the magnetic field (A, B, C)	S.	$V_A - V_C \neq 0$
		T.	The energy of the system dissipates

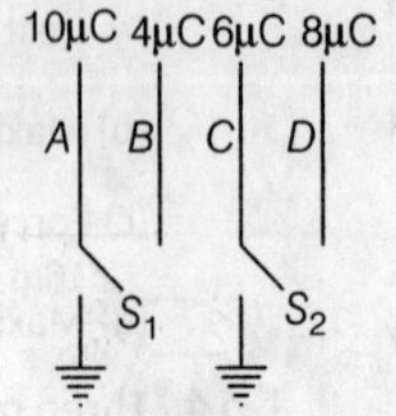

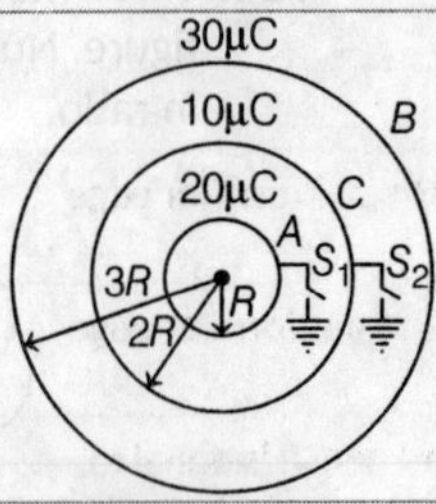

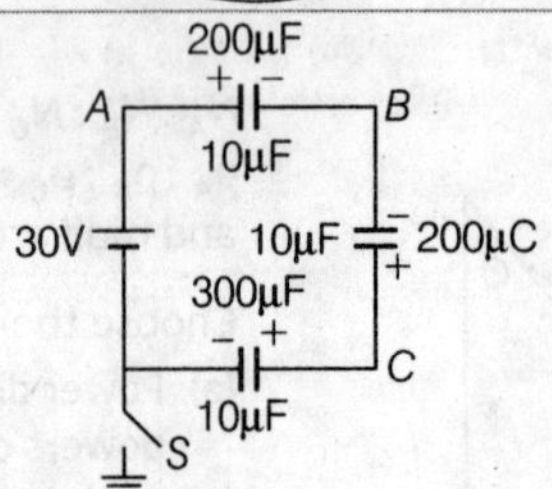

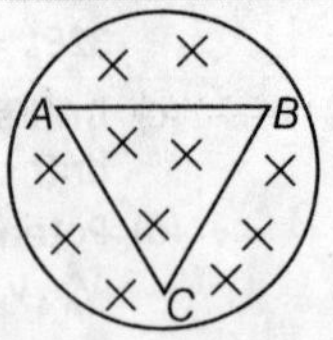

Which one of the following options is correct?

	I	II	III	IV		I	II	III	IV
(a)	R	Q	T	T	(b)	Q	P	P	T
(c)	P	R	T	S	(d)	T	Q	P	P

16. When we write expression for energy of electron in nth orbit of helium ion (He^+) we take zero potential energy for $n = \infty$, but the potential energy depends on reference. If we take total energy of atom for $n = 1$ orbit as zero, then

	List-I		List-II
I.	Total energy of electron in $n = 2$ (in eV)	P.	54.4
II.	Ionisation energy in ground state	Q.	40.8
III.	Energy required to excite electron from $n = 1$ to $n = 2$ (in J)	R.	depends on reference level
IV.	Negative of potential energy of electron in $n = 1$ (in eV)	S.	independent of reference level
		T.	65.28×10^{-19}

Which one of the following options is correct?

	I	II	III	IV		I	II	III	IV
(a)	R	S	T	Q	(b)	P	R	T	S
(c)	Q	S	T	P	(d)	T	S	R	P

17. A square platform of side length 8 m is situated in X-Z plane such that it is at 16 m from the X-axis and 8m from the Z-axis as shown in figure. A particle is projected with velocity $\mathbf{v} = (v_2\hat{\mathbf{i}} + 25\hat{\mathbf{j}})$ m/s relative to wind from origin and at the same instant, the platform starts with acceleration $\mathbf{a} = (2\hat{\mathbf{i}} + 2.5\hat{\mathbf{j}})$ m/s^2. Wind is blowing with velocity $v_1\hat{\mathbf{k}}$. (Take, $g = 10$ m/s^2)

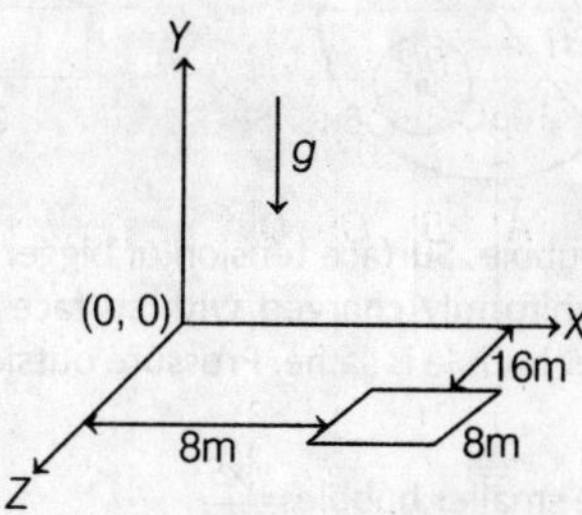

	List-I		List-II
I.	Least possible values of v_2 (in m/s) so that particle hits the platform or edge of platform is	P.	4
II.	Least possible value of v_1 (in m/s), so that particle hits the platform or edge of platform is	Q.	6
III.	If t is the time (in second) after particle hits the platform, then $2t$ is equal to	R.	8
IV.	Value of displacement with respect to ground (in m) of the particle in y-direction, when v_2 has its minimum possible value is (till particle hits the platform or edge of platform)	S.	20
		T.	40

Which one of the following options is correct?

	I	II	III	IV		I	II	III	IV
(a)	Q	P	T	S	(b)	S	P	R	T
(c)	Q	T	R	S	(d)	Q	P	R	S

18. List-I shows a system for which two quantities x and y are defined, List-II shows several relations between x and y.

	List-I		List-II
I.	A_2 A_1 ρ 3ρ A uniform solid cylinder of height h and density ρ is floating in a liquid of density 3ρ as shown.Cylinder is slightly displaced and released. Time period of SHM of cylinder (if $A_1 = 3A_2$) $= 2\pi\sqrt{\frac{2h}{xg}}$ Time period of SHM of cylinder (if $A_1 >>>> A_2$) $= 2\pi\sqrt{\frac{h}{yg}}$	P.	$x = y^y$

	List-I		List-II

II. 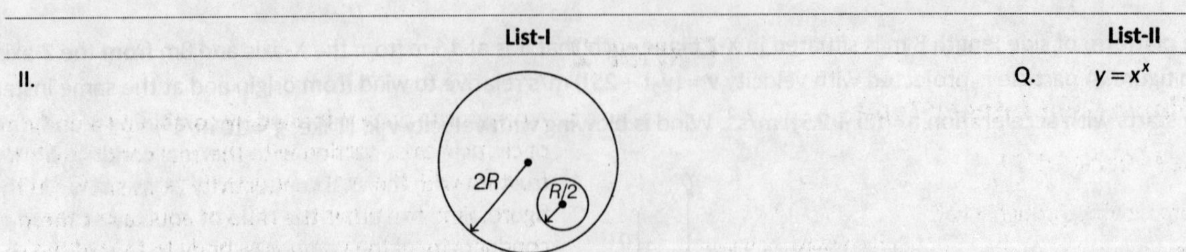

There is a small bubble inside a bigger bubble. Surface tension of bigger bubble is S and of smaller bubble is $2S$. Inner bubble is uniformly charged with surface charge density σ. Pressure inside bigger bubble and smaller bubble is same. Pressure outside bigger bubble is p_0.

Excess pressure (in addition to p_0) inside smaller bubble $= \dfrac{xS}{R}$

Value of $\sigma = y\sqrt{\dfrac{2\varepsilon_0 S}{R}}$

Q. $y = x^x$

III. 

Rod PQR is of uniform linear mass density and cross section A.

Young modulus of rod is σ.

In natural state $PQ = QR = \dfrac{l}{2}$

Elongation in part $PQ = \dfrac{xFl}{8A\sigma}$

Elongation in part $QR = \dfrac{9Fl}{yA\sigma}$

R. $x = y^2$

IV. 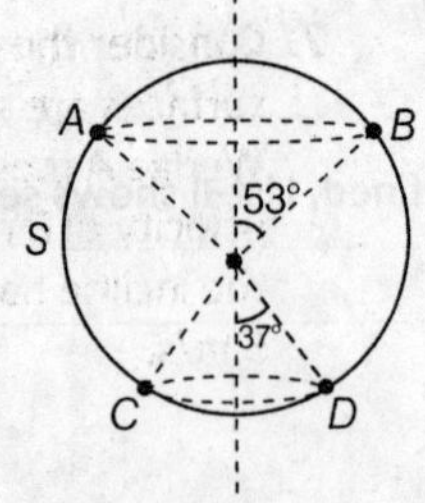

We have a spherical bubble of radius R, made up by liquid having surface tension S. AB and CD are two parallel planes as shown in figure. Net force of surface tension on part $ABCD$ due to rest of the part is $\dfrac{\alpha\pi RS}{\beta}$. There is no common factor in α and β. x is defined as $x = \dfrac{3\alpha}{14}$ y is defined as $y = \dfrac{\beta}{5}$

S. $5y = 6x$

T. $x - y = 3$

Which one of the following options is correct?

	I	II	III	IV		I	II	III	IV
(a)	P	Q	R	S	(b)	R	Q	P	S
(c)	T	P	T	Q	(d)	R	Q	T	S

Answers

1 (2.50)	2 (0.75)	3 (54.00)	4 (0.69)	5 (1.25)	6 (0.41)	7 (14)	8 (56)	9 (b,c)	10. (a,d)
11 (b,c,d)	12 (a,b,c)	13 (a,b,c,d)	14 (a,b,d)	15 (d)	16 (c)	17 (d)	18 (d)		

See detailed explanations on page no. 346

Paper 2

Section I *Single Digit Integer Type*

Instructions *See knockout 11*

1. A laser beam moving through a half cylinder (of refractive index $\frac{5}{4}$) strikes a screen as shown. The situation shown is at $t = 0$.

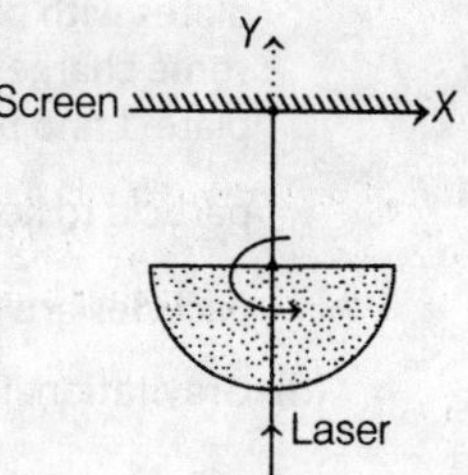

The cylinder now starts rotating with angular speed $\omega = \frac{53\pi}{540}$ rad/s, at $t = 0$. Find average speed (in cm/s) of the laser spot on the screen between $t = 0$ till the instant it disappears.

It is given that, axis of rotation is along z-direction with points on axis having y-coordinate equal to -20 cm.

2. Two identical imaginary open cones shown in the figure have flux ϕ_1 and ϕ_2, respectively through them. The flux is due to a semi-infinite uniformly charged wire oriented along axis of the cone such that one end of the wire coincides with common centre O of the common base. Find $\frac{\phi_2}{\phi_1}$, if heights of the cones are double of their radii.

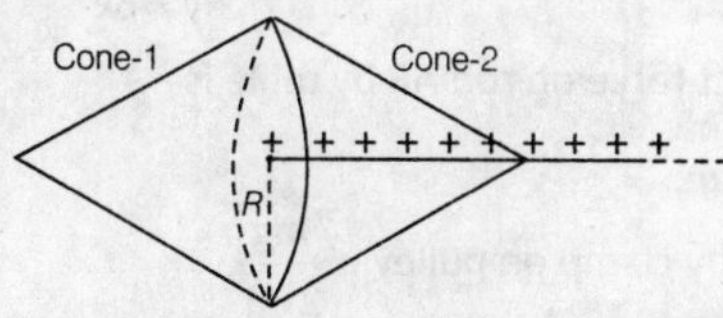

3. Ratio of de-Broglie wavelength to orbital radius of an electron in Li^{2+} in first excited state is $\frac{6\pi}{x}$. Find x.

4. A massless cork is connected to a perfectly conducting tube (with a small orifice) of length 60 cm and cross-sectional area 1.6 cm^2 with a piston fitted at the other end. It requires force F to be applied normal to the surface of cork to move it out of the tube. If the orifice is now closed and piston slides slowly by a distance of 12 cm towards the cork, the cork pops out. If atmospheric pressure p_0 is 10^5 N/m^2, find F (in N).

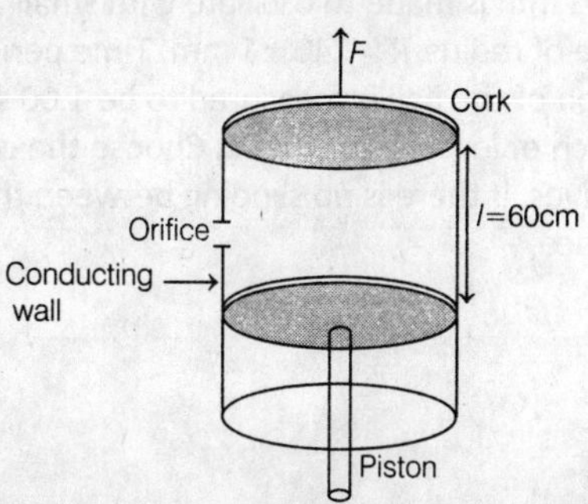

5. A composite body is formed by combining a uniform rod of circular cross-section with thermal conductivity K and a frustum with thermal conductivity $2K$ as shown in the figure. Find five times the ratio of equivalent thermal conductivity of the composite body to that of the rod.

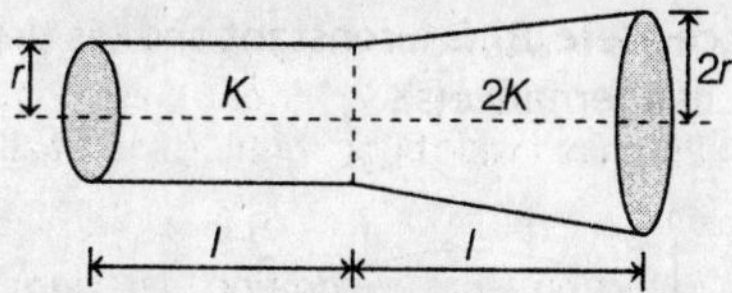

6. A coordinate axis system taking X-axis along horizontal smooth floor is shown in figure. Two small balls of masses m and $3m$ attached with a string are released from some heights on Y-axis as shown in figure. The balls may collide head on or obliquely. After a certain time, mass m is at (9 cm, 20 cm) while mass $3m$ is 25 cm above the X-axis and the string is taut. The balls always remain in XY-plane. If the length of string in cm is $x^2 - x + 1$, find x.

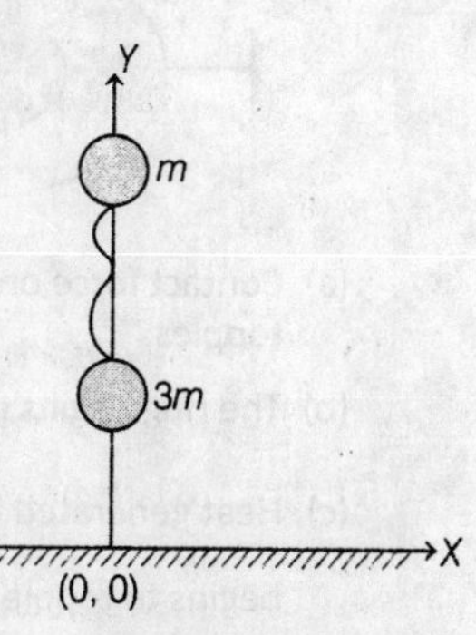

7. Consider the system shown in the figure, All contact surfaces are smooth and string is light and inextensible. Wedge A moves towards right with speed 10 m/s and velocity of B relative to A is in downward direction along the incline having magnitude 5 m/s.

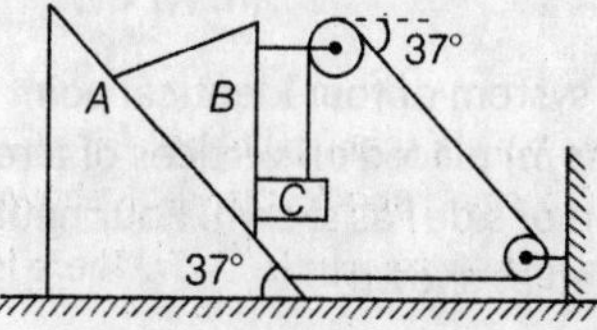

Ratio of x-component of velocity to y-component of velocity of C is $a : 13$. Find a.

8. The square shown in the figure is a superconducting loop of mass 0.9 g and side 0.1 m lying in a horizontal plane with its centre at origin, in a non-uniform magnetic field given by $B_x = -\pi x$, $B_y = 0$ and $B_z = \pi z + B_0$ (B_0 = constant). The induction of loop is 10 milli henry. The loop is released from rest under gravity. The time (in s) at which loop is at $z = -\frac{z_0}{2}$, is $\frac{T}{10}$, where z_0 is extreme value of z-coordinate of loop. Find T.

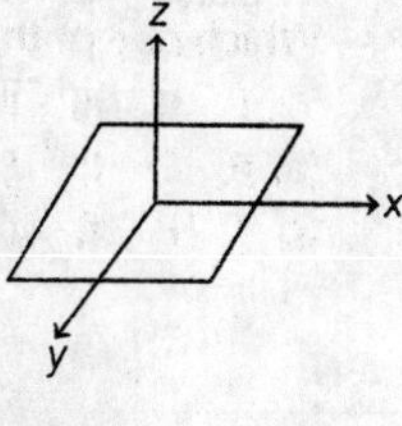

Section II *One or more than one correct options*

Instructions *See knockout 11*

9. A uniform conducting ring of mass m, radius r and resistance R is kept on the horizontal circular surface shown in figure. A uniform but time varying magnetic field, $B_0(\hat{i}+t^2\hat{j})$ is switched on in the region bounded by the surface. Here, B_0 is a constant and t is time. Choose the correct alternative(s).

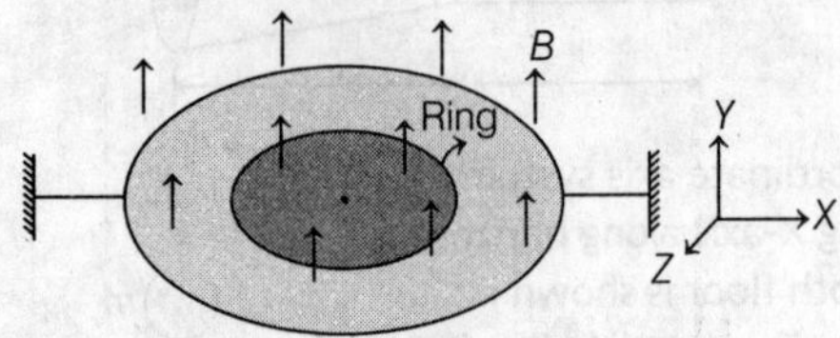

(a) Contact force on the ring increases with time before it topples.

(b) The ring begins to topple after $t=\dfrac{mgR}{2B_0^2\pi^2r^3}$.

(c) Heat generated in the ring till the instant t_0 after which it begins to topple is $\dfrac{4B_0^2\pi^2r^4t^3}{3R}$.

(d) The ring would slip before it topples, if the surface was smooth.

10. A small metal ball is released at the top of a long vertical column of glycerine of height $2h$. The ball falls through a height h in time t_1, and then the remaining height with terminal speed in time t_2. W_1 and W_2 represent work done against viscous force over these heights. Choose the correct alternative(s).

(a) $t_1=t_2$ (b) $t_1>t_2$
(c) $W_1=W_2$ (d) $W_1<W_2$

11. Consider a system of four identical point masses (each having mass m) placed on vertices of a regular tetrahedron of side l as shown. Four neutral metal plates are also fixed as shown

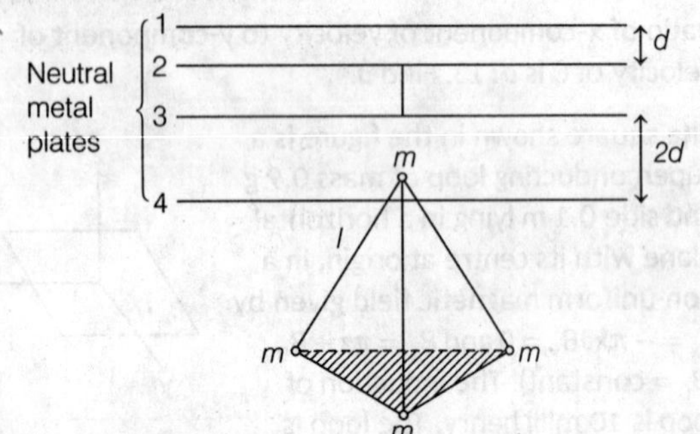

(a) Minimum work to be done to slowly disassemble the system is $\dfrac{6Gm^2}{l}$.

(b) Gravitational field at centre of the system is zero.

(c) Out of four large identical fixed horizontal neutral metal plates with plate-2 and 3 connected, plate-1 is given some charge such that potential difference between plate-1 and plate-2 is V. Magnitude of charge on topmost particle to keep it at rest is $\dfrac{\sqrt{6}Gm^2d}{Vl^2}$ (assuming other particles are fixed).

(d) Gravitational potential at centre of tetrahedron is $-\dfrac{4Gm}{l}$.

12. A uniform rod AB of mass m and length l in contact with a table edge and another non-uniform rod CD of mass m' having linear mass density varying as function of distance x from right hinged end D as, $\lambda=\lambda_0x$ are connected *via* a light string as shown. If the system shown is in equilibrium, choose the correct alternatives (λ_0 = constant).

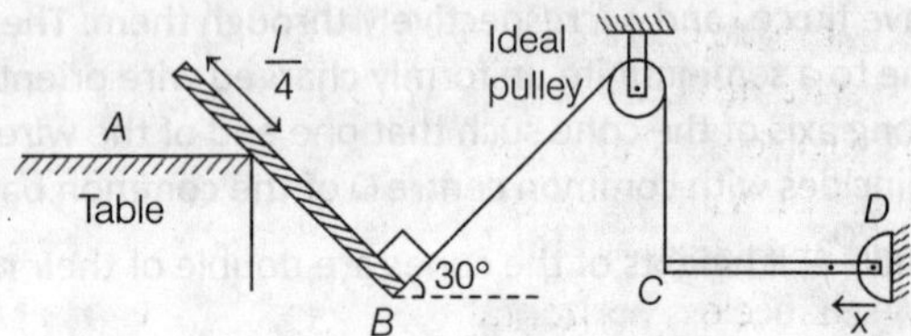

(a) Contact force on rod AB by table is $\dfrac{mg}{3}$.

(b) $4m'=m$.

(c) Force by clamp on pulley is $\dfrac{mg}{2\sqrt{3}}$.

(d) Reaction at hinge is equal to $\dfrac{5mg}{6}$.

13. A metal ball emits radiation which has maximum spectral intensity at wavelength λ. If thermodynamic temperature of the body is doubled,

(a) maximum spectral intensity will be at wavelength 2λ.

(b) maximum spectral intensity will be at wavelength $\dfrac{\lambda}{2}$

(c) total power emitted will increase by factor of 16

(d) total power emitted will increase by a factor of 2

14. In an experiment to find g, a small solid ball of radius $r=40\pm1$ mm is made to oscillate with small amplitude on a surface of radius, $R=240\pm1$ mm. Time period of oscillation of the ball is measured to be 1.00 s, using a stopwatch of least count 0.01 s. Choose the correct alternatives, if there is no slipping between the ball and the surface.

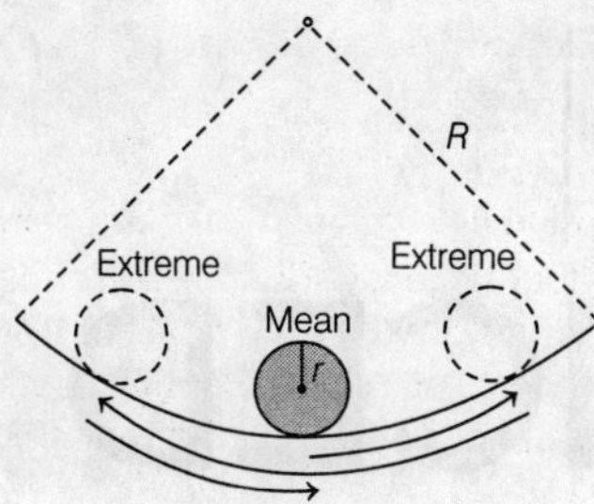

(a) Time period of oscillation is given by $T = 2\pi\sqrt{\dfrac{7(R-r)}{5g}}$.

(b) Error in measurement of r is 2.5%.

(c) Error in measurement of R is 0.4%.

(d) Error in determination of g is 2%.

Section III *Only one correct option*

Instructions *See knockout 11*

15. A parabolic conducting wire frame PQ of negligible resistance and mass m is at rest on a pair of smooth resistanceless horizontal rails, having its ends connected by an inductor of inductance L in a region of transverse inward magnetic field B. Shape of the frame is given by $y = x^2$ with vertex at origin O, at $t = 0$ with y-coordinate of end P equal to l. The key K is now closed for an instant thereby sending an impulsive current i in PQ for time t.

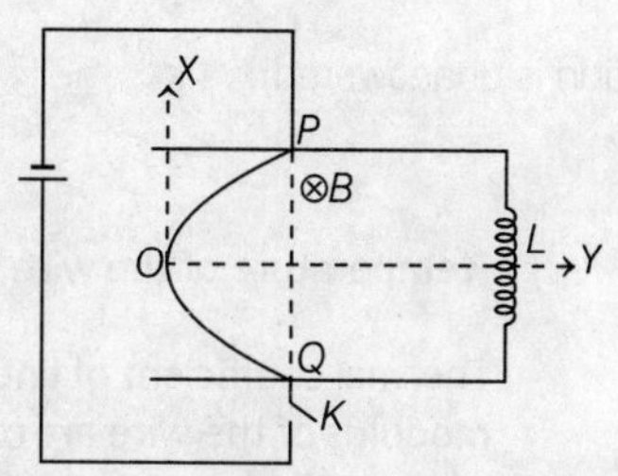

Maximum displacement of PQ from the shown position is

(a) $it\sqrt{\dfrac{L}{m}}$ (b) $it\sqrt{\dfrac{L}{2m}}$

(c) $\dfrac{i}{t}\sqrt{\dfrac{L}{m}}$ (d) $\dfrac{i}{t}\sqrt{\dfrac{2L}{m}}$

16. Sound of frequency 16 kHz is being emitted by two coherent point sources of sound, placed 2m apart, along side the centre of a track of radius $\dfrac{1000}{\pi}$ m. Passenger of a train running on the track with speed 36 km/h observes N maxima per second on an average. Here, N is (speed of sound in air = 320 m/s)

(a) 2 (b) 4

(c) 6 (d) 8

17. A straight infinite wire carrying current I produces magnetic field B at point A shown in the Fig.1. The wire is now bent creating a semi-circular segment. If point A is now at bottom of circle of the bent segment, magnetic induction of A will be

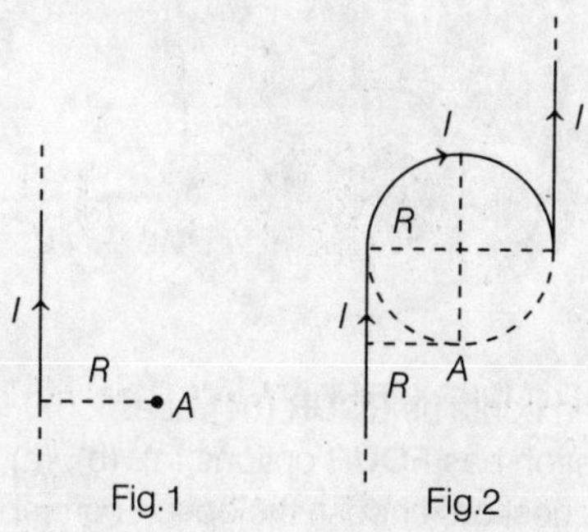

(a) $B[\sqrt{2} + \ln(\sqrt{2}+1)]$ (b) $B\left[\dfrac{1}{\sqrt{2}} + \ln(\sqrt{2}+1)\right]$

(c) $B\left[\dfrac{1}{\sqrt{2}} + \ln(\sqrt{\sqrt{2}+1})\right]$ (c) $B[\sqrt{2} + \ln(\sqrt{\sqrt{2}+1})]$

18. Consider the arrangement shown. Light of intensity I coming from an infinite sheet source falls on a perfectly black cone of base diameter l and semi-vertex angle $\theta = \tan^{-1}\dfrac{1}{2}$. The same light is incident on a perfectly reflecting square mirror of side l and is keeping it in equilibrium as shown. If mass of the mirror is same as that of the cone, acceleration of the cone is

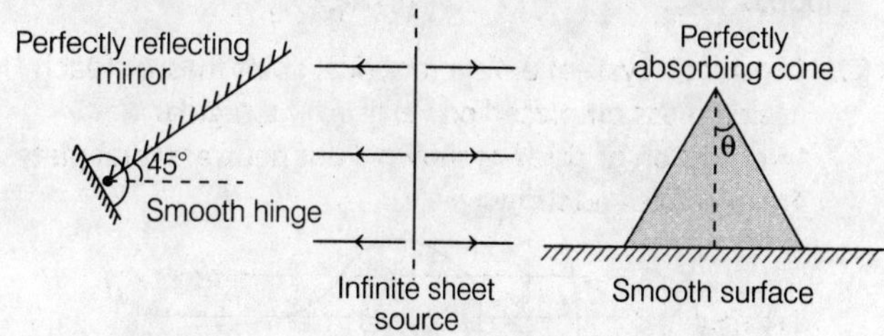

(a) g (b) $\dfrac{g}{2}$

(c) $\dfrac{g}{\sqrt{2}}$ (d) $\dfrac{g}{2\sqrt{2}}$

Answers

1	(5)	2	(3)	3	(6)	4	(4)	5	(6)	6	(4)	7	(7)	8	(1)	9	(b,c)	10.	(b,d)
11	(a,b,c)	12	(b,c)	13	(b,c)	14	(a,b,c)	15	(a)	16	(a)	17	(c)	18	(d)				

See detailed explanations on page no. 352

Knockout 14

JEE ADVANCED

Physics

Paper 1

Section I

- This section contains **FOUR (04)** questions.
- Each question has **FOUR** options (a), (b), (c) and (d). **ONLY ONE** of these four options is the correct answer.
- For each question, choose the option corresponding to the correct answer.
- Answer to each question will be evaluated according to the following marking scheme:

Full Marks : +3 If ONLY the correct option is chosen;
Zero Marks : 0 If none of the options is chosen (i.e., the question is unanswered);
Negative Marks: −1 In all other cases.

1. Consider a uniformly charged ring of charge Q and radius R initially at rest in YZ-plane and centred at origin O. Variation of electric field due to ring along its axis is as shown in the figure. The graph has it maxima at $x = d$. The ring is now rotated about X-axis with constant angular speed ω. A metal loop having radius $r(<< R)$ co-axial and parallel to the ring is moved from $x = -\infty$ towards O with constant speed as shown. Maximum emf induced in the loop is

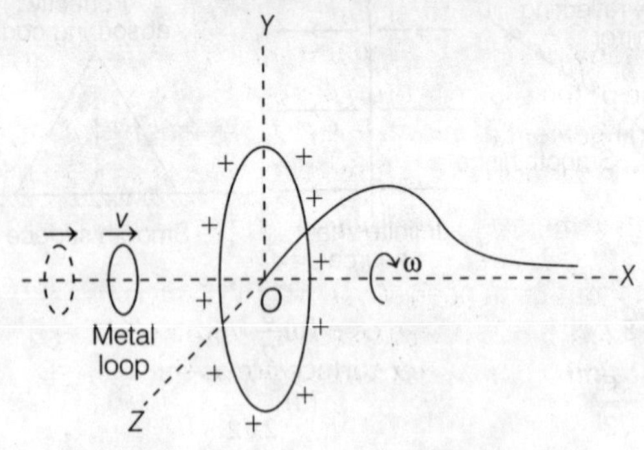

(a) $\frac{6\mu_0 Q\omega r^2 v}{25\sqrt{5}\,d^2}$ (b) $\frac{\mu_0 Q\omega r^2 v}{d^2}$

(c) $\frac{2\mu_0 Q\omega r^2 v}{3\sqrt{3}\,R^2}$ (d) $\frac{\mu_0 Q\omega^2 r^2 v}{6R^2}$

2. A wire of density ρ is stretched between two rigid supports having separation equal to natural length l at temperature T_0 equal to ambient temperature. Temperature of the wire is now decreased by $\frac{T_0}{9}$. Thermal coefficient of linear expansion and Young's modulus of the wire are α and Y, respectively. Frequency of tuning fork to set up standing wave in the string in second overtone is

(a) $\sqrt{\frac{2Y\alpha T_0}{\rho l^2}}$ (b) $\sqrt{\frac{8Y\alpha T_0}{9\rho l^2}}$

(c) $\sqrt{\frac{3Y\alpha T_0}{\rho l^2}}$ (d) $\sqrt{\frac{4Y\alpha T_0}{9\rho l^2}}$

3. Consider the figures shown, showing relevant specifications of the systems.

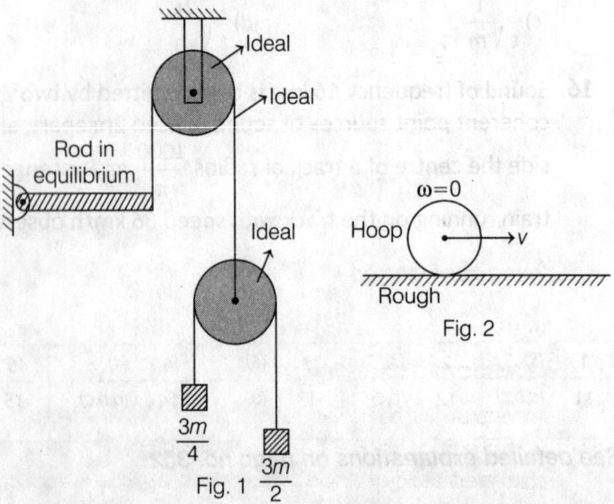

If the rod and the hoop have same masses, heat dissipated due to friction acting on the hoop during long time is (v = Initial speed of CM of hoop)

(a) mv^2
(b) $0.5mv^2$
(c) $2\ mv^2$
(d) zero

4. For a twin star system with identical stars, escape speed at mid-point of line joining the stars is v. If separation between the stars is L, time period of revolution of a star in CM frame of the system of stars is

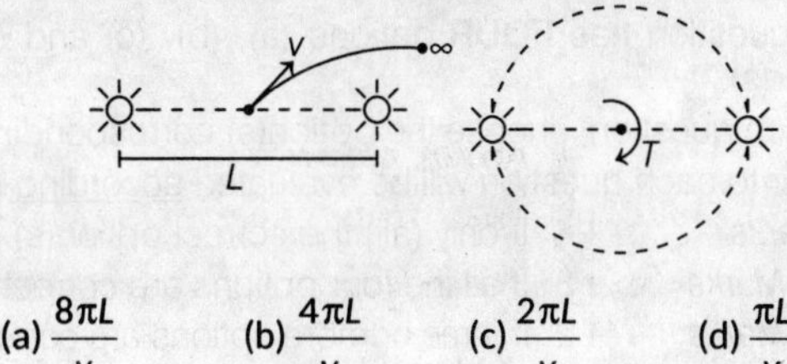

(a) $\frac{8\pi L}{v}$ (b) $\frac{4\pi L}{v}$ (c) $\frac{2\pi L}{v}$ (d) $\frac{\pi L}{v}$

Section II

- This section contains **THREE (03)** question stems.
- There are **TWO (02)** questions corresponding to each question stem.
- The answer to each question is a **NUMERICAL VALUE.**
- If the numerical value has more than two decimal places, **truncate/round-off** the value to **TWO** decimal places.
- Answer to each question will be evaluated according to the following marking scheme:

Full Marks : +2 If ONLY the correct numerical value is entered at the designated place;
Zero Marks : 0 In all other cases.

Questions stem for 5 and 6

n moles of oxygen is contained in an adiabatic vessel with two smooth pistons of cross-sectional areas A_1 and A_2 connected by a light string. Knob of the smaller piston carries charge $-q$ while the larger piston is connected to a block of mass m through a system of ideal strings and pulleys. The region has an infinite uniform non-conducting sheet S of charge density σ. The system is initially in equilibrium. On supplying heat slowly to the oxygen, the block descends by d and gas temperature increases by ΔT.

Consider, $n = 4$, $A_2 - A_1 = 10\ \text{cm}^2$, $q = \frac{1}{400\pi}\ \mu\text{C}$,

$m = 20$ kg, $\sigma = (20/9)\ \text{C/m}^2$, $d = 12.5$ cm, $g = 10\ \text{m/s}^2$,

p_0 = atmospheric pressure $= 10^5\ \text{N/m}^2$, $R = 25/3$ J/mol-K

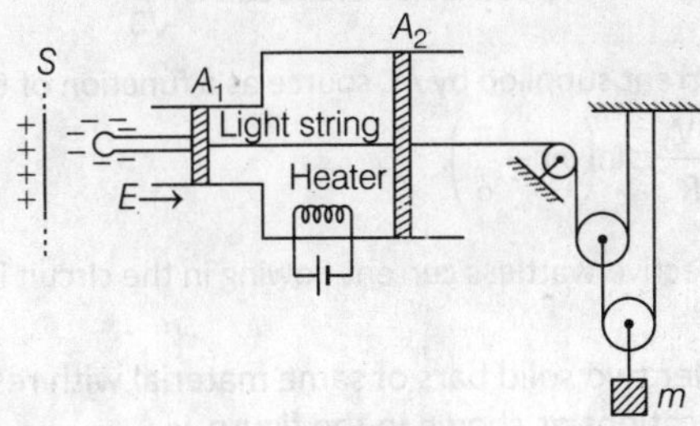

5. Pressure of oxygen is ...... atm.

6. ΔT is ...... °C.

Questions stem for 7 and 8

A neutron with kinetic energy 70 eV collides inelastically with a stationary He^+ ion in ground state. The neutron is scattered at right angle to original direction of motion on collision. Due to collision, the electron in He^+ ion is excited to third excited state. It is given that mass of He^+ ion is approximately four times that of neutron.

7. Difference in kinetic energies of He^+ ion and neutron after the collision is .... eV.

8. Maximum possible number of different types of wavelengths emitted during de-excitation of He^+ ion is ....

Questions stem for 9 and 10

Three isosceles right angled prism with respective refractive indices labelled in the Fig.1 are kept in contact. As shown, a ray entering the system normally leaves the system undeviated. A slab of thickness 3 cm and a thin bi-convex lens of focal length 60 cm in air made up of material of refractive index n (which is refractive index of one of the shown prisms) are used in the other arrangement as shown in Fig. 2. The lens is silvered at one of the surfaces and is fitted at bottom of a vessel filled with water (refractive index $\frac{4}{3}$) up to height 30 cm. A luminous point object O, separated from water surface by the slab, has its image coinciding with itself. Distances of slab and O from water surface are as shown in Fig. 2.

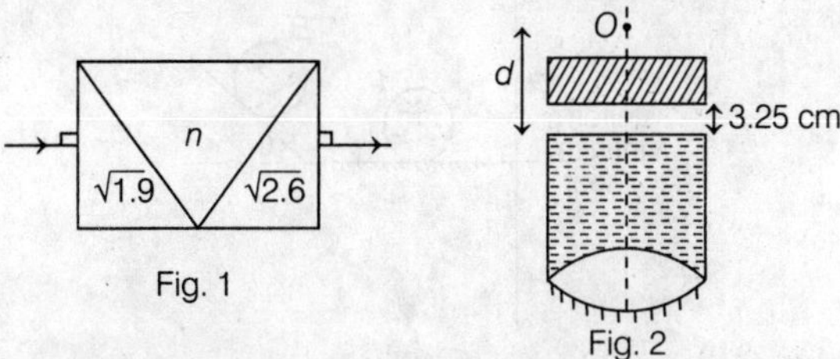

Fig. 1 Fig. 2

9. The value of n is ....

10. The value of d is .... cm.

Section III

- This section contains **SIX (06)** questions.
- Each question has **FOUR** options (a), (b), (c) and (d). **ONE OR MORE THAN ONE** of these four option(s) is (are) correct answer(s).
- For each question, choose the option(s) corresponding to (all) the correct answer(s).
- Answer to each question will be evaluated <u>according to the following marking scheme:</u>

Full Marks : +4 If only (all) the correct option(s) is(are) chosen;
Partial Marks : +3 If all the four options are correct but ONLY three options are chosen;
Partial Marks : +2 If three or more options are correct but ONLY two options are chosen, both of which are correct;
Partial Marks : +1 If two or more options are correct but ONLY one option is chosen and it is a correct option;
Zero Marks : 0 If unanswered;
Negative Marks : – 2 In all other cases.

11. Choose the correct alternative(s), considering the circuit given in the figure. It is given that resistance r_0 is equal to resistance of potentiometer wire AB.

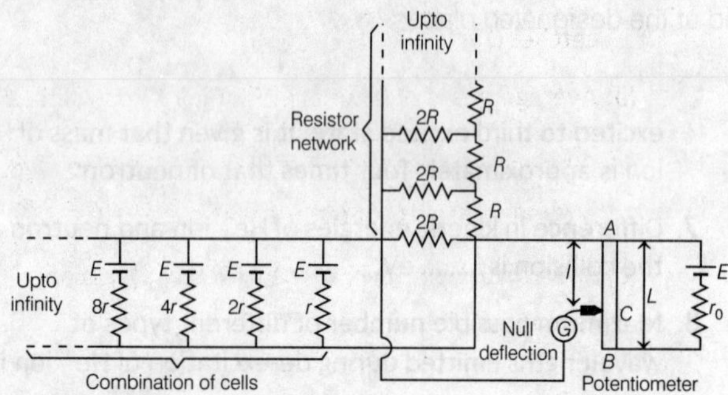

(a) For a given r, if $r = 2R$, resistor network consumes maximum power.

(b) For a given R, if $r = 2R$, resistor network consumes maximum power.

(c) For $r = 4R, l = \dfrac{2L}{3}$ in balanced state.

(d) For $r = R$, no balancing length is obtained.

12. Two identical solid spheres A and B of mass m and radius r each have short light identical dipoles embedded at their respective centres. B is in equilibrium on an incline of inclination θ as shown such that its dipole moment is parallel to the incline. Sphere A is released, in the position shown, on a rough horizontal surface.

Both A and B are located in electric field of a uniform infinite sheet of surface charge density σ. If friction between A and horizontal surface is sufficient to prevent slipping,

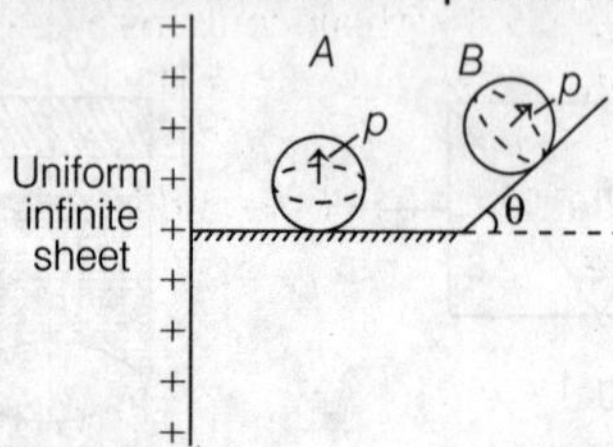

(a) its acceleration is $\dfrac{5g}{7}$, just after its release

(b) friction acting on it is $\dfrac{2mg}{7}$, just after its release

(c) its angular speed at the instant, when it has angularly displaced by $\dfrac{\pi}{2}$ is $\sqrt{\dfrac{10p\sigma}{7mr^2\varepsilon_0}}$

(d) friction acting on it, when the dipole becomes parallel to horizontal surface is zero

13. Consider the AC circuit shown and choose correct alternative(s).

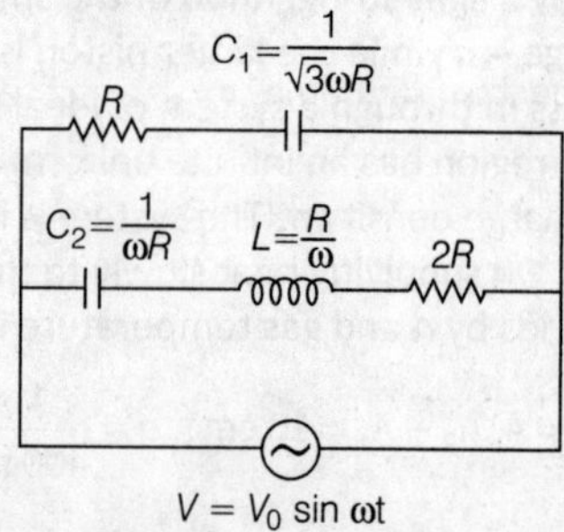

(a) Effective reactance of the circuit is $\sqrt{3}R$.

(b) Effective impedance of the circuit is $\dfrac{2R}{\sqrt{3}}$.

(c) Current supplied by AC source as a function of time is $\dfrac{\sqrt{3}V_0}{2R} \cdot \sin\left(\omega t + \dfrac{\pi}{6}\right)$.

(d) Effective wattless current flowing in the circuit is $\dfrac{\sqrt{3}\,V_0}{4R}$.

14. Consider two solid bars of same material with respective specifications as shown in the figure.

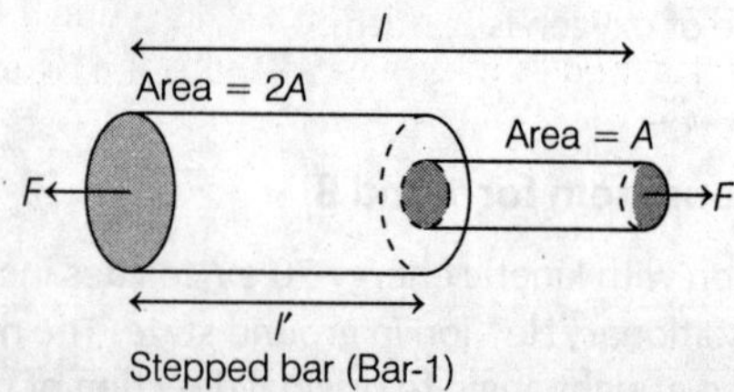

Stepped bar (Bar-1)

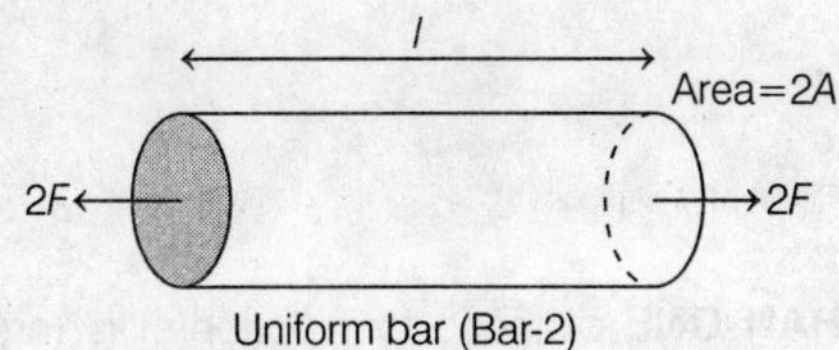

Choose the correct alternative(s) for $l' = 0.4l$.

(a) Maximum stresses in the two bars are equal.
(b) Elastic strain energy of Bar-2 is 2.5 times that of Bar-1.
(c) Elastic potential energy of shorter portion of stepped bar is 3 times that of the longer portion.
(d) Ratio of breaking force of Bar-1 to that of Bar-2 is 1 : 2.

15. A radioactive sample has equal number of nuclei of A and B. A decays into X with decay constant λ. B may decay into X or Y with decay constant λ and 2λ, respectively. Initial ($t = 0$) number of nuclei of A and B are both equal to N_0. Number of nuclei of A, B, X and Y are N_A, N_B, N_X and N_Y, respectively at any later instant. Choose the correct alternative(s).

(a) $\frac{N_B}{N_A} = e^{-2\lambda t}$

(b) $N_X = \frac{N_0}{3}(4 - e^{-3\lambda t})$

(c) N_B is equal to N_Y at time, $t = \frac{\ln 2.5}{3\lambda}$

(d) N_Y is equal to $\frac{N_0}{3}$ at time, $t = \frac{\ln 2}{3\lambda}$

16. Three particles P, Q and R initially located at vertices of an equilateral triangle of side l start moving with constant speeds v each such that P always chases (moves towards) Q, Q always chases R and R always chases P. Trajectory followed by P is shown in the figure.

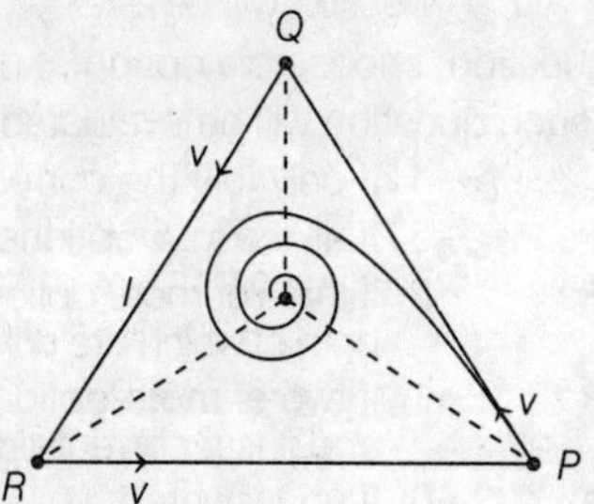

Choose the correct alternative(s).

(a) Average velocity of P for its motion till the instant it catches Q is $\frac{\sqrt{3}v}{2}$.
(b) Average speed of P for its motion till it completes one revolution around centroid O is v.
(c) Distance covered by P when it completes one revolution around centroid O of the triangle is $\frac{2l}{3}(1 - e^{-2\sqrt{3}\pi})$.
(d) Separation between P and Q as P completes one revolution around O is $\frac{2l}{3}e^{-2\sqrt{3}\pi}$.

Section IV

- This section contains **THREE (03)** questions.
- The answer to each question is a **NON-NEGATIVE INTEGER.**
- Answer to each question will be evaluated according to the following marking scheme:

Full Marks : +4 If ONLY the correct integer is entered;
Zero Marks : 0 In all other cases.

17. A solid cylinder of height $l = 36$ cm floating in a water tank shown oscillates with time period $T = \frac{5\pi}{3}\sqrt{\frac{l}{g}}$, when disturbed slightly. A thin rod (of same material as that of cylinder) of length $d = 48$ cm is tied to bottom of the tank by a vertical string. Find $h + b$ (in cm), if spring attached to the rod is relaxed. The figure is indicative.

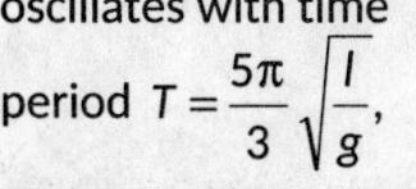

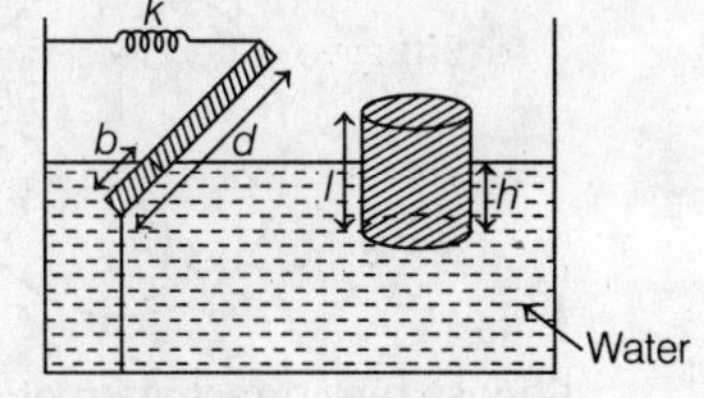

18. A metal plate has a circular hole of radius $r = 8$ cm. A metal sphere of radius $R = 10$ cm is kept on the hole such that its extending part beyond level of plate remains at h cm (constant), even on increasing temperature of the system. Coefficients of linear expansion of material of plate and sphere are α and α', respectively. Find $\frac{8\alpha}{\alpha'}$.

19. A container filled with air contains a soap bubble. On reducing air pressure isothermally in vessel by 50% radius of the bubble increases by 25%. Find the ratio of initial air pressure outside the bubble and initial excess pressure in the bubble.

Answers

1 (a)	2 (a)	3 (a)	4 (b)	5 (1.5)	6 (2.25)	7 (16.6)	8 (3)	9 (1.5)	10 (14.5)
11 (a,c,d)	12 (a,d)	13 (b,c)	14 (a,b,d)	15 (a,c,d)	16 (a,b,c)	17 (65)	18 (5)	19 (24)	

See detailed explanations on page no. 357

Paper 2

Section I

- This section contains **SIX (06)** questions.
- Each question has **FOUR** options (a), (b), (c) and (d). **ONE OR MORE THAN ONE** of these four option(s) is (are) correct answer(s).
- For each question, choose the option(s) corresponding to (all) the correct answer(s).
- Answer to each question will be evaluated according to the following marking scheme:

Full Marks : +4 If only (all) the correct option(s) is(are) chosen;
Partial Marks : +3 If all the four options are correct but ONLY three options are chosen;
Partial Marks : +2 If three or more options are correct but ONLY two options are chosen, both of which are correct;
Partial Marks : +1 If two or more options are correct but ONLY one option is chosen and it is a correct option;
Zero Marks : 0 If unanswered;
Negative Marks : −2 In all other cases.

1. Consider the circuit shown. The key k shown in the figure is closed at $t = 0$. Before k is closed, the circuit was in steady state.

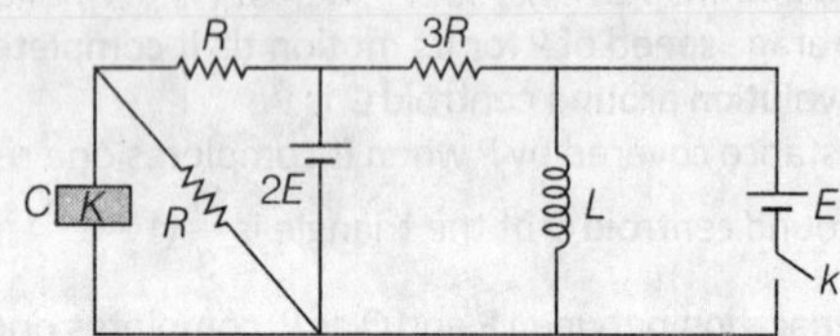

Which of the following statement(s) is/are correct for given situation?

(a) At $t < 0$, power delivered by the cell of emf $2E$ is $\frac{10E^2}{3R}$.

(b) At $t < 0$, electric field between the plates of capacitor with plate separation d is $\frac{E}{Kd}$. Here, K is dielectric constant of dielectric completely filling space between plates.

(c) Just after closing the switch, current in $3R$ is $\frac{E}{3R}$.

(d) At $t = \frac{L}{R}$, power consumed by the inductor is $\frac{E^2}{2R}$.

2. m mass of a gas sample of molar mass M contained in an insulating light box of length l on a smooth horizontal surface is attached to a block of mass m placed on an incline of inclination 53°. Coefficient of kinetic friction between block and incline is 1. The system is released from rest. Choose the correct alternative(s), if string and pulleys are ideal and temperature of gas sample is T. (Take, $g = 10\ \text{m/s}^2$)

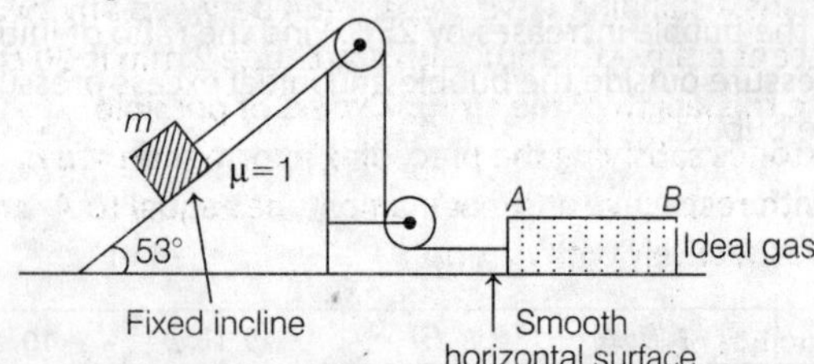

(a) Acceleration of the system is $g/5$.

(b) Gas pressure at end B is greater than that at end A of the box.

(c) Ratio of pressures at the ends of the box is $e^{\frac{Ml}{RT}}$.

(d) If pressure difference between the ends A and B is p and cross-sectional area of the tube is A', then number of moles of the gas is $\frac{pA'}{M}$.

3. Consider a cylindrical region of radius R having a uniform transverse magnetic field B as shown in the figure centred at C. An L-shaped conducting wire CDE is located in the field as shown in figure. Resistances of the segments CD and DE of the wire are $1\,\Omega$ and $1\,\Omega$, respectively. Two voltmeters x (ideal) and y (resistance $= 10\,\Omega$) are connected as shown. Magnetic field is given as a function of time t as, $B = B_0 t$, where $B_0 = \frac{192}{\pi R^2}$ T/s.

Choose the correct alternative(s).

(a) Reading of x is 2 V

(b) Reading of y is 20 V

(c) $\left|\int_C^D \mathbf{E}\cdot d\mathbf{l}\right|$ is equal to 2V

(d) $\left|\int_C^E \mathbf{E}\cdot d\mathbf{l}\right|$ is equal to 2 V

4. A uniform magnetic field $B\hat{\mathbf{k}}$ exists in a region $y \geq 0$. A particle having mass m and charge q is travelling with speed u along y-axis initially at origin. The particle experiences a drag given by $\mathbf{F} = -c\mathbf{v}$, here c is equal to $\frac{qB}{2}$ and $\mathbf{v}$ is velocity. Consider the motion of the particle till it finally stops at (x, y). Choose the correct option(s).

(a) $x = \frac{2mu}{5c}$ (b) $y = \frac{u}{5c}$

(c) Work done by magnetic force is $-\frac{1}{4}mu^2$

(d) Work done by drag is $-\frac{1}{2}mu^2$

5. Consider a uniform sphere of density ρ and radius R having a spherical cavity of radius $\frac{R}{2}$ centred at C_1 as shown. A point mass m is released at end of a diameter of the cavity at position shown.

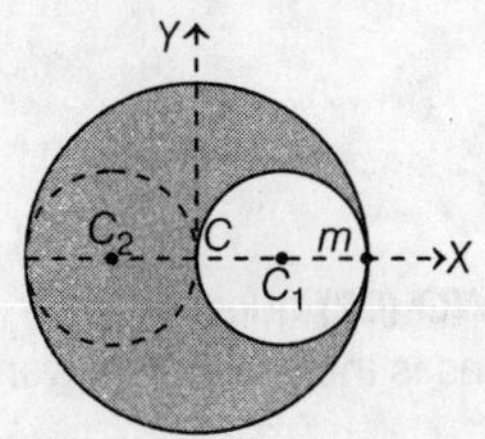

The diameter passes through centre C of the sphere. Choose the correct alternative(s).

(a) Gravitational field inside the cavity is non-uniform.

(b) Time taken by the particle to strike surface of the cavity is $\sqrt{\frac{6R}{\pi G\rho}}$.

(c) If another identical cavity is created centered at C_2, gravitational field at C_1 changes from $\mathbf{E}_1$ to $\mathbf{E}_2$ such that $4\mathbf{E}_2 = 3\mathbf{E}_1$.

(d) Work done in moving a point mass from C_1 to C_2 is zero if another identical cavity centred at C_2 is created.

6. Which of the following pairs of quantities have same dimensional formula?

(a) Stress and pressure

(b) Coefficient of viscosity (η) and Reynold's number (R)

(c) $\frac{L}{R}$ and R-C. Here, L, R and C are inductance, resistance and capacitance, respectively

(d) $\frac{1}{\sqrt{\mu_0 \varepsilon_0}}$ and terminal speed, here μ_0 is permeability and ε_0 is permittivity

Section II

- This section contains **THREE (03)** question stems.
- There are **TWO (02)** questions corresponding to each question stem.
- The answer to each question is a **NUMERICAL VALUE.**
- If the numerical value has more than two decimal places, **truncate/round-off** the value to **TWO** decimal places.
- Answer to each question will be evaluated according to the following marking scheme:

Full Marks : +2 If ONLY the correct numerical value is entered at the designated place;

Zero Marks : 0 In all other cases.

Questions stem for 7 and 8

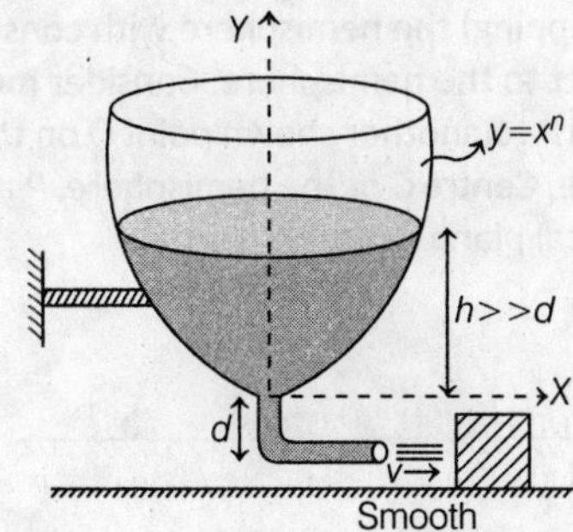

A water tank is designed such that its section in XY-plane can be described by $y = x^n$, considering origin at its bottom, which has a small orifice of cross-sectional area a. Value of n is chosen such that, $\frac{dh}{dt}$ does not depend on h. Also, if h is maintained constant by replenishing lost water by a source from top, velocity of efflux also becomes constant equal to v. If the ejecting jet (almost horizontal) strikes surface of a block on smooth horizontal surface (initially at rest), the block begins to accelerate and the maximum power delivered to the block is $\frac{\rho a v^3}{x}$ during subsequent motion. Here, ρ is density of water. Assume that the water instantly comes to rest after it strikes the block's surface.

7. The value of n is ... .

8. The value of x is ... .

Questions stem for 9 and 10

A uniform string of length 2.4 m clamped at both ends sustains a standing wave. Separation between any two adjacent points vibrating with amplitude 2 mm is 20 cm along the length of the string. Orders of possible overtones satisfying the preceding information are n_1 and n_2 with respective anti-node amplitudes equal to A_1 and A_2, respectively with $n_1 > n_2$.

9. The value of $\frac{n_1}{n_2}$ is ... .

10. The value of $\frac{A_2}{A_1}$ is ....

Questions stem for 11 and 12

Twelve light rods are hinged to each other as shown in the arrangement in the figure geometrically resembling three rhombuses of sides in the ratio 3 : 2 : 1. Hinge A is fixed to a vertical wall while hinge B is connected to centre of an oscillating disc (amplitude of centre = A) of mass m by a light rigid rod. The disc is connected to two identical springs of spring constant k each. Friction between disc and horizontal surface in its contact is sufficient to prevent slipping of the disc. It is given that,

$A = 0.2$ mm, $m = \frac{1}{3}$ kg, $k = 90$ N/m, $\theta = 45°$ (when the disc is at mean position).

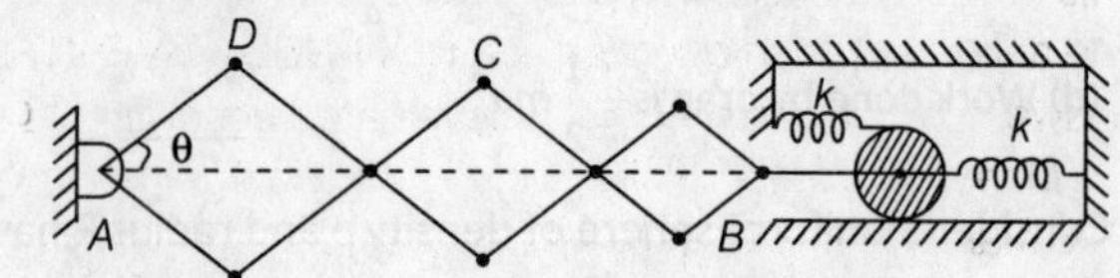

11. Speed of hinge C, at the instant $\theta = 45°$, is .... mm/s.

12. Angular speed of rod AD of length $L = \sqrt{2}$ mm, at the instant, $\theta = 45°$, is ... rad/s.

Section III

- This section contains **TWO (02) paragraphs**. Based on each paragraph, there are **TWO (02)** questions.
- Each question has **FOUR** options (a), (b), (c) and (d). **ONLY ONE** of these four options is the correct answer.
- For each question, choose the option corresponding to the correct answer.
- Answer to each question will be evaluated according to the following marking scheme:

Full Marks : +3 If ONLY the correct option is chosen;
Zero Marks : 0 If none of the options is chosen (i.e., the question is unanswered);
Negative Marks : – 1 In all other cases.

Paragraph for 13 and 14

A small metallic disc of radius a mounted on a thin axle is rotating with constant angular speed ω inside a long/ideal solenoid of inductance L having its two ends connected to the disc by two brushes as shown. Electrical resistance of the circuit is R. A small magnetic disturbance is initiated making current grow in the solenoid. This arrangement is popularly known as self excited magnetic dynamo.

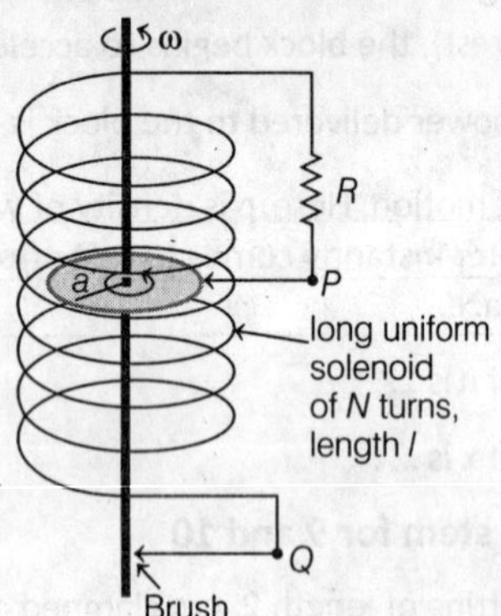

13. Minimum value of angular speed that ensures growth of current is

(a) $\frac{IR}{\mu_0 Na^2}$ (b) $\frac{NlR}{\mu_0 a^2}$ (c) $\frac{2lR}{\mu_0 Na^2}$ (d) $\frac{2NlR}{\mu_0 a^2}$

14. External torque applied to the axle to make the disc rotate with constant angular speed ω is (Here, i_0 = initial current and $c = \frac{\mu_0 Na^2\omega}{2lL} - \frac{R}{L}$)

(a) $\frac{\mu_0 Na^2 i_0^2}{2l} e^{ct}$ (b) $\frac{\mu_0 N^2 a^2 i_0^2 e^{2ct}}{2l}$

(c) $\frac{\mu_0 N^2 a^2 i_0^2}{l} e^{ct}$ (d) $\frac{\mu_0 Na^2 i_0^2 e^{2ct}}{2l}$

Paragraph for 15 and 16

A uniform hemisphere of mass $2m$ and radius R is placed at rest on a smooth horizontal surface. A small insect of mass m is at rest at a point P of the hemisphere near ground as shown. Now, the insect begins to climbing up (without slipping) the hemisphere with constant speed v with respect to the hemisphere. Consider motion of the insect from P to another shown point Q on the hemisphere. Centre C of the hemisphere, P and Q lie in same vertical plane.

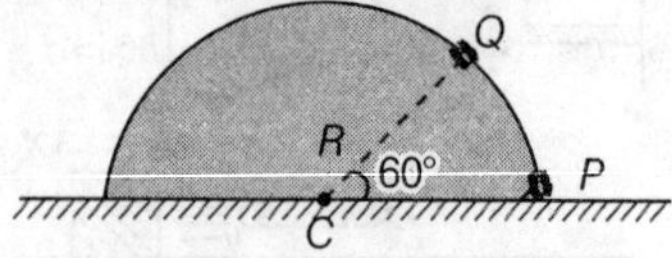

15. Displacement of the hemispherical bowl is

(a) $\frac{R}{3}$ (b) $\frac{R}{6}$

(c) $\frac{\sqrt{3}R}{2}$ (d) zero

16. Acceleration of the hemisphere at the instant, the insect is at Q, is

(a) $\frac{v^2}{3R}$ (b) $\frac{v^2}{6R}$ (c) $\frac{\sqrt{3}v^2}{2R}$ (d) zero

Section IV

- This section contains **THREE (03)** questions.
- The answer to each question is a **NON-NEGATIVE INTEGER.**
- Answer to each question will be evaluated according to the following marking scheme:

Full Marks : +4 If ONLY the correct integer is entered;
Zero Marks : 0 In all other cases.

17.

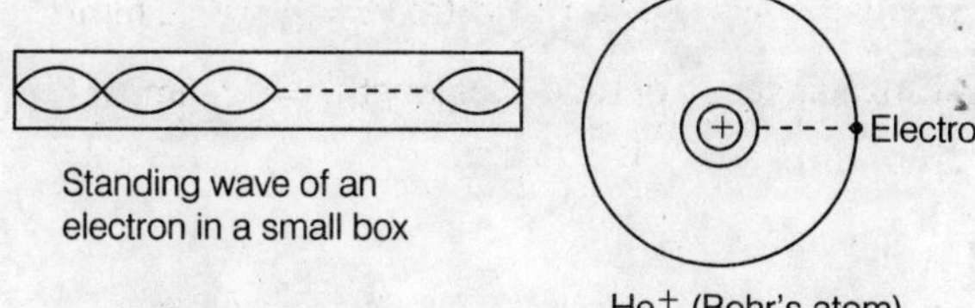

Standing wave of an electron in a small box

He$^+$ (Bohr's atom)

Electrons shown in the two figures are in same quantum state. Magnitude of electron's energy in the box is $\frac{2h^2}{ml^2}$.

Here, h is Planck's constant, m is mass of electron, l is length of the box. Considering that magnitude of electron's energy in 1st orbit of hydrogen atom is E_0, potential energy of electron in the Bohr's atom shown is $\frac{E_0}{x}$. Find x.

18. A solid conducting sphere of radius, $R = 2$ m and carrying a charge of $q = 12\,\mu$C is rotating about a vertical cylindrical axle with angular speed of 6 rad/s in a region with uniform horizontal magnetic field of $B = 3$T. Ends P and Q of the axle are attached to two horizontal strings with the help of rings and are separated by $l = 8$ m. Find tension in the upper string in μN neglecting gravity.

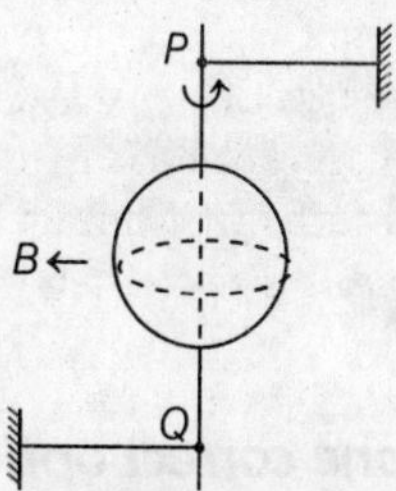

19. Capillary-1 having a semi-circular bend of radius 8 mm has liquid rising in it up to height 40 mm as shown. Another capillary (capillary-2 of same radius as capillary-1) is dipped in the same liquid as shown in the figure, such that it has length 50 mm outside the liquid surface and is inclined at 30° with horizontal.

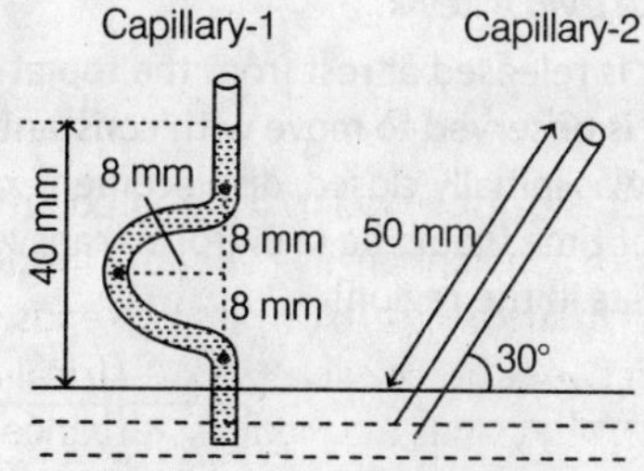

Find the length of liquid (in mm) that rises in capillary-2

Answers

1 *(a,c)*	2 *(b,c,d)*	3 *(a,b,c)*	4 *(a,d)*	5 *(c,d)*	6 *(a,c,d)*	7 *(4.00)*	8 *(6.75)*	9 *(2.20)*	10 *(1.41)*
11 *(4.12)*	12 *(1.5)*	13 *(c)*	14 *(d)*	15 *(b)*	16 *(b)*	17 *(2)*	18 *(36)*	19 *(50)*	

See detailed explanations on page no. 363

Knockout 15

JEE ADVANCED

Physics

Paper 1

Section I Only one correct option

Instructions *See knockout 14*

1. Consider the arrangements shown in the figures. A conducting slider of mass m and length l can slide freely on the shown pair of long smooth rails in vertical plane. The rails are connected at one end by a capacitor of capacitance C while connected at the other end by an inductor of inductance L *via* a key k.

The slider is released at rest from the top at $t = 0$. If k is open, the slider is observed to move with constant acceleration $g/2$. If k was initially closed, displacement x of the slider as function of time would be (a uniform transverse magnetic field B exists in the region)

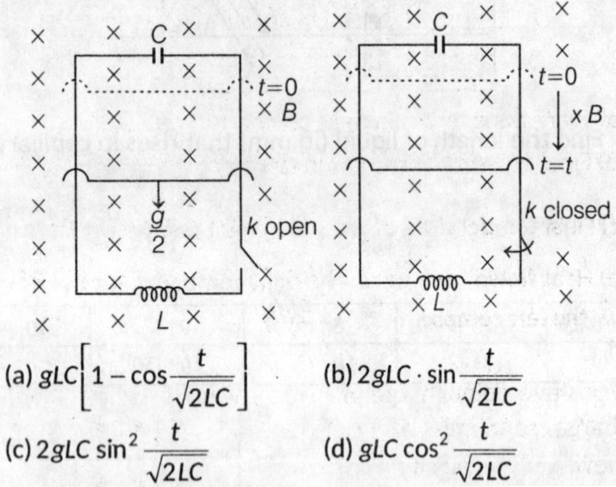

(a) $gLC\left[1-\cos\frac{t}{\sqrt{2LC}}\right]$ (b) $2gLC\cdot\sin\frac{t}{\sqrt{2LC}}$

(c) $2gLC\sin^2\frac{t}{\sqrt{2LC}}$ (d) $gLC\cos^2\frac{t}{\sqrt{2LC}}$

2. Consider the arrangements shown.

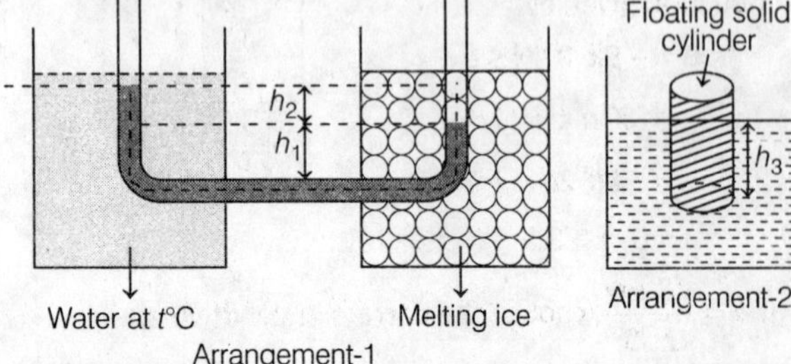

Liquid in U-tube in Arrangement-1 is same as that in Arrangement-2. If on increasing temperature of Arrangement-2, h_3 remains unchanged, coefficient of cubical expansion of the cylinder is

(a) $\frac{(h_2+h_1)}{h_1 t}$ (b) $\frac{3h_2}{2h_1 t}$ (c) $\frac{2(h_1+h_2-h_3)}{3t}$ (d) $\frac{h_2}{h_1 t}$

3. A satellite is transferred from one circular orbit to another circular orbit by Hohmann Transfer orbit manoeuvre, by temporarily entering in an intermediate elliptical orbit by increasing speed instantly by firing propeller. To transfer a satellite in circular orbit of radius r to another orbit of radius $3r$, its speed at point P (in orbit of radius r) has to be increased by (M = Mass of planet)

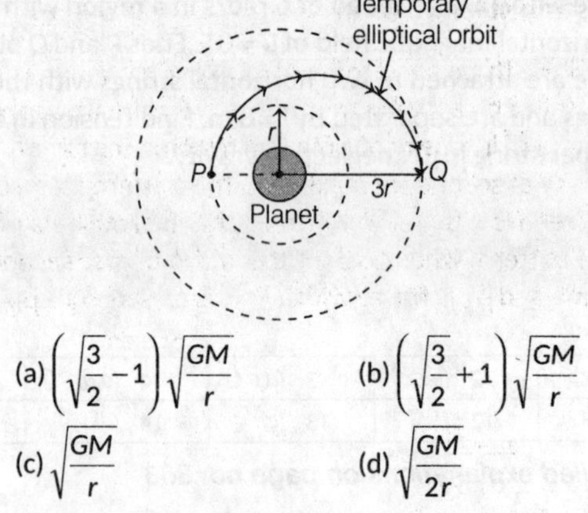

(a) $\left(\sqrt{\frac{3}{2}}-1\right)\sqrt{\frac{GM}{r}}$ (b) $\left(\sqrt{\frac{3}{2}}+1\right)\sqrt{\frac{GM}{r}}$

(c) $\sqrt{\frac{GM}{r}}$ (d) $\sqrt{\frac{GM}{2r}}$

4. The figure here shows a closed surface enclosing a point charge q comprised of cylindrical surface-1, spherical surface-2 and flat surface-3. Difference in flux through surface-1 (ϕ_1) and surface-2 (ϕ_2) is

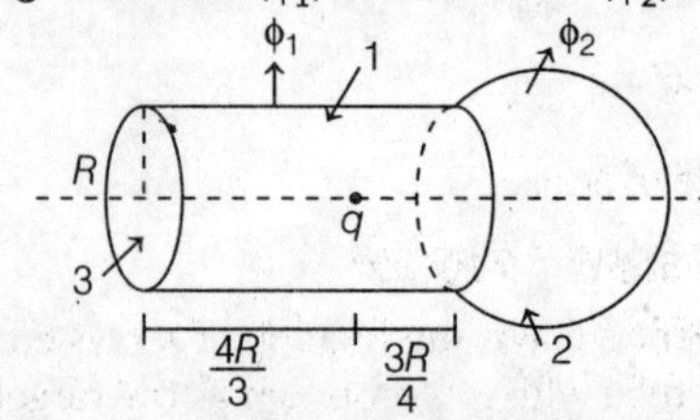

(a) $\frac{q}{2\varepsilon_0}$ (b) $\frac{3q}{5q_0}$ (c) $\frac{7q}{10\varepsilon_0}$ (d) $\frac{q}{5\varepsilon_0}$

Section II *Numerical Value Type*

Instructions *See knockout 14*

Question stem (5 to 6)

Consider the shown arrangement in which a solid cylinder of mass $m = 0.67$ kg is placed on a rough horizontal table. An ideal thread A wound around the cylinder is attached to an ideal movable pulley P going over ideal pulley Q. Another ideal thread B, connecting blocks of masses $3m$ and $6m$, passes over P. The arrangement is released from rest. Assuming that the cylinder does not slip w.r.t. its contact with thread A and the horizontal surface, tension in thread A is T and minimum coefficient of friction between the cylinder and the horizontal surface is μ. (Take, $g = 10$ m/s^2)

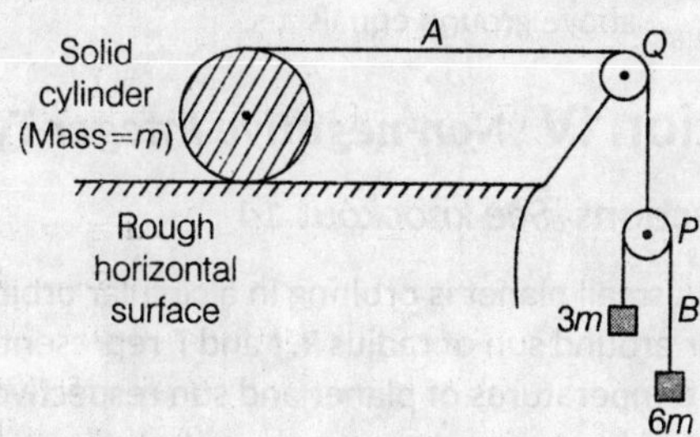

5. The value of T is .... N.

6. The value of μ^{-1} is ....

Question stem (7 to 8)

Slits in the three slit interference experimental set up is illuminated by a monochromatic parallel beam as shown. The ratio of intensity of principal maxima to that of intensity of secondary maxima in the pattern formed on the screen is r. β_1 is the width of principal maxima of the fringe pattern, whereas β_2 is the width of first secondary maxima and β_3 is fringe width if S_2 is closed. $\beta_1 - \beta_2 = n\beta_3$.

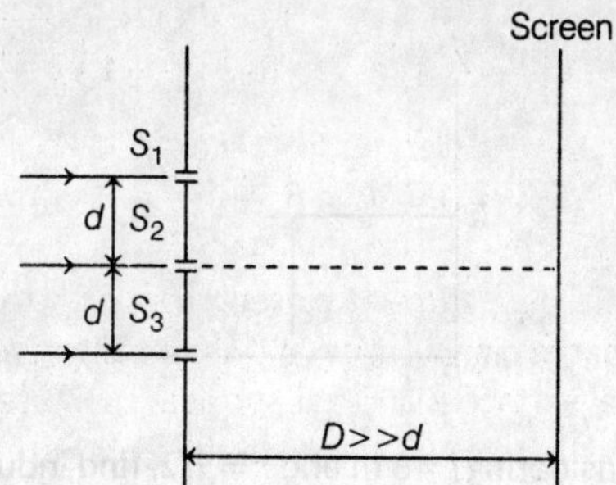

7. The value of r is ....

8. The value of n is ....

Question Stem (9 to 10)

Intensity *versus* wavelength graph of X-rays emitted from a coolidge tube with molybdenum as the target metal is as shown in the figure. The graph is indicative and may not be up to scale.

Cut-off wavelength λ_c is equal to 0.4 Å. Peaks in the graph correspond to k_α and k_β X-rays with respective wavelengths $\lambda_2 = 0.71$ Å and $\lambda_1 = 0.63$Å

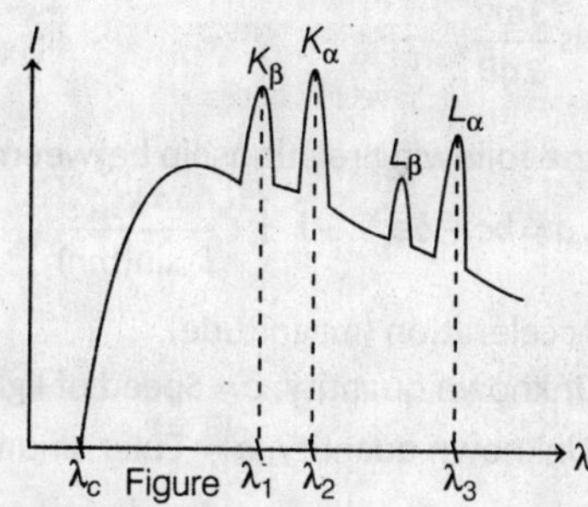

Figure

Take $hc = 12400$ eV-Å

9. λ_3 is equal to .... Å.

10. Accelerating voltage across the tube is .... kV.

Section III *One or more than one correct options*

Instructions *See knockout 14*

11. A cylinder with adiabatic walls having volume $2V_0$ contains an ideal monoatomic gas as shown. The cylinder is divided into two equal parts by a fixed perfectly conducting partition. Initial pressures and temperatures of gases in the two parts are shown. During long time,

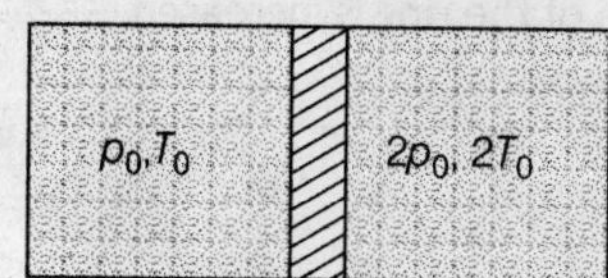

(a) Work done by gas in right compartment is p_0V_0

(b) Final pressure of the gas in left compartment is $\frac{3p_0}{2}$

(c) Final temperature of the gas in right compartment is $\frac{3T_0}{2}$.

(d) Heat flown from gas in the right compartment to gas in the left compartment is $\frac{3p_0V_0}{4}$

12. A positive point charge of charge q and mass m moving with velocity $v\hat{i}$ enters a region of magnetic induction given by

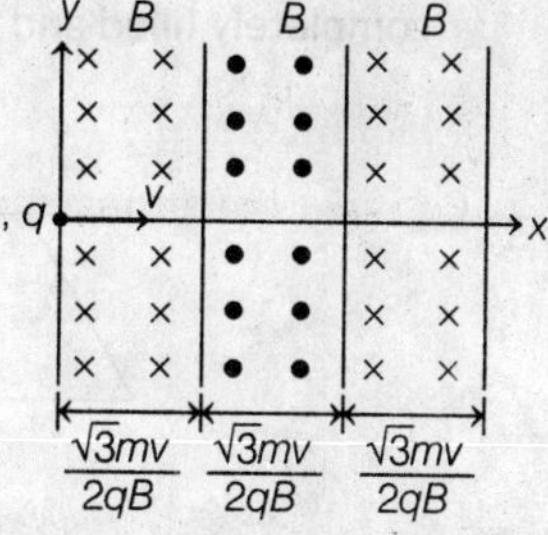

$$\mathbf{B} = -B\hat{\mathbf{k}} \quad 0 \le x \le d$$
$$= B\hat{\mathbf{k}} \quad d < x \le 2d$$
$$= -B\hat{\mathbf{k}} \quad 2d < x \le 3d$$
$$= 0 \quad x > 3d$$

If $d = \frac{\sqrt{3}\,mv}{2qB}$, choose the correct alternative(s).

(a) Time of motion of the particle in magnetic field is $\frac{\pi m}{qB}$.

(b) Average force experienced by the particle during its motion in magnetic field is qvB.

(c) Average force experienced by the particle during its motion in magnetic field is $\frac{qvB}{\pi}$.

(d) y-coordinate of the point where particle exits magnetic field region is $\frac{3mv}{2qB}$.

13. Consider the following relationship between different physical quantities $a = bc + de^{fgh} + \hat{\mathbf{i}} \cdot \hat{\mathbf{j}} + \frac{k}{l \cdot \sin(mn)}$

Here a = Acceleration (magnitude),

b = Unknown quantity, c = Speed of light,

d = Unknown quantity, e = Euler's number,

f = Unknown quantity, g = Acceleration due to gravity (magnitude),

h = Height, $\hat{\mathbf{i}}$ = Unit vector in x direction,

$\hat{\mathbf{j}}$ = Unit vector in y direction, k = Unknown quantity,

l = Length, m = Mass and n = Unknown quantity

Choose the correct alternative(s)

(a) $\left[\frac{d}{b}\right] = [LT^{-1}]$

(b) Product of k and f is dimensionless

(c) $[n] = M^{-1}$

(d) The given relation can't be established by dimensional analysis.

14. The figure here shows a metallic ring with a small gap (t). If temperature of the ring is increased.

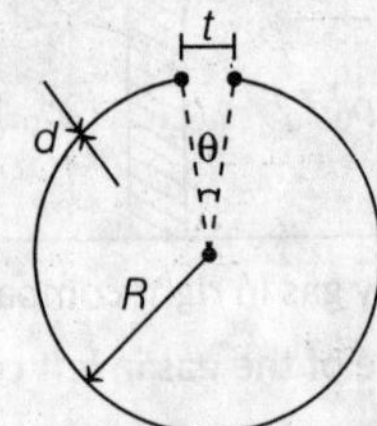

(a) t increases (b) d increases

(c) R increases (d) θ remains constant

15. A thin hollow cone of mass M confines m mass of water between itself and a horizontal table such that the cone is completely filled and is at rest. Choose correct alternative(s).

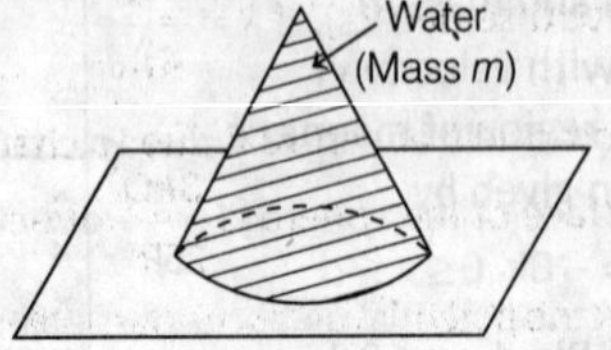

(a) Contact force by water on table is mg.

(b) Contact force by water on table is $3mg$.

(c) If $M = 3mg$, normal force on cone by table is mg.

(d) Minimum value of M is just greater than $2mg$.

16. A balloon released from rest near earth's surface starts rising vertically upwards with acceleration 5 m/s^2. Given that acceleration of balloon decreases linearly with its height above ground and it attains maximum speed at a height of 20 m above ground. Choose the correct alternative(s)

(a) Maximum height attained by the balloon is 40 m

(b) Motion of balloon is SHM.

(c) Speed of balloon at a height of 10 m above ground is $5\sqrt{3}$ m/s.

(d) Time taken by balloon to reach height of 10 m above ground equals π s.

Section IV *Non-negative Integer Type*

Instructions *See knockout 14*

17. A small planet is orbiting in a circular orbit of radius r around sun of radius R. t and T represent surface temperatures of planet and sun respectively. If $\left(\frac{t}{T}\right)^x = \frac{R}{yr}$, find $x + y$ considering planet and sun as black bodies. Here x and y are positive integers.

18. A radioactive element is being produced at a constant rate k. The element has a decay constant λ. At $t = 0$, number of nuclei of the element is N_0. If $k = 7\lambda N_0$, number of nuclei of the element after one half life of the element is xN_0. Find x.

19. The shown conducting square loop $PQRS$ of side l and resistance r is located in a region of transverse magnetic field $\mathbf{B}$ given by $\mathbf{B} = (x + y)t\hat{\mathbf{k}}$.

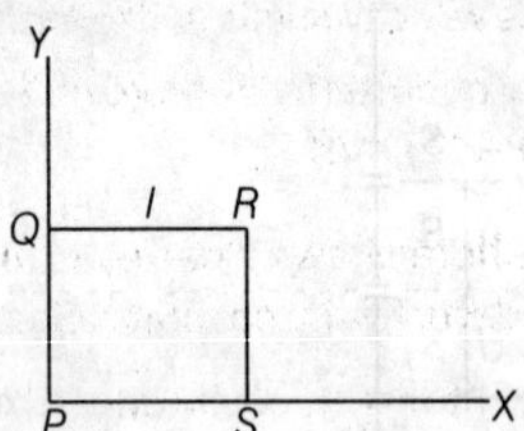

Considering $l = 3$ m and $r = 9\Omega$, find induced current (in A) in the loop at $t = 8$ s.

Answers

1	(a)	2	(b)	3	(a)	4	(a)	5	(2.40)	6	(8.38)	7	(9.00)	8	(0.67)	9	(5.59)	10	(31.00)
11	(b,c,d)	12	(a, c, d)	13	(a,b,c,d)	14	(a,b,c,d)	15	(b,c,d)	16	(a,b,c)	17	(4)	18	(4)	19	(3)		

See detailed explanations on page no. 368

Paper 2

Section I *One or more than one correct options*

Instructions *See knockout 14*

1. Each of the resistors shown in the network is R. Centre of symmetry of the network is maintained at positive potential V. Current flowing in various branches will be

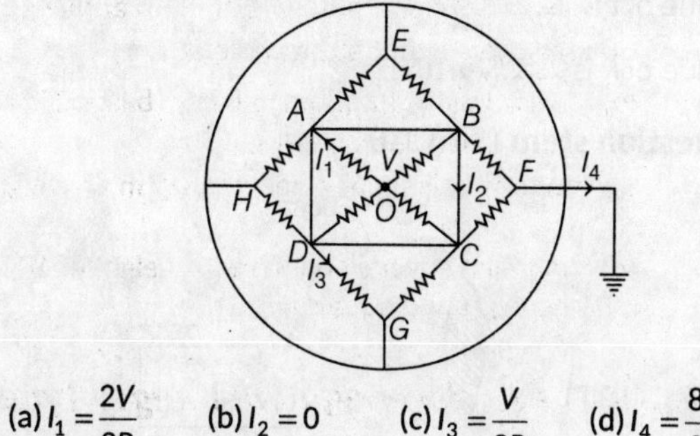

(a) $I_1 = \frac{2V}{3R}$ (b) $I_2 = 0$ (c) $I_3 = \frac{V}{3R}$ (d) $I_4 = \frac{8V}{3R}$

2. Considering the set-up shown, choose the correct alternatives considering rays to be approximately paraxial.

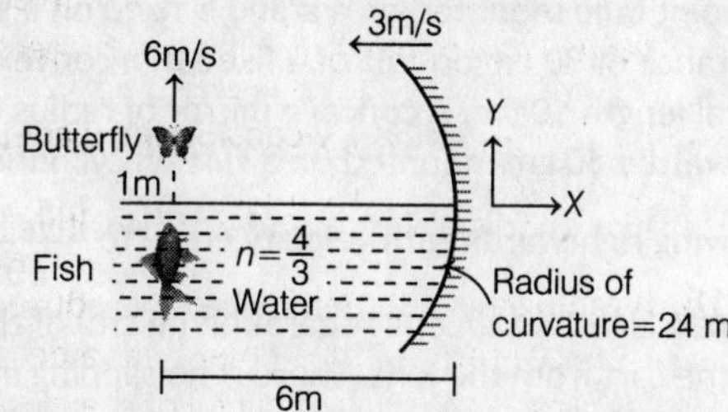

(a) Velocity of butterfly's image (direct reflection) in mirror is $-15\hat{i} + 11\hat{j}$ m/s.

(b) Velocity of butterfly's image (direct reflection) w.r.t. butterfly is at angle $\tan^{-1}\frac{1}{3}$ w.r.t. horizontal.

(c) Velocity of butterfly w.r.t. fish is parallel to butterfly's image's velocity in mirror if velocity of fish is $7.5\hat{i} + 5.5\hat{j}$ m/s.

(d) Velocity of butterfly's (direct reflection) image in mirror is $-12\hat{i} + 11\hat{j}$ m/s.

3. The figure here shows a narrow tube with a fixed sound source. A detector is moving in circular path with constant speed equal to $\frac{1}{20}$ th of the speed of sound. When the detector is diametrically opposite to the source as shown in figure, then

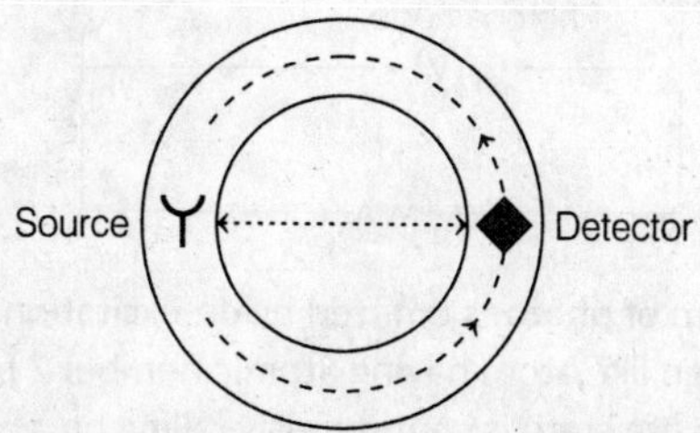

(a) no doppler effect is observed by the detector

(b) ratio of frequencies observed by the detector is 21 : 19

(c) beat frequency observed by the detector is $0.1f$

(d) if the detector stops instantly, it will observed local maxima of sound

4. A sample of argon is undergoing a cyclic process as indicated by a T-V indicator diagram here. Which of the following alternative(s) is/are correct? (Symbols have usual meaning)

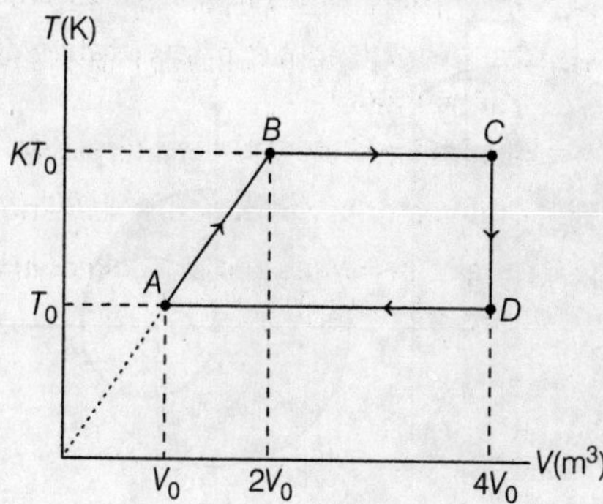

(a) $p_A = p_B$ (b) $|Q_{BC}| = |Q_{DA}|$

(c) $p_{max} = 4p_{min}$ (d) $U_B = 2U_A$

5.

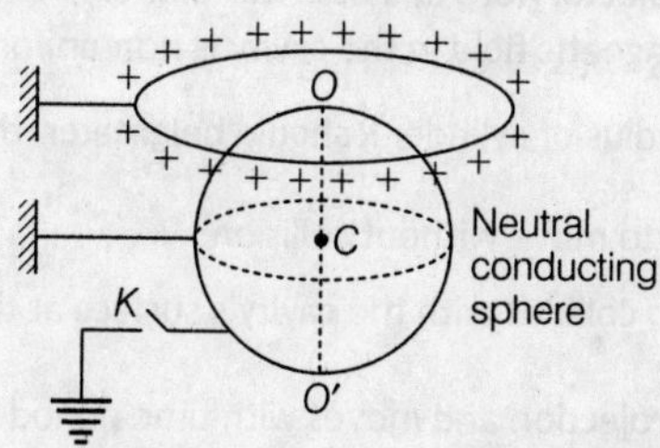

The arrangement here shows a fixed neutral conducting sphere of radius $r' = 3R$ and non-conducting ring of positive charge Q and radius $r = 4R$ fixed, so that centre O of the ring coincides with topmost point of surface of the sphere. The two stands are insulating and line joining O and centre C of the sphere is axis of the ring. Choose the correct statement(s), if $k = \frac{1}{4\pi\varepsilon_0}$.

(a) Electric field at centre C due to charges induced on surface of the sphere is $\frac{3kQ}{25R^2}$ directed from C to O.

(b) Electric potential on bottomost point O' of the sphere is $\frac{kQ}{5R}$.

(c) Electric potential at O due to charges induced on sphere's surface is $-\frac{kQ}{20R}$.

(d) If the sphere is grounded by closing the shown key K, number of electrons flowing from ground to the sphere during long duration is $\frac{3Q}{5e}$, here e is electronic charge.

6. The figure shows a cylindrical cavity of radius $\frac{R}{2}$ in a long cylinder of radius R such that axis of the two are parallel and surface of the cavity touches axis of the cylinder. A direct current of current density $J\hat{k}$ flows along the remaining cylinder as shown in views in the figure. A positive point charge $+q$ at C and a negative point charge $-q$ at C are imparted velocities $v\hat{i}$ and $v\hat{j}$ respectively. Choose the correct alternative(s). (Assume subsequent collisions as elastic).

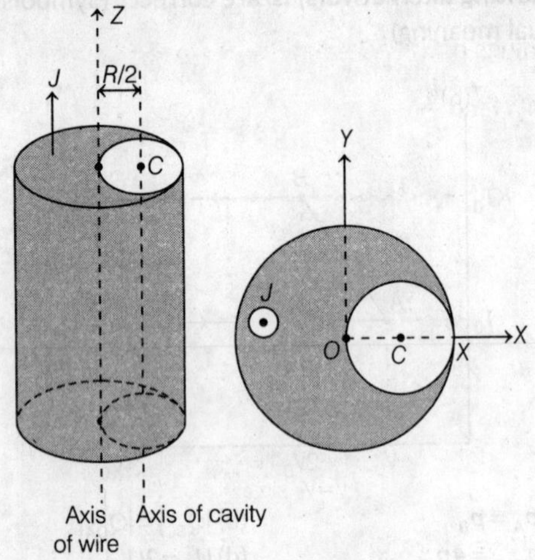

(a) Trajectory of $+q$ lies in XZ- plane.

(b) Magnetic field in the cavity is non-uniform.

(c) radius of cylinder R should be greater than $\sqrt{\frac{8mv}{q\mu_0 J}}$, if $+q$ is to move without collision.

(d) $-q$ collides with the cavity's surface at time $\frac{R}{2v}$ after projection and moves with time period of $\frac{2R}{v}$.

Section II *Numerical Value Type*

Instructions *See knockout 14*

Question stem (7 to 8)

Two identical balls A and B of mass m and charge $+q$ each are connected by a light rigid rod of length l. The rod is hinged at centre O and is initially at rest in a gravity free space as shown in Fig.1. A third uncharged ball C identical to the two balls is resting at a distance $\frac{l}{2}$ from centre of the rod in the position shown. The system is placed in a transverse uniform magnetic field B_0 in cylindrical region having its axis passing through O. The magnetic field is suddenly switched off making the rod rotate and particle A collide perfectly inelastically with C. The ball A collides with the ball C at time $t = t$. Reaction at hinge just after the collision is R. It is given that $q = 2\mu C$, $m = 1\,\mu g$, $B_0 = 10$ T, $l = 3$ m.

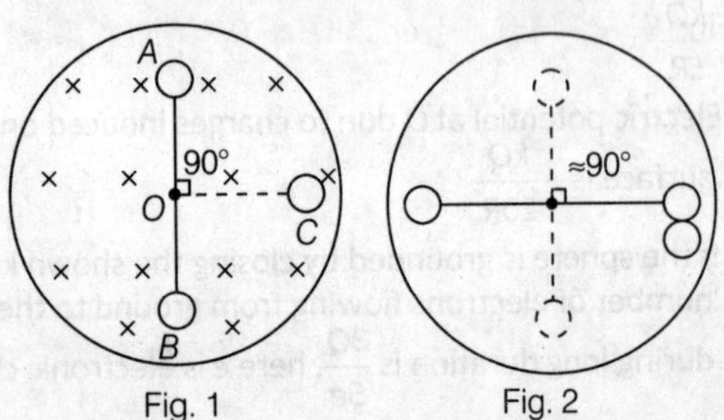

Fig. 1 Fig. 2

7. Value of t is .... s.

8. Value of R is .... (in μN).

Question stem (9 to 10)

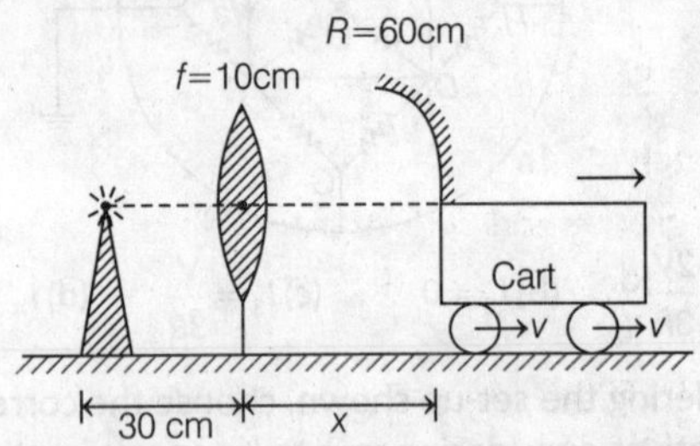

A point bulb mounted on a stand is fixed on a ground at a distance of 30 cm on axis of a fixed thin convex lens of focal length 10 cm. A concave mirror of radius of curvature 60 cm mounted on a cart on cylindrical rollers moving rightwards with velocity equal to $\frac{(45-x)^2}{600}$ cm/s. Here x is instantaneous separation (in cm) of the left end of the cart from the lens. There is no slipping at contact points of rollers with other surfaces. Considering image after refraction from lens followed by reflection from mirror, velocity of image and magnification are v_i and m respectively for $x = 60$ cm.

9. The value of v_i is ...... cm/s.

10. The value of m is ....

Question stem (11 to 12)

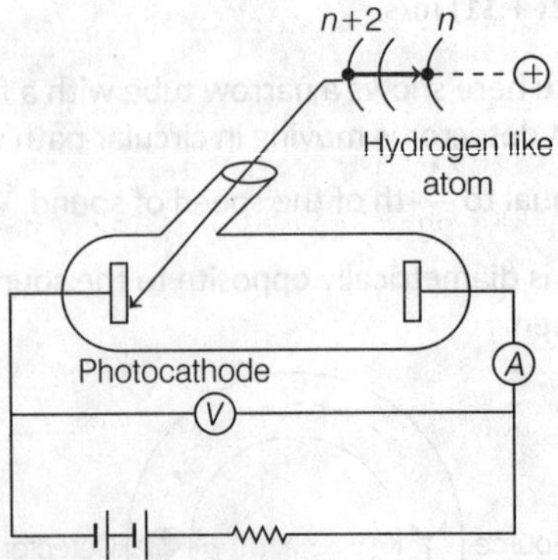

A stream of photons emitted by de-excitation of a hydrogen like atom having atomic number Z from $(n+2)$ th state to nth state is continuously falling on a photocathode ($\phi = 4.2$ eV) in photoelectric cell as shown in figure. To register zero photocurrent in the circuit, negative anode potential corresponds to a reading for which the emitted photoelectrons have minimum de-Broglie wavelength of 5 Å. Take, $\pi = 3.14$ and Bohr's radius equal to 0.53 Å.

11. $\frac{Z}{n}$ is equal to ....

12. de-Broglie wavelength of electron before it de-excites is .... Å.

Section III *Paragraph Based Questions*

Instructions *See knockout 14*

Paragraph (13 to 14)

A bicycle has pedal rods of length 16 cm connected to sprocketed disc of radius 10 cm. The bicycle wheels are 70 cm in diameter and the chain runs over a gear of radius 4 cm. The speed of the cycle is constant and the cyclist applies 150 N force that is always perpendicular to the pedal rod, as shown. Assume tension in the lower part of chain negligible. The cyclist is peddling at a constant rate of two revolutions per second. Assume that the force applied by other foot is zero when one foot is exerting 150 N force. Neglect friction within cycle parts and rolling friction.

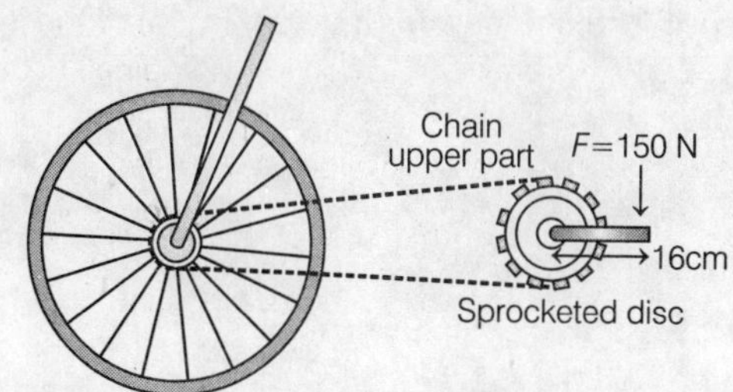

13. The tension in the upper portion of the chain is equal to

(a) 100 N (b) 120 N (c) 160 N (d) 240 N

14. The power delivered by the cyclist is equal to

(a) 280 W (b) 100 W (c) 96 π W (d) 32 W

Paragraph (15 to 16)

Refractive index of a medium is related to wavelength of radiation as $\mu = a + \frac{b}{\lambda^2}$. This relation is called Cauchy's formula, here a and b are constants for a given medium. If, for a given medium $a = 1.105$

15. A radiation of $\lambda = 4000$ Å incident on the medium's boundary (at 60° with normal) with vacuum emerges grazingly in vacuum. Value of b is

(a) 1 $(Å)^2$ (b) 8×10^6 $(Å)^2$ (c) 0.8×10^6 $(Å)^2$ (d) 0.8 $(Å)^2$

16. Refractive index of the medium for $\lambda = 6000$ Å is

(a) 1.155 (b) 1.127 (c) 1.19 (d) 1.157

Section IV *Non-negative Integer Type*

Instructions *See knockout 14*

17. Readings of the AC ammeter for $\omega \to 0$ and $\omega \to \infty$ are I_1 and I_2. Find $\frac{I_1}{I_2}$.

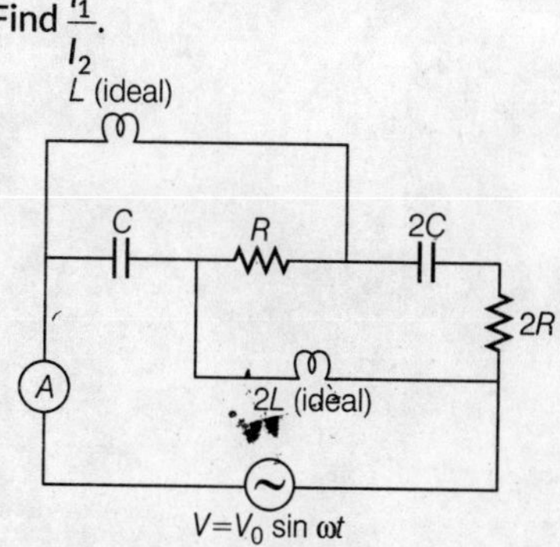

18. A uniform string of length, $l = 1$ m rotates about one of its ends P on a smooth horizontal table about a vertical axis passing through end P with constant angular speed $\omega = 10\sqrt{6}$ rad/s. A transverse pulse is generated at end Q as shown. Find speed of the wave pulse (in m/s) as it reaches mid point of the string.

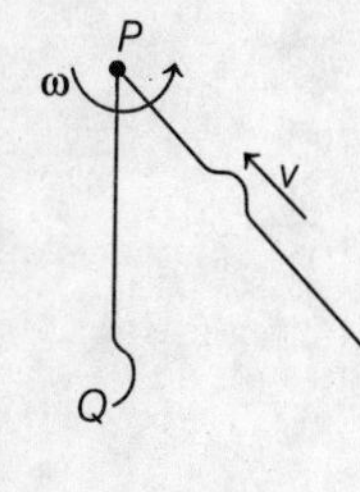

19.

Consider the shown arrangement of two identical prism, having refractive indices $\mu = \frac{4}{3}$. θ is chosen such that the total deviation suffered by ray is double of the deviation produced by prism-1 only. If possible values of θ are θ_1 and θ_2. Find $\theta_1 - \frac{\theta_2}{2}$ (in degrees) if $\theta_1 > \theta_2$. Given that $\sin 53° = \frac{4}{5}$.

Answers

1	(a,b,c,d)	2	(a,b,c)	3	(b,c,d)	4	(a,b,c,d)	5	(b,c,d)	6	(a,c,d)	7	(0.16)	8	(66.67)	9	(3.75)	10	1.00
11	(1)	12	(6.66)	13	(d)	14	(c)	15	(c)	16	(b)	17	(3)	18	(15)	19	(53)		

See detailed explanations on page no. 371

The Real Nuts

Past Year's JEE Main & Advanced Question Papers

Now you are ready for exam, so attempt these Past Exams' Papers and compare your score with the Cut Off Score of that year.

The Real Nuts

JEE Main 2022

(Real Nut 1-24 June 2022, Shift-I)

Physics

Instructions

1. This question paper contains of 30 Questions of Physics, divided into two Sections : **Section A** Objective Type Questions and **Section B** Numerical Value Questions.
2. Section A contains 20 Objective questions and all Questions are compulsory (Marking Scheme : Correct + 4, Incorrect −1) .
3. Section B contains 10 Numerical value questions out of which only 5 questions are to be attempted (Marking Scheme : Correct + 4, Incorrect 0)

Section A *Objective Type Questions*

1 The bulk modulus of a liquid is 3×10^{10} Nm^{-2}. The pressure required to reduce the volume of liquid by 2 % is

(a) 3×10^{8} Nm^{-2}

(b) 9×10^{8} Nm^{-2}

(c) 6×10^{8} Nm^{-2}

(d) 12×10^{8} Nm^{-2}

2 Given below are two statements, one is labelled as Assertion (A) and the other is labelled as Reason (R).

Assertion (A) In a uniform magnetic field, speed and energy remains the same for a moving charged particle.

Reason (R) Moving charged particle experiences magnetic force perpendicular to its direction of motion.

(a) Both A and R are true and R is the correct explanation of A.

(b) Both A and R are true but R is NOT the correct explanation of A.

(c) A is true but R is false.

(d) A is false but R is true.

3 Two identical cells each of emf 1.5 V are connected in parallel across a parallel combination of two resistors each of resistance 20 Ω. A voltmeter connected in the circuit measures 1.2 V. The internal resistance of each cell is

(a) 2.5 Ω (b) 4 Ω (c) 5 Ω (d) 10 Ω

4 Identify the pair of physical quantities which have different dimensions.

(a) Wave number and Rydberg's constant

(b) Stress and coefficient of elasticity

(c) Coercivity and magnetisation

(d) Specific heat capacity and latent heat

5 A projectile is projected with velocity of 25 m/s at an angle θ with the horizontal. After t seconds its inclination with horizontal becomes zero. If R represents horizontal range of the projectile, the value of θ will be [use, $g = 10$ m/s^2]

(a) $\frac{1}{2}\sin^{-1}\left(\frac{5t^2}{4R}\right)$ (b) $\frac{1}{2}\sin^{-1}\left(\frac{4R}{5t^2}\right)$

(c) $\tan^{-1}\left(\frac{4t^2}{5R}\right)$ (d) $\cot^{-1}\left(\frac{R}{20t^2}\right)$

6 A block of mass 10 kg starts sliding on a surface with an initial velocity of 9.8 ms^{-1}. The coefficient of friction between the surface and block is 0.5. The distance covered by the block before coming to rest is [use, $g = 9.8$ ms^{-2}]

(a) 4.9 m (b) 9.8 m

(c) 12.5 m (d) 19.6 m

7 A boy ties a stone of mass 100 g to the end of a 2m long string and whirls it around in a horizontal plane. The string can withstand the maximum tension of 80 N. If the maximum speed with which the stone can revolve is $\frac{K}{\pi}$ rev/min. The value of K is (Assume the string is massless and unstretchable)

(a) 400 (b) 300

(c) 600 (d) 800

8 A vertical electric field of magnitude 4.9×10^{5} N/C just prevents a water droplet of a mass 0.1 g from falling. The value of charge on the droplet will be (given, $g = 9.8$ m/s^2)

(a) 1.6×10^{-9} C (b) 2.0×10^{-9} C

(c) 3.2×10^{-9} C (d) 0.5×10^{-9} C

9 A particle experiences a variable force $\mathbf{F} = (4x\hat{\mathbf{i}} + 3y^2\hat{\mathbf{j}})$ in a horizontal X-Y plane. Assume, distance in metre and force in newton. If the particle moves from point (1, 2) to point (2, 3) in the XY-plane, then kinetic energy changes by

(a) 50.0 J (b) 12.5 J
(c) 25.0 J (d) 0 J

10 The approximate height from the surface of earth at which the weight of the body becomes $\frac{1}{3}$ of its weight on the surface of earth is [Radius of earth, $R = 6400$ km and $\sqrt{3} = 1.732$]

(a) 3840 km (b) 4685 km
(c) 2133 km (d) 4267 km

11 A resistance of 40 Ω is connected to a source of alternating current rated 220 V, 50 Hz. Find the time taken by the current to change from its maximum value to the rms value

(a) 2.5 ms (b) 1.25 ms
(c) 2.5 s (d) 0.25 s

12 The equations of two waves are given by

$$y_1 = 5\sin 2\pi(x - vt) \text{ cm}$$
$$y_2 = 3\sin 2\pi(x - vt + 1.5) \text{ cm}$$

These waves are simultaneously passing through a string. The amplitude of the resulting wave is

(a) 2 cm (b) 4 cm
(c) 5.8 cm (d) 8 cm

13 A plane electromagnetic wave travels in a medium of relative permeability 1.61 and relative permittivity 6.44. If magnitude of magnetic intensity is 4.5×10^{-2} Am^{-1} at a point, what will be the approximate magnitude of electric field intensity at that point?

(Given, permeability of free space $\mu_0 = 4\pi \times 10^{-7}$ NA^{-2}, speed of light in vacuum, $c = 3 \times 10^8$ ms^{-1})

(a) 16.96 Vm^{-1} (b) 2.25×10^{-2} Vm^{-1}
(c) 8.48 Vm^{-1} (d) 6.75×10^6 Vm^{-1}

14 Choose the correct option from the following options given below

(a) In the ground state of Rutherford's model, electrons are in stable equilibrium while in Thomson's model electrons always experience a net-force.
(b) An atom has a nearly continuous mass distribution in a Rutherford's model but has a highly non-uniform mass distribution in Thomson's model.
(c) A classical atom based on Rutherford's model is doomed to collapse.
(d) The positively charged part of the atom possesses most of the mass in Rutherford's model but not in Thomson's model.

15 Nucleus A is having mass number 220 and its binding energy per nucleon is 5.6 MeV. It splits in two fragments B and C of mass numbers 105 and 115. The binding energy of nucleons in B and C is 6.4 MeV per nucleon. The energy Q released per fission will be

(a) 0.8 MeV (b) 275 MeV
(c) 220 MeV (d) 176 MeV

16 A baseband signal of 3.5 MHz frequency is modulated with a carrier signal of 3.5 GHz frequency using amplitude modulation method. What should be the minimum size of antenna required to transmit the modulated signal?

(a) 42.8 m (b) 42.8 mm
(c) 21.4 mm (d) 21.4 m

17 A Carnot engine whose heat sink is at 27°C, has an efficiency of 25%. By how many degrees should the temperature of the source be changed to increase the efficiency by 100 % of the original efficiency?

(a) Increases by 18°C
(b) Increases by 200°C
(c) Increases by 120°C
(d) Increases by 73°C

18 A parallel plate capacitor is formed by two plates, each of area 30π cm^2 separated by 1 mm. A material of dielectric strength 3.6×10^7 Vm^{-1} is filled between the plates. If the maximum charge that can be stored on the capacitor without causing any dielectric breakdown is 7×10^{-6} C, the value of dielectric constant of the material is

$\left\{\text{Use, } \frac{1}{4\pi\varepsilon_0} = 9 \times 10^9 \text{ Nm}^2\text{C}^{-2}\right\}$

(a) 1.66 (b) 1.75
(c) 2.25 (d) 2.33

19 The magnetic field at the centre of a circular coil of radius r, due to current I flowing through it, is B. The magnetic field at a point along the axis at a distance $r/2$ from the centre is

(a) $B/2$ (b) $2B$
(c) $\left(\frac{2}{\sqrt{5}}\right)^3 B$ (d) $\left(\frac{2}{\sqrt{3}}\right)^3 B$

20 Two metallic blocks M_1 and M_2 of same area of cross-section are connected to each other (as shown in figure). If the thermal conductivity of M_2 is K, then the thermal conductivity of M_1 will be : [Assume steady state heat conduction]

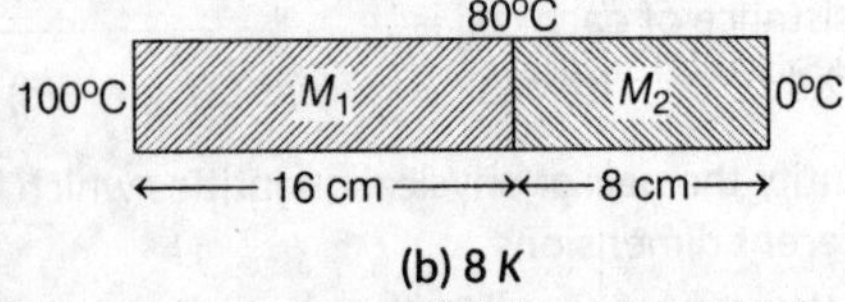

(a) $10K$ (b) $8K$
(c) $12.5K$ (d) $2K$

Section II *Numerical Value Questions*

21 0.056 kg of Nitrogen is enclosed in a vessel at a temperature of 127°(C). The amount of heat required to double the speed of its molecules is ...... k cal.

(Take, $R = 2$ cal mol^{-1}K^{-1})

22 Two identical thin biconvex lenses of focal length 15 cm and refractive index 1.5 are in contact with each other. The space between the lenses is filled with a liquid of refractive index 1.25. The focal length of the combination is ...... cm.

23 A transistor is used in common-emitter mode in an amplifier circuit. When a signal of 10 mV is added to the base-emitter voltage, the base current changes by 10 μA and the collector current changes by 1.5 mA. The load resistance is 5 kΩ. The voltage gain of the transistor will be ....

24 As shown in the figure, an inductor of inductance 200 mH is connected to an AC source of emf 220 V and frequency 50 Hz. The instantaneous voltage of the source is 0 V when the peak value of current is $\frac{\sqrt{a}}{\pi}$ A. The value of a is ....

L=200 mH

25 Sodium light of wavelengths 650 nm and 655 nm is used to study diffraction at a single slit of aperture 0.5 mm. The distance between the slit and the screen is 2.0 m. The separation between the positions of the first maxima of diffraction pattern obtained in the two cases is ...... $\times 10^{-5}$ m.

26 When light of frequency twice the threshold frequency is incident on the metal plate, the maximum velocity of emitted electron is v_1. When the frequency of incident radiation is increased to five times the threshold value, the maximum velocity of emitted electron becomes v_2. If $v_2 = x\, v_1$, the value of x will be ....

27 From the top of a tower, a ball is thrown vertically upward which reaches the ground in 6 s. A second ball thrown vertically downward from the same position with the same speed reaches the ground in 1.5 s. A third ball released, from the rest from the same location, will reach the ground in .... s.

28 A ball of mass 100 g is dropped from a height, $h = 10$ cm on a platform fixed at the top of vertical spring (as shown in figure). The ball stays on the platform and the platform is depressed by a distance $h/2$. The spring constant is .... Nm^{-1}. (Use, $g = 10$ ms^{-2})

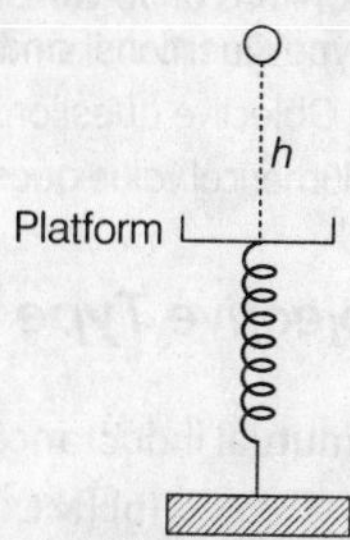

29 In a potentiometer arrangement, a cell gives a balancing point at 75 cm length of wire.

This cell is now replaced by another cell of unknown emf. If the ratio of the emf's of two cells, respectively is 3 : 2, the difference in the balancing length of the potentiometer wire in above two cases will be ...... cm.

30 A metre scale is balanced on a knife edge at its centre. When two coins, each of mass 10 g are put one on the top of the other at the 10.0 cm mark the scale is found to be balanced at 40.0 cm mark.

The mass of the metre scale is found to be $x \times 10^{-2}$ kg. The value of x is ....

Answers

1 (c)	2 (a)	3 (c)	4 (d)	5 (d)	6 (b)	7 (c)	8 (b)	9 (c)	10 (b)
11 (a)	12 (a)	13 (c)	14 (c)	15 (d)	16 (c)	17 (b)	18 (d)	19 (c)	20 (b)
21 12	22 10	23 750	24 242	25 3	26 2	27 3	28 120	29 25	30 6

See detailed explanations on page no. 376

The Real Nuts

JEE Main 2022

(Real Nut 2-26 June 2022, Shift-II)

Physics

Instructions

1. This question paper contains of 30 Questions of Physics, divided into two Sections : **Section A** Objective Type Questions and **Section B** Numerical Value Questions.
2. Section A contains 20 Objective questions and all Questions are compulsory (Marking Scheme : Correct + 4, Incorrect –1) .
3. Section B contains 10 Numerical value questions out of which only 5 questions are to be attempted (Marking Scheme : Correct + 4, Incorrect 0)

Section A *Objective Type Questions*

1 The dimension of mutual inductance is

(a) $[ML^2T^{-2}A^{-1}]$ (b) $[ML^2T^{-3}A^{-1}]$
(c) $[ML^2T^{-2}A^{-2}]$ (d) $[ML^2T^{-3}A^{-2}]$

2 **In the arrangement shown in figure a_1, a_2, a_3 and a_4 are the accelerations of masses m_1, m_2, m_3 and m_4, respectively. Which of the following relation is true for this arrangement?**

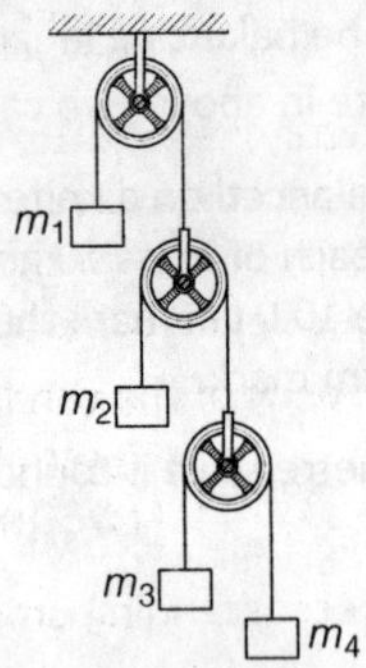

(a) $4a_1 + 2a_2 + a_3 + a_4 = 0$ (b) $a_1 + 4a_2 + 3a_3 + a_4 = 0$
(c) $a_1 + 4a_2 + 3a_3 + 2a_4 = 0$ (d) $2a_1 + 2a_2 + 3a_3 + a_4 = 0$

3 **Arrange the four graphs in descending order of total work done, where W_1, W_2, W_3 and W_4 are the work done corresponding to figures A, B, C and D, respectively**

A.
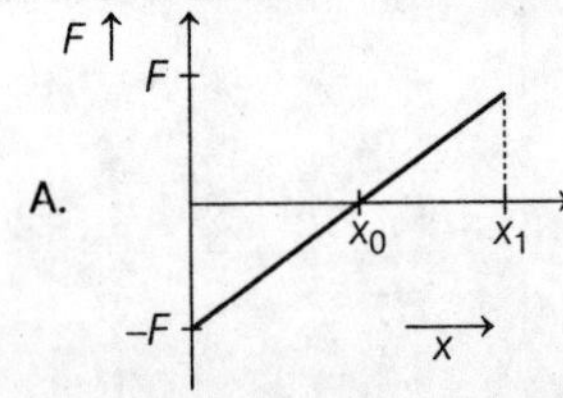

B.
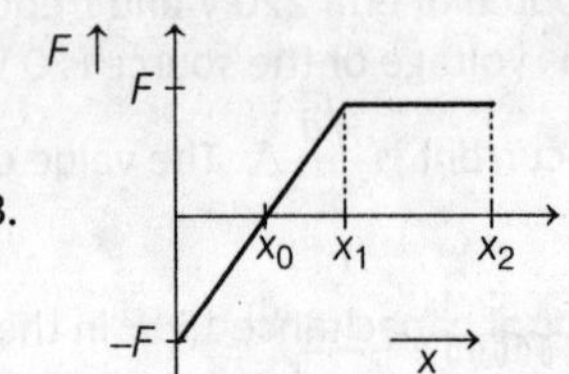

C.
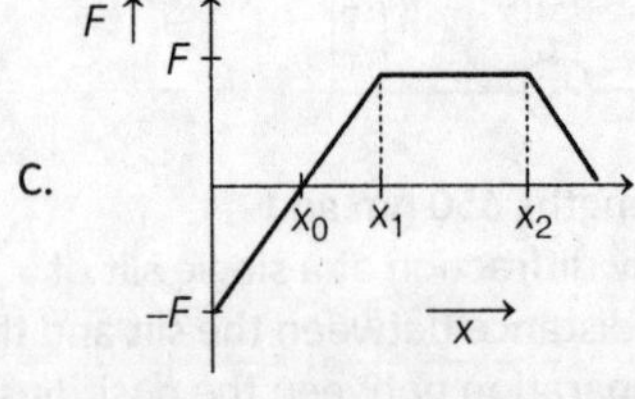

D.
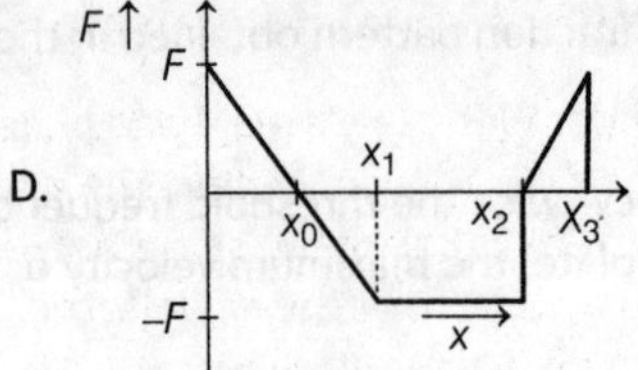

(a) $W_3 > W_2 > W_1 > W_4$ (b) $W_3 > W_2 > W_4 > W_1$
(c) $W_2 > W_3 > W_4 > W_1$ (d) $W_2 > W_3 > W_1 > W_4$

4 **A solid spherical ball is rolling on a frictionless horizontal plane surface about its axis of symmetry. The ratio of rotational kinetic energy of the ball to its total kinetic energy is**

(a) $\frac{2}{5}$ (b) $\frac{2}{7}$ (c) $\frac{1}{5}$ (d) $\frac{7}{10}$

5 **Given below are two statements. One is labelled as Assertion A and the other is labelled as Reason R.**

Assertion (A) If we move from poles to equator, the direction of acceleration due to gravity of earth always points towards the centre of earth without any variation in its magnitude.

Reason (R) At equator, the direction of acceleration due to the gravity is towards the centre of earth.

In the light of above statements, choose the correct answer from the options given below

(a) Both A and R are true and R is the correct explanation of A.

(b) Both A and R are true but R is not the correct explanation of A.

(c) A is true but R is false.

(d) A is false but R is true.

6 If ρ is the density and η is coefficient of viscosity of fluid which flows with a speed v in the pipe of diameter d, the correct formula for Reynolds number R_e is

(a) $R_e = \frac{\eta d}{\rho v}$ (b) $R_e = \frac{\rho v}{\eta d}$

(c) $R_e = \frac{\rho v d}{\eta}$ (d) $R_e = \frac{\eta}{\rho v d}$

7 A flask contains argon and oxygen in the ratio of 3 : 2 in mass and the mixture is kept at 27°C. The ratio of their average kinetic energy per molecule respectively, will be

(a) 3 : 2 (b) 9 : 4

(c) 2 : 3 (d) 1 : 1

8. The charge on capacitor of capacitance 15μF in the figure given below is :

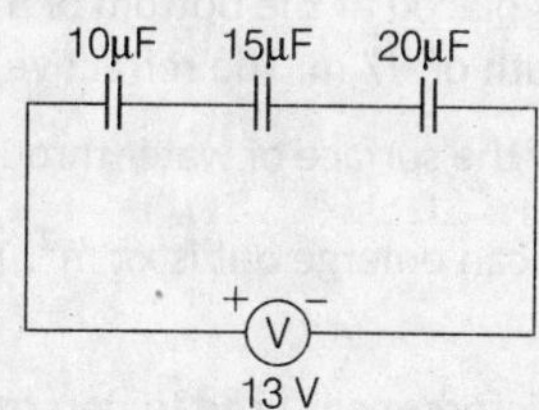

(a) 60 μC (b) 130 μC (c) 260 μC (d) 585 μC

9 A parallel plate capacitor with plate area A and plate separation $d = 2$ m has a capacitance of 4μF. The new capacitance of the system, if half of the space between them is filled with a dielectric material of dielectric constant, $K = 3$ (as shown in figure) will be

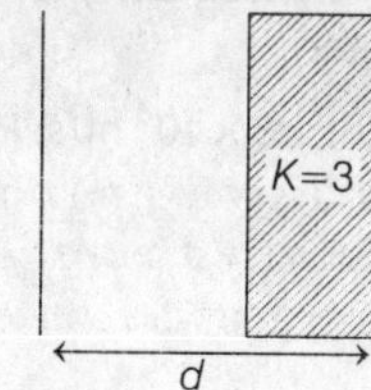

(a) 2 μF (b) 32 μF (c) 6 μF (d) 8 μF

10 Sixty four conducting drops each of radius 0.02 m and each carrying a charge of 5 μC are combined to form a bigger drop. The ratio of surface density of bigger drop to the smaller drop will be

(a) 1 : 4 (b) 4 : 1 (c) 1 : 8 (d) 8 : 1

11 The equivalent resistance between points A and B in the given network is

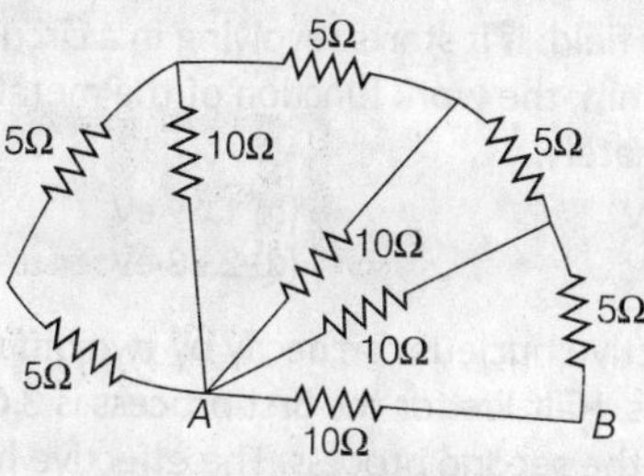

(a) 65 Ω (b) 20 Ω

(c) 5 Ω (d) 2 Ω

12 A bar magnet having a magnetic moment of 2.0×10^5 JT^{-1}, is placed along the direction of uniform magnetic field of magnitude, $B = 14 \times 10^{-5}$ T. The work done in rotating the magnet slowly through 60° from the direction of field is

(a) 14 J (b) 8.4 J

(c) 4 J (d) 1.4 J

13 Two coils of self-inductance L_1 and L_2 are connected in series combination having mutual inductance of the coils as M. The equivalent self-inductance of the combination will be

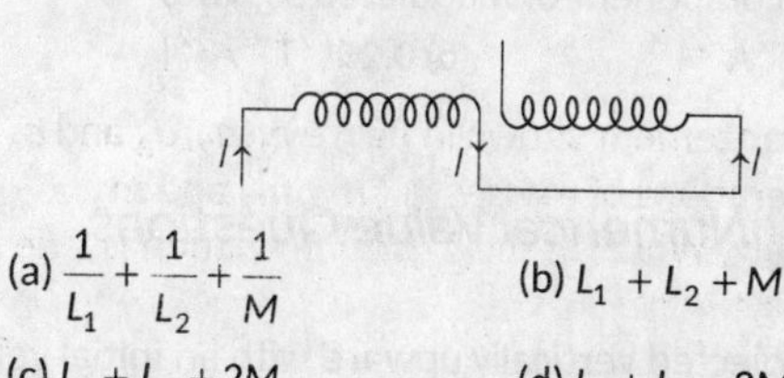

(a) $\frac{1}{L_1} + \frac{1}{L_2} + \frac{1}{M}$ (b) $L_1 + L_2 + M$

(c) $L_1 + L_2 + 2M$ (d) $L_1 + L_2 - 2M$

14 A metallic conductor of length 1m rotates in a vertical plane parallel to East-West direction about one of its end with angular velocity 5 rad/s. If the horizontal component of earth's magnetic field is 0.2×10^{-4} T, then emf induced between the two ends of the conductor is

(a) 5 μV (b) 50 μV

(c) 5 mV (d) 50 mV

15 Which is the correct ascending order of wavelengths?

(a) $\lambda_{visible} < \lambda_{X\text{-}ray} < \lambda_{gamma\text{-}ray} < \lambda_{microwave}$

(b) $\lambda_{gamma\text{-}ray} < \lambda_{X\text{-}ray} < \lambda_{visible} < \lambda_{microwave}$

(c) $\lambda_{X\text{-}ray} < \lambda_{gamma\text{-}ray} < \lambda_{visible} < \lambda_{microwave}$

(d) $\lambda_{microwave} < \lambda_{visible} < \lambda_{gamma\text{-}ray} < \lambda_{X\text{-}ray}$

16 For a specific wavelength 670 nm of light coming from a galaxy moving with velocity v, the observed wavelength is 670.7 nm.

The value of v is

(a) 3×10^8 ms^{-1}

(b) 3×10^{10} ms^{-1}

(c) 3.13×10^5 ms^{-1}

(d) 4.48×10^5 ms^{-1}

17 A metal surface is illuminated by a radiation of wavelength 4500 Å. The ejected photo-electron enters a constant magnetic field of 2 mT making an angle of 90° with the magnetic field. If it starts revolving in a circular path of radius 2 mm, the work function of the metal is approximately.

(a) 1.36 eV (b) 1.69 eV
(c) 2.78 eV (d) 2.23 eV

18 A radioactive nucleus can decay by two different processes. Half-life for the first process is 3.0 h while it is 4.5 h for the second process. The effective half-life of the nucleus will be

(a) 3.75 h (b) 0.56 h (c) 0.26 h (d) 1.80 h

19 The positive feedback is required by an amplifier to act an oscillator. The feedback here means

(a) external input is necessary to sustain AC signal in output.
(b) a portion of the output power is returned back to the input.
(c) feedback can be achieved by *L-R* network.
(d) the base-collector junction must be forward biased.

20 A sinusoidal wave $y(t) = 40\sin(10 \times 10^6 \pi t)$ is amplitude modulated by another sinusoidal wave $x(t) = 20\sin(1000\pi t)$. The amplitude of minimum frequency component of modulated signal is

(a) 0.5 (b) 0.25
(c) 20 (d) 10

Section II *Numerical Value Questions*

21 A ball is projected vertically upward with an initial velocity of 50 ms^{-1} at $t = 0$ s. At $t = 2$ s, another ball is projected vertically upward with same velocity. At $t =$ ...... s, second ball will meet the first ball (Take, $g = 10\ ms^{-2}$).

22 A batsman hits back a ball of mass 0.4 kg straight in the direction of the bowler without changing its initial speed of 15 ms^{-1}. The impulse imparted to the ball is ...... N-s.

23 A system to 10 balls each of mass 2 kg are connected *via* massless and unstretchable string. The system is allowed to slip over the edge of a smooth table as shown in figure. Tension on the string between the 7th and 8th ball is ...... N, when 6th ball just leaves the table.

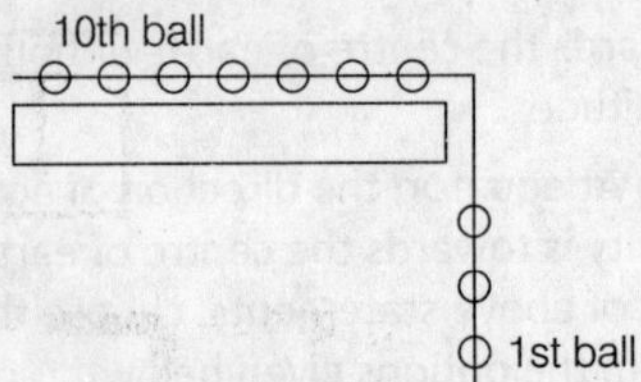

24 A geyser heats water flowing at a rate of 2.0 kg per minute from 30°C to 70°C. If geyser operates on a gas burner, the rate of combustion of fuel will be ...... g min^{-1}.
[Heat of combustion $= 8 \times 10^3\ Jg^{-1}$,
Specific heat of water $= 4.2\ Jg^{-1}°C^{-1}$]

25 A heat engine operates with the cold reservoir at temperature 324 K. The minimum temperature of the hot reservoir, if the heat engine takes 300 J heat from the hot reservoir and delivers 180 J heat to the cold reservoir per cycle, is ...... K.

26 A set of 20 tuning forks is arranged in a series of increasing frequencies. If each fork gives 4 beats with respect to the preceding fork and the frequency of the last fork is twice the frequency of the first, then the frequency of last fork is ...... Hz.

27 Two 10 cm long, straight wires, each carrying a current of 5 A are kept parallel to each other. If each wire experienced a force of 10^{-5} N, then separation between the wires is ...... cm.

28 A small bulb is placed at the bottom of a tank containing water to a depth of $\sqrt{7}$ m. The refractive index of water is $\frac{4}{3}$. The area of the surface of water through which light from the bulb can emerge out is $x\pi\ m^2$. The value of x is ....

29 A travelling microscope is used to determine the refractive index of a glass slab. If 40 divisions are there in 1 cm on main scale and 50 vernier scale divisions are equal to 49 main scale divisions, then least count of the travelling microscope is ...... $\times 10^{-6}$ m.

30 The stopping potential for photoelectrons emitted from a surface illuminated by light of wavelength 6630 Å is 0.42 V. If the threshold frequency is $x \times 10^{13}\ s^{-1}$, where x is ...... (nearest integer).
(Given, speed of light $= 3 \times 10^8$ m/s, Planck's constant $= 6.63 \times 10^{-34}$ J-s)

Answers

1 (c)	2 (a)	3 (a)	4 (b)	5 (d)	6 (c)	7 (*)	8 (a)	9 (c)	10 (b)
11 (c)	12 (a)	13 (d)	14 (b)	15 (b)	16 (c)	17 (a)	18 (d)	19 (b)	20 (d)
21 6	22 12	23 36	24 42	25 540	26 152	27 5	28 9	29 5	30 35

See detailed explanations on page no. 380

The Real Nuts

JEE Main 2022

[Real Nut 3-29 June 2022, Shift-I]

Physics

Instructions

1. This question paper contains of 30 Questions of Physics, divided into two Sections : **Section A** Objective Type Questions and **Section B** Numerical Value Questions.
2. Section A contains 20 Objective questions and all Questions are compulsory (Marking Scheme : Correct + 4, Incorrect −1).
3. Section B contains 10 Numerical value questions out of which only 5 questions are to be attempted (Marking Scheme : Correct + 4, Incorrect 0)

Section A *Objective Type Questions*

1 Two balls A and B are placed at the top of 180 m tall tower. Ball A is released from the top at $t=0$ s. Ball B is thrown vertically down with an initial velocity u at $t=2$ s. After a certain time, both balls meet 100 m above the ground. Find the value of u (in ms^{-1}). [Use $g=10\,ms^{-2}$]

(a) 10 (b) 15 (c) 20 (d) 30

2 A body of mass M at rest explodes into three pieces, in the ratio of masses 1 : 1 : 2. Two smaller pieces fly off perpendicular to each other with velocities of 30 ms^{-1} and 40 ms^{-1}, respectively. The velocity of the third piece will be

(a) 15 ms^{-1} (b) 25 ms^{-1} (c) 35 ms^{-1} (d) 50 ms^{-1}

3 The activity of a radioactive material is 2.56×10^{-3} Ci. If the half-life of the material is 5 days, after how many days the activity will become 2×10^{-5} Ci?

(a) 30 days (b) 35 days (c) 40 days (d) 25 days

4 A spherical shell of 1 kg mass and radius R is rolling with angular speed ω on horizontal plane as shown in figure. The magnitude of angular momentum of the shell about the origin O is $\frac{a}{3}R^2\omega$. The value of a will be

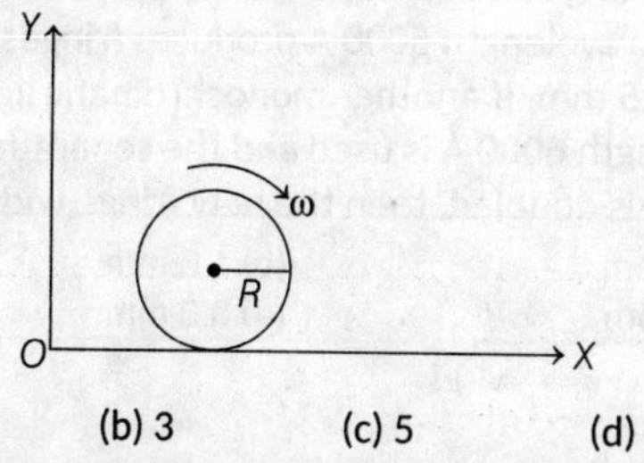

(a) 2 (b) 3 (c) 5 (d) 4

5 A cylinder of fixed capacity of 44.8 L contains helium gas at standard temperature and pressure. The amount of heat needed to raise the temperature of gas in the cylinder by 20.0°C will be
(Given, gas constant, $R=8.3\,JK^{-1}\text{-}mol^{-1}$)

(a) 249 J (b) 415 J
(c) 498 J (d) 830 J

6 A wire of length L is hanging from a fixed support. The length changes to L_1 and L_2 when masses 1kg and 2 kg are suspended respectively from its free end, then the value of L is equal to

(a) $\sqrt{L_1 L_2}$ (b) $\frac{L_1+L_2}{2}$
(c) $2L_1-L_2$ (d) $3L_1-2L_2$

7 Given below are two statements : one is labelled as Assertion A and the other is labelled as Reason R.

Assertion A The photoelectric effect does not takes place, if the energy of the incident radiation is less than the work function of a metal.

Reason R Kinetic energy of the photoelectrons is zero, if the energy of the incident radiation is equal to the work function of a metal.

In the light of the above statements, choose the most appropriate answer from the options given below.

(a) Both A and R are correct and R is the correct explanation of A.

(b) Both A and R are correct but R is not the correct explanation of A.

(c) A is correct but R is not correct.

(d) A is not correct but R is correct.

8 A particle of mass 500 g is moving in a straight line with velocity, $v = bx^{5/2}$. The work done by the net force during its displacement from $x = 0$ to $x = 4$ m is (Take, $b = 0.25\ m^{-3/2}\ s^{-1}$)

(a) 2 J (b) 4 J (c) 8 J (d) 16 J

9 A charged particle moves along circular path in a uniform magnetic field in a cyclotron. The kinetic energy of the charged particle increases to 4 times its initial value. What will be the ratio of new radius to the original radius of circular path of the charged particle

(a) 1 : 1 (b) 1 : 2 (c) 2 : 1 (d) 1 : 4

10 For a series *L-C-R* circuit, *I* versus ω curve is shown

(A) to the left of ω_r, the circuit is mainly capacitive.

(B) to the left of ω_r, the circuit is mainly inductive.

(C) at ω_r, impedance of the circuit is equal to the resistance of the circuit.

(D) at ω_r, impedance of the circuit is 0.

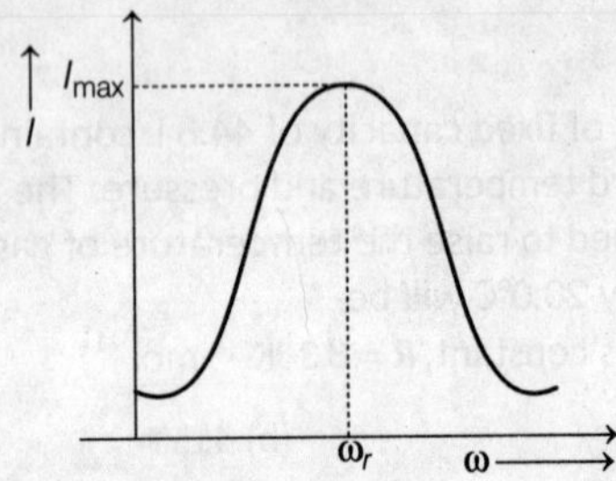

Choose the most appropriate answer from the options given below.

(a) (A) and (D) only (b) (B) and (D) only

(c) (A) and (C) only (d) (B) and (C) only

11 A block of metal weighing 2 kg is resting on a frictionless plane as shown in figure. It is struck by a jet releasing water at a rate of 1 kgs^{-1} and at a speed of 10 ms^{-1}. Then, the initial acceleration of the block (in ms^{-2}) will be

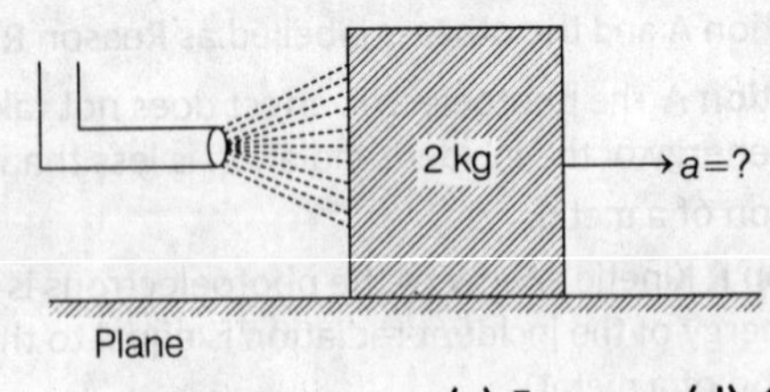

(a) 3 (b) 6 (c) 5 (d) 4

12 In van der Waal's equation $\left[p + \frac{a}{V^2}\right][V - b] = RT$ where, *p* is pressure, *V* is volume, *R* is universal gas constant and *T* is temperature. The ratio of constants $\frac{a}{b}$ is dimensionally equal to

(a) $\frac{p}{V}$ (b) $\frac{V}{p}$ (c) pV (d) pV^3

13 To vectors **A** and **B** have equal magnitudes. If magnitude of **A** + **B** is equal to two times the magnitude of **A** − **B**, then the angle between **A** and **B** will be

(a) $\sin^{-1}\left(\frac{3}{5}\right)$ (b) $\sin^{-1}\left(\frac{1}{3}\right)$

(c) $\cos^{-1}\left(\frac{3}{5}\right)$ (d) $\cos^{-1}\left(\frac{1}{3}\right)$

14 The escape velocity of a body on a planet *A* is 12 kms^{-1}. The escape velocity of the body on another planet *B*, whose density is four times and radius is half of the planet *A* is

(a) 12 kms^{-1} (b) 24 kms^{-1}

(c) 36 kms^{-1} (d) 6 kms^{-1}

15 At a certain place, the angle of dip is 30° and the horizontal component of earth's magnetic field is 0.5 G. The earth's total magnetic field (in G), at that certain place is

(a) $\frac{1}{\sqrt{3}}$ (b) $\frac{1}{2}$ (c) $\sqrt{3}$ (d) 1

16 A longitudinal wave is represented by $y = 10 \sin 2\pi\left(nt - \frac{x}{\lambda}\right)$ cm. The maximum particle velocity will be four times the wave velocity, if the determined value of wavelength is equal to

(a) 2π (b) 5π (c) π (d) $\frac{5\pi}{2}$

17 A parallel plate capacitor filled with a medium of dielectric constant 10, is connected across a battery and is charged. The dielectric slab is replaced by another slab of dielectric constant 15, then the energy of capacitor will

(a) increased by 50% (b) decreased by 15%

(c) increased by 25% (d) increased by 33%

18 A positive charge particle of 100 mg is thrown in opposite direction to a uniform electric field of strength $1 \times 10^5\ NC^{-1}$. If the charge on the particle is 40 μC and the initial velocity is 200 ms^{-1}, how much distance it will travel before coming to the rest momentarily

(a) 1 m (b) 5 m

(c) 10 m (d) 0.5 m

19 Using Young's double slit experiment, a monochromatic light of wavelength 5000 Å produces fringes of fringe width 0.5 mm. If another monochromatic light of wavelength 6000 Å is used and the separation between the slits is doubled, then the new fringe width will be

(a) 0.5 mm (b) 1.0 mm

(c) 0.6 mm (d) 0.3 mm

20 Only 2% of the optical source frequency is the available channel bandwidth for an optical communicating system operating at 1000 nm. If an audio signal requires a bandwidth of 8 kHz, how many channels can be accommodated for transmission

(a) 375×10^7 (b) 75×10^7

(c) 375×10^8 (d) 75×10^9

Section II *Numerical Value Questions*

21 Two coils require 20 min and 60 min, respectively to produce same amount of heat energy when connected separately to the same source. If they are connected in parallel arrangement to the same source, the time required to produce same amount of heat by the combination of coils, will be ...... min.

22 The intensity of the light from a bulb incident on a surface is 0.22 W/m^2. The amplitude of the magnetic field in this light wave is ...... $\times 10^{-9}$ T.

(Given, permittivity of vacuum, $\varepsilon_0 = 8.85 \times 10^{-12}$ C^2 N^{-1} - m^{-2}, speed of light in vacuum, $c = 3 \times 10^8$ ms^{-1})

23 As per the given figure, two plates *A* and *B* of thermal conductivity *K* and 2*K* are joined together to form a compound plate. The thickness of plates are 4.0 cm and 2.5 cm, respectively and the area of cross-section is 120 cm^2 for each plate. The equivalent thermal conductivity of the compound plate is $\left(1 + \frac{5}{\alpha}\right)$K, then the value of α will be ______.

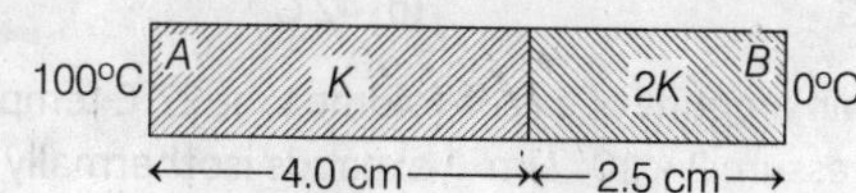

24 A body is performing simple harmonic with an amplitude of 10 cm. The velocity of the body was tripled by air jet when it is at 5 cm from its mean position. The new amplitude of vibration is $\sqrt{x}$ cm. The value of *x* is ....

25 The variation of applied potential and current flowing through a given wire is shown in figure. The length of wire is 31.4 cm. The diameter of wire is measured as 2.4 cm. The resistivity of the given wire is measured as $x \times 10^{-3}$ Ω-cm. The value of *x* is .... (Take, $\pi = 3.14$)

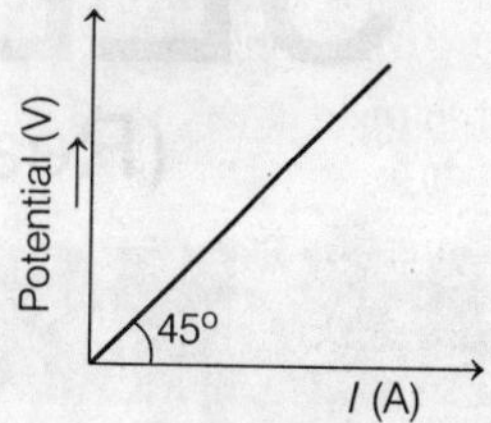

26 300 cal of heat is given to a heat engine and it rejects 225 cal of heat. If source temperature is 227°C, then the temperature of sink will be ...... 0°C.

27 $\sqrt{d_1}$ and $\sqrt{d_2}$ are the impact parameters corresponding to scattering angles 60° and 90° respectively, when an α-particle is approaching a gold nucleus. For $d_1 = x\, d_2$, the value of *x* will be ....

28 A transistor is used in an amplifier circuit in common emitter mode. If the base current changes by 100 μA, it brings a change of 10 mA in collector current. If the load resistance is 2 kΩ and input resistance is 1 kΩ, the value of power gain is $x \times 10^4$. The value of *x* is ______.

29 A parallel beam of light is allowed to fall on a transparent spherical globe of diameter 30 cm and refractive index 1.5. The distance from the centre of the globe at which the beam of light can converge is ______ mm.

30 For the network shown below, the value of $V_B - V_A$ is ______ V.

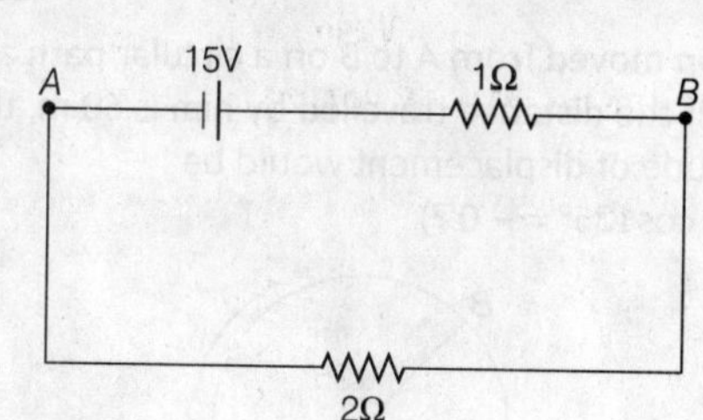

Answers

1 (d)	2 (b)	3 (b)	4 (c)	5 (c)	6 (c)	7 (b)	8 (d)	9 (c)	10 (c)
11 (c)	12 (c)	13 (c)	14 (a)	15 (a)	16 (b)	17 (a)	18 (d)	19 (d)	20 (b)
21 15	22 43	23 21	24 700	25 144	26 102	27 3	28 2	29 225	30 10

See detailed explanations on page no. 384

The Real Nuts

JEE Main 2022

(Real Nut 4-25 July 2022, Shift-I)

Physics

Instructions

1. This question paper contains of 30 Questions of Physics, divided into two Sections : **Section A** Objective Type Questions and **Section B** Numerical Value Questions.
2. Section A contains 20 Objective questions and all Questions are compulsory (Marking Scheme : Correct + 4, Incorrect −1).
3. Section B contains 10 Numerical value questions out of which only 5 questions are to be attempted (Marking Scheme : Correct + 4, Incorrect 0)

Section A *Objective Type Questions*

1 If momentum (*p*), area (*A*) and time (*t*) are taken as fundamental quantities, then the dimensional formula for coefficient of viscosity is

(a) $[pA^{-1}T^{0}]$ (b) $[pAT^{-1}]$ (c) $[pA^{-1}T]$ (d) $[pA^{-1}T^{-1}]$

2 Which of the following physical quantities have the same dimensions?

(a) Electric displacement and surface charge density
(b) Displacement current and electric field
(c) Current density and surface charge density
(d) Electric potential and energy

3 A person moved from A to B on a circular path as shown in figure. If the distance travelled by him is 60 m, then the magnitude of displacement would be (Given, $\cos 135° = -0.7$)

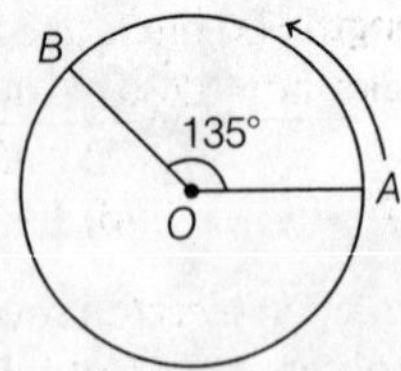

(a) 42 m (b) 47 m (c) 19 m (d) 40 m

4 A body of mass 0.5 kg travels on straight line path with velocity $v = (3x^2 + 4)$ m/s. The net work done by the force during its displacement from $x = 0$ to $x = 2$ m is

(a) 64 J (b) 60 J (c) 120 J (d) 128 J

5 A solid cylinder and a solid sphere, having same mass *M* and radius *R*, roll down the same inclined plane from top without slipping. They start from rest. The ratio of velocity of the solid cylinder to that of the solid sphere, with which they reach the ground, will be

(a) $\sqrt{\frac{5}{3}}$ (b) $\sqrt{\frac{4}{5}}$ (c) $\sqrt{\frac{3}{5}}$ (d) $\sqrt{\frac{14}{15}}$

6 Three identical particles *A*, *B* and *C* of mass 100 kg each are placed in a straight line with $AB = BC = 13$ m. The gravitational force on a fourth particle *P* of the same mass is *F*, when placed at a distance 13 m from the particle *B* on the perpendicular bisector of the line *AC*. The value of *F* will be approximately

(a) 21 G (b) 100 G
(c) 59 G (d) 42 G

7 A certain amount of gas of volume V at 27°C temperature and pressure 2×10^7 Nm^{-2} expands isothermally until its volume gets doubled. Later it expands adiabatically until its volume gets redoubled. The final pressure of the gas will be (Use, $\gamma = 1.5$)

(a) 3.536×10^5 N/m^2 (b) 3.536×10^6 N/m^2
(c) 1.25×10^6 N/m^2 (d) 1.25×10^5 N/m^2

8 Following statements are given

(A) The average kinetic energy of a gas molecule decreases when the temperature is reduced.
(B) The average kinetic energy of a gas molecule increases with increase in pressure at constant temperature.
(C) The average kinetic energy of a gas molecule decreases with increase in volume.
(D) Pressure of a gas increases with increase in temperature at constant volume.
(E) The volume of gas decreases with increase in temperature.

Choose the correct answer from the options given below.
(a) (A) and (D) only
(b) (A), (B) and (D) only
(c) (B) and (D) only
(d) (A), (B) and (E) only

9 In Fig. (A), mass 2 m is fixed on mass m which is attached to two springs of spring constant k. In Fig. (B), mass m is attached to two springs of spring constant k and $2k$. If mass m in Fig. (A) and in Fig. (B) are displaced by distance x horizontally and then released, then time period T_1 and T_2 corresponding to Fig. (A) and Fig. (B) respectively follow the relation.

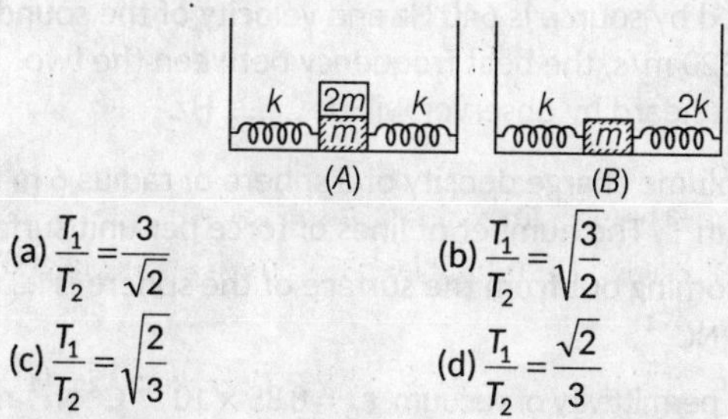

(a) $\frac{T_1}{T_2}=\frac{3}{\sqrt{2}}$ (b) $\frac{T_1}{T_2}=\sqrt{\frac{3}{2}}$
(c) $\frac{T_1}{T_2}=\sqrt{\frac{2}{3}}$ (d) $\frac{T_1}{T_2}=\frac{\sqrt{2}}{3}$

10 A condenser of 2 μF capacitance is charged steadily from 0 to 5 C. Which of the following graph represents correctly the variation of potential difference (V) across it's plates with respect to the charge (Q) on the condenser?

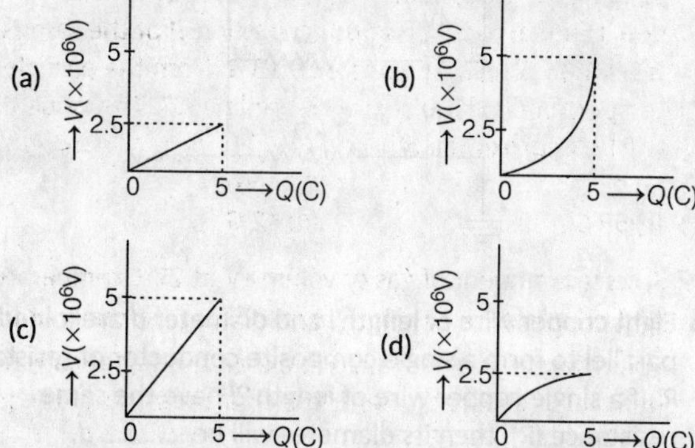

11 Two charged particles, having same kinetic energy, are allowed to pass through a uniform magnetic field perpendicular to the direction of motion. If the ratio of radii of their circular path is 6 : 5 and their respective masses ratio is 9 : 4. Then, the ratio of their charges will be
(a) 8 : 5 (b) 5 : 4
(c) 5 : 3 (d) 8 : 7

12 To increase the resonant frequency in series *L-C-R* circuit,
(a) source frequency should be increase(d)
(b) another resistance should be added in series with the first resistance
(c) another capacitor should be added in series with the first capacitor
(d) the source frequency should be decreased

13 A small square loop of wire of side l is placed inside a large square loop of wire $L(L >> l)$. Both loops are coplanar and their centres coincide at point O as shown in figure. The mutual inductance of the system is

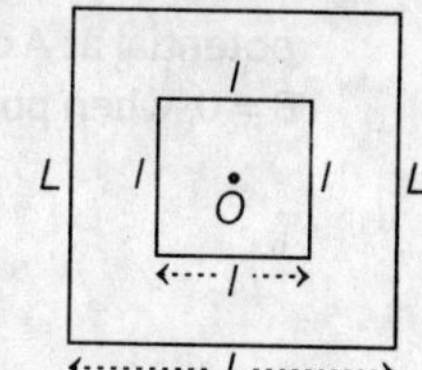

(a) $\frac{2\sqrt{2}\mu L^2}{\pi l}$ (b) $\frac{\mu_0 l^2}{2\sqrt{2}\pi L}$
(c) $\frac{2\sqrt{2}\mu_0 l^2}{\pi L}$ (d) $\frac{\mu_0 L^2}{2\sqrt{2}\pi l}$

14 The rms value of conduction current in a parallel plate capacitor is 6.9 μA. The capacity of this capacitor, if it is connected to 230 V AC supply with an angular frequency of 600 rad/s, will be
(a) 5 pF (b) 50 pF
(c) 100 pF (d) 200 pF

15 Which of the following statement is correct?
(a) In primary rainbow, observer sees red colour on the top and violet on the bottom.
(b) In primary rainbow, observer sees violet colour on the top and red on the bottom.
(c) In primary rainbow, light wave suffers total internal reflection twice before coming out of water drops.
(d) Primary rainbow is less bright than secondary rainbow.

16 Time taken by light to travel in two different materials A and B of refractive indices μ_A and μ_B of same thickness is t_1 and t_2, respectively. If $t_2 - t_1 = 5\times10^{-10}$s and the ratio of μ_A to μ_B is 1 : 2. Then, the thickness of material in metre is (Given, v_A and v_B are velocities of light in A and B materials, respectively.)
(a) $(5\times10^{-10}\times v_A)$ m (b) (5×10^{-10}) m
(c) (1.5×10^{-10}) m (d) $(5\times10^{-10}\times v_B)$ m

17 A metal exposed to light of wavelength 800 nm and emits photoelectrons with a certain kinetic energy. The maximum kinetic energy of photoelectron doubles when light of wavelength 500 nm is used. The work function of the metal is (Take, hc = 1230 eV-nm)
(a) 1.537 eV (b) 2.46 eV
(c) 0.615 eV (d) 1.23 eV

18 The momentum of an electron revolving in nth orbit is given by (Symbols have their usual meanings)
(a) $\frac{nh}{2\pi r}$ (b) $\frac{nh}{2r}$ (c) $\frac{nh}{2\pi}$ (d) $\frac{2\pi r}{nh}$

19 The magnetic moment of an electron (e) revolving in an orbit around nucleus with an orbital angular momentum is given by
(a) $\mu_L = \frac{e\mathbf{L}}{2m}$ (b) $\mu_L = -\frac{e\mathbf{L}}{2m}$
(c) $\mu_L = -\frac{e\mathbf{L}}{m}$ (d) $\mu_L = \frac{2e\mathbf{L}}{m}$

20 In the circuit, the logical value of $A = 1$ or $B = 1$ when potential at A or B is 5 V and the logical value of $A = 0$ or $B = 0$, when potential at A or B is 0 V.

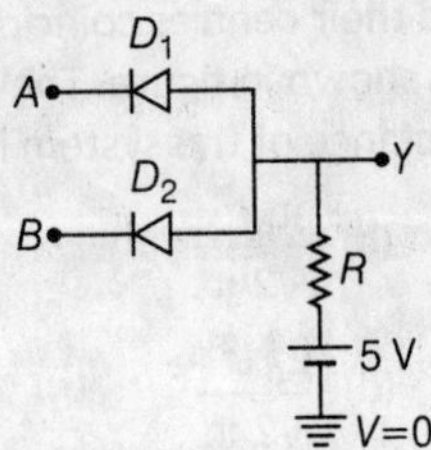

The truth table of the given circuit will be

(a)

A	B	Y
0	0	0
1	0	0
0	1	0
1	1	1

(b)

A	B	Y
0	0	0
1	0	1
0	1	1
1	1	1

(c)

A	B	Y
0	0	0
1	0	0
0	1	0
1	1	0

(d)

A	B	Y
0	0	1
1	0	1
0	1	1
1	1	0

Section II *Numerical Value Questions*

21 A car is moving with speed of 150 km/h and after applying the break it will move 27 m before it stops. If the same car is moving with a speed of one-third the reported speed, then it will stop after travelling ...... m distance.

22 For forces are acting at a point P in equilibrium as shown in figure. The ratio of force F_1 to F_2 is $1 : x$, where $x =$ ....

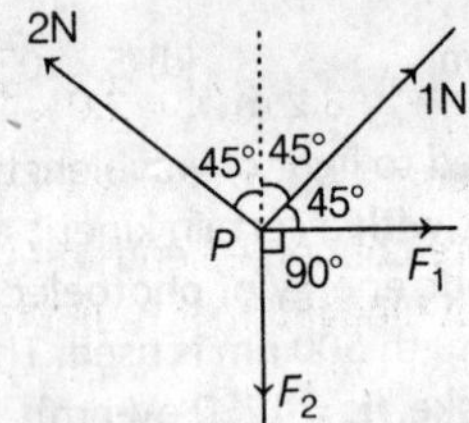

23 A wire of length L and radius r is clamped rigidly at one end. When the other end of the wire is pulled by a force F, its length increases by 5 cm. Another wire of the same material of length $4L$ and radius $4r$ is pulled by a force $4F$ under same conditions. The increase in length of this wire is .... cm.

24 A unit scale is to be prepared whose length does not change with temperature and remains 20 cm, using a bimetallic strip made of brass and iron each of different length. The length of both components would change in such a way that difference between their lengths remains constant. If length of brass is 40 cm and length of iron will be .... cm.

($\alpha_{iron} = 1.2 \times 10^{-5}$ K^{-1} and $\alpha_{brass} = 1.8 \times 10^{-5}$ K^{-1}).

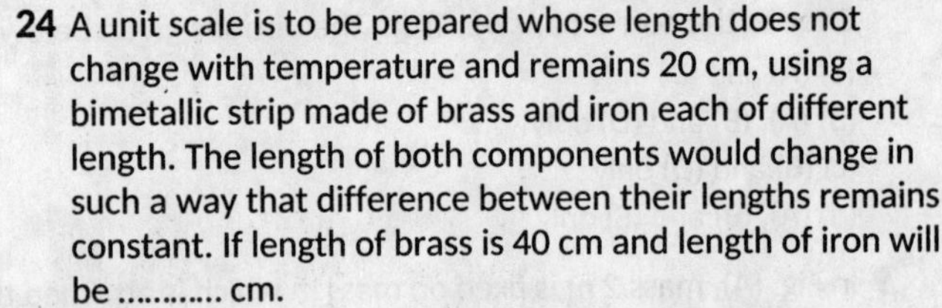

25 An observer is riding on a bicycle and moving towards a hill at 18 kmh^{-1}. He hears a sound from a source at some distance behind him directly as well as after its reflection from the hill. If the original frequency of the sound as emitted by source is 640 Hz and velocity of the sound in air is 320 m/s, the beat frequency between the two sounds heard by observer will be .... Hz.

26 The volume charge density of a sphere of radius 6 m is 2 μC cm^{-3}. The number of lines of force per unit surface area coming out from the surface of the sphere is .... $\times 10^{10}$ NC^{-1}.

[Given, permittivity of vacuum, $\varepsilon_0 = 8.85 \times 10^{-12}$ C^2 N^{-1}-m^{-2}].

27 In the given figure, the value of V_0 will be .... V.

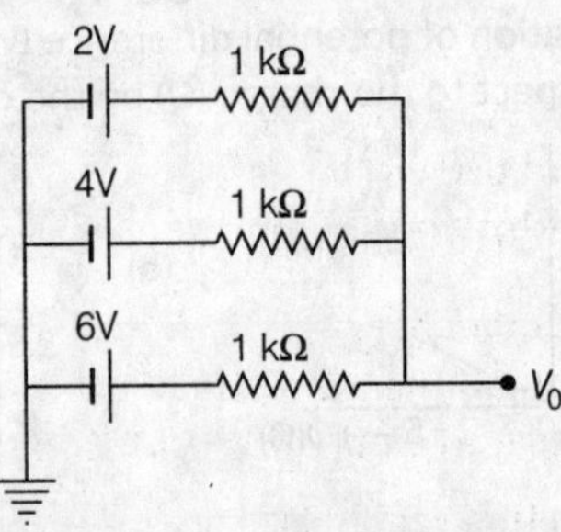

28 Eight copper wire of length l and diameter d are joined in parallel to form a single composite conductor of resistance R. If a single copper wire of length $2l$ have the same resistance (R), then its diameter will be .... d.

29 The energy band gap of semiconducting material to produce violet (wavelength = 4000 Å) LED is .... eV. (Round off to the nearest integer).

30 The required height of a TV tower which can cover the population of 6.03 lakh is h. If the average population density is 100 per square km and the radius of earth is 6400 km, then the value of h will be .... m.

Answers

1 (a)	2 (a)	3 (b)	4 (b)	5 (d)	6 (b)	7 (b)	8 (a)	9 (a)	10 (a)
11 (b)	12 (c)	13 (c)	14 (b)	15 (a)	16 (a)	17 (c)	18 (a)	19 (b)	20 (a)
21 3	22 3	23 5	24 60	25 20	26 45	27 4	28 4	29 3	30 150

See detailed explanations on page no. 388

JEE Main 2022

(Real Nut 5-27 July 2022, Shift-II)

Physics

Instructions

1. This question paper contains of 30 Questions of Physics, divided into two Sections :
Section A Objective Type Questions and **Section B** Numerical Value Questions.
2. Section A contains 20 Objective questions and all Questions are compulsory (Marking Scheme : Correct + 4, Incorrect –1) .
3. Section B contains 10 Numerical value questions out of which only 5 questions are to be attempted (Marking Scheme : Correct + 4, Incorrect 0)

Section A *Objective Type Questions*

1 An expression of energy density is given by $u = \frac{\alpha}{\beta} \sin\left(\frac{\alpha x}{kt}\right)$, where α, β are constants, x is displacement, k is Boltzmann constant and t is the temperature. The dimensions of β will be

(a) $[ML^{-2}T^{-1}\theta^{-1}]$ (b) $[M^0L^2T^{-2}]$ (c) $[M^0L^0T^0]$ (d) $[M^0L^2T^0]$

2 A body of mass 10 kg is projected at an angle of 45° with the horizontal. The trajectory of the body is observed to pass through a point (20, 10). If T is the time of flight, then its momentum vector, at time $t = \frac{T}{\sqrt{2}}$, is ....

(Take, $g = 10\ m/s^2$)

(a) $100\hat{i} + (100\sqrt{2} - 200)\hat{j}$ (b) $100\sqrt{2}\,\hat{i} + (100 - 200\sqrt{2})\hat{j}$

(c) $100\hat{i} + (100 - 200\sqrt{2})\hat{j}$ (d) $100\sqrt{2}\,\hat{i} + (100\sqrt{2} - 200)\hat{j}$

3 A block of mass M slides down on a rough inclined plane with constant velocity. The angle made by the incline plane with horizontal is θ. The magnitude of the contact force will be

(a) Mg (b) $Mg \cos\theta$

(c) $\sqrt{Mg \sin\theta + Mg \cos\theta}$ (d) $Mg \sin\theta\sqrt{1 + \mu}$

4 A block A takes 2 s to slide down a frictionless incline of 30° and length l, kept inside a lift going up with uniform velocity v. If the incline is changed to 45°, the time taken by the block to slide down the incline, will be approximately

(a) 2.66 s (b) 0.83 s (c) 1.68 s (d) 0.70 s

5 The velocity of the bullet becomes one-third after it penetrates 4 cm in a wooden block. Assuming that bullet is facing a constant resistance during its motion in the block. The bullet stops completely after travelling at $(4 + x)$ cm inside the block. The value of x is

(a) 2.0 (b) 1.0 (c) 0.5 (d) 1.5

6 A body of mass m is projected with velocity $\lambda\, v_e$ in vertically upward direction from the surface of the earth into space. It is given that v_e is escape velocity and $\lambda < 1$. If air resistance is considered to be negligible, then the maximum height from the centre of earth, to which the body can go, will be (R is radius of earth)

(a) $\frac{R}{1 + \lambda^2}$ (b) $\frac{R}{1 - \lambda^2}$ (c) $\frac{R}{1 - \lambda}$ (d) $\frac{\lambda^2 R}{1 - \lambda^2}$

7 A steel wire of length 3.2 m ($Y_s = 2.0 \times 10^{11}\ Nm^{-2}$) and a copper wire of length 4.4 m ($Y_c = 1.1 \times 10^{11}\ Nm^{-2}$), both of radius 1.4 mm are connected end-to-end. When stretched by a load, the net elongation is found to be 1.4 mm.

The load applied, (in Newton), will be $\left(\text{Given}, \pi = \frac{22}{7}\right)$

(a) 360 (b) 180

(c) 1080 (d) 154

8 In first case, Carnot engine operates between temperatures 300 K and 100 K. In second case, as shown in the figure, a combination of two engines is used. The efficiency of this combination (in second case) will be

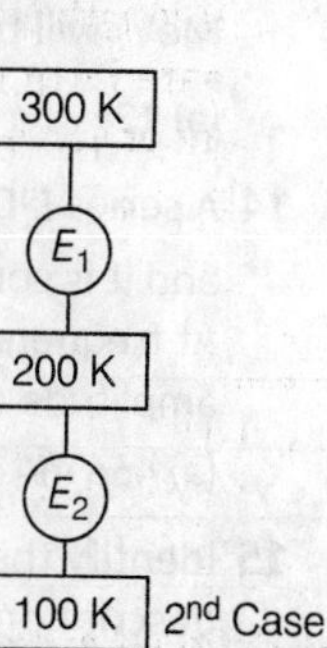

(a) same as the first case

(b) always greater than the first case

(c) always less than the first case

(d) may increase with respect to the first case

9 Which statements are correct about degrees of freedom?

A. A molecule with n degrees of freedom has n^2 different ways of storing energy.

B. Each degree of freedom is associated with $\frac{1}{2}RT$ average energy per mole.

C. A monoatomic gas molecule has 1 rotational degree of freedom whereas diatomic molecule has 2 rotational degrees of freedom.

D. CH_4 has a total of 6 degrees of freedom.

Choose the correct answer from the option given below.

(a) B and C only (b) B and D only
(c) A and B only (d) C and D only

10 A charge of $4\,\mu C$ is to be divided into two. The distance between the two divided charges is constant. The magnitude of the divided charges so that the force between them is maximum, will be

(a) $1\,\mu C$ and $3\,\mu C$ (b) $2\,\mu C$ and $2\,\mu C$
(c) 0 and $4\,\mu C$ (d) $1.5\,\mu C$ and $2.5\,\mu CC$

11 (A) The drift velocity of electrons decreases with the increase in the temperature of conductor.

(B) The drift velocity is inversely proportional to the area of cross-section of given conductor.

(C) The drift velocity does not depend on the applied potential difference to the conductor.

(D) The drift velocity of electron is inversely proportional to the length of the conductor.

(E) The drift velocity increases with the increase in the temperature of conductor.

Choose the correct answer from the options given below.

(a) (A) and (B) only (b) (A) and (D) only
(c) (B) and (E) only (d) (B) and (C) only

12 A compass needle of oscillation magnetometer oscillates 20 times per minute at a place P of dip 30°. The number of oscillations per minute become 10 at another place Q of 60° dip. The ratio of the total magnetic field at the two places $(B_Q : B_P)$ is

(a) $\sqrt{3}:4$ (b) $4:\sqrt{3}$ (c) $\sqrt{3}:2$ (d) $2:\sqrt{3}$

13 A cyclotron is used to accelerate protons. If the operating magnetic field is 1.0 T and the radius of the cyclotron dees is 60 cm, the kinetic energy of the accelerated protons (in MeV) will be (Use, $m_p = 1.6 \times 10^{-27}$ kg, $e = 1.6 \times 10^{-19}$ C)

(a) 12 (b) 18 (c) 16 (d) 32

14 A series L-C-R circuit has $L = 0.01$ H, $R = 10\,\Omega$ and $C = 1\,\mu F$ and it is connected to AC voltage of amplitude (V_m) 50 V. At frequency 60% lower than resonant frequency, the amplitude of current will be approximately

(a) 466 mA (b) 312 mA (c) 238 mA (d) 196 mA

15 Identify the correct statements from the following descriptions of various properties of electromagnetic waves.

(A) In a plane electromagnetic wave electric field and magnetic field must be perpendicular to each other and direction of propagation of wave should be along electric field or magnetic field.

(B) The energy in electromagnetic wave is divided equally between electric and magnetic fields.

(C) Both electric field and magnetic field are parallel to each other and perpendicular to the direction of propagation of wave.

(D) The electric field, magnetic field and direction of propagation of wave must be perpendicular to each other.

(E) The ratio of amplitude of magnetic field to the amplitude of electric field is equal to speed of light.

Choose the most appropriate answer from the options given below.

(a) (D) only (b) (B) and (D) only
(c) (B), (C) and (E) only (d) (A), (B) and (E) only

16 Two coherent sources of light interfere. The intensity ratio of two sources is 1 : 4. For this interference pattern if the value of $\frac{I_{max} + I_{min}}{I_{max} - I_{min}}$ is equal to $\frac{2\alpha + 1}{\beta + 3}$, then $\frac{\alpha}{\beta}$ will be

(a) 1.5 (b) 2 (c) 0.5 (d) 1

17 With reference to the observations in photoelectric effect, identify the correct statements from below.

(A) The square of maximum velocity of photoelectrons varies linearly with frequency of incident light.

(B) The value of saturation current increases on moving the source of light away from the metal surface.

(C) The maximum kinetic energy of photoelectrons decreases on decreasing the power of LED (Light Emitting Diode) source of light.

(D) The immediate emission of photoelectrons out of metal surface can not be explained by particle nature of light/electromagnetic waves.

(E) Existence of threshold wavelength cannot be explained by wave nature of light/electromagnetic waves.

Choose the correct answer from the options given below.

(a) (A) and (B) only (b) (A) and (E) only
(c) (C) and (E) only (d) (D) and (E) only

18 The activity of a radioactive material is 6.4×10^{-4} curie. Its half-life is 5 days. The activity will become 5×10^{-6} curie after

(a) 7 days (b) 15 days (c) 25 days (d) 35 days

19 For a constant collector-emitter voltage of 8 V, the collector current of a transistor reached to the value of 6 mA from 4 mA, whereas base current changed from $20\,\mu A$ to $25\,\mu A$ value. If transistor is in active state, small signal current gain (current amplification factor) will be

(a) 240 (b) 400 (c) 00025 (d) 200

20 A square wave of the modulating signal is shown in the figure. The carrier wave is given by $c(t) = 5\sin(8\pi t)$ V. The modulation index is

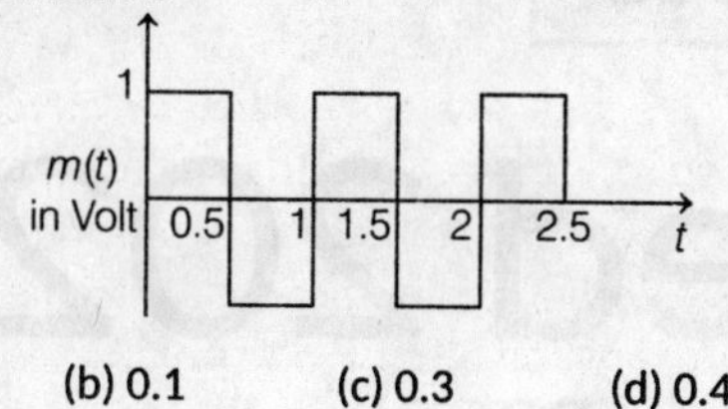

(a) 0.2 (b) 0.1 (c) 0.3 (d) 0.4

Section B *Numerical Value Questions*

21 In an experiment to determine the Young's modulus, steel wires of five different lengths (1, 2, 3, 4 and 5 m) but of same cross-section (2 mm^2) were taken and curves between extension and load were obtained. The slope (extension/load) of the curves were plotted with the wire length and the following graph is obtained. If the Young's modulus of given steel wires is $x \times 10^{11}$ Nm^{-2}, then the value of x is ....

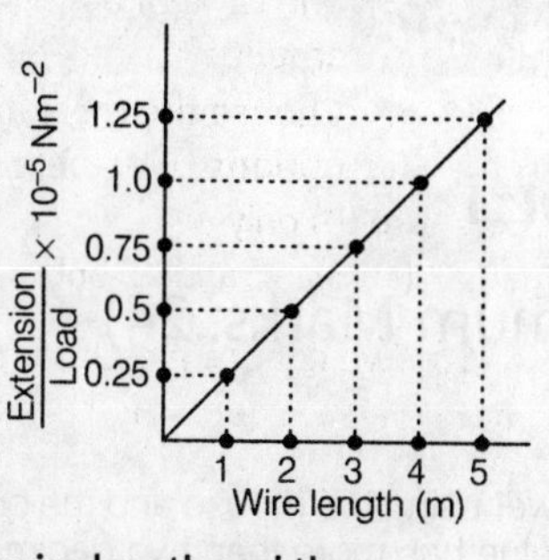

22 In the given figure of meter bridge experiment, the balancing length AC corresponding to null deflection of the galvanometer is 40 cm. The balancing length, if the radius of the wire AB is doubled, will be .... cm.

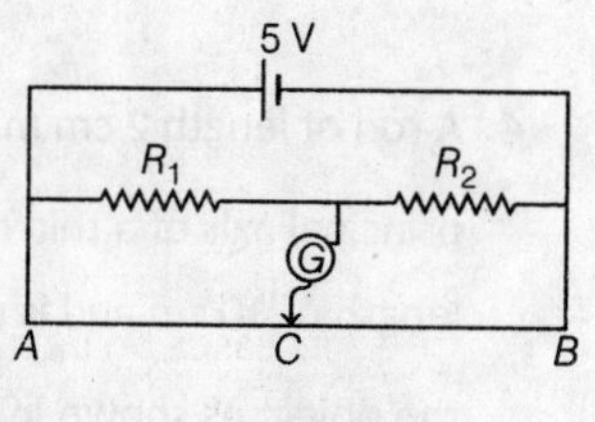

23 A thin prism of angle 6° and refractive index for yellow light (n_Y) 1.5 is combined with another prism of angle 5° and $n_Y = 1.55$. The combination produces no dispersion. The net average deviation (δ) produced by the combination is $\left(\frac{1}{x}\right)$. The value of x is ....

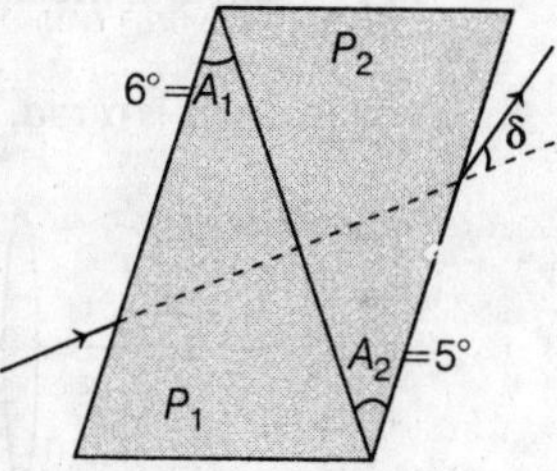

24 A conducting circular loop is placed in XY-plane in presence of magnetic field $\mathbf{B} = (3t^3\hat{\mathbf{j}} + 3t^2\hat{\mathbf{k}})$ in SI unit. If the radius of the loop is 1 m, the induced emf in the loop, at time $t = 2$ s is $n\pi$ V. The value of n is ....

25 As shown in the figure, in the steady state, the charge stored in the capacitor is .... $\times 10^{-6}$ C.

26 A parallel plate capacitor with width 4 cm, length 8 cm and separation between the plates of 4 mm is connected to a battery of 20 V. A dielectric slab of dielectric constant 5 having length 1 cm, width 4 cm and thickness 4 mm is inserted between the plates of parallel plate capacitor. The electrostatic energy of this system will be .... ε_0J. (where, ε_0 is the permittivity of free space)

27 A wire of length of 30 cm, stretched between rigid supports, has it's nth and $(n+1)$th harmonics at 400 Hz and 450 Hz, respectively. If tension in the string is 2700 N, its linear mass density is .... kg/m.

28 A spherical soap bubble of radius 3 cm is formed inside another spherical soap bubble of radius 6 cm. If the internal pressure of the smaller bubble of radius 3 cm in the above system is equal to the internal pressure of the another single soap bubble of radius r cm. The value of r is ....

29 A solid cylinder length is suspended symmetrically through two massless strings, as shown in the figure. The distance from the initial rest position, the cylinder should be unbinding the strings to achieve a speed of 4 m/s, is .... cm. (Take, $g = 10$ m/s^2).

30 Two inclined planes are placed as shown in figure. A block is projected from the point A of inclined plane AB along its surface with a velocity just sufficient to carry it to the top point B at a height 10 m. After reaching the point B, the block slides down on inclined plane BC. Time it takes to reach to the point C from point A is $t(\sqrt{2}+1)$s. The value of t is .... cm. (Take, $g = 10$ m/s^2).

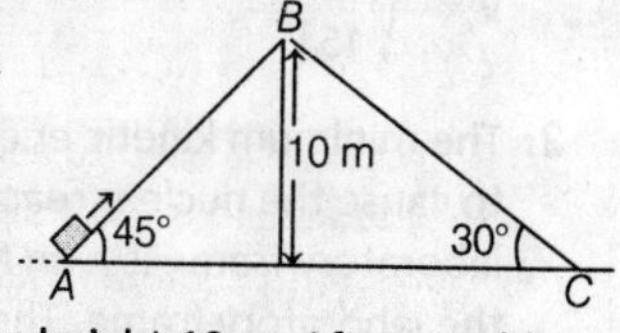

Answers

1 (d)	2 (d)	3 (a)	4 (c)	5 (c)	6 (b)	7 (d)	8 (c)	9 (b)	10 (b)
11 (a)	12 (a)	13 (b)	14 (c)	15 (b)	16 (b)	17 (b)	18 (d)	19 (b)	20 (a)
21 2	22 40	23 4	24 12	25 10	26 240	27 3	28 2	29 120	30 2

See detailed explanations on page no. 392

The Real Nuts

JEE Advanced 2022

(Real Nut 6-Solved Paper 2022)

Physics

Paper 1

SECTION 1 (Maximum Marks: 24)

- This section contains **EIGHT (08)** questions.
- The answer to each question is a **NUMERICAL VALUE**.
- For each question, enter the correct numerical value of the answer using the mouse and the on-screen virtual numerical keypad in the place designated to enter the answer. If the numerical value has more than two decimal places, **truncate/round-off** the value of **TWO** decimal places.
- Answer to each question will be evaluated according to the following marking scheme:

Full Marks : +3 **ONLY** if the correct numerical value is entered;
Zero Marks : 0 In all other cases.

1. Two spherical stars A and B have densities ρ_A and ρ_B, respectively. A and B have the same radius, and their masses M_A and M_B are related by $M_B = 2M_A$. Due to an interaction process, star A loses some of its mass, so that its radius is halved, while its spherical shape is retained, and its density remains ρ_A. The entire mass lost by A is deposited as a thick spherical shell on B with the density of the shell being ρ_A. If v_A and v_B are the escape velocities from A and B after the interaction process, the ratio $\frac{v_B}{v_A} = \sqrt{\frac{10n}{15^{\frac{1}{3}}}}$. The value of n is ....

2. The minimum kinetic energy needed by an alpha particle to cause the nuclear reaction ${}^{16}_{7}N + {}^{4}_{2}He \longrightarrow {}^{1}_{1}H + {}^{19}_{8}O$ in a laboratory frame is n (in MeV). Assume that ${}^{16}_{7}N$ is at rest in the laboratory frame. The masses of ${}^{16}_{7}N$, ${}^{4}_{2}He$, ${}^{1}_{1}H$ and ${}^{19}_{8}O$ can be taken to be 16.006 u, 4.003 u , 1.008 u and 19.003 u respectively, where 1 u = 930 MeVC^{-2}. The value of n is ....

3. In the following circuit $C_1 = 12\,\mu F$, $C_2 = C_3 = 4\,\mu F$ and $C_4 = C_5 = 2\,\mu F$. The charge stored in C_3 is .... μC.

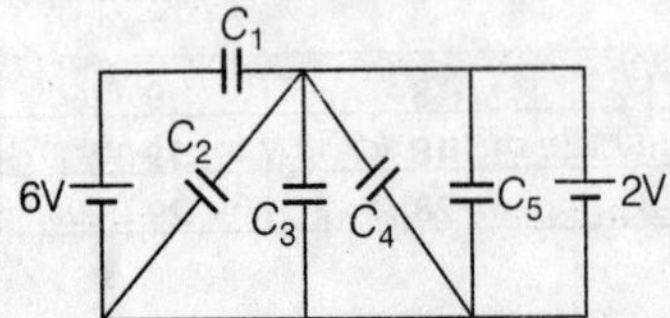

4. A rod of length 2 cm makes an angle $\frac{2\pi}{3}$ rad with the principal axis of a thin convex lens. The lens has a focal length of 10 cm and is placed at a distance of $\frac{40}{3}$ cm from the object as shown in the figure. The height of the image is $\frac{30\sqrt{3}}{13}$ cm and the angle made by it with respect to the principal axis is α rad. The value of α is $\frac{\pi}{n}$ rad, where n is

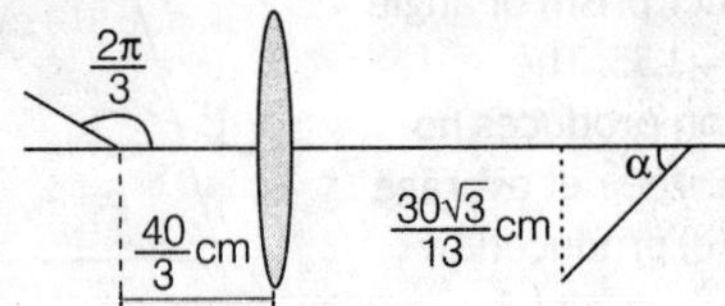

5. At time $t = 0$, a disk of radius 1 m starts to roll without slipping on a horizontal plane with an angular acceleration of $\alpha = \frac{2}{3}$ rad s^{-2}. A small stone is stuck to the disk. At $t = 0$, it is at the contact point of the disk and the plane. Later, at time $t = \sqrt{\pi}$ s, the stone detaches itself and flies off tangentially from the disk. The maximum height (in m) reached by the stone measured from the plane is $\frac{1}{2} + \frac{x}{10}$.

The value of x is ....
[Take, $g = 10\ ms^{-2}$]

6. A solid sphere of mass 1 kg and radius 1 m rolls without slipping on a fixed inclined plane with an angle of inclination $\theta = 30°$ from the horizontal. Two forces of magnitude 1 N each, parallel to the incline, act on the sphere, both at distance $r = 0.5$ m from the centre of the sphere, as shown in the figure. The acceleration of the sphere down the plane is .... ms^{-2}. (Take, $g = 10\ ms^{-2}$)

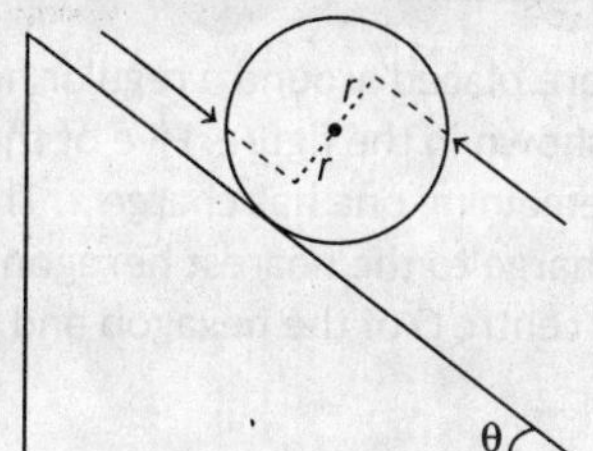

7. Consider an *L-C* circuit, with inductance $L = 0.1$ H and capacitance $C = 10^{-3}$ F, kept on a plane. The area of the circuit is 1 m^2. It is placed in a constant magnetic field of strength B_0 which is perpendicular to the plane of the circuit. At time $t = 0$, the magnetic field strength starts increasing linearly as $B = B_0 + \beta t$ with $\beta = 0.04\ Ts^{-1}$. The maximum magnitude of the current in the circuit is .... mA.

8. A projectile is fired from horizontal ground with speed *v* and projection angle θ. When the acceleration due to gravity is *g*, the range of the projectile is *d*. If at the highest point in its trajectory, the projectile enters a different region, where the effective acceleration due to gravity is $g' = \frac{g}{0.81}$, then the new range is $d' = nd$. The value of *n* is ....

SECTION 2 (Maximum Marks: 24)

- This section contains **SIX (06)** questions.
- Each question has **FOUR** options (a), (b), (c) and (d). **ONE OR MORE THAN ONE** of these four option(s) is(are) correct answer(s).
- For each question, choose the option(s) corresponding to all the correct answer(s).
- Answer to each question will be evaluated according to the following marking scheme:

Full Marks	: +4	**ONLY** if (all) the correct option(s) is(are) chosen;
Partial Marks	: +3	If all the four options are correct but **ONLY** three options are chosen;
Partial Marks	: +2	If three or more options are correct but **ONLY** two options are chosen, both of which are correct;
Partial Marks	: +1	If two or more options are correct but **ONLY** one option is chosen and it is a correct option;
Zero Marks	: 0	If none of the options is chosen (i.e. the question is unanswered);
Negative Marks	: −2	In all other cases.

9. A medium having dielectric constant $K > 1$ fills the space between the plates of a parallel plate capacitor. The plates have large area, and the distance between them is *d*. The capacitor is connected to a battery of voltage *V*, as shown in Fig. (a). Now, both the plates are moved by a distance of $d/2$ from their original positions, as shown in Fig. (b).

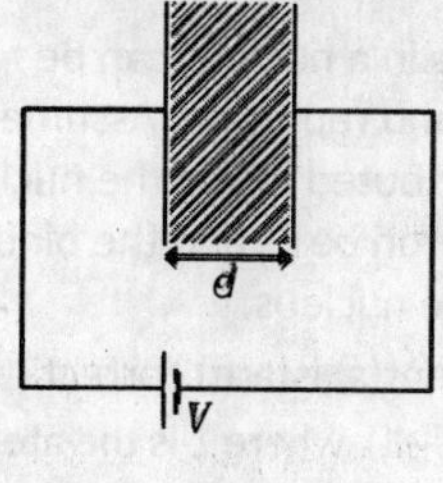

Fig. (a)

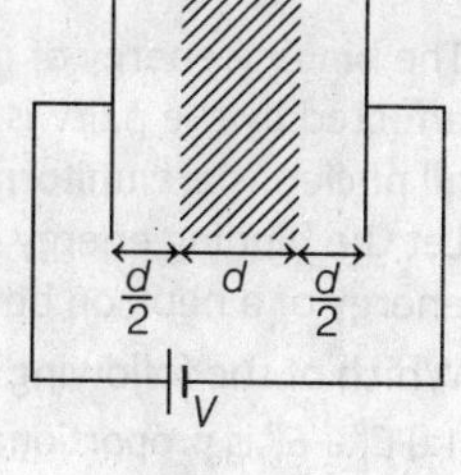

Fig. (b)

In the process of going from the configuration depicted in Fig. (a) to that in Fig. (b), which of the following statement(s) is (are) correct?

(a) The electric field inside the dielectric material is reduced by a factor of 2*K*.

(b) The capacitance is decreased by a factor of $\frac{1}{K+1}$.

(c) The voltage between the capacitor plates is increased by a factor of $(K + 1)$.

(d) The work done in the process does not depend on the presence of the dielectric material.

10. The figure shows a circuit having eight resistances of 1 Ω each, labelled R_1 to R_8, and two ideal batteries with voltages $\varepsilon_1 = 12$ V and $\varepsilon_2 = 6$ V.

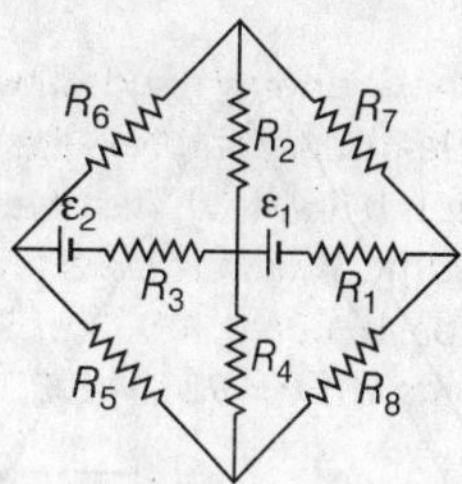

Which of the following statement(s) is(are) correct?

(a) The magnitude of current flowing through R_1 is 7.2 A.

(b) The magnitude of current flowing through R_2 is 1.2 A.

(c) The magnitude of current flowing through R_3 is 4.8 A.

(d) The magnitude of current flowing through R_5 is 2.4 A.

11. An ideal gas of density $\rho = 0.2 \text{ kg m}^{-3}$ enters a chimney of height h at the rate of $\alpha = 0.8 \text{ kg s}^{-1}$ from its lower end, and escapes through the upper end as shown in the figure. The cross-sectional area of the lower end is $A_1 = 0.1 \text{ m}^2$ and the upper end is $A_2 = 0.4 \text{ m}^2$. The pressure and the temperature of the gas at the lower end are 600 Pa and 300 K, respectively, while its temperature at the upper end is 150 K. The chimney is heat insulated, so that the gas undergoes adiabatic expansion. Take, $g = 10 \text{ ms}^{-2}$ and the ratio of specific heats of the gas $\gamma = 2$. Ignore atmospheric pressure.

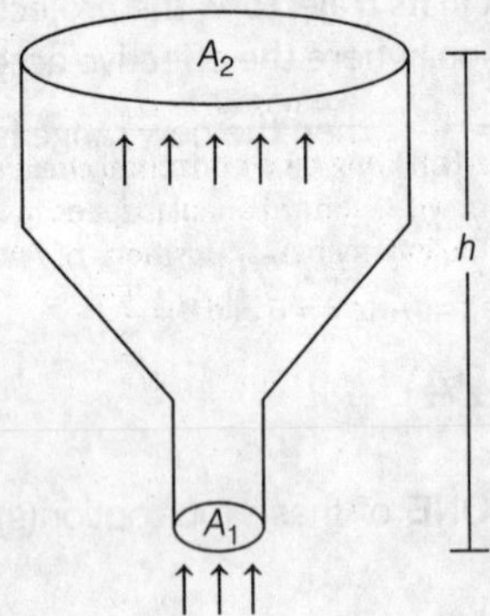

Which of the following statement(s) is(are) correct?

(a) The pressure of the gas at the upper end of the chimney is 300 Pa.

(b) The velocity of the gas at the lower end of the chimney is 40 ms^{-1} and at the upper end is 20 ms^{-1}.

(c) The height of the chimney is 590 m.

(d) The density of the gas at the upper end is 0.05 kg m^{-3}.

12. Three plane mirrors form an equilateral triangle with each side of length L. There is a small hole at a distance $l > 0$ from one of the corners as shown in the figure. A ray of light is passed through the hole at an angle θ and can only come out through the same hole. The cross-section of the mirror configuration and the ray of light lie on the same plane.

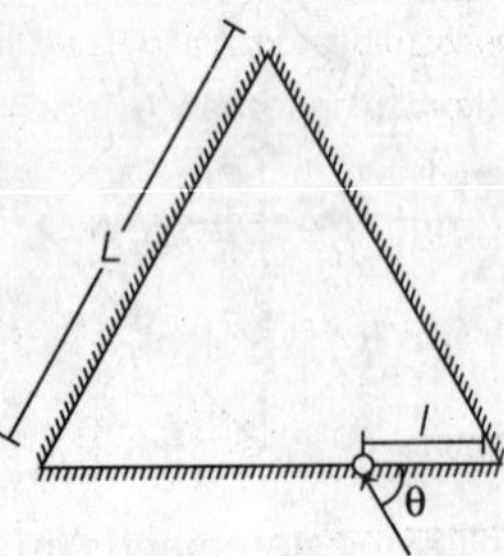

Which of the following statement(s) is(are) correct?

(a) The ray of light will come out for $\theta = 30°$, for $0 < l < L$.

(b) There is an angle for $l = \frac{L}{2}$ at which the ray of light will come out after two reflections.

(c) The ray of light will never come out for $\theta = 60°$, and $l = \frac{L}{3}$.

(d) The ray of light will come out for $\theta = 60°$, and $0 < l < \frac{L}{2}$ after six reflections.

13. Six charges are placed around a regular hexagon of side length a as shown in the figure. Five of them have charge q, and the remaining one has charge x. The perpendicular from each charge to the nearest hexagon side passes through the centre O of the hexagon and is bisected by the side.

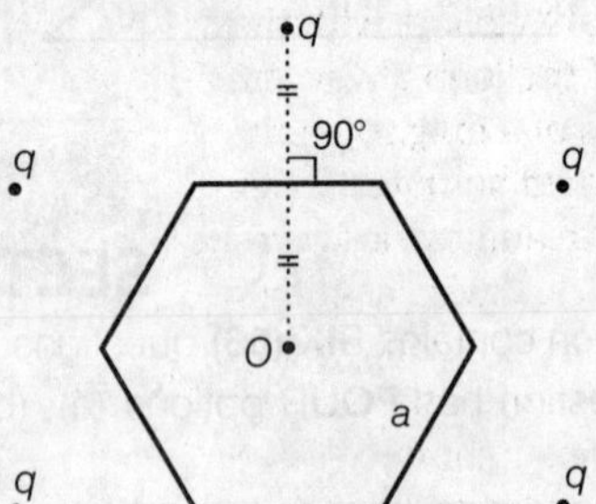

Which of the following statement(s) is(are) correct in SI units?

(a) When $x = q$, the magnitude of the electric field at O is zero.

(b) When $x = -q$, the magnitude of the electric field at O is $\frac{q}{6\pi\varepsilon_0 a^2}$.

(c) When $x = 2q$, the potential at O is $\frac{7q}{4\sqrt{3}\pi\varepsilon_0 a}$.

(d) When $x = -3q$, the potential at O is $-\frac{3q}{4\sqrt{3}\pi\varepsilon_0 a}$.

14. The binding energy of nucleons in a nucleus can be affected by the pairwise Coulomb repulsion. Assume that all nucleons are uniformly distributed inside the nucleus. Let the binding energy of a proton be E_b^p and the binding energy of a neutron be E_b^n in the nucleus.

Which of the following statement(s) is(are) correct?

(a) $E_b^p - E_b^n$ is proportional to $Z(Z-1)$, where Z is the atomic number of the nucleus.

(b) $E_b^p - E_b^n$ is proportional to $A^{-\frac{1}{3}}$, where A is the mass number of the nucleus.

(c) $E_b^p - E_b^n$ is positive.

(d) E_b^p increases, if the nucleus undergoes a beta decay emitting a positron.

SECTION 3 (Maximum Marks: 12)

- This section contains **FOUR (04)** Matching List sets.
- Each set has **ONE** Multiple Choice Question.
- Each set has **TWO** columns: **Column-I** and **Column-II**.
- **Column-I** has **Four** entries (I), (II), (III) and (IV) and **Column-II** has **Five** entries (P), (Q), (R), (S) and (T).
- **FOUR** options are given in each Multiple Choice Question based on **Column-I** and **Column-II** and **ONLY ONE** of these four options satisfies the condition asked in the Multiple Choice Question.
- Answer to each question will be evaluated according to the following marking scheme:

Full Marks	:	+3 **ONLY** if the option corresponding to the correct combination is chosen;
Zero Marks	:	0 If none of the options is chosen (i.e., the question is unanswered);
Negative Marks	:	−1 In all other cases.

15. A small circular loop of area A and resistance R is fixed on a horizontal XY-plane with the centre of the loop always on the axis $\hat{\mathbf{n}}$ of a long solenoid. The solenoid has n turns per unit length and carries current I counter clockwise as shown in the figure. The magnetic field due to the solenoid is in $\hat{\mathbf{n}}$ direction. Column-I gives time dependences of $\hat{\mathbf{n}}$ in terms of a constant angular frequency ω.

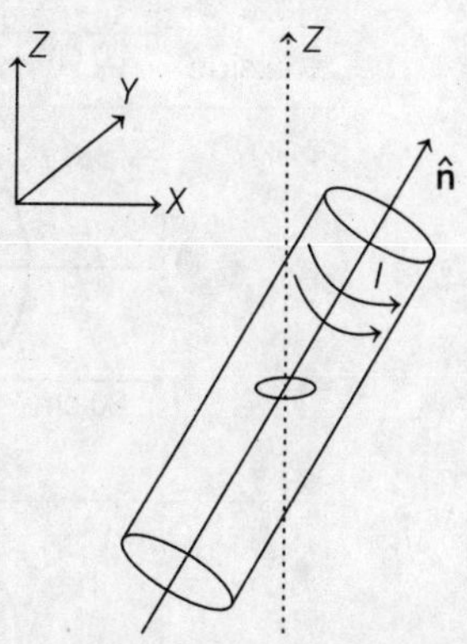

Column-II gives the torques experienced by the circular loop at time $t = \frac{\pi}{6\omega}$. Let $\alpha = \frac{A^2\mu_0^2 n^2 I^2 \omega}{2R}$.

	Column-I		Column-II
I.	$\frac{1}{\sqrt{2}}(\sin\omega t\,\hat{\mathbf{j}} + \cos\omega t\,\hat{\mathbf{k}})$	P.	0
II.	$\frac{1}{\sqrt{2}}(\sin\omega t\,\hat{\mathbf{i}} + \cos\omega t\,\hat{\mathbf{j}})$	Q.	$-\frac{\alpha}{4}\hat{\mathbf{i}}$
III.	$\frac{1}{\sqrt{2}}(\sin\omega t\,\hat{\mathbf{i}} + \cos\omega t\,\hat{\mathbf{k}})$	R.	$\frac{3\alpha}{4}\hat{\mathbf{i}}$
IV.	$\frac{1}{\sqrt{2}}(\cos\omega t\,\hat{\mathbf{j}} + \sin\omega t\,\hat{\mathbf{k}})$	S.	$\frac{\alpha}{4}\hat{\mathbf{j}}$
		T.	$-\frac{3\alpha}{4}\hat{\mathbf{i}}$

Which one of the following option is correct?

	I	II	III	IV
(a)	Q	P	S	T
(b)	S	T	Q	P
(c)	Q	P	S	R
(d)	T	Q	P	R

16. Column-I describes four systems, each with two particles A and B in relative motion as shown in figures. Column-II gives possible magnitudes of their relative velocities (in ms^{-1}) at time $t = \frac{\pi}{3}$ s.

	Column-I		Column-II
I.	A and B are moving on a horizontal circle of radius 1 m with uniform angular speed $\omega = 1$ rad s^{-1}. The initial angular positions of A and B at time $t = 0$ are $\theta = 0$ and $\theta = \frac{\pi}{2}$, respectively. 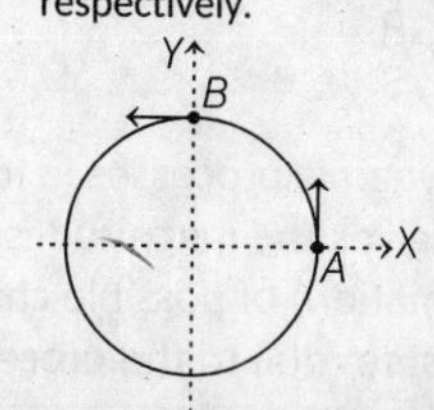	P.	$\frac{\sqrt{3}+1}{2}$
II.	Projectiles A and B are fired (in the same vertical plane) at $t = 0$ and $t = 0.1$ s respectively, with the same speed $v = \frac{5\pi}{\sqrt{2}}\ \text{ms}^{-1}$ and at 45° from the horizontal plane. The initial separation between A and B is large enough, so that they do not collide. ($g = 10\ \text{ms}^{-2}$) 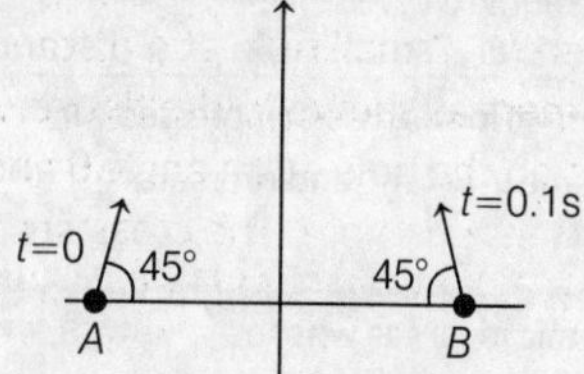	Q.	$\frac{(\sqrt{3}-1)}{\sqrt{2}}$
III.	Two harmonic oscillators A and B moving in the x-direction according to $x_A = x_0 \sin\frac{t}{t_0}$ and $x_B = x_0 \sin\left(\frac{t}{t_0} + \frac{\pi}{2}\right)$ respectively, starting from $t = 0$. Take $x_0 = 1$ m, $t_0 = 1$ s. 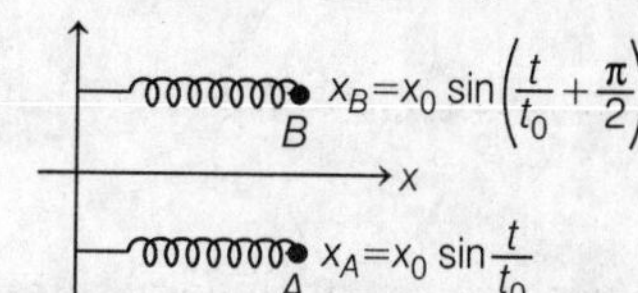	R.	$\sqrt{10}$

	Column-I		Column-II
IV.	Particle *A* is rotating in a horizontal circular path of radius 1 m on the *XY*-plane, with constant angular speed $\omega = 1\text{ rad s}^{-1}$. Particle *B* is moving up at a constant speed 3 ms^{-1} in the vertical direction as shown in the figure. (Ignore gravity.)	S.	$\sqrt{2}$
		T.	$\sqrt{25\pi^2 + 1}$

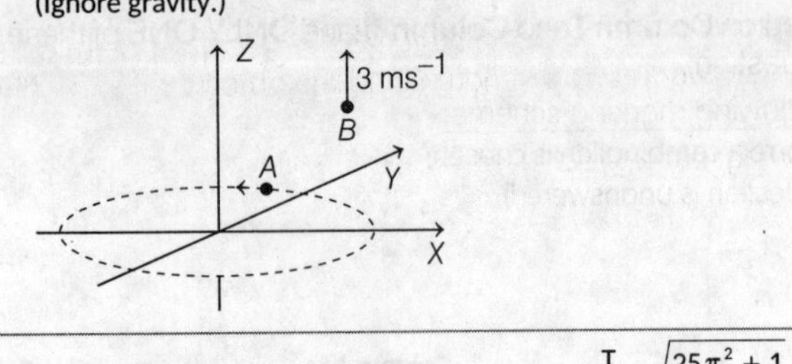

Which one of the following options is correct?

	I	II	III	IV
(a)	R	T	P	S
(b)	S	P	Q	R
(c)	S	T	P	R
(d)	T	P	R	S

17. Column-I describes thermodynamic processes in four different systems. Column-II gives the magnitudes (either exactly or as a close approximation) of possible changes in the internal energy of the system due to the process.

	Column-I		Column-II
I.	10^{-3} kg of water at 100°C is converted to steam at the same temperature, at a pressure of 10^5 Pa. The volume of the system changes from 10^{-6} m^3 to 10^{-3} m^3 in the process. Latent heat of water = 2250 kJ/kg.	P.	2 kJ
II.	0.2 moles of a rigid diatomic ideal gas with volume *V* at temperature 500 K undergoes an isobaric expansion to volume 3*V*. Assume $R = 8.0\text{ J mol}^{-1}\text{ K}^{-1}$.	Q.	7 kJ
III.	One mole of a monoatomic ideal gas is compressed adiabatically from volume $V = \frac{1}{3}\text{ m}^3$ and pressure 2 kPa to volume $V/8$.	R.	4 kJ
IV.	Three moles of a diatomic ideal gas whose molecules can vibrate, is given 9 kJ of heat and undergoes isobaric expansion.	S.	5 kJ
		T.	3 kJ

Which one of the following options is correct?

	I	II	III	IV
(a)	T	R	S	Q
(b)	S	P	T	P
(c)	P	R	T	Q
(d)	Q	R	S	T

18. Column-I contains four combinations of two lenses (1 and 2) whose focal lengths (in cm) are indicated in the figures. In all cases, the object is placed 20 cm from the first lens on the left, and the distance between the two lenses is 5 cm. Column-II contains the positions of the final images.

	Column-I		Column-II
I.	*f* = +10, +15; O; 20 cm, 1, 5 cm, 2	P.	Final image is formed at 7.5 cm on the right side of lens 2.
II.	*f* = +10, −10; O; 20 cm, 1, 5 cm, 2	Q.	Final image is formed at 60.0 cm on the right side of lens 2.
III.	*f* = +10, −20; O; 20 cm, 1, 5 cm, 2	R.	Final image is formed at 30.0 cm on the left side of lens 2.
IV.	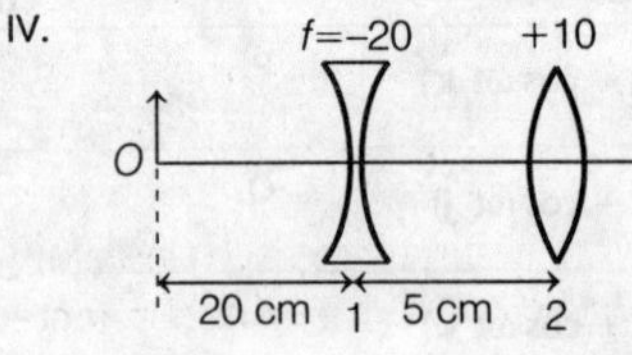	S.	Final image is formed at 6.0 cm on the right side of lens 2.
		T.	Final image is formed at 30.0 cm on the right side of lens 2.

Which one of the following options is correct?

	I	II	III	IV
(a)	P	R	Q	T
(b)	Q	P	T	S
(c)	P	T	R	Q
(d)	T	S	Q	R

Answers

1 *2.30*	2 *2.32*	3 *8*	4 *6*	5 *0.52*	6 *2.86*	7 *4*	8 *0.95*	9 *(b)*	10 *(a,b,c,d)*
11 *(b)*	12 *(a,b)*	13 *(a,b,c)*	14 *(a,b,d)*	15 *(c)*	16 *(c)*	17 *(c)*	18 *(a)*		

See detailed explanations on page no. 397

Paper 2

SECTION 1 (Maximum Marks: 24)

- This section contains **EIGHT (08)** questions.
- The answer to each question is a **SINGLE DIGIT INTEGER ranging from 0 TO 9, BOTH INCLUSIVE.**
- For each question, enter the correct integer corresponding to the answer using the mouse and the on-screen virtual numeric keypad in the place designated to enter the answer.
- Answer to each question will be evaluated according to the following marking scheme:

Full Marks : +3 If **ONLY** the correct integer is entered;
Zero Marks : 0 If the question is unanswered;
Negative Marks : −1 In all other cases.

1. A particle of mass 1 kg is subjected to a force which depends on the position as $\mathbf{F} = -k(x\hat{\mathbf{i}} + y\hat{\mathbf{j}})$ kg-ms^{-2} with $k = 1$ kg s^{-2}. At time $t = 0$, the particle's position $\mathbf{r} = \left(\frac{1}{\sqrt{2}}\hat{\mathbf{i}} + \sqrt{2}\hat{\mathbf{j}}\right)$ m and its velocity $\mathbf{v} = \left(-\sqrt{2}\hat{\mathbf{i}} + \sqrt{2}\hat{\mathbf{j}} + \frac{2}{\pi}\hat{\mathbf{k}}\right)$ ms^{-1}. Let v_x and v_y denote the x and the y-components of the particle's velocity, respectively. (Ignore gravity). When $z = 0.5$ m, the value of $(x\,v_y - y\,v_x)$ is .... m^{2}s^{-1}.

2. In a radioactive decay chain reaction, $^{230}_{90}\mathrm{Th}$ nucleus decays into $^{214}_{84}\mathrm{Po}$ nucleus. The ratio of the number of α to number of β^{-1} particles emitted in this process is ....

3. Two resistances $R_1 = X\Omega$ and $R_2 = 1\,\Omega$ are connected to a wire AB of uniform resistivity, as shown in the figure. The radius of the wire varies linearly along its axis from 0.2 mm at A to 1 mm at B. A galvanometer (G) connected to the centre of the wire, 50 cm from each end along its axis, shows zero deflection when A and B are connected to a battery. The value of X is ....

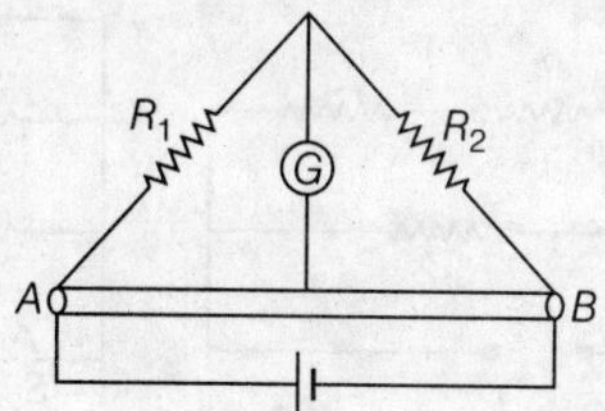

4. In a particular system of units, a physical quantity can be expressed in terms of the electric charge e, electron mass m_e, Planck's constant h and Coulomb's constant $k = \frac{1}{4\pi\varepsilon_0}$, where ε_0 is the permittivity of vacuum. In terms of these physical constants, the dimension of the magnetic field is $[B] = [e]^{\alpha}[m_e]^{\beta}[h]^{\gamma}[k]^{\delta}$. The value of $\alpha + \beta + \gamma + \delta$ is ....

5. Consider a configuration of n identical units, each consisting of three layers. The first layer is a column of air of height $h = \frac{1}{3}$ cm and the second and third layers are of equal thickness $d = \frac{\sqrt{3}-1}{2}$ cm and refractive indices $\mu_1 = \sqrt{\frac{3}{2}}$ and $\mu_2 = \sqrt{3}$, respectively. A light source O is placed on the top of the first unit, as shown in the figure. A ray of light from O is incident on the second layer of the first unit at an angle of $\theta = 60°$ to the normal. For a specific value of n, the ray of light emerges from the bottom of the configuration at a distance $l = \frac{8}{\sqrt{3}}$ cm, as shown in the figure. The value of n is ....

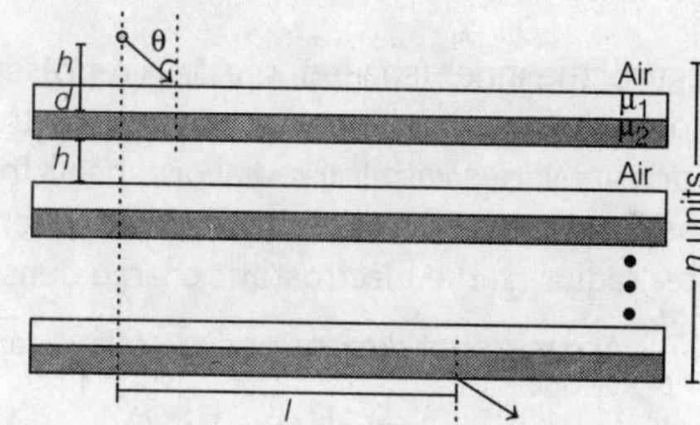

6. A charge q is surrounded by a closed surface consisting of an inverted cone of height h and base radius R, and a hemisphere of radius R as shown in the figure. The electric flux through the conical surface is $\frac{nq}{6\varepsilon_0}$ (in SI units). The value of n is ....

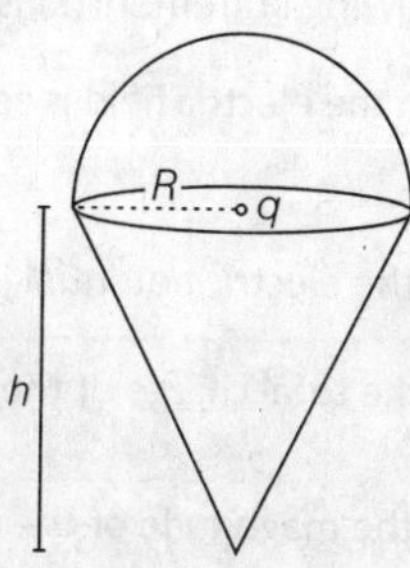

7. On a frictionless horizontal plane, a bob of mass $m = 0.1$ kg is attached to a spring with natural length $l_0 = 0.1$ m. The spring constant is $k_1 = 0.009$ N m^{-1} when the length of the spring $l > l_0$ and is $k_2 = 0.016$ N m^{-1} when $l < l_0$. Initially, the bob is released from $l = 0.15$ m. Assume that Hooke's law remains valid throughout the motion. If the time period of the full oscillation is $T = (n\pi)$ s, then the integer closest to n is ....

8. An object and a concave mirror of focal length $f = 10$ cm both move along the principal axis of the mirror with constant speeds. The object moves with speed $v_0 = 15$ cm s^{-1} towards the mirror with respect to a laboratory frame.

The distance between the object and the mirror at a given moment is denoted by u. When $u = 30$ cm, the speed of the mirror v_m is such that the image is instantaneously at rest with respect to the laboratory frame and the object forms a real image. The magnitude of v_m is .... cm s^{-1}.

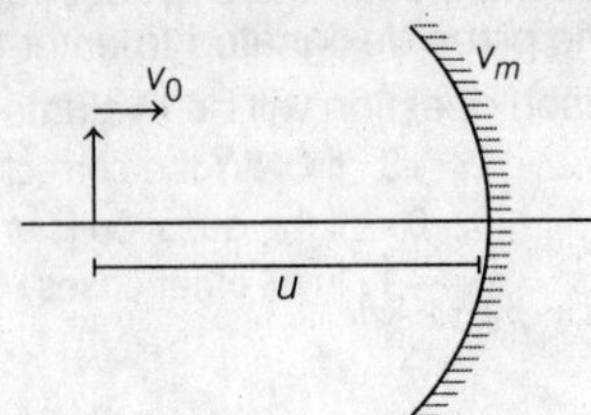

SECTION 2 (Maximum Marks: 24)

- This section contains **SIX (06)** questions.
- Each question has **FOUR** options (a), (b), (c) and (d). **ONE OR MORE THAN ONE** of these four option(s) is(are) correct answer(s).
- For each question, choose the option(s) corresponding to all the correct answer(s).
- Answer to each question will be evaluated according to the following marking scheme:

Full Marks : +4 **ONLY** if (all) the correct option(s) is/are chosen;
Partial Marks : +3 If all the four options are correct but **ONLY** three options are chosen;
Partial Marks : +2 If three or more options are correct but **ONLY** two options are chosen, both of which are correct;
Partial Marks : +1 If two or more options are correct but **ONLY** one option is chosen and it is a correct option;
Zero Marks : 0 If unanswered);
Negative Marks : – 2 In all other cases.

9. In the figure, the inner (shaded) region A represents a sphere of radius $r_A = 1$, within which of the electrostatic charge density varies with the radial distance r from the centre as $\rho_A = kr$, where k is positive. In the spherical shell B of outer radius r_B, the electrostatic charge density varies as $\rho_B = \frac{2k}{r}$. Assume that dimensions are taken care of. All physical quantities are in their SI units.

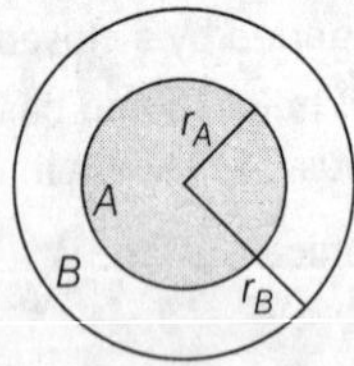

Which of the following statement(s) is(are) correct?

(a) If $r_B = \sqrt{\frac{3}{2}}$, then the electric field is zero everywhere outside B.

(b) If $r_B = \frac{3}{2}$, then the electric potential just outside B is $\frac{k}{\varepsilon_0}$.

(c) If $r_B = 2$, then the total charge of the configuration is $15\pi k$.

(d) If $r_B = \frac{5}{2}$, then the magnitude of the electric field just outside B is $\frac{13\pi k}{\varepsilon_0}$.

10. In Circuit-1 and Circuit-2 shown in the figures, $R_1 = 1\ \Omega$, $R_2 = 2\ \Omega$ and $R_3 = 3\ \Omega$. P_1 and P_2 are the power dissipations in Circuit-1 and Circuit-2 when the switches S_1 and S_2 are in open conditions, respectively.

Q_1 and Q_2 are the power dissipations in Circuit-1 and Circuit-2 when the switches S_1 and S_2 are in closed conditions, respectively.

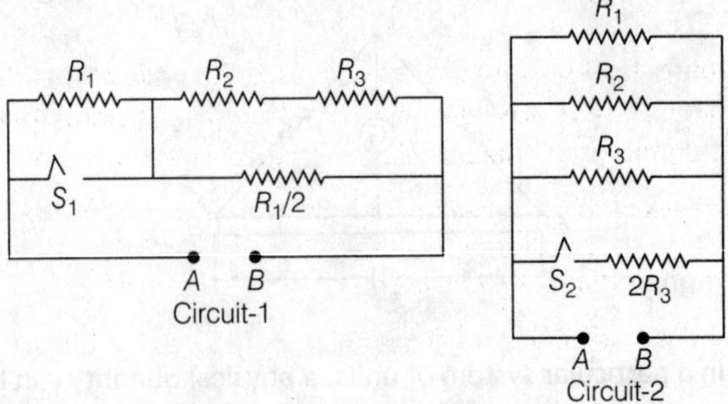

Which of the following statement(s) is(are) correct?

(a) When a voltage source of 6 V is connected across A and B in both circuits, $P_1 < P_2$.

(b) When a constant current source of 2 A is connected across A and B in both circuits, $P_1 > P_2$.

(c) When a voltage source of 6 V is connected across A and B in Circuit-1, $Q_1 > P_1$.

(d) When a constant current source of 2 A is connected across A and B in both circuits, $Q_2 < Q_1$.

11. A bubble has surface tension S. The ideal gas inside the bubble has ratio of specific heats $\gamma = \frac{5}{3}$. The bubble is exposed to the atmosphere and it always retains its spherical shape. When the atmospheric pressure is p_{a_1}, the radius of the bubble is found to be r_1 and the temperature of the enclosed gas is T_1. When the atmospheric pressure is p_{a_2}, the radius of the bubble and the temperature of the enclosed gas are r_2 and T_2, respectively.

Which of the following statement(s) is(are) correct?

(a) If the surface of the bubble is a perfect heat insulator, then $\left(\frac{r_1}{r_2}\right)^5 = \frac{p_{a_2} + \frac{2S}{r_2}}{p_{a_1} + \frac{2S}{r_1}}$.

(b) If the surface of the bubble is a perfect heat insulator, then the total internal energy of the bubble including its surface energy does not change with the external atmospheric pressure.

(c) If the surface of the bubble is a perfect heat conductor and the change in atmospheric temperature is negligible, then $\left(\frac{r_1}{r_2}\right)^3 = \frac{p_{a_2} + \frac{4S}{r_2}}{p_{a_1} + \frac{4S}{r_1}}$.

(d) If the surface of the bubble is a perfect heat insulator, then $\left(\frac{T_2}{T_1}\right)^{\frac{5}{2}} = \frac{p_{a_2} + \frac{4S}{r_2}}{p_{a_1} + \frac{4S}{r_1}}$.

12. A disk of radius R with uniform positive charge density σ is placed on the XY-plane with its centre at the origin. The Coulomb potential along the Z-axis is

$$V(z) = \frac{\sigma}{2\varepsilon_0}\left(\sqrt{R^2 + z^2} - z\right).$$

A particle of positive charge q is placed initially at rest at a point on the Z-axis with $z = z_0$ and $z_0 > 0$. In addition to the Coulomb force, the particle experiences a vertical force $\mathbf{F} = -c\hat{\mathbf{k}}$ with $c > 0$. Let $\beta = \frac{2c\varepsilon_0}{q\sigma}$. Which of the following statement(s) is/are correct?

(a) For $\beta = \frac{1}{4}$ and $z_0 = \frac{25}{7}R$, the particle reaches the origin.

(b) For $\beta = \frac{1}{4}$ and $z_0 = \frac{3}{7}R$, the particle reaches the origin.

(c) For $\beta = \frac{1}{4}$ and $z_0 = \frac{R}{\sqrt{3}}$, the particle returns back to $z = z_0$.

(d) For $\beta > 1$ and $z_0 > 0$, the particle always reaches the origin.

13. A double slit set up is shown in the figure. One of the slit is in medium-2 of refractive index n_2. The other slit is at the interface of this medium with another medium-1 of refractive index $n_1 (\neq n_2)$. The line joining the slits is perpendicular to the interface and the distance between the slits is d. The slit widths are much smaller than d. A monochromatic parallel beam of light is incident on the slits from medium-1. A detector is placed in medium-2 at a large distance from the slits and at an angle θ from the line joining them, so that θ equals the angle of refraction of the beam. Consider two approximately parallel rays from the slits received by the detector.

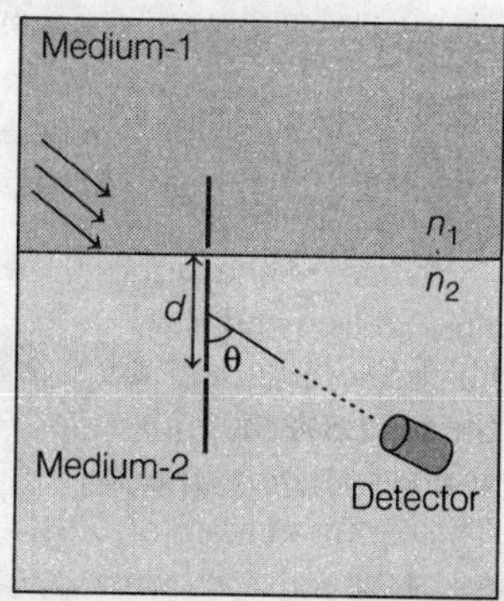

Which of the following statement(s) is(are) correct?

(a) The phase difference between the two rays is independent of d.

(b) The two rays interfere constructively at the detector.

(c) The phase difference between the two rays depends on n_1 but is independent of n_2.

(d) The phase difference between the two rays vanishes only for certain values of d and the angle of incidence of the beam, with θ being the corresponding angle of refraction.

14. In the given p-V diagram, a monoatomic gas $\left(\gamma = \frac{5}{3}\right)$ is first compressed adiabatically from state A to state B. Then, it expands isothermally from state B to state C. [Given, $\left(\frac{1}{3}\right)^{0.6} \simeq 0.5$, $\ln 2 \simeq 0.7$].

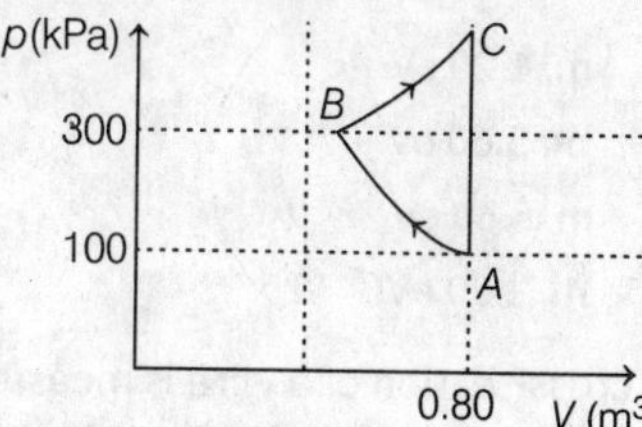

Which of the following statement(s) is(are) correct?

(a) The magnitude of the total work done in the process $A \to B \to C$ is 144 kJ.

(b) The magnitude of the work done in the process $B \to C$ is 84 kJ.

(c) The magnitude of the work done in the process $A \to B$ is 60 kJ.

(d) The magnitude of the work done in the process $C \to A$ is zero.

SECTION 3 (Maximum Marks: 12)

- This section contains **FOUR (04)** questions.
- Each question has **FOUR** options (a), (b), (c) and (d). **ONLY ONE** of these four options is the correct answer.
- Four each question, choose the option corresponding to the correct answer.
- Answer to each question will be evaluated according to the following marking scheme:

Full Marks : +3 If **ONLY** correct option is chosen;
Zero Marks : 0 If none of the options is chosen (i.e. the question is unanswered);
Negative Marks : –1 In all other cases.

15. A flat surface of a thin uniform disk *A* of radius *R* is glued to a horizontal table. Another thin uniform disk *B* of mass *M* and with the same radius *R* rolls without slipping on the circumference of *A*, as shown in the figure. A flat surface of *B* also lies on the plane of the table. The centre of mass of *B* has fixed angular speed ω about the vertical axis passing through the centre of *A*. The angular momentum of *B* is $nM\omega R^2$ with respect to the centre of *A*. Which of the following is the value of *n*?

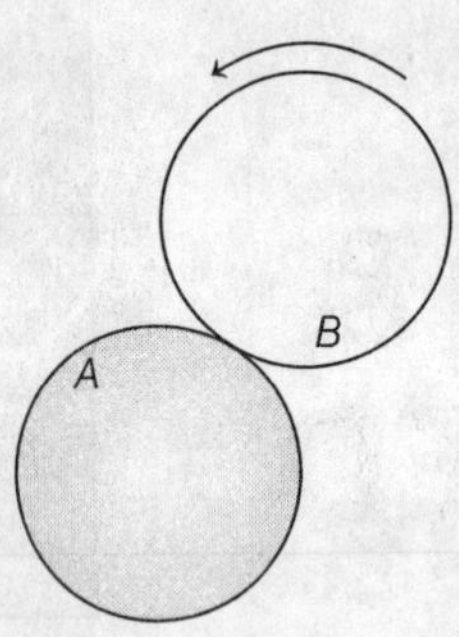

(a) 2 (b) 5
(c) $\frac{7}{2}$ (d) $\frac{9}{2}$

16. When light of a given wavelength is incident on a metallic surface, the minimum potential needed to stop the emitted photoelectrons is 6.0 V. This potential drops to 0.6 V, if another source with wavelength four times that of the first one and intensity half of the first one is used. What are the wavelength of the first source and the work function of the metal, respectively?

[Take, $\frac{hc}{e} = 1.24\times 10^{-6}$ JmC^{-1}]

(a) 1.72×10^{-7} m, 1.20 eV
(b) 1.72×10^{-7} m, 5.60 eV
(c) 3.78×10^{-7} m, 5.60 eV
(d) 3.78×10^{-7} m, 1.20 eV

17. Area of the cross-section of a wire is measured using a screw gauge. The pitch of the main scale is 0.5 mm. The circular scale has 100 divisions and for one full rotation of the circular scale, the main scale shifts by two divisions. The measured readings are listed below.

Measurement condition	Main scale reading	Circular scale reading
Two arms of gauge touching each other without wire	0 division	4 divisions
Attempt-1: With wire	4 divisions	20 divisions
Attempt-2: With wire	4 divisions	16 divisions

What are the diameter and cross-sectional area of the wire measured using the screw gauge?

(a) 2.22 ± 0.02 mm, π (1.23 ± 0.02) mm^2
(b) 2.22 ± 0.01 mm, π (1.23 ± 0.01) mm^2
(c) 2.14 ± 0.02 mm, π (1.14 ± 0.02) mm^2
(d) 2.14 ± 0.01 mm, π (1.14 ± 0.01) mm^2

18. Which one of the following options represents the magnetic field **B** at *O* due to the current flowing in the given wire segments lying on the *XY*-plane?

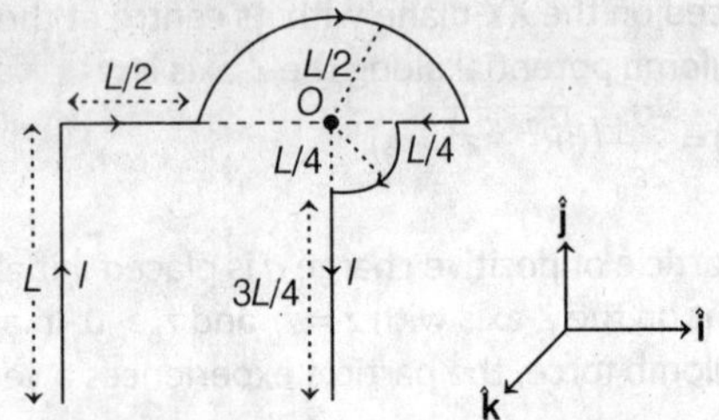

(a) $\mathbf{B} = \frac{-\mu_0 I}{L}\left(\frac{3}{2} + \frac{1}{4\sqrt{2}\pi}\right)\hat{k}$ (b) $\mathbf{B} = \frac{\mu_0 I}{L}\left(\frac{3}{2} + \frac{1}{2\sqrt{2}\pi}\right)\hat{k}$

(c) $\mathbf{B} = \frac{-\mu_0 I}{L}\left(1 + \frac{1}{4\sqrt{2}\pi}\right)\hat{k}$ (d) $\mathbf{B} = \frac{-\mu_0 I}{L}\left(1 + \frac{1}{4\pi}\right)\hat{k}$

Answers

1 3	2 2	3 5	4 4	5 4	6 3	7 6	8 3	9 (b)	10 (a,b,c)
11 (c,d)	12 (a,c,d)	13 (a,b)	14 (b,c,d)	15 (b)	16 (a)	17 (c)	18 (c)		

See detailed explanations on page no. 400

JEE MAIN & ADVANCED

Explanations

Qualifiers, Part Tests, Knockouts, Real Nuts

THE QUALIFIERS

Qualifier 1 (Physics & Measurement and Experimental Skills)

1. To find area of nine plates, we need to add area of triangular plate 9 times. So, the required area,

$A = 3.24 + 3.24 + \ldots$ upto 9 times
$= 29.16\ m^2$ (upto correct significant figures)

2. Given, $A_1 = 24.46, B_1 = 0.0724$ and $C_1 = 256.2$

$\therefore A_1 + B_1 + C_1 = 280.7324$

As sum contains same number of digits after decimal as present in the number having the least number of decimal places, so

$A_1 + B_1 + C_1 = 280.7$

Similarly, $A_2 + B_2 + C_2 = 280.7$

$A_3 + B_3 + C_3 = 280.7$ (rounded off)

$A_4 + B_4 + C_4 = 280.8$ (rounded off)

So, $A_1 + B_1 + C_1 = A_2 + B_2 + C_2 = A_3 + B_3 + C_3 < A_4 + B_4 + C_4$

3. Equivalent resistance for parallel combination is given by

$$\frac{1}{R} = \frac{1}{a} + \frac{1}{b} \quad \ldots \text{(i)}$$

$$\Rightarrow \frac{\Delta R}{R^2} = \frac{\Delta a}{a^2} + \frac{\Delta b}{b^2}$$

$$\Rightarrow \Delta R = R^2\left(\frac{\Delta a}{a^2} + \frac{\Delta b}{b^2}\right) \quad \ldots \text{(ii)}$$

Also, from Eq. (i), $R = \frac{ab}{a+b}$ ... (iii)

From Eqs. (ii) and (iii), we get

$$\Delta R = \left(\frac{ab}{a+b}\right)^2\left(\frac{\Delta a}{a^2} + \frac{\Delta b}{b^2}\right)$$

4. As, $\rho = \frac{RA}{l} = \frac{VA}{li} = \frac{V\pi d^2}{4li}$

$$\Rightarrow \frac{\Delta\rho}{\rho}\times 100 = \frac{2\Delta d}{d}\times 100 + \frac{\Delta V}{V}\times 100 + \frac{\Delta l}{l}\times 100 + \frac{\Delta i}{i}\times 100$$

$$\Rightarrow \frac{\Delta\rho}{\rho}\times 100 = 2\times\frac{0.01}{2.50}\times 100 + \frac{0.1}{20.0}\times 100 + \frac{0.2}{10.0}\times 100 + \frac{0.01}{2.0}\times 100$$

$$\Rightarrow \frac{\Delta\rho}{\rho}\times 100 = 3.8\%$$

5. As argument of exponential function is dimensionless, so $\frac{bx^2}{kT}$ is dimensionless

$\Rightarrow [bx^2] = [kT]$ ... (i)

As energy of gas molecule in ideal gas is given by

Energy, $E = \frac{3}{2}kT \Rightarrow [kT] = [E]$ ... (ii)

From Eqs. (i) and (ii), we get

$[bx^2] = [kT] = [\text{Energy}]$

$\Rightarrow [bx^2] = [U]$

$\Rightarrow \frac{bx^2}{U}$ is dimensionless.

Also argument of sine function is dimensionless.

$\Rightarrow \frac{x}{f} =$ Dimensionless

$\Rightarrow [x] = [f]$ ... (iii)

Also, from principle of homogeneity,

$[U] = [cx] = [a^2b] = [d]$ ... (iv)

From Eq. (iv), $[cx] = d$

$\Rightarrow [cf] = [d]$ [using Eq. (iii)]

$\therefore \frac{cf}{d}$ is dimensionless.

From Eq. (iv), $[a^2b] = [d]$

$\therefore \frac{a^2b}{d}$ is dimensionless.

From Eq (iv), $[U] = [d]$

$\therefore \frac{U}{d}$ is dimensionless.

$\Rightarrow \frac{fd}{U}$ is not dimensionless.

6. All options are given in the format,

$F = a \log b$

Therefore, $[F] = [a][\log b]$

$\Rightarrow [F] = [a]$, as log is dimensionless.

Considering options (a) and (b), for both these options,

$a = 2\rho Av^2$

$\Rightarrow [a] = [\rho][A][v]^2$
$= [ML^{-3}][L^2][LT^{-1}]^2$
$= [MLT^{-2}] = [F]$

So, out of options (a) and (b), one of the choices is correct.

Consider argument of option (a). That is

$b = \frac{\rho Ar}{\pi m}$

Therefore, $[b] = \frac{[\rho][A][r]}{[\pi][m]}$
$= \frac{[ML^{-3}][L^2][L]}{[M]}$
$=$ Dimensionless

So, option (a) is dimensionally consistent.

7. Let the bond number B be related to other quantities as $B = \rho^a g^b l^c S^d$

Here, a, b, c and d are constants.

Dimensional formulae of various quantities are

$[B] = [M^0L^0T^0]$ (as it is dimensionless)

$[\rho] = [ML^{-3}], [g] = [LT^{-2}]$

$[l] = [L], [S] = [ML^0T^{-2}]$

Putting these dimensions in the assumed relation, we get

$[M^0L^0T^0] = [ML^{-3}]^a [LT^{-2}]^b [L]^c [ML^0T^{-2}]^d$

$\Rightarrow [M^0L^0T^0] = [M]^{a+d}[L]^{-3a+b+c}[T]^{-2b-2d}$

Comparing dimensions on both sides, we get

$a + d = 0$ ... (i)

$-3a + b + c = 0$ ... (ii)

$-2b - 2d = 0$ ... (iii)

From Eq. (i), $a = -d$ ... (iv)

and from Eq. (iii), $b = -d$ ... (v)

Thus, putting $a = b = -d$ in Eq. (ii), we get

$-3(-d) + (-d) + c = 0$

$\Rightarrow c = -2d$ ... (vi)

From Eqs. (iv), (v) and (vi), we get

$a : b : c : d = 1 : 1 : 2 : -1$

According to above relation, option (a) is correct.

8. Dimensional formulae of different quantities are

$[h] = [ML^2T^{-1}], [c] = [LT^{-1}]$

$[k] = [ML^2T^{-2}\theta^{-1}]$

$[G] = [M^{-1}L^3T^{-2}]$

Let Planck's temperature be $\theta_P = h^a c^b k^c G^d$

Here, a, b, c and d are constants.

$\Rightarrow \quad [\theta_P] = [h]^a [c]^b [k]^c [G]^d$

$= [ML^2T^{-1}]^a [LT^{-1}]^b [ML^2T^{-2}\theta^{-1}]^c [M^{-1}L^3T^{-2}]^d$

$[\theta_P] = [M]^{a+c-d} [L]^{2a+b+2c+3d} [T]^{-a-b-2c-2d} [\theta]^{-c}$

Comparing dimensions of θ on both sides, we get

$$-c = 1 \Rightarrow c = -1$$

Only option for which power of k is -1 is option (b).

9. Time period of a pendulum of length l is given by

$$T = 2\pi\sqrt{\frac{l}{g}} \Rightarrow g = \frac{4\pi^2 l}{T^2}$$

$$\Rightarrow \frac{\Delta g}{g} = \frac{\Delta l}{l} + 2\frac{\Delta T}{T}$$

$$\Rightarrow \frac{\Delta g}{g} \times 100 = \frac{\Delta l}{l} \times 100 + 2\frac{\Delta T}{T} \times 100$$

$$= \frac{0.1}{50.0} \times 100 + 2 \times \frac{1}{40} \times 100$$

$$= 0.2 + 5 = 5.2$$

10. As per the given law, $I = e^{2V} - 1$ ... (i)

Differentiating Eq. (i) w.r.t. V on both sides, we get

$$\frac{dI}{dV} = 2 \cdot e^{2V} = 2(I + 1)$$

[Using Eq (i).]

$$\Rightarrow \quad dI = 2(I + 1)\, dV$$

$$\Rightarrow \quad \frac{dI}{I} = \frac{2(I + 1)\, dV}{I}$$

$$\Rightarrow \frac{dI}{I} \times 100 = \frac{2(I + 1)\, dV}{I} \times 100 \quad \text{... (ii)}$$

Putting given values of $I = 3$ mA and $dV = \pm\ 0.02$ V in Eq. (ii), we get

$$\frac{dI}{I} \times 100 = 2\frac{(3 + 1)}{3} \times 0.02 \times 100$$

$$= \frac{16}{3} = 5.33\%$$

11. As 9 divisions of main scale (equal to 9 mm) coincide with 10 divisions of vernier scale, so 1 vernier scale division = 0.9 mm. Therefore, least count = Main scale division − Vernier scale division

$$= 1\text{mm} - 0.9\text{mm} = 0.1\text{ mm}$$

In question, Fig.1 shows some reading, which means that the callipers has zero error given by

Zero error = Main scale reading + (Vernier scale reading) × Least count

$$= -1\text{ mm} + 6 \times 0.1\text{ mm}$$

$\Rightarrow$ Zero error = − 0.4 mm ... (i)

In question, Fig. 2 shows reading given by

Reading = Main scale Reading + (Vernier scale reading) × Least count

$$= 11\text{ mm} + 7 \times 0.1\text{ mm}$$

$\Rightarrow$ Reading = 11.7 mm ... (ii)

Measured diameter = Reading − Zero error

$= 11.7 - (-0.4)$ [Using Eqs. (i) and (ii)]

$= 12.1$ mm

12. Let the liquid rise upto a height h (as measured for the lower meniscus B) and let the meniscus ABC have hemispherical shape.

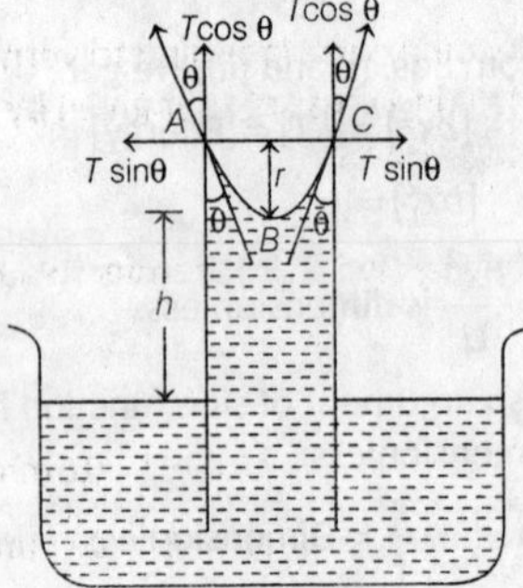

Then, volume of the liquid risen upto lower meniscus $= \pi r^2 h$

Volume of liquid in meniscus above B = Volume of cylinder of radius r and height h − Volume of hemisphere of radius r

$$= \pi r^2 \cdot r - \frac{2}{3}\pi r^3 = \frac{\pi r^3}{3}$$

Total volume of the liquid risen

$$= \pi r^2 h + \frac{\pi r^3}{3} = \pi r^2\left(h + \frac{r}{3}\right)$$

If liquid has a density ρ, then mass of liquid risen

$$= \pi r^2 \times \left(h + \frac{r}{3}\right)\rho$$

and weight of the liquid risen

$$= \pi r^2\left(h + \frac{r}{3}\right)\rho g$$

For equilibrium,

$$\pi r^2\left(h + \frac{r}{3}\right)\rho g = 2\,\pi\, rT\cos\theta$$

or $\quad h = \dfrac{2T\cos\theta}{r\rho g} - \dfrac{r}{3}$

(From above, we find that $h \propto \frac{1}{r}$, i.e. liquid rises more in a capillary tube of small radius)

$$\Rightarrow \quad T = \frac{(h + r/3)r\rho g}{2\cos\theta}$$

$$= \frac{(3h + r)\rho rg}{6\cos\theta}$$

13. Let v and e are speed of sound and end correction, respectively.

As effective length for 1st resonance (fundamental mode), as shown in figure, is

$$L = L_1 + e$$

$$\Rightarrow \quad f = f_0 = \frac{v}{4L} = \frac{v}{4(L_1 + e)}$$

(Here, f_0 is fundamental frequency)

$$\Rightarrow \quad L_1 + e = \frac{v}{4f} \quad \text{... (i)}$$

For second resonance (3rd harmonic) effective length,

$$L' = L_2 + e$$

Therefore, frequency of second resonance (3rd harmonic) is

$$f = 3f_0 = \frac{3v}{4L'} = \frac{3v}{4(L_2 + e)}$$

$$\Rightarrow \quad L_2 + e = \frac{3v}{4f} \quad \text{... (ii)}$$

Dividing Eq. (ii) by Eq. (i), we get

$$\frac{L_2 + e}{L_1 + e} = 3 \Rightarrow L_2 + e = 3L_1 + 3e$$

$$\Rightarrow \quad e = \frac{L_2 - 3L_1}{2} = \frac{73 - 3 \times 23}{2} = 2\text{ cm} \quad \text{... (iii)}$$

As per Rayleigh's relation between end correction and radius, $e = 0.6\, r$

$\Rightarrow \quad 0.6\, r = 2$ cm $\Rightarrow r = 3.33$ cm

From Eq (i), $\quad v = 4f(L_1 + e)$

$$v = 4 \times 330\left(\frac{23}{100} + \frac{2}{100}\right) = 330\text{ m/s}$$

[Using Eq. (iii)]

14. Galvanometer resistance (G) is related to R and S by the relation,

$$G = \frac{RS}{R - S} = \frac{R\left(\frac{R}{3}\right)}{R - \frac{R}{3}} = \frac{R}{2}$$

15. If a capacitor is put between probes of a multimeter, then during charging a current flows in circuit, so there is a deflection which becomes soon zero.

$\therefore$ Statement in option (c) is not correct.

16. Density is mass per unit volume,

$$\Rightarrow \rho = \frac{m}{\left(\frac{\pi d^2}{4}\right)l} \Rightarrow \left(\frac{\Delta\rho}{\rho}\right) = 2\frac{\Delta d}{d} + \frac{\Delta l}{l}$$

Δd = least count of screw gauge

$$= \frac{1\text{ mm}}{100} = 0.01 \text{ mm}$$

$d = 3.07$ mm from the figure

$$\Rightarrow \left(\frac{\Delta\rho}{\rho}\right)_{max} = \left(2 \times \frac{0.01}{3.07} + \frac{1}{100}\right) \times 100\% = 1.65\%$$

17. On hanging load mg, the wire undergoes extension x as shown.

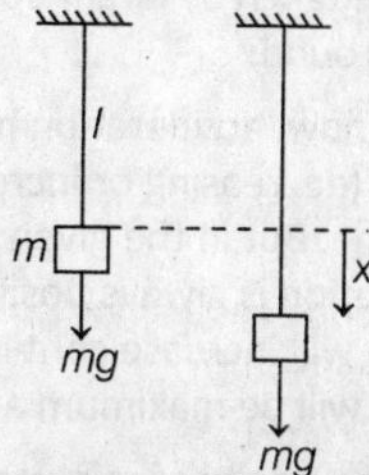

By Hooke's law,

$$Y = \frac{\text{Stress}}{\text{Strain}}$$

$$\Rightarrow \quad Y = \frac{mg \cdot l}{\pi r^2 \cdot x}$$

where, r is radius of wire.

Taking ln on both sides, we get

$$\ln Y = \ln m + \ln g + \ln l - \ln r^2 - \ln x - \ln \pi$$

$$\Rightarrow \ d(\ln Y) = d(\ln m) + d(\ln g) + d(\ln l) - d(2\ln r) - d(\ln x) - d(\ln \pi)$$

$$\Rightarrow \frac{dY}{Y} = \frac{dm}{m} + \frac{dg}{g} + \frac{dl}{l} - \frac{2dr}{r} - \frac{dx}{x}$$

As g and l are known exactly, so dg and dl are zero.

$$\Rightarrow \frac{dY}{Y} = \frac{dm}{m} - \frac{2dr}{r} - \frac{dx}{x}$$

$$\Rightarrow \pm\frac{\Delta Y}{Y} = \pm\frac{\Delta m}{m} - 2\left(\pm\frac{\Delta r}{r}\right) - \left(\pm\frac{\Delta x}{x}\right)$$

$$\Rightarrow (\Delta Y)_{max} = Y\left[\frac{\Delta m}{m} + 2\frac{\Delta r}{r} + \frac{\Delta x}{x}\right]$$

$$\Rightarrow (\Delta Y)_{max} = Y\left[\frac{\Delta m}{m} + 2\frac{\Delta D}{D} + \frac{\Delta x}{x}\right]$$

(as, diameter $D = 2r$, therefore $\Delta D = 2\,\Delta r$ and so $\frac{\Delta D}{D} = \frac{2\Delta r}{2r} = \frac{\Delta r}{r}$)

Putting given values in the expression, we get

$$(\Delta Y)_{max} = 2 \times 10^{11} \left[\frac{0.1}{2.0} + 2 \times \frac{0.01}{0.5} + \frac{0.1}{1.6}\right]$$

$$= 0.305 \times 10^{11} \text{ N/m}^2$$

or $\quad \Delta Y = 3.05 \times 10^{10} \text{ N/m}^2$

$\because \quad x + y = 3.05 + 10 = 13.05$

18. Separation of markings on vernier scale from zero are as shown.

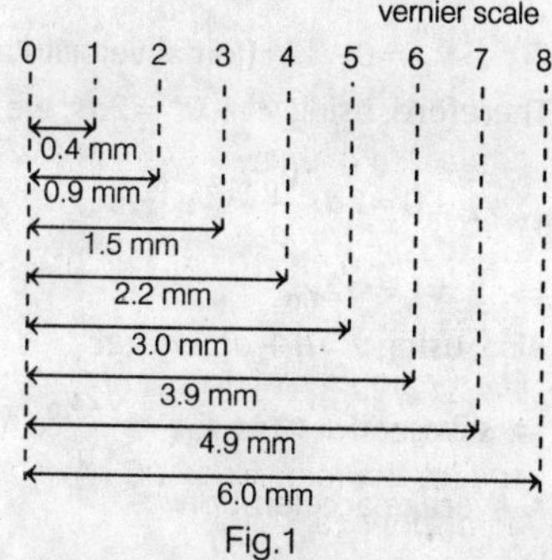

Fig.1

Reading corresponding to vernier scale in excess of that given by main scale will be

Vernier Division Coinciding	Vernier Reading
0	0
1	$\|0.4 - 1\| = 0.6$ mm
2	$\|0.9 - 1\| = 0.1$ mm
3	$\|1.5 - 2\| = 0.5$ mm
4	$\|2.2 - 3\| = 0.8$ mm
5	$\|3.0 - 3\| = 0$ mm
6	$\|3.9 - 4\| = 0.1$ mm
7	$\|4.9 - 5\| = 0.1$ mm
8	$\|6.0 - 6\| = 0$ mm

y=0.1mm
0 1 2 3 4 5 6 7 8
D 3.9 mm

Fig. 2

From the Fig. 2

$$D = 4 + 0.1 = 4.1 \text{ mm} \quad \text{... (i)}$$

Taking into account the zero error, we get

$$\text{Diameter} = D - x = 4.1 - (-0.2) = 4.3 \text{ mm}$$

19. At balance point,

$$\frac{E_1}{E_2} = \frac{l_1}{l_2} = \frac{3 \times 100 + (100 - 40)}{7 \times 100 + 50} = \frac{36}{75}$$

$\therefore \quad a = 36$

20. Given, balance length, $l = 25$ cm

At balance point, $\frac{R}{l} = \frac{S}{100 - l}$

$$\Rightarrow \frac{R}{25} = \frac{S}{75} \Rightarrow R = \frac{S}{3}\,\Omega \quad \text{... (i)}$$

When R is replaced by some other resistance of half length and half diameter, then resistance in left gap,

$$R' = \frac{\rho\frac{l}{2}}{\frac{\pi}{4}\left(\frac{d}{2}\right)^2} = 2\left\{\frac{\rho l}{\left(\frac{\pi}{4}d^2\right)}\right\}$$

$$\Rightarrow \quad R' = 2R$$

Now, if balance is obtained at length l', then

$$\frac{R'}{l'} = \frac{S}{(100 - l')}$$

$$\Rightarrow \quad \frac{2R}{l'} = \frac{S}{100 - l'}$$

Substituting for S from Eq. (i), we get

$$\frac{2R}{l'} = \frac{3R}{100 - l'}$$

$$\Rightarrow 200 - 2l' = 3l'$$

or $\quad l' = 40$ cm

Qualifier 2 (Kinematics)

1. According to the question, final speed of the car, $v = 0$

Initial speed of the car,

$$u = \frac{5}{18} \times 36 = 10 \text{ m/s}$$

Retardation of the car, $a = 2 \text{ m/s}^2$

Using $v = u + at$, we get

$$0 = 10 - 2t$$

$$\Rightarrow \quad t = 5 \text{ s}$$

Though, the time interval between timer's readings 34 s and 28 s is 6 s. But as the car stops before that, so we have to find the distance travelled by the car in 5 s only.

Now, using $s = ut + \frac{1}{2}at^2$, we get

$$s = 10 \times 5 + \frac{1}{2} \times (-2) \times 5^2 = 25 \text{ m}$$

2. Suppose retardation due to air drag is b and maximum height attained is H. For upward journey or ascent, displacement is H, retardation is $g + b$ and final velocity (at highest point) is zero.

$$\Rightarrow \quad H = \frac{1}{2}(g + b)T^2 \quad \text{.... (i)}$$

Similarly, for descent, displacement is H, retardation is $g-b$ while initial velocity (at highest point) is zero.

$$\Rightarrow \quad H=\frac{1}{2}(g-b)(nT)^2 \quad \text{... (ii)}$$

From Eqs. (i) and (ii), we get

$$(g+b)T^2=(g-b)(nT)^2$$

$$\Rightarrow \quad \frac{g+b}{g-b}=n^2 \quad \text{... (iii)}$$

Now, distance moved in 1st second of descent,

$$s=ut+\frac{1}{2}at^2=\frac{1}{2}(g+b) \quad \text{... (iv)}$$

and distance moved in last second of ascent,

$$s'=vt-\frac{1}{2}at^2=\frac{1}{2}(g-b) \quad \text{... (v)}$$

Dividing Eq. (iv) by Eq. (v), we get

$$\frac{s}{s'}=\frac{g+b}{g-b}=n^2 \quad \text{[from Eq. (iii)]}$$

3. According to the question, retardation, $a=-bv$

(Here, $b=$ constant)

$$\Rightarrow \quad \frac{dv}{dt}=-bv$$

Integrating both sides, we get

$$\Rightarrow \quad \int_{v_0}^{v}\frac{dv}{v}=-b\int_0^t dt \Rightarrow v=v_0e^{-bt}$$

$$\Rightarrow \quad |a|=bv_0e^{-bt}$$

At $t=1$ s, $v=\frac{v_0}{2}$ (Given) $\Rightarrow e^{-b}=\frac{1}{2}$

At $t=3$ s, $v=v_0(e^{-b})^3=\frac{v_0}{8}$

As $a\propto v$, it will also become (1/8)th.

4. Let particle start its motion from rest ($u=0$) at A, speed up at rate a till point B acquiring speed v_0.

$\overrightarrow{a}$ $\overrightarrow{v_0}$ $\overleftarrow{a}$

A B C

$t=0$

At B, if direction of acceleration is reversed, the speed of particle will decrease gradually such that it comes to rest at C instantly. Thereafter, particle will begin moving in opposite direction, i.e. from C towards A.

For motion from A to B, time of motion, $t_{AB}=\frac{v-u}{a}=\frac{v_0-0}{a}=\frac{v_0}{a}$

and displacement, $s_{AB}=\frac{v^2-u^2}{2a}=\frac{v_0^2}{2a}$

Similarly for B to C, $t_{BC}=\frac{v_0}{a}$, $s_{BC}=\frac{v_0^2}{2a}$

For motion from C to A,

$$s_{AC}=s_{AB}+s_{BC}=\frac{v_0^2}{a}$$

$$v_C=0 \quad \text{(Initial velocity at C)}$$

Therefore, using $v^2-u^2=2as$, we get

$$v_A^2-0=2a\cdot\frac{v_0^2}{a}$$

$$\Rightarrow \quad v_A=\sqrt{2}v_0$$

Also, using $v=u+at$, we get

$$\Rightarrow \sqrt{2}v_0=0+at \Rightarrow t_{CA}=\frac{\sqrt{2}v_0}{a}$$

$\therefore$ Average acceleration

$$=\frac{v_A-0}{t_{AB}+t_{BC}+t_{CA}}$$

$$=\frac{\sqrt{2}v_0}{\frac{v_0}{a}+\frac{v_0}{a}+\frac{\sqrt{2}v_0}{a}}=\frac{a}{\sqrt{2}+1}$$

5. As we know, slope of graph $=\frac{dx}{dt}$

$=$ velocity which is decreasing in magnitude from B to C. So, we can say particle is retarding.

For upward concave x-t graph, a is positive. So, from D to E, a is positive. In first half of the interval slope/velocity is negative while slope/velocity is positive in second half.

Displacement from A to D, $\Delta x=0$

$\Rightarrow$ Average velocity from A to D

$$=\frac{\Delta x}{\Delta t}=0$$

Similarly, average velocity from A to E $=0$

As x-t graph between B and D is parabolic, so motion will be uniformly accelerated. Hence, statement of option (d) is incorrect.

6. As, mass of sphere,

$$m=\rho\times\frac{4}{3}\pi\left(\frac{A}{4\pi}\right)^{\frac{3}{2}}$$

(as area of sphere, $A=4\pi r^2$)

Therefore, $m\propto A^{\frac{3}{2}}$

It is given that, acceleration is directly proportional to mass.

$$\Rightarrow \quad a=CA^{\frac{3}{2}}$$

Using $s=ut+\frac{1}{2}at^2$, as $u=0$ for dropping, we get

$$s=\frac{1}{2}CA^{\frac{3}{2}}t^2$$

$$\Rightarrow \quad t\propto A^{-\frac{3}{4}} \text{ or } t=KA^{-\frac{3}{4}}$$

$$\Rightarrow \frac{dt}{t}\times100=-\frac{3}{4}\times\frac{dA}{A}\times100$$

$$=-\frac{3}{4}\times4=-3\%$$

$\Rightarrow$ Smaller sphere takes 0.97 times, the time taken by larger sphere to reach ground.

7. As we know, acceleration may be varying (decreasing or increasing) with time. But in the given graph, acceleration is always positive, so velocity will increase continuously. Thus, it will be maximum at $t=t_3$.

8. Relative velocity of rain w.r.t. Shruti is shown at different instants. As velocity v of Shruti increases, relative velocity of rain rotates continuously towards Shruti as shown.

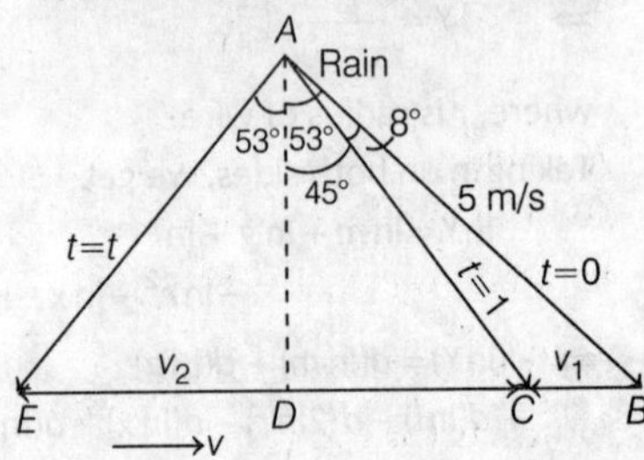

At $t=1$ s, let velocity is v_1 and at $t=t$, let velocity is v_2 when rain is again at 53° with vertical.

From ΔABD, $DB=5\sin53°$

$$=5\times\frac{4}{5}=4 \text{ m/s} \quad \text{...(i)}$$

and $AD=5\cos53°=5\times\frac{3}{5}=3$ m/s

From ΔADC, $DC=AD\tan45°$

$$=3 \text{ m/s} \quad \text{...(ii)}$$

From Eqs. (i) and (ii),

$CB=v_1=DB-DC=1$ m/s

Therefore, acceleration of Shruti

$$=\frac{v-u}{t}=\frac{1-0}{1}=1 \text{ m/s}^2$$

Now, from triangle ADE,

$$ED=AD\tan53°=3\times\frac{4}{3}=4 \text{ m/s}$$

So, velocity at time t,

$$v_2=DB+ED$$

$$=4+4=8 \text{ m/s}$$

$$\Rightarrow \quad t=\frac{v-u}{a}=\frac{8-0}{1}=8 \text{ s}$$

So, according to the question, required time $=8-1=7$ s

9. Motion (path) of the three particles is roughly sketched as in figure.

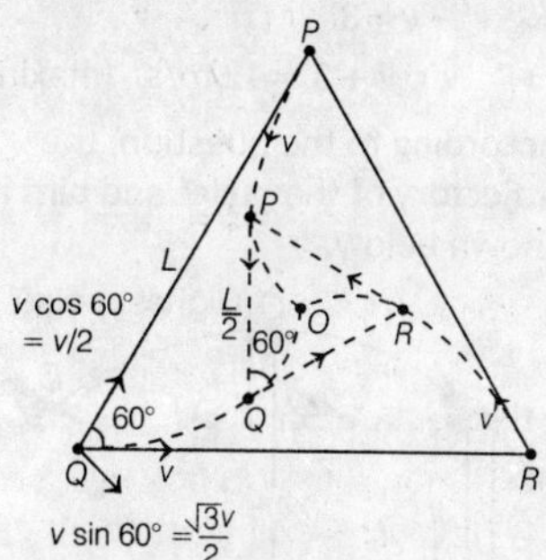

By symmetry, all the particles will meet at centre O of the triangle. At any instant, the particles lie on an equilateral triangle.

Let us consider line joining P and Q. Taking component of velocity of Q along PQ, velocity of approach of Q towards P is given by

$$v_{\text{approach}} = v - \left(-\frac{v}{2}\right) = \frac{3v}{2}$$

According to the question, we have to consider interval in which separation becomes half of initial i.e. $\frac{L}{2}$. So, relative displacement of Q with respect to P is $D_{\text{relative}} = L - \frac{L}{2} = \frac{L}{2}$

Therefore, required time is given by

$$t = \frac{D_{\text{relative}}}{v_{\text{approach}}} = \frac{\frac{L}{2}}{\frac{3v}{2}} = \frac{L}{3v}$$

10. According to the question, velocity components of the swimmers are as shown.

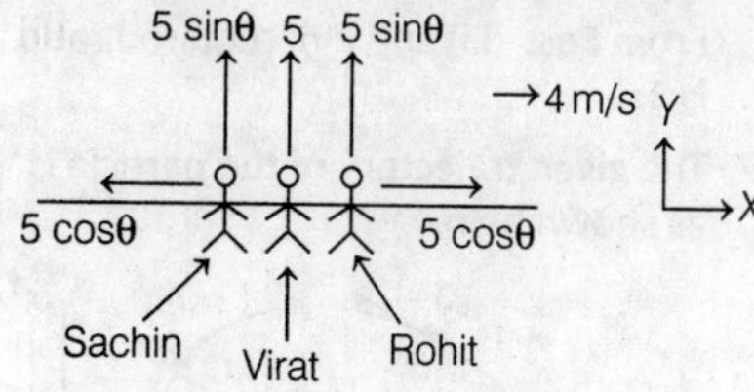

As, it is given that Sachin reaches directly opposite on the other bank.

⇒ Net velocity of Sachin in x-direction (along river) = 0

$$\Rightarrow \quad 5\cos\theta = 4 \Rightarrow \cos\theta = \frac{4}{5}$$

$$\Rightarrow \quad \theta = 37°$$

Components of net velocities of the swimmers will therefore be, as shown, resultant of swimmer's self velocity and river's velocity.

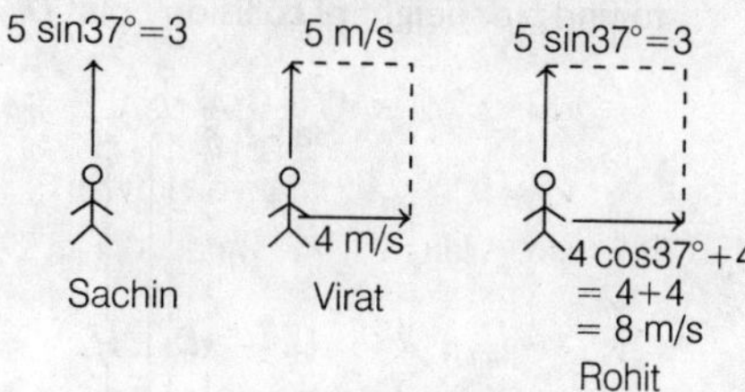

Now, t = Time taken to cross river

$$= \frac{d}{v_y}$$

and displacement along river or drift,

$$D = v_x \cdot t$$

Using above formula, we can calculate t and D for Virat and Rohit as

$$t_V = \frac{60}{5} = 12\text{ s}$$

$$\Rightarrow \quad D_V = 4 \times 12 = 48\text{ m}$$

and $t_R = \frac{60}{3} = 20\text{ s}$

$$\Rightarrow \quad D_R = 8 \times 20 = 160\text{ m}$$

$\therefore$ Virat's speed $= \frac{48\text{m}}{t} = v$ ...(i)

and Rohit's speed $= \frac{160\text{m}}{t} = v'$ ...(ii)

Dividing Eq. (i) by Eq. (ii), we get

$$\frac{v}{v'} = \frac{48}{160} = \frac{3}{10}$$

11. Relative to Dhoni,

u_y = initial velocity of ball = 5 m/s

v_y = final velocity of ball = 35 m/s

$\therefore$ a_y = acceleration of ball

$= a_{\text{ball}} + a_{\text{Dhoni}} = 10 + 5 = 15\text{ m/s}^2$

So, $t = \frac{v_y - u_y}{a_y} = \frac{35 - 5}{15} = 2\text{ s}$

⇒ Relative displacement of Salman = Initial separation = Relative velocity × Time

$= 15 \times 2 = 30\text{ m}$

12. The given situation in the question is as shown below at the instant of firing of shells at B.

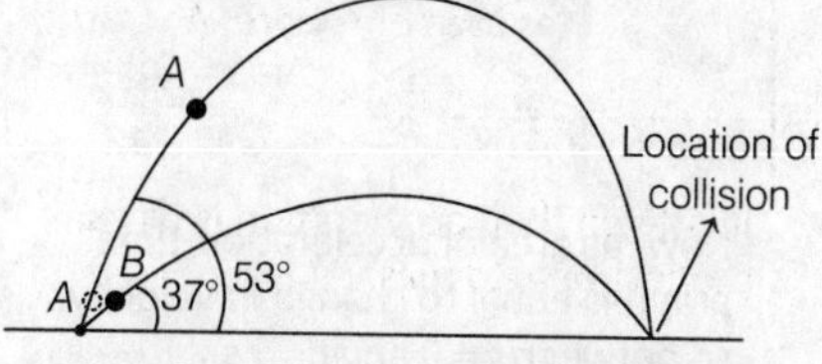

Angle of projection of shell with horizontal $= 90° - 53° = 37°$.

So, the two shells are fired at complementary angles, therefore range will be same. So, if collision happens between A and B, it must be at point of landing.

Time of flight of $A = \frac{2u\sin 53°}{g} = \frac{4u}{25}$

$(\because \sin 53° = 4/5)$

and time of flight of B

$$= \frac{2u\sin 37°}{g} = \frac{3u}{25} \quad (\because \sin 37° = 3/5)$$

$\therefore$ Time interval between firing should be equal to difference in times of flight $= \frac{4u}{25} - \frac{3u}{25} = 6\text{ s}$ (Given)

$$\Rightarrow \quad u = 150\text{ m/s}$$

13. Let the direction in which plane is heading makes an angle θ with line AB. For net velocity of plane to be along AB, velocity components perpendicular to line AB should cancel. Therefore,

$$v\sin\theta = v_{\text{wind}} = \frac{v}{2}$$

$$\Rightarrow \quad \theta = 30°$$

⇒ Velocity (net) of plane along AB

$$= v\cos 30° = \frac{\sqrt{3}v}{2}$$

⇒ Time of motion from A to B

$$T = \frac{d}{\frac{\sqrt{3}v}{2}} = \frac{2d}{\sqrt{3}v} \quad \text{...(i)}$$

For motion along BC, net velocity of plane $= v + \frac{v}{2} = \frac{3v}{2}$ as velocity of wind is in same direction as that of plane.

⇒ Time of motion from B to C

$$T' = \frac{d}{\frac{3v}{2}} = \frac{2d}{3v} \quad \text{...(ii)}$$

Dividing Eq. (ii) by Eq. (i), we get

$$\frac{T'}{T} = \frac{1}{\sqrt{3}}$$

$$\Rightarrow \quad T' = \frac{T}{\sqrt{3}}$$

14. Let speed of projection of balls = u

For motion of ball B, using $v = u + at$, we get

$$0 = u + (-g)t$$

$$\Rightarrow \quad t = \frac{u}{g} = \text{Time of ascent of } B \quad \text{...(i)}$$

Also, using $v^2 - u^2 = 2as$, we get

$$\Rightarrow \quad 0^2 - u^2 = 2(-g)(H)$$

$\Rightarrow H = \frac{u^2}{2g}$ = Maximum height attained by B ... (ii)

Displacement of A in same time as that calculated for B, can be calculated as

$$\Rightarrow \quad \mathbf{s}_A = -u\hat{\mathbf{i}}\left(\frac{u}{g}\right) + \frac{1}{2}(-g\hat{\mathbf{j}})\left(\frac{u}{g}\right)^2$$

$$= -\frac{u^2}{g}\hat{\mathbf{i}} - \frac{u^2}{2g}\hat{\mathbf{j}}$$

$$= -2H\hat{\mathbf{i}} - H\hat{\mathbf{j}}$$

[using Eqs. (i) and (ii)]

Similarly, displacement of C,

$$\mathbf{s}_C = 2H\hat{\mathbf{i}} - H\hat{\mathbf{j}}$$

So, the balls A, B, C will lie at vertices of a triangle as shown. Therefore, area of triangle ABC will be equal to

$$= \frac{1}{2} \times 4H \times 2H = 4H^2$$

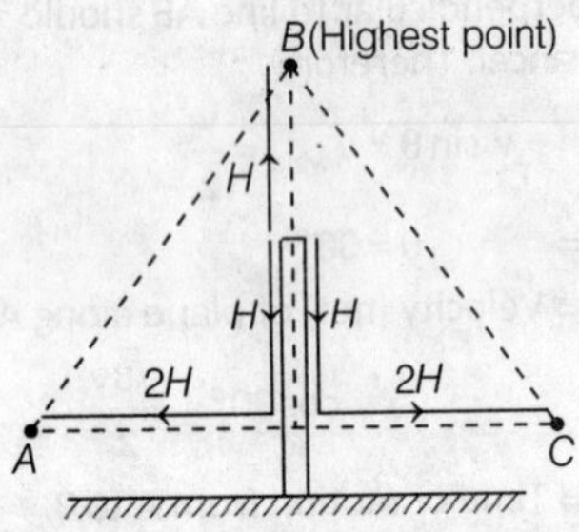

15. Considering origin at point of projection, coordinates of basketball at location of basket will be as shown.

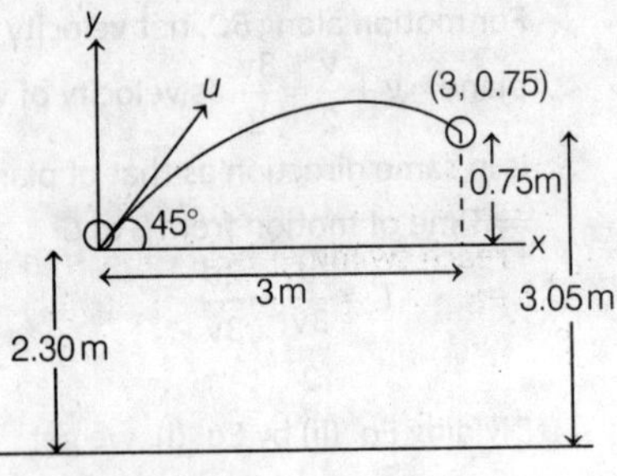

As equation of trajectory of projectile is given by

$$y = \tan\theta \cdot x - \frac{gx^2}{2u^2\cos^2\theta}$$

Let us put coordinates and θ in this equation, we get

$$0.75 = (\tan 45°)3 - \frac{10(3)^2}{2u^2\cos^2 45°}$$

$$\Rightarrow \quad 0.75 = 3 - \frac{90}{u^2}$$

$$\Rightarrow \quad u^2 = \frac{90}{2.25} = 40$$

$$\Rightarrow \quad u = 2\sqrt{10} \text{ m/s}$$

16. Situation can be depicted as shown w.r.t. ground frame. We are required to find h or height of collision point D.

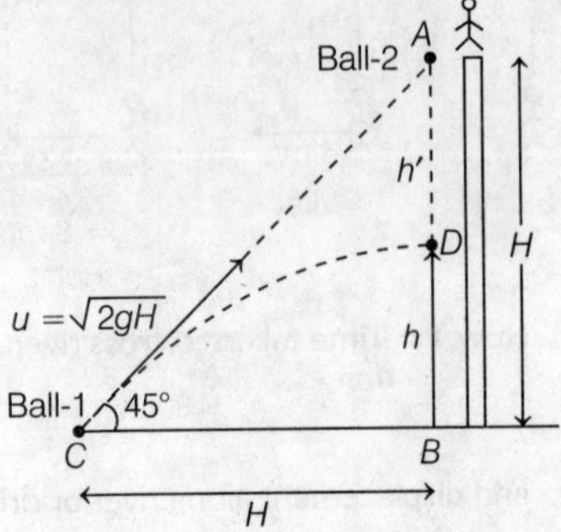

Relative initial velocity of ball-1 w.r.t. ball-2, $u_{12} = \sqrt{2gH}$

Relative acceleration of ball-1 w.r.t. ball-2, $\mathbf{a}_{12} = (-g\hat{\mathbf{j}}) - (-g\hat{\mathbf{j}}) = 0$

$\Rightarrow$ Relative velocity

$$= u_{12} = \sqrt{2gH} = \text{Constant}$$

To collide with ball-2, ball-1 has to cover $\sqrt{2}H$ as per the diagram. So, time of collision

$$t = \frac{\sqrt{2}H}{\sqrt{2gH}} = \sqrt{\frac{H}{g}}$$

$\therefore$ Displacement of ball-2 before collision in ground frame

$$AD = h' = \frac{1}{2}at^2 = \frac{1}{2}g\left(\sqrt{\frac{H}{g}}\right)^2 = \frac{H}{2}$$

17. As acceleration is equal to $\frac{dv}{dt}$ = Slope of v-t graph.

$\Rightarrow$ Acceleration at $t = 0$ is $\tan\alpha = 2$ m/s^2 and at $t = 9$ s is $-\tan\beta = -4$ m/s^2

Also, acceleration at $t = 3$ s is zero. Therefore, acceleration-time graph will be as shown

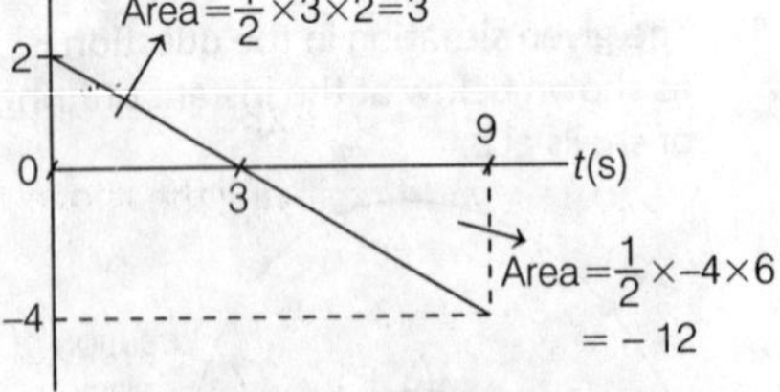

Now, as area of acceleration-time graph is equal to change in velocity, so between $t = 0$ and $t = 9$ s,

Change in velocity = Net area of a-t graph

$$\Rightarrow \quad 0 - v = 3 - 12$$

$$\Rightarrow \quad v = 9 \text{ m/s (initial)}$$

Similarly, between $t = 0$ and $t = 3$ s

$$\Rightarrow \quad v' - v = 3$$

$$\Rightarrow \quad v' = v + 3 = 12 \text{ m/s (maximum)}$$

18. According to the question, the trajectory of the bullet and bird is as shown below.

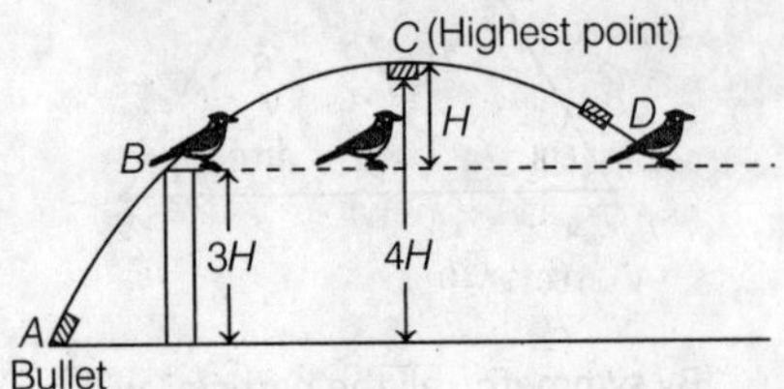

Let maximum height attained by the bullet = $4H$

$\Rightarrow$ Height of tower $= \frac{3}{4} \times 4H = 3H$

As formula for time of ascent $= \sqrt{\frac{2h}{g}}$

For bullet,

Time of flight from A to C

$$= \sqrt{\frac{2(4H)}{g}} = 2T \qquad \text{...(i)}$$

$$\left(\text{Assuming } \sqrt{\frac{2H}{g}} = T\right)$$

Time of flight from B to C = Time of flight from C to D

$$= \sqrt{\frac{2H}{g}} = T \qquad \text{...(ii)}$$

From Eqs. (i) and (ii), time of flight of bullet till it hits the bird $= 3T$ ...(iii)

As bird starts flying when bullet reaches B, so time of flight of bird = time of flight of bullet from C to D

$$= 2T \qquad \text{...(iv)}$$

From Eqs. (iii) and (iv), required ratio is 3 : 2.

19. The given trajectory of the particle is as shown below.

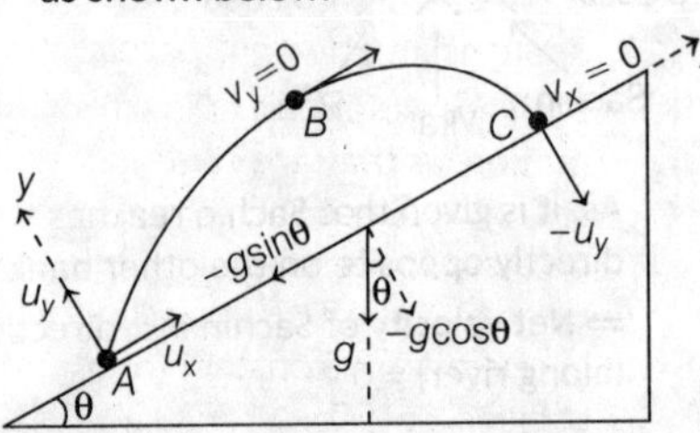

Let initial velocity components at A equal to u_x and u_y as shown.

At B, as y is maximum, therefore

$$\frac{dy}{dt}=v_y=0$$

As particle hits the incline normally at C, therefore $v_x=0$ at C.

For motion from A to C, $s_y=0$

$$\Rightarrow v_y^2-u_y^2=2a_ys_y=0$$

$$\Rightarrow \quad v_y=\pm u_y$$

Out of the two values, $v_y=-u_y$ is acceptable, as clearly direction of motion at C is negative y-direction.

For motion from A to B,

$$T_1=\frac{v_y-u_y}{a_y}$$

$$=\frac{0-u_y}{-g\cos\theta}$$

$$=\frac{u_y}{g\cos\theta} \quad \text{...(i)}$$

Similarly, for B to C

$$T_2=\frac{-u_y-0}{-g\cos\theta}=\frac{u_y}{g\cos\theta} \quad \text{...(ii)}$$

From Eqs. (i) and (ii),

$$T_1=T_2=T \text{ (say)}$$

Now, for A to C, time of motion $=2T$

Using $s_x=v_xt-\frac{1}{2}a_xt^2$, we get

$$\Rightarrow d_1+d_2=0-\frac{1}{2}(-g\sin\theta)(2T)^2$$

$$\Rightarrow d_1+d_2=2g\sin\theta\, T^2 \quad \text{...(iii)}$$

For B to C, $d_2=0-\frac{1}{2}(-g\sin\theta)T^2$

$$\Rightarrow \quad d_2=\frac{1}{2}g\sin\theta T^2 \quad \text{...(iv)}$$

Subtracting Eq. (iv) from Eq. (iii), we get

$$d_1=\frac{3}{2}g\sin\theta T^2 \quad \text{...(v)}$$

Dividing Eq. (v) by Eq. (iv), we get

$$\frac{d_1}{d_2}=3 \text{ or } d_1=3d_2$$

20. Though, speed (v) and acceleration (a) both are variable in uniform circular motion, as they are continuously changing direction but variable acceleration is not caused by variable velocity. Velocity is variable even if acceleration is constant (as in projectile motion).

So, Statement II is not correct explanation of statement I.

21. Let parachutist switches on propeller at position B as shown

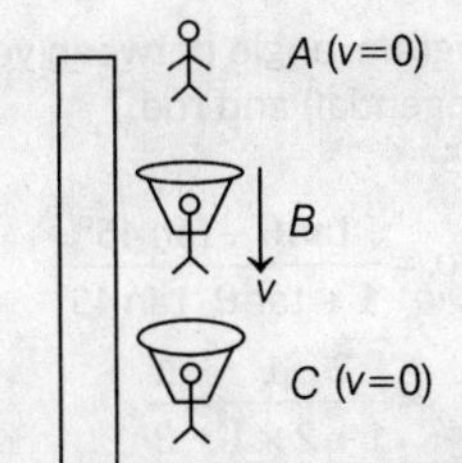

Velocity at B,

$v=u+at=0+10\times4=40$ m/s

Distance moved from A to B,

$$s=\frac{1}{2}\times10\times4^2=80\text{ m}=AB \quad \text{...(i)}$$

For B to C, $a=-v$ (given)

$$\Rightarrow v\frac{dv}{dx}=-v\Rightarrow \Delta v=-\Delta x$$

$$\Rightarrow 0-40=-\Delta x$$

$$\Rightarrow \quad \Delta x=40\text{ m}=BC \quad \text{...(ii)}$$

Height of building

$=AB+BC=80+40=120$ m

[Using Eqs. (i) and (ii)]

22. Position vector of a particle is given as

$$\mathbf{r}=x\hat{\mathbf{i}}+y\hat{\mathbf{j}}$$

Here, $x=3t$, $y=3t(1-t)$

$$\Rightarrow \quad \mathbf{r}=3t\hat{\mathbf{i}}+(3t-3t^2)\hat{\mathbf{j}}$$

Differentiating the above equation w.r.t. time, we get

$$\frac{d\mathbf{r}}{dt}=\mathbf{v}=3\hat{\mathbf{i}}+(3-6t)\hat{\mathbf{j}}$$

Differentiating the above w.r.t. time, we get

$$\mathbf{a}=-6\hat{\mathbf{j}}$$

Dot product of **a** and **v** $=\mathbf{a}\cdot\mathbf{v}=av\cos\theta$

$$\Rightarrow \cos30^\circ=\frac{-6\times(3-6t)}{6\sqrt{3^2+(3-6t)^2}}$$

$$\Rightarrow \quad \frac{\sqrt{3}}{2}=\frac{6t-3}{3\sqrt{1+(2t-1)^2}}$$

$$\Rightarrow \sqrt{3}\cdot\sqrt{1+(2t-1)^2}=2(2t-1)$$

Let $2t-1=p$

$$\Rightarrow \quad \sqrt{3}\cdot\sqrt{1+p^2}=2p$$

Squaring and simplifying the above equation, we get

$$p=\pm\sqrt{3}$$

$$\Rightarrow \quad t=\frac{\sqrt{3}+1}{2}=\frac{2.73}{2}=1.36\text{ s}$$

23. According to the question, the velocity vector of the particle at points P and Q are as follows

$$\mathbf{u}=u\hat{\mathbf{i}}+0\hat{\mathbf{j}}$$

$$\mathbf{v}=0\hat{\mathbf{i}}-v\hat{\mathbf{j}}$$

$$\Rightarrow \quad \mathbf{a}=a_x\hat{\mathbf{i}}+a_y\hat{\mathbf{j}}$$

$$=-g\sin53^\circ\hat{\mathbf{i}}-g\cos53^\circ\hat{\mathbf{j}}$$

$$=-8\hat{\mathbf{i}}-6\hat{\mathbf{j}}$$

By $\mathbf{v}=\mathbf{u}+\mathbf{a}t$

$$-v\hat{\mathbf{j}}=u\hat{\mathbf{i}}-8t\hat{\mathbf{i}}-6t\hat{\mathbf{j}}=(u-8t)\hat{\mathbf{i}}-6t\hat{\mathbf{j}}$$

Comparing the components of $\hat{\mathbf{i}}$ and $\hat{\mathbf{j}}$ on both sides, we get

$$u-8t=0\Rightarrow u=8t \quad \text{...(i)}$$

and $\quad v=6t \quad$ ...(ii)

Dividing Eq. (ii) by Eq. (i), we get

$$\frac{v}{u}=\frac{3}{4}=0.75$$

24. Let us analyse situation w.r.t. river stream. Relative velocity of wind w.r.t. river will be

$$\mathbf{v}_{wr}=\mathbf{v}_w-\mathbf{v}_r=-12\hat{\mathbf{j}}-16\hat{\mathbf{i}}$$

$\Rightarrow v_{wr}=20$ m/s making angle 37° with shore as shown

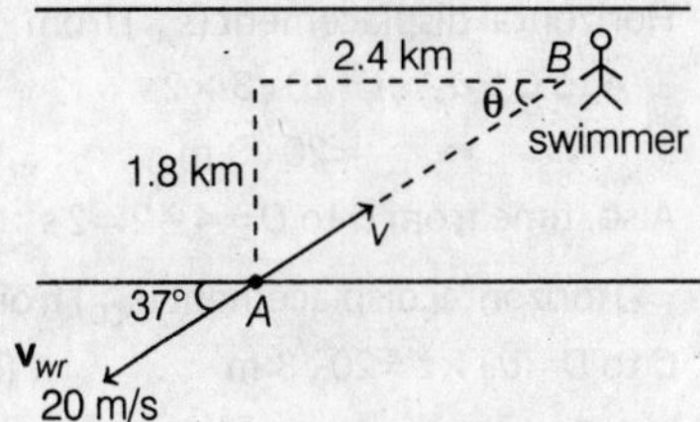

$$\text{As } \theta=\tan^{-1}\left(\frac{1.8}{2.4}\right)$$

$$=\tan^{-1}\left(\frac{3}{4}\right)=37^\circ$$

i.e. Line AB also makes 37° with shore, so wind is along AB. Therefore, to reach swimmer helicopter should fly from A to B as shown. Net velocity of helicopter, $v=80-20=60$ m/s

As, distance $AB=\sqrt{1.8^2+2.4^2}=3$ km

$$\text{Time of flight}=\frac{AB}{v}=\frac{3000}{60}=50\text{ s}$$

25. Initial velocity components of the ball are as shown

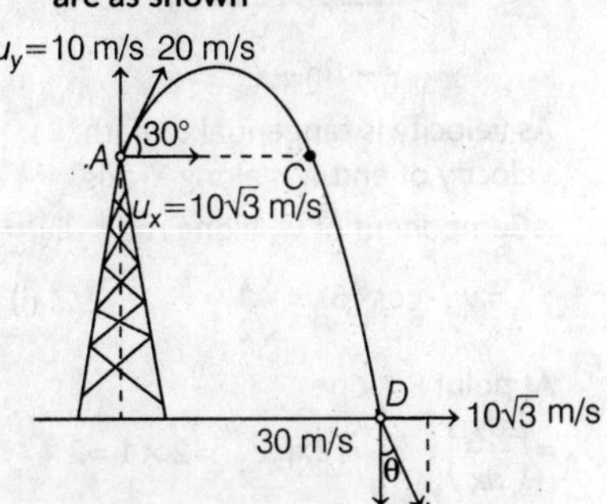

For motion from A to D,

$$s_y = u_y t + \frac{1}{2} a_y t^2$$

$$\Rightarrow \quad -40 = 10t + \frac{1}{2}(-10)t^2$$

$$\Rightarrow t^2 - 2t - 8 = 0$$

$$\Rightarrow (t-4)(t+2) = 0 \Rightarrow t = 4, -2$$

As, t can't be negative, $t = 4$

$\Rightarrow$ At point $D, v_y = u_y + a_y t$

$$= 10 - 10(4) = -30 \text{ m/s}$$

$$\Rightarrow \quad \tan\theta = \left|\frac{v_x}{v_y}\right|$$

$$= \frac{10\sqrt{3}}{30} = \frac{1}{\sqrt{3}}$$

$$\Rightarrow \quad \theta = \frac{\pi}{6} \Rightarrow x = 6 \quad \text{... (i)}$$

Now, time of motion from A to C

$$= \frac{2u\sin\theta}{g} = \frac{2 \times 20 \times \frac{1}{2}}{10} = 2 \text{ s}$$

Horizontal displacement (s_{AC}) from A to $C = u_x \times t = 10\sqrt{3} \times 2$

$$= 20\sqrt{3} \text{ m} \quad \text{...(ii)}$$

Also, time from C to $D = 4 - 2 = 2$ s

$\Rightarrow$ Horizontal displacement (s_{CD}) from C to $D = u_x \times t = 20\sqrt{3}$ m ...(iii)

From Eqs. (ii) and (iii), $\frac{s_{AC}}{s_{CD}} = y = 1$ ...(iv)

$\therefore$ From Eqs. (i) and (iv),

$$x + y = 6 + 1 = 7$$

Qualifier 3 (Laws of Motion)

1. Angle made by rod with X-axis

$$= \tan^{-1}\left(\frac{BC}{AC}\right) = 45°$$

As velocity is tangential to path, velocity of end A is along X-axis.

$\therefore$ Component of v_A along rod

$$= v_A \cdot \cos 45° = \frac{v_A}{\sqrt{2}} \quad \text{... (i)}$$

At point B, slope

$$= \left(\frac{dy}{dx}\right)_{\text{at } x=1} = 2x|_{x=1} = 2 \times 1 = 2$$

$$\Rightarrow \quad \tan\theta = 2$$

From diagram, angle between velocity of B (tangential) and rod,

$$\alpha = \theta - 45°$$

$$\Rightarrow \quad \tan\alpha = \frac{\tan\theta - \tan 45°}{1 + \tan\theta \cdot \tan 45°}$$

$$= \frac{2-1}{1 + 2 \times 1} = \frac{1}{3}$$

$$\therefore \quad \cos\alpha = \frac{3}{\sqrt{10}}$$

$\therefore$ Component of v_B along rod

$$= v_B \cos\alpha = \frac{3v_B}{\sqrt{10}} \quad \text{... (ii)}$$

As for a rigid body, components of velocities of any points along line joining the points are equal,

From Eqs. (i) and (ii), we get

$$\frac{v_A}{\sqrt{2}} = \frac{3v_B}{\sqrt{10}} \Rightarrow \frac{v_A}{v_B} = \frac{3}{\sqrt{5}} = 1.32$$

2. By symmetry, forces in string and spring are equal (say F). Using Lami's theorem,

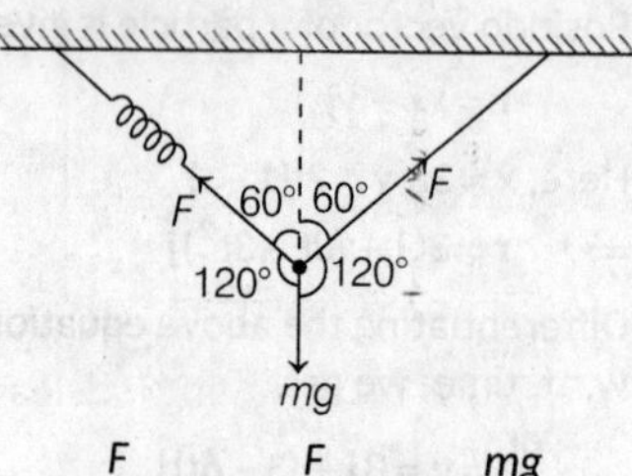

$$\frac{F}{\sin 120°} = \frac{F}{\sin 120°} = \frac{mg}{\sin 120°}$$

$$\Rightarrow \quad F = mg$$

Just after the spring is cut, acceleration is tangential,

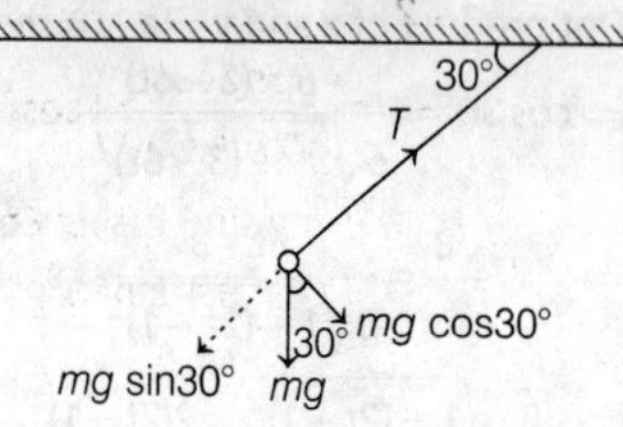

$$a_1 = \frac{\text{Tangential force}}{\text{Mass}}$$

$$= \frac{mg\cos 30°}{m} = \frac{\sqrt{3}g}{2}$$

Just after string is cut, spring force remains unchanged. So acceleration,

$$a_2 = \frac{\text{Net force}}{\text{Mass}} = \frac{mg}{m} = g$$

$$\therefore \quad \frac{a_1}{a_2} = \frac{\sqrt{3}g}{2} \times \frac{1}{g} = \frac{\sqrt{3}}{2}$$

3. As the block is at rest, net force on the block is zero,

$\Rightarrow$ According to FBD, $N = mg$

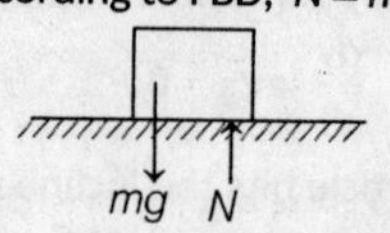

Statement-II is always true by Newton's third law.

Note N and mg are not action-reaction pair.

4. As leftward pull is greater, so system will accelerate left

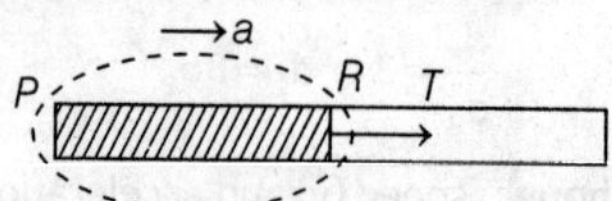

For 6 kg block By $F = ma$, we get

$$20 - T = 6a \quad \text{...(i)}$$

For 4 kg block, we get

$$T - 10 = 4a \quad \text{...(ii)}$$

Solving Eqs. (i) and (ii), we get

$$\therefore \quad a = 1 \text{ and } T = 14 \text{ N}$$

$\Rightarrow$ Reading $= T = 14$ N

5. Linear mass density varies with x as shown in graph.

Mass of the rope, $m = \int \lambda \cdot dx$

$$= \text{Area under the graph}$$

$$= \frac{1}{2}(\lambda_0 + 2\lambda_0)L = \frac{3\lambda_0 L}{2}$$

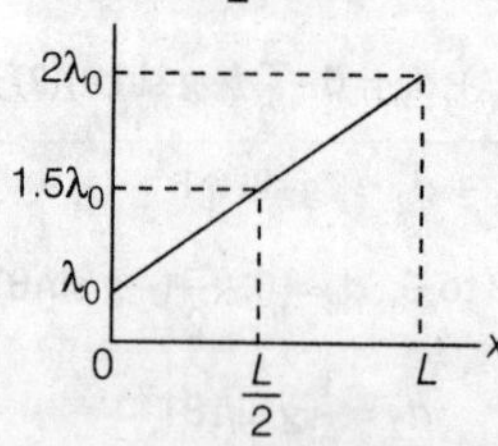

Therefore, acceleration of rope,

$$a = \frac{F}{m} = \frac{2F}{3\lambda_0 L}$$

To find tension at mid-point (say R), we draw FBD of PR as shown

Mass of PR, m' = Area under graph between P and $R = \frac{1}{2}(\lambda_0 + 1.5\lambda_0)\frac{L}{2}$

$$= \frac{5\lambda_0 L}{8}$$

Therefore,

$$T = m'a = \frac{5\lambda_0 L}{8} \times \frac{2F}{3\lambda_0 L} = \frac{5F}{12}$$

6. From FBD of the block, horizontal acceleration, $a = \frac{F}{m} = \frac{mg}{m} = g$

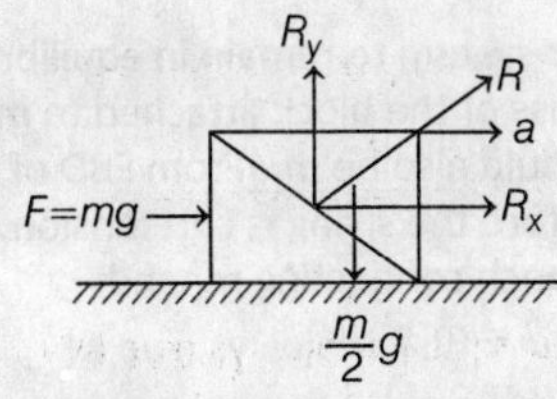

Let contact force by A on B has components R_x and R_y as shown. For horizontal direction, using $F = ma$, we get

$$R_x = \frac{m}{2}g$$

For vertical direction, $R_y = \frac{m}{2}g$

Therefore, net contact force $= R$

$$= \sqrt{R_x^2 + R_y^2} = \frac{mg}{\sqrt{2}}$$

7. Various forces acting on the system are shown below

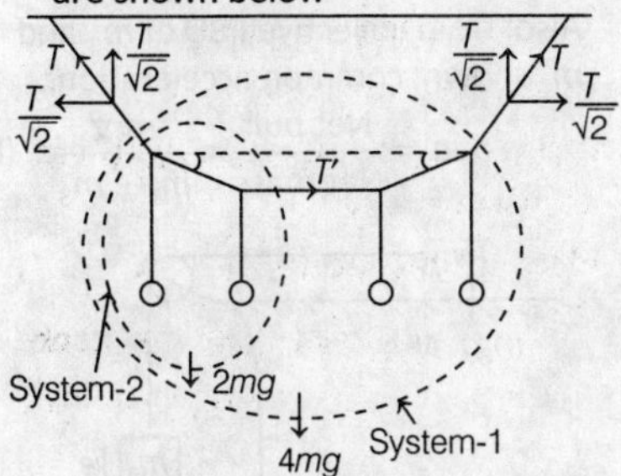

For vertical equilibrium of system-1,

$$\frac{2T}{\sqrt{2}} = 4mg \Rightarrow \sqrt{2}T = 4mg \quad \text{...(i)}$$

For horizontal equilibrium of system-2,

$$\frac{T}{\sqrt{2}} = T' \quad \text{... (ii)}$$

Dividing Eq. (ii) by Eq. (i), we get

$$T' = 2mg$$

8. From FBD of block A, in direction perpendicular to the incline.

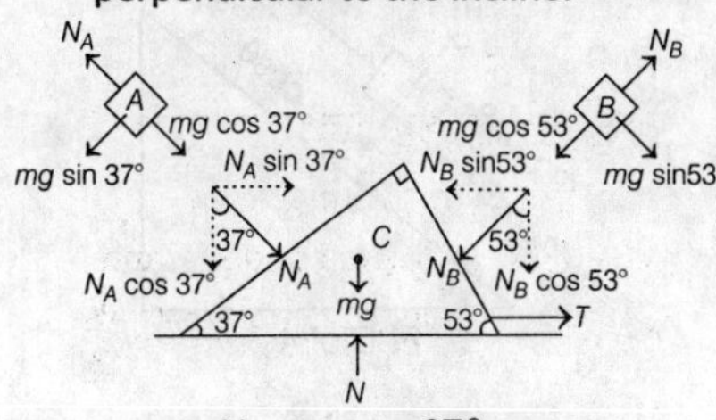

$$N_A = mg\cos 37°$$

Similarly, from FBD of block B,

$$N_B = mg\cos 53°$$

From FBD of wedge C, resultant of normal forces in horizontal direction is

$$N_H = N_A \sin 37° - N_B \sin 53°$$
$$= mg\cos 37° \sin 37° - mg\cos 53° \sin 53°$$
$$= mg\left(\frac{4}{5}\right)\left(\frac{3}{5}\right) - mg\left(\frac{3}{5}\right)\left(\frac{4}{5}\right) = 0$$

Therefore, the wedge does not have tendency to move. So, both tensions in rope and friction from ground will be zero.

From FBD of the wedge, in vertical direction, as the wedge is in equilibrium,

Upward force = Downward force

$$\Rightarrow N = N_A\cos 37° + N_B \cos 53° + mg$$
$$= mg\cos^2 37° + mg\cos^2 53° + mg$$
$$= mg\cos^2 37° + mg\sin^2 37° + mg$$
$$= 2mg$$

Therefore,

$$|\mathbf{N} + 2\mathbf{T} - 3\mathbf{f}| = |2mg\,\mathbf{j} + 0 - 0| = 2mg$$

9. Acceleration of wedge,

$$a = \frac{dv}{dt} = \frac{d(kt^2\hat{\mathbf{i}})}{dt} = 2kt\,\hat{\mathbf{i}}$$

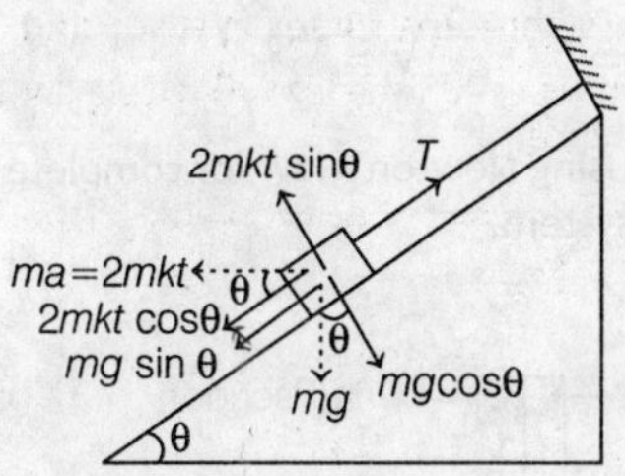

From FBD of block, when block leaves contact

$$2mkt\sin\theta = mg\cos\theta$$

$$\Rightarrow \quad t = \frac{mg\cos\theta}{2mk\sin\theta} \quad \text{... (i)}$$

At this instant, along the incline,

$$T = 2mkt\cos\theta + mg\sin\theta$$
$$= 2mk\left(\frac{mg\cos\theta}{2mk\sin\theta}\right)\cos\theta + mg\sin\theta \text{ [using Eq. (i)]}$$
$$= mg\left(\frac{\cos^2\theta + \sin^2\theta}{\sin\theta}\right)$$
$$= \frac{mg}{\sin\theta} = mg\,\text{cosec}\,\theta$$

10. From FBD of pulley, tension T in string is given by

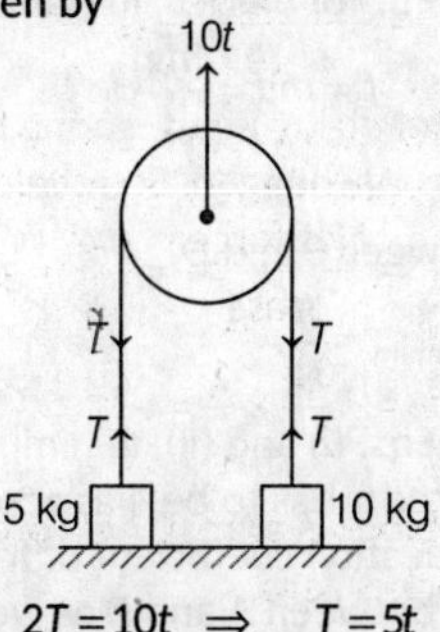

$$2T = 10t \Rightarrow T = 5t$$

For lifting of 5 kg block, tension should just exceed its weight

$$\Rightarrow \quad T = 5t \approx 50 \Rightarrow t \approx 10 \text{ s}$$

Similarly, block of 10 kg lifts at $t = 20$ s

In between, the situation is as shown.

From FBD, acceleration of 5 kg block,

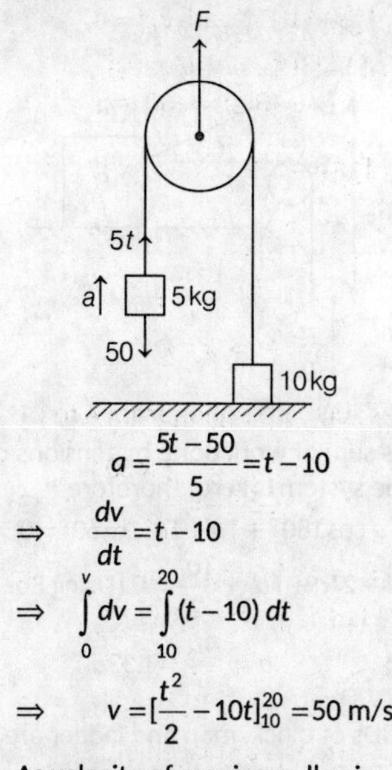

$$a = \frac{5t - 50}{5} = t - 10$$

$$\Rightarrow \quad \frac{dv}{dt} = t - 10$$

$$\Rightarrow \quad \int_0^v dv = \int_{10}^{20} (t - 10)\,dt$$

$$\Rightarrow \quad v = \left[\frac{t^2}{2} - 10t\right]_{10}^{20} = 50 \text{ m/s}$$

As velocity of moving pulley is average of velocity of ends, therefore

$$v_{\text{pulley}} = \frac{50 + 0}{2} = 25 \text{ m/s}$$

11. Let tension in strings connecting A and B is T. From FBD of block A and pulley to which it is attached, For vertical equilibrium, we get

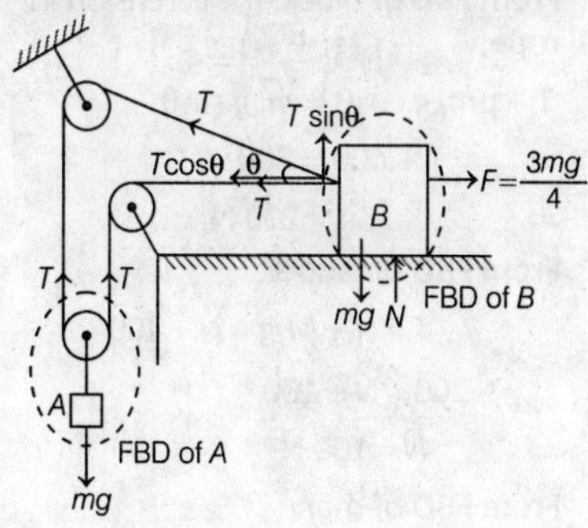

$$2T = mg \Rightarrow T = \frac{mg}{2} \quad \text{...(i)}$$

From FBD of B, for horizontal equilibrium, we get

$$T + T\cos\theta = \frac{3}{4}mg$$

Substituting value of T from Eq. (i), we get

$$\Rightarrow \frac{mg}{2} + \frac{mg}{2}\cos\theta = \frac{3}{4}mg$$

$\Rightarrow \quad \cos\theta = \frac{1}{2} \Rightarrow \theta = 60°$

Just after F is withdrawn, the block will accelerate as shown. Lets assume tension in string connected to A be T'. From FBD of pulley connected to block A, $T' = 2T$ ... (ii)

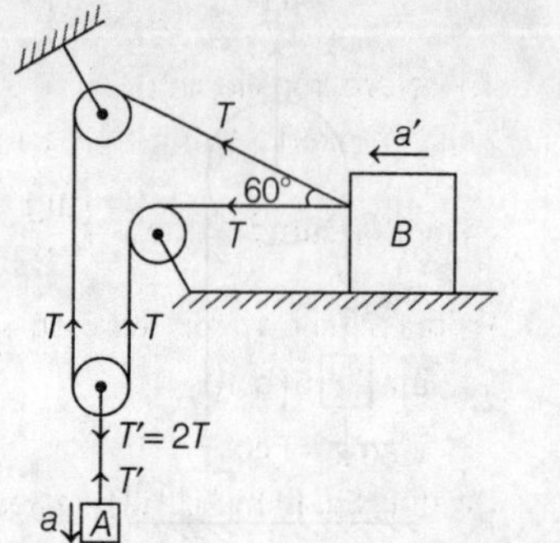

As sum of work done by tensions on the system is zero, therefore

$T' a\cos 180° + Ta' + Ta' \cos 60° = 0$

$\Rightarrow -2Ta + Ta' + \frac{Ta'}{2} = 0$ [Using Eq. (ii)]

$\Rightarrow \quad a' = \frac{4a}{3} = 1.33a$

12. FBDs of block, man and ladder are as shown.

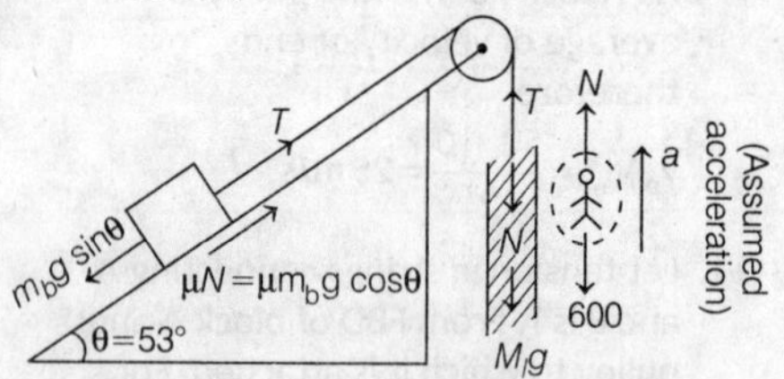

From FBD of block, if T is tension in rope,

$T + \mu m_b g \cos\theta = m_b g \sin\theta$

$\Rightarrow \quad T + 600 = 800$

$\Rightarrow \quad T = 200$ N

From FBD of ladder,

$T = N + M_l g = N + 100$

$200 = N + 100$

$\Rightarrow \quad N = 100$ N

From FBD of man,

$N - M_m g = M_m \times a$

$\Rightarrow 100 - 600 = 60a$

$\Rightarrow \quad a = -\frac{25}{3}$ m/s^2

13. As block A is imparted velocity u_0 initially but block B is at rest, so string will become loose. But as B is freely falling and speeding down, there will come an instant at which displacements of both blocks will become equal in magnitude and string will become taut. Let it happens after time t,

i.e. $\quad s_A = s_B$

$\Rightarrow \quad u_0 t = \frac{1}{2} g t^2$

$\Rightarrow \quad t = \frac{2u_0}{g}$

Velocity of block B just before string become taut,

$$v = u + at = 0 + g\left(\frac{2u_0}{g}\right) = 2u_0$$

As the string becomes taut the two blocks acquire common speed (say v').

Now, by conservation of magnitude of momentum,

$mu_0 + m(2u_0) = mv' + mv'$

$\Rightarrow \quad 2mv' = 3mu_0$

$\Rightarrow \quad v' = \frac{3u_0}{2}$

14. Using Newton's law for complete system,

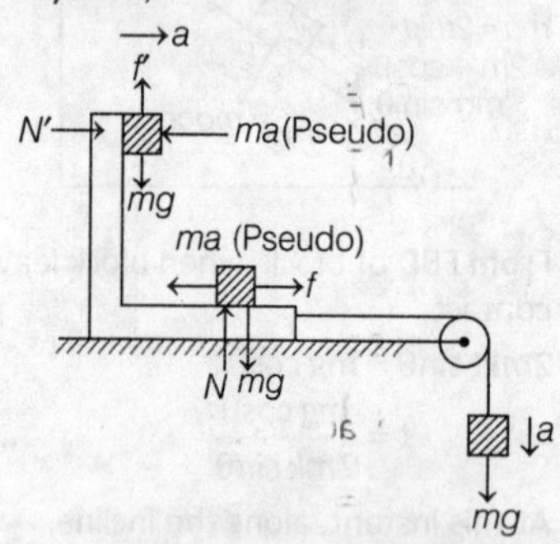

$$a = \frac{\text{Net pull}}{\text{Net mass}} = \frac{mg}{m + m + m + m} = \frac{g}{4}$$

From FBD of block A, in frame of D,

$f' = mg$

$N' = ma = \frac{mg}{4}$

$\therefore$ Between A and D,

$\mu_{\text{minimum}} = \frac{f'}{N'} = 4$ ... (i)

From FBD of block B, in frame of D,

$f = ma = \frac{mg}{4}$

$N = mg$

$\therefore$ Between B and D,

$\mu_{\text{minimum}} = \frac{f}{N} = \frac{1}{4}$ ...(ii)

From Eqs. (i) and (ii), minimum required μ has to be 4 as according to the question coefficient of friction is same between A and D as well as B and D.

15. For system to remain in equilibrium mass of the block attached to m_3 should also be m_1. From FBD of m_1 before the string is cut, tension in branch connecting m_1 and m_2, $T = m_1 g$

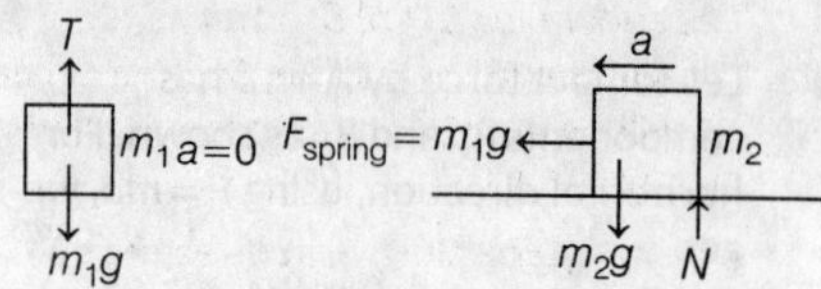

Just after the string connecting the blocks on table is cut, FBD of m_2 is shown above.

As, spring force (equal to T) cannot change suddenly due to cutting of string, acceleration of m_2 will be

$a = \frac{m_1 g}{m_2}$ ... (i)

Also, from collective FBD of m_3 and m_1 shown, common acceleration,

$a' = \frac{\text{Net pull}}{\text{Net mass}} = \frac{m_1 g}{m_1 + m_3}$ ... (ii)

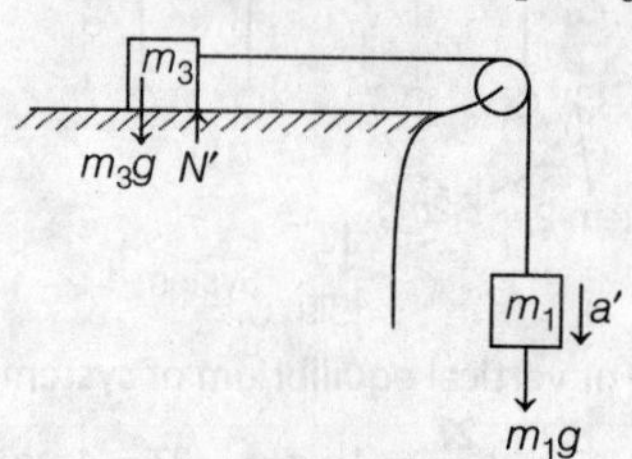

As it is given that, $a = 2a'$

$\Rightarrow \quad \frac{m_1 g}{m_2} = \frac{2m_1 g}{m_1 + m_3}$

[using Eqs. (i) and (ii)]

$\Rightarrow \quad 2m_2 = m_1 + m_3 \Rightarrow m_2 = m_3$

16. FBD of the two blocks are as shown.

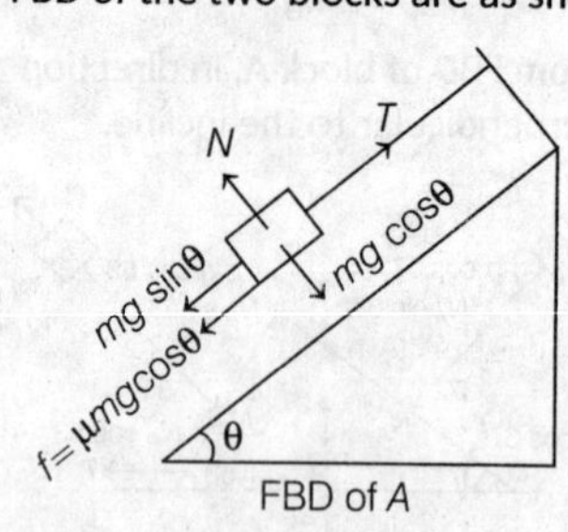

FBD of A

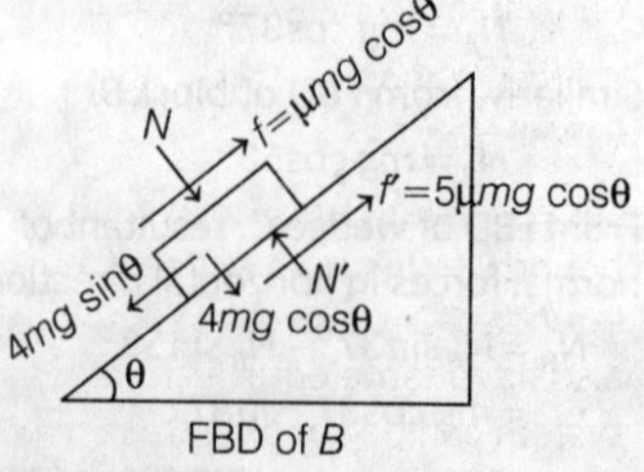

FBD of B

From FBD of A, in direction perpendicular to incline,

$$N = mg\cos\theta \quad \text{... (i)}$$

$\Rightarrow$ Friction on block B by block A, f

$$= \mu N = \mu mg\cos\theta \quad \text{...(ii)}$$

As shown in FBD of B, it has tendency to slip down the incline. So, friction on A will be equal and opposite as shown in FBD of A.

From FBD of block B, in direction perpendicular to incline,

$$N' = N + 4mg\cos\theta$$
$$= 5mg\cos\theta \quad \text{[From Eq. (i)]}$$

Therefore, friction from incline on B,

$$f' = \mu N' = 5\mu mg\cos\theta$$

Thus, along the incline, for B,

$$4mg\sin\theta = f + f'$$
$$= \mu mg\cos\theta + 5\mu mg\cos\theta$$

$\Rightarrow \quad 4\sin\theta = 6\mu\cos\theta$

$\Rightarrow \quad \tan\theta = \frac{3}{2}\mu = \frac{3}{2}\times\frac{2}{3} = 1$

$\Rightarrow \quad \theta = 45°$

17. For the shown system of blocks m_1 and m_2 connected by string, by $F = ma$

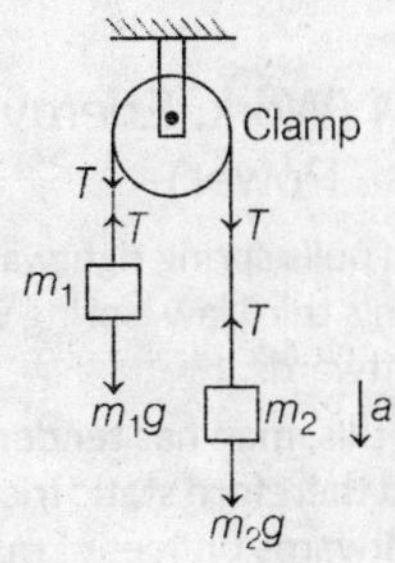

For m_1, $T - m_1g = m_1a$ ...(i)

For m_2, $m_2g - T = m_2a$ ...(ii)

(Assuming $m_2 > m_1$)

Solving Eqs. (i) and (ii), we get

$$T = \frac{2m_1m_2g}{m_1 + m_2} \quad \text{... (iii)}$$

Therefore, downward pulling force on ceiling pulley $= 2T = \frac{4m_1m_2g}{m_1 + m_2}$ ...(iv)

[Using Eq. (iii)]

So, the system of two blocks is equivalent to a single block of mass $\left(\frac{4m_1m_2}{m_1 + m_2}\right)$.

Let equivalent mass of system in boundary- 1 is x. As system in boundary-2 is also the same, it will also have same equivalent mass. So, system can be simplified as shown.

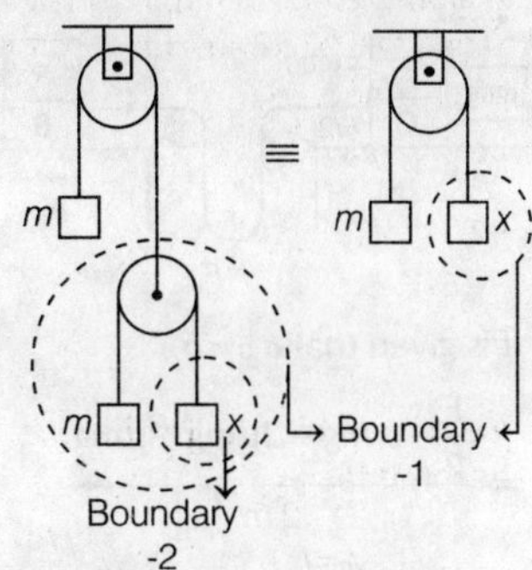

For system in boundary-1, by concept of equivalent mass

$$x = \frac{4mx}{m + x} \Rightarrow x = 3m$$

Therefore, using Eq. (iv), downward pulling force on clamp

$$= \frac{4\times m\times 3m\times g}{m + 3m} = 3mg$$

18. As, tension in strings equal to applied external force on string. Forces on A and B will be as shown.

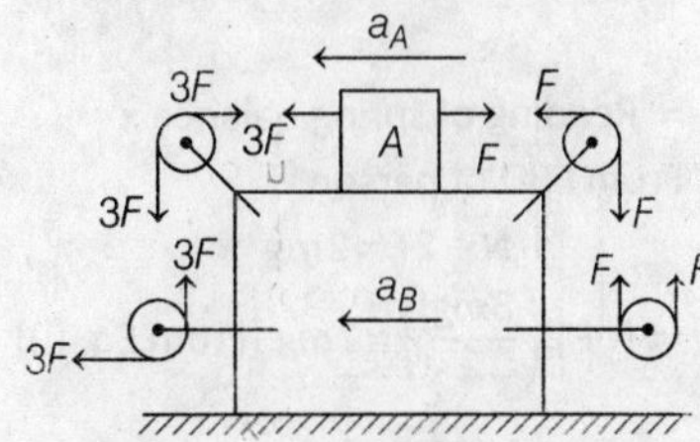

Therefore, acceleration of A,

$$a_A = \frac{3F - F}{m} = \frac{2F}{m}$$

Acceleration of B,

$$a_B = \frac{3F - 3F + F}{m} = \frac{F}{m}$$

So, acceleration of A relative to B,

$$a_{AB} = a_A - a_B = \frac{F}{m}$$

With respect to B, using

$$s = ut + \frac{1}{2}at^2, \text{ we get}$$

$$L = 0 + \frac{1}{2}\times\frac{F}{m}\times t^2$$

$$\Rightarrow \quad t = \sqrt{\frac{2Lm}{F}}$$

$\therefore$ Displacement of block B in same time,

$$s_B = u_Bt + \frac{1}{2}a_Bt^2$$

$$= 0 + \frac{1}{2}\times\frac{F}{m}\times\left(\sqrt{\frac{2Lm}{F}}\right)^2 = L$$

19. Under influence of greater centrifugal force, block B has tendency to move right and so A has tendency to move left. So, frictions on A and B will be acting as shown.

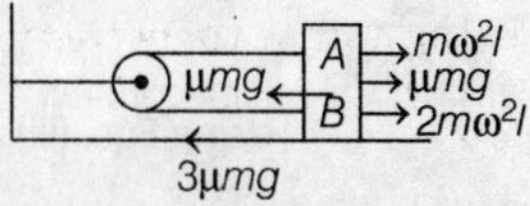

Therefore, for slipping

$$2m\omega^2 l - m\omega^2 l > 3\mu mg + \mu mg + \mu mg$$

$$\Rightarrow m\omega^2 l > 5\mu mg \Rightarrow \omega > \sqrt{\frac{5\mu g}{l}}$$

20. From FBD shown for first case,

$$m\omega^2 r = T\sin\theta \quad \text{...(i)}$$

$$mg = T\cos\theta \quad \text{...(ii)}$$

Dividing Eq. (i) by Eq. (ii), we get

$$\frac{\omega^2 r}{g} = \tan\theta$$

$$\Rightarrow \quad \omega = \sqrt{\frac{g\tan\theta}{r}} = \sqrt{\frac{g}{l\cos\theta}} \quad \text{... (iii)}$$

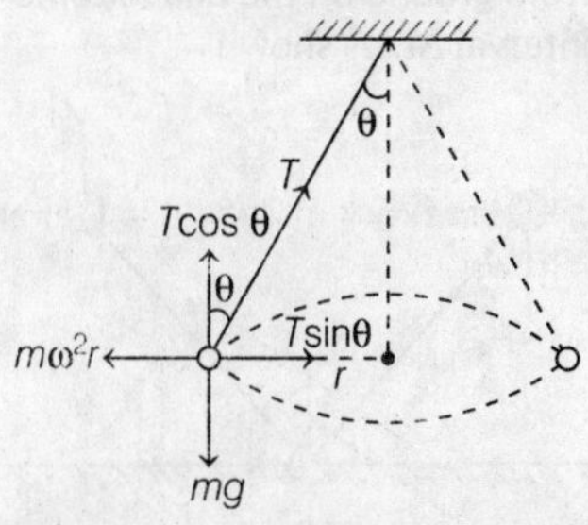

From the given diagram, direction of resultant of mg and pseudo force (ma) is as shown. Therefore, $\tan 45° = \frac{ma}{mg}$

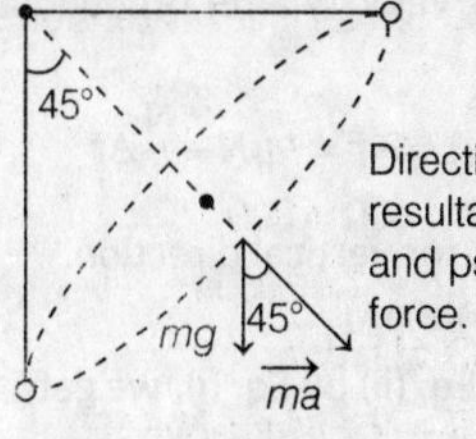

$\Rightarrow \quad a = g$

$\therefore$ Resultant of mg and ma

$$= \sqrt{(mg)^2 + (ma)^2}$$
$$= \sqrt{2}\, mg$$

$\therefore$ Effective gravity $= \sqrt{2}\, g = g'$

Doing similar analysis as done for pendulum attached to ceiling, we get

Angular speed,

$$\omega' = \sqrt{\frac{g'}{l\cos 45°}}$$

$$= \sqrt{\frac{\sqrt{2}\, g}{l\times\frac{1}{\sqrt{2}}}} = \sqrt{\frac{2g}{l}} \quad \text{... (iv)}$$

As time periods of the two pendulums are equal, angular speeds should also be equal. Thus, $\omega = \omega'$

$$\Rightarrow \sqrt{\frac{g}{l\cos\theta}} = \sqrt{\frac{2g}{l}}$$

[Using Eqs. (iii) and (iv)]

$$\Rightarrow \cos\theta = \frac{1}{2} \Rightarrow \theta = 60°$$

21. It is given that, F at $t_1 = F$ at t_2

$$\Rightarrow \left(\frac{dp}{dt}\right)_{t_1} = \left(\frac{dp}{dt}\right)_{t_2}$$

$$\Rightarrow 16t = 8 \Rightarrow t = \frac{1}{2}\text{ s}$$

$$\text{As, } p\left(\text{at } t = \frac{1}{2}\text{ s}\right) = 8\left(\frac{1}{2}\right)^2 = 2$$

Therefore, required average force,

$$F_{av} = \frac{\Delta p}{\Delta t} = \frac{2}{1/2} = 4$$

22. Let normal force N and friction f act from ground on the ball for time interval Δt, as shown

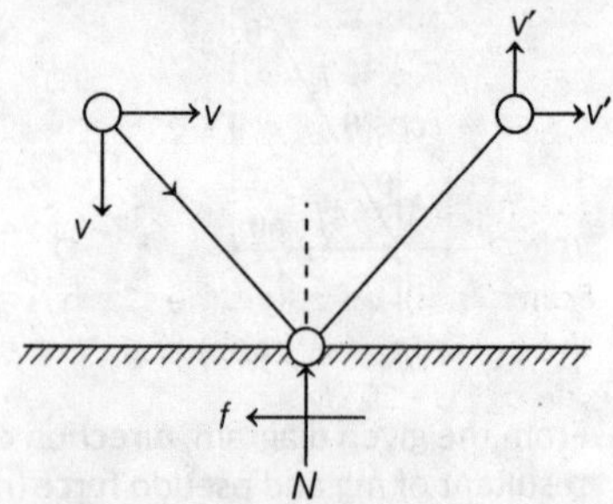

As $\Delta \mathbf{p} = \mathbf{F}\Delta t$, for horizontal direction, assuming velocity after rebound as $v'\hat{\mathbf{i}} + v'\hat{\mathbf{j}}$

$$m(v' - v) = -f = -\mu N - \frac{N}{2}\Delta t \quad \text{...(i)}$$

Similarly, for vertical direction,

$$m(v' + v) = N\Delta t \quad \text{... (ii)}$$

Dividing Eq. (ii) by Eq. (i), we get

$$\frac{v' + v}{v' - v} = -2$$

$$\Rightarrow v' = \frac{v}{3}$$

$\therefore$ Speed just after rebound

$$= \sqrt{v'^2 + v'^2}$$

$$= \sqrt{2}v' = \frac{\sqrt{2}v}{3}$$

$$\Rightarrow x = 3$$

23. From FBD of pulley, $2T = F$

$$\Rightarrow T = \frac{F}{2}$$

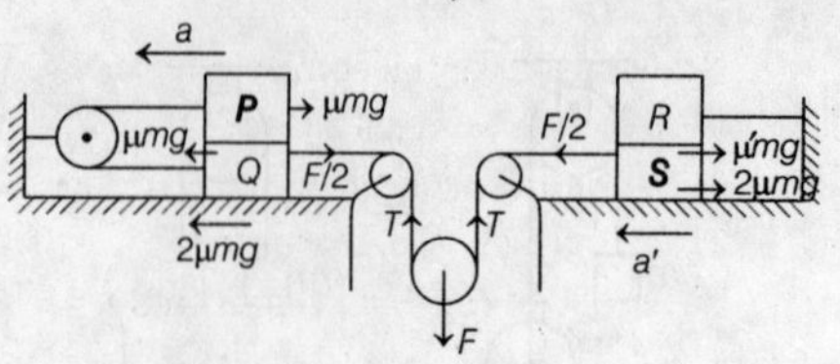

It is given that $a_p = a_s$

$$\Rightarrow \frac{\frac{F}{2} - \mu mg - 2\mu mg - \mu mg}{2m}$$

$$= \frac{\frac{F}{2} - \mu mg - 2\mu mg}{m}$$

$$\Rightarrow \frac{F}{2} = 4\mu mg = F - 6\mu mg$$

$$\Rightarrow F = 4\mu mg = x^2\mu mg \text{ (given)}$$

$$\therefore x = 2$$

24. Let mass of lift and man be m and $2m$. From combined FBD, as acceleration is zero, $4T = 3mg$

$$\Rightarrow \text{Tension in string, } T = \frac{3mg}{4} \quad \text{...(i)}$$

= Reading of spring balance x

From FBD of person,

$$N + 2T = 2mg$$

$$\Rightarrow N + 2\left(\frac{3mg}{4}\right) = 2mg \text{ [From Eq. (i)]}$$

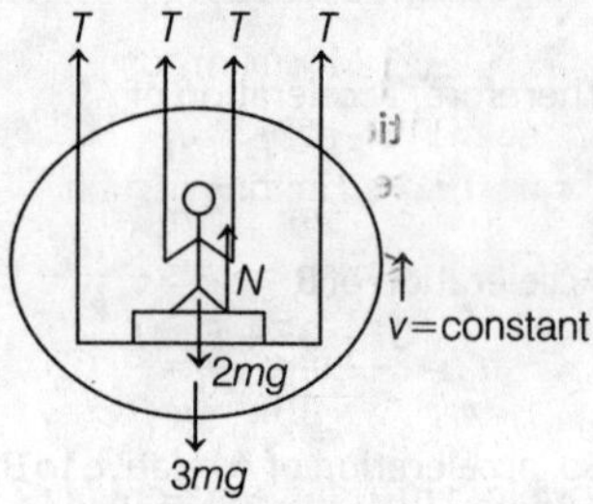

$$\Rightarrow N = \frac{mg}{2} = \text{Reading of weighing machine } y \text{ ... (ii)}$$

$$\Rightarrow \frac{x}{y} = \frac{3mg}{4} \times \frac{2}{mg} = 1.5$$

25. FBDs of the two particles are as shown.

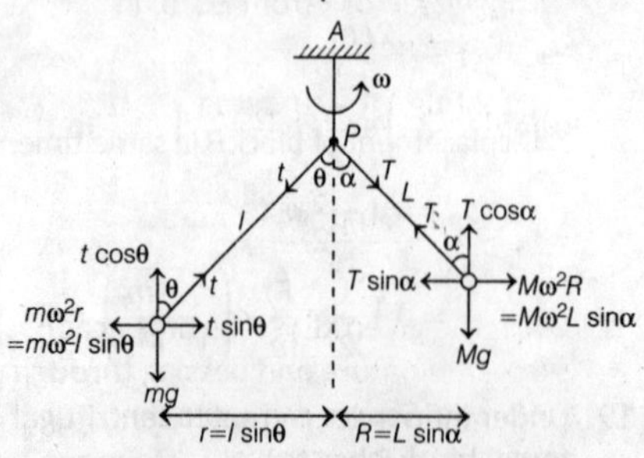

From FBD of m, by balancing forces in horizontal and vertical,

$$t\sin\theta = m\omega^2 l\sin\theta \Rightarrow t = m\omega^2 l \quad \text{... (i)}$$

$$\text{and } t\cos\theta = mg \quad \text{... (ii)}$$

Similarly, for M,

$$T = M\omega^2 L \quad \text{... (iii)}$$

$$\text{and } T\cos\alpha = Mg \quad \text{... (iv)}$$

Also, for rod to be vertical, horizontal components of tensions at P should be equal.

$$\Rightarrow t\sin\theta = T\sin\alpha \quad \text{... (v)}$$

Squaring and subtracting Eq. (iv) from Eq. (ii), we get

$$t^2\cos^2\theta - T^2\cos^2\alpha = (m^2 - M^2)g^2 \quad \text{... (vi)}$$

Squaring Eq. (v), we get

$$\Rightarrow t^2\sin^2\theta - T^2\sin^2\alpha = 0 \quad \text{... (vii)}$$

Adding Eqs. (vi) and (vii), we get

$$t^2 - T^2 = (m^2 - M^2)g^2$$

$$\Rightarrow m^2\omega^4 l^2 - M^2\omega^4 L^2 = (m^2 - M^2)g^2$$

$$\Rightarrow \omega^4 = \frac{(m^2 - M^2)g^2}{(m^2 l^2 - M^2 L^2)}$$

$$= \left(\frac{4-2}{16-2}\right)100 = \frac{100}{7} \Rightarrow x = 7$$

Qualifier 4 (Work, Energy and Power)

1. As man pulls spring rightwards, by Newton's third law, spring will pull man leftwards.

Due to this, man has tendency to slip left and therefore static friction will act rightwards on feet of man. As velocity of system is constant or acceleration is zero, net force on man is zero.

$$\Rightarrow F = f$$

$$\therefore \text{Work by friction} = fs\cos\theta$$

$$= Fvt\cos 180° = -Fvt$$

2. Let (p, q) are coordinates of particle A of mass m as shown in figure. So, components of velocity of the particle will be

$$\dot{p} = \frac{dp}{dt} = v_P \quad \text{...(i)}$$

$$\dot{q} = \frac{dq}{dt} = v_Q \quad \text{... (ii)}$$

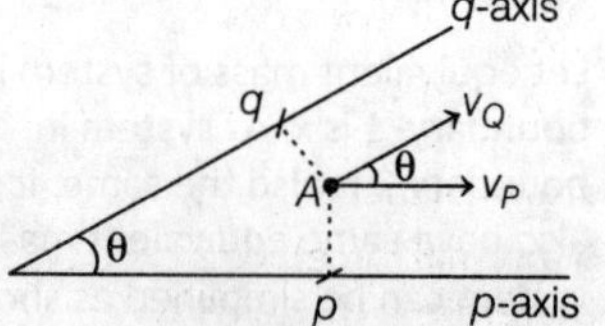

By parallelogram law of vector addition, velocity v of the particle is given as

$$v = v_P^2 + v_Q^2 + 2v_P v_Q \cos\theta$$

$$v = \dot{p}^2 + \dot{q}^2 + 2\dot{p}\,\dot{q}\cos\theta$$

[using Eqs. (i) and (ii)]

$\Rightarrow$ Kinetic energy $= \frac{1}{2}mv^2$

$$= \frac{1}{2}m(\dot{p}^2 + \dot{q}^2 + 2\dot{p}\dot{q}\cos\theta) = K$$

So, quantity K represent kinetic energy of the particle.

Let initial momentum is p, so K will be

$$K = \frac{p^2}{2m} \quad \text{... (iii)}$$

If momentum is increased by 100%. It means momentum is doubled, so new kinetic energy is given by,

$$K' = \frac{(2p)^2}{2m} = 4 \times \frac{p^2}{2m} = 4K \quad \text{... (iv)}$$

[using Eq. (iii)]

$\Rightarrow$ Percentage increase in kinetic energy

$$= \frac{K' - K}{K} \times 100 = \frac{4K - K}{K} \times 100$$

[using Eq. (iv)]

$= 300\%$

3. When the chain in pulled slowly, work done by person will go into increasing potential energy only as kinetic energy is not changing.

$$\Rightarrow \quad W = \int F dx = \Delta PE \quad \text{... (i)}$$

But when person is applying four times the force, a part of work done by person will increase kinetic energy of the chain as well

$$\Rightarrow \quad W' = \Delta KE + \Delta PE$$

$$\Rightarrow 4\int F dx = \Delta KE + \Delta PE \quad \text{... (ii)}$$

From Eqs. (i)and (ii),

$$\Rightarrow \quad 4W = \Delta KE + W \Rightarrow \Delta KE = 3W$$

4. Consider any position C during motion and small displacement ds for the block as shown in figure

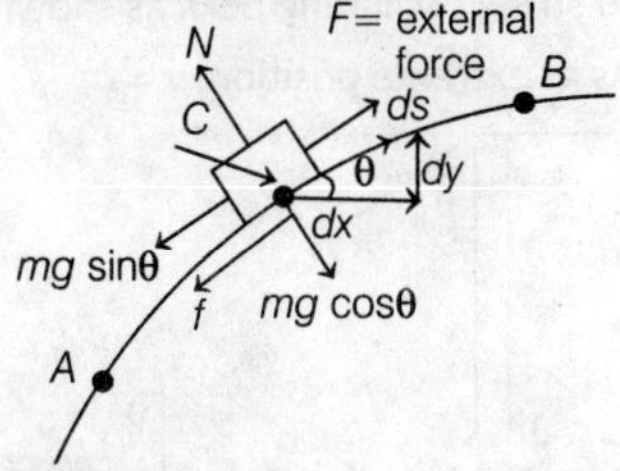

From FBD at C,

N (normal force) $= mg\cos\theta$ and therefore f (friction)

$$= \mu N = \mu\, mg\cos\theta \quad \text{... (i)}$$

Now, as tangential component of mg is opposing external agent.

$\Rightarrow$ Work done by external force against gravity (i.e. increase in potential energy) $= \int mg\sin\theta\, ds$

$$= \int mg.\frac{dy}{ds}ds = mg\int_{y_A}^{y_B} dy$$

$$= mg(y_B - y_A) \quad \text{... (ii)}$$

Also, work done against friction (i.e. heat dissipated)

$$= \int f\,ds = \int \mu mg\cos\theta\, ds$$

[from Eq (i)]

$$= \int \mu\, mg.\frac{dx}{ds}.ds$$

$$= \int_{x_A}^{x_B} \mu\, mg\, dx = \mu\, mg(x_B - x_A)$$

$$= \mu\, mg(y_B^2 - y_A^2)$$

As it is given that, Increase in potential energy = Heat dissipated

$$\Rightarrow \; mg(y_B - y_A) = \mu\, mg(y_B^2 - y_A^2)$$

$$\Rightarrow \quad y_B + y_A = \frac{1}{\mu}$$

5. The system of blocks and spring is as shown below.

For no motion of m_2,

Spring force $\le$ Limiting friction

$$\Rightarrow \quad kx \le \mu m_2 g \Rightarrow x \le \frac{2\mu mg}{k}$$

$$\Rightarrow x_{\text{maximum}} = \frac{2\mu mg}{k} \quad \text{... (i)}$$

For block m, using work-energy theorem,

$$W_{\text{friction}} + W_{\text{spring}} = \Delta KE$$

$$\Rightarrow -\mu mgx - \frac{1}{2}kx^2 = \frac{1}{2}m(0^2 - u^2)$$

$$\Rightarrow \mu mgx + \frac{1}{2}kx^2 = \frac{1}{2}mu^2 \quad \text{... (ii)}$$

Putting value of x from Eq. (i) in Eq. (ii), we get

$$\mu mg\left(\frac{2\mu mg}{k}\right) + \frac{1}{2}k\left(\frac{2\mu mg}{k}\right)^2 = \frac{1}{2}mu^2$$

$$\Rightarrow \quad u^2 = \frac{8m\mu^2 g^2}{k}$$

6. Since, the given KE *versus* time graph is linear in nature and passing through the origin. So, we can write the equation of the graph as

KE $= mt$ (Here m = slope)

$$\Rightarrow \frac{1}{2}Mv^2 = mt \Rightarrow v = \sqrt{\frac{2m}{M}t}$$

$$\Rightarrow \text{Acceleration, } a = \frac{dv}{dt} = \sqrt{\frac{m}{2Mt}}$$

$\Rightarrow$ Force acting on the body,

$$F = Ma = \sqrt{\frac{Mm}{2t}}$$

Therefore, at $t = 1$ s, $F = \sqrt{\frac{Mm}{2}}$ ... (i)

Also, at $t = 4$, $F' = \sqrt{\frac{Mm}{8}} = \frac{1}{2}\sqrt{\frac{Mm}{2}} = \frac{F}{2}$

[Using eq (i)]

7. Given, velocity of a block,

$$v = (20 - 10t) \text{ m/s} \quad \text{... (i)}$$

$$\Rightarrow \text{Acceleration, } a = \frac{dv}{dt} = -10 \text{ m/s}^2$$

$$\Rightarrow \text{Force, } F = ma = -20 \text{ N} \quad \text{...(ii)}$$

$$\Rightarrow \text{Power, } P = Fv = -20(20 - 10t)$$

$$= (200t - 400) \text{ W} \quad \text{... (iii)}$$

From Eq. (ii), at $t = 3$ s, $|F| = 20$ N

From Eq. (iii), at $t = 3$ s,

$P = 200 \times 3 - 400 = 200$ W

From Eq. (i) at $t = 2$s, $v = 20 - 20 = 0$

$$\Rightarrow \text{Kinetic energy} = \frac{1}{2}mv^2 = 0$$

From Eq. (i), velocity-time graph is as shown. From the graph, at $t_1 = 3$ s, velocity is -10 m/s

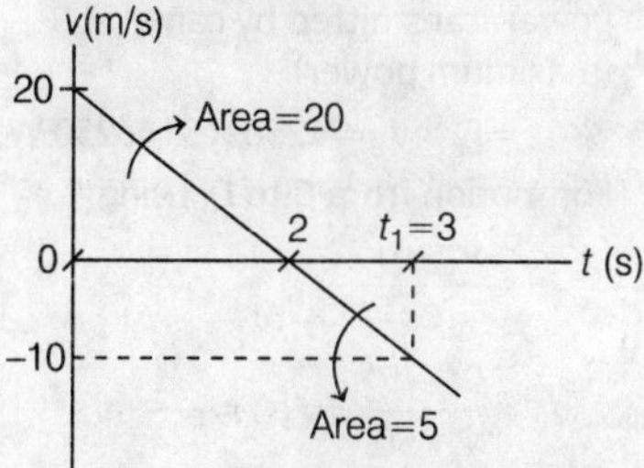

Work done by force in this interval is equal to change in kinetic energy

$$= \frac{1}{2}m(v^2 - u^2)$$

$$= \frac{1}{2} \times 2 \times (10^2 - 20^2) = -300 \text{ J}$$

From the given options, statement in option (d) is incorrect but rest are correct.

8. Given that, $P = v^2$

$$\Rightarrow \quad Fv = v^2 \Rightarrow F = v$$

$$\Rightarrow \quad a = v \quad (\text{as, } m = 1)$$

$$\Rightarrow \quad \frac{dv}{dt} = v$$

Integrating the above equation on both sides within the limits, we get

$$\Rightarrow \int_u^v \frac{dv}{v} = \int_0^t dt$$

$$\Rightarrow \ln\frac{v}{u} = t \Rightarrow v = ue^t \Rightarrow v \propto e^t$$

So, the graph between v and t will be exponential in nature. So, the correct option is (b).

9. The position of the block pulled by the camel at different instants is as shown below

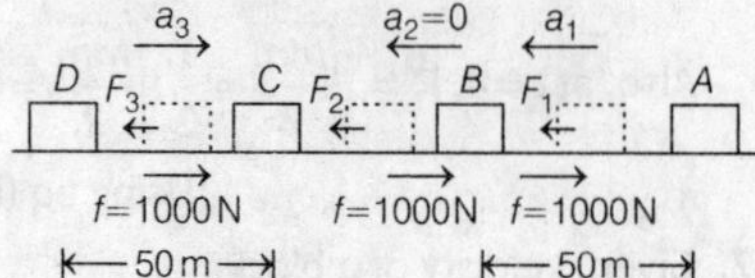

Let motion is accelerated with uniform rate from A to B, it is uniform motion from B to C and retarded from C to D. Pulling forces by the camel in the intervals are shown as F_1, F_2 and F_3. From the above figure, we have friction equal to

$\mu mg = 0.1 \times 1000 \times 10 = 1000$ N

For motion from A to B, acceleration

$$= a_1 = \frac{v^2 - u^2}{2s} = \frac{5^2 - 0^2}{2 \times 50} = \frac{1}{4} \text{ m/s}^2$$

$$\Rightarrow F_1 - 1000 = 1000 \times \frac{1}{4} \text{ (using } F_{\text{net}} = ma)$$

$$\Rightarrow \quad F_1 = 1250 \text{ N} \quad \text{... (i)}$$

Power transmitted by camel at B (maximum power)

$$= F_1 \times v_B = 1250 \times 5 = 6250 \text{ W}$$

For motion from C to D, using

$$a = \frac{v^2 - u^2}{2s}$$

$$a_3 = \frac{0^2 - 5^2}{2 \times 50} \Rightarrow a_3 = -\frac{1}{4} \text{ m/s}^2$$

$$\Rightarrow F_3 - 1000 = 1000 \times \left(\frac{1}{4}\right)$$

(using $F_{\text{net}} = ma$)

$$\Rightarrow F_3 = 750 \text{ N} \quad \text{...(ii)}$$

Now, work done from A to B,

$$W_{AB} = F_1 \times s_1 = 1250 \times 50 \quad \text{... (iii)}$$

[using Eq. (i)]

Work done from C to D,

$$W_{CD} = F_3 \times s_2 = 750 \times 50 \quad \text{... (iv)}$$

[using Eq. (ii)]

Dividing Eq. (iii) by (iv), we get

$$\frac{W_{AB}}{W_{CD}} = \frac{5}{3} = 1.67$$

10. The given system of pulley and block, with the components of forces on them and their direction is as shown in the figure.

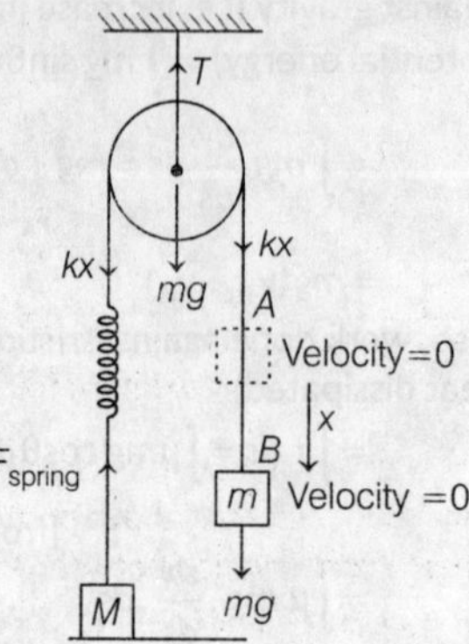

If maximum downward displacement of m is x, by energy conservation,

Loss in gravitational potential energy = Gain in spring potential energy

$$\Rightarrow \quad mgx = \frac{1}{2}kx^2 \Rightarrow x = \frac{2mg}{k} \quad \text{... (i)}$$

$\Rightarrow$ Spring force on M, $F_{\text{spring}} = kx = 2mg$

For just lifting of M, $F_{\text{spring}} \approx Mg$

$$\Rightarrow \quad 2mg \approx Mg$$

$$\Rightarrow \quad 2m \approx M \quad \text{... (ii)}$$

Now, from FBD of pulley, force by rod,

$$T = mg + 2kx = mg + 2k\left(\frac{2mg}{k}\right)$$

[using Eq. (i)]

$$= mg + 4mg = mg + 2Mg$$

[using Eq. (ii)]

$$= (2M + m)\,g$$

11. Let the speed of block and wedge be v and V, respectively when the block reaches bottom. By conservation of energy for the system,

Gain in KE = Loss in PE

$$\Rightarrow \frac{1}{2}mv^2 + \frac{1}{2}MV^2 = mgh \quad \text{... (i)}$$

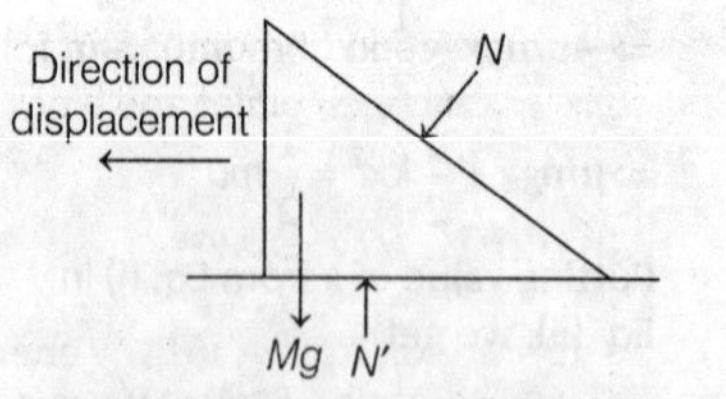

By work-energy theorem for the wedge,

$$W_N + W_{N'} + W_{mg} = \Delta\text{KE}$$

$$\Rightarrow \quad W_N + 0 + 0 = \frac{1}{2}MV^2$$

$$\Rightarrow \quad W_N = \frac{1}{2}MV^2 \quad \text{... (ii)}$$

Adding Eqs. (i) and (ii), we get

$$W_N + \frac{1}{2}mv^2 + \frac{1}{2}MV^2 = mgh + \frac{1}{2}MV^2$$

$$\Rightarrow \quad W_N = mgh - \frac{1}{2}mv^2 \quad \text{... (iii)}$$

Also, $W_{N'} = N' \cdot s \cos 90° = 0$ ... (iv)

Adding Eqs. (iii) and (iv), we get

$$W_N + W_{N'} = mgh - \frac{1}{2}mv^2 < mgh$$

12. Assuming that the block reaches top of the wedge after it is released and speed of block equal to v at top of the wedge.

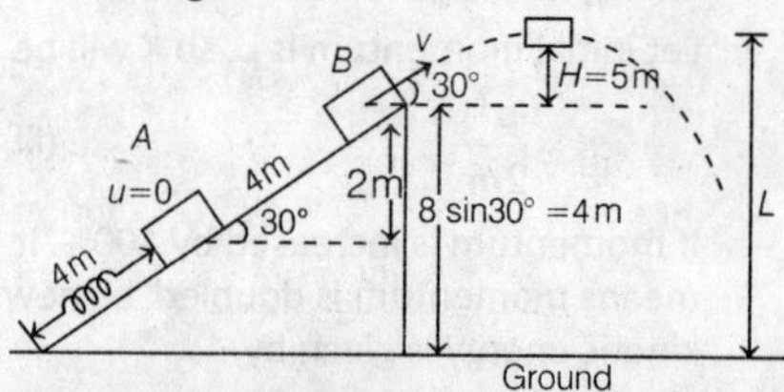

By energy conservation for motion from A to B (i.e. when it reaches the highest point on the wedge)

Energy at A = Energy at B

$$\frac{1}{2}kx^2 = mgh + \frac{1}{2}mv^2$$

Substituting the given values, we get

$$\Rightarrow \frac{1}{2} \times 110 \times 2^2 = 1 \times 10 \times 2 + \frac{1}{2} \times 1 \times v^2$$

$$\Rightarrow \quad v = 20 \text{ m/s}$$

As per our assumption, the block leaves the wedge with speed 20 m/s at 30° with horizontal as shown. After leaving, it will follow a parabolic path like a projectile. Therefore, maximum height,

$$H = \frac{v^2 \sin^2\theta}{2g} = \frac{20^2 \times \left(\frac{1}{2}\right)^2}{2 \times 10} = 5 \text{ m}$$

So, from diagram, maximum height of the block above ground

$$= L = 4 + 5 = 9 \text{ m}$$

13. Let angle between mean and either extreme position of the ball attached to string oscillating be θ, as shown.

As at extreme position, $v = 0$

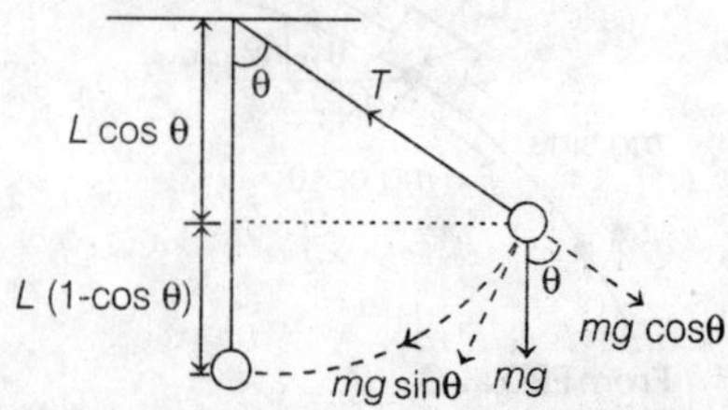

$\Rightarrow a_{centripetal} = \frac{v^2}{L} = 0$

So, the ball has only tangential acceleration,

$$a_T = \frac{F_T}{m} = \frac{mg\sin\theta}{m}$$

$$= g\sin\theta = a \quad \text{(say) ... (i)}$$

As the ball moves from extreme to mean, let it acquires speed v. By conservation of energy,

Gain in KE = Loss in PE

$$\Rightarrow \frac{1}{2}mv^2 = mgh = mgL(1-\cos\theta)$$

$$\Rightarrow \quad v^2 = 2gL(1-\cos\theta)$$

As there is no tangential force, $a_T = 0$ but

$$a_C = \frac{v^2}{L} = \frac{2gL(1-\cos\theta)}{L}$$

$$= 2g(1-\cos\theta) = a' \quad \text{(say) ... (ii)}$$

It is given that, $a = \frac{a'}{2}$

$$\Rightarrow g\sin\theta = \frac{2g(1-\cos\theta)}{2}$$

[using Eqs. (i) and (ii)]

$$\Rightarrow \quad \sin\theta = 1-\cos\theta$$

$$\Rightarrow \quad 2\sin\frac{\theta}{2}\cos\frac{\theta}{2} = 2\sin^2\frac{\theta}{2}$$

$$\Rightarrow \quad \tan\frac{\theta}{2} = 1$$

$$\Rightarrow \quad \theta = 90°$$

Therefore, the ball oscillates as shown.

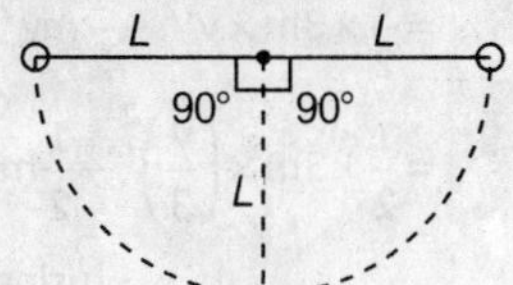

The area swept is semi-circular $= \frac{\pi L^2}{2}$

So, comparing with the value given in question, KL^2, the value of K is $\pi/2$.

14. The positions and motion of the given arrangement at different instants is as shown in the figure below

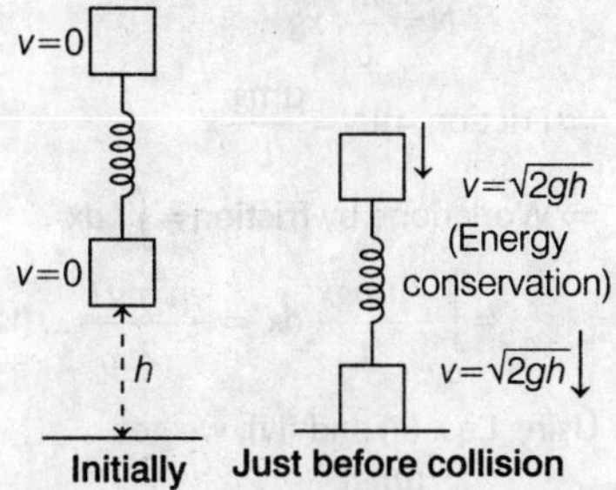

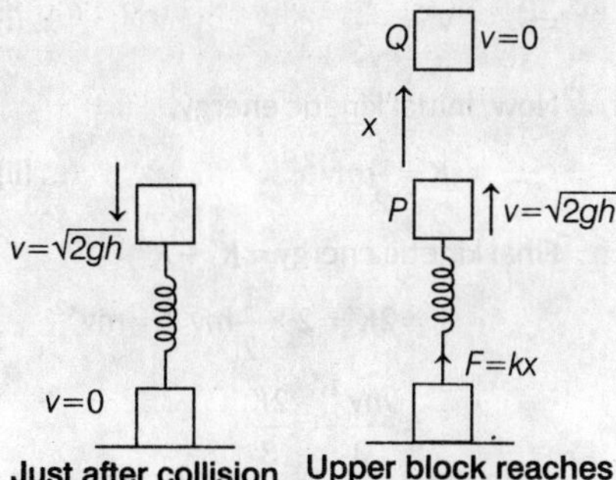

Consider when upper block reaches maximum height x (above position P). By energy conservation between P and Q,

Energy at P = Energy at Q

$$\frac{1}{2}m(\sqrt{2gh})^2 = \frac{1}{2}kx^2 + mgx$$

$$\Rightarrow \quad mgh = \frac{1}{2}kx^2 + mgx \quad \text{... (i)}$$

Also, for lifting of lower block, spring force should just exceed its weight

$$\Rightarrow \quad F_{spring} = kx \approx 2mg$$

$$\Rightarrow \quad x = \frac{2mg}{k} \quad \text{... (ii)}$$

Putting x from Eq. (ii) in Eq. (i), we get

$$mgh = \frac{1}{2}k\left(\frac{2mg}{k}\right)^2 + mg\left(\frac{2mg}{k}\right)$$

$$\Rightarrow \quad mgh = \frac{4m^2g^2}{k} \Rightarrow h = \frac{4mg}{k}$$

15. Initial extension in spring (x_0), which can be calculated by balancing forces on block, i.e. $kx_0 = mg$.

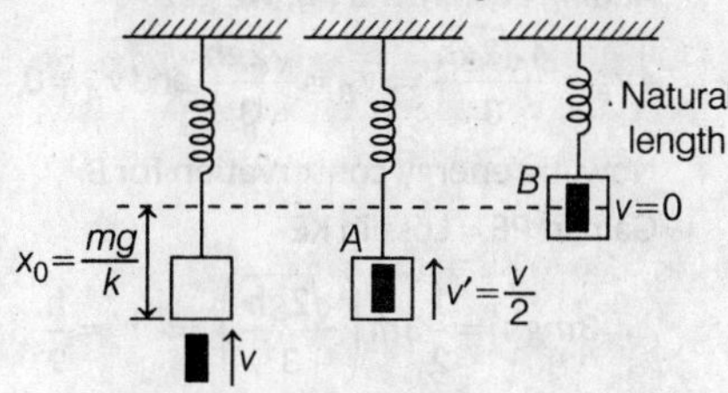

By conservation of momentum for collision between bullet and block, we get

$$2mv' = mv \Rightarrow v' = \frac{v}{2}$$

So, for motion from A to B, by energy conservation, for bullet-block system,

$$\frac{1}{2}\cdot 2m\left(\frac{v}{2}\right)^2 + \frac{1}{2}k\left(\frac{mg}{k}\right)^2 = 2mg\cdot\frac{mg}{k}$$

$$\Rightarrow \quad \frac{1}{4}mv^2 = \frac{3}{2}\frac{m^2g^2}{k} \quad \text{... (i)}$$

Now, kinetic energy before collision

$$= \frac{1}{2}mv^2$$

Kinetic energy after collision

$$= \frac{1}{2}\cdot 2m\left(\frac{v}{2}\right)^2 = \frac{1}{4}mv^2$$

$\therefore$ Loss = Initial KE − Final KE

$$= \frac{1}{2}mv^2 - \frac{1}{4}mv^2 = \frac{1}{4}mv^2$$

$$= \frac{3}{2}\frac{m^2g^2}{k} \quad \text{[from Eq. (i)]}$$

16. Let B be the position till which the jumper is falling freely as shown in the figure below. As length $AB = l$, by energy conservation from A to B,

Gain in kinetic energy = Loss in potential energy

$$\Rightarrow \quad \frac{1}{2}mv_B^2 = mgl \Rightarrow v_B = \sqrt{2gl} \quad \text{... (i)}$$

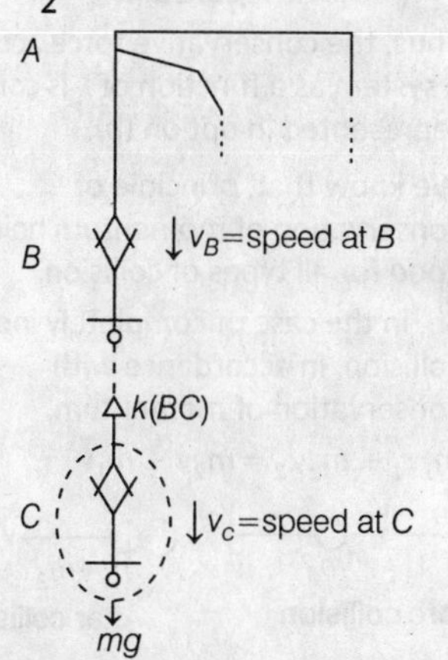

After B, the bungee begins to stretch and as per Hooke's law $(F = kx)$, its force will keep on increasing. Till the instant bungee's force is lesser than mg, the jumper will keep on speeding up. An instant will come (shown as C in diagram), when bungee's force will become equal to mg. After this instant, due to further extension of bungee, its force will exceed mg and jumper will begin speeding down.

At C, as mg is equal to bungee's force, we get

$$k(BC) = mg \Rightarrow \frac{mg}{l}(BC) = mg$$

$\Rightarrow BC$ = extension in bungee $= l$ ... (ii)

Now, by energy conservation,

Energy at B = Energy at C

$$\frac{1}{2}mv_B^2 = \frac{1}{2}mv_C^2 - mg(BC) + \frac{1}{2}k(BC)^2$$

Putting values of v_B and BC from Eqs. (i) and (ii) as well as $k = \frac{mg}{l}$, we get

$$\frac{1}{2}m(\sqrt{2gl})^2 = \frac{1}{2}mv_C^2 - mgl + \frac{1}{2}\frac{mg}{l}\cdot l^2$$

⇒ $mgl = \frac{1}{2}mv_C^2 - mgl + \frac{mgl}{2}$

⇒ $v_C = \sqrt{3gl}$

17. From the given U *versus* x graph, between $x = 0$ and $x = x_1$, assuming $U = kx^2$ (since, the graph is parabolic in nature)

So, force, $F = -\frac{dU}{dx} = -\frac{d(kx^2)}{dx} = -2kx$

⇒ $F \propto -x$

So, the graph between F and x between $x = 0$ and $x = x_1$ will be a straight line with negative slope between $x = x_1$ to $x = x_2$.

$F = -\frac{dU}{dx} = -$ (Slope of U-x graph)

$= -(-k') = k' =$ constant

Thus, the conservative force acting on a system as a function of x is correctly represented in option (b).

18. We know that, principle of conservation of momentum holds good for all types of collision.

So, in the case of completely inelastic collision, in accordance with conservation of momentum,

$m_1v_1 + m_2v_2 = m_2v + m_1v$

v_1 v_2 v
m_1 m_2 m_1+m_2
Before collision **After collision**

⇒ $v = \frac{m_1v_1 + m_2v_2}{m_1 + m_2} \neq 0$

Therefore, total KE cannot be completely lost.

Hence, both statements I and II are true.

19. Let the speed of the ball A before collision be v and after collision both the balls A and B have speed v'. So, the given situation in question is as shown in the figure below.

A → v B
→ K
Before collision

K' v' v'sin30° 30° v'cos30°
30° v'cos30° K' v' v'sin30°
After collision

So, by conservation of momentum in x-direction,

$mv' \cos 30° + mv' \cos 30° = mv$

⇒ $v' = \frac{v}{\sqrt{3}}$ ... (i)

Now, initial kinetic energy,

$K = \frac{1}{2}mv^2$ ... (ii)

Final kinetic energy $= K' + K'$

$= 2K' = 2 \times \frac{1}{2}mv'^2 = mv'^2$

$= \frac{mv^2}{3} = \frac{2K}{3}$ [using Eqs. (i) and (ii)]

$= 0.67\, K$

20. The positions of the balls before and after the collision is as shown below

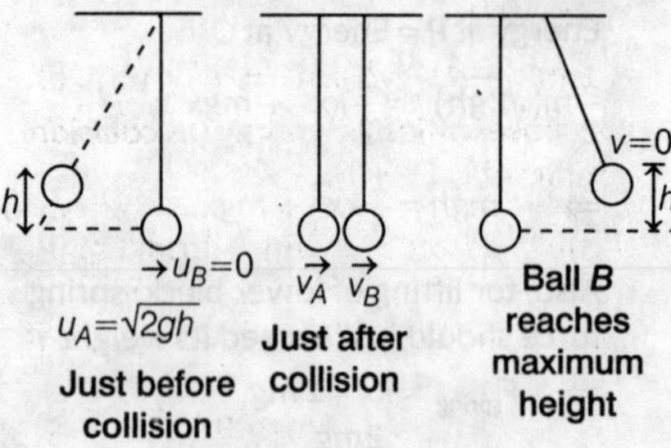

For collision, by conservation of momentum,

$m \cdot v_A + 3m \cdot v_B = m\sqrt{2gh}$

$\Rightarrow v_A + 3v_B = \sqrt{2gh}$ ... (i)

By Newton's law of restitution,

$v_B - v_A = e(u_A - u_B)$, where e is coefficient of restitution.

⇒ $v_B - v_A = \frac{\sqrt{2gh}}{3}$ ... (ii)

Adding Eqs. (i) and (ii), we get

$4v_B = \frac{4\sqrt{2gh}}{3} \Rightarrow v_B = \frac{\sqrt{2gh}}{3}$ and $v_A = 0$

Now, by energy conservation for B,

Gain in PE = Loss in KE

$3mgh' = \frac{1}{2}3m\left(\frac{\sqrt{2gh}}{3}\right)^2 \Rightarrow h' = \frac{h}{9}$

21. Given, potential energy of particle,

$U = 30 + (x - 3)^2$

So, the variation of U *versus* x is as shown below.

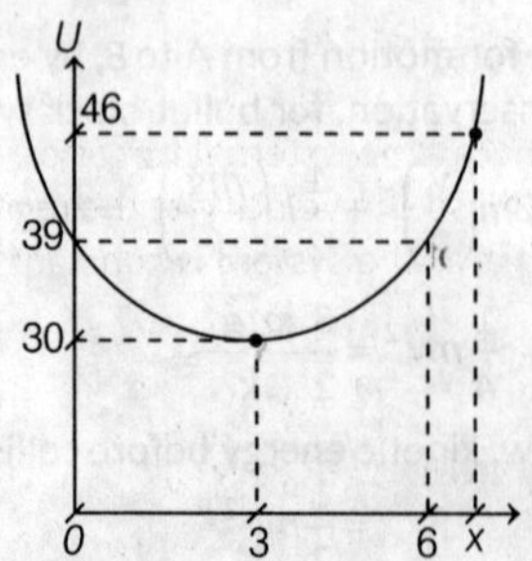

For $x = 6, U = 30 + (6 - 3)^2 = 39$ J

Similarly, for $x = 3, U = 30$ J

Given, $K = 7$J

⇒ For $x = 6$, total energy,

$T = U + K = 46$ J ... (i)

As particle moves from $x = 6$ to $x = x$ shown, U increases as can be seen from graph. As T is constant, so K will decrease. However, at extreme position, K will become zero.

⇒ For $x = x, U = T - K = 46 - 0 = 46$ [using Eq. (i)]

$\Rightarrow 30 + (x - 3)^2 = 46$

$\Rightarrow x - 3 = \pm 4 \Rightarrow x = -1, 7$

∴ Required difference $= 7 - (-1) = 8$

22. Motion of the system is as shown.

→ v
A
B C
v=0 v=0
Initially

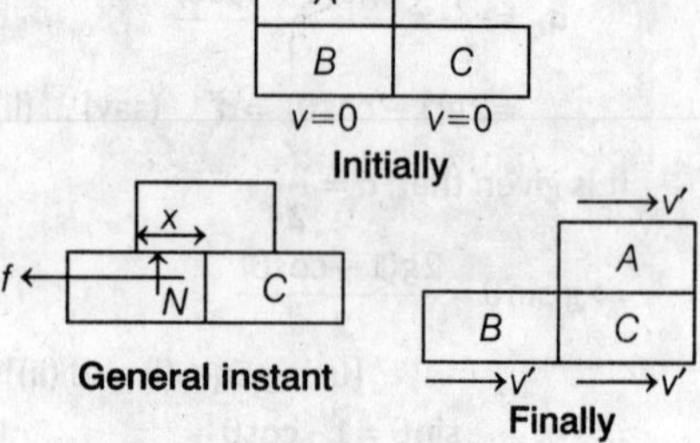

As final velocities of all blocks are equal (say v') by conservation of momentum,

$3mv' = mv \Rightarrow v' = \frac{v}{3}$ ... (i)

By work-energy theorem,

$W_{\text{friction}} =$ change in kinetic energy

$= \frac{1}{2} \times 3m \times v'^2 - \frac{1}{2}mv^2$

$= \frac{1}{2} \times 3m \times \left(\frac{v}{3}\right)^2 - \frac{1}{2}mv^2$ [using Eq. (i)]

$= -\frac{1}{3}mv^2 = -\frac{1}{3} \times 1 \times (6)^2$

$= -12$ J ... (ii)

⇒ Heat dissipated, $H = 12$ J ... (iii)

Also, as shown at general instant, assuming x length of A is in contact with B, normal force at contact

$N = \frac{m}{L} \cdot xg$

⇒ Friction $= \mu N = \frac{\mu mg}{L}x$

⇒ Work done by friction $= \int f\, dx$

$= \int_0^L -\frac{\mu mgx}{L} dx = \frac{-\mu\, mg\, L}{2}$ ... (iv)

Using Eqs. (ii) and (iv), we get

$\frac{\mu mgL}{2} = 12$

$$\Rightarrow \quad \frac{\mu \times 1 \times 10 \times 2}{2} = 12$$

$$\Rightarrow \quad \mu = 1.2 \quad \text{... (v)}$$

From Eqs. (iii) and (v), $\frac{H}{\mu} = \frac{12}{1.2} = 10$

23. Assuming l to be natural length of spring. Initial and final positions of the spring and bead system during its motion over incline are as shown in figure.

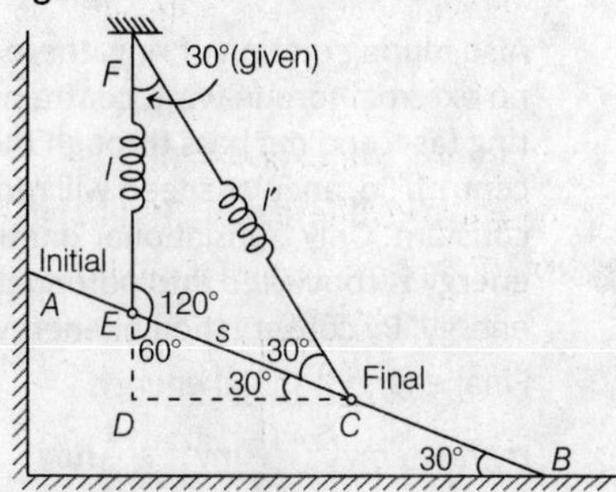

Let s is displacement of bead and l' is final spring's length.

By sine rule in triangle EFC,

$$\frac{l'}{\sin 120°} = \frac{s}{\sin 30°} = \frac{l}{\sin 30°}$$

$$\Rightarrow l' = \sqrt{3} l \text{ and } s = l \quad \text{... (i)}$$

From ΔEDC, $ED = s \sin 30° = \frac{l}{2}$ ... (ii)

So, by conservation of energy for motion of spring-bead system.

$$\Rightarrow \frac{1}{2} k (\sqrt{3} l - l)^2 = mg \frac{l}{2}$$

[using Eqs. (i) and (ii)]

$$\Rightarrow k = \frac{mg}{(\sqrt{3}-1)^2 l}$$

$$= \frac{(\sqrt{3}-1) \times 10}{(\sqrt{3}-1)^2 (\sqrt{3}+1) \times 2} = 2.5 \text{ N/m}$$

24. Given, power supplied by a force on a particle, $P = \text{constant} = C$ (say)

$$\Rightarrow \quad F.v = C \Rightarrow mav = C$$

$$\Rightarrow \quad mv \frac{dv}{dx} v = C$$

Integrating both sides of the above relation within the limits, we get

$$\Rightarrow \int_0^v v^2 dv = \frac{C}{m} \int_0^x dx \Rightarrow \frac{v^3}{3} = \frac{Cx}{m}$$

$$\Rightarrow \quad v \propto x^{1/3} \quad \text{... (i)}$$

$$\Rightarrow \quad KE = \frac{1}{2} mv^2 \propto x^{2/3}$$

[using Eq. (i)]

As x increases from $x = 1$ to $x = 8$

KE becomes $8^{2/3}$ times, i.e. 4 times.

25. Let the direction of the velocities of the ball during its motion over the hemispherical surface is as shown in figures.

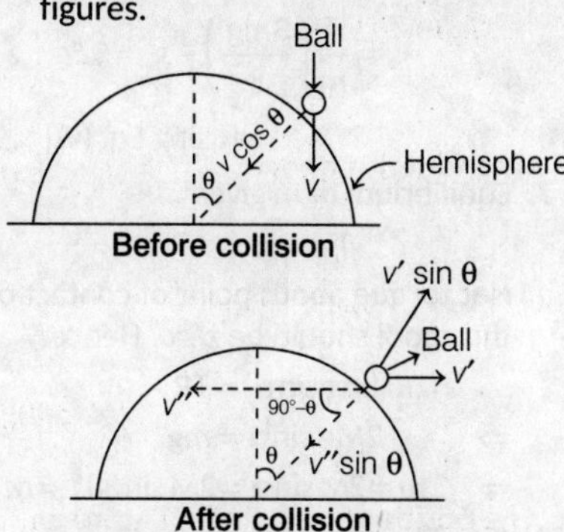

By conservation of momentum in horizontal,

$$mv' + m(-v'') = 0 \Rightarrow v'' = v' \quad \text{... (i)}$$

By conservation of energy (as collision is elastic)

$$\frac{1}{2} mv'^2 + \frac{1}{2} mv'^2 = \frac{1}{2} mv^2 \text{ [from Eq. (i)]}$$

$$\Rightarrow \quad \frac{v'}{v} = \frac{1}{\sqrt{2}} \quad \text{... (ii)}$$

By Newton's law of restitution,

$$v_{\text{separation}} = ev_{\text{approach}}$$

$$\Rightarrow v'' \sin\theta - (-v' \sin\theta) = v \cos\theta$$

$$\Rightarrow 2v' \sin\theta = v \cos\theta \quad (\text{as } v'' = v)$$

$$\Rightarrow \quad \cot\theta = \frac{2v'}{v} = \sqrt{2} \text{ [using Eq. (ii)]}$$

$$\Rightarrow \quad \theta = \cot^{-1} \sqrt{2} \Rightarrow x = 2$$

Qualifier 5 (Rotational Motion)

1. If A, A_1, A_2, A_3 are areas of complete disc, disc of radius r, disc of radius $\sqrt{2}r$, disc of radius $2r$ respectively, position vector of remaining disc will be

$$\mathbf{r} = \frac{A \times 0 - A_1 \mathbf{a} - A_2 \mathbf{b} - A_3 \mathbf{c}}{A - A_1 - A_2 - A_3} = 0 \text{ (given)}$$

$$\Rightarrow \quad A_1 \mathbf{a} + A_2 \mathbf{b} + A_3 \mathbf{c} = 0$$

$$\Rightarrow \pi r^2 \mathbf{a} + \pi (\sqrt{2} r)^2 \mathbf{b} + \pi (2r)^2 \mathbf{c} = 0$$

$$\Rightarrow \quad \mathbf{a} + 2\mathbf{b} + 4\mathbf{c} = 0$$

2. At $t = 0$, position of CM is

$$R_0 = \frac{M(0) + M(L/2)}{M + M} = \frac{L}{4}$$

$$\Rightarrow \quad \mathbf{R}_0 = 0\hat{\mathbf{i}} + \frac{L}{4} \hat{\mathbf{j}}$$

As, there is no external forces on the system, so the velocity of the centre of mass of the system is constant.

$$\mathbf{v}_{CM} = \frac{Mv_0 \hat{\mathbf{i}} + M(0)}{M + M} = \frac{v_0}{2} \hat{\mathbf{i}}$$

At time t, $\mathbf{R}_{CM} = \mathbf{R}_0 + \mathbf{v}_{CM} t$

$$= \frac{L}{4} \hat{\mathbf{j}} + \frac{v_0}{2} t \hat{\mathbf{i}}$$

3.

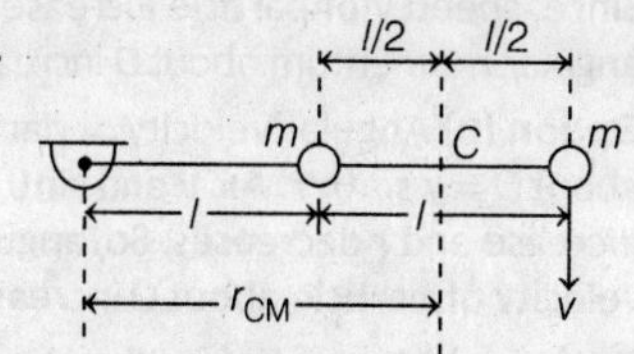

The distance of the centre of mass from the hinge,

$$r_{CM} = \frac{ml + m(2l)}{m + m} = \frac{3}{2} l$$

The angular velocity of the system,

$$\omega = \frac{v}{2l}$$

The velocity of the centre of mass of the system,

$$v_{CM} = r_{CM} \cdot \omega = \frac{3l}{2} \omega = \frac{3}{4} v$$

$$\Rightarrow \quad K_{CM} = \frac{1}{2} 2mv_{CM}^2 = \frac{9mv^2}{16}$$

The moment of inertia of the system about the hinge,

$$I = ml^2 + m(2l)^2 = 5ml^2$$

The rotational kinetic energy of the system,

$$K_R = \frac{1}{2} I\omega^2 = \frac{1}{2} 5ml^2 \left(\frac{v}{2l}\right)^2 = \frac{5mv^2}{8}$$

$$\therefore \quad \frac{K_{CM}}{K_R} = \frac{9mv^2}{16} \times \frac{8}{5mv^2} = 0.9$$

4. As, it is given that, $I_{\text{sphere}} = I_{\text{cylinder}}$

$$\Rightarrow \quad \frac{2}{3} mR^2 = \frac{mR^2}{2} + \frac{mL^2}{12}$$

$$\Rightarrow \quad \frac{mL^2}{12} = \frac{mR^2}{6} \Rightarrow L = \sqrt{2} R \quad \text{...(i)}$$

Radius of gyration K of a body of moment of inertia I and mass m is given by

$$K = \sqrt{\frac{I}{m}} = \sqrt{\frac{\frac{2}{3} mR^2}{m}} = \frac{\sqrt{2}R}{\sqrt{3}} = \frac{L}{\sqrt{3}}$$

[using Eq. (i)]

5. The situation can be shown as

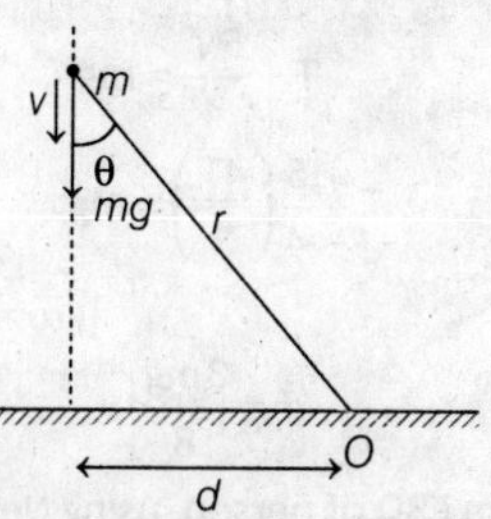

Option (a) The magnitude of angular momentum of particle about $O = mvd$

Since, speed v of particle increases, its angular momentum about O increases.

Option (b) Angular velocity of particle about $O = v\sin\theta / r$. As, v and $\sin\theta$ increase and r decreases. So, angular velocity of particle about O increases.

Option (c) Moment of inertia of particle about $O = mr^2$. Hence, moment of inertia of particle about O decreases.

Option (d) Magnitude of torque of gravitational force about $O = mgd$ = constant.

6. FBD of cylinder is as shown in the figure.

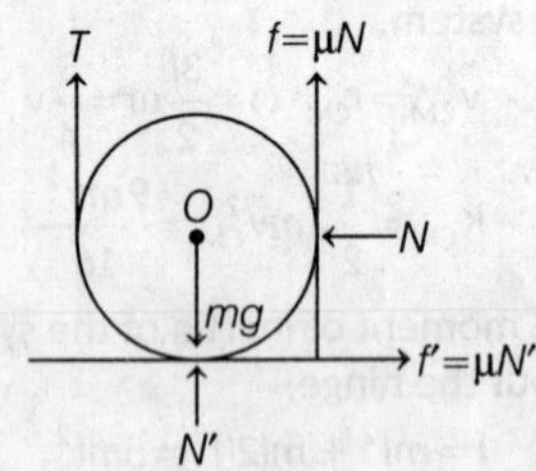

For rotational limiting equilibrium about centre O of the cylinder, when T is maximum.

Torque of tension = Torque of friction

$$T \cdot R = (f + f')R$$

$$\Rightarrow \quad T = \mu(N + N') \quad \text{...(i)}$$

For horizontal equilibrium

$$N = \mu N' \quad \text{...(ii)}$$

For vertical equilibrium,

$$T + N' + \mu N = mg \quad \text{...(iii)}$$

From Eqs. (i) and (ii), we get

$$T = \mu(\mu N' + N') = \mu(\mu + 1)N'$$

$$\Rightarrow \quad T = \frac{1}{2}\left(\frac{1}{2} + 1\right)N' = \frac{3}{4}N'$$

$$\Rightarrow \quad N' = \frac{4T}{3} \quad \text{...(iv)}$$

From Eqs. (ii) and (iii), we get

$$T + N' + \mu^2 N' = mg$$

$$\Rightarrow \quad T + N' + \frac{1}{4}N' = mg$$

$$\Rightarrow \quad T + \frac{5N'}{4} = mg$$

$$\Rightarrow \quad T + \frac{5}{4}\left(\frac{4T}{3}\right) = mg \quad \text{[From Eq. (iv)]}$$

$$\Rightarrow \quad T = \frac{3mg}{8} \quad \text{...(v)}$$

From FBD of person, using Newton's second law, we get

$$T - \frac{mg}{4} = \frac{m}{4}a$$

$$\Rightarrow \quad a = \frac{4T}{m} - g$$

$$= \frac{4}{m}\left(\frac{3mg}{8}\right) - g = 0.5g \quad \text{[using Eq. (v)]}$$

7. Equilibrium of m gives

$$T = mg$$

Net torque about point of contact of the spool should be zero. Hence,

$$(2R)(mg\sin\alpha) = TR$$

$$\Rightarrow \quad 2Mg\sin\alpha = mg$$

$$\Rightarrow \quad m = 2M\sin\alpha = 2M\sin 30° = M$$

8. Consider FBD of the cylinder.

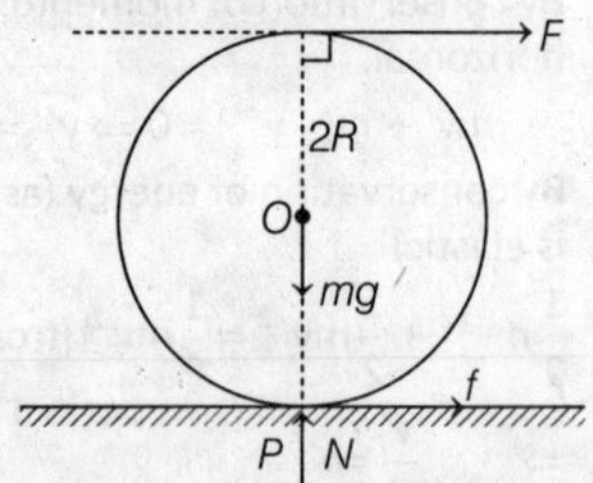

About instantaneous axis through P, angular acceleration,

$$\alpha = \frac{\tau_P}{I_P} = \frac{F(2R)}{\frac{mR^2}{2} + mR^2} = \frac{4F}{3mR}$$

$$\Rightarrow \quad a_{CM} = \alpha R = \frac{4F}{3m}$$

$$= \frac{4 \times 12}{3 \times 1} = 16 \text{ m/s}^2 \quad \text{...(i)}$$

$$\therefore \quad \mathbf{a}_{CM} = 16\hat{\mathbf{i}}$$

Using $F_{net} = ma_{CM}$, we get

$$\therefore \quad f + F = m\left(\frac{4F}{3m}\right) \quad \text{[using Eq. (i)]}$$

$$\Rightarrow \quad f = \frac{F}{3} = \frac{12}{3} = 4 \text{ N} \quad \text{...(ii)}$$

$\therefore$ Torque of force,

$$= fR\hat{\mathbf{j}} = 4 \times 3 = 12\hat{\mathbf{j}} \quad \text{...(iii)}$$

Also, as cylinder is not rotating about Z-axis, so torque of friction is equal but opposite of torque of F about Z-axis equal to

$$\Rightarrow \quad \tau' = \frac{-Fl}{2}\hat{\mathbf{k}} = -\frac{12 \times 2}{2}\hat{\mathbf{k}}$$

$$= -12\hat{\mathbf{k}} \quad \text{...(iv)}$$

From Eqs. (iii) and (iv), we get

$$\tau_{net} = 12\hat{\mathbf{j}} - 12\hat{\mathbf{k}}$$

9. In case 1 When the ring A reaches at maximum height then, its velocity relative to B is zero.

So, if velocity of B is assumed v' at this instant, velocity of A is also v'.

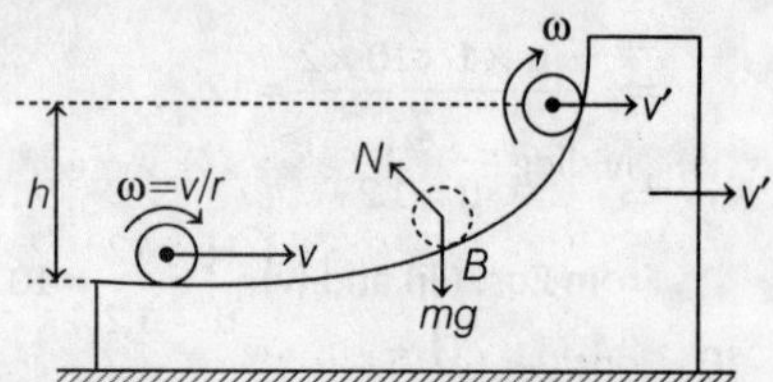

By conservation of momentum for the system in horizontal direction,

$$2mv' = mv \Rightarrow v' = \frac{v}{2} \quad \text{...(i)}$$

Also, during motion of ring, there is no external torque w.r.t. centre of the ring (as N and mg pass through the centre). So, angular speed will remain constant. Only translational kinetic energy is converted into potential energy. By conservation of energy,

Final energy = Initial energy

$$mgh + \frac{1}{2}mv'^2 + \frac{1}{2}mv'^2 + \frac{1}{2}I\omega^2$$

$$= \frac{1}{2}mv^2 + \frac{1}{2}I\omega^2$$

$$\Rightarrow \quad mgh = \frac{1}{2}mv^2 - mv'^2$$

$$= \frac{1}{2}mv^2 - m\left(\frac{v}{2}\right)^2 \quad \text{[using Eq. (i)]}$$

$$\Rightarrow \quad h = \frac{v^2}{4g} \quad \text{...(ii)}$$

In case 2 As the friction is sufficient to prevent slipping, the ring will be rolling without slipping continuously. At highest point, it will at rest relative to B. So, its angular speed will be zero at highest point. Also, its speed will also be $v' = \frac{v}{2}$ as determined in case 1.

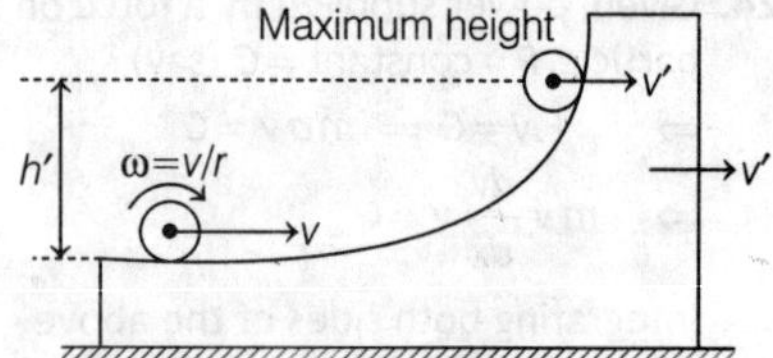

By conservation of energy,

Final energy = Initial energy

$$\frac{1}{2}mv'^2 + \frac{1}{2}mv'^2 + mgh'$$

$$= \frac{1}{2}mv^2 + \frac{1}{2}I\omega^2$$

$$\Rightarrow m\left(\frac{v}{2}\right)^2 + mgh' = \frac{1}{2}mv^2 + \frac{1}{2}(mr^2)\left(\frac{v}{r}\right)^2 \quad \text{[using Eq. (i)]}$$

$$\Rightarrow \quad h' = \frac{3v^2}{4g} \quad \text{...(iii)}$$

Dividing Eq. (iii) by Eq. (ii), we get

$$\frac{h'}{h} = 3 \Rightarrow h' = 3h$$

10. Consider the figure showing FBD of the ball (radius $= r$) at position B. Normal force is zero at B as the ball leaves contact.

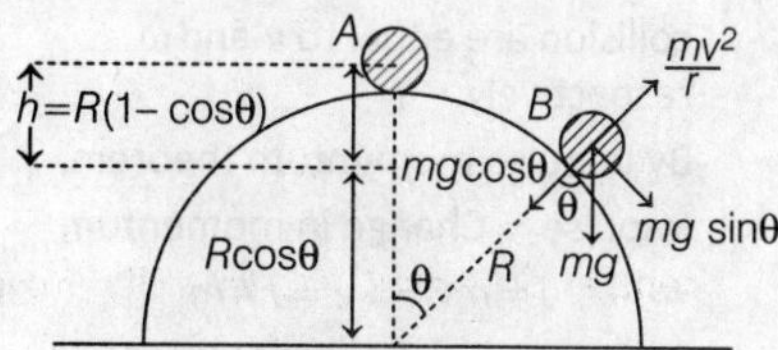

For radial direction at B,

$$\frac{mv^2}{R} = mg\cos\theta$$

$$\Rightarrow \quad v = \sqrt{gR\cos\theta} \quad \text{...(i)}$$

By energy conservation for motion from A to B,

Gain in KE = Loss in PE

$$\frac{1}{2}mv^2 + \frac{1}{2}I_{CM}\omega^2 = mgh \quad \text{...(ii)}$$

Putting value of I_{CM} of solid sphere, $\omega = \frac{v}{r}$ and h from figure in Eq. (ii), we get

$$\Rightarrow \frac{1}{2}mv^2 + \frac{1}{2}\cdot\frac{2}{5}mr^2\left(\frac{v}{r}\right)^2 = mgR(1-\cos\theta)$$

$$\Rightarrow \frac{7}{10}mv^2 = mgR(1-\cos\theta)$$

$$\Rightarrow \frac{7}{10}m(\sqrt{gR\cos\theta})^2 = mgR(1-\cos\theta)$$

[using Eq. (i)]

$$\Rightarrow \quad \frac{7\cos\theta}{10} = 1-\cos\theta$$

$$\Rightarrow \quad \cos\theta = \frac{10}{17}$$

Therefore, gain in KE = loss in PE

$$= mgh = mgR(1-\cos\theta)$$

$$= mgR\left(1-\frac{10}{17}\right) = \frac{7mgR}{17}$$

11. Consider motion of bob during descent (as in Fig.1).

By conservation of energy,

Gain in KE = Loss in PE

$$\Rightarrow \frac{1}{2}mv^2 = mgh$$

$$\Rightarrow \quad v = \sqrt{2gh}$$

As from Fig.1, $h = l\sin 30° = \frac{l}{2}$

$$\Rightarrow \quad v = \sqrt{2g\frac{l}{2}} = \sqrt{gl}$$

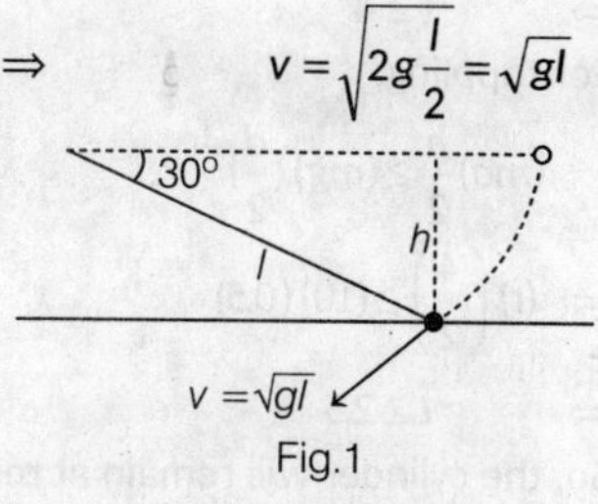

Fig.1

Components of v along and perpendicular to the surface are as shown in Fig.2.

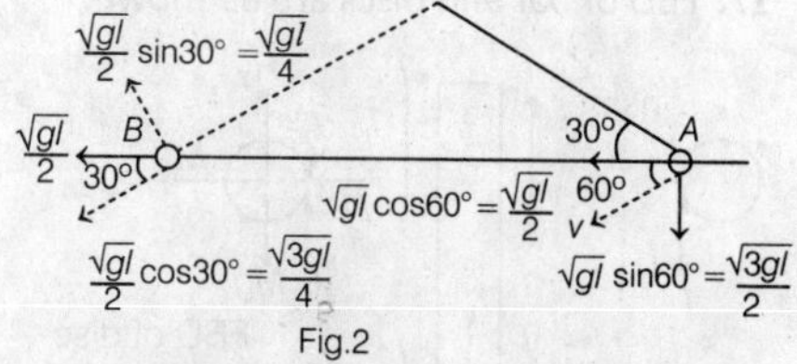

Fig.2

Component perpendicular to the surface will become zero, as the collision is given to be perfectly inelastic. The bob will graze along the surface with velocity $\frac{\sqrt{gl}}{2}$ moving from position A to B till the string is taut again.

Just before the string is taut, components of velocity along and perpendicular to the string in position-B are as shown in Fig.2. Just after the string is taut, velocity component along the string reduces to zero, as shown in Fig.3. The bob ascends from B to C (position of maximum height) till its velocity becomes zero.

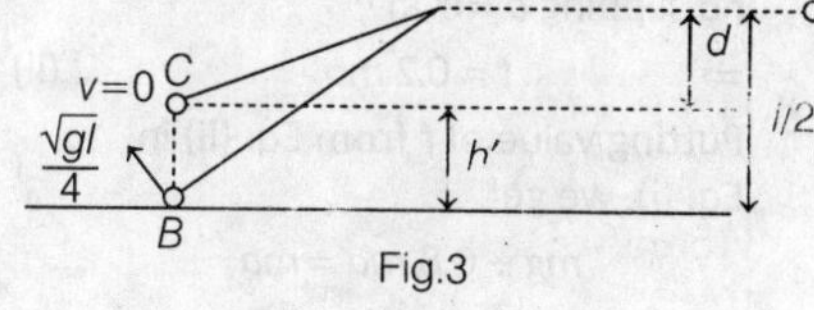

Fig.3

By conservation of energy for motion from B to C,

Gain in PE = Loss in KE

$$mgh' = \frac{1}{2}m\left(\frac{\sqrt{gl}}{4}\right)^2$$

$$\Rightarrow \quad h' = \frac{l}{32}$$

Therefore, height fallen w.r.t. position of release,

$$d = \frac{l}{2} - h' = \frac{l}{2} - \frac{l}{32} = \frac{15l}{32}$$

Work done by gravity will therefore be

$$W = mgd$$

$$= mg\left(\frac{15l}{32}\right) = \frac{15mgl}{32}$$

12. Using the principle of conservation of angular momentum,

$$m\sqrt{2gl} \times R = \left[\frac{(2m)R^2}{2} + mR^2\right] \times \omega$$

$$[\because v = \sqrt{2gl}]$$

$$\Rightarrow \quad \omega = \sqrt{\frac{gl}{2R^2}}$$

$$\because \quad v = \omega R$$

$$\therefore \quad = \sqrt{\frac{gl}{2}}$$

13. Given $\frac{dR}{R} \times 100 = \frac{(507.5 - 500.0)}{500.0} \times 100 = 1.5\%$

Now, $K = \frac{1}{2}I\omega^2 = \frac{1}{2I}(I\omega)^2 = \frac{L^2}{2I}$

or $K = \frac{L^2}{2\left(\frac{MR^2}{2}\right)} = \frac{L^2}{MR^2}$

Taking log and differentiating,

$$\frac{dK}{K} = -\frac{2dR}{R}$$

or the percentage change in K

$$= \frac{dK \times 100}{K} = -\frac{2dR}{R} \times 100$$

$$= -2 \times 1.5\% = -3\%$$

14. The larger disc will move along line of impact (LI)

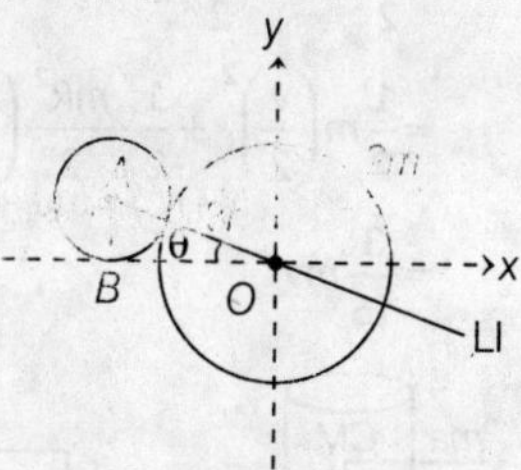

As $e = 0$, so velocity of larger disc,

$$v' = \frac{mv\cos\theta}{m+2m} = \frac{v\cos\theta}{3}$$

Velocity of larger disc

$$= v'\cos\theta\,\hat{i} - v'\sin\theta\,\hat{j}$$

$$= \frac{v}{3}\cos^2\theta\,\hat{i} - \frac{v}{3}\sin\theta\cos\theta\,\hat{j}$$

(from the ΔOAB, we can calculate $\cos\theta = \frac{2\sqrt{2}}{3}$ and $\sin\theta = \frac{1}{3}$)

$$= \frac{8}{27}v\hat{i} - \frac{2\sqrt{2}}{27}v\hat{j}$$

15. As velocity of moving pulley is average velocity of ends. Therefore, velocity of pulley-1,

$$v' = \frac{v + (-3v)}{2} = -v = v \text{ (downwards)}$$

As plank-1 is attached to pulley-1, so it will also move with velocity v'. Also as roller is not slipping, it will be the velocity of roller contact point with plank as well. Top point of the roller, as in contact with plank-2, at rest will have zero velocity.

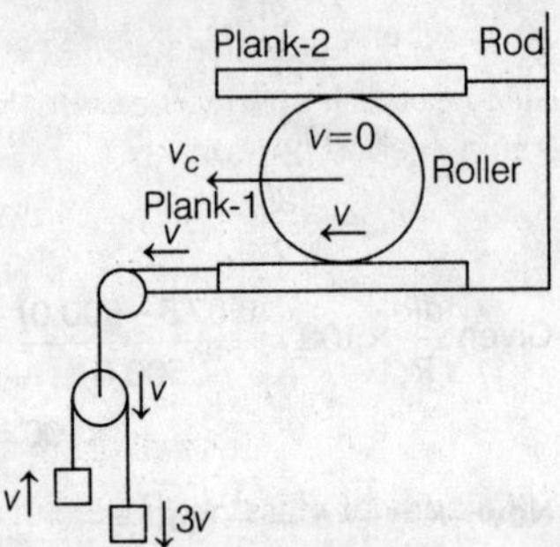

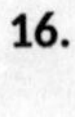

As, velocity of centre of rolling object is average of velocities of top and bottom.

Therefore, velocity of centre of roller,

$$v_c = \frac{v + 0}{2} = \frac{v}{2} \quad \text{...(i)}$$

Also, $\omega = \frac{v_c}{R} = \frac{v}{2R}$ ... (ii)

(by condition of pure rolling)

Therefore, kinetic energy

$$= \text{KE}_{\text{translation}} + \text{KE}_{\text{rotation}}$$

$$= \frac{1}{2} m v_c^2 + \frac{1}{2} I_{\text{CM}} \omega^2$$

$$= \frac{1}{2} m \left(\frac{v}{2}\right)^2 + \frac{1}{2} \cdot \frac{mR^2}{2} \left(\frac{v}{2R}\right)^2$$

$$= \frac{3}{16} mv^2$$

16.

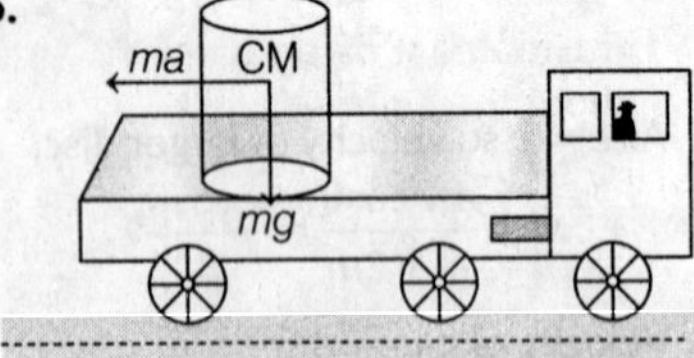

Given, $(x = t^3 + t)/6$,

$\mu = 0.4$, $d = 1$ m and $h = 4$ m

Acceleration, $a = \frac{d^2x}{dt^2}$

$$= \frac{d^2}{dt^2}\left(\frac{t^3 + t}{6}\right) = t$$

For sliding,

$$ma \geq \mu_s mg$$

$\Rightarrow \quad t \geq 0.4 \times 10$

$\Rightarrow \quad t \geq 4$

For toppling,

$$(ma)\frac{h}{2} \geq (mg)\left(\frac{d}{2}\right)$$

$$\Rightarrow (t)\left(\frac{4}{2}\right) \geq (10)(0.5)$$

$\Rightarrow \quad t \geq 2.5$

So, the cylinder will remain at rest relative to the truck and after some time, it will topple before sliding.

17. FBD of bar and discs are as shown.

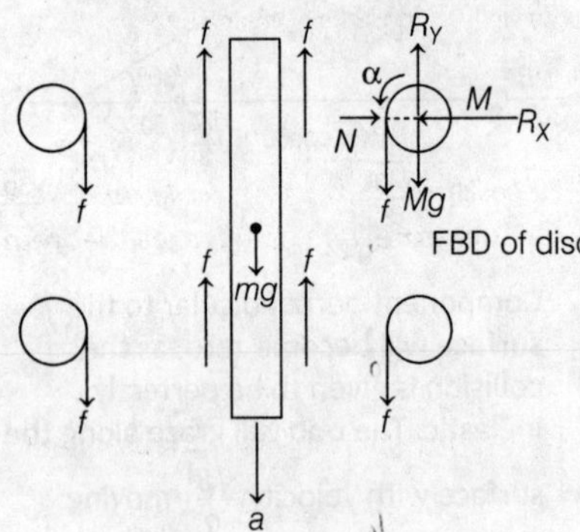

For the rod, by Newton's second law

$$mg - 4f = ma, \quad \text{...(i)}$$

For any of the discs, using $\tau = I\alpha$, we get

$$fR = \frac{MR^2}{2} \cdot \alpha$$

$$\Rightarrow f = \frac{M\alpha R}{2} = \frac{(0.4\,m)\left(\frac{a}{R}\right)R}{2}$$

(As, M is given equal to 0.4 m and for no slipping $a = \alpha R$)

$$\Rightarrow \quad f = 0.2\,ma \quad \text{...(ii)}$$

Putting value of f from Eq. (ii) in Eq. (i), we get

$$mg - 0.8\,ma = ma$$

$$\Rightarrow \quad a = \frac{5g}{9}$$

Using this value of a in Eq. (ii), we get

$$f = 0.2\,ma = 0.2\,m\left(\frac{5g}{9}\right) = \frac{mg}{9} \quad \text{... (iii)}$$

From FBD of disc,

$$R_Y = Mg + f$$

$$= 0.4\,mg + \frac{mg}{9}$$

[using Eq. (iii)]

$$= \frac{23mg}{45}$$

18. Let the ball hits the rod at distance x from centre of the rod as shown.

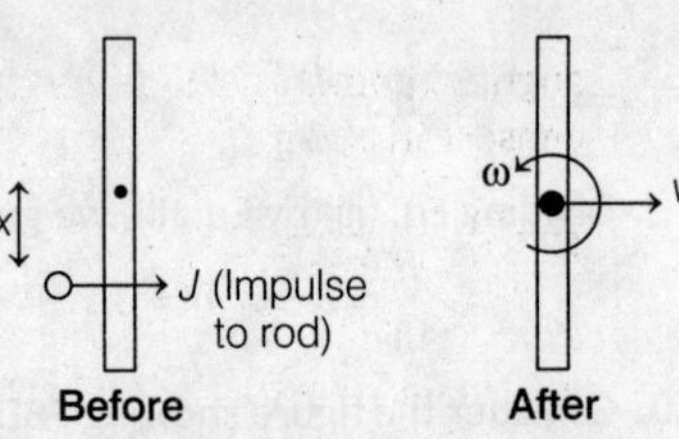

Let J be the impulse imparted to the rod by the ball. Let velocity and angular velocity of the rod just after collision are equal to v and ω, respectively.

By impulse momentum theorem,

Impulse = Change in momentum

$$\Rightarrow \quad J = mv \Rightarrow v = J/m \quad \text{...(i)}$$

By angular impulse-angular momentum theorem about CM,

Angular impulse = Change in angular momentum

$$\Rightarrow \quad Jx = \frac{ml^2}{12}\omega$$

$$\Rightarrow \quad \omega = \frac{12\,Jx}{ml^2} \quad \text{...(ii)}$$

For the man to not experience any jerk, net velocity of the top point should be zero.

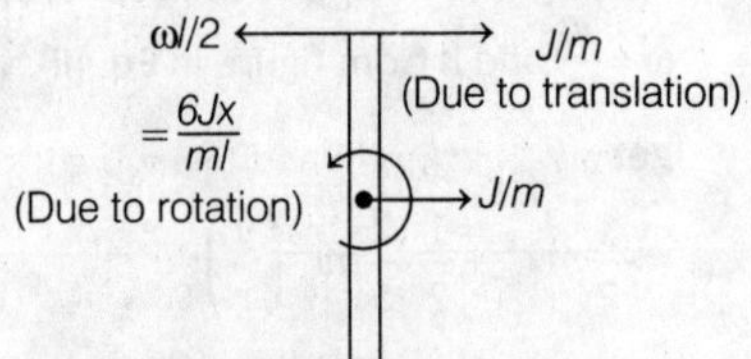

Therefore, velocities due to translation and rotation (shown in diagram) should cancel. i.e.

$$\frac{J}{m} = \frac{6Jx}{ml}$$

$$\Rightarrow \quad x = \frac{l}{6}$$

$$\Rightarrow \quad AC = \frac{l}{2} + \frac{l}{6} = \frac{2l}{3}$$

19. Here, the figures show velocities and angular velocity just before and just after the collision. As, there is no slipping between bullet and cylinder, if velocity of bullet is assumed v after collision, velocity of cylinder's top will also be v. As velocity of bottommost point of cylinder will be zero owing to no slipping, angular velocity of cylinder will be

$$\omega = \frac{v - 0}{2R} = \frac{v}{2R} \quad \text{...(i)}$$

Though friction acts at bottom point O, its torque about O is zero and so angular momentum L of the sphere is conserved about O.

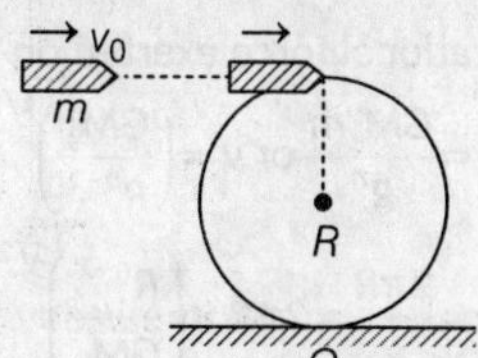

Before and during collision

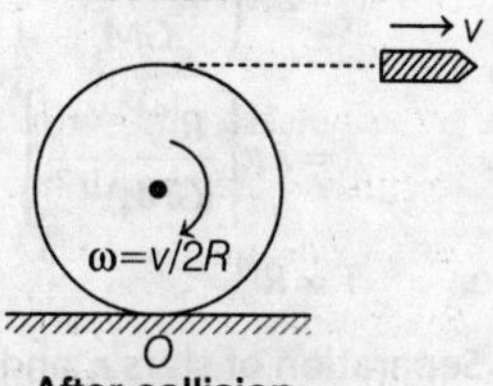

After collision

Therefore, $L_{final} = L_{initial}$

$$2mvR + I_0\omega = 2mv_0R \quad \text{...(ii)}$$

Moment of inertia about O, using parallel axes theorem,

$$I_0 = I_{CM} + MR^2 = \frac{MR^2}{2} + MR^2$$

$$= \frac{3MR^2}{2} = 4mR^2 \quad \text{...(iii)}$$

(as, $M = 8m/3$)

From Eqs. (i), (ii) and (iii), we get

$$2mvR + 4mR^2\left(\frac{v}{2R}\right) = 2mv_0R$$

$$\Rightarrow \quad v = \frac{v_0}{2}$$

20. As, the sphere does not have tendency of slipping. So, it will keep on rolling without slipping with constant speed v.

Therefore, time of motion,

$$t = \frac{\text{Displacement}}{\text{Velocity}} = \frac{\pi r}{v}$$

⇒ Angle rotated by sphere,

$$\theta = \omega t = \frac{v}{r} \cdot \frac{\pi r}{v} = \pi$$

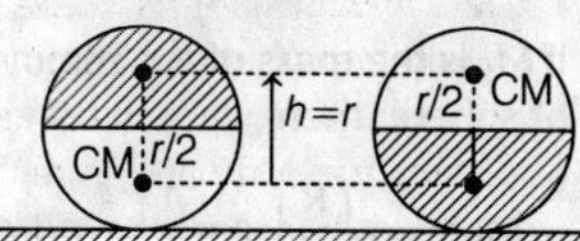

The centre of mass of a hemisphere is at a distance $\frac{r}{2}$ from its base. As, the sphere rotates by π, centre of mass of the non-shaded portion gains height $h = r$ as shown.

Therefore, work done by gravity on non-shaded portion,

$$W_{gravity} = \frac{-mgr}{2} \quad \text{...(i)}$$

(As work done by gravity on body of mass M, if its centre of mass gains height h is $-Mgh$)

Also, moment of inertia of hemisphere about axis through O,

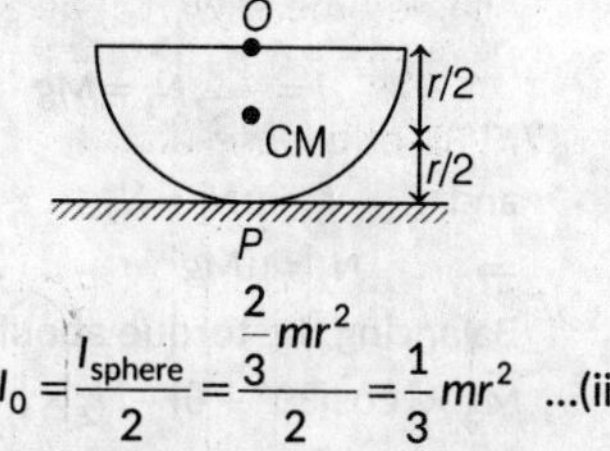

$$I_0 = \frac{I_{sphere}}{2} = \frac{\frac{2}{3}mr^2}{2} = \frac{1}{3}mr^2 \quad \text{...(ii)}$$

Therefore, by parallel axes theorem at CM,

$$I_{CM} = I_0 - \frac{m}{2}\left(\frac{r}{2}\right)^2 \quad \text{...(iii)}$$

Again by parallel axes theorem at P,

$$I_P = I_{CM} + \frac{m}{2}\left(\frac{r}{2}\right)^2 \quad \text{...(iv)}$$

Adding Eqs. (iii) and (iv), we get

$$I_P = I_0 = \frac{1}{3}mr^2 \quad \text{...(v)}$$

[using Eq. (ii)]

Initial kinetic energy of lower non-shaded portion will therefore be (considering axis through P as instantaneous axis)

$$K_1 = \frac{1}{2}I_P\omega^2 = \frac{1}{2}\left(\frac{1}{3}mr^2\right)\left(\frac{v}{r}\right)^2$$

[using Eq. (v)]

$$= \frac{1}{6}mv^2 \quad \text{...(vi)}$$

Also, total kinetic energy of the sphere,

$$K = K_{translation} + K_{rotation}$$

$$= \frac{1}{2}mv^2 + \frac{1}{2}I_{CM}\omega^2$$

$$= \frac{1}{2}mv^2 + \frac{1}{2}\left(\frac{2}{3}mr^2\right)\left(\frac{v}{r}\right)^2$$

$$K = \frac{5}{6}mv^2 \quad \text{...(vii)}$$

Subtracting Eq. (vi) from Eq. (vii), we get

$$K_2 = K - K_1$$

$$= \frac{5}{6}mv^2 - \frac{1}{6}mv^2$$

$$K_2 = \frac{2}{3}mv^2 \quad \text{...(viii)}$$

As lower non-shaded hemisphere moves in upper position its kinetic energy will increase from K_1 to K_2.

$$\therefore \quad \Delta K = K_2 - K_1$$

$$= \frac{2}{3}mv^2 - \frac{1}{6}mv^2$$

$$= \frac{1}{2}mv^2 \quad \text{...(ix)}$$

[using Eqs. (vi) and (viii)]

As per work-energy theorem, for non-shaded portion,

$$W_{contact} + W_{gravity} = \Delta K$$

$$\Rightarrow \quad W_{contact} = \Delta K - W_{gravity}$$

$$= \frac{1}{2}mv^2 + \frac{mgr}{2}$$

[using Eqs. (i) and (ix)]

21. If a body of mass m_1 (having y-coordinate of CM $= y_1$) is removed from body of mass m_2 (having y-coordinate of CM $= y_2$). y_{CM} coordinate of remaining body,

$$y_{CM} = \frac{m_2y_2 - m_1y_1}{m_2 - m_1}$$

$$= \frac{V_2y_2 - V_1y_1}{V_2 - V_1}$$

Here, V_1 and V_2 are respective volumes.

$$\Rightarrow y_{CM} = \frac{\frac{4}{3}\pi(2R)^3\, 0 - \frac{2}{3}\pi R^3 \frac{3R}{8}}{\frac{4}{3}\pi(2R)^3 - \frac{2}{3}\pi R^3} = -\frac{R}{40}$$

$$\therefore \quad x = 40$$

22. The moment of inertia of the system about the point O,

$$I_0 = 3\left[\frac{2}{5}M\left(\frac{d}{2}\right)^2 + M\left(\frac{d}{\sqrt{3}}\right)^2\right] = \frac{13}{10}Md^2$$

The moment of inertia of the system about the point A,

$$I_A = 2\left[\frac{2}{5}M\left(\frac{d}{2}\right)^2 + M(d)^2\right] + \frac{2}{5}M\left(\frac{d}{2}\right)^2$$

$$= \frac{23}{10}Md^2$$

So, the ratio $= \frac{13}{23} = \frac{n}{23}$ (Given)

$$\Rightarrow \quad n = 13$$

23.

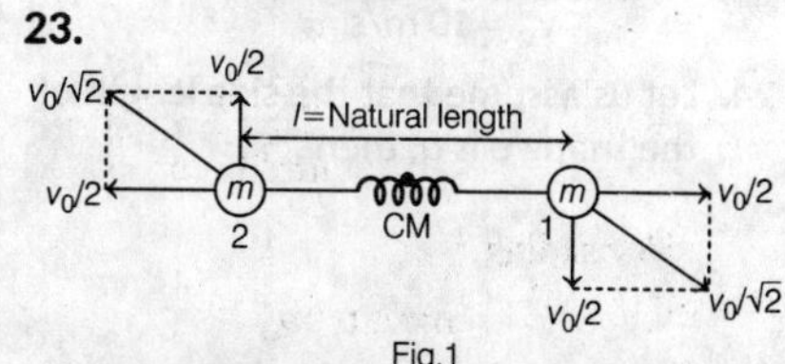

Fig.1

Magnitudes of velocities of both the spheres will be $\frac{v_0}{\sqrt{2}}$ as shown in CM frame.

Due to velocity components along the spring, the spring starts elongating. At the instant of maximum extension, velocity components along the spring will be zero.

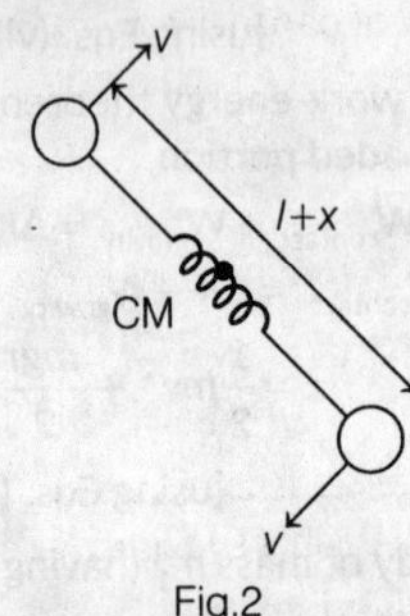

Fig.2

By conservation of energy,

Initial energy = Final energy

$$\Rightarrow \frac{1}{2}mv_0^2 = mv^2 + \frac{1}{2}kx^2 \quad \text{...(i)}$$

By conservation of angular momentum in CM frame,

$$L_{\text{final}} = L_{\text{initial}}$$

$$2 \cdot mv\frac{(l+x)}{2} = 2 \cdot m\frac{v_0}{2}\frac{l}{2}$$

$$\Rightarrow mv(l+x) = \frac{mv_0 l}{2}$$

$$\Rightarrow \quad v = \frac{v_0 l}{2(l+x)} \quad \text{...(ii)}$$

Putting value of v from Eq. (ii) into Eq. (i), we get

$$\Rightarrow \frac{1}{2}mv_0^2 = \frac{mv_0^2 l^2}{4(l+x)^2} + \frac{1}{2}kx^2 \quad \text{...(iii)}$$

It is given that,

$m = 2$ kg, $l = 1$ m,
$x = 1$ m and $k = 175$ N/m.

Putting these values in Eq. (iii), we get

$$\frac{1}{2} \times 2 \times v_0^2 = \frac{2v_0^2}{4(1+1)^2} + \frac{1}{2} \times 175$$

$$\Rightarrow \quad v_0^2 = \frac{v_0^2}{8} + \frac{175}{2}$$

$$\Rightarrow \quad \frac{7v_0^2}{8} = \frac{175}{2}$$

$$\Rightarrow \quad v_0 = 10 \text{ m/s}$$

24. Let us assume that the side length of the triangle is a, then

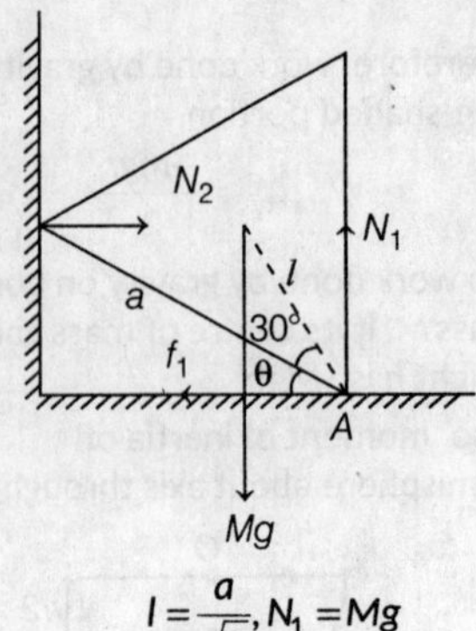

$$l = \frac{a}{\sqrt{3}}, N_1 = Mg$$

and $\quad f_1 = \mu N_1 = N_2$

$\Rightarrow \quad N_2 = \mu Mg$

Balancing the torque about point A,

$$Mg \times l\cos(30° + \theta) - N_2 \times a\sin\theta = 0$$

$$\Rightarrow Mg \times \frac{a}{\sqrt{3}}\cos(30° + \theta) - \mu Mg \times a\sin\theta = 0$$

$$\Rightarrow \frac{1}{\sqrt{3}}\left(\frac{\sqrt{3}}{2}\cos\theta - \frac{1}{2}\sin\theta\right) = \mu \sin\theta$$

On solving further, we get

$$\theta = \cot^{-1}\left[2\mu + \frac{1}{\sqrt{3}}\right]$$

$\Rightarrow \quad x = 2$ and $y = 3$

$\Rightarrow \quad x + y = 5$

25. Work done

$$= F \times \Delta r = 5.625 \times 0.8 \text{ m}$$
$$= 4.5 \text{ J}$$

Also, as per work-energy theorem,

$$\text{Work done} = \Delta K = \frac{1}{2}I\omega_f^2 - \frac{1}{2}I\omega_i^2$$

$$\therefore \quad 4.5 = \frac{1}{2} \times 4 \times 10^{-4} \times \omega^2 - 0$$

($\because$ top starts from rest, $\omega_i = 0$)

$\Rightarrow \quad \omega = 150$ rad/s

$$\frac{\omega}{10} = 15$$

Qualifier 6 (Gravitation)

1. The field lines show the direction of force on a small test mass. The gravitational force is attractive, hence for masses, gravitational feld lines always point towards the mass as shown in option (c). Also at mid-point of line joining them (equal masses), gravitational field is zero. So, there must be no field lines passing through mid point.

2. The necessary centripetal force required for a planet to move around the sun

= Gravitational force exerted on it

i.e. $\frac{mv^2}{R} = \frac{GM_s m}{R^n}$ or $v = \left(\frac{GM_s}{R^{n-1}}\right)^{1/2}$

Now, $T = \frac{2\pi R}{v} = 2\pi R \times \left(\frac{R^{n-1}}{GM_s}\right)^{1/2}$

$$= 2\pi\left(\frac{R^2 \times R^{n-1}}{GM_s}\right)^{1/2}$$

$$= 2\pi\left[\frac{R^{(n+1)/2}}{(GM_s)^{1/2}}\right]$$

or $\quad T \propto R^{(n+1)/2}$

3. Separation of stars r_1 and r_2 from CM are in the ratio,

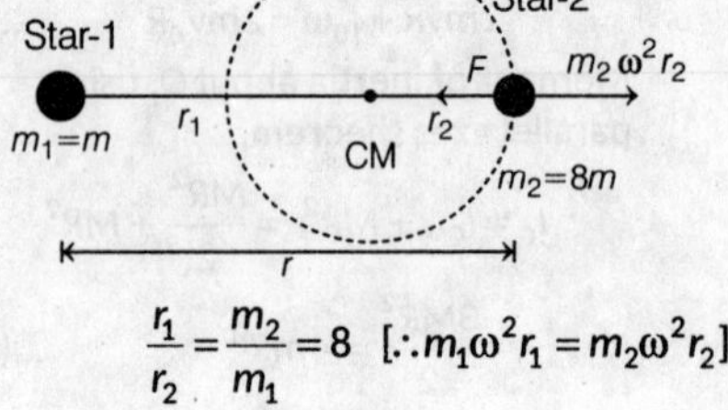

$$\frac{r_1}{r_2} = \frac{m_2}{m_1} = 8 \quad [\because m_1\omega^2 r_1 = m_2\omega^2 r_2]$$

$\Rightarrow \quad r_1 = 8r_2 \quad$ ...(i)

Also, $\quad r_1 + r_2 = r \quad$ ...(ii)

From Eqs. (i) and (ii), $r_2 = \frac{r}{9}$ ...(iii)

From FBD of star-2,

Gravitational force = Centrifugal force

$$\Rightarrow \frac{Gm_1 m_2}{r^2} = m_2\omega^2 r_2$$

$$\Rightarrow \omega = \sqrt{\frac{Gm_1}{r^2 r_2}} = \sqrt{\frac{Gm}{r^2\left(\frac{r}{9}\right)}} = \sqrt{\frac{9Gm}{r^3}}$$

[using Eq. (iii)]

4. Gravitational force between sphere of mass M and the particle of mass m is

$$F_1 = \frac{GMm}{d^2}$$

If M_1 is the mass of the removed part of sphere, then

$$M_1 = \frac{4}{3}\pi\left(\frac{R}{2}\right)^3\rho = \frac{1}{8}\left(\frac{4}{3}\pi R^3\rho\right) = \frac{M}{8}$$

$$\left(\because \rho = \frac{M}{\frac{4}{3}\pi R^3}\right)$$

Gravitational force between the removed part and the particle of mass m,

$$F_2 = \frac{GM_1 m}{(d-R/2)^2} = \frac{GMm}{8(d-R/2)^2}$$

∴Required force,

$$F = F_1 - F_2 = \frac{GMm}{d^2} - \frac{GMm}{8[d-(R/2)]^2}$$

$$= \frac{GMm}{d^2}\left[1 - \frac{1}{8\left(1-\frac{R}{2d}\right)^2}\right]$$

5. If F be the force applied by each sun on the planet as shown, then net force on the planet,

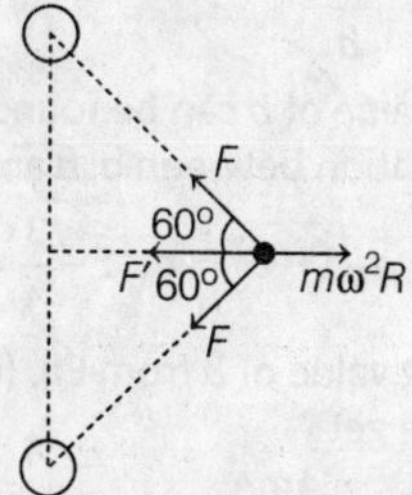

$$F' = \sqrt{F^2 + F^2 + 2FF\cos 120°} = F \quad ...(i)$$

From FBD of earth-sun system,

$$F' = m\omega^2 R = F \text{ [using Eq. (i)]}$$

Using Newton's law of gravitation,

$$\frac{GMm}{(2R)^2} = m\omega^2 R$$

$$\Rightarrow \quad \omega = \sqrt{\frac{GM}{4R^3}} = \frac{1}{2}\sqrt{\frac{GM}{R^3}} \quad ...(ii)$$

∴ Time period of earth in imaginary situation,

$$T' = \frac{2\pi}{\omega} = 4\pi\sqrt{\frac{R^3}{GM}} = 2T$$

(As for earth in our solar system, time period is $T = 2\pi\sqrt{\frac{R^3}{GM}}$)

6. As, acceleration due to gravity earth's surface, $g = \frac{GM}{R^2}$

When radius shrinks by 1%, then

$$R' = \left(1 - \frac{1}{100}\right)R = \frac{99}{100}R$$

So, value of g becomes

$$g' = \frac{GM}{R'^2} = \frac{GM(100)^2}{(99)^2 R^2}$$

$$\therefore \text{\% increase in } g = \frac{(g'-g)\times 100}{g}$$

$$= \left(\frac{g'}{g} - 1\right)\times 100 = \left[\left(\frac{100}{99}\right)^2 - 1\right]\times 100$$

$$= \left[\left(1 + \frac{1}{99}\right)^2 - 1\right]\times 100$$

$$= (1.02 - 1)\times 100 \approx 2\%$$

7. From FBD of block,

$$kx = mg$$

$$\Rightarrow \quad x = \frac{mg}{k} \quad ...(i)$$

⇒ Potential energy of spring

$$U = \frac{1}{2}kx^2 = \frac{1}{2}k\left(\frac{mg}{k}\right)^2$$

[using Eq. (i)]

$$= \frac{m^2 g^2}{2k} \Rightarrow U \propto g^2 \quad ...(ii)$$

Now, g at earth's surface,

$$g_1 = \frac{GM}{R^2} \quad ...(iii)$$

while g at height R (which is equal to distance $2R$ from earth's centre),

$$g_2 = \frac{GM}{(2R)^2} \quad ...(iv)$$

Dividing Eq. (iv) by Eq (iii), we get

$$\frac{g_2}{g_1} = \frac{1}{4} \quad ...(v)$$

Therefore, from Eq. (ii),

$$\frac{U_2}{U_1} = \left(\frac{g_2}{g_1}\right)^2 = \frac{1}{16}$$

[using Eqs. (ii) and (v)]

Therefore, $U_2 = \frac{U_1}{16} = \frac{E}{16}$

8. Given, $3\sigma = 7\rho$

Mass of material of density σ,

$$m_1 = \sigma\frac{4}{3}\pi R^3 \quad ...(i)$$

Mass of material of density ρ,

$$m_2 = \rho\frac{4}{3}\pi(R'^3 - R^3)$$

$$= \frac{3\sigma}{7}\cdot\frac{4\pi}{3}(R'^3 - R^3) \quad ...(ii)$$

Acceleration due to gravity at surface will be due to $m_1 + m_2$ while at interface, it will only be due to m_1 as per Shell theorem. As the two are given equal, $g_{surface} = g_{interface}$

$$\Rightarrow \quad \frac{G(m_1+m_2)}{R'^2} = \frac{Gm_1}{R^2}$$

$$\Rightarrow \quad \left(\frac{R'}{R}\right)^2 = \frac{m_2}{m_1} + 1 = \frac{3}{7}\left(\frac{R'^3}{R^3} - 1\right) + 1$$

[using Eqs. (i) and (ii)]...(iii)

Out of the given values, only $\frac{R'}{R} = 2$, satisfies Eq. (iii).

9. As acceleration due to gravity depends on height h and is given by

$$g' = g\left(1 - \frac{2h}{R}\right) \quad ...(i)$$

its value will be different at different location of pans (say g_1 and g_2 as shown)

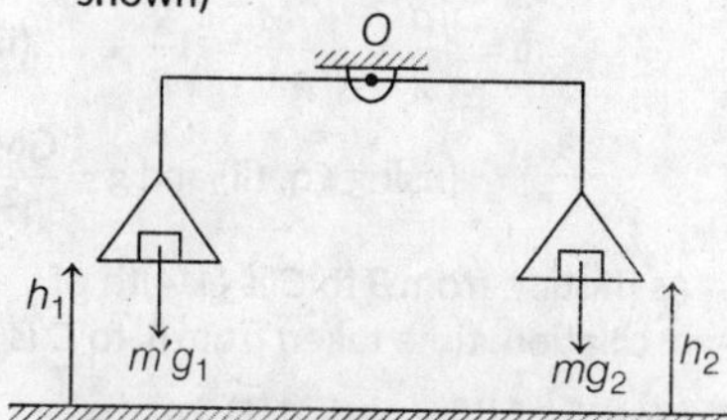

In equilibrium, $m' g_1 = mg_2$

$$\Rightarrow \text{Measured mass, } m' = \frac{mg_2}{g_1}$$

$$\therefore \text{ Error, } \Delta m = m' - m = \frac{mg_2}{g_1} - m$$

$$= m\left(\frac{g_2}{g_1} - 1\right) \quad ...(ii)$$

Putting values of g_1 and g_2 using Eqs. (i) and (ii), we get

$$\Delta m = m\left[\frac{g\left(1 - \frac{2h_2}{R}\right)}{g\left(1 - \frac{2h_1}{R}\right)} - 1\right]$$

$$= m\left[\left(1 - \frac{2h_2}{R}\right)\left(1 - \frac{2h_1}{R}\right)^{-1} - 1\right]$$

$$\approx m\left[\left(1 - \frac{2h_2}{R}\right)\left(1 + \frac{2h_1}{R}\right) - 1\right]$$

$$\Rightarrow \Delta m = m\left[1 + \frac{2(h_1 - h_2)}{R} - \frac{4h_1h_2}{R^2} - 1\right]$$

$$\approx \frac{2m(h_1 - h_2)}{R}$$

(neglecting $\frac{4h_1h_2}{R^2}$, as it is very small)

$$= \frac{2ml}{R} \quad (\because h_1 - h_2 = 2l - l = l)$$

10. For motion from A to B,

$$s = ut + \frac{1}{2}at^2$$

$$\Rightarrow \quad h = 0 + \frac{1}{2}gt^2$$

$$\Rightarrow \quad t = \sqrt{\frac{2h}{g}} \quad ...(i)$$

Consider the particle at a general position P distant x from C. Force on the particle,

$F = mE = \dfrac{mGMx}{R^3}$ directed towards centre

∴ Acceleration of particle,

$$a = \frac{F}{m} = \frac{GM}{R^3}x \quad \text{... (ii)}$$

As force and acceleration are always towards centre and proportional to x, particle will execute SHM while inside earth. For SHM,

$$\omega = \sqrt{\frac{a}{x}} = \sqrt{\frac{GM}{R^3}} = \sqrt{\frac{g}{R}} \quad \text{...(iii)}$$

$$\left[\text{using Eq. (ii) and } g = \frac{GM}{R^2}\right]$$

As motion from B to C is (1/4)th of oscillation, time taken from B to C is (1/4)th of time period (T). i.e. $t' = \dfrac{T}{4}$

$$= \frac{\pi}{2\omega} = \frac{\pi}{2}\sqrt{\frac{R}{g}} \quad \text{...(iv)}$$

[using Eq (iii)]

Dividing Eq. (iv) by Eq. (i), we get

$$t' = \frac{\pi}{2}\sqrt{\frac{R}{2h}}\,t = \pi\sqrt{\frac{R}{8h}}\,t$$

11. Lets imagine an identical hemispherical shell (shell B) below the given hemispherical shell (shell A) as shown, thereby completing a hollow sphere of mass $2M$. At point Q net field due to the sphere

$$\frac{G(2M)}{(2R)^2} = \frac{GM}{2R^2}$$

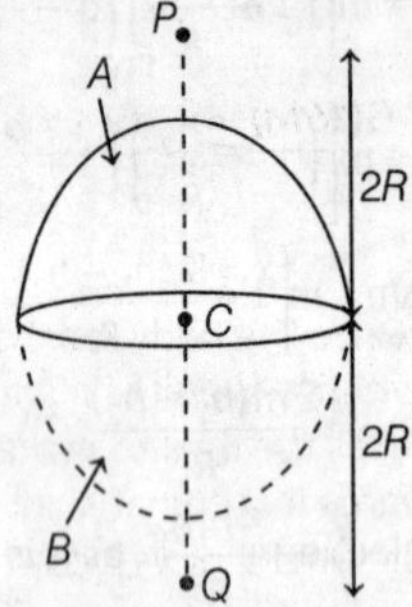

$$\Rightarrow E_A + E_B = \frac{GM}{2R^2}$$

$$\Rightarrow E_A = \frac{GM}{2R^2} - E_B = \frac{GM}{2R^2} - I$$

(As by symmetry, field at P due to hemisphere A is same as field at Q due to hemisphere B)

12. Potential at O due to element dm,

$$dV = -\frac{Gdm}{R}$$

$$\Rightarrow V = -\frac{G}{R}\int dm = -\frac{Gm}{R} \quad \text{...(i)}$$

Likewise, consider an element on wire at distance y from O having thickness dy as shown.

(From ΔOAP, $OA = OP \cot 45° = R$.
From ΔOBP, $OB = OP \cot\theta = 2R$)

Mass of element

$$= \frac{m}{l}dy = \frac{m}{2R - R}dy = \frac{m}{R}dy$$

Potential due to element of wire,

$$dV = -\frac{Gdm}{y} = -\frac{Gm}{R}\frac{dy}{y}$$

$$\Rightarrow V = -\frac{Gm}{R}\int_R^{2R}\frac{dy}{y} = -\frac{Gm}{R}\ln 2 \quad \text{...(ii)}$$

We get the potential at O by adding Eqs. (i) and (ii),

$$V_{\text{net}} = \frac{-Gm}{R}(1 + \ln 2)$$

13. The given situation can be shown below, where mass m is at distance x from the elementary part of rod dx.

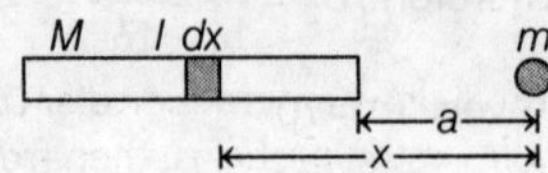

Then, the potential energy due to this elementary part can be given as

$$dU = \frac{-Gm\left(\dfrac{M}{l}dx\right)}{x}$$

Integrating above equation, we get

$$\Rightarrow \int dU = \frac{-GmM}{l}\int_a^{a+l}\frac{dx}{x}$$

$$\Rightarrow U = \frac{-GmM}{l}\log_e\left(\frac{a+l}{a}\right)$$

14. Even if gravitational force does not depend inversely on square of separation, torque of gravitational force about sun would still be zero as line of action would pass through sun. It results in conservation of angular momentum L of planet about sun.

∴ Areal speed $\left(= \dfrac{L}{2m}\right)$ will also be constant.

Hence, Kepler's second law is valid here.

15. If we assume b as semi-minor axis, angular momentum of the planet w.r.t. sun is $L = mvb = pb$

$$\Rightarrow \quad p = \frac{L}{b} \quad \text{...(i)}$$

Also, as angular momentum of planet w.r.t. sun is constant, it will be same at P and Q. It is related to areal speed A by the relation

$$L = 2mA \quad \text{...(ii)}$$

Putting value of L from Eq. (ii) in Eq. (i), we get

$$p = \frac{2mA}{b} \quad \text{...(iii)}$$

Also, value of b can be found using the relation between a, b and e. i.e.

$$b = a\sqrt{1 - e^2} = a\sqrt{1 - \frac{3}{4}} = \frac{a}{2} \quad \text{...(iv)}$$

Putting value of b from Eq. (iv) in Eq. (iii), we get

$$p = \frac{4mA}{a}$$

16. Energy at P = Kinetic energy + Potential energy

$$= \frac{1}{2}mv^2 - \frac{GMm}{\infty} = \frac{1}{2}mv^2 \quad \text{...(i)}$$

$$\text{Energy at } Q = \frac{1}{2}mv'^2 - \frac{GMm}{r} \quad \text{...(ii)}$$

By energy conservation, from Eqs. (i) and (ii), we get

$$\frac{1}{2}mv^2 = \frac{1}{2}mv'^2 - \frac{GMm}{r}$$

$$\Rightarrow \frac{1}{2}mv^2 = \frac{1}{2}m\left(\frac{vl}{r}\right)^2 - \frac{GMm}{r}$$

(as by conservation of angular momentum, $mvl = mv'r$ or $v' = \dfrac{vl}{r}$)

$$\Rightarrow \left(\frac{v^2l^2}{2}\right)\frac{1}{r^2} - GM\left(\frac{1}{r}\right) - \frac{v^2}{2} = 0$$

This is a quadratic equation of $\dfrac{1}{r}$.

Roots of this equation will therefore be

$$\frac{1}{r} = \frac{GM \pm \sqrt{(GM)^2 - 4\left(\dfrac{v^2l^2}{2}\right)\left(\dfrac{-v^2}{2}\right)}}{2\left(\dfrac{v^2l^2}{2}\right)}$$

$$=\frac{GM \pm \sqrt{(GM)^2 + v^4 l^2}}{v^2 l^2} \quad \text{...(iii)}$$

Putting given value of $v^2 = \frac{\sqrt{3}GM}{l}$ in Eq. (iii), we get

$$\frac{1}{r} = \frac{GM \pm \sqrt{(GM)^2 + 3(GM)^2}}{\sqrt{3}GMl}$$

$$\Rightarrow \frac{1}{r} = \frac{\sqrt{3}}{l} \text{ and } -\frac{1}{\sqrt{3}l}$$

$\therefore$ Acceptable value of $r = \frac{l}{\sqrt{3}}$

17. The potential energy of a particle of mass m and element dM of ring-1 is

$$dU = -\frac{GdMm}{2R}$$

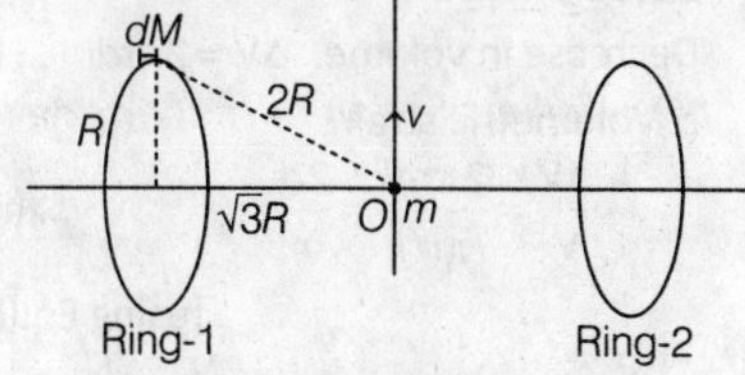

$$\Rightarrow \text{Potential energy, } U_0 = \frac{-Gm}{2R}\int dM$$

$$= -\frac{GMm}{2R} \quad \text{...(i)}$$

Similarly, potential energy of particle with ring-2 will also be same. Thus, total potential energy,

$$U = 2U_0 = -\frac{GMm}{R} \quad \text{...(ii) [using Eq. (i)]}$$

By conservation of energy,

Energy at O = Energy at infinity

$$\Rightarrow \frac{1}{2}mv^2 - \frac{GMm}{R} = 0 \quad \text{[using Eq. (ii)]}$$

$$\Rightarrow v = \sqrt{\frac{2GM}{R}}$$

18. Acceleration of a satellite (or any particle) in gravitational field of earth is equal to F/m which is equal to gravitational field of earth. So, acceleration is independent of speed and mass of particle. Therefore, it will remain unchanged and so $\frac{a_1}{a_2} = 1$

19. It is given that, $v_o = \frac{v_e}{2}$

$$\Rightarrow \sqrt{\frac{GM}{r}} = \frac{1}{2}\sqrt{\frac{2GM}{R}}$$

$$\Rightarrow r = 2R$$

$\therefore$ By energy conservation between P and Q, Gain in KE = Loss in PE

$$\Rightarrow K = \left(-\frac{GMm}{2R}\right) - \left(-\frac{GMm}{R}\right)$$

$$= \frac{GMm}{2R} \quad \text{...(i)}$$

Also, by energy conservation between positions T and S,

Kinetic energy at T = Energy at S

$$\Rightarrow K' = -\frac{GMm}{4R} + K = \frac{-K}{2} + K = 0.5K$$

[using Eq. (i)]

20. Angular speed ω of a satellite is related to orbital radius r as $r = \sqrt[3]{\frac{GM}{\omega^2}}$

When angular speed of earth becomes 8 times to keep the satellite geo-stationary, then its angular speed should also become 8 times.

Therefore, new orbital radius,

$$r' = \sqrt[3]{\frac{GM}{(8\omega)^2}} = \frac{1}{4}\sqrt[3]{\frac{GM}{\omega^2}} = \frac{r}{4}$$

So, orbital radius decreases by

$$r - \frac{r}{4} = \frac{3r}{4}$$

21. Let orbital radius be R.

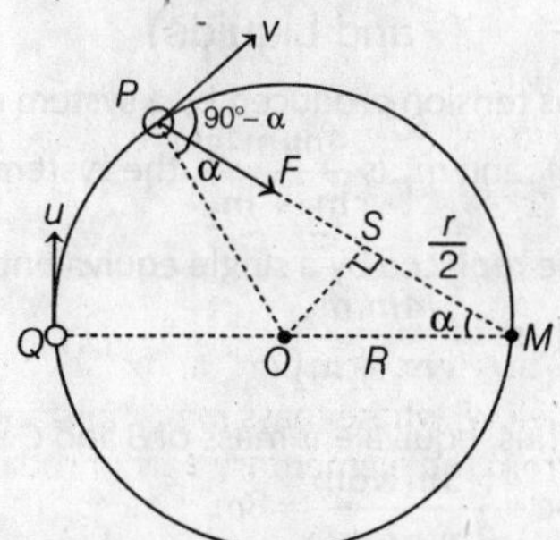

If we draw a perpendicular OS on line joining the particles, then from ΔOSM,

$$SM = \frac{r}{2} = R\cos\alpha$$

$$\Rightarrow \cos\alpha = \frac{r}{2R} \quad \text{...(i)}$$

As shown in the problem, line of force at any instant passes through fixed mass M, so torque of F about M is zero. Hence, angular momentum (L) of particle about M is conserved. Now, about M, lets equate angular momentum in positions Q and P.

$$L_Q = L_P$$

$$\Rightarrow mu(2R) = mvr\sin(90 - \alpha)$$

(as angle between velocity and relative position vector is $90° - \alpha$)

$$\Rightarrow v = \frac{2uR}{r\cos\alpha} = \frac{2uR}{r \cdot r/2R} = \frac{4uR^2}{r^2} \quad \text{...(ii)}$$

[using Eq. (i)]

Now, radial component of force in circular motion is equal to $\frac{mv^2}{r}$.

$$\Rightarrow F\cos\alpha = \frac{mv^2}{R}$$

$$\Rightarrow F = \frac{mv^2}{R\cos\alpha} = \frac{m\left(\frac{4uR^2}{r^2}\right)^2}{R\frac{r}{2R}}$$

[using Eqs. (i) and (ii)]

$$\Rightarrow F = \frac{32mu^2R^4}{r^5}$$

$$\Rightarrow F \propto \frac{1}{r^5} \quad \therefore \quad n = 5$$

22. For points inside earth, $g = \frac{g_0 r}{R}$

$$\Rightarrow \frac{g_0}{2} = \frac{g_0 r_1}{R}$$

$$\Rightarrow r_1 = \frac{R}{2} = 0.5R \quad \text{...(i)}$$

For points outside earth, $g = \frac{g_0 R^2}{r^2}$

$$\Rightarrow \frac{g_0}{2} = \frac{g_0 R^2}{r_2^2}$$

$$\Rightarrow r_2 = \sqrt{2}R = 1.41R \quad \text{...(ii)}$$

Adding Eqs. (i) and (ii), we get

$$r_1 + r_2 = 1.91R$$

Hence, $x = 1.91$

23. First we have to find a point where the resultant field due to both is zero. Let the point P be at a distance x from centre of bigger star.

$$\Rightarrow \frac{G(16M)}{x^2} = \frac{GM}{(10a - x)^2}$$

$$\Rightarrow x = 8a$$

i.e. Once the body reaches P, the gravitational pull of attraction due to M takes the lead to make m move towards it automatically. So, minimum KE or velocity has to be imparted to m from surface of $16M$ such that it is just able to cross point P

By law of conservation of energy,

Total mechanical energy at A

= Total mechanical energy at P

$$\Rightarrow \frac{1}{2}mv_{min}^2 + \left[-\frac{G(16M)m}{2a} - \frac{G(M)m}{8a}\right]$$

$$= 0 + \left[-\frac{GMm}{2a} - \frac{G(16M)m}{8a}\right]$$

$$\Rightarrow \frac{1}{2}mv_{min}^2 = \frac{GMm}{8a}(45)$$

$$\Rightarrow \quad v_{min} = \frac{3}{2}\sqrt{\frac{5GM}{a}}$$

Comparing with given value, we get

$$k = 5$$

24. Time period of revolution of planet in circular orbit is given by

$$T = 2\pi\sqrt{\frac{r^3}{GM}} \quad \text{...(i)}$$

When the planet is suddenly stopped, it is attracted by sun and the planet strikes sun following a straight path. This path can be perceived as super highly eccentric elliptical orbit followed by planet having major axis equal to initial orbital radius r as shown. Time of motion from A to B is approximately equal to half of the time period in this orbit as AB is approximately half of ellipse.

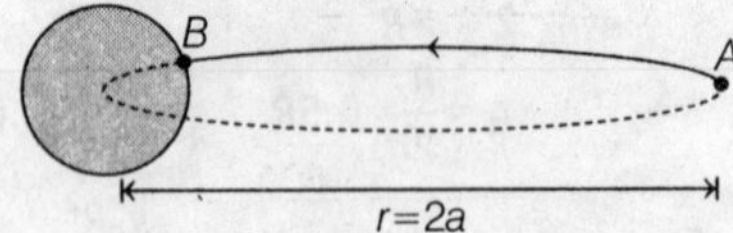

As, time period of planet in terms of semi-major axis is given by

$$T' = 2\pi\sqrt{\frac{a^3}{GM}}$$

$$\Rightarrow \quad T' = 2\pi\sqrt{\frac{\left(\frac{r}{2}\right)^3}{GM}} = \frac{2\pi}{2^{3/2}}\cdot\sqrt{\frac{r^3}{GM}} \quad \text{...(ii)}$$

Therefore, time of motion from A to B,

$$T'' = \frac{T'}{2} = \frac{2\pi}{2^{5/2}}\sqrt{\frac{r^3}{GM}}$$

[using Eq. (ii)] ...(iii)

Dividing Eq. (iii) by Eq (i), we get

$$\frac{T''}{T} = \frac{1}{2^{5/2}} \Rightarrow T'' = \frac{T}{2^{5/2}}$$

$$\Rightarrow \quad x = \frac{5}{2} = 2.5$$

25. Time period of a planet in circular orbit around sun of mass M is related to orbital radius R by the following relation

$$T = 2\pi\sqrt{\frac{R^3}{GM}}$$

$$\Rightarrow \quad T^2 = 4\pi^2\cdot\frac{R^3}{GM}$$

$$\Rightarrow \quad R^3 = \frac{GM}{4\pi^2}\cdot T^2$$

Taking log on both sides, we get

$$3\log R = 2\log T + \log\frac{GM}{4\pi^2}$$

$$\Rightarrow \quad \log R = \frac{2}{3}\log T + \frac{1}{3}\log\frac{GM}{4\pi^2}$$

Comparing it with equation of straight line

$$y = mx + C$$

we get, y intercept,

$$C = \frac{1}{3}\log\frac{GM}{4\pi^2} \Rightarrow \frac{GM}{4\pi^2} = 10^{3C}$$

From given graph, $C = 7$

$$\Rightarrow \quad \frac{GM}{4\pi^2} = 10^{21}$$

$$\Rightarrow \quad M = \frac{4\pi^2 \times 10^{21}}{G}$$

Substituting given values, we get

$$M = \frac{4 \times 10 \times 10^{21}}{\frac{20}{3}\times 10^{-11}} = 6 \times 10^{32} \text{ kg}$$

$$\Rightarrow \quad a = 6, \; b = 32$$

So, $\frac{b}{a} = \frac{32}{6} = 5.33$

Qualifier 7 (Properties of Soilds and Liquids)

1. As tension produced by a system of m_1 and m_2 is $\frac{4m_1m_2g}{m_1 + m_2}$, the system can be replaced by a single equivalent mass of $\frac{4m_1m_2}{m_1 + m_2}$.

Thus, equivalent mass of B and C will be $\frac{4 \times 3m \times 6m}{3m + 6m} = 8m$

Therefore, on equivalent basis, the FBD of this system is as shown. Acceleration of the blocks will be

$$a = \frac{(12m - 8m)g}{12m + 8m}$$

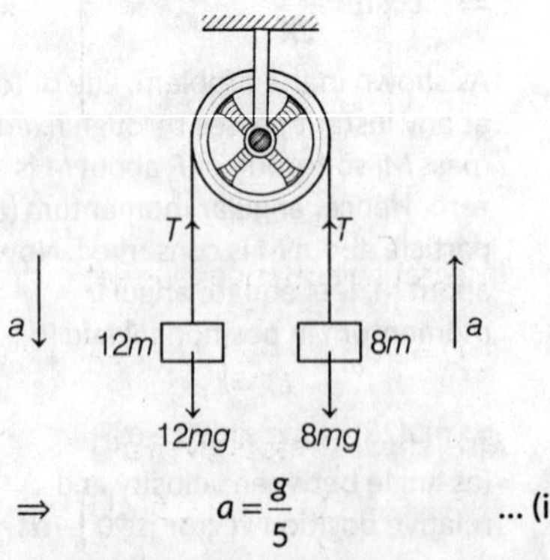

$$\Rightarrow \quad a = \frac{g}{5} \quad \text{... (i)}$$

From FBD of $12m$, using $F_{net} = m \times a$

$$\Rightarrow \quad 12\,mg - T = 12m \times \frac{g}{5}$$

[using Eq. (i)]

$$\Rightarrow \quad T = \frac{48mg}{5}$$

$$\Rightarrow \text{Stress in wire} = \frac{T}{A} = \frac{48mg}{5A} \quad \text{... (ii)}$$

Also, strain in wire $= \frac{\Delta l}{l}$ ... (iii)

By Hooke's law,

$$\text{Young's modulus} = Y = \frac{\text{Stress}}{\text{Strain}} \quad \text{... (iv)}$$

Putting values from Eqs. (ii) and (iii) in Eq. (iv), we get

$$Y = \frac{48mgl}{5A\Delta l} \Rightarrow \Delta l = \frac{48mgl}{5AY}$$

2. Decrease in radius of cork, when in bottle's mouth $= d$

Decrease in volume, $\Delta V = 2\pi r d l$ ... (i)

$\therefore$ Volumetric strain,

$$\frac{\Delta V}{V} = \frac{2\pi r d l}{\pi r^2 l} = \frac{2d}{r} \quad \text{... (ii)}$$

[using Eq.(i)]

Also, volumetric stress $= \frac{N}{A} = \frac{N}{2\pi r l}$ ... (iii)

Now, compressibility,

$$K = \frac{1}{\text{Bulk Modulus}} = \frac{\text{Strain}}{\text{Stress}}$$

$$\Rightarrow K = \frac{\frac{2d}{r}}{\frac{N}{2\pi r l}} \quad \text{[using Eqs. (ii) and (iii)]}$$

$$\Rightarrow \quad N = \frac{4\pi d l}{K} \quad \text{...(iv)}$$

$$\therefore \text{ Limiting friction, } f_l = \mu N = \frac{4\pi\mu d l}{K}$$

[using Eq. (iv)]

It is the minimum pulling force needed to pull the cork out.

3. Assuming V as volume of each triangular plate, weight of triangular plate DAB equal to ρV will act at its centre of mass C_1 which is at (1/3) rd of height $\left(\frac{l}{\sqrt{2}}\right)$ from base.

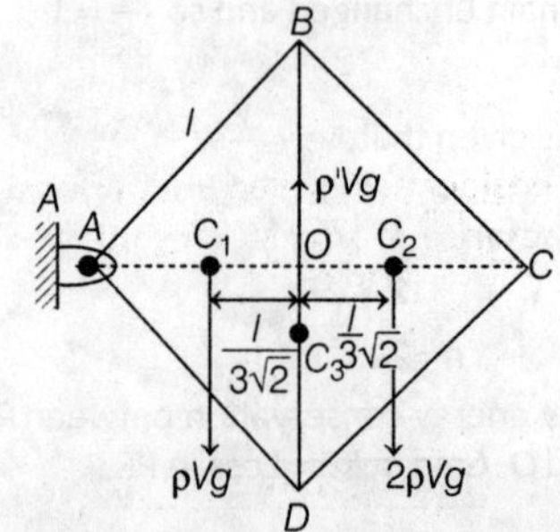

Similarly, weight of plate BCD acts at its centre of mass C_2. Buoyancy is equal to weight of displaced fluid $(=\rho' Vg)$.

It acts at centre of buoyancy C_3 or centre of mass of displaced fluid.

For equilibrium, net torque about $A =$ zero

$$\Rightarrow \rho Vg(AC_1)+2\rho Vg(AC_2) - \rho' Vg(AO)=0$$

$$\Rightarrow \rho Vg\left(\frac{2l}{3\sqrt{2}}\right)+2\rho Vg\left(\frac{4l}{3\sqrt{2}}\right)-\rho' Vg\left(\frac{l}{\sqrt{2}}\right)=0$$

$$\Rightarrow \quad \rho'=\frac{10}{3}\rho=3.33\,\rho$$

4. Acceleration at any instant is the slope of v-t graph. Therefore, accelerations will be as shown in FBD of ball at various instants. By $F_{net}=ma$

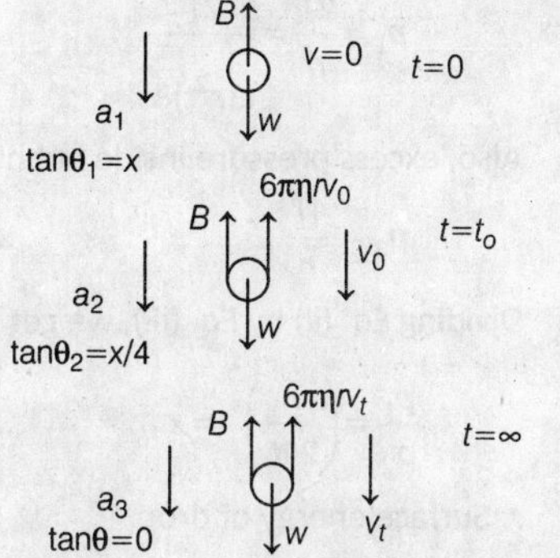

At $t=0$, $w - B = ma_1 = mx$ ... (i)

At $t=t_0$, $w - B - 6\pi\eta r v_0 = m\dfrac{x}{4}$ ... (ii)

At $t\to\infty$, $w - B - 6\pi\eta r v_t = 0$ ...(iii)

From Eqs. (i) and (ii), we get

$$6\pi\eta r v_0=\frac{3mx}{4} \quad \text{... (iv)}$$

From Eqs. (i) and (iii), we get

$$6\pi\eta r v_t = mx \quad \text{...(v)}$$

From Eqs. (iv) and (v), we get

$$v_t=\frac{4}{3}v_0 \quad \text{... (vi)}$$

From Eq. (iii), $\eta=\dfrac{w-\dfrac{w}{1.5}}{6\pi r v_t}=\dfrac{w}{18\pi r v_t}$

$$=\frac{w}{18\pi r\times\frac{4}{3}v_0}=\frac{w}{24\pi r v_0}$$

[using Eq. (vi)]

5. (c) Consider a fluid element of mass dm before and after striking the bend.

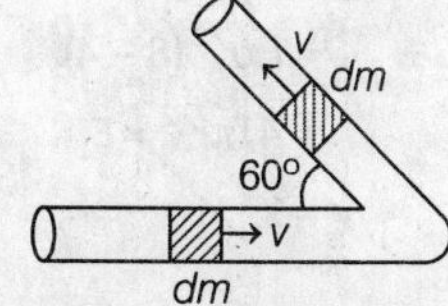

Change in momentum of the element,

$$dp = dm\sqrt{v^2+v^2-2vv\cos 120°}$$

$$\Rightarrow \quad dp = dm\sqrt{3}v$$

$$\Rightarrow \quad F=\frac{dp}{dt}=\frac{dm\sqrt{3}v}{dt}$$

$$=\rho av\,\sqrt{3}v=\sqrt{3}\rho av^2$$

$$\left(\because \text{ mass flow rate, } \frac{dm}{dt}=\rho av\right)$$

6. Consider a disc element of radius x and thickness dx as shown. Velocity of any particle of the element is $v(=\omega x)$ as shown.

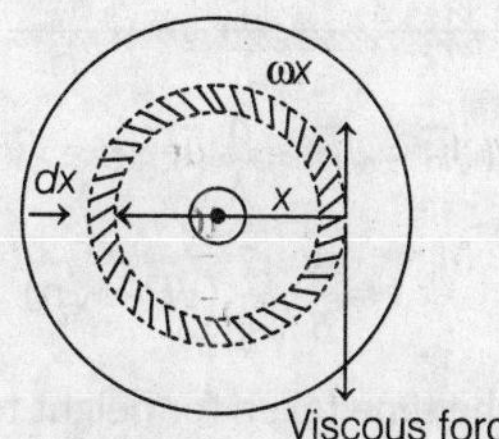

Viscous force will act opposite to velocity tangentially as shown. Torque of viscous force df,

$$d\tau = df\cdot x=\eta\cdot A\cdot\frac{v}{t}\cdot x$$

$$\Rightarrow d\tau=\eta\cdot 2\pi x\,dx\cdot\frac{\omega x}{t}\cdot x$$

Integrating both sides, we get

$$\text{Total torque, } \tau=\frac{2\pi\eta\omega}{t}\int_0^r x^3\,dx=\frac{\pi\eta\omega r^4}{2t}$$

7. Consider a rectangular strip of unit width (as shown) in between plates at a height y from central line.

Volume flow rate through strip,

$dQ = v\cdot dA$

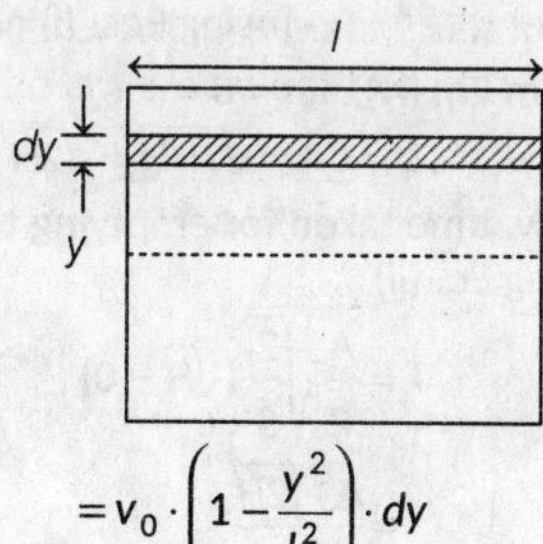

$$=v_0\cdot\left(1-\frac{y^2}{l^2}\right)\cdot dy$$

Integrating both sides, we get

$$Q=\int_{-l}^{l} v_0\left(1-\frac{y^2}{l^2}\right)dy=\frac{4v_0 l}{3} \quad \text{... (i)}$$

Also, shear stress is given by

$$\tau=-\eta\frac{dv}{dy}=-\eta\cdot\left(-\frac{2v_0 y}{l^2}\right)$$

$$=\frac{2v_0\eta y}{l^2}$$

At $y=\dfrac{l}{2}$, $\tau=\dfrac{2v_0\eta\frac{l}{2}}{l^2}=\dfrac{v_0\eta}{l}$ ...(ii)

Dividing Eq. (ii) by Eq. (i), we get

$$\frac{\tau}{Q}=\frac{3\eta}{4l^2}\Rightarrow \tau=\frac{3\eta Q}{4l^2}$$

8. Given, volume flow rate,

$$Q=100\text{ L min}^{-1}=\frac{1}{600}\text{m}^3/\text{ s}$$

$$r=\frac{5}{\pi}\times 10^{-2}\text{m}, \eta=10^{-3}\text{ Pa-s}$$

$$\rho=10^3\text{ kg/m}^3$$

Reynold's number, $R_e=\dfrac{\rho vD}{\eta}$

Using velocity, $v=\dfrac{Q}{\text{Area}}$ and diameter $D=2r$ in above equation, we get

$$R_e=\frac{\rho Q\cdot 2r}{\eta\cdot\pi r^2}=\frac{2\rho Q}{\pi\eta r}$$

$$\Rightarrow R_e=\frac{2\times 10^3\times\frac{1}{600}}{\pi\times 10^{-3}\times\frac{5}{\pi}\times 10^{-2}}$$

$$=6.67\times 10^4$$

9. Lets draw FBD of water portion between the manometers.

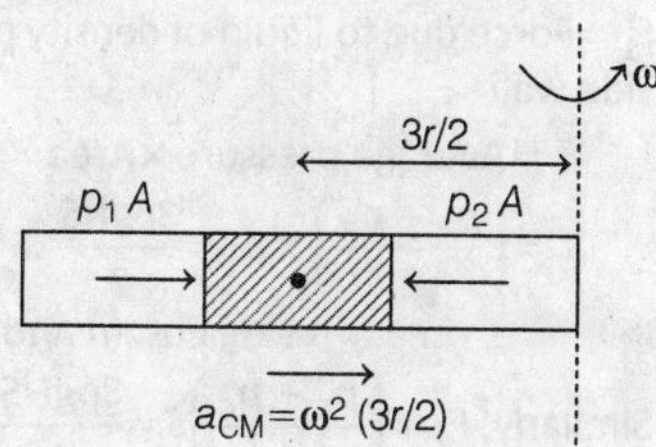

$$F_{net}=ma_{CM}$$

$$\Rightarrow p_1A-p_2A=\rho\cdot A\cdot r\cdot\omega^2\left(\frac{3r}{2}\right)$$

$$\Rightarrow \quad p_1-p_2=\frac{3\rho\omega^2 r^2}{2}=1.5\rho\omega^2 r^2$$

10. By applying Bernoulli's theorem for air flow between points P and Q,

Energy density at $P =$ Energy density at Q

$$\Rightarrow \quad p_1=p_2+\frac{1}{2}\sigma v^2$$

where, p_1 and p_2 are air pressure at P and Q respectively which will also be pressures on mercury surfaces.

$$\Rightarrow \quad p_1-p_2=\frac{1}{2}\sigma v^2$$

$$\Rightarrow \quad \rho gH=\frac{1}{2}\sigma v^2\Rightarrow v=\sqrt{\frac{2\rho gH}{\sigma}}$$

11. Consider the figure shown, pressure at point A is sum of pressures due to all liquid columns above point A.

$$p_A = \rho gH + \frac{\rho}{2}gH + \frac{\rho}{4}gH + \ldots$$

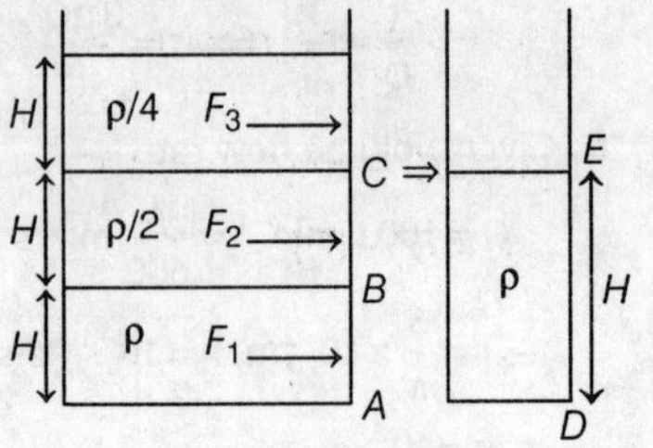

$$= \rho gH\left(1 + \frac{1}{2} + \frac{1}{4} + \ldots \infty \text{ terms}\right)$$

$$= \rho gH\left(\frac{1}{1-1/2}\right) \quad \left[\text{using, } s = \frac{a}{1-r}\right]$$

$$\Rightarrow \quad p_A = 2\rho gH \quad \ldots \text{(i)}$$

Similarly, $p_B = \frac{\rho}{2}gH + \frac{\rho}{4}gH + \ldots =$

$$\frac{\rho gH}{2}\left(1 + \frac{1}{2} + \ldots\right) = \rho gH \quad \ldots \text{(ii)}$$

$$p_C = \frac{\rho}{4}gH + \frac{\rho}{8}gH + \ldots =$$

$$\frac{\rho gH}{4}\left(1 + \frac{1}{2} + \ldots\right) = \frac{\rho gH}{2} \quad \ldots \text{(iii)}$$

and so on.

F_1 = Force due to liquid of density ρ on side wall

= Average pressure × Area

$$= \left(\frac{p_A + p_B}{2}\right) \times S = \frac{3\rho gHS}{2} \quad \ldots \text{(iv)}$$

[using Eqs. (i) and (ii)]

Similarly, $F_2 = \left(\frac{p_B + p_C}{2}\right)S = \frac{3\rho gHS}{4}$

[using Eqs. (ii) and (iii)] ... (v)

and so on.

So, net force on side wall is given by

$$F = F_1 + F_2 + \ldots = \frac{3\rho gHS}{2} + \frac{3\rho gHS}{4} + \ldots$$

[using Eqs. (iv) and (v)]

$$\Rightarrow F = \frac{3\rho gHS}{2}\left(1 + \frac{1}{2} + \ldots\right) = 3\rho gHS \quad \ldots \text{(vi)}$$

If the system is replaced by single liquid of height H'

$$F = \frac{(p_E + p_D)}{2} \times S = \frac{\rho gH'S}{2} \quad \ldots \text{(vii)}$$

From Eqs. (vi) and (vii), we get

$$H' = 6H$$

12. If at any instant, v = velocity of efflux

⇒ Velocity of liquid surface,

$$v' = \frac{av}{A} = \frac{a}{A}\sqrt{2gh}$$

(by continuity equation)

$$\Rightarrow \quad -\frac{dh}{dt} = \frac{a}{A}\sqrt{2gh}$$

$$\Rightarrow \quad \frac{dh}{\sqrt{h}} = \frac{a}{A}\sqrt{2g} \cdot dt$$

$$\Rightarrow \quad -\int_H^h \frac{dh}{\sqrt{h}} = \frac{a}{A}\sqrt{2g}\int_0^t dt$$

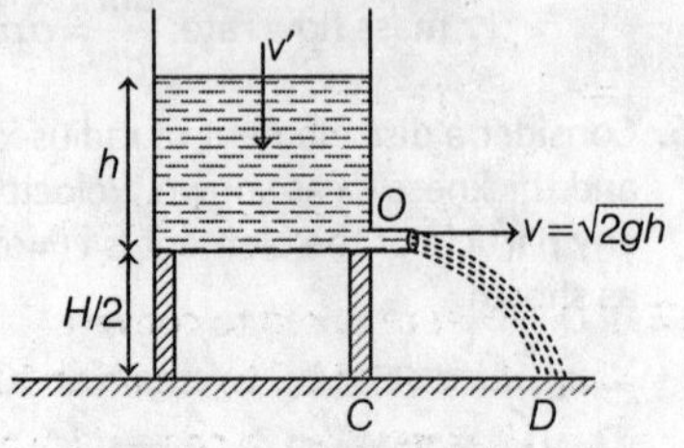

$$\Rightarrow 2(\sqrt{H} - \sqrt{h}) = \frac{a}{A}\sqrt{2g}\,t$$

$$\Rightarrow \quad t = \frac{A}{a}\sqrt{\frac{2}{g}}(\sqrt{H} - \sqrt{h}) \quad \ldots \text{(ii)}$$

It is the time taken for height to reduce from H to h.

Also, for motion of liquid drops from orifice O to point D at which the liquid drops strike the ground

$$s_y = u_y t + \frac{1}{2}a_y t^2$$

$$\Rightarrow \quad \frac{H}{2} = 0 + \frac{1}{2}gt'^2$$

⇒ Time of motion from O to D,

$$t' = \sqrt{\frac{H}{g}} \quad \ldots \text{(iii)}$$

∴ Horizontal displacement of liquid drops = $CD = v \cdot t'$

$$= \sqrt{2gh} \cdot \sqrt{\frac{H}{g}} = \sqrt{2hH} \quad \ldots \text{(iv)}$$

[using Eqs. (i) and (iii)]

From Eq. (iv), at $t = 0$,

$$CD = CA = \sqrt{2HH} = \sqrt{2}H \quad \ldots \text{(v)}$$

Now, time taken for emptying tank using Eq. (ii),

$$T = \frac{A}{a}\sqrt{\frac{2}{g}}(\sqrt{H} - 0)$$

$$= \frac{A}{a}\sqrt{\frac{2H}{g}} \quad \ldots \text{(vi)}$$

Therefore, at $t = \frac{T}{2}$, height of liquid H' is given by Eq. (ii),

$$\frac{T}{2} = \frac{A}{a}\sqrt{\frac{2}{g}}(\sqrt{H} - \sqrt{H'})$$

$$\Rightarrow \frac{A}{2a}\sqrt{\frac{2H}{g}} = \frac{A}{a}\sqrt{\frac{2}{g}}(\sqrt{H} - \sqrt{H'})$$

[using Eq. (vi)]

$$\Rightarrow \quad H' = \frac{H}{4} \quad \ldots \text{(vii)}$$

Thus, at $t = \frac{T}{2}$, $CD = CB = \sqrt{2H'H}$

[using Eqs. (iv) and (vii)]

$$= \sqrt{2\frac{H}{4}H} = \frac{H}{\sqrt{2}} \quad \ldots \text{(viii)}$$

$$\therefore CA - CB = \sqrt{2}H - \frac{H}{\sqrt{2}} = \frac{H}{\sqrt{2}}$$

[using Eqs. (v) and (viii)]

13. Let radius of drop is r'. By volume conservation in formation of drop,

$$V_{\text{bubble}} = V_{\text{drop}}$$

$$\Rightarrow \quad 4\pi r^2 t = \frac{4}{3}\pi r'^3$$

$$\Rightarrow \quad r' = (3r^2t)^{\frac{1}{3}} \quad \ldots \text{(i)}$$

⇒ Excess pressure inside drop,

$$p_1 = \frac{2T}{r'} = \frac{2T}{(3r^2t)^{\frac{1}{3}}} \quad \ldots \text{(ii)}$$

Also, excess pressure inside bubble,

$$p_2 = \frac{4T}{r} \quad \ldots \text{(iii)}$$

Dividing Eq. (ii) by Eq. (iii), we get

$$\frac{p_1}{p_2} = \left(\frac{r}{24t}\right)^{\frac{1}{3}} = x \quad \ldots \text{(iv)}$$

∴ Surface energy of drop,

$$E_1 = T \times A$$

$$= T \times 4\pi r'^2 \quad \ldots \text{(v)}$$

By volume conservation during breaking of drop into droplets

$$V_{\text{drop}} = V_{\text{droplets}}$$

$$\Rightarrow \quad \frac{4}{3}\pi r'^3 = 8 \times \frac{4}{3}\pi r''^3$$

Here, r'' = radius of droplet

$$\Rightarrow \quad r'' = \frac{r'}{2}$$

∴ Total surface area of droplets,

$$E_2 = 8 \times 4\pi r''^2$$

$$= 8 \times 4\pi\left(\frac{r'}{2}\right)^2 = 8\pi r'^2$$

∴ Surface energy of droplets

$$E_2 = T \times 8\pi r'^2 \quad \ldots \text{(vi)}$$

From Eqs. (vi) and (v), increase in surface energy,

$$\Delta E = E_2 - E_1$$

$$= T\pi r'^2(8 - 4)$$

$$= 4T\pi r'^2 = E_1$$

$$\therefore \quad y = 1$$

14. The trapped drop has curvature diameter equal to distance between plates d, so radius of curvature of liquid surface, $r = \frac{d}{2}$. ...(i)

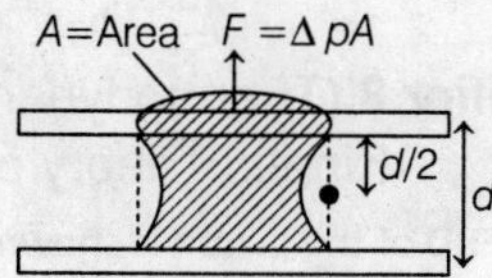

In a cylindrical curved surface, excess pressure,

$$\Delta p = \frac{T}{r} = \frac{2T}{d} \quad \text{... (ii) [using Eq. (i)]}$$

Thus, pressure inside drop is lesser by Δp or $\frac{2T}{d}$ compared to atmospheric pressure. So, glass plate 2 is sticking to it. To overcome it, a force F has to applied as shown.

$$\Rightarrow \quad F = \Delta p \cdot A = \frac{2TA}{d} = \frac{2TAd}{d^2} = \frac{2Tm}{\rho d^2}$$

$$\Rightarrow \quad T = \frac{F\rho d^2}{2m} \quad \text{... (iii)}$$

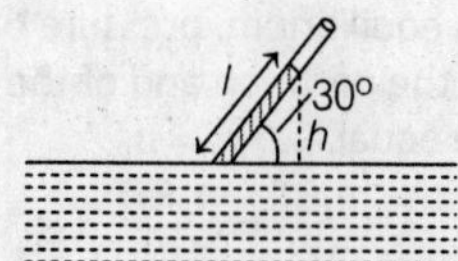

$$\text{So, } l = h \operatorname{cosec} 30° = 2h = \frac{4T}{\rho dg} = \frac{2Fd}{mg}$$

[using $h = 2T/\rho dg$ and Eq. (iii)]

15. Given, $L = 3$ m, $d = 1$ mm

$$\Rightarrow \quad r = \frac{1}{2} \times 10^{-3} \text{ m and } m = 10 \text{ kg.}$$

The contraction in the length of the wire due to change in temperature is given as

$$\Delta L_1 = \alpha L \Delta T$$
$$= 1.2 \times 10^{-5} \times 3 \times (-170 - 30)$$
$$= -7.2 \times 10^{-3} \text{ m}$$
$$A = 3.14 \times \left(\frac{1}{2} \times 10^{-3}\right)^2$$
$$\approx 0.75 \times 10^{-6} \text{m}^2$$

The expansion in the length of wire due to stretching force is given as

$$\Delta L_2 = \frac{FL}{AY} = \frac{mgL}{AY}$$
$$= \frac{(10 \times 10) \times 3}{(0.75 \times 10^{-6})(2 \times 10^{11})}$$
$$= 2 \times 10^{-3} \text{ m}$$

Resultant change in length,

$$\Delta L_1 + \Delta L_2 = -7.2 \times 10^{-3} + 2 \times 10^{-3}$$
$$\Delta L = -5.2 \times 10^{-3} = -5.2 \text{ mm}$$

Negative sign shows a contraction in the length of the wire.

16. Variation of density with temperature

$$\rho' = \rho(1 - \gamma \Delta T)$$
$$60 = 50[1 - \gamma(100 - 50)]$$
$$\frac{60}{50} = [1 - \gamma(50)]$$
$$\Rightarrow \quad 50\gamma = 1 - \frac{6}{5}$$
$$\gamma = -\frac{1}{250} \simeq -0.005/°\text{C}$$

17. If Q = Heat required to convert 3 kg of ice at −12°C to steam at 100°C.

Q_1 = Heat required to convert ice at −12°C to ice at 0°C

$$= ms_i \, \Delta T_1 = 3 \times 2100 \times [0 - (-12)]$$
$$= 75600 \text{ J}$$

Q_2 = Heat required to melt ice at 0°C to water at 0°C

$$= mL_i = 3 \times (3.35 \times 10^5) = 1005000 \text{ J}$$

Q_3 = Heat required to convert water at 0°C to water at 100°C

$$= ms_w \Delta T_2 = (3)$$
$$(4186 \text{ J kg}^{-1}\text{K}^{-1}) \times (100°\text{C})$$
$$= 1255800$$

Q_4 = Heat required to convert water at 100°C to steam at 100°C

$$= mL_s = 3 \times (2.256 \times 10^6) = 6768000 \text{ J}$$

So, $Q = Q_1 + Q_2 + Q_3 + Q_4$

$$= 75600 \text{ J} + 1005000 \text{ J} + 1255800 \text{ J} + 6768000 \text{ J}$$
$$= 9.1 \times 10^6 \text{ J}$$

18.

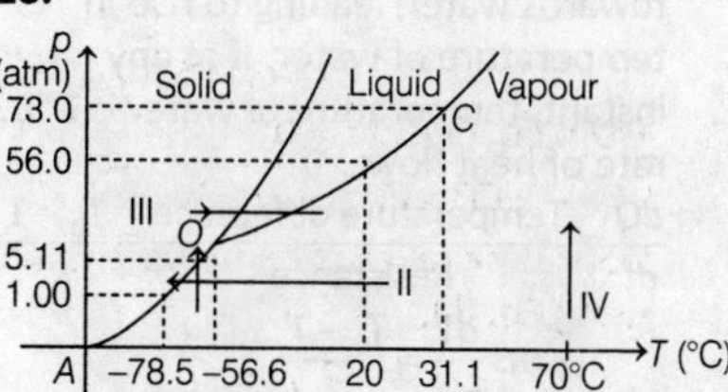

Here, statement II and III are correct and rest can be corrected as

I. From graph, it is clear that when CO_2 at 1 atm and −60°C is compressed isothermally, then it is converted into solid state directly without changing liquid state.

IV. When CO_2 is compressed at 70°C isothermally, then it cannot liquify because for liquification of CO_2 first it is cooled below critical temperature.

19. It is given that the first and third plate are maintained at temperature $2T$ and $3T$, respectively.

If T' be the temperature of second plate, then under steady state,

Rate of energy received = Rate of energy emitted

$$\sigma A(3T)^4 - \sigma A(T')^4 = \sigma A(T')^4 - \sigma A(2T)^4$$
$$\Rightarrow \quad (3T)^4 - (T')^4 = (T')^4 - (2T)^4$$
$$\Rightarrow \quad T' = \left(\frac{97}{2}\right)^{1/4} T$$

20. Rate of cooling as per Newton's law of cooling,

$$R = \frac{4e\sigma A T_0^3}{ms}(T - T_0)$$
$$R = \frac{4e\sigma \cdot 4\pi r^2 T_0^3}{\rho \cdot \frac{4}{3}\pi r^3 \cdot s}(T - T_0)$$
$$\Rightarrow \quad R \propto r^{-1}$$

21. As temperature is constant. For air inside bubble,

$$p_{\text{final}} V_{\text{final}} = p_{\text{initial}} V_{\text{initial}} \quad \text{... (i)}$$

As pressure inside bubble in terms of surrounding pressure p is

$$p_{\text{inside}} = p + \frac{4T}{r} \quad \text{... (ii)}$$

Now, air inside cylinder is compressed making volume $\frac{1}{8}$th or radius half, i.e. $\frac{r}{2}$. Also, assuming outside pressure equal to p'. Using Eq. (ii), final pressure inside bubble,

$$p_{\text{final}} = p' + \frac{4T}{r/2} = p' + \frac{8T}{r} \quad \text{... (iii)}$$

Also, $V_{\text{initial}} = 8V_{\text{final}}$ .... (iv)

Using value of Eqs. (ii), (iii) and (iv) in Eq. (i), we get

$$\left(p' + \frac{8T}{r}\right) V_{\text{final}} = \left(p + \frac{4T}{r}\right) 8V_{\text{final}}$$
$$\Rightarrow \quad p' + \frac{8T}{r} = 8p + \frac{32T}{r}$$
$$\Rightarrow \quad p' = 8p + \frac{24T}{r}$$

$\therefore$ Increment in pressure

$$= p' - p$$
$$= 7p + \frac{24T}{r}$$
$$\therefore \quad x = 7, y = 24$$

and $\frac{y}{x} = \frac{24}{7} = 3.42$

22. FBDs of block and ball are as shown.

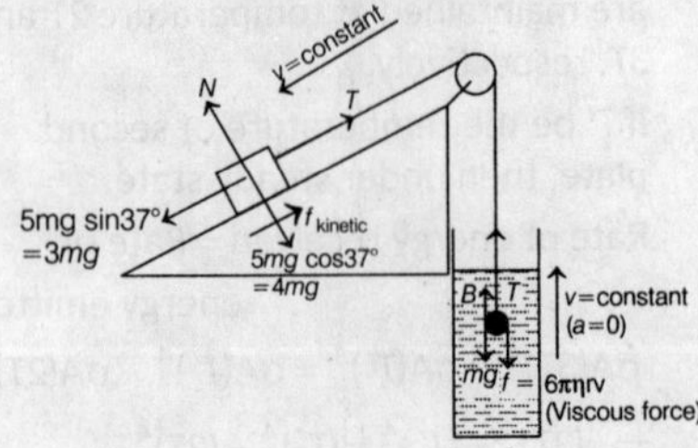

From FBD of block, as acceleration and net force are zero,

$$3mg = T + f_{\text{kinetic}}$$
$$= T + 0.02\,(4\,mg)$$
$$\Rightarrow \quad T = 2.92\,mg \quad \text{...(i)}$$

From FBD of ball,

$$B + T = mg + 6\pi\eta rv$$
$$\Rightarrow \frac{\rho}{2}vg + 2.92\,mg = mg + 6\pi\eta rv$$
$$\Rightarrow \frac{mg}{2} + 2.92\,mg = mg + 6\pi\eta rv$$
$$\Rightarrow \quad v = \frac{12.1\,mg}{30\pi\eta r} \quad \therefore \; x = 12.1$$

23. By continuity equation between A and B,

$$av = \frac{a}{5}v' \Rightarrow v' = 5v \quad \text{... (i)}$$

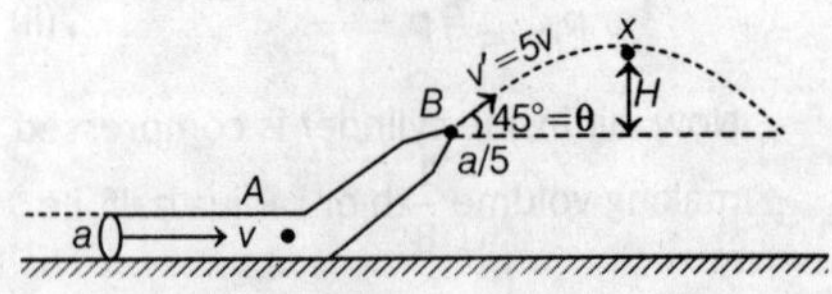

Using Bernoulli's equation between A and B,

$$\frac{1}{2}\rho v^2 + 2p_0 = \frac{1}{2}\rho(5v)^2 + p_0 + \rho g\left(\frac{p_0}{2\rho g}\right)$$

[using Eq. (i) and $h = \frac{p_0}{2\rho g}$]

$$\Rightarrow \; 12\rho v^2 = \frac{p_0}{2} \Rightarrow v = \sqrt{\frac{p_0}{24\rho}} \quad \text{... (i)}$$

Maximum height w.r.t. nozzle,

$$H = \frac{v'^2 \sin^2\theta}{2g}$$
$$= \frac{(5v)^2 \sin^2 45°}{2g} = \frac{25h}{48} \quad \text{... (ii)}$$

[using Eq. (i)]

$\therefore$ Maximum height of liquid particle from ground,

$$H_{\max} = H + h = \frac{25h}{48} + h = \frac{73h}{48}$$

Comparing with given value, we get

$$\alpha = 73 \text{ and } \beta = 48$$

$$\therefore \quad \alpha - \beta = 73 - 48 = 25$$

24. Thermal strain $= \frac{\Delta l}{l} = \alpha\,\Delta T$

Stress $= Y \times$ Strain $= Y\alpha\,\Delta T$

$$\frac{T}{A} = Y\alpha\,\Delta T$$
$$\Rightarrow m = \frac{YA\alpha\,\Delta T}{g} \quad (\because T = mg)$$
$$= \frac{1.5\times10^{11}\times8\times10^{-6}\times2\times10^{-5}\times5}{10}$$
$$= 12\text{ kg} \quad \text{... (i)}$$

Also, elastic potential energy,

$$U = \frac{1}{2}\times\text{stress}\times\text{strain}\times\text{volume}$$
$$= \frac{1}{2}\times\frac{mg}{A}\times\alpha\,\Delta T\times Al$$
$$= \frac{1}{2}\times12\times10\times1\times2\times10^{-5}\times5$$
$$= 0.006\text{ J} = 6\text{ mJ} \quad \text{... (ii)}$$

From Eqs. (i) and (ii), we get

$$m + U = 12 + 6 = 18$$

25. Lets first find resistance of shell. Consider a thin shell element of radius r and thickness dr.

Resistance of element,

$$dR = \frac{dr}{k\cdot4\pi r^2}$$

Resistance of shell,

$$R' = \frac{1}{4\pi k}\int_R^{2R}\frac{1}{r^2}dr = \frac{1}{4\pi k}\left[-\frac{1}{r}\right]_R^{2R}$$
$$\Rightarrow \quad R' = \frac{1}{8\pi kR} \quad \text{... (i)}$$

Heat will flow from hot air in chamber towards water, leading to rise in temperature of water. If at any instant, temperature of water is T °C, rate of heat flow,

$$\frac{dQ}{dt} = \frac{\text{Temperature difference}}{\text{Resistance}} = \frac{T_0 - T}{R'}$$
$$ms\frac{dT}{dt} = \frac{T_0 - T}{R'}$$
$$\Rightarrow \quad \frac{dT}{T_0 - T} = \frac{1}{msR'}dt$$

Integrating both sides, we get

$$\Rightarrow \quad \int_0^{\frac{T_0}{2}}\frac{dT}{T_0 - T} = \frac{1}{msR'}\int_0^t dt$$
$$\Rightarrow \quad \ln T_0 - \ln\left(T_0 - \frac{T_0}{2}\right) = \frac{t}{msR'}$$
$$\Rightarrow \quad t = msR'\ln 2 = \frac{ms}{8\pi kR}\ln 2$$

[using Eq. (i)]

$$\rho\cdot\frac{4}{3}\pi R^3 s$$
$$= \frac{\rho\cdot\frac{4}{3}\pi R^3 s}{8\pi\ln 2R}\ln 2 = \frac{\rho R^2 s}{6}$$

Comparing with the given value, we get $x = 6$

Qualifier 8 (Thermodynamics & Kinetic Theory of Gases)

1. FBD of the piston is shown as

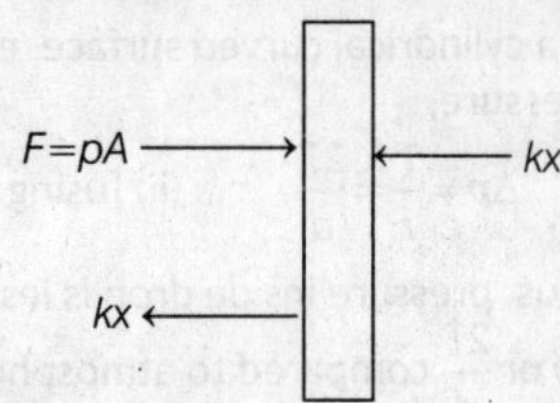

In equilibrium, net force on the piston becomes zero, so

$$pA - kx = kx$$
$$\Rightarrow \quad p = \frac{2kx}{A} \;\left(\text{Here, } x = \frac{L}{2}\right)$$
$$\therefore \quad p = \frac{2kL}{2A} = \frac{kL}{A}$$

2. In equilibrium, pressure on both sides of the partition and of the stopper will be equal, i.e. $p_1 = p_2$

$$\Rightarrow \quad \frac{n_1RT}{V_1} = \frac{n_2RT}{V_2}$$

As, $n = \frac{m}{M}$, where m is given mass and M is molar mass.

$$\Rightarrow \quad \frac{m}{M_1V_1} = \frac{m}{M_2V_2} \text{ or } \frac{V_2}{V_1} = \frac{M_1}{M_2}$$

Here, $M_1 = 32$ and $M_2 = 28$

$$\Rightarrow \quad \frac{V_2}{V_1} = \frac{32}{28} = \frac{8}{7}$$

So, the angle θ is $= \left[\frac{360°}{(8+7)}\right]\times8 = 192°$

3. FBD of the piston and block are as shown.

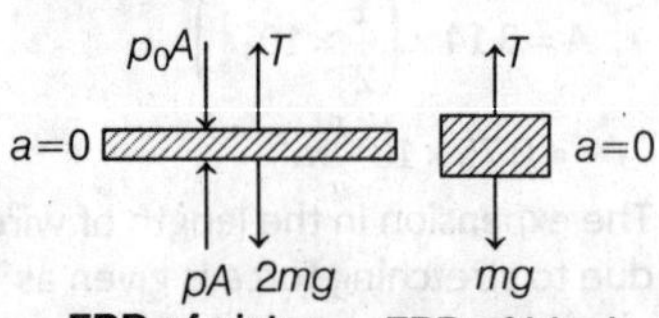

FBD of piston FBD of block

As acceleration of block is zero

$$T = mg \quad \text{... (i)}$$

Also, as acceleration of piston is zero,

$$pA + T = p_0A + 2mg \quad \text{... (ii)}$$

Subtracting Eq. (i) from Eq. (ii), we get

$$pA = p_0A + mg \quad \text{... (iii)}$$

As p_0 and mg are constants. So, p (gas pressure) is also constant and therefore the process is isobaric. By first law of thermodynamics, heat supplied,

$$dQ = dU + dW$$

$$\Rightarrow \quad dQ = \frac{f}{2} p \cdot dV + p \cdot dV$$

$$= \frac{f}{2} p \cdot A \cdot dx + p \cdot A \cdot dx$$

$$= p \cdot A \cdot dx\left(\frac{f}{2} + 1\right)$$

$$= 4p \cdot A \cdot dx$$

[As, f for ammonia is 6] ... (iv)

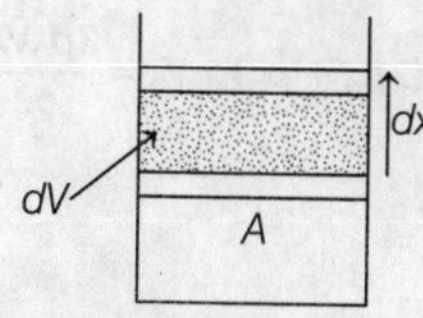

Dividing Eq. (iv) by time taken dt, we get

$$\frac{dQ}{dt} = 4pA\frac{dx}{dt}$$

$$\Rightarrow \quad p' = 4pAv$$

$$\Rightarrow \quad v = \frac{p'}{4pA}$$

$$\Rightarrow \quad v = \frac{p'}{4(p_0 A + mg)}$$

[using Eq. (iii)]

4. Let vessel volume is V and gas pressure is p.

Work done by surroundings applying constant pressure p while pushing the gas (n moles) into container

$$W = pV$$

$$\Rightarrow \quad W = nRT$$

(using ideal gas equation) ... (i)

Also, as the gas is suddenly pushed in, the process is adiabatic ($Q = 0$).

By first law of thermodynamics, if ΔU is change in internal energy,

$$W + Q = \Delta U$$

$$\Rightarrow \quad nRT + 0 = \frac{nR}{\gamma - 1}(T' - T)$$

[using Eq. (i)]

[here, T' = final temperature]

$$\Rightarrow \quad T' = \gamma T$$

5. As the walls of the containers are adiabatic (insulated), internal energy of the system will be conserved. Therefore,

Final internal energy (U_{final}) = Initial internal energy (U_{final})

$$\Rightarrow U_{\underset{\text{(final)}}{\text{He}}} + U_{\underset{\text{(final)}}{O_2}} = U_{\underset{\text{(initial)}}{\text{He}}} + U_{\underset{\text{(initial)}}{O_2}}$$

$$\Rightarrow \quad \frac{3}{2}pV_0 + \frac{5}{2}p(2V_0)$$

$$= \frac{3}{2}p_0V_0 + \frac{5}{2}(2p_0)(2V_0)$$

Here, p = final pressure and internal energies are written using formula $U = \frac{f}{2}pV$ (where, f or degree of freedom is 3 for monoatomic and 5 for diatomic)

$$\Rightarrow \quad \frac{13}{2}pV_0 = \frac{23p_0V_0}{2}$$

$$\Rightarrow \quad p = \frac{23p_0}{13}$$

6. On tilting vertical, mercury length and pressure will reduce, so oxygen will expand. Also, as tube is conducting, so expansion will be isothermal (T = constant). Therefore,

$$pV = nRT = \text{constant}.$$

$$\Rightarrow \quad pAl = \text{constant}$$

(Here, A = cross-sectional area of tube and l = oxygen column length)

$$\Rightarrow \quad pl = \text{constant}$$

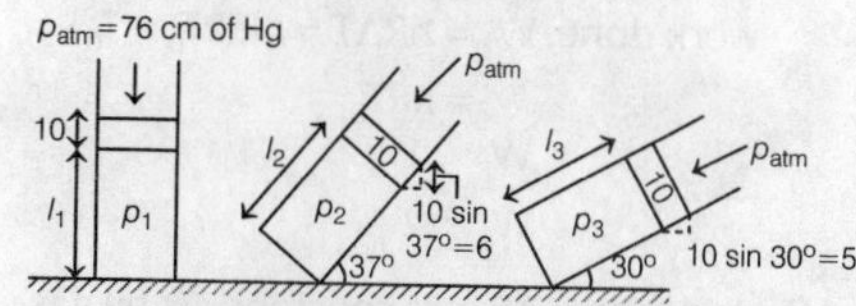

Oxygen pressure in three cases shown will be atmosphere pressure plus pressure due to vertical height of mercury. Therefore, oxygen pressures (as marked in figure) are

$$p_1 = 76 \text{ cm} + 10 \text{ cm} = 86 \text{ cm} \quad \text{... (i)}$$

$$p_2 = 76 \text{ cm} + 6 \text{ cm} = 82 \text{ cm} \quad \text{... (ii)}$$

$$p_3 = 76 \text{ cm} + 5 \text{ cm} = 81 \text{ cm} \quad \text{... (iii)}$$

As $\quad pl = \text{constant}$

$$\Rightarrow \quad p_1l_1 = p_2l_2 = p_3l_3$$

$$\Rightarrow \quad l_2 = \frac{p_1l_1}{p_2} \quad \text{... (iv)}$$

and $\quad l_3 = \frac{p_1l_1}{p_3}$ ... (v)

Subtracting Eq. (iv) from Eq. (v), we get $l_3 - l_2 = p_1l_1\left(\frac{1}{p_3} - \frac{1}{p_2}\right)$

$$= 86 \times 66.42\left(\frac{1}{81} - \frac{1}{82}\right)$$

$$= 0.86 \text{ cm}$$

7. As we know, molar heat capacity,

$$C = C_V + W'$$

where, C_V is molar heat capacity and W' is the work done by the gas per unit mole per unit rise in temperature.

$$\Rightarrow \quad C = C_V + \frac{dW}{ndT}$$

Given, $C = \alpha T$

$$\Rightarrow \quad W' = \alpha T - C_V$$

$$= \alpha T - \frac{5R}{2} \quad \text{... (i)}$$

[$\because$ For a diatomic gas, $C_V = \frac{5R}{2}$]

$$\Rightarrow \quad \Delta W = \int W' dT$$

$$= \int_{T_0}^{3T_0}\left(\alpha T - \frac{5R}{2}\right)dT$$

[using Eq. (i)]

$$= \left[\frac{\alpha T^2}{2} - \frac{5RT}{2}\right]_{T_0}^{3T_0} = (4\alpha T_0 - 5R)T_0$$

8. In an adiabatic process, $T \propto p^{1-\frac{1}{\gamma}}$

$$\Rightarrow \quad T \propto p^{\frac{1}{3}} \text{ (As, } \gamma = 1.5) \quad \text{... (i)}$$

As the gas samples in two compartments are undergoing adiabatic processes from same initial state, if T_L and T_R are final temperature of gases in left and right compartments respectively, p_L and p_R are respective pressures, U_L and U_R are respective internal energies.

$$\Rightarrow \quad \frac{U_L}{U_R} = \frac{\frac{f}{2}nRT_L}{\frac{f}{2}nRT_R} = \frac{T_L}{T_R}$$

$$\Rightarrow \quad \frac{U_L}{U_R} = \left(\frac{p_L}{p_R}\right)^{\frac{1}{3}} \quad \text{[using Eq. (i)]}$$

$$= \left(\frac{1}{8}\right)^{\frac{1}{3}} = \frac{1}{2} = 0.5 \quad \left(\because \frac{p_R}{p_L} = 8\right)$$

9. For any process shown, for which T-V graph passes through O,

$$T \propto V$$

$$\Rightarrow \quad T = mV \quad \text{... (i)}$$

(Here, m = slope of graph)

$$\Rightarrow \quad V = \frac{T}{m}$$

$$\Rightarrow \quad \frac{dV}{dT} = \frac{1}{m} \quad \text{... (ii)}$$

$$\Rightarrow \quad \gamma = \frac{dV}{VdT} = \frac{1}{m \cdot \frac{T}{m}} = \frac{1}{T} \quad \text{... (iii)}$$

[using Eqs. (i) and (ii)]

Now, from ΔOQA,

$$V_0 = T_0 \cot 30° = \sqrt{3}\, T_0 \quad \text{... (iv)}$$

From ΔOSA,

$$T_S = V_0 \tan 60° = \sqrt{3}\, T_0 \cdot \sqrt{3} \quad \text{[using Eq. (i)]}$$

$$\Rightarrow \quad T_S = 3T_0 \quad \text{... (v)}$$

Using Eq. (iii), $\gamma_R = \dfrac{1}{T_0}$

(As $T_R = T_0$ from graph)

$\gamma_Q = \dfrac{1}{T_0}$ (As $T_Q = T_0$ from graph)

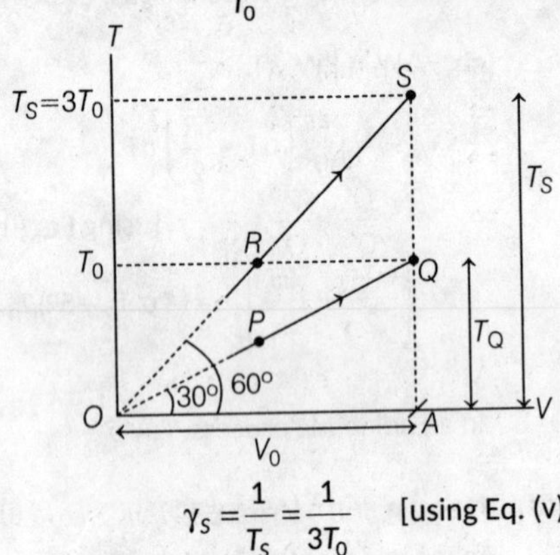

$$\gamma_S = \frac{1}{T_S} = \frac{1}{3T_0} \quad \text{[using Eq. (v)]}$$

Therefore, $\dfrac{\gamma_R}{\gamma_Q} = 1$ and $\dfrac{\gamma_S}{\gamma_Q} = \dfrac{1}{3}$

10. For process-1 (isobaric),

$$\Delta U_1 = \frac{f}{2}(p_{\text{final}}V_{\text{final}} - p_{\text{initial}}V_{\text{initial}})$$

$$= \frac{5}{2}(p_0 \cdot 2V_0 - p_0V_0)$$

$$= 2.5\, p_0V_0 \quad \text{... (i)}$$

As slope of isotherm is lesser in magnitude than adiabat, so process-2 must be isothermal. Therefore,

$$\Delta U_2 = \frac{f}{2} nR\Delta T = 0 \quad \text{... (ii)}$$

For any adiabatic process, $Q = 0$

$$\Rightarrow \quad |\Delta U| = W = \text{Area}$$

From graph, $|\Delta U_4| < |\Delta U_3| < p_0V_0$ ... (iii)

From Eqs. (i), (ii) and (iii), option (b) is correct.

11. For isobaric condition, we know that, heat absorbed/released, $\Delta Q = nC_p\Delta T$, Work done, $W = nR\Delta T$

$$\Rightarrow \frac{\Delta Q}{W} = \frac{nC_p\Delta T}{nR\Delta T} \Rightarrow \Delta Q = \frac{C_p}{R} W$$

For a diatomic gas, $C_p = \dfrac{7}{2}R$

$$\therefore \quad \Delta Q = \frac{7R}{2R} W = \frac{7}{2} W$$

Given, $W = 10$ J

$$\Rightarrow \quad \Delta Q = \frac{7}{2} \times 10 = 7 \times 5 = 35 \text{ J}$$

12. Since, for first process, the equation of the process can be given as

$$T \propto \frac{1}{V} \text{ or } T = \frac{C}{V} \quad \text{... (i)}$$

(where, C is a proportionality constant)

This is not equation of adiabatic/isentropic process.

As, $p = \dfrac{nRT}{V} = \dfrac{nRC}{V(V)} = \dfrac{nRC}{V^2}$

$$\therefore \text{Work done, } W_1 = \int_{V_0}^{2V_0} p \cdot dV = \int_{V_0}^{2V_0} \frac{nRC}{V^2} \cdot dV = \frac{nRT_0}{2}$$

Similarly for second process, since it represents a isobaric process, so work done, $W_2 = nR\Delta T = nR(2T_0 - T_0) = nRT_0$

$$\Rightarrow \quad \frac{W_1}{W_2} = \frac{1}{2}$$

13. In process AB, p is constant. As by gas equation $pV = nRT$ and since p, n, R are constants, V will be proportional to T. So, T-V graph is straight line passing through origin.

In process BC, p-V graph is straight line through origin.

Therefore, $p \propto V$

$$\Rightarrow \quad \frac{nRT}{V} \propto V \Rightarrow T \propto V^2$$

$\Rightarrow$ T-V graph is upward concave parabola with vertex at O.

Also, equation of process CA can be written by using two point form equation of straight line as

$$\frac{p - 4p_0}{V - 2V_0} = \frac{4p_0 - 2p_0}{2V_0 - 4V_0}$$

$$\Rightarrow \quad p = \left(-\frac{p_0}{V_0}\right)V + 6p_0$$

$$\Rightarrow \quad \frac{nRT}{V} = \left(-\frac{p_0}{V_0}\right)V + 6p_0$$

$$\Rightarrow \quad T = \left(-\frac{p_0}{V_0 nR}\right)V^2 + \frac{6p_0V}{nR}$$

which is equation of downward concave parabola.

14. First, considering y is pressure and V is volume, value of Q (heat) for the three steps are

AB (Isochoric) : $Q = \Delta U + W$

$$= \frac{f}{2}(p_{\text{final}} \cdot V_{\text{final}} - p_{\text{final}} \cdot V_{\text{final}}) + 0$$

$$= \frac{6}{2}(2p_0 \cdot V_0 - p_0 \cdot V_0) = 3p_0V_0 \quad \text{... (i)}$$

BC : $\Delta U = \dfrac{6}{2} \cdot (p_0 \cdot 2V_0 - 2p_0 \cdot V_0) = 0$

W = Area under p-V graph

$$= \frac{1}{2} \times \text{Sum of parallel sides} \times \text{Distance}$$

$$= \frac{1}{2} \times (2p_0 + p_0) \times V_0 = \frac{3p_0V_0}{2}$$

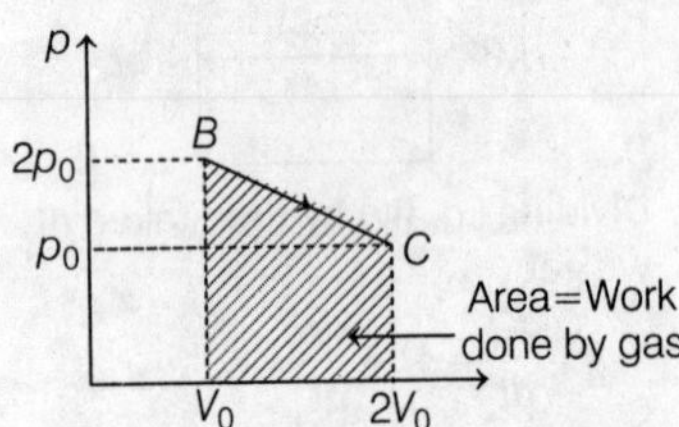

So, $Q_{BC} = \Delta U + W = 0 + \dfrac{3p_0V_0}{2}$

$$= \frac{3}{2} p_0V_0 \quad \text{... (ii)}$$

CA (Isobaric) : $\Delta U = \dfrac{6}{2}(p_0V_0 - p_0 \cdot 2V_0) = -3p_0V_0$

W = Area under p-V graph $= -p_0V_0$

So, $Q_{CA} = \Delta U + W = -3p_0V_0 - p_0V_0 = -4p_0V_0$ ... (iii)

Thus, for cycle $ABCA$,

$$W_{\text{cycle}} = Q_{\text{cycle}} - \Delta U_{\text{cycle}} = Q_{\text{cycle}} - 0 = Q_{\text{cycle}}$$

$$\Rightarrow \quad W_{\text{cycle}} = Q_{AB} + Q_{BC} + Q_{CA} = \frac{1}{2} p_0V_0 \quad \text{... (iv)}$$

[using Eqs. (i), (ii) and (iii)]

Also, heat input, Q_{input} = sum of positive Q

$$= Q_{AB} + Q_{BC} = 3p_0V_0 + \frac{3}{2} p_0V_0$$

[using Eqs. (i) and (ii)]

$$=\frac{9}{2}p_0V_0 \quad \text{... (v)}$$

Therefore, efficiency,

$$\eta=\frac{W_{cycle}}{Q_{input}}=\frac{\frac{1}{2}p_0V_0}{\frac{9}{2}p_0V_0}=\frac{1}{9} \quad \text{... (vi)}$$

If the graph is *T-S* graph, value of *Q* for the three steps can be calculated keeping in mind that area under the graph represent *Q* as

***AB* (Isochoric) :** $Q_{AB}=0$ ... (vii)

***BC* :** Here, area $Q_{BC}=\frac{1}{2}(2T_0+T_0)\times S_0$

$$=\frac{3}{2}T_0S_0 \quad \text{... (viii)}$$

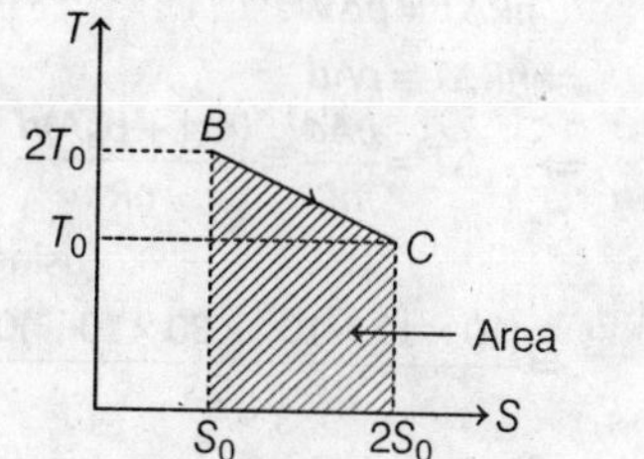

***CA* :** Here, area $=Q_{CA}=-T_0S_0$ ... (ix)

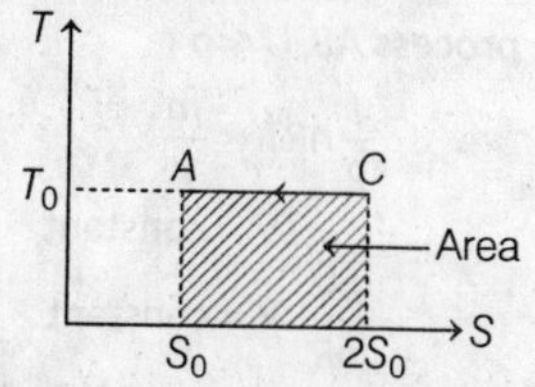

Note that, when entropy decreases, heat has been extracted and so we put a minus sign.

Thus, efficiency $=\eta'=\frac{W_{cycle}}{Q_{input}}$

$$=\frac{\frac{3}{2}T_0S_0-T_0S_0}{\frac{3}{2}T_0S_0}=\frac{1}{3} \quad \text{... (x)}$$

Dividing Eq. (x) by Eq. (vi), we get

$$\eta'=3\eta$$

15. For $x=0$, $pV^0=$ constant or $p=$ constant. So, the process is isobaric. Therefore,

$$C=C_p=p \quad \text{... (i)}$$

For $x=1$, $pV=$ constant or $nRT=$ constant. So, the process is isothermal. Therefore,

$$C=C_T=\frac{Q}{n\Delta T}=\infty$$

Thus, *r* corresponding to $C\rightarrow\infty$ should be equal to 1.

Therefore, $r=1$ ... (ii)

For $x=\gamma$, $pV^{\gamma}=$ constant i.e. the process is adiabatic. Therefore,

$$C=\frac{Q}{n\Delta T}=0, \text{ thus } s=\gamma. \quad \text{... (iii)}$$

For $x\rightarrow\infty$, $p^{\infty}V=$ constant (As $pV^x=$ constant can be written as $p^{\frac{1}{x}}V=$ constant) or $V=$ constant.

Therefore, $C=C_V=q$ ... (iv)

From Eqs. (i), (ii), (iii) and (iv), various options can be reduced as

Option (a) $p-q=C_p-C_V=R$ (as per Mayer's relation)

Option (b) $p-qs=C_p-C_V\cdot\gamma$

$$=C_p-C_V\cdot\frac{C_p}{C_V}=C_p-C_p=0$$

Option (c) $r=1$

Option (d) $ps-r=C_p\cdot\gamma-1=\frac{\gamma^2R}{\gamma-1}-1$

Clearly, option (d) depends on γ or depends on nature of gas.

16. Lets consider the options one-by-one.

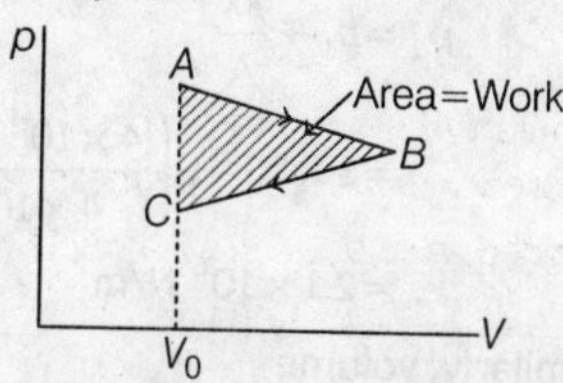

Option (a) In the shown example process, initial volume is same as final volume (V_0) and work is done equal to area shown. So, the statement is correct.

Option (b) In sudden bursting of tyre, air in the tyre expands suddenly. So, the expansion is adiabatic ($dQ=0$) in which energy used for expansion comes at the expense of internal energy. Thus, internal energy and temperature decrease. So, the statement is correct.

Option (c) Internal energy is given by

$$U=\frac{f}{2}pV$$

As atmospheric pressure and room volume are constants, internal energy is constant even if room air temperature increases. So, statement is incorrect.

Option (d) Statement is correct as per second law of thermodynamics.

17. Assuming temperature of common reservoir equal to *T*, heat at various steps are assumed as shown.

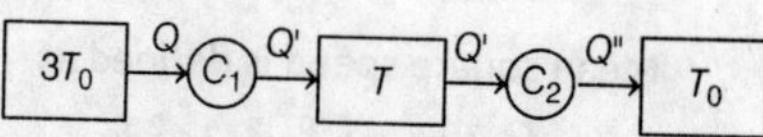

Note that,

$Q=$ heat supplied by hot reservoir to C_1,

$Q'=$ heat supplied by C_1 to C_2 *via* common reservoir

$Q''=$ heat supplied to cold reservoir by C_2.

So, $W_1=$ work output by

$$C_1=Q-Q'$$

$W_2=$ work output by

$$C_2=Q'-Q''$$

It is given that, $W_1=W_2$

$$\Rightarrow \quad Q-Q'=Q'-Q''$$

$$\Rightarrow \quad Q+Q''=2Q'$$

$$\Rightarrow \quad \frac{Q}{Q'}+\frac{Q''}{Q'}=2$$

$$\Rightarrow \quad \frac{3T_0}{T}+\frac{T_0}{T}=2$$

(As *Q*'s are in ratio of reservoir temperatures for Carnot engine)

$$\Rightarrow \quad T=2T_0$$

18. Average time between successive collisions or relaxation time, is given as

$$\Rightarrow \quad \tau\propto\frac{v_{rms}^{-1}}{n}$$

($n=$ number density)

$$\Rightarrow \quad \tau\propto\frac{v_{rms}^{-1}}{N/V}$$

$$\Rightarrow \quad \tau\propto v_{rms}^{-1}V \quad \text{... (i)}$$

As the compression is sudden, heat exchange with surroundings is zero or the process is adiabatic. As for adiabatic process, $TV^{\gamma-1}=$ constant and γ for argon is $\frac{5}{3}$.

Therefore, $TV^{5/3-1}=$ constant

$$\Rightarrow \quad TV^{2/3}=\text{constant}$$

$$\Rightarrow \quad v_{rms}^2V^{2/3}=\text{constant}$$

$$\left(\text{As } v_{rms}=\sqrt{\frac{3RT}{M}}\Rightarrow T\propto v_{rms}^2\right)$$

$$\Rightarrow \quad V\propto v_{rms}^{-3} \quad \text{... (ii)}$$

From Eqs. (i) and (ii), $\tau\propto v_{rms}^{-4}$

Therefore, as v_{rms} doubles, τ becomes $\frac{1}{16}$th.

19. Let $\frac{dN}{dv}=kv^2$ ... (i)

Here, *k* is constant (as for upward concave parabolic curve with vertex at *O*, $y\propto x^2$).

Mean square speed is defined as

$$v_{ms} = \frac{\int v^2 dN}{\int dN} = \frac{\int_0^{v_0} v^2 \cdot kv^2 dv}{\int_0^{v_0} kv^2 dv}$$

[from Eq. (i), $dN = kv^2 dv$]

$$= \frac{\frac{kv_0^5}{5}}{kv_0^3/3} = \frac{3v_0^2}{5} = 0.6{v_0}^2$$

20. Before the gas container is stopped, it has organised kinetic energy $\frac{1}{2}mv^2$.

On stopping, this organised kinetic energy is converted into random kinetic energy or internal energy of gas. Therefore,

$$\frac{1}{2}mv^2 = U_{final} - U_{initial} \quad \text{... (i)}$$

As, internal energy, $U = \frac{f}{2}nRT$

$$\Rightarrow \quad U_{final} = \frac{f}{2}nRT = \frac{3}{2}\frac{m}{M/2}RT$$

$$= \frac{3mRT}{M} \quad \text{... (ii)}$$

(For monoatomic, $f = 3$ and on dissociation molar mass becomes half)

Also, $U_{initial} = \frac{f}{2}nRT = \frac{5}{2}\frac{m}{M}RT \quad \text{... (iii)}$

(For diatomic gas, $f = 5$)

From Eqs. (i), (ii) and (iii), we get

$$\frac{1}{2}mv^2 = \frac{3mRT}{M} - \frac{5mRT}{2M}$$

$$\Rightarrow \quad \frac{1}{2}v^2 = \frac{RT}{2M}$$

$$\Rightarrow \quad M = \frac{RT}{v^2}$$

21. Heat will flow from Part 2 at higher temperature to Part 1 till final common temperature T is attained. As the vessel is insulated, internal energy of the system is conserved. So, final internal energy = initial internal energy

$$\Rightarrow \frac{f}{2}n_1RT + \frac{f}{2}n_2RT = \frac{f}{2}n_1RT_1 + \frac{f}{2}n_2RT_2$$

$$\Rightarrow \quad T = \frac{n_1T_1 + n_2T_2}{n_1 + n_2} = \frac{\frac{p_1V_1}{R} + \frac{p_2V_2}{R}}{\frac{p_1V_1}{RT_1} + \frac{p_2V_2}{RT_2}}$$

$$= \frac{2T_1T_2}{T_1 + T_2} = \frac{2 \times 200 \times 800}{200 + 800} = 320\text{K}$$

Here, symbols have usual meaning.

For Part 1, final pressure

$$p'_1 = \frac{n_1RT}{V_1} = \frac{p_1T}{T_1} = \frac{10^5 \times 320}{200}$$

$$= 1.6 \times 10^5 \text{ Pa}$$

For Part 2, final pressure

$$p'_2 = \frac{n_2RT}{V_2} = \frac{p_2T}{T_2} = \frac{10^5 \times 320}{800}$$

$$= 0.4 \times 10^5 \text{ Pa}$$

As $p'_2 < p'_1$, so external force F is required for equilibrium as shown.

For equilibrium,

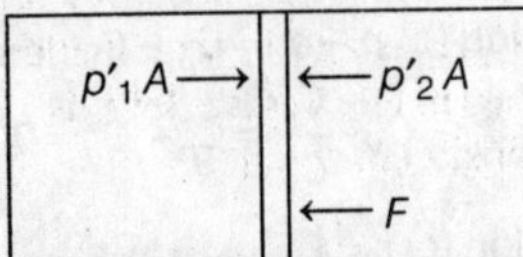

$$F = (p'_1 - p'_2)A$$

$$= (1.6 \times 10^5 - 0.4 \times 10^5)(2 \times 10^{-4}\text{m}^2)$$

$$= 24 \text{ N}$$

22. When the piston is moved out, then pressure,

$$p_2 = p_1 + \frac{kx}{A}$$

$$= 1 \times 10^5 + \left(\frac{4 \times 10^4 \times 0.2}{4 \times 10^{-3}}\right)$$

$$= 2.1 \times 10^6 \text{ N/m}^2$$

Similarly, volume

$$V_2 = V_1 + Ax$$

$$= 1.2 \times 10^{-3} + 4 \times 10^{-3} \times 0.2$$

$$= 2 \times 10^{-3} \text{ m}^3$$

In equilibrium, in accordance with ideal gas equation,

$$\frac{p_1V_1}{T_1} = \frac{p_2V_2}{T_2}$$

$$\Rightarrow \quad \frac{1 \times 10^5 \times 1.2 \times 10^{-3}}{100} = \frac{2.1 \times 10^6 \times 2 \times 10^{-3}}{T_2}$$

$$\Rightarrow \quad T_2 = \frac{2.1 \times 10^6 \times 2 \times 10^{-3} \times 100}{1 \times 10^5 \times 1.2 \times 10^{-3}}$$

$$= 3500 \text{ K} = 35 \times 10^2 \text{ K}$$

23. Let cross-section of upper and lower pistons are A_1 and A_2 respectively and gas pressure equal to p. FBD of the system of pistons will be as shown.

As the arrangement is moving slowly without acceleration, net force on the arrangement is zero.

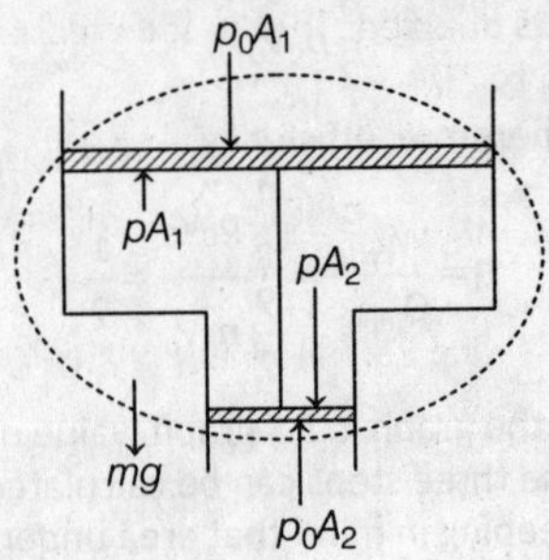

$$\Rightarrow pA_1 + p_0A_2 = pA_2 + p_0A_1 + mg$$

$$\Rightarrow p(A_1 - A_2) = mg + p_0(A_1 - A_2)$$

$$\Rightarrow \quad pA = mg + p_0A = \text{constant} \quad \text{... (i)}$$

So, the process is isobaric. Now, by ideal gas equation,

$$nR\Delta T = p\Delta V$$

$$\Rightarrow nR\Delta T = pAd$$

$$\Rightarrow \quad \Delta T = \frac{pAd}{nR} = \frac{(mg + p_0A)d}{nR}$$

[using Eq. (i)]

$$= \frac{(10 \times 10 + 10^5 \times 30 \times 10^{-4})0.4}{3 \times \frac{25}{3}}$$

$$= 6.4 \text{ K}$$

24. In process AB, $U \propto \rho$

$$\Rightarrow \quad \frac{f}{2}nRT \propto \frac{m}{V}$$

$$\Rightarrow \quad TV = \text{constant}$$

$$\Rightarrow \quad \frac{pV}{nR} \cdot V = \text{constant}$$

$$\Rightarrow \quad pV^2 = \text{constant}$$

So, the process is polytropic with index $x = 2$ ... (i)

Also, as ρ becomes four times, U will also become 4 times. As U is proportional to T, T will also become 4 times. That is, if initial T is T_0, then finally it will be $4T_0$. As work done in polytropic process is $W = \frac{nR\Delta T}{1 - x}$ ... (ii)

Using Eqs. (i) and (ii), we get

$$W_{AB} = \frac{nR(4T_0 - T_0)}{1 - 2} = -3nRT_0 \quad \text{... (iii)}$$

In process CD, $v \propto V$

$$\Rightarrow \quad \sqrt{T} \propto V$$

$$\Rightarrow \quad T \propto V^2$$

$$\Rightarrow \quad \frac{pV}{nR} \propto V^2$$

$$\Rightarrow \quad pV^{-1} = \text{constant}$$

$$\Rightarrow \quad x = -1 \quad \text{... (iv)}$$

Also, as volume becomes $\sqrt{2}$ times, average speed becomes $\sqrt{2}$ times and

T is doubled. That is, it increases from T_0 to $2T_0$.

Using Eqs. (ii) and (iv), we get

$$W_{CD} = \frac{nR(2T_0 - T_0)}{1-(-1)} = \frac{nRT_0}{2} \quad \text{... (v)}$$

Dividing Eq. (iii) by Eq. (v), we get

$$\frac{W_{AB}}{W_{CD}} = -6 \Rightarrow \frac{|W_{AB}|}{|W_{CD}|} = 6$$

25. In states A, B and C degrees of freedom are experimentally deduced to be $f_A = 3, f_B = 5, f_C = 7$, respectively.

As internal energy, $U = \frac{f}{2} nRT$,

therefore internal energies in the three states are equal to

$$U_A = \frac{3}{2} nRT_0 \quad \text{... (i)}$$

$$U_B = \frac{5}{2} nR(10T_0) \quad \text{... (ii)}$$

$$U_C = \frac{7}{2} nR(xT_0) \quad \text{... (iii)}$$

It is given that, $U_C = 14(U_A + U_B)$

$$\Rightarrow \frac{7}{2} nR(xT_0) = 14\left[\frac{3}{2} nRT_0 + \frac{5}{2} nR(10T_0)\right]$$

[using Eqs. (i), (ii) and (iii)]

$$\Rightarrow \quad x = 106$$

Qualifier 9 (Oscillations and Waves)

1. For particle A, at $t = 0$, $x_A = \frac{A}{\sqrt{2}}$

Putting these values in given equation for A, we get

$$\frac{A}{\sqrt{2}} = A\sin(0 + \alpha)$$

$$\Rightarrow \sin\alpha = \frac{1}{\sqrt{2}} \Rightarrow \alpha = \frac{\pi}{4} \text{ or } \frac{3\pi}{4} \quad \text{...(i)}$$

Now, if we differentiate x_A w.r.t. t, we get

$$\frac{dx_A}{dt} = A\omega\sin(\omega t + \alpha)$$

$\Rightarrow$ Velocity of A, $v_A = A\omega\sin(\omega t + \alpha)$

At, $t = 0$, we get

$$v_A = A\omega\sin\alpha = \text{positive (given)}$$

$\Rightarrow \sin\alpha =$ positive

$\therefore$ Out of values of α suggested in Eq. (i), correct value is $\frac{\pi}{4}$.

Similarly, for particle B, at $t = 0$,

$$x_B = \frac{\sqrt{3}A}{2}$$

$$\Rightarrow -\frac{\sqrt{3}A}{2} = A\cos(0 + \beta)$$

$$\Rightarrow \cos\beta = -\frac{\sqrt{3}}{2}$$

$$\Rightarrow \beta = -\frac{5\pi}{6} \text{ or } \frac{5\pi}{6} \quad \text{...(ii)}$$

Also, $v_B = \frac{dx_B}{dt} = -A\omega\sin(\omega t + \beta)$

$= -A\omega\sin\beta$ (at $t = 0$)

= Negative (given)

$\therefore$ Out of given values of β suggested in Eq. (ii), correct value of β is $\frac{5\pi}{6}$.

Thus, $\alpha + \beta = \frac{\pi}{4} + \frac{5\pi}{6} = \frac{13\pi}{12}$

2. Let the ball is displaced by x and the rod rotates by θ in arrangement-1 as shown in Fig. 1. Also, let x' is extension in spring B.

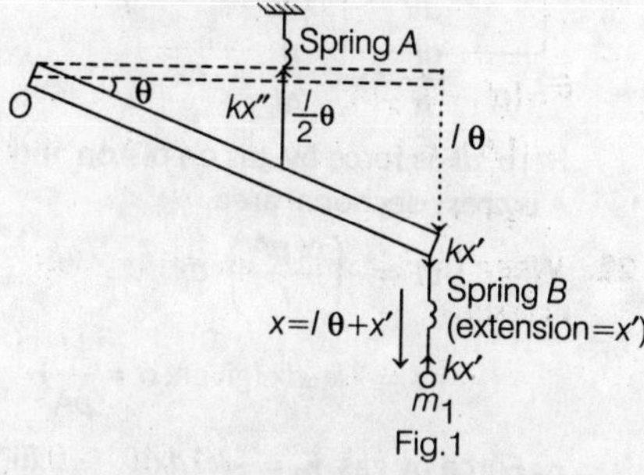

Fig.1

Due to rotation θ of end of rod, the ball will move $l\theta$ downwards and due to extension x' in spring also it moves downwards. So, displacement of ball,

$$x = l\theta + x'$$

$$\Rightarrow \quad x' = x - l\theta \quad \text{...(i)}$$

$\therefore$ Force by spring B on end of rod is kx' downwards as shown in Fig. 1

Also, centre of the rod is displaced by

$$x'' = \frac{l}{2}\theta \quad \text{...(ii)}$$

(thereby extending the spring A by same amount).

Thus, rod will experience a force of kx'' upwards at its centre. As, the rod is massless, its moment of inertia will be zero and therefore net torque on it is zero. Therefore,

$$\tau \text{ of } kx'' = \tau \text{ of } kx'$$

$$\Rightarrow \quad kx''\frac{l}{2} = kx'l$$

$$\Rightarrow \quad x'' = 2x'$$

$$\Rightarrow \quad \frac{l}{2}\theta = 2(x - l\theta)$$

$$\Rightarrow \quad l\theta = \frac{4x}{5} \quad \text{...(iii)}$$

Restoring force on the ball,

$$F = kx'$$

$$= k(x - l\theta) \quad \text{[using Eq. (i)]}$$

$$= k\left(x - \frac{4x}{5}\right)$$

[using Eq. (iii)]

$$\Rightarrow \quad F = \frac{kx}{5}$$

As restoring force in SHM is $m\omega^2 x$, so

$$m_1\omega^2 x = \frac{kx}{5} \Rightarrow \omega = \sqrt{\frac{k}{5m_1}}$$

$$\Rightarrow \quad T_1 = \text{Time period} = \frac{2\pi}{\omega}$$

$$= 2\pi\sqrt{\frac{5m_1}{k}} \quad \text{...(iv)}$$

Now, consider arrangement-2. If the ball is displaced slightly downwards by x in vertical direction, as shown in Fig. 2, components of displacement along both the springs will be $x/\sqrt{2}$.

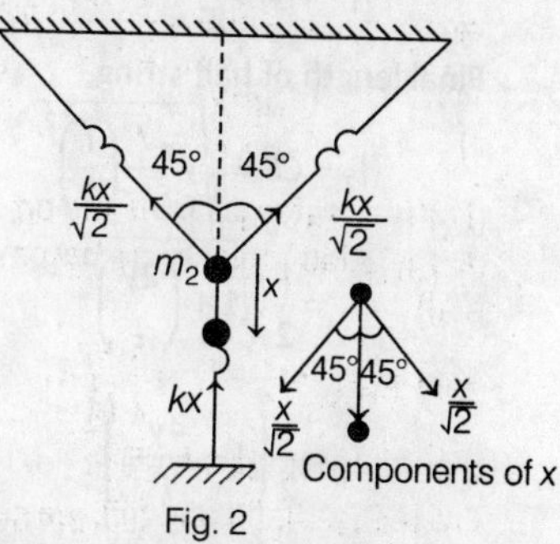

Fig. 2

Therefore, vertical spring due to its compression will apply x upwards while the inclined springs will pull with $\frac{kx}{\sqrt{2}}$ each along their lengths as shown.

Net force on the ball will be resultant of the three forces which will be as shown in Fig. 3. equal to,

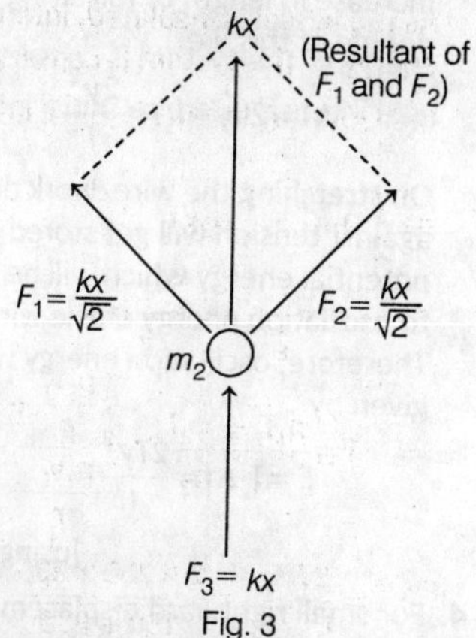

Fig. 3

$$F = 2kx$$

$$\Rightarrow \quad m_2\omega^2 x = 2kx$$

$$\Rightarrow \quad \omega = \sqrt{\frac{2k}{m_2}}$$

$$\Rightarrow \quad T_2 = \frac{2\pi}{\omega} = 2\pi\sqrt{\frac{m_2}{2k}} \quad \text{...(v)}$$

As it is given that $T_1 = T_2$, therefore using Eqs. (iv) and (v), we get

$$2\pi\sqrt{\frac{5m_1}{k}} = 2\pi\sqrt{\frac{m_2}{2k}}$$

$$\Rightarrow \quad m_1 = 0.1\, m_2$$

3. The figure can be labelled as shown below.

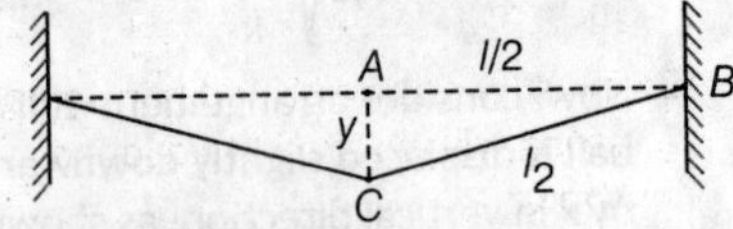

Initial length of half string,

$$l_1 = AB = \frac{l}{2} \quad \text{...(i)}$$

Final length of half string,

$$l_2 = CB = \sqrt{y^2 + \left(\frac{l}{2}\right)^2}$$

$$= \frac{l}{2}\sqrt{1 + \left(\frac{2y}{l}\right)^2}$$

$$= \frac{l}{2}\left(1 + \frac{4y^2}{l^2}\right)^{\frac{1}{2}}$$

$$\Rightarrow \quad l_2 \approx \frac{l}{2}\left(1 + \frac{2y^2}{l^2}\right) \quad \text{...(ii)}$$

[Using binomial approximation $(1+x)^n \approx 1 + nx$, if $x << 1$]

Subtracting Eq. (i) from Eq. (ii), we get, Increase in length of half string

$$= l_2 - l_1 = \frac{y^2}{l}$$

Increase in length of full string will be double of this. i.e.

$$\Delta l = 2(l_2 - l_1) = \frac{2y^2}{l} \quad \text{...(iii)}$$

On stretching the wire, work done against tension will get stored as potential energy which will be equal to oscillation energy of the wire. Therefore, oscillation energy will be given by

$$E = T\,\Delta l = \frac{2Ty^2}{l}$$

[using Eq. (iii)]

4. For small rightward displacement dx, spring will exert leftward force as shown in figure, given by

$$F_1 = -k \cdot dx \quad \text{...(i)}$$

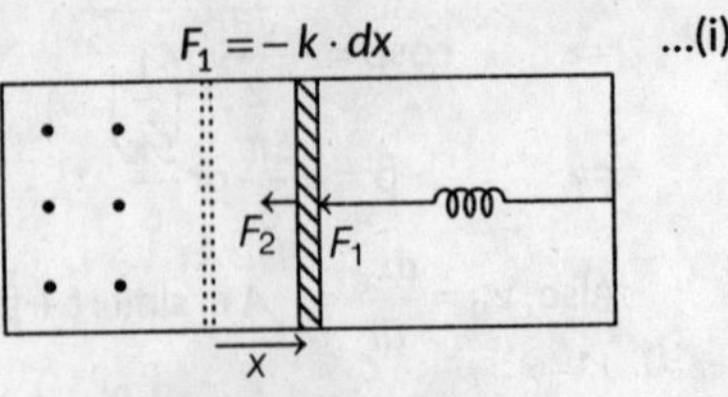

Also, as the cylinder is non-conducting, the gas will expand adiabatically.

For adiabatic process,

$$pV^{\alpha} = \text{constant} \quad \text{...(ii)}$$

Here, p is pressure, V is volume and α is adiabatic exponent.

Differentiating Eq. (ii) with respect to V, we get

$$\frac{d(pV^{\alpha})}{dV} = 0 \Rightarrow dp = -\frac{\alpha p}{V} \cdot dV$$

$$\Rightarrow \quad \frac{dF}{A} = -\alpha \frac{p}{Al} \cdot A \cdot dx$$

Here, dF is force by gas on piston and A is cross-sectional area.

$$\Rightarrow \quad dF = -\left(\frac{\alpha\, pA}{l}\right) \cdot dx$$

$$= -k \cdot dx \;(\text{given}, \alpha = \frac{kl}{pA})$$

$\Rightarrow$ Force by gas, $F_2 = -k \cdot dx$ ...(iii)

Adding Eqs. (i) and (iii), we get

Restoring force, $F = F_1 + F_2 = -2k \cdot dx$

$$= -m\omega^2\, dx$$

$$\Rightarrow \quad \omega = \sqrt{\frac{2k}{m}}$$

5. Energy density of wave is given by $\frac{1}{2}\rho A^2 \omega^2$

Equating energy densities at $x = 0$ and $x = 1$, we get

$$\frac{1}{2}(1+0)A^2 = \frac{1}{2}(1+1)A'^2$$

$$\Rightarrow \quad A' = \frac{A}{\sqrt{2}} = 0.707\, A$$

6. As, water does not stick to walls of sphere and so does not rotate during oscillation.

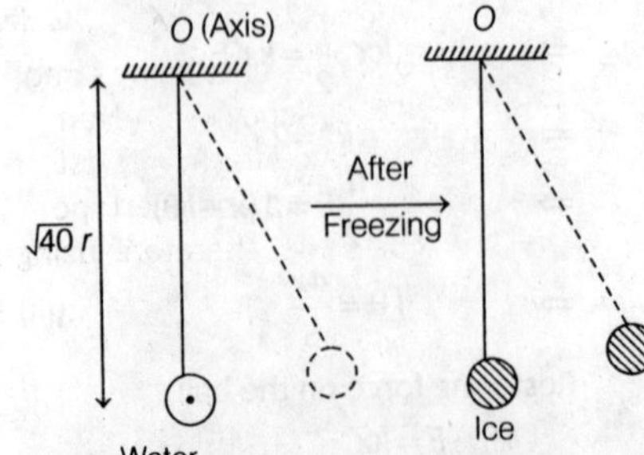

Moment of inertia of water about axis of oscillation through O is calculated assuming water as point mass at centre of sphere,

$$I_1 = m(\sqrt{40}\, r)^2 = 40\, mr^2$$

But after the water freezes into ice, it sticks to walls of sphere and rotates with sphere. Moment of inertia about axis,

$$I_2 = \frac{2}{5}mr^2 + m(\sqrt{40}r)^2$$

$$= 40.4\, mr^2$$

Thus, percentage increase in moment of inertia is

$$\frac{\Delta I}{I} \times 100 = \frac{I_2 - I_1}{I_1} \times 100$$

$$= \frac{40.4 - 40}{40} \times 100 = 1\% \quad \text{...(i)}$$

As, time period of oscillation of a physical pendulum is proportional to $\sqrt{I}$.

i.e. $T \propto \sqrt{I}$

$$\Rightarrow \frac{\Delta T}{T} \times 100 = \frac{1}{2} \times \frac{\Delta I}{I} \times 100$$

$$= \frac{1}{2} \times 1 = 0.5\%$$

(increase) [using Eq. (i)]

7. Velocity of sound in a gas is given by

$$\Rightarrow \quad v \propto \sqrt{\frac{\gamma}{M}}$$

For H_2 $(\gamma = 1.4, M = 2)$, $\sqrt{\frac{\gamma}{M}} = \sqrt{\frac{1.4}{2}}$

For N_2 $(\gamma = 1.4, M = 28)$, $\sqrt{\frac{\gamma}{M}} = \sqrt{\frac{1.4}{28}}$

For He $(\gamma = 1.67, M = 4)$, $\sqrt{\frac{\gamma}{M}} = \sqrt{\frac{1.67}{4}}$

For CO_2 $(\gamma = 1.34, M = 44)$, $\sqrt{\frac{\gamma}{M}} = \sqrt{\frac{1.34}{44}}$

As for CO_2, M is highest while γ is least. So, $\sqrt{\frac{\gamma}{M}}$ is least and as $v \propto \sqrt{\frac{\gamma}{M}}$.

Hence, v is least for CO_2.

8. On displacement x of the tube B, path of sound wave travelling through B increases by $2x$ as can be seen in the figure.

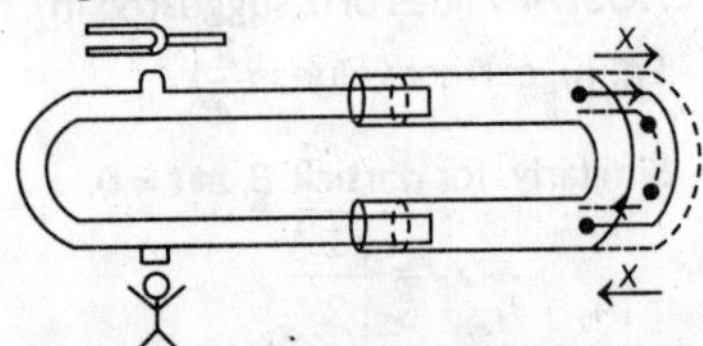

Therefore, for displacement of $x = 12$ cm of the tube, change in path difference is equal to $2x = 24$ cm. Also, as while moving from one minima to another minima intensity becomes maximum 12 times. So, by condition of maxima path difference must have changed by 12 λ.

Therefore,

$$24 \text{ cm} = 12\lambda$$

$$\Rightarrow \lambda = 2 \text{ cm}$$

9. Equations can be written as

Wave-1 $y_1 = 2A\cos\left(kx - \omega t + \frac{\pi}{3} + \frac{\pi}{2}\right)$

Wave-2 $y_2 = \sqrt{3}A\cos\left(kx - \omega t - \frac{\pi}{3}\right)$

Wave-3 $y_3 = 2\sqrt{3}A\cos\left(kx - \omega t + \frac{\pi}{3}\right)$

So, with respect to wave-3, wave-1 leads in phase by $\frac{\pi}{2}$ while wave-2 lags in phase by $\frac{\pi}{3} - \left(-\frac{\pi}{3}\right) = \frac{2\pi}{3}$.

Therefore, phasors representing the waves can be drawn as

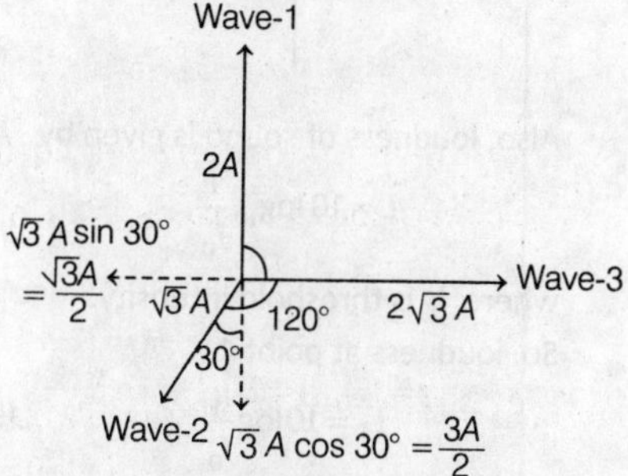

To find resultant amplitude, add these phasors treating them as vectors. By resolving phasor of wave-2, we get corresponding vector as

$$\mathbf{A}_2 = \frac{-\sqrt{3}A}{2}\hat{\mathbf{i}} - \frac{3A}{2}\hat{\mathbf{j}} \quad \text{...(i)}$$

Vectors corresponding to wave-1 and wave-3 respectively are

$$\mathbf{A}_1 = 2A\,\hat{\mathbf{j}} \quad \text{...(ii)}$$

$$\mathbf{A}_3 = 2\sqrt{3}A\,\hat{\mathbf{i}} \quad \text{...(iii)}$$

Adding Eqs. (i), (ii) and (iii), we get,

$$\mathbf{A}_1 + \mathbf{A}_2 + \mathbf{A}_3 = \left(\frac{-\sqrt{3}A}{2} + 2\sqrt{3}A\right)\hat{\mathbf{i}} + \left(2A - \frac{3A}{2}\right)\hat{\mathbf{j}}$$

$$= \frac{3\sqrt{3}}{2}A\,\hat{\mathbf{i}} + \frac{A}{2}\hat{\mathbf{j}}$$

$$\therefore |\mathbf{A}_1 + \mathbf{A}_2 + \mathbf{A}_3| = \sqrt{\left(\frac{3\sqrt{3}}{2}\right)^2 + \left(\frac{1}{2}\right)^2}\,A$$

$$= \sqrt{\frac{28}{4}} = \sqrt{7}\,A$$

10. Equation of displacement of progressive wave is of the form

$$s = A\sin(\omega t - \mathbf{k}\cdot\mathbf{r} + \phi)$$

On comparison with given wave equation, we get

$$\mathbf{k}\cdot\mathbf{r} = -3x + 4y - 12z$$

$$\Rightarrow \mathbf{k}\cdot(x\hat{\mathbf{i}} + y\hat{\mathbf{j}} + z\hat{\mathbf{k}}) = -3x + 4y - 12z$$

$$\Rightarrow \mathbf{k} = -3\hat{\mathbf{i}} + 4\hat{\mathbf{j}} - 12\hat{\mathbf{k}}$$

$$\Rightarrow k = |\mathbf{k}| = \sqrt{3^2 + 4^2 + 12^2} = 13$$

$$\Rightarrow \frac{2\pi}{\lambda} = 13$$

$$\Rightarrow \lambda = \frac{2\pi}{13}$$

11. On decreasing temperature of a wire fixed at both ends, decrease in its natural length is

$$\Delta l = l\,\alpha\,\Delta T \quad \text{...(i)}$$

But if the wire is fixed and cannot contract, thermal strain will be developed in the wire as given by

$$\varepsilon = \frac{\Delta l}{l} = \alpha\,\Delta T \quad \text{[using Eq. (i)] ...(ii)}$$

As per Hooke's law, thermal stress

$$\sigma = \varepsilon Y$$

where, Y is Young's modulus

$$\Rightarrow \sigma = Y\alpha\,\Delta T \quad \text{[using Eq. (ii)]}$$

$$\Rightarrow \frac{T}{A} = Y\alpha\,\Delta T$$

$$\Rightarrow T = YA\alpha\,\Delta T \quad \text{...(iii)}$$

where, T is tension developed in wire and A is its cross-sectional area.

If a wire is vibrating in nth harmonic, frequency of vibration/source is given by

$$f = \frac{n}{2l}\sqrt{\frac{T}{\mu}}$$

$$\Rightarrow f = \frac{n}{2l}\sqrt{\frac{YA\alpha\,\Delta T}{\mu}}$$

$$\Rightarrow f \propto n\sqrt{\Delta T} \quad \text{...(iv)}$$

Now, as waves are created by same tuning fork, frequency in all given cases, i.e. fundamental ($n = 1$), 1st overtone ($n = 2$) and 2nd overtone ($n = 3$) will be same. Therefore, using Eq. (iv), we get

$$1\cdot\sqrt{x} = 2\cdot\sqrt{y} = 3\cdot\sqrt{z}$$

$$\Rightarrow x = 4y = 9z$$

$$\Rightarrow y = \frac{x}{4} \text{ and } z = \frac{x}{9} \quad \text{... (v)}$$

Considering LHS of option (a),

$$5x + 27z = 5x + 27\cdot\frac{x}{9} \quad \text{[using Eq. (v)]}$$

$$= 8x$$

Now, consider RHS of option (a),

$$32y = 32\cdot\frac{x}{4} = 8x \quad \text{[Using Eq. (v)]}$$

As, RHS and LHS of option (a) are equal, it is correct option.

Similarly, we can check for other options, but they are seen to be incorrect.

12. In 1st overtone or 2nd harmonic, string will vibrate in two loops as shown

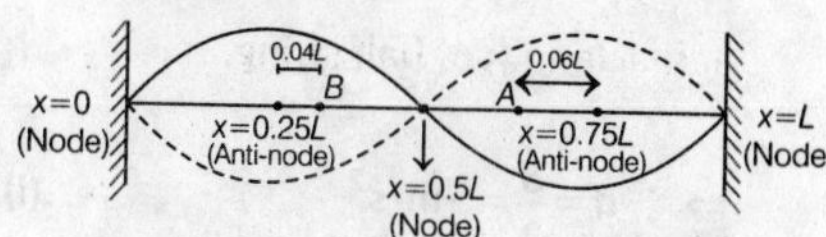

Amplitude is maximum at anti-nodes and as we move towards node, it decreases. As $x = 0.69\,L$ (point A) is at a distance $0.06\,L$ from anti-node while $x = 0.29\,L$ (point B) is at a distance $0.04\,L$ from anti-node as shown, point B is closer to anti-node and so amplitude at B will be greater. As, maximum kinetic energy of oscillation is proportional to square of amplitude, it will be greater for B. So, option (c) is correct. Other points given in other options are closer to anti-node compared to $x = 0.29\,L$.

13. Angular frequency,

$$\omega = 2\pi f = 120 \text{ rad/s}$$

Linear mass density,

$$\mu = 90 \text{ g/m}$$

$$= 9\times10^{-2} \text{ kg/m}$$

Maximum power in string wave is given by

$$P_{max} = \sqrt{\mu T}\,A^2\omega^2$$

$$\Rightarrow P_{max} = \sqrt{9\times10^{-2}\times900}\,(10^{-2})^2\,(120)^2$$

$$= 12.96 \text{ W} \approx 13 \text{ W}$$

14. Consider FBD of portion of string below wave pulse (having length x). If mass per unit length of string is μ, weight of the portion is μxg.

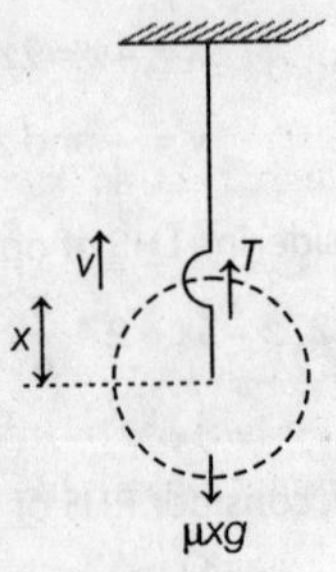

Therefore, tension at location of wave pulse, $T = \mu x g$

Speed of wave,

$$v = \sqrt{\frac{T}{\mu}} = \sqrt{\frac{\mu x g}{\mu}} = \sqrt{gx}$$

$\Rightarrow$ Acceleration of wave,

$$a = v \cdot \frac{dv}{dx} = \sqrt{gx} \cdot \frac{d(\sqrt{gx})}{dx}$$

$$= \sqrt{gx} \cdot \sqrt{g} \cdot \frac{1}{2\sqrt{x}}$$

$$\Rightarrow \quad a = \frac{g}{2} = 5 \text{ m/s}^2 \quad \text{...(i)}$$

Now, wave travels 5 m to reach the mid-point. Using $s = ut + \frac{1}{2}at^2$ for wave motion till mid of rope, we can get time of motion t_1. i.e.

$$5 = 0 + \frac{1}{2} \times 5 \times t_1^2 \quad \text{[using Eq. (i)]}$$

$$\Rightarrow \quad t_1 = \sqrt{2} \text{ s} \quad \text{...(ii)}$$

For ball, using $s = ut + \frac{1}{2}at^2$, we can obtain time t_2 to reach mid of rope.

i.e. $$5 = 0 + \frac{1}{2} \times 10 \times t_2^2$$

$$\Rightarrow \quad t_2 = 1 \text{ s} \quad \text{...(iii)}$$

Therefore, time gap t after which the ball should be dropped, so that both the ball and the pulse reach the mid-point at same time is given by

$$t = t_1 - t_2$$

$$= \sqrt{2} - 1 = 0.41 \text{ s}$$

15. Fundamental frequency is given by

$$f = \frac{v}{4l} = \frac{1}{4l}\sqrt{\frac{\gamma RT}{M}} \quad \text{...(i)}$$

$\Rightarrow f \propto \sqrt{T}$ so, when temperature rises, fundamental frequency will increase. So, option (a) is correct. But if pressure rises, temperature may be constant and so fundamental frequency may remain constant. So, option (d) is incorrect. Also, second overtone or fifth harmonic has frequency five times that of the fundamental frequency. So, option (b) is correct. If length of the open pipe is l', its fundamental frequency will be

$$f' = \frac{v}{2l'} \quad \text{...(ii)}$$

As per option (c), $f = f'$

$$\Rightarrow \quad \frac{v}{4l} = \frac{v}{2l'} \Rightarrow l' = 2l$$

So, option (c) is also correct.

16. Fundamental frequency of a wire fixed at both ends is given by $f = \frac{v}{2l}$

Therefore, $$f \propto \frac{1}{l} \Rightarrow l \propto \frac{1}{f}$$

So, ratio of lengths of three segments will be

$$l_1 : l_2 : l_3 = 1 : \frac{1}{2} : \frac{1}{3}$$

$$\Rightarrow \quad l_1 : l_2 : l_3 = 6 : 3 : 2 \quad \text{...(i)}$$

Also, length of the wire,

$$l_1 + l_2 + l_3 = L \quad \text{(given) ...(ii)}$$

From Eqs. (i) and (ii), length of largest segment l_1 will be

$$l_1 = \frac{6}{6+3+2} \times L = \frac{6L}{11}$$

17. 1st and 2nd resonances are as shown in the figure. e represents end correction or distance of anti-node from ends.

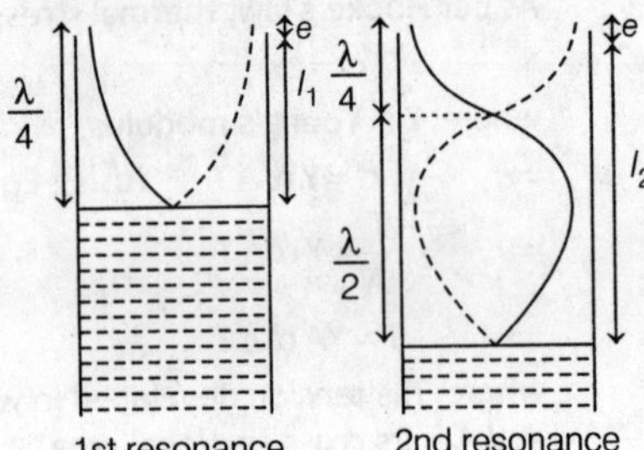

Distance between two consecutive nodes is $\frac{\lambda}{2}$, while distance between adjacent node and anti-node is $\frac{\lambda}{4}$. So, for first resonance as per figure,

$$\frac{\lambda}{4} = l_1 + e \quad \text{...(i)}$$

For second resonance,

$$\frac{\lambda}{4} + \frac{\lambda}{2} = l_2 + e$$

$$\Rightarrow \quad \frac{3\lambda}{4} = l_2 + e \quad \text{...(ii)}$$

Dividing Eq. (ii) by Eq. (i), we get

$$3 = \frac{l_2 + e}{l_1 + e}$$

$$\Rightarrow \quad e = \frac{l_2 - 3l_1}{2} \quad \text{...(iii)}$$

As per Rayleigh's suggestion, end correction in terms of radius,

$$e = 0.6\,r \quad \text{...(iv)}$$

From Eqs (iii) and (iv),

$$0.6\,r = \frac{l_2 - 3l_1}{2}$$

$$\Rightarrow \quad r = \frac{5}{6}(l_2 - 3l_1)$$

18. Intensity at a distance r from a point source of power P is given by

$$I = \frac{P}{4\pi r^2} \Rightarrow I \propto \frac{1}{r^2}$$

$$\frac{I_1}{I_2} = \frac{r_2^2}{r_1^2} \quad \text{...(i)}$$

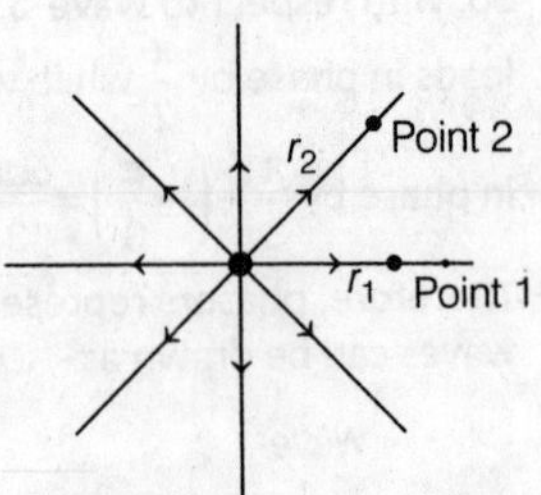

Also, loudness of sound is given by

$$L = 10 \log_{10} \frac{I}{I_0}$$

where, I_0 is threshold intensity.

So, loudness at point 1,

$$L_1 = 10 \log \frac{I_1}{I_0} \quad \text{...(ii)}$$

and loudness at point 2,

$$L_2 = 10 \log \frac{I_2}{I_0} \quad \text{... (iii)}$$

Subtracting Eq. (iii) from Eq. (ii), we get

$$L_1 - L_2 = 10 \log \frac{I_1}{I_2}$$

$$\Rightarrow \quad 6 = 10 \log \left(\frac{r_2}{r_1}\right)^2 \quad \text{[using Eq. (i)]}$$

$$\Rightarrow \quad 6 = 20 \log \frac{r_2}{r_1}$$

$$\Rightarrow \quad \log \frac{r_2}{r_1} = 0.3 \Rightarrow \frac{r_2}{r_1} = 2$$

19. For no observation of beats, apparent frequencies of sounds from the car and the siren should be equal

$$\Rightarrow \quad f_{car} = f_{siren}$$

$$\Rightarrow 176\left(\frac{330 - v}{330 - 22}\right) = 165\left(\frac{330 - (-v)}{330 - 0}\right)$$

$$\Rightarrow v = 22 \text{ m/s}$$

20. The situation is as shown in the figure here.

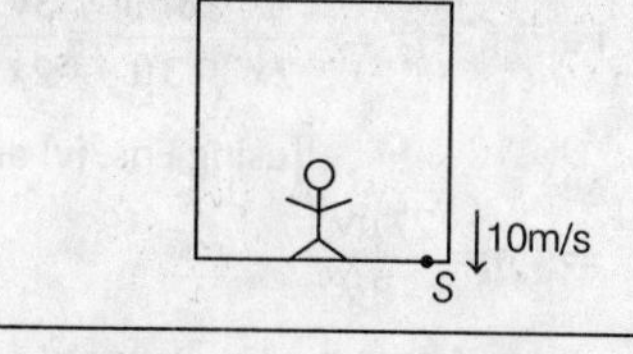

The person hears sound directly from the source having frequency equal to actual given by $f_1 = 30$ Hz ...(i)

Sound heard by person after reflection from medium's surface can be interpreted as coming from image source as shown.

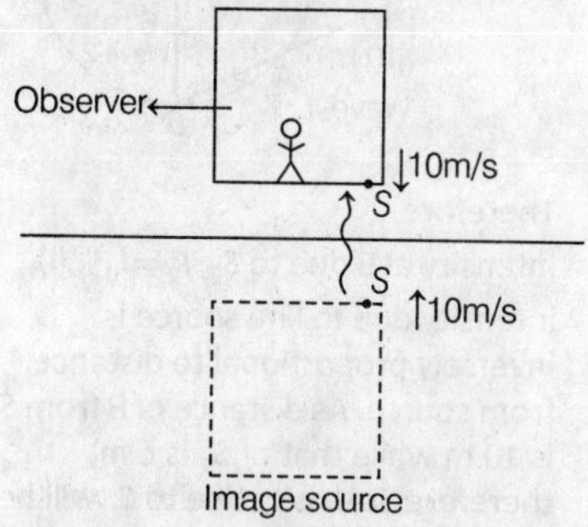

Apparent frequency of the reflected sound heard by the person can be found using formula of apparent frequency, $f' = f\left(\frac{v - v_o}{v - v_s}\right)$ ...(ii)

Here, v is velocity of sound, v_o is velocity of observer and v_s is velocity of source.

$$\Rightarrow f_2 = 30\left[\frac{310-(-10)}{310-10}\right] = 32 \text{ Hz} \quad ...(iii)$$

Note that observer velocity (v_o) is negative as it is opposite to direction of motion of sound while velocity of source is positive, as it is in same direction as direction of sound.

Beat frequency is difference of frequencies of simultaneous sound reaching observer.

So, using Eqs. (i) and (iii), we get

$$f_{beat} = f_2 - f_1 = 32 - 30 = 2$$

Now, apparent frequency of sound incident on medium's surface using Eq. (ii), is

$$f_3 = 30\left(\frac{310-0}{310-10}\right) = 31 \text{ Hz} \quad ...(iv)$$

Detector D detects this sound as coming from surface as shown in Fig. 2. So, surface is source. Using Eq. (ii), apparent frequency detected by detector,

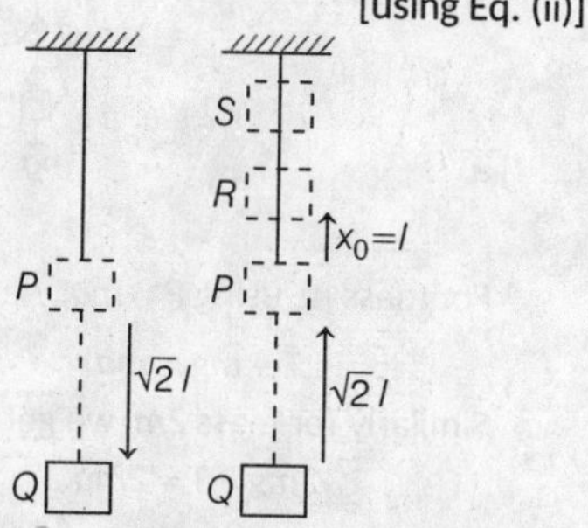

$$f_4 = 31\left[\frac{1240-(-20)}{1240-0}\right] = 31.5 \text{ Hz}$$

21. Initial extension in the string x_0 is given by balancing forces,

$$kx_0 = mg$$

$$\Rightarrow \quad x_0 = \frac{mg}{k} = \frac{mg}{\frac{mg}{l}} = l \quad ...(i)$$

Also, angular frequency of the system,

$$\omega = \sqrt{\frac{k}{m}} = \sqrt{\frac{mg}{l \cdot m}} = \sqrt{\frac{g}{l}} \quad ...(ii)$$

Block is imparted velocity, $v = \sqrt{2gl}$ at equilibrium position. As velocity at equilibrium is given by

$$v = A\omega$$

$$\Rightarrow \quad A = \frac{v}{\omega} = \frac{\sqrt{2gl}}{\sqrt{\frac{g}{l}}} = \sqrt{2}\, l \quad ...(iii)$$

[using Eq. (ii)]

Therefore, the block first moves down $\sqrt{2}\, l$ from P to Q, then returns back to P. Then, it moves l from P to R, where the string extension becomes zero. Thereafter, string becomes slack and block moves under influence of gravity only from R to S (where its velocity becomes zero). Then, it returns from S to R to P completing one oscillation.

Time from P to Q, $t_1 = \frac{T}{4}$ (as the motion is $\frac{1}{4}$ th oscillation)

Time from Q to P, $t_2 = \frac{T}{4}$

For P to R, using $x = A \sin \omega t$, we get

$$l = \sqrt{2}\, l \sin \omega t \quad \text{[using Eq. (iii)]}$$

$$\Rightarrow \sin \omega t = \frac{1}{\sqrt{2}} \Rightarrow \omega t = \frac{\pi}{4}$$

$\therefore$ Time of motion from P to R,

$$t = \frac{\pi}{4\omega} = \frac{\pi}{4 \cdot \frac{2\pi}{T}} = \frac{T}{8} = t_3 \text{ (say)}$$

For SHM, speed as function of position x is given by

$$v = \omega\sqrt{A^2 - x^2}$$

Therefore, speed at R,

$$v = \sqrt{\frac{g}{l}}\sqrt{2l^2 - l^2} = \sqrt{gl}$$

For R to S, as string becomes slack, acceleration is due to gravity only.

Using, $v_{final} = v_{initial} + at$, we get

$$0 = \sqrt{gl} - gt$$

$\therefore$ Time of motion from R to S

$$t_4 = \sqrt{\frac{l}{g}}$$

By symmetry, for motion from S to R time is t_4 and from R to P time is t_3.

Therefore, time period of oscillation,

$$t = t_1 + t_2 + t_3 + t_4 + t_4 + t_3$$
$$= t_1 + t_2 + 2t_3 + 2t_4$$
$$= \frac{T}{4} + \frac{T}{4} + 2 \times \frac{T}{8} + 2\sqrt{\frac{l}{g}}$$
$$= \frac{3T}{4} + 2\sqrt{\frac{l}{g}} = \frac{3}{4} \cdot \frac{2\pi}{\omega} + 2\sqrt{\frac{l}{g}}$$
$$= \frac{3}{4}\frac{2\pi}{\sqrt{\frac{g}{l}}} + 2\sqrt{\frac{l}{g}} \quad \text{[using Eq. (ii)]}$$
$$= \left(\frac{3\pi}{2} + 2\right)\sqrt{\frac{l}{g}}$$
$$= 6.71\sqrt{\frac{l}{g}} = x\sqrt{\frac{l}{g}} \quad \text{(given)}$$

$\therefore \quad x = 6.71$

22. Let the plank be displaced right by amount x. FBD of the plank and the cylinder, at this instant will be as shown in Fig. 1. f, a, a', α and k represent friction, acceleration of cylinder's centre of mass, acceleration of plank, angular acceleration of cylinder and spring constant, respectively.

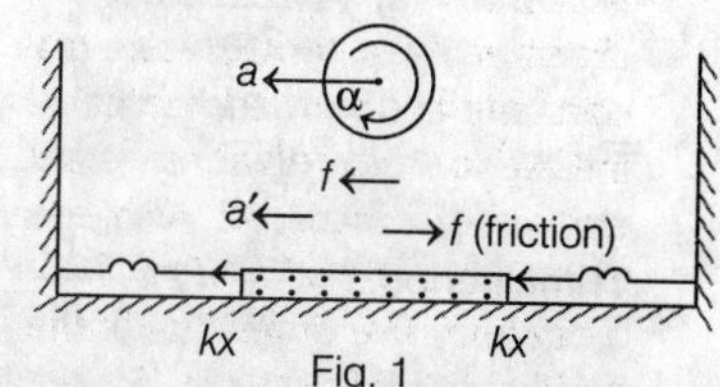

Fig. 1

For plank, using $F = ma$, we get

$$2kx - f = ma' \quad \text{...(i)}$$

Similarly for cylinder, $f = ma$ ...(ii)

For cylinder, using $\tau = I\alpha$, we get

$$fR = \frac{mR^2}{2}\alpha$$

$$\Rightarrow \quad f = \frac{m\alpha R}{2}$$

$$\Rightarrow \quad 2f = m\alpha R \quad \text{...(iii)}$$

Now, consider Figure-2

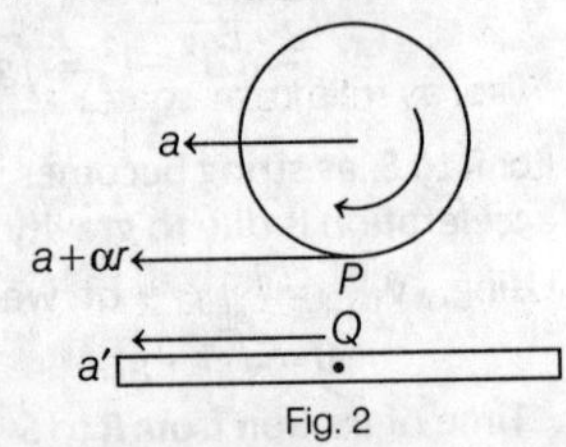

Fig. 2

Acceleration of bottomost point P of the cylinder is a (due to translation) and αR (due to rotation). So, its net horizontal acceleration,

$$a_P = a + \alpha R$$

For contact point Q of plank, acceleration,

$$a_Q = a'$$

As, there is no slipping between cylinder and plank.

i.e. $\quad a_P = a_Q$

$$\Rightarrow \quad a + \alpha R = a'$$

$$\Rightarrow \quad ma + m\alpha R = ma' \quad \text{...(iv)}$$

Putting values from Eqs. (i), (ii) and (iii) in Eq. (iv), we get

$$f + 2f = 2kx - f$$

$$\Rightarrow \quad f = \frac{kx}{2} \quad \text{... (v)}$$

From Eq. (i), acceleration of plank,

$$a' = \frac{2kx - f}{m}$$

$$\Rightarrow \quad a' = \frac{2kx - \frac{kx}{2}}{m} \quad \text{[using Eq. (v)]}$$

$$\Rightarrow \quad a' = \frac{3kx}{2m} \quad \text{... (vi)}$$

Comparing Eq. (vi) with acceleration in SHM (equal to $\omega^2 x$), we get

$$\omega^2 x = \frac{3kx}{2m}$$

$$\Rightarrow \quad \omega = \sqrt{\frac{3k}{2m}}$$

$$\therefore \text{Time period, } T = \frac{2\pi}{\omega} = 2\pi\sqrt{\frac{2m}{3k}}$$

$$= 2\pi\sqrt{\frac{m}{x\,k}} \text{ (given)}$$

$$\Rightarrow \quad x = \frac{3}{2} = 1.5$$

23. Time period of torsional pendulum is given by

$$T = 2\pi\sqrt{\frac{I}{C}}$$

where, I is moment of inertia and C is torsional constant.

$$\Rightarrow \quad I \propto T^2$$

If time period has doubled, moment of inertia must become 4 times

i.e. $\quad I_{final} = 4 I_{initial}$

$$\Rightarrow \quad \frac{ml^2}{12} + 2mx^2 = 4\frac{ml^2}{12}$$

$$\Rightarrow \quad 2mx^2 = \frac{ml^2}{4}$$

$$\Rightarrow \quad \frac{l}{x} = \sqrt{8} = 2\sqrt{2} = 2.82$$

24. Consider FBD of blocks.

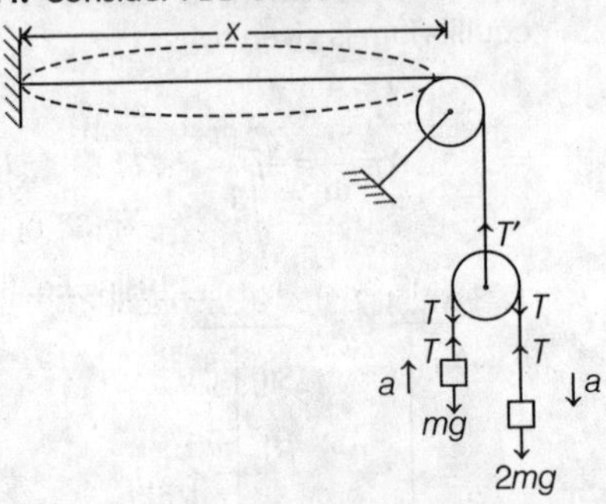

For mass m, using $F = ma$, we get

$$T - mg = ma \quad \text{...(i)}$$

Similarly for mass $2m$, we get

$$2mg - T = 2ma \quad \text{...(ii)}$$

From Eqs. (i) and (ii), $T = \dfrac{4mg}{3}$ ...(iii)

From FBD of pulley,

$$T' = 2T = \frac{8mg}{3} \quad \text{...(iv)}$$

[using Eq. (iii)]

Therefore, frequency of vibration of wire in fundamental mode,

$$f_1 = \frac{1}{2l}\sqrt{\frac{T'}{\mu}} = \frac{1}{2x}\sqrt{\frac{8mg}{3\mu}} \quad \text{... (v)}$$

[using Eq. (iv)]

Also, frequency of vibration of air in 1st overtone (3rd harmonic),

$$f_2 = \frac{3v}{4l} = \frac{3v}{4\frac{x}{2}} = \frac{3v}{2x} \quad \text{...(vi)}$$

As, resonance implies frequencies are equal.

i.e. $\quad f_1 = f_2 \Rightarrow \dfrac{1}{2x}\sqrt{\dfrac{8mg}{3\mu}} = \dfrac{3v}{2x}$

[using Eqs. (v) and (vi)]

$$\Rightarrow \quad m = \frac{27\mu v^2}{8g}$$

$$= \frac{27(0.2 \times 10^{-3})(400)^2}{8 \times 10}$$

$$= 10.8 \text{ kg}$$

25. Intensity of sound due to S_2 at B is same as that at A as both points are at same distance from S_2.

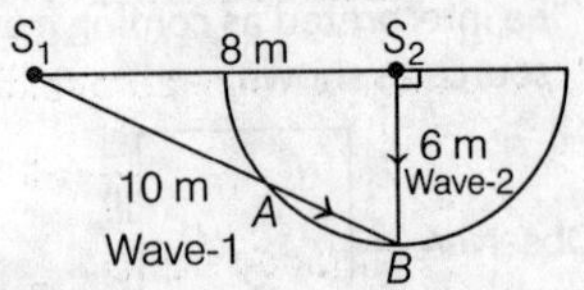

Therefore,

intensity at B due to S_2, $I_2 = I_0$ ...(i)

intensity due to line source is inversely proportional to distance from source. As distance of B from S_1 is 10 m while that of S_2 is 6 m, therefore, intensity due to S_1 will be $\dfrac{6}{10}$ or $\dfrac{3}{5}$ times of that due to S_2. So,

intensity at B due to S_1, $I_1 = \dfrac{3I_0}{5}$ ...(ii)

Clearly from diagram, paths of waves from S_2 and S_1 are 6 m and 8 m, respectively. So, path difference is 2 m, which is integral multiple of given wavelength of 2 m. So, resultant intensity is maximum and given by

$$I_{max} = (\sqrt{I_1} + \sqrt{I_2})^2$$

$$= \left(\sqrt{I_0} + \sqrt{\frac{3I_0}{5}}\right)^2$$

[Using Eqs. (i) and (ii)]

$$= I_0\left(1 + \sqrt{\frac{3}{5}}\right)^2$$

$$= I_0\left(1 + \frac{3}{5} + 2\sqrt{\frac{3}{5}}\right)$$

$$= I_0\left(\frac{8}{5} + 2\sqrt{\frac{3}{5}}\right) = 3.14\, I_0$$

$$\therefore \text{ Ratio} = \frac{I_{max}}{I_0} = 3.14$$

Hence, greatest integral value is 3.

Qualifier 10 (Electrostatics)

1. E_{net} at any general point P on X axis between $x = -\frac{r}{2}$ and $x = \frac{r}{2}$.

$\mathbf{E} = \mathbf{E}_1 + \mathbf{E}_2$, here $\mathbf{E}_1$ and $\mathbf{E}_2$ are electric fields due to $64Q$ and $-Q$, respectively.

$$\Rightarrow \quad E = \frac{k(64Q)}{(r-l)^2} + \frac{kQ}{l^2}$$

At location of minimum field,

$$\frac{dE}{dl} = 0$$

$$\Rightarrow \quad \frac{2k(64Q)}{(r-l)^3} - \frac{2kQ}{l^3} = 0$$

$$\Rightarrow \quad \left(\frac{l}{r-l}\right)^3 = \frac{1}{64}$$

$$\Rightarrow \quad \frac{l}{r-l} = \frac{1}{4} = \frac{r}{5}$$

$$\Rightarrow \quad l = \frac{r}{5}$$

If E_{net} at point $R = 0$

$$\frac{k(64Q)}{(r+l')^2} = \frac{kQ}{l'^2}$$

$$\Rightarrow \quad \frac{r+l'}{l'} = 8 \Rightarrow l' = \frac{r}{7}$$

From diagram, $x_2 - x_1 = PR = l + l'$

$$\frac{r}{5} + \frac{r}{7} = \frac{12r}{35}$$

2. Consider a general element of wire at distance y from end P of the wire PQ as shown in figure.

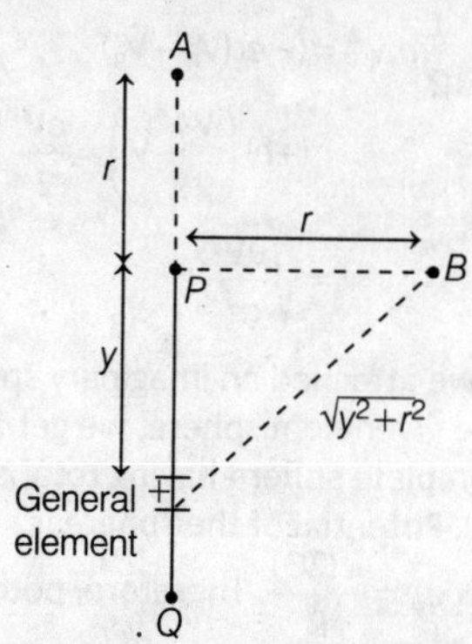

From figure, separation between the element and $A = r_A = r + y$

Separation between the element A and B,

$$r_B = \sqrt{r^2 + y^2}$$

Clearly, $r_A > r_B$. As, $V \propto \frac{1}{r}$, so $V_A < V_B$

$$\Rightarrow \int_A^B \mathbf{E} \cdot d\mathbf{s} = V_A - V_B = \text{Negative.}$$

3. From triangle shown, $r = R\cos 37° = \frac{4R}{5}$

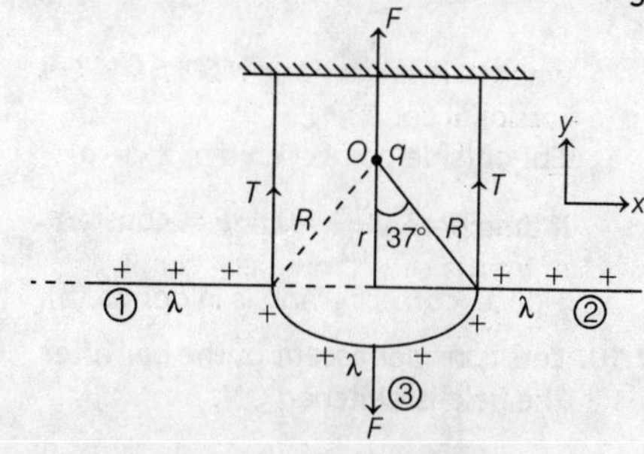

(a) Field at O due to segment (1),

$$\mathbf{E}_1 = \frac{k\lambda}{r}(\cos 37° - \cos 90°)\hat{\mathbf{i}} + \frac{k\lambda}{r}(\sin 90° - \sin 37°)\hat{\mathbf{j}}$$

(b) Field at O due to segment (2),

$$\mathbf{E}_2 = \frac{k\lambda}{r}(\cos 90° - \cos 37°)\hat{\mathbf{i}} + \frac{k\lambda}{r}(\sin 90° - \sin 37°)\hat{\mathbf{j}}$$

(c) Field at O due to segment (3),

$$\mathbf{E}_3 = \frac{2k\lambda}{R}\sin 37°\,\hat{\mathbf{j}}$$

$$\mathbf{E}_{net} = \left(\frac{4k\lambda}{5r} + \frac{6k\lambda}{5R}\right)\hat{\mathbf{j}} = \frac{2.2k\lambda}{R}\hat{\mathbf{j}}$$

Force on $q = \frac{2.2k\lambda q}{R}\hat{\mathbf{j}}$

By Newton's 3rd law, wire experiences equal but opposite force which is balanced by tension.

$$\Rightarrow \quad 2T = \frac{2.2\,k\lambda q}{R}$$

$$\Rightarrow \quad T = \frac{1.1\,k\lambda q}{R}$$

4. As we know, electric field is perpendicular to equipotential surface. So, electric field line will be perpendicular to given circle at P, as shown.

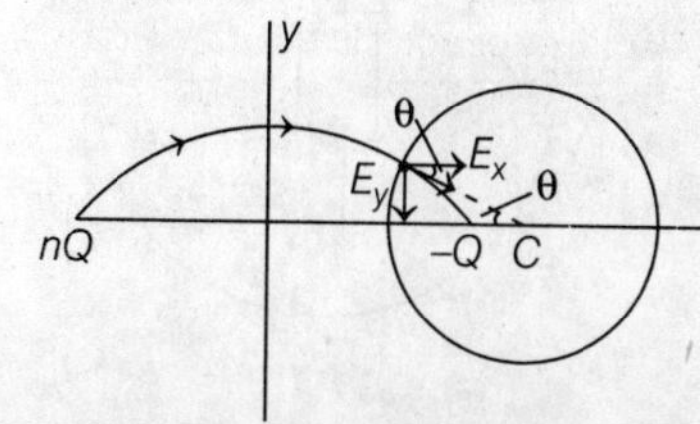

So, from diagram, $\tan\theta = \frac{-E_y}{E_x}$

$$\therefore \quad \frac{E_x}{E_y} = -\cot\theta$$

5. Induced charge on conducting surface is equivalent to equal and opposite image charge, as shown. Thus, field at point P = field of dipole formed by $+q$ and $-q = \frac{kq(2d)}{r^3}$

Also, as field near conductor is equal to $\frac{\sigma}{\varepsilon_0}$.

$$\Rightarrow \quad \frac{\sigma_P}{\varepsilon_0} = \frac{kq(2d)}{r^3}$$

$$\Rightarrow \quad \sigma_P \propto r^{-3}$$

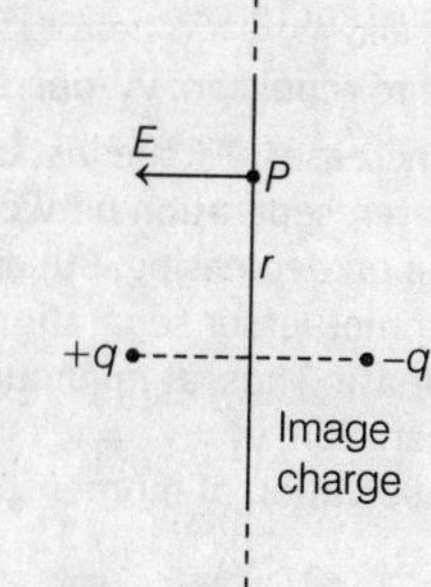

6.

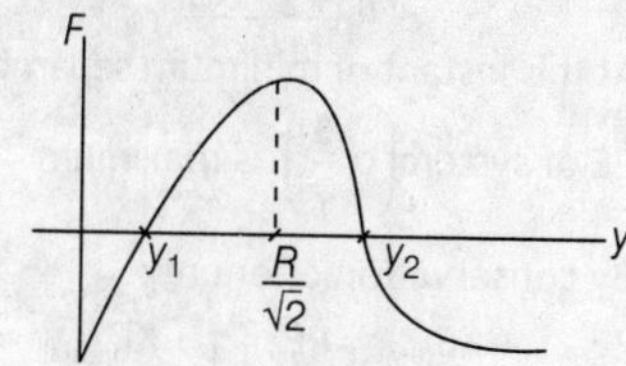

F

y_1 $\frac{R}{\sqrt{2}}$ y_2 y

At general position shown, net force on particle, $F = qE - mg$ ...(i)

Also, electric field on axis of ring,

$$E = \frac{kQy}{(R^2 + y^2)^{3/2}} \quad \text{...(ii)}$$

Substituting E from Eq. (ii) in Eq. (i), we get

$$F = \frac{qkQy}{(R^2 + y^2)^{3/2}} - mg$$

Graph of F with y is as shown. From this graph, particle can remain in equilibrium for $y = y_1$ (Unstable) and for $y = y_2$ (Stable).

Thus, for stable equilibrium,

$$y = y_2 > \frac{R}{\sqrt{2}}$$

$$\Rightarrow \quad \frac{R}{y} < \sqrt{2} \Rightarrow \tan\theta < \sqrt{2}$$

So, out of given choices only possible θ is 45°.

7. Here, dipole is placed in non-uniform electric field of sphere, which is given by $E = \frac{kQr}{R^3}$

In non-uniform field, dipole experiences force given by

$$F = p\frac{dE}{dr} = p\frac{d\left[\frac{kQr}{R^3}\right]}{dr} = \frac{kQp}{R^3}$$

As, force does not depend on r, so it is a constant force.

8. Due to repulsion, v_1 decreases while v_2 increases. Till the instant v_1 is greater, separation between blocks keep on decreasing. But after v_1 becomes lesser separation begins to increase. Thus, at minimum separation, $v_1 = v_2 = v'$ (say). By conservation of momentum,

$\rightarrow K_1$ $\rightarrow v_1$ $\rightarrow K_2$ $\rightarrow v_2$

$F \leftarrow$ + + + + $\rightarrow F$

$$mv' + mv' = mv$$

$$\Rightarrow \quad v' = \frac{v}{2}$$

$$\Rightarrow \quad K_1 = K_2 = \frac{1}{2}mv'^2$$

$$= \frac{1}{4} \times \frac{1}{2}mv^2 = \frac{K}{4}$$

At this instant of minimum separation, PE of system $\left(\alpha \frac{1}{r}\right)$ is maximum.

By conservation of energy

$$PE_{final} + KE_{final} = PE_{initial} + KE_{initial}$$

$$\Rightarrow PE_{final} + 2\left(\frac{K}{4}\right) = 0 + K$$

$$\Rightarrow \quad PE_{final} = \frac{K}{2}$$

9. As per Gauss law,

$$\rho = \varepsilon_0 \frac{dE}{dx}$$

$$\Rightarrow \rho_0 x = \varepsilon_0 \frac{dE}{dx} \quad \text{(for inside point)}$$

where, ρ_0 = slope of ρ *versus* x graph

$$\Rightarrow \int_0^E dE = \frac{\rho_0}{\varepsilon_0}\int_0^x x\,dx$$

$$\Rightarrow \quad E = \frac{\rho_0 x^2}{2\varepsilon_0}$$

E-x graph is parabolic for inside region. Taking direction into account,

$$\mathbf{E} = \frac{\rho_0 x^2}{2\varepsilon_0}\hat{\mathbf{j}} \quad 0 \le x \le a$$

$$= -\frac{\rho_0 x^2}{2\varepsilon_0}\hat{\mathbf{j}} \quad -a \le x \le 0$$

For outside points ($x > a$ or $x < -a$)

$$\rho = 0 \Rightarrow \varepsilon_0 \frac{dE}{dx} = 0 \Rightarrow E = \text{constant.}$$

Hence, correct graph is in option (b).

10. Lets consider ascent of the ball after the field is switched ON.

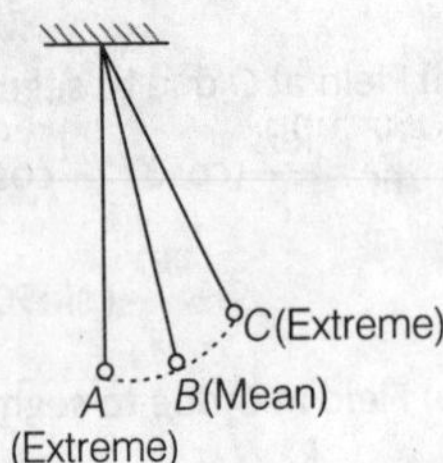

$$t_a = \text{Time of ascent}$$

$$= t_{AB} + t_{BC}$$

$$= \frac{T}{4} + \frac{T}{4} = \frac{T}{2}$$

$$= \pi\sqrt{\frac{l}{g'}} \quad \text{...(i)}$$

$$g' = \sqrt{g^2 + \left(\frac{qE}{m}\right)^2} > g$$

Next, consider descent of the ball after switching OFF the field.

$$t_d = \text{Time of descent}$$

$$= t_{CA} = \frac{T}{4} = \frac{\pi}{2}\sqrt{\frac{l}{g}} \quad \text{...(ii)}$$

From Eqs. (i) and (ii), we get

$$t_d > \frac{t_a}{2}$$

11. Lets complete the outer hemisphere by placing identical hemisphere as shown.

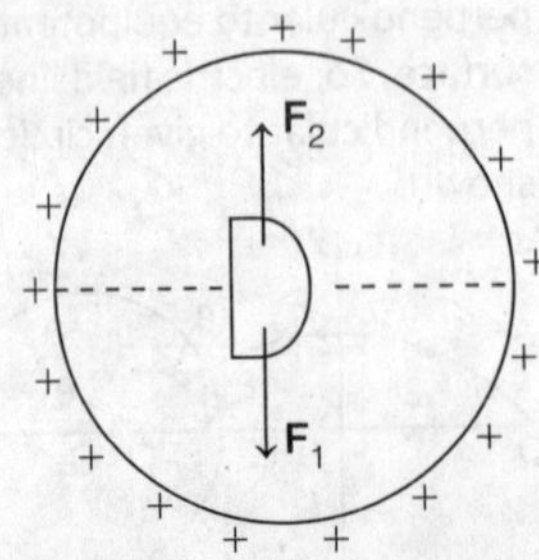

$\mathbf{F}_{net}$ on inner sphere = 0 as in this case net field inside hollow sphere is zero. Thus, forces on inner sphere due to upper and lower halves of outer sphere should be equal and opposite shown as $\mathbf{F}_1$ and $\mathbf{F}_2$ respectively.

So, due to only upper half portion, F_y = – ve.

and $F_x = 0$.

12. Imagine 7 more identical cubes as shown, thereby creating a charged cube of side $2l$ and charge $8Q$ (here l = side of original/smaller cube and Q = charge of original cube).

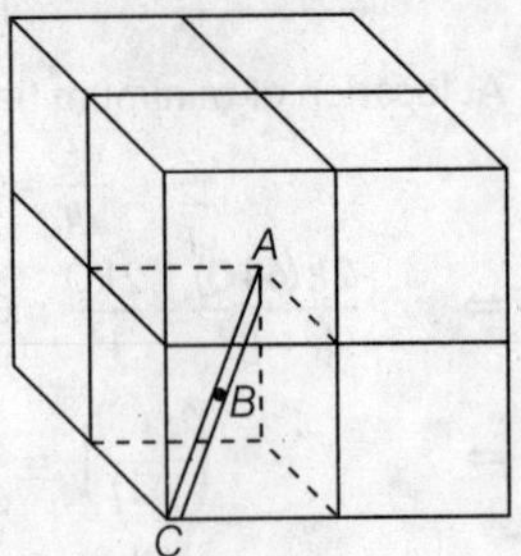

For small/original cube, at centre,

$$V \propto \frac{Q}{l}$$

For large cube, at centre (point A)

$$V \propto \frac{8Q}{2l}$$

$$\Rightarrow V' = 4V \text{ (due to 8 small cubes)}$$

$$\Rightarrow V_A = \frac{V'}{8} = \frac{V}{2}$$

(due to one original small cube)

Now, electron released at A will be attracted towards centre of positive cube.

In its motion from A to B, it gains KE at expense of PE. Therefore,

Gain in KE = Loss in PE

$$\frac{1}{2}mv^2 = (-e)(V_A - V_B)$$

$$= (-e)\left(\frac{V}{2} - V\right) = \frac{eV}{2}$$

$$\Rightarrow \quad v = \sqrt{\frac{eV}{m}}$$

13. If we attached an imaginary sphere to the given hemisphere, we get a complete sphere having total charge 2Q. Potential of the sphere is $V_{sphere} = \frac{k(2Q)}{R}$. Therefore, potential due to hemisphere at A,

$$V_A = \frac{V_{sphere}}{2}$$

$$= \frac{k(2Q)}{2R} = \frac{kQ}{R} \quad \text{...(i)}$$

Similarly, potential at C,

$$V_C = \frac{V_{\text{sphere}}}{2} = \frac{k(2Q)}{2r}$$

$$= \frac{kQ}{r} = \frac{3kQ}{5R} \quad \text{...(ii)}$$

Therefore, work done in moving $-q$ from A to C,

$$W = -q(V_C - V_A)$$

$$= (-q)\left(\frac{3kQ}{5R} - \frac{kQ}{R}\right)$$

$$= \frac{2kQq}{5R} \quad \text{[using Eqs. (i) and (ii)]}$$

14. By superposition, potential of innermost sphere,

$$V = \frac{kQ_1}{R/3} + \frac{kQ_2}{R/2} + \frac{kQ_3}{R}$$

and potential of outermost sphere,

$$V' = \frac{kQ_1}{R} + \frac{kQ_2}{R} + \frac{kQ_3}{R}$$

For no heat to dissipate, no current should flow on closing the key

$$\Rightarrow \quad V = V'$$

$$\Rightarrow \quad \frac{3kQ_1}{R} + \frac{2kQ_2}{R} + \frac{kQ_3}{R} = \frac{kQ_1}{R} + \frac{kQ_2}{R} + \frac{kQ_3}{R}$$

$$\Rightarrow \quad 2Q_1 + Q_2 = 0$$

15. As net charge on ball's surface is zero, potential due to induced charges at ball's centre $= 0$

$\Rightarrow V$ at ball's centre $= V$ due to dipole

$$= \frac{kp}{R^2}$$

As metal body is equipotential

$$V_P = V_{\text{centre}} = \frac{kp}{R^2}$$

$$\Rightarrow V_{\text{dipole}} + V_{\text{induced charges}} = \frac{kp}{R^2}$$

$$\Rightarrow \quad \frac{kp\cos\theta}{r^2} + V_{\text{in}} = \frac{kp}{R^2}$$

$$\Rightarrow \quad \frac{kpR}{r^3} + V_{\text{in}} = \frac{kp}{R^2}\left[\because \cos\theta = \frac{R}{r}\right]$$

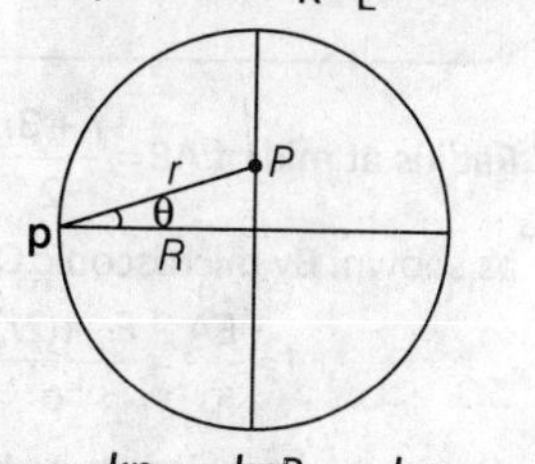

$$\Rightarrow \quad V_{\text{in}} = \frac{kp}{R^2} - \frac{kpR}{(\sqrt[3]{2}R)^3} = \frac{kp}{2R^2}$$

16. As proton is located at focus its distance from origin is $ae = \frac{a}{2}$.

Here, e is eccentricity.

At nearest position shown,

$$\text{potential energy, PE} = \frac{kQ_1Q_2}{r}$$

As distance r between particles is $\frac{a}{2}$

$$\Rightarrow \text{PE} = -\frac{ke^2}{\frac{a}{2}} = -\frac{2ke^2}{a} \quad \text{...(i)}$$

$$\text{Also, total energy, TE} = \frac{kQ_1Q_2}{2a} = \frac{-ke^2}{2a} \quad \text{...(ii)}$$

Subtracting Eq. (i) from Eq. (ii), we get kinetic energy

$$\text{KE} = \text{TE} - \text{PE}$$

$$= \left(\frac{-ke^2}{2a}\right) - \left(\frac{-2ke^2}{a}\right) = \frac{3}{2}\frac{ke^2}{a}$$

$$\text{Therefore, } \frac{|\text{PE}|}{|\text{KE}|} = \frac{4}{3}$$

17. $W = \int F_x dx + \int F_y \, dy$

$$= \int (-2xyq)\,dx + \int (-x^2 q)\,dy$$

Putting $y = x^2$,

$$W = -\int 2x^3 q\,dx - \int (yq)\,dy$$

$$= -\frac{qx^4}{2} - \frac{qy^2}{2} + C$$

$$= -\frac{qx^4}{2} - \frac{qx^4}{2} + C = -qx^4 + C$$

$$\Rightarrow \quad |W| = q[x^4]_{-2}^{3} = 10^{-6}[3^4 - (-2)^4]$$

$$= 65\,\mu\text{J}$$

18. The electric field due to hollow cylinder of charge density ρ, $E = \frac{\rho R^2}{2\varepsilon_0 r}$

Work done against field in moving charge from r_1 to $r_2 = -\int_{r_1}^{r_2} qE dr$

$$= -\int_{r_1}^{r_2} q \cdot \frac{\rho R^2}{2\varepsilon_0 r} dr = \frac{\rho R^2 q}{2\varepsilon_0} \ln\left(\frac{r_1}{r_2}\right)$$

As it is given that $W_{AB} = W_{BC}$

$$\Rightarrow \quad \frac{\rho R^2 q}{2\varepsilon_0} \ln\frac{r_A}{r_B} = \frac{\rho R^2 q}{2\varepsilon_0} \ln\frac{r_B}{r_C}$$

$$\Rightarrow \quad r_B = \sqrt{r_A r_C}$$

19. If we assume x charge flows from left plate to right plate in certain time interval, then charges on plates will be as shown.

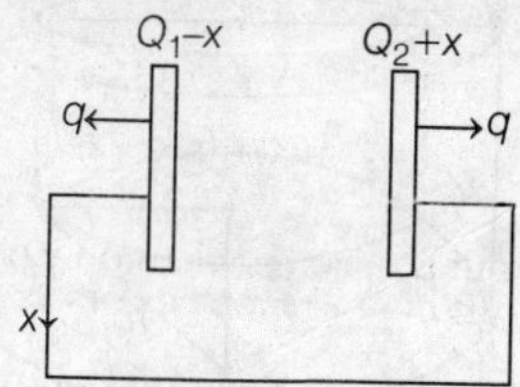

As charges on outer surfaces of plates are equal to half of total charge of system

$$\Rightarrow \quad q = \frac{(Q_1 - x) + (Q_2 + x)}{2}$$

$$= \frac{Q_1 + Q_2}{2} = \text{constant}$$

20. With electric field,

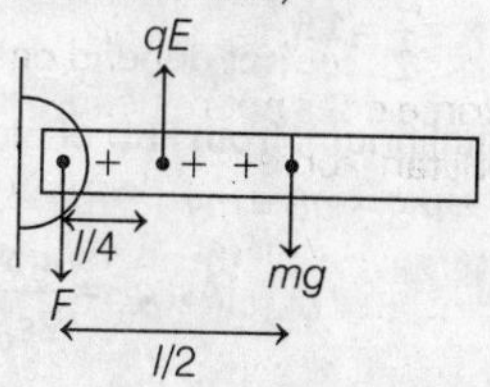

$$\tau_{\text{clockwise}} = \tau_{\text{anticlockwise}}$$

$$mg\frac{l}{2} = qE\frac{l}{4} \Rightarrow \quad qE = 2mg$$

If F is force by hinge, for equilibrium,

$$qE = mg + F \Rightarrow \quad F = mg$$

When electric field is turned OFF

$$\alpha = \frac{\tau}{I} = \frac{mg\frac{l}{2}}{\frac{ml^2}{3}} = \frac{3g}{2l}$$

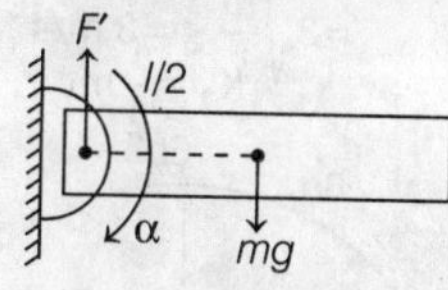

$$a_{\text{CM}} = \alpha r = \frac{3g}{2l} \cdot \frac{l}{2} = \frac{3g}{4}$$

By $\quad F_{\text{net}} = ma_{\text{cm}}$

$$mg - F' = m\left(\frac{3g}{4}\right) \Rightarrow \quad F' = \frac{mg}{4}$$

$$\Rightarrow \text{Decrease} = \frac{3mg}{4}$$

$$\% \text{ decrease} = \left(\frac{\frac{3}{4}mg}{mg} \times 100\right)\%$$

$$= 75\% = p\%$$

$$\therefore \quad p = 75$$

21. Electrostatic pressure and is given by the formula $p = \frac{\sigma^2}{2\varepsilon_0}$.

Force experienced by surface = Electrostatic pressure × Projected Area

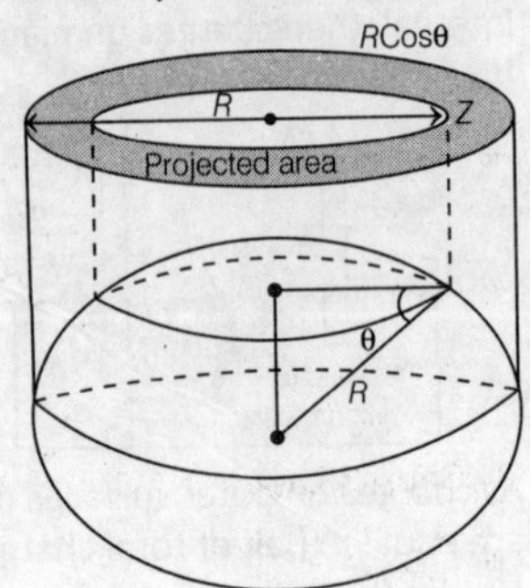

$$=\frac{\sigma^2}{2\varepsilon_0}\cdot \pi R^2\,[1-\cos^2\theta]$$

$$=\frac{\pi\sigma^2R^2}{2\varepsilon_0}\sin^2\theta=\frac{\pi\sigma^2R^2}{2\varepsilon_0}\times\frac{3}{\pi}=\frac{3\sigma^2R^2}{2\varepsilon_0}$$

$$\Rightarrow\quad x=\frac{3}{2}=1.5$$

22. At equilibrium, from FBD of block

$$kx=mg+qE=mg+2mg=3mg$$

$$\left(\text{As, } qE=\frac{q\sigma}{2\varepsilon_0}=2mg\right)$$

$$\Rightarrow\quad x=\frac{3mg}{k}=A$$

$$v_{max}=A\omega=\frac{3mg}{k}\sqrt{\frac{k}{m}}$$

$$=3\sqrt{\frac{m}{k}}\,g=3\text{ m/s}$$

23.

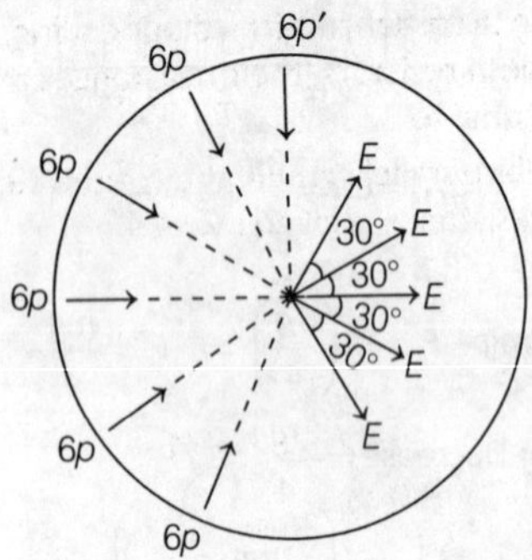

System can be reduced to system of six dipoles as shown. As fields of diametrically opposite dipoles are opposite to each other. Fields of dipoles other than that of $6p'$ are shown.

E_1 be the resultant of field of dipoles of $6p$, which will be horizontal as shown.

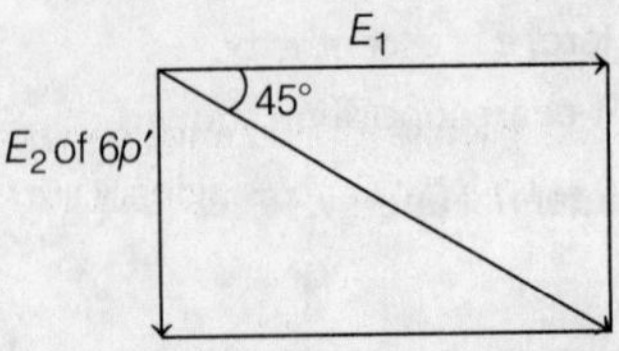

$$E_1=E+2E\cos 30^\circ+2E\cos 60^\circ=E(2+\sqrt{3})$$

For net field to be directed along hour hand at 4 : 30, field of $6p'$ should be same along vertical. Thus, $E_2=E_1$

$$\frac{2k(6p')}{r^3}=\frac{2k(6p)(2+\sqrt{3})}{r^3}$$

$$\Rightarrow\quad \frac{p'}{p}=2+\sqrt{3}=3.73$$

24.

Lets construct a cone as shown. By field picture, ϕ through lateral surface is zero.

$$\Rightarrow\quad \phi_{section}=\phi_{cone}=\frac{q_{inside}}{\varepsilon_0}$$

$$=\frac{\rho\cdot\frac{1}{3}\pi\left(\frac{R}{\sqrt{2}}\right)^2\left(\frac{R}{\sqrt{2}}\right)}{\varepsilon_0}$$

$$=\frac{\left(\frac{Q}{\frac{4}{3}\pi R^3}\right)\cdot\left(\frac{1}{3}\pi\frac{R^3}{2\sqrt{2}}\right)}{\varepsilon_0}$$

$$=\frac{Q}{8\sqrt{2}\varepsilon_0}=\frac{Q}{(11.28)\,\varepsilon_0}$$

$$\therefore\quad x=11.28$$

25. FBD of particle A is as shown. F is electric repulsion on A due to each of B and C. D is centre of triangle.

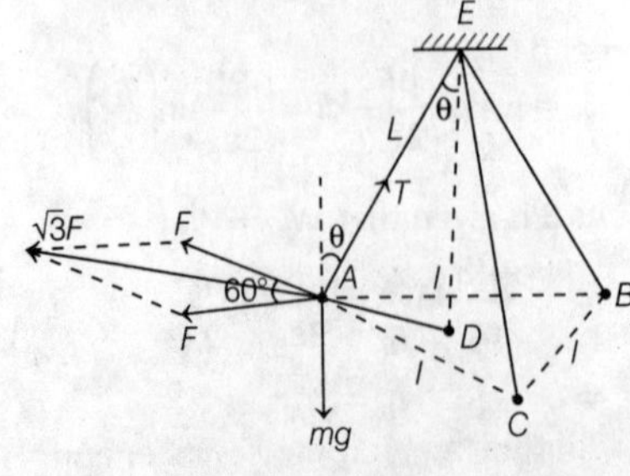

For vertical, $T\cos\theta=mg$ ...(i)

For horizontal, $T\sin\theta=\sqrt{3}F$ ...(ii)

Divide Eq. (ii) by Eq. (i),

$$\tan\theta=\frac{AD}{L}=\frac{\sqrt{3}F}{mg}\quad (\text{As}, l<<L, ED\approx L)$$

$$\Rightarrow\quad \frac{l}{\sqrt{3}L}=\frac{\sqrt{3}kq^2}{l^2mg}$$

or $\quad l\propto q^{2/3}$

$$\text{PE of system}=3\times\frac{kq^2}{l}\ (\text{initially})$$

If q is now made $8q$, then l becomes 4 times, so new potential energy will be

$$3\times\frac{k(8q)^2}{4l}=16\text{ times of }U$$

Qualifier 11 (Current Electricity)

1. As we know, |slope| of V-x graph

$$=\left|\frac{dV}{dx}\right|=|E|=\rho J$$

For the given wires, we can say, slope of V-x graph from l to $2l$ = Half of slope of V-x graph from $x=0$ to $x=l$ besides being constant for both wires as resistivities and current densities are constants.

$\therefore \tan\theta_{AB}>\tan\theta_{BC}\Rightarrow\theta_{AB}>\theta_{BC}$

Hence, option (b) is correct.

2. Inside a conductor, average speed due to random thermal motion of electrons and speed due to their drifting are of the order of 10^6 m/s and 10^{-3} m/s, respectively.

3. The given wire ABC can be drawn as shown,

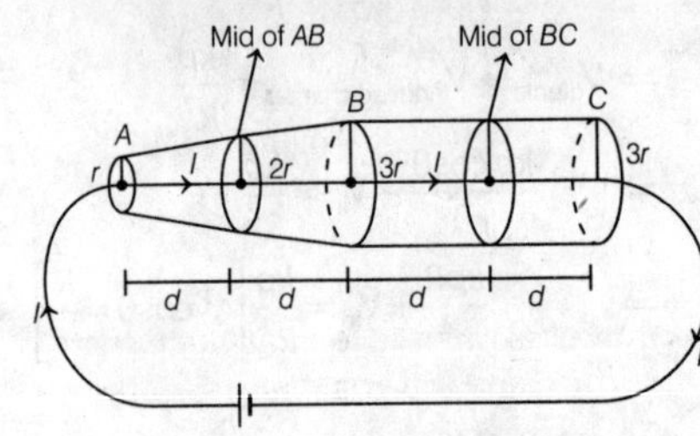

$$\text{Radius at mid of } AB=\frac{r+3r}{2}=2r$$

as shown. By microscopic Ohm's law,

$$I=\frac{EA}{\rho}=\frac{E\cdot\pi(2r)^2}{\rho}\quad ...(i)$$

If we assume resistivity to be ρ' at mid of BC, by Ohm's law, $I=\dfrac{E\cdot\pi(3r)^2}{\rho'}$ ...(ii)

(As E is given to be same as that at mid of AB)

From Eqs. (i) and (ii), we get

$$\frac{E\cdot\pi(2r)^2}{\rho}=\frac{E\cdot\pi(3r)^2}{\rho'}\Rightarrow\rho'=\frac{9\rho}{4}$$

As, resistivity is increasing linearly from B to C,

ρ' = average of resistivity at B and C

$$\Rightarrow\quad\rho'=\frac{\rho_B+\rho_C}{2}$$

$$\Rightarrow\quad\rho_C=2\rho'-\rho_B=\frac{9\rho}{2}-\rho=\frac{7\rho}{2}=3.5\rho$$

4. Cross-section of the cylinder is as shown. If inner surface is assumed at higher potential, current will flow as shown in radially outward direction.

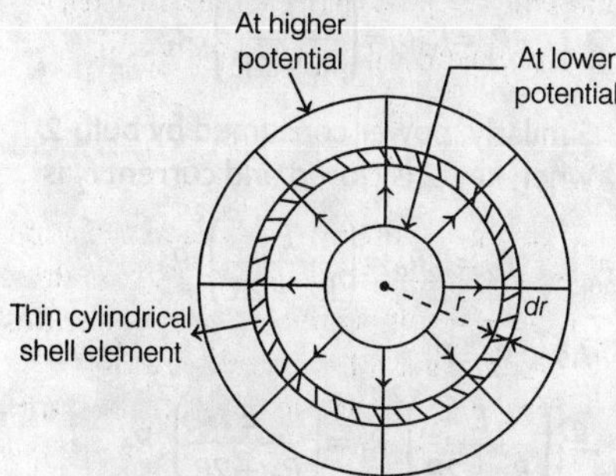

Let us consider a small element dr for the given shell as shown in the figure.

$\therefore$ Resistance of the shell element shown $=\frac{\rho\cdot dr}{2\pi rl}$

Integrating the above expression with in the limits,
Resistance of cylinder

$$=\frac{\rho}{2\pi l}\int_{r_1}^{r_2}\frac{1}{r}dr=\frac{\rho}{2\pi l}\ln\frac{r_2}{r_1}\quad\text{...(i)}$$

Let radius of an imaginary co-axial cylindrical surface shown, where potential is $\frac{V_1+V_2}{2}$ be x.

Potential difference between inner surface and the imaginary surface

$$=V_1-\left(\frac{V_1+V_2}{2}\right)=\frac{V_1-V_2}{2}$$

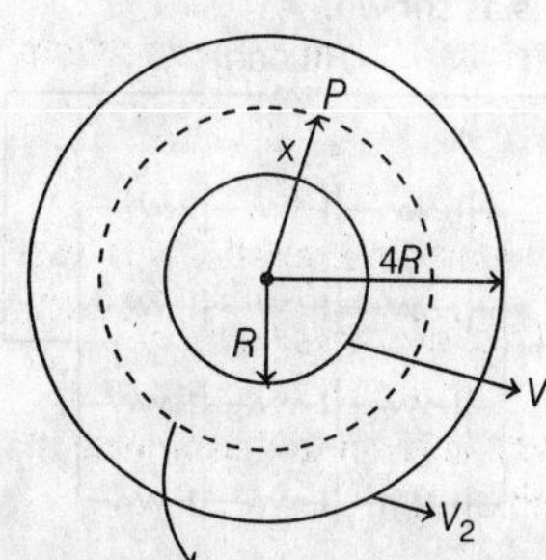

Imaginary cylindrical surface

Also, potential difference between outer surface and imaginary surface

$$=\frac{V_1+V_2}{2}-V_2=\frac{V_1-V_2}{2}$$

As the above two potential differences are equal, corresponding resistances should also be equal

$$\Rightarrow\quad\frac{\rho}{2\pi l}\ln\frac{x}{R}=\frac{\rho}{2\pi l}\ln\frac{4R}{x}$$

(using earlier derived expression of resistance)

$$\Rightarrow\quad\frac{x}{R}=\frac{4R}{x}$$

$$\Rightarrow\quad x=2R$$

5. Due to low value of thermal coefficient of resistance of metal alloys, resistance does not vary significantly with fluctuations/ variations of temperature which is practically desired. Thus, metal alloys are used in making standard resistance coils.

6. As the elements are in series, current through elements will be equal as per conservation of current. Resistance is inversely proportional to area. So, resistance of element-1 will be more and therefore, power $=P=i^2R$ will be more.

Hence, statement-I is true but statement-II is false.

7. Resistance of wire between A and D is resistance of wire AB added to resistance of wire BD (which is half of resistance of wire BC)

$$\Rightarrow\quad R_{AD}=R_{AB}+R_{BD}=R+2R=3R$$

Also, in balanced condition, potential difference between points A and D equals emf of cell, $E=V_{AD}$

So, by Ohm's law, current in potentiometer wire,

$$I=\frac{V_{AD}}{R_{AD}}=\frac{E}{3R}$$

By microscopic Ohm's law, electric field in wire -1,

$$E_1=\rho J=\frac{\rho I}{A}=\frac{\rho E}{3AR}$$

and electric field in wire-2

$$E_2=\rho' J=\frac{4\rho E}{3AR}\left(\text{As, }\frac{\rho'}{\rho}=\frac{R'}{R}=4\right)$$

Consider an imaginary cylinder and apply

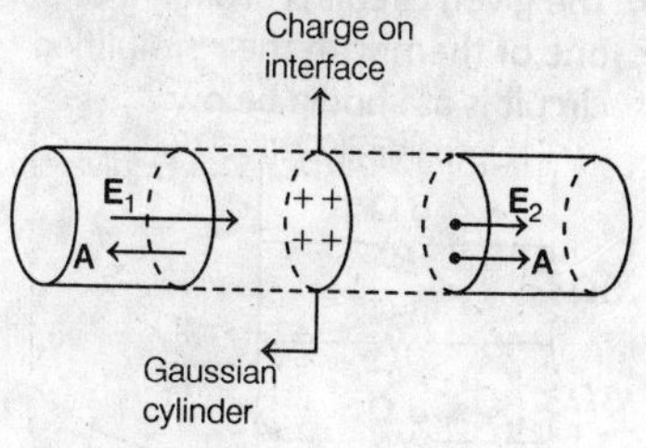

By Gauss's Law,

$$\phi_{\text{cylinder}}=\frac{q}{\varepsilon_0}$$

$$\Rightarrow\quad q=\phi_{\text{cylinder}}\,\varepsilon_0$$
$$=(\mathbf{E}_2\cdot\mathbf{A}+\mathbf{E}_1\cdot\mathbf{A})\varepsilon_0$$
$$=(E_2A\cos 0^\circ+E_1A\cos 180^\circ)\varepsilon_0$$
$$=(E_2-E_1)A\varepsilon_0$$
$$=\left(\frac{4\rho E}{3AR}-\frac{\rho E}{3AR}\right)A\varepsilon_0$$
$$=\frac{\rho\varepsilon_0 E}{R}$$

8. When N identical bulbs of resistance R each is connected in parallel, then equivalent resistance is given as,

$$R_{eq}=\frac{R}{N}$$

$\therefore$ For $N=5, 6, 7$ respective equivalent resistances will be $\frac{R}{5},\frac{R}{6},\frac{R}{7}$. According to the question for $N=6$ or $R_{eq}=\frac{R}{6}$, power P is maximum.

Thus, resistance of cell should lie between $\frac{R}{7}$ and $\frac{R}{5}$ as per maximum power theorem.

9. In accordance with colour coding, for both resistors, their resistances are equal to $82\pm5\%\,\Omega$.

For parallel combination, equivalent resistance is given by

$$\frac{1}{R}=\frac{1}{R_1}+\frac{1}{R_2}$$

$$=\frac{1}{82}+\frac{1}{82}=\frac{1}{41}\quad\text{...(i)}$$

$$\Rightarrow\quad R=41\,\Omega\quad\text{...(ii)}$$

Also, $\frac{\Delta R}{R}\times100$

$$=R\left[\frac{\Delta R_1}{R_1^2}\times100+\frac{\Delta R_2}{R_2^2}\times100\right]$$

$$=41\left[\frac{5}{82}+\frac{5}{82}\right]=5\%\quad\text{...(iii)}$$

From Eqs. (ii) and (iii), we get

$$R_{eq}=41\pm5\%\,\Omega$$

10. The given circuit is broken into parts, one of them with their simplified circuit is as shown below

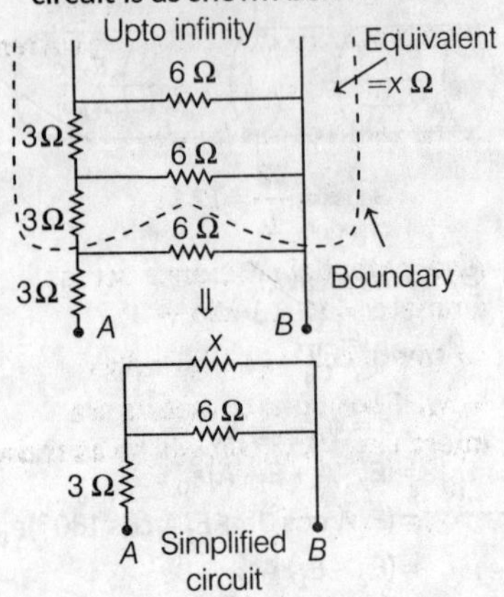

Thus, $R_{AB} = \dfrac{6x}{6+x} + 3 = x$

$\Rightarrow \quad x^2 - 3x - 18 = 0 \Rightarrow x = 6\ \Omega$

For the other infinite circuit, let $R_{CD} = y$

C D 6 Ω 2 Ω 4 Ω 12 Ω 8 Ω 24 Ω Equivalent=2y

⇓

C D 2Ω 6Ω 2y Simplified circuit

Thus, $R_{CD} = y = \dfrac{6 \cdot 2y}{6+2y} + 2$

$\Rightarrow \quad y^2 - 5y - 6 = 0 \Rightarrow y = 6\ \Omega$

Given circuit can be redrawn which represents a balanced Wheatstone bridge. As, 15 Ω resistor will not carry any current, it can be removed.

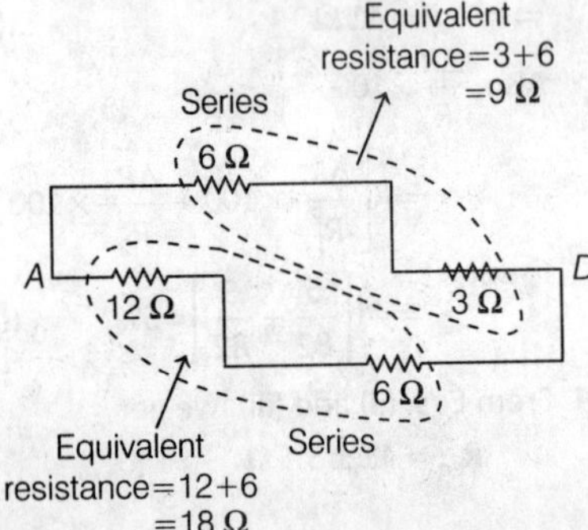

Net resistance of the above mentioned circuit,

$$R_{eq} = \frac{9 \times 18}{9+18} = 6\Omega$$

Therefore, as per maximum power theorem,

$$r = R_{eq} = 6\Omega$$

11. If r_1 and r_2 are internal resistances of two cells and E_1 and E_2 are their respective emf, so their equivalent emf,

$E = \dfrac{E_1 r_2 + E_2 r_1}{r_1 + r_2}$, which is weighted average of E_1 and E_2. So, it should lie between E_1 and E_2.

12. With key open, the given branch is as shown below.

A D C R B 10 V ε r 2 V

The potential of point $D = 10 - \varepsilon$.

So, depending on emf ε, D may be at higher, lower or at same potential compared to B. Thus, corresponding current may be rightwards, leftwards or zero. With key closed, equivalent emf of the cells in parallel $= \dfrac{E(r) + (-E)(r)}{r+r} = 0$

and equivalent resistance $= \dfrac{r}{2}$.

As we know, in resistances, the current must flow from higher potential to lower potential. So, current must flow from A to B.

13. If cells are connected in supporting manner, circuit is as shown below.

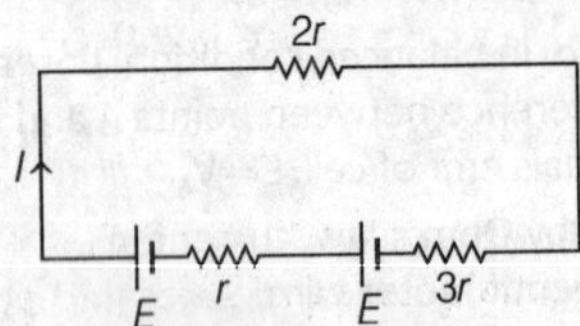

Current in circuit,

$$I = \frac{E_{net}}{R + r_{net}}$$

$$\Rightarrow \quad I = \frac{E+E}{2r + (r+3r)} = \frac{E}{3r}$$

Potential difference across cell of internal resistance $3r$

$$= E - \left(\frac{E}{3r}\right)3r = 0$$

If cells are connected in opposing manner, as shown in the circuit below

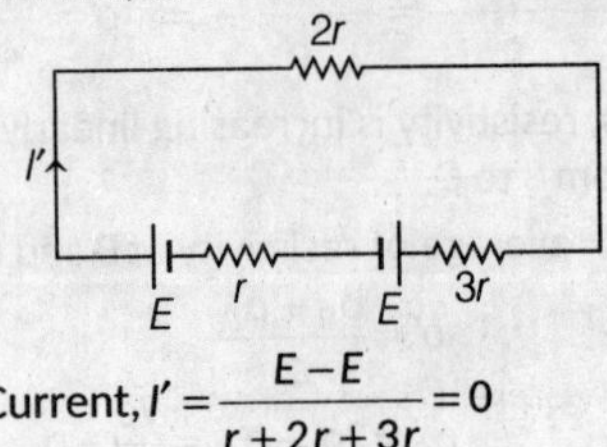

Current, $I' = \dfrac{E - E}{r + 2r + 3r} = 0$

Potential difference across cell of internal resistance $3r = E$

14. Let resistances of bulb-1 and bulb-2 be R_1 and R_2, respectively. Power consumed by bulb-1, when key-1 is closed and current I_1 flows through it will be

$$P_1 = I_1^2 R_1 = \left(\frac{E}{R_1 + 2R}\right)^2 R_1$$

Similarly, power consumed by bulb-2 when key-2 is closed and current I_2 is

$$P_2 = I_2^2 R_2 = \left(\frac{E}{R_2 + 2R}\right)^2 R_2$$

As, $P_1 = P_2$ (given)

$\Rightarrow \left(\dfrac{E}{R_1 + 2R}\right)^2 R_1 = \left(\dfrac{E}{R_2 + 2R}\right)^2 R_2$

$\Rightarrow \quad R_2 R_1^2 + 4R^2 R_2 = R_1 R_2^2 + 4R^2 R_1$

$\Rightarrow \quad R_1 R_2 (R_1 - R_2) = 4R^2 (R_1 - R_2)$

$\Rightarrow \quad R_1 R_2 = 4R^2$

$\Rightarrow \quad R_2 = 4R \quad (\because \text{Given that, } R_1 = R)$

Considering (V_1, P_1) and (V_2, P_2) as ratings of the two bulbs and using the relation, $R = \dfrac{V^2}{P}$

We can write the above relation as

$$\frac{V_2^2}{P_2} = 4\left(\frac{V_1^2}{P_1}\right)$$

Only option (b) satisfies the above relation and is therefore the correct choice.

15. Initially, the cells are arranged as shown. If internal resistance and emf of each cells are r and ε respectively, equivalent cell is as shown.

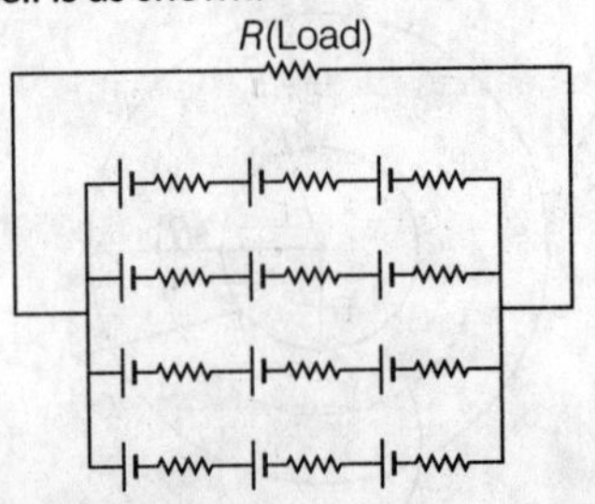

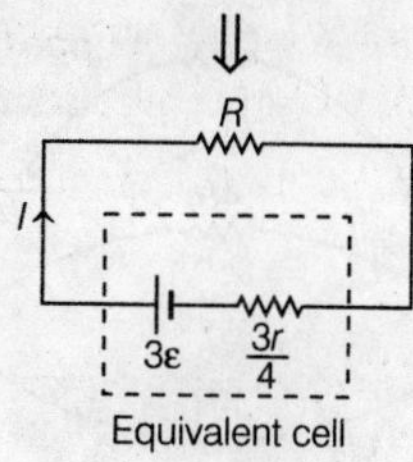

Equivalent cell

Therefore, current drawn,

$$I = \frac{E_{net}}{R + r_{net}}$$

$$= \frac{3\varepsilon}{R + \frac{3r}{4}} \quad \text{...(i)}$$

As per maximum power theorem, to draw maximum power,

Load resistance (R) = Internal resistance of cell R

$$= \frac{3r}{4}$$

So, Eq. (i) can be written as

$$\Rightarrow \quad I = \frac{3\varepsilon}{\frac{3r}{4} + \frac{3r}{4}} = \frac{2\varepsilon}{r}$$

After restructuring, the arrangement and its equivalent are as shown.

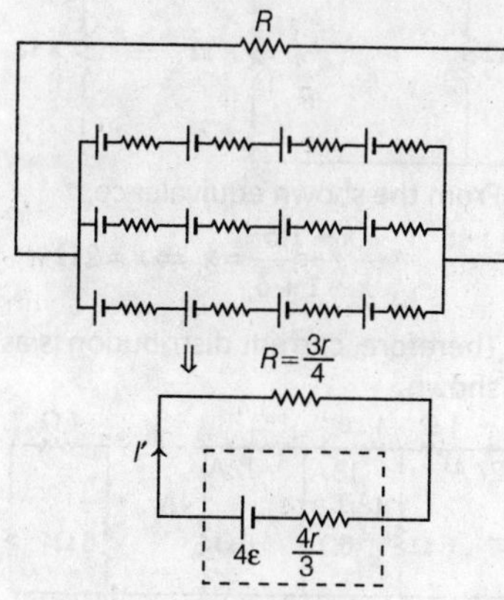

Similarly, current drawn,

$$I' = \frac{4\varepsilon}{\frac{4r}{3} + \frac{3r}{4}}$$

$$= \frac{48\varepsilon}{25r} = \frac{1.92\varepsilon}{r}$$

Percentage change in current,

$$\left(\frac{I' - I}{I}\right) \times 100 = \left(\frac{\frac{1.92\varepsilon}{r} - \frac{2\varepsilon}{r}}{\frac{2\varepsilon}{r}}\right) \times 100$$

$$= \left(\frac{1.92 - 2}{2}\right) \times 100 = -4\%$$

16. *ABCD* is a plane of symmetry for the circuit shown.

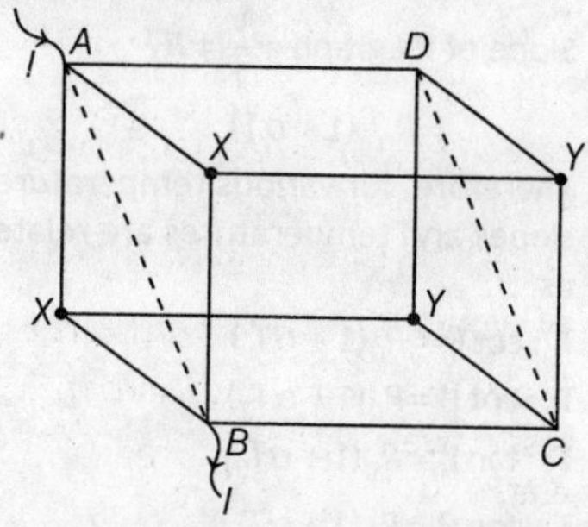

Points located symmetrically w.r.t. this plane are at same potential and thus, can be assigned same alphabet as done in the diagram. Two 20 Ω resistors between points *A* and *X* are in parallel and can be replaced by a single resistor of 10 Ω.

Likewise, 40 Ω resistors between *X* and *B* are in parallel and can be replaced by a single resistor of 20 Ω between *X* and *B*.

By similar simplification, circuit reduces to following equivalent and current distribution in the circuit is as shown.

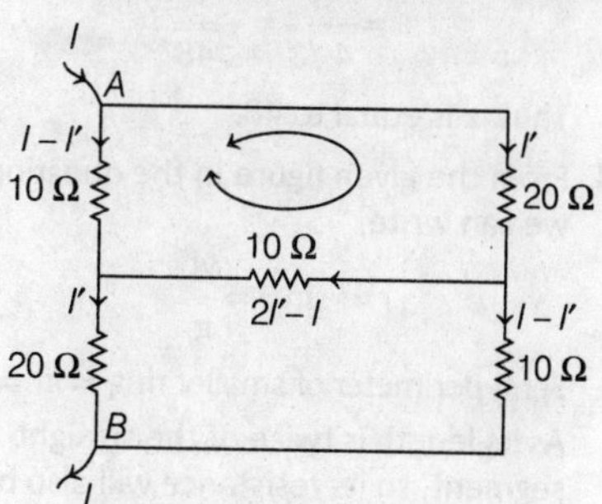

Applying KVL, in upper loop, we get

$$-20I' - 10(2I' - I) + 10(I - I') = 0$$

$$\Rightarrow \quad -50I' + 20I = 0$$

$$\Rightarrow \quad I' = \frac{2I}{5} = 0.4I$$

17. Let us first analyse initial set-up shown. Meters can be replaced by their respective resistances.

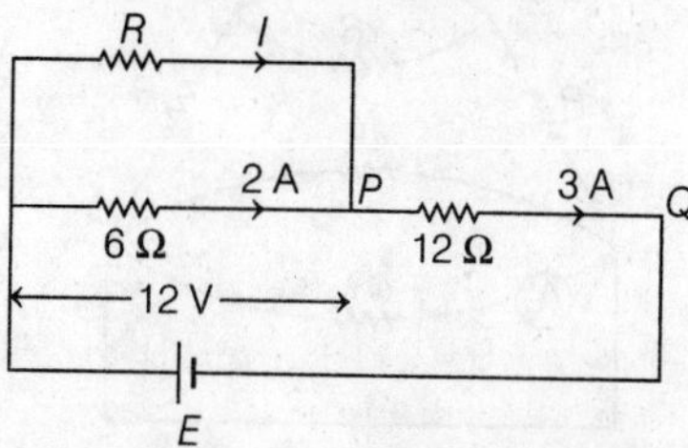

From the information given, current in voltmeter using Ohm's law is

$$\frac{V}{R} = \frac{12}{6} = 2\text{ A}$$

Applying KCL, at point *P*, we get

Incoming current = Outgoing current

$$\Rightarrow \quad I + 2 = 3 \Rightarrow I = 1\text{ A}$$

∴ The value of resistance,

$$R = \frac{12}{1} = 12\ \Omega$$

Also, potential difference across ammeter $= 12 \times 3 = 36$ V

⇒ Emf of cell $= 12 + 36 = 48$ V

Now, if positions of meters are interchanged, circuit will be as shown.

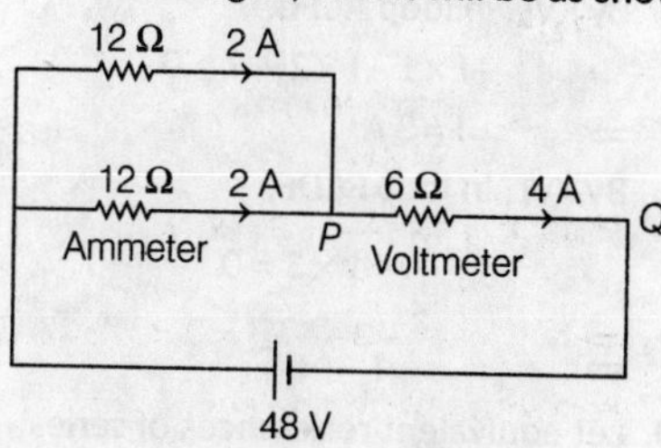

Reading of voltmeter $= V_{PQ}$

$$= 6 \times 4 = 24\text{ V}$$

18. Let the circuit at the time *t* is as shown

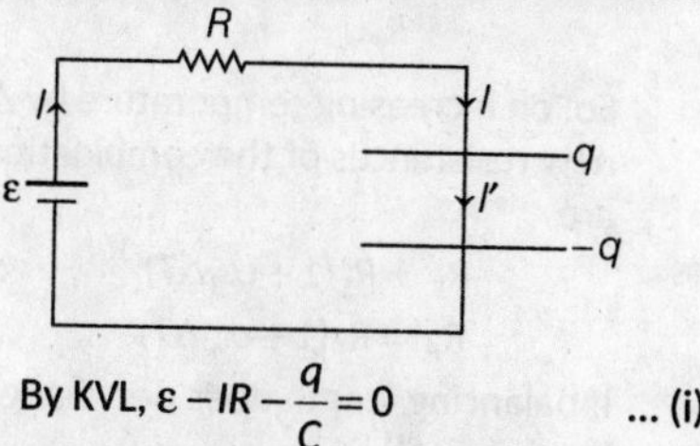

By KVL, $\varepsilon - IR - \frac{q}{C} = 0$ ... (i)

Also, by conservation of current for dielectric, we get

$$I = I' + \frac{dq}{dt} = \frac{q}{RC} + \frac{dq}{dt} \quad \text{... (ii)}$$

From (i) and (ii), we get

$$\varepsilon - \left(\frac{q}{RC} + \frac{dq}{dt}\right)R - \frac{q}{C} = 0$$

$$\Rightarrow \varepsilon C - 2q - RC\frac{dq}{dt} = 0$$

$$\Rightarrow \int_0^q \frac{dq}{\varepsilon C - 2q} = \int_0^t \frac{dt}{RC}$$

$$\Rightarrow -\frac{1}{2}\ln\left(\frac{C\varepsilon - 2q}{C\varepsilon}\right) = \frac{t}{RC}$$

$$\Rightarrow \quad q = \frac{1}{2}C\varepsilon(1 - e^{-2t/RC})$$

Thus, at $t = RC\ln 2$, we get,

$$q = \frac{1}{2}C\varepsilon(1 - e^{-2\ln 2}) = \frac{1}{2}C\varepsilon\left(1 - \frac{1}{4}\right)$$

$$= \frac{3C\varepsilon}{8}$$

19. In steady state, capacitor behaves as open switch. Also, branch of 3Ω and 6Ω is shorted by plain wire and will carry no current. So, current will flow as shown.

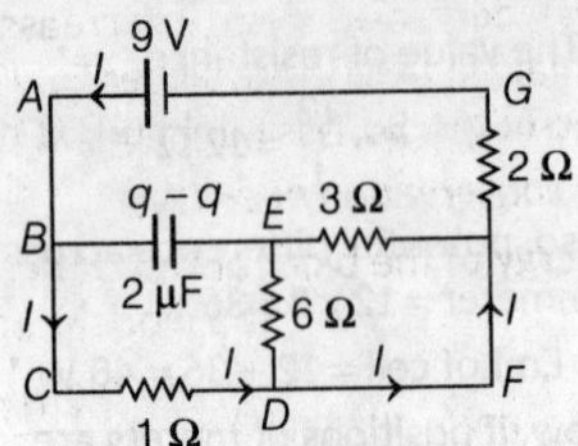

By KVL, in loop $ACFG$,

$$-I\times1-I\times2+9=0$$

$$\Rightarrow \quad I=3\text{ A}$$

By KVL, in loop $BCDE$,

$$\frac{q}{2}-1\times3=0$$

$$\Rightarrow \quad q=6\,\mu\text{C}$$

20. Let equivalent resistances of series and parallel combination of R_1 and R_2 be R_S and R_P. In balanced condition of a meter bridge,

$$\frac{R_S}{R_P}=\frac{100-l}{l} \quad \text{...(i)}$$

So, on increasing temperature by ΔT, new resistances of the combinations are

$$R_S'=R_S(1+\alpha_S\Delta T) \quad \text{...(ii)}$$

$$R_P'=R_P(1+\alpha_P\Delta T) \quad \text{...(iii)}$$

If balancing length does not change, then

$$\frac{R_S(1+\alpha_S\Delta T)}{R_P(1+\alpha_P\Delta T)}=\frac{R_S}{R_P} \quad \left(\because \frac{R_S'}{R_P'}=\frac{R_S}{R_P}\right)$$

[from Eqs. (ii) and (iii)]

$$\Rightarrow \quad 1+\alpha_S\Delta T=1+\alpha_P\Delta T$$

$$\Rightarrow \quad \alpha_S=\alpha_P$$

$$\Rightarrow \frac{R_1\alpha_1+R_2\alpha_2}{R_1+R_2}=\frac{R_1\alpha_2+R_2\alpha_1}{R_1+R_2}$$

$$\Rightarrow R_1(\alpha_1-\alpha_2)=R_2(\alpha_1-\alpha_2)$$

Above relation is not satisfied only for option (d).

21. We know that, relaxation time is given as, $\tau=\dfrac{m}{ne^2\rho}$

Substituting the given values in the above relation, we get

$$\tau=\frac{9.11\times10^{-31}}{(8.5\times10^{28})\,(1.6\times10^{-19})^2\,(1.72\times10^{-8})}$$

$$=2.4\times10^{-14}\text{ s}$$

Thus, order of τ is 10^{-14} s, which implies that magnitude of x is 14.

22. Slope of V-I graph $=\dfrac{V}{I}=R$

$$=R_0\cdot(1+\alpha T)$$

Therefore, for various temperatures, slopes and temperatures are related as

$$T_1:\cot\theta=R_0(1+\alpha T_1) \quad \text{...(i)}$$

$$T_2:\cot\beta=R_0(1+\alpha T_2) \quad \text{...(ii)}$$

$$T_3:\tan\beta=R_0(1+\alpha T_3) \quad \text{...(iii)}$$

$$T_4:\tan\theta=R_0(1+\alpha T_4) \quad \text{...(iv)}$$

Subtracting Eq. (i) from Eq. (iv), we get

$$\cot\theta-\tan\theta=R_0\alpha\,(T_1-T_4)$$

$$\frac{\cos^2\theta-\sin^2\theta}{\sin\theta\cos\theta}=R_0\alpha(T_1-T_4)$$

$$\Rightarrow R_0\alpha(T_1-T_4)=\frac{2\cos2\theta}{\sin2\theta}=2\cot2\theta \quad \text{...(v)}$$

Similarly, $R_0\alpha(T_2-T_3)=2\cot2\beta$ ...(vi)

[from Eqs. (ii) and (iii)]

Dividing Eq. (vi) by Eq. (v),

$$\frac{T_2-T_3}{T_1-T_4}=\frac{\cot2\beta}{\cot2\theta}=\frac{\cot53^\circ}{\cot30^\circ}$$

$$=\frac{3}{4\sqrt{3}}=\frac{3}{\sqrt{48}}$$

Thus, x is equal to 48.

23. From the given figure in the question, we can write,

$$r=l\sin\theta=\frac{2l}{\pi}$$

Semi-perimeter of smaller ring $=\pi r=2l$

As its length is twice of the straight segment, so its resistance will also be doubled. i.e. $2R$. Thus, semi-perimeter and resistance of larger ring will be $4R$ (as it's radius is twice as that of the smaller ring). Circuit can be represented as

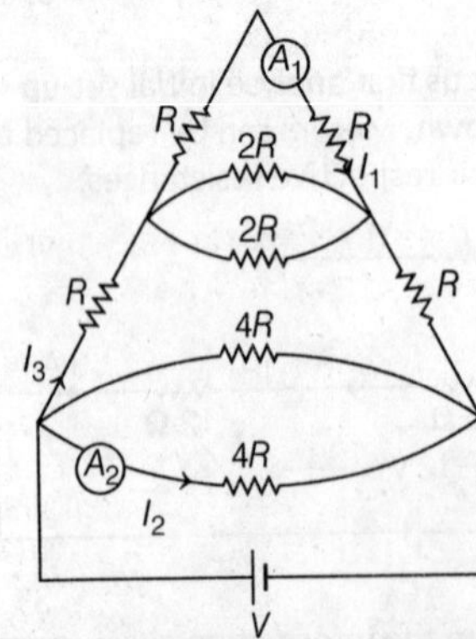

This circuit can further be simplified to

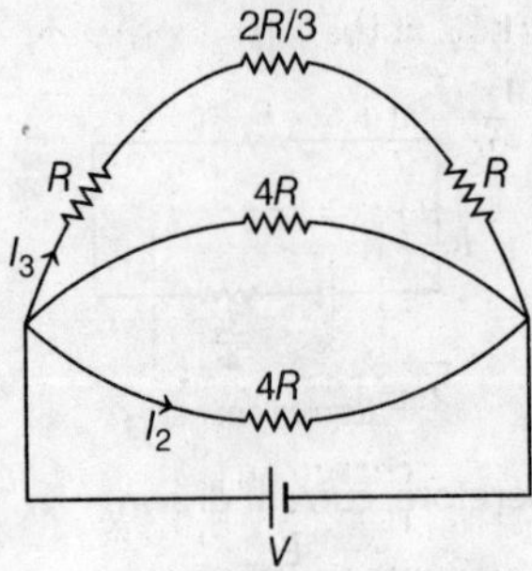

From circuit here, by Ohm's law

$$I_2=\frac{V}{4R}$$

and $\quad I_3=\dfrac{V}{R+R+\dfrac{2R}{3}}=\dfrac{3V}{8R}$

$$\Rightarrow \quad I_1=\frac{I_3}{3}=\frac{V}{8R} \quad \text{(By symmetry)}$$

So, $\quad I_2-I_1=\dfrac{V}{8R}\Rightarrow x=8$

24. Power consumed is independent of number of sections, if equivalent resistance is independent of number of sections. Therefore,

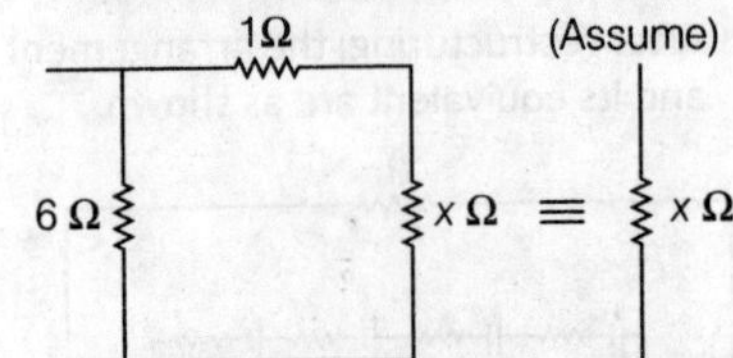

From the shown equivalence,

$$\frac{(x+1)6}{x+1+6}=x\Rightarrow x=2\Omega$$

Therefore, current distribution is as shown.

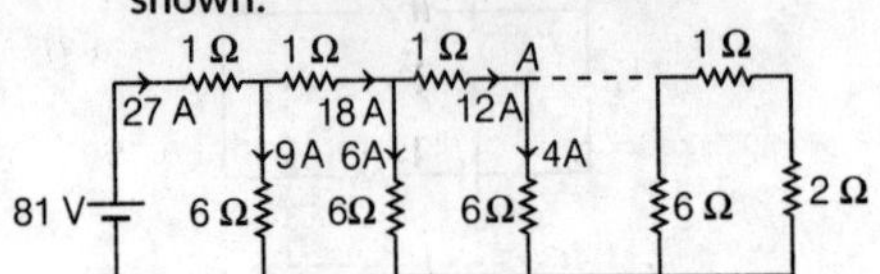

$$\therefore \quad I_{AB}=4\text{ A}$$

25. Let at any time t charge flown through the plate B to plate A is q and instantaneous current is I.

So, effective charge on the capacitor at instant shown in

$$\frac{(-Q_0+q)-(-q)}{2}=\frac{2q-Q_0}{2}$$

By KCL, at the instant t shown, we get

$$\left(\frac{2q-Q_0}{2C}\right)+IR-\varepsilon=0$$

$$\Rightarrow \quad R\frac{dq}{dt}=\frac{-2q+2\varepsilon C+Q_0}{2C}$$

$$\Rightarrow \quad \frac{dq}{2\varepsilon C+Q_0-2q}=\frac{dt}{2RC}$$

Now, for charge on plate A at time t to be zero, $q=Q_0$. So, by integrating taking these values, we get

$$\int_0^{Q_0}\frac{dq}{2\varepsilon C+Q_0-2q}=\int_0^t\frac{dt}{2RC}$$

$$\Rightarrow \quad t=RC\ln\left[\frac{2\varepsilon C+Q_0}{2\varepsilon C-Q_0}\right]$$

$$=RC\ln\left[\frac{2EC+EC}{2EC-EC}\right]$$

$$=RC\ln 3$$

$$\Rightarrow \quad x=3$$

Qualifier 12 (Magnetic Effects of Current and Magnetism)

1. Magnetic field at a distance r from axis of solid cylinder are

$$B_{\text{outside}}=\frac{\mu_0 I}{2\pi r} \quad \text{...(i)}$$

$$B_{\text{inside}}=\frac{\mu_0 Ir}{2\pi R^2} \quad \text{...(ii)}$$

Magnetic field at P using Eq. (i) is

$$B=\frac{\mu_0 I}{2\pi(2R)}=\frac{\mu_0 I}{4\pi R} \quad \text{...(iii)}$$

Magnetic field at Q inside cylinder is also B, so using Eq. (ii),

$$B=\frac{\mu_0 Ir}{2\pi R^2} \quad \text{...(iv)}$$

Equating RHS of Eqs. (iii) and (iv), we get

$$\frac{\mu_0 Ir}{2\pi R^2}=\frac{\mu_0 I}{4\pi R}$$

$$\Rightarrow \quad r=\frac{R}{2}$$

So, distance of mid-point of P and Q from axis is $\frac{2R+\frac{R}{2}}{2}=\frac{5R}{4}$, which is an outside point.

Therefore, using Eq. (i), we get

$$B'=\frac{\mu_0 I}{2\pi\left(\frac{5R}{4}\right)}=\frac{2\mu_0 I}{5\pi R} \quad \text{...(v)}$$

Dividing Eq. (v) by Eq. (iii), we get

$$\frac{B'}{B}=\frac{8}{5}\Rightarrow B'=1.6B$$

2. For $0<r<R$, there is no current in cylinder. So, as per Ampere's law,

$$\oint \mathbf{B}\cdot d\mathbf{l}=\mu_0 I=0$$

For $R<r<2R$, to find current through shown amperian loop consider a ring element of radius x and thickness dx

current through element $=J\cdot dA$

$\Rightarrow$ Total current, $I=\int J\,dA$

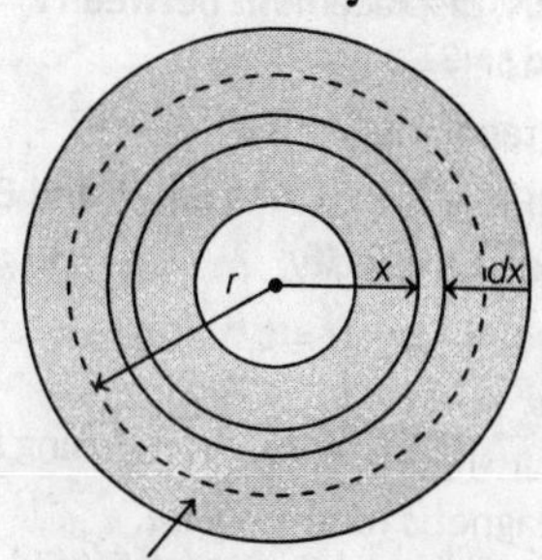

Amperian loop

$$=\int_R^r\frac{k}{x}\cdot 2\pi x\,dx=2\pi k(r-R)$$

$$\Rightarrow \oint \mathbf{B}\cdot d\mathbf{l}=\mu_0 I=2\pi\mu_0 k(r-R)$$

$\Rightarrow \oint \mathbf{B}\cdot d\mathbf{l}$ increases linearly from zero for $R<r<2R$

For $r>2R$, $I=$ constant

$$\Rightarrow \quad \oint \mathbf{B}\cdot d\mathbf{l}=\text{constant}$$

3. As current distribution for the given thin long uniformly charged hollow cylinder is similar to solenoid, magnetic field B is axial as shown. Considering amperian loop $PTRS$ and applying Ampere's law to it, we get

$$Bl=\mu_0 I=\frac{\mu_0 Ql\omega}{2\pi}$$

$$\Rightarrow \quad B=\frac{\mu_0 Q\omega}{2\pi}$$

4. Assume the speed at any general position of the block be v.

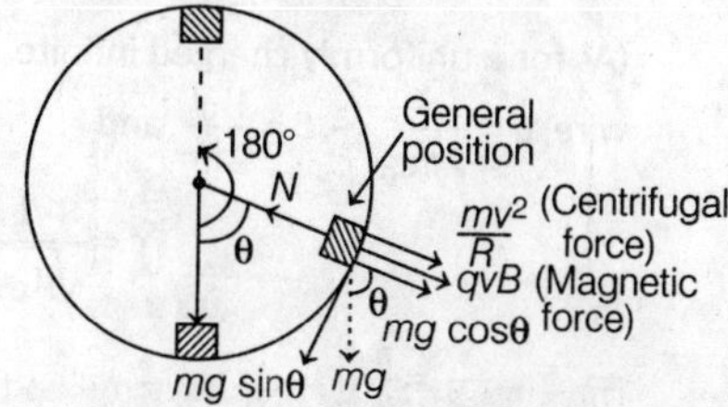

So, from FBD of block at general position,

$$N=mg\cos\theta+\frac{mv^2}{R}+qvB \quad \text{...(i)}$$

As block moves up, θ increases and so $\cos\theta$ decreases. Also, v decreases due to gain in height. So, as per Eq. (i), N decreases. So, N is minimum at top.

By conservation of energy,

Energy of the block at top = Energy of the block at bottom

$$\Rightarrow \frac{1}{2}mv_{\text{top}}^2+mg(2R)=\frac{1}{2}m\left(\frac{2mg}{qB}\right)^2$$

Putting given value of $B=\frac{mg}{q\sqrt{2gR}}$ in above equation, we get

$$\frac{1}{2}mv_{\text{top}}^2+2mgR=4mgR$$

$$\Rightarrow \quad v_{\text{top}}=\sqrt{4gR}$$

Putting this value of speed and $\theta=180°$ in Eq. (i), we get

$$N=mg\cos 180°+\frac{m(\sqrt{4gR})^2}{R}+q\sqrt{4gR}\cdot\frac{mg}{q\sqrt{2gR}}$$

$$=(3+\sqrt{2})mg=4.4\,mg$$

5. The sheet produces magnetic field in region of P equal to

$$B_{\text{sheet}}=\frac{\mu_0\lambda}{2} \quad \text{...(i)}$$

As velocity is constant, net force should be zero. Therefore,

$$F_{\text{magnetic}}=mg$$

$$\Rightarrow \quad qvB=mg$$

$$\Rightarrow \quad v=\frac{mg}{qB}=\frac{2mg}{\mu_0 q\lambda} \quad \text{...(ii)}$$

In a transverse uniform field path of particle is circle. So, if gravity disappears at P, then

$$F_{\text{magnetic}}=\frac{mv^2}{r}$$

$$\Rightarrow \quad qvB=\frac{mv^2}{r}$$

$$\Rightarrow \quad r=\frac{mv}{qB}=\frac{4m^2g}{q^2\mu_0^2\lambda^2}$$

[Putting values of v and B from Eqs. (i) and (ii)]

6. The given situation is as shown in the figure below

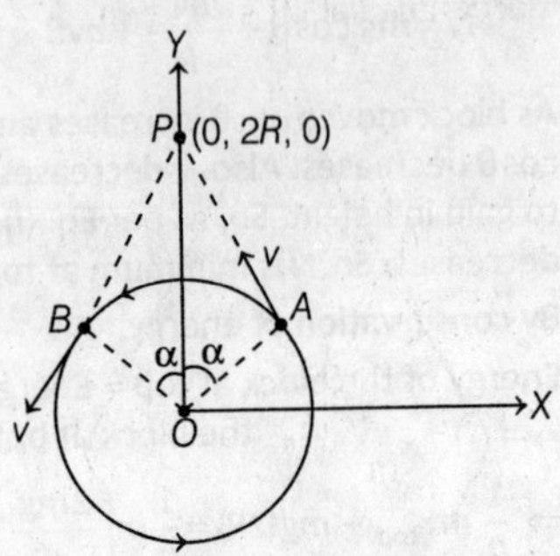

Let tangents from P intersect circle at A and B. When positron is at A, its velocity is towards P, so angle between v and relative position vector of P is 0°. So, as per Biot-Savart's law, magnetic field,

$$B = \frac{\mu_0}{4\pi}\frac{qv\sin 0°}{r^2} = 0$$

Similarly, magnetic field is zero when positron is at B. Now, from triangle OAP,

$$\cos\alpha = \frac{OA}{OP} = \frac{R}{2R} = \frac{1}{2} \Rightarrow \alpha = \frac{\pi}{3} \quad ...(i)$$

So, time of motion from A to $B = \frac{2\alpha}{\omega}$

$$= \frac{\frac{2\pi}{3}}{\frac{2\pi}{T}} = \frac{T}{3} \quad \text{[using Eq. (i)]}$$

7. By work energy theorem,

$$W_{electric} + W_{magnetic} = \Delta KE$$

$$qE_y + 0 = \frac{1}{2}mv^2$$

(As magnetic force $q\mathbf{v} \times \mathbf{B}$ is perpendicular to $\mathbf{v}$, work done by it is always zero).

$$\Rightarrow \quad v = \sqrt{\frac{2qE_y}{m}}$$

8. Before the electric field is switched ON proton will move on circle in YZ-plane. After proton returns to origin at $t = T$, on switching ON electric field, proton will experience electric force in x-direction and will start displacing simultaneously in x-direction in accordance with Lorentz force. Thus, it will follow helical path.

Acceleration of proton in x-direction,

$$a = \frac{eE}{m} = \text{constant} \quad [\because E \text{ is constant}]$$

So, displacement between $t = T$ and $t = 2T$ can be found using

$$s_x = u_x t + \frac{1}{2}a_x t^2$$

$$= 0 + \frac{1}{2}aT^2 = \frac{1}{2}aT^2 \quad ...(i)$$

So, average velocity,

$$v = \frac{s_x}{T} = \frac{1}{2}aT \quad ...(ii)$$

Similarly, between $t = T$ and $t = 3T$

$$s_x' = \frac{1}{2}a(2T)^2 = 2aT^2 \quad ...(iii)$$

Thus, displacement between $t = 2T$ and $t = 3T$

$$s_x'' = s_x' - s_x = 1.5\,aT^2$$

[Using Eq. (i) and Eq. (iii)]

Average velocity,

$$v' = \frac{s_x''}{T} = \frac{3aT}{2} = 3v$$

[using Eq. (ii)]

9. Magnetic force on wire,

$$\mathbf{F}_m = I\mathbf{l} \times \mathbf{B} = I(l\hat{\mathbf{j}}) \times (-B\hat{\mathbf{k}})$$

$$= -BIl\hat{\mathbf{i}} \quad ...(i)$$

As this force is uniform, it can be assumed to be acting at centre. Thus,

$$\text{torque}, \tau = BIl \cdot \frac{l}{2} = \frac{BIl^2}{2}$$

Moment of inertia, $I_P = \frac{ml^2}{3}$

So, angular acceleration,

$$\alpha = \frac{\tau}{I_P} = \frac{3BI}{2m}$$

Acceleration of centre of mass $= \alpha r$

$$= \frac{3BI}{2m} \times \frac{l}{2} = \frac{3}{4}\frac{BIl}{m} \quad ..(ii)$$

By Newton's law,

$$F_{net} = ma$$

$$\Rightarrow F_{magnetic} - R = ma$$

$$\Rightarrow \quad BIl - R = m\left(\frac{3BIl}{4m}\right)$$

[using Eqs. (i) and (ii)]

$$\Rightarrow \quad R = \frac{BIl}{4}$$

10. As velocity is constant, so

$$F_{electric} = F_{magnetic}$$

$$\Rightarrow \quad qE = qvB$$

$$\Rightarrow \quad v = \frac{E}{B} = \frac{\lambda c^2}{I}$$

(As for a uniformly charged infinite wire, $E = \frac{1}{2\pi\varepsilon_0}\frac{\lambda}{r}, B = \frac{\mu_0 I}{2\pi r}$ and $c = \frac{1}{\sqrt{\mu_0\varepsilon_0}}$)

$$\Rightarrow \quad \frac{v}{c^2} = \frac{\lambda}{I}$$

11. The trajectory of the particle is as shown below.

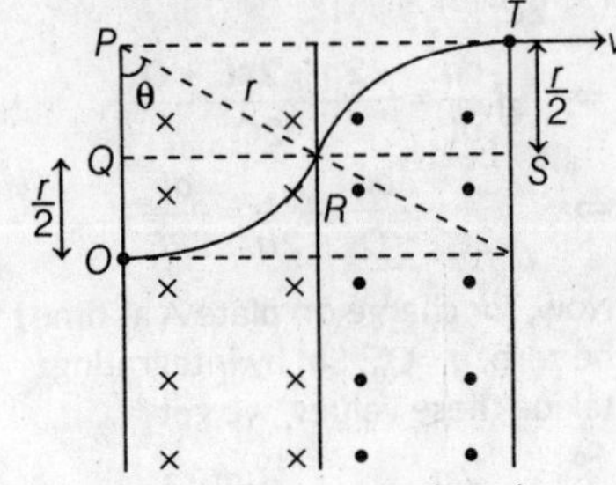

$$\text{From } \Delta PQR, \theta = \sin^{-1}\left(\frac{\frac{\sqrt{3}r}{2}}{r}\right) = 60°$$

$$\Rightarrow \quad PQ = r\cos 60° = \frac{r}{2}$$

$$\Rightarrow \quad QO = PO - PQ = r - \frac{r}{2} = \frac{r}{2}$$

Similarly, $ST = \frac{r}{2}$

So, angular momentum w.r.t. O

$$= mvr_\perp = mv(OP) = mvr$$

12. As we know, magnetic energy density $= \frac{B^2}{2\mu_0}$

Putting value of B due to straight infinite wire in above expression,

$$\text{Magnetic energy density} = \frac{\left(\frac{\mu_0 I}{2\pi r}\right)^2}{2\mu_0}$$

$$= \frac{\mu_0 I^2}{8\pi^2 r^2} \propto \frac{1}{r^2}$$

13. Torque on loop, τ

$$= \mathbf{M} \times \mathbf{B} = IL^2\hat{\mathbf{i}} \times B\hat{\mathbf{j}}$$

$$= BIL^2\hat{\mathbf{k}} \text{ (anti-clockwise)}$$

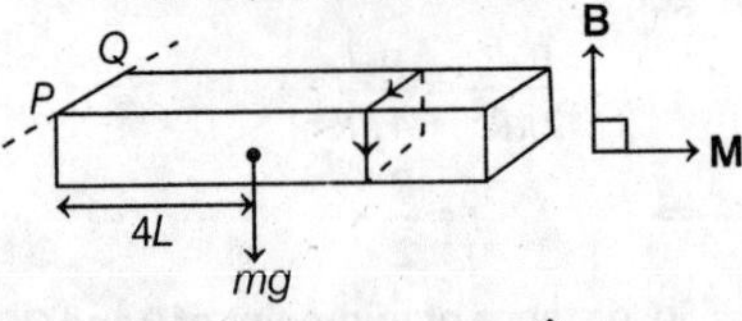

Torque of $mg = -mg(4L)\hat{\mathbf{k}}$ (clockwise)

For equilibrium, these two torques should be in balance

$$\Rightarrow \quad BIL^2 = 4mgL \Rightarrow I = \frac{4mg}{BL}$$

14. As length of wire is constant, on doubling number of turns, radius will be halved. So, magnetic field will be

$$B' = \frac{\mu_0 I}{2\left(\frac{R}{2}\right)} \cdot 2N = 4\left(\frac{N\mu_0 I}{2R}\right) = 4B$$

As magnetic moment, $M = NI\pi R^2$

$\Rightarrow \quad M' = 2NI\pi\left(\frac{R}{2}\right)^2 = \frac{NI\pi R^2}{2} = \frac{M}{2}$

15. The given situation is as shown in the figure below

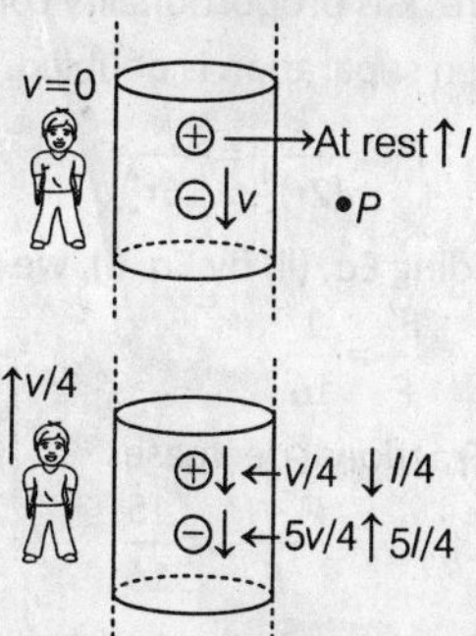

For stationary observer, current I is constituted by electrons drifting with speed v, while protons are fixed and don't contribute to current.

So, for a moving observer, relative velocity of electrons $= v - \left(-\frac{v}{4}\right) = \frac{5v}{4}$.

As, $\quad I \propto v$

So, corresponding current $= \frac{5I}{4}$, upwards. While, in observer's frame protons also have relative velocity $= \frac{v}{4}$, downwards. So, protons constitute $\frac{I}{4}$ downward current.

Net current will be $\frac{5I}{4} - \frac{I}{4} = I$ upwards

As current remains unchanged, B will remain same.

16. For stable equilibrium, angle between **M** and **B** is zero.

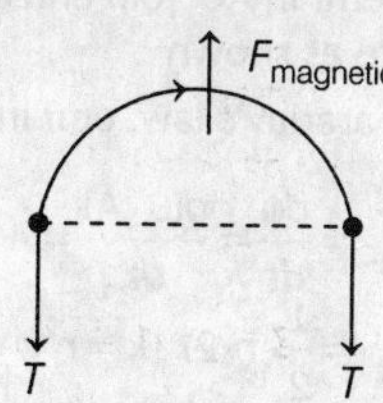

FBD of upper half of the circular loop is as shown in figure. In equilibrium,

$F_{magnetic} = 2T$

$\Rightarrow \quad BI(2R) = 2T$

$\Rightarrow \quad T = BIR = B \cdot \frac{M}{\pi R^2} \cdot R$

$= \frac{BM}{\pi R} = \frac{2BM}{L}$

17. Ratio of magnetic moment (M) to angular momentum (L),

$\frac{M}{L} = \frac{q}{2m} \Rightarrow M = L \times \frac{q}{2m} = I\omega \times \frac{q}{2m}$ ...(i)

So, $M_{\text{solid sphere}} = \frac{2}{5} mR^2 \times \omega \times \frac{q}{2m}$

$= \frac{q\omega R^2}{5} = M$ ...(ii)

[using Eq. (i)]

Charge on a conducting solid sphere lies on surface, so it will have same magnetic moment as that of hollow sphere. So, $M_{\text{conducting sphere}}$

$= \frac{2}{3} mR^2 \times \omega \times \frac{q}{2m} = \frac{q\omega R^2}{3} = \frac{5}{3} M$

$= 1.67M$ [using Eq. (ii)]

18. If M is the magnetic moment of bar magnet PR, half PQ has magnetic moment $\frac{M}{2}$.

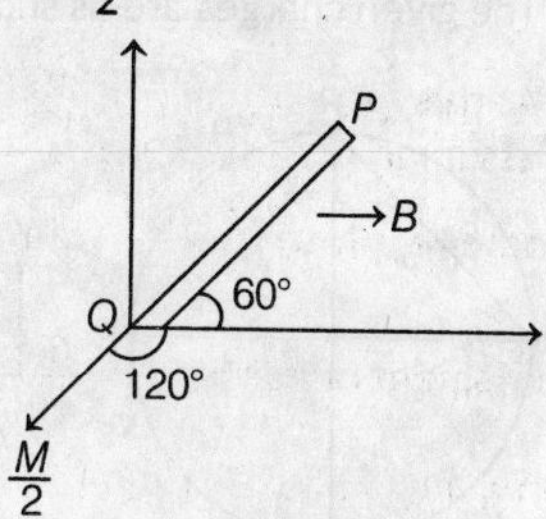

As we know, potential energy of dipole $= -MB\cos\theta$

$\Rightarrow$ Initial potential energy of

$PQ = -\frac{M}{2} B\cos 0° = -\frac{MB}{2}$

Final potential energy

$= -\frac{M}{2} B\cos 120° = \frac{MB}{4}$

Work done $= \Delta$ PE

$= \frac{MB}{4} - \left(-\frac{MB}{2}\right) = \frac{3MB}{4}$

19. Relation between apparent inclination/dip, in two mutually perpendicular vertical planes and true dip is

$$\cot\phi = \sqrt{\cot^2\phi_1 + \cot^2\phi_2}$$

Here, $\phi_1 = 45°$, $\phi_2 = \cot^{-1}\sqrt{2}$

$\Rightarrow \cot\phi = \sqrt{\cot^2 45° + (\sqrt{2})^2} = \sqrt{3}$

$\Rightarrow \quad \phi = 30°$

20. Diamagnetic materials are magnetised opposite to external field. So, the end near magnetic pole has same polarity, resulting in repulsion.

21. Let current I divides as shown. To find magnetic field due to PQ drop perpendicular OT as shown.

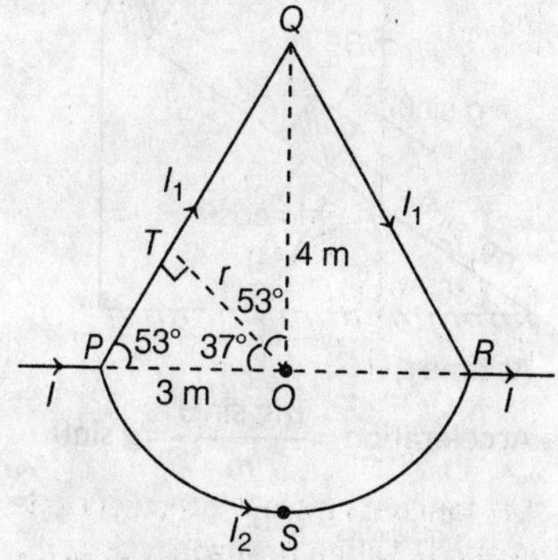

Angle P in $\Delta POQ = \tan^{-1}\frac{4}{3} = 53°$.

So, angle subtended by ends P and Q w.r.t. OT are $\theta_1 = 37°$ and $\theta_2 = 53°$.

Also, from ΔPTO, $r = 3\sin 53° = \frac{12}{5}$ m

So, magnetic field due to PQ

$B_{PQ} = \frac{\mu_0 I_1}{4\pi r}(\sin\theta_1 + \sin\theta_2)$

$= \frac{\mu_0 I_1}{4\pi\left(\frac{12}{5}\right)}\left(\frac{3}{5} + \frac{4}{5}\right) = \frac{7\mu_0 I_1}{48\pi}$ ...(i)

(directed inwards by right hand rule)

$B_{QR} = B_{PQ} = \frac{7\mu_0 I_1}{48\pi}$ ...(ii)

Magnetic field due to semicircular wire

$B_{PSR} = \frac{\mu_0 I}{4R} = \frac{\mu_0 I_2}{4(3)} = \frac{\mu_0 I_2}{12}$ ...(iii)

(directed outwards by right hand rule)

As net magnetic field is given to be zero, fields of straight and circular wires should cancel. So,

$B_{\text{straight}} = B_{\text{semi-circular}} \Rightarrow B_{PQ} + B_{QR} = B_{PSR}$

Using Eqs. (i), (ii) and (iii), we get

$\Rightarrow \quad \frac{7\mu_0 I_1}{48\pi} + \frac{7\mu_0 I_1}{48\pi} = \frac{\mu_0 I_2}{12} \Rightarrow \frac{I_1}{I_2} = \frac{2\pi}{7}$

As for wires in parallel, currents are in inverse ratio of resistances (say R_1 and R_2)

$\frac{R_2}{R_1} = \frac{2\pi}{7}$

So, $\quad \frac{\frac{\rho_2 l_2}{A}}{\frac{\rho_1 l_1}{A}} = \frac{2\pi}{7}$

$\Rightarrow \frac{\rho_2}{\rho_1} = \frac{2\pi}{7} \times \frac{l_1}{l_2} = \frac{2\pi}{7} \times \frac{10}{\pi(3)} = \frac{20}{21}$

$\Rightarrow x + y = 20 + 21 = 41$

22. The FBD of the block is as shown below.

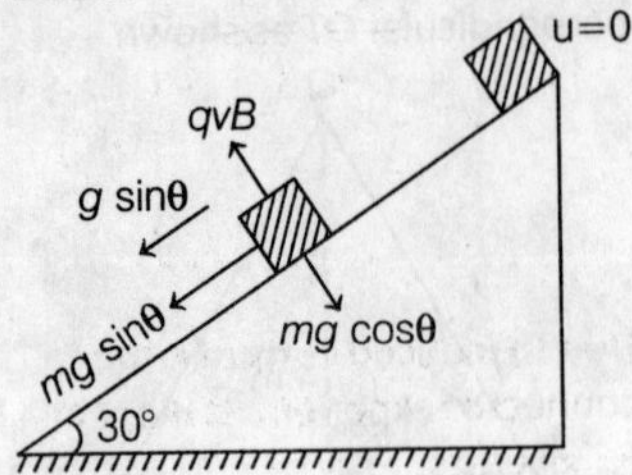

At time t,

$$\text{Acceleration} = \frac{mg \sin\theta}{m} = g\sin\theta$$

$$F_{\text{magnetic}} = qvB$$

$\Rightarrow$ Velocity, $v = u + at = g\sin\theta t$

$\Rightarrow$ Magnetic force shown $= qvB$

$$= q\,g\sin\theta Bt$$

For leaving contact, it should just exceed $mg\cos\theta$

$$\Rightarrow \quad q\,g\sin\theta\, Bt \approx mg\cos\theta$$

$$\Rightarrow \quad t \approx \frac{m\cot\theta}{qB}$$

$$= 10\sqrt{3} = 17.32\text{s}$$

23. For initial equilibrium,

$$F_{\text{magnetic}} = mg$$

$$\Rightarrow \frac{\mu_0 I_1 I_2}{2\pi l} = mg \quad \text{...(i)}$$

Net force on slight displacement x upwards,

$$F = \frac{\mu_0 I_1 I_2}{2\pi(l+x)} - mg$$

$$= \frac{\mu_0 I_1 I_2}{2\pi l}\left(1+\frac{x}{l}\right)^{-1} - mg$$

$$= mg\left(1-\frac{x}{l}\right) - mg = \frac{-mgx}{l}$$

[using Eq. (i)]

(– sign signifies restoring force)

$$\Rightarrow \quad a = -\frac{gx}{l} = -\omega^2 x$$

$$\Rightarrow \quad \omega = \sqrt{\frac{g}{l}}$$

$$\Rightarrow \quad T = 2\pi\sqrt{\frac{l}{g}} \quad \text{...(ii)}$$

Torque of gravity on slightly disturbance in other arrangement

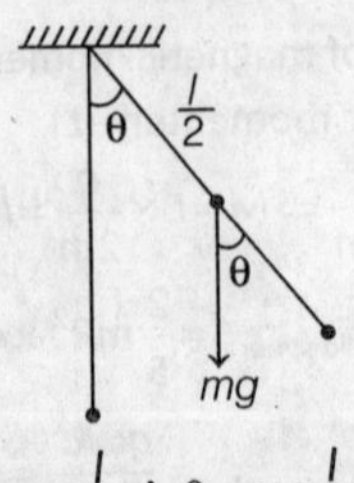

$$\tau = mg\frac{l}{2}\sin\theta \approx mg\frac{l}{2}\theta$$

$$I = \text{Moment of inertia of wire} = \frac{ml^2}{3}$$

$$\text{So, } \alpha = \frac{\tau}{I} = \frac{3g}{2l}\theta = \omega^2\theta$$

$$\Rightarrow \quad \omega = \sqrt{\frac{3g}{2l}} \quad \Rightarrow T' = 2\pi\sqrt{\frac{2l}{3g}} \quad \text{...(iii)}$$

Dividing Eq. (iii) by Eq. (ii), we get

$$\frac{T'}{T} = \sqrt{\frac{2}{3}} \Rightarrow \left(\frac{T'}{T}\right)^2 = 0.67$$

24. The given charges are as shown below

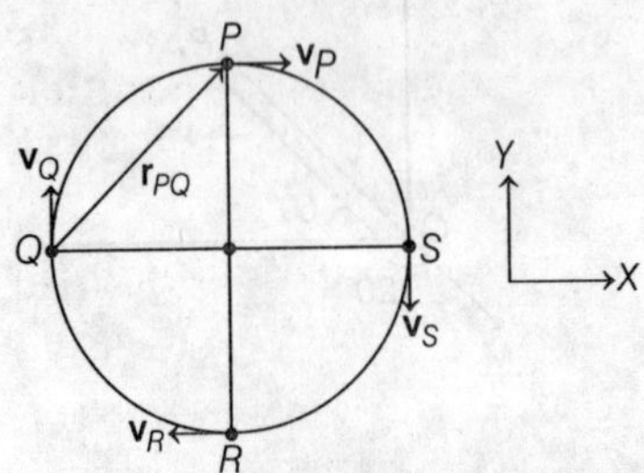

Let us find magnetic field at location of P due to Q, R and S, using Biot-Savart's law.

$$\textbf{Due to Q}: \mathbf{B}_Q = \frac{\mu_0 q}{4\pi}\frac{\mathbf{v}_Q \times \mathbf{r}_{PQ}}{r_{PQ}^3}$$

$$= \frac{\mu_0 q}{4\pi}\frac{\omega R\hat{\mathbf{j}} \times (R\hat{\mathbf{i}} + R\hat{\mathbf{j}})}{(\sqrt{2}R)^3}$$

$$= -\frac{\mu_0 q\omega}{8\sqrt{2}\pi R}\hat{\mathbf{k}}$$

Similarly, due to S :

$$\mathbf{B}_S = -\frac{\mu_0 q\omega}{8\sqrt{2}\,\pi R}\hat{\mathbf{k}}$$

$$\textbf{Due to R}: \mathbf{B}_R = -\frac{\mu_0 q\omega}{16\pi R}\hat{\mathbf{k}}$$

$$\text{So, } \mathbf{B}\text{ (net)} = \mathbf{B} = \mathbf{B}_Q + \mathbf{B}_S + \mathbf{B}_R$$

$$= -\frac{\mu_0 q\omega}{8\sqrt{2}\pi R}\left(2+\frac{1}{\sqrt{2}}\right)\hat{\mathbf{k}}$$

$$\Rightarrow \text{Force on } P = q\cdot\mathbf{v}\times\mathbf{B}$$

$$= q\omega R\hat{\mathbf{i}} \times \left\{-\frac{\mu_0 q\omega}{8\sqrt{2}\pi R}\left(2+\frac{1}{\sqrt{2}}\right)\hat{\mathbf{k}}\right\}$$

$$= \frac{\mu_0 q^2\omega^2}{\pi}\left(\frac{2\sqrt{2}+1}{16}\right)\hat{\mathbf{j}}$$

25. Force between magnetic dipoles is inversely proportional to fourth power of separation. i.e.

$$F \propto \frac{1}{r^4} \text{ or } F = \frac{k}{r^4} \quad \text{...(i)}$$

(Here, k is proportionality constant)

When separation is doubled,

$$F' = \frac{k}{(2r)^4} = \frac{k}{16r^4} \quad \text{...(ii)}$$

Dividing Eq. (ii) by Eq. (i), we get

$$\frac{F'}{F} = \frac{1}{16}$$

$\Rightarrow$ Fractional decrease

$$= \frac{F - F'}{F} = \frac{15}{16}$$

$$\Rightarrow \quad x = \frac{15}{16} \times 2 = 1.87$$

Qualifier 13 (Electromagnetic Induction & Alternating Current)

1. Due to time varying (increasing) magnetic field, circular electric field will be induced as shown in figure. Direction of field lines can be determined by Lenz's law, which is anti-clockwise.

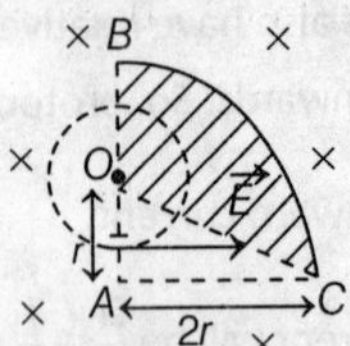

As $\mathbf{E}$ is perpendicular to segment AB, emf induced in any general element having length vector dl is

$$e_{AB} = -E\cdot dl = -Edl\cos 90° = 0 \quad \text{... (i)}$$

To find emf in AC, join ends A and C to centre as shown

As per Faraday's law, emf induced in side AC,

$$e_{AC} = \frac{d\phi}{dt} = \frac{d(B\cdot A)}{dt} = A\cdot\frac{dB}{dt}$$

$$= \frac{1}{2}\cdot r\cdot 2r\cdot k = r^2 k \quad \text{...(ii)}$$

$$\left(\text{Given, } \frac{dB}{dt} = k\right)$$

To find emf in arc BC, join ends B and C to centre O as shown.

Area of the loop OBC,

A' = Area of quarter circle ABC – Area of triangle OAC

$$= \frac{\pi(2r)^2}{4} - \frac{1}{2}\times r\times 2r$$

$\Rightarrow \quad A' = r^2(\pi - 1)$ ...(iii)

As per Faraday's law, emf induced in segment BC,

$$e_{BC} = \frac{d\phi}{dt} = \frac{d(BA')}{dt} = A'\frac{dB}{dt}$$

$$= r^2(\pi - 1)\, k \quad \text{... (iv)}$$

[using Eq. (iii)]

2. Let length of wire PQ be l and AQ be x at any general instant.

Area of triangle PAQ will be

$$A = \frac{1}{2} \times PA \times AQ$$

$$= \frac{1}{2} \times \sqrt{l^2 - x^2} \cdot x \quad \text{...(i)}$$

Flux through loop PAQ,

$$\phi = B \cdot A = \frac{B}{2}\sqrt{l^2 - x^2} \cdot x \quad \text{...(ii)}$$

As per Faraday's law, induced emf,

$$E = -\frac{d\phi}{dt}$$

$$\Rightarrow \quad E = -\frac{B}{2}\frac{d(\sqrt{l^2 - x^2} \cdot x)}{dt}$$

[using Eq. (ii)]

$$\Rightarrow E = -\frac{B}{2}\left[-\frac{vx^2}{\sqrt{l^2 - x^2}} + \sqrt{l^2 - x^2} \cdot v\right] \quad \text{...(iii)}$$

At the instant $E = 0$, using Eq. (iii), we get

$$0 = \frac{-vx^2}{\sqrt{l^2 - x^2}} + \sqrt{l^2 - x^2} \cdot v$$

$$\Rightarrow \quad x = \frac{l}{\sqrt{2}}$$

$$\Rightarrow \quad \alpha = \cos^{-1}\frac{x}{l} = 45°$$

3. Flux linked with the ring,

$$\phi = (B_{\text{solenoid}})(A_{\text{solenoid}})$$

$$= \mu_0 nI \times \pi R^2$$

So, $\phi = \mu_0 \pi R^2 \times nI_0 \cdot t \cdot (1 - t)$

Magnitude of induced emf in the ring,

$$V_R = |E| = \frac{d\phi}{dt}$$

$$= \frac{d}{dt}[\mu_0 \pi R^2 \times nI_0 t(1 - t)]$$

$$= \mu_0 \pi R^2 nI_0 (1 - 2t)$$

Clearly, induced emf is zero, when

$$1 - 2t = 0$$

$$\Rightarrow \quad t = \frac{1}{2}\,\text{s} = 0.5\,\text{s}$$

So, induced emf and induced current are zero at $t = 0.5$ s and their direction also reverses.

4. By Faraday's law, $e = BA\omega \sin\omega t$

As $\quad B = \frac{\mu_0 I}{2b}$ and $A = \pi a^2$

$$\therefore \quad e = \frac{\mu_0 I}{2b}(\pi a^2)\,\omega \sin \omega t$$

$$= \frac{\pi a^2 \mu_0 I}{2b}\,\omega \sin\omega t$$

5. A motional emf is induced between ends of the rod with A at higher potential. As the ring is resistanceless, so point C will be at same potential as B.

Rotational motional emf between ends A and B is equal to

$$V = |V_B - V_A| = \frac{B\omega r^2}{2}$$

Therefore, current in the bulb,

$$I = \frac{V}{R} = \frac{B\omega r^2}{2R}$$

(directed from A to C) ... (i)

In rod, current will flow from B to A.

Magnetic force F_m on the rod is given by

$$F_m = BIl = B\left(\frac{B\omega r^2}{2R}\right) r \quad \text{[using Eq. (i)]}$$

$$\Rightarrow \quad F = F_m = \frac{B^2\omega r^3}{2R}$$

(As $\omega =$ constant) ...(ii)

Power delivered by any force,

$$P = \mathbf{F} \cdot \mathbf{v} = Fv \cos 90° = fv \quad \text{... (iii)}$$

Velocity of centre,

$$v = \omega\frac{r}{2} \quad \text{... (iv)}$$

Putting F and v from Eqs. (ii) and (iv) in Eq. (iii), we get

$$P = \frac{B^2\,\omega\, r^3}{2R} \cdot \frac{\omega\, r}{2}$$

$$= \frac{B^2\,\omega^2\,r^4}{4R} = \frac{B^s\,\omega^p\,r^q}{tR}$$

Therefore, $\sqrt{p \times q \times s \times t}$

$$= \sqrt{2 \times 4 \times 2 \times 4} = 8$$

6. As the connector begins to accelerate downwards, at any later instant, let it acquire velocity v as shown.

Due to B_H, motional emf is induced in connector equal to

$$\varepsilon = B_H vl \quad \text{... (i)}$$

Due to this emf, current begins to flow in the circuit as shown.

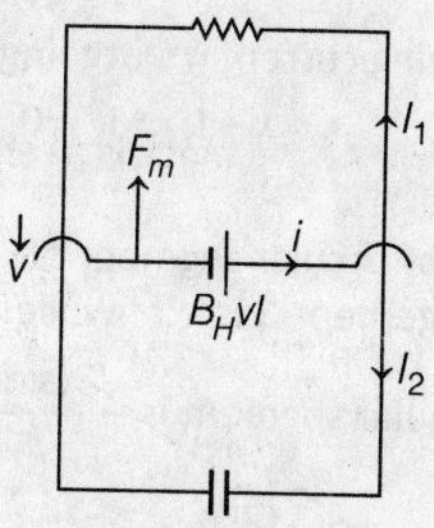

Due to induced current I, the connector experiences magnetic force F_m given as

$$F_m = B_H Il \quad \text{... (ii)}$$

Let steady state speed of connector be v_0.

By Ohm's law, current in resistor,

$$I_1 = \frac{\varepsilon}{R} = \frac{B_H v_0 l}{R} \quad \text{... (iii)}$$

[using Eq. (i)]

Charge on capacitor in steady state will be

$$Q = CV = CB_H v_0 l \quad \text{... (iv)}$$

[using Eq. (i)]

As Q is constant, current through capacitor, $I_2 = \frac{dQ}{dt} = 0$ ... (v)

From Eqs. (iii) and (v), we get

$$I = I_1 + I_2 = \frac{B_H v_0 l}{R}$$

Therefore, from Eq. (ii),

$$F_m = B_H Il = B_H\left(\frac{B_H v_0 l}{R}\right) l$$

$$= \frac{B_H^2 v_0 l^2}{R} \quad \text{... (vi)}$$

As in steady state, $F_m = mg$

$$\Rightarrow \quad \frac{B_H^2 v_0 l^2}{R} = mg \quad \text{[using Eq. (vi)]}$$

$$\Rightarrow \quad v_0 = \frac{mgR}{B_H^2 l^2} \quad \text{... (vii)}$$

Therefore, from Eqs. (iv) and (vii), charge on capacitor is

$$Q = C\,B_H v_0 l = CB_H\left(\frac{mgR}{B_H^2 l^2}\right) l$$

$$= \frac{mgRC}{Bl\cos\theta} \quad (\because B_H = B\cos\theta)$$

7. Let induced current in triangular segment of arrangement-1 is x as shown. Thus, by KCL for point P,

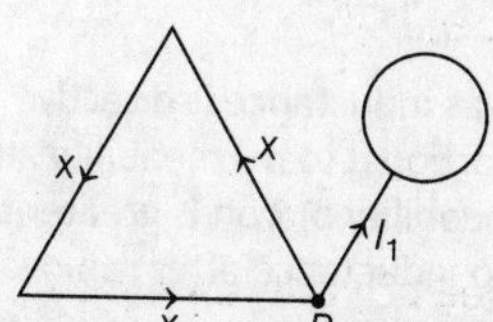

Incoming current = Outgoing current

$\Rightarrow \quad x = x + I_1 \Rightarrow I_1 = 0$

Similarly, $I_2 = 0$

Area of circular segment of arrangement-3 is πr^2 while that of triangular segment is $\dfrac{\sqrt{3}(\text{side})^2}{4}$

$$= \frac{\sqrt{3}\,(2r)^2}{4} = \sqrt{3}\,r^2$$

As magnetic flux is inward and increasing by Lenz's law, flux of induced current should be perpendicularly outwards. So, by right hand rule, induced current should be anti-clockwise in circular segment (as it has larger area) and so, it will be clockwise in triangular segment as shown.

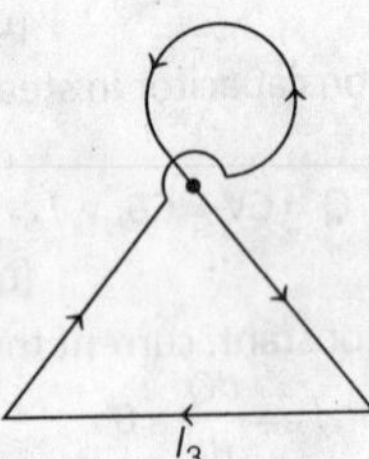

So, the direction shown is correct.

In arrangement-4, induced currents in both the loops will be anti-clockwise and equal (say I) as shown.

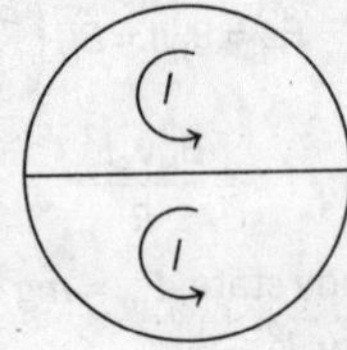

So, net current in diametrical wire will be zero.

i.e. $I_4 = 0$

8. As per Faraday's law, flux (ϕ) through a coil cannot change abruptly. Therefore,

$\phi_{\text{Just after removal}} = \phi_{\text{Just before removal}}$

$\Rightarrow \quad L'I' = LI$

Here, L and L' are inductances before and after removal of the rod. I and I' are currents before and just after removal of the rod.

$$\Rightarrow \quad I' = \frac{LI}{L'} \quad \text{... (i)}$$

Also, as inductance is directly proportional to permeability and permeability of iron is greater than air, so inductance after removal is lesser. Thus, $L' < L$ ... (ii)

Using Eqs. (i) and (ii), $I' > I$.

Therefore, current increases abruptly. But in steady state, current in LR circuit is $\dfrac{E}{R}$ and is independent of L.

So, current will decrease back to same value I.

This variation is correctly shown in option (d).

9. As masses of ball and rod are equal, their velocities will be interchanged, So, velocities of rod and ball will be v and zero respectively after the collision.

Given that, later the velocity becomes $\dfrac{v}{2}$. By conservation of energy,

Magnetic energy = Loss in kinetic energy

$$= \frac{1}{2}mv^2 - \frac{1}{2}m\left(\frac{v}{2}\right)^2 = \frac{3}{8}mv^2$$

10. Current I in superconducting loop is induced such that flux through the loop is constant. Therefore,

Final flux = Initial flux

$$LI = \phi A \Rightarrow I = \frac{\phi A}{L}$$

Therefore, work done in rotation

= increase in potential energy

$$= \frac{1}{2}LI^2 = \frac{1}{2}L\left(\frac{\phi A}{L}\right)^2 = \frac{\phi^2 A^2}{2L}$$

11. Energy Density is given by

$$\text{ED} = \frac{B^2}{2\mu_0} \quad \text{... (i)}$$

$$\Rightarrow \quad \text{ED} = \frac{(\mu_0 nI)^2}{2\mu_0} \quad [\because B = \mu_0 nI]$$

$$\Rightarrow \quad \text{ED} \propto I^2 \quad \text{... (ii)}$$

At any instant, as P and Q are in parallel, potential difference across the two will be equal.

$$\Rightarrow \quad \frac{d\phi_P}{dt} = \frac{d\phi_Q}{dt}$$

$$\Rightarrow \phi_P = \phi_Q$$

$$\Rightarrow L_P I_1 = L_Q I_2$$

$$\Rightarrow \quad \frac{I_1}{I_2} = \frac{L_Q}{L_P} = \frac{\mu_0 n^2 A l_2}{\mu_0 n^2 A l_1} = \frac{l_2}{l_1} \quad \text{...(iii)}$$

$(\because L = \mu_0 n^2 Al)$

The ratio of energy density is

$$\frac{(\text{ED})_P}{(\text{ED})_Q} = \frac{I_1^2}{I_2^2} = \left(\frac{l_2}{l_1}\right)^2 = \frac{25}{4}$$

[using Eq. (iii)]

12. Current in L-R circuit as function of time t is $I = \dfrac{E}{R}\left(1 - e^{\frac{-Rt}{L}}\right)$

Current at $t = \dfrac{L}{R}\ln 2$,

$$I = \frac{E}{R}(1 - e^{-\ln 2}) = \frac{E}{2R} \quad \text{... (i)}$$

Magnetic force on the coil, $F = BIl$

$$\Rightarrow \quad F = \frac{BEl}{2R} \quad \text{... (ii)}$$

[using Eq. (i)]

For sliding, magnetic force should be just greater than limiting friction.

$$F \approx \mu\, mg$$

$$\Rightarrow \quad \frac{BEl}{2R} \approx \mu\, mg \quad \text{[using Eq. (ii)]}$$

$$\Rightarrow \quad \mu \approx \frac{BEl}{2mgR}$$

13. If we assume current I in hexagonal loop, magnetic field at centre of loop,

$d = \dfrac{l}{2}\cot 30° = \dfrac{\sqrt{3}\,l}{2}$

$l/2$, i, 30°, 30°

$$B = \frac{\mu_0 I}{4\pi d}(\sin\theta_1 + \sin\theta_2)$$

$$= \frac{\mu_0 I}{4\pi\left(\frac{\sqrt{3}l}{2}\right)}(\sin 30° + \sin 30°)$$

$$= \frac{\mu_0 I}{2\sqrt{3}\,\pi\, l}$$

Magnetic field due to loop will be

$$B' = 6B = \frac{\sqrt{3}\mu_0\, I}{\pi\, l}$$

Therefore, flux through circular loop is

$$\phi = B' \cdot \pi r^2$$

$$= \frac{\sqrt{3}\,\mu_0 I\,\pi\, r^2}{\pi\, l} = \frac{\sqrt{3}\,\mu_0\, r^2\, I}{l}$$

Mutual inductance of the system,

$$M = \frac{\phi}{I} = \frac{\sqrt{3}\,\mu_0 r^2}{l} \quad \text{... (i)}$$

As induced emf is given by

$$E = M\frac{dI}{dt} \quad \text{... (ii)}$$

E in hexagonal loop due to current in circular loop,

Using Eqs. (i) and (ii), we get

$$E = \frac{\sqrt{3}\,\mu_0 r^2}{l} \cdot \frac{d(I_0 t)}{dt}$$

$$= \frac{\sqrt{3}\,\mu_0 I_0 r^2}{l} \quad \text{... (iii)}$$

Also, power dissipated is given by

$$P = \frac{E^2}{R}$$

$$\text{So, } P = \frac{\left(\frac{\sqrt{3}\mu_0 I_0 r^2}{l}\right)^2}{R} = \frac{3\mu_0^2 I_0^2 r^4}{l^2 R}$$

[using Eq. (iii)]

Power dissipated in one side of loop,

$$P' = \frac{P}{6} = \frac{\mu_0^2 I_0^2 r^4}{2 l^2 R}$$

14. Due to change in magnetic flux, currents are induced on the surface of hollow cylinder.

These currents oppose downward motion of the magnet by applying magnetic force F_m upwards.

As, the magnet speeds up in downward direction, induced currents and F_m keep on increasing.

But when F_m becomes equal to mg, net force and acceleration of magnet becomes zero. Thereafter, the magnet moves uniformly or with constant speed.

15. The voltage across an inductor is

$$V = L\frac{dI}{dt} = L \times \text{Slope}$$

16. As, $Z = \sqrt{R^2 + \frac{1}{(\omega C)^2}}$

and $Z' = \sqrt{R^2 + \frac{1}{(\omega 4C)^2}}$

Now, $I_R^A = \frac{V}{Z}$ and $I_R^B = \frac{V}{Z'}$

As, $Z' < Z \Rightarrow I_R^A < I_R^B$

$\Rightarrow$ Option (b) is correct .

Also, as $V_R = IR$, we wil have

$$V_R^A < V_R^B$$

$\Rightarrow V_C^A > V_C^B$ (As total voltage is constant)

17. As resistance is related to power specification by $R = \frac{V^2}{P} \Rightarrow R \propto \frac{1}{P}$

$\therefore$ Resistance of 50 W bulb (bulb-2)

$= 2 \times$ Resistance of 100 W bulb

or $R_{50} = 2R_{100}$

When switch/key is opened,

Power consumption of bulb-1 will be 100 W as current has not changed, i.e. $P_1 = 100$ W.

But as the same current I is flowing in 50 W bulb, so its power consumption becomes

$$P_2 = I^2 R_{50} = I^2 \times 2R_{100} = 2 \times I^2 R_{100}$$

$$= 2P_1 = 2 \times 100 = 200 \text{ W}$$

$\therefore$ Total power consumed,

$$P = P_1 + P_2 = 100 + 200 = 300 \text{ W}$$

18. From given equation of AC source,

$\omega = 100\pi$

$\Rightarrow$ Inductive reactance,

$$X_L = \omega L = 100\pi \times \frac{1}{\pi} = 100\,\Omega$$

$\Rightarrow$ Capacitance reactance,

$$X_C = \frac{1}{\omega C} = \frac{1}{100\pi \times \frac{50}{\pi} \times 10^{-6}} = 200\,\Omega$$

When only S_1 is closed circuit will be as shown.

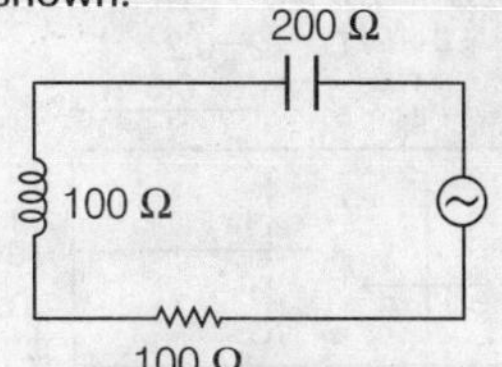

Impedance of the circuit,

$$Z = \sqrt{(X_L - X_C)^2 + R^2}$$

$$= \sqrt{(100-200)^2 + 100^2}$$

$$= 100\sqrt{2}\,\Omega \quad \text{...(i)}$$

$$\therefore \quad V_{rms} = \frac{V_{max}}{\sqrt{2}} = \frac{400\sqrt{2}}{\sqrt{2}} = 400 \text{ V} \quad \text{...(ii)}$$

From Eqs. (i) and (ii), rms current in the circuit

$$I_1 = \frac{V_{rms}}{Z} = \frac{400}{100\sqrt{2}} = 2\sqrt{2} \text{ A} \quad \text{...(iii)}$$

Also, the current in series *L-C-R* leads the voltage by phase of

$$\phi = \tan^{-1}\left(\frac{X_C - X_L}{R}\right) \quad \text{...(iv)}$$

$$\Rightarrow \phi_1 = \tan^{-1}\left(\frac{200-100}{100}\right) = 45^\circ \quad \text{...(v)}$$

When only S_2 is closed, the circuit is as shown. rms current in branch *CD* is given by $I_{CD} = \frac{V_{rms}}{R} = \frac{400}{100} = 4$ A

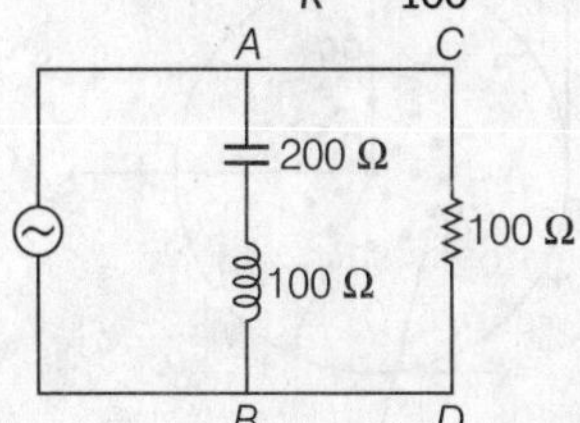

Current I_{CD} lead the voltage by

$$\phi = \tan^{-1}\left(\frac{0-0}{100}\right) = 0^\circ$$

Also, rms current in branch *AB*,

$$I_{AB} = \frac{V_{rms}}{Z} = \frac{V_{rms}}{\sqrt{(X_L - X_C)^2 + R^2}}$$

$$= \frac{400}{\sqrt{(100-200)^2 + 0^2}} = 4 \text{ A}$$

Current I_{AB} lead the voltage by

$$\phi = \tan^{-1}\left(\frac{X_C - X_L}{R}\right)$$

$$= \tan^{-1}\left(\frac{200-100}{0}\right) = 90^\circ$$

To find net current I_2 through source, we draw phasors of I_{AB} and I_{CD} and take the resultant. From the phasor diagram shown,

$$I_2 = \sqrt{I_{AB}^2 + I_{CD}^2} = 4\sqrt{2} \text{ A} \quad \text{... (vi)}$$

$$\text{and } \phi_2 = \tan^{-1}\frac{I_{AB}}{I_{CD}} = 45^\circ \quad \text{... (vii)}$$

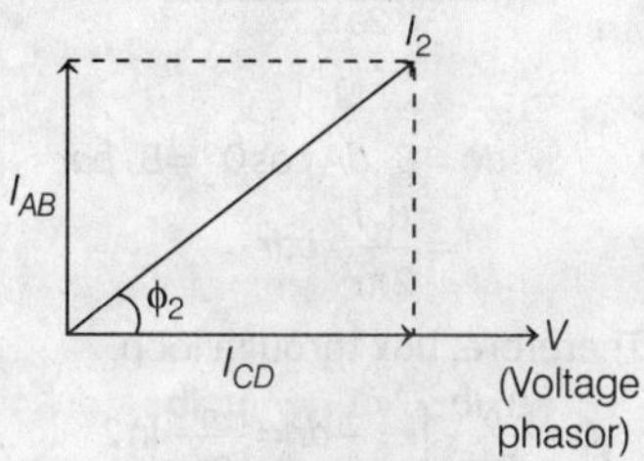

From Eqs. (iii) and (vi), we get

$$I_2 = 2I_1$$

From Eqs. (v) and (vii), we get

$$\phi_1 = \phi_2$$

19. If I_1 is original current, I_2 is current after replacing inductor by plain wire and I_3 is current after replacing capacitor by plain wire, it is given that

$$I_2 = I_3 = \frac{I_1}{2}$$

$$\Rightarrow \quad \frac{V}{\sqrt{X_C^2 + R^2}} = \frac{V}{\sqrt{X_L^2 + R^2}} = \frac{V}{2R}$$

$$\Rightarrow \quad X_L = X_C = \sqrt{3}R$$

$$\therefore \text{Q-factor} = \frac{X_L}{R} = \sqrt{3}$$

20. Output power,

$$P_2 = I_2 V_2$$

$$\Rightarrow \quad V_2 = \frac{P_2}{I_2} = \frac{2.2 \times 10^3}{10} = 220 \text{ V} \quad \text{... (i)}$$

We know that,

$$\frac{N_1}{N_2} = \frac{\text{Input voltage}}{\text{Output voltage}} = \frac{V_1}{V_2}$$

$$\Rightarrow \quad V_1 = \left(\frac{N_1}{N_2}\right)V_2 = \left(\frac{300}{150}\right)\times(220\text{ V})$$

[using Eq. (i)]

$$= 440\text{ V} \quad \text{... (ii)}$$

Again, $\frac{V_1}{V_2} = \frac{I_2}{I_1}$ (As P = constant)

$$\Rightarrow I_1 = \left(\frac{V_2}{V_1}\right)I_2 = \frac{220}{440}\times 10 = 5\text{ A}$$

[using Eqs. (i) and (ii)]

21. First consider a rectangular strip at a distance r having thickness dr, as shown in Fig. 1.

Flux through the strip, assuming area vector of strip in direction of field **B** (i.e. inwards)

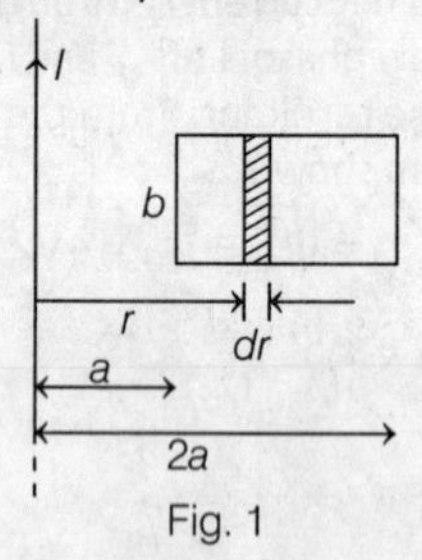

Fig. 1

$$d\phi = B\cdot dA\cos 0° = B\cdot bdr$$

$$= \frac{\mu_0 I}{2\pi r}\cdot bdr$$

Therefore, flux through loop,

$$\phi = \frac{\mu_0 Ib}{2\pi}\int_a^{2a}\frac{1}{r}\,dr = \frac{\mu_0 Ib}{2\pi}\ln 2 \quad \text{... (i)}$$

Similarly, when the loop is turned by 180° flux is equal to

$$\phi' = -\frac{\mu_0 Ib}{2\pi}\ln\frac{3}{2} \quad \text{... (ii)}$$

As per Faraday's law

$$\text{Induced current} = \frac{\text{Induced emf}}{\text{Resistance}}$$

$$\Rightarrow \frac{dq}{dt} = \frac{d\phi}{dt\cdot R}$$

$\Rightarrow$ Charge flow on turning loop,

$$q = \frac{|\Delta\phi|}{R} = \frac{\mu_0 I\,b}{2\pi R}\left[\ln 2 + \ln\frac{3}{2}\right]$$

$$= \frac{\mu_0 I_0 b}{2\pi R}[\ln 3] \quad (\text{As } I = I_0)$$

[using Eqs. (i) and (ii)] ... (iii)

Now, lets consider the second situation in which $I = I_0 e^{-t}$ ... (iv)

Flux through loop, as given by Eqs.(i) and (iv) is

$$\therefore \quad \phi = \frac{\mu_0 I_0 e^{-t} b}{2\pi}\ln 2$$

$\Rightarrow$ Induced emf,

$$E = -\frac{d\phi}{dt} = \frac{\mu_0 I_0 b}{2\pi}\ln 2\, e^{-t}$$

$$\Rightarrow \text{Induced current} = \frac{E}{R} = \frac{\mu_0 I_0 b\ln 2}{2\pi R}e^{-t}$$

$\Rightarrow$ At $t = 0$,

$$\text{Induced current, } c = \frac{\mu_0 I_0 b\ln 2}{2\pi R} \quad \text{...(v)}$$

Dividing Eq. (iii) by Eq. (v), we get

$$\frac{q}{c} = \frac{\ln 3}{\ln 2} = 1.57$$

22. Induced emf, $E = \frac{d\phi}{dt}$

$$= \frac{dB}{dt}\cdot A + \frac{dA}{dt}\cdot B$$

$$= \frac{dB}{dt}\cdot Id + \frac{d(lx)}{dt}\cdot B$$

$$= \frac{d(4t)}{dt} I\cdot d + IvB \quad \left(\because \frac{dx}{dt} = v\right)$$

$$= 4\times(0.4) + 0.4\times 0.1\times 8$$

$$= 1.6 + 0.32 = 1.92\text{ m} \quad \text{... (i)}$$

Also, resistance of loop,

R = resistance per unit length × length

$$= r(2d + l) = 0.8\,(2 + 0.4) = 1.92\ \Omega \quad \text{...(ii)}$$

From Eqs. (i) and (ii),

$$\text{Induced current, } I = \frac{E}{R} = \frac{1.92}{1.92} = 1\text{ A}$$

Direction of I is anti-clockwise as per Lenz's law. Opposing magnetic force, $F_m = BIl = 8\times 1\times 0.4 = 3.2$ N. As, rod is moving with constant velocity, so force of external agent is equal but opposite.

Therefore, $F = 3.2$ N

23. Due to sudden switching ON of the field, an electric field is induced in the region outside the magnetic field region.

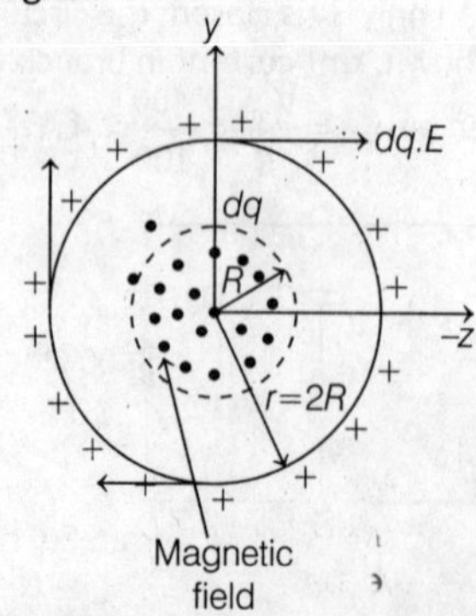

Induced electric field in a cylindrical region with time varying magnetic field is given by

$$E = \frac{R^2}{2r}\frac{dB}{dt} \quad (\text{for } r > R)$$

Therefore, at location of ring

$$E = \frac{R^2}{2(2R)}\frac{dB}{dt} = \frac{R}{4}\frac{dB}{dt} \quad \text{... (i)}$$

Electric force due to this field on an element of the ring having charge dq is

$$dF = dq\cdot E$$

Thus, torque on element,

$$d\tau = dF\cdot 2R$$

$$= dq\cdot E\cdot 2R$$

$$= dq\cdot\frac{R}{4}\frac{dB}{dt}\cdot 2R \quad [\text{using Eq. (i)}]$$

Integrating both sides, we get

$$\tau = \frac{R^2}{2}\frac{dB}{dt}\int dq$$

$$= \frac{R^2}{2}\frac{dB}{dt}\cdot q = \frac{qBR^2}{2t} \quad \text{... (ii)}$$

($\because$ Magnetic field changes from 0 to B in time t)

If L and I are angular momentum and moment of inertia of the ring.

$$\Delta L = \tau\,\Delta t$$

(Newton's second law in rotation)

$$\Rightarrow \quad \Delta\omega = \frac{\tau\,\Delta t}{I} \quad (\text{As, } L = I\omega)$$

Using Eq. (ii), we get

$$\omega = \frac{\frac{qBR^2}{2t}\times t}{m(2R)^2} = \frac{qB}{8m}$$

$$= \frac{\sigma(4\pi R)B}{8m} = \frac{\sigma\pi RB}{2m}$$

$$\therefore \quad n = \frac{2}{\pi} = 0.63$$

24. Here, maximum value of voltage,

$$V_{max} = 10\text{ V}$$

$$\Rightarrow V_{rms} = \sqrt{V_{av}}$$

$$= \sqrt{\frac{1}{T}\int_0^T V^2 dt}$$

$$= \sqrt{\frac{1}{T}\int_0^T 10^2 dt}$$

$$\therefore \quad V = 10\text{ V}$$

25. It is given that, PF of arrangement-1 is 0.6.

$$\Rightarrow \frac{R_1}{\sqrt{(X_L - 0)^2 + R_1^2}} = 0.6$$

$$\Rightarrow \quad X_L = \frac{4}{3}R_1 \quad \text{... (i)}$$

Also, for arrangement-3, PF is 1.

$$\Rightarrow \frac{R_1+R_2}{\sqrt{(X_L-X_C)^2+(R_1+R_2)^2}}=1$$

$$\Rightarrow \quad X_L = X_C$$

$$\Rightarrow \quad X_C = \frac{4}{3}R_1 \quad \text{... (ii)}$$

[using Eq. (i)]

For arrangement-2, using Eq. (i), we get

$$\text{PF} = \frac{R_2}{\sqrt{X_C^2+R_2^2}} = \frac{8R_1}{\sqrt{X_C^2+64R_1^2}}$$

(As, $R_2 = 8R_1$)

$$= \frac{8R_1}{\sqrt{\left(\frac{4}{3}R_1\right)^2+64R_1^2}}$$

[using Eq.(ii)]

$$= \sqrt{\frac{36}{37}} = \sqrt{\frac{6^2}{6^2+1}}$$

Therefore, $x = 6$

Qualifier 14 (Electromagnetic Waves & Communication Systems)

1. The situation can be shown as

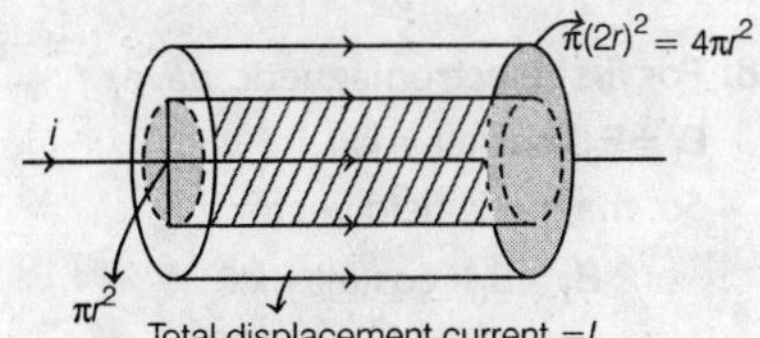

Total displacement current $= I$

As per theory of displacement current, total displacement current flowing from one plate to the other is equal to conduction current I.

Therefore, λ = Displacement current per unit area $= \dfrac{I}{\pi(2r)^2}$

$$\Rightarrow \quad \lambda = \frac{I}{4\pi r^2} \quad \text{... (i)}$$

As area of cross-section of the imaginary cylinder is $A = \pi r^2$, displacement current through it will be

$$I' = \lambda \times A = \frac{I}{4\pi r^2} \times \pi r^2 = \frac{I}{4}$$

[using Eq. (i)]

2. Refractive index n is related to relative permittivity ε_r and relative permeability μ_r by the relation

$$n = \sqrt{\mu_r \varepsilon_r}$$

$$\Rightarrow \quad n = \sqrt{\varepsilon_r} \quad (\because \mu_r = 1)$$

$$\Rightarrow \quad \varepsilon_r = n^2 \quad \text{... (i)}$$

Speed of wave in medium, $v = \dfrac{c}{n}$ ... (ii)

Also, power transmitted (per unit area) along the wave is $P = \dfrac{1}{2}\varepsilon_0 E_0^2 c$ (in vacuum) or $\dfrac{1}{2}\varepsilon_r \varepsilon_0 E^2 v$ (in medium). As there is no loss,

$$P_{\text{vacuum}} = P_{\text{medium}}$$

$$\Rightarrow \quad \frac{1}{2}\varepsilon_0 E_0^2 c = \frac{1}{2}\varepsilon_r \varepsilon_0 E^2 v$$

$$\Rightarrow \quad \frac{1}{2}\varepsilon_0 E_0^2 c = \frac{1}{2}n^2 \varepsilon_0 E^2 \frac{c}{n}$$

[using Eqs. (i) and (ii)]

$$\Rightarrow \quad E = \frac{E_0}{\sqrt{n}} = \frac{E_0}{\sqrt{2}} \quad \text{... (iii)}$$

As, B is related to E by relation

$$\frac{E}{B} = v \quad (v = \text{Speed of wave})$$

As, B is related to E by relation

$$\frac{E}{B} = v \quad (v = \text{Speed of wave})$$

$$\Rightarrow \quad B = \frac{E}{v}$$

$$\Rightarrow \quad B = \frac{E_0/\sqrt{n}}{c/n}$$

[using Eqs. (ii) and (iii)]

$$\Rightarrow \quad B = \sqrt{n}\frac{E_0}{c} = \sqrt{n}\,B_0 = \sqrt{2}\,B_0$$

3. Direction of wave propagation/velocity is given by $\mathbf{E} \times \mathbf{B}$.

$$\mathbf{E} \times \mathbf{B} = (\sqrt{3}\,\hat{\mathbf{i}} + \hat{\mathbf{j}}) \times \hat{\mathbf{k}}$$

$$= -\sqrt{3}\,\hat{\mathbf{j}} + \hat{\mathbf{i}} = \hat{\mathbf{i}} - \sqrt{3}\,\hat{\mathbf{j}}$$

So, unit vector along $\mathbf{E} \times \mathbf{B}$ will be

$$\hat{\mathbf{n}} = \frac{\mathbf{E} \times \mathbf{B}}{|\mathbf{E} \times \mathbf{B}|} = \frac{\hat{\mathbf{i}} - \sqrt{3}\,\hat{\mathbf{j}}}{2}$$

4. Poynting vector or energy carried by EM wave per unit area per unit time is given by

$$\mathbf{S} = \frac{\mathbf{E} \times \mathbf{B}}{\mu_0} \quad \text{... (i)}$$

Also, direction of $\mathbf{B}$ is given by the unit vector

$$\hat{\mathbf{B}} = \frac{\mathbf{c} \times \mathbf{E}}{cE}$$

$$\Rightarrow \quad \mathbf{B} = B\hat{\mathbf{B}} = \frac{B(\mathbf{c} \times \mathbf{E})}{cE}$$

$$\Rightarrow \quad \mathbf{B} = \frac{\mathbf{c} \times \mathbf{E}}{c^2} \quad \left(\because \frac{E}{B} = c\right) \quad \text{... (ii)}$$

Putting the value of $\mathbf{B}$ from Eq. (ii) in Eq. (i), we get

$$\mathbf{S} = \frac{\mathbf{E} \times (\mathbf{c} \times \mathbf{E})}{\mu_0 c^2}$$

$$= \varepsilon_0 \mathbf{E} \times (\mathbf{c} \times \mathbf{E}) \quad \left(\because c^2 = \frac{1}{\mu_0 \varepsilon_0}\right)$$

5. Radiation pressure, if light of intensity I is incident on perfect reflector, is

$$P = \frac{2I}{c} \quad \text{[Here, } c = \text{Speed of light]}$$

$$= \left(\frac{2}{c}\right)\left(\frac{1}{2}\varepsilon_0 E_0^2 c\right)$$

$$= \varepsilon_0 E_0^2 = 8.85 \times 10^{-12} \times \left(\frac{1}{\sqrt{8.85}}\right)^2$$

$$= 10^{-12} \text{ pascal}$$

6. Intensity at distance from the bulb is

$$I = \frac{\eta P}{4\pi r^2} \quad \text{... (i)}$$

Also, intensity of EM wave is given by

$$I = \frac{1}{2}c\,\varepsilon_0 E_0^2 \quad \text{... (ii)}$$

From Eqs. (i) and (ii), we get

$$\frac{\eta P}{4\pi r^2} = \frac{1}{2}c\,\varepsilon_0 E_0^2$$

$$\Rightarrow \quad E_0 = \sqrt{\frac{\eta P}{2\pi\varepsilon_0 c r^2}}$$

7. (a) Infrared waves are used to treat muscular strain.

(b) Radiowaves are used for broadcasting purposes.

(c) X-rays are used to detect fracture of bones.

(d) Ultraviolet rays are absorbed by ozone layer of the atmosphere.

So, correct match is A-1, B-2, C-3, D-4.

8. If h_R and h_T are heights of receiving and transmitting antennas, then range d is given by

$$d = \sqrt{2Rh_T} + \sqrt{2Rh_R}$$

$$\Rightarrow \quad d = \sqrt{2R(9h)} + \sqrt{2R(4h)}$$

$$\Rightarrow \quad d = 3\sqrt{2Rh} + 2\sqrt{2Rh}$$

$$\Rightarrow \quad \sqrt{2Rh} = \frac{d}{5}$$

$$\Rightarrow \quad h = \frac{d^2}{50R}$$

Height of transmitting antenna

$$= 9h = \frac{9d^2}{50R}$$

9. Loss in dB is given by

$$L = 10\log\frac{P_{\text{input}}}{P_{\text{output}}} \quad \text{... (i)}$$

So, loss between transmitter and mid-way is

$$L_1 = 10\log\frac{P}{P_m} \quad \text{... (ii)}$$

and loss between mid-way and receiver is

$$L_2 = 10\log\frac{P_m}{P'} \quad \text{... (iii)}$$

As L_1 is given equal to L_2. So, from Eqs. (ii) and (iii), we get

$$L_1 = L_2$$

$$\Rightarrow 10\log\frac{P}{P_m} = 10\log\frac{P_m}{P'}$$

$$\Rightarrow \frac{P}{P_m} = \frac{P_m}{P'}$$

$$\Rightarrow P_m = \sqrt{PP'}$$

10. Range in terms of height of transmitting antenna (h) and height of receiving antenna (h') is given by

$$\text{Range} = \sqrt{2Rh} + \sqrt{2Rh'} \quad \text{... (i)}$$

Here, R is earth's radius. [using Eq. (i)]

Initial range,

$$R_1 = \sqrt{2R(80)} + \sqrt{2R(20)} \quad \text{... (ii)}$$

[using Eq (i)]

Final range,

$$R_2 = \sqrt{2R(80)} \quad \text{...(iii)}$$

Subtracting Eq. (iii) from Eq. (ii), we get

Decrease in range,

$$\Delta R = R_1 - R_2 = \sqrt{2R(20)} \quad \text{... (iv)}$$

From Eqs. (iv) and (ii),

Percentage decrease in range is

$$\frac{\Delta R}{R_1} \times 100 = \frac{\sqrt{2R(20)}}{\sqrt{2R(80)} + \sqrt{2R(20)}} \times 100$$

$$= 33.33\%$$

11. If a carrier wave is modulated by several waves having $n_1, n_2, n_3, \ldots$, as modulation indices, then modulation index of AM wave is

$$n = \sqrt{n_1^2 + n_2^2 + n_3^2 + \ldots}$$

$$\Rightarrow n = \sqrt{\left(\frac{1}{4}\right)^2 + \left(\frac{1}{4\sqrt{2}}\right)^2 + \left(\frac{1}{8}\right)^2 + \ldots}$$

$$= \frac{1}{4}\sqrt{1 + \frac{1}{2} + \frac{1}{4} + \frac{1}{8} + \ldots}$$

$$= \frac{1}{4}\sqrt{\frac{1}{1 - \frac{1}{2}}}$$

(using formula for summation of infinite GP i.e. $s_\infty = \frac{a}{1-r}$)

$$= \frac{1}{2\sqrt{2}}$$

12. If the equation of AM wave is given by

$$V = (A_c + A_m \sin\omega_m t)\sin(\omega_c t + \phi)$$

Comparing the given equation with this, we get

$$A_c = a\text{ V}, A_m = 4\text{ V}, \omega_m = 10^4\pi,$$
$$\omega_c = 10^7\pi$$

$$\Rightarrow f_m = \frac{\omega_m}{2\pi} = 5\text{ kHz}$$

$$\text{and } f_c = \frac{\omega_c}{2\pi} = \frac{10^7\pi}{2\pi} = 5000\text{ kHz}$$

Also, A_m = Modulation index $\times A_c$

$$\Rightarrow \quad 4 = 0.5 \times a \Rightarrow a = 8\text{ V}$$

Hence, graph showing in option (d) is correct.

13. For satisfactory working of envelope detector, $f_c >> \frac{1}{RC}$

$$\Rightarrow \quad f_c >> \frac{1}{0.5 \times 10^3 \times 2 \times 10^{-6}}$$

$$\Rightarrow \quad f_c >> 1\text{kHz}$$

$\therefore$ Most appropriate option is (d).

14. Critical/Maximum frequency that can be reflected by F_1 layer or any other layer of the ionosphere is given by

$$f_{max} = 9\sqrt{N_{max}}$$

Here, N_{max} is maximum number density of electrons in the layer.

$$\Rightarrow N_{max} = \frac{f_{max}^2}{81} = \frac{(6 \times 10^6)^2}{81}$$

$$= 4.4 \times 10^{11}\text{ m}^{-3}$$

15. If h_T and h_R are heights of transmitting and receiving antennas range (l) is

$$l = \sqrt{2Rh_T} + \sqrt{2Rh_R} \quad \text{... (i)}$$

Also, given that $h_T + h_R = 40$ m ...(ii)

From Eqs. (i) and (ii) we get

$$l = \sqrt{2Rh_T} + \sqrt{2R(40 - h_T)}$$

For range to be maximum

$$\frac{dl}{dh_T} = 0 \Rightarrow \frac{1}{\sqrt{h_T}} = \frac{1}{\sqrt{40 - h_T}}$$

$$\Rightarrow \quad h_T = 40 - h_T \Rightarrow \quad h_T = 20\text{ m}$$

$$\Rightarrow h_R = 20\text{ m} \quad \text{[using Eq. (ii)]}$$

Putting these values in Eq. (i), we get 0-32 km.

16.

C, $V = 18\sin\Omega t$

From the given information,

$$C = \frac{\varepsilon_0 A}{d} = \frac{\varepsilon_0 \times 1}{2 \times 10^{-3}}\text{ F}$$

$$\therefore X_C = \frac{1}{\omega C} = \frac{2 \times 10^{-3}}{2 \times 50\pi \times \varepsilon_0} = \frac{2 \times 10^{-3}}{25 \times 4\pi\varepsilon_0}$$

$$\therefore X_C = \frac{2 \times 10^{-3}}{25} \times 9 \times 10^9$$

$$= \frac{18}{25} \times 10^6\ \Omega$$

$$\therefore \quad I_0 = \frac{V_0}{X_C} = \frac{18 \times 25}{18} \times 10^{-6}\text{ A}$$

$$= 25\mu\text{A}$$

The value of amplitude of displacement current will be same as value of amplitude of conventional current.

17. As $\mathbf{F} = q(\mathbf{v} \times \mathbf{B})$

$$\Rightarrow \quad \mathbf{F}_1 = 6\pi\left[0.25c\,\hat{\mathbf{i}} \times B_0\left(\frac{\hat{\mathbf{i}} + \hat{\mathbf{j}}}{\sqrt{2}}\right)\cos\left(k.\frac{\pi}{k} - 0\right)\right]$$

$$= -6\pi\left[0.25c\,\hat{\mathbf{i}} \times B_0\left(\frac{\hat{\mathbf{i}} + \hat{\mathbf{j}}}{\sqrt{2}}\right)\right]$$

and $\mathbf{F}_2 =$

$$2\pi\left[0.25c\,\hat{\mathbf{i}} \times B_0\left(\frac{\hat{\mathbf{i}} + \hat{\mathbf{j}}}{\sqrt{2}}\right)\cos\left(k.\frac{3\pi}{k} - 0\right)\right]$$

$$= -2\pi\left[0.25c\,\hat{\mathbf{i}} \times B_0\left(\frac{\hat{\mathbf{i}} + \hat{\mathbf{j}}}{\sqrt{2}}\right)\right]$$

As $\cos\pi = -1$, $\cos 3\pi = -1$,

$$\therefore \quad \frac{F_1}{F_2} = 3$$

18. For first electromagnetic wave,

$$\mathbf{E}_1 = \mathbf{E}_0\hat{\mathbf{j}}\cos(\omega t - kx)$$

So, magnetic field vector,

$$\mathbf{B}_1 = \mathrm{B}_0\hat{\mathbf{k}}\cos(\omega t - kx)$$

$$= \frac{E_0}{c}\hat{\mathbf{k}}\cos(\omega t - kx)$$

Also, for second electromagnetic wave,

$$\mathbf{E}_2 = \mathrm{E}_0\hat{\mathbf{k}}\cos(\omega t - ky)$$

$$\Rightarrow \quad \mathbf{B}_2 = \frac{\mathrm{E}_0}{c}\hat{\mathbf{i}}\cos(\omega t - ky)$$

Force on charged particle under influence of both electric and magnetic fields, $F = q(\mathbf{v} \times \mathbf{B} + \mathbf{E})$ ...(i)

Here, $\mathbf{v} = 0.8\,c\,\hat{\mathbf{j}}$

$$\text{Now, } \mathbf{B} = \mathbf{B}_1 + \mathbf{B}_2 = \frac{\mathrm{E}_0}{c}\hat{\mathbf{k}}\cos(\omega t - kx) + \frac{E_0}{c}\hat{\mathbf{i}}\cos(\omega t - ky)$$

Therefore, at $t = 0$, at origin ($x = 0$, $y = 0$ and $z = 0$), we have

$$\mathbf{B} = \frac{E_0}{c}(\hat{\mathbf{i}} + \hat{\mathbf{k}}) \quad \text{...(ii)}$$

Similary, $\mathbf{E} = \mathbf{E}_1 + \mathbf{E}_2$

$$= E_0\hat{\mathbf{j}}\cos(\omega t - kx) + E_0\hat{\mathbf{k}}\cos(\omega t - ky)$$

Therefore, at $t=0$ and at origin,
$\mathbf{E}=E_0(\hat{\mathbf{j}}+\hat{\mathbf{k}})$ ... (ii)

So, from Eqs. (i), (ii) and (iii), we get

$$\mathbf{F}=q\left[0.8c\hat{\mathbf{j}}\times\frac{E_0}{c}(\hat{\mathbf{i}}+\hat{\mathbf{k}})+E_0(\hat{\mathbf{j}}+\hat{\mathbf{k}})\right]$$
$$=E_0q\,[0.8\hat{\mathbf{j}}\times(\hat{\mathbf{i}}+\hat{\mathbf{k}})+(\hat{\mathbf{j}}+\hat{\mathbf{k}})]$$
$$=E_0q\,[0.8(-\hat{\mathbf{k}}+\hat{\mathbf{i}})+(\hat{\mathbf{j}}+\hat{\mathbf{k}})]$$
$$=E_0q\,(0.8\hat{\mathbf{i}}+\hat{\mathbf{j}}+0.2\hat{\mathbf{k}})\text{ N}$$

Comparing this equation with given equation, we get

$$A=0.8, B=0.2$$
$$\Rightarrow \frac{A}{B}=\frac{0.8}{0.2}=4$$

19. Given, modulating frequency,

$$f_m=8\text{ kHz}$$

Frequency deviation, $\Delta f=52$ kHz

$\therefore$ Carrier Swing,

$$\text{CS}=\frac{\text{Frequency deviation }(\Delta f)}{\text{Modulating frequency }(f_m)}$$
$$=\frac{52}{8}=6.5$$

20. Only 10% of 10 GHz is utilised for transmission.

$\therefore$ Band available for transmission

$$=\frac{10}{100}\times 10\times 10^9\text{ Hz}$$
$$=10^9\text{ Hz}$$

Now, if there are n channels each using 5 kHz, then

$$n\times 5\times 10^3=10^9$$
$$\Rightarrow \quad n=2\times 10^5$$
$$\therefore \quad x=2$$

Qualifier 15 (Optics)

1. Let the bulb is placed at point O.

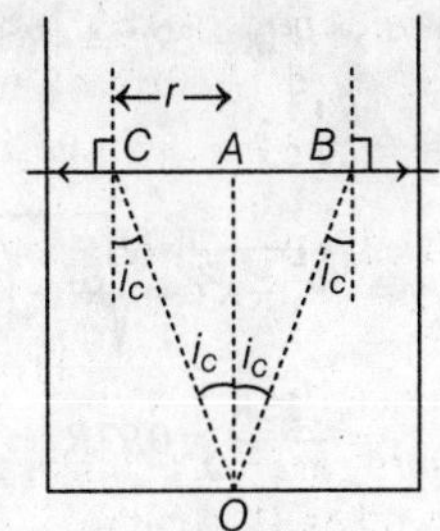

If angle of incidence is less than the critical angle, light will refract into air and when angle of incidence is greater than critical angle, then it will be reflected back in water.

The source of light is 80 cm below the surface of water, i.e. $AO=80$ cm, $\mu_w=1.33$

Using the formula for critical angle,

$$\sin i_c=\frac{1}{\mu_w}$$
$$\sin i_c=\frac{1}{1.33}=0.75=\frac{3}{4}$$
$$\Rightarrow \quad r=l\tan i_c$$
$$=80\frac{3}{\sqrt{7}}=\frac{240}{\sqrt{7}}\text{ cm}$$

Area of circular surface of water through which light will emerge,

$$A=\pi r^2$$
$$=3.14\times\left(\frac{240}{\sqrt{7}}\right)^2$$
$$\approx 2.6\text{m}^2$$

2. Image I formed after reflection from concave mirror will be as shown.

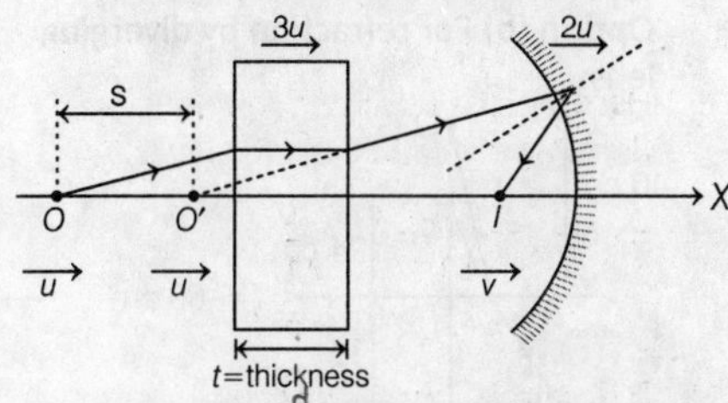

O' is the intermediate image formed after refraction from the slab, shifted w.r.t. object O by

$$S=t\left(1-\frac{1}{n}\right)$$

Therefore, irrespective of position of slab, distance between O and O' is constant. So velocity of O' is equal to that of O i.e. u.

Now, for reflection, velocity of image w.r.t. mirror (v_{im}) is related to velocity of object w.r.t. mirror (v_{om}) by the relation $v_{im}=-m^2 v_{om}$

(m = magnification)

$$\Rightarrow v_i-v_m=-m^2(v_o-v_m)$$
$$\Rightarrow \quad v_i=-m^2v_o+v_m(1+m^2)\quad \text{... (i)}$$

As per sign convention,

Velocity of object, $v_o=+u$ ... (ii)

Velocity of mirror, $v_m=+2u$ ... (iii)

Putting values of v_o and v_m from Eq. (ii) and Eq. (iii) in Eq. (i), we get

$$\Rightarrow v_i=-m^2(+u)+(+2u)(1+m^2)$$
$$=+2u+um^2=+u(2+m^2)$$

$\therefore$ Speed of image $=|v_i|=u(2+m^2)>u$

3. For formation of final image of the object, rays should be incident normally on the mirror as shown in figure.

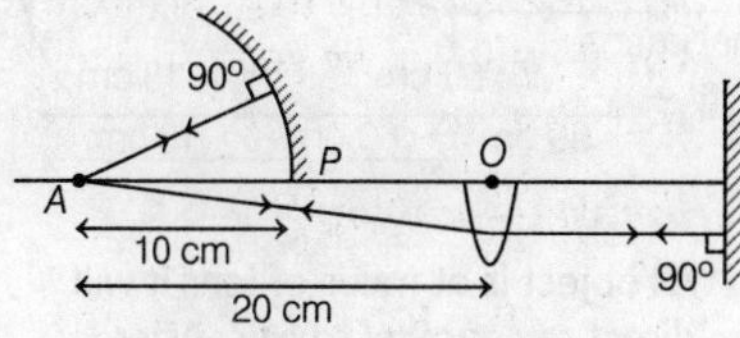

From diagram, A should be centre of curvature of concave mirror.

Therefore, its radius of curvature,

$$R=PA=10\text{ cm}$$
$$\Rightarrow \text{Focal length}=f=\frac{R}{2}=5\text{ cm}$$

Also, ray after refraction from lens should become parallel to axis. Therefore, A is focus of the lens and OA is equal to focal length of lens which is equal to 20 cm.

4. As for complete lens, object and image distances are both equal to 60 cm. So, object must be at $2F$. Therefore, focal length of the lens will be 30 cm. After the lens is cut, its power will be halved or focal length will be doubled. So, new focal length will be 60 cm.

Using lens Maker's formula, for concave lens,

$$\frac{1}{f_1}=\left(\frac{3}{2}-1\right)\left(\frac{1}{-10}-\frac{1}{+15}\right)=-\frac{1}{12}\quad \text{... (i)}$$

For convex lens in combination,

$$\frac{1}{f_2}=\left(\frac{4}{3}-1\right)\left(\frac{1}{15}-\frac{1}{-15}\right)=\frac{2}{45}\quad \text{... (ii)}$$

And for mirror,

$$\frac{1}{f_m}=\frac{2}{R_m}=\frac{2}{-15}\quad \text{... (iii)}$$

For combination of lenses and mirrors equivalent focal length is given by

$$\frac{1}{f}=\frac{1}{f_{\text{mirror}}}-2\,\Sigma\frac{1}{f_{\text{lens}}}$$
$$\Rightarrow \quad \frac{1}{f}=\frac{1}{f_m}-2\left(\frac{1}{f_1}+\frac{1}{f_2}\right)$$

[using Eqs. (i), (ii) and (iii)]

$$\Rightarrow \quad \frac{1}{f}=\frac{2}{-15}-2\left(-\frac{1}{12}+\frac{2}{45}\right)=-\frac{1}{18}$$
$$\Rightarrow \quad f=-18\text{ cm}$$

So, the combination is equivalent to a concave mirror of focal length 18 cm.

Thus, the given system can be represented on equivalent basis as

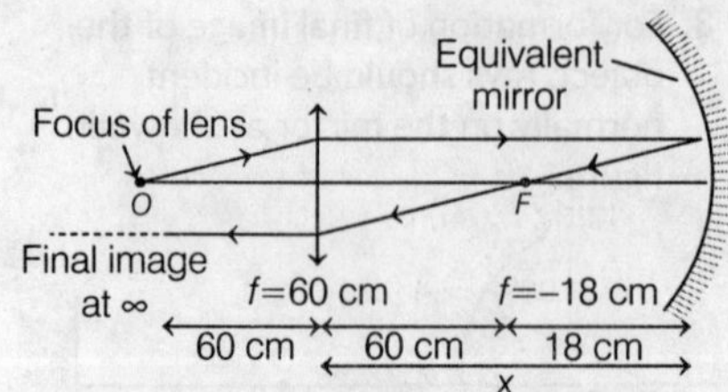

As object is at focus of lens it will direct ray parallel to axis. After reflection equivalent mirror will reflect ray towards its focus F as shown. For final image to be at infinity, the ray should be directed parallel to principal axis by the lens. So, the point F from where the ray is coming should be the focus of the lens, distant 60 cm from the lens. From diagram,

$$x = 60 + 18 = 78 \text{ cm}$$

5. Magnification, from given figure,

$$|m| = \left|\frac{v}{u}\right| = \frac{OB}{OA} = \frac{OC \cdot \cot 60°}{OC \cdot \cot 30°}$$

$$= \cot^2 60° = 1/3$$

Velocity of image (v_i) is related to velocity of object (v_o) by the relation

$$v_i = m^2 v_o = \left(\frac{1}{3}\right)^2 v_o = \frac{v_o}{9}$$

6. Consider a ray incident grazingly on top of the elliptical cross-section as shown

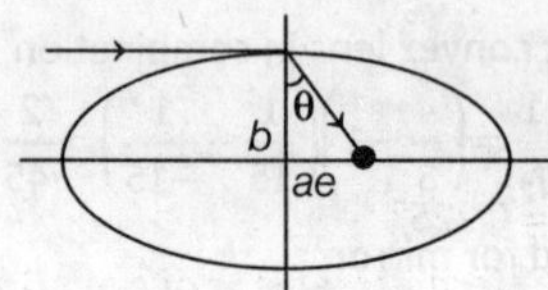

By Snell's law,

$$n_1 \sin 90° = n_2 \sin\theta$$

$$n_1 = n_2 \cdot \frac{ae}{\sqrt{b^2 + (ae)^2}}$$

$$\frac{n_2}{n_1} = \sqrt{\frac{b^2}{a^2 e^2} + 1}$$

$$= \sqrt{\frac{1 - e^2}{e^2} + 1} = \frac{1}{e}$$

$$\Rightarrow \quad e = \frac{n_1}{n_2}$$

7. Lets consider every option one by one.

Option (a) For refraction by converging lens

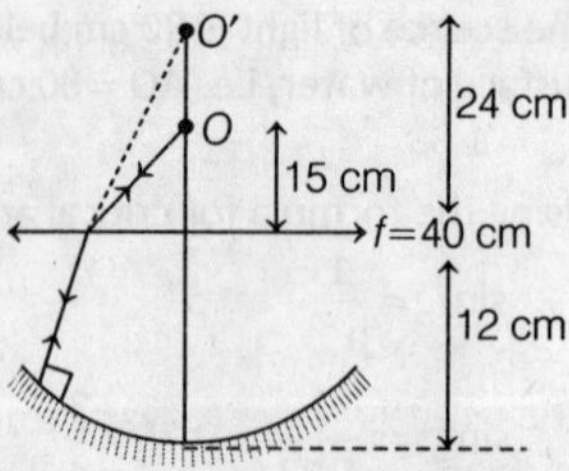

Radius of curvature = 36 cm

$$\frac{1}{v} - \frac{1}{u} = \frac{1}{f} \Rightarrow \frac{1}{v} - \frac{1}{-15} = \frac{1}{40}$$

$\Rightarrow$ Position of image O', $v = -24$ cm

As distance of O' from mirror will be equal to 12 cm + 24 cm = 36 cm which is same as radius of curvature of the mirror, O' will be at centre of curvature of the mirror. So, rays from O' will be incident normally on the mirror, as shown. The rays will retrace their path and so image will coincide with object.

Option (b) For refraction by diverging lens

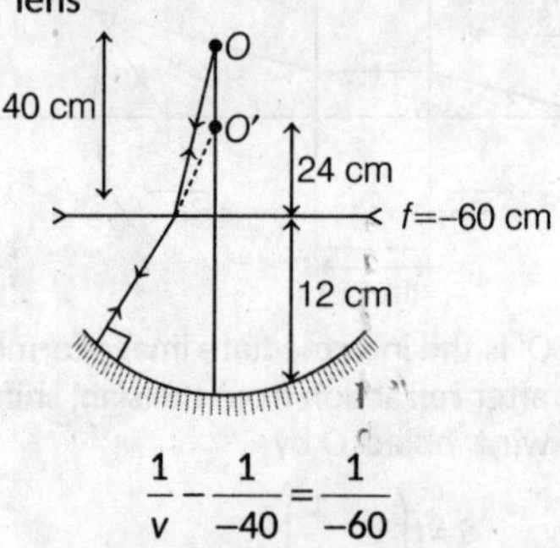

$$\frac{1}{v} - \frac{1}{-40} = \frac{1}{-60}$$

$\Rightarrow$ Position of image O', $v = -24$ cm

Similar to situation in option (a), image object coincidence will happen.

Option (c) Shift produced by glass slab

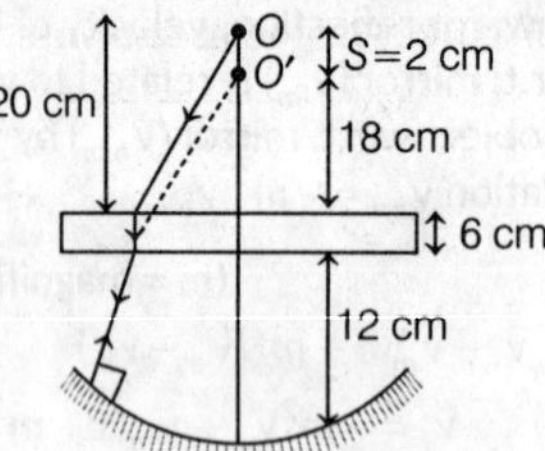

$$S = t\left(1 - \frac{1}{n}\right) = 6\left(1 - \frac{1}{1.5}\right) = 2 \text{ cm}$$

Distance of image of slab O' from upper surface is equal to $20 - S = 18$ cm (as shown). Again O' is at centre of curvature of mirror. Similar to options (a) and (b), object image coincidence will take place.

So, option (d) is correct.

8. The figure shows a strip at a distance x of thickness dx. As μ of material increases with x, ray will continuously bend towards normal as shown. By Snell's law, between O and A,

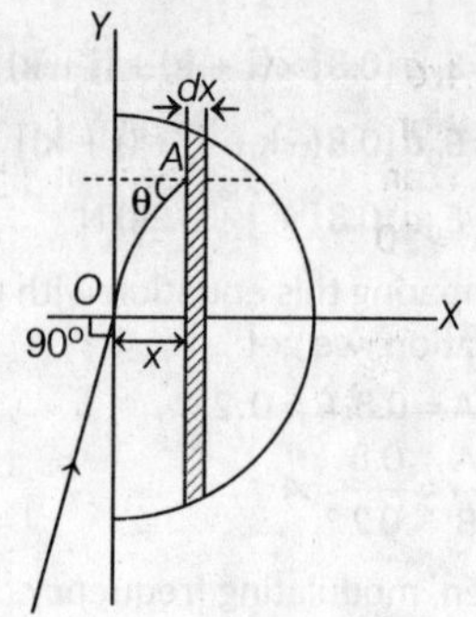

$$1 \times \sin 90° = \frac{2R}{2R - x} \times \sin\theta$$

$$\Rightarrow \quad \tan\theta = \frac{2R - x}{\sqrt{(2R)^2 - (2R - x)^2}}$$

$$\Rightarrow \quad \frac{dy}{dx} = \frac{2R - x}{\sqrt{(2R)^2 - (2R - x)^2}}$$

Integrating above relation, we get

$$\Rightarrow \quad \int_0^y dy = \int_0^x \frac{2R - x}{\sqrt{(2R)^2 - (2R - x)^2}} dx$$

$$\Rightarrow \quad y = \sqrt{(2R)^2 - (2R - x)^2}$$

$$\Rightarrow \quad y^2 + (x - 2R)^2 = (2R)^2$$

Which is equation of circle of radius $2R$ centred at $(2R, 0)$

Also, equation of hemispherical surface is $x^2 + y^2 = (R)^2$

$$\Rightarrow \quad y^2 = R^2 - x^2$$

Putting this value of y^2 in equation of trajectory we can find coordinates of point where the ray comes out of hemisphere, as shown

$$R^2 - x^2 + (x - 2R)^2 = 4R^2$$

$$\Rightarrow \quad x = \frac{R}{4}$$

and $\quad y = \sqrt{R^2 - x^2} = \sqrt{R^2 - \left(\frac{R}{4}\right)^2}$

$$= \frac{\sqrt{15}R}{4} = 0.97R$$

9. Clearly, the graph is discontinuous for $i = C$. Therefore, x is equal to critical angle C.

By Snell's law, for grazing emergence

$$n_{glass} \cdot \sin C = n_{air} \cdot \sin 90°$$

$\Rightarrow \quad \sin C = \frac{n_{air}}{n_{glass}}$

$= \frac{1}{2/\sqrt{3}} = \frac{\sqrt{3}}{2}$

$\Rightarrow \quad C = x = 60°$ ... (i)

Also, from the given graph, y is deviation corresponding to $i = x = C$, which can be calculated from figure as

$y = \delta = 90° - C = 90° - 60° = 30°$ ... (ii)

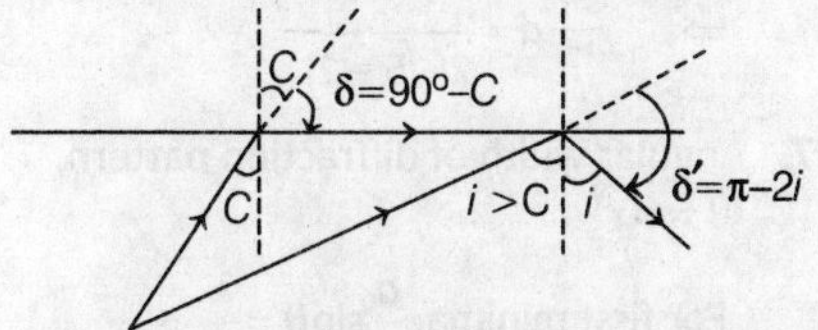

And z is the deviation corresponding to i just greater than C, which can be calculated from figure as

$z = \delta' = \pi - 2C$

$= 180° - 2 \times 60° = 60°$ ...(iii)

10. The given situation can be shown as

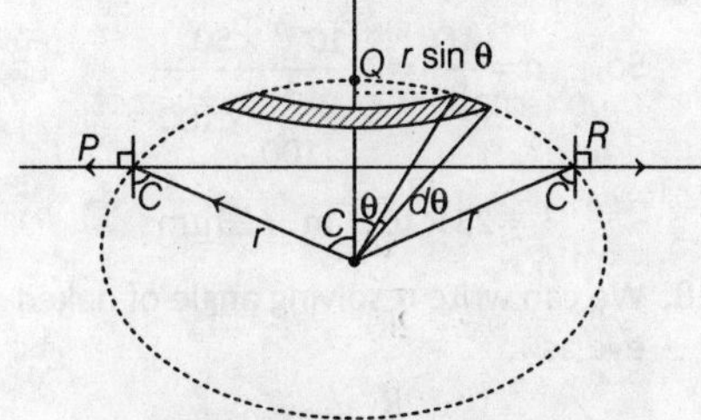

Energy crossing through PQR will emerge in air, as at P and R incidence angles are equal to critical angle. To find rate of transfer of energy through surface, we need to find surface area of cap PQR. To do this, consider an element of cap at angle θ and angular thickness $d\theta$.

Area of element, $dA = (2\pi r \sin\theta) r d\theta$

$dA = 2\pi r^2 \sin\theta \, d\theta$

Integrating it, we get

$A = 2\pi r^2 \int_0^C \sin\theta \, d\theta$

$= 2\pi r^2 (1 - \cos C)$

$\therefore$ Power crossing the surface,

$P_s = \frac{2\pi r^2 (1 - \cos C)}{4\pi r^2} \times P$

$= \left(\frac{1 - \cos C}{2}\right) \times P$ ... (i)

As, $\mu = \frac{1}{\sin C} \Rightarrow \sin C = \frac{1}{\mu} = \frac{\sqrt{8}}{3}$

$\Rightarrow \quad \cos C = \sqrt{1 - \sin^2 C} = \sqrt{1 - \frac{8}{9}} = \frac{1}{3}$

Putting these values in Eq. (i), we get

$$P_s = \left(\frac{1 - \frac{1}{3}}{2}\right) \times 6 = \frac{1}{3} \times 6 = 2 \text{ W}$$

11. Power of lens P is related to refractive index n and radii of curvature of the lens by the relation.

$P = (n - 1)\left(\frac{1}{R_1} - \frac{1}{R_2}\right)$ ... (i)

For violet, if $n = n_v$, using Eq. (i)

$P = a = (n_v - 1)\left(\frac{1}{R_1} - \frac{1}{R_2}\right)$ ... (ii)

For yellow, if $n = n_y$, using Eq. (i)

$P = b = (n_y - 1)\left(\frac{1}{R_1} - \frac{1}{R_2}\right)$ ... (iii)

For red, if $n = n_R$, using Eq. (i)

$P = c = (n_R - 1)\left(\frac{1}{R_1} - \frac{1}{R_2}\right)$ ... (iv)

Subtracting Eq. (iv) from Eq. (ii), we get

$a - c = (n_v - n_R)\left(\frac{1}{R_1} - \frac{1}{R_2}\right)$ ... (v)

Dividing Eq. (v) by Eq. (iii), we get

$\frac{a - c}{b} = \frac{n_v - n_R}{n_y - 1}$ ... (vi)

Dispersive power (ω) is related to n_v, n_R and n_y by the relation

$\omega = \frac{n_v - n_R}{n_y - 1}$ ...(vii)

From Eqs. (vi) and (vii), we get

$\omega = \frac{a - c}{b} = (a - c)b^{-1}$.

12. To produce no deviation, prisms should be oriented as shown, so that

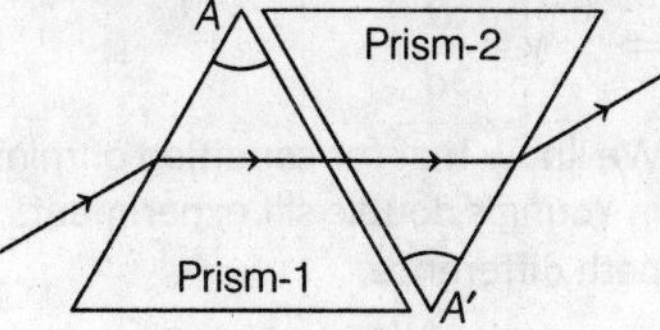

Clockwise deviation (Prism-1) = Anticlockwise deviation(Prism-2)

$\Rightarrow \quad A(\mu_y - 1) = A'(\mu_y' - 1)$

$\Rightarrow \quad 5(1.3 - 1) = A'(1.5 - 1)$

$\Rightarrow \quad A' = 3°$

$\therefore$ Statement of option (a) is correct.

Angular dispersion is given by the formula

$\theta = A(n_V - n_R)$ ... (i)

Also, dispersive power is defined as

$\omega = \frac{n_V - n_R}{n_Y - 1}$ ...(ii)

Dividing Eq. (i) by Eq. (ii), we get

$\frac{\theta}{\omega} = A(n_y - 1)$

$\Rightarrow \quad \theta = A\omega(n_y - 1)$ ... (iv)

As prims-2 is inverted it will anti-disperse while prism-1 will disperse. If θ_1 and θ_2 are dispersions of prism-1 and prism-2 respectively, net dispersion

$\theta_{net} = \theta_1 - \theta_2$

$= |A\omega(n_y - 1) - A'\omega'(n_y' - 1)|$

$= |5(0.07)(1.3 - 1) - 3(0.08)(1.5 - 1)|$

$= 0.015°$

Therefore, statement of option (b) is correct.

If the prisms are similarly, directed as shown

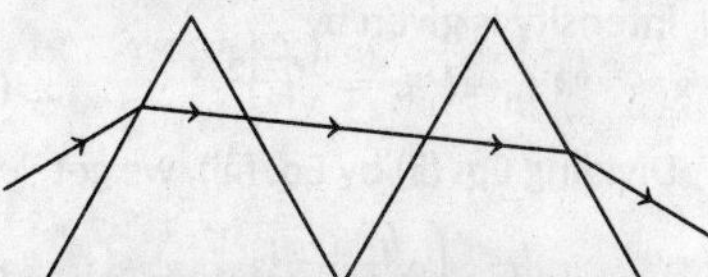

Net deviation $= \delta_{net} = \delta_1 + \delta_2$

$= A(n_y - 1) + A'(n_y' - 1)$

$= 5(1.3 - 1) + 3(1.5 - 1)$

$= 1.5 + 1.5 = 3°$

Therefore, statement of option (c) is correct. Net dispersion

$\theta_{net} = \theta_1 + \theta_2$

$= A\omega(n_y - 1) + A'\omega'(n_y' - 1)$

$= 5(0.07)(1.3 - 1) + 3(0.08)(1.5 - 1)$

$= 0.225°$

Therefore, statement of option (d) is incorrect.

13. For the objective,

$\therefore \frac{1}{v_o} - \frac{1}{-1/3.8} = \frac{1}{1/4}$

or $\quad \frac{1}{v_o} = 0.2 = \frac{1}{5}$

or $\quad v_o = 5$ cm

Now, $\quad m_o = \frac{5}{-\frac{1}{3.8}} = -19$

Total magnification,

$m = m_o \times m_e$

$-190 = -19 \times m_e$

or $\quad m_e = \frac{190}{19} = 10$

14. Consider that at every interface 25% light is reflected and 75% is transmitted. Intensities at different locations is as shown.

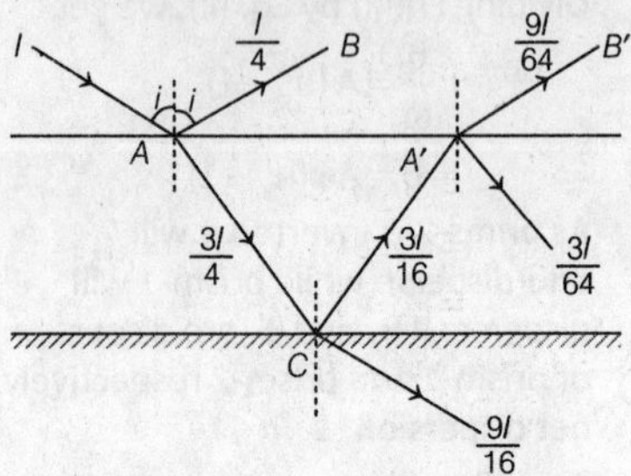

Intensities of AB and $A'B'$ will be

$$I_1 = \frac{I}{4} \text{ and } I_2 = \frac{9I}{64} \quad \text{... (i)}$$

For constructive interference, resultant intensity is given by

$$I_C = (\sqrt{I_1} + \sqrt{I_2})^2 \quad \text{... (ii)}$$

For destructive interference, resultant intensity is given by

$$I_D = (\sqrt{I_1} - \sqrt{I_2})^2 \quad \text{... (iii)}$$

Dividing Eq. (ii) by Eq. (iii), we get

$$\frac{I_C}{I_D} = \left(\frac{\sqrt{I_1} + \sqrt{I_2}}{\sqrt{I_1} - \sqrt{I_2}}\right)^2 \quad \text{... (iv)}$$

Putting values of I_1 and I_2 from Eq. (i) in Eq. (iv), we get

$$\frac{I_C}{I_D} = \left(\frac{\sqrt{\frac{I}{4}} + \sqrt{\frac{9I}{64}}}{\sqrt{\frac{I}{4}} + \sqrt{\frac{9I}{64}}}\right)^2$$

$$= \left(\frac{\sqrt{16I} + \sqrt{9I}}{\sqrt{16I} - \sqrt{9I}}\right)^2$$

$$= \left(\frac{4+3}{4-3}\right)^2 = 49$$

$$\Rightarrow \quad I_C = 49 I_D = 49 I_0 \text{ (As } I_D = I_0) \quad \text{... (v)}$$

Therefore, increase in resultant intensity is equal to

$$\Delta I = I_C - I_D = 49 I_0 - I_0 = 48 I_0$$

[using Eq. (v)]

15. Let central maxima is formed at point P at a distance y from centre O of the screen as shown.

As geometrical path difference is given by the formula $\frac{dy}{D}$. So, extra geometrical path of wave-1 compared to wave-2.

$$\Delta x = \frac{dy}{D} \quad \text{... (i)}$$

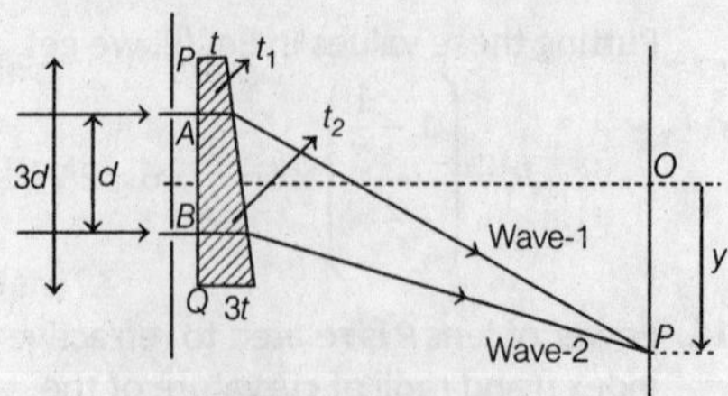

Let thickness of the film in front of slit-1 and slit-2 be t_1 and t_2, respectively. As optical path difference created by slab of thickness t and refractive index μ is given by $t(\mu - 1)$. Optical, path dfference for wave-1 is

$$\Delta x_1 = t_1(\mu - 1) \quad \text{... (ii)}$$

and for wave-2 is

$$\Delta x_2 = t_2(\mu - 1) \quad \text{...(iii)}$$

Therefore, optical path difference between the two waves is obtained by subtracting Eq. (ii) from Eq. (iii),

$$\Delta x' = \Delta x_2 - \Delta x_1 = (t_2 - t_1)(\mu - 1) \quad \text{... (iv)}$$

Also, from given geometry of the slab,

$$t_2 - t_1 = \frac{\text{Change in thickness}}{PQ} \times AB$$

$$\Rightarrow \quad t_2 - t_1 = \frac{3t - t}{3d} \times d = \frac{2t}{3} \quad \text{... (v)}$$

Using Eqs. (iv) and (v), we get

$$\Delta x' = \frac{2t}{3}\left(\frac{3}{2} - 1\right) = \frac{t}{3} \quad \text{...(vi)}$$

$$\left(\text{Given, } \mu = \frac{3}{2}\right)$$

Now, as at location of central maxima, net path difference is zero.

Extra geometrical path of wave-1

= Extra optical path of wave-2

$$\Rightarrow \quad \Delta x = \Delta x'$$

$$\Rightarrow \quad \frac{dy}{D} = \frac{t}{3} \quad \text{[using Eqs. (i) and (vi)]}$$

$$\Rightarrow \quad y = \frac{tD}{3d}$$

16. We know that for condition of minima in Young's double slit experiment, path difference,

$$\Delta x = (2n - 1)\lambda / 2$$

For first minima,

$$n = 1$$

$$\Rightarrow \quad \Delta x = \lambda / 2 \quad \text{... (i)}$$

Path difference between the rays coming from virtual sources S_1 and S_2 at point P will be

$$\Delta x = S_2P - S_1P \quad \text{... (ii)}$$

From triangle S_1S_2P,

$$S_1P = 2d \quad \text{... (iii)}$$

and $(S_2P)^2 = (S_1S_2)^2 + (S_1P)^2$

$$= d^2 + (2d)^2 = 5d^2$$

or $\quad S_2P = \sqrt{5}\, d \quad$ ...(iv)

Substituting the values from Eqs. (iii) and (iv) in Eq. (ii), we get

$$\Delta x = \sqrt{5}\, d - 2d \quad \text{...(v)}$$

From Eqs. (i) and (v), we get

$$\sqrt{5}\, d - 2d = \lambda / 2$$

$$\Rightarrow \quad d = \frac{\lambda}{2(\sqrt{5} - 2)}$$

17. Angular width of diffraction pattern, $\theta = 60°$

For first minima, $\frac{a}{2}\sin\theta = \frac{\lambda}{2}$,

$$\Rightarrow \quad \lambda = 10^{-6} \times \sin 30° = \frac{10^{-6}}{2} \text{m}$$

Now, in case of interference caused by bringing second slit,

$$\therefore \text{ Fringe width, } \beta = \frac{\lambda D}{d}$$

$$\text{So,} \quad d = \frac{\lambda D}{\beta} = \frac{10^{-6} \times 50}{2 \times \frac{1}{100} \times 100}$$

$$= 25 \times 10^{-6} \text{ m} = 25 \mu\text{m}$$

18. We can write resolving angle of naked eye as

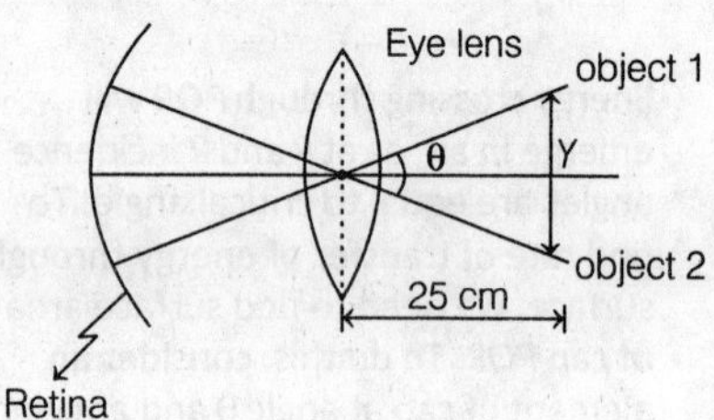

$$\theta = 1.22 \frac{\lambda}{D}$$

(where, D is the diameter of eye lens)

$$\Rightarrow \quad \frac{Y}{25 \times 10^{-2}} = \frac{1.22 \times 750 \times 10^{-9}}{0.25 \times 2 \times 10^{-2}}$$

$$\Rightarrow \quad Y = 45 \times 10^{-6} \text{ m} = 45 \mu\text{m}$$

19. The aperture (D) of the telescope is given as

$$D = \frac{1.22\,\lambda}{\theta}$$

$$= \frac{1.22 \times 5460 \times 10^{-10}}{4.6 \times 10^{-6}} = 0.1448 \text{ m}$$

20. If I_0 is intensity of unpolarised light, then from 1st Nicol prism, $I_1 = \frac{I_0}{2}$

From 2nd Nicol prism,

$$I_2 = I_1 \cos^2(90° - 60°)$$

$$= \frac{I_0}{2}\left(\frac{\sqrt{3}}{2}\right)^2 = \frac{3}{8} I_0$$

$$\Rightarrow \frac{I_2}{I_0} = 0.375 = 37.5\,\%$$

21. Consider the figure shown.

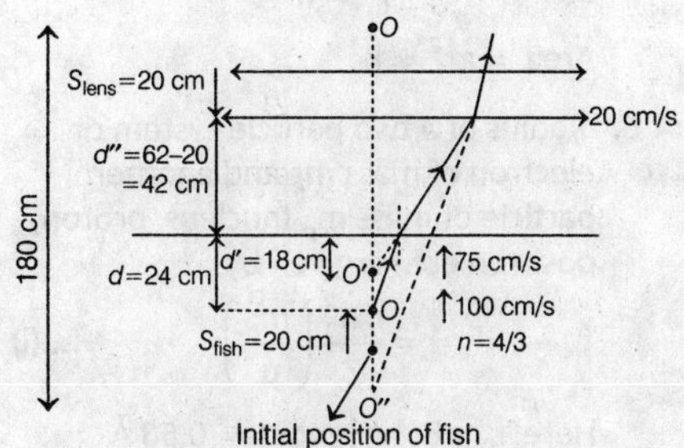

Displacement of fish in 0.2 s is

$$S_{fish} = V_{fish} \times t = 100 \times 0.2 = 20 \text{ cm}$$

So distance of fish at O from surface of water at $t = 0.2$s is

$$d = 44 - 20 = 24 \text{ cm} \quad \text{... (i)}$$

Rays coming from fish undergo refraction at surface forming image at O'. Apparent depth of fish or depth of image O' of fish can be found as

$$d' = \frac{d}{n} = \frac{24}{4/3} = 18 \text{ cm}$$

[using Eq. (i)] ...(ii)

Also, displacement of lens is given by

$$s_{lens} = ut + \frac{1}{2}at^2 = 0 + \frac{1}{2} \times 10 \times (0.2)^2$$

$$= 20 \text{ cm}$$

So, distance of lens from surface

$$d'' = 62 - 20 = 42 \text{ cm} \quad \text{...(iii)}$$

As O' is object for refraction at lens its distance from lens

$$|u| = d' + d'' = 18 + 42 = 60 \text{ cm} \quad \text{... (iv)}$$

[using Eqs. (ii) and (iii)]

So, for refraction from lens,

$$\frac{1}{v} - \frac{1}{u} = \frac{1}{f}$$

$$\Rightarrow \frac{1}{v} - \frac{1}{-60} = \frac{1}{90}$$

$$\Rightarrow v = -180 \text{ cm} \quad \text{...(v)}$$

So, final image is formed at O'' as shown.

Its magnification is given by

$$m = \frac{v}{u} = \frac{-180}{-60} = 3 \quad \text{... (vi)}$$

[using Eqs. (iv) and (v)]

Also, velocity of O' (object for lens) is given by formula for apparent velocity

$$v' = \frac{v}{n} = \frac{100}{4/3} = 75 \text{ cm/s} \quad \text{... (vii)}$$

Velocity of lens at $t = 0.2$s is

$$v_{lens} = u + at = 0 + 10 \times 0.2 = 2 \text{ m/s}$$

... (viii)

As for lens, relative velocity of object (w.r.t. lens) and image (w.r.t. lens) are related as

$$v_{il} = + m^2 v_{ol}$$

$$\Rightarrow v_i - v_l = + m^2(v_o - v_l)$$

$$\Rightarrow v_i = (1 - m^2)v_l + m^2 v_o$$

$$= (1 - 3^2)(-2) + 3^2(+0.75) = 22.75 \text{ m/s}$$

Therefore, velocity of fish's image w.r.t, observer

$$= 22.75 - (-2.5) = 25.25 \text{ m/s}$$

22. According to Fermat's principle, when a ray going from P to Q i.e. from one medium to the other, it takes the least time path for which Snell's law is satisfied. i.e.

$$\frac{v_1}{\sin\theta_1} = \frac{v_2}{\sin\theta_2} \quad \text{... (i)}$$

Therefore, for the boy, $\frac{4}{\sin\theta_1} = \frac{3}{6/10}$

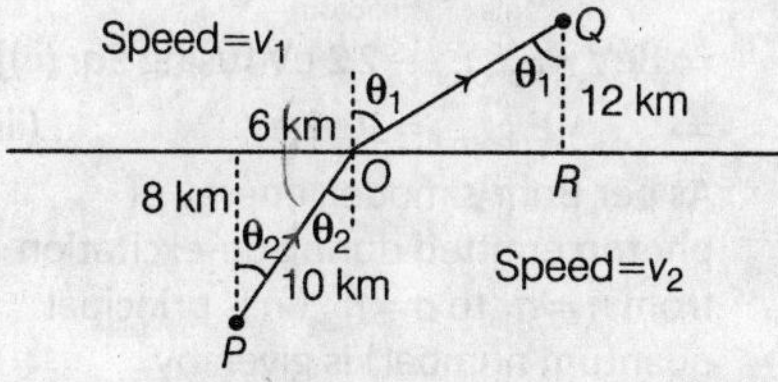

$$\Rightarrow \sin\theta_1 = \frac{4}{5}$$

$$\Rightarrow \theta_1 = 53°$$

$\Rightarrow$ In ΔOQR,

$$OQ = 12 \sec 53° = 20 \text{ km}$$

Therefore, time of motion from P to Q is

$$\frac{OQ}{v_1} + \frac{OP}{v_2} = \frac{20}{4} + \frac{10}{3} = 8.33 \text{ h}$$

23. Given, $R = 10$ cm

Applying Snell's law, $\frac{\sin\theta}{\sin r} = \frac{3}{4} \Rightarrow r = 53°$

By Sine law in ΔABC,

$$\frac{\sin(r - \theta)}{10} = \frac{\sin(\pi - r)}{(10 + x)}$$

$$\frac{10 + x}{10} = \frac{4}{5(\sin r \cos\theta - \cos r \sin\theta)}$$

$$= \frac{4}{5\left(\frac{4}{5} \times \frac{4}{5} - \frac{3}{5} \times \frac{3}{5}\right)}$$

$$10 + x = \frac{200}{7} \Rightarrow x = \frac{200 - 70}{7} = 18.57$$

24. The number of fringes on either side of C of screen is

$$n_1 = \left[\frac{AC}{\beta}\right] = \left[\frac{0.5}{0.021}\right] = [23.8] \approx 24$$

Total number of fringes

$$= 2n_1 + \text{Fringe at centre}$$
$$= 2n_1 + 1$$
$$= 2 \times 24 + 1$$
$$= 48 + 1 = 49$$

25. By Snell's law, at surface-1

$$1 \cdot \sin 45° = \sqrt{2} \cdot \sin r_1$$

$$\Rightarrow r_1 = 30° \quad \text{...(i)}$$

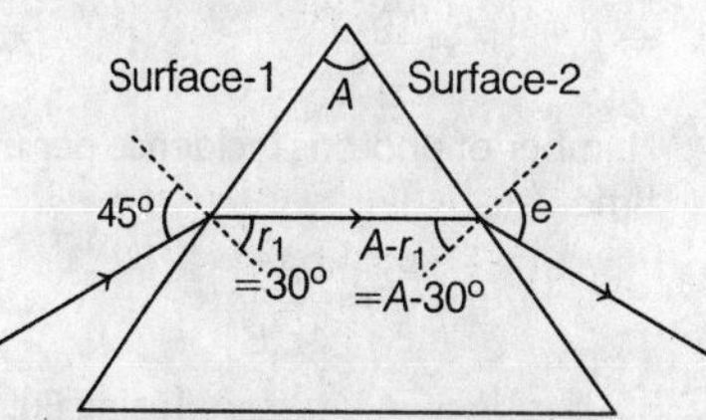

Angle of incidence at surface -2 will be

$$r_2 = A - r_1 = A - 30°$$

[using Eq. (i)] ...(ii)

For refraction at surface -2, by Snell's law

$$1 \cdot \sin e = \sqrt{2}\sin(A - 30°) \quad \text{... (iii)}$$

Differentiating both sides w.r.t. t, we get

$$\Rightarrow \cos e \frac{de}{dt} = \sqrt{2}\cos(A - 30°)\frac{dA}{dt}$$

$$\Rightarrow \frac{de}{dt} = \frac{\sqrt{2}\cos(A - 30°)\frac{dA}{dt}}{\cos e} \quad \text{... (iv)}$$

Also, for $A = 60°$, using Eq. (iii),

$$\sin e = \sqrt{2}\sin(60° - 30°) = \frac{1}{\sqrt{2}}$$

$$\Rightarrow e = 45° \quad \text{... (v)}$$

As $\frac{dA}{dt} = -3$ rad/s (Given) ... (vi)

Put values in Eq. (iv) from Eqs. (v) and (vi), we get

$$\frac{de}{dt} = \frac{\sqrt{2}\cos(60° - 30°)(-3)}{\cos 45°}$$

$$= -3\sqrt{3} \text{ rad/s} \quad \text{... (vii)}$$

Now, deviation,

$$\delta = i + e - A$$
$$= 45° + e - A$$

Differentiating w.r.t. time, we get

$$\frac{d\delta}{dt} = \frac{de}{dt} - \frac{dA}{dt} = (-3\sqrt{3}) - (-3)$$
$$= -3(\sqrt{3} - 1)$$
$$= -2.19 \text{ rad/s}$$

[using Eqs. (vi) and (vii)]

Qualifier 16 Modern Physics (Dual Nature of Matter and Radiation & Atoms and Nuclei)

1. Intensity of light from source at location of sphere,

$$I = \frac{P}{4\pi r^2} \quad \text{...(i)}$$

Power received by sphere,

$$P' = I \times \text{Projected Area}$$

$$\Rightarrow \quad P' = \frac{P}{4\pi r^2} \times \pi R^2 \quad \text{[using Eq. (i)]}$$

$$\Rightarrow \quad P' = \frac{PR^2}{4r^2} \quad \text{...(ii)}$$

Number of photons incidence per unit time

$$n = \frac{P'}{E} = \frac{PR^2}{4r^2E} \quad \text{...(iii)}$$

[using Eq. (ii)]

As efficiency is $\frac{1}{\eta}$, so number of photoelectrons emitted per unit time

$$N = \frac{n}{\eta} = \frac{PR^2}{4r^2E\eta} \quad \text{...(iv)}$$

Thus, positive charge acquired by sphere after time t,

$$Q = Net = \frac{PR^2et}{4r^2E\eta} \quad \text{...(v)}$$

[using Eq. (iv)]

When potential due to the charge becomes equal to stopping potential, emission stops, i.e.

$$V_{sphere} = V_{stopping} \Rightarrow \frac{kQ}{R} = \frac{E - \phi}{e}$$

($\because$ By Einstein's equation, $V_{stopping} = \frac{E-\phi}{e}$)

$$\Rightarrow \quad \frac{kPR^2et}{4r^2E\eta R} = \frac{E-\phi}{e} \quad \text{[using Eq. (v)]}$$

$$\Rightarrow \quad E - \phi = \frac{kPRe^2t}{4\eta Er^2}$$

2. As stopping potential from the diagram is least for *r*, so its work function will be highest while it will be least for *p*.

As saturation photocurrents are different for the three metals despite same beams being incident on the three metals the only possibility is beam of wavelength 3λ (having least energy photon) must be able to eject electrons only from least work function metal (*r*). While beam of wavelength 2λ must have ejected electrons from *q* and *p*. Beam of wavelength λ (having highest energy photon) must have ejected electrons from all three metals.

3. The curves given in List II are empirical curves for photoelectric effect experiment.

So, correct match is A $\rightarrow$ 3, B $\rightarrow$ 4, C $\rightarrow$ 1, D $\rightarrow$ 2

4. de Broglie or matter wavelength (in Å) of electron is given by

$$\lambda = \sqrt{\frac{150}{K}} \quad \text{...(i)}$$

Here, *K* is kinetic energy of electron in eV.

It is given that, $\lambda_{minimum} = \frac{5\sqrt{3}}{2}$ Å

or $\quad \lambda \geq \frac{5\sqrt{3}}{2}$ Å $\Rightarrow \sqrt{\frac{150}{K}} \geq \frac{5\sqrt{3}}{2}$ [using Eq. (i)]

$$\Rightarrow \quad K \leq 8 \text{ eV}$$

Maximum kinetic energy of photoelectrons,

$$K_{max} = 8 \text{ eV} \quad \text{...(ii)}$$

Now, by Einstein's equation,

$$K_{max} = E_{photon} - \phi$$

$$\Rightarrow 8\text{eV} = E_{photon} - 2.2 \text{ eV} \quad \text{[using Eq. (ii)]}$$

$$\Rightarrow \quad E_{photon} = 10.2 \text{ eV} \quad \text{...(iii)}$$

As per Bohr's model, energy of photon emitted during de-excitation from $n = n_1$ to $n = n_2$ (*n* is principal quantum number) is given by

$$E_{photon} = 13.6\, Z^2\left(\frac{1}{n_2^2} - \frac{1}{n_1^2}\right) \quad \text{...(iv)}$$

Putting the given values of $n_1 = Z + 4$; $n_2 = Z$ and E_{photon} in Eq. (iv), we get

$$10.2 = 13.6\, Z^2\left(\frac{1}{Z^2} - \frac{1}{(Z+4)^2}\right)$$

$$\Rightarrow \quad 10.2 = 13.6\left(1 - \frac{Z^2}{(Z+4)^2}\right)$$

$$\left(\frac{Z}{Z+4}\right)^2 = \frac{3.4}{13.6} \Rightarrow \frac{Z+4}{Z} = 2$$

$$\Rightarrow \quad Z = 4$$

$\therefore$ Gas sample corresponds to Be^{3+} ions.

5. Given that, $U = kr^2$

$$\Rightarrow \quad |F| = \left|-\frac{dU}{dr}\right| = 2kr \quad \text{...(i)}$$

As this force provides necessary centripetal force $|F| = \frac{mv^2}{r}$

$$\Rightarrow \quad 2kr = \frac{mv^2}{r} \quad \text{[using Eq. (i)]}$$

$$\Rightarrow \quad r = \sqrt{\frac{m}{2k}}\, v \quad \text{...(ii)}$$

By Bohr's quantisation rule,

$$mvr = \frac{nh}{2\pi}$$

$$\Rightarrow \quad m\frac{r\,r}{\sqrt{\frac{m}{2k}}} = \frac{nh}{2\pi} \quad \text{[using Eq. (ii)]}$$

$$\Rightarrow \quad r^2 \propto n$$

$$\text{Area} = \pi r^2 \propto n$$

6. Radius of a two particle system of electron of mass m_e and another particle of mass m_p (nucleus, proton, positron etc.) is given by

$$r = \frac{r_0 n^2}{Z}\left(\frac{m_e}{\mu}\right) \quad \text{...(i)}$$

Here, r_0 = Bohr's radius= 0.53 Å

μ = Reduced mass of the system

$$= \frac{m_e m_p}{m_e + m_p} = \frac{m_e \times m_e}{m_e + m_e} = \frac{m_e}{2}$$

(As positron has same mass as that of electron)

For positronium in first excited state,

$$n = 2 \text{ and } Z = 1$$

Putting these values in Eq. (i), we get

$$r = \frac{r_0 2^2}{1}\left(\frac{m_e}{m_e/2}\right) = 8r_0$$

7. As radius of nucleus, $R \propto A^{\frac{1}{3}}$

$$\Rightarrow \quad \frac{R_{Ge}}{R_{Be}} = \left(\frac{X}{9}\right)^{\frac{1}{3}}$$

$$\Rightarrow \quad 2 = \left(\frac{X}{9}\right)^{\frac{1}{3}} \Rightarrow X = 72$$

$\therefore$ Number of neutrons $= 72 - 32 = 40$

8. Energy of an electron

$$= \frac{E}{n^2} = \frac{-2.18 \times 10^{-18}}{n^2} \text{ J}$$

Hence, energy associated with the fifth orbit of hydrogen atom,

$$E_5 = -\frac{2.18 \times 10^{-18}}{(5)^2} = -8.72 \times 10^{-20} \text{ J}$$

As, radius of Bohr's *n*th orbit for hydrogen atom is given by

$$r_n = 0.053\, n^2$$

For $n = 5$, $r_5 = 0.053\,(5)^2 = 1.32$ nm

9. As wavelength λ emitted in any transition is inversely proportional to reduced/effective mass μ of the system,

$$\lambda = \frac{k}{\mu} \quad \text{...(i)}$$

(Here, k is proportionality constant)

Reduced mass of two particle system of m_1 and m_2 is given by

$$\mu = \frac{m_1 m_2}{m_1 + m_2} \quad \text{...(ii)}$$

If mass of electron is assumed m, then mass of proton is approximately 1836 times m. So, reduced mass of hydrogen is

$$\mu_H = \frac{m(1836\,m)}{m + 1836\,m} = \frac{1836}{1837} m \quad \text{...(iii)}$$

[using Eq. (ii)]

As, mass of neutron is also approximately equal to m, so reduced mass of deuterium will be

$$\mu_D = \frac{m(2 \times 1836\,m)}{m + 2 \times 1836\,m} = \frac{1836}{1836.5} m \quad \text{...(iv)}$$

Differentiating Eq. (i) w.r.t μ, we get

$$\frac{d\lambda}{d\mu} = \frac{-k}{\mu^2} \quad \text{...(v)}$$

Dividing Eq. (v) by Eq. (i)

$$\frac{d\lambda}{\lambda} = -\frac{d\mu}{\mu}$$

$$\Rightarrow \quad |d\lambda| = \frac{d\mu}{\mu} \times \lambda = \frac{\mu_D - \mu_H}{\mu_H} \times \lambda$$

$$\Rightarrow \quad \Delta\lambda = \left(\frac{\mu_D}{\mu_H} - 1\right)\lambda \quad \text{...(vi)}$$

As for any transition from n_2 to n_1

$$\text{Wavelength emitted, } \lambda = \frac{912\,\text{Å}}{\frac{1}{n_1^2} - \frac{1}{n_2^2}}$$

For first line of Lyman's series ($n_1 = 1$, $n_2 = 2$), we get

$$\lambda = \frac{912\,\text{Å}}{\frac{1}{1^2} - \frac{1}{2^2}} = 1216\,\text{Å} \quad \text{...(vii)}$$

Putting values of μ_H, μ_D and λ from Eqs. (iii), (iv) and (vii) in Eq. (vi), we get

$$\Delta\lambda = \left(\frac{1837}{1836.5} - 1\right)(1216\,\text{Å})$$

$$= 0.33\,\text{Å} = 33\,\text{pm}$$

10. If angle of **L** with **B** is assumed θ, angle between μ and **B** will be 5θ.

As **L** and μ are opposite, therefore

$$\theta + 5\theta = 180°$$

$$\Rightarrow \quad \theta = 30° \quad \text{...(i)}$$

Gyromagnetic ratio of a current carrying loop or atom is given by

$$\frac{\mu}{L} = \frac{q}{2m}$$

$$\Rightarrow \quad \mu = \frac{q}{2m} \times L$$

So, for electron in first orbit of Bohr's atom

$$\mu = \frac{e}{2m} \times \frac{h}{2\pi} = \frac{eh}{4\pi m} \quad \text{...(ii)}$$

As, magnetic torque is given by

$$\tau = \mu B \sin\theta = \frac{eh}{4\pi m} B \sin 30°$$

[using Eqs. (i) and (ii)]

$$= \frac{ehB}{8\pi m}$$

11. The moment and kinetic energies of the particles before and after collision are shown below.

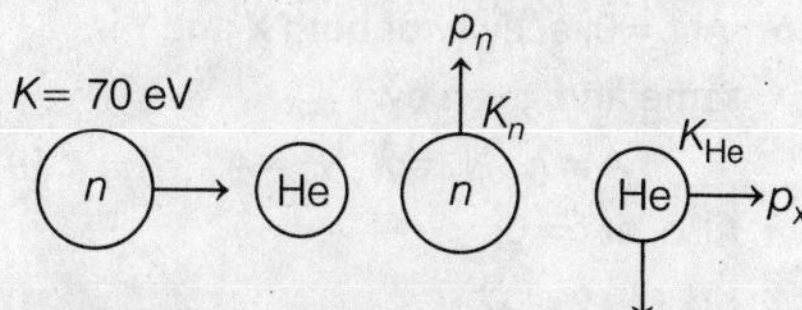

Just before collision **Just after collision**

Also, assume $m_{He} = 4m_n = 4m$

By conservation of momentum in x-direction

$$p_x = \sqrt{2mK}$$

By conservation of momentum in y-direction

$$p_y = p_n = \sqrt{2mK_n}$$

Also,

$$K_{He} = \frac{p_{He}^2}{2m_{He}} = \frac{p_x^2 + p_y^2}{2m_{He}}$$

$$= \frac{2mK + 2mK_n}{2(4m)}$$

$$\Rightarrow 4K_{He} - K_n = K = 70\,\text{eV} \quad \text{...(i)}$$

Now, energy in atomic inelastic collisions is lost due to excitation/ionisation. It is given that electron in He^+ is excited to third excited state ($n = 4$). So, energy spent in this process is equal to energy loss in collision.

$$E = 13.6 \times 2^2\left(1 - \frac{1}{4^2}\right) = 51\,\text{eV} \quad \text{...(ii)}$$

In terms of kinetic energies loss E can be written as

$$K - (K_{He} + K_n) = E$$

$$\Rightarrow \quad K_{He} + K_n = K - E$$

$$= 70 - 51 = 19\,\text{eV} \quad \text{...(iii)}$$

[using Eq. (ii)]

Solving Eqs. (i) and (ii), we get

$$K_{He} = 17.8\,\text{eV and } K_n = 1.2\,\text{eV}$$

Also, maximum number of different wavelengths emitted in de-excitation from nth orbit to ground state

$$= \frac{n(n-1)}{2} = \frac{4(4-1)}{2} = 6$$

12. Wavelength emitted in transition from n_2 to n_1,

$$\lambda = \frac{1}{Rz^2\left(\frac{1}{n_1^2} - \frac{1}{n_2^2}\right)} \quad \text{...(i)}$$

For series limit of Balmer series in H-spectrum $n_1 = 2$ and $n_2 = \infty$ and $z = 1$

$$\Rightarrow \quad \lambda_0 = \frac{1}{R\left(\frac{1}{2^2} - \frac{1}{\infty}\right)} = \frac{4}{R}$$

[using Eq. (i)] ...(ii)

For sixth line of Paschen series in Li^{2+}; $n_1 = 3, n_2 = 9$ and $z = 3$

$$\Rightarrow \quad \lambda = \frac{1}{R \cdot 3^2\left(\frac{1}{3^2} - \frac{1}{9^2}\right)} = \frac{9}{8R}$$

[using Eq. (i)] ...(iii)

Dividing Eq. (iii) by Eq. (ii), we get

$$\frac{\lambda}{\lambda_0} = \frac{9}{32} \Rightarrow \lambda = \frac{9\lambda_0}{32}$$

13. Option (a) For de-excitation from $n = n_2$ to $n = n_1$, wavelength of photon emitted is given by

$$\lambda = \frac{912\,\text{Å}}{z^2\left(\frac{1}{n_1^2} - \frac{1}{n_2^2}\right)} \quad \text{...(i)}$$

For transition A, $n_2 = \infty$, $n_1 = 1$, therefore

$$\lambda = \frac{912\text{Å}}{z^2\left(\frac{1}{1^2} - \frac{1}{\infty^2}\right)} = \frac{912\text{Å}}{z^2}$$

$\Rightarrow$ For $Z \geq 1, \lambda \leq 912$ Å. Therefore, photon cannot be an infrared photon.

Option (b) As per quantisation rule, angular momentum, $L = \frac{nh}{2\pi}$

As in transition B, n decreases from 5 to 2,

$$L_1 = \frac{5h}{2\pi} \text{ and } L_2 = \frac{2h}{2\pi}$$

$$\Delta L = \frac{3h}{2\pi}$$

$\therefore$ Percentage change in

$$\Delta L = \frac{\Delta L}{L_1} \times 100 = \frac{3h/2\pi}{5h/2\pi} \times 100$$

$$= \frac{300}{5}\% = 60\%$$

Option (c) If energy gap corresponding to D (between $n=2$ and $n=4$) is in visible region, definitely energy gap corresponding to C (between $n=5$ to $n=3$) being even lesser, cannot be in ultraviolet region.

Option (d) For C (n decreases from 5 to 3)

$$\therefore \quad \lambda_C = \frac{912 \text{ Å}}{\frac{1}{3^2} - \frac{1}{5^2}} = \frac{912 \text{ Å}}{\frac{16}{225}} \quad \text{[using (i)] ...(ii)}$$

For D (n increases from 2 to 4)

$$\therefore \quad \lambda_D = \frac{912 \text{ Å}}{\frac{1}{2^2} - \frac{1}{4^2}} = \frac{912 \text{ Å}}{\left(\frac{3}{16}\right)} \quad \text{...(iii)}$$

Dividing Eq. (ii) by Eq. (iii), we get

$$\frac{\lambda_C}{\lambda_D} = \frac{225}{16} \times \frac{3}{16} = 2.63$$

$\therefore$ Photon emitted in C has more than double the wavelength of the photon absorbed in D.

14. Various X-ray photons correspond to the transitions are shown below.

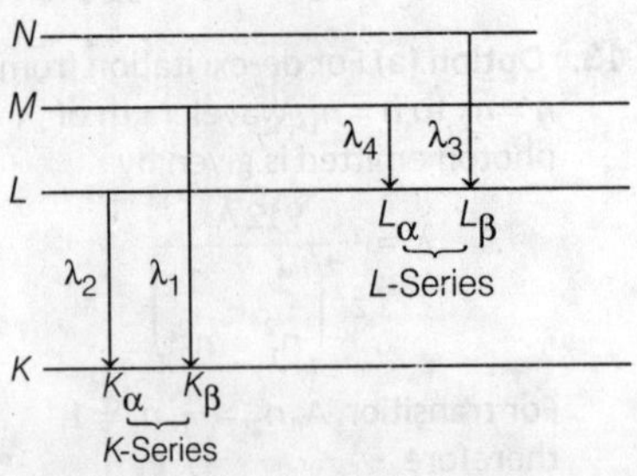

As K series photons have greater energies as clear from energy level diagram, so they have lesser wavelengths. Therefore, X-series corresponds to K-series and Y-series corresponds to L-series. Also, K_β has higher energy and so lesser wavelength. Also, from diagram,

$$E_{L_\alpha} = E_{k_\beta} - E_{k_\alpha}$$

$$\Rightarrow \frac{hc}{\lambda_4} = \frac{hc}{\lambda_1} - \frac{hc}{\lambda_2}$$

$$\Rightarrow \lambda_4 = \frac{\lambda_1\lambda_2}{\lambda_2 - \lambda_1}$$

Also, cut-off wavelength,

$$\lambda_0 = \frac{hc}{eV}$$

$$\Rightarrow V = \frac{hc}{e\lambda_0}$$

15. The standing waves formed by the electron are as shown below.

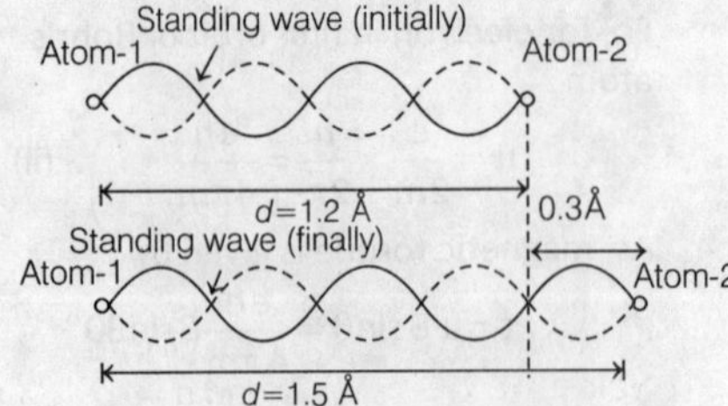

In subsequent loop there will be one more loop as shown in the figures. Clearly, from the diagram size of one loop is 0.3 Å. So in the basic mode of standing wave formation, distance between atoms should atleast be 0.3 Å.

16. At $t=0$, activity of both X and Y is same and given by

$$A = \lambda_x N_x = \lambda_y N_y = A_0 \quad \text{...(i)}$$

Also, at $t=0$,

$$\lambda_x N_y = \frac{\lambda_x}{\lambda_y} \cdot N_y \lambda_y$$

$$= \frac{\lambda}{2\lambda} \cdot A_0 = \frac{A_0}{2} \quad \text{...(ii)}$$

[using Eq. (i)]

From the relation given in problem,

$$\lambda_y N_y = \lambda_x N_x + \lambda_x N_y + Ce^{-\lambda_y t} \quad \text{...(iii)}$$

For $t=0$, putting values from Eqs. (i) and (ii) in Eq. (iii), we get

$$A_0 = A_0 + \frac{A_0}{2} + C$$

$$\Rightarrow \quad C = -\frac{A_0}{2}$$

Thus, putting $\lambda_x = \lambda, \lambda_y = 2\lambda$ and $C = -\frac{A_0}{2}$ in Eq. (iii), we get

$$N_y = \frac{A_0}{2\lambda}(2e^{-\lambda t} - e^{-2\lambda t})$$

17. Given, $\frac{N_B}{N_A} = 0.3 = \frac{3}{10} = \frac{30}{100}$

So, $N_0 = 100 + 30 = 130$ atoms

By using $N = N_0 e^{-\lambda t}$, we have

$$100 = 130e^{-\lambda t} \Rightarrow \frac{1}{1.3} = e^{-\lambda t}$$

Taking log of both sides, we get

$$\Rightarrow \quad \log_e 1.3 = \lambda t \quad \text{...(i)}$$

If T is half-life, then $\lambda = \frac{\log_e 2}{T}$

$$\Rightarrow \log_e 1.3 = \frac{\log_e 2}{T} \cdot t \quad \text{[using Eq. (i)]}$$

$$\therefore \quad t = \frac{T \cdot \log_e(1.3)}{\log_e 2}$$

18. The decay processes can be shown as

$$\underset{\text{Radioactive}}{P} \xrightarrow{\lambda} \underset{\text{(Stable)}}{R} \xleftarrow{\lambda} \underset{\text{(Radioactive)}}{Q} \xrightarrow{2\lambda} \underset{\text{(Stable)}}{S}$$

$t=0$	N_0	0	N_0	0
$t=t$	N_P	N_R	N_Q	N_S

Number of nuclei decayed,

$$N' = N_0(1 - e^{-\lambda t}) \quad \text{...(i)}$$

As Q is simultaneously decaying into R and S, effective decay constant,

$$\lambda_{\text{effective}} = \lambda + 2\lambda$$

Using Eq. (i), we get

$$\text{and} \quad N'_Q = N_0(1 - e^{-3\lambda t}) \quad \text{...(ii)}$$

Also, ratio of nuclei of Q decayed into R and S are in same ratio as respective decay constants 1 : 2.

Therefore, number of nuclei of S,

$$N_s = \frac{2}{3}N'_Q = \frac{2N_0}{3}(1 - e^{-3\lambda t}) \quad \text{...(iii)}$$

[using Eq. (ii)]

and number of nuclei of R produced by disintegration of

$$Q = \frac{N_Q'}{3} = \frac{N_0}{3}(1 - e^{-3\lambda t}) \quad \text{...(iv)}$$

[using Eq. (ii)]

Also, number of nuclei of R produced by disintegration of

$$P = N_p' = N_0(1 - e^{-\lambda t}) \quad \text{...(v)}$$

Thus, total number of nuclei of R produced can be obtained by adding Eqs. (iv) and (v).

$$\therefore \quad N_R = \frac{N_0}{3}(1 - e^{-3\lambda t}) + N_0(1 - e^{-\lambda t})$$

$$= N_0\left(\frac{4}{3} - e^{-\lambda t} - \frac{e^{-3\lambda t}}{3}\right)$$

19. Reaction under consideration is

$${}_1^2\text{H} + {}_1^2\text{H} \longrightarrow {}_2^4\text{He} + Q$$

Here, $BE_H = 1.1$ MeV and

$BE_{He} = 7$ MeV

As Q value $= \Sigma BE_{\text{products}} - \Sigma BE_{\text{reactants}}$

$$Q = 4 \times 7 - (2 \times 1.1 + 2 \times 1.1)$$
$$= 23.6 \text{ MeV}$$
$$= 23.6 \times 10^6 \times 1.6 \times 10^{-19} \text{ J}$$
$$= 37.76 \times 10^{-13} \text{ J}$$

20. Decay can be represented as

$${}_{11}^{22}\text{Na} \longrightarrow {}_{10}^{22}\text{Ne} + {}_b^aX + {}_0^0\nu$$

From above equation, we get

$$a = 0, b = 1$$

So, the unknown particle is positron or β^+ and the decay is β^+ decay.

Mass of Na nucleus,

$$m = m_1 - 11m_e \quad ...(i)$$

Mass of products,

$$m' = m_{Ne_{nucleus}} + m_x + m_v$$
$$= (m_2 - 10m_e) + m_e + 0$$
$$= m_2 - 9m_e \quad ...(ii)$$

Mass lost/defect, $\Delta m = m - m'$

$$= (m_1 - 11m_e) - (m_2 - 9m_e)$$
[from Eqs. (i) and (ii)]
$$= m_1 - m_2 - 2m_e$$

$\therefore$ Q-value $= \Delta mc^2 = (m_1 - m_2 - 2m_e)c^2$

21. From Einstein's photoelectric equation, $KE = \frac{hc}{\lambda} - \phi$

For case I, $\frac{1}{2}mv_1^2 = 4 - \phi \quad ...(i)$

For case II, $\frac{1}{2}mv_2^2 = 2.5 - \phi \quad ...(ii)$

Given, $\frac{v_1}{v_2} = 2$

Dividing Eq. (i) by Eq. (ii), we get

$$\frac{v_1^2}{v_2^2} = \frac{4-\phi}{2.5-\phi}$$

$$\Rightarrow \quad (2)^2 = \frac{4-\phi}{2.5-\phi}$$

$$\Rightarrow \quad \phi = \frac{6}{3} = 2 \text{ eV}$$

22. Frequency of revolution of electron,

$$f = \frac{v}{2\pi r} = \frac{v_0 \frac{Z}{n}}{2\pi r_0 \frac{n^2}{Z}} = \frac{v_0 Z^2}{2\pi r_0 n^3} \quad ...(i)$$

Number of revolutions in time t will be

$$N = ft = \frac{v_0 Z^2 t}{2\pi r_0 n^3} \quad \text{[using Eq. (i)]} ...(ii)$$

As we know, Bohr's radius

$r_0 = 0.53 \text{ Å} = 0.53 \times 10^{-10}$ m

v_0 = Bohr's speed $= 2.2 \times 10^6$ m/s

Putting these values in Eq. (ii), we get

$$N = \frac{2.2 \times 10^6 \times 1^2 \times 10^{-8}}{2 \times 3.14 \times 0.53 \times 10^{-10} \times 2^3}$$

$$\approx 8 \times 10^6.$$

Comparing with given value, we get $x = 6$

23. As per the equation of Moseley's law, $\sqrt{f} = a(Z - b)$

Here, $b = 1$ for k_α X-ray,

$\Rightarrow \quad f \propto (Z-1)^2$

so, for given metals,

$$\frac{f_{La}}{f_{Cu}} = \left(\frac{Z_{La}-1}{Z_{Cu}-1}\right)^2$$

or $\quad f_{La} = f_{Cu}\left(\frac{Z_{La}-1}{Z_{Cu}-1}\right)^2$

$$= 1.88 \times 10^{18}\left(\frac{57-1}{29-1}\right)^2$$

$$= 7.52 \times 10^{18} \text{ Hz}$$

Comparing this value with given value, we get $m = 7.52$ and $n = 18$

$\Rightarrow \quad n - m = 10.48$

Greatest integral value of $n - m$ is 10.

24. As ratio of Ar atoms to K atoms is 7 : 1, lets assume number of respective atoms equal to $7x$ and x. If N_0 is initial number of K atoms, by conservation principle,

$$x + 7x = N_0$$

$$\Rightarrow \quad x = \frac{N_0}{8} = \frac{N_0}{2^3} \quad ...(i)$$

In general, number of nuclei of a radioactive sample after n half lives is

$$N = \frac{N_0}{2^n} \quad ...(ii)$$

Comparing Eqs. (i) and (ii), we get

$$n = 3$$

Therefore, age of the rock = 3 half-lives

$= 3 \times 1.25 \times 10^9$ yrs. $= 3.75$ billion yrs.

25. When 1 ng of antimatter annihilates 1 ng of matter, a total of 2 ng is converted into energy thereby producing energy equal to

$E = mc^2$ (from Einstein's equation)

$\Rightarrow E = (2 \times 10^{-12})(3 \times 10^8)^2 = 18 \times 10^4$ J

If energy E is used to lift mass m, E should be equal to increase in potential energy of m. Therefore

$$E = mgh$$

$$\Rightarrow m = \frac{E}{gh} = \frac{18 \times 10^4}{10 \times 10^3} = 18 \text{ kg}$$

Qualifier 17 (Electronic Devices)

1. At $T > 0$ K as some electrons are part of covalent bond they are in VB while some electrons are free and are part of CB. So, both VB and CB are partially filled.

Also, due to doping an extra energy level having energy slightly greater than highest energy level of VB (0.01 eV to 0.05 eV) is created corresponding to energy of holes contributed by the acceptor atoms.

2. Current I through diode as function of voltage is given by

$$I = I_s\left[\exp\left(\frac{eV}{2kT}\right) - 1\right] \quad ...(i)$$

$$\frac{dI}{dV} = \frac{I_s e}{2kT}\exp\left(\frac{eV}{2kT}\right) \quad ...(ii)$$

Dividing Eq. (ii) by Eq. (i), we get (for $V \to \infty$)

$$\frac{dI}{IdV} = \frac{e}{2kT} \Rightarrow dI = \left(\frac{e \cdot dV}{2kT}\right)I$$

3. Number density of electrons ≈ Number density of donor impurity

$\Rightarrow n_e = n_D = 2$ ppm

$$= 2 \times 5 \times 10^{28} \times 10^{-6} \text{ m}^{-3}$$
$$= 10^{23} \text{ m}^{-3}$$

As per law of mass action, number density of holes, $n_h = n_i^2 / n_e$

$$= \frac{(1.6 \times 10^{16})^2}{10^{23}} = 2.56 \times 10^9 \text{ m}^{-3}$$

4. On closing key k_1, the circuit will be as shown in figure. As D_3 is reverse biased, current passes through D_1.

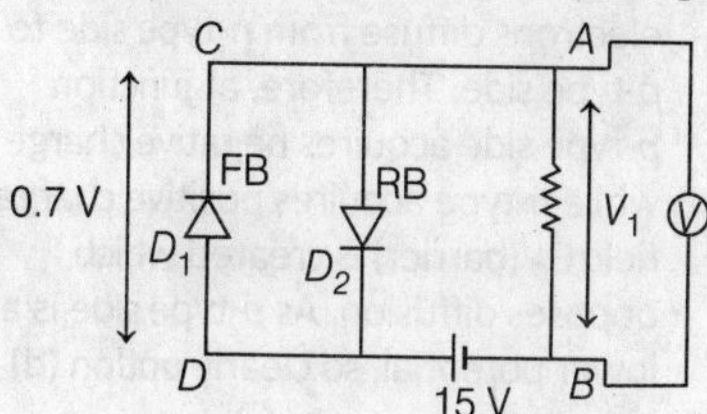

So, $\quad V_1 = 15 - 0.7 = 14.3$V $\quad ...(i)$

On closing K_2, the circuit will be as shown

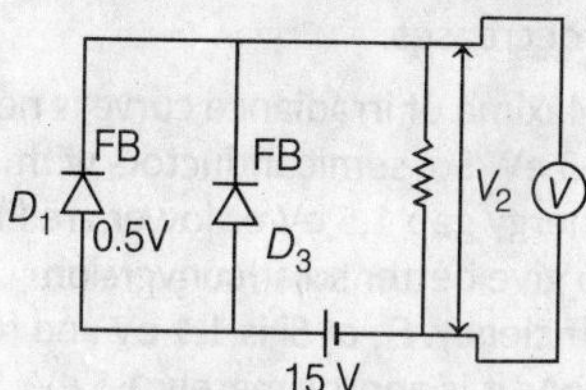

As D_3 has lesser barrier, current will pass through it. So,

$$V_2 = 15 - 0.5 = 14.5 \text{ V} \quad ...(ii)$$

From Eqs. (i) and (ii), we get

$$V_2 - V_1 = 0.2\text{V}$$

5. Conductivity of an intrinsic/pure semiconductor is $\sigma = en_i(\mu_e + \mu_h)$

$$\Rightarrow \sigma = 1.6 \times 10^{-19} \times 2.5 \times 10^{19} (0.4 + 0.2)$$

$$\Rightarrow \sigma = 2.4 \ \Omega^{-1}\text{m}^{-1} \quad ...(i)$$

Resistance of a straight conductor between ends,

$$R = \frac{l}{\sigma A} \quad \text{[using Eq. (i)]}$$

$$\Rightarrow R = \frac{6 \times 10^{-3}}{2.4 \times 2 \times 10^{-6}}$$

$$= 1.25 \times 10^3 \ \Omega$$

$$= 1.25 \text{k}\Omega$$

6. Intrinsic charge carrier density at temperature T is given by

$$n_i = n_0\, e^{-\frac{E_g}{2kT}} \quad \text{...(i)}$$

where, n_0 is a constant.

On doubling temperature, it will change to

$$n_i' = n_0 e^{-\frac{E_g}{4kT}} \quad \text{...(ii)}$$

Dividing Eq. (ii) by Eq. (i), equal to

$$\frac{n_i'}{n_i} = \frac{e^{-\frac{E_g}{4kT}}}{e^{-\frac{E_g}{2kT}}} = e^{\frac{E_g}{4kT}}$$

As, conductivity is proportional to n_i, so it will also increase by same factor.

7. When a *p-n* junction is fabricated holes diffuse from *p*-type side (where they are in majority) to *n*-type side (to region of lower concentration). Likewise, free electrons diffuse from *n*-type side to *p*-type side. Therefore, at junction *p*-type side acquires negative charge while *n*-type acquires positive charge. A field E_b (barrier) is created which opposes diffusion. As *p*-type side is at lower potential, so clearly option (d) is incorrect.

8. On decreasing temperature of semiconductor (silicon) resistivity increases while for metal (aluminium) it decreases.

9. Maxima of irradiance curve is near 1.5 eV. So, semiconductors with energy gap 1.5 eV or lower are likely to give better solar conversion efficiency. E_g of Si is 1.1 eV and for GaAs it is approximately 1.5 eV.

10. In this case, $E \geq E_g$

$$\Rightarrow \quad \frac{hc}{\lambda} \geq E_g \Rightarrow \lambda \leq \frac{hc}{E_g}$$

As $hc = 12400$ eV-Å and E_g is given 2 eV, we get

$$\lambda \leq \frac{12400}{2} \Rightarrow \lambda \leq 6200\ \text{Å}$$

$$\Rightarrow \quad \lambda_{max} = 620\ \text{nm}$$

11. The arrangement is a combination of full wave bridge rectifier followed by centre tap full wave rectifier.

So, output is given as

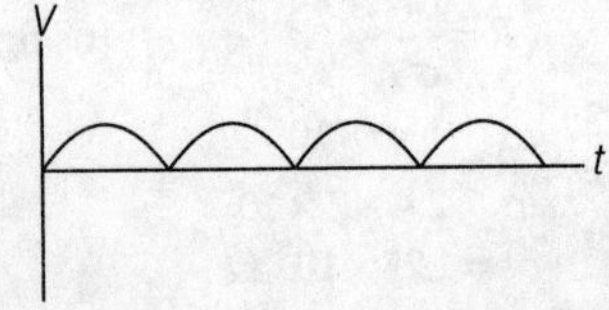

12. Zener current will be maximum when the unregulated voltage acquires maximum value. Thus, considering it equal to 15 V the circuit is as shown. As voltage across load resistor R_L is equal to V_Z, current in it is

$$I = \frac{V_Z}{R_L} = \frac{5}{5 \times 10^3} = 1\ \text{mA}$$

$R_L = 5\ \text{k}\Omega$, $V_Z = 5$ V, $R_S = 2.5\ \text{k}\Omega$, Unregulated voltage (Maximum 15 V)

Also, for loop *ABCD* by KVL, we get

$$15 - (2.5 \times 10^3)I' - 5 = 0$$

$$\Rightarrow \quad I' = \frac{10}{2.5 \times 10^3} = 4\ \text{mA}$$

Thus, by KCL for junction *B*, we get, current through zener diode equal to

$$I'' = I' - I = 4 - 1 = 3\ \text{mA}$$

13. For LED (Operating in forward biasing) correct curves are

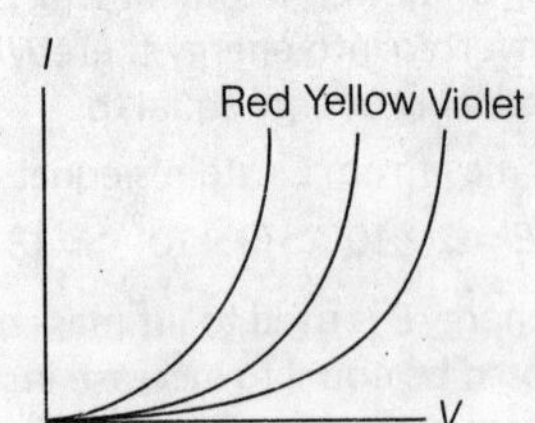

14. Transistor saturation happens when $V_{CE} = V_2 = 0$

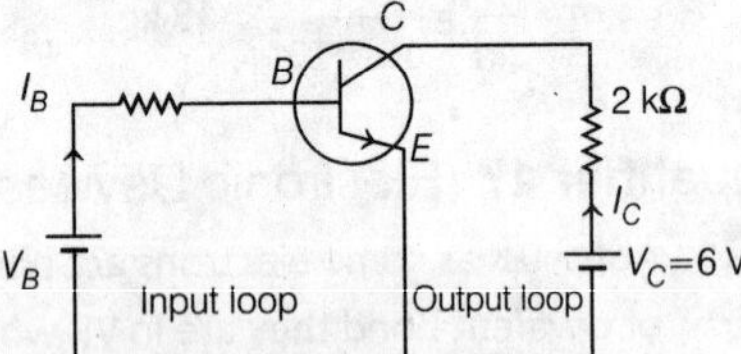

For output loop, by KVL,

$$V_{CE} = V_C - I_C R_C$$

$$\Rightarrow \quad 0 = 6 - I_C(2 \times 10^3) \Rightarrow I_C = 3\ \text{mA}$$

As input current is given by $I_B = \frac{I_C}{\beta}$

$$\Rightarrow \quad I_B = \frac{3 \times 10^{-3}}{150} = 20\ \mu\text{A}$$

Now, by KVL, for input loop,

$$V_B = I_B R_B + V_{BE}$$

$$\Rightarrow \quad V_B = (20 \times 10^{-6}) \times 0.1 \times 10^6 + 1 = 3\ \text{V}$$

15. Voltage gain (A_V) typically varies with frequency (f) as shown.

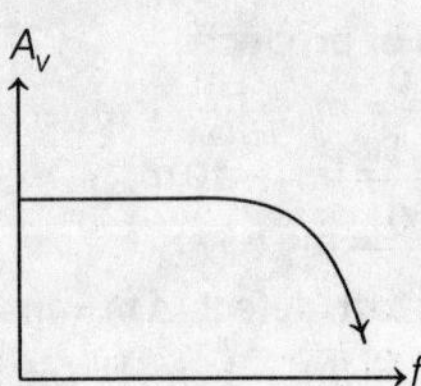

So, voltage gain remains constant with increasing frequency initially, while decreases later.

16. Power gain (A_P) is given by the relation

$$A_P = \beta^2 \left(\frac{R_{output}}{R_{input}}\right)$$

$$\Rightarrow A_P = (100\sqrt{2})^2 \left(\frac{9 \times 10^3}{90}\right) = 2 \times 10^6$$

Corresponding value in dB is

$$A'_P = 10 \log_{10} A_P = 10 \log_{10}(2 \times 10^6)$$
$$= 10[\log_{10} 2 + \log_{10} 10^6]$$
$$= 10[0.3 + 6] = 63\ \text{dB}$$

17. Here, the emitter-base junction of the *n-p-n* transistor is forward biased with battery V_{BB} through resistance *R*. When the value of *R* is reduced, then the base current i_b will increase. As result, the collector current will also increase ($i_c = \beta i_b$). Due to increase in i_c potential difference across *L* increases and hence, the reading of voltmeter will increase.

18. Outputs through different gates and hence, the final output *Y* are as shown.

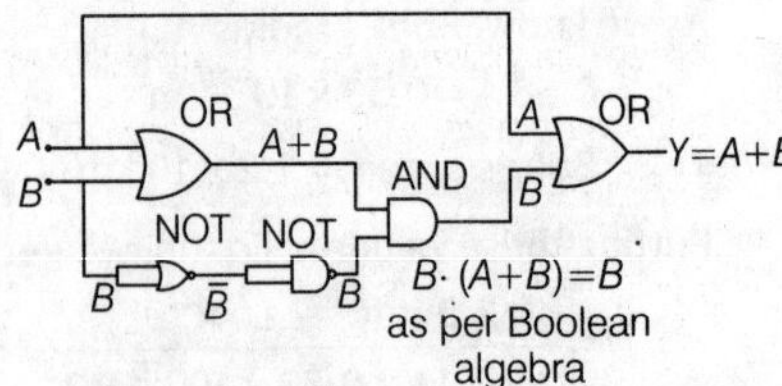

19. Output of the given arrangement of gates and final output *Y* will be as shown in the figure.

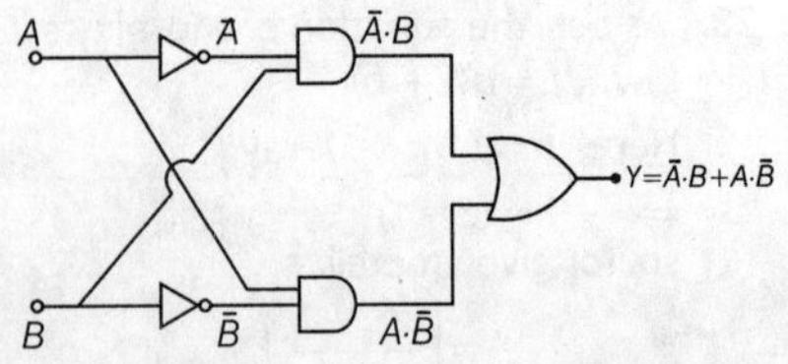

Truth table of the arrangement

A	B	$\bar{A}$	$\bar{B}$	$\bar{A}\cdot B$	$A\cdot\bar{B}$	$Y=\bar{A}\cdot B + A\cdot\bar{B}$
0	0	1	1	0	0	0
1	0	0	1	0	1	1
0	1	1	0	1	0	1
1	1	0	0	0	0	0

As output 1 is only obtained when either of input is 1, this arrangement is called exclusive OR (XOR) gate. Therefore for given waveforms output will be 1 only between t_2 to t_3 (when only input at A is 1) and between t_3 to t_4 (when only input at B is 1).

20. Outputs at various points is as shown

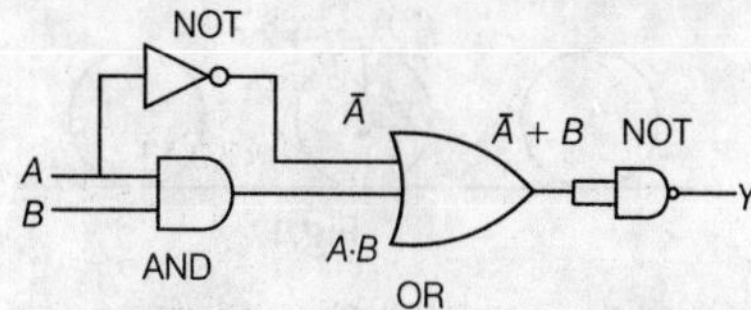

$Y=\overline{\bar{A}+B}$

$=\bar{\bar{A}}\cdot\bar{B}$ (using De-Morgan theorem)

$=A\cdot\bar{B}$

As final output $=A\cdot\bar{B}$, so truth table is as shown,

A	B	$\bar{B}$	$Y=A\cdot\bar{B}$
0	0	1	0
1	0	1	1
0	1	0	0
1	1	0	0

21. Dynamic resistance of a non-Ohmic device is given by $R=\dfrac{\Delta V}{\Delta I}$

$$\Rightarrow \quad R=\frac{0.8-0.7}{(22-7)\times10^{-3}}=6.67\,\Omega$$

22. When S_1 is closed, then circuit will be as shown in Fig.1. Resistors constitute balanced Wheatstone bridge.

i.e. $\dfrac{R_1}{R_2}=\dfrac{R_3}{R_4}=\dfrac{1}{2}$.

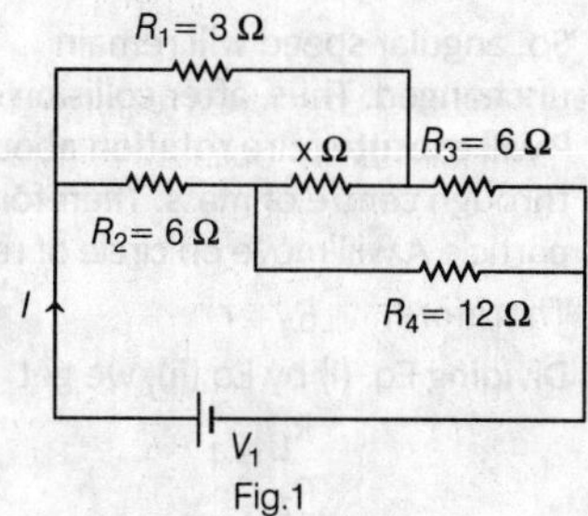

Fig.1

Current in $x\,\Omega$ will be zero and so, $x\,\Omega$ can be removed.

Equivalent resistance of network will be parallel equivalent of R_1, R_3 and R_2, R_4

i.e. $\quad R=\dfrac{9\times18}{9+18}=6\,\Omega$

By Ohm's law, $I=\dfrac{V}{R}=\dfrac{V_1}{6}$ ...(i)

When S_2 is closed, then the circuit will be as shown in Fig.2 in which $6\,\Omega$, $x\,\Omega$ and $6\,\Omega$ will be in series. So, equivalent resistance will be $R'=12\,\Omega+x\,\Omega$.

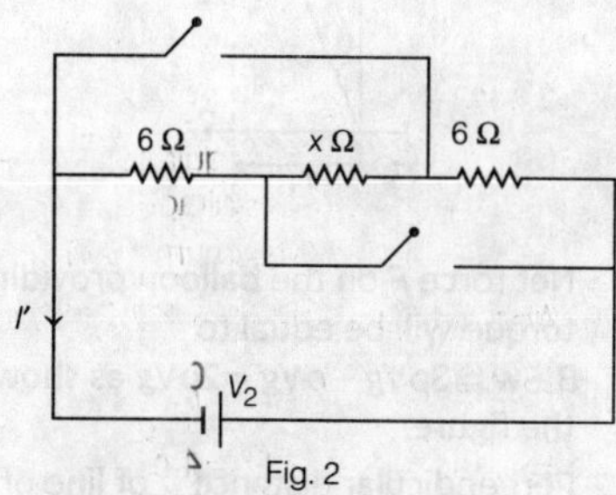

Fig. 2

By Ohm's law, current supplied by cell

$$I'=\frac{V}{R'}=\frac{V_2}{12+x}$$

$$=\frac{3V_1}{12+x} \quad \text{...(ii)}$$

As I is given to be equal to I', from Eqs. (i) and (ii), we get

$$\frac{V_1}{6}=\frac{3V_1}{12+x}$$

$$\Rightarrow \quad x=6\,\Omega$$

23. Current gain,

$$\alpha=\frac{I_C}{I_E}$$

$$\Rightarrow \quad I_C=\alpha I_E=\frac{60}{61}\times7.32$$

$$=7.2\text{ mA}$$

$$\Rightarrow \quad x=7.2 \quad \text{...(i)}$$

Also, current amplification factor for CE configuration is given by

$$\beta=\frac{I_C}{I_B}=\frac{I_C}{I_E-I_C}$$

$(\text{As } I_E=I_C+I_B)$

$$=\frac{7.2}{7.32-7.2}$$

$$\Rightarrow \beta=60 \quad \text{...(ii)}$$

From Eqs. (i) and (ii), we get

$$x+\beta=7.2+60=67.2$$

24. Resistances R, $2R$, $4R$ ... etc. are in parallel. Equivalent resistance of the combination will be

$$\frac{1}{r}=\frac{1}{R}+\frac{1}{2R}+\frac{1}{4R}+\dots$$

$$\Rightarrow \quad \frac{1}{r}=\frac{1}{R}\left(1+\frac{1}{2}+\frac{1}{4}+\dots\right)$$

$$=\frac{1}{R}\left(\frac{1}{1-\frac{1}{2}}\right)=\frac{2}{R}$$

$$\Rightarrow \quad r=\frac{R}{2}=\frac{1400}{2}=700\,\Omega$$

So, the given circuit can be shown as

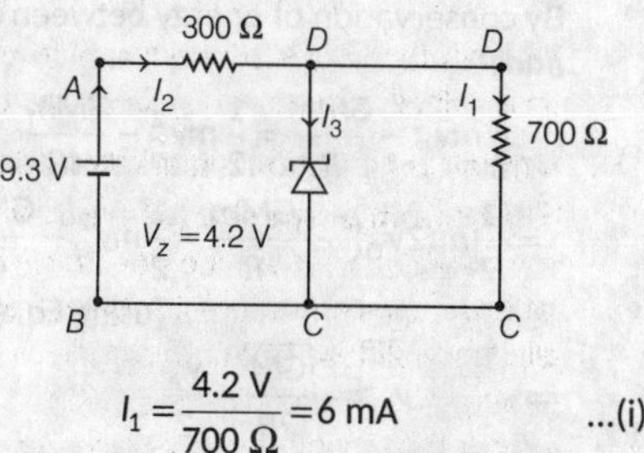

$$I_1=\frac{4.2\text{ V}}{700\,\Omega}=6\text{ mA} \quad \text{...(i)}$$

By KVL, in loop $ABCD$, we get

$$9.3-300\,I_2-4.2=0$$

$$\Rightarrow \quad I_2=\frac{5.1}{300}=17\text{ mA} \quad \text{...(ii)}$$

By KCL, for junction D, we get current through diode equal to

$$I_3=I_2-I_1$$

$$=17-6\text{ mA}$$

[using Eqs. (i) and (ii)]

$$=11\text{ mA}$$

25. Current gain

$$=\beta=\frac{I_c}{I_b}=\frac{9\text{ mA}}{150\,\mu\text{A}}$$

or we can also find it as

$$\beta=\frac{15\text{mA}}{250\,\mu\text{A}}=60$$

Resistance gain,

$$R_g=\frac{R_{\text{output}}}{R_{\text{input}}}$$

$$=\frac{85\times10^3\,\Omega}{85\,\Omega}=10^3$$

As power $=(\text{current})^2\times$ resistance, therefore power gain $=\beta^2\times R_g$

$$=(60)^2\times10^3=3.6\times10^6$$

$\therefore \; P=3.6$

PART TESTS

Part Test 01

1. Distance of particle from earth's centre at Q and P are

$$r_Q = 4R \quad \text{...(i)}$$
$$r_P = R \quad \text{...(ii)}$$

By conservation of angular momentum between positions Q and P,

$$mv_P r_P = mv_Q r_Q \sin 150°$$
$$\Rightarrow \quad v_P = 2v_Q \quad \text{...(iii)}$$

[using Eqs. (i) and (ii)]

By conservation of energy between Q and P,

$$\frac{1}{2}mv_P^2 - \frac{GMm}{R} = \frac{1}{2}mv_Q^2 - \frac{GMm}{4R}$$
$$\Rightarrow \frac{1}{2}m(2v_Q)^2 - \frac{GMm}{R} = \frac{1}{2}mv_Q^2 - \frac{GMm}{4R}$$

[using Eq. (iii)]

$$\Rightarrow \quad v_Q = \sqrt{\frac{GM}{2R}} = \frac{v_e}{2}$$

(as escape velocity is given by formula $v_{\text{escape}} = \sqrt{\frac{2GM}{R}}$)

2. The situation can be shown as

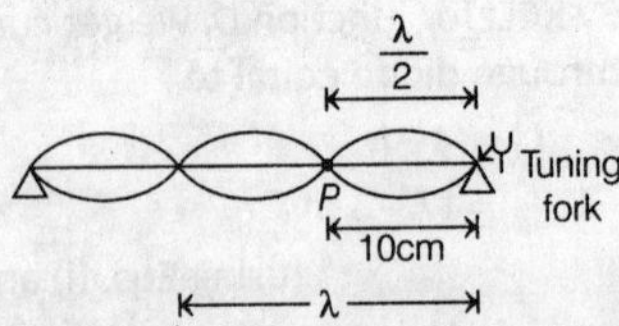

For no vibration at P, a node should be formed at it.

From figure, $\frac{\lambda}{2} = 10 \times 10^{-2}$ m

$$\Rightarrow \quad \lambda = 20 \times 10^{-2} \text{ m}$$
$$\Rightarrow \quad f = \frac{v}{\lambda} \quad \text{...(i)}$$

For string, $v = \sqrt{\frac{T}{\mu}}$

$$\Rightarrow \quad v = \sqrt{\frac{40}{0.1}} = 20 \text{ m/s}$$

$\therefore$ From Eq. (i), we get

$$f = \frac{20}{20 \times 10^{-2}} = 100 \text{ Hz}$$

So, the rider will not vibrate at frequency having multiple value of 100 Hz, i.e. 300 Hz.

3. Let, volume of the balloon is V.

Weight of the balloon $= w = \rho V g$

Also, buoyancy by surrounding air $= 3\rho V g$

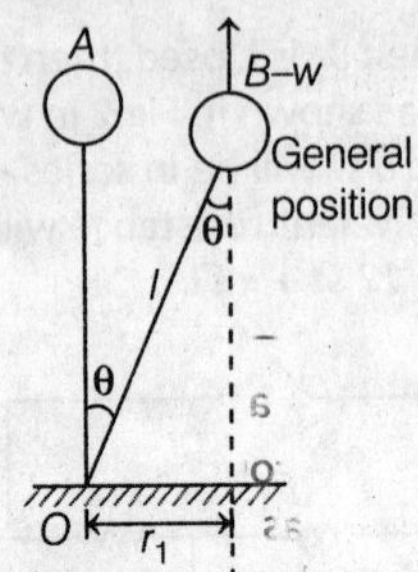

Net force F on the balloon providing torque will be equal to $B - w = 3\rho V g - \rho V g = 2\rho V g$ as shown in the figure.

Perpendicular distance r_1 of line of action of force from axis O at general position is $r_1 = l \sin\theta \approx l\theta$ as θ is given to be small. Therefore, restoring torque,

$$\tau = F \cdot r_1 = 2\rho V g l\theta$$

$\Rightarrow$ Angular acceleration of balloon (having moment of inertia I equal to ml^2) is

$$\alpha = \frac{\tau}{I} = \frac{2\rho V g l\theta}{ml^2} = \frac{2\rho V g\theta}{ml}$$

As mass m of balloon/gas is ρV, therefore

$$\alpha = \frac{2\rho V g}{ml}\theta = \frac{2\rho V g}{\rho V l}\theta = \frac{2g}{l}\theta$$

As in angular oscillation, $\alpha = \omega^2\theta$, where, ω is angular frequency, we get

$$\omega^2\theta = \frac{2g}{l}\theta \Rightarrow \omega = \sqrt{\frac{2g}{l}}$$

As, time to move from B (one extreme) to the other extreme is half of time period of oscillation.

$$\therefore \quad t = \frac{T}{2} = \frac{\frac{2\pi}{\omega}}{2}$$
$$= \frac{\pi}{\omega} = \pi\sqrt{\frac{l}{2g}}$$

4. As intensity due to point source is inversely proportional to square of distance from source.

$\Rightarrow$ I at $r = 1$ m is four times that at 2 m

So, at $r = 2$ m,

$$L = 10 \log \frac{I}{I_0} \quad \text{...(i)}$$

While at $r = 1$ m,

$$L' = 10 \log\left(\frac{4I}{I_0}\right) \quad \text{...(ii)}$$

Subtracting Eq. (i) from Eq. (ii),

$$L' - L = 10 \log 4$$
$$\Rightarrow L' - 10 = 20 \log 2$$
$$\Rightarrow L' - 10 = 6 \Rightarrow L' = 16 \text{ dB}$$

5. Point on periphery of a rolling sphere follows cycloid, as shown in Fig.1

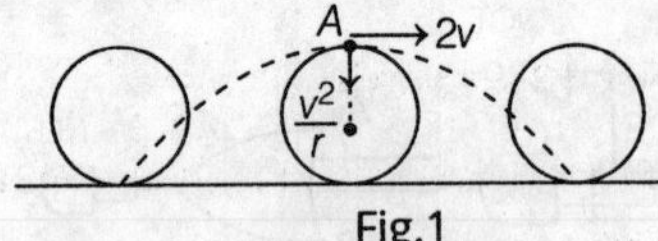

Fig.1

While at top (position A) velocity of the point is $2v$ while acceleration is $\frac{v^2}{r}$ in terms of radius r of the sphere. Radius of curvature of a path is given by

$$R = \frac{(\text{Speed})^2}{\text{Normal acceleration}}$$

Therefore, $R_1 = \frac{(2v)^2}{\frac{v^2}{r}} = 4r \quad \text{...(i)}$

As in elastic collision of identical objects velocities are exchanged. So, on collision, sphere P will come at rest while sphere Q will start moving with v but as normal force (during collision) will pass through centre of mass of sphere (as shown in Fig.2) it will provide no torque.

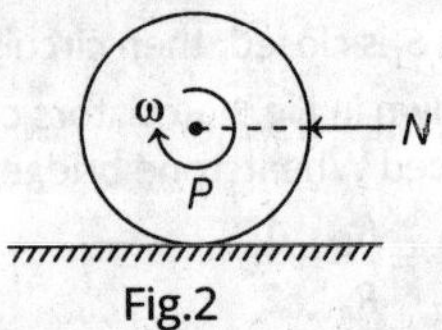

Fig.2

So, angular speed will remain unchanged. Thus, after collision sphere P will execute pure rotation about axis through centre of mass. Therefore, top particle A will move on circle of radius r.

Therefore, $\quad R_2 = r \quad \text{...(ii)}$

Dividing Eq. (i) by Eq (ii), we get

$$\frac{R_1}{R_2} = 4$$

6. A block on rough horizontal surface is as shown below

$\to v_0$ $a \leftarrow$ $\to v$

$t = 0$

According to the question, retardation, $a = -bv$ (Here, b = constant)

$$\Rightarrow \quad \frac{dv}{dt} = -bv$$

Integrating both sides, we get

$$\Rightarrow \quad \int_{v_0}^{v} \frac{dv}{v} = -b\int_0^t dt \Rightarrow v = v_0 e^{-bt}$$

At $t = 1$ s, $v = \frac{v_0}{2}$ (given)

$$\Rightarrow \quad e^{-b} = \frac{1}{2}$$

At $t = 3$ s, $v = v_0(e^{-b})^3 = \frac{v_0}{8}$

As $a \propto v$, it will also become (1/8)th.

7. FBD of block is as shown

Note that there is no spring force, as spring is relax

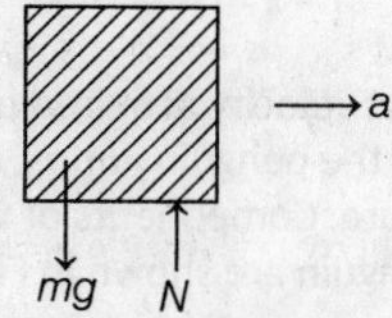

For vertical equilibrium,

$$N = mg = 2 \times 10 = 20 \text{ N}$$

FBD of box is as shown

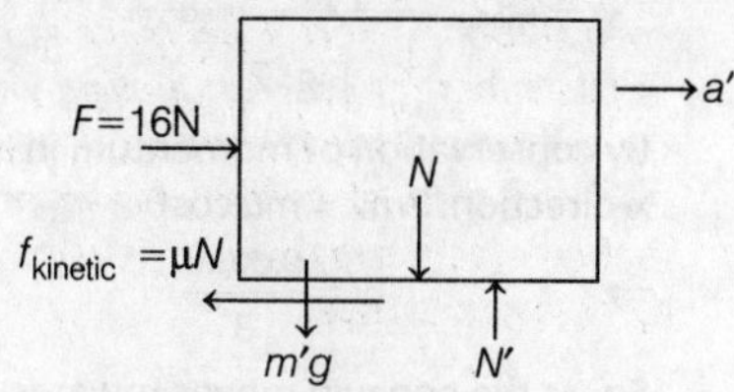

For vertical equilibrium,

$$N' = N + m'g$$
$$= 20 + 30 = 50 \text{ N}$$

Limiting friction between box and ground $= \mu N' = 0.2 \times 50 = 10$ N

As, external force, $F = 16 \text{ N} > f_{\text{limiting}}$ block will slip and therefore it will experience kinetic friction as given by

$$f_K = \mu N' = 0.2 \times 50 = 10 \text{ N}$$

Therefore, acceleration of box,

$$a' = \frac{F - f_K}{\text{Mass of box}} = \frac{16 - 10}{3} = 2 \text{ m/s}^2$$

While acceleration (a) of block is zero, as there is no horizontal force on it.

8. From the given U *versus* x graph, between $x = 0$ and $x = x_1$, assuming $U = kx^2$ (since, the graph is parabolic in nature)

So, force, $F = -\frac{dU}{dx} = -\frac{d(kx^2)}{dx} = -2kx$

$$\Rightarrow \quad F \propto -x$$

$\Rightarrow$ So, the graph between F and x between $x = 0$ and $x = x_1$ will be a straight line with negative slope.

Between $x = x_1$ to $x = x_2$.

$$F = -\frac{dU}{dx} = -(\text{slope of } U\text{-}x \text{ graph})$$
$$= -(-k') = k' = \text{constant}$$

$\Rightarrow$ Force is a positive constant.

Thus, the conservative force acting on a system as a function of x is correctly represented in option (b).

9. As, the sphere does not have tendency of slipping. So, it will keep on rolling without slipping with constant speed v.

Therefore, time of motion,

$$t = \frac{\text{displacement}}{\text{velocity}} = \frac{\pi r}{v}$$

$\Rightarrow$ Angle rotated by sphere,

$$\theta = \omega t = \frac{v}{r} \cdot \frac{\pi r}{v} = \pi$$

Therefore, upper shaded portion will take position of lower non-shaded portion finally as shown.

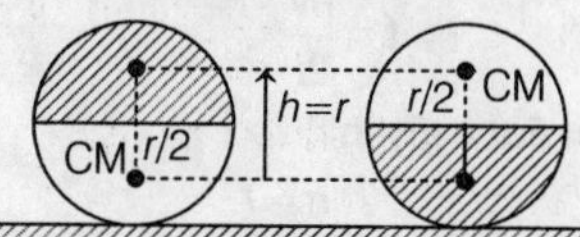

The centre of mass of a hemisphere is at a distance $\frac{r}{2}$ from its base. As the sphere rotates by π centre of mass, the non-shaded portion gains height, $h = r$ as shown.

Therefore, work done by gravity on non-shaded portion,

$$W_{\text{gravity}} = -\frac{m}{2} g \cdot r = \frac{-mgr}{2} \quad \text{...(i)}$$

(As work done by gravity on body of mass m, if its centre of mass gains height h is $-mgh$)

Also, moment of inertia of hemisphere about axis through O,

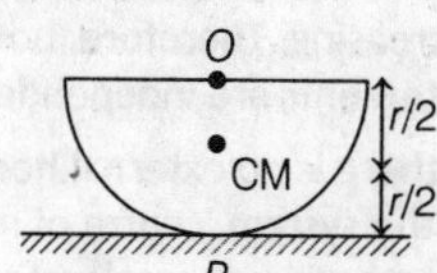

$$I_0 = \frac{I_{\text{sphere}}}{2} = \frac{\frac{2}{3}mr^2}{2} = \frac{1}{3}mr^2 \quad \text{...(ii)}$$

Therefore, by parallel axes theorem at CM,

$$I_{\text{CM}} = I_0 - \frac{m}{2}\left(\frac{r}{2}\right)^2$$

Again by parallel axes theorem at P,

$$I_P = I_{\text{CM}} + \frac{m}{2}\left(\frac{r}{2}\right)^2 \quad \text{...(iv)}$$

Adding Eqs. (iii) and (iv), we get

$$I_P = I_0 = \frac{1}{3}mr^2 \quad \text{...(v)}$$

[using Eq. (ii)]

Initial kinetic energy of lower non-shaded portion will therefore be (considering axis through P as instantaneous axis)

$$K_1 = \frac{1}{2}I_P\omega^2 = \frac{1}{2}\left(\frac{1}{3}mr^2\right)\left(\frac{v}{r}\right)^2$$

[using Eq. (v)]

$$= \frac{1}{6}mv^2 \quad \text{...(vi)}$$

Also, total kinetic energy of the sphere,

$$K = K_{\text{translation}} + K_{\text{rotation}}$$
$$= \frac{1}{2}mv^2 + \frac{1}{2}I_{\text{CM}}\omega^2$$
$$= \frac{1}{2}mv^2 + \frac{1}{2}\left(\frac{2}{3}mr^2\right)\left(\frac{v}{r}\right)^2$$
$$K = \frac{5}{6}mv^2 \quad \text{...(vii)}$$

Therefore, kinetic energy of the upper shaded portion can be obtained by subtracting K_1 from K

Subtracting Eq. (vi) from Eq. (vii), we get

$$K_2 = K - K_1 = \frac{5}{6}mv^2 - \frac{1}{6}mv^2$$
$$K_2 = \frac{2}{3}mv^2 \quad \text{...(viii)}$$

As lower non-shaded hemisphere moves in upper position its kinetic energy will increase from K_1 to K_2. Increase in kinetic energy will therefore be

$$\Delta K = K_2 - K_1 = \frac{2}{3}mv^2 - \frac{1}{6}mv^2$$
$$= \frac{1}{2}mv^2 \quad \text{...(ix)}$$

[using Eqs. (vi) and (viii)]

As per work-energy theorem, for non-shaded portion

$$W_{\text{contact}} + W_{\text{gravity}} = \Delta K$$

$$\Rightarrow W_{contact} = \Delta K - W_{gravity}$$
$$= \frac{1}{2}mv^2 + \frac{mgr}{2}$$
[using Eqs. (ix) and (i)]

10. Let $\frac{dN}{dv} = kv^2$ ... (i)

Here, k is constant (as for upward concave parabolic with vertex at O, $y \propto x^2$)

Mean square speed is defined as

$$v_{mean} = \frac{\int v^2 dN}{\int dN} = \frac{\int_0^{v_0} v^2 \cdot kv^2 dv}{\int_0^{v_0} kv^2 dv}$$
[from Eq. (i), $dN = kv^2 dv$]
$$= \frac{\frac{kv_0^5}{5}}{kv_0^3/3} = \frac{3v_0^2}{5} = 0.6{v_0}^2$$

11. Apparent frequency f' is given by
$$f' = f\left(\frac{v - v_o}{v - v_s}\right)$$
Let speed of the train equal to u.

Therefore, apparent frequency for stationary observer in case of approach,
$$f' = f\left(\frac{v}{v-u}\right) = 6F \text{ (given)} \quad ...(i)$$

While apparent frequency for stationary observer in case of receding,
$$f' = f\left[\frac{v}{v-(-u)}\right]$$
$$= f\left(\frac{v}{v+u}\right) = 3F \quad \text{(given)}...(ii)$$
Dividing Eq. (i) by Eq. (ii), we get
$$\frac{v+u}{v-u} = 2 \Rightarrow u = \frac{v}{3}$$
Using this value in Eq. (i), we get
$$f\left(\frac{v}{v - \frac{v}{3}}\right) = 6F$$
$$\Rightarrow \quad f = 4F$$
As for passenger in the train, source is relatively at rest, means there is no Doppler effect and so apparent frequency is same as actual frequency, i.e. $4F$.

12. Excess reading (Zero error) = (–1mm) + (92) (0.01) = –0.08 mm

It is giving 7.97 mm in which there is –0.07 mm excess reading , which has to be removed (subtracted). So, actual reading = 7.97 –(–0.08) = 8.05 mm

13. As the graph is given to be parabola (rightward concave), relation between T and $\frac{1}{V}$ will be of the form
$$\Rightarrow \quad \frac{1}{V} = kT^2$$
$$\Rightarrow \quad TV^{1/2} = \text{constant} \quad ... (i)$$
Also, in adiabatic process,
$$TV^{\gamma-1} = \text{constant} \quad ... (ii)$$
Comparing Eqs. (i) and (ii), we get
$$\gamma - 1 = \frac{1}{2}$$
$$\Rightarrow \quad \gamma = 1.5 \quad ... (iii)$$
Now, $$v_{rms} = \sqrt{\frac{3RT}{M}} \quad ... (iv)$$
While $$v_{sound} = \sqrt{\frac{\gamma RT}{M}} \quad ... (v)$$
Dividing Eq. (iv) by Eq. (v), we get
$$\frac{v_{rms}}{v_{sound}} = \sqrt{\frac{3}{\gamma}}$$
$$\Rightarrow \left(\frac{v_{rms}}{v_{sound}}\right)^2 = \frac{3}{1.5} = 2 \quad \text{[using Eq. (iii)]}$$

14. Dimension of ψ from first term of expression = $[L^2]$

So, dimension of coefficient of ψ in second term = $[L^{-2}]$

15. Frequency of nth harmonic for open pipe,
$$f = \frac{nv}{2l}$$
$\Rightarrow$ For a given f,
$$n \propto l$$
Therefore, $$\frac{n'}{n} = \frac{l'}{l} = \frac{2}{3}$$
$$\Rightarrow n' = \frac{2n}{3} = \frac{2 \times 6}{3} = 4 \text{ (3rd overtone)}$$

16. For limiting condition, $\mu = \frac{m_B}{m_A + m_C}$
$$\Rightarrow \quad 0.25 = \frac{5}{10 + m_C}$$
$$\Rightarrow \quad m_C = 10\text{kg}$$

17. Even if tangential acceleration is decreasing speed of particle can increase resulting in increase of centripetal acceleration. Hence if speed increases we can't say acceleration of particle is increasing or decreasing. Therefore, both statements are independently true.

18. As there is no external horizontal force on the system, centre of mass of the system will not accelerate and so will remain at rest. Therefore, displacement of CM will be zero. So, statement given in option (c) is correct. Also, displacement of CM can be written as $s_{CM} = \frac{m_p s_p + m_s s_s}{m_p + m_s}$

Assuming displacement of sled equal to x as shown in the Fig. 1, we can put respective values. Using the figure, we get
$$\Rightarrow 0 = \frac{-m(l-x) + 3mx}{m + 3m}$$
$$\Rightarrow x = \frac{l}{4} = \text{Displacement of sled}$$

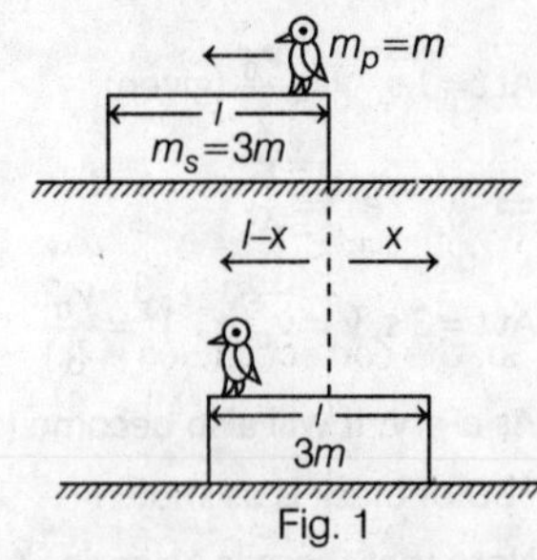

Fig. 1

Therefore, displacement of penguin is
$$l - x = l - \frac{l}{4} = \frac{3l}{4}$$
Now, let velocity acquired by the sled be v as the penguin jumps, as shown in the figure. Components of velocity of the penguin are shown in Fig. 2

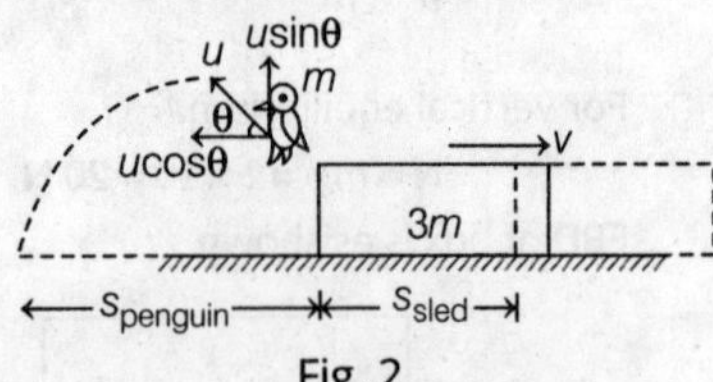

Fig. 2

By conservation of momentum in x-direction, $3mv = mu\cos\theta$
$$\Rightarrow \quad v = \frac{u\cos\theta}{3}$$
So, as the penguin moves towards the ground the sled moves rightwards as shown in Fig 2.

Thus, after jumping, the penguin falls on the ground at a distance (from the left end of the sled) given by
$$d = s_{penguin} + s_{sled}$$
$$= \frac{u^2 \sin 2\theta}{g} + \frac{u\cos\theta}{3} \times T$$
$$= \frac{u^2 \sin 2\theta}{g} + \frac{u\cos\theta}{3} \times \frac{2u\sin\theta}{g}$$
$$= \frac{4u^2 \sin 2\theta}{3g}$$
So, clearly, statement given in option (b) is incorrect.

19. (A) $W_{gravity}$ = loss in gravitational potential energy

$= mgh = 2\times 10\times 0.2\sin 30° = 2\text{ J}$

(B) W_{spring} = loss in spring potential energy

$= \frac{-k}{2}(x^2_{initial} - x^2_{final})$

$= -\frac{1000}{2}(0-400)\times 10^{-4}$

$= -20\text{ J}$

(C) As per work-energy theorem,

$W = \Delta KE$

$\Rightarrow W_{gravity} + W_{spring} + W_{external} = \Delta KE$

$\Rightarrow 2 + (-20) + W_{external} = 0$

$\Rightarrow W_{external} = 18\text{ J}$

(D) $W_{contact} = W_{spring} + W_{external}$

$= -20 + 18 = -2\text{J}$

So, the correct choice is (c).

20. Sharpness in such a graph is measure of accuracy. As graph I has highest sharpness, it has to be most accurate.

21. First we have to find a point where the resultant field due to both is zero. Let the point P be at a distance x from centre of bigger star.

$$\Rightarrow \frac{G(16M)}{x^2} = \frac{GM}{(10a-x)^2}$$

$$\Rightarrow x = 8a \quad (\text{from } O_1)$$

i.e. Once the body reaches P, the gravitational pull of attraction due to M takes the lead to make m move towards it automatically. So, a minimum KE or velocity has to be imparted to m from surface of 16 M such that it is just able to cross P. By law of conservation of energy,

Total mechanical energy at surface of bigger star

= Total mechanical energy at P

$$\Rightarrow k_{min} + \left[\frac{G(16M)m}{2a} - \frac{GMm}{8a}\right] = 0 + \left[\frac{GMm}{2a} - \frac{G(16M)m}{8a}\right]$$

$$\Rightarrow |k_{min}| = \frac{GMm}{8a}(45)$$

Comparing with given value, we get

$k = 8$

22. Let velocity of pulley be v. By pulley constraint relation, velocity of block will be $2v$. FBD of block and disc are as shown. As acceleration for block and disc is zero, from FBD of disc, $2T = mg$

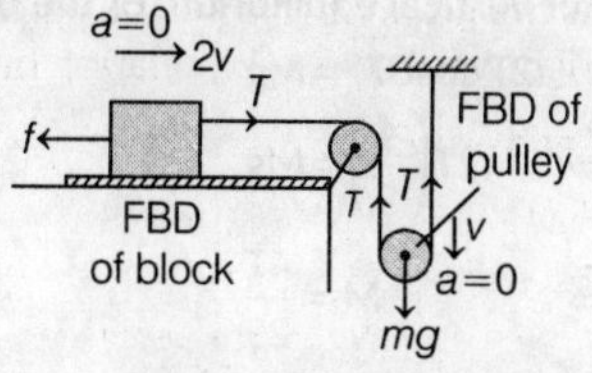

$$\Rightarrow T = \frac{mg}{2} \quad \text{... (i)}$$

From FBD of block, we get

$$T = f \quad \text{... (ii)}$$

From Eqs. (i) and (ii), we get

$$mg/2 = f$$

$$\Rightarrow \frac{mg}{2} = \eta A\frac{2v}{d} \Rightarrow \eta = \frac{mgd}{4Av}$$

$$= \frac{20\times 10^{-3}\times 10\times 0.2\times 10^{-3}}{4\times 10^3\times 10^{-4}\times 2\times 10^{-2}}$$

$$= 5\times 10^{-3}\text{ Pa-s}$$

$$\Rightarrow x = 5$$

23. Stress is zero at free ends and maximum at middle so rod will rupture at middle.

By Newton's second law for the element shown in the figure,

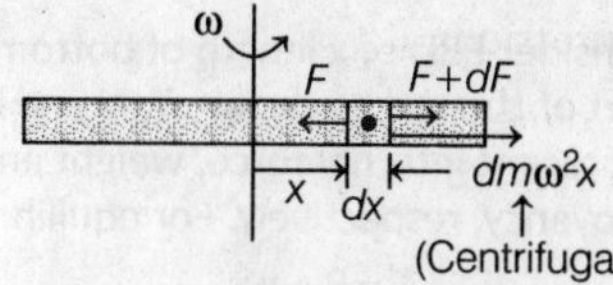

$$F - (F + dF) = dmx\omega^2$$

$$-\int dF = \int \rho A\omega^2 x dx$$

where, ω is the speed of rotation and F is internal force.

$$\Rightarrow -[F]_0^F = \rho A\omega^2\left[\frac{x^2}{2}\right]_{l/2}^{x}$$

$$\Rightarrow F = \rho\frac{A\omega^2}{2}\left[\left(\frac{l}{2}\right)^2 - x^2\right]$$

At $x = 0$, $F = \frac{\rho A\omega^2 l^2}{8} \Rightarrow \frac{F}{A} = \frac{\rho\omega^2 l^2}{8}$

For rupture, $\frac{F}{A} = \sigma \Rightarrow \frac{\rho\omega^2 l^2}{8} = \sigma$

$$\Rightarrow \omega = \sqrt{\frac{8\sigma}{\rho l^2}}$$

$\Rightarrow$ Rotation frequency,

$$f = \frac{\omega}{2\pi} = \frac{1}{2\pi}\sqrt{\frac{8\sigma}{\rho l^2}}$$

$$\Rightarrow f = \frac{1}{2\pi}\sqrt{\frac{8\times 2.5\times 10^8}{9\times 10^3\times\left(\frac{2\sqrt{2}}{3\pi}\right)^2}} = 250\text{ s}^{-1}$$

$= 25n$ (given) $\Rightarrow n = 10$

24. If centre of mass is at A,

$$A_{square}\, x_{square} = A_{triangle}\, x_{triangle}$$

$$a^2\frac{a}{2} = \frac{1}{2}ab\sin\theta\times\frac{1}{3}b\sin\theta$$

or $\frac{b}{a} = \sqrt{\frac{13}{4}}$ $\left[\because \sin^2\theta = \left(1 - \frac{a^2}{4b^2}\right)\right]$

$\therefore \quad m + n = 13 + 4 = 17$

25. Efficiency of Carnot engine is given by

$$\eta = \frac{W}{Q_1} = \frac{T_1 - T_2}{T_1}$$

$$\Rightarrow W = Q_1\left(\frac{T_1 - T_2}{T_1}\right) \quad \text{... (i)}$$

Also, coefficient of performance of refrigerator is given by

$$\alpha = \frac{Q_4}{W} = \frac{T_4}{T_3 - T_4}$$

$$\Rightarrow \frac{Q_3 - W}{W} = \frac{T_4}{T_3 - T_4}$$

(as $Q_4 + W = Q_3$)

$$\Rightarrow W = Q_3\left(\frac{T_3 - T_4}{T_3}\right) \quad \text{... (ii)}$$

From Eqs. (i) and (ii), we get

$$Q_1\left(\frac{T_1 - T_2}{T_1}\right) = Q_3\left(\frac{T_3 - T_4}{T_3}\right)$$

$$\Rightarrow Q_1\left(\frac{400 - 150}{400}\right) = Q_3\left(\frac{325 - 225}{325}\right)$$

$$\Rightarrow \frac{Q_3}{Q_1} = 2.03 \Rightarrow X = 2.03$$

26. Given that, $a_C = kt$

$$\Rightarrow \frac{v^2}{r} = kt \Rightarrow v = \sqrt{krt}$$

Tangential acceleration, $a_t = \frac{dv}{dt} = \frac{\sqrt{kr}}{2\sqrt{t}}$

So, power of resultant force, $P = \mathbf{F}\cdot\mathbf{v}$

$= [ma_C + ma_t]\cdot\mathbf{v} = 0 + ma_t v$

$$= m\frac{\sqrt{kr}}{2\sqrt{t}}\cdot\sqrt{krt} = \frac{mkr}{2} = \frac{2\times 1\times 3}{2} = 3\text{W}$$

27. As string does no work on the ball, energy conservation can be applied. i.e. Loss in kinetic energy = Gain in potential energy

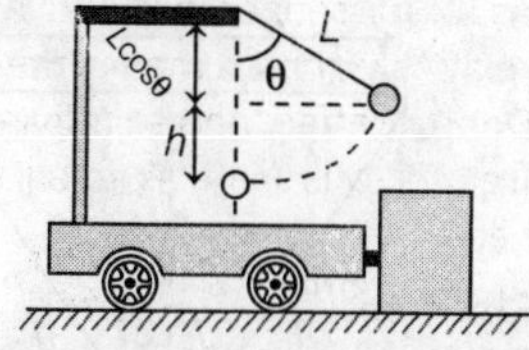

$$\Rightarrow \frac{1}{2}mv^2 = mgh = mg(L - L\cos\theta)$$

$$\Rightarrow v = \sqrt{2gL(1 - \cos\theta)}$$

On putting values, we get

$$v = \sqrt{10} \text{ m/s}.$$

Therefore, square of speed is $10 \text{ m}^2/\text{s}^2$.

28. Applying Bernoulli theorem at points A and B, when the flow is stopped

$$p_a + 0 + 0 = p + \rho g(h - l) + 0$$

where, l is the distance by which the water level has descended.

$$\Rightarrow \quad p = p_a - \rho g(h - l) \quad \text{...... (i)}$$

As process can be taken as isothermal for air,

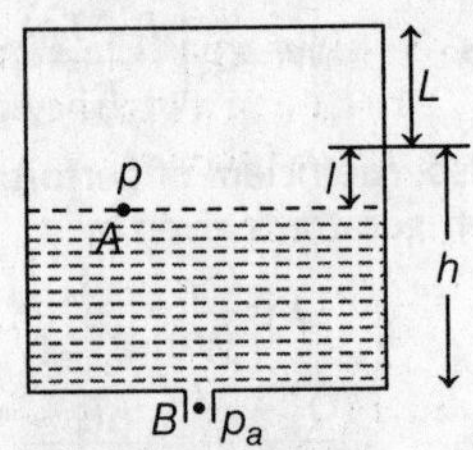

$$p_a(AL) = pA(L + l)$$

$$\Rightarrow \quad L(p_a - p) = pl \quad \text{... (ii)}$$

Using Eqs. (i) and (ii), we get

$$L = \frac{(p_a - \rho gh + \rho gl)l}{\rho g(h - l)}$$

$$= \frac{10^4(10 - 4.5 + 0.5)0.5}{10^4[4.5 - 0.5]} = 0.75 \text{ m}$$

29. The change in length of rod due to increase in temperature in absence of walls,

$$\Delta l = l\alpha\Delta T = 1000 \times 10^{-4} \times 20 \text{ mm}$$

$$= 2 \text{ mm}$$

But the rod can expand upto 1001 mm only.

At that temperature, its natural length $= 1002$ mm.

So, compression $= 1$ mm

$\therefore$ Mechanical stress

$$= Y\frac{\Delta l}{l} = 10^{11} \times \frac{1}{1000} = 10^8 \text{ N/m}^2$$

$$\Rightarrow x = 8$$

30. Consider FBD of block shown in the figure.

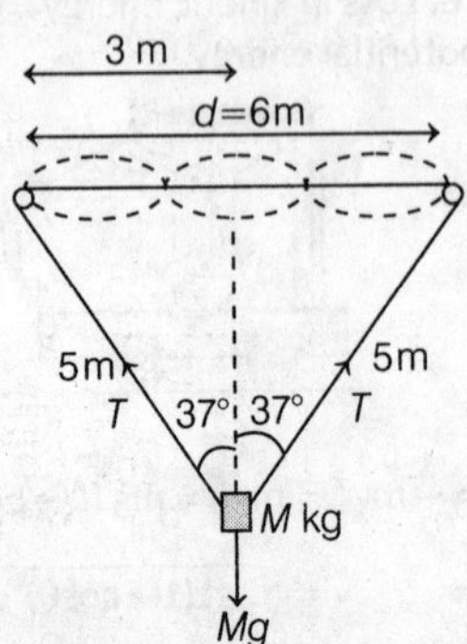

For vertical equilibrium of the block,

$$2T\cos 37° = Mg$$

$$\Rightarrow \quad 2T\left(\frac{4}{5}\right) = Mg$$

$$\Rightarrow \quad M = \frac{4T}{25} \quad \text{... (i)}$$

Also, for standing wave formed in 3rd harmonic, frequency of vibration,

$$f = \frac{3}{2d}\sqrt{\frac{T}{\mu}}$$

$$\Rightarrow T = \frac{4d^2f^2\mu}{9} = \frac{4(6)^2 \times (25)^2 \times 0.01}{9}$$

$$= 100 \text{ N}$$

Putting in Eq. (i), we get

$$M = 16 \text{ kg}$$

Part Test 02

1.

Consider FBD of x length of bottom part of the rod as shown. T, w and B represent internal force, weight and buoyancy, respectively. For equilibrium,

$$T = B - w$$

$$\Rightarrow \quad T = 2\rho gAL - \rho gAx$$

$$= \rho gA(2L - x)$$

$$\Rightarrow \text{Compression} = \int \frac{Tdx}{AY}$$

$$= \int_0^L \frac{\rho g(2L - x)}{Y}dx$$

$$= \frac{3\rho gL^2}{2Y}$$

2. At a small incremental time dt, the mass dm that is poured onto the conveyor belt is given by

$$dm = \mu dt$$

This implies that the change in momentum dp is given by (v is the velocity of the conveyor belt that is pulling the sand up)

$$dp = dmv = \mu v dt$$

By Newton's second law, the amount of force that is directed upwards on crane is given by

$$F_{\text{up}} = \frac{dp}{dt} = \frac{\mu v dt}{dt} = \mu v$$

We note that there is a force of gravity that directed downwards. The total mass of all the sand grains on the conveyor belt with length l is given by $m = \frac{\mu}{v}l$, thus the force directed downwards is given by

$$F_{\text{down}} = mg\sin\alpha = \frac{\mu g}{v}l\sin\alpha$$

This gives us the total force to bring sand grains up on a conveyor belt as

$$F = \mu v + \frac{\mu g}{v}l\sin\alpha$$

Minimising this function by differentiating with respect to v gives us

$$\mu - \frac{\mu g}{v^2}l\sin\alpha = 0$$

$$\Rightarrow \quad v = \sqrt{gl\sin\alpha}$$

Substituting this expression back into our expression for force gives us

$$F_{\min} = \mu\sqrt{gl\sin\alpha} + \frac{\mu g}{\sqrt{gl\sin\alpha}}l\sin\alpha$$

$$= 2\mu\sqrt{gl\sin\alpha}$$

$\Rightarrow$ The minimum torque is given by

$$\tau = F_{\min} \cdot R = 2\mu R\sqrt{gl\sin\alpha}$$

3. By the equation of continuity, we have

$$\mu_i = \mu_1 + \mu_2 \quad \text{...(i)}$$

By Bernoulli's theorem, the velocity of both the left and the right compartments is same and equal to v.

Now, by conservation of momentum in the horizontal direction, we get

$$\mu_i\rho(v\cos 2\alpha) = \mu_1\rho(v) - \mu_2\rho(v)$$

$$\mu_i\cos 2\alpha = \mu_1 - \mu_2 \quad \text{... (ii)}$$

Adding Eqs. (i) and (ii), we get

$$\mu_i(1 + \cos 2\alpha) = 2\mu_1$$

$$\Rightarrow \mu_1 = \frac{\mu_i(1 + \cos 2\alpha)}{2} = \mu_i\cos^2\alpha \quad \text{...(iii)}$$

From Eqs. (i) and (iii), we get

$$\mu_2 = \mu_i - \mu_1 = \mu_i - \mu_i\cos^2\alpha$$

$$\Rightarrow \quad \mu_2 = \mu_i\sin^2\alpha \quad \text{...(iv)}$$

Dividing Eq. (iii) by Eq. (iv), we get

$$\frac{\mu_1}{\mu_2} = \cot^2\alpha$$

4. Path difference = Path B − Path A

$$\Delta x = 7d - 3d = 4d$$

(Note that there is no phase change in reflections from mirror in case of sound)

For minima,

$$\Delta x = 4d = \frac{\lambda}{2}; \frac{3\lambda}{2}; \ldots\ldots$$

$\Rightarrow$ For minimum value of d,

$$4d = \frac{\lambda}{2}$$

$$\Rightarrow \quad d = \frac{\lambda}{8}$$

5. The situation can be shown as,

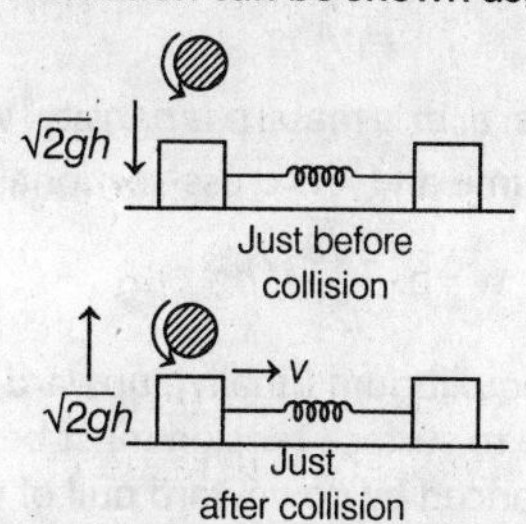

For ball in vertical direction,

$$\int N dt = 2m\sqrt{2gh} \quad \text{...(i)}$$

For left block in horizontal direction,

$$\mu \int N dt = mv \quad \text{...(ii)}$$

As $\mu = 1 \Rightarrow v = 2\sqrt{2gh}$

[using Eqs. (i) and (ii)]

For subsequent motion, till maximum compression,

$$\frac{1}{2}\mu v_{rel}^2 = \frac{1}{2}kx^2$$

(here, μ is reduced mass)

$$\Rightarrow \quad x = \sqrt{\frac{\mu}{k}}\, v_{rel} = \sqrt{\frac{m}{2k}} \cdot 2\sqrt{2gh}$$

$$= 2\sqrt{\frac{mgh}{k}}$$

Time taken for maximum compression

$$= \frac{T}{4} = \frac{2\pi\sqrt{\frac{m}{2k}}}{4} = \frac{\pi}{2}\sqrt{\frac{m}{2k}}$$

6. Case 1 $v = u$

If r is instantaneous separation and velocity of dog makes α with X-axis,

$$v - u\cos\alpha = -\frac{dr}{dt}$$

Integrating both sides, we get

$$\Rightarrow u\int_0^t dt - u\int_0^t \cos\alpha\, dt = -\int_l^d dr \quad (\because v = u)$$

Here, d = final separation

$$\Rightarrow ut - u\int_0^l \cos\alpha\, dt = l - d \quad \text{...(i)}$$

For displacements along X-axis, displacement of cat = displacement of dog + d

$$ut = u\int_0^l \cos\alpha\, dt + d \quad \text{...(ii)}$$

From Eqs. (i) and (ii), we get

$$d = \frac{l}{2}$$

Case 2 If $v = 2u$ and t is time of catching, then

$$vt - u\int_0^t \cos t\, dt = l \quad \text{...(i)}$$

Also, displacement of cat

= displacement of dog

$$ut = v\int_0^t \cos\alpha\, dt$$

$$\Rightarrow \int_0^t \cos\alpha\, dt = \frac{u}{v}t \quad \text{...(ii)}$$

From Eqs. (i) and (ii), we get

$$vt - u\left(\frac{u}{v}t\right) = l$$

$$\Rightarrow \quad t = \frac{vl}{v^2 - u^2} = \frac{2l}{3u} \quad (\because v = 2u)$$

$\Rightarrow$ Distance moved by dog $= \frac{4l}{3}$

$$\text{Average velocity of dog } = \sqrt{\frac{l^2 + \left(\frac{2l}{3}\right)^2}{2l/3u}}$$

$$= \frac{\sqrt{13}}{2}u$$

7. Kinetic energy of rod = Loss in PE = mgl

As rotational kinetic energy $\propto I$

(Moment of inertia)

$$\propto ml^2$$

$\Rightarrow$ Kinetic energy of $AC = \frac{mgl}{8}$

$\Rightarrow$ KE of $CB = \frac{7mgl}{8}$

By work-energy theorem, work done by CB on AC

$$= \Delta K - W_{gravity}$$

$$= \frac{mgl}{8} - \frac{m}{2}g\frac{l}{2}$$

$$= -\frac{mgl}{8}$$

$\Rightarrow$ Work done by AC on $CB = \frac{mgl}{8}$

8. Speed of wave $= \sqrt{\frac{T}{\mu}} = \sqrt{\frac{4\mu gx}{\mu}}$

$$= \sqrt{4gx} \quad \text{(w.r.t. string)}$$

$\Rightarrow a$ (w.r.t. string) of wave pulse $= 2g$

Note that acceleration in B is w.r.t. ground. So, it is incorrect.

Also, $\quad t = \sqrt{\frac{2l}{g}} = \sqrt{\frac{l}{g}}$

$$= \frac{T}{2\pi} = \frac{T}{6.28}$$

$\therefore$ Pendulum released from extreme should be between extreme and mid position B.

9. (a) As potentials at centres of the two spheres will be different, work done by gravitational force will be

$$W = m\Delta V \neq 0$$

(b) Consider a particle of mass m in YZ-plane at a distance y from origin, as shown

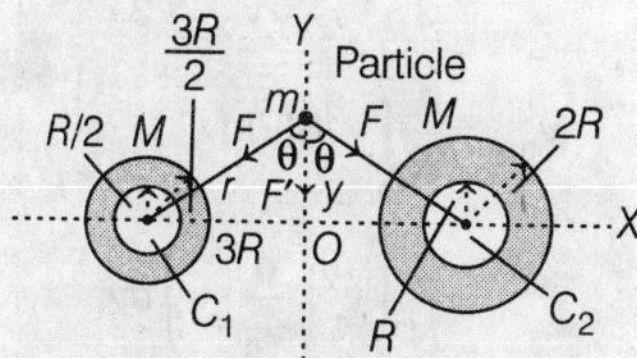

Force on the particle by each sphere is F towards respective centre (same in magnitude by symmetry). Thus, resultant force will be

$$F' = 2F\cos\theta = 2\cdot\frac{GMm}{r^2}\cdot\frac{y}{r}$$

$$= \frac{2GMmy}{r^3} = \frac{2GMmy}{(9R^2 + y^2)^{3/2}} \quad \text{...(i)}$$

For small displacement $(y \to 0)$, $9R^2 + y^2 \approx 9R^2$

Therefore, $\quad F' = \frac{2GMmy}{27R^3}$

Comparing it with $F' = ky$, we get

$$k = \frac{2GMm}{27R^3}$$

$$\Rightarrow \text{Frequency} = \frac{1}{2\pi}\sqrt{\frac{k}{m}} = \frac{1}{2\pi}\sqrt{\frac{2GM}{27R^3}}$$

(c) $y^2 + z^2 = 16R^2 = (4R)^2$ is equation of circle with radius $4R$.

As, gravitational force provides the necessary centripetal force.

i.e. $F = m\omega^2(4R)$

$$\Rightarrow \quad \frac{2GMm(4R)}{[9R^2 + (4R)^2]^{3/2}} = m\omega^2(4R)$$

[using Eq. (i)]

$$\Rightarrow \quad \omega = \sqrt{\frac{2GM}{125R^3}}$$

$$\Rightarrow \quad T = \frac{2\pi}{\omega} = 10\pi\sqrt{\frac{5R^3}{2GM}}$$

(d) Potential decreases in magnitude as distance of point from spheres' centre increases.

10. Area under the curve is equal to number of molecules of the gas sample, hence

$$N = \frac{1}{2} \cdot a \cdot v_0 \Rightarrow av_0 = 2N$$

$$v_{avg} = \frac{1}{N}\int_0^\infty vN(v)dv$$

$$= \frac{1}{N}\int_0^{v_0} v \cdot \left(\frac{a}{v_0} \cdot v\right) dv$$

$$= \frac{2}{3}v_0 \Rightarrow \frac{v_{avg}}{v_0} = \frac{2}{3}$$

$$v_{rms}^2 = \frac{1}{N}\int_0^\infty v^2 N(v)dv$$

$$= \frac{1}{N}\int_0^{v_0} v^2\left(\frac{a}{v_0} \cdot v\right) dv$$

$$= \frac{v_0^2}{2} \Rightarrow \frac{v_{rms}}{v_0} = \frac{1}{\sqrt{2}}$$

Area under the curve from 0.5 v_0 to v_0 is $\frac{3}{4}$th of total area.

11. FBD of the beam balance is as shown.

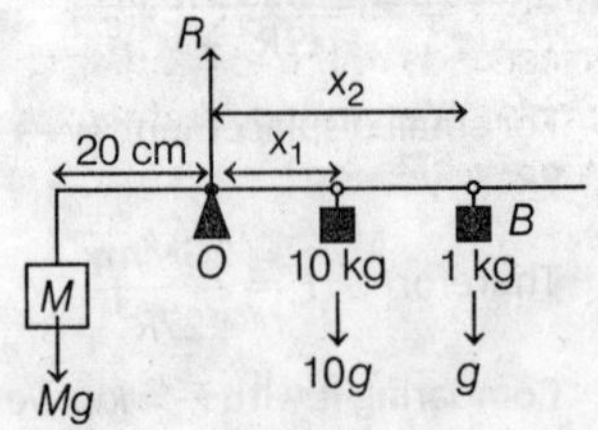

(A) Balancing torques of various forces about O, we get

$$20M = 10x_1 + x_2$$

$$\Rightarrow \quad M = \frac{1}{20}(10x_1 + x_2)$$

$$\Rightarrow \quad \Delta M = \frac{1}{20}(10\Delta x_1 + \Delta x_2)$$

$\Rightarrow \Delta M$ does not depend on absolute values of x_1 and x_2.

(B) $\Delta M = \frac{1}{20}(10 \times 0.1 + 0.1) = \frac{1.1}{20}$

$$= 0.055 \text{ kg}$$

(C) $M = \frac{1}{20}(10 \times 10 + 20) = 6$ kg

$$\Rightarrow \frac{\Delta M}{M} \times 100 = \frac{0.055}{6} \times 100 = 0.9\%$$

12. In horizontal direction, as final velocity is vertical, so horizontal velocity component is zero.

$$\Rightarrow \quad 0 = u - (g/2)t$$

$$\Rightarrow \quad t = \frac{2u}{g}$$

In vertical direction, final velocity will be

$$v = u + at = 0 + g \cdot \frac{2u}{g} = 2u$$

Also, $h = 0 + \frac{1}{2}g\left(\frac{2u}{g}\right)^2 = \frac{2u^2}{g}$

and work done by wind, $\Delta KE_{horizontal} = -\frac{1}{2}mu^2$

13. Fundamental frequency of wire,

$$f_{wire} = \frac{v}{2l}$$

(a) $f = \frac{v}{4l}, \frac{3v}{4l}, \frac{5v}{4l}$ can't match with f_{wire}

(b) $f = \frac{v}{2(2l)}, \frac{2v}{2(2l)}, \frac{3v}{2(2l)}$, its second harmonic $\frac{2v}{2(2l)}$ matches with f_{wire}

(c) $f = \frac{v}{2\left(\frac{l}{2}\right)}, \frac{2v}{2\left(\frac{l}{2}\right)},$

can't match with f_{wire}

(d) $f = \frac{v}{4\left(\frac{l}{2}\right)}, \frac{3v}{4\left(\frac{l}{2}\right)}, \ldots$

its fundamental frequency matches with f_{wire}

14. The equivalent p-V curve of the process is shown below.

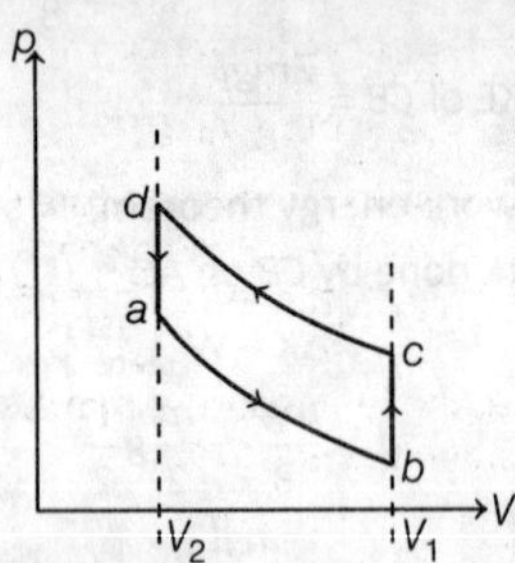

From the equivalent p-V curve, bc is isochoric and so, work in it is zero, cd is isothermal compression and so work in it is negative. As the cycle is anti-clockwise, work done in cycle is negative.

15. As angle of contact is given to be θ and side of cross-section is l, vertical component of force due to surface tension is $T\cos\theta \times l$. As there are six sides, therefore upward pull of surface tension,

$$F = 6T\cos\theta l \quad \ldots(i)$$

As the liquid rises by height h in the tube, weight of liquid in the tube,

$$w = mg = \rho Vg$$
$$= \rho Ahg$$

where, m is mass, ρ is density, V is volume and A is cross-sectional area.

$$\Rightarrow \quad w = \rho \cdot \frac{3\sqrt{3}}{2}l^2hg \quad \ldots(ii)$$

In equilibrium (finally), upward pull due to surface tension must be balanced by downward pull of weight. i.e. $F = w$

$$\Rightarrow 6T\cos\theta l = \frac{\rho \cdot 3\sqrt{3}\, l^2 hg}{2}$$

[using Eqs. (i) and (ii)]

$$\Rightarrow \quad h = \frac{4T\cos\theta}{\sqrt{3}\rho gl} = \frac{\sqrt{x}\,T\cos\theta}{\rho gl} \quad \text{(given)}$$

$$\Rightarrow \sqrt{x} = \frac{4}{\sqrt{3}} = \sqrt{\frac{16}{3}} \Rightarrow \quad x = \frac{16}{3} = 5.33$$

16. The total amount of heat Q liberated by the space object per unit time is proportional to its volume.

$$\Rightarrow \quad Q \propto R^3 \quad \ldots(i)$$

Also, since the amount of heat given away per unit surface area is proportional to T^4 as per Stefan's law, and in equilibrium, the entire amount of the liberated heat is dissipated into space, we can write

$$\Rightarrow \quad Q \propto R^2T^4 \quad \ldots(ii)$$

Thus, from Eqs. (i) and (ii), we get

$$R^2T^4 \propto R^3$$

$$\Rightarrow \quad T \propto \sqrt[4]{R}$$

If R becomes 16 times, T will be doubled, i.e. $2T$.

17. Suppose the radius of the cylinder is R and length of rod is $2l$.

Consider the case when the end A has sliding tendency up.

Forces acting on the rod are shown in the figure.

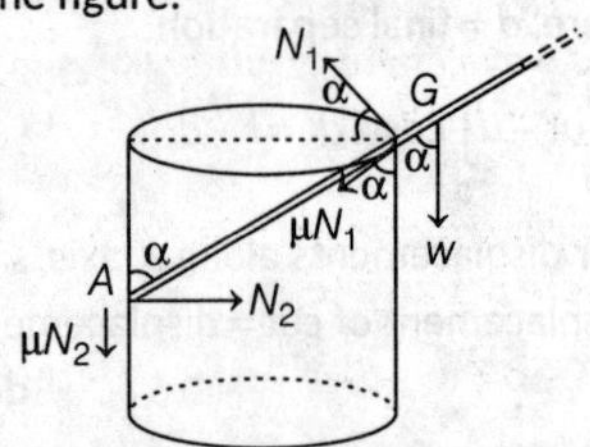

Resolving forces horizontally and vertically, we have

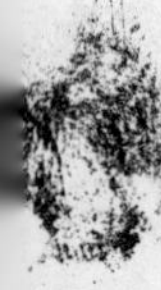

$N_2 = N_1 \cos\alpha + \mu N_1 \sin\alpha$ ...(i)

and $N_1 \sin\alpha = \mu N_2 + \mu N_1 \cos\alpha + w$ ...(ii)

Taking moment about A,

$$N_1(2R\operatorname{cosec}\alpha) = w(l \sin\alpha) \quad ...(iii)$$

From Eqs. (i), (ii) and (iii), we get

$$2R = l[1-\mu^2]\sin\alpha - 2\mu\cos\alpha]\sin^2\alpha \quad ...(iv)$$

Similarly, when the rod makes least angle β, we get A will have sliding tendency downward.

$$2R = l[(1-\mu^2)\sin\beta + 2\mu\cos\beta]\sin^2\beta \quad ...(v)$$

From Eqs. (iv) and (v), we get

$$\mu = \tan\left[\frac{1}{2}\tan^{-1}\left(\frac{\sin^3\alpha - \sin^3\beta}{\sin^2\alpha\cos\alpha + \sin^2\beta\cos\beta}\right)\right]$$

After substituting the values, we get

$$\mu = \tan\left[\frac{1}{2}\tan^{-1}\left(\frac{37}{84}\right)\right] \Rightarrow n = 3$$

18. As $\Delta S = 2.303\, nR\log\left(\frac{V_{\text{final}}}{V_{\text{initial}}}\right)$, between points Q and P shown on the graph,

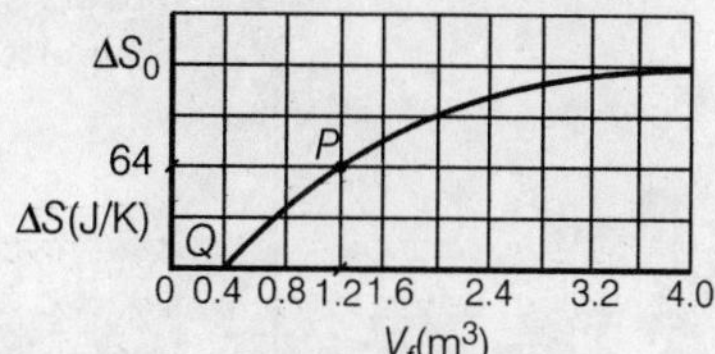

$$64 = 2.303\,n\,(8.314)\log\left(\frac{1.2}{0.4}\right)$$

$$\Rightarrow n = \frac{64}{2.303 \times 8.314 \times \log 3} = 7$$

19. The sound wave bifurcates at the junction of the straight and the semi-circular parts. The wave through the straight part travels a distance $p_1 = 2 \times 10$ cm and the wave through the curved part travels a distance $p_2 = \pi \times 10 = 31.4$ cm before they meet again and travel to the receiver.

The path difference between the two waves received, therefore

$\Delta p = p_2 - p_1 = 31.4 - 20 = 11.4$ cm

The wavelength of either wave is $\frac{v}{\nu} = \frac{330\text{ m/s}}{\nu}$.

For constructive interference, $\Delta p = n\lambda$, where n is an integer.

or $\Delta p = n \cdot \frac{v}{f}$

$$\Rightarrow f = \frac{n \cdot v}{\Delta p} = \frac{n \cdot 342}{0.114} = 3000n$$

Thus, frequencies for which constructive interference takes place are integral multiple of 3 kHz, *viz.* 3 kHz, 6 kHz and so on. Only 6 kHz falls in the range given in the question statement.

20.

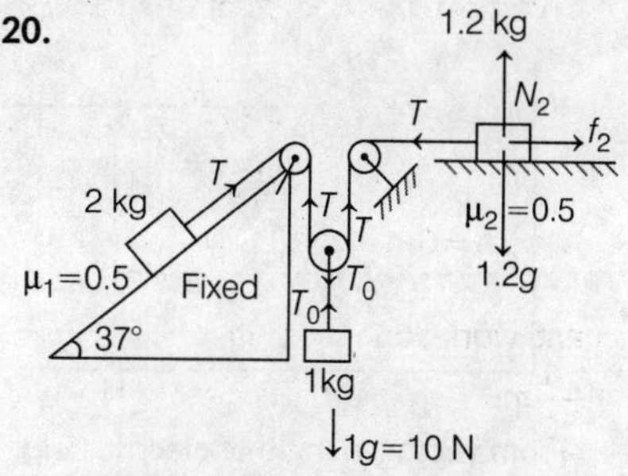

Friction force between blocks and surfaces is sufficient to prevent motion of blocks.

From FBD of 1 kg, we get

$$T_0 = 1g = 10\text{ N}$$

From FBD of pulley, we get

$$2T = T_0 \Rightarrow T = 5\text{ N}$$

From FBD of 1.2 kg, we get

$$N_2 = 1.2\,g = 12\text{ N}$$

Also, $f_2 = T = 5$ N

Contact force between 1.2 kg and surface

$$R = \sqrt{N_2^2 + f_2^2} = \sqrt{12^2 + 5^2} = 13\text{ N}$$

So, $\frac{R}{T} = 2.60$

21. Let density changes from ρ_1 at θ_1 to ρ_2 at θ_2.

For floatation of balloon,

Final weight = Buoyancy

$$\Rightarrow V_B \cdot \rho_2 g + mg = V_B \cdot \rho_1 g$$

(ρ_2 is density at temperature θ_2)

$$\Rightarrow \rho_2 = \rho_1 - \frac{m}{V_B} = 1.2 - \frac{0.187}{1.1} = 1.03$$

Then, the temperature may be obtained from

$$\frac{\rho_1}{\rho_2} = \frac{\theta_2}{\theta_1}$$

(As at constant pressure $\rho \propto \frac{1}{\theta}$)

$$\Rightarrow \theta_2 = \frac{\rho_1}{\rho_2}\theta_1 = \frac{1.2}{1.03} \times 293.15$$

$$= 341.53\text{ K} = 68.38^\circ\text{C}$$

22. The tension F_B in the rope is the difference between the buoyant force F_A and the weight force F_G.

$F_B = V_B \cdot \rho_1 \cdot g - (V_B \cdot \rho_3 + m) \cdot g$ ...(i)

Also, $\rho_3 \cdot \theta_3 = \rho_1 \cdot \theta_1$ ...(ii)

From Eqs. (i) and (ii), we get

$$F_B = V_B \cdot \rho_1 \cdot g \cdot \left(1 - \frac{\theta_1}{\theta_3}\right) - m \cdot g$$

$$= 1.21\text{ N}$$

23-24.

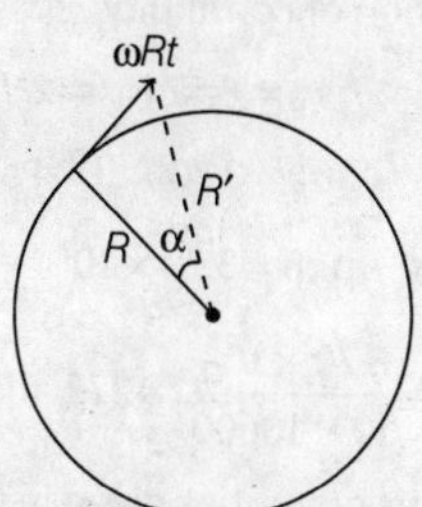

In the free-falling frame, all the particles move with constant velocities, each particle had initial velocity equal to the wheel's velocity at the releasing point, i.e. tangential to the wheel and equal to ωR. Hence, the ensemble of particle expands as a circle, the radius of which can be calculated from the pythagoras theorem,

$$R'^2 = R^2 + \omega^2 R^2 t^2$$

$$\Rightarrow \quad R' = R\sqrt{1 + \omega^2 t^2}$$

In the ground frame, the centre of the circle performs a free fall $d = \frac{1}{2}gt^2 - R$.

A droplet reaching the point A corresponds to the expanding circle touching the ground, therefore setting $R' = d$ gives us

$$R\sqrt{1 + \omega^2 t^2} = \frac{1}{2}gt^2 - R$$

$$\Rightarrow \frac{1}{4}g^2 t^4 - gRt^2 + R^2 = R^2 + R^2\omega^2 t^2$$

$$\Rightarrow \frac{1}{4}g^2 t^2 - gR = R^2\omega^2$$

$$\Rightarrow t = 2\sqrt{\frac{R}{g}\left(1 + \frac{R\omega^2}{g}\right)} = 2\sqrt{2}\sqrt{\frac{R}{g}}$$

$$= 2.82\omega^{-1}$$

We can also tell from the given diagram that,

$$\alpha = \tan^{-1}\left(\frac{\omega Rt}{R}\right) \Rightarrow \alpha = \tan^{-1}(\omega t)$$

$$\Rightarrow x = 2\sqrt{2} = 2.82$$

25-26.

Applying Bernoulli's theorem between points A and C that are at same horizontal level.

$$\frac{1}{2}\rho \cdot v_A^2 + p_A = \frac{1}{2}\rho \cdot v_C^2 + p_{\text{atm}}$$

$$\Rightarrow \quad p_A = (1.01 \times 10^5 + \frac{1}{2} \times 13600(8^2 - 4^2)$$

$$= 4.27 \times 10^5 \text{ Pa}$$

Also, by applying Bernoulli's equation between points B and C and using equation of continuity

$$v_B = 8.57 \text{ m/s}$$

and $$p_B = 3.70 \times 10^4 \text{ Pa}$$

$$\Rightarrow \rho g h = 3.70 \times 10^4$$

$$\Rightarrow h = \frac{3.70 \times 10^4}{10 \times 13600} = 272 \text{ mm} = 0.27 \text{ m}$$

27. Various quantities given in the problem are related to mass of planet (M), mass of satellite (m) and radius of satellite (r) by the following relations

$$v_0 = \sqrt{\frac{GM}{r}}$$

$$T_0 = 2\pi\sqrt{\frac{r^3}{GM}}$$

$$K_0 = \frac{GMm}{2r}$$

$$P_0 = -\frac{GMm}{r}$$

$$B_0 = \frac{GMm}{2r}$$

$$E_0 = -\frac{GMm}{2r}$$

$$L_0 = mvr = m\sqrt{GMr}$$

Therefore,

$$v_0 K_0 \propto r^{-3/2}$$

$$B_0 L_0 \propto r^{-1/2}$$

$$P_0 E_0 L_0^4 \propto r^0$$

$$\frac{T_0}{L_0^3} \propto r^0$$

Part Test 03

1. Potential at a distance r outside sphere is given by

$$V = \frac{kq}{r} \quad \text{...(i)}$$

Field at a distance r outside sphere is given by,

$$E = \frac{kq}{r^2} \quad \text{...(ii)}$$

Dividing Eq. (i) by Eq. (ii), we get

$$\frac{V}{E} = r$$

$$\Rightarrow r = \frac{V}{E} = \frac{900}{\sqrt{54^2 + 72^2}} = 10 \text{ m}$$

$$\Rightarrow 900 = \frac{9 \times 10^9 \times q}{10} \quad \text{[using Eq. (i)]}$$

$$\Rightarrow q = 1\,\mu\text{C}$$

Hence, option (a) is correct.

Now, consider the figure shown

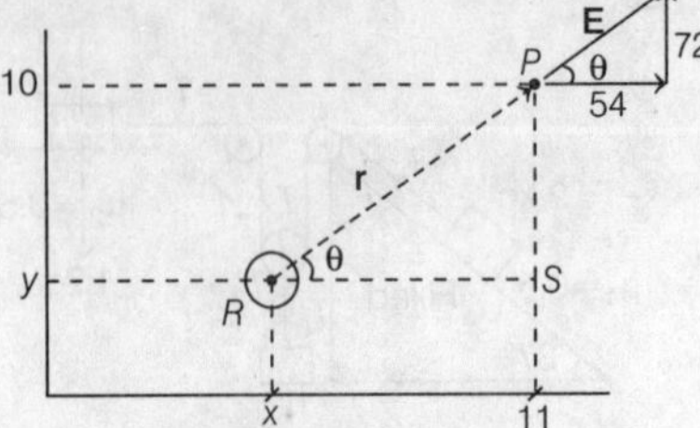

From vector triangle of electric field,

$$\tan\theta = \frac{72}{54} = \frac{4}{3}$$

$$\Rightarrow \theta = 53°$$

Therefore, in triangle PRS,

$PS = r\sin\theta = 10 \times \sin 53° = 8$ m

and $RS = r\cos\theta = 10 \times \cos 53° = 6$ m

Thus, from diagram, coordinates of centre of the sphere are

$$x = 11 - RS = 11 - 6 = 5 \text{ m}$$

and $y = 10 - PS = 10 - 8 = 2$ m

Hence, option (b) is correct.

Now, dielectric strength of any medium is the maximum electric field (E_{max}) that can be sustained by the medium without breaking down.

Therefore, using

$$E = \frac{kq}{R^2}$$

We get, $$R_{min}^2 = \frac{kq}{E_{max}} = \frac{9 \times 10^9 \times 10^{-6}}{3 \times 10^6}$$

$$= 3 \times 10^{-3} = 30 \times 10^{-4} \text{ m}^2$$

$$\Rightarrow R_{min} = \sqrt{30} \times 10^{-2} \text{ m}$$

$$= \sqrt{30} \text{ cm}$$

Hence, option (c) is correct.

Thus, most appropriate option is (d).

2. Let us first find general expression of flux (through disc) of point charge on axis of disc. To do this, consider a ring element of radius r and thickness dr as shown. Flux through the element

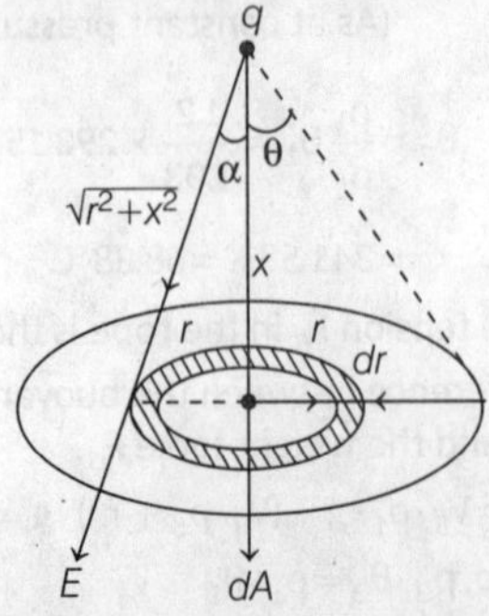

$$d\phi = EdA\cos\alpha$$

$$= \frac{q}{4\pi\varepsilon_0(r^2 + x^2)} \cdot 2\pi r dr \cdot \frac{x}{\sqrt{r^2 + x^2}}$$

$$\Rightarrow \phi = \int d\phi = \frac{qx}{2\varepsilon_0}\int_0^R \frac{r}{\sqrt{r^2 + x^2}}dr$$

$$= \frac{q}{2\varepsilon_0}\left[1 - \frac{x}{\sqrt{R^2 + x^2}}\right]$$

$$= \frac{q}{2\varepsilon_0}(1 - \cos\theta) \quad \text{...(i)}$$

A : By Gauss' law, $\phi_{cone} = \frac{q_{inside}}{\varepsilon_0} = 0$

$$\Rightarrow \phi_{lateral} + \phi_{flat} = 0$$

$$\Rightarrow \phi_{lateral} = -\phi_{flat}$$

$$= -\frac{q}{2\varepsilon_0}(1 - \cos 53°)$$

[using Eq. (i)]

$$= -\frac{q}{5\varepsilon_0}$$

B : From diagram, no field line crosses lateral surface.

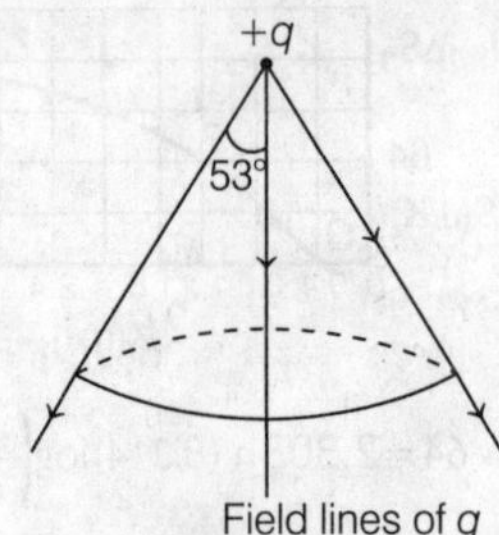

Field lines of q

$$\Rightarrow \phi_{lateral} = 0$$

C : By Gauss' law, $\phi_{cone} = \frac{q}{\varepsilon_0}$

$$\Rightarrow \phi_{lateral} + \phi_{flat} = \frac{q}{\varepsilon_0}$$

$$\Rightarrow \phi_{lateral} + \frac{q}{2\varepsilon_0}(1 - \cos 53°) = \frac{q}{\varepsilon_0}$$

[using Eq. (i)]

$$\Rightarrow \phi_{lateral} = \frac{4q}{5\varepsilon_0}$$

3. The given circuit diagram and its equivalent is as shown below.

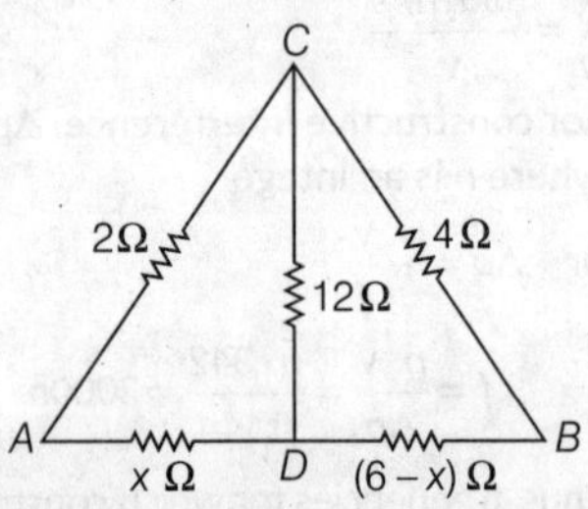

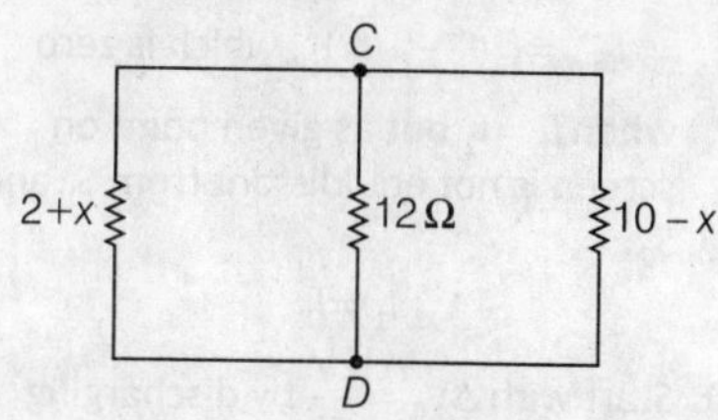

Equivalent resistance of the circuit between C and D is given by,

$$\frac{1}{R}=\frac{1}{12}+\frac{1}{2+x}+\frac{1}{10-x}$$

For R to be maximum or I to be minimum $\frac{d\left(\frac{1}{R}\right)}{dx}=0$

$$\Rightarrow \frac{1}{(2+x)^2}-\frac{1}{(10-x)^2}=0$$

$$\Rightarrow 2+x=10-x$$

$$\Rightarrow x=4\,\Omega$$

$$\Rightarrow \frac{AD}{AB}=\frac{4}{6}$$

$$\Rightarrow AD=\frac{2L}{3}$$

Option (c) is correct.

4. To go undeflected in velocity filter

$$qvB=qE$$

$$\Rightarrow v=\frac{E}{B}=\frac{100}{0.1}=10^3 \text{ m/s}$$

Only the particle having velocity 10^3 m/s, can go straight and emerge through slit S_2.

After that the particle will perform circular motion.

Radius of the path is given by,

$$R=\frac{mv}{qB}$$

$$\Rightarrow 2R=\frac{2mv}{qB}$$

$$\Rightarrow 0.42\times10^{-3}=\frac{2m(10^3)}{q(0.1)}$$

$$\Rightarrow \frac{q}{m}=4.8\times10^7 \text{ C/kg}$$

So, the particle must be α-particle.

5. Given, focal length of the objective $=60$ cm

Focal length of the eyepiece $=5$ cm

From the formula of magnification,

$$M=\frac{f_o}{f_e}=\frac{60}{5}=12$$

Hence, angular width of the image is given by,

$\beta=\alpha\times M=1\times12=12°$

6. Final output for various inputs are as shown

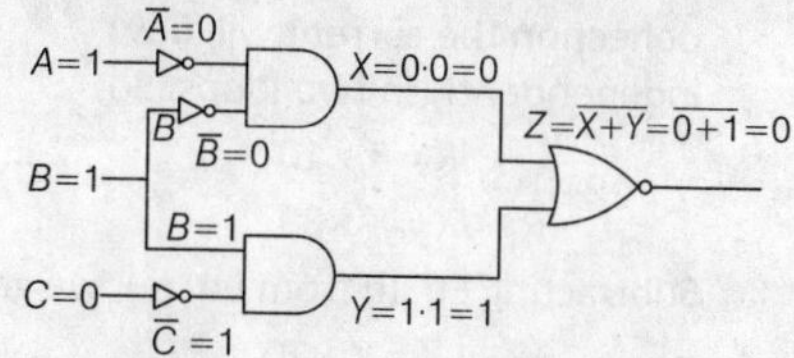

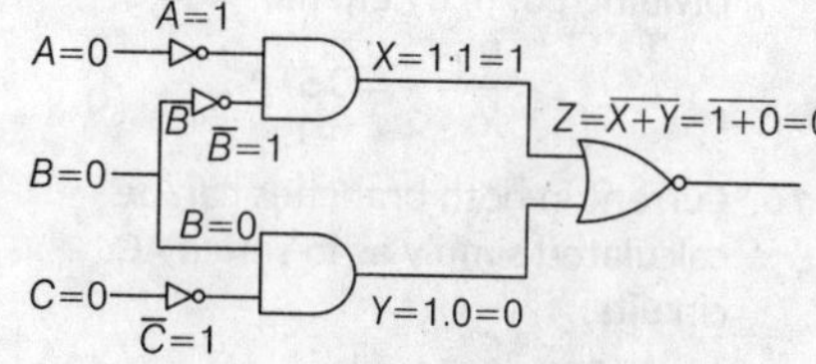

7. We first take a cylindrical element to find its capacitance and then integrate it to obtain the net capacitance and equivalent K.

$$\frac{\varepsilon_0 A}{d}\cdot K_{eq}=\int_0^R \frac{\varepsilon_0}{d}(2\pi r dr).k_0 r^n$$

$$K_{eq}\propto R^n$$

8. By Faraday's law,

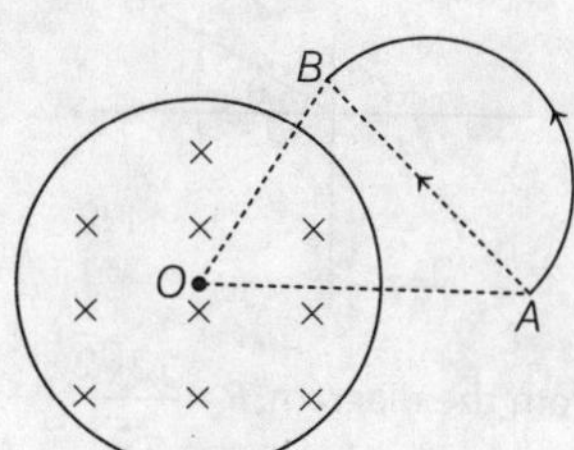

$$\oint \mathbf{E}\cdot d\mathbf{l}=\frac{d\phi}{dt}$$

$$\Rightarrow q\oint \mathbf{E}\cdot d\mathbf{l}=q\frac{d\phi}{dt}$$

$$\Rightarrow \oint \mathbf{F}\cdot d\mathbf{l}=q\frac{d\phi}{dt}$$

$$\Rightarrow W_{AB}+W_{OA}+W_{BO}=q\frac{d\phi}{dt}$$

$W_{AO}=W_{OB}=0$ (Since, electric field and dl are perpendicular) $W_{AB}=q\frac{d\phi}{dt}$

ϕ is same for both closed path.

So, work will also be same, so Statement I is false. But this is not necessarily true for all the paths as induced electric field is non-conservative in nature. So, Statement II is also false.

9. A. Point contact diodes are used to detect microwaves.

B. 1nm to 10^{-3} nm corresponds to X-rays.

C. UV radiations can be focused into very narrow beams for high precision applications such as LASIK (Laser assisted in situ keratomileusis) eye surgery.

D. Infrared detectors are used in earth's satellite, both for military purposes and to observe growth of crops.

10. Velocity of projection of the particle can be written as

$$\mathbf{u}=u_x\hat{\mathbf{i}}+u_y\hat{\mathbf{j}}$$

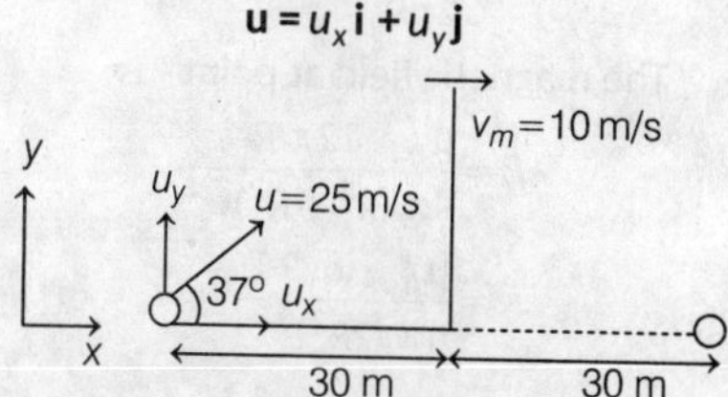

$$u_x=25\cos37°=20 \text{ m/s}$$

$$u_y=25\sin37°=15 \text{ m/s}$$

$\Rightarrow$ Velocity of image in x-direction

$$u_{I_x}=2v_m-u_x=2\times10-20=0$$

$$u_{I_y}=u_y=15 \text{ m/s}$$

$$a_{I_y}=a_{py}=-g$$

$$u_{IP}=(0-20)\hat{\mathbf{i}}+(15-15)\hat{\mathbf{j}}=-20\hat{\mathbf{i}}$$

$\Rightarrow$ Relative velocity of image w.r.t. object is constant. So,

$$\mathbf{a}_{IP}=-g\hat{\mathbf{j}}-(-g\hat{\mathbf{j}})=0$$

Separation at $t=2$ s is

$$=60+(-20)\times2=20 \text{ m}$$

11. For v_{min}, collision should be completely inelastic.

According to energy conservation principle,

$$\therefore \frac{1}{2}mv_{min}^2=\frac{1}{2}mv^2+\frac{1}{2}mv^2+\Delta E \quad \text{... (i)}$$

According to momentum conservation principle,

$$mv_{min}=mv+mv$$

$$\therefore v=\frac{v_{min}}{2} \quad \text{... (ii)}$$

After solving Eqs. (i) and (ii), we get

$$\frac{1}{2}mv_{min}^2=2\Delta E$$

$$\therefore v_{min}=\sqrt{\left(\frac{4\Delta E}{m}\right)}$$

Here, $\Delta E=$ minimum excitation energy $=10.2$ eV

$$m=1.67\times10^{-27} \text{ kg}$$

$$\therefore v_{min}=\sqrt{\left(\frac{4\times10.2\times1.6\times10^{-19}}{1.67\times10^{-27}}\right)}$$

$$=6.25\times10^4 \text{ ms}^{-1}$$

12. Let q be the charge on the ring. The electric field at point P is

$$E = \frac{1}{4\pi\varepsilon_0}\frac{qx}{(x^2+R^2)^{3/2}}$$

$$= \frac{1}{4\pi\varepsilon_0}\frac{qR}{(2R^2)^{3/2}}$$

The rotating charged (q) ring is equivalent to a ring in which current I flows, such that

$$I = \frac{qv}{2\pi R}$$

The magnetic field at point P is

$$B = \frac{\mu_0}{4\pi}\frac{2\pi IR^2}{(x^2+R^2)^{3/2}}$$

$$= \frac{\mu_0}{4\pi}\frac{qvR}{(2R^2)^{3/2}}$$

$$\therefore \quad \frac{E}{B} = \frac{1}{\mu_0\varepsilon_0 v} = \frac{c^2}{v}$$

13. From the given transfer characteristics of a common emitter transistor, we note that,

(i) When $V_i = 0.4$ V, there is no collector current. The transistor circuit is in cut off state and is used as a switch.

(ii) When $V_i = 1$ V (this is in between 0.6 V to 2 V), the transistor circuit is in active state and is used as an amplifier.

(iii) When $V_i = 0.5$ V, there is no collector current. The transistor is in cut off state. The transistor circuit can be used as a switch turned OFF.

(iv) When $V_i = 2.5$ V, the collector current becomes maximum and transistor is in saturation state and can be used as switch turned ON state.

14. As per the given information,

$$L = L_1 + L_2 + 2M = 1.9 \quad \text{...(i)}$$

$$L = L_1 + L_2 - 2M = 0.7 \quad \text{...(ii)}$$

Subtracting Eq. (ii) from Eq (i), we get

$$4M = 1.2 \Rightarrow M = 0.3$$

Putting this value in Eq.(i), we get

$$L_1 + L_2 = 1.3 \quad \text{... (iii)}$$

As, $\quad M = K\sqrt{L_1L_2}$

$$\therefore \quad L_1L_2 = 0.36 \quad \text{... (iv)}$$

Solving Eqs. (iii) and (iv), we get

$$L_1 = 0.9 \text{ H}, \; L_2 = 0.4 \text{ H}$$

15. Let potential drop unit length of a potentiometer wire be K. For zero deflection the current will flow independently in two loops. So,

$$IR = K \times 10 \quad \text{... (i)}$$

$$IR + IX = K \times 30 \quad \text{... (ii)}$$

Subtracting Eq. (i) from Eq. (ii), we get

$$\Rightarrow \quad IX = K \times 20 \quad \text{... (iii)}$$

Dividing Eq. (i) by Eq. (iii), we get

$$\frac{R}{X} = \frac{1}{2} = 0.5$$

16. Current in both branches can be calculated simply as in series AC circuits.

$$i_1 = \frac{200\sqrt{2}}{\sqrt{30^2+40^2}}\sin\left[\omega t - \tan^{-1}\left(\frac{40}{30}\right)\right]$$

$$= 4\sqrt{2}\sin(100\pi t - 53°)$$

$$i_2 = \frac{200\sqrt{2}}{50}\sin\left(\omega t + \frac{\pi}{2}\right)$$

To find resultant current R and its phase difference with voltage, draw phasor diagram as shown.

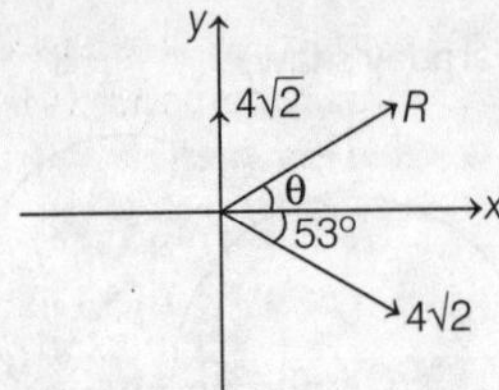

From the diagram, $R = \frac{12\sqrt{2}}{5}\hat{\mathbf{i}} + \frac{4\sqrt{2}}{5}\hat{\mathbf{j}}$

$$\therefore \quad \tan\theta = \frac{R_y}{R_x} = \frac{1}{3}$$

$$\text{Power factor} = \cos\theta = \frac{3}{\sqrt{10}}$$

17. Once the saturation is achieved, decreasing temperature will not affect magnetisation.

18. Suppose after earthing charge on inner shell becomes q', then for its potential to become zero,

$$\frac{kq'}{r} + \frac{kq}{3r} = 0$$

$$\Rightarrow \quad q' = -\frac{q}{3}$$

So, charge flown from shell to earth is $+\frac{q}{3}$ or $0.33\,q$

19. $I_p = I_1 + I_2 + \sqrt{2I_1I_2}\cos\phi$

Intensity is minimum, when $\cos\phi = -1$

$\Rightarrow I_{\min} = (\sqrt{I_1} - \sqrt{I_2})^2$, which is zero when $I_1 = I_2$ but as given point on screen is not equidistant from S_1 and S_2

$$I_1 \neq I_2$$

20. Start with $\Delta V_C = \frac{2V}{3}$ by discharging formula $\Delta V_C(t) = \frac{2}{3}Ve^{-t/R_2C}$

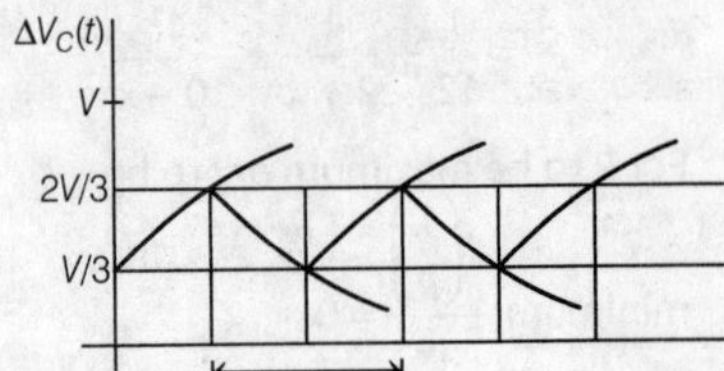

For $\Delta V_C(t) = \frac{V}{3}$, we get $t_1 = R_2C\ln 2$.

After the switch opens voltage is $\frac{V}{3}$ increasing towards V with time constant $(R_1 + R_2)\,C$, so

$$V_C(t) = V - \frac{2}{3}Ve^{-t_2/(R_1+R_2)C}$$

$$\Rightarrow \quad t_2 = (R_1 + R_2)C\ln 2$$

Time period of the waveform will therefore be $t_1 + t_2 = (R_1 + 2R_2)C\ln 2$.

21. Cross-section of cylinder is as shown. To find magnetic field at $r = 2R$, consider an amperian loop of radius $2R$ as shown.

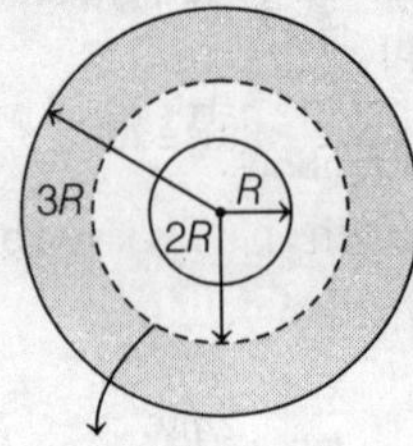

Current crossing the loop,

$$i = \frac{I}{\text{Area}} \times \text{Area of loop}$$

$$\Rightarrow \quad i = \frac{I}{\pi[(3R)^2 - R^2]} \times \pi[(2R)^2 - R^2]$$

$$\Rightarrow \quad i = \frac{3I}{8} \quad \text{...(i)}$$

By Ampere's law, $\oint \mathbf{B}\cdot d\mathbf{l} = \mu_0 i$

$$\Rightarrow \quad B(2\pi r) = \mu_0 i$$

$$\Rightarrow \quad B(2\pi \cdot 2R) = \mu_0 \cdot \frac{3I}{8}$$

[putting value of i From Eq. (i)]

$$\Rightarrow \quad B=\frac{3\mu_0 I}{32\pi R}$$

$$\Rightarrow \quad x=\frac{32}{3}=10.67$$

22. In a Bohr's atom,

Orbital velocity, $v \propto \frac{Z}{n}$ ...(i)

Orbital radius, $r \propto \frac{n^2}{Z}$ ...(ii)

So, for circular motion of electron, acceleration is given by

$$a=\frac{v^2}{r} \propto \frac{\left(\frac{Z}{n}\right)^2}{\frac{n^2}{Z}} \quad \text{[using Eqs. (i) and (ii)]}$$

$$\Rightarrow \quad a \propto Z^3$$

So, for hydrogen ($Z_1=1$) and helium ($Z_2=2$), ratio of corresponding electronic accelerations is

$$\frac{a_2}{a_1}=\left(\frac{Z_2}{Z_1}\right)^3$$

$$=\left(\frac{2}{1}\right)^3=8$$

$$\Rightarrow \quad x=8 \quad \text{...(iii)}$$

By Einstein's equation, stopping potential (V) is given by

$$V=\frac{hc}{e\lambda}-\frac{\phi}{e} \quad \text{...(iv)}$$

Here, $\lambda=$ wavelength of incident radiation, $\phi=$ work function

h, c, e are constants.

So, for wavelength equal to $(x-5)\lambda=(8-5)\lambda=3\lambda$ [using Eq. (iii)]

Stopping potential according to Eq. (iv) is

$$\frac{V}{5}=\frac{hc}{e(3\lambda)}-\frac{\phi}{e}$$

$$\Rightarrow \quad V=\frac{5hc}{3e\lambda}-\frac{5\phi}{e} \quad \text{...(v)}$$

As LHS of Eqs. (iv) and (v) are equal, by equating RHS, we get

$$\frac{hc}{e\lambda}-\frac{\phi}{e}=\frac{5hc}{3e\lambda}-\frac{5\phi}{e}$$

$$\Rightarrow \quad \frac{4\phi}{e}=\frac{2hc}{3e\lambda}$$

$$\Rightarrow \quad \phi=\frac{hc}{6\lambda}=\frac{hc}{y\lambda} \text{ (given)}$$

$$\Rightarrow \quad y=6 \quad \text{...(vi)}$$

From Eqs. (iii) and (vi), we get

$$\frac{x}{y}=\frac{8}{6}=\frac{4}{3}=1.33$$

23. No. of nuclei of a radioactive material with decay constant λ is given by

$$N=N_0 e^{-\lambda t}$$

Here, N_0 is initial number of nuclei.

As at $t=t_0$, $N_A=N_B$, therefore,

$$2N_0 e^{-\lambda_A t_0}=N_0 e^{-\lambda_B t_0}$$

$$\Rightarrow e^{(\lambda_A-\lambda_B)t_0}=2 \quad \text{...(i)}$$

At time $t=2t_0$, the required ratio will be

$$\frac{N_B}{N_A}=\frac{N_0 e^{-\lambda_B \cdot 2t_0}}{2N_0 e^{-\lambda_A \cdot 2t_0}}=\frac{e^{2(\lambda_A-\lambda_B)t_0}}{2}$$

$$=\frac{2^2}{2}=2 \quad \text{[using Eq. (i)]}$$

24. From the given diagram, S is linear gap between central maxima to second minima. For nth minima, this gap is equal to $n\lambda D/a$. Therefore, for $n=2$, we get s equal to

$$\frac{2\lambda D}{a}=\frac{2\times 600\times 10^{-9}\times 2}{4\times 10^{-4}}=6\times 10^{-3}\text{ m}$$

which is equal to 6 mm.

25. True dip at a place related to apparent dips in mutually perpendicular planes by the following relation .

$$\cot^2\delta=\cot^2\delta_1+\cot^2\delta_2$$

$$=(\cot 30^\circ)^2+(\cot 45^\circ)^2$$

$$=3+1=4$$

$$\Rightarrow \quad \cot\delta=2$$

$$\Rightarrow \quad \delta=2$$

26. For L-C_1 system,

$$\omega_1=\frac{1}{\sqrt{LC_1}}=\frac{100}{3}\text{ rad/s}$$

$$\Rightarrow \quad T_1=2\pi\sqrt{LC_1}=\frac{6\pi}{100}\text{ s}$$

For L-C_2 system,

$$\omega_2=\frac{1}{\sqrt{LC_2}}=100\text{ rad/s}$$

$$\Rightarrow \quad T_2=2\pi\sqrt{LC_2}=\frac{2\pi}{100}\text{ s}$$

Circuit L-C_1 is ON for $\frac{1.5\pi}{100}=\frac{T_1}{4}$ s

The charge on capacitor C_1 will be zero. So, the entire energy $\left(\frac{1}{2}C_1V_1^2\right)$ will go in inductor.

Now, after $t=\frac{0.5\pi}{100}=\frac{T_2}{4}$ s, current in the inductor will be zero. So, now all the energy $\left(\frac{1}{2}C_1V_1^2\right)$ will go in the capacitor C_2.

$$\Rightarrow \quad \frac{1}{2}C_1V_1^2=\frac{1}{2}C_2V_2^2$$

$$\Rightarrow \quad \frac{1}{2}(900\,\mu\text{F})(1)^2=\frac{1}{2}(100\,\mu\text{F})V_2^2$$

$$\Rightarrow \quad V_2=3\text{ V}$$

27. By Moseley's law,

$$\sqrt{v}=a(Z-b)$$

$$\Rightarrow \quad \sqrt{\frac{\lambda_2}{\lambda_1}}=\frac{Z_1-1}{Z_2-1}$$

$$\Rightarrow \quad 2=\frac{36}{Z_2-1}$$

$$\Rightarrow Z_2-1=18 \Rightarrow Z_2=19$$

28. Let N denotes the total number of nuclei. Initially,

$$N=N_u+N_s \quad \text{... (i)}$$

After a time T since the activity decreased to one-third, number of unstable nuclei will also become one-third. So, after a time T

$$N/2=N_u/3+N_s \quad \text{... (ii)}$$

Solving Eqs. (ii) and (ii) we get

$$N_u/N_s=3$$

29. Focal length doubles on cutting perpendicular to axis as power is halved, i.e. it will be 60 cm for each piece.

For 1st refraction,

$$\frac{1}{u}-\frac{1}{-20}=\frac{1}{60}$$

$$\therefore \quad u=-30\text{ cm}$$

This acts as an object for second refraction.

2nd refraction,

$$\frac{1}{v}-\frac{1}{-30}=\frac{1}{60}$$

$$v=-60\text{ cm}$$

$$m=\frac{v}{u}=\frac{-60}{-30}=2$$

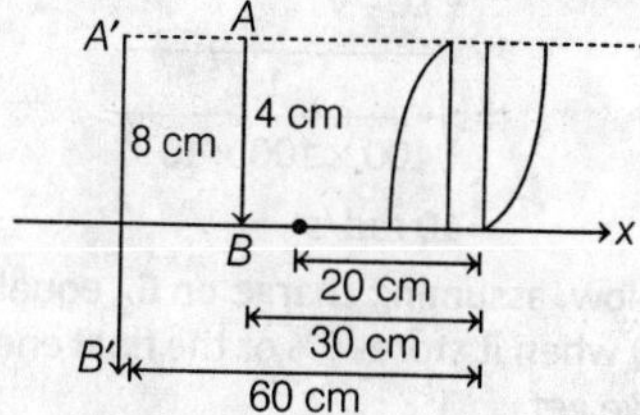

Coordinates of final image are (–40 cm, –4 cm).

$\therefore \quad x = -40$ and $y = -4$

$\Rightarrow \left|\frac{x}{10} + y\right| = \left|\frac{-40}{10} - 4\right| = 8$

30. Percentage modulation $= \frac{A_m}{A_c} \times 100 = (15/60) \times 100 = 25\%$

Part Test 04

1. Power transmitted across the slit is

$$P_1 = \frac{3.2}{4\pi(80)^2} \times \pi \times (0.8)^2 \times 0.8 = 6.4 \times 10^{-5}\ \text{W}$$

$\Rightarrow$ Number of photons falling on sphere per second

$$\frac{P_1}{E_{photon}} = \frac{6.4 \times 10^{-5}}{5 \times 1.6 \times 10^{-19}} = 8 \times 10^{13}$$

Number of electrons ejected per second

$$N = 10^{-4} \times 8 \times 10^{13} = 8 \times 10^{9}$$

$$\Rightarrow \quad i = Ne = 8 \times 10^{9} \times 1.6 \times 10^{-19} = 12.8 \times 10^{-10} = 1.28\ \text{nA}$$

2. Initially, for L-C circuit

$$\omega = \frac{1}{\sqrt{LC_1}} = \frac{1}{\sqrt{400 \times 10^{-6} \times 100}} = 5\ \text{rad/s}$$

Charge on capacitor is given by

$$q = q_0 \cos(\omega t)$$

$\Rightarrow$ At $t = \frac{\pi}{10}$ s,

$$q = q_0 \cos\left(5 \times \frac{\pi}{10}\right) = 0$$

So, at $t = \frac{\pi}{10}$ s, all the energy of capacitor C_1 would be stored in inductor.

Now, $\omega' = \sqrt{\frac{1}{LC_2}} = \sqrt{\frac{1}{100 \times 100 \times 10^{-6}}} = 10\ \text{rad/s}$

Now, assuming charge on C_2 equal to Q when it stores 9% of the final energy, we get

$$9\% \text{ of } \frac{Q_0^2}{2C_2} = \frac{Q^2}{2C_2}$$

$$Q = \frac{3}{10} Q_0$$

$$\Rightarrow \quad \frac{3Q_0}{10} = Q_0 \sin(10t)$$

$$\Rightarrow \sin(10t) = 0.3 = \sin\frac{\pi}{10}$$

$$\Rightarrow \quad t = \frac{\pi}{100}\ \text{s}$$

$$\text{Total time} = \frac{\pi}{10} + \frac{\pi}{100} = \frac{11\pi}{100}$$

3. In azimuthal direction, induced electric field $E_\phi(r) = \frac{r}{2} \cdot \frac{dB_z}{dt}$

This field acts on the charged cylindrical shell to produce azimuthal torque (per unit length),

$$\tau_\phi = I\frac{d\omega}{dt} = aE_\phi(a) 2\pi a \sigma$$

$$\Rightarrow \quad d\omega = -\frac{\sigma \pi a^3}{I} dB_z$$

$$\Rightarrow \quad \omega = -\frac{\sigma \pi a^3}{I} \int_{B_i}^{B_f} dB_z = \frac{\sigma \pi a^3}{I}(B_i - B_f)$$

$B_i = B_{ex}$ and B_f is the non-zero magnetic field produced by the rotating charged cylinder. For the rotating cylinder, compare with solenoid, the magnetic field will be along Z-axis and equal to

$$\mathbf{B}_f = \mu_0 n i \hat{z} = \mu_0 j_\phi \hat{z}$$

where, $j_\phi = a\sigma\omega$ is azimuthal current per unit length. Thus,

$$\mathbf{B}_f = \mu_0 a \sigma \omega \hat{z}$$

$$\therefore \quad \omega = \frac{\sigma \pi a^3}{I}(B_{ex} - \mu_0 a \sigma \omega)$$

$$\Rightarrow \quad \omega = \frac{\sigma \pi a^3}{I}\left(1 + \frac{\mu_0 \sigma^2 a^4 \pi}{I}\right)^{-1} B_{ex}$$

4. Flux will be maximum when maximum length of ring is inside the sphere.

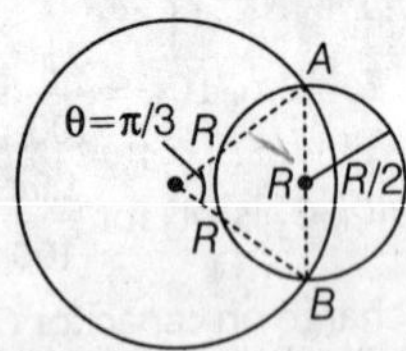

This will occur when the chord AB is maximum. Now, maximum length of chord AB = diameter of sphere. In this case the arc of ring inside the sphere subtends an angle of $\frac{\pi}{3}$ at the centre of ring.

$\Rightarrow$ Charge on this arc $= \frac{R\pi}{3}\lambda$

$$\therefore \quad \phi = \frac{\frac{R\pi}{3}\lambda}{\varepsilon_0} = \frac{R\pi\lambda}{3\varepsilon_0}$$

5. Due to the surface tension force by outside film, loop will expand and finally convert into a circular loop, as it has maximum area for a given perimeter, so that the film has minimum area and surface energy. As area of the loop increases, inward flux through the loop increases. To oppose this increase in inward flux, induced current should have outward flux as per Lenz's law and so, the induced current will be in anti-clockwise direction.

Also, as per Faraday's law, charge flown will be equal to $Q = \frac{\phi_f - \phi_i}{R}$

$$= \frac{B\left[\pi\left(\frac{l}{2\pi}\right)^2 - \frac{l^2}{8\pi}\right]}{R} = \frac{Bl^2}{8\pi R}$$

6. Consider the following relations :

$i = neAv_d \Rightarrow i \propto v_d \Rightarrow$ (A) is correct.

$P = \frac{V^2}{R} = E^2 \frac{l^2}{R} \Rightarrow P \propto E^2 \Rightarrow$ (B) is correct

$P = i^2 R \Rightarrow P \propto i^2 \Rightarrow$ (D) is correct

But as $P \propto i^2 \propto v_d^2$, so P-v_d graph will be parabolic.

$\Rightarrow$ (c) is incorrect.

7. (a) $KE_{max} = W_{\text{electric field}}$

$$= qE \cdot \frac{4R}{\pi} = \frac{\pi \times 1 \times 4 \times 1}{\pi}$$

$= 4$ J, when the ring is in Y-Z plane.

(b) $KE_{max} = W_{\text{electric field}}$

$$= \left|q_1 E \cdot \frac{2R}{\pi}\right| + \left|q_2 E \cdot \frac{2R}{\pi}\right|$$

$$= \frac{2ER}{\pi}[|q_1| + |q_2|]$$

$$= \frac{2 \times 1 \times 1}{\pi} \times 3\pi = 6\ \text{J}$$

(c) As, $\tau = pE\sin\theta$ is not proportional to angular displacement, so oscillation is not SHM.

(d) $\tau = pE\sin\theta \approx \frac{4qR}{\pi} E\theta$

$$\Rightarrow T = 2\pi\sqrt{\frac{I}{pE}} = 2\pi\sqrt{\frac{mR^2/2}{\frac{4qRE}{\pi}}} = 2\pi\ \text{s}$$

$\Rightarrow$ Required time $= \frac{\tau}{2} = \pi$ s

8. Fringe width, $\beta = \frac{\lambda D}{d} = \frac{\lambda_0 D}{n_2 d}$

If angular position of CM ($\Delta x = 0$) is θ, for $t = 0$.

θ (initial) is positive, while θ at $t = 2$ s is 0 as $n_1 = n_2$ and θ at $t = 2.5$ s is negative.

9. From Fig. A

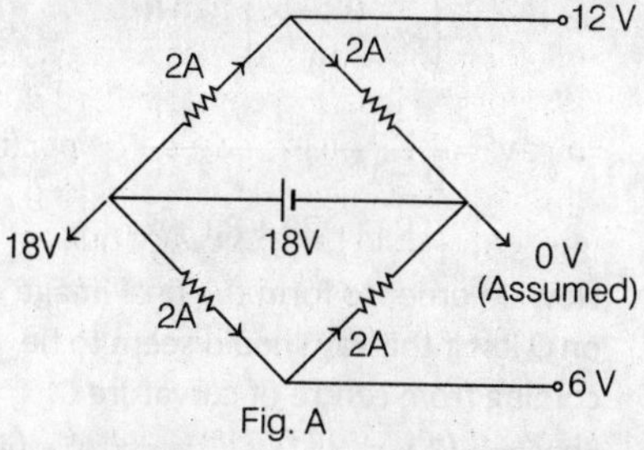

Fig. A

E_{eq} = Open circuit voltage = 6 V

From Fig. B,

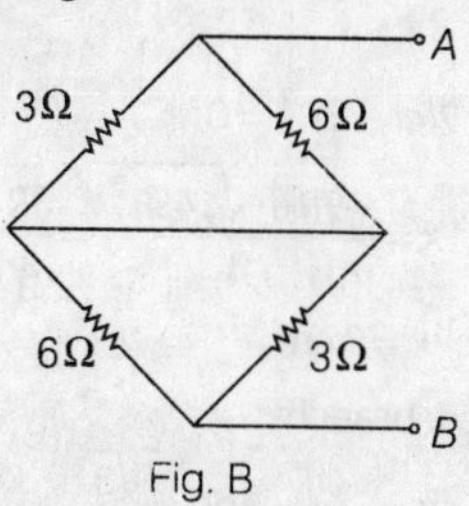

Fig. B

$r_{eq} = 4\,\Omega$

Thus, short circuit current,

$$= \frac{E_{eq}}{r_{eq}} = \frac{6}{4} = 1.5\text{ A}$$

By maximum power theorem,

$$P_{max} = \frac{E_{eq}^2}{4r_{eq}} = \frac{36}{4 \times 4} = 2.25\text{ W}$$

10. As S_1 is closed for long time, so the circuit is in steady state with charge on capacitor equal to $C\varepsilon$.

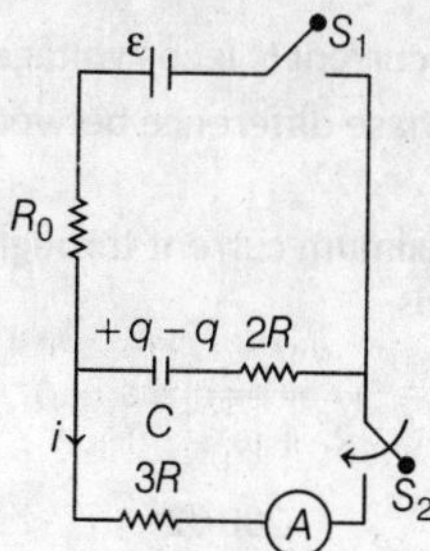

Now, the capacitor will be discharging through S_2 as shown, with time constant of the circuit equal to $5RC$. Thus, charge as function of time will be

$$q = q_0 e^{-\frac{t}{\tau}}$$

$$\Rightarrow \quad q = C\varepsilon e^{-\frac{t}{5RC}} \quad \text{...(i)}$$

$$\Rightarrow \quad i = -\frac{dq}{dt} = \frac{\varepsilon}{5R} e^{-\frac{t}{5RC}} \quad \text{...(ii)}$$

From Eq. (ii),

At $t = 0, i = \frac{\varepsilon}{5R}$

Also, heat dissipated = loss in PE

$$= \frac{1}{2}C\varepsilon^2 - \frac{1}{8}C\varepsilon^2 = \frac{3}{8}C\varepsilon^2$$

In series, resistor carry same current, so the heat dissipation in B is proportional to resistance.

Heat dissipated in $3R$ will be given by

$$H = \frac{3R}{3R + 2R} \times \frac{3}{8}C\varepsilon^2 = \frac{9C\varepsilon^2}{40}$$

11. The wavelength of the K_α-radiation from Nb is

$$\lambda = \frac{4}{3R}\frac{1}{(Z-1)^2}$$

$$= \frac{4}{3R}\frac{1}{40^2} = 0.76\text{°A}$$

$$\Rightarrow \quad E_{K_\alpha} = \frac{hc}{\lambda} = \frac{12400}{0.76}$$

$$\Rightarrow \quad E_{K_\alpha} = 16.3\text{ keV}$$

$\Rightarrow$ Ionisation energy of gas

$$= 16.3 - 2.7 = 13.6\text{ keV}$$

$$\Rightarrow \quad 13.6 Z^2 = 13.6 \times 10^3$$

$$\therefore \quad Z_{gas}^2 = 1000; Z_{gas} = 32$$

If the momentum of the electrons is doubled, then the KE is increased by 4 times.

$\therefore$ The minimum energy of the X-rays is $(16.3 + 3 \times 2.7)$ keV $= 24.4$ keV

The voltage across the tube should be greater than 24.4 keV

Since, $E_{K_\alpha} \propto (Z-1)^2$

$$\Rightarrow \quad \left(\frac{Z-1}{40}\right)^2 = \left(\frac{24.4}{16.3}\right) : Z = 50$$

The number of X-rays photons incident

$$= \frac{100 \times 10^{-3} \times 10^{19}}{1.6 \times 24.4 \times 10^3} \text{ per m}^2$$

$\Rightarrow$ Number of ions produced in 1 s

$$= \frac{100 \times 10^{-3} \times 10^{-2} \times 10^{19}}{1.6 \times 24.4 \times 10^3 \times 3 \times 10^8} \text{ per m}^3$$

$$\approx 850 \text{ per m}^3$$

12. From FBD of the sphere shown

$$\therefore \quad qE - T = 0$$

$$\Rightarrow \quad T = qE \quad \text{...(i)}$$

From FBD of the loop, when it is totally inside the magnetic field.

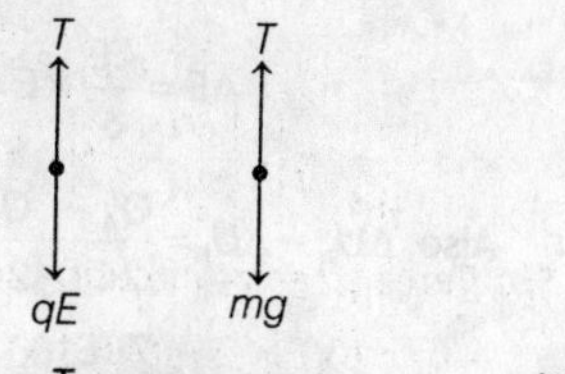

$$T - mg = ma \quad \text{...(ii)}$$

From Eqs. (i) and (ii), we get

$$a = \frac{qE}{m} - g$$

$$\Rightarrow \quad a = 10 \text{ m/s}^2$$

At $t = 2$ s, let speed of the loop be u,

$$\Rightarrow \quad u = v_0 + at$$

$$= 0 + 10 \times 2$$

$$\Rightarrow \quad u = 20 \text{ m/s}$$

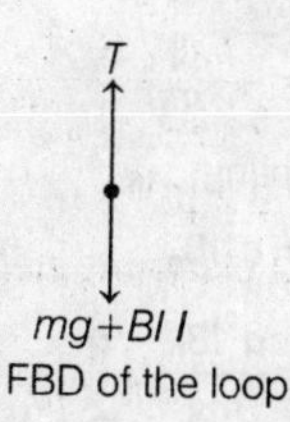

FBD of the loop

Let at any time t, speed of the loop be v, emf induced in the loop is $\varepsilon = Bvl$

Hence, current in the loop, $I = \frac{Bvl}{R}$ ...(iii)

$$\Rightarrow \quad m\frac{dv}{dt} = T - mg - BIl$$

$$\Rightarrow \quad m\frac{dv}{dt} = qE - mg - \frac{B^2l^2v}{R}$$

[using Eqs.(i) and (iii)]

$$\Rightarrow \quad \frac{dv}{dt} = \left(\frac{qE}{m} - g\right) - \frac{B^2l^2v}{mR}$$

$$= 10 - 2v$$

$$\Rightarrow \quad \frac{dv}{10 - 2v} = dt$$

$$\Rightarrow \quad v = 5[1 + 3e^{-(2t-4)}]$$

$\Rightarrow$ Terminal speed = 5 m/s

13.

Initial: C, C

$+\frac{CE}{2}$ $-\frac{CE}{2}$ $+\frac{CE}{2}$ $-\frac{CE}{2}$

Final: C, 2C

$+\frac{2CE}{3}$ $-\frac{2CE}{3}$ $+\frac{2CE}{3}$ $-\frac{2CE}{3}$

$$\therefore \quad \Delta Q = \frac{2CE}{3} - \frac{CE}{2} = \frac{CE}{6}$$

$$\Delta E = \frac{CE}{6} \times E = \frac{CE^2}{6}$$

Also, $\Delta U_A - \Delta U_i = \frac{Q_A'^2}{2C} - \frac{Q_A^2}{2C}$

$$= \frac{7CE^2}{72}$$

14. Consider FBD of the block

$$\tau_M = a^2 IB_0$$

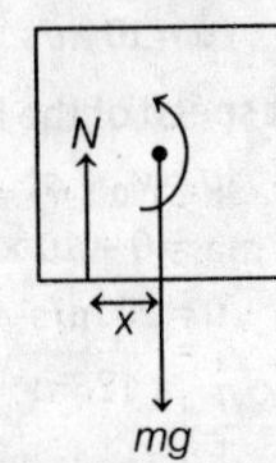

For no toppling,

$$mgx = a^2 IB_0$$

$$\Rightarrow \quad x = \frac{a^2 IB_0}{mg} \le \frac{a}{2}$$

$$\Rightarrow \quad \frac{aIB_0}{mg} \le \frac{1}{2} \Rightarrow I \le \frac{mg}{2aB_0}$$

Also, $x = \frac{a}{4} = \frac{a^2 IB_0}{mg} \Rightarrow I = \frac{mg}{4aB_0}$

15. When magnetic flux (ϕ) through a coil is changed, charge flown through the coil is given by

$$Q = \frac{\Delta\phi}{R}$$

$$\Rightarrow \quad Q = \frac{NBA}{R} = \frac{n(2\pi r) \cdot \frac{\mu_0 i}{2\pi r} \cdot S}{R}$$

$$\frac{\mu_0 nSi}{QR} = 1$$

16. $\lambda = \frac{0.693}{T_{1/2}} = \frac{0.693}{5730y}$

$$= 1.209 \times 10^{-4} y^{-1}$$

As $\quad N = N_0 e^{-\lambda t}$

$\Rightarrow \quad 0.29 = e^{-\lambda t}$

$\Rightarrow \quad t = -\ln(0.29)/\lambda$

$\Rightarrow \quad t \approx \frac{-\ln(0.29)}{1.209 \times 10^{-4} y^{-1}}$

$= 1.0 \times 10^4 y = A \times 10^B y$ (Given)

$\Rightarrow \quad A = 1$ and $B = 4$

$\Rightarrow \quad A + B = 5$

17. By Ohm's law in microscopic from, we get

$$|\mathbf{J}| = \frac{1}{\rho} |\mathbf{E}| \sin 37^\circ$$

$$\Rightarrow \quad |\mathbf{J}| = 10^5 \times 10^{-4} \times \frac{3}{5} = 6 \text{ A/m}^2$$

18. Let vertices 1 and 2 be adjacent. Consider the setup, where a current 1A enters through vertex 1, and a current $\left(\frac{1}{11}\right)$A leaves through the other 11 vertices. Note that, due to symmetry, a current $\left(\frac{1}{5}\right)$A flows through each of the 5 edges leaving vertex 1. Hence, the voltage difference between vertices 1 and 2 is

$$V_1 - V_2 = \left(\frac{1}{5}\text{A}\right)(1\Omega) = \frac{1}{5}\text{V} \quad \text{...(i)}$$

Consider a second setup, where a current 1 A leaves through vertex 2 and a current $\left(\frac{1}{11}\right)$A enters through the other 11 vertices. Again, not that a current $\left(\frac{1}{5}\right)$A flows through each of the 5 edges entering vertex 2. Hence, the voltage difference between vertices 1 and 2 is

$$V_1 - V_2 = \left(\frac{1}{5}\text{A}\right)(1\Omega) = \frac{1}{5}\text{V} \quad \text{...(ii)}$$

If we superimpose these two setups on each other, then arrive at the setup where,

a current $\left(\frac{12}{11}\right)$A enters through vertex 1,

a current $\left(\frac{12}{11}\right)$A leaves through vertex 1,

no current enters or leaves through the other 10 vertices, and

the potential difference between vertices 1 and 2 is

$$V_1 - V_2 = \frac{1}{5}\text{V} + \frac{1}{5}\text{V} = \frac{2}{5}\text{V} \quad \text{...(iii)}$$

The effective resistance between vertices 1 and 2 is therefore given by

$$V = IR \Rightarrow \frac{2}{5}\text{V} = \left(\frac{12}{11}\text{A}\right)R_{\text{eff}}$$

$$\Rightarrow \quad R_{\text{eff}} = \frac{11}{30}\Omega \quad \text{...(iv)}$$

$$\Rightarrow \quad x = 2.67$$

19. For refraction at plane surface,

$$u = -(2R + x)$$

$$\Rightarrow \quad \frac{1}{v} - \frac{\mu}{-(2R + x)} = 0$$

$$\Rightarrow \quad v = -\frac{(2R + x)}{\mu}$$

For refraction at curved surface,

$$\Rightarrow \quad u = -\left(R + \frac{2R + x}{\mu}\right)$$

$$\Rightarrow \quad \frac{\mu}{v'} - \frac{1}{-\left(R + \frac{2R + x}{\mu}\right)} = \frac{\mu - 1}{-R}$$

$$\Rightarrow \quad v' = \frac{-\mu}{\frac{\mu - 1}{R} + \frac{\mu}{2R + R\mu + x}} \quad \text{...(i)}$$

Now, in order to form the final image on O itself this ray should seem to be coming from centre of curvature C.

So $v' = -(R + x)$ ...(ii)

From Eqs. (i) and (ii) and substituting $\mu = \frac{3}{2}$

$$2x^2 + 9Rx - 8R^2 = 0$$

$$\Rightarrow \quad x = \frac{-9R + \sqrt{145R^2}}{4} = \frac{3R}{4}$$

$$x = 3 \text{ cm}$$

20. For R_1-L branch

$$X_L = \omega L = 100 \times \frac{\sqrt{3}}{10}$$

$$= 10\sqrt{3}\,\Omega, R_1 = 10\Omega$$

$$\therefore \quad \tan\phi = \frac{X_L}{R_1} = \sqrt{3}$$

Hence, current I_1 lags voltage by 60°.

For R_2-C branch

$$X_C = \frac{1}{\omega C} = \frac{1}{100 \times \frac{\sqrt{3}}{2} \times 10^{-3}} = \frac{20}{\sqrt{3}}\Omega$$

$$\therefore \tan\phi = \frac{X_C}{R_2} = \frac{1}{\sqrt{3}} \text{ or } \phi = 30^\circ$$

Hence, current I_2 leads voltage by 30°.

$\therefore$ The phase difference between I_1 and I_2 is 90°.

The maximum current through R_1-L branch is

$$= \frac{V_0}{\sqrt{R_1^2 + \omega^2 L^2}}$$

$$= \frac{200\sqrt{2}}{\sqrt{10^2 + (10\sqrt{3})^2}}$$

$$= 10\sqrt{2} \text{ A}$$

Hence, when current through R_1-L branch is $10\sqrt{2}$ A (maximum), the current through R_2-C branch will be zero (minimum).

21. Just after the switch is closed the voltage V_5 across the capacitor is zero and there is also no current through the inductor, so $V_3 = 0$.

$V_2 + V_3 = V_4 = V_5$ and since, $V_5 = 0$ and $V_3 = 0$, V_4 and V_2 are also zero. $V_4 = 0$ means V_3 reads zero. V_1 then must be equal to 40.0 V, and this means the current read by A_1 is $\frac{(40.0\text{V})}{50.0\Omega} = 0.800\text{A}$.

$A_2 + A_3 + A_4 = A_1$ but $A_2 = A_3 = 0$, so $A_4 = A_1 = 0.800$ A.

$$\Rightarrow \frac{V_1 + V_2 + V_3 + V_4 + V_5}{A_1 + A_2 + A_3 + A_4} = \frac{40}{1.6} = 25.00\ \Omega$$

22. After a long time the capacitor is fully charged, so $A_4 = 0$. The current through the inductor is not changing, so $V_2 = 0$. The currents can be calculated from the equivalent circuit that replaces the inductor by a short circuit, as shown in figure.

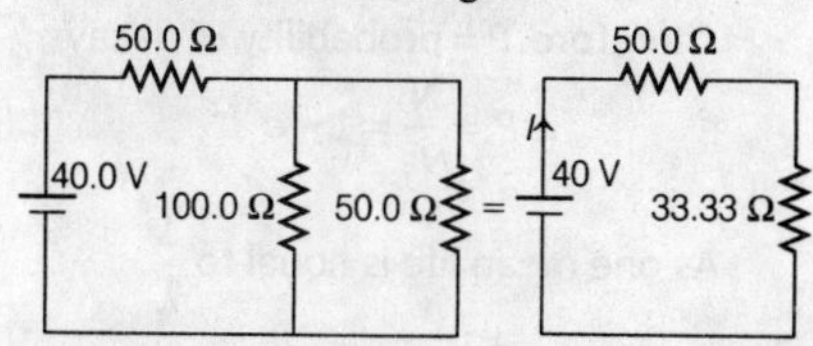

$$A_1 = I = \frac{40}{83.33} = 0.48\text{A}$$

$$V_1 = I \times 50 = 24\text{ V}$$

$$A_2 = \frac{I}{3} = 0.16\text{A}$$

$$A_3 = \frac{2I}{3} = 0.32\text{A}$$

$$V_3 = \frac{I}{3} \times 100 = 16\text{V}$$

$$V_4 = A_3 \times 50$$

$$= 0.32 \times 50 = 16\text{ V}$$

$$\Rightarrow \frac{V_1 + V_2 - V_3 + V_4}{2A_1 - A_2 - A_3 + 7A_4} = 50\ \Omega$$

23. For small angles of incidence on the prism, Snell's law tells us that, an incident angle of θ on the flat side of the prism enters the prism at an angle of $\frac{\theta}{n}$, where n is the index of refraction of the prism. Similarly, on leaving the prism, the in going angle is $\frac{\theta}{n-A}$ from the normal and the outgoing angle, relative to the prism is $n\left(\frac{\theta}{n-A}\right)$. So, the beam leaving the prism is at an angle of $\theta' = n\left(\frac{\theta}{n-A}\right) + A$ from the optical axis. So, $\theta - \theta' = (n-1)A$. At the plane of the source S_0, we can calculate the height of one image above the source

$$\frac{d}{2} = \tan(\theta - \theta')a \approx (\theta - \theta')a = (n-1)Aa$$

$$\Rightarrow d = 2aA(n-1)$$

$$= 2(0.200)(3.50 \times 10^{-3})(1.50 - 1.00)$$

$$= 0.7\text{mm}$$

24. To find the spacing of fringes on a screen, we use

$$\Delta y = \frac{R\lambda}{d} = \frac{R\lambda}{2aA(n-1)}$$

$$= \frac{(2.00 + 0.200)(5.00 \times 10^{-7})}{2(0.200)(3.50 \times 10^{-3})(1.50 - 1.00)}$$

$$= 1.57 \times 10^{-3}\text{ m} = 1.57\text{ mm}$$

25. Here, the two particles have the same mass m, so the reduced mass is

$$m' = \frac{mM}{m+M} = \frac{m^2}{2m} = \frac{m}{2} \quad \text{...(i)}$$

As energy is proportional to mass, so ratio of energy of positronium in nth excited state to that of hydrogen will be proportional to masses, i.e.

$$\frac{E'_n}{E_n} = \frac{m'}{m} = \frac{1}{2} \quad \text{[using Eq. (i)]}$$

$$\Rightarrow \quad E'_n = \frac{E_n}{2} = \frac{13.6}{2n^2}\text{eV} = \frac{6.8}{n^2}\text{eV}$$

For 1st excited state, $n = 2$. So,

$$E'_n = \frac{6.8}{2^2} = 1.7\text{eV}$$

26. Here, $m = 207\,m_e$ and $M = 1836m_e$ so the reduced mass is,

$$m' = \frac{mM}{m+M}$$

$$= \frac{(207m_e)(1836m_e)}{207m_e + 1836m_e} = 186m_e$$

The orbit radius corresponding to $n = 1$ is

$$r_1 = \frac{h^2\varepsilon_0}{\pi m_e e^2}$$

where, $r_1 = a_0 = 5.29 \times 10^{-11}$ m

Hence, the radius r' that correspond to the reduced mass m' is

$$r'_1 = \left(\frac{m}{m'}\right)r_1 = \left(\frac{m}{186m_e}\right)a_0$$

$$= 2.85 \times 10^{-13} \approx 3 \times 10^{-13}\text{ m}$$

$\Rightarrow \quad A = 3$ and $B = 13$

$$\Rightarrow \quad \frac{B}{A} = \frac{13}{3} = 4.33$$

27. Charges induced on various surfaces are as shown

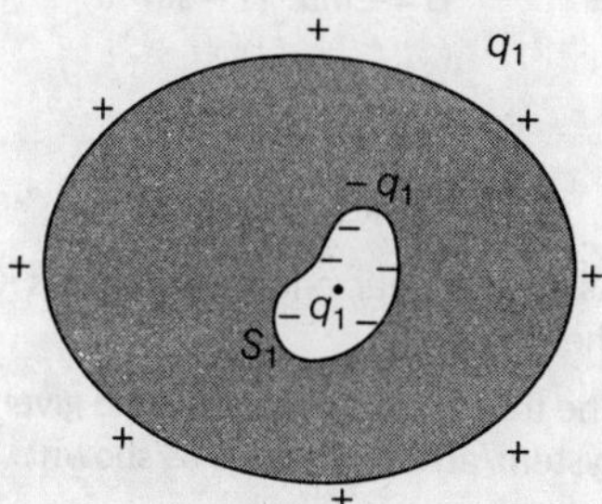

Also, as per Gauss' law, for any closed imaginary surface,

$$\oint \mathbf{E} \cdot d\mathbf{a} = \frac{q_{\text{inside}}}{\varepsilon_0}$$

For S_1, $\oint \mathbf{E}_{\text{in}} \cdot \mathbf{da} = -\frac{q_1}{\varepsilon_0}$, $\oint \mathbf{E}_{\text{net}} \cdot \mathbf{da} = 0$

For S_2,

$\oint \mathbf{E}_{\text{out}} \cdot \mathbf{da} = \frac{q_1}{\varepsilon_0}$, $\oint \mathbf{E}_{\text{net}} \cdot d\mathbf{a} = \frac{q_1 + q_2}{\varepsilon_0}$

THE KNOCKOUTS

Knockout 01

1. Let speed of projection is u. Initial velocity components will be as shown in the figure. We know that, at highest point on the trajectory for a projectile, there is only horizontal component of velocity as shown below.

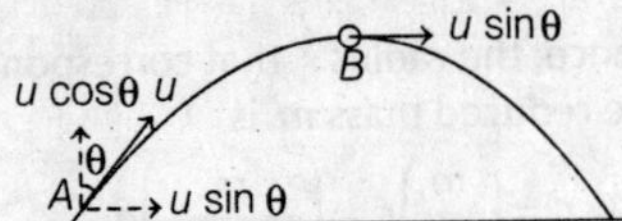

Assuming potential energy at B (highest point) equals to U. By conservation of energy for motion from A to B,

Energy at A = Energy at B

$$\Rightarrow \frac{1}{2}mu^2 = \frac{1}{2}mu^2\sin^2\theta + U$$

$$\Rightarrow U = \frac{1}{2}mu^2(1-\sin^2\theta)$$

$$= \frac{1}{2}mu^2\cos^2\theta$$

$$U = K\cos^2\theta$$

As initial kinetic energy is given as K in the question.

2. The free body diagram for the given system/arrangement is as shown below.

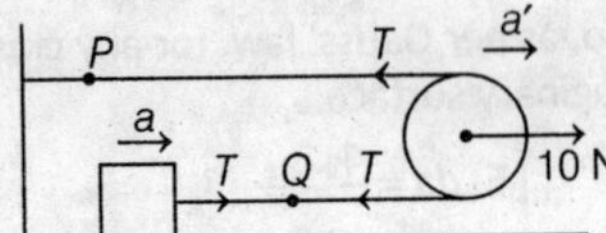

Acceleration of $P = 0$

(as attached to wall)

From the FBD of pulley,

$$2T = 10$$

$$\Rightarrow T = 5\,\text{N}$$

Limiting friction between block and ground $= \mu N$

$$= \mu mg$$

$$= 0.2 \times 1 \times 10$$

$$= 2\,\text{N}$$

As tension acting on block is greater than f_{limiting}, block will move and experience kinetic friction as shown.

So, a = acceleration of block

$$= \frac{5-2}{1} = 3\,\text{m/s}^2 \quad \text{...(i)}$$

As acceleration of pulley is average of acceleration of ends of thread going over it,

$$a' = \frac{a_P + a_Q}{2} = \frac{0+a}{2} = \frac{3}{2}\,\text{m/s}^2 \quad \text{...(ii)}$$

Relative acceleration,

$$a_{\text{rel}} = a - a' = 3 - \frac{3}{2}$$

$$= 1.5\,\text{m/s}^2 \text{[from Eqs. (i) and (ii)]}$$

3. Velocity of a particle executing SHM at mean position, $v_{\text{mean}} = A\omega$

Velocity of the particle at extreme position, $v_{\text{extreme}} = 0$

Time of motion for the particle from mean to extreme $= \frac{T}{4}$

$$= \frac{\pi}{2\omega} \quad \left(\because T = \frac{2\pi}{\omega}\right)$$

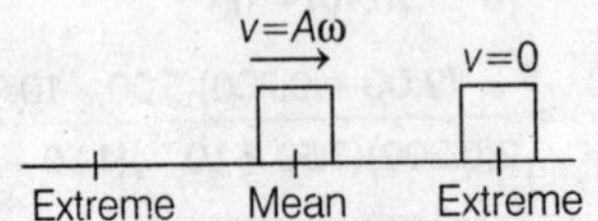

As, average acceleration is defined as

$$a_{\text{av}} = \frac{\Delta v}{\Delta t}$$

$$\Rightarrow |a_{\text{av}}| = \frac{|A\omega - 0|}{\frac{\pi}{2\omega}} = \frac{2A\omega^2}{\pi}$$

4. Assume potential at point D is equal to zero. As we know potential of all points on a plane wire are equal, so potential at B will also be equal to 0 V. Also potential difference across cell is 24 V, so potential at A will be 24 V. Similarly, potential at C is also 24 V.

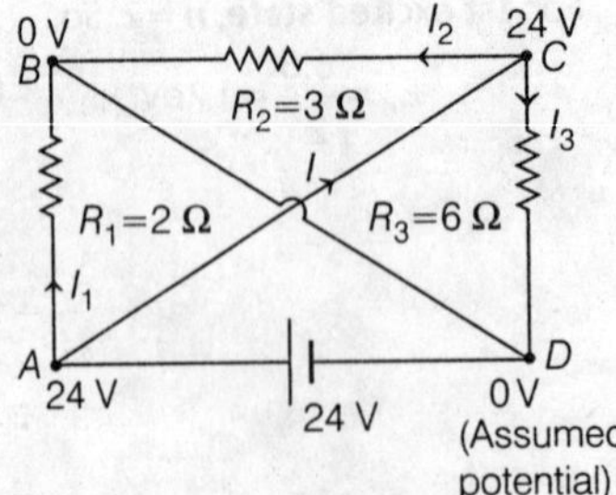

Using Ohm's law for branch AB,

$$I_1 = \frac{V_A - V_B}{R_1}$$

$$= \frac{24-0}{2} = 12\,\text{A}$$

For branch CB,

$$I_2 = \frac{V_C - V_B}{R_2} = \frac{24-0}{3} = 8\,\text{A}$$

For branch CD,

$$I_3 = \frac{V_C - V_D}{R_3} = \frac{24-0}{6} = 4\,\text{A}$$

By KCL for junction C,

$$I = I_2 + I_3 = 8 + 4 = 12\,\text{A}$$

5. Number of nuclei decayed as per Rutherford's and Soddy decay law is $N = N_0(1 - e^{-\lambda t})$

where, N_0 = initial number of nuclei, λ = decay constant and t = time

Therefore, P = probability of decay

$$P = \frac{N}{N_0} = 1 - e^{-\lambda t} \quad \text{...(i)}$$

As one mean life is equal to $\frac{1}{\lambda}$.

Putting $t = \frac{1}{\lambda}$ in Eq. (i),

$$P = 1 - e^{-1} = 1 - 0.37$$

$$= 0.63 = 63\%$$

6. Given that T^3V^2 = constant

$$\Rightarrow \left(\frac{pV}{nR}\right)^3 V^2 = \text{constant}$$

$$\left(\because \text{using ideal gas equation, } pV = nRT \text{ or } T = \frac{pV}{nR}\right)$$

$$\Rightarrow p^3V^5 = \text{constant} \Rightarrow pV^{\frac{5}{3}} = \text{constant} \quad \text{......(i)}$$

Differentiating Eq. (i) with respect to volume V on both sides, we get

$$\Rightarrow \frac{dp}{dV}\cdot V^{\frac{5}{3}} + p\cdot\frac{5}{3}\cdot V^{\frac{2}{3}} = 0$$

$$\Rightarrow \frac{dp}{dV} = -\frac{5}{3}\frac{p}{V} \quad \text{...(ii)}$$

Bulk modulus is defined as,

$$B = \frac{\text{Volumetric stress}}{\text{Volumetric strain}}$$

$$= \frac{dp}{-\frac{dV}{V}} = -V\frac{dp}{dV}$$

$$= -V\left(-\frac{5}{3}\frac{p}{V}\right) \quad \text{[using Eq. (ii)]}$$

$$= \frac{5}{3}p$$

7. Average energy (electric or magnetic) in electromagnetic wave is given by

$$\frac{1}{4}\varepsilon_0 E_0^2 = \frac{B_0^2}{4\mu_0} \quad ...(i)$$

$$\Rightarrow \quad \varepsilon_0 E_0^2 = \frac{B_0^2}{\mu_0} \quad ...(ii)$$

Consider option (b),

$$\frac{1}{8}\varepsilon_0 E_0^2 + \frac{B_0^2}{8\mu_0}$$

$$\Rightarrow \quad \frac{1}{8}\varepsilon_0 E_0^2 + \frac{1}{8}\varepsilon_0 E_0^2 \quad \text{[using Eq. (ii)]}$$

$$= \frac{1}{4}\varepsilon_0 E_0^2$$

which is average electric energy as per Eq. (i).

8. As we know,

Range of tower, $r = \sqrt{2Rh}$ ...(i)

where, R = radius of earth,

and h = height of tower.

Also, as volume $= \frac{\text{mass}}{\text{density}}$

Since, shape of Earth is considered as spherical.

So, $\frac{4}{3}\pi R^3 = \frac{m}{\rho}$

As mass is constant, $R = \frac{k}{\rho^{\frac{1}{3}}}$ ...(ii)

where, k is proportionality constant.

Putting value of R from Eq. (ii) in Eq. (i), we get

$$r = \sqrt{\frac{2kh}{\rho^{\frac{1}{3}}}}$$

As k and h are constants, $r = \frac{C}{\rho^{\frac{1}{6}}}$ ...(iii)

where, C is proportionality constant.

Differentiating the above relation w.r.t. ρ, we get

$$\frac{dr}{d\rho} = -\frac{1}{6}C\rho^{-\frac{7}{6}} \quad ...(iv)$$

Dividing Eq. (iv) by Eq. (iii), we get

$$\frac{dr}{r} = -\frac{1}{6}\frac{d\rho}{\rho}$$

$\Rightarrow$ % change in the range of telecommunication,

$$\frac{\Delta r}{r} \times 100 = -\frac{1}{6} \times \frac{\Delta\rho}{\rho} \times 100$$

$$= -\frac{1}{6} \times 3 = -0.5\%$$

The range of a telecommunication tower on earth's surface will decreases by 0.5%.

9. If n_1 and n_2 are the number of moles of air in the two bubbles while n is number of moles in resulting bubble. By conservation of mass, $n = n_1 + n_2$

$$\Rightarrow \quad \frac{pV}{RT} = \frac{p_1V_1}{RT} + \frac{p_2V_2}{RT}$$

(using ideal gas equation)

$$\Rightarrow \quad pV = p_1V_1 + p_2V_2 \quad ...(i)$$

As bubbles are in vacuum, so outside pressure is zero ($p_o = 0$). As excess pressure inside bubble is given by

$$p - p_O = \frac{4T}{R}$$

$$\Rightarrow \quad p = \frac{4T}{R} \quad ...(ii)$$

Also, $V = \frac{4}{3}\pi R^3$ ...(iii)

Using Eqs. (ii) and (iii), Eq. (i) can be written as

$$\frac{4T}{R}\cdot\frac{4}{3}\pi R^3 = \frac{4T}{R_1}\cdot\frac{4}{3}\pi R_1^3 + \frac{4T}{R_2}\cdot\frac{4}{3}\pi R_2^3$$

$$\Rightarrow \quad R^2 = R_1^2 + R_2^2$$

$$\Rightarrow \quad \pi R^2 = \pi R_1^2 + \pi R_2^2$$

$$\Rightarrow \quad A = A_1 + A_2 = A + 2A = 3A$$

10. Given, potential at point C is zero, this means potential at O is zero as surface of metal bodies is equipotential in nature

$\Rightarrow V_0 = 0 \Rightarrow V_{\text{dipole}} + V_{\text{point}} = 0$

$$\Rightarrow \frac{Kp}{(2R)^2}\cos 180° + \frac{Kq}{(2R)} = 0$$

$$\Rightarrow \quad p = 2qR \quad ...(i)$$

Now, as net field inside metal ball = 0. So, at O

$$\Rightarrow \quad \mathbf{E}_{\text{dipole}} + \mathbf{E}_{\text{point}} + \mathbf{E}_{\text{induced}} = 0$$

$$\Rightarrow -\frac{2Kp}{(2R)^3}\hat{\mathbf{i}} - \frac{Kq}{(2R)^2}\hat{\mathbf{i}} + \mathbf{E}_{\text{induced}} = 0 \quad ...(ii)$$

$$\Rightarrow \mathbf{E}_{\text{induced}} = \frac{3}{8}\frac{Kp}{R^3}\hat{\mathbf{i}} = \frac{3}{4}\frac{Kq}{R^2}\hat{\mathbf{i}}$$

[using Eqs. (i) and (ii)]

11. Since, force applied is same

$\Rightarrow k_1x_1 = k_2x_2 = k_{\text{eq}}x_0$, where

$$k_{\text{eq}} = \frac{k_1k_2}{k_1 + k_2}$$

$$\Rightarrow x_2 = \frac{k_1x_1}{k_2} \text{ and } x_0 = \left(\frac{k_1 + k_2}{k_2}\right)x_1$$

W_1 = Work done by F on block,

$$W_1 = \frac{1}{2}k_{\text{eq}}x_0^2$$

$$= \frac{1}{2}\frac{k_1k_2}{k_1 + k_2} \times \left(\frac{k_1 + k_2}{k_2}\right)^2 x_1^2$$

$$= \frac{1}{2}\frac{k_1(k_1 + k_2)x_1^2}{k_2}$$

As change in KE of block is zero, work done by S_2 on block

$$= -W_1 = -\frac{1}{2}\frac{k_1(k_1 + k_2)x_1^2}{k_2}$$

Work done by S_2 on S_1 = Change in PE of $S_1 = \frac{1}{2}k_1x_1^2$

As displacement of wall is zero, work done by S_1 on wall = 0

12. If $v_1, v_2, v_3, ..., v_n$ are molecular speeds, then average molecular kinetic (translational) energy will be

$$K = \frac{\frac{1}{2}m(v_1^2 + v_2^2 + v_3^2 + ... + v_n^2)}{n}$$

$$= \frac{1}{2}m\left[\sqrt{\frac{v_1^2 + v_2^2 + ... + v_n^2}{n}}\right]^2 = \frac{1}{2}mv_{\text{rms}}^2$$

13. Given, $f_o = 2$ cm, $f_e = 5$ cm

$|v_o| + |u_e| = 20$ cm,

$v_e = -25$ cm

From lens formula, $\frac{1}{f_e} = \frac{1}{v_e} - \frac{1}{u_e}$

$$\frac{1}{u_e} = \frac{1}{v_e} - \frac{1}{f_e} = -\frac{1}{25} - \frac{1}{5}$$

$$\therefore u_e = -\frac{25}{6} \text{ cm}$$

Distance of real image from objective,

$$v_o = 20 - |u_e| = 20 - \frac{25}{6}$$

$$= \frac{120 - 25}{6} = \frac{95}{6} \text{ cm}$$

Now, $\frac{1}{f_o} = \frac{1}{v_o} - \frac{1}{u_o}$

$$\Rightarrow \quad \frac{1}{u_o} = \frac{1}{v_o} - \frac{1}{f_o} = \frac{1}{(95/6)} - \frac{1}{2}$$

$$= \frac{6}{95} - \frac{1}{2} = \frac{12 - 95}{190} = -\frac{83}{190}$$

$$\therefore \quad u_o = -\frac{190}{83} = -2.3 \text{ cm}$$

Magnifying power,

$$M = -\frac{v_o}{u_o}\left(1 + \frac{D}{f_e}\right)$$

$$= -\frac{95/6}{2.3}\left(1 + \frac{25}{5}\right) = -41.5$$

It is close to 40.

14. On dividing a bar magnet along its length, as its pole strength of m will be halved, so dipole moment μ will also be halved.

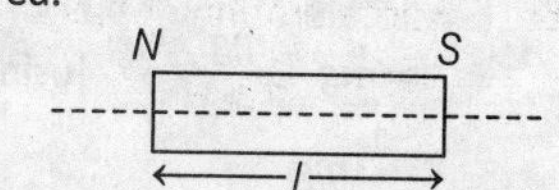

$(\because \mu = ml)$

Also, moment of inertia of the magnet,

$$I = \frac{ml^2}{12}$$

As mass m is halved, so I is also halved. Time period of oscillation is given by

$$T = 2\pi\sqrt{\frac{I}{\mu B}} \quad \text{...(i)}$$

Time period of half of the magnet,

$$T' = 2\pi\sqrt{\frac{\frac{I}{2}}{\frac{\mu}{2}B}} = 2\pi\sqrt{\frac{I}{\mu B}} \quad \text{...(ii)}$$

From Eqs. (i) and (ii), we get $T' = T$

So, time period of oscillation on slight disturbance will still be T.

15. As per Einstein's photoelectric equation, $V_s = \frac{hf}{e} - \frac{\phi}{e}$ ... (i)

If f is doubled, new stopping potential,

$$V_s' = \frac{2hf}{e} - \frac{\phi}{e}$$

$$= 2\left(\frac{hf}{e} - \frac{\phi}{e}\right) + \frac{\phi}{e}$$

$$= 2V_s + \frac{\phi}{e} \quad \text{[from Eq. (i)]}$$

which is more than double or an increase of more than 100%.

16. Free body diagram of rain drop falling with terminal speed is as shown alongside

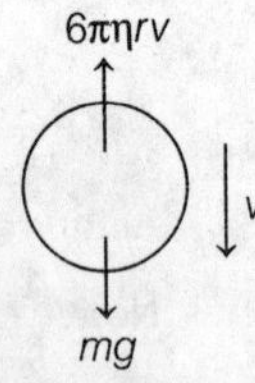

In this condition, its acceleration and net force are zero, i.e.

$6\pi\eta rv$ (drag force) $= mg$ (weight) ... (i)

where, η = coefficient of viscosity and r = radius of the rain drop.

For a rain drop of mass (m) falling with (1/4)th speed, free body diagram is as shown.

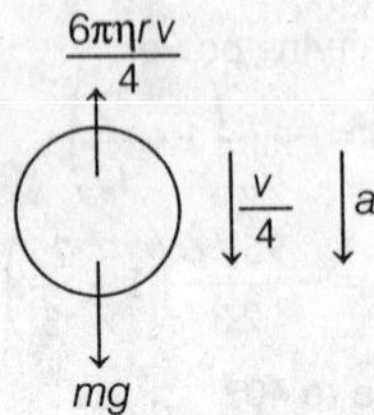

Net force on the drop,

$$F = mg - \frac{6\pi\eta rv}{4}$$

$$= mg - \frac{mg}{4} \quad \text{[using Eq. (i)]}$$

$$= \frac{3mg}{4}$$

17. As per triangle law, relative velocity (v_{BA}) of B w.r.t. A will be as shown in the figure.

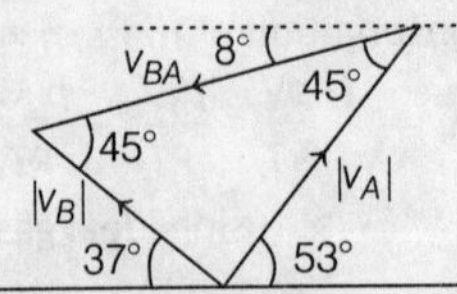

From the triangle using sine rule, we get

$$\frac{v_B}{\sin 45^\circ} = \frac{60}{\sin 45^\circ}$$

$$\Rightarrow \quad v_B = 60 \text{ m/s}$$

18. Diode 1 is forward biased as its p-side is connected to higher potential terminal of cell. So, it behaves as plane wire while Diode 2 is reverse biased. So, it will act like an open switch. Therefore, equivalent circuit is as shown.

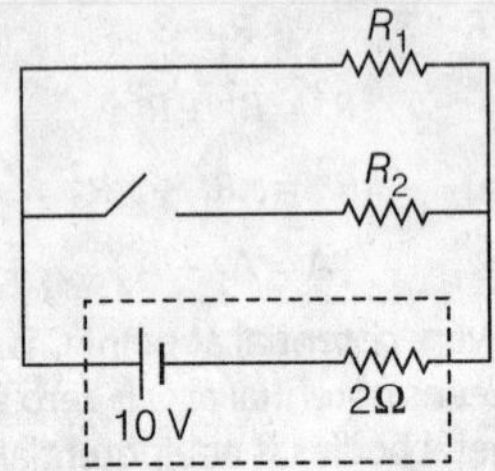

So, effective resistance of external circuit is R_1. For maximum power consumption, $R_{external} = R_{internal}$ as per maximum power theorem

$\Rightarrow \quad R_1 = 2\Omega$

and R_2 may be any value, hence option (d) is correct.

19. When a charged particle enters a region of a uniform magnetic field, such that the angle it makes with the direction of $B \neq 90^\circ$, then it follows a helical path as shown below

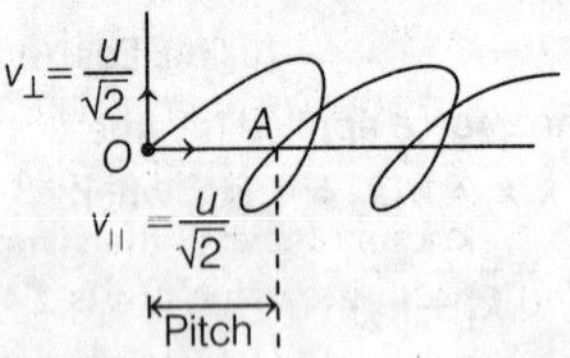

Radius of helix,

$$R = \frac{mv_\perp}{qB} = \frac{mu}{\sqrt{2}qB} \quad \text{...(i)}$$

where, $v_\perp$ = component of velocity perpendicular to field.

Also, pitch, P = Displacement along field in one revolution (OA)

$$= v_{\parallel} \times T = \frac{u}{\sqrt{2}} \times \frac{2\pi m}{qB} \quad \text{...(ii)}$$

Dividing Eq. (ii) by Eq. (i), $\frac{P}{R} = 2\pi$

20. In a series L-C-R circuit at resonance,

Capacitive reactance = Inductive reactance

$$\Rightarrow \quad X_C = X_L \Rightarrow \omega L = \frac{1}{\omega C}$$

where, ω is angular frequency, C is capacitance and L is inductance.

As, $\omega = 2\pi f$

where, f is frequency.

$\Rightarrow$ At resonance, frequency is given as

$$f_r = \frac{1}{2\pi\sqrt{LC}}$$

Now, the frequency of the source is half of f_r.

$$\Rightarrow \quad f = \frac{1}{2}f_r = \frac{1}{4\pi\sqrt{LC}}$$

$$\Rightarrow \quad f < f_r$$

$$\Rightarrow \quad f < \frac{1}{2\pi\sqrt{LC}}$$

$$\Rightarrow \quad (2\pi\sqrt{LC})f < 1$$

$$\Rightarrow \quad (2\pi fL)(2\pi fC) < 1$$

$$\Rightarrow \quad X_L < X_C$$

This means that the nature of the circuit is essentially capacitive.

21. Wavelength of photon/line for transition of electron from $n = n_2$ to $n = n_1$ is given by

$$\lambda = \frac{R^{-1}}{\frac{1}{n_1^2} - \frac{1}{n_2^2}}$$

where, R is Rydberg's constant.

For first line of Lyman series, $n_1 = 1$ and $n_2 = 2$

$$\Rightarrow \lambda_1 = \frac{R^{-1}}{1 - \frac{1}{2^2}} = \frac{4}{3R} \quad \text{...(i)}$$

For series limit of Brackett series, $n_1 = 4$ and $n_2 = \infty$

$$\Rightarrow \lambda_2 = \frac{R^{-1}}{\frac{1}{4^2} - \frac{1}{\infty^2}} = \frac{16}{R} \quad \text{...(ii)}$$

Dividing Eq. (ii) by Eq. (i), we get

$$\frac{\lambda_2}{\lambda_1} = \frac{\frac{16}{R}}{\frac{4}{3R}} = \frac{16}{R} \times \frac{3R}{4} = 12$$

22. As per Stefan's law, power emitted,

$$P = \sigma AT^4$$

where, σ is Stefan's constant, A is surface area and T is temperature of black body.

$$\Rightarrow \quad P = \sigma(4\pi r^2)\left(\frac{b}{\lambda}\right)^4$$

As black body is spherical in nature, so surface area $= 4\pi r^2$ and according to Wien's law $\lambda T = b$,
where, b is Wien's constant.

$$\Rightarrow \quad P \propto \frac{r^2}{\lambda^4} \Rightarrow \frac{P_A}{P_B} = \left(\frac{r_A}{r_B}\right)^2\left(\frac{\lambda_B}{\lambda_A}\right)^4$$

Substituting the given values, we get

$$\frac{P_A}{P_B} = 2^2(1.01)^4$$

$$= 4(1+0.01)^4$$

$$\approx 4(1+0.04) = 4.16$$

(using binomial approximation)

23. As we know,
Frequency of string $\propto \sqrt{\text{Tension}}$

$$\Rightarrow \quad \frac{\Delta f}{f} \times 100 = \frac{1}{2}\frac{\Delta T}{T} \times 100 = \frac{1}{2} \times 4$$

$$\left(\because \text{given}, \frac{\Delta T}{T} \times 100 = 4\%\right)$$

$$= 2\%$$

Here, $\quad f = 100 \text{ Hz} \Rightarrow \Delta f = 2 \text{ Hz}$

$\Rightarrow$ Frequency of string after tightening

$$= 100 + 2 = 102 \text{ Hz}$$

Beat frequency = Difference in frequency of sources

$$= 102 - 100 = 2$$

24. Planck's length will have dimensional formula of length,

$$\Rightarrow \quad [\text{L}] = [\text{M}^0\text{LT}^0] = \left[\sqrt{\frac{hG}{c^3}}\right] = [\text{M}^x\text{L}^y\text{T}^z]$$

Comparing the powers of M, L and T on both sides, we get

$$\Rightarrow \quad x = 0, y = 1, z = 0$$

So, $x + y + z = 1$

25. A system of pulleys attached with two blocks of masses m_1 and m_2 is as shown below,

m_1 m_2 $\equiv$ m

Equivalent mass of the above mentioned system, $m_{eq} = \dfrac{4m_1m_2}{m_1 + m_2}$

So, equivalent of 2 kg and 3 kg system given in the question,

$$m_{eq} = \frac{4 \times 2 \times 3}{2+3} = 4.8$$

Given system can therefore be represented as

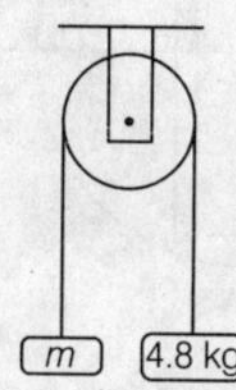

Therefore, for equilibrium m must equal to 4.8 kg.

26. For maxima, path difference $= n\lambda$

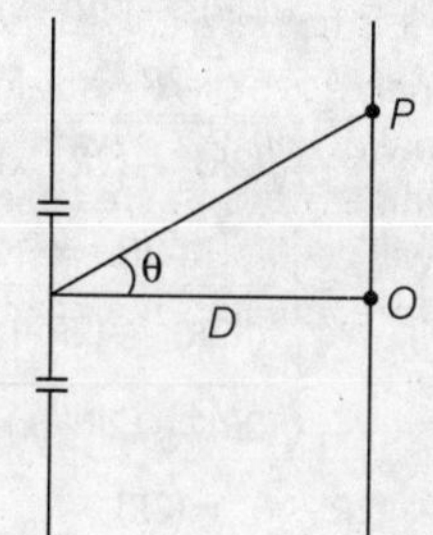

$$\Rightarrow d\sin\theta = n\lambda \quad \Rightarrow \sin\theta = \frac{n\lambda}{d}$$

Substituting the given values, we get

$$\sin\theta = \frac{2000 \times 5000 \times 10^{-10}}{2 \times 10^{-3}} = \frac{1}{2}$$

$$\Rightarrow \quad \theta = 30°$$

According to the figure,

$$OP = D\tan\theta = 1 \cdot \tan 30° = \frac{1}{\sqrt{3}}$$

$$= 0.58 \text{ m}$$

27. As sphere is not slipping, instantaneous displacement of point of contact of sphere with incline is zero. Work is done only by $mg = mg \times$ vertical displacement $= mgh$

So, by work-energy theorem,

$$W_{\text{friction}} + W_{\text{normal}} + W_{mg} = \Delta\,\text{KE}$$

$$0 + 0 + mgh = \Delta\,\text{KE}$$

$$\Rightarrow \quad \Delta\text{KE} = mgh$$

So, by comparing with the given value in question, the value of x is 1.

28. The given circuit can be shown as follows

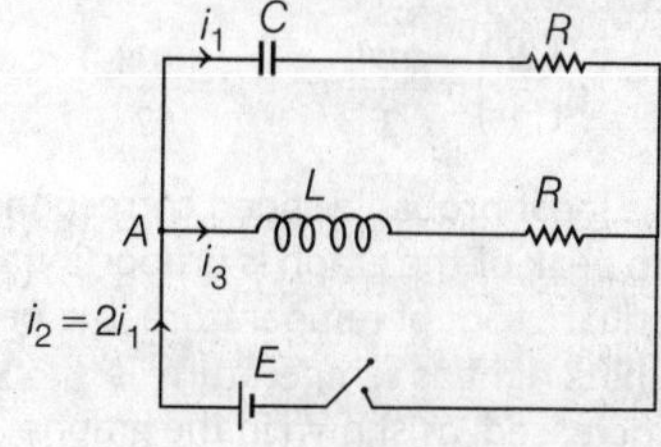

Applying KCL at node A,

$$2i_1 = i_1 + i_3$$

$$\Rightarrow \quad i_1 = i_3$$

$$\Rightarrow \quad \frac{E}{R}e^{-\frac{t}{RC}} = \frac{E}{R}\left(1 - e^{-\frac{Rt}{L}}\right)$$

Substituting the given values, we get

$$\Rightarrow \quad e^{-t} = 1 - e^{-t}$$

$$\Rightarrow \quad e^{-t} = \frac{1}{2}$$

$$\Rightarrow \quad t = \ln 2 = 0.69$$

29. Acceleration due to gravity at height $h << R$ is given by

$$g_1 = g\left(1 - \frac{2h}{R}\right) \quad \text{...(i)}$$

where, $g = 9.8 \text{ m/s}^2$ and R is the radius of the earth.

Also, acceleration due to gravity at depth d is given by

$$g_2 = g\left(1 - \frac{d}{R}\right) \quad \text{...(ii)}$$

Given that, $g_1 = g_2$

From Eqs. (i) and (ii), we get

$$g\left(1 - \frac{2h}{R}\right) = g\left(1 - \frac{d}{R}\right)$$

$$\Rightarrow \quad h = \frac{d}{2} = \frac{15}{2}$$

$$= 7.5 \text{ km}$$

30. The position of the bullet and rod during its motion is as shown below

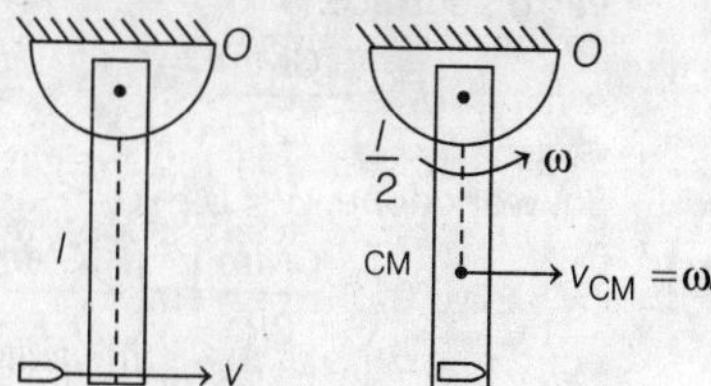

By conservation of angular momentum about hinge O,

$$L_{\text{final}} = L_{\text{initial}}$$

$$\Rightarrow \quad I\omega = mvl$$

$$\Rightarrow \quad \left(\frac{ml^2}{3} + ml^2\right)\omega = mvl$$

$$\Rightarrow \quad \omega = \frac{3v}{4l}$$

$$\Rightarrow \quad v_{CM} = \omega r = \left(\frac{3v}{4l}\right) \cdot \frac{l}{2} = \frac{3v}{8}$$

$$\Rightarrow \quad x = \frac{8}{3} = 2.67$$

Knockout 02

1. At any general time t, potential difference across inductor is equal to emf of cell. So, for inductor,

$$\frac{Ldi}{dt}=E$$

$$\Rightarrow \quad di=\frac{E}{L}dt$$

Integrating both sides, we get

$$\Rightarrow \quad i=\frac{E}{L}t \quad \text{...(i)}$$

So, magnetic energy stored in an inductor,

$$U=\frac{1}{2}Li^2=\frac{1}{2}L\left(\frac{E}{L}t\right)^2$$

[using Eq. (i)]

$$\Rightarrow \quad U \propto t^2$$

$\Rightarrow$ Graph between U and t will be upward concave parabola.

2. Potential energy of a particle at a distance r outside the earth surface is given by

$$U=-\frac{GMm}{r}$$

where, M = mass of earth

and m = mass of particle.

Therefore, potential energy at earth's surface,

$$U_i=-\frac{GMm}{R} \quad \text{...(i)}$$

While potential energy at height R from earth's surface,

$$U_f=-\frac{GMm}{2R} \quad \text{...(ii)}$$

So, work done, $W=U_f-U_i$

$$=\left(-\frac{GMm}{2R}\right)-\left(-\frac{GMm}{R}\right)$$

[from Eqs. (i) and (ii)]

$$W=\frac{GMm}{2R} \quad \text{...(iii)}$$

At final position,

$$g=\frac{GM}{r^2}=\frac{GM}{(2R)^2}=\frac{GM}{4R^2} \quad \text{...(iv)}$$

Dividing Eq. (iii) by Eq. (iv), we get

$$\frac{W}{g}=2mR$$

$$\Rightarrow \quad W=2mgR$$

3. The figure shows a strip at a distance x of thickness dx. As μ of material increases with x, ray continuously bends as shown.

By Snell's law between O and A,

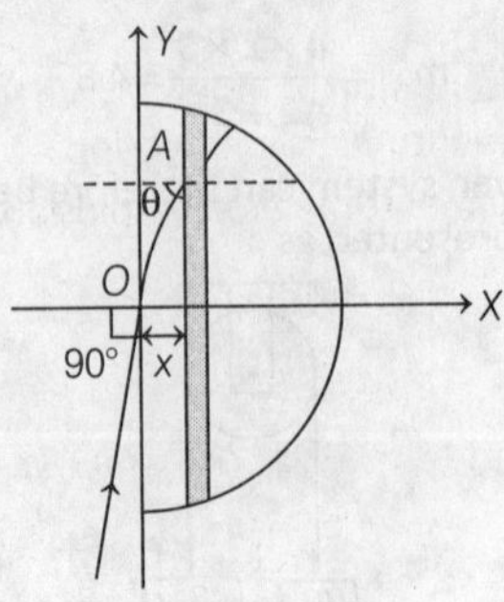

$$1\times\sin 90°=\frac{2R}{2R-x}\times\sin\theta$$

$$\Rightarrow \quad \tan\theta=\frac{2R-x}{\sqrt{(2R)^2-(2R-x)^2}}$$

$$\Rightarrow \quad \frac{dy}{dx}=\frac{2R-x}{\sqrt{(2R)^2-(2R-x)^2}}$$

$$\Rightarrow \quad \int_0^y dy=\int_0^x \frac{2R-x}{\sqrt{(2R)^2-(2R-x)^2}}dx$$

$$\Rightarrow \quad y=\sqrt{(2R)^2-(2R-x)^2}$$

$$\Rightarrow y^2+(2R-x)^2=(2R)^2$$

which is equation of circle of radius $2R$ centred at $(2R, 0)$.

4. FBD of the rod is as shown

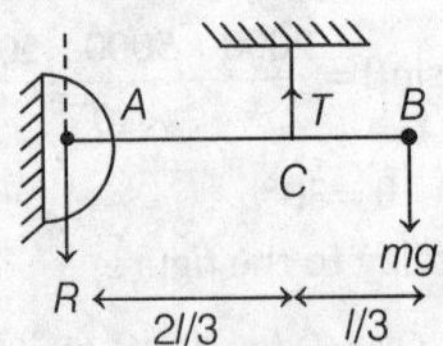

About point C, torque of tension is zero as its line of action is passing through C only.

Torque of mg about $C=mg(BC)$

$=\frac{mgl}{3}$ clockwise, as shown in diagram.

As the rod is in equilibrium, torque of reaction at hinge must be equal and opposite to torque of mg. So, R will be downward as shown. Similarly, torque of R about $C=R(AC)=R\left(\frac{2l}{3}\right)$, anti-clockwise.

Equating magnitudes of the two torques, we get

$$R\left(\frac{2l}{3}\right)=\frac{mgl}{3} \Rightarrow R=\frac{mg}{2}$$

5. As most probable speed corresponding to peak of the graph is proportional to square root of temperature, the peak shifts right as temperature, is increased, as shown in the graphs here. But as area under the graph represents total number of gas molecules, it does not change.

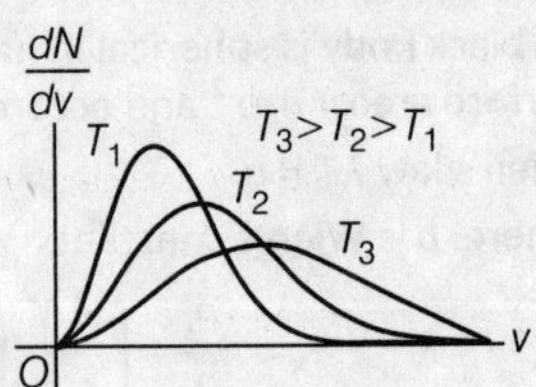

6. As we know, work done by gas in a thermodynamic process = area under p-V graph

Also, work done by gas is positive in expansion and negative in compression. So, works in steps AC, CD and DB can be calculated from area under graph as shown.

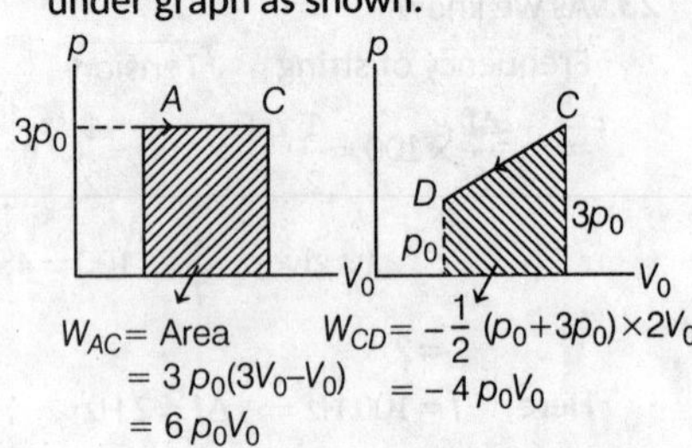

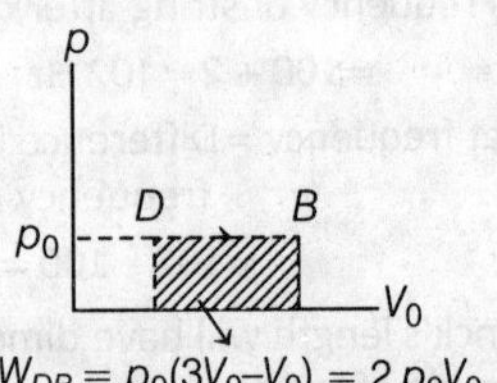

So, total work, $W=W_{AC}+W_{CD}+W_{DB}$

$$=6p_0V_0-4p_0V_0+2p_0V_0$$

or $\quad =4p_0V_0 \quad$ ...(i)

Also, change in internal energy,

$$\Delta U=\frac{f}{2}(p_fV_f-p_iV_i)$$

$$=\frac{f}{2}(p_0 3V_0-3p_0V_0)=0 \quad \text{...(ii)}$$

By first law of thermodynamics,

Heat $=W+\Delta U=4p_0V_0+0$

$=4p_0V_0$ [using Eqs. (i) and (ii)]

7. For paramagnetic substances, as per Curie's law, magnetic susceptibility,

$$\chi \propto \frac{1}{T}$$

where, T = temperature in kelvin.

$$\Rightarrow \quad \frac{\chi_{\text{final}}}{\chi_{\text{initial}}}=\frac{T_{\text{initial}}}{T_{\text{final}}}=\frac{27+273}{327+273}$$

$$=\frac{300}{600}=\frac{1}{2}$$

8. The gate shown here is an exclusive OR(XOR) gate which gives 1 as an output only when one of the inputs (i.e. either A or B) is 1.

9. As per law of radioactive decay, number of nuclei at time $t = N_0 e^{-\lambda t}$

$$\Rightarrow \quad N_A = N_0 e^{-\lambda t} \quad \text{...(i)}$$

As at $t = 6$, $N_A = \dfrac{N_0}{8}$.

where, N_0 = initial number of nuclei

From Eq. (i),

$$\frac{N_0}{8} = N_0 e^{-\lambda(6)}$$

$$\Rightarrow \quad e^{6\lambda} = \ln 8 \Rightarrow \lambda = \frac{\ln 8}{6} \quad \text{...(ii)}$$

Also, at $t = t_1$, $N_A = \dfrac{N_0}{5}$.

From Eq. (i),

$$\frac{N_0}{5} = N_0 e^{-\lambda t_1}$$

$$\Rightarrow \quad \ln 5 = \lambda t_1 = \frac{\ln 8}{6} t_1 \text{ [using Eq. (ii)]}$$

$$\Rightarrow \quad t_1 = \frac{6 \ln 5}{\ln 8} \quad \text{...(iii)}$$

Also, number of nuclei remaining,

$$\Rightarrow \quad N_B = N_0(1 - e^{-\lambda t}) \quad \text{...(iv)}$$

As at $t = t_2$, $N_B = \dfrac{9N_0}{10}$.

From Eq. (iv),

$$\frac{9N_0}{10} = N_0(1 - e^{-\lambda t_2})$$

$$\Rightarrow e^{-\lambda t_2} = \frac{1}{10}$$

$$\Rightarrow \quad t_2 = \frac{\ln 10}{\lambda} = \frac{6 \ln 10}{\ln 8}$$

[using Eq. (ii)] ...(v)

Subtracting Eq. (iii) from Eq. (v), we get

$$t_2 - t_1 = \frac{6(\ln 10 - \ln 5)}{\ln 8} = 2\text{s}$$

10. Let the bomb (of mass m) is projected with speed u. Velocity components at initial point are as shown.

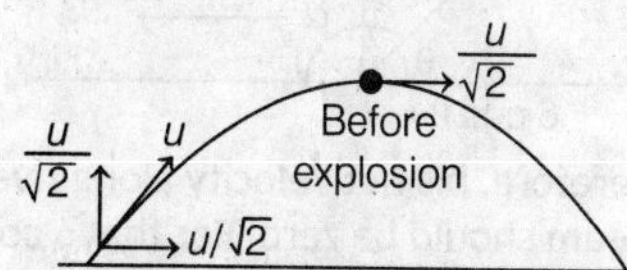

At highest point, only horizontal component, i.e. $\dfrac{u}{\sqrt{2}}$ is present before explosion. Velocity of one of the pieces is given to be zero after explosion. Let velocity of the other piece be v. By conservation of momentum,

momentum after explosion = momentum before explosion

$$\Rightarrow \quad \frac{m}{2} v = m \frac{u}{\sqrt{2}}$$

$$\Rightarrow \quad v = \sqrt{2} u \quad \text{...(i)}$$

Kinetic energy before explosion

$$K_1 = \frac{1}{2} m \left(\frac{u}{\sqrt{2}}\right)^2 = \frac{1}{4} mu^2 \quad \text{...(ii)}$$

Kinetic energy after explosion

$$K_2 = \frac{1}{2}\frac{m}{2} v^2 = \frac{1}{2}\frac{m}{2}(\sqrt{2}u)^2$$

[using Eq. (i)]

$$\Rightarrow \quad K_2 = \frac{1}{2} mu^2 \quad \text{...(iii)}$$

Using Eqs. (iii) and (ii), kinetic energy released in explosion

$$= K_2 - K_1 = \frac{1}{4} mu^2 = \frac{1}{2} K$$

11. Let energy of electron in energy levels K, L, M be E_K, E_L, E_M, respectively.

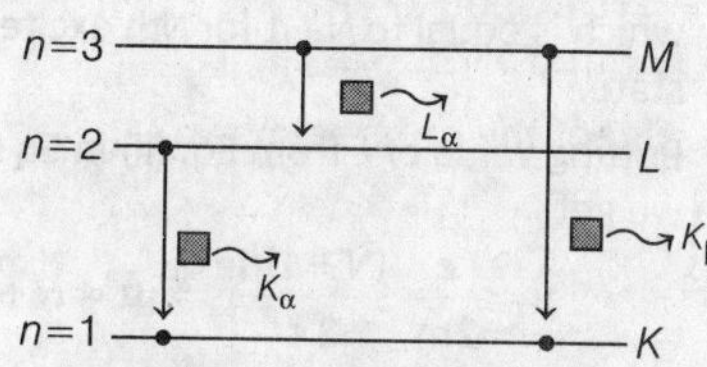

So, from energy level diagram,

$$\frac{hc}{\lambda_1} = \text{energy of } K_\alpha \text{ X-ray photon}$$

$$= E_L - E_K \quad \text{...(i)}$$

$$\frac{hc}{\lambda_2} = \text{energy of } K_\beta \text{ X-ray photon}$$

$$= E_M - E_K \quad \text{...(ii)}$$

$$\frac{hc}{\lambda_3} = \text{energy of } L_\alpha \text{ X-ray photon}$$

$$= E_M - E_L \quad \text{...(iii)}$$

Subtracting Eq. (i) from Eq. (ii), we get

$$\frac{hc}{\lambda_2} - \frac{hc}{\lambda_1} = E_M - E_L \quad \text{...(iv)}$$

From Eqs. (iii) and (iv), we get

$$\frac{hc}{\lambda_2} - \frac{hc}{\lambda_1} = \frac{hc}{\lambda_3}$$

$$\Rightarrow \quad \lambda_3 = \frac{\lambda_1 \lambda_2}{\lambda_1 - \lambda_2}$$

12. Before the block is placed on the block executing SHM, time period,

$$T = 2\pi\sqrt{\frac{m}{k}} \quad \text{...(i)}$$

where, m is mass of the block and k is spring constant.

After the block is placed, both blocks execute SHM together. So, mass of system $= 2m$

Therefore, time period,

$$T' = 2\pi\sqrt{\frac{2m}{k}} \quad \text{...(ii)}$$

Dividing Eq. (ii) by Eq. (i), we get

$$\frac{T'}{T} = \sqrt{2}$$

$$\Rightarrow \quad T' = \sqrt{2}T$$

Before the block is placed, if we assume p to be momentum at mean position, energy of oscillation is given as

$$\frac{p^2}{2m} = \frac{1}{2} kA^2 \quad \text{...(iii)}$$

After the block is placed, momentum remains unchanged as force between blocks is internal force, mass becomes $2m$ and assume A' as new amplitude. So, energy of oscillation can be written as

$$\frac{p^2}{2(2m)} = \frac{1}{2} kA'^2 \quad \text{...(iv)}$$

Dividing Eq. (iv) by Eq. (iii), we get

$$\frac{1}{2} = \left(\frac{A'}{A}\right)^2 \Rightarrow A' = \frac{A}{\sqrt{2}}$$

13. It is given that, $l_1 - l_2$ = constant

Taking change (Δ) on both sides, we get

$$\Delta l_1 - \Delta l_2 = \Delta \text{ constant} = 0$$

$$\Rightarrow \quad \Delta l_1 = \Delta l_2$$

$$\Rightarrow \quad l_1 \alpha_1 \Delta T = l_2 \alpha_2 \Delta T$$

$$\Rightarrow \quad l_1 \alpha_1 = l_2 \alpha_2$$

14. The given circular platform and ball is as shown below

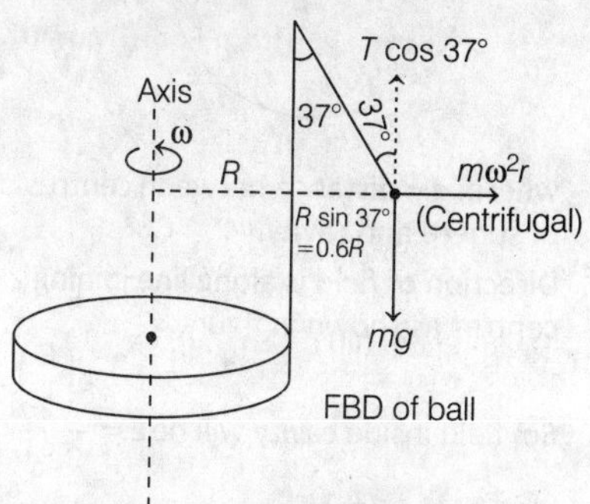

Distance of ball from axis of rotation,

$$r = R + R\sin 37° = 1.6R = 4.8 \text{ m} \quad \text{...(i)}$$

From FBD of ball, in

Horizontal : $m\omega^2 r = T \sin 37°$ ...(i)

Vertical : $mg = T \cos 37°$ ...(ii)

Dividing Eq. (i) by Eq. (ii), we get

$$\frac{\omega^2 r}{g} = \tan 37°$$

$$\Rightarrow \quad \omega = \sqrt{\frac{g \tan 37°}{r}}$$

$$= \sqrt{\frac{10 \times 0.75}{4.8}} = 1.25 \text{ rad/s}$$

15. **For interference at A** S_2 is behind S_1 by a distance of $100\lambda + \frac{\lambda}{4}$ (equal to phase difference $\frac{\pi}{2}$). Further S_2 lags S_1 by $\frac{\pi}{2}$.

Hence, the waves from S_1 and S_2 interfere at A with a phase difference of $200.5\pi + 0.5\pi = 201\pi$

Hence, the net amplitude at A is

$$2a - a = a$$

For interference at B S_2 is ahead of S_1 by a distance of $100\lambda + \frac{\lambda}{4}$ (equal to phase difference $\frac{\pi}{2}$). Further S_2 lags S_1 by $\frac{\pi}{2}$. Hence, the waves from S_1 and S_2 interfere at B with a phase difference of $200.5\pi - 0.5\pi = 200\pi$

Hence, the net amplitude at A is

$$2a + a = 3a$$

Hence, $\left(\frac{I_A}{I_B}\right) = \left(\frac{a}{3a}\right)^2 = \frac{1}{9}$

16. Field inside spherical cavity in a sphere

$$= \frac{\rho a}{3\varepsilon_0}$$

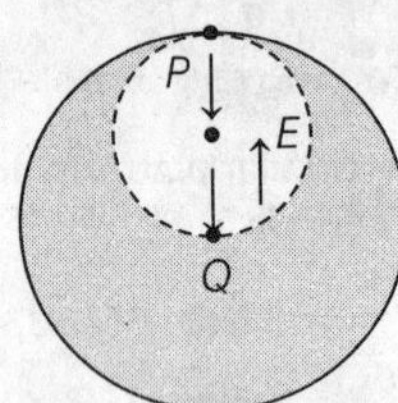

where, a = distance between centres of sphere and cavity.

Direction of field is along line joining centres as shown in figure.

So, field inside cavity will be $E = \dfrac{\rho\left(\frac{R}{2}\right)}{3\varepsilon_0}$

$$= \frac{\rho R}{6\varepsilon_0} \text{ (as shown)}$$

Under influence of field, electron will accelerate down with acceleration,

$$a = \frac{eE}{m} = \frac{\rho Re}{6\varepsilon_0 m} \quad \text{...(i)}$$

As electrons move from P to Q, striking the cavity at Q, its displacement will be equal to $PQ = R = s$ ... (ii)

So, by using, $s = ut + \frac{1}{2}at^2$, we get

$$R = 0 + \frac{1}{2}\frac{\rho Re}{6\varepsilon_0 m}t^2$$

[using Eqs. (i) and (ii)]

$$\Rightarrow \quad t = \sqrt{\frac{12\varepsilon_0 m}{\rho e}}$$

17. Ratio of magnetic moment to angular momentum is called Gyromagnetic ratio and is given by

$\frac{\mu}{L} = \frac{e}{2m}$ (Here e = electronic charge and m = electronic mass)

$$\Rightarrow \quad \mu = \frac{eL}{2m} \quad \text{...(i)}$$

By Bohr's quantisation rule,

$$L = \frac{nh}{2\pi} = \frac{(N+1)h}{2\pi} \quad \text{...(ii)}$$

where, n is principal quantum number which is equal to $N+1$ for Nth excited state.

Putting value of L from Eq. (ii) in Eq (i), we get

$$\mu = \frac{e}{2m} \cdot \frac{(N+1)h}{2\pi} \Rightarrow \mu \propto N+1$$

18. As the capillary is dipped in liquid, force F of surface tension begins pulling the liquid up till equilibrium is reached. In equilibrium, weight of liquid balances the force due to surface tension.

i.e. $\quad F = mg$

$\therefore$ Work done, $W = Fh$ ...(i)

ΔU = Increase in potential energy of liquid

$= mg \times$ height gained by centre of mass

$$= mg\frac{h}{2} \quad \text{...(ii)}$$

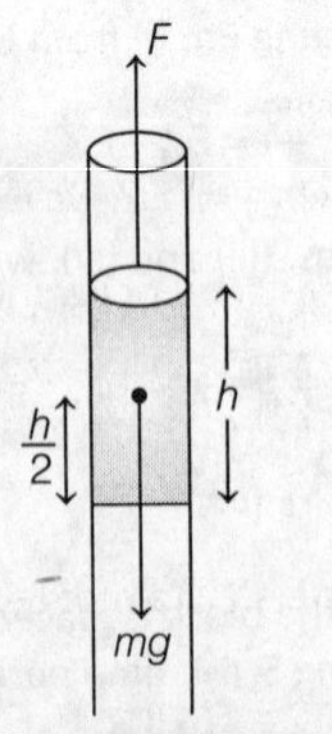

A part of work which is not converted to potential energy must have dissipated as heat. So, heat

$$= W - \Delta U = mgh - mg\frac{h}{2} = mg\frac{h}{2}$$

[using Eqs. (i) and (ii)]

19. Stress at left and right ends of the given rod is $\frac{F}{A}$ and $\frac{2F}{A}$ respectively, so

$$\text{average stress} = \frac{\frac{F}{A} + \frac{2F}{A}}{2} = \frac{3F}{2A} = \sigma \quad \text{...(i)}$$

As per Hooke's law,

$$Y = \frac{\text{Stress}}{\text{Strain}} = \frac{\sigma}{\frac{\Delta l}{l}}$$

$$\Rightarrow \text{Extension} = \Delta l = \frac{\sigma l}{Y} = \frac{3Fl}{2AY}$$

[using Eq. (i)]

20. Given, $f_c = 1.5 \text{ MHz} = 1500 \text{ kHz}$,

$$f_m = 10 \text{ kHz}$$

$\therefore$ Lower side band frequency

$$= f_c - f_m = 1500 \text{ kHz} - 10 \text{ kHz}$$
$$= 1490 \text{ kHz}$$

Upper side band frequency

$$= f_c + f_m = 1500 \text{ kHz} + 10 \text{ kHz}$$
$$= 1510 \text{ kHz}$$

21. Density $= \frac{\text{Mass}}{\text{Volume}}$

$$\Rightarrow \quad \rho = \frac{m}{l^3}$$

$$\Rightarrow \quad \frac{d\rho}{\rho} = \frac{dm}{m} - \frac{3dl}{l}$$

$$\Rightarrow \quad \left|\left(\frac{\Delta\rho}{\rho}\right)_{min}\right| = |1 - 3 \times 2| = 5$$

22. Let swimmer makes angle θ with upstream. Velocity components of swimmer's velocity w.r.t. river are as shown in figure. To reach directly opposite point (i.e. from P to Q), velocity of swimmer should be along PQ.

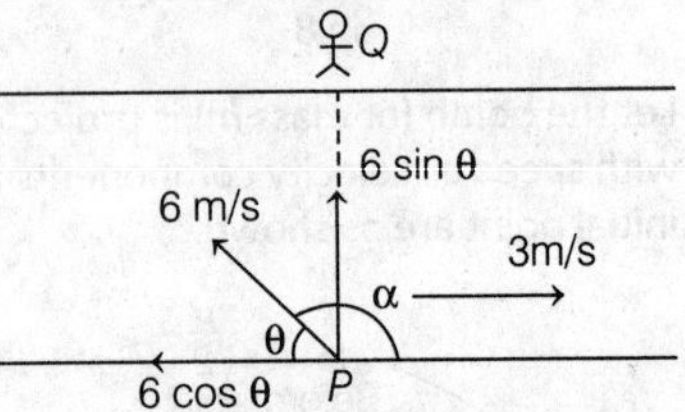

Therefore, his net velocity along river stream should be zero. For that $6\cos\theta$ (velocity component of swimmer in x-direction) should cancel river's velocity,

$$\Rightarrow \quad 6\cos\theta = 3$$

$$\Rightarrow \quad \cos\theta = \frac{1}{2}$$

$\Rightarrow \quad \theta = \dfrac{\pi}{3}$

$\therefore \alpha$ = Angle of stroking with downstream

$= \pi - \theta = \pi - \dfrac{\pi}{3} = \dfrac{2\pi}{3}$

$= 2.09$ rad

23. Inductive reactance,

$X_L = \omega L$

$= 100\pi \times \dfrac{3}{100\pi} = 3\Omega$

Capacitive reactance,

$X_C = \dfrac{1}{\omega C} = \dfrac{1}{100\pi \times \dfrac{1}{700\pi}} = 7\Omega$

Impedance, $Z = \sqrt{(X_C - X_L)^2 + R^2}$

$= \sqrt{(7-3)^2 + 3^2} = 5\Omega$

$i_{rms} = \dfrac{V_{rms}}{Z} = \dfrac{50\sqrt{2}}{5} = 10\sqrt{2}$ A ...(i)

So, $\tan\phi = \dfrac{X_C - X_L}{R} = \dfrac{7-3}{3} = \dfrac{4}{3}$

$\Rightarrow \quad \phi = 53°$ ...(ii)

$\therefore$ Wattless component

$= i_{rms} \sin\phi$

$= 10\sqrt{2} \times \sin 53°$

[using Eqs. (i) and (ii)]

$= 10\sqrt{2} \times \dfrac{4}{5} = (\sqrt{2})^7$ A

24. To find flux through infinite Plane -1, let us construct an infinite Plane-2 at same distance from q on other side. If electric flux through Plane-1 is ϕ, then flux through Plane-2 will be also ϕ.

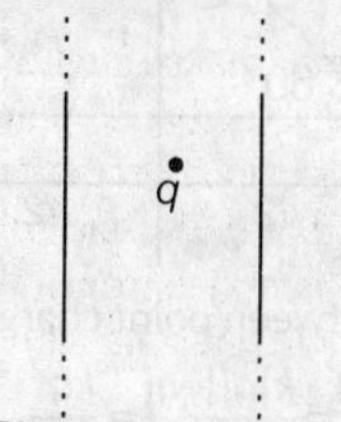

By Gauss's Law,

$\phi_{total} = 2\phi = \dfrac{q}{\varepsilon_0}$

$\Rightarrow \quad \phi = \dfrac{q}{2\varepsilon_0} = \dfrac{1}{8\pi\varepsilon_0}$

$= \dfrac{9 \times 10^9}{2}$

$= 4.5 \times 10^9$

$\Rightarrow \quad a = 4.5, b = 9$

$\Rightarrow \quad a + b = 13.5$

25. Let temperature of junction is T as shown in the figure.

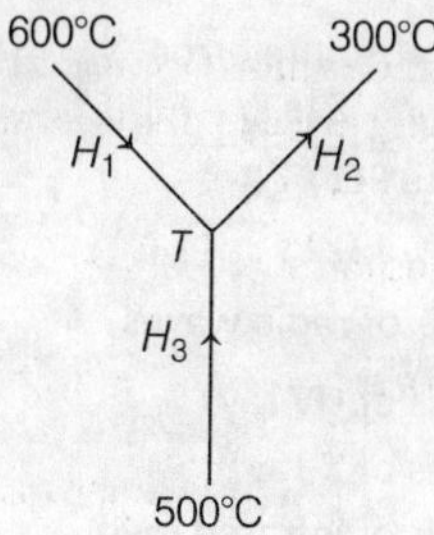

By conservation of thermal current,

$H_1 + H_3 = H_2$

$\Rightarrow \dfrac{KA(600-T)}{l} + \dfrac{3KA(500-T)}{l} = \dfrac{2KA(T-300)}{l}$

$\Rightarrow 600 - T + 3(500 - T) = 2(T - 300)$

$\Rightarrow \quad T = 450°$ C

$\therefore \quad \dfrac{H_1 + H_2}{H_3}$

$= \dfrac{\dfrac{KA(600-450)}{l} + \dfrac{2KA(450-300)}{l}}{\dfrac{3KA(500-450)}{l}} = 3$

26. Consider an element at a distance x from axis having thickness dx as shown. Velocity of element, $v = \omega x$.

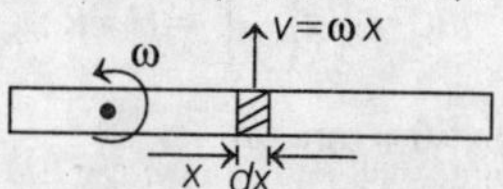

$\Rightarrow$ Motional emf in element $= B \cdot \omega x \cdot dx$

$(\because e = Bvl)$

$\Rightarrow$ Motional emf induced between ends of the rod

$= \displaystyle\int_{-\frac{l}{3}}^{\frac{2l}{3}} B\omega x\, dx = B\omega \left[\dfrac{x^2}{2}\right]_{-\frac{l}{3}}^{\frac{2l}{3}}$

$= \dfrac{B\omega}{2}\left[\left(\dfrac{2l}{3}\right)^2 - \left(-\dfrac{l}{3}\right)^2\right] = \dfrac{B\omega l^2}{6}$

$\Rightarrow \quad x = 6$

27. From theory of EM wave, $\mu_0 \varepsilon_0 = \dfrac{1}{c^2}$

Here, c is speed of light in vacuum

$\Rightarrow [\mu_0\varepsilon_0] = \left[\dfrac{1}{c^2}\right] = [c]^{-2} = [LT^{-1}]^{-2}$

$= [L^{-2}T^2]$ ...(i)

Also, time constant of L-R circuit is $\dfrac{L}{R}$

$\Rightarrow \quad \left[\dfrac{L}{R}\right] = T$ ...(ii)

As, argument $\dfrac{\mu_0\varepsilon_0 L}{Rs}$ is dimensionless.

$\Rightarrow [s] = \left[\dfrac{\mu_0\varepsilon_0 L}{R}\right] = [L^{-2}T^2 \cdot T] = [L^{-2}T^3]$

...(iii)

[using Eqs. (i) and (ii)]

Also, exponent $\dfrac{rk}{sE}$ is dimensionless.

Also,

$[E] = [ML^2T^{-2}]$

$\Rightarrow [rk] = [s]\,[E]$

$= [L^{-2}T^3 ML^2T^{-2}] = [MT]$ ...(iv)

By principle of homogeneity,

$\Rightarrow [p] = [q \cdot e^{\frac{rk}{sE}}] = \left[rk \cdot \sin\left(\dfrac{\mu_0\varepsilon_0 L}{Rs}\right)\right]$

$\Rightarrow \quad [p] = [q] = [rk] = [MT]$

[using Eq. (iv)]

Comparing with the given value in the question, $x = 1, y = 1 \Rightarrow x + y = 2$

28. The given circuit can be redrawn as

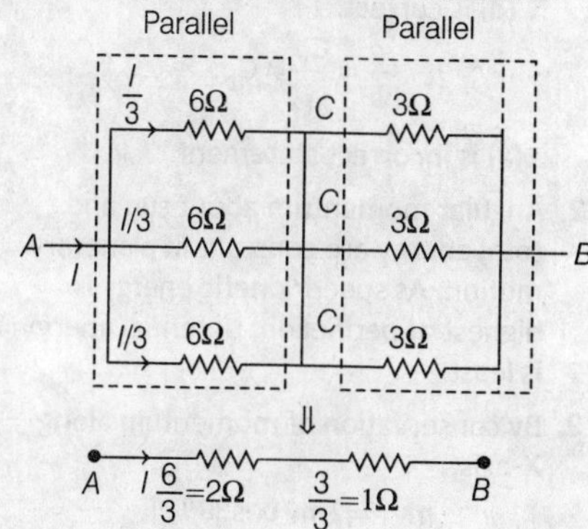

So, current flowing between points A and B will be

$I = \dfrac{V}{R_{net}} = \dfrac{24}{2+1} = 8$ A

So, current in all 6Ω resistors $= \dfrac{I}{3} = \dfrac{8}{3}$ A

$\therefore$ Power dissipated

$= I^2 R = \left(\dfrac{8}{3}\right)^2 \times 6 = 42.67$ W

29. Given that, $P_{capacitor} = P_{resistor}$

$\Rightarrow \quad V_C i = V_R i \Rightarrow V_C = V_R$

$\Rightarrow \quad \varepsilon(1 - e^{-\frac{t}{RC}}) = \varepsilon e^{-\frac{t}{RC}} \Rightarrow e^{\frac{t}{RC}} = 2$

$\Rightarrow \quad t = RC \ln 2 = 0.69\,RC$

30. To convert a galvanometer into ammeter, a low shunt resistance is connected to it, whose value is given by

$S = \dfrac{i_g R_g}{i - i_g} = \dfrac{20 \times 10^{-3} \times 20}{4 - 20 \times 10^{-3}}$

$= \dfrac{20}{199}\,\Omega \Rightarrow \quad x = 20$

Knockout 03

1. As, we know, specific heat capacity,

$C = C_V + \frac{R}{1-x}$, for polytropic process

So, from graph,

$p = C_p, q = C_V,$

$r = 1, s = \gamma$

$\Rightarrow \quad p = q \cdot s$

and $\quad pr = q \cdot s$

So, $(p - q)$ does not depend on nature or atomicity of gas.

$\therefore$ (b), (c) are correct.

For $TV^{\frac{1}{2}} =$ constant, $pV^{\frac{3}{2}} =$ constant

$\Rightarrow \quad x = \frac{3}{2} \quad$ (i.e. $1 < x < \gamma$)

$\Rightarrow \quad C = -$ve or temperature of gas decreases on supplying heat.

$\therefore$ (d) is correct.

$$\frac{q}{s} = \frac{C_v}{\gamma} \neq C_p$$

$\therefore$ (a) is incorrect statement.

2. Angular momentum about sun and total energy are constant in planetary motion. As speed/kinetic energy is highest at perihelion, potential energy is least.

3. By conservation of momentum along X-axis,

$mv_1 = 2mv \cos 30°$

$\Rightarrow \quad v_1 = \sqrt{3}\, v$

By conservation of momentum along Y-axis,

$mv_2 = 2mv \sin 30°$

$\Rightarrow \quad v_2 = v$

$\Rightarrow v_1 = \sqrt{3}\, v_2$, but it is incorrect to write $\mathbf{v}_1 = \sqrt{3}\mathbf{v}_2$

P_{system} in frame of centre of mass

$= m_1(\mathbf{v}_1 - \mathbf{v}_{CM}) + m_2(\mathbf{v}_2 - \mathbf{v}_{CM})$

$= m_1\mathbf{v}_1 + m_2\mathbf{v}_2 - \mathbf{v}_{CM}(m_1 + m_2)$

$= 0$

Kinetic energy of system after explosion

$= \frac{1}{2} m[(\sqrt{3}v)^2 + v^2]$

$= 2mv^2$

Kinetic energy before explosion

$= \frac{1}{2} \cdot 2m \cdot v^2 = mv^2$

$\Rightarrow$ Minimum energy released $= mv^2$.

4. Least count of measuring instrument $= 0.1$ s

Mean absolute error

$= \frac{\Sigma |t_{avg} - t_i|}{3}$

≈ 0.2 s

5. (i) λ_1 is of radio waves
   (ii) λ_2 is of UV rays
   (iii) λ_3 is of X-ray
   (iv) λ_4 is of infrared rays

$\therefore \lambda_3 < \lambda_2 < \lambda_4 < \lambda_1$

6. The gases carbon monoxide (CO) and nitrogen (N_2) are diatomic, so both have equal kinetic energy of $\frac{5}{2} kT$, i.e. $E_1 = E_2$

7. Displacement at any time t,

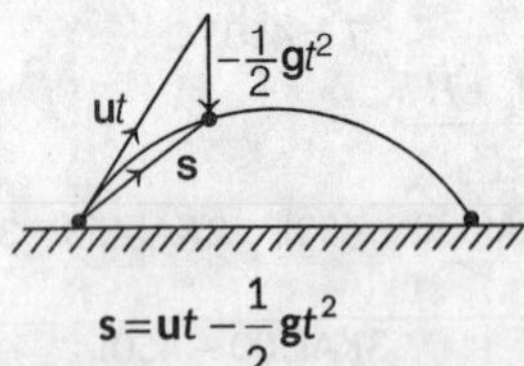

$$\mathbf{s} = \mathbf{u}t - \frac{1}{2}\mathbf{g}t^2$$

It can be interpreted as vector sum of $\mathbf{u}t$ and $-\frac{1}{2}\mathbf{g}t^2$ as shown.

$\Rightarrow \quad BC = \frac{1}{2} g\left(\frac{T}{2}\right)^2 = H = R$

for $\quad \theta = \tan^{-1} 4$

Also, $DE = \frac{1}{2} gT^2 = 4BC$, irrespective of θ.

8. For a uniform acceleration, path is straight or parabolic, i.e. curved.
For $\mathbf{a} = \mathbf{k} \times \mathbf{v}$, path is circular or helical.
$\mathbf{a}$ is constant only in magnitude in a uniform circular motion.
In damped oscillation,

$A = A_0 e^{-kt}$

Given, $A = \frac{A_0}{2}$ at $t = 2$s

$\Rightarrow \quad \frac{A_0}{2} = A_0 e^{-k(2)}$, so $A = A_0 e^{-k(3)}$

$= A_0 \left[\frac{1}{2}\right]^{\frac{3}{2}} = \frac{A_0}{2\sqrt{2}}$

9. $I_C = \frac{10 - V_{CE}}{1000} = 5$ mA

$\beta = \frac{I_C}{I_B} \Rightarrow I_B = \frac{I_C}{\beta}$

$\Rightarrow I_B = \frac{5 \times 10^{-3}}{100} = 5 \times 10^{-5}$ A

$\Rightarrow R_B = \frac{10 - V_{BE}}{I_B} = \frac{10 - 0}{5 \times 10^{-5}} = 2 \times 10^5\ \Omega$

10. Magnitude will remain unchanged, if sum of dimensions in fundamental quantities is zero.
For gravitational energy, the dimensional formula is

$[E] = [ML^2T^{-2}]$

So, when units of mass, length and time are doubled. The magnitude of E will become 2 times.

11. For amplitude of message signal greater than that of carrier wave distortion happens .

12. Given, $U = -\frac{k}{r^3}$

$\Rightarrow \quad F = -\frac{dU}{dr} = \frac{3k}{r^4} = \frac{mv^2}{r}$

$\Rightarrow \quad mv^2 = \frac{3k}{r^3} \quad$ ...(i)

Also, $mvr = \frac{nh}{2\pi} \quad$ ...(ii)

From Eqs. (i) and (ii), we get

$r \propto \frac{1}{n^2}$ and $v \propto n^3$

also, $\quad E \propto v^2 \Rightarrow E \propto n^6$

$\therefore \quad v / r = n^3 \times n^2 = n^5$

and $\frac{v^2 \cdot r}{\sqrt{E}} \propto \frac{n^6 \cdot n^{-2}}{n^3} \propto n$

13. Equivalent set-up is

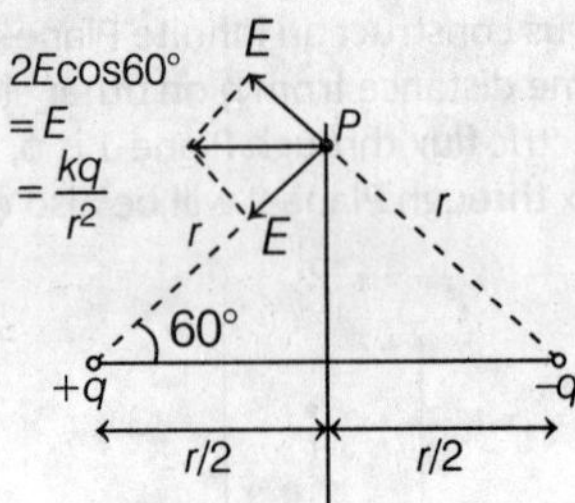

Force between point charges,

$$F = \frac{k|q||-q|}{r^2} = \frac{kq^2}{r^2}$$

Electric field at $P = 2E \cos 60° = E = \frac{kq}{r^2}$

14. Tension in AC is F.
So, extension produced,

$x_1 = \frac{F \times l/2}{AY}$

Tension in CB is $3F$.
So, extension produced,

$x_2 = \frac{3F \times l/2}{AY}$

Total extension in rod,

$x = x_1 + x_2 = \frac{Fl}{2AY} + \frac{3Fl}{2AY} = \frac{2Fl}{AY}$

As stress ∝ force, so stress in portion CB is thrice of that in AC.

Also strain ∝ stress, so strain produced in portion CB is thrice of that in AC.

Elastic potential energy,

$$U \propto (\text{extension})^2$$

$\therefore U$ in CB is 9 times of that in AC.

15. Initially, $V_C = V_R = i_0 R_0$

Also, $i = i_0 e^{-t/RC}$

$\Rightarrow \frac{i_0}{2} = i_0 e^{-t/RC}$

$\Rightarrow e^{t_0/RC} = 2$

$\Rightarrow C = \frac{t_0}{R\ln 2}$

$\Rightarrow \tau = RC = \frac{t_0}{\ln 2} > t_0$

$\therefore t_1$ cannot possibly be time constant.

At $t = t_0,\ q = \frac{q_0}{2}$

Potential energy of capacitor

$$= \frac{1}{4} \times \text{Initial potential energy}$$

$\therefore \frac{3}{4}$th is dissipated

16. Using lens Maker's formula,

$$\frac{1}{f_{\text{concave}}} = \left(\frac{3}{2} - 1\right)\left(-\frac{1}{10} - \frac{1}{15}\right) = -\frac{1}{12}$$

Similarly,

$$\frac{1}{f_{\text{convex}}} = \left(\frac{4}{3} - 1\right)\left(\frac{1}{15} + \frac{1}{15}\right) = \frac{2}{45}$$

$$\therefore \frac{1}{f_{eq}} = \frac{1}{f_{\text{mirror}}} - 2\left(\frac{1}{f_{\text{concave}}} + \frac{1}{f_{\text{convex}}}\right)$$

$$= -\frac{1}{18} \Rightarrow f_{eq} = -18 \text{ cm}$$

As magnification,

$$m = \frac{f}{f-u} = \frac{-18}{(-18)-(-27)} = -2$$

$$\Rightarrow v_{\text{image}} = -m^2 v_{\text{object}} = -8 \text{ m/s}$$

17. The situation can be shown as

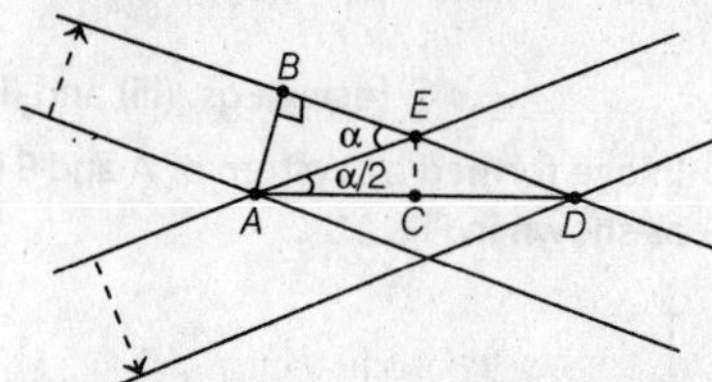

In time t, distance moved by rod,

$$AB = vt$$

$\Rightarrow$ By geometry, distance moved by contact point $= AD = 2 \cdot AC$

$$= 2 \cdot AE \cdot \cos\frac{\alpha}{2}$$

$$= 2 \cdot \frac{AB}{\sin\alpha} \cdot \cos\frac{\alpha}{2}$$

$$= vt \operatorname{cosec}\frac{\alpha}{2}$$

$\Rightarrow$ Speed of $O = v \operatorname{cosec}\frac{\alpha}{2}$

$$= 3 \operatorname{cosec} 30° = 6 \text{ m/s}.$$

18. By string constraint,

$$\text{acceleration} \propto \frac{1}{\text{tension}}$$

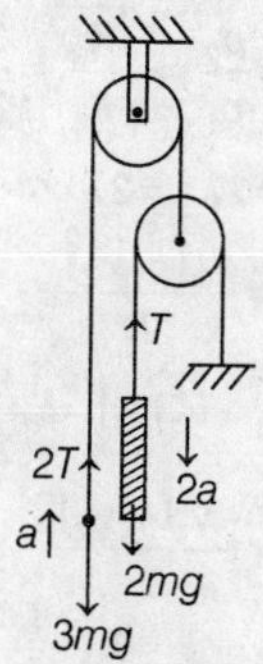

$\Rightarrow$ Accelerations will be as shown

For ball,

$$2T - 3mg = 3ma \quad \text{...(i)}$$

For rod,

$$2mg - T = 4ma \quad \text{...(ii)}$$

From Eqs. (i) and (ii), $a = \frac{g}{11}$

$\Rightarrow$ Relative acceleration of ball w.r.t. rod,

$$a' = 3a = \frac{3g}{11}$$

$$\Rightarrow t = \sqrt{\frac{2l}{a'}} = \sqrt{\frac{2\left(\frac{15}{11}\right)}{\frac{3 \times 10}{11}}} = 1 \text{ s}$$

19. For hollow sphere, $\frac{M}{L} = \frac{q}{2m}$

For solid sphere (conducting),

$$\frac{M'}{L'} = \frac{M}{\frac{3}{5}L} = \frac{5}{3} \cdot \frac{q}{2m} \quad (\text{as } L \propto I)$$

$$= \frac{5}{6} \cdot \frac{q}{m} = \frac{5}{6} \times 6 = 5$$

20. Considering that to find mass of parent and daughter nuclei mass of electron needs to be subtracted from atomic masses,

$$Q = (m_{\text{reactant}} - m_{\text{product}})c^2$$

$$= [(m_1 - Zm_3) - \{(m_2 - Zm_3 + m_3) + m_3\}]c^2$$

$$= (m_1 - m_2 - 2m_3)c^2$$

$$\therefore k + 1 = 2 + 1 = 3$$

21. If v is the assumed minimum speed in nearest position B, corresponding speed in farthest position C is zero.

By conservation of energy between B and C, loss in KE = gain in PE

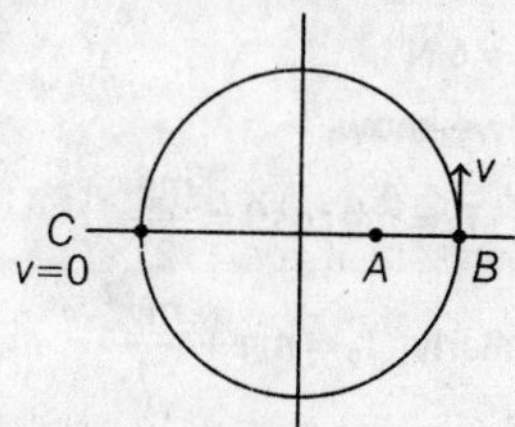

$$\frac{1}{2}(1)v^2 = \int \frac{3}{r^2} dr = \left[-\frac{3}{r}\right]_1^3$$

$$= (-1) - (-3) = 2$$

$$\Rightarrow v = 2 \text{ m/s}$$

22. For O, $\Delta x = 2l = 2\lambda$ which will be the point of destructive interference, as due to reflection condition of destructive and constructive interferences are interchanged, so nearest point for destructive interference should have $\Delta x = \lambda$.

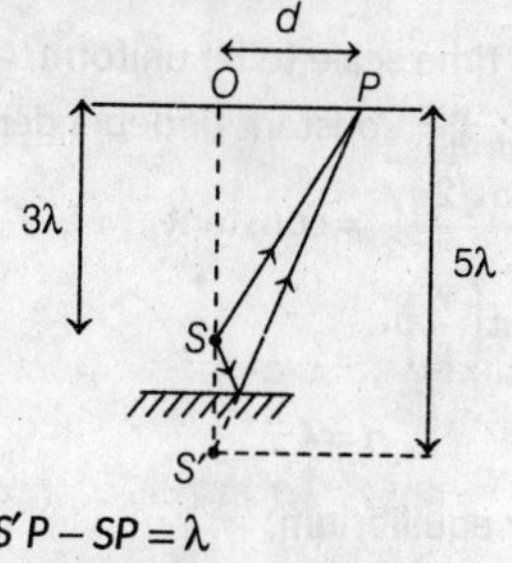

$$\Rightarrow S'P - SP = \lambda$$

$$\Rightarrow \sqrt{(5\lambda)^2 + d^2} - \sqrt{(3\lambda)^2 + d^2} = \lambda$$

$$\Rightarrow 25\lambda^2 + d^2 = \lambda^2 + 9\lambda^2 + d^2 + 2\lambda\sqrt{9\lambda^2 + d^2}$$

$$\Rightarrow 15\lambda^2 = 2\lambda\sqrt{9\lambda^2 + d^2}$$

$$\Rightarrow d = \sqrt{\frac{189}{4}}\lambda$$

$$= \sqrt{\frac{189}{4}} \cdot \frac{2}{\sqrt{21}} = 3 \text{ m}$$

23. Force on rod in magnetic field is given by

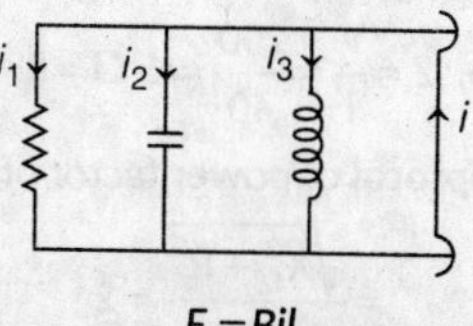

$$F = Bil$$

$$=B(i_1+i_2+i_3)l$$
$$=B\left[\frac{Bvl}{R}+C\cdot Bal+\frac{Bvl}{L}t\right]l$$
$$=B^2l^2v\left[\frac{1}{R}+\frac{t}{L}\right] \quad \text{(as, } a=0\text{)}$$
$$=2^2\cdot 1^2\cdot 2\left[\frac{1}{2}+\frac{2}{8}\right]$$
$$=6\text{ N}$$

24. As, we know,

$$T_1=mg\cos\theta=\frac{mg}{2}$$

Similarly, $T_2=mg+\frac{mv^2}{l}$

$$=mg+\frac{m}{l}\{\sqrt{2gl(1-\cos 60^\circ)}\}^2=2mg$$

$$\therefore \quad \frac{T_2}{T_1}=\frac{2mg}{mg/2}=4$$

25. Given, $f'=f_{\text{fundamental}}$

$$\Rightarrow \frac{3u}{4l}\left\{\frac{u-v}{u}\right\}=\frac{u}{4l}$$
$$\Rightarrow \frac{v}{u}=\frac{2}{3}=\frac{a}{b}$$
$$\Rightarrow a+b=5$$
$$\Rightarrow (a+b)^2=25$$

26. For time scale to be uniform,

$v_{\text{surface}}=$ constant (independent of y)

$$\Rightarrow \frac{a\sqrt{2gy}}{\pi\left(\frac{y}{k}\right)^{\frac{2}{n}}}=\text{constant}$$
$$\Rightarrow \quad n=4$$

27. For equilibrium,

$$\tau_{\text{anticlockwise}}=\tau_{\text{clockwise}}$$
$$\Rightarrow BIN\pi R^2=v\cdot\frac{dm}{dt}\cdot\frac{3L}{4}$$
$$\Rightarrow BIN\pi R^2=v\cdot\rho RLv\cdot\frac{3L}{4}$$
$$\Rightarrow \quad I=\frac{3\rho v^2L^2}{4N\pi RB}=3\text{ A}$$

28. $X_C=\frac{1}{\omega C}=\frac{1}{100\cdot\frac{1}{500\sqrt{3}}}=5\sqrt{3}\,\Omega$

As, power factor $=1$

$$\Rightarrow \quad X_L=X_C=5\sqrt{3}\,\Omega$$

Also, $Z=\frac{V}{I}=\frac{200}{40}=5\,\Omega=R$

Reciprocal of power factor of box

$$=\frac{\sqrt{X_L^2+R^2}}{R}=2$$

29. As, $K=\frac{12400}{3100}-2$

$$=2\text{ eV}=K_1$$

$$\Rightarrow \quad K_2=K-1.5=0.5$$

Since, $\lambda\propto p$

$$\Rightarrow \quad \frac{\lambda_1}{\lambda_2}=\frac{p_2}{p_1}=\sqrt{\frac{K_2}{K_1}}=\frac{1}{2}$$
$$\Rightarrow \quad \lambda_2=2\lambda_1=2\lambda$$
$$\mathbf{v}_{\text{CM}}=\frac{v_1\hat{\mathbf{i}}+v_2\hat{\mathbf{j}}}{2}$$
$$\Rightarrow \quad \mathbf{v}_{2,\text{ CM}}=v_2\mathbf{j}-\left(\frac{v_1\mathbf{i}+v_2\mathbf{j}}{2}\right)$$
$$=\frac{-v_1\mathbf{i}+v_2\mathbf{j}}{2}$$
$$\Rightarrow \lambda_{2,\text{ CM}}=\frac{h}{m\sqrt{\frac{v_1^2+v_2^2}{4}}}=\frac{2\lambda_1\lambda_2}{\sqrt{\lambda_1^2+\lambda_2^2}}$$
$$=\frac{2\cdot\lambda\cdot 2\lambda}{\sqrt{\lambda^2+(2\lambda)^2}}=\frac{4\lambda}{\sqrt{5}}$$
$$\therefore \quad x=\sqrt{5}=2.24$$

30. By work-energy theorem,

$$W_{\text{gravity}}+W_{\text{friction}}=\Delta\text{KE}$$
$$\Rightarrow \quad mgh-\mu mgs=0$$
$$\Rightarrow \quad \mu=\frac{h}{s}=\frac{1}{3}=\frac{2}{6}$$
$$\therefore \quad x=6$$

Knockout 04

1. From free body diagram of element (of mass dm) shown

$$(p+dp)A-pA=dma$$

Here, p is pressure and A is cross-sectional area of tube

$$\Rightarrow \quad dp\cdot A=\rho A\,dxa$$
$$\Rightarrow \quad dp=\frac{pM}{RT}a\,dx$$

[using ideal gas equation]

$$\Rightarrow \quad \frac{dp}{p}=\frac{Ma}{RT}dx$$

Integrating both sides, we get

$$\Rightarrow \quad \int_{p_0}^{2p_0}\frac{dp}{p}=\frac{Ma}{RT}\int_0^L dx$$
$$\Rightarrow \quad \ln 2=\frac{MaL}{RT}$$
$$\Rightarrow \quad a=\frac{RT\ln 2}{ML}$$

2. For disc to be at rest, contact force F by the insect on the disc should pass through centre O of the disc. From free body diagam shown, for horizontal direction,

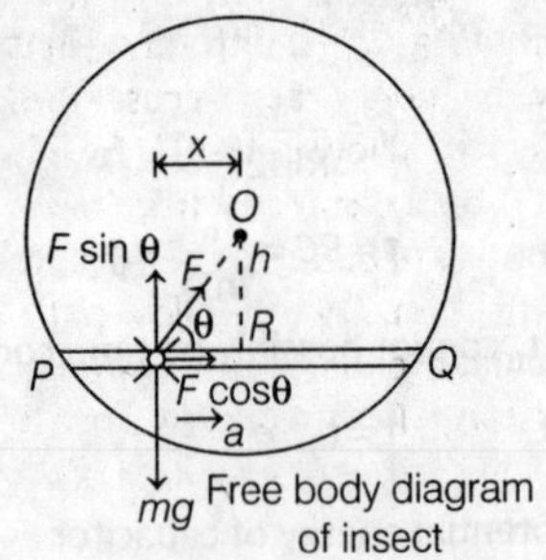

Free body diagram of insect

$$F\cos\theta=ma \quad \text{...(i)}$$

For vertical direction,

$$F\sin\theta=mg \quad \text{...(ii)}$$

Dividing Eq. (i) by Eq. (ii), we get

$$\cot\theta=\frac{a}{g}\Rightarrow a=g\cot\theta=\frac{gx}{h}$$

where, $x=$ Distance of insect from centre of groove.

As acceleration is comparable to $a=\omega^2x$ and is directed towards centre of the groove, so motion of the insect is SHM, with angular frequency,

$$\omega=\sqrt{\frac{g}{h}} \quad \text{...(iii)}$$

Also, amplitude of SHM is equal to maximum distance of the insect from centre R of the groove, so amplitude is $A=RQ=h$ (using trigonometry) ...(iv)

Maximum speed in SHM is at mean position equal to

$$v=A\omega=h\sqrt{\frac{g}{h}}=\sqrt{gh}$$

[using Eqs. (iii) and (iv)]

3. Image formed by system of A and B is as shown in Fig. 1.

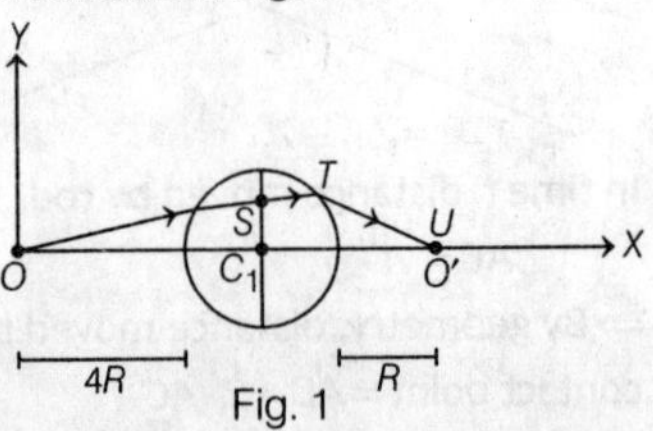

Fig. 1

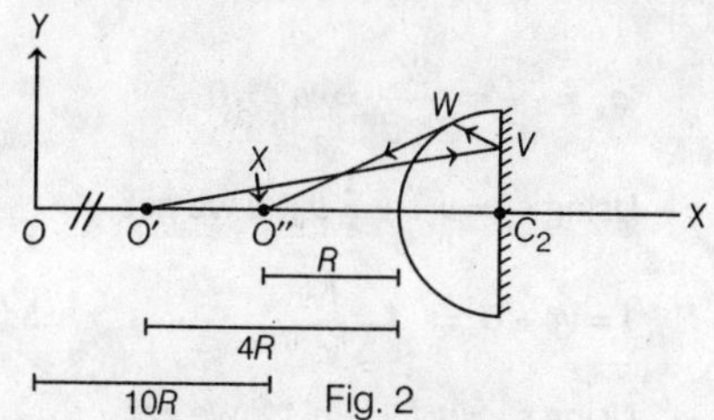

For C, object O' is at a distance $4R$ which is same as the distance of O from surface of A. So, rays from O' will undergo refraction on entering C as that experienced by rays from O on entering A. The difference in cases in two figures is that in case-1 (of Fig. 1) ray will follow path STU forming image at O' at a distance R from curved surface of B. But in case-2, after reflection, ray will follow path VWX (similar to STU) forming image O'' at a distance R from curved surface of C. Therefore, x-coordinate of O'' will be $10R$.

4. The given circuit can be simplified first as shown in Fig.1 and finally as in Fig.2

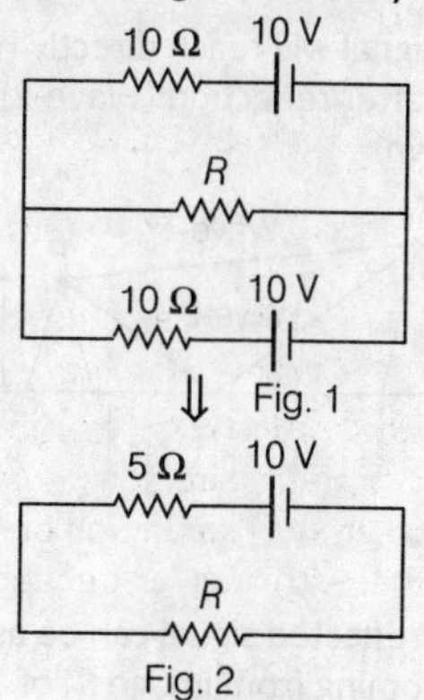

As per maximum power theorem, for maximum power consumption, R should have value equal to resistance of remaining circuit which is 5Ω. As rate of change of resistance is $1\Omega/°C$, therefore $\frac{\Delta R}{\Delta T}=1$.

$$\Rightarrow \frac{5-15}{\Delta T}=1 \Rightarrow \Delta T=-10°C$$

$\Rightarrow$ Final temperature of R

$$=50-10=40°C$$

As per Newton's law of cooling,

$$T_f - T_{surrounding} = (T - T_{surrounding})\, e^{-kt}$$

$$\Rightarrow 40-20=(50-20)e^{-kt}$$

$$\Rightarrow \quad t=\frac{\ln\frac{3}{2}}{k}=\frac{\ln\frac{3}{2}}{\frac{\ln\frac{9}{4}}{100}}=\frac{\ln\frac{3}{2}}{\frac{2\cdot\ln\frac{3}{2}}{100}}=50\text{ s}$$

5. Free body diagram of ball (in block's frame) and block (showing only horizontal forces) are as shown in figures.

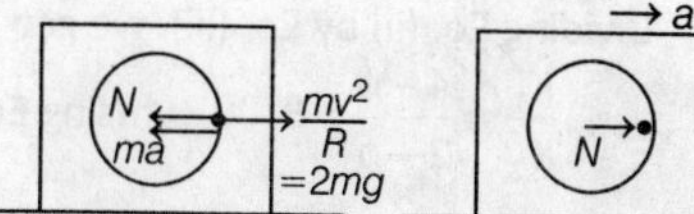

From free body diagram of the ball,

$$N+ma=2mg \quad \text{...(i)}$$

From free body diagram of the block, using $F_{net}=ma$,

$$N=2ma \quad \text{...(ii)}$$

From Eqs. (i) and (ii), we get

$$2ma+ma=2mg \Rightarrow a=\frac{2g}{3}$$

6. If e is eccentricity of the ellipse, b is semi-minor axis and a is semi-major axis, coordinates of sun at focus of ellipse will be $(-ae, 0)$.

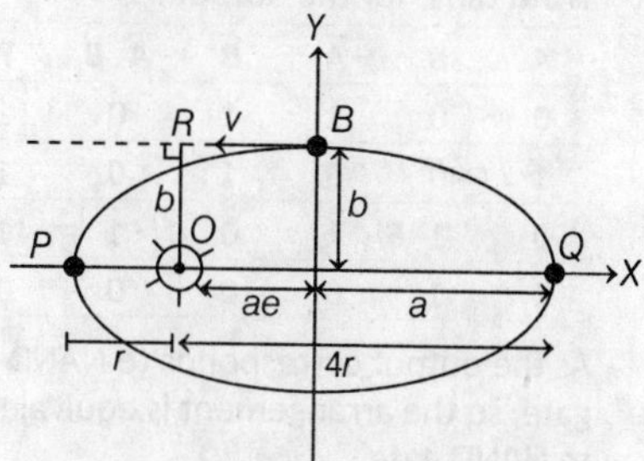

Therefore, from the figure,

$$r_{minimum}=OP=r=a-ae$$
$$=a(1-e) \quad \text{...(i)}$$
$$r_{maximum}=OQ=4r=a+ae$$
$$=a(1+e) \quad \text{...(ii)}$$

Now, semi-minor axis is given by

$$b=a\sqrt{1-e^2}=\sqrt{a^2(1+e)(1-e)}$$
$$=\sqrt{4r\cdot r} \quad \text{[using Eqs. (i) and (ii)]}$$
$$=2r \quad \text{...(iii)}$$

Therefore, angular momentum of the planet is $L=mv(OR)=2mvr$

As angular momentum of the planet is constant w.r.t. sun, so angular momentum in position A will also be the same, that is $2mvr$.

7. For Amperian loop around A in Arrangement-1, by Ampere's law,

$$\oint \mathbf{B}_1\cdot d\mathbf{l}=\mu_0 i \Rightarrow B_1(2\pi r)=\mu_0 i$$

$$\Rightarrow \quad B_1=\frac{\mu_0 i}{2\pi r} \quad \text{...(i)}$$

For Amperian loop around B in Arrangement-2, by Ampere's law,

$$\oint \mathbf{B}_2\cdot d\mathbf{l}=\mu_0 i \Rightarrow B_2=\frac{\mu_0 i}{2\pi r} \quad \text{...(ii)}$$

From Eqs. (i) and (ii), we get

$$B_1=B_2$$

So, required ratio is 1.

8. At time t, distances moved by sliders GH and EF will be $3vt$ and vt respectively as shown.

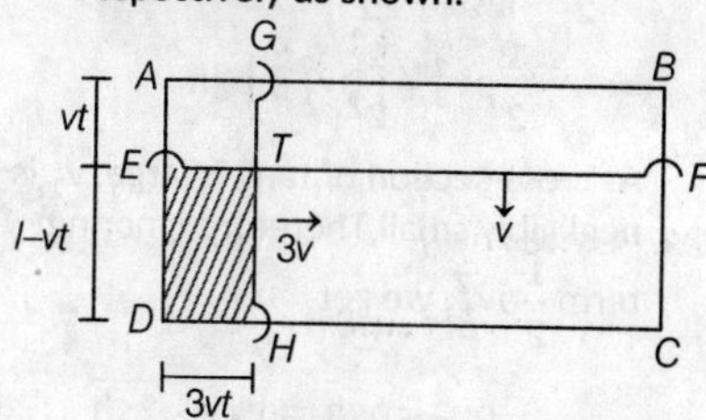

Therefore, area of loop $ETHD$ will be

$$A=3vt(l-vt)=3vlt-3v^2t^2$$

$$\Rightarrow \quad \frac{dA}{dt}=3vl-6v^2t \quad \text{...(i)}$$

At the instant, the loop is square, its two sides will be equal. Therefore,

$$3vt=l-vt \Rightarrow t=\frac{l}{4v} \quad \text{...(ii)}$$

By Faraday's law, emf induced in the loop

$$\varepsilon=\frac{d\phi}{dt}=\frac{d(B_0\cdot A)}{dt}=B_0\cdot\frac{dA}{dt}$$
$$=B_0(3vl-6v^2t) \quad \text{[using Eq. (i)]}$$
$$=B_0\left[3vl-6v^2\left(\frac{l}{4v}\right)\right] \quad \text{[using Eq. (ii)]}$$
$$=\frac{3B_0vl}{2}=1.5\,B_0vl$$

9. Total time taken by the ball to reach at bottom $=\sqrt{\frac{2H}{g}}=\sqrt{\frac{2\times 80}{10}}=4\text{ s}$

Let time taken in one collision is t, then

$$t\times 10=7 \Rightarrow t=0.7\text{ s}$$

No. of collisions $=\frac{4}{0.7}=5\frac{5}{7}$

(5th collisions from wall B)

Horizontal distance travelled in between 2 successive collisions = 7m

$\therefore$ Horizontal distance travelled in 5/7 part of collisions $=\frac{5}{7}\times 7=5\text{m}$, from wall B.

10. Consider the figure shown. Let fluid velocities at points 1, 2, 3 be v_1, v_2 and v_3 respectively.

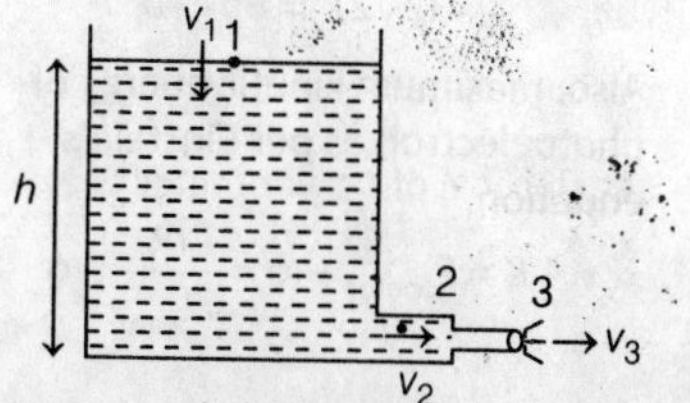

Using Bernoulli's theorem between points 1 and 3, as pressures at points 1 and 3 is equal to atmospheric pressure p_0, we get

$$\Rightarrow \frac{1}{2}\rho v_3^2 + p_0 = \frac{1}{2}\rho v_1^2 + p_0 + \rho g h$$

$$\Rightarrow \quad \frac{1}{2}\rho v_3^2 = \frac{1}{2}\rho v_1^2 + \rho g h$$

As cross-section of tank is large, v_1 is negligibly small. Therefore ignoring term $\frac{1}{2}\rho v_1^2$, we get

$$\frac{1}{2}\rho v_3^2 = \rho g h \Rightarrow v_3 = \sqrt{2gh} \quad \text{...(i)}$$

If A_2 and A_3 are cross-sectional areas at points 2 and 3, by continuity equation,

$$A_2 v_2 = A_3 v_3 \Rightarrow \quad v_2 = \frac{A_3 v_3}{A_2}$$

$$= \frac{v_3}{\sqrt{2}} \quad \text{(given, } A_2 = \sqrt{2}A_3\text{)}$$

$$\Rightarrow \quad v_2 = \sqrt{gh} \quad \text{...(ii) [using Eq. (i)]}$$

By Bernoulli's theorem, between points 1 and 2,

$$\Rightarrow \frac{1}{2}\rho v_2^2 + p = \frac{1}{2}\rho v_1^2 + p_0 + \rho g h$$

$$\Rightarrow p - p_0 = \rho g h + \frac{1}{2}\rho v_1^2 - \frac{1}{2}\rho v_2^2 \quad \text{...(iii)}$$

Ignoring $\frac{1}{2}\rho v_1^2$, and putting value of v_2 from Eq. (ii) into Eq. (iii), we get,

Gauge pressure,

$$p - p_0 = \rho g h - \frac{1}{2}\rho(\sqrt{gh})^2 = \frac{\rho g h}{2}$$

11. As the collision of molecules is elastic, decrease in energy of one molecule must correspond to equal increase in energy for the other molecule. So, Statement 1 is true.
Also, as velocity distribution is random, so statistical average of velocity is zero. Hence, Statement 2 is also true.

12. de-Broglie wavelength λ of electron having kinetic energy K is given by

$$\lambda = \frac{h}{\sqrt{2mK}} \Rightarrow K \propto \frac{1}{\lambda^2}$$

$$\frac{K_1}{K_2} = \left(\frac{\lambda_2}{\lambda_1}\right)^2$$

$$= (2\sqrt{2})^2 = 8 \quad \text{...(i)}$$

Also, maximum kinetic energy of photoelectron as per Einstein's equation,

$$K = E_{\text{photon}} - \phi = \frac{hc}{\lambda_{\text{wave}}} - \phi$$

$$\Rightarrow \quad K_1 = \frac{12400}{3100} - \phi = 4 - \phi \quad \text{...(ii)}$$

$$\text{and } K_2 = \frac{12400}{6200} - \phi = 2 - \phi \quad \text{...(iii)}$$

Dividing Eq. (ii) by Eq. (iii), we get

$$\frac{K_1}{K_2} = \frac{4-\phi}{2-\phi} = 8 \quad \text{[using Eq. (i)]}$$

$$\Rightarrow 4 - \phi = 8(2 - \phi)$$

$$\Rightarrow \quad \phi = \frac{12}{7}\text{ eV} = 1.7\text{ eV}$$

13. The final output of the arrangement as shown below is

$$Y = \overline{Z \cdot B} = \overline{(A+\overline{B})\cdot B} = \overline{(A+\overline{B})} + \overline{B}$$

$$= \overline{A}\cdot B + \overline{B}$$

(using de Morgan's theorem)

Truth table for the output Y is

A	B	$\overline{A}$	$\overline{B}$	$\overline{A}\cdot B$	Y
0	0	1	1	0	1
1	0	0	1	0	1
0	1	1	0	1	1
1	1	0	0	0	0

As the output corresponds to NAND gate, so the arrangement is equivalent to NAND gate.

14. Capacitance of capacitor-1 $= \frac{\varepsilon_0 A}{d}$

Capacitance of capacitor-2

$$= \frac{K\varepsilon_0 A}{2d} = \frac{\varepsilon_0 A}{d} \quad (\because K = 2)$$

As the two capacitors have same capacitance, potential difference across the two capacitors will be equal, each equal to $\frac{V}{2}$. Now consider motion of electron in between plates of capacitor-1, from A to B, assuming it just escapes hitting the plates.

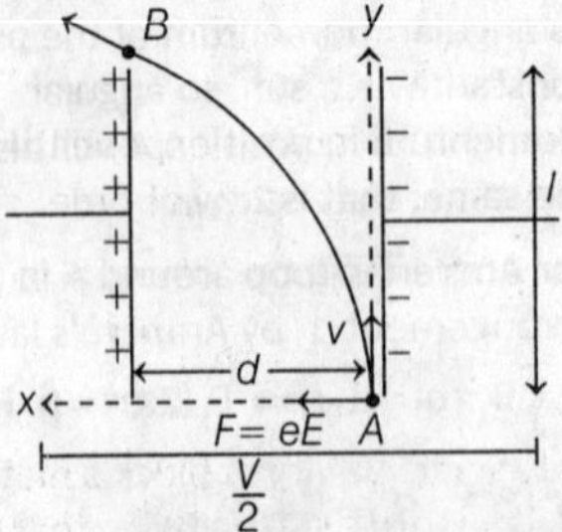

The electron experiences electric force eE towards the positive plate as shown. So acceleration components of the electron are

$$a_x = \frac{eE}{m} = \frac{eV}{2md} \Rightarrow a_y = 0$$

Using $s_y = u_y t + \frac{1}{2}a_y t^2$, we get

$$l = vt + 0 \Rightarrow t = \frac{l}{v} \quad \text{... (i)}$$

Using $s_x = u_x t + \frac{1}{2}a_x t^2$, we get

$$d = 0 + \frac{1}{2}\left(\frac{eV}{2md}\right)\left(\frac{l}{v}\right)^2 \quad \text{[using Eq. (i)]}$$

$$\Rightarrow mv^2 = \frac{eVl^2}{4d^2}$$

$$\text{Kinetic energy} = \frac{1}{2}mv^2 = \frac{eVl^2}{8d^2}$$

15. Electron capture is equivalent to removal of K-shell electron, in which energy equal to binding energy E is consumed. Also, mass lost in the transformation $(m_x - m_y)$ converts into energy given by Einstein's energy-mass equivalence equation, $E = mc^2$ equal to $(m_x - m_y)c^2$.
Therefore, energy released is effectively equal to $Q = (m_x - m_y)c^2 - E$

16. (*b*) Signal will reach directly (Wave-1) and after reflection (Wave-2) as shown.

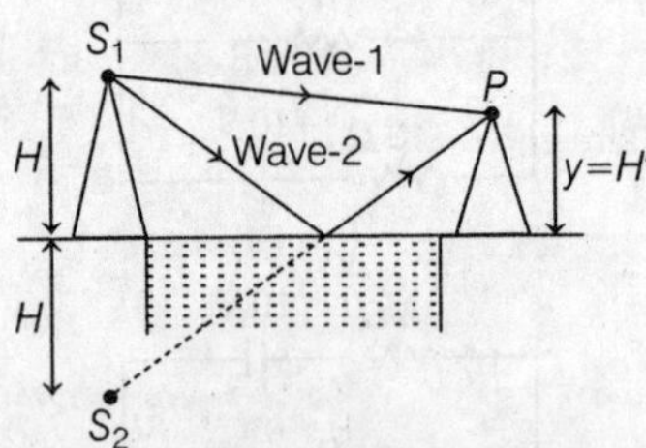

The reflected signal can be assumed to be coming from image S_2 of transmitter S_1 as shown in the figure. So, the geometry is similar to Young's double slit experiment (YDSE).
Also, due to reflection of Wave-2 at water surface, it undergoes phase change of π which is equivalent to path difference of $\frac{\lambda}{2}$. Therefore, net path

$$\text{difference} = \frac{2HH'}{D} + \frac{\lambda}{2}$$

$$\text{For maxima,} \quad \frac{2HH'}{D} + \frac{\lambda}{2} = n\lambda$$

$$\Rightarrow \frac{2HH'}{D} = \left(n - \frac{1}{2}\right)\lambda$$

Only option satisfying above equation is option (b) for $n = 2$

$$\Rightarrow H' = \left(2 - \frac{1}{2}\right)\lambda \times \frac{D}{2H} = \frac{3\lambda D}{4H}$$

17. At highest point of track, normal force becomes zero (if speeds at bottom is just sufficient). So, at highest point

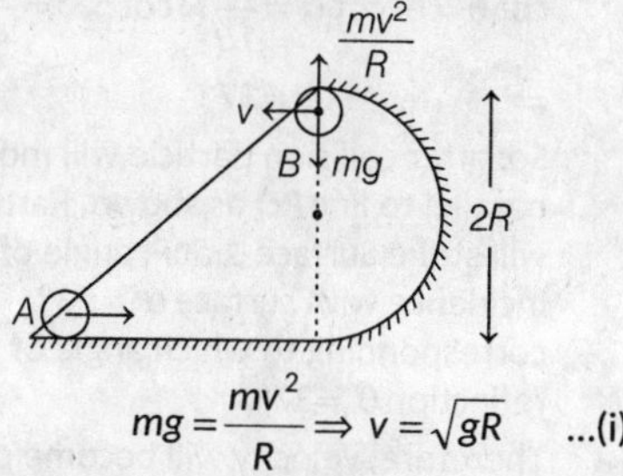

$$mg = \frac{mv^2}{R} \Rightarrow v = \sqrt{gR} \quad \text{...(i)}$$

For track-1, by conservation of energy,

Energy at A = Energy at B

$$\Rightarrow \frac{1}{2}mv_1^2 = \frac{1}{2}mv^2 + mg(2R)$$

$$= \frac{1}{2}m(\sqrt{gR})^2 + 2mgR$$

[using Eq. (i)]

$$\Rightarrow \frac{1}{2}mv_1^2 = \frac{5mgR}{2} \Rightarrow v_1 = \sqrt{5gR}$$

For track-2, by conservation of energy for pure rolling as the track is highly rough,

Energy at A = Energy at B

$$\frac{1}{2}mv_2^2 + \frac{1}{2}I_{CM}\omega_A^2 = \frac{1}{2}mv^2 + \frac{1}{2}I_{CM}\omega_B^2 + mg(2R)$$

Here, $\omega_A = \frac{v_A}{r} = \frac{v_2}{r}$, $\omega_B = \frac{v_B}{r} = \frac{v}{r}$

$$\Rightarrow \frac{1}{2}mv_2^2 + \frac{1}{2}mr^2\left(\frac{v_2}{r}\right)^2 = \frac{1}{2}mv^2 + \frac{1}{2}mr^2\left(\frac{v}{r}\right)^2 + 2mgR$$

$$\Rightarrow v_2^2 = v^2 + 2gR$$

$$= (\sqrt{gR})^2 + 2gR \quad \text{[using Eq. (i)]}$$

$$\Rightarrow v_2 = \sqrt{3gR}$$

Therefore, $\frac{v_1}{v_2} = \frac{\sqrt{5gR}}{\sqrt{3gR}} = \sqrt{\frac{5}{3}}$

18. Frequency received directly by observer, $f_1 = f$ ...(i)

As per formula of apparent frequency,

$$f' = f\left(\frac{v - v_o}{v - v_s}\right) \quad \text{...(ii)}$$

where, v_o = velocity of observer and v_s = velocity of source.

Using Eq. (ii), frequency received by wall

$$f_2 = f\left(\frac{v - \frac{v}{k}}{v}\right) = f\left(\frac{k-1}{k}\right) \quad \text{...(iii)}$$

Wall will reflect this frequency f_2 towards observer, so, wall will be treated as source. Apparent frequency observed [using Eq. (ii)]

$$f_3 = f_2\left(\frac{v - v_o}{v - v_s}\right) = f\left(\frac{k-1}{k}\right)\left(\frac{v - 0}{v + \frac{v}{k}}\right)$$

$$= f\left(\frac{k-1}{k+1}\right) \quad \text{...(iv)}$$

(Note that as wall is moving opposite to velocity of reflected sound so, it is taken negative or $v_s = -\frac{v}{k}$)

$$\text{Beat frequency} = f_1 - f_3 = f - f\left(\frac{k-1}{k+1}\right)$$

$$= \frac{2f}{k+1} \quad \text{[using Eqs. (i) and (iv)]}$$

19. In null deflection state, potential difference across PQ is same as that across AC.

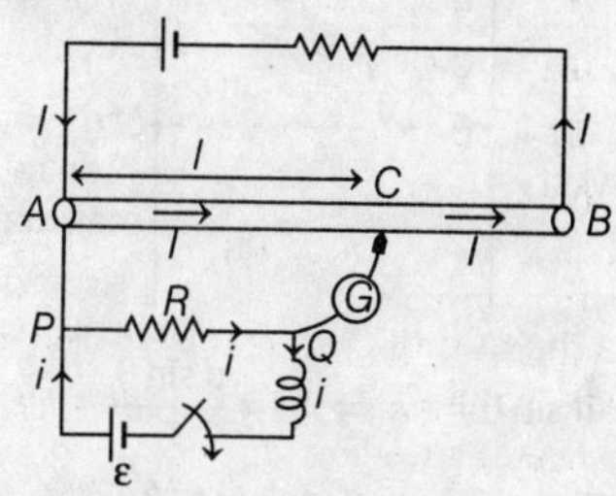

$$\Rightarrow V_{AC} = V_{PQ} \Rightarrow kl = iR \quad \text{...(i)}$$

where, k is potential gradient.

In L-R circuit, current is given by

$$i = \frac{\varepsilon}{R}\left(1 - e^{-\frac{Rt}{L}}\right) \quad \text{...(ii)}$$

Putting i from Eq. (ii) in Eq. (i), we get

$$kl = \frac{\varepsilon}{R}\left(1 - e^{-\frac{Rt}{L}}\right)R \Rightarrow l = \frac{\varepsilon}{k}\left(1 - e^{-\frac{Rt}{L}}\right)$$

Differentiating w.r.t. time, we get

$$\frac{dl}{dt} = v = \frac{\varepsilon}{k}\cdot\frac{R}{L}e^{-\frac{Rt}{L}}$$

Therefore, velocity is exponentially decreasing as function of time.

20. Buoyancy acting on A is equal to

$$B = \rho Vg = \rho\cdot\frac{m}{2\rho}\cdot g = \frac{mg}{2} \quad \text{...(i)}$$

(As specific gravity of block's material is 2, its density will be twice that of water, i.e. 2ρ).

Free body diagram of the two blocks will be as shown

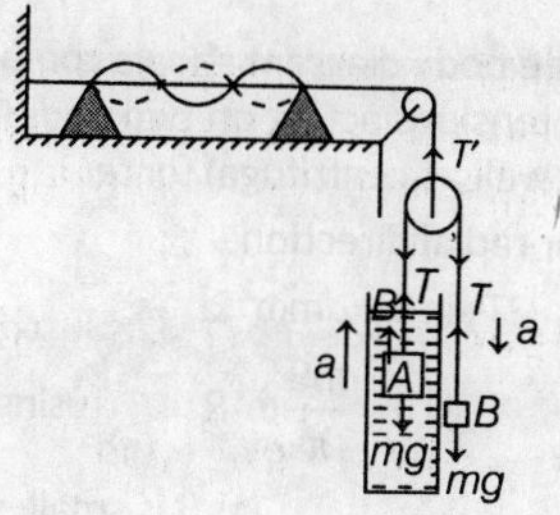

For block A Using $F = ma$, we get

$$T + B - mg = ma$$

$$\Rightarrow T + \frac{mg}{2} - mg = ma \quad \text{[Using Eq. (i)]}$$

$$\Rightarrow \quad T - \frac{mg}{2} = ma \quad \text{...(ii)}$$

For block B $mg - T = ma$ ...(iii)

From Eqs. (ii) and (iii), we get

$$T - \frac{mg}{2} = mg - T$$

$$\Rightarrow \quad T = \frac{3mg}{4} \quad \text{...(iv)}$$

From free body diagram of pulley,

$$T' = 2T = \frac{3mg}{2} \quad \text{...(v)}$$

[using Eq. (iv)]

Frequency of nth harmonic in string wave is given by

$$f = \frac{n\sqrt{\frac{T}{\mu}}}{2l} \Rightarrow l = \frac{n\sqrt{\frac{T}{\mu}}}{2f}$$

As string is vibrating in 3 loops, so $n = 3$. Also, putting value of tension from Eq. (v), we get

$$l = \frac{3\sqrt{\frac{3mg}{2\mu}}}{2f} = \sqrt{\frac{27mg}{8\mu f^2}}$$

21. Consider an infinitesimally small element PQ on ring (as shown) of angular thickness 2θ.

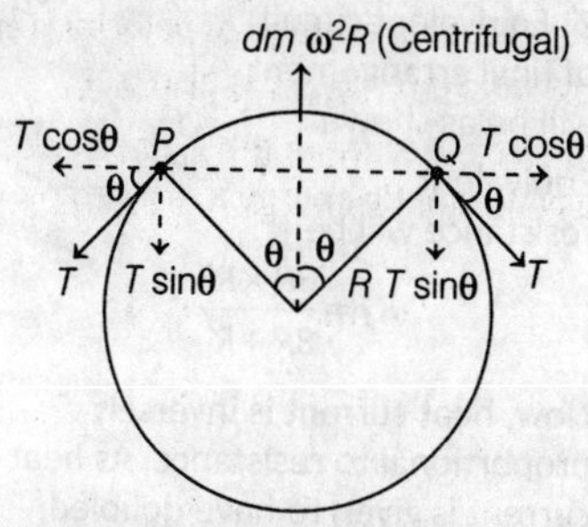

Length of element $= R(2\theta)$

$$dm = \text{Mass of element} = \frac{m}{2\pi R}\cdot R(2\theta)$$

$$\Rightarrow dm = \frac{m\theta}{\pi} \quad \text{...(i)}$$

Free body diagram shows components of tensions acting on two ends P and Q as well as centrifugal force.

For radial direction,

$$2T\sin\theta = dm\omega^2 R$$

$$\Rightarrow \quad 2T\theta = \frac{m\theta}{\pi}\omega^2 R \quad \text{[using Eq. (i)]}$$

(as θ is small, $\sin\theta \approx \theta$)

$$\Rightarrow \quad T = \frac{m\omega^2 R}{2\pi} \quad \text{...(ii)}$$

Elastic energy is given by

$$U = \frac{1}{2}\times\frac{(\text{Stress})^2}{Y}\times\text{Volume}$$

$$\Rightarrow \quad U = \frac{1}{2}\times\frac{\left(\frac{T}{A}\right)^2}{Y}\times A\times 2\pi R$$

$$= \frac{T^2\pi R}{YA} \quad \text{...(iii)}$$

Putting value of tension from Eq. (ii) and cross-sectional area $A = \pi r^2$ in Eq. (iii), we get

$$U = \frac{m^2\omega^4 R^3}{4\pi^2 r^2 Y} = \frac{m^2\omega^4 R^3}{40 r^2 Y}$$

$\therefore \quad a = 2, b = 4, c = 3, d = 40, e = 2$

$\Rightarrow a + b + c + d + e = 51$

22. Let resistance of minor arc $PQ = R$. As resistance is proportional to length, so resistance of major arc $PQ = 3R$.

Equivalent circuit will be as shown in Fig. 1. As the two resistors are in parallel, equivalent resistance,

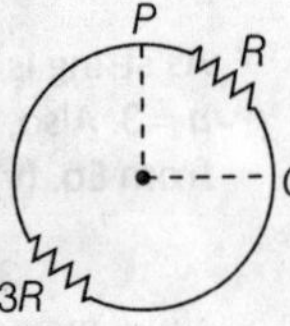

$$R_1 = \frac{R\times 3R}{R+3R} = \frac{3R}{4} \quad \text{...(i)}$$

Let resistance of straight segment is R'. Equivalent circuit of final arrangement will be as shown.

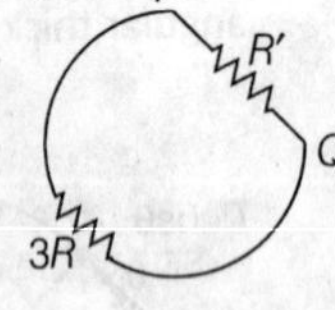

Equivalent resistance will be

$$R_2 = \frac{3R\times R'}{3R+R'} \quad \text{...(ii)}$$

Now, heat current is inversely proportional to resistance. As heat current is given to have doubled, resistance must have halved in the process. Therefore, $R_1 = 2R_2$

$$\Rightarrow \quad \frac{3R}{4} = 2\cdot\frac{3RR'}{3R+R'}$$

[using Eqs. (i) and (ii)]

$$\Rightarrow \quad R' = \frac{3R}{7} \quad \text{...(iii)}$$

As thermal resistance is $\frac{l}{KA}$,

so from Eq. (iii),

$$\frac{l'}{K'A} = \frac{3l}{7KA}$$

$$\Rightarrow \quad \frac{K'}{K} = \frac{7}{3}\frac{l'}{l} \quad \text{...(iv)}$$

If r is radius of ring, then l' and l will be $\sqrt{2}r$ and $\frac{\pi r}{2}$, respectively. Substituting these values in Eq. (iv), we get

$$\frac{K'}{K} = \frac{7}{3}\cdot\frac{\sqrt{2}r}{\frac{\pi r}{2}} = \frac{14\sqrt{2}}{3\pi} = x\frac{\sqrt{2}}{\pi} \text{ (given)}$$

$$\Rightarrow \quad x = \frac{14}{3} = 4.67$$

23. Angular position θ of nth order minima is given by

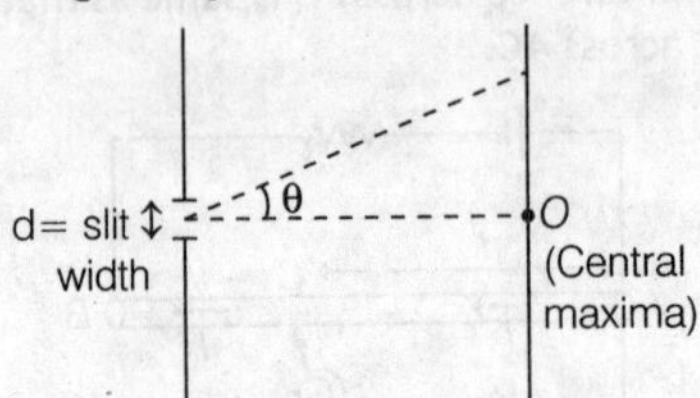

$$d\sin\theta = n\lambda \Rightarrow n = \frac{d\sin\theta}{\lambda}$$

$$\Rightarrow \quad n_{\max} = \frac{d}{\lambda} = \frac{30\times 10^{-6}}{6000\times 10^{-10}} = 50$$

$\therefore$ 50 minimas will be above central maxima O, while 50 minimas will be below O. So, a total of 100 minimas will be observed.

24. As radius of path followed is $\frac{mv}{qB}$, so particle will strike the surface at Q as shown just outside the magnetic field. From geometry, velocity will make $\alpha = 53°$ with surface before collision with Surface-2.

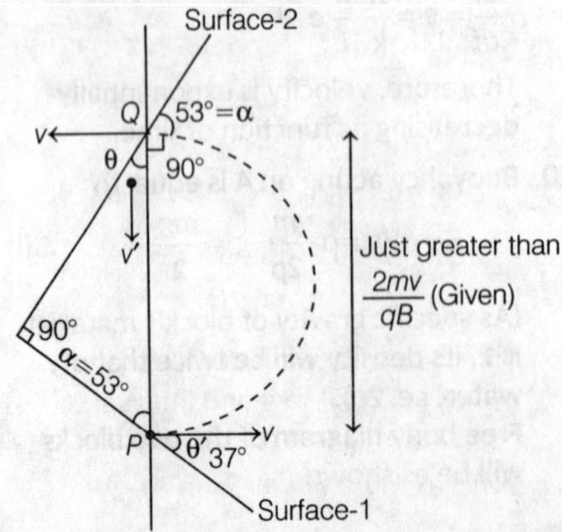

Angle θ made by velocity after collision with the surface will be given by

$$\cot\theta = e\cdot\cot\alpha = \frac{9}{16}\times\cot 53° = \frac{3}{4}$$

$$\Rightarrow \quad \theta = 37°$$

So, after collision particle will move parallel to line PQ as shown. Particle will strike Surface-1 at P, angle of incidence with surface $\alpha' = 53°$, corresponding to which angle of reflection $\theta' = 37°$.

Therefore, velocity will become parallel to initial after collision at P.

Time of motion in magnetic field,

$$t_1 = \frac{\text{Distance}}{\text{Speed}} = \frac{\pi r}{v} = \frac{\pi\frac{mv}{qB}}{v} = \frac{\pi m}{qB}$$

Time of motion from Q to P,

$$t_2 = \frac{\text{Distance}}{\text{Speed}} = \frac{2r}{v'} = \frac{2\left(\frac{mv}{qB}\right)}{v'} = \frac{2mv}{qBv'}$$

Total time of motion, from P back to P,

$$t = t_1 + t_2 = \frac{\pi m}{qB} + \frac{2mv}{qBv'} = \frac{m}{qB}\left(\pi + \frac{2v}{v'}\right)$$

$\therefore \quad x = \pi = 3.14$ and $y = 2$

$\Rightarrow \quad x + y = 5.14$

25. For series circuit in Fig. 1 of question, impedance,

$$Z_1 = \sqrt{R^2 + (X_L - X_C)^2}$$

$$= \sqrt{3^2 + (8-4)^2} = 5\Omega$$

Consider the circuit in Fig.2 of question. Equivalent impedance of inductor and capacitor is given by

$$\frac{1}{X} = \frac{1}{X_L} + \frac{1}{X_C} = \frac{1}{8j} + \frac{1}{-4j} = -\frac{1}{8j}$$

$$\Rightarrow \quad X = -8j$$

So, circuit can be redrawn as

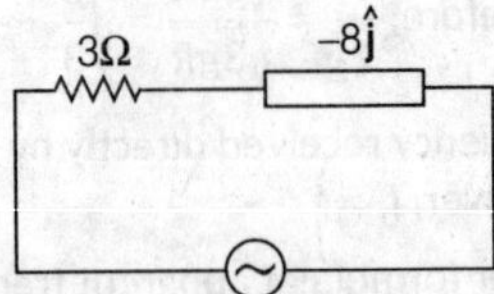

Equivalent impedance,

$$Z_2 = \sqrt{R^2 + X^2} = \sqrt{3^2 + 8^2}$$

$$\Rightarrow \quad Z_2 = \sqrt{73}\ \Omega$$

Therefore, current in circuit-1 is

$$I_1 = \frac{V}{Z_1} = \frac{V}{5}$$

Similarly, current in circuit-2 is

$$I_2 = \frac{V}{Z_2} = \frac{V}{\sqrt{73}}$$

Current decreases by factor

$$=\frac{I_1}{I_2}=\frac{\frac{V}{5}}{\frac{V}{\sqrt{73}}}=\sqrt{2.92}$$

$\therefore$ $x=2.92$

26. Work done, $W=\int \mathbf{F}\cdot d\mathbf{s}=\int(3t\hat{\mathbf{i}})\cdot(4t\,dt\hat{\mathbf{i}})$

$$=\int_0^2 12t^2dt=\frac{12[t^3]_0^2}{3}=32\text{ J}$$

27. As, angular frequency (coefficient of time) does not depend on medium.

$$\Rightarrow \omega=\frac{\omega'}{2}\Rightarrow \frac{\omega}{\omega'}=0.5 \quad ...(i)$$

Also, coefficient of x represent angular wave number. So, for electric field wave in liquid, angular wave number,

$$\frac{2\pi}{\lambda'}=\frac{6\pi}{\lambda}$$

where, λ' is wavelength in liquid.

$$\Rightarrow \lambda'=\frac{\lambda}{3}$$

$\therefore$ Refractive index of liquid $n=\frac{\lambda}{\lambda'}=3$

Also, as refractive index in terms of relative permittivity ε_r is given by

$$n=\sqrt{\varepsilon_r\mu_r}\Rightarrow \varepsilon_r\propto n^2$$

$$\Rightarrow \frac{(\varepsilon_r)_{\text{liquid}}}{(\varepsilon_r)_{\text{air}}}=\left(\frac{n_{\text{liquid}}}{n_{\text{air}}}\right)^2=\left(\frac{3}{1}\right)^2=9$$

As $(\varepsilon_r)_{\text{air}}=1$, therefore $(\varepsilon_r)_{\text{liquid}}=9$.

As, relative permittivity is same as dielectric constant,

$\therefore$ Dielectric constant,

$$C=(\varepsilon_r)_{\text{liquid}}=9 \quad ...(ii)$$

From Eqs. (i) and (ii), we get

$$C-\frac{\omega}{\omega'}=9-0.5=8.5$$

28. Time period of a pendulum is given by

$$T=2\pi\sqrt{\frac{l}{g}}\Rightarrow g=\frac{4\pi^2 l}{T^2}$$

$$\Rightarrow\left(\frac{\Delta g}{g}\times100\right)_{\max}=\frac{\Delta l}{l}\times100+2\times\frac{\Delta T}{T}$$

$$=1+2\times2=5\%$$

29. Velocity of CM of a system of two particles of masses m_1 and m_2 moving with velocities $\mathbf{v}_1$ and $\mathbf{v}_2$ respectively is given by

$$\mathbf{v}_{\text{CM}}=\frac{m_1\mathbf{v}_1+m_2\mathbf{v}_2}{m_1+m_2}$$

$$\Rightarrow m_1\mathbf{v}_{\text{CM}}+m_2\mathbf{v}_{\text{CM}}=m_1\mathbf{v}_1+m_2\mathbf{v}_2$$

$$\Rightarrow m_1(\mathbf{v}_1-\mathbf{v}_{\text{CM}})+m_2(\mathbf{v}_2-\mathbf{v}_{\text{CM}})=0$$

$\therefore$ Momentum of system is zero in CM frame irrespective of given information.

30. Force on Dipole-2

= Force due to Dipole-1 + Force due to ring

$$=p\frac{dE_1}{dx}+p\frac{dE_2}{dx}$$

$$=\frac{pd\left[\frac{2Kp}{x^3}\right]}{dx}+0 \text{ (as field of ring is maximum at } x=\frac{R}{\sqrt{2}})$$

$$=\frac{6Kp^2}{x^4}=\frac{6\left(\frac{1}{4\pi\varepsilon_0}\right)p^2}{(\sqrt{2}R)^4}$$

$$=\frac{3p^2}{8\pi\varepsilon_0R^4}$$

$$\Rightarrow x=\frac{8}{3}=2.67$$

Knockout 05

1.

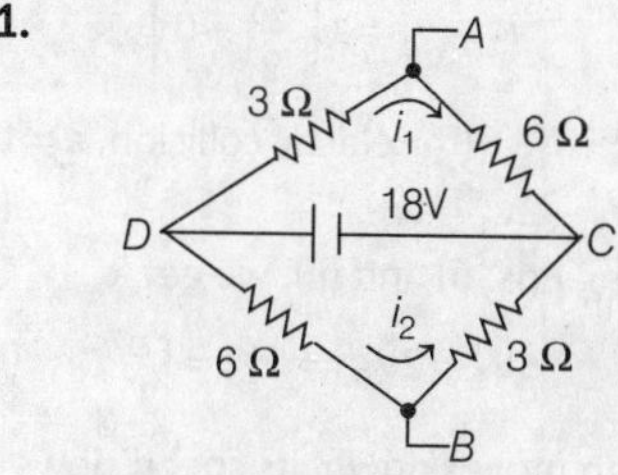

Applying KCL in $CDAC$,

$$18-3i_1-6i_1=0$$

$\therefore$ $i_1=2\text{A}$

Applying KCL in $CDBC$,

$$18-6i_2-3i_2=0$$

$$i_2=2\text{A}$$

Now,

$$V_D-V_A=3\times2=6\text{ V} \quad ...(i)$$

$$V_D-V_B=6\times2=12\text{V} \quad ...(ii)$$

Subtracting Eq. (i) from Eq. (ii), we get

$$V_A-V_B=6\text{V}$$

Also, as ideal cell has zero resistance, to find effective resistance between A and B replace cell by plain (resistance less) wire, we get

$$\frac{3\times6}{3+6}=2\Omega \qquad \frac{3\times6}{3+6}=2\Omega \qquad \equiv 4\Omega$$

Thus, given circuit is equivalent to a cell of emf $V_{AB}=6$ V and internal resistance $R_{AB}=4\,\Omega$ as shown.

For maximum power,

$$R_{\text{external}}=R_{\text{internal}}$$

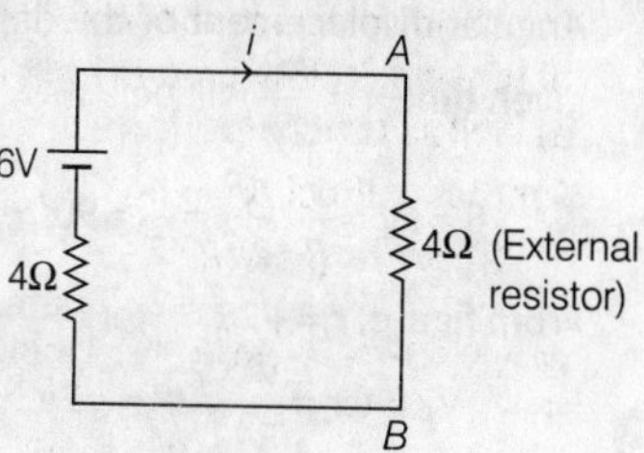

Current i supplied to external resistor, by Ohm's law,

$$i=\frac{6}{4+4}=\frac{3}{4}\text{ A}$$

Therefore, power consumed

$$=i^2R=\left(\frac{3}{4}\right)^2\times4=2.25\text{ W}$$

2. In pure rolling, bottomost point (O in figure) is instantly at rest and so, we can assume an instantaneous axis. Assume distance between bottomost point O and point charge at P equal to r. Considering pure rolling as pure rotation about instantaneous axis through O, velocity of point charge v_P is perpendicular to line joining point charge and O, is given by

$$v_P=\omega r \quad ...(i)$$

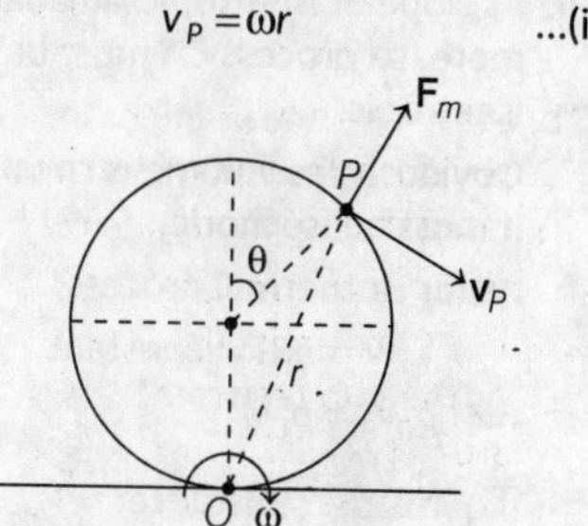

Now, magnetic force on point charge,

$$F_m=qv_PB\sin90^\circ=qv_PB \text{ (as shown)} \quad ...(ii)$$

$$\Rightarrow \text{About } O,\ \alpha=\frac{\tau}{I}=\frac{F_m\times0}{I}=0$$

$$\Rightarrow \omega=\text{constant}$$

As in pure rolling, $v_{\text{CM}}=\omega R$ and ω is constant, so v_{CM} is also constant and acceleration of CM is zero. So, ring rolls with constant speed v and angular speed, $\omega=\frac{v_{\text{CM}}}{R}=\frac{v}{R}$ ...(iii)

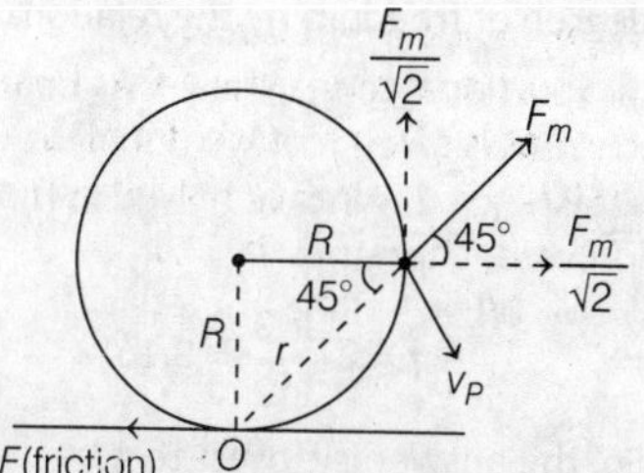

Angular displacement of the ring in given time, $t = \frac{\pi R}{2v}$ will be

$$\theta = \omega t = \frac{v}{R} \cdot \frac{\pi R}{2v} = \frac{\pi}{2} = 90^\circ$$

From figure, $r = \sqrt{2}R$ ...(iv)

$$\Rightarrow \quad v_P = \omega r = \frac{v}{R} \cdot \sqrt{2}R = \sqrt{2}v \quad \text{...(v)}$$

[using Eqs. (i), (iii) and (iv)]

By Newton's law

$$\Sigma F_x = m a_x$$

$$\Rightarrow -f + \frac{F_m}{\sqrt{2}} = 0 \qquad [\because a_x = a_{CM} = 0]$$

$$\Rightarrow \quad f = \frac{F_m}{\sqrt{2}}$$

$$= \frac{qv_P B}{\sqrt{2}}$$

$$= q\sqrt{2}vB / \sqrt{2}$$

$$= qvB \text{ [using Eqs. (ii) and (v)]}$$

3. As work done by applied downward force is positive, so potential energy of the chain should increase and therefore centre of mass should move up, i.e. it ascends.

4. As slope of isentropic/adiabatic is more, so process *CA* must be isentropic.

Obviously, as volume is constant in *AB*, it must be isochoric.

As for isothermal process,

$$pV = nRT = \text{constant}$$

$$\Rightarrow \quad p_B V_B = p_C V_C$$

$$\Rightarrow \quad p_0 V_0 = 3p_0 V_1$$

$$\Rightarrow \quad V_1 = \frac{V_0}{3}$$

For adiabatic process *CA*,

$$pV^\gamma = \text{constant}$$

$$\Rightarrow \quad p_C V_C^\gamma = p_A V_A^\gamma$$

$$\Rightarrow 3p_0 \left(\frac{V_0}{3}\right)^\gamma = \frac{p_0}{2} V_0^\gamma$$

$$\Rightarrow \quad 3^\gamma = 6$$

$$\Rightarrow \quad \gamma = \log_3 6 = \frac{\ln 6}{\ln 3}$$

As adiabatic exponent γ is related to degree of freedom by the relation,

$$\gamma = 1 + \frac{2}{f}$$

$$\Rightarrow \quad 1 + \frac{2}{f} = \frac{\ln 6}{\ln 3}$$

$$\Rightarrow \quad f = 2 \cdot \frac{\ln 3}{\ln 2} \approx 3.16$$

So, the answer is closest to π.

5. The collision process is shown below.

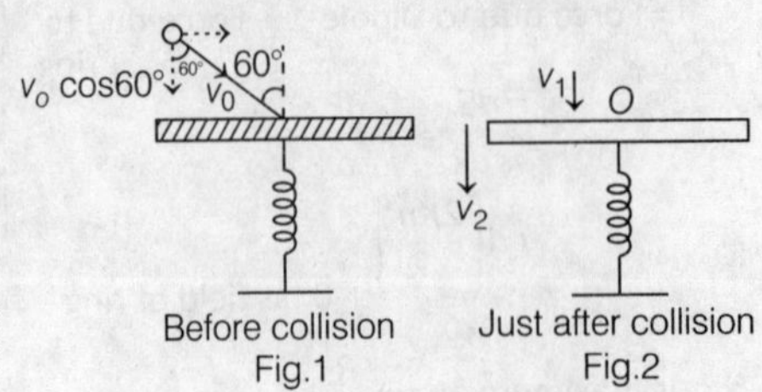

Velocity components of ball just before collision are as shown, vertical component being $\frac{v}{2}$. Assuming velocities in vertical direction as shown in Fig.2, by conservation of momentum

$$2mv_2 + mv_1 = \frac{mv_0}{2}$$

$$\Rightarrow \quad 4v_2 + 2v_1 = v_0 \quad \text{...(i)}$$

Also, by Newton's law of restitution,

$$v_2 - v_1 = e(u_1 - u_2)$$

$$\Rightarrow \quad v_2 - v_1 = 1\left(\frac{v_0}{2} - 0\right)$$

(for elastic collision, $e = 1$)

$$\Rightarrow 2v_2 - 2v_1 = v_0 \quad \text{...(ii)}$$

Adding Eqs. (i) and (ii), we get

$$6v_2 = 2v_0 \Rightarrow v_2 = \frac{v_0}{3} \quad \text{...(iii)}$$

As pan moves down, its speed slows down due to opposing force by spring and comes to rest instantly at distance A and subsequently perform SHM.

As, velocity at mean/equilibrium position is

$$v_{\text{mean}} = A\omega$$

$$\Rightarrow \quad v_2 = A\sqrt{\frac{k}{2m}}$$

$$\Rightarrow \quad A = v_2\sqrt{\frac{2m}{k}} = \frac{v_0}{3}\sqrt{\frac{2m}{k}}$$

[using Eq. (iii)]

6. Escape speed for a planet of mass *M* at a distance *r* from its centre is given by

$$v = \sqrt{\frac{2GM}{r}}$$

So, assuming mass of the planet be *M*, then escape speed at height *h*,

$$v = \sqrt{\frac{2GM}{R+h}} \quad \text{...(i)}$$

Now, mass of earth

$$= \text{density} \times \text{volume}$$

$$= \rho_e \times \frac{4}{3}\pi R_e^3$$

Here, $\rho_p = \frac{\rho_e}{2}$ and $R_e = \frac{R}{2}$

$$\Rightarrow \quad M_e = 2\rho_p \times \frac{4}{3}\pi\left(\frac{R}{2}\right)^3$$

$$= \frac{1}{4} \cdot \rho_p \times \frac{4}{3}\pi R^3 = \frac{M}{4}$$

Thus, escape speed at earth's surface,

$$v_e = \sqrt{\frac{2GM_e}{R_e}}$$

$$= \sqrt{\frac{2G\left(\frac{M}{4}\right)}{\frac{R}{2}}} = \sqrt{\frac{GM}{R}} \quad \text{...(ii)}$$

Equating the escape speeds in Eqs. (i) and (ii), we get

$$v = v_e$$

$$\sqrt{\frac{2GM}{R+h}} = \sqrt{\frac{GM}{R}}$$

$$\Rightarrow \quad R + h = 2R$$

$$\Rightarrow \quad h = R$$

7. After the key is closed at $t = 0$, potential difference across inductor oscillates as given by

$$V_L = V_0 \cos\omega t \quad \text{...(i)}$$

(As it is oscillatory circuit and potential difference across inductor is maximum initially in such circuits)

Also, at any time *t*, potential difference across capacitor, is

$$V_C = E - V_L$$

$$\Rightarrow \quad V_C = E - V_0 \cos\omega t \quad \text{...(ii)}$$

As at $t = 0$, capacitor is uncharged, therefore $V_C = 0$.

$$\Rightarrow \quad 0 = E - V_0 \cos 0^\circ$$

$$\Rightarrow \quad V_0 = E$$

So, from Eq. (ii), we get

$$V_C = E(1 - \cos\omega t)$$

For $\cos\omega t = -1$, V_C is maximum equal to $2E$.

Therefore maximum charge

$$= CV_C = C(2E) = 2CE$$

8. In case of source approaching observer, apparent wavelength is given by

$$\lambda_{\text{apparent}} = \frac{v_{\text{sound}} - v_{\text{source}}}{f_{\text{source}}}$$

So apparent wavelength observed by the child is

$$\lambda_{\text{apparent}} = \frac{5v - v}{f} = \frac{4v}{f} \quad \text{...(i)}$$

Also, apparent frequency is given by the relation

$$f_{\text{apparent}} = f\left(\frac{v_{\text{sound}} - v_{\text{observer}}}{v_{\text{sound}} - v_{\text{source}}}\right) \quad \text{...(ii)}$$

To find, frequency observed by diver, we have to first find frequency incident at water surface (say f_1), using Eq. (ii),

$$f_1 = f\left(\frac{5v-0}{5v-v}\right) = \frac{5f}{4} \quad ...(iii)$$

This frequency f_1 will be transmitted into water from water surface and for diver, water surface will thus be the source. Apparent frequency observed by the diver, corresponding to f_1 is

$$f_2 = f_1\left[\frac{20v-(-v)}{20v}\right] = \frac{21f_1}{20} \quad ...(iv)$$

(Note that as diver is moving opposite to sound, its velocity is taken as negative.)

Putting value of f_1 from Eq. (iii) in Eq. (iv), we get

$$f_2 = \frac{21}{20}\times\frac{5f}{4} = \frac{21f}{16} \quad ...(v)$$

Therefore, required product is

$$\lambda_{\substack{\text{apparent}\\\text{(for child)}}} \times f_2 = \frac{4v}{f}\times\frac{21f}{16} = \frac{21v}{4}$$

$$= 5.25\,v \quad \text{[Using Eqs. (i) and (v)]}$$

9. The ball experiences centrifugal force F_c and electric force F_e both in radially outward direction.

$$\Rightarrow \quad F = F_c + F_e = m\omega^2 x + q\cdot\left(\frac{KQx}{R^3}\right)$$

$$= \left(m\omega^2 + \frac{KQq}{R^3}\right)x$$

$\Rightarrow$ Acceleration relative to sphere

$$a = \left(\omega^2 + \frac{KQq}{mR^3}\right)x$$

$$\Rightarrow v_r\frac{dv_r}{dx} = \left(\omega^2 + \frac{KQq}{mR^3}\right)x$$

where v_r = radial velocity.

Integrating both sides, we get

$$\Rightarrow \int_0^{v_r} v_r\,dv_r = \int_0^R \left(\omega^2 + \frac{KQq}{mR^3}\right)x\,dx$$

$$\Rightarrow \quad \frac{v_r^2}{2} = \frac{\omega^2R^2}{2} + \frac{KQq}{2mR}$$

$$= \frac{\omega^2R^2}{2} + \frac{\omega^2R^2}{2}$$

$$\left(\because \frac{KQq}{R} = m\omega^2R^2\right)$$

$$\Rightarrow \quad v_r = \sqrt{2}\,\omega R \quad ...(i)$$

At point of leaving, the ball will also be having tangential velocity

$$v_t = \omega R \quad ...(ii)$$

From Eqs. (i) and (ii), we get

$$v = \sqrt{v_r^2 + v_t^2} = \sqrt{3}\,\omega R$$

10. The particles are as shown in the figure below,

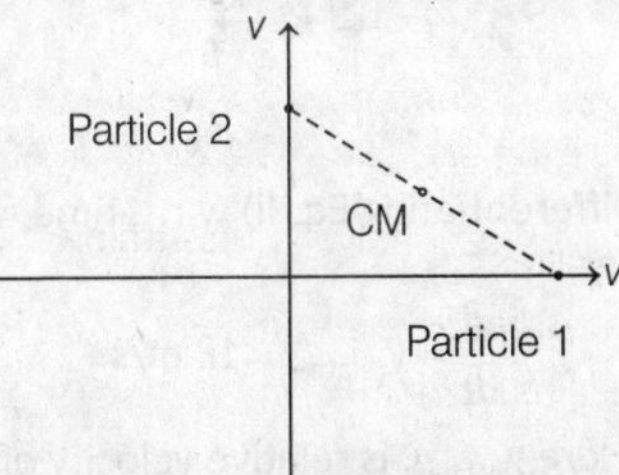

As, de-Broglie wavelengths,

$\lambda = \frac{h}{mv}$ i.e, $\lambda \propto \frac{1}{v}$ are given to be same, so particles must be moving with same speed as shown. Velocity of CM,

$$\mathbf{v}_{CM} = \frac{mv\hat{\mathbf{i}} + mv\hat{\mathbf{j}}}{m+m} = \frac{v\hat{\mathbf{i}} + v\hat{\mathbf{j}}}{2}$$

Therefore, velocity of particle-1 w.r.t. CM

$$\mathbf{v}_{1CM} = \mathbf{v}_1 - \mathbf{v}_{CM} = v\hat{\mathbf{i}} - \frac{v\hat{\mathbf{i}} + v\hat{\mathbf{j}}}{2}$$

$$= \frac{v\hat{\mathbf{i}} - v\hat{\mathbf{j}}}{2}$$

$\Rightarrow$ Relative speed $(v_{1C}) = \frac{v}{\sqrt{2}}$

$\Rightarrow$ Wavelength of one of the particle in CM frame is

$$\lambda_{1C} = \frac{h}{m\frac{v}{\sqrt{2}}} = \frac{\sqrt{2}h}{mv} = \sqrt{2}\lambda$$

11. Let A_c is amplitude of carrier wave and A_m is amplitude of message signal.

For AM wave,

$$A_{max} = A_c + A_m = 20\text{ V (given)} \quad ...(i)$$

$$A_{min} = A_c - A_m = 10\text{ V (given)} \quad ...(ii)$$

Adding Eqs. (i) and (ii), we get

$$2A_c = 30\text{ V} \Rightarrow A_c = 15\text{ V}$$

Putting $A_c = 15$ V in Eq. (i), we get

$$A_m = 5\text{V}$$

Percentage modulation

$$= \frac{A_m}{A_c}\times 100 = 33.33\%$$

12. Here, X_L = Inductive reactance

$$= \omega L = 100\pi\times\frac{10}{\pi}\times 10^{-3} = 1\,\Omega$$

X_C = Capacitive reactance

$$= \frac{1}{\omega C} = \frac{1}{100\pi\times\frac{2}{\pi}\times 10^{-3}} = 5\,\Omega$$

As $X_C > X_L$, current leads voltage by

$$\phi = \tan^{-1}\left(\frac{X_C - X_L}{R}\right) = \tan^{-1}\frac{4}{3} = 53° \quad ...(i)$$

Between points A and B, voltage lags behind current by

$$\phi' = \tan^{-1}\left(\frac{X_C - X_L}{R}\right)$$

$$= \tan^{-1}\left(\frac{5-1}{0}\right) = 90° \quad ...(ii)$$

So, from Eq. (i), phase of current = phase of AC source voltage

$$+\phi = 100\pi t + 53°$$

and from Eq. (ii), phase of V_{AB} = phase of current $-\phi' = 100\pi t + 53° - 90°$

$$= 100\pi t - 37°$$

Therefore, V_{AB} lags behind V of AC source by 37°.

13. Let ρ is density of water. As specific gravity of solid is 8, its density will be 8ρ.

In equilibrium, downward weight must be balanced by upward buoyancy,

$$W = B$$

$$\Rightarrow 8\rho(V - V')g = \rho Vg$$

$$\Rightarrow \quad V' = V - \frac{V}{8} = \frac{7V}{8}$$

14. If n_1th order minima is coinciding with n_2th order minima, position of coinciding point can be written as

$$y = \frac{(2n_1-1)\,\lambda_1 D}{2d} = \frac{(2n_2-1)\lambda_2 D}{2d}$$

$$\Rightarrow \quad \frac{2n_1-1}{2n_2-1} = \frac{\lambda_2}{\lambda_1} = \frac{650}{520} = \frac{5}{4}$$

As $(2n_1-1)$ and $(2n_2-1)$ are both odd, their ratio cannot be $\frac{5}{4}$ (i.e. $\frac{\text{odd}}{\text{even}}$)

So, no real values of n_1 and n_2 satisfy above equation. Therefore, dark fringes do not coincide at any point.

15. Assume currents as shown in figure. As zener diode operates in breakdown mode, voltage across it (between P and Q) is zener voltage equal to 5 V.

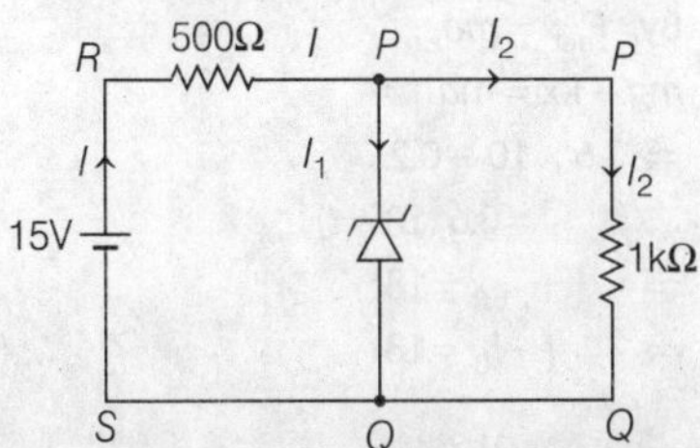

Therefore, current in 1 kΩ resistor, by Ohm's law, is

$$I_2 = \frac{5V}{1000\,\Omega} = 5\text{ mA} \quad ...(i)$$

Also, by KVL in loop *RPQS* with Zener diode (starting at *S* and moving around the loop clockwise)

$$15 - 500I - 5 = 0$$

$$\Rightarrow \quad I = \frac{10}{500} = 20\text{ mA} \quad ...(ii)$$

By KCL, for junction at *P*,

$$I = I_1 + I_2$$

$$\Rightarrow \quad I_1 = I - I_2$$

$$= 20 - 5 = 15\text{ mA} \quad ...(iii)$$

[using Eqs. (i) and (ii)]

Dividing Eq. (ii) by Eq. (iii), we get

$$\frac{I}{I_1} = \frac{20}{15} = \frac{4}{3} = 1.33$$

16. The emf generated in the ring is,

$$V = -\frac{d\phi}{dt} = -\frac{d}{dt}(B \cdot A)$$

$$= -A\frac{d}{dt}(2t^2)$$

$$= -\pi R^2 \times 4t = -4\pi R^2 t \quad ...(i)$$

Minimum force required to move ring is,

$$F_{\min} = \mu mg \quad ...(ii)$$

where, μ is the coefficient of friction.

At $t = 4$ s, emf $(V) = 16\pi R^2$

[using Eq. (i)]

Force on ring,

$$F_{\min} = qE = \frac{qV}{2\pi R} = \frac{16q\pi R^2}{2\pi R}$$

$$= 8qR \quad ...(iii)$$

From Eqs. (ii) and (iii), we get

$$\mu mg = 8qR$$

$$\Rightarrow \quad \mu = \frac{8qR}{mg}$$

17. As atmospheric pressure and volume of air in the room are constant, so internal energy given by $fpV/2$ is also constant.

18. Let extension in spring at time *t* is equal to *x*. Free body diagram of block will be as shown.

By $F_{net} = ma$,

$$mg - kx = ma$$

$$\Rightarrow 3.6 \times 10 - 0.2x$$

$$= 3.6\,(10 - t)$$

$$\Rightarrow \quad x = 18t$$

$$\Rightarrow \quad l - l_0 = 18t \quad ....(i)$$

Here *l* is the length of spring at shown time *t* and l_0 is *natural* length of spring.

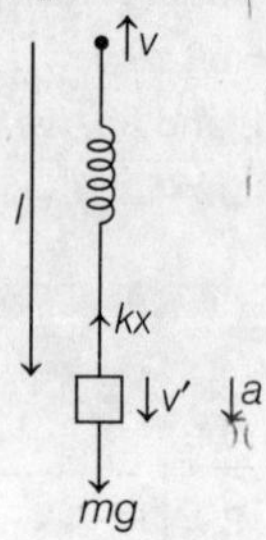

Differentiating Eq. (i) w.r.t. time, we get

$$\frac{dl}{dt} = v_{\text{relative}} = 18\text{ m/s}$$

(Here v_{relative} is relative velocity of block w.r.t. upper end of spring)

$$\Rightarrow v + v' = 18 \quad ...(ii)$$

(Here *v* and *v′* are velocities of upper end of spring and block respectively).

Now, as acceleration of block is given to be

$$a = 10 - t$$

$$\Rightarrow \quad dv' = (10 - t)\,dt$$

Integrating both sides, we get

$$\Rightarrow \quad v' = 10t - \frac{t^2}{2} \quad ...(iii)$$

Putting value of *v′* from Eq. (iii) in Eq. (ii), we get

$$\Rightarrow \quad v = \frac{t^2}{2} - 10t + 18 \quad ...(iv)$$

At rest, $v = 0$

$$\Rightarrow \quad v = \frac{t^2}{2} - 10t + 18$$

$$\Rightarrow t^2 - 20t + 36 = 0$$

$$\Rightarrow t = 2\text{ s or }18\text{ s}$$

At $t = 2$ s, velocity of end of spring becomes zero for the first time.

19. The rate of accumulation of *X* is given by

$$\frac{dN_x}{dt} = r - \lambda N_x$$

Solving this, we get

$$\Rightarrow \quad N_x = \frac{r}{\lambda}(1 - e^{-\lambda t})$$

With the passage of time, the value of N_x increases first and then becomes constant

So, the brightness of bulb increases with time in beginning and then becomes constant.

20. In the diagram shown, *A* is object (fish), *B* is image in mirror, *C* is final fish's image formed after refraction, *D* is water air interface.

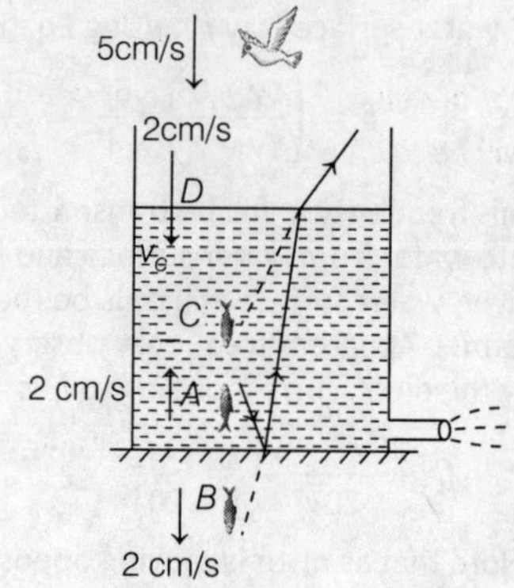

So, relative velocity of *B* w.r.t. interface *D*,

$$v_{BD} = v_B - v_D = 2 - 2 = 0 \quad ...(i)$$

As, in refraction at plane surface,

$$v_{\text{image}} = \frac{v_{\text{object}}\, n_r}{n_i}$$

Here velocities are relative to interface, n_r is refractive index of medium of refraction and n_i is refractive index of medium of incidence.

⇒ Velocity of *C* w.r.t. *D*,

$$v_{CD} = \frac{v_{BD} \cdot n_{\text{air}}}{n_{\text{water}}} \quad ...(ii)$$

Putting $v_{BD} = 0$ from Eq. (i) in Eq. (ii), we get

$$v_{CD} = v_C - v_D = 0$$

$$\Rightarrow \quad v_C = v_D = 2\text{ cm/s} \quad ...(iii)$$

We are required to find velocity of final image as observed by the bird which will be relative velocity equal to

$$v_{C,\text{Bird}} = v_C - v_{\text{Bird}}$$

$$= (-2) - (-5)$$

$$= 3\text{ cm/s}$$

21. The extension in the left rod;

$$\Delta l_1 = l_0 \alpha \Delta\theta$$

where, $\Delta\theta$ = change in temperature

The extension in the right rod,

$$\Delta l_2 = 2\Delta l_1 = 2l_0 \alpha \Delta\theta$$

As, the centre of mass of two rod system will not shift, the junction will shift by *x* as shown.

Taking moment of mass about original centre of mass *C*.

•C_1	•C •C_2
α	2α

(x shown by arrow ← above the junction)

$$m \times \left[\frac{(l_0 + \Delta l)}{2} + x\right] = m\left[\frac{(l_0 + 2\Delta l)}{2} - x\right]$$

Solving it, we get

$$\therefore \quad \frac{\Delta l}{x} = 4$$

22. v_{AB} or velocity of A with respect to B will be as shown

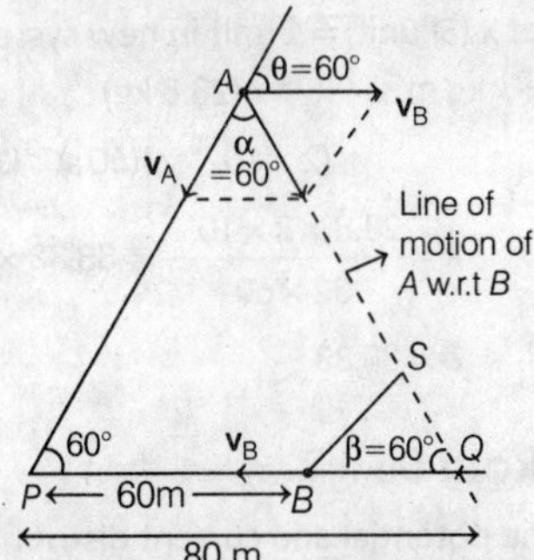

In ΔBSQ, $BQ = PQ - PB$

$$= 80 - 60 = 20 \text{ m}$$

Therefore, $BS = BQ \sin 60°$

$$= 20 \times \frac{\sqrt{3}}{2} = 17.32 \text{ m},$$

minimum distance.

23. In Arrangement-1, let for small displacement x of the block, extension in springs is x' as shown

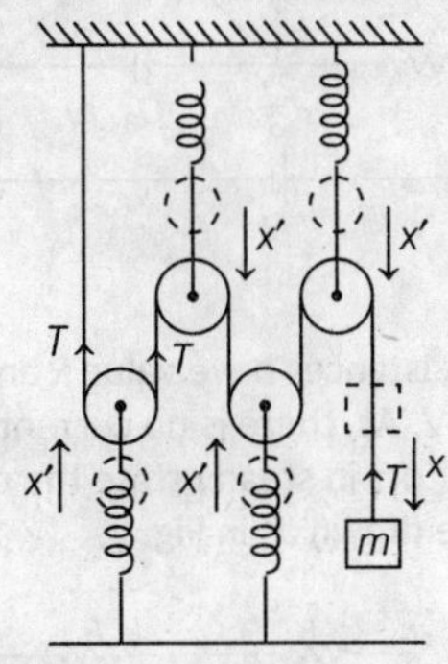

As for displacement x' of pulley, length of thread going over pulley reduces by $2x'$, so total reduction in length going over the four pulleys is $8x'$.

$$\Rightarrow \quad 8x' = x$$

$$\Rightarrow \quad x' = \frac{x}{8} \quad \text{...(i)}$$

From free body diagram of any of the pulleys, say the leftmost pulley, if T is restoring tension

$$2T = kx'$$

$$\Rightarrow \quad T = \frac{kx'}{2} = \frac{kx}{16} \quad \text{...(ii)}$$

[using Eq. (i)]

From Eq. (ii), force constant $= \dfrac{k}{16}$

$$\text{Time period, } t_1 = 2\pi\sqrt{\frac{\text{Mass}}{\text{Force constant}}}$$

$$= 2\pi\sqrt{\frac{m}{k/16}} = 8\pi\sqrt{\frac{m}{k}} \quad \text{...(iii)}$$

For Arrangement-2, consider the instant shown (P). When block is at mean position and moving rightward at $t = 0$

R P Q
$x = 2x_0$ $t=0$, $x=0$ $x=\sqrt{3}x_0$

As amplitude of oscillation is $2x_0$, $x - t$ equation will be,

$$x = 2x_0 \sin \omega t \quad \text{...(iv)} \quad \left(\omega = \sqrt{\frac{k}{m}}\right)$$

To find time taken to move to Q,

Put $x = \sqrt{3}x_0$ in Eq. (iv), we get

$$\Rightarrow \sin \omega t_{PQ} = \frac{\sqrt{3}}{2}$$

$$\Rightarrow \quad t_{PQ} = \frac{\pi}{3\omega} = \frac{T}{6} \text{ ... (v)} \left(\because T = \frac{2\pi}{\omega}\right)$$

Time to move back to P is same

$$\Rightarrow \quad t_{QP} = \frac{T}{6} \quad \text{...(vi)}$$

As motion from P (mean) to R (extreme) is one-fourth of oscillation, so time of motion from P to R or from R to P

$$t_{RP} = t_{PR} = \frac{T}{4} \quad \text{...(vii)}$$

Adding Eqs (v), (vi) and (vii), we get time period of oscillation,

$$t_2 = \frac{T}{6} + \frac{T}{6} + \frac{T}{4} + \frac{T}{4} = \frac{5T}{6}$$

$$= \frac{5}{6} \times 2\pi\sqrt{\frac{k}{m}} = \frac{5\pi}{3}\sqrt{\frac{k}{m}} \quad \text{...(viii)}$$

Dividing Eq. (iii) by Eq. (viii), we get

$$\frac{t_1}{t_2} = \frac{24}{5} \quad \text{...(ix)}$$

If after n_1 and n_2 oscillations of arrangement-1 and 2 respectively, the two blocks are at release positions, total time of oscillation of the blocks can be written as

$$t = n_1 t_1 = n_2 t_2$$

$$\Rightarrow \quad \frac{n_1}{n_2} = \frac{t_2}{t_1} = \frac{5}{24} \quad \text{[using Eq. (ix)]}$$

$\therefore$ After 5 oscillations of Arrangement – 1 both blocks will be at release positions again.

24. For the screw gauge shown,

$$\text{LC} = \frac{\text{Pitch}}{\text{No. of circular scale divisions}}$$

$$= \frac{0.5 \text{ mm}}{50} = 0.01 \text{ mm}$$

For first wire shown in diagram,

Reading (Thickness) = MSR + LC × CSR

$$= 7 + 0.01 \times 47 = 7.47 \text{ mm}$$

$\Rightarrow$ Actual thickness of first wire,

$$t_1 = 7.47 - e \text{ mm} \quad \text{...(i)}$$

Here, e = zero error

For second wire,

Reading (Thickness) = MSR + LC × CSR

$$= 13 + 0.01 \times 49$$

$$= 13.49 \text{ mm}$$

$\Rightarrow$ Actual thickness of second wire, t_2

$$= 13.49 - e \text{ mm} \quad \text{...(ii)}$$

It is given that $t_2 = 2t_1$

$$\Rightarrow 13.49 - e = 2(7.47 - e)$$

[using Eqs. (i) and (ii)]

$$\Rightarrow \quad e = 1.45$$

25. Energy conservation at A and P gives PE at A = (PE + KE) at P

$$\Rightarrow \quad U_A = U_P + K_P$$

$$mgh_A = mgh_P + K_P$$

$$1 \times 10 \times 2 = 1 \times 10 \times 1 + K_P$$

$$\therefore \quad K_P = 10 \text{ J}$$

26. By Stefan's law, rate of radiant energy emission is given by

$$\frac{dQ}{dt} = \sigma A T^4$$

$$\Rightarrow -ms\frac{dT}{dt} = \sigma A T^4$$

$\Rightarrow$ Rate of cooling, R

$$= \left|\frac{dT}{dt}\right| = \frac{\sigma A T^4}{ms} = \frac{\sigma A T^4}{\rho V s}$$

As material, surface area σ and temperatures are given to be same for the two objects.

$$R \propto \frac{1}{V}$$

$$\Rightarrow \quad x = \frac{R_{\text{sphere}}}{R_{\text{cube}}} = \frac{V_{\text{cube}}}{V_{\text{sphere}}} \quad \text{...(i)}$$

Also, as buoyant force is given by

$$B = \rho_l V g$$

(Here ρ_l is density of liquid and V is volume of immersion).

$$\Rightarrow \quad B \propto V$$

$\therefore$ Ratio of buoyancies experienced

$$y = \frac{B_{\text{cube}}}{B_{\text{sphere}}} = \frac{V_{\text{cube}}}{V_{\text{sphere}}} \quad \text{...(ii)}$$

From Eqs. (i) and (ii), we get

$$x \cdot y = \left(\frac{V_{\text{cube}}}{V_{\text{sphere}}}\right)^2 \quad \text{...(iii)}$$

Assuming l be side of cube and r be radius of sphere.

$$\frac{V_{\text{cube}}}{V_{\text{sphere}}}=\frac{l^3}{\frac{4}{3}\pi r^3}=\frac{3}{4\pi}\left(\frac{l}{r}\right)^3 \quad \text{...(iv)}$$

As surface areas are given to be equal,

$$A_{\text{cube}}=A_{\text{sphere}} \Rightarrow 6l^2=4\pi r^2$$

$$\Rightarrow \frac{l}{r}=\sqrt{\frac{2\pi}{3}} \quad \text{...(v)}$$

Putting value of $\frac{l}{r}$ from Eq. (v) in Eq. (iv), we get

$$\frac{V_{\text{cube}}}{V_{\text{sphere}}}=\frac{3}{4\pi}\left(\sqrt{\frac{2\pi}{3}}\right)^3=\sqrt{\frac{\pi}{6}} \quad \text{...(vi)}$$

Putting value of Eq. (vi) in Eq. (iii), we get

$$x\cdot y=\left(\sqrt{\frac{\pi}{6}}\right)^2=\frac{\pi}{6}=0.52$$

27. $s_7-s_6=\left(7u+\frac{1}{2}a(49)\right)-\left(6u+\frac{1}{2}a(36)\right)$

$$\Rightarrow u+\frac{13}{2}a=20$$

$$\Rightarrow 2u+13a=40 \quad \text{... (i)}$$

$$\Rightarrow s_9-s_8=\left(9u+\frac{1}{2}a(81)\right)-\left(8u+\frac{1}{2}a(64)\right)$$

$$\Rightarrow \quad u+\frac{17}{2}a=24$$

$$\Rightarrow \quad 2u+17a=48 \quad \text{...(ii)}$$

Solving Eqs. (i) and (ii), we get

$$a=2\text{ m/s}^2 \text{ and } u=7\text{ m/s}$$

$$\Rightarrow s_{10}-s_9=\left[10u+\frac{1}{2}a(100)\right]-\left[9u+\frac{1}{2}a(81)\right]$$

$$=u+\frac{19}{2}a=26\text{ m}$$

28. The situation can be shown as,

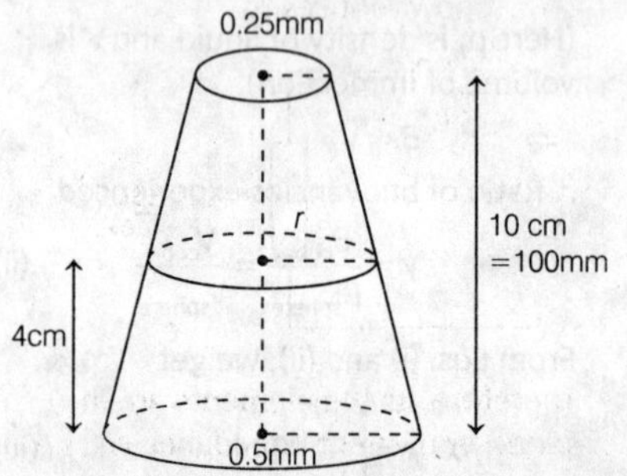

Decrease in radius (as we move up) per unit length

$$\frac{\Delta r}{\Delta l}=\frac{\text{Decrease in radius}}{\text{Change in length}}$$

$$=\frac{0.25\text{ mm}}{100\text{ mm}}=\frac{1}{400} \quad \text{...(i)}$$

$\therefore$ Decrease in radius as we move up by 4 cm

$$=\frac{\Delta r}{\Delta l}\times 4\text{ cm}=\frac{1}{400}\times 40\text{ mm [using Eq. (i)]}$$

$$=0.1\text{ mm}$$

$\therefore$ Radius at height 4 cm is equal to

$$r=0.5\text{ mm}-0.1\text{ mm}=0.4\text{ mm} \quad \text{...(ii)}$$

By ascent formula, the liquid height in capillary is given by

$$h=\frac{2T\cos\theta}{\rho r g}$$

$$\Rightarrow \quad T=\frac{\rho r g h}{2\cos\theta}$$

$$\Rightarrow T=\frac{10^3\times 0.4\times 10^{-3}\times 10\times 4\times 10^{-2}}{2\times\cos 0^\circ}$$

$$\Rightarrow \quad T=8\times 10^{-2}\text{ N/m}=80\text{ N/km}$$

29. From diagram,

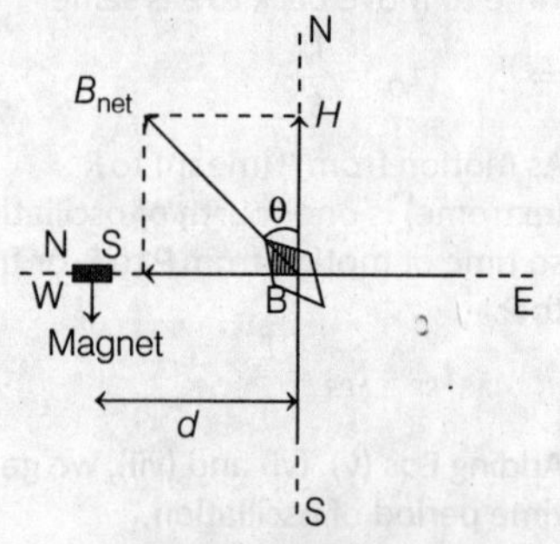

$$\tan\theta=\frac{B}{H}=\frac{2\mu_0 M}{4\pi d^3 H} \quad \text{...(i)}$$

Here, M = magnetic moment of magnet

d = distance of magnet from magnetometer

When d is doubled, θ will change to θ'. Similar to Eq. (i), we can write

$$\tan\theta'=\frac{B'}{H}=\frac{2\mu_0 M}{4\pi(2d)^3 H} \quad \text{...(ii)}$$

Dividing Eq. (ii) by Eq. (i), we get

$$\frac{\tan\theta'}{\tan\theta}=\frac{1}{8}$$

$$\Rightarrow \quad \tan\theta'=\frac{\tan 30^\circ}{8}$$

$$=\frac{\tan 30^\circ}{8}=\frac{0.57}{8}$$

$$\therefore \quad x=0.57$$

30. Thermal current H (Heat flowing per unit time) in a conductor of length l, area of cross-section A and temperature difference ΔT between ends is given by $H=KA\frac{\Delta T}{\Delta l}$

$$\Rightarrow [K]=\frac{[H][\Delta l]}{[A][\Delta T]}=\frac{[\text{ML}^2\text{T}^{-3}\cdot\text{L}]}{[\text{L}^2\cdot\theta]}$$

$$=[\text{MLT}^{-3}\theta^{-1}]$$

Let x (SI unit) = 1 unit in new system

$$\Rightarrow x\text{ kg m s}^{-3}\text{ K}^{-1}=(28.8\text{ kg})(2\times 10^{-2}\text{ m})(60\text{ s})^{-3}(32\text{K})^{-1}$$

$$\Rightarrow \quad x=\frac{28.8\times 2\times 10^{-2}}{32\times 60^3}=83.33\times 10^{-9}$$

$$\therefore \quad a=83.33$$

Knockout 06

1. The potential and current distribution for given circuit shown below can be understood by assuming potential of point E equal to zero by following calculations.

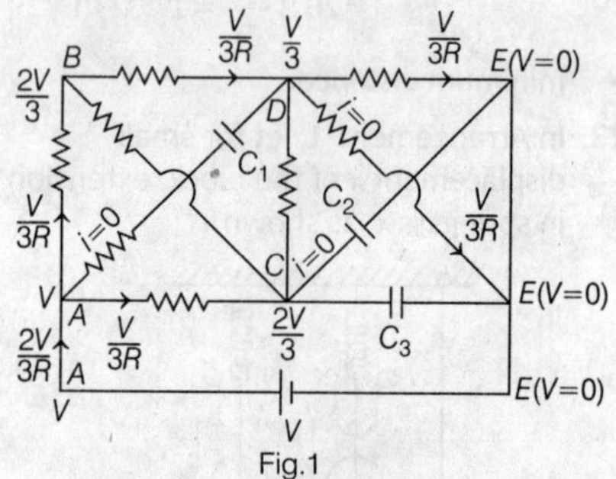

Fig.1

Let resistances have value R and emf of cell is V. As, there is no current in capacitors in steady state the circuit can be drawn as in Fig. 2.

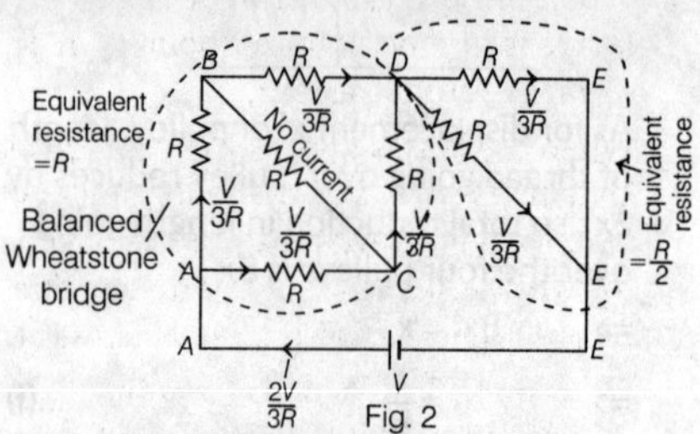

Fig. 2

As, resistors between D and E are in parallel. Equivalent resistance of the circuit, therefore, is

$$R_{\text{eq}}=R+\frac{R}{2}=\frac{3R}{2}$$

So, using Ohm's law, current supplied by cell,

$$I=\frac{V}{R_{\text{eq}}}=\frac{V}{\frac{3R}{2}}=\frac{2V}{3R}$$

There is no current in capacitors in steady state. Consider Fig. 1 now. Using Ohm's law for resistor between points A and B,

$$V_A - V_B = \frac{V}{3R} \times R = \frac{V}{3}$$

$$\Rightarrow \quad V_B = V_A - \frac{V}{3}$$

$$= V - \frac{V}{3} = \frac{2V}{3}$$

So, for C_1, potential difference between ends,

$$V_1 = V_A - V_D = V - \frac{V}{3} = \frac{2V}{3} \quad \text{...(i)}$$

Similarly, potential differences across C_2 and C_3 are

$$V_2 = V_3 = \frac{2V}{3} - 0 = \frac{2V}{3} \quad \text{...(ii)}$$

So, energy stored by C_1,

$$U_1 = \frac{1}{2} C_1 V_1^2 = \frac{1}{2} \cdot 4C \cdot \left(\frac{2V}{3}\right)^2 \quad \text{...(iii)}$$

[using Eq. (i)]

and energy stored by C_2,

$$U_2 = \frac{1}{2} C_2 V_2^2 = \frac{1}{2} \cdot 2C \cdot \left(\frac{2V}{3}\right)^2 \quad \text{...(iv)}$$

[using Eq. (ii)]

and energy stored by C_3,

$$U_3 = \frac{1}{2} C_3 V_3^2 = \frac{1}{2} \cdot 3C \left(\frac{2V}{3}\right)^2 \quad \text{...(v)}$$

[using Eq. (ii)]

From Eqs. (iii), (iv) and (v), we get

$U_1 : U_2 : U_3 = 4 : 2 : 3$

2. When the lens is at mean position image is formed at focus (point P) at a distance f from the lens.

When the lens is at extreme position as shown in figure, axis of the lens tilts by θ, so incident wave makes angle θ with the axis. As per rules of ray tracing this beam will be focussed in focal plane at point which can be located using the incident ray passing through optical centre of the lens.

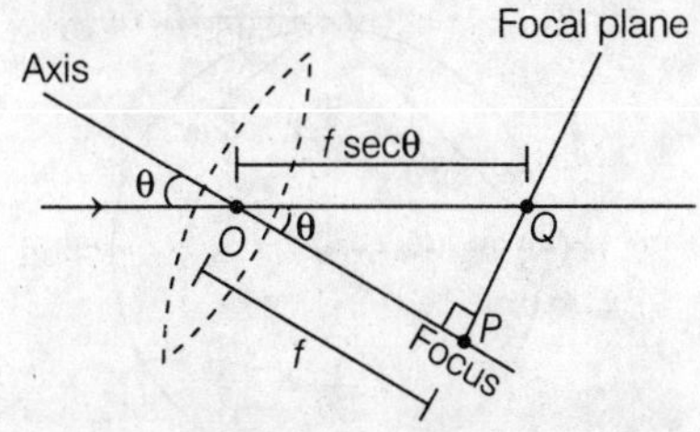

So, distance travelled by point of convergence as lens moves from mean to extreme position ($\frac{1}{4}$th oscillation) is

$$OQ - OP = f \sec\theta - f = f(\sec\theta - 1)$$

Therefore, in one oscillation, the convergence or image point moves 4 times this distance.

$\therefore$ Required distance $= 4f(\sec\theta - 1)$

$$= 4f\left(\frac{1-\cos\theta}{\cos\theta}\right)$$

3. Consider FBD of any electron (say Electron-1) in the given system as shown in figure.

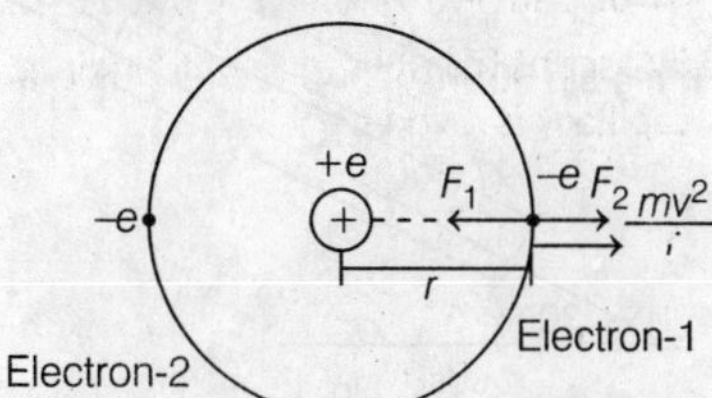

By balancing the forces, we get

$$F_1 = F_2 + \frac{mv^2}{r}$$

$$\Rightarrow \quad \frac{ke^2}{r^2} = \frac{ke^2}{4r^2} + \frac{mv^2}{r}$$

$$\Rightarrow \quad \frac{mv^2}{r} = \frac{3ke^2}{4r^2}$$

$$\Rightarrow \quad (mvr)v = \frac{3ke^2}{4}$$

As per Bohr's quantisation rule, angular momentum,

$$mvr = \frac{h}{2\pi} \quad \text{...(i)}$$

$$\Rightarrow \quad \frac{h}{2\pi} v = \frac{3ke^2}{4}$$

$$\Rightarrow \quad v = \frac{3\pi ke^2}{2h} = \frac{3e^2}{8\varepsilon_0 h} \quad \text{...(ii)}$$

Dividing Eq. (i) by Eq. (ii), we get

$$mr = \frac{4\varepsilon_0 h^2}{3\pi e^2}$$

$$\Rightarrow \quad r = \frac{4\varepsilon_0 h^2}{3\pi me^2} = \frac{4}{3} r_0$$

4. Acceleration of accelerometer, if heights of liquid in limbs are l_1 and l_2 is

$$a = \frac{l_1 - l_2}{l_1 + l_2} g$$

$$\Rightarrow \quad a = \frac{\frac{7l}{2} - \frac{l}{2}}{\frac{7l}{2} + \frac{l}{2}} g = \frac{3g}{4} \quad \text{...(i)}$$

Therefore, effective acceleration due to gravity w.r.t. cart is

$$\mathbf{g}' = \mathbf{g} - a = -g\hat{\mathbf{j}} - \frac{3g}{4}\hat{\mathbf{i}}$$

$$\Rightarrow \quad g' = \sqrt{g^2 + \left(\frac{3g}{4}\right)^2} = \frac{5g}{4} \quad \text{...(ii)}$$

[using Eq. (i)]

Thus effective highest and lowest positions of looping are A and B having maximum and minimum speeds, respectively. As, minimum speed at highest point in vertical looping is $\sqrt{gl}$, so minimum speed (at P) in accelerating frame of cart is

$$\sqrt{g'l} = \sqrt{\frac{5gl}{4}} = \frac{\sqrt{5gl}}{2} \quad \text{[using Eq. (ii)]}$$

5. Let equivalent impedance of the circuit is Z (inductive) as shown below.

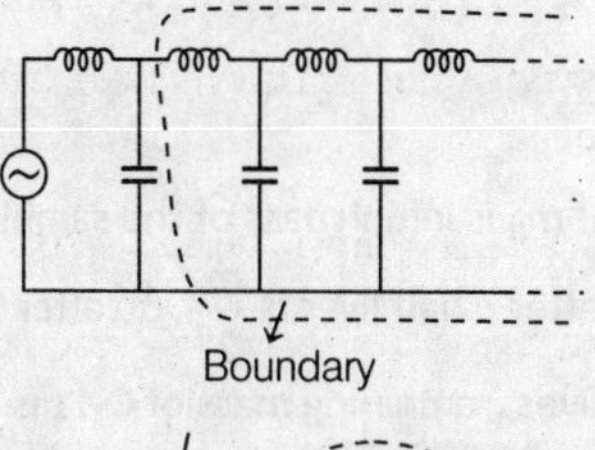

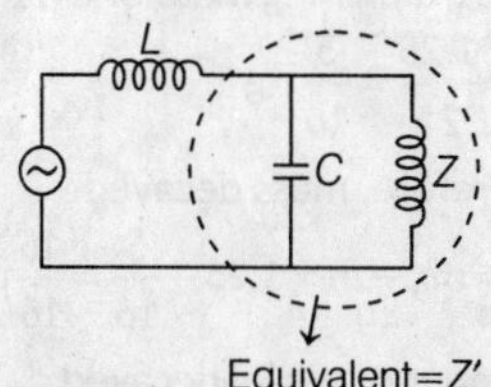

As the circuit portion in boundary is same as original circuit. So, its impedance will also be Z. Therefore, portion in boundary can be replaced by element of impedance Z (inductive) as shown in figure.

Now as capacitor and the equivalent inductive element are in parallel, their equivalent impedance Z' can be calculated by formula for parallel combination. So,

$$\frac{1}{Z'} = \frac{1}{Z} + \frac{1}{X_C} = \frac{1}{Z\hat{\mathbf{j}}} + \frac{1}{\left(-\frac{1}{\omega C}\right)\hat{\mathbf{j}}}$$

$$\Rightarrow \quad Z' = \frac{Z}{1 - Z\omega C}\hat{\mathbf{j}} \quad \text{...(i)}$$

Circuit now reduces to

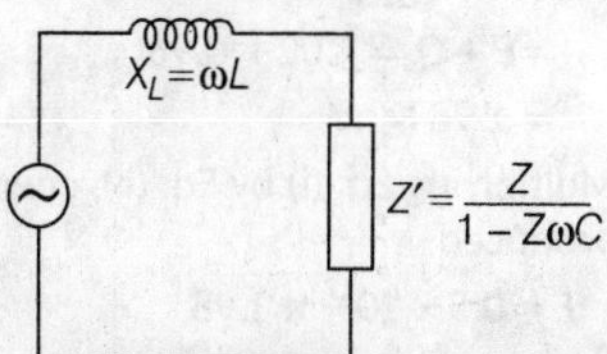

Therefore, as the elements are in series, equivalent impedance will be

$$Z = X_L + Z'$$

$$\Rightarrow \quad Z\hat{j} = \omega L\hat{j} + \frac{Z}{1 - Z\omega C}\hat{j} \text{ [using Eq. (i)]}$$

$$\Rightarrow \quad C \cdot Z^2 - \omega LC \cdot Z + L = 0$$

Solving the above quadratic equation, we get

$$Z = \frac{\omega LC \pm \sqrt{\omega^2 L^2 C^2 - 4LC}}{2C}$$

For circuit to be purely inductive impedance of the circuit should be independent of C. This will happen when term inside square root is zero. Therefore,

$$\omega^2 L^2 C^2 - 4LC = 0$$

and $\quad Z = \frac{\omega LC}{2C} = \frac{\omega L}{2} = \omega L_{eq}$

$$\Rightarrow \quad L_{eq} = \frac{L}{2}$$

6. If m_0 is initial mass of the sample, mass after n half lives is $\frac{m_0}{2^n}$. So after 2 half lives, remaining mass of C-11 is

$$m = \frac{1.25}{2^2} = \frac{5}{16} \mu g$$

Therefore, mass decayed

$$m' = m_0 - m = 1.25 - \frac{5}{16} = \frac{15}{16} \mu g$$

Number of nuclei decayed

$$N = \frac{m'}{m} \times N_0 = \frac{\frac{15}{16} \times 10^{-6}}{11} \times 6.023 \times 10^{23}$$

$$= 0.5 \times 10^{17} \quad \text{...(i)}$$

$\therefore$ Mass lost in annihilation of positron (β^+) with electron is

$$m = m_e + m_e = 2m_e$$

$$= 2 \times 9.1 \times 10^{-31} \text{ kg}$$

$\Rightarrow$ Energy produced, E (in one annihilation)

$$= mc^2 = 2 \times 9.1 \times 10^{-31} \times (3 \times 10^8)^2$$

$$= \frac{2 \times 9.1 \times 10^{-31} \times (3 \times 10^8)^2}{1.6 \times 10^{-19}}$$

$$= 1.02 \text{ MeV}$$

Also, Q of decay $= 0.96$ MeV

Thus, energy produced in every decay

$$= E + Q = 1.02 + 0.96$$

$$= 1.98 \text{ MeV} \quad \text{...(ii)}$$

Multiplying Eq. (i) by Eq. (ii), energy produced

$$E = 0.5 \times 10^{17} \times 1.98$$

$$\approx 10^{17} \text{ MeV}$$

7. Work done in closed path is zero for conservative and constant forces but not for non-conservative and variable forces. As at higher temperatures, extra degrees of freedom(modes of energy)get activated, internal energy can become more than doubled even though thermodynamic temperature is doubled.

8. Assuming friction between the cylinder and the plank equal to f and acceleration of the plank equal to a, FBD of the two bodies are as shown in Fig 1.

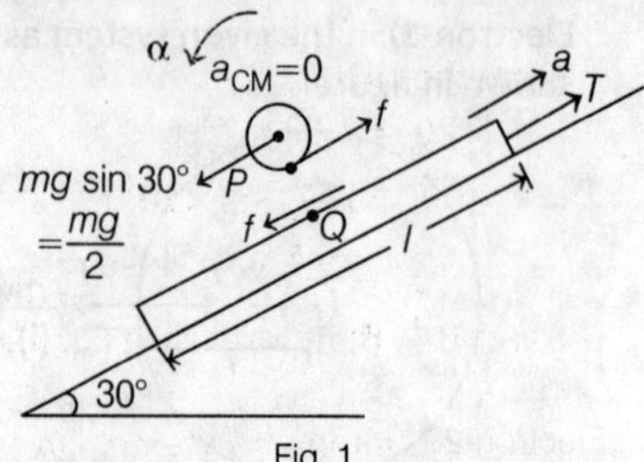

Fig. 1

As for cylinder, acceleration of CM is zero,

$$f = \frac{mg}{2} \quad \text{...(i)}$$

Using, $\tau = I\alpha$, (about CM) for cylinder, we get

$$fR = \frac{mR^2}{2}\alpha$$

$$\Rightarrow \quad \alpha = \frac{2f}{mR} = \frac{2\left(\frac{mg}{2}\right)}{mR} = \frac{g}{R} \quad \text{...(ii)}$$

[using Eq. (i)]

As there is no slipping between contact points P and Q as shown in figure.

$$a_P = a_Q$$

$$\Rightarrow \quad \alpha R = a$$

$$\Rightarrow \quad a = \frac{g}{R} \cdot R = g \quad \text{...(iii)}$$

Using equation of motion for the plank, we get,

$$s = ut + \frac{1}{2}at^2$$

$$\Rightarrow \quad l = 0 + \frac{1}{2}gt^2 \quad \text{[using Eq. (iii)]}$$

$$\Rightarrow \quad t = \sqrt{\frac{2l}{g}} \quad \text{...(iv)}$$

Angle rotated by the cylinder in same time can be found using

$$\theta = 0 + \frac{1}{2}\left(\frac{g}{R}\right)\left(\sqrt{\frac{2l}{g}}\right)^2$$

[using Eqs. (ii) and (iv)]

$$\Rightarrow \quad \theta = \frac{l}{R}$$

9. Putting dimensions of various quantities in given relation, we get

$$[ML^2T^{-3}] = [T^{-1}]^a [MLT^{-2}A^{-2}]^b [AL^2]^c [LT^{-1}]^d$$

$$\Rightarrow [ML^2T^{-3}]A^0 = M^b L^{b+2c+d} T^{-a-2b-d} A^{-2b+c}$$

Comparing dimensional powers of LHS and RHS, we get

$$b = 1 \quad \text{...(i)}$$

$$b + 2c + d = 2 \quad \text{...(ii)}$$

$$-a - 2b - d = -3 \quad \text{...(iii)}$$

$$-2b + c = 0 \quad \text{...(iv)}$$

Solving Eqs. (i), (ii), (iii) and (iv), we get $a = 4, b = 1, c = 2, d = -3$. These values satisfy the relation given in option (c) only.

10. Speed of wave relative to string

$$v = \sqrt{\frac{T}{\mu}} = \sqrt{\frac{\mu\omega^2 r^2}{\mu}} = \omega r$$

Suppose the string is disturbed at point A thereby creating two wave pulses travelling in opposite sense relative to string as shown in Fig.1 with speed ωr. Also, as point A of string is in circular motion, its speed will be ωr.

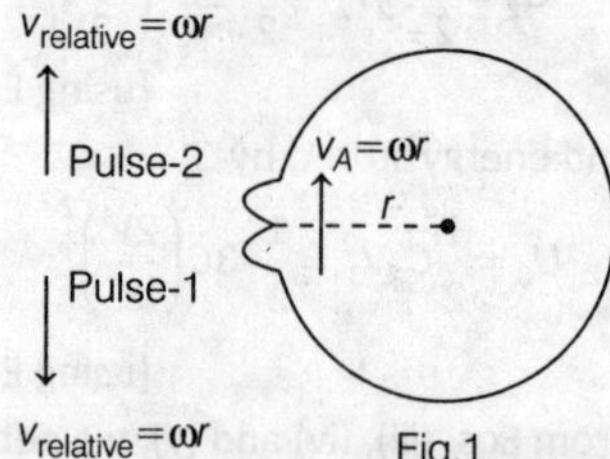

Fig.1

As velocity of point A of string is equal and opposite to relative velocity of wave pulse-1, its net velocity will be zero, while velocity of point A is in same direction as that of relative velocity of pulse 2, so, its net velocity will be $2\omega r$.

Situation at a later instant, given in the question will therefore be as shown in Fig. 2.

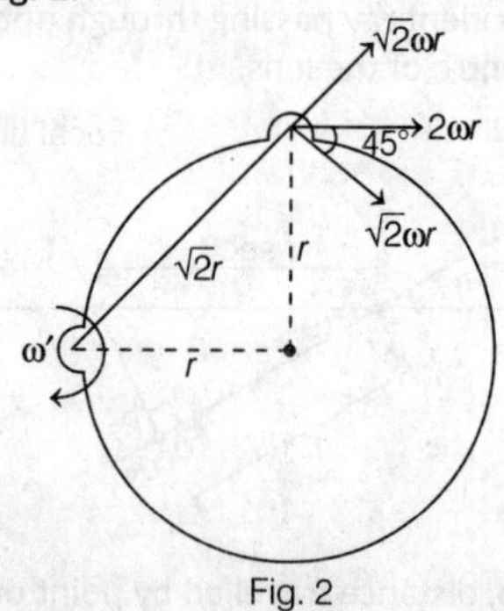

Fig. 2

Thus, angular velocity of pulse-2 relative to pulse-1,

$$\omega' = \frac{\text{Component of velocity perpendicular to line joining}}{\text{Distance between pulses}}$$

$$= \frac{\sqrt{2}\omega r}{\sqrt{2}r} = \omega$$

11. Shunt (S) to convert galvanometer of range i and resistance R into an ammeter of range I is given by

$$S = \frac{iR}{I - i}$$

As I is given equal to $2i$, therefore

$$S = \frac{iR}{2i - i} = R$$

So, ammeter will have equivalent resistance equal to $\frac{R}{2}$.

By condition of balancing,

$$\frac{l}{100 - l} = \frac{R_{\text{ammeter}}}{R_{\text{galvanometer}}}$$

$$\Rightarrow \frac{l}{100 - l} = \frac{\frac{R}{2}}{R}$$

$$\Rightarrow \quad l = \frac{100}{3} \text{ cm} \quad \text{...(i)}$$

When ammeter is modified by connecting one more shunt across it, equivalent resistance will be $\frac{R}{3}$.

Again, by the condition of balancing,

$$\frac{l'}{100 - l'} = \frac{\frac{R}{3}}{R}$$

$$\Rightarrow \quad l' = \frac{100}{4} \text{ cm} \quad \text{...(ii)}$$

Dividing Eq. (ii) by Eq. (i), we get

$$\frac{l'}{l} = \frac{3}{4}$$

$$\Rightarrow \quad l' = \frac{3l}{4}$$

$$\Rightarrow \quad \text{Shift} = l - l' = l - \frac{3l}{4} = \frac{l}{4}$$

12. The current gain for CE configuration, using the relation,

$$\beta = \frac{\alpha}{1 - \alpha}$$

Here, α gain is for CB and β gain is for CE.

$$\Rightarrow \quad \beta = \frac{\frac{100}{101}}{1 - \frac{100}{101}} = 100 \quad \text{...(i)}$$

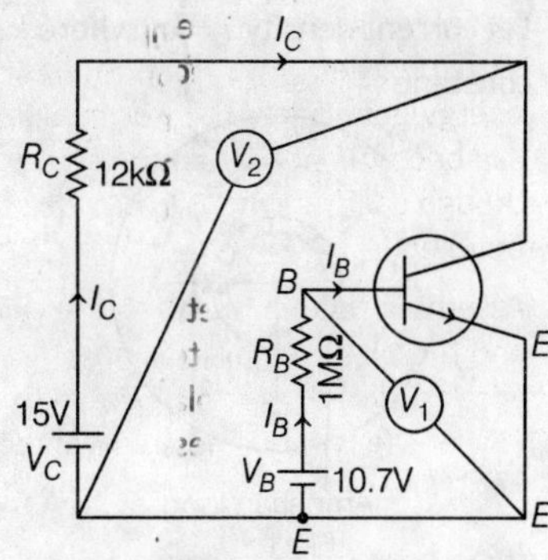

From the circuit,

$$V_1 = V_B - I_B R_B$$

$$\Rightarrow \quad 0.7 = 10.7 - I_B \times 10^6$$

$$\Rightarrow \quad I_B = 10^{-5} \text{ A}$$

As $I_C = \beta I_B$, therefore using Eq. (i), we get

$$I_C = 100 \times 10^{-5} = 10^{-3} \text{ A}$$

Also, from the circuit,

$$V_2 = V_C - I_C R_C$$

$$= 15 - (10^{-3} \times 12 \times 10^3) = 3\text{V}$$

13. Temperature of the shell will be constant in steady state, so power P incident from the point source on inner surface of the shell will be equal to thermal current I flowing through the shell. Therefore,

$$P = I \quad \text{...(i)}$$

Also, thermal current is given by

$$I = \frac{KA\Delta T}{t} \quad \text{...(ii)}$$

Here, A is area through which current is flowing.

From Eqs. (i) and (ii), $P = \frac{KA\Delta T}{t}$

$$\Rightarrow \quad \Delta T = \frac{Pt}{KA} = \frac{Pt}{\frac{KS}{2}} = \frac{2Pt}{KS}$$

(As total surface area S in terms of radius R is $8\pi R^2$ while surface area A through which current is flowing is $4\pi R^2$).

14. At a later instant, due to electric force qE the system begins to move acquiring velocity v as shown.

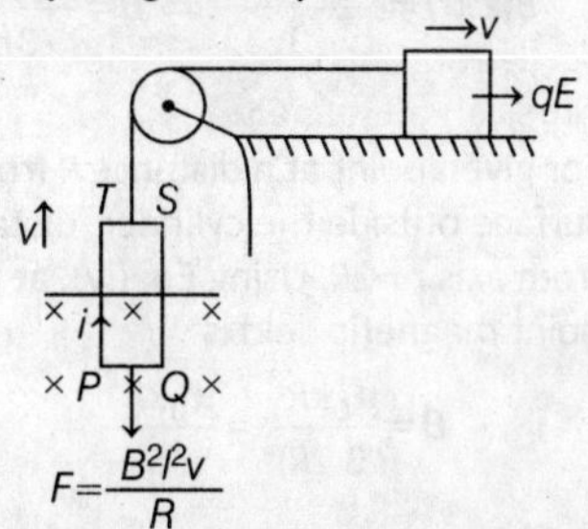

Due to movement of loop in magnetic field, current induced in the loop is equal to

$$i = \frac{Bvl}{R} \quad \text{...(i)}$$

Magnitude of magnetic force

$$F = \frac{B^2 l^2}{R} v$$

Finally, when magnetic force F becomes equal to electric force qE, net pull on the system becomes zero and velocity becomes constant. So,

$$F = qE \Rightarrow \frac{B^2 l^2 v}{R} = qE$$

$$\Rightarrow \quad v = \frac{qER}{B^2 l^2} \quad \text{...(ii)}$$

Using Eqs. (i) and (ii), we get

$$i = \frac{B\left(\frac{qER}{B^2 l^2}\right) l}{R} = \frac{qE}{Bl}$$

Thus, in steady state power consumed is

$$P = I^2 R = \frac{q^2 E^2 R}{B^2 l^2}$$

15. For motion of stone from A to B,

$$s = ut + \frac{1}{2} at^2$$

$$\Rightarrow \quad h = 0 + \frac{1}{2} gt^2$$

$$\Rightarrow \quad t_1 = \sqrt{\frac{2h}{g}} \quad \text{...(i)}$$

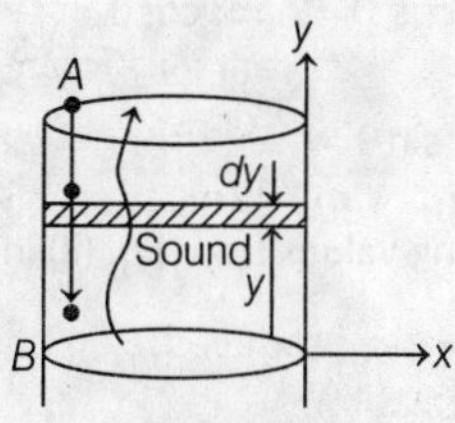

As temperature profile is linear, temperature at height y from water's surface can be found using two point form equation.

$$\frac{T - 9T_0}{T_0 - 9T_0} = \frac{y - 0}{h - 0}$$

$$\Rightarrow \quad T = 9T_0 - \frac{8T_0 y}{h} \quad \text{...(ii)}$$

As speed of sound is given to be $v = C\sqrt{T}$ time taken by sound to move through air strip of thickness dy shown is $dt = \frac{dy}{v} = \frac{dy}{C\sqrt{T}} = \frac{dy}{C\sqrt{9T_0 - \frac{8T_0}{h} y}}$

$\Rightarrow$ Time for sound to move from B to A,

$$t_2 = \frac{1}{C}\int_0^h \frac{dy}{\sqrt{9T_0 - \frac{8T_0}{h}y}} = \frac{h}{2C\sqrt{T_0}} \quad ...(iii)$$

From Eqs. (i) and (iii), total time

$$t_{total} = t_1 + t_2 = \sqrt{\frac{2h}{g}} + \frac{h}{2C\sqrt{T_0}}$$

16. On passing through polaroids A, B, C the intensity of light becomes,

$$I = \frac{I_0}{2} \times \cos^2\theta \times \cos^2\theta$$

As polaroid B and D are crossed their axis PQ and TU are perpendicular. So, angle between TU and RS is $90° - \theta$. Intensity, therefore, will become $\cos^2(90° - \theta)$ or $\sin^2\theta$ times on passing through D. So emergent intensity

$$I = I_0 \times \frac{1}{2} \times \cos^2\theta \times \cos^2\theta \times \sin^2\theta$$

$$= \frac{I_0(\sin\theta \cdot \cos^2\theta)^2}{2} \quad ...(i)$$

For I to be maximum, $\frac{dI}{d\theta} = 0$

$$\Rightarrow \frac{d[\sin\theta \cdot \cos^2\theta]}{d\theta} = 0$$

$$\Rightarrow -\cos\theta \cdot \cos^2\theta + \sin\theta \cdot 2\cos\theta \cdot \sin\theta = 0$$

$$\Rightarrow -\cos^2\theta + 2\sin^2\theta = 0$$

$$\Rightarrow -\cos^2\theta + 2(1 - \cos^2\theta) = 0$$

$$\Rightarrow 3\cos^2\theta = 2 \Rightarrow \cos\theta = \sqrt{\frac{2}{3}}$$

and $\sin\theta = \frac{1}{\sqrt{3}}$ ...(ii)

Putting values from Eq. (ii) in Eq. (i), we get

$$I = \frac{2I_0}{27}$$

17. As, $dS = \frac{dQ}{T}$

$$\Rightarrow dQ = T \cdot dS$$

$$\Rightarrow Q = \int T \cdot dS = \text{Area under } T\text{-}S \text{ graph}$$

$$= T_0 S_0$$

As for cyclic process, internal energy change (ΔU) is zero, so, by first law of thermodynamics.

$$W = Q - \Delta U = Q = T_0 S_0$$

Also, heat input (H) = Sum of positive Q_S $= +2T_0S_0$

∴ Efficiency,

$$\eta = \frac{W}{H} \times 100 = \frac{T_0 S_0}{2T_0 S_0} \times 100 = 50\%$$

18. Let current density $J = kr$, where k is a constant.

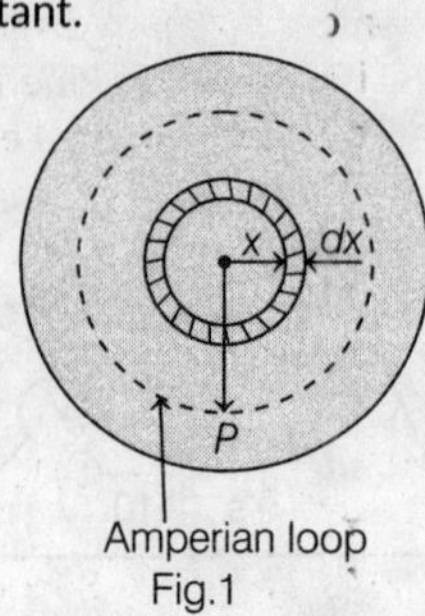

Amperian loop
Fig.1

To find magnetic field at P inside cylinder consider an Amperian loop of radius r as shown in Fig. 1.

Current through ring element of radius x and thickness dx.

$$di = JdA = kx2\pi x dx$$

∴ Current crossing Amperian loop,

$$i = \int di = 2\pi k \int_0^r x^2 dx = \frac{2\pi k r^3}{3} \quad ...(i)$$

As per Ampere's law, $\oint \mathbf{B} \cdot d\mathbf{l} = \mu_0 i$

Using this law, for loop in Fig. 1, we get

$$B(2\pi r) = \frac{\mu_0 \cdot 2\pi k r^3}{3} \quad \text{[using Eq. (i)]}$$

$$\Rightarrow B = \frac{\mu_0 k r^2}{3} \quad ...(ii)$$

Current crossing the Amperian loop as shown in Fig. 2.

$$i = \int_0^R kx2\pi x dx = \frac{2\pi k R^3}{3} \quad ...(iii)$$

Amperian loop
Fig. 2

Using Ampere's law, for the loop in Fig. 2, we get

$$B(2\pi r) = \frac{\mu_0 2\pi k R^3}{3} \Rightarrow B = \frac{\mu_0 k R^3}{3r} \quad ...(iv)$$

For given point at a distance R from surface outside the cylinder, distance from axis $r = 2R$. Using Eq. (iv), at this point magnetic field is

$$B = \frac{\mu_0 k R^3}{3(2R)} = \frac{\mu_0 k R^2}{6} \quad ...(v)$$

To find r which has same B as that given by Eq. (v), on equating Eqs. (ii) and (v), we get

$$\frac{\mu_0 k r^2}{3} = \frac{\mu_0 k R^2}{6} \Rightarrow r = \frac{R}{\sqrt{2}}$$

19. Velocities of different points will be as shown

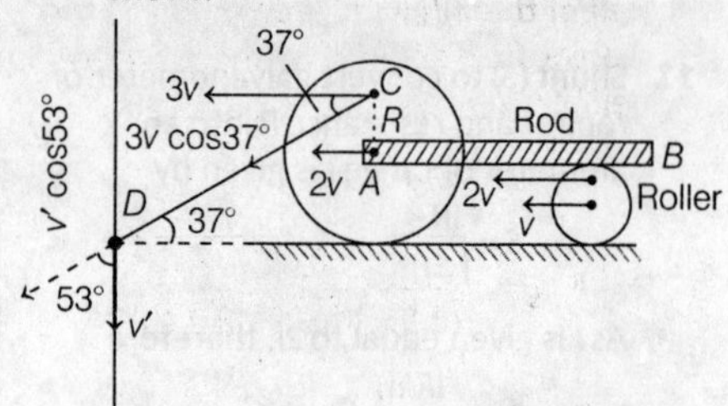

Components of velocities of ends C and D will be equal along length of the rod. Therefore,

$$3v\cos 37° = v'\cos 53°$$

$$\Rightarrow v' = 4v$$

20. de-Broglie wavelength of electron is given by

$$\lambda = \frac{h}{p} = \frac{h}{\sqrt{2mk}}$$

$$= \frac{h}{\sqrt{2meV}}$$

$$\Rightarrow \lambda \propto \frac{1}{\sqrt{V}}$$

As resolving power is inversely proportional to λ

∴ Resolving power $\propto \sqrt{V}$

21. As the system is rotating freely, there is no external torque so by conserving angular momentum

$$L_{final} = L_{initial}$$

$$\Rightarrow I_f\omega_f = I_i\omega_i$$

Here I_f, I_i, ω_f and ω_i are final and initial moment of inertia, final and initial angular speed respectively.

$$\Rightarrow (I_{cone} + I_{insect})\omega_f = (I_{cone} + I_{insect})\omega_i$$

$$\Rightarrow \left(\frac{3}{10}mR^2 + mR^2\right)\omega_f = \left(\frac{3}{10}mR^2 + m \times 0^2\right)\omega_0$$

$$\Rightarrow \omega_f = \frac{3}{13}\omega_0 = \frac{3}{13} \times \frac{13}{4}$$

$$= 0.75 \text{ rad/s}$$

22. The bulb, as a point source, radiates light in all directions uniformly. At a distance of 3 m, the surface area of the surrounding sphere is

$$A = 4\pi r^2 = 4\pi(3)^2 = 113 \text{ m}^2$$

The intensity at this distance

$$= \frac{\text{Power}}{\text{Area}}$$
$$= \frac{100 \times 2.5\%}{113}$$
$$= 0.022\ \text{W/m}^2$$

Half of this intensity is provided by the electric field and half by the magnetic field. So,

$$\frac{1}{2} I = \frac{1}{2} (\varepsilon_0 E_{rms}^2 c)$$

$$\Rightarrow E_{rms} = \sqrt{\frac{0.022}{(8.85 \times 10^{-12})(3 \times 10^8)}}$$
$$= 2.9\ \text{V/m}$$

The peak electric field, E_0 is

$$E_0 = \sqrt{2}\, E_{rms} = \sqrt{2} \times 2.9\ \text{V/m}$$
$$= 4.07\ \text{V/m}$$

which is approximately 4 V/m.

23. Let x be the distance of null point P from sphere X.

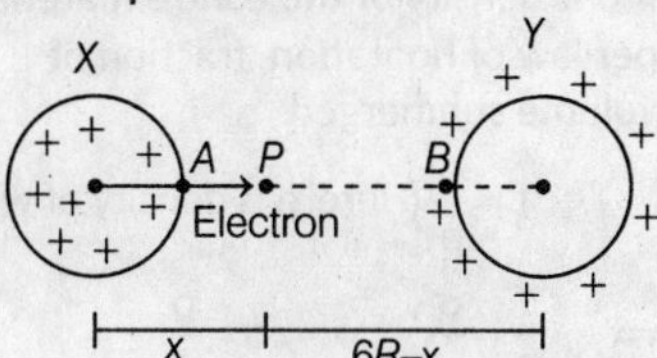

At P, force on electron is zero. So, force due to X = force due to Y

$$\Rightarrow \frac{k \cdot Q}{x^2} = \frac{k \cdot 4Q}{(6R - x)^2}$$

$$\Rightarrow 4x^2 = (6R - x)^2$$

$$\Rightarrow 2x = 6R - x$$

$$\Rightarrow x = 2R$$

To reach point B, the electron should just cross point P or speed of electron at P should be just greater than zero. So, by conservation of energy for motion from P to B (surface point of sphere Y)

$$KE_P + PE_P = KE_B + PE_B$$

$$0 + \frac{kQ(-e)}{2R} + \frac{k \cdot 4Q(-e)}{4R}$$
$$= KE_B + \frac{kQ(-e)}{5R} + \frac{k \cdot 4Q(-e)}{R}$$

$$\Rightarrow KE_B = \frac{2.7\, kQe}{R} = \frac{xkQe}{R} \text{ (given)}$$

$$x = 2.7$$

24. Velocity components of bead before collision are as shown in figure. Let velocity of (bead + particle) equal to v' after collision. By conservation of momentum along rod,

$$2mv' = m \cdot 10\sqrt{2}$$

$$\Rightarrow \quad v' = 5\sqrt{2}\ \text{m/s} \quad \text{...(i)}$$

At position of maximum displacement (B), speed is zero. So, all kinetic energy converts to spring potential energy.

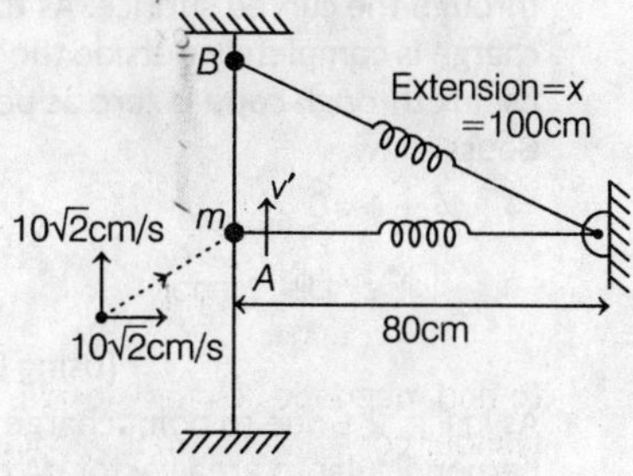

$\Rightarrow$ Gain in PE = Loss in KE

$$\Rightarrow \frac{1}{2} kx^2 = \frac{1}{2} 2m \cdot v'^2$$

$$\Rightarrow x = \sqrt{\frac{2m}{k}} v' = \sqrt{\frac{2 \times 1}{100}} \times 5\sqrt{2}$$
$$= 1\text{m} = 100\ \text{cm}$$

$\therefore$ Max displacement,

$$AB = \sqrt{100^2 - 80^2} = 60\ \text{cm}$$

25. For two perpendicular magnets of magnetic moment M_0 and moment of inertia I_0 each, equivalent magnetic moment, $M = \sqrt{2} M_0$ ...(i)

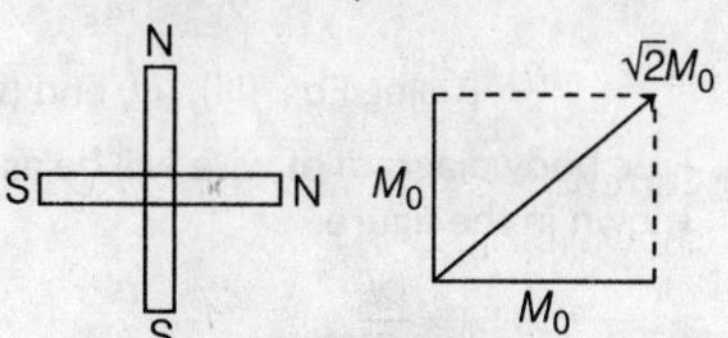

and total moment of inertia

$$I = 2I_0 \quad \text{...(ii)}$$

Also, time period of oscillation of magnet in magnetic field is given by

$$T = 2\pi \sqrt{\frac{I}{MB}} \quad \text{...(iii)}$$

Time period of the system, using Eqs. (i), (ii) and (iii), we get

$$T = 2\pi \sqrt{\frac{2I_0}{\sqrt{2} M_0 B}} = 2\pi \sqrt{\frac{\sqrt{2} I_0}{M_0 B}} \quad \text{...(iv)}$$

Also, using Eq. (iii) time period of single magnet,

$$T' = 2\pi \sqrt{\frac{I_0}{M_0 B}} \quad \text{...(v)}$$

Dividing Eq. (v) by Eq. (iv), we get

$$\frac{T'}{T} = \frac{1}{2^{\frac{1}{4}}}$$

$$\Rightarrow T' = \frac{T}{2^{\frac{1}{4}}} = \frac{32^{\frac{1}{4}}}{2^{\frac{1}{4}}} = 16^{\frac{1}{4}} = 2\ \text{s}$$

26. Equation of an AM wave is given by

$$V = (A_c + A_m \cos \omega_m t) \cos \omega_c t$$

Comparing it with the given equation, we get

$$A_c = 10\ \text{V and } A_m = 8\ \text{V}$$

As $A_{max} = A_c + A_m$

and $A_{min} = A_c - A_m$, so desired ratio

$$a = \frac{A_{max}}{A_{min}} = \frac{10 + 8}{10 - 8} = 9$$

Also, $\omega_m = 1.57 \times 10^8\ \text{rad s}^{-1}$

$$\Rightarrow \text{Bandwidth} = 2f_m = 2\left(\frac{\omega_m}{2\pi}\right) = \frac{\omega_m}{\pi}$$
$$= \frac{1.57 \times 10^8}{3.14} = 50\ \text{MHz}$$
$$= b\ \text{MHz} \quad \text{(given)}$$

$$\Rightarrow b = 50$$

$$\therefore a + b = 59$$

27. Magnification of the object

$$m = \frac{f}{f - u} = \frac{f}{f - (-f)} = \frac{1}{2} \quad \text{...(i)}$$

As velocity component of image along axis is given by

$$v_i = -m^2 v_0 \quad \text{...(ii)}$$

$$\Rightarrow v_i = -\left(\frac{1}{2}\right)^2 4 \cos 30° = -\frac{\sqrt{3}}{2}\ \text{cm/s}$$

[using Eq. (i)]

Also velocity component of image perpendicular to axis is given by

$$v'_i = mv'_0 = \frac{1}{2} \cdot 4 \sin 30° = 1\ \text{cm/s}$$

[using Eq. (i)]

Therefore, net velocity of image is

$$v'_{net} = \sqrt{v_i^2 + v_i'^2}$$
$$= \sqrt{\frac{3}{4} + 1} = \frac{\sqrt{7}}{2}\ \text{cm/s}$$
$$= 5\sqrt{7} \text{ or } 13.2\ \text{mm/s}$$

28. Energy required to disassemble a solid sphere is equal to magnitude of its self energy given by

$$E = \frac{3}{5} \frac{GM^2}{R} \quad \text{...(i)}$$

Also, acceleration due to gravity at a height h above surface is

$$g = \frac{GM}{(R + h)^2}$$

$$\Rightarrow g = \frac{GM}{4R^2} \quad (\because h = R) \text{...(ii)}$$

Dividing Eq. (i) by Eq. (ii), we get

$$\frac{E}{g} = \frac{12\ MR}{5} \Rightarrow E = 2.4\, MgR$$

$$\therefore \quad x = 2.4$$

29. It is given that volume of air in the flask is constant.

$\Rightarrow$ Change in volume of mercury = Change in volume of flask

$\Rightarrow V_M \gamma_M \Delta T = V_F \gamma_F \Delta T$

$\Rightarrow$ Initial volume of mercury,

$$V_M = \frac{V_F \gamma_F}{\gamma_M} = \frac{V_F (1.5\,\beta_F)}{\gamma_M}$$

$$= \frac{0.1 \times 1.5 \times 18 \times 10^{-6}}{1.8 \times 10^{-4}}$$

$$= 15 \times 10^{-3}\ \text{L} = 15\ \text{cc}$$

$\therefore$ Volume of air = Volume of flask − Volume of mercury

$$= 100 - 15 = 85\ \text{cc}$$

30. From first figure, excess reading (zero error) = 0.02 mm

From the second figure, the screw gauge gives a reading of 7.67 mm in which there is 0.02 mm excess reading, which has to be removed (subtracted).

So, actual reading or thickness of the wire = 7.67 − 0.02 = 7.65 mm

Knockout 07

1. To find flux of wire through the base consider a ring element of radius r and thickness dr as shown in Fig. 1. Out of x and y components flux will only be due to x component of field equal to

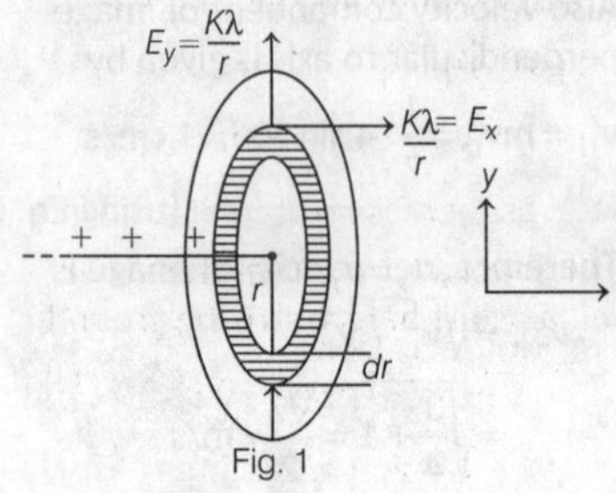

Fig. 1

$$d\phi = EdA = \frac{K\lambda}{r} \cdot 2\pi r dr = 2\pi k \lambda dr$$

$\therefore$ Flux through base will be

$$\phi = \int EdA = 2\pi k\lambda \int_0^R dr = 2\pi k \lambda R$$

$$\Rightarrow \phi = \frac{\lambda R}{2\varepsilon_0} \quad \text{...(i)} \quad \left(\text{as, } k = \frac{1}{4\pi\varepsilon_0}\right)$$

Also, flux due to point charge Q placed on axis of a disc (as in Fig. 2) is given by

$$\phi' = \frac{Q}{2\varepsilon_0}(1 - \cos 60°) = \frac{Q}{4\varepsilon_0} \quad \text{... (ii)}$$

As, net flux through base is given zero, flux due to line charge must be cancelling the flux due to point charge

$\Rightarrow \quad \phi = \phi'$

$$\Rightarrow \frac{\lambda R}{2\varepsilon_0} = \frac{Q}{4\varepsilon_0} \quad \text{[using Eqs. (i) and (ii)]}$$

$$Q = 2\lambda R \quad \text{...(iii)}$$

Let ϕ'' be flux due to line charge through the curved surface. As the line charge is completely outside the cone, its flux through cone is zero as per Gauss's law.

$\Rightarrow \quad \phi'' + \phi = 0$

$$\Rightarrow \quad |\phi''| = |\phi| = \frac{\lambda R}{2\varepsilon_0} \quad \text{...(iv)}$$

[using Eq. (i)]

As in Fig. 2, **E** due to point charge is perpendicular to area vector $d\mathbf{A}$ of element on curved surface, so flux of point charge

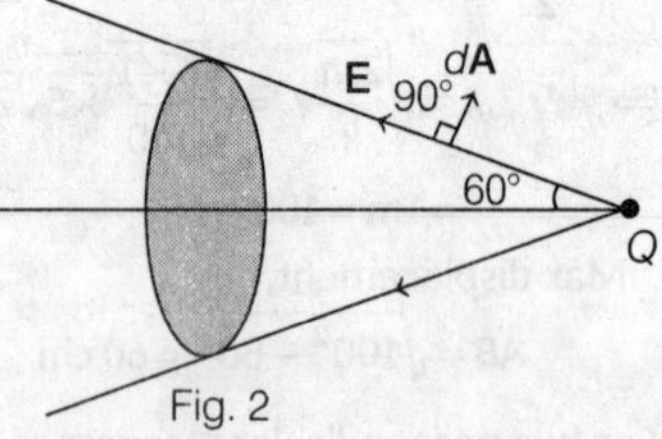

Fig. 2

$$\phi''' = \int \mathbf{E} \cdot d\mathbf{A} = 0 \quad \text{...(v)}$$

$$\Rightarrow \text{Net flux} = \phi'' + \phi''' = \frac{\lambda R}{2\varepsilon_0} = \frac{Q}{4\varepsilon_0}$$

[Using Eqs. (iii), (iv) and (v)]

2. Free body diagram of wire will be as shown in the figure.

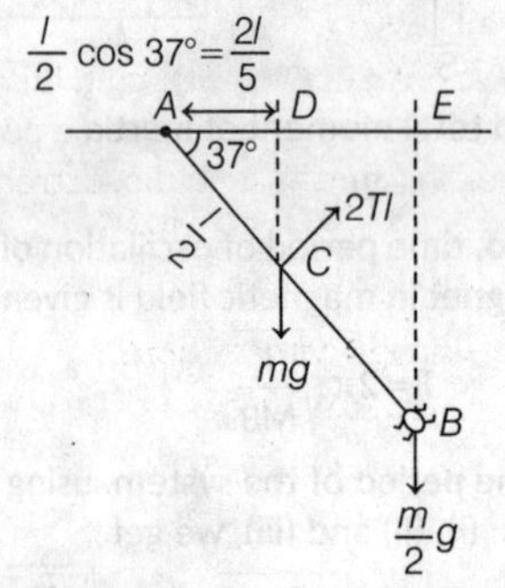

As soap film has two surfaces, forces due to surface tension will be $2Tl$ acting uniformly perpendicular to length of the wire. Being uniform, it can be assumed to be acting at CM of the wire. Gravitational forces on the wire and the insect are also shown.

Torque of $2Tl$ about A, $\tau_1 = 2Tl \cdot \frac{l}{2}$

$= Tl^2$, anti-clockwise

Torque of mg about A,

$$\tau_2 = mg \times AD = mg \times \frac{2l}{5}$$

$$= \frac{2mgl}{5}, \text{ clockwise}$$

Torque of $\frac{mg}{2}$ about A, $\tau_3 = \frac{mg}{2} \times AE$

$$= \frac{mg}{2} \times \frac{4l}{5} = \frac{2mgl}{5}, \text{ clockwise}$$

For equilibrium, anti-clockwise torque is balanced by clockwise torque

$\Rightarrow \quad \tau_1 = \tau_2 + \tau_3$

$$\Rightarrow \quad Tl^2 = \frac{2mgl}{5} + \frac{2mgl}{5}$$

$$\Rightarrow \quad T = \frac{4mg}{5l}$$

3. Time taken to pass one spoke

$$t = \frac{\theta}{\omega} = \frac{\pi}{4\omega} \quad \text{...(i)}$$

$\Rightarrow$ Velocity of arrow will be

$$v = \frac{\text{Distance}}{\text{Time}} = \frac{l}{t} = \frac{l}{\frac{\pi}{4\omega}} = \frac{4\omega l}{\pi}$$

4. If σ is density of the cone's material, as per law of floatation, fraction of volume submerged

$$f = \frac{\sigma}{\rho} \text{ (Here, } \rho \text{ is density of water)}$$

$$\Rightarrow \quad \frac{1}{2} = \frac{\sigma}{\rho} \quad \Rightarrow \quad \sigma = \frac{\rho}{2} \quad \text{...(i)}$$

On slight vertical downward displacement x, increase in buoyancy or restoring upward force

$$F = \rho \cdot dV \cdot g$$

Here, dV = Extra volume of cone submerged $= \pi r^2 x$

$$\Rightarrow \quad F \approx \rho \pi r^2 x g \quad \text{...(ii)}$$

Also, mass of the composite body

$$m = \sigma \times V = \frac{\rho}{2} \times 2 \times \frac{1}{3}\pi r^2 h$$

[using Eq. (i)]

$$\Rightarrow \quad m = \frac{\rho \pi r^2 h}{3} \quad \text{...(iii)}$$

Dividing Eq. (ii) by Eq. (iii), we get Acceleration of cone equal to

$$a = \frac{F}{m} = \frac{3g}{h} \cdot x$$

Comparing this with acceleration in SHM, $a = \omega^2 x$, we get

$$\omega^2 = \frac{3g}{h} \quad \Rightarrow \omega = \sqrt{\frac{3g}{h}}$$

5. Let length of each tube $= \frac{l}{2} = d$

As fundamental frequency of a closed pipe is lesser than that of an open pipe, a given mode of closed pipe can be in unison will a lower mode of an open pipe. Thus, seventh harmonic and sixth overtone (13th harmonic) in unison must correspond to open and closed pipe respectively. Therefore,

$$\frac{7v}{2(d+2e)}=\frac{13v}{4(d+e)}$$

Here, e is end correction.

$$\Rightarrow 14(d+e)=13(d+2e) \Rightarrow e=\frac{d}{12}$$

As per Rayleigh's end correction, e is equal to 0.6 times radius of tube

$$\Rightarrow \quad 0.6r=\frac{d}{12}$$

$$\Rightarrow \quad r=\frac{5d}{36}=\frac{5l}{72}\approx 0.07\,l$$

6. On rotation $d\theta$ of the slab about O, rotational work done W by torque τ, is equal to change in potential energy U

$$\Rightarrow \quad dW=\tau d\theta=|dU|$$

$$\Rightarrow \quad \tau=\left|\frac{dU}{d\theta}\right| \quad \text{...(i)}$$

Also, potential energy of the arrangement is $U=\frac{1}{2}CV^2$ ...(ii)

Now, the capacitor can be seen as parallel combination of air-cored and dielectric-cored portions.

So, the equivalent capacitance will be

$$C=C_{\text{air}}+C_{\text{dielectric}}$$

$$=\frac{\varepsilon_0 R^2\theta}{2d}+\frac{K\cdot\varepsilon_0 R^2(\pi-\theta)}{2d}$$

$$\Rightarrow \quad C=-\frac{(K-1)\,\varepsilon_0 R^2\theta}{2d}+\frac{K\varepsilon_0 R^2\pi}{2d} \quad \text{...(iii)}$$

From Eqs. (i) and (ii), we get

$$\tau=\left|\frac{dU}{d\theta}\right|=\frac{1}{2}V^2\cdot\left|\frac{dC}{d\theta}\right| \quad \text{...(iv)}$$

Differentiating Eq. (iii) w.r.t. θ, we get

$$\frac{dC}{d\theta}=-\frac{(K-1)\,\varepsilon_0 R^2}{2d}$$

$$\Rightarrow \left|\frac{dC}{d\theta}\right|=\frac{(K-1)\,\varepsilon_0 R^2}{2d} \quad \text{...(v)}$$

From Eqs. (iv) and (v), we get

$$\tau=\frac{1}{2}V^2\cdot\frac{(k-1)\,\varepsilon_0 R^2}{2d}=\frac{(k-1)\varepsilon_0 R^2 V^2}{4d}$$

$$=\frac{(4\pi+1-1)\,\varepsilon_0\left(\frac{2A}{\pi}\right)V^2}{4d}$$

(As A is $\frac{\pi R^2}{2}$ and K is given equal to $4\pi+1$)

$$\Rightarrow \quad \tau=\frac{2\varepsilon_0 AV^2}{d}$$

7. As per statistical law of radioactive decay, rate of change of number of nuclei,

$$\frac{dN}{dt}=-\lambda N$$

$\Rightarrow$ Fraction of nuclei decayed,

$$\left|\frac{dN}{N}\right|=|-\lambda dt|=\lambda dt$$

$\Rightarrow$ Fraction of nuclei survived

$$=1-\left|\frac{dN}{N}\right|=1-\lambda\cdot dt$$

which is same as probability of survival.

8. If I is current in the DC circuit, by KCL for point P, $I=I'+I \Rightarrow I'=0$

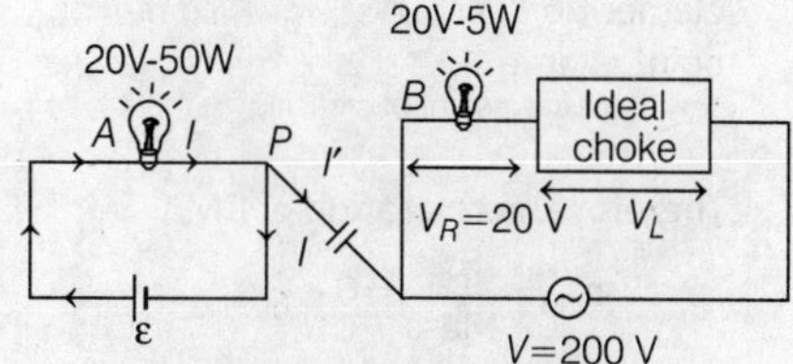

$\therefore$ No current will go in capacitor's branch. So, the two circuits (DC and AC) will be independent.

As, $\quad P=\frac{V^2}{R} \Rightarrow V\propto\sqrt{P}$.

As bulb A is consuming one-fourth power compared to specification, voltage across it is half of specification. Therefore,

emf of cell, $\varepsilon=\frac{20}{2}=10\text{V}$ ...(i)

Now, consider the AC circuit. It is given that bulb B is consuming same power as design specification. So, current is

$$I=\frac{P}{V}=\frac{5}{20}=\frac{1}{4}\text{A} \quad \text{...(ii)}$$

Also, voltage across bulb B,

$$V_R=20\text{ V} \quad \text{...(iii)}$$

Now, as net voltage (V) is

$$V^2=V_L^2+V_R^2$$

$$\Rightarrow \quad 200^2=V_L^2+20^2 \quad \text{[using Eq. (iii)]}$$

$$\Rightarrow \quad V_L=20\sqrt{99}\text{ V}$$

$$\Rightarrow I\cdot 2\pi f\cdot L=20\sqrt{99} \quad (\text{as } \omega=2\pi f)$$

Putting the given values of f and I, we get

$$\frac{1}{4}\times 2\pi\times\frac{50}{\pi}\sqrt{11}\times L=20\sqrt{99}$$

$$\Rightarrow \quad L=2.4\text{ H}$$

9. In general, a standing wave of n loops can be formed as shown in figure. As distance between adjacent nodes is $\frac{\lambda}{2}$.

$$\therefore \quad \frac{n\lambda}{2}=l \Rightarrow \lambda=\frac{2l}{n} \quad \text{...(i)}$$

As per de-Broglie hypothesis, wavelength of matter wave in terms of momentum p is

$$\lambda=\frac{h}{p} \Rightarrow p=\frac{h}{\lambda} \quad \text{...(ii)}$$

From Eqs. (i) and (ii), we get

$$p=\frac{nh}{2l}$$

Kinetic energy of particle,

$$\text{KE}=\frac{p^2}{2m}=\frac{n^2h^2}{8ml^2}$$

$\therefore$ For first excited state ($n=2$),

$$K_1=\frac{4h^2}{8ml^2} \quad \text{...(iii)}$$

and for second excited state ($n=3$),

$$K_2=\frac{9h^2}{8ml^2} \quad \text{...(iv)}$$

Subtracting Eq. (iii) from Eq. (iv), we get

$$K_2-K_1=\frac{5h^2}{8ml^2}$$

10. For motion in gravitational field, range is given by

$R=$ Horizontal velocity $\times$ Time of flight

$$\Rightarrow \quad R=v_1\sqrt{\frac{2h}{g}}=\frac{v_1}{g}\sqrt{2gh} \quad \text{...(i)}$$

Let v_x and v_y are velocity components of velocity just before the particle strikes ground. Using $v_y=\sqrt{u_y^2+2a_y s_y}$, we get

$$v_y=\sqrt{0^2+2gh}=\sqrt{2gh}$$

Also, as there is no acceleration in x-direction, $v_x=v_1$. Therefore, net velocity just before striking ground

$$\mathbf{v}_2=v_x\hat{\mathbf{i}}+v_y\hat{\mathbf{j}}=v_1\hat{\mathbf{i}}+\sqrt{2gh}\,\hat{\mathbf{j}}$$

$$=\mathbf{v}_1+\sqrt{2gh}\,\hat{\mathbf{j}}$$

$$\Rightarrow \mathbf{v}_2-\mathbf{v}_1=\sqrt{2gh}\,\hat{\mathbf{j}}$$

$$\Rightarrow \quad \sqrt{2gh}=|\mathbf{v}_2-\mathbf{v}_1| \quad \text{...(ii)}$$

From Eqs. (i) and (ii), we get

$$R=\frac{v_1}{g}|\mathbf{v}_2-\mathbf{v}_1| \quad \text{...(iii)}$$

Now, for motion in magnetic field, as particle strikes the ground perpendicularly, range is equal to radius given by

$$R=\frac{mv}{qB}$$

As specific charge (S) is $\frac{q}{m}$, we get

$$R=\frac{v}{SB} \Rightarrow S=\frac{v}{BR} \quad \text{...(iv)}$$

Putting expression of R from Eq. (iii) in Eq. (iv), we get

$$S = \frac{g}{B|\mathbf{v}_2 - \mathbf{v}_1|} \text{ (As, } v = v_1 = v_3)$$

11. Current due to electron is given by

$$i_e = n_e eAv_e \quad \text{...(i)}$$

Similarly, current due to holes is given by

$$i_h = n_h eAv_h \quad \text{...(ii)}$$

Also, total current is given by

$$i = i_e + i_h \quad \text{...(iii)}$$

$$\Rightarrow \frac{4i_e}{3} = i_e + i_h \quad \left(\because i = \frac{4}{3}i_e\right)$$

$$\Rightarrow i_e = 3i_h \quad \text{...(iv)}$$

Using Eqs. (i), (ii) and (iv), we get

$$n_e eAv_e = 3n_h eAv_h$$

$$\Rightarrow \frac{n_h}{n_e} = \frac{v_e}{3v_h} = \frac{11}{12} \text{ or } 11:12$$

(As $\frac{v_e}{v_h}$ is given equal to $\frac{11}{4}$)

12. Free body diagram of insect in frame of particle on which the insect is sitting is as shown. If assumed acceleration of the string particle is a, pseudo force experienced by the insect is ma upwards.

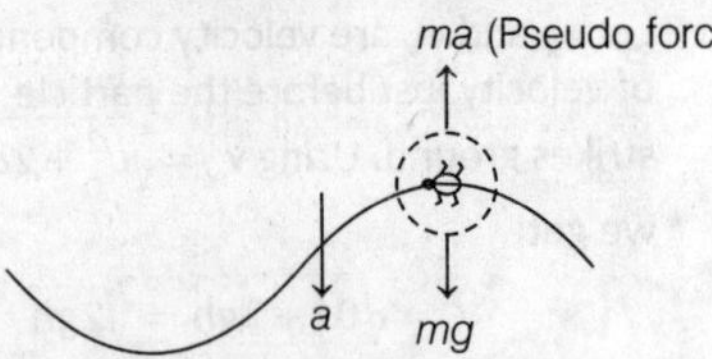

For weightlessness, $ma \geq mg \Rightarrow a \geq g$

Also, maximum particle acceleration in SHM is equal to $A\omega^2$, where ω is angular frequency of SHM, so

$$A\omega^2 \geq g \Rightarrow A \geq \frac{g}{\omega^2}$$

$$\Rightarrow A_{\min} = \frac{g}{\omega^2} \quad \text{...(i)}$$

Also, $\omega = 2\pi f = \frac{2\pi v}{\lambda}$ ...(ii)

Now, fundamental frequency of a string fixed at both ends is given by

$$f = \frac{v}{2l} \Rightarrow v = 2fl \quad \text{...(iii)}$$

From Eqs. (ii) and (iii), we get

$$\omega = \frac{4\pi fl}{\lambda} \quad \text{...(iv)}$$

For Eqs. (i) and (iv), we get

$$A_{\min} = \frac{g\lambda^2}{16\pi^2 f^2 l^2} = \left(\frac{\lambda}{4fl}\right)^2 \quad (\because g = \pi^2)$$

$$\Rightarrow \sqrt{A_{\min}} = \frac{\lambda}{4fl}$$

13. As the ring and the particle move under influence of each other's attraction, net external force on the system is zero.

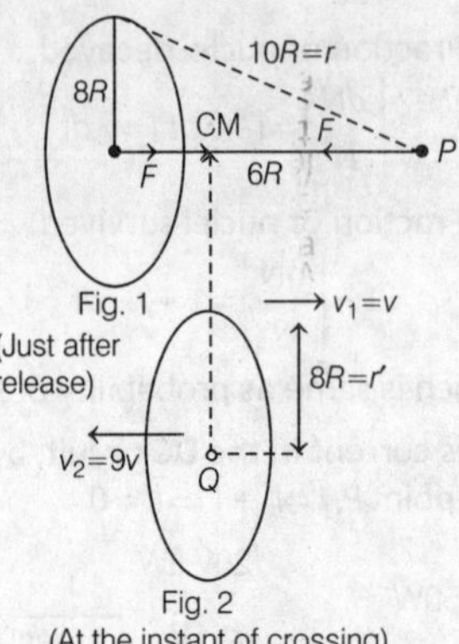

Therefore, acceleration of CM

$$a_{CM} = \frac{\mathbf{F}_{\text{net}}}{\text{Mass}} = 0$$

So, centre of mass of the system will not move. Therefore, ring and particle will cross each other at location of CM. Also by conservation of momentum,

Final momentum = Initial momentum

$$m_1 v_1 + m_2(-v_2) = 0$$

Here, v_1 and v_2 are speeds of ring and particle, respectively.

$$\Rightarrow m_1 v_1 = m_2 v_2$$

$$\Rightarrow \frac{v_2}{v_1} = \frac{m_1}{m_2} = \frac{900}{100} = 9$$

$\Rightarrow$ If v_1 is assumed equal to v, v_2 will be equal to $9v$

Initial potential energy of particle at point P is given by

$$U_{\text{initial}} = -\frac{Gm_1m_2}{r} = -\frac{Gm_1m_2}{10R} \quad \text{...(i)}$$

Final potential energy at point Q is

$$U_{\text{final}} = -\frac{Gm_1m_2}{8R} \quad \text{...(ii)}$$

By conservation of energy for system,

Gain in kinetic energy = Loss in potential energy

$$\Rightarrow \frac{1}{2} \times 900 \times v^2 + \frac{1}{2} \times 100 \times (9v)^2 = \left(-\frac{Gm_1m_2}{10R}\right) - \left(-\frac{Gm_1m_2}{8R}\right)$$

[using Eqs. (i) and (ii)]

$$\Rightarrow 4500v^2 = \frac{Gm_1m_2}{40R}$$

$$\Rightarrow 4500\, v^2 = \frac{G(900)(100)}{40R}$$

$$\Rightarrow v = \sqrt{\frac{G}{2R}}$$

14. Free body diagram of hollow cone (in frame of trolley) is as shown in fig.-1 pseudo force on the cone acts at CM of the cone which it at a height $\frac{h}{3}$.

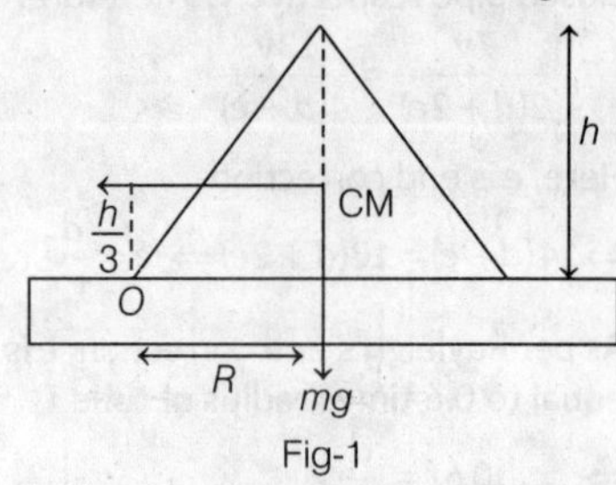

Fig-1

Torque (about O) of pseudo force

$$= ma \times \frac{h}{3} \text{ (anti-clockwise)}$$

Torque (about O) of mg

$$= mg \times R \text{ (clockwise)}$$

For toppling, torque of pseudo force must be just greater than the torque of mg.

$$\Rightarrow \frac{mah}{3} > mgR$$

$$\Rightarrow a_{\min} = \frac{3gR}{h}$$

$$\Rightarrow g\tan\theta = \frac{3gR}{2R} \quad \text{(As } h = 2R)$$

$$\Rightarrow \tan\theta = \frac{3}{2} \quad \text{... (i)}$$

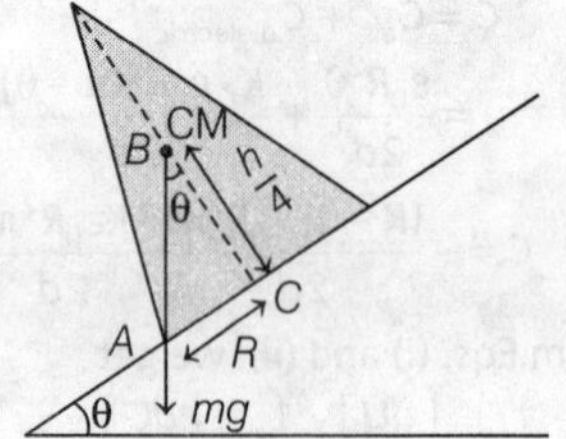

mg on solid cone acts at it CM B at a height $\frac{h}{4}$ as shown. From ΔABC,

$$\tan\theta = \frac{R}{\frac{h}{4}} = \frac{4R}{h} \quad \text{...(ii)}$$

From Eqs. (i) and (ii), we get

$$\frac{4R}{h} = \frac{3}{2}$$

$$\Rightarrow h = \frac{8R}{3} = 2.67R$$

15. Consider free body diagram of half of the cube. For equilibrium of this half, contact forces on this half due to the other half will be equal and opposite to the external forces.

That is $\mathbf{F}'_1 = F_1$ and $\mathbf{F}'_2 = F_2$

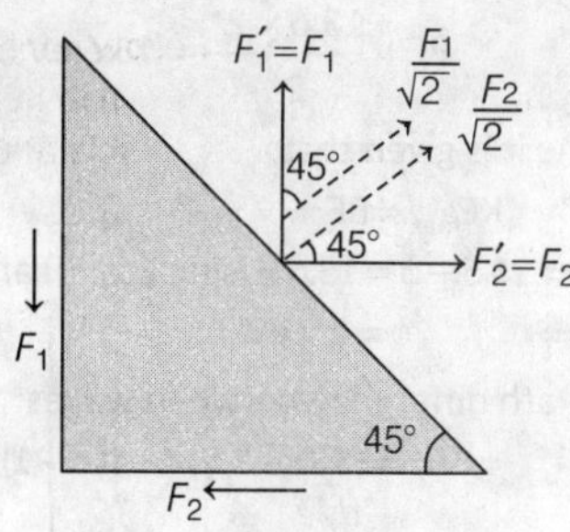

Thus, normal force on the surface is

$$F=\frac{F_1}{\sqrt{2}}+\frac{F_2}{\sqrt{2}}=\frac{F_1+F_2}{\sqrt{2}} \quad ...(i)$$

Also, as face diagonal has length $\sqrt{2}\,L$, surface area of XX' is equal to

$$A=\sqrt{2}L^2 \quad ...(ii)$$

Dividing Eq. (i) by Eq. (ii), we get

$$\text{Normal stress}=\frac{F}{A}=\frac{F_1+F_2}{2L^2}$$

As per question,

$$\frac{F}{L^2}=\frac{F_1+F_2}{2L^2} \Rightarrow F=\frac{F_1+F_2}{2}$$

16. Angle of incidence at which reflected ray is 100% polarised called Brewster angle α is related to refractive index n as

$$n=\tan\alpha$$

$$\Rightarrow \quad n=\frac{5}{3} \quad (\text{As } \alpha=\tan^{-1}\frac{5}{3})$$

Now, corresponding to minimum value of y for which ray parallel to X-axis emerges in air from OB in grazing emergence as shown. Therefore, incidence angle will be critical angle C.

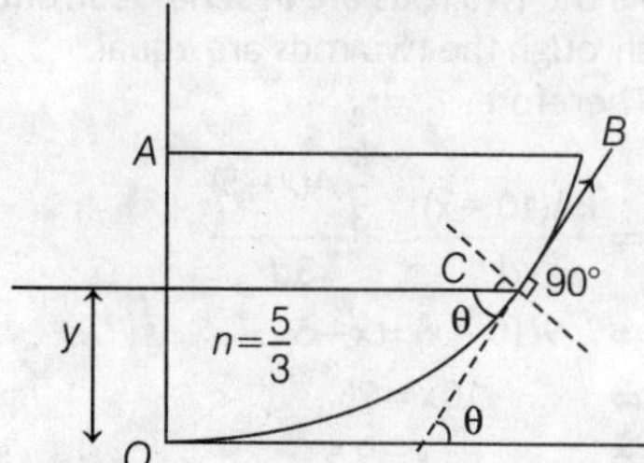

By Snell's law, $\frac{5}{3}\sin C=1\cdot\sin 90°$

$$\Rightarrow \quad \sin C=\frac{3}{5}$$

$$\Rightarrow \quad C=37°$$

$$\Rightarrow \quad \theta=90°-C=53°$$

$$\Rightarrow \quad \tan\theta=\tan 53°$$

$$\Rightarrow \quad \frac{dy}{dx}=\frac{4}{3} \quad (\text{As, slope}=\frac{dy}{dx})$$

$$\Rightarrow \quad \frac{d(x^2)}{dx}=\frac{4}{3} \quad (\because y=x^2)$$

$$\Rightarrow \quad 2x=\frac{4}{3} \Rightarrow x=\frac{2}{3}$$

$$\therefore \quad y=\frac{4}{9}$$

17. Lymann alpha emission line corresponds to de-excitation from $n=2$ to $n=1$. As wavelength emitted due to de-excitation is given by

$$\lambda=\frac{R^{-1}}{Z^2\left(\frac{1}{n_1^2}-\frac{1}{n_2^2}\right)}$$

$$\Rightarrow \lambda=\frac{912}{26^2\left(1-\frac{1}{2^2}\right)}=1.8\text{Å}\approx 2\text{Å}$$

18. Flux through the semi-circular loop at general instant

$$\phi=BA\cos\theta=B\cdot\frac{\pi r^2}{2}\cos\omega t$$

As per Faraday's law of electro-magnetic induction, induced emf is

$$\varepsilon=-\frac{d\phi}{dt}=\frac{B\pi r^2\omega}{2}\sin\omega t \quad ...(i)$$

As angular frequency ω is resonant angular frequency, so impedance of the circuit is equal to $Z=R$. From Eq. (i), electrical power consumed by the circuit,

$$P=\frac{\varepsilon^2}{R}=\left(\frac{\pi B\omega r^2}{2\sqrt{R}}\right)^2\cdot\sin^2\omega t \quad ...(ii)$$

To maintain angular speed of the rotating wire external agent should supply power equal to electrical power. So, its maximum value is

$$P_{\max}=\left(\frac{\pi B\omega r^2}{2\sqrt{R}}\right)^2 \quad [\text{from Eq. (ii)}]$$

19. Assuming potential of point P and Q equal to 0 volt and x volt respectively, potential of various points are as shown.

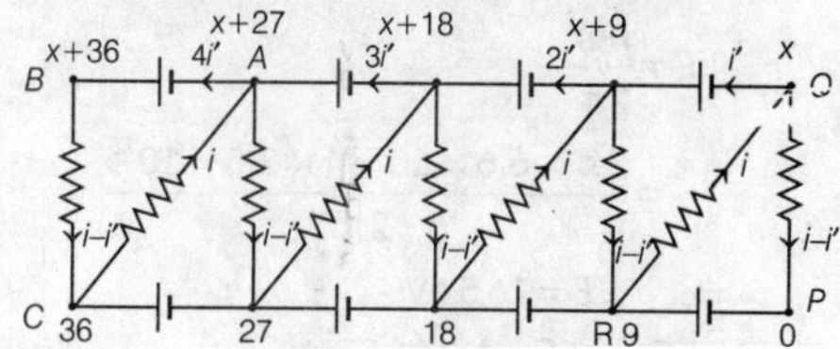

Currents in various resistors can be assumed as shown. For branch ABC, current flowing through cell is same as the current through resistor, since the two are in series

$$\Rightarrow \quad 4i'=i-i'$$

$$\Rightarrow \quad i'=\frac{i}{5} \quad ...(i)$$

Also, for resistance between Q and P, by Ohm's law, $V=IR$, we get

$$x-0=(i-i')\times 1$$

$$\Rightarrow \quad x=i-i'$$

$$\Rightarrow \quad x=\frac{4i}{5} \quad [\text{Using Eq. (i)}] \; ...(ii)$$

Similarly, for resistance between R and Q,

$$9-x=i\times 1$$

$$\Rightarrow \quad 9-x=i \quad ...(iii)$$

Dividing Eq. (iii) by Eq. (ii), we get

$$\frac{9-x}{x}=\frac{5}{4}$$

$$\Rightarrow 36-4x=5x$$

$$\Rightarrow \quad x=4\text{ V}$$

Putting $x=4$ V in Eq. (ii), we get

$$4=\frac{4i}{5}$$

$$\Rightarrow \quad i=5\text{ A}$$

$$\Rightarrow \quad i'=1\text{ A} \quad [\text{Using Eq. (i)}]$$

As current through the cell in boundary is $3i'$, it will be equal to

$$I=3i'=3\text{ A}$$

Also, emf of cell $=9$ V

$\therefore$ Power delivered by cell

$$=VI=9\times 3=27\text{ W}$$

20. Consider the critical case shown in which the ray is incident at angle just greater than critical angle at core cladding interface.

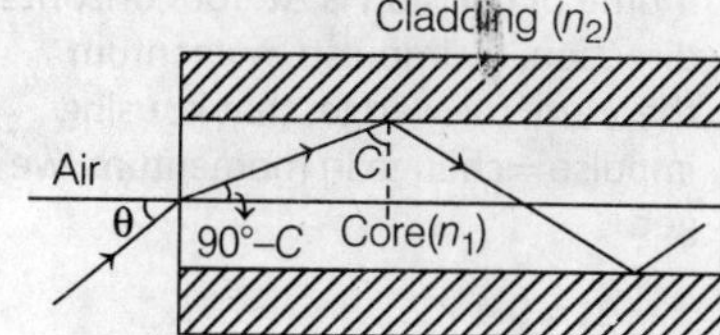

For refraction at air core interface

$$1\cdot\sin\theta=n_1\sin(90°-C)$$

$$\Rightarrow \sin\theta=n_1\cos C$$

$$=n_1\frac{\sqrt{n_1^2-n_2^2}}{n_1} \quad (\text{As }\sin C=\frac{n_2}{n_1})$$

$$\Rightarrow \quad \theta=\sin^{-1}(\sqrt{n_1^2-n_2^2})$$

If θ is increased beyond this value, incidence angle at core-cladding interface will become less than C and TIR will not take place. Also, very high frequency EM signals of range 10^8 to 10^9 MHz is typically transmitted through optical fibres. Optical fibres have advantage of not facing interference from outside and extremely low losses.

21. As the mercury air (trapped) interface moves a distance of $5L$ in the process work done against atmosphere is

$$W_1 = \text{Force} \times \text{Displacement}$$
$$= p_0 A \times 5L$$
$$\Rightarrow \quad W_1 = 5p_0 AL \quad \text{...(i)}$$

Also, work done against gravity is equal to increase in potential energy of the liquid,

$$W_2 = 7\rho A L^2 g \quad \text{...(ii)}$$

Also, pressure in horizontal part is equal to

$$2p_0 = p_0 + \rho g L$$
$$\Rightarrow \quad p_0 = \rho g L \quad \text{...(iii)}$$

From Eqs. (ii) and (iii), we get

$$W_2 = 7p_0 AL \quad \text{...(iv)}$$

From Eqs. (i) and (iv), total work done is

$$W = W_1 + W_2 = 12p_0 AL$$
$$\therefore \quad x = 12$$

22. Normal impulsive force between the ball and the wedge acts as shown, during collision

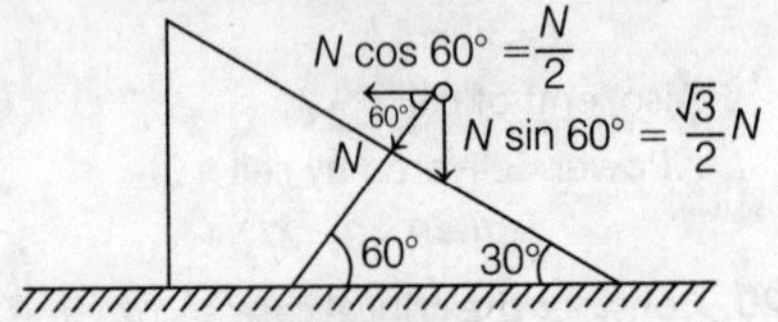

Horizontal component of the normal force $= N\cos 60° = \frac{N}{2}$

If time of collision is Δt, for horizontal direction, by impulse momentum theorem, for wedge, that is, using impulse = change in momentum, we get

$$\frac{N}{2}\Delta t = 0.4 \times 2$$

$\therefore$ Impulse of normal force

$$= N\Delta t = 1.6 \text{ N-s}$$

23. For screw gauge, number of circular scale divisions is given by

$$N = \frac{\text{Main scale division}}{\text{Least count}} = \frac{\text{MSD}}{\text{LC}}$$

To measure 10 μm diameter, least count should be 10 μm or lesser. Also, main scale division is given to be 0.5 mm. Therefore, minimum value of N is

$$N_{\text{minimum}} = \frac{0.5 \times 10^{-3}}{10 \times 10^{-6}} = 50$$

24. Inward current of 2 A can be assumed as superposition of inward 3 A and outward 1 A current as shown in Fig. 1 and Fig. 2

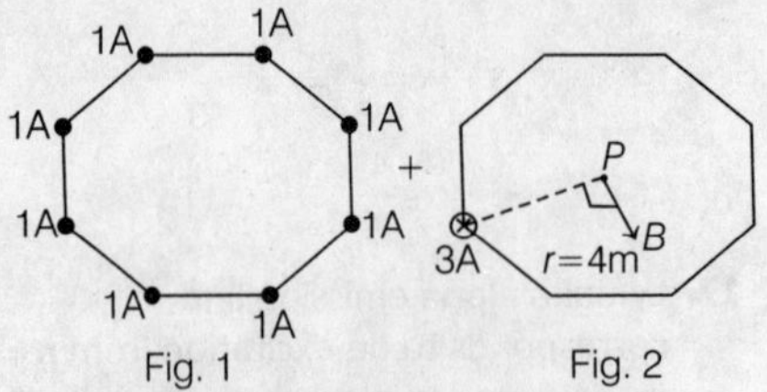

Fig. 1 Fig. 2

Net magnetic field due to currents in Fig. 1, by symmetry, is zero.

Magnetic field due to $I = 3\text{A}$ wire is directed as shown (by Right hand rule) in Fig. 2

Magnetic field at point P will be

$$B = \frac{\mu_0 I}{2\pi r} = \frac{2 \times 10^{-7} \times 3}{4}$$
$$= 1.5 \times 10^{-7} \text{ T}$$
$$\therefore \quad x = 1.5$$

25. The circuit can be drawn as

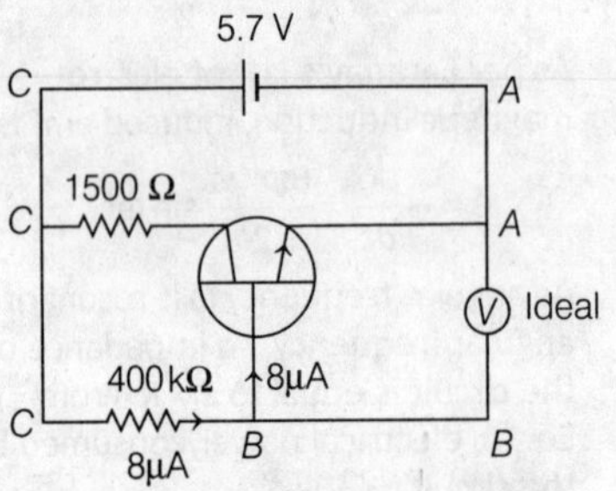

$$V_{BA} = V_B - V_A = (V_B - V_C) + (V_C - V_A)$$
$$= (-8 \times 10^{-6})(4 \times 10^5) + 5.7 = 2.5 \text{ V}$$

26. Electric field is given to be

$$E = E_0(1 + \cos\omega_1 t)\cos\omega_2 t$$
$$= E_0[\cos\omega_2 t + \cos\omega_1 t \cos\omega_2 t]$$
$$= E_0\left[2\cos\omega_2 t + \frac{\cos(\omega_1 - \omega_2)t + \cos(\omega_1 + \omega_2)t]}{2}\right.$$

Clearly, maximum angular frequency,

$$\omega = \omega_1 + \omega_2$$
$$= 5 \times 10^{15} + 2 \times 10^{16} = 2.5 \times 10^{16} \text{ s}^{-1}$$

Energy of photon,

$$E = \frac{h\omega}{2\pi}$$
$$= \frac{2\pi \times 6.6 \times 10^{-16} \times 2.5 \times 10^{16}}{2\pi}$$
$$\Rightarrow \quad E = 16.5 \text{ eV}$$
$$\therefore \text{KE}_{\text{max}} = E - \phi = 16.5 - \phi \quad \text{...(i)}$$

Also, binding energy of hydrogen like atom in nth state is

$$\text{BE} = \frac{13.6 Z^2}{n^2} \text{ (in eV)}$$

So, for $He^+ (Z = 2)$ in first excited state $(n = 2)$, binding energy is

$$\text{BE} = \frac{13.6 \times 2^2}{2^2} = 13.6 \text{ eV} \quad \text{...(ii)}$$

As it is given that,

$$\text{KE}_{\text{max}} = \text{BE}$$
$$\Rightarrow 16.5 - \phi = 13.6 \text{ [Using Eqs. (i) and (ii)]}$$
$$\Rightarrow \quad \phi = 2.9 \text{ eV}$$

27. Path difference between waves

$$\Delta x = (S_2P - S_1P)n + t(n-1)$$
$$= \frac{dy}{D} \cdot n + t(n-1)$$

As for point P, $y = \frac{d}{2}$

$$\Rightarrow \quad \Delta x = \frac{d^2 n}{2D} + t(n-1)$$

As for maxima, Δx is integral multiple of λ, therefore

$$N\lambda = \frac{d^2 n}{2D} + t(n-1)$$
$$\Rightarrow \quad \lambda_{\text{max}} = \frac{d^2 n}{2D} + t(n-1)$$
$$= \frac{(2 \times 10^{-3})^2 \times 1.4}{2 \times 10} + 0.2 \times 10^{-6}(1.4 - 1)$$
$$= 2.8 \times 10^{-7} + 0.8 \times 10^{-7}$$
$$= 3.6 \times 10^{-7} \text{ m}$$
$$\therefore \quad x = 3.6$$

28. Let temperature of the interface is x °C

10°C → x°C → 5°C (l_1, l_2)

As the two rods are in series, currents through the two rods are equal.

Therefore, $I_1 = I_2$

$$\Rightarrow \frac{kA(10 - x)}{d} = \frac{\frac{k}{3}A(x - 5)}{3d}$$
$$\Rightarrow \quad 9(10 - x) = x - 5$$
$$\Rightarrow \quad 10x = 95$$
$$\Rightarrow \quad x = 9.5$$

29. For complete cycle,

$$Q_{\text{cycle}} = W_{\text{cycle}} = 400 + 100 + Q_{C \to A}$$
$$= \frac{1}{2}(2 \times 10^{-3})(4 \times 10^4)$$
$$\Rightarrow Q_{C \to A} = -460 \text{ J}$$
$$\Rightarrow Q_{A \to C} = +460 \text{ J}$$

So, x will be 46.

30. Moment of inertia of two particles system about axis through CM,

$$I = \mu l^2 = \frac{m_1 m_2}{m_1 + m_2} l^2 = 2ml^2 \quad \text{...(i)}$$

As per Bohr's quantisation rule,

$$L = \frac{nh}{2\pi}$$

$$\Rightarrow \quad I\omega = \frac{nh}{2\pi}$$

$$\Rightarrow \quad \omega = \frac{nh}{4\pi ml^2} \quad \text{[using Eq. (i)]}$$

For 2nd excited state, $n = 3$, so we get

$$\omega = \frac{3h}{4\pi ml^2}$$

$$\therefore \quad x = \frac{4}{3} = 1.33$$

Knockout 08

1. When the insect sticks itself to the ring, centre of mass of the system will be as shown in Fig. 1. CM will exactly be mid-way between point A (where insect sticks to ring) and centre O of the ring. Let velocity of CM and angular velocity about CM be v' and ω respectively as shown in Fig. 2.

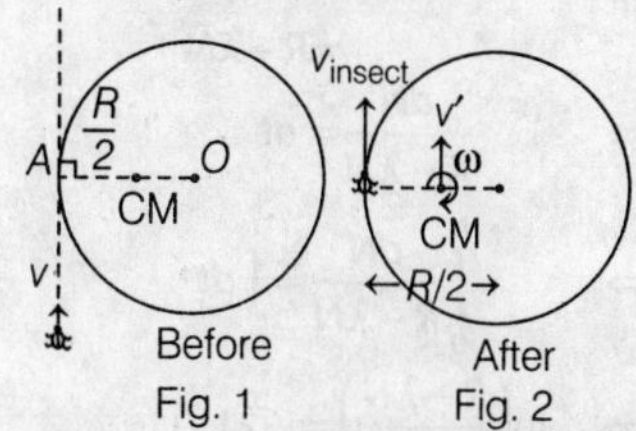

Fig. 1 Fig. 2

As there is no external torque, angular momentum of the system will be conserved about CM of the system.

Therefore, $L_{after} = L_{before}$

$$I_{CM}\,\omega = mv\frac{R}{2}$$

$$\Rightarrow (I_{ring} + I_{insect})\,\omega = mv\frac{R}{2}$$

$$\Rightarrow \left\{mR^2 + m\left(\frac{R}{2}\right)^2 + m\left(\frac{R}{2}\right)^2\right\}\omega = \frac{mvR}{2}$$

$$\Rightarrow \quad \frac{3}{2}mR^2\omega = \frac{mvR}{2}$$

$$\Rightarrow \quad \omega = \frac{v}{3R} \quad \text{...(i)}$$

Also by conservation of linear momentum, as there is no external force, we get,

$$p_{after} = p_{before}$$

$$\Rightarrow \quad 2mv' = mv$$

$$\Rightarrow \quad v' = \frac{v}{2} \quad \text{...(ii)}$$

Now, velocity of insect due to translation is same as that of CM equal to v', as shown. Also, velocity due to rotation is $\frac{\omega R}{2}$. So

$$v_{insect} = v' + \frac{\omega R}{2} = \frac{v}{2} + \left(\frac{v}{3R}\right)\frac{R}{2} = \frac{2v}{3}$$

[using Eqs. (i) and (ii)]

2. The given δ-i graph becomes discontinuous when angle of incidence increases just beyond critical angle. Thus, the given deviation of 45° in the graph corresponds to critical angle of incidence C as shown in the Fig. 1 for which grazing emergence takes place.

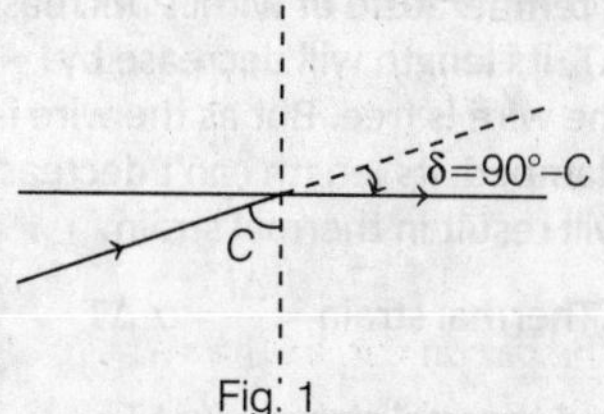

Fig. 1

From the figure, deviation is

$$\delta = 90° - C$$

$$\Rightarrow \quad 45° = 90° - C \Rightarrow C = 45°$$

So, by Snell's law for the refraction shown in the figure,

$$\mu \cdot \sin 45° = 1 \cdot \sin 90°$$

$$\Rightarrow \quad \mu = \sqrt{2}$$

Now, for maximum deviation, the angles of incidences should be near to 90°. So, for refraction at surface PQ, by Snell's law,

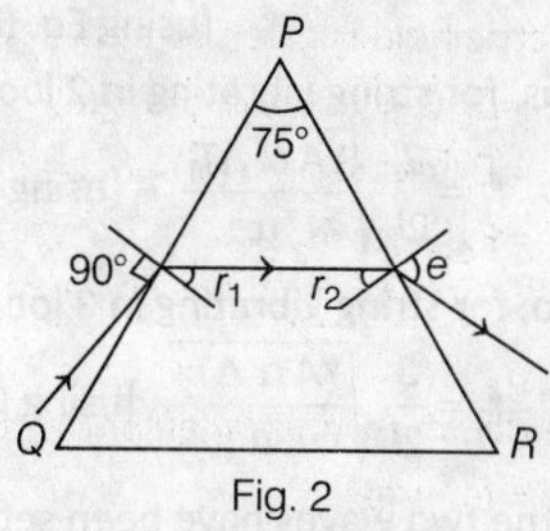

Fig. 2

$$1 \cdot \sin 90° = \sqrt{2} \cdot \sin r_1$$

$$\Rightarrow \quad r_1 = 45°$$

As $\quad r_1 + r_2 = A$

$$\Rightarrow \quad 45° + r_2 = 75°$$

$$\Rightarrow \quad r_2 = 30°$$

So, by Snell's law for refraction at surface PR

$$\sqrt{2} \cdot \sin 30° = 1 \cdot \sin e$$

$$\Rightarrow \quad \sin e = \frac{1}{\sqrt{2}} \Rightarrow e = 45°$$

As deviation is given by the formula

$$\delta = i + e - A$$

So, the maximum deviation will be

$$\delta = 90° + 45° - 75° = 60°$$

3. Tension in a ring of linear mass density μ and radius R rotating with angular speed ω is given by,

$$T = \mu\omega^2R^2 \quad \text{...(i)}$$

By Hooke's law, extension in a wire having tension T, cross-sectional area A, length l and Young's modulus Y is given by,

$$\Delta l = \frac{Tl}{AY} \quad \text{...(ii)}$$

As for ring, length is given by

$$l = 2\pi R$$

$\therefore$ Increase in length $= \Delta l = 2\pi\Delta R$

Therefore, Eq. (ii) reduces to

$$2\pi\Delta R = \frac{\mu\omega^2R^2 \cdot 2\pi R}{AY} \quad \text{[using Eq. (i)]}$$

$$\Delta R = \frac{\mu\omega^2R^3}{AY}$$

$\therefore$ Fractional change

$$= \frac{\Delta R}{R} = \frac{\mu\omega^2R^2}{AY} \propto R^2$$

4. If the two pieces having lengths in ratio 1:2 have lengths l_1 and l_2 respectively,

$$\frac{l_1}{l_2} = \frac{1}{2} \quad \text{...(i)}$$

Also, $\quad l_1 + l_2 = l \quad$ ...(ii)

From Eqs. (i) and (ii), we get

$$l_1 = \frac{l}{3} \text{ and } l_2 = \frac{2l}{3}$$

As spring constant is inversely proportional to length, spring-1 having length $\frac{l}{3}$ will have spring constant 3 times the original i.e. $3k$. Similarly the longer piece has spring constant $\frac{3k}{2}$.

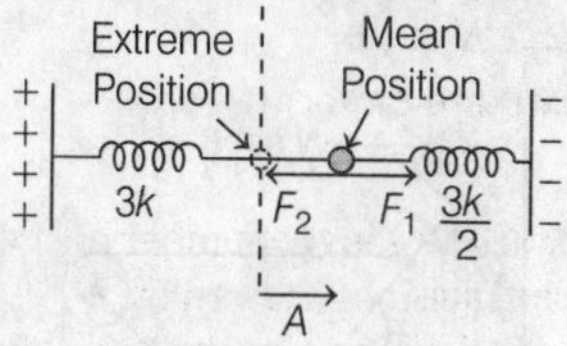

On leaving the particle in extreme or rest position, it experiences electric force due to electric field between sheets, equal to

$$F_1 = q(E_1 + E_2)$$

Here, E_1 and E_2 are fields due to Sheet-1 and Sheet-2

$$\Rightarrow \quad F_1 = q\left(\frac{\sigma}{2\varepsilon_0} + \frac{3\sigma}{2\varepsilon_0}\right) = \frac{2q\sigma}{\varepsilon_0}$$

At certain position to the right of this position, say at a distance A, electric force is balanced by spring force. This position is equilibrium or mean position. Spring force in this position,

$$F_2 = 3kA + \frac{3k}{2}A = \frac{9kA}{2}$$

For equilibrium, $F_1 = F_2$

$$\Rightarrow \quad \frac{2q\sigma}{\varepsilon_0} = \frac{9kA}{2} \Rightarrow A = \frac{4q\sigma}{9\varepsilon_0 k} \quad \text{...(iii)}$$

A is separation between extreme and mean positions and therefore will be amplitude of resulting SHM. As at any general position, spring force is given by

$$F = 3kx + \frac{3kx}{2} = \frac{9kx}{2}$$

Force constant of SHM $= C = \frac{9k}{2}$

Now, angular frequency of SHM is given by

$$\Rightarrow \quad \omega = \sqrt{\frac{C}{m}} = \sqrt{\frac{9k}{2m}} \quad \text{...(iv)}$$

As maximum speed in SHM is given by

$$v = A\omega$$

$$\Rightarrow \quad v = \frac{4q\sigma}{9\varepsilon_0 k}\sqrt{\frac{9k}{2m}} = \frac{2\sqrt{2}}{3}\frac{q\sigma}{\varepsilon_0\sqrt{km}}$$

5. As tangential component of weight (F_T) and speed are maximum at point just before striking the ground, power delivered $= F_T v$ is also maximum. So, Statement-1 is true.
As angle between velocity and weight is continuously changing, tangential acceleration is variable. So, Statement-2 is false.

6. As there is no slipping between B and C, all the bodies will have same magnitude of acceleration (say a). FBD of the bodies will be as shown in the figures.

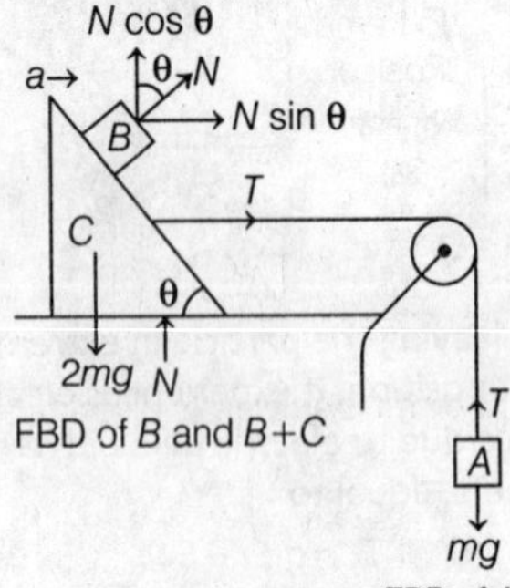

FBD of B and $B+C$

FBD of A

From FBD of A, using $F_{Net} = ma$, we get

$$mg - T = ma \quad \text{...(i)}$$

From FBD of $B + C$, we get

$$T = 2ma \quad \text{...(ii)}$$

From Eqs. (i) and (ii), we get

$$\Rightarrow \quad a = \frac{g}{3} \quad \text{...(iii)}$$

From FBD of B, in horizontal direction

$$N\sin\theta = ma \quad \text{....(iv)}$$

and in vertical direction,

$$N\cos\theta = mg \quad \text{...(v)}$$

Dividing Eq. (iv) by Eq. (v), we get

$$\tan\theta = \frac{a}{g} = \frac{\frac{g}{3}}{g} \quad \text{[using Eq. (i)]}$$

$$\Rightarrow \quad \theta = \cot^{-1} 3$$

7. If temperature of wire is decreased by ΔT, its length will decrease by $l \propto \Delta T$, if the wire is free. But as the wire is clamped, its length can't decrease and will result in thermal strain.

$$\therefore \text{Thermal strain} = \frac{\Delta l}{l} = \alpha\,\Delta T$$

and thermal stress $= Y\alpha\Delta T$

here, Y is Young's modulus. Now, as stress is tension per unit area, therefore, we get

$$\Rightarrow \quad \frac{T}{A} = Y\alpha\Delta T$$

$$\therefore \text{Tension, } T = YA\,\alpha\,\Delta T \quad \text{...(i)}$$

For string of linear mass density μ vibrating in n loops, frequency of vibration is given by

$$f = \frac{n}{2l}\sqrt{\frac{T}{\mu}} = \frac{n}{2l}\sqrt{\frac{YA\,\alpha\,\Delta T}{\mu}}$$

[using Eq. (i)] ...(ii)

Thus, for string vibrating in 2 loops

$$f_1 = \frac{2}{2l}\sqrt{\frac{YA\,\alpha\,\Delta T_1}{\mu}} \quad \text{[using Eq. (ii)]}$$

Also, for string vibrating in 3 loops,

$$f_2 = \frac{3}{2l}\sqrt{\frac{YA\,\alpha\,\Delta T_2}{\mu}} \quad \text{[using Eq. (iii)]}$$

As the two waves have been set up using some source, frequencies of the two waves are same.

$$\therefore \quad f_1 = f_2$$

$$\Rightarrow \frac{2}{2l}\sqrt{\frac{YA\,\alpha\Delta T_1}{\mu}} = \frac{3}{2l}\sqrt{\frac{YA\,\alpha\,\Delta T_2}{\mu}}$$

$$\Rightarrow \quad \frac{\Delta T_1}{\Delta T_2} = \frac{9}{4}$$

8. By careful observation following relations can be co-related to conclude that option (c) is dimensionless.

$$[\text{Energy}]_{(\text{Magnetic})} = \left[\frac{1}{2}Li^2\right] = [Li^2]$$

$$\left[\frac{\text{Energy}}{\text{Volume}}\right]_{(\text{Electrical})} = \left[\frac{1}{2}\varepsilon_0 E^2\right] = [\varepsilon_0 E^2]$$

$$= \left[\frac{\text{Energy}}{H^3}\right]$$

$$\left[\frac{\text{Energy}}{\text{Volume}}\right]_{(\text{Magnetic})} = \left[\frac{B^2}{2\mu_0}\right]$$

$$= \left[\frac{B^2}{\mu_0}\right] = \left[\frac{\text{Energy}}{H^3}\right]$$

$$[c^2] = \left[\frac{1}{\mu_0\varepsilon_0}\right]$$

$$[\text{Resistance}] = \left[\frac{\rho l}{A}\right] = \left[\frac{\rho}{H}\right] = \sqrt{\frac{\mu_0}{\varepsilon_0}}$$

$$\Rightarrow \quad [\rho] = \left[H\sqrt{\frac{\mu_0}{\varepsilon_0}}\right]$$

9. For the sample having N_0 nuclei and decaying, number of nuclei as function of time t will be

$$N_1 = N_0 e^{-\lambda t} \quad \text{...(i)}$$

The sample being produced in lab, rate of change of number of nuclei will be

$$\frac{dN}{dt} = \text{Rate of production} + \text{Rate of decay}$$

$$= R - \lambda N$$

$$\Rightarrow \quad \frac{dN}{R - \lambda N} = dt$$

$$\Rightarrow \quad \int_0^N \frac{dN}{R - \lambda N} = \int_0^t dt$$

$$\Rightarrow \quad \ln\left(\frac{R - \lambda N}{R}\right) = -\lambda t$$

$$\Rightarrow \quad N = \frac{R}{\lambda}(1 - e^{-\lambda t}) = N_2 \text{ (say)} \quad \text{...(ii)}$$

According to the given graph, at $t = 2T$

$$N_1 = N_2$$

$$\Rightarrow N_0 e^{-\lambda(2T)} = \frac{R}{\lambda}(1 - e^{-\lambda \cdot 2T})$$

[using Eqs. (i) and (ii)]

$$\Rightarrow N_0 e^{-2\lambda \cdot \frac{\ln 2}{\lambda}} = \frac{R}{\lambda}\left(1 - e^{-2\lambda \cdot \frac{\ln 2}{\lambda}}\right)$$

$$\left(\text{As } T = \frac{\ln 2}{\lambda}\right)$$

$$\Rightarrow \quad \frac{N_0}{4} = \frac{R}{\lambda}\left(1 - \frac{1}{4}\right)$$

$$\Rightarrow \quad R = \frac{\lambda N_0}{3} = \frac{\ln 2 N_0}{3T} = \frac{\ln 2^{\frac{1}{3}} N_0}{T}$$

10. Initial equivalent capacitance is

$$C_{eq} = \frac{C_1 C_2}{C_1 + C_2} = \frac{C \times C}{C + C} = \frac{C}{2}$$

Therefore, charge stored by system

$$Q = C_{eq}E = \frac{CE}{2} \quad \text{...(i)}$$

Now, capacitance of parallel plate capacitor is

$$C = \frac{\varepsilon_0 A}{d} \Rightarrow C \propto \frac{1}{d}$$

$\Rightarrow$ As separation between plates is doubled, capacitor will become half. Therefore, we get

$$C'_1 = \frac{C}{2}$$

Also, capacitance of a dielectric capacitor is given by

$$C = \frac{k\varepsilon_0 A}{d} \Rightarrow C \propto k$$

Therefore, we get $C'_2 = 2C$

So, final equivalent capacitance of the system is

$$C'_{eq} = \frac{C'_1 C'_2}{C'_1 + C'_2} = \frac{\left(\frac{C}{2}\right)(2C)}{\frac{C}{2} + 2C} = \frac{2C}{5}$$

Therefore, charge stored by the system is

$$Q' = C'_{eq} E = \frac{2CE}{5} \quad \text{...(ii)}$$

Charge flown through the cell,

$$q = Q' - Q = \frac{2CE}{5} - \frac{CE}{2} = -\frac{CE}{10}$$

[using Eqs. (i) and (ii)]

$\therefore$ Work done by cell $= |q|E = \frac{CE^2}{10}$

11. Thermal power dissipated in the wire

$$P_1 = i^2 R = i^2 \frac{l}{\sigma A} = \frac{i^2 l}{\sigma A} \quad \text{...(i)}$$

Power radiated by the wire can be found using Stefan's law equal to

$$P_2 = ec \cdot 2\pi rl \cdot (T^4 - T_0^4) \quad \text{...(ii)}$$

Here e is emissivity, c is Stefan's constant, r is radius, T is temperature of wire and T_0 is temperature of surroundings. As in steady state, thermal power is equal to power radiated, we get

$$P_1 = P_2 \Rightarrow \frac{i^2 l}{\sigma A} = ec \cdot 2\pi rl(T^4 - T_0^4)$$

As l will cancel from both LHS and RHS equilibrium temperature is independent of l.

12. Heat supplied to gas in isothermal process is given by

$$Q = nRT \ln \frac{V_{\text{final}}}{V_{\text{initial}}}$$

So, for increase in volume from V_0 to V

$$Q_1 = nRT \ln \frac{V}{V_0} \quad \text{...(i)}$$

While for increase in volume from V_0 to $2V_0$

$$Q_2 = nRT \ln \frac{2V_0}{V_0}$$

$$\Rightarrow \quad 2Q_1 = nRT \ln 2 \quad \text{...(ii)}$$

Dividing Eq. (i) by Eq. (ii), we get

$$\frac{1}{2} = \frac{\ln \frac{V}{V_0}}{\ln 2} \Rightarrow \ln \frac{V}{V_0} = \ln \sqrt{2}$$

$$\Rightarrow \quad V = \sqrt{2} V_0 = 1.414\, V_0$$

So, V is closest to $1.4\, V_0$.

13. Viscous force on a solid in contact with liquid is given by

$$f = \eta A \frac{dv}{dy} \text{ or } \eta A \frac{\Delta v}{\Delta y} \quad \text{...(i)}$$

So, if we consider a ring element of radius r and thickness dr as shown in the figure, for a disc particle (as A) velocity is ωr while particle of fixed surface (as B) is at rest.

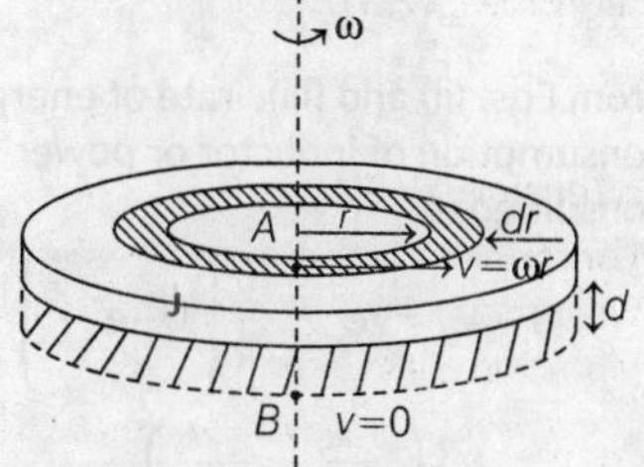

So, $\quad \Delta v = \omega r - 0 = \omega r \quad$ ...(ii)

Also, difference in height of A and B

$$\Delta y = d \quad \text{...(iii)}$$

And surface area of ring element

$$dA = 2\pi r dr \quad \text{...(iv)}$$

Using Eqs. (i), (ii), (iii) and (iv),

$$\text{Torque on element} = fr = \eta A \frac{\Delta v}{\Delta y} r$$

$$= \eta \cdot 2\pi r dr \cdot \frac{\omega r}{d} \cdot r$$

$$\Rightarrow \text{Torque on disc} = \int_0^R \eta \cdot 2\pi r\, dr \cdot \frac{\omega r}{d} \cdot r$$

$$= \frac{2\pi\eta\omega}{d} \int_0^R r^3 dr$$

$$= \frac{\pi\eta\omega R^4}{2d}$$

14. Range in terms of radius of earth r, height of transmitter tower H_T and height of receiver tower H_R is given by

$$R = \sqrt{2rH_T} + \sqrt{2rH_R}$$

As for the two cases R is same

$$\Rightarrow \sqrt{2rH} + \sqrt{2rH} = \sqrt{2 \cdot r \cdot \frac{H}{4}} + \sqrt{2rH_R}$$

$$\Rightarrow \left(2\sqrt{2} - \frac{1}{\sqrt{2}}\right)\sqrt{rH} = \sqrt{2rH_R}$$

$$\Rightarrow \quad \frac{3}{\sqrt{2}}\sqrt{rH} = \sqrt{2rH_R}$$

$$\Rightarrow \quad H_R = \frac{9}{4} H = 2.25\, H$$

15. As the Particle-1 has to travel double the distance, so its speed and thereby momentum will be double that of Particle-2. So, lets assume momentum of the Particle-1 and Particle-2 equal to $2p$ and p respectively.

As de-Broglie wavelength of Particle-2,

$$\lambda = \frac{h}{p} \quad \text{...(i)}$$

For Particle-1, as momentum is $2p$ de-Broglie wavelength is $\lambda' = \frac{h}{2p}$ ...(ii)

Clearly, $\lambda > \lambda'$, so higher of the two wavelengths is λ given by Eq. (i). The two particles collide at vertex Q as shown in the figure.

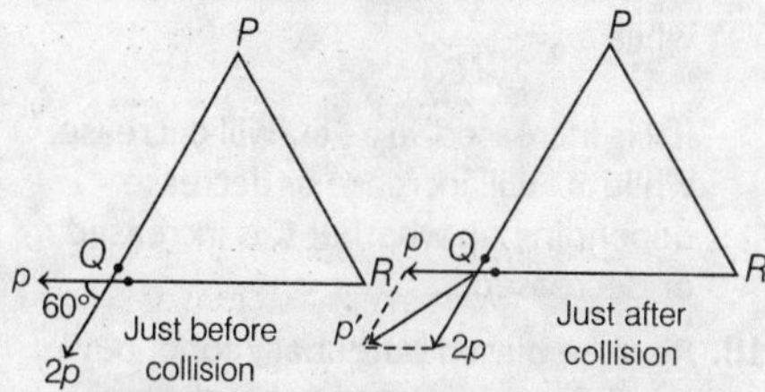

Momentum of the composite mass formed on collision will be, vector resultant of momenta of the two particles. Therefore,

$$p' = \sqrt{p^2 + (2p)^2 + 2 \cdot p \cdot 2p \cdot \cos 60°}$$

$$= \sqrt{7}p$$

$\therefore$ de-Broglie wavelength of composite body

$$\lambda'' = \frac{h}{p'} = \frac{h}{\sqrt{7}p} = \frac{\lambda}{\sqrt{7}} \quad \text{[using Eq. (i)]}$$

16.

Apparent frequency is given by

$$f' = f\left(\frac{v - v_0}{v - v_s}\right)$$

For A Frequency received directly from source

$$f_1 = 300\left(\frac{350 - 0}{350 - 50}\right) = 350 \text{ Hz}$$

As reflected sound can be considered to be coming from image of source, frequency received after reflection from wall

$$f_2=300\left(\frac{350-0}{350-50}\right)=350\text{ Hz}$$

$\Rightarrow$ Beat frequency $=f_1-f_2=0$ Hz

For B f_1(direct) $=300\left(\frac{350-5}{350-50}\right)=345$ Hz

f_2(reflected) $=300\left(\frac{350+5}{350-50}\right)=355$ Hz

$\Rightarrow$ Beat frequency $=f_2-f_1=10$ Hz

For C f_2(reflected) $=300\left(\frac{350-(-50)}{350-50}\right)$

$$=400\text{ Hz}$$

and $v_{relative}=350-(-50)=400$ m/s

$$\Rightarrow \quad \lambda=\frac{v_{rel}}{f_2}=\frac{400}{400}=1\text{ m}$$

Speed of sound emitted w.r.t. ground is same as that w.r.t. air equal to 350 m/s.

17. $\omega_2-\omega_1=$ band width $=\frac{R}{L}$

while $\omega_0=\frac{1}{\sqrt{LC}}$

If R is increased, $\omega_2-\omega_1$ will decrease, while ω_0 will increase or decrease depending on whether C is increased or decreased.

18. Reverse biased potential V for breakdown is related to breakdown field E and thickness of depletion layer by the relation $V=Ed$

$$\Rightarrow \quad V=1.2\times10^6\times2\times10^{-6}=2.4\text{ V}$$

19. As C has acceleration $\frac{F}{m}$, it must be CM of the body. If height of cone is assumed h, CM of the cone will be of height $\frac{h}{4}$. Also CM of sphere is at a distance $\frac{3r}{8}$ from centre of sphere.

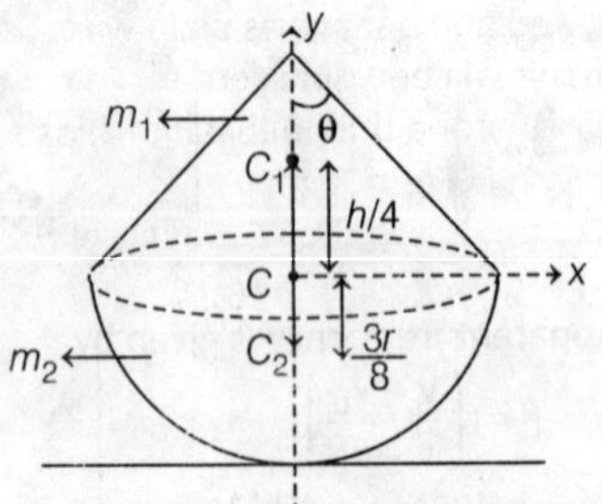

As coordinate of CM of composite body is given by $y=\frac{m_1y_1+m_2y_2}{m_1+m_2}$

$$\Rightarrow \quad 0=\rho\cdot\frac{1}{3}\pi r^2h\cdot\frac{h}{4}-\rho\cdot\frac{2}{3}\pi r^3\cdot\frac{3r}{8}$$

(here ρ is density)

$$\Rightarrow \quad h=\sqrt{3}r \quad \Rightarrow \tan\theta=\frac{r}{h}=\frac{1}{\sqrt{3}}$$

$$\Rightarrow \quad \theta=30^\circ$$

20. Intensity of nth maxima is given by

$$I=\left(\frac{2}{(2n+1)\pi}\right)^2 I_0$$

For $n=2$, $I=\left(\frac{2}{5\pi}\right)^2 I_0\approx\frac{I_0}{61}$

21. Effective length of the wire PQS is $l=4r$

So motional emf induced in it will be

$$V=Bvl=4Bvr \quad \text{...(i)}$$

As current flowing in an L-R growth circuit is given by

$$I=\frac{V}{R}\left(1-e^{-\frac{Rt}{L}}\right) \quad \text{...(ii)}$$

Potential difference across inductor

$$V_L=L\frac{dI}{dt}=L\cdot\frac{V}{R}\cdot\frac{R}{L}\cdot e^{-\frac{Rt}{L}}$$

$$=Ve^{-\frac{Rt}{L}} \quad \text{...(iii)}$$

From Eqs. (ii) and (iii), rate of energy consumption of inductor or power consumed is

$$P=V_LI=Ve^{-\frac{Rt}{L}}\cdot\frac{V}{R}\left(1-e^{-\frac{Rt}{L}}\right)$$

$$\Rightarrow \quad P=\frac{V^2}{R}\left(e^{-\frac{Rt}{L}}-e^{-\frac{2Rt}{L}}\right) \quad \text{...(iv)}$$

For P to be maximum, $\frac{dP}{dt}=0$

$$\Rightarrow \left(-\frac{R}{L}\right)e^{-\frac{Rt}{L}}-\left(-\frac{2R}{L}\right)e^{-\frac{2Rt}{L}}=0$$

$$\Rightarrow \quad e^{\frac{Rt}{L}}=2 \Rightarrow t=\frac{L}{R}\ln 2=0.693\frac{L}{R} \quad \text{...(v)}$$

$$\Rightarrow \quad a=0.69 \quad \text{...(vi)}$$

Also, the maximum power consumed will be

$$P=\frac{V^2}{R}(e^{-\ln 2}-e^{-2\ln 2})$$

[using Eqs. (iv) and (v)]

$$\Rightarrow \quad P=\frac{V^2}{4R}=\frac{16(Bvr)^2}{4R}=\frac{4(Bvr)^2}{R}$$

[using Eq. (i)]

$$\Rightarrow \quad b=4 \quad \text{...(vii)}$$

From Eqs. (vi) and (vii), $a+b=4.69$

22. Let M be the mass of each star and radius of orbit is R.

From FBD of Star-2 shown in the figure, if F and F' are forces on it due to Star-3 and Star-1 respectively.

Star-1 ---- Star-3 ---- Star-2, F, F', $M\omega^2R$; distances R, $2R$

$$F+F'=M\omega^2R$$

$$\Rightarrow \frac{GM\cdot M}{R^2}+\frac{GM\cdot M}{(2R)^2}=M\omega^2R$$

(using Newton's law of gravitation)

$$\Rightarrow \omega=\sqrt{\frac{5}{4}\frac{GM}{R^3}}$$

$$\text{Time period}=\frac{2\pi}{\omega}=2\pi\sqrt{\frac{R^3}{GM}}\times\sqrt{\frac{4}{5}}=T\sqrt{\frac{4}{5}}$$

(As $2\pi\sqrt{\frac{R^3}{GM}}$ represents time period of earth around sun)

$$=\frac{2T}{\sqrt{5}}=\frac{2T}{\sqrt{x}} \text{ (given)}$$

$$\therefore \quad x=5$$

23. Velocity of Q due to translation $=v$

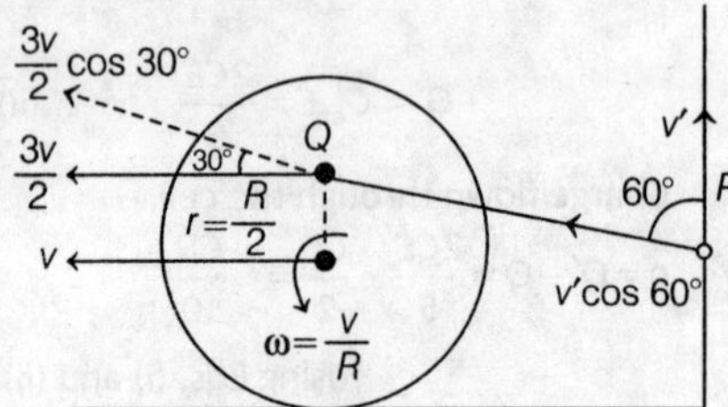

Velocity of Q due to rotation

$$=\omega r=\frac{v}{2}$$

So, net velocity of $Q=\frac{3v}{2}$

If velocity of ring is v', equating velocity components of P and Q along the rod, as it is rigid, we get

$$v'\cos 60^\circ=\frac{3v}{2}\cos 30^\circ$$

$$\Rightarrow \quad v'=\frac{3\sqrt{3}v}{2}=\frac{3\sqrt{3}\times\sqrt{3}}{2}=4.5\text{ m/s}$$

24. When bubbles combine isothermally in vacuum, surface area and energy are conserved.

$$\Rightarrow \quad A_{film}=A_{bubble\text{-}1}+A_{bubble\text{-}2}$$

$$\Rightarrow \quad 2l^2=2+6$$

$$\Rightarrow \quad l=2\text{ cm}$$

25. Let charge on surface of the ball be Q. As the ball is grounded, potential of the ball is zero. Therefore,

$$\frac{kq}{r'}+\frac{kp\cos 180^\circ}{r^2}+\frac{kQ}{R}=0$$

$$\Rightarrow \quad \frac{Q}{R}=\frac{p}{r^2}-\frac{q}{r'}$$

Differentiating w.r.t. t, we get

$$\frac{i}{R}=\frac{2pv}{r^3}+\frac{qv}{r'^2}$$

$$\Rightarrow \quad |i|=R\left|\frac{q}{r'^2}+\frac{2p}{r^3}\right|v$$

$$=0.5\left|\frac{1}{1}+\frac{2\times5}{1}\right|2=11\text{ A}$$

26. Range in such case can be written as

$$R=\frac{u^2\sin2\theta}{\frac{mg+F}{m}}=\frac{u^2\sin2\theta}{\frac{mg+qE}{m}}$$

As for A, $q=0$, we get

$$R_A=\frac{u^2\sin2\theta}{g}=R \quad \text{(given) ...(i)}$$

For B, $q=q$, so, we get

$$R_B=\frac{u^2\sin2\theta}{g+\frac{qE}{m}}=\frac{R}{2} \quad \text{(given) ...(ii)}$$

Dividing Eq. (i) by Eq. (ii), we get

$$1+\frac{qE}{mg}=2 \Rightarrow qE=mg \quad \text{...(iii)}$$

Therefore, for C, range will be

$$R_C=\frac{u^2\sin2\theta}{g+\frac{qE}{2m}}=\frac{u^2\sin2\theta}{g+\frac{g}{2}}$$

[using Eq. (iii)]

$$=\frac{2u^2\sin2\theta}{3g}=\frac{2R}{3} \quad \text{[using Eq. (i)]}$$

$\therefore \quad x=3$

27. Energy density of EM wave is given by

$$\text{ED}=\frac{1}{2}\varepsilon_0E^2=\frac{1}{2}\varepsilon_0E_0^2\sin^2(\omega t-kx)$$

As average of $\sin^2(\omega t-kx)$ over a cycle is $\frac{1}{2}$, therefore

$$\text{Average ED}=\frac{1}{2}\varepsilon_0E_0^2\times\frac{1}{2}=\frac{1}{4}\varepsilon_0E_0^2$$

$\Rightarrow \quad x=1$

28. Corresponding to maximum height, θ is equal to angle of repose i.e. $\tan^{-1}\mu$

$$\Rightarrow h=r\tan\theta=r\cdot\mu=\sqrt{3}\cdot\sqrt{3}=3$$

29. As velocity of CM is given by

$$\mathbf{v}_{cm}=\frac{m_1\mathbf{v}_1+m_2\mathbf{v}_2+...}{m_1+m_2+...}$$

$$\Rightarrow m_1(\mathbf{v}_1-\mathbf{v}_{cm})+m_2(\mathbf{v}_2-\mathbf{v}_{cm})+...=0$$

$\therefore$ Momentum of system of particles in CM frame is 0.

30. As ranges are same, height of circular hole from ground is same as depth of square hole from top.

$$\frac{Q_C}{Q_S}=\frac{V_C\cdot A_C}{V_S\cdot A_S}=\frac{\sqrt{4gh}\cdot\pi r^2}{\sqrt{2gh}\cdot l^2}=\frac{\sqrt{2}\pi r^2}{l^2}$$

$$=\sqrt{2}\pi\left(\frac{1}{\frac{1}{2^{\frac{1}{4}}}}\right)^2=\pi=3.14$$

Knockout 09

1. For thin lens, object distance (u) and image distance (v) are related as

$$\frac{1}{f}=\frac{1}{v}-\frac{1}{u}$$

Putting, $u=-OA$ and $v=OB$ (as given by the figure), we get

$$\frac{1}{f}=\frac{1}{OB}-\frac{1}{-OA}=\frac{1}{OB}+\frac{1}{OA} \quad \text{...(i)}$$

$$\text{From } \Delta OCA,\ OA=\frac{L}{\tan\theta}\approx\frac{L}{\theta} \quad \text{...(ii)}$$

(as θ is very small for paraxial rays)

$$\text{Similarly, from } \Delta OCB,\ OB=\frac{L}{2\theta} \quad \text{...(iii)}$$

Putting values of OA and OB from Eqs. (ii) and (iii) into Eq. (i), we get

$$\frac{1}{f}=\frac{2\theta}{L}+\frac{\theta}{L}=\frac{3\theta}{L}\Rightarrow f=\frac{L}{3\theta}$$

2. The SI unit of power, $u=\text{kg m}^2\text{s}^{-3}$. If unit of mass, length and time are tripled, new unit of power will be

$$u'=(3\text{ kg})\ (3\text{ m})^2\ (3\text{ s})^{-3}$$

$$=\frac{3\times3^2}{3^3}\text{kg m}^2\text{s}^{-3}=\text{kg m}^2\text{s}^{-3}$$

(unaltered)

SI unit of $G=u=\text{kg}^{-1}\text{m}^3\text{s}^{-2}$ and new unit

$$=u'=(3\text{ kg})^{-1}(3\text{m})^3\ (3\text{ s})^{-2}$$

$$=\text{kg}^{-1}\text{m}^3\text{s}^{-2}\ \text{(unaltered)}$$

Also, as Reynold's number is dimensionless/unitless, so its unit is always unaltered.

3. Let Q and R be charge and radius of the ring respectively. From ΔPOS, distance of P from centre O of the ring

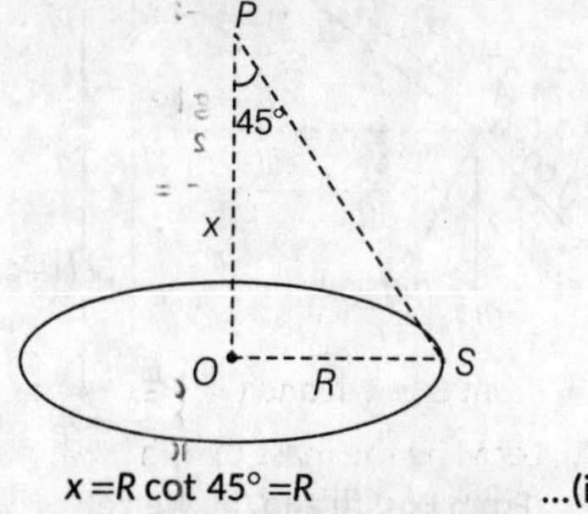

$$x=R\cot45°=R \quad \text{...(i)}$$

Now, electric field on axis of a uniformly charged ring at P is given by

$$E=\frac{Qx}{4\pi\varepsilon_0(R^2+x^2)^{\frac{3}{2}}}$$

$$=\frac{QR}{4\pi\varepsilon_0(R^2+R^2)^{3/2}}$$

[using Eq. (i)]

$$\Rightarrow \quad E=\frac{QR}{4\pi\varepsilon_0(2R^2)^{\frac{3}{2}}} \quad \text{...(ii)}$$

Also, equivalent current in a rotating ring is given by

$$I=\frac{Q}{T}=\frac{Q}{\frac{2\pi R}{v}}=\frac{Qv}{2\pi R} \quad \text{...(iii)}$$

Here, v is speed of ring particles.

This rotating circular current produces magnetic field given by

$$B=\frac{\mu_0IR^2}{2(R^2+x^2)^{\frac{3}{2}}} \quad \text{...(iv)}$$

Putting values of x and I from Eqs. (i) and (iii) in Eq. (iv), we get

$$B=\frac{\mu_0\cdot\frac{Qv}{2\pi R}R^2}{2(R^2+R^2)^{\frac{3}{2}}}$$

$$B=\frac{\mu_0QvR}{4\pi(2R^2)^{3/2}} \quad \text{...(v)}$$

Dividing Eq. (ii) by Eq. (v), we get

$$\frac{E}{B}=\frac{1}{\mu_0\varepsilon_0v}$$

As v is given to be pc and $\frac{1}{\mu_0\varepsilon_0}$ is c^2 as per Maxwell's theory, we get

$$\frac{E}{B}=\frac{c^2}{pc}=\frac{c}{p} \Rightarrow Ep=Bc$$

4. If $V_A>V_B$, both diodes are forward biased and behave as plain wire. So, circuit will be equivalent to Wheatstone bridge (balanced) as shown in Fig. 1.

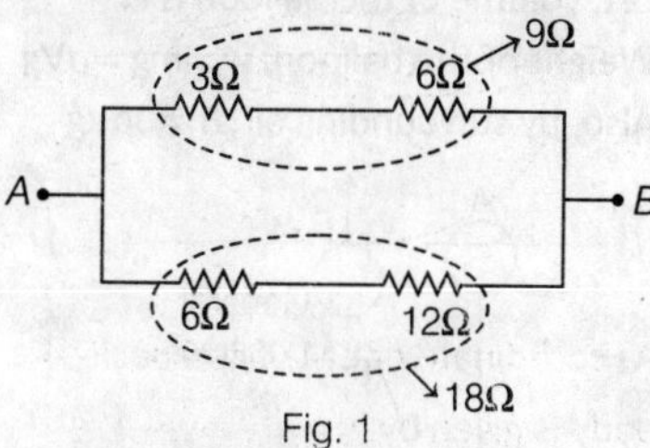

Fig. 1

Equivalent resistance between A and B will therefore be

$$R_{AB}=\frac{9\times18}{9+18}=6\ \Omega \quad \text{...(i)}$$

If $V_A < V_B$ both diodes are reverse biased and will impose infinite resistance. Equivalent circuit will be as shown

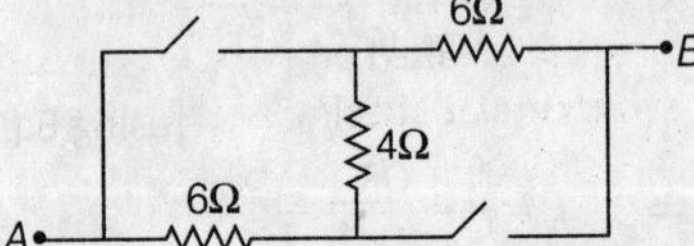

As three resistors will be in series, equivalent resistance between A and B will be

$$R'_{AB} = 6 + 4 + 6 = 16\ \Omega \quad \text{...(ii)}$$

From Eqs. (i) and (ii), difference in equivalent resistance is

$$x\ \Omega = |R'_{AB} - R_{AB}| = 16 - 6 = 10\Omega$$

$\therefore \quad x = 10$

Considering the frequency given to be x MHz, which will be 10 MHz, wavelength of the wave is

$$\lambda = \frac{c}{f} = \frac{3\times 10^8 \text{ m/s}}{10\times 10^6 \text{ Hz}} = 30 \text{ m}$$

Minimum length of antenna is

$$l = \frac{\lambda}{4} = \frac{30}{4} = 7.5 \text{ m}$$

5. Only force acting on the sphere is viscous force given by Stoke's law equal to $-6\pi\eta rv$.

Due to this force, the sphere retards and stops finally.

So, at general position, acceleration,

$$a = -\frac{6\pi\eta rv}{m}$$

$$\Rightarrow \quad v\frac{dv}{dx} = \frac{-6\pi\left(\frac{1}{2\pi}\right)rv}{m}$$

$$\Rightarrow \quad mdv = -3rdx$$

$$\Rightarrow \quad m\int_u^0 dv = -3r\int_0^x dx \Rightarrow -mu = -3xr$$

$$\Rightarrow \quad x = \frac{mu}{3r} = \frac{p}{3r}$$

6. Let, volume of the balloon is V.

Weight of the balloon, $w = mg = \rho Vg$

Also, by surrounding air, $B = 3\rho Vg$

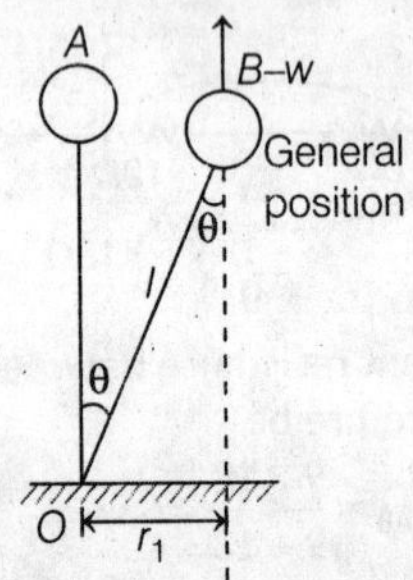

Net force F on the balloon providing torque will be equal to $B - w = 3\rho Vg - \rho Vg = 2\rho Vg$ as shown in the figure.

Perpendicular distance r_1 of line of action of force from axis O at general position is $r_1 = l\sin\theta \approx l\theta$ as θ is given to be small. Therefore, restoring torque

$$\tau = F\cdot r_1 = 2\rho Vgl\theta$$

Angular acceleration of balloon (having moment of inertia I equal to ml^2) is

$$\alpha = \frac{\tau}{I} = \frac{2\rho Vgl\theta}{ml^2} = \frac{2\rho Vg\theta}{ml}$$

$$= \frac{2\rho Vg}{\rho Vl}\theta = \frac{2g}{l}\theta$$

As in angular oscillation, $\alpha = \omega^2\theta$,

$$\Rightarrow \quad \omega^2\theta = \frac{2g}{l}\theta$$

$$\Rightarrow \quad \omega = \sqrt{\frac{2g}{l}}$$

As, time to move from B to A is $\frac{1}{4}$th of time period of oscillation,

$$\therefore \quad t = \frac{T}{4} = \frac{\frac{2\pi}{\omega}}{4} = \frac{\pi}{2\omega} = \frac{\pi}{2}\sqrt{\frac{l}{2g}}$$

$$= \pi\sqrt{\frac{l}{8g}}$$

7. By condition of looping at point B, speed at B

$$v_B \geq \sqrt{5gl} \quad \text{...(i)}$$

Also, by conservation of energy for motion from A and B,

Gain in KE = Loss is PE

$$\Rightarrow \quad \frac{1}{2}mv_B^2 = mg\cdot 5l\,(1-\cos\theta)$$

(using figure)

$$\Rightarrow \quad v_B = \sqrt{10gl(1-\cos\theta)} \quad \text{...(ii)}$$

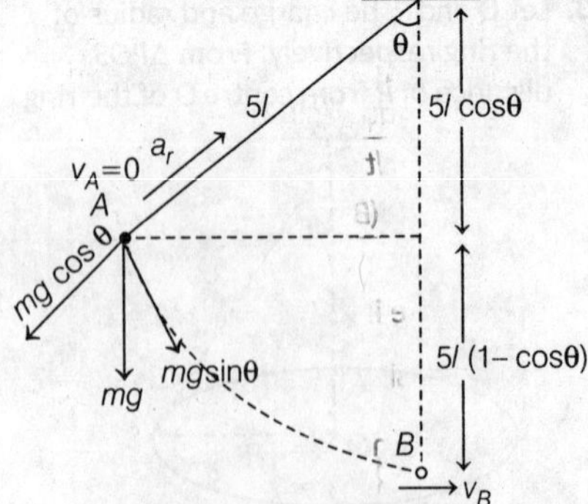

From Eqs. (i) and (ii), we get

$$\sqrt{10gl(1-\cos\theta)} \geq \sqrt{5gl}$$

$$\Rightarrow 1-\cos\theta \geq \frac{1}{2} \Rightarrow \cos\theta \leq \frac{1}{2} \Rightarrow \theta \geq 60°$$

$\Rightarrow \theta$ (minimum) $= 60°$

Thus, from the FBD of bob in position A.

$$a_T = \text{Tangential acceleration}$$

$$= \frac{\text{Tangential force}}{\text{Mass}}$$

$$= \frac{mg\sin 60°}{m} = \frac{\sqrt{3}g}{2}$$

$$a_R = \text{Radial acceleration}$$

$$= \frac{v^2}{r} = 0 \text{ (as } v_A = 0\text{)}$$

Thus, net acceleration

$$= a = \sqrt{a_T^2 + a_R^2} = \frac{\sqrt{3}g}{2}$$

8. As thermal expansion is photographic, all linear dimensions increase by same factor while angular dimension remains unchanged.

9. Wavelength of sound,

$$\lambda = \frac{v}{f} = \frac{336}{112} = 3 \text{ m} \quad \text{...(i)}$$

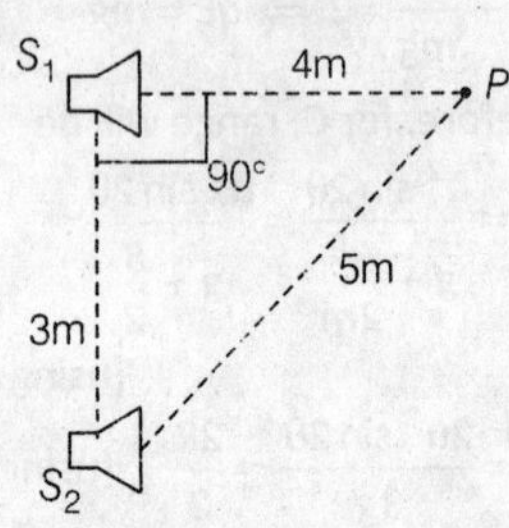

Path difference between waves reaching P,

$$\Delta x = S_2P - S_1P = 5 - 4 = 1 \text{ m} \quad \text{...(ii)}$$

As phase difference is given by

$$\phi = \frac{2\pi}{\lambda}\Delta x = \frac{2\pi}{3}\times 1 = \frac{2\pi}{3} \quad \text{...(iii)}$$

[using Eqs. (i) and (ii)]

As resultant intensity on interference of two coherent waves is given by

$$I = I_1 + I_2 + 2\sqrt{I_1 I_2}\cos\phi$$

Let $I_1 = I_0$ and $I_2 = kI_0$

Therefore,

$$3I_0 = I_0 + kI_0 + 2\sqrt{I_0\cdot kI_0}\cos\frac{2\pi}{3}$$

[using Eq. (iii)]

$$\Rightarrow \quad 3 = 1 + k - \sqrt{k}$$

$$\Rightarrow k - \sqrt{k} - 2 = 0$$

$$\Rightarrow \quad k = 4 \Rightarrow I_2 = 4I_0$$

Now, intensity I of a point source of power P at a distance r is given by

$$I = \frac{P}{4\pi r^2} \Rightarrow P = 4\pi r^2 I$$

Thus, ratio of powers will be

$$\frac{P_1}{P_2} = \frac{r_1^2 I_1}{r_2^2 I_2} = \frac{4^2\times I_0}{5^2\times 4I_0} = \frac{4}{25}$$

10. Voltage applied,

$$V = 100(\sin 100t + \cos 100t)$$

$$V = 100\sqrt{2}\sin\left(100t + \frac{\pi}{4}\right) \quad \text{...(i)}$$

$\therefore$ Peak voltage, $V_0 = 100\sqrt{2}$ V ...(ii)

Inductive reactance

$$= X_L = \omega L = 100 \times 1 = 100\,\Omega \quad \text{...(iii)}$$

Capacitive reactance

$$= X_C = \frac{1}{\omega C} = \frac{1}{100 \times 0.2 \times 10^{-3}}$$

$$= 50\,\Omega \quad \text{...(iv)}$$

So, peak current through inductor is

$$I_1 = \frac{V_0}{X_L} = \frac{100\sqrt{2}}{100} = \sqrt{2}\text{ A}$$

[using Eqs. (ii) and (iii)]

Also, peak current through capacitor is

$$I_2 = \frac{V_0}{X_C} = \frac{100\sqrt{2}}{50} = 2\sqrt{2}\text{ A}$$

[using Eqs. (ii) and (iv)]

Peak current through resistor is

$$I_3 = \frac{V_0}{R} = \frac{100\sqrt{2}}{100} = \sqrt{2}\text{ A}$$

Considering that current in inductor, capacitor and resistor lag, lead and are in phase w.r.t voltage respectively. So, phasor diagram will be as shown in Fig.1. As from Fig.-2, resultant current I is sum of I_1, I_2, I_3. So, we add phasors of I_1, I_2, I_3 in Fig. 1 to get maximum net current I.

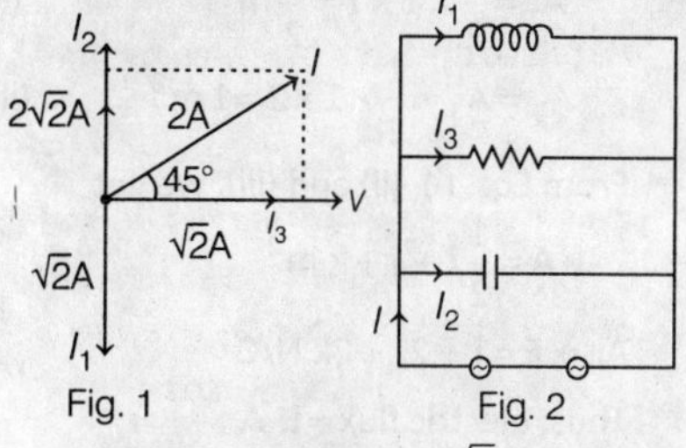

Fig. 1 Fig. 2

Resultant of I_2 and I_1 is $\sqrt{2}$ A upwards and its final resultant with I_3 is as shown in Fig.1.

From phasor diagram, resultant current has peak value of 2A and leads voltage by $\frac{\pi}{4}$. Thus, current function would be

$$I = 2\sin\left(\omega t + \frac{\pi}{4} + \frac{\pi}{4}\right) = 2\cos\omega t$$

11. The fringe width is given by

$$\beta = \frac{\lambda D}{nd}$$

As for vacuum, n is exactly one while for air, n is slightly greater than one. So, when air from a YDSE set-up is pumped out, the value of β will increase.

12. For earth to become black hole, escape speed on its surface should be just greater than speed of light. Therefore,

$$v_e \approx c$$

$$\Rightarrow \sqrt{\frac{2GM}{R}} \approx c$$

$$\Rightarrow \sqrt{\frac{2 \times 6.67 \times 10^{-11} \times 6 \times 10^{24}}{R}} = 3 \times 10^8$$

$$\Rightarrow R = 0.9\text{ cm} \approx 1\text{ cm}$$

13. FBD of the body is as shown

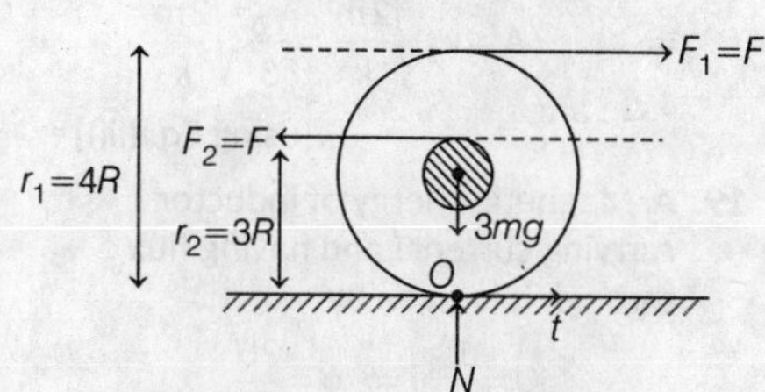

As the body is not slipping, so O is the instantaneous axis of rotation.

Moment of inertia about O, using parallel axis theorem,

$$I = I_{CM} + (\text{Mass}) \times d^2$$

$$= \frac{2mR^2}{2} + \frac{m(2R)^2}{2} + 3m \times (2R)^2$$

$$= 15mR^2$$

Using $\alpha = \frac{\tau}{I}$ about O, we get

$$\alpha = \frac{F_1(r_1) - F_2(r_2)}{15\,mR^2}$$

$$= \frac{F(4R) - F(3R)}{15mR^2} = \frac{F}{15mR}$$

Using $a = \alpha r$ about instantaneous axis O, we get, acceleration of A equals to

$$a = \frac{F}{15mR} \times 4R = \frac{4F}{15m}$$

14. As per Faraday's law, induced emf

$$\varepsilon = \frac{d\phi}{dt} = \frac{d(BA)}{dt}$$

$$= \frac{d(B \cdot \pi r^2)}{dt} = \pi B \cdot 2r \cdot \frac{dr}{dt}$$

In the time interval $t = t_0$ to $t = 2t_0$

r is increasing linearly with time, $\frac{dr}{dt}$ is constant. Therefore,

$$\varepsilon \propto r$$

So, ε-t graph will be similar to r-t graph. But in the time intervals $t = 0$ to $t = t_0$ and $t = 2t_0$ to $t = 5t_0$, r is constant and so $\frac{dr}{dt}$ is zero. Therefore, induced emf is also zero.

Most appropriate graph representing this is shown in option (c).

15. pV^x = Constant is the given general equation of the processes. Such a process is called polytropic process for which molar specific heat is given by

$$C = \frac{R}{\gamma - 1} - \frac{R}{x - 1}$$

Clearly, it is negative for $1 < x < \gamma$, that is for the process C between adiabatic and isotherm in p-V diagram.

16. Time period of a physical pendulum of mass m is given by

$$T = 2\pi\sqrt{\frac{I}{mgx}} \quad \text{...(i)}$$

Here, I is moment of inertia about axis of oscillation and x is the distance between point of suspension O from centre of mass C.

If K is radius of gyration about axis passing through CM

$$\Rightarrow I = I_{CM} + mx^2$$

(by parallel axes theorem)

$$\Rightarrow I = m(K^2 + x^2) \quad (\because I_{CM} = mR^2) \text{...(ii)}$$

From Eqs. (i) and (ii), we get

$$T = 2\pi\sqrt{\frac{m(K^2 + x^2)}{mgx}}$$

$$\Rightarrow T = 2\pi\sqrt{\left(\frac{K^2}{x} + x\right)\frac{1}{g}}$$

$$\Rightarrow \frac{K^2}{x} + x = \frac{T^2 g}{4\pi^2}$$

$$\Rightarrow x^2 - \frac{T^2 g}{4\pi^2}x + K^2 = 0$$

From above equation, for a given time period, we will have two values of x, that are given in graph as a and b. As product of roots of quadratic is constant term divided by coefficient of x^2. Therefore,

$$a \times b = \frac{K^2}{1} \Rightarrow b = \frac{K^2}{a} \quad \text{...(iii)}$$

As I_{CM} for rod is $\frac{ml^2}{12}$, so,

$$\frac{ml^2}{12} = mK^2$$

$$\Rightarrow K^2 = \frac{l^2}{12}$$

Putting, $K^2 = \frac{l^2}{12}$ and $a = \frac{l}{4}$ (given) in Eq. (iii), we get

$$b = \frac{l^2}{12 \times \frac{l}{4}} = \frac{l}{3}$$

17. Activity as function of time t is given by $A = A_0 e^{-\lambda t}$

Taking ln on both sides

$\ln A = -\lambda t + \ln A_0$

Above equation is of the form

$$y = mx + c$$

On comparing, we get

$$m = \text{slope} = -\lambda \quad \text{...(i)}$$

Also, from the graph,

$$m = \text{slope} = \frac{\ln A_1 - \ln A_2}{t_1 - t_2} \quad \text{...(ii)}$$

From Eqs. (i) and (ii), we get

$$-\lambda = \frac{\ln A_1 - \ln A_2}{t_1 - t_2}$$

$$\Rightarrow \quad \lambda = \frac{\ln A_1 - \ln A_2}{t_2 - t_1}$$

$$\Rightarrow \text{Half-life} = \frac{\ln 2}{\lambda} = \ln 2\left(\frac{t_2 - t_1}{\ln A_1 - \ln A_2}\right)$$

$$= \ln 2\left(\frac{t_2 - t_1}{\ln \frac{A_1}{A_2}}\right)$$

18. The collision process is shown below.

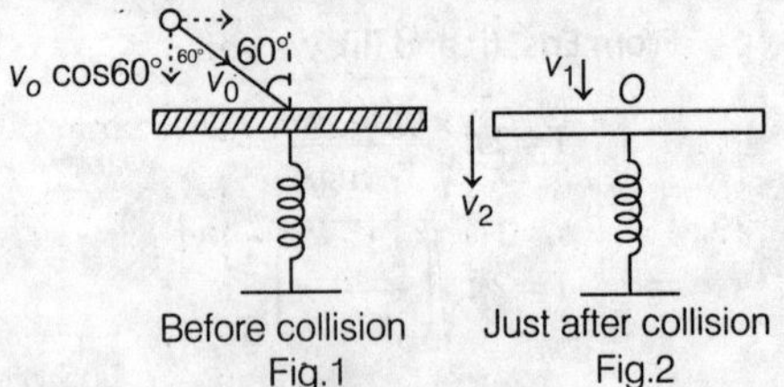

Before collision Fig.1 Just after collision Fig.2

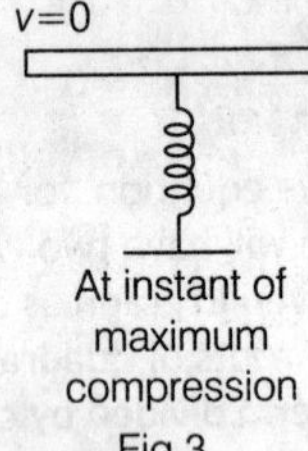

At instant of maximum compression Fig.3

Velocity components of ball just before collision are as shown, vertical component being $\frac{v}{2}$. Assuming velocities in vertical direction as shown in Fig.2, by conservation of momentum

$$2mv_2 + mv_1 = \frac{mv_0}{2}$$

$$\Rightarrow \quad 4v_2 + 2v_1 = v_0 \quad \text{...(i)}$$

Also, by Newton's law of restitution,

$$v_2 - v_1 = e(u_1 - u_2)$$

$$\Rightarrow \quad v_2 - v_1 = 1\left(\frac{v_0}{2} - 0\right)$$

(for elastic collision, $e = 1$)

$$\Rightarrow 2v_2 - 2v_1 = v_0 \quad \text{...(ii)}$$

Adding Eqs. (i) and (ii), we get

$$6v_2 = 2v_0 \Rightarrow v_2 = \frac{v_0}{3} \quad \text{...(iii)}$$

As pan moves down, its speed slows down due to opposing force by spring and comes to rest instantly at distance A shown in Fig.3 and subsequently perform SHM.

As velocity at mean/equilibrium position is SHM,

$$v_{\text{mean}} = A\omega \Rightarrow v_2 = A\sqrt{\frac{k}{2m}}$$

$$\Rightarrow \quad A = v_2\sqrt{\frac{2m}{k}} = \frac{v_0}{3}\sqrt{\frac{2m}{k}}$$

[using Eq. (iii)]

19. A. Magnetic energy of inductor carrying current i and having flux ϕ through it is given by

$$U = \frac{1}{2}\phi i \Rightarrow \phi = \frac{2U}{i}$$

$$\Rightarrow [\phi] = \frac{[U]}{[i]} = \frac{[ML^2T^{-2}]}{[I]}$$

$$= [ML^2T^{-2}I^{-1}]$$

Dimensions of mass, length and current are 1, 2 and -1 respectively. Therefore, sum $= 1 + 2 - 1 = 2$

B. Work done by gravity is independent of path.

C. Range $= \frac{u^2 \sin^2 \theta}{g}$

(Here u and θ are speed and angle of projection)

Range $\propto u^2$

If u is doubled, range becomes four times.

D. Speed at highest point $= u\cos\theta$

Kinetic energy at highest point

$$K' = \frac{1}{2}m(u\cos\theta)^2 = \frac{1}{2}mu^2\cos^2\theta$$

$$= \frac{1}{4}\left[\frac{1}{2}mu^2\right] = \frac{K}{4} \quad \text{... (i)}$$

By conservation of energy, potential energy at highest point is

U = loss in kinetic energy

$$= K - K' = K - \frac{K}{4}$$

$$\Rightarrow U = \frac{3K}{4} \quad \text{... (ii)}$$

Dividing Eq. (ii) by Eq. (i), we get

$$\frac{U}{K'} = 3$$

20. As per Einstein's equation,

$KE_{max} = h\nu - \phi$

Therefore, $0.5\,\text{eV} = h\nu - \phi$ ... (i)

$0.8\text{ eV} = 1.2\,h\nu - \phi$ ... (ii)

Solving Eqs. (i) and (ii), we get

$$\phi = 1\text{ eV}$$

21. Total perimeter of the blade

$$P = 60 + 80 = 140\text{ cm} = 1.4\text{ m}$$

Therefore, surface tension force on the blade is

$$F = T \times P = \frac{1}{140} \times 1.4 = \frac{1}{100}\text{ N}$$

$$= 10\text{ mN}$$

22. Triangular surface will be as shown in figure. If A_1, A_2, A_3 are projected areas OQR, ORP and OPQ respectively, area vector of triangle PQR can be written as

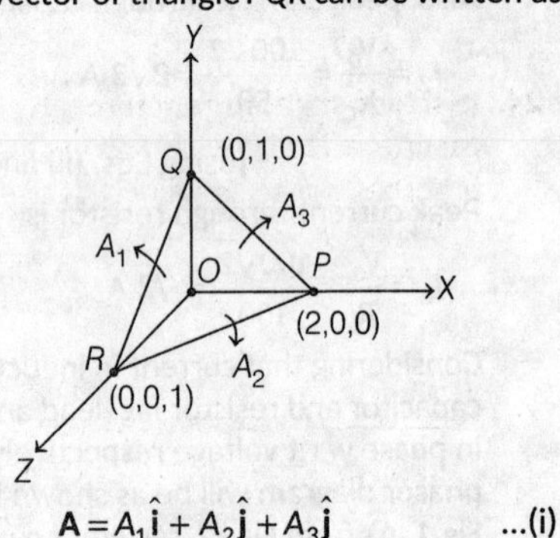

$$\mathbf{A} = A_1\hat{\mathbf{i}} + A_2\hat{\mathbf{j}} + A_3\hat{\mathbf{j}} \quad \text{...(i)}$$

Using coordinates of P, Q and R, we can find areas as

$$A_1 = \frac{1}{2} \times 1 \times 1 = \frac{1}{2}\text{ m}^2 \quad \text{...(ii)}$$

$$A_2 = A_3 = \frac{1}{2} \times 1 \times 2 = 1\text{ m}^2 \quad \text{...(iii)}$$

From Eqs. (i), (ii) and (iii), we get

$$\mathbf{A} = \frac{1}{2}\hat{\mathbf{i}} + \hat{\mathbf{j}} + \hat{\mathbf{k}}\text{ m}^2$$

Also, $\mathbf{E} = \hat{\mathbf{i}} + 2\hat{\mathbf{j}} + 3\hat{\mathbf{k}}$ N/C

Thus, electric flux $= \mathbf{E}\cdot\mathbf{A}$

$$= \frac{1}{2} \times 1 + 1 \times 2 + 1 \times 3 = 5.5\text{V-m}$$

23. Consider FBD of the system shown. As the blocks move together, common acceleration of the blocks is

$$a = \frac{F_{\text{Net}}}{m_{\text{Net}}} = \frac{F - \mu(3mg)}{3m} \quad \text{...(i)}$$

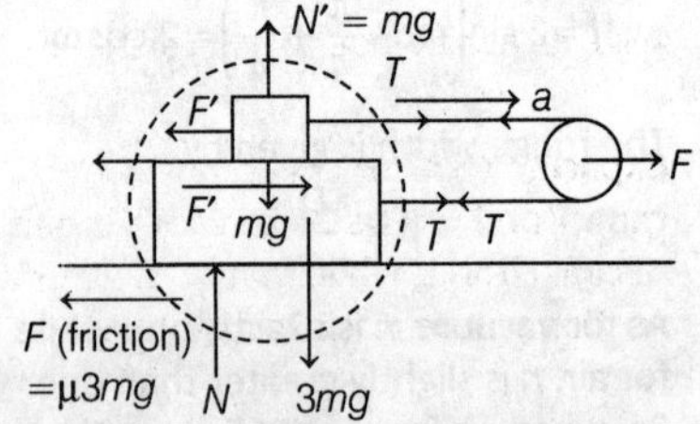

From FBD of pulley, we get

$$2T = F \Rightarrow T = \frac{F}{2} \quad ...(ii)$$

As F is the maximum force for which there is no slipping between the blocks, friction between the blocks will be maximum static/limiting friction. So, from FBD of block P, using Newton's 2nd law, we get

$$\frac{F}{2} - 5\mu\, mg = ma \quad \text{(as, } F' = 5\mu mg)$$

$$\Rightarrow \quad F = 2ma + 10\mu mg \quad ...(iii)$$

Putting value of F from Eq. (iii) in Eq. (i), we get

$$a = \frac{2ma + 10\mu mg - 3\mu mg}{3m}$$

$$\Rightarrow 3ma = 2ma + 7\mu mg$$

$$\Rightarrow \quad a = 7\mu g = x\mu g \text{ (given)}$$

$$\therefore \quad x = 7$$

24. In steady state, current through capacitors is zero while current in other branches will be as shown in Fig.1.

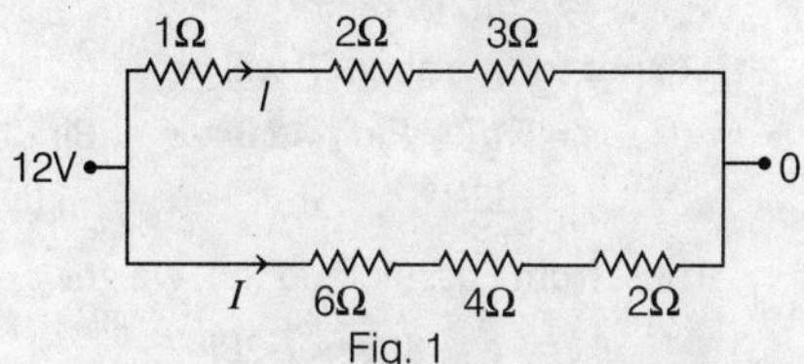

Fig. 1

As resistors in upper branch are in series, so

$$I = \frac{V}{R} = \frac{12 - 0}{1 + 2 + 3} = 2\text{ A}$$

Similarly, current in lower branch

$$I' = \frac{V}{R'} = \frac{12 - 0}{6 + 4 + 2} = 1\text{ A}$$

Now, using Ohm's law for 1Ω resistor (refer Fig.2)

Fig. 2

$$V_P - V_Q = I \times R$$

$$\Rightarrow 12 - V_Q = 2 \times 1 \Rightarrow V_Q = 10\text{ V}$$

Similarly, using Ohm's law, potentials of different points will be as shown in Fig.2

Also, if capacitance of capacitor-1 is

$$C_1 = C \quad ...(i)$$

Capacitance of air portion of capacitor-2 will be $2C$ as width is half of capacitor-1, while that of dielectric portion will be $K \times 2C$ equal to $6C$, as in Fig.2. As air and dielectric are in series effective capacitance will be

$$\frac{1}{C_2} = \frac{1}{2C} + \frac{1}{6C}$$

$$\Rightarrow \quad C_2 = 1.5C \quad ...(ii)$$

Also, for capacitor-3,

$$C_3 = KC = 3C \quad ...(iii)$$

From Fig. 2, potential difference across C_1, C_2, C_3 respectively are

$$V_1 = |12 - 10| = 2 \quad ...(iv)$$

$$V_2 = 6 - 6 = 0 \quad ...(v)$$

$$V_3 = |2 - 0| = 2 \quad ...(vi)$$

Using Eqs. (i) to (vi), ratio of charges

$$Q_1 : Q_2 : Q_3 = C_1V_1 : C_2V_2 : C_3V_3$$

$$= C \times 2 : 1.5C \times 0 : 3C \times 2$$

$$= 2 : 0 : 6 \Rightarrow y = 6, x = 0$$

$$\therefore \quad y - x = 6$$

25. As per Biot Savart law, magnetic field at nucleus

$$B = \frac{\mu_0}{4\pi}\frac{ev}{r^2} \quad ...(i)$$

Angular momentum of electron,

$$L = mvr = \frac{h}{2\pi}$$

(as per Bohr's quantisation rule)

$$\Rightarrow \quad v = \frac{h}{2\pi mr} \quad ...(ii)$$

Putting value of v from Eq. (ii) in Eq. (i), we get

$$B = \frac{\mu_0 e}{4\pi r^2}\left(\frac{h}{2\pi mr}\right)$$

$$\Rightarrow \quad B = \frac{\mu_0 eh}{8\pi^2 mr^3} = \frac{\mu_0 eh}{80 mr^3}$$

Comparing with given expression, we get $x = 80$ and $y = 3$

Therefore, $\frac{x}{y} = \frac{80}{3} = 26.67$

26. After releasing, the situation can be shown as

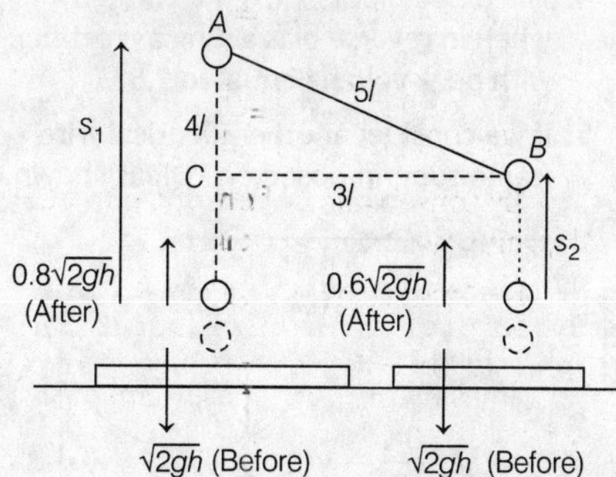

As velocity just after collision is e times the incident velocity, therefore velocities of balls after collision will be as shown. Let the string becomes taut at time t in position AB.

From ΔABC,

$$AC = \sqrt{(5l)^2 - (3l)^2} = 4l$$

$\Rightarrow$ Displacement of ball-1 will be $4l$ greater than ball-2

$$\Rightarrow \quad s_1 = s_2 + 4l$$

$$\Rightarrow 0.8\sqrt{2gh}\,t - \frac{1}{2}gt^2 = 0.6\sqrt{2gh}\,t - \frac{1}{2}gt^2 + 4l$$

$$\Rightarrow 0.2\sqrt{2gh} = 4l$$

$$\Rightarrow \quad t = \frac{20l}{\sqrt{2gh}}$$

$$\therefore \quad x = 20, y = 2 \Rightarrow \frac{x}{y} = \frac{20}{2} = 10$$

27. It is given that

$$v_{\text{average}} \text{ of gas-1} = v_{\text{rms}} \text{ of gas-2}$$

$$\sqrt{\frac{8kT}{\pi m_1}} = \sqrt{\frac{3kT}{m_2}}$$

$$\Rightarrow \quad \frac{m_2}{m_1} = \frac{3\pi}{8} = 1.17$$

28. $\quad LC = 1\text{ MSD} - 1\text{ VSD}$

$$\Rightarrow \quad LC = 1\text{ MSD} - \frac{19}{20}\text{ MSD} = \frac{\text{MSD}}{20}$$

$$\Rightarrow \text{MSD} = 20 \times LC = 20 \times 0.05 = 1\text{ mm}$$

29. $\quad \phi = B \cdot A = \int_0^l xt \cdot l\,dx + \int_0^l yt \cdot l\,dy = l^3 t$

$$\therefore \quad i = \frac{\varepsilon}{R} = \frac{\frac{d\phi}{dt}}{R} = \frac{l^3}{R} = \frac{(3)^3}{9} = 3\text{ A}$$

30. In thermal equilibrium,

$$\sigma(4\pi R^2)T^4 \frac{\pi R_p^2}{4\pi r^2} = \sigma(4\pi R_p^2)t^4$$

$$\Rightarrow \quad \left(\frac{t}{T}\right)^2 = \frac{R}{2r}$$

$$\therefore \quad x + y = 2 + 2 = 4$$

Knockout 10

1. As slab of dielectric constants, $K = 2$ and air are in series the arrangement can be considered as shown.

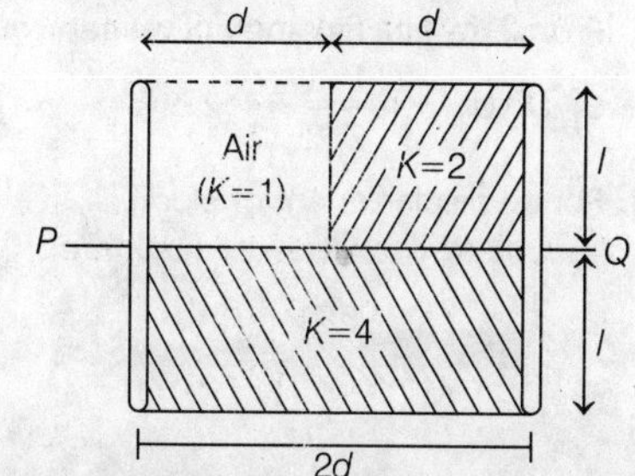

Equivalent diagram of the arrangement is

$$C_0=\frac{\varepsilon_0 A}{d} \qquad C_0=\frac{K\varepsilon_0 A}{d}=\frac{2\varepsilon_0 A}{d}=2C_0$$

$K=1$ $K=2$

P V_1 V_2 Q

$K=4$

$$\frac{K\varepsilon_0 A}{2d}=\frac{4\varepsilon_0 A}{2d}=2C_0$$

V

Respective capacitance are as shown.

As, potential differences for capacitors in series are in inverse ratio of capacitances, therefore

$$\frac{V_1}{V_2}=\frac{2C_0}{C_0}=2$$

$$\Rightarrow \quad V_1=2V_2 \quad \text{...(i)}$$

Also, $V_1+V_2=V$ ...(ii)

From Eqs. (i) and (ii), we get

$$2V_2+V_2=V$$

$$\Rightarrow \quad V_2=\frac{V}{3}$$

$$\Rightarrow \quad V_1=\frac{2V}{3}$$

Therefore, energy density of air is

$$U_1=\frac{\text{Energy}}{\text{Volume}}=\frac{\frac{1}{2}\cdot C_0\cdot V_1^2}{lbd}$$

$$=\frac{\frac{1}{2}C_0\left(\frac{2V}{3}\right)^2}{lbd}=\frac{2C_0V^2}{9lbd} \quad \text{...(iii)}$$

(Here, b is width of capacitor)

Similarly, energy density in capacitor with dielectric of dielectric constant 2 is

$$U_2=\frac{\frac{1}{2}\cdot 2C_0V_2^2}{lbd}$$

$$=\frac{C_0\left(\frac{V}{3}\right)^2}{lbd}=\frac{C_0V^2}{9lbd} \quad \text{...(iv)}$$

$$\text{and } U_3=\frac{\frac{1}{2}\cdot 2C_0\cdot V^2}{lb\cdot 2d}=\frac{C_0V^2}{2lbd} \quad \text{...(v)}$$

From Eqs. (iii), (iv) and (v), we get

$$U_1:U_2:U_3=\frac{2}{9}:\frac{1}{9}:\frac{1}{2}=4:2:9$$

2. For no displacement of block,

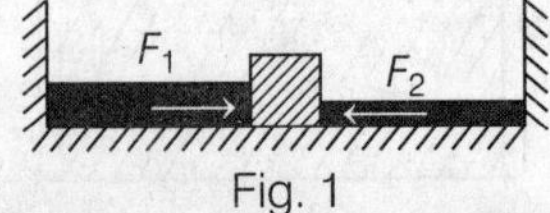

Fig. 1

$$F_1=F_2$$

$$\Rightarrow Y_1A_1\alpha_1\,\Delta T=Y_2A_2\alpha_2\Delta T$$

$$\Rightarrow \quad Y_2=\frac{Y_1A_1\alpha_1}{A_2\alpha_2}=\frac{YA\alpha}{\frac{A}{2}\frac{\alpha}{2}}=4Y$$

As, stiffness constant of rod is $\frac{YA}{l}$, so the system in Fig. 2 is equivalent to series arrangement of blocks as shown in figure. Equivalent spring constant is

$K_1=\frac{YA}{l}$

$K_2=\frac{2YA}{l}$

m

Fig. 2

$$K=\frac{K_1K_2}{K_1+K_2}=\frac{2YA}{3l}$$

$$\Rightarrow \quad T=2\pi\sqrt{\frac{m}{K}}=2\pi\sqrt{\frac{3ml}{2YA}}$$

3. If the frequency is halved it may become lesser than threshold frequency, photoelectric emission will stop and so current will become zero.

Also, photocurrent is given by

$$i=\frac{\eta PA}{4\pi hfr^2}$$

Here, η = quantum efficiency, P = power of point source, A = plate area, h = Planck's constant, f = frequency, r = distance between source and plate. Thus, if both r and f become half and f is still greater than threshold frequency, new current will be

$$i'=\frac{\eta PA}{4\pi h\left(\frac{f}{2}\right)\left(\frac{r}{2}\right)^2}=8i$$

4. The diode blocks/clips the voltage when in reverse bias acting as rectifier with peak voltage equal to 2.5 V.

5. If we consider another identical wire frame superimposed on PQR as shown

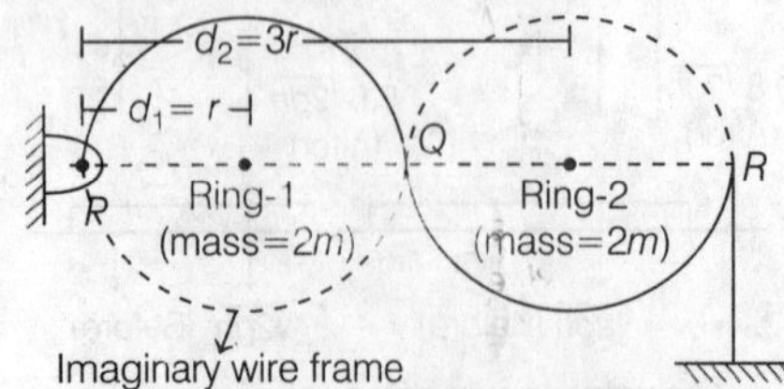

Moment of inertia of both the rings (mass $=2m$ each) about axis through centre and perpendicular to plane will be I_{CM} equal to $2\,mr^2$. Therefore, for Ring-1, moment of inertia about axis through P, by parallel axis theorem, will be

$$I_1=I_{CM}+2md_1^2=2mr^2+2mr^2$$

$$\Rightarrow \quad I_1=4mr^2 \quad \text{...(i)}$$

Similarly, for Ring-2, we get

$$I_2=2mr^2+2m(3r)^2=20mr^2 \quad \text{...(ii)}$$

Thus, moment of inertia of composite body is

$I_C=I_1+I_2=24mr^2$ [using Eqs. (i) and (ii)]

Thus, for PQR, moment of inertia will be

$$I=\frac{I_C}{2}=12mr^2 \quad \text{...(iii)}$$

Also, magnetic force in uniform field is given by $F=Bil$

(Here, l is effective length or distance between ends)

So, force on PQ is $F_1=Bi(2r)=2Bir$

and force on QR is

$$F_2=Bi(2r)=2Bir$$

So, net torque about P will be

$$\tau=F_1d_1+F_2d_2=2\,Bir\cdot r+2Bir\cdot 3r$$
$$=8Bir^2 \quad \text{...(iv)}$$

Thus, from Eqs. (iii) and (iv), we get

$$\alpha=\frac{\tau}{I}=\frac{8Bir^2}{12mr^2}=\frac{2Bi}{3m}$$

6. Energy radiated by sun per unit time

$$P=\sigma\cdot 4\pi R^2\cdot T^4$$

Intensity at location of planet will be

$$I=\frac{P}{A}=\frac{\sigma\cdot 4\pi R^2T^4}{4\pi r^2}=\frac{\sigma R^2T^4}{r^2}$$

Thus, energy received by planet per unit time

$P_1=I\times$ Projected area of planet

$$P_1=\frac{\sigma R^2T^4}{r^2}\times\pi r_p^2 \quad \text{...(i)}$$

Here, r_p is planet's radius.

Assuming surface temperature of planet equal to T' power radiated by planet as per Stefan's law is

$$P_2=\sigma\cdot 4\pi r_p^2T'^4 \quad \text{...(ii)}$$

In equilibrium, $P_1=P_2$

$$\Rightarrow \frac{\sigma R^2T^4}{r^2}\pi r_p^2=\sigma\cdot 4\pi r_p^2T'^4$$

$$\Rightarrow \quad T'=\sqrt[4]{\frac{R^2}{4r^2}}\,T=\sqrt{\frac{R}{2r}}\,T$$

7. To move the mass slowly, external force equal and opposite to the gravitational force needs to be applied.

So, force on 3 kg mass at a general point is

$$\mathbf{F} = -m\mathbf{E}$$

$$\Rightarrow \quad \mathbf{F} = -[3(z^2 - y^2)\hat{\mathbf{j}} + 6yz\hat{\mathbf{k}}]$$

$$\Rightarrow \quad \mathbf{F} = 3(y^2 - z^2)\hat{\mathbf{j}} - 6yz\hat{\mathbf{k}}$$

As gravitational force is conservative, so work can be calculated by motion along any path of choice. We choose path $OABC$ as shown in figure. For motion along OA, $y = 0$, $z = 0 \Rightarrow W_{OA} = 0$. For path AB, $z = 0$, therefore

$$\mathbf{F} = 3y^2\hat{\mathbf{j}}$$

$$\Rightarrow \quad W_{AB} = \int F_y dy = \int_0^2 3y^2 dy$$

$$= [y^3]_0^2 = 8 \text{ J}$$

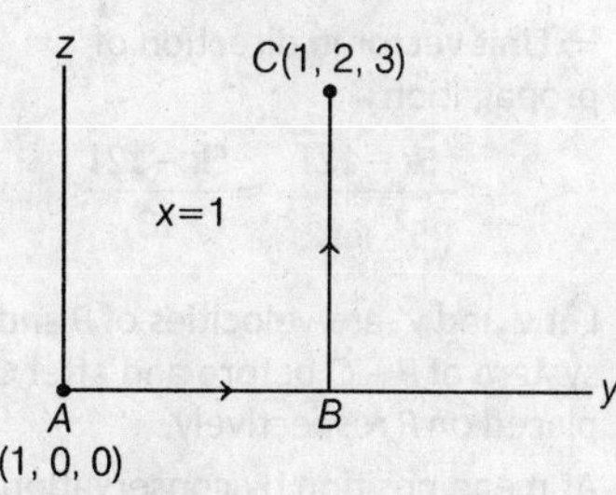

For path BC, $y = 2$, therefore

$$\mathbf{F} = 3(4 - z^2)\hat{\mathbf{j}} - 12z\hat{\mathbf{k}}$$

$$\Rightarrow W_{BC} = \int F_z dz = \int_0^3 -12z dz = -6[z^2]_0^3$$

$$= -54 \text{ J}$$

Thus, total work $= W_{AB} + W_{BC}$

$$= 8 - 54 = -46 \text{ J}$$

8. For refraction by slab, shift produced,

$$s = t\left(1 - \frac{1}{\mu}\right) = 3\left(1 - \frac{1}{\frac{3}{2}}\right) = 1 \text{ cm}$$

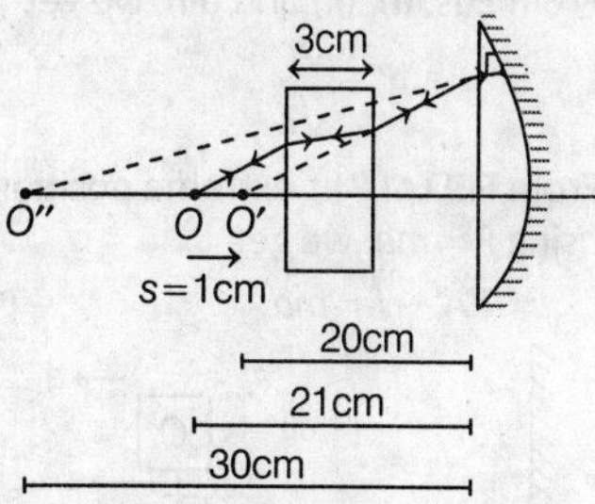

Image of slab is at O' at a distance 20 cm from the lens.

For refraction at plane surface of lens,

Image distance = Object distance $\times \mu$

$$= 20 \times 1.5 = 30 \text{ cm}$$

This image O'' acts as object for reflection at curved surface. As, for object image coincidence rays should be incident normally on curved surface, O'' should be at centre of curvature.

So, radius of curvature of curved surface should be 30 cm.

9. In 1st overtone, string will vibrate in 2 loops. Consider a small element of thickness dx as shown in figure.

dm = mass of element $= \lambda \cdot dx$ ...(i)

Also, amplitude of oscillation is given by

$$A' = A \sin kx \quad \text{...(ii)}$$

Thus, as per formula of oscillation energy in SHM i.e. $\frac{1}{2}m\omega^2 A^2$,

oscillation energy of element is

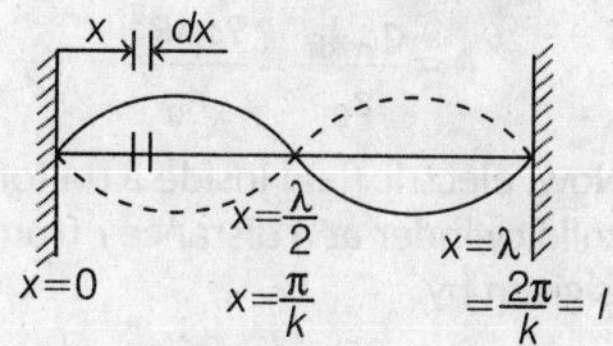

$$dE = \frac{1}{2}dm\omega^2 A'^2 = \frac{1}{2}\lambda dx \omega^2 A^2 \sin^2 kx$$

[using Eqs. (i) and (ii)]

$$\therefore \text{ Total energy, } E = \frac{1}{2}\lambda\omega^2 A^2 \int_0^l \sin^2 kx dx$$

$$= \frac{1}{2}\frac{T}{v^2}\omega^2 A^2 \int_0^l \left(\frac{1 - \cos 2kx}{2}\right)dx$$

$$\left(\because v = \sqrt{\frac{T}{\lambda}}\right)$$

$$= \frac{1}{2}T\left(\frac{2\pi}{l}\right)^2 A^2 \frac{l}{2} = \frac{T\pi^2 A^2}{l}$$

$$\left(\because \frac{2\pi}{l} = k\right)$$

10. FBD of a ball of radius r, moving with terminal speed is as shown in Fig. 1. From FBD,

$$mg = B + 6\pi\eta rv$$

Here, m is mass of ball, B is buoyancy, η is coefficient of viscosity.

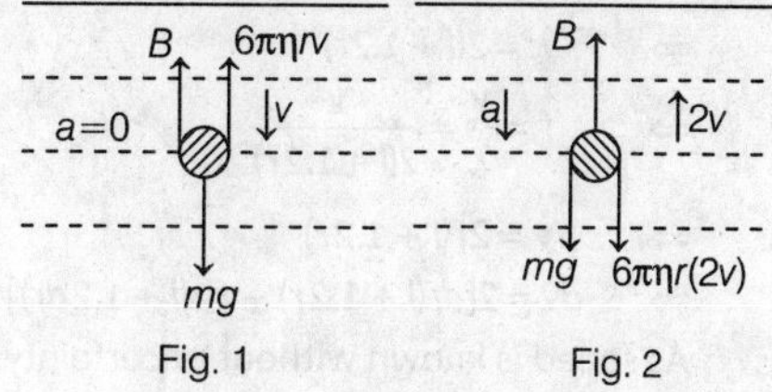

If ρ is density of water and σ is density of ball, we get

$$mg = \rho Vg + 6\pi\eta rv$$

$$\Rightarrow \quad mg = \frac{\sigma}{3}Vg + 6\pi\eta rv$$

$$(\because \sigma = S\rho = 3\rho)$$

$$\Rightarrow \quad mg = \frac{mg}{3} + 6\pi\eta rv$$

$$\Rightarrow 6\pi\eta rv = \frac{2mg}{3} \quad \text{...(i)}$$

FBD of ball when projected with speed $2v$ is as shown in Fig.2.

From the FBD, acceleration of the ball is

$$a = \frac{mg - B + 12\pi\eta rv}{m}$$

$$= \frac{mg - \frac{mg}{3} + \frac{4mg}{3}}{m} = 2g$$

[using Eq. (i)]

11. Let impulse J be applied as shown in figure due to which CM acquires speed v and the rod acquires angular speed ω, as shown in the figure.

By impulse-momentum theorem,

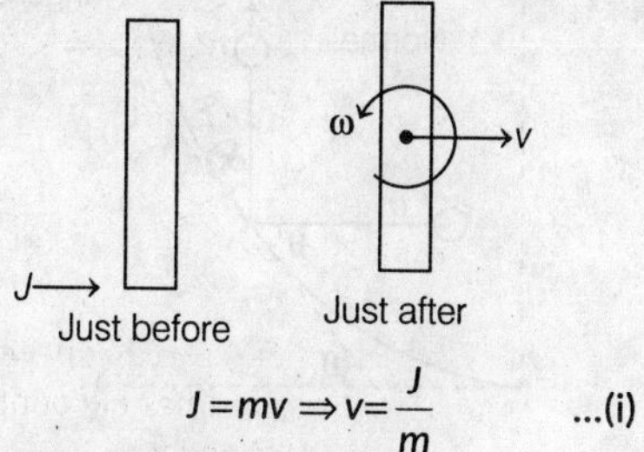

$$J = mv \Rightarrow v = \frac{J}{m} \quad \text{...(i)}$$

By angular impulse-angular momentum theorem, about CM

$$J \cdot r = I_{CM}\omega$$

$$\Rightarrow \quad \frac{Jl}{2} = \frac{ml^2}{12}\omega \Rightarrow \omega = \frac{6J}{ml} \quad \text{...(ii)}$$

Therefore, kinetic energy

$$= \frac{1}{2}mv^2 + \frac{1}{2}I_{CM}\omega^2$$

$$\Rightarrow \quad K = \frac{1}{2}m\left(\frac{J}{m}\right)^2 + \frac{1}{2}\frac{ml^2}{12}\left(\frac{6J}{ml}\right)^2$$

[using Eq. (ii)]

$$\Rightarrow \quad J = \sqrt{\frac{mK}{2}}$$

12. From FBD of any of the particles, in direction normal to the incline

N, a, f=μN, O, mg sin 45°, mg cos45°, 45°

$$N = mg\cos 45° = \frac{mg}{\sqrt{2}} \quad \text{...(i)}$$

Along the incline, using $F = ma$, we get

$$mg \sin 45° - \mu N = ma$$

$$\Rightarrow \frac{mg}{\sqrt{2}} - \frac{\mu mg}{\sqrt{2}} = ma \quad \text{[using Eq. (i)]}$$

$\Rightarrow \quad a = \frac{g}{\sqrt{2}}(1-\mu)$ ...(ii)

Thus, by using $s = ut + \frac{1}{2}at^2$, for any general particle released at $x = x$, we get

$$y = 0 + \frac{1}{2}\frac{g}{\sqrt{2}}(1-\mu)\left(\frac{1}{\sqrt{5}}\right)^2$$

[using Eq. (ii)]

$\Rightarrow \quad \sqrt{2}x^2 = \frac{1}{\sqrt{2}}(1-\mu) \Rightarrow \mu = 1 - 2x^2$

13. Let tangent at P make θ with horizontal, incident velocity is u and velocity after collision is v. As surface is smooth, velocity component along tangent will remain same.

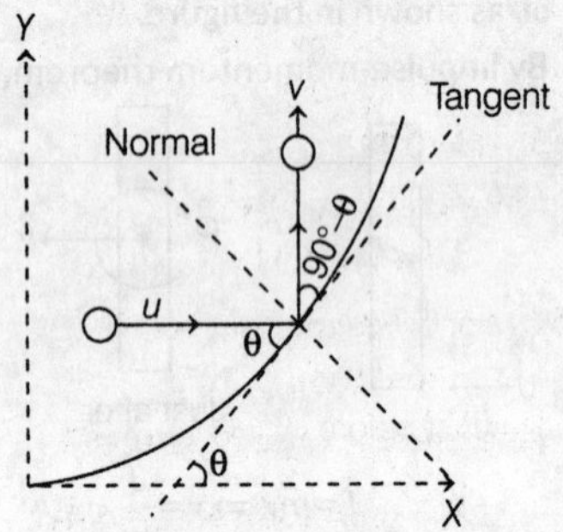

So, $u\cos\theta = v\sin\theta$ ..(i)

Also, velocity component perpendicular to surface will become $\frac{1}{2}$ times. Therefore,

$\frac{1}{2}\cdot u\sin\theta = v\cos\theta$ ...(ii)

Dividing Eq (ii) by Eq. (i), we get

$\tan^2\theta = 2$

$\Rightarrow \quad \left(\frac{dy}{dx}\right)^2 = 2 \Rightarrow (2x)^2 = 2$

$\Rightarrow \quad x^2 = \frac{1}{2} \Rightarrow y = \frac{1}{2}$

14. To find flux through $PQRS$, join PS and QR with axis O as shown forming a closed surface.

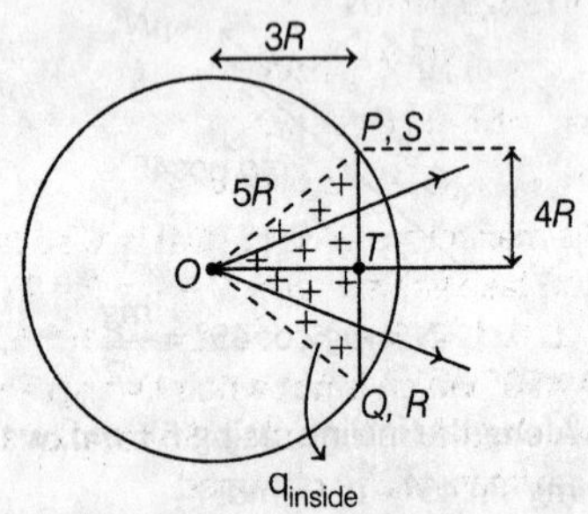

As field lines are crossing only $PQRS$, flux through it will be

$\phi = \frac{q_{\text{inside}}}{\varepsilon_0}$ (as per Gauss' Law) ...(i)

By Pythagoras theorem,

$$OT = \sqrt{OP^2 - PT^2} = 3R$$

So, volume of closed surface is

$$V = \frac{1}{2} \times PQ \times OT \times PS$$

$$= \frac{1}{2} \times 8R \times 3R \times 8R = 96R^3$$

$\Rightarrow q_{\text{inside}} = \rho V = 96\rho R^3$ ...(ii)

From Eqs. (i) and (ii), we get

$\phi = \frac{q_{\text{inside}}}{\varepsilon_0} = \frac{96\rho R^3}{\varepsilon_0}$ ...(iii)

Now, electric field inside a uniform solid cylinder at a distance r from axis is given by

$$E = \frac{\rho r}{2\varepsilon_0}$$

It will be minimum for r minimum equal to $3R$ for surface $PQRS$,

$\Rightarrow \quad E_0 = \frac{\rho(3R)}{2\varepsilon_0}$

$\Rightarrow \quad \frac{\rho R}{\varepsilon_0} = \frac{2E_0}{3}$ ...(iv)

From Eqs. (iii) and (iv), we get,

$$E = 96R^2 \cdot \frac{\rho R}{\varepsilon_0} = 96R^2\left(\frac{2E_0}{3}\right)$$

$$= 64E_0R^2 = E_0(8R)^2 = E_0A$$

15. Separation between antinodes

$$= \frac{\lambda}{2} = l + 1.2r$$

λ/2

Antinode Antinode

0.6r 0.6r

End correction

$\Rightarrow \quad \lambda = 2(l + 1.2r)$

$\Rightarrow \quad f = \frac{v}{\lambda} = \frac{v}{2(l + 1.2r)}$

$\Rightarrow \quad v = 2f(l + 1.2r)$

$\Rightarrow \quad dv = 2[df(l + 1.2r) + f(dl + 1.2dr)]$

As speed is known without uncertainty, dv will be zero.

$\Rightarrow \quad \left|\frac{df}{f}\right| = \frac{dl + 1.2dr}{l + 1.2r}$

$$= \frac{0.1 + 1.2 \times 0.05}{95.2 + 1.2 \times 4} = \frac{0.16}{100}$$

$\Rightarrow \quad \left|\frac{df}{f}\right| \times 100 = 0.16$

16. Standard equation of EM wave's magnetic component is of the form

$$\mathbf{B} = B_0 \sin(\omega t - \mathbf{k}\cdot\mathbf{r} + \phi)\,\mathbf{n}$$

For $\phi = \frac{\pi}{2}$, it reduces to

$$\mathbf{B} = B_0 \cos(\omega t - \mathbf{k}\cdot\mathbf{r})\hat{\mathbf{n}}$$

Here, **k** is propagation vector directed along direction of propagation.

Given, equation can be written as

$$\mathbf{B} = B_0 \cos[\omega t - (5\hat{\mathbf{k}} - 12\hat{\mathbf{i}}) \cdot (x\hat{\mathbf{i}} + y\hat{\mathbf{j}} + z\hat{\mathbf{k}})]\hat{\mathbf{n}}$$

$\Rightarrow \quad \mathbf{k} = 5\hat{\mathbf{k}} - 12\hat{\mathbf{i}}$

$\Rightarrow$ Unit vector in direction of propagation

$$= \frac{5\hat{\mathbf{k}} - 12\hat{\mathbf{i}}}{\sqrt{5^2 + 12^2}} = \frac{5\hat{\mathbf{k}} - 12\hat{\mathbf{i}}}{13}$$

17. Let v and v' are velocities of P and system of $P + Q$ before and after Q is placed on P respectively.

At mean position by conservation of momentum,

$$2mv' = mv$$

$\Rightarrow \quad v' = \frac{v}{2}$ ...(i)

Also, velocity at mean position in terms of amplitude A, mass m and spring constant K is given by

$v = A\sqrt{\frac{K}{m}}$ ...(ii)

If A' is the new amplitude, after placing Q

$v' = A'\sqrt{\frac{K}{2m}}$ ...(iii)

From Eqs. (i), (ii) and (iii), we get

$A' = \frac{A}{\sqrt{2}}$ ...(iv)

From FBD of P at extreme position, using $F = ma$, we get

$KA' - f = ma$ ...(v)

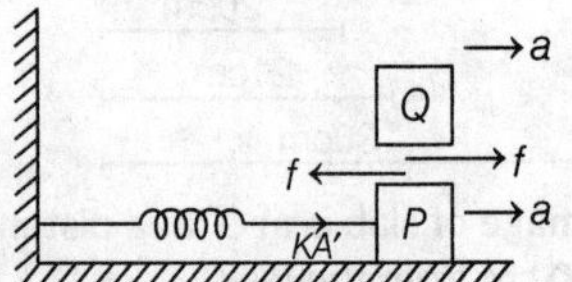

From FBD of Q, we get

$f = ma$ ...(vi)

From Eqs. (iv), (v) and (vi), we get

$$f = \frac{KA}{2\sqrt{2}}$$

18. As there is no current through galvanometer, the current I flows as shown in figure. By Ohm's law,

$$I = \frac{50}{3+2} = 10\text{ A}$$

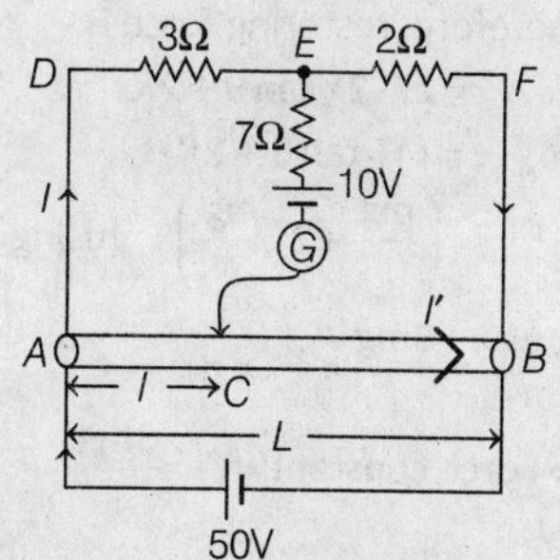

Thus, by KVL in loop $ADECA$, we get

$V_{AC} - 10 \times 3 - 10 = 0$

$\Rightarrow \quad V_{AC} = 40\text{ V}$ ...(i)

Also, by Ohm's law, if resistances between AC and AB are R_{AC} and R_{AB} respectively, we get,

$$V_{AC} = I' R_{AC} = I' \frac{\rho l}{A} \quad \text{...(ii)}$$

and $V_{AB} = I' R_{AB} = I' \dfrac{\rho L}{A}$ ...(iii)

Here, ρ is resistivity and A is cross-sectional area.

Dividing Eq. (ii) by Eq. (iii), we get

$$\frac{V_{AC}}{V_{AB}} = \frac{l}{L}$$

$$\Rightarrow \quad l = \left(\frac{V_{AC}}{V_{AB}}\right) L = \left(\frac{40}{50}\right) L = 0.8\,L$$

[using Eq. (i)]

19. Equation of v-x graph will be

$$v = kx$$

Here, k is slope of the graph

$$\Rightarrow \quad \frac{dx}{dt} = kx$$

$$\Rightarrow \quad \int_{x_0}^{x} \frac{dx}{x} = k\int_0^t dt$$

$$\Rightarrow \quad \ln\frac{x}{x_0} = kt$$

$$\Rightarrow \quad x = x_0 e^{kt}$$

$$\Rightarrow \quad v = \frac{dx}{dt} = x_0 k e^{kt} = v_0 e^{kt}$$

Here, $x_0 k = v_0 =$ initial velocity

As at, $t = t_0$, $v = 2v_0$, we get

$$2v_0 = v_0 e^{kt_0}$$

$$\Rightarrow \quad e^{kt_0} = 2$$

Thus, at $t = 2t_0$, velocity will be

$$v = v_0 e^{k(2t_0)} = v_0 [e^{kt_0}]^2$$

$$= v_0 2^2 = 4v_0$$

So, velocity increases from v_0 to $4v_0$ between $t = t_0$ and $t = 2t_0$

$\Rightarrow$ Average acceleration

$$= \frac{\Delta v}{\Delta t} = \frac{4v_0 - v_0}{2t_0 - t_0} = \frac{3v_0}{t_0}$$

20. Minimum separation for resolved observation is called limit of resolution and is given by

$$d = \frac{0.61\lambda}{\text{NA}}$$

$$= \frac{0.61 \times 400 \times 10^{-9}}{1.2} = 0.2\,\mu\text{m}$$

21. The various forces acting in the arrangement are shown below.

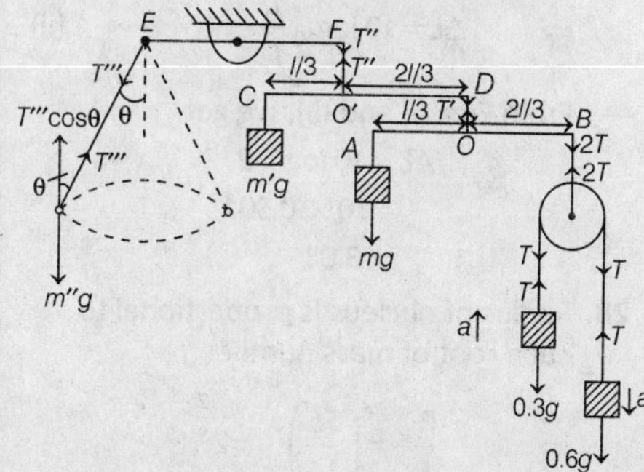

For 0.6 kg block, by $F = ma$, we get

$$0.6g - T = 0.6a \quad \text{...(i)}$$

For 0.3 kg block, we get,

$$T - 0.3g = 0.3a \quad \text{...(ii)}$$

Solving Eqs. (i) and (ii), we get

$$T = 0.4g$$

For rod AB to be equilibrium,

τ of $mg = \tau$ of tension

$$\Rightarrow \quad mg\frac{l}{3} = 0.8g \times \frac{2l}{3} \quad \text{[using Eq. (iii)]}$$

$$\Rightarrow \quad m = 1.6\text{ kg} \quad \text{...(iv)}$$

Similarly, by considering equilibrium of CD, we get, $m' g\dfrac{l}{3} = T' \times \dfrac{2l}{3}$

$$\Rightarrow m' g\frac{l}{3} = (mg + 2T)\frac{2l}{3}$$

$$\Rightarrow m' g\frac{l}{3} = (1.6g + 2 \times 0.4g)\frac{2l}{3}$$

[using Eq. (iii) and (iv)]

$$\Rightarrow m' = 4.8\,kg$$

For equilibrium of EF, we get

$$T''' \cos\theta\frac{l}{3} = T'' \times \frac{2l}{3}$$

$$\Rightarrow \quad m''g\frac{l}{3} = (m' g + T')\frac{2l}{3}$$

$$\Rightarrow \quad m''g = 2(4.8 \times g + 2.4g)$$

$$\Rightarrow \quad m'' = 14.4\text{ kg}$$

22. Max amplitude $= A_c + A_m = 9$ ...(i)

Here, A_c and A_m are amplitudes of carrier wave and message signal.

Also, $\mu =$ Modulation index $= \dfrac{A_m}{A_c}$

$$\Rightarrow \quad A_m = \mu A_c = 0.8A_c \quad \text{...(ii)}$$

From Eqs. (i) and (ii),

$$A_c + 0.8A_c = 9$$

$$\Rightarrow \quad A_c = 5$$

$$\Rightarrow \quad A_m = 4$$

Minimum amplitude $A = A_c - A_m = 1$ ...(iii)

Lower side band frequency

$$= \text{central frequency} - \frac{\text{BW}}{2}$$

$$= 1 - \frac{20 \times 10^{-3}}{2} = 1 - 10^{-2}$$

$$= 0.99\text{ MHz}$$

$\Rightarrow \quad f = 0.99$ ...(iv)

From Eqs. (ii) and (iv),

$$f + A = 1.99 \approx 2$$

23. Angular frequency of source,

$$\omega = 100\pi$$

Inductive reactance of solenoid,

$$X_L = \omega L = 100\pi \times \frac{1}{25\pi} = 4\Omega$$

Impedance of solenoid,

$$Z = \sqrt{X_L^2 + R^2} = \sqrt{4^2 + 3^2} = 5\Omega$$

Maximum current in solenoid

$$= \frac{V_{\max}}{Z} = \frac{5}{5} = 1\text{ A}$$

$$\therefore \quad i = 1 \cdot \sin(100\pi t + \phi)$$

Emf induced in ring, $\varepsilon = |M - L|\dfrac{di}{dt}$

$$= \frac{1}{50\pi} \cdot 100\pi\cos(100\pi t + \phi)$$

$$= 2\cos(100\pi t + \phi)$$

$$\Rightarrow \quad \varepsilon_{\max} = 2$$

$\therefore$ Maximum current $= \dfrac{\varepsilon_{\max}}{R} = \dfrac{2}{2} = 1\text{ A}$

24. For maxima at point P of screen in Arrangement-1

$$d\sin\theta = \pm n\lambda$$

$$\Rightarrow \quad 6\lambda\sin\theta = \pm n\lambda$$

$$\Rightarrow \quad n = \pm 6\sin\theta$$

As maximum value of $\sin\theta$ is 1, so n can take values $-6, -5, -4, -3, -2, -1, 0, 1, 2, 3, 4, 5, 6$. But for $n = \pm 6$, $\theta = 90°$ which is not a point on screen, so, should be excluded. So total of 11 maximas will be obtained.

$$\therefore \quad n_1 = 11$$

In Arrangement-2 owing to symmetry about X-axis, circular fringes are obtained, as shown in figure. Path difference at O (centre of screen) is 3.5 λ. As we move from O to ∞ on screen, path differences of 3λ, 2λ and λ are obtained. Corresponding to these, three bright circular fringes will be observed.

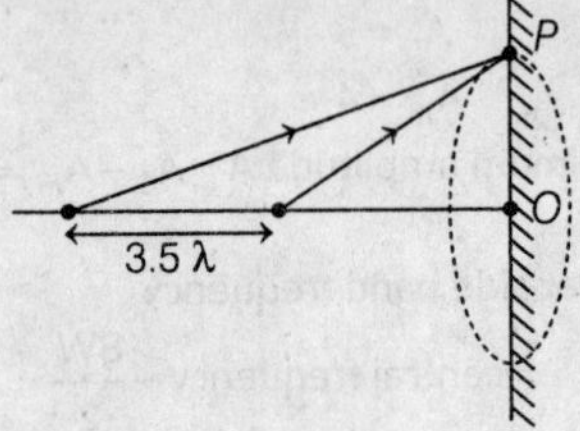

$$\Rightarrow \quad n_2 = 3$$

Therefore, $\frac{n_1}{n_2} = \frac{11}{3} = 3.67$

25. It is given that, $\rho^2 U^3 = \text{constant}$

$$\Rightarrow \left(\frac{m}{V}\right)^2 \cdot \left(\frac{f}{2} nRT\right)^3 = \text{constant}$$

Here, m is mass and f is degree of freedom

$$\Rightarrow \quad \frac{T^3}{V^2} = \text{constant}$$

$$\Rightarrow \frac{(pV)^3}{V^2} = \text{constant (As, } T = \frac{pV}{nR})$$

$$\Rightarrow \quad pV^{\frac{1}{3}} = \text{constant}$$

So, polytropic index of process $(\gamma) = \frac{1}{3}$

As for polytropic process

$pV^x = \text{constant}$

Molar specific heat is given by

$$C = \frac{f}{2}R + \frac{R}{1-\gamma}$$

Therefore, as f of CO_2 is 5, we get

$$C = \frac{5}{2}R + \frac{R}{1-\frac{1}{3}} = 4R$$

$$= 4 \times 8.31$$

$$= 33.24$$

26. The two liquids apply forces as shown in figure.

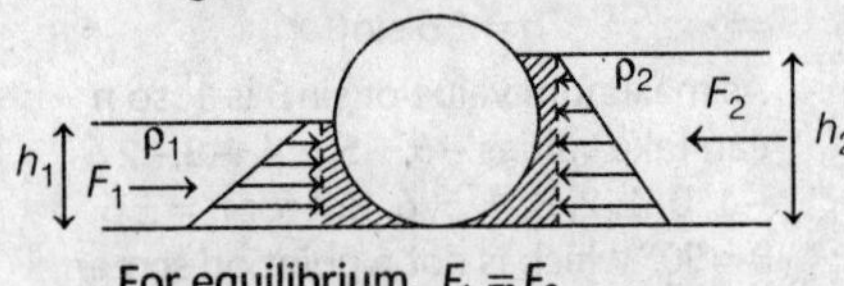

For equilibrium, $F_1 = F_2$

$$\Rightarrow (\rho_{\text{average}})_1 \times A_1 = (\rho_{\text{average}})_2 \times A_2$$

$$\Rightarrow \frac{\rho_1 g h_1}{2} \times h_1 \times l = \frac{\rho_2 g h_2}{2} \times h_2 \times l$$

Here, l is length of cylinder.

$$\Rightarrow \quad h_2 = \sqrt{\frac{\rho_1}{\rho_2}}\, h_1 = \sqrt{\frac{1.69}{1}} \times 1.6 = 2.08$$

27. Intensity due to a line source is inversely proportional to perpendicular distance r from source. So, ratio of intensity at $r_1 = 3$ m to $r_2 = 6$ m is

$$\frac{I_1}{I_2} = \frac{r_2}{r_1} = 2 \quad \text{...(i)}$$

Also, loudness for intensity I is given by

$$L = 10 \log_{10} \frac{I}{I_0}$$

$$\Rightarrow \quad L_1 - L_2 = 10\left[\log_{10}\frac{I_1}{I_0} - \log_{10}\frac{I_2}{I_0}\right]$$

$$\Rightarrow \quad \Delta L = 10 \log_{10} \frac{I_1}{I_2} \quad \text{...(ii)}$$

From Eqs. (i) and (ii), we get

$$\Delta L = 10 \log_{10} 2$$

$$= 10 \times 0.301$$

$$= 3.01$$

28. Radius of nucleus is proportional to cube root of mass number

$$\Rightarrow \quad \frac{R_{Fe}}{R_N} = \left(\frac{56}{14}\right)^{\frac{1}{3}} = 2^{\frac{2}{3}}$$

$$\Rightarrow \quad x = 2$$

29. For equilibrium of wire AB shown in Fig.1,

Surface tension force = Weight

$$\Rightarrow \quad F = mg$$

$$\Rightarrow 2T \cdot 2l \tan\theta = mg$$

$$\Rightarrow \quad \tan\theta = \frac{mg}{4Tl} \quad \text{...(i)}$$

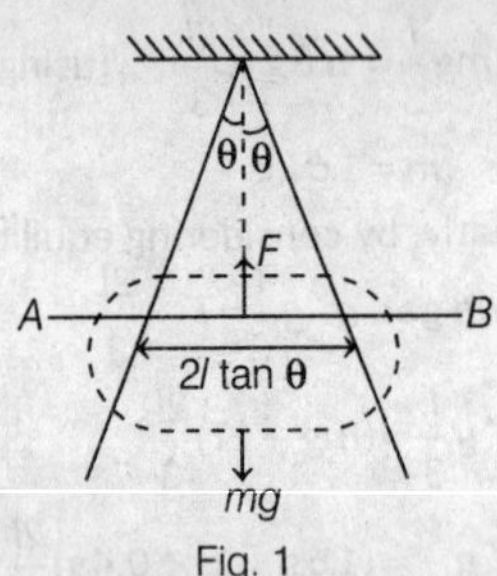

Fig. 1

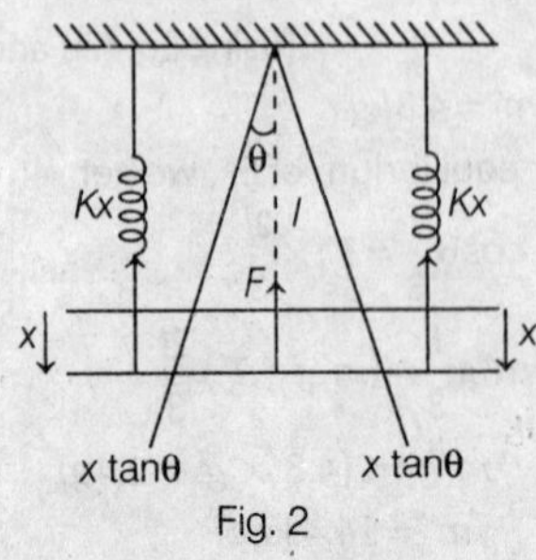

Fig. 2

Now, if the wire is displaced by amount x as shown in Fig. 2, increase in length of wire in contact with soap film $= 2x \tan\theta$.

Also, increase in lengths of spring $= x$

Therefore, restoring force is

$$F' = 2T \cdot 2x \tan\theta + 2Kx$$

$$= (4T \tan\theta + 2K)x$$

$$= \left(\frac{mg}{l} + 2 \cdot \frac{mg}{l}\right)x \quad \text{[using Eq. (i)]}$$

$$= \frac{3mg}{l} x = Cx$$

$$\Rightarrow \text{Force constant} = C = \frac{3mg}{l}$$

As time period is given by $2\pi\sqrt{\frac{m}{C}}$

Therefore, we get

$$T = 2\pi\sqrt{\frac{m}{\frac{3mg}{l}}} = \pi\sqrt{\frac{4l}{3g}}$$

$$\therefore \quad x = \frac{4}{3} = 1.33$$

30. As, displacement of wall is always zero, work done by the spring is zero.

Knockout 11 (Paper 1)

1. Consider ΔABC in Star-1.

As angle of a regular pentagon is

$$\left(\frac{n-2}{n}\right)\pi = \frac{5-2}{5} \times 180° = 108°$$

So, angle B and C will be 72° as shown in Fig. 1, so angle A will be $180° - 2 \times 72°$ equal to 36°.

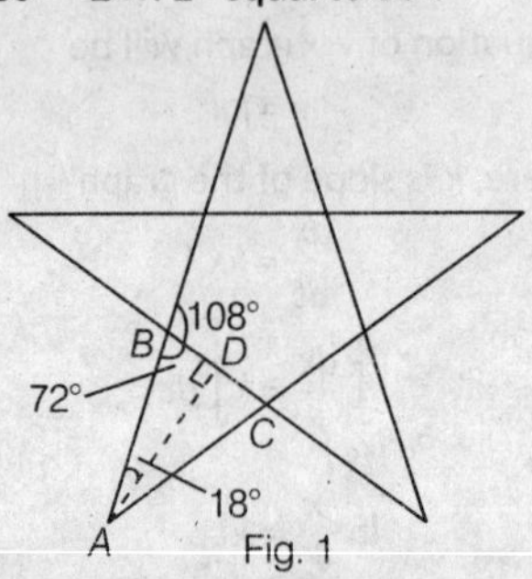

Fig. 1

In isosceles triangle ABC, we now draw perpendicular from A on side BC. Half of angle A will thus be 18°. By trigonometry, $BD = AB \sin 18° = \frac{AB}{3}$

$$\Rightarrow \quad BC = 2 \times BD = \frac{2AB}{3}$$

(As triangle is isosceles, so $BD = CD$)

Length of segment BC is (2/3)rd of AB and as resistance is proportional to length, resistance of BC will also be

(2/3)rd of that of AB, therefore

$$R_{BC}=\frac{2}{3}\times R_{AB}=\frac{4}{3}\,\Omega$$

So, the circuit can be visualised as shown in Fig. 2 with AP as line of symmetry.

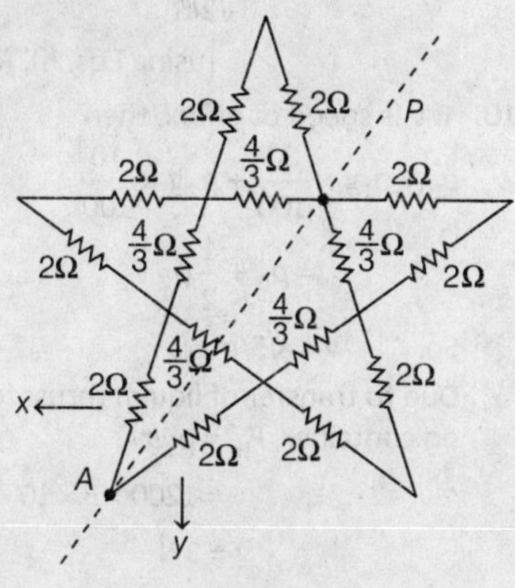

Fig.2

As mirror image resistors (for example resistors like x and y marked in Fig. 2) are in parallel, so one half can be folded on other half thereby reducing circuit to that shown in Fig. 3.

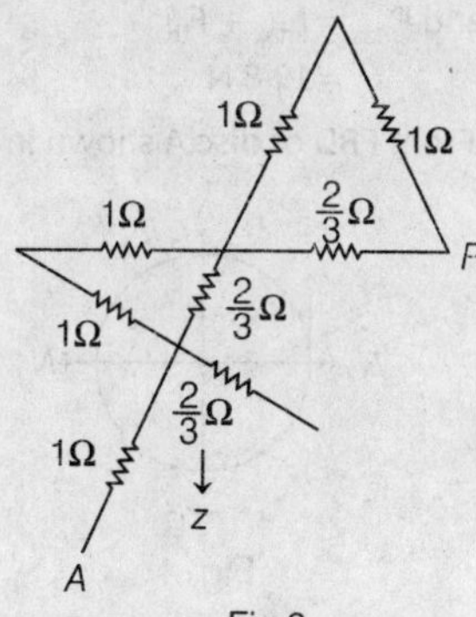

Fig.3

Resistor marked z is in open circuit and so can be ignored. Remaining resistors can be reduced by using formulae of series and parallel equivalents as shown in Figs. 4 and 5.

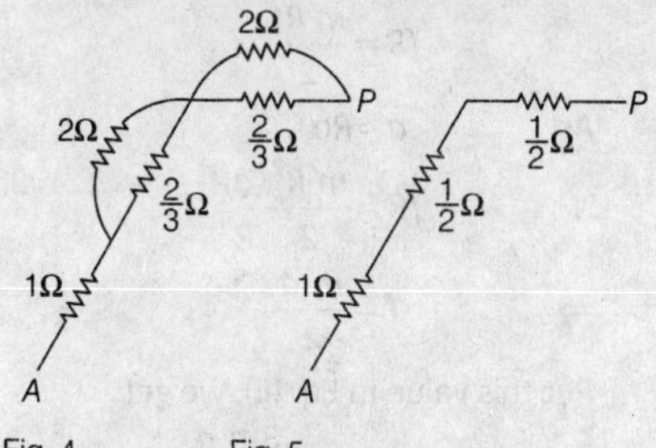

Fig. 4 Fig. 5

So, equivalent resistance will be

$$R_{AP}=1+\frac{1}{2}+\frac{1}{2}=2\,\Omega$$

Similarly, equivalent capacitance between Q and F can be found as

$$C_{QF}=3\,\mu F$$

Thus, the circuit is equivalent to circuit shown in Fig. 6

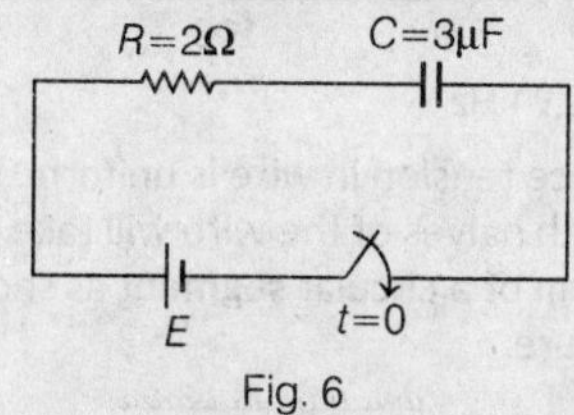

Fig. 6

Energy stored by capacitor is given by

$$U=\frac{Q^2}{2C}$$

$$\Rightarrow \quad Q\propto\sqrt{U}$$

When energy is (1/4)th of final energy, charge will be half of steady state charge (Q_0).

As, for RC charging circuit,

$$Q=Q_0\,(1-e^{-t/RC})$$

(Here, Q_0 is final charge)

$$\Rightarrow \quad \frac{Q_0}{2}=Q_0(1-e^{-t/RC})$$

$$\Rightarrow \quad e^{-t/RC}=\frac{1}{2}$$

$$\Rightarrow \quad t=RC\ln 2$$

$$=2\times 3\times 10^{-6}\times 0.693$$

$$=4.16\,\mu s$$

2. Take clockwise to be positive. As, angular momentum is conserved.

$$I\omega_i-mv_id=I\omega_f+mv_fd$$

$$\Rightarrow \quad 0.30(\omega)-0.15(50)(0.8)$$

$$=0.3(0.35\,\omega)+0.15(40)(0.8)$$

$$\Rightarrow \quad \omega=55.4\text{ rad/s}$$

$$\therefore \text{ Period, } T=\frac{2\pi}{\omega}=0.11\text{s}$$

3. The image shall coincide with object O, if the ray starting from O is incident normally on mirror (Fig. 1). For Fig.1,

$$x=4\times\frac{4}{3}=\frac{16}{3}\text{ cm}$$

$$\Rightarrow \quad R=40+\frac{16}{3}=\frac{136}{3}\text{ cm}$$

In second case, the image shall coincide with object O, if ray starting from O is incident normally on mirror (Fig. 2)

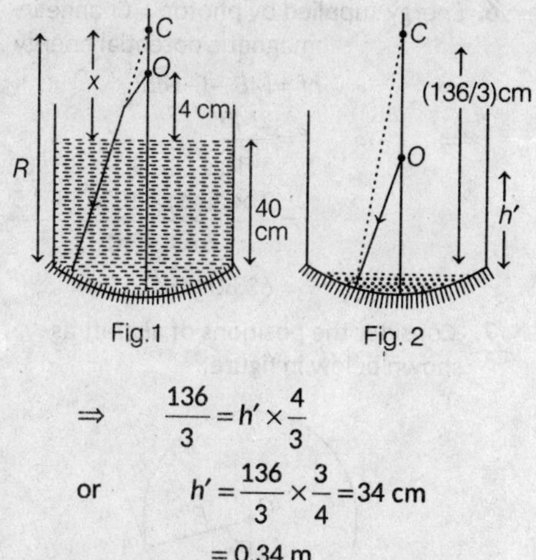

Fig.1 Fig. 2

$$\Rightarrow \quad \frac{136}{3}=h'\times\frac{4}{3}$$

$$\text{or} \quad h'=\frac{136}{3}\times\frac{3}{4}=34\text{ cm}$$

$$=0.34\text{ m}$$

4. Potential energy of electron in nth orbit is given by

$$\text{PE (in eV)}=-27.2/n^2$$

$$\Rightarrow \quad -6.8\text{ eV}=-27.2/n^2$$

$$\Rightarrow \quad n=2$$

$$\text{Orbital period}=\frac{2\pi r_n}{v_n}$$

$$=\frac{2\varepsilon_0 n^2h^2/me^2}{e^2/2\varepsilon_0 nh}=\frac{4\varepsilon_0^2n^3h^3}{me^4}$$

As $T\propto n^3$, for $n=2$,

$$T_2=T_1(2)^3=1.22\times 10^{-15}\text{ s}$$

Therefore, number of orbits

$$=\frac{1.0\times 10^{-8}}{1.22\times 10^{-15}}$$

$$=8.19\times 10^6=8.19\text{ million}$$

5. In parallel combination, the equivalent resistance is

$$\frac{1}{R_{eq}}=\frac{1}{R_1}+\frac{1}{R_2}+\frac{1}{R_3}$$

$$\Rightarrow \quad \frac{dR_{eq}}{R_{eq}^2}=\frac{dR_1}{R_1^2}+\frac{dR_2}{R_2^2}+\frac{dR_3}{R_3^2}$$

$$\Rightarrow \quad \frac{dR_{eq}}{R_{eq}}\times 100$$

$$=R_{eq}\left(\frac{1}{R_1}\frac{dR_1}{R_1}\times 100+\frac{1}{R_2}\frac{dR_2}{R_2}\times 100+\frac{1}{R_3}\frac{dR_3}{R_3}\times 100\right)$$

$$\Rightarrow \frac{dR_{eq}}{R_{eq}}\times 100$$

$$=\pm 1\left[\frac{1}{3}\times 1+\frac{1}{6}\times 2+\frac{1}{2}\times 1\right]$$

$$\Rightarrow \frac{dR_{eq}}{R_{eq}}\times 100=\pm\frac{7}{6}\%=1.16$$

6. Energy supplied by photon = Change in magnetic potential energy

$\Rightarrow \quad hf = MB - (-MB)$

$\Rightarrow \quad f = \frac{2MB}{h}$

$= \frac{2 \times 1.41 \times 10^{-26} \times 1.5}{6.63 \times 10^{-34}}$

$= 63.80$ MHz

7. Consider the positions of aircraft as shown below in figure.

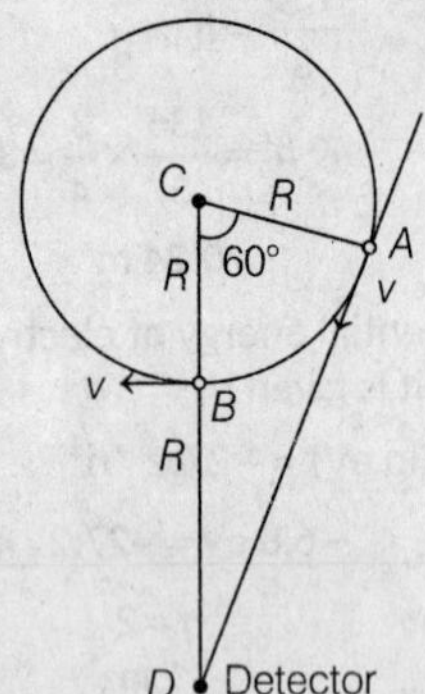

From triangle ACD,

Time taken by plane to travel by 60°

$= \frac{2\pi R}{v} \times \frac{60°}{360°} = \frac{2\pi R}{v} \times \frac{1}{6}$

Time taken by sound to travel $\sqrt{3}R$ distance $= \frac{\sqrt{3}R}{v_w}$

Now, $\frac{2\pi R}{v} \times \frac{1}{6} = \frac{\sqrt{3}R}{v_w}$

$\Rightarrow \frac{v}{v_w} = \frac{2\pi}{(\sqrt{3})6} = \frac{\pi}{3\sqrt{3}}$

which is equal to mach number = 0.60

8. Change in length of string due to increase in temperature,

$\Delta l = l\alpha\Delta T$ ...(i)

Also, by Hooke's law, change in tension (F),

$\Delta F = \frac{\Delta l \cdot Y \cdot A}{l}$ ...(ii)

From Eqs. (i) and (ii), we get

$\Delta F = YA\alpha\Delta T$ ...(iii)

Also, frequency is related to tension F by the relation

$f = \frac{1}{2l}\sqrt{\frac{F}{\mu}}$ ...(iv)

Here, l = length of string

and μ = linear mass density.

$\Rightarrow \quad \frac{df}{dF} = \frac{1}{2l\sqrt{\mu}} \cdot \frac{1}{2\sqrt{F}}$ ...(v)

Dividing Eq. (v) by Eq. (iv), we get

$\frac{df}{f} = \frac{1}{2} \cdot \frac{dF}{F} \Rightarrow \Delta f = \frac{1}{2} \cdot \frac{\Delta F}{F} \cdot f$

$\Rightarrow \Delta f = \frac{1}{2} \frac{YA\alpha\Delta T}{F} f$ [using Eq. (iii)]

$= \frac{1}{2} \times \frac{2 \times 10^{11} \times 0.1 \times 10^{-6} \times 1.2 \times 10^{-5} \times 10 \times 245}{100}$

$= 2.94$ Hz

9. Since tension in wire is uniform, so both halves of the wire will take the form of a circular segment as shown in figure.

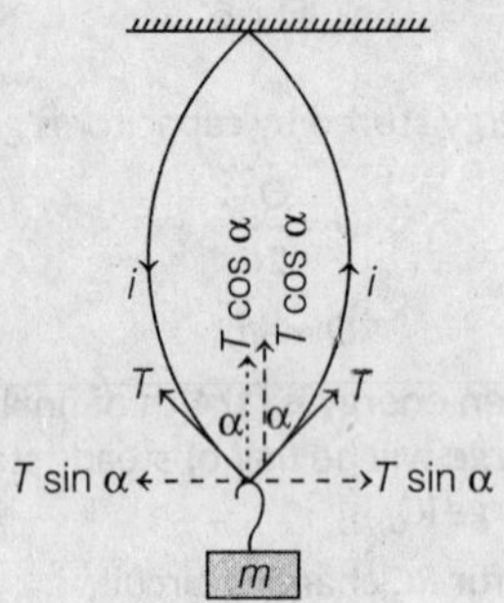

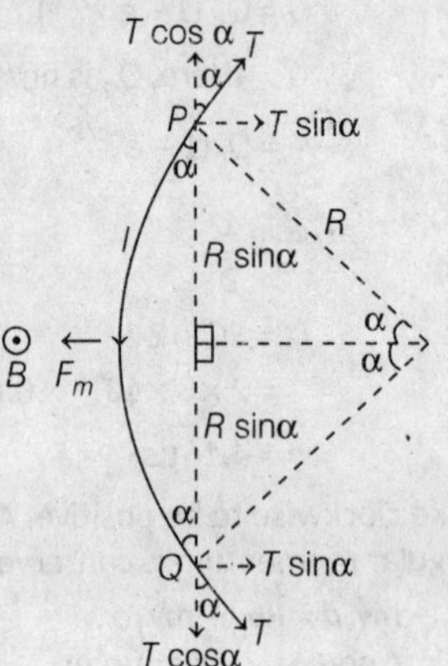

From FBD of block, in vertical direction,

$2T\cos\alpha = mg$ ...(i)

From FBD of left half of wire, in horizontal direction,

$2T\sin\alpha = F_m = Bi(PQ) = 2BiR\sin\alpha$

$\Rightarrow \quad T = BiR$ ...(ii)

Also, length of half of string from diagram,

$l = 2R\alpha$

$\Rightarrow \quad R = \frac{l}{2\alpha}$ ...(iii)

So, height by which block is lifted,

$\Delta h = l - 2R\sin\alpha = l\left(1 - \frac{\sin\alpha}{\alpha}\right)$ ...(iv)

Also, for $\Delta h = l\left(1 - \frac{3}{\pi}\right)$, we get

$l\left(1 - \frac{\sin\alpha}{\alpha}\right) = l\left(1 - \frac{3}{\pi}\right)$ [using Eq. (iv)]

$\Rightarrow \quad \frac{\sin\alpha}{\alpha} = \frac{3}{\pi}$

$\Rightarrow \quad i = \frac{mg\pi}{3\sqrt{2}lB}$

[using Eqs. (i), (ii), (iii)]

10. If v is speed of efflux, then

$p_0 + \rho_1 g \times \frac{30}{100} + \rho_2 g \times \frac{10}{100} = p_0 + \frac{1}{2}\rho_2 v_2^2$

So, $\quad v = \sqrt{5}$ m / s

Due to transfer of liquid, thrust force on container, $F_{th} = \rho_2 a v^2$

$= 1200 \times 5 \times 10^{-4} \times 5$

$= 3$ N

Normal force from surface,

$N = (\rho_1 A \times 0.3)\, g + (\rho_2 A \times 0.2) g = 420$ N

So, $\quad f_{max} = 0.04 \times 420 = 16.8$ N

As $f_{max} > F_{th}$, the vessel will be in equilibrium.

So, $\quad F_{min} = 0$

and $F_{max} = f_{max} + F_{th}$

$= 19.8$ N

11. From FBD of disc A shown in Fig. 1,

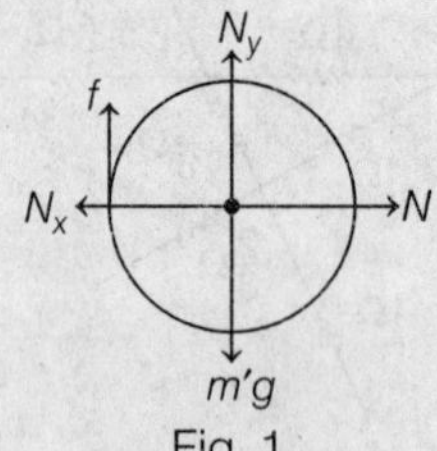

Fig. 1

In horizontal direction

$N = N_x$ ...(i)

In vertical direction,

$m'g - f - N_y = m'a$ ...(ii)

Torque due to friction,

$fR = \frac{m'R^2}{2}\alpha$

As, $\quad a = R\alpha$

$\therefore \quad fR = \frac{m'R^2}{2}\frac{a}{R}$

$\Rightarrow \quad f = \frac{m'a}{2}$

Put this value in Eq. (ii), we get

$m'g - N_y = \frac{3m'a}{2}$

$\Rightarrow \quad N_y = m'g - \frac{3m'a}{2}$ ...(iii)

Also, from FBD of bar shown in Fig. 2.

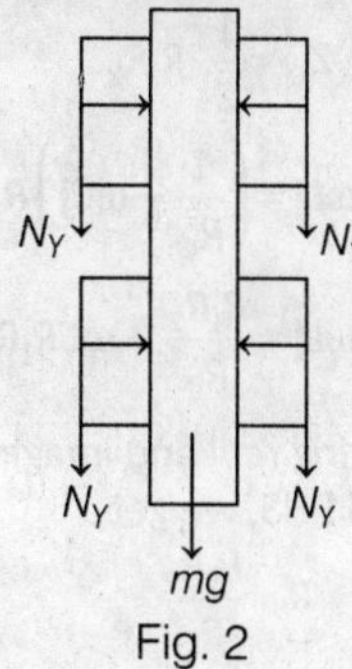

Fig. 2

$$4N_y + mg = ma$$

Put N_y from Eq. (iii), we get

$$4m'g - 6m'a + mg = ma \quad \text{...(iv)}$$

As, $m' = 2$ kg and $m = 5$ kg

$\therefore \quad 8g - 12a + 5g = 5a$

$$a = \frac{13g}{17} \downarrow$$

From Eq. (iv) (neglecting m'), $a = g \downarrow$

From Eq. (iv) (neglecting m), $a = \frac{2g}{3} \downarrow$

12. Since F-r curve is continuous, so

$\left.\frac{dF}{dr}\right|_{P^+} = \left.\frac{dF}{dr}\right|_{P^-} = \left.\frac{dF}{dr}\right|_P = -\alpha$ and F (At P) $= 0$, so Hooke's law is valid near point P.

Energy required to separate the atoms $|\Delta U| = |\int \mathbf{F} \cdot d\mathbf{r}| =$ Area enclosed between curve and r-axis (between actual separation and infinity).

13. Power delivered by tension to the bead, $P = Tv \cos 90° = 0$.

So, work done by tension on bead is 0. Hence, speed and kinetic energy of bead will remain constant and so its average speed will be v_0 only.

Also, let the length of string that winds on the string at time t be x as shown in the figure.

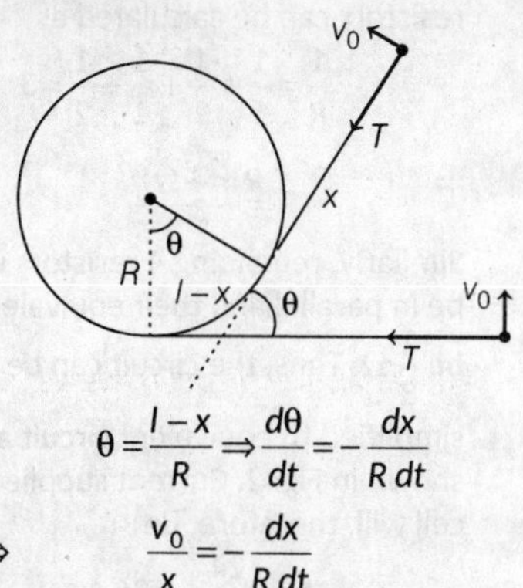

$$\theta = \frac{l-x}{R} \Rightarrow \frac{d\theta}{dt} = -\frac{dx}{R\,dt}$$

$$\Rightarrow \quad \frac{v_0}{x} = -\frac{dx}{R\,dt}$$

$$\Rightarrow \quad x\,dx = -Rv_0\,dt \Rightarrow t = \frac{l^2}{2Rv_0}$$

14. The figure shows a strip at a distance x of thickness dx, As μ of material increases with x, ray will deviate continuously as shown. By Snell's law, between O and A,

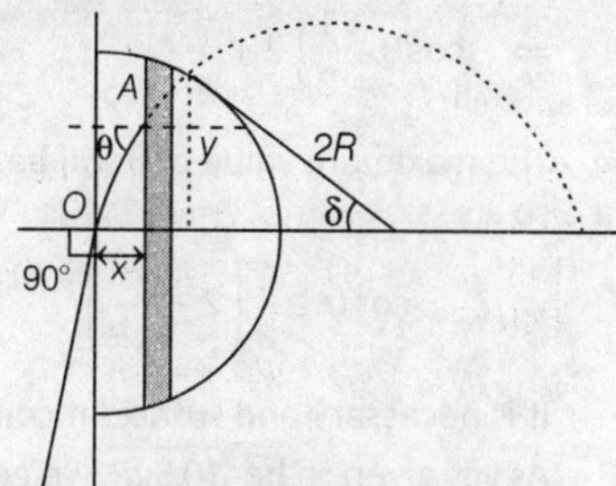

$$1 \times \sin 90° = \frac{2R}{2R - x} \times \sin\theta$$

$$\Rightarrow \quad \tan\theta = \frac{2R - x}{\sqrt{(2R)^2 - (2R - x)^2}}$$

$$\Rightarrow \quad \frac{dy}{dx} = \frac{2R - x}{\sqrt{(2R)^2 - (2R - x)^2}}$$

$$\Rightarrow \quad \int_0^y dy = \int_0^x \frac{2R - x}{\sqrt{(2R)^2 - (2R - x)^2}}\,dx$$

$$\Rightarrow \quad y = \sqrt{(2R)^2 - (2R - x)^2}$$

$$\Rightarrow \quad y^2 + (x - 2R)^2 = (2R)^2$$

which is equation of circle of radius $2R$ centred at $(2R, 0)$. Also, equation of hemispherical surface is

$$x^2 + y^2 = R^2 \Rightarrow y^2 = R^2 - x^2$$

Putting this value of y^2 in equation of trajectory, we can find coordinates of point where the ray comes out of hemisphere, as

$$R^2 - x^2 + (x - 2R)^2 = 4R^2$$

$$\Rightarrow \quad x = \frac{R}{4} \Rightarrow y = \sqrt{R^2 - x^2}$$

$$= \sqrt{R^2 - \left(\frac{R}{4}\right)^2} = \frac{\sqrt{15}R}{4}$$

$$= 0.97R$$

From the diagram,

$$\sin\delta = \frac{y}{2R} = \frac{\sqrt{15}}{8} \simeq \frac{\sqrt{16}}{8} = \frac{1}{2}$$

$$\Rightarrow \quad 0 < \delta < 30°$$

15. I. FBDs of block and wedge are as shown

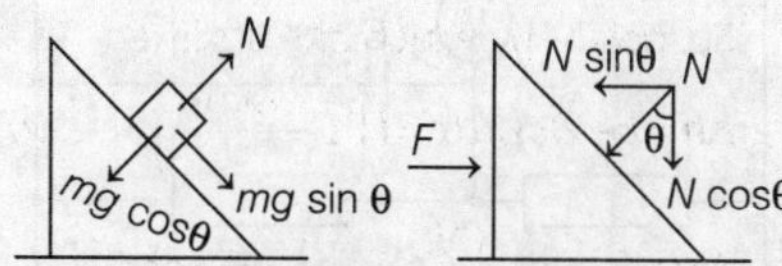

If wedge was at rest but block was slide down, for the block

$$N = mg\cos\theta \quad \text{...(i)}$$

Therefore, for the wedge

$$F = N\sin\theta = mg\cos\theta\sin\theta$$

[using Eq. (i)]

II. Limiting friction at ground,

$$f_l = \mu_s N$$

$$\Rightarrow \quad f_l = 0.6 \times 15 \times 10 = 90\text{N}$$

But as the total force acting on the system (besides friction) is 60 N, so the lower block will not slide on the ground and friction acting on it will be 60 N as shown.

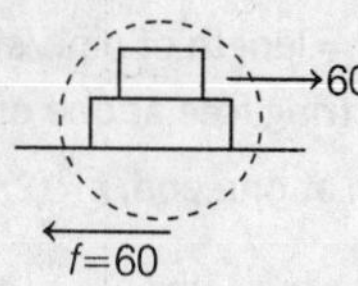

Limiting friction between blocks,

$$f_l' = 0.4 \times 5 \times 10 = 20\text{N}$$

As force on upper block is 40 N ($> f_l'$), it will slide relative to the lower block. Friction acting on it will be kinetic friction.

So, friction on the lower block is not limiting.

III.

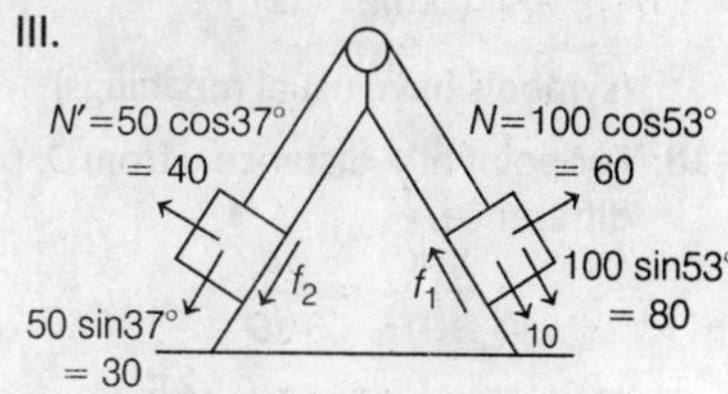

Limiting friction for the system,

$$f_l = f_1 + f_2$$

$$= 0.6 \times 60 + 0.6 \times 40 = 60\text{N}$$

External pulling force along the branch

$$= 80 + 10 - 30 = 60\text{N}$$

So, the system will remain in limiting equilibrium.

IV.

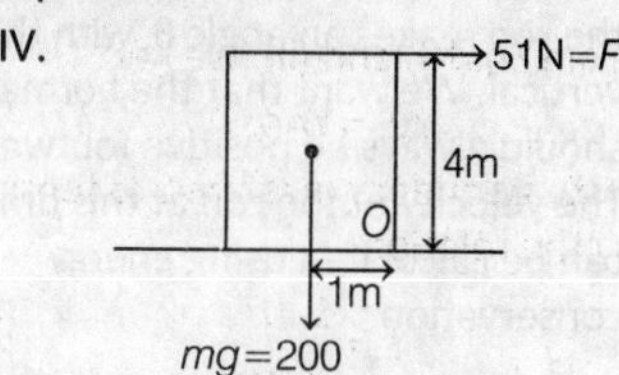

$$f_{\text{limiting}} = 0.4 \times 20 \times 10 = 80\text{N}$$

As $F < f_{\text{limiting}}$ block will not slide

Also, torque of F about O,

$$\tau_1 = 51 \times 4 = 204 \text{ N-m (clockwise)}$$

Torque of mg about O,

$\tau_2 = 200 \times 1 = 200$ N-m (anti-clockwise)

So, the block will rotate clockwise.

Its CM will move as shown

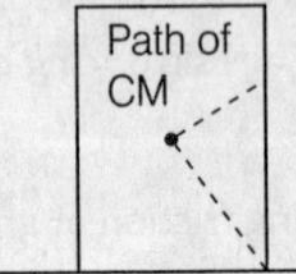

16. For string fixed at both ends and for organ pipe open/closed at both ends, resonance frequencies are given by

$$f = n\left(\frac{v}{2l}\right)$$

where, v = speed of wave

and l = length of pipe/string.

For string free at one end or for pipe open at one end, $f = (2n-1)\frac{v}{4l}$

17. I. $L = mvr = \frac{nh}{2\pi}$

II. $v = \frac{e^2}{2\varepsilon_0 h}\left(\frac{Z}{n}\right)$

III. $U = -\frac{me^4}{4\varepsilon_0^2 h^2}\left(\frac{Z^2}{n^2}\right)$

IV. $\sqrt{r} = \sqrt{\frac{\varepsilon_0 h^2}{\pi m e^2}\left(\frac{n^2}{Z}\right)}$

(symbols have usual meanings)

18. For point at a distance y from O, path difference,

$$\Delta x = \frac{dy}{D}$$

Phase difference, $\Delta\phi = \frac{2\pi}{\lambda}\Delta x$

and resultant intensity,

$$I = I_1 + I_2 + 2\sqrt{I_1 I_2}\cos\Delta\phi$$

(Paper 2)

1. Consider the time when the angle between the line joining the edge to the rod makes an angle θ, with the vertical. We want that the normal should always be positive (outwards). The velocity of the rod at this time is v, can be calculated using energy conservation

$$\frac{1}{2}mv'^2 = \frac{1}{2}mv^2 + mgR(1-\cos\theta)$$

Setting total forces along the line joining the rod to the edge to O, we get

$$\frac{mv'^2}{R} + N = mg\cos\theta$$

$$\Rightarrow N = mg\cos\theta - \frac{2\cdot\frac{1}{2}mv'^2}{R}$$

$$= mg\cos\theta - \frac{mv^2 + 2mgR(1-\cos\theta)}{R}$$

$$\Rightarrow 0 \le 3\,mg\cos\theta - \frac{mv^2 + 2mgR}{R}$$

$$\Rightarrow \cos\theta \ge \frac{1}{3}\left(2 + \frac{v^2}{gR}\right)$$

The maximum value of θ will be alpha, so

$$\Rightarrow \cos\alpha \ge \frac{1}{3}\left(2 + \frac{v^2}{gR}\right)$$

It is necessary and sufficient condition, As v is given to be $\sqrt{0.5gR}$, we get

$$\cos\alpha \ge \frac{1}{3}\left(2 + \frac{0.5gR}{gR}\right)$$

$$\Rightarrow \cos\alpha \ge \frac{5}{6} \Rightarrow 6\cdot\cos\alpha \ge 5$$

2. As the two halves are in parallel

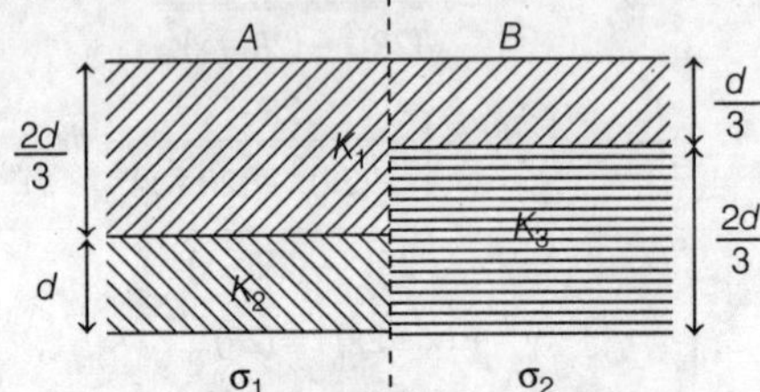

Potential difference will be same on both sides.

$$\Rightarrow \frac{\sigma_1}{2\varepsilon_0}\left(\frac{2d}{3}\right) + \frac{\sigma_1}{4\varepsilon_0}\times\frac{d}{3} = \frac{\sigma_2}{2\varepsilon_0}\left(\frac{d}{3}\right) + \frac{\sigma_2}{6\varepsilon_0}\times\frac{2d}{3}$$

where, σ_1 and σ_2 are surface charge densities as shown in the figure.

$$\Rightarrow \frac{\sigma_2}{\sigma_1} = \frac{\frac{2}{3}+\frac{1}{6}}{\frac{1}{3}+\frac{2}{9}} = \frac{5}{6}\times\frac{9}{5} = 3:2 = \beta:\alpha$$

$$\Rightarrow \alpha + \beta = 5$$

3. Let impedance of coil and $R_C \cdot C$ combination be Z_C and Z, respectively. Also, assume angular frequency of source equal to ω.

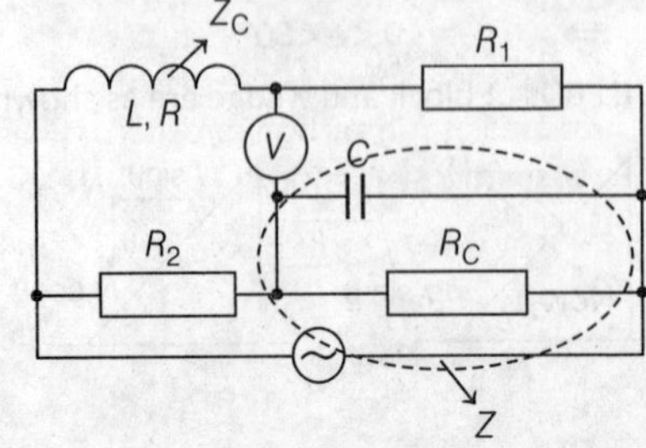

By condition of balancing of bridge,

$$Z_C = \frac{1}{Z}\cdot R_1 R_2$$

$$\Rightarrow R + \omega L\hat{j} = \left(\frac{1}{R_C} + \omega C\hat{j}\right)R_1 R_2$$

$$\Rightarrow R + \omega L\hat{j} = \frac{R_1 R_2}{R_C} + \omega C R_1 R_2\,\hat{j}$$

Comparing real and imaginary parts of LHS and RHS, we get

$$R = \frac{R_1 R_2}{R_C} \qquad \text{...(i)}$$

and $\qquad L = CR_1R_2 \qquad$ ...(ii)

As time constant of LR circuit is $\frac{L}{R}$.

Dividing Eq. (ii) by Eq. (i), we get

$$\frac{L}{R} = C\cdot R_C = (2\mu\text{F})(3\,\Omega) = 6\,\mu\text{s}$$

4. LC of screw gauge

$$= \frac{(1/2)\text{ mm}}{50} = 0.01\text{ mm}$$

Diameter of wire is measured by the screw gauge

$$= 8\times\frac{1}{2} + 10\times 0.01 = 4.1\text{ mm}$$

As, $\qquad \rho = \frac{R\pi\frac{d^2}{4}}{l}$

$$\Rightarrow \left(\frac{\Delta\rho}{\rho}\right)_{max} = \frac{\Delta R}{R} + \frac{2\,\Delta d}{d} - \frac{\Delta l}{l}$$

$$\Rightarrow \left(\frac{\Delta\rho}{\rho}\right)_{max}\times 100$$

$$= \left(\frac{1.5}{100} + \frac{2\times 0.01}{4.1} + \frac{1}{100}\right)\times 100 = 3\%$$

5. As the ammeters are ideal or resistanceless, points P, Q, R and S shown in Fig. 1 are at same potential. Resistors 1 Ω, 2 Ω, 1 Ω and 2 Ω connected to B will be in parallel. Equivalent resistance of these four resistors can be calculated as

$$\frac{1}{R} = \frac{1}{1} + \frac{1}{2} + \frac{1}{1} + \frac{1}{2} = 3$$

$$\Rightarrow \quad R = \frac{1}{3}\,\Omega$$

Similarly, remaining 4 resistors will also be in parallel and their equivalent will be $\frac{1}{3}$ Ω. Thus, the circuit can be simplified to equivalent circuit as shown in Fig. 2. Current supplied by cell will, therefore, be

$$I = \frac{24}{\frac{1}{3}+\frac{1}{3}} = 36\text{ A}$$

So, potential difference between B and P,

$$V_{BP} = 36 \times \frac{1}{3} = 12\text{ V} \quad \text{...(i)}$$

Also, potential difference between A and P,

$$V_{AP} = 36 \times \frac{1}{3} = 12\text{ V} \quad \text{...(ii)}$$

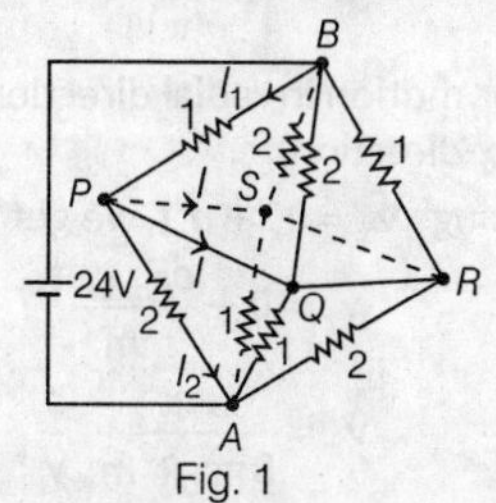

Fig. 1

|||

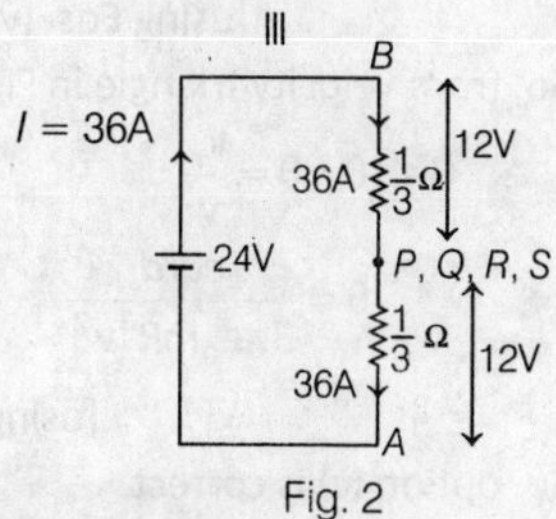

Fig. 2

By Ohm's law, current flowing in 1 Ω resistor between B and P,

$$I_1 = \frac{V_{BP}}{1\,\Omega} = \frac{12\text{ V}}{1\,\Omega} = 12\text{A} \quad \text{...(iii)}$$

[using Eq. (i)]

Similarly, current in 2 Ω resistor between A and P,

$$I_2 = \frac{V_{AP}}{2\,\Omega} = \frac{12\text{ V}}{2\,\Omega} = 6\text{A} \quad \text{...(iv)}$$

By symmetry, currents in ammeter connected to P can be assumed to be equal (suppose I). Thus, by applying KCL at point P,

$$I_2 + I + I = I_1$$

$$\Rightarrow \quad I = \frac{I_1 - I_2}{2} = \frac{12-6}{2} = 3\text{ A}$$

6. In Region-1, kinetic energy,

$$K_1 = 2a - a = a \quad \text{...(i)}$$

While in Region-2, kinetic energy,

$$K_2 = 2a$$

As, de-Broglie wavelength is given by

$$\lambda = \frac{h}{\sqrt{2mK}}$$

$$\Rightarrow \quad \frac{\lambda_1}{\lambda_2} = \sqrt{\frac{K_2}{K_1}} = \sqrt{2}$$

[using Eqs. (i) and (ii)]

$$\Rightarrow \quad \left(\frac{\lambda_1}{\lambda_2}\right)^2 = 2$$

7. Rate of formation of nuclei at time t is $\frac{dN}{dt} = \alpha - \lambda N$, where N = number of nuclei at that time.

$$\Rightarrow \quad N = \frac{\alpha}{\lambda}(1 - e^{-\lambda t})$$

Number of nuclei disintegrated in time t,

$$N_d = \alpha t - \frac{\alpha}{\lambda}(1 - e^{-\lambda t})$$

∴ Energy released till time t,

$$E = E_0 N_d = E_0\left[\alpha t - \frac{\alpha}{\lambda}(1 - e^{-\lambda t})\right]$$

20% of this energy is used for heating water,

$$0.2E_0\left[\alpha t - \frac{\alpha}{\lambda}(1 - e^{-\lambda t})\right] = ms\Delta\theta$$

$$\Delta\theta = \frac{0.2E_0\left[\alpha t - \frac{\alpha}{\lambda}(1 - e^{-\lambda t})\right]}{ms}$$

At $t = T_{1/2}$,

$$\Delta\theta = \frac{0.2E_0\left[2\lambda T_{1/2} - \frac{2\lambda}{\lambda}\left(1 - \frac{1}{2}\right)\right]}{ms}$$

$$\Rightarrow \quad \Delta\theta = \frac{0.2E_0\,(0.386)}{ms}$$

$$= 772\text{ K} = 193\,n\text{K}$$

$$\Rightarrow \quad n = 4$$

8. $\left(p_0 + \frac{4S}{R}\right)\left(\frac{4}{3}\pi R^3\right)$

$$= \left(\frac{p_0}{2} + \frac{4S \times 4}{5R}\right) \times \frac{4}{3}\pi\left(\frac{5R}{4}\right)^3$$

$$\Rightarrow \quad p_0 + \frac{4S}{R} = \left(\frac{p_0}{2} + \frac{16S}{5R}\right)\frac{125}{64}$$

$$\Rightarrow \quad p_0 = \frac{96S}{R}$$

$$\Rightarrow \quad 12n = 96 \Rightarrow n = 8$$

9. Equating the potential gravitational energy to the kinetic energy at the instant before impact, we can arrive at the pre-impact velocity v_0.

$$mgh = \frac{mv_0^2}{2} \quad \text{...(i)}$$

$$\Rightarrow \quad v_0 = \sqrt{2gh} \quad \text{...(ii)}$$

Let v_{2x} and v_{2y} be the horizontal and vertical components respectively, of the velocity of the mass centre at instant after impact. The height attained in the vertical direction will be αh and then $v_{2y}^2 = 2g\alpha h$ ...(iii)

$$\Rightarrow \quad v_{2y} = \sqrt{2g\alpha h} = cv_0 \quad \text{...(iv)}$$

Now, we have

$$I_y = \int_{t_1}^{t_2} N(t)dt = mv_0 + mv_{2y}$$

(N is the normal force)

$$= m(1+c)\sqrt{2gh} \quad \text{...(v)}$$

$$I_x = \int_{t_1}^{t_2} f_r(t)\,dt = mv_{2x} \quad \text{...(vi)}$$

$$I_\theta = \int_{t_1}^{t_2} Rf_r(t)\,dt = I(\omega_0 - \omega_2) \quad \text{...(vii)}$$

where I_x, I_y and I_θ are the linear and angular impulses of the acting forces and ω_2 is the angular velocity after impact. The times t_1 and t_2 correspond to the beginning and end of impact.

$$f_r = \mu_k N(t) \quad \text{...(viii)}$$

Substituting Eq. (viii) in Eqs. (vi) and (vii) and using Eq. (v), we find that

$$I_x = \mu_k \int_{t_1}^{t_2} N(t)\,dt = \mu_k I_y$$

$$= \mu_k m(1+c)\sqrt{2gh} = mv_{2x} \quad \text{...(ix)}$$

and $I_\theta = R\mu_k \int_{t_1}^{t_2} N(t)\,dt$

$$= R\mu_k m(1+c)\sqrt{2gh}$$

$$= I(\omega_0 - \omega_2) \quad \text{...(x)}$$

which can give us the horizontal component of the velocity v_2 and the final angular velocity in the form

$$v_{2x} = \mu_k(1+c)\sqrt{2gh} \quad \text{...(xi)}$$

$$\omega_2 = \omega_0 - \frac{\mu_k mR(1+c)}{I}\sqrt{2gh} \quad \text{...(xii)}$$

The range of validity of the solution under consideration may be obtained from Eqs. (xi) and (xii). This solution will be valid whenever at the end of the impact, the contact point has a velocity in the direction of the negative X-axis. i.e. $\omega_2 R > v_{2x}$

$$\omega_0 - \frac{\mu_k\, mR(1+c)}{I}\sqrt{2gh} > \frac{\mu_k(1+c)}{R}\sqrt{2gh}$$

$$\Rightarrow \omega_0 > \frac{\mu_k\sqrt{2gh}}{R}(1+c)\left(\frac{mR^2}{I} + 1\right)$$

...(xiii)

$$\Rightarrow \omega_{0\min} = \frac{\mu_k(1+c)\sqrt{2gh}\left(1 + \frac{mR^2}{I}\right)}{R}$$

$$\Rightarrow \quad \omega_{0\min} = \frac{7\mu_k(1+c)\sqrt{2gh}}{2R}$$

Also,

For $\tan\theta$ from Eqs. (iv) and (xi), we get

$$\tan\theta = \frac{v_{2x}}{v_{2y}} = \frac{\mu_k(1+c)\sqrt{2gh}}{c\sqrt{2gh}}$$

$$= \mu_k\frac{(1+c)}{c}$$

and the rising and falling time of the ball, $t_v = 2\frac{v_{2y}}{g} = \frac{2c\sqrt{2gh}}{g} = 2c\sqrt{\frac{2h}{g}}$

The distance to be found,

$d_1 = v_{2x}t_v = \mu_k(1+c)\sqrt{2gh}\,2c\sqrt{\frac{2h}{g}}$

$\Rightarrow \quad d_1 = 4\mu_k(1+c)\,ch$

which is independent of ω_0.

10. Regarding option (a)

Treating the arrangement of plates as parallel plate capacitor, charge on capacitor will be $Q = CV$

$\Rightarrow \quad ne = \frac{\varepsilon_0 A}{d}V$

$\Rightarrow n = \frac{8.85 \times 10^{-12} \times 10}{0.5 \times 10^{-3} \times 1.6 \times 10^{-19}} \times 16$

$\Rightarrow n = 8.85 \times 10^9$

Regarding option (b)

Incident power can be written as

$P = \frac{nhc}{\lambda}$

where, n = number of photons incident per unit time.

Also, saturation current,

$I = ne \Rightarrow P = \frac{Ihc}{e\lambda} \Rightarrow \lambda = \frac{Ihc}{eP}$

$= \frac{(2\times10^{-6})(6.6\times10^{-34})(3\times10^{8})}{(4\times10^{-6})(1.6\times10^{-19})}$

$= \frac{9.9}{1.6} \times 10^{-7}\,\text{m} = 6187\text{Å}$

which corresponds to given range of orange.

Regarding option (c)

As seen in option (b), orange is ejecting but as wavelength range of red is greater than that of orange it may or may not eject but as wavelength of violet is lesser it must.

Regarding option (d)

Stopping potential, $V_s = 8$ V

$\therefore KE_{max} = 8$ eV while $KE_{min} = 0$, so average energy will be 4 eV.

11. Electric field at a distance z from centre of ring is given by

$E_{axis} = \frac{qz}{4\pi\varepsilon_0(R^2+z^2)^{3/2}}$, along axis.

For points very near to centre, we have $z << R$

$\Rightarrow E_{axis} = \frac{qz}{4\pi\varepsilon_0(R^2)^{3/2}} = \frac{qz}{4\pi\varepsilon_0 R^3} \quad$ ...(i)

So, option (a) is correct.

To find non-axial component of field near centre of the ring, consider a small cylindrical Gaussian surface of length $2z << R$ and radius $r << R$ having its axis and centre same as the ring, as shown.

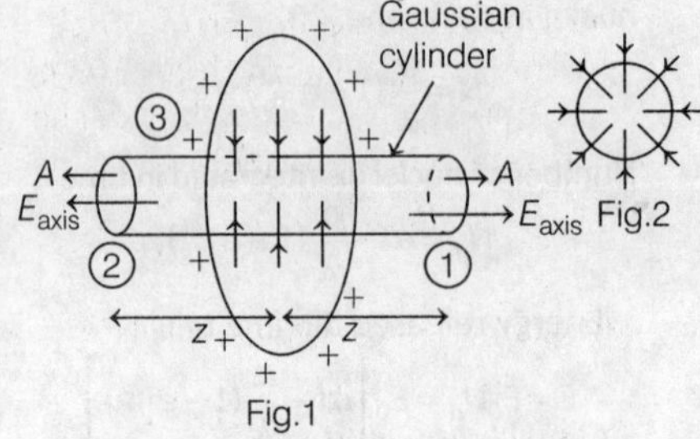

Fig.1

As there is no charge enclosed by the surface, so by Gauss law,

$\Rightarrow \quad \phi = 0 \quad$ ...(ii)

Let fluxes through flat surfaces from Eqs. (i) and (ii) are ϕ_1 and ϕ_2 while flux through the curved surface is ϕ_3.

From Fig. 1, $\phi_1 = \phi_2 = EA\cos\theta$

$= \frac{qz}{4\pi\varepsilon_0 R^3}(\pi r^2)\cos 0°$

[using Eqs. (i) and (ii)]

$\Rightarrow \quad \phi_1 = \phi_2 = \frac{qz\,\pi r^2}{4\pi\varepsilon_0 R^3} \quad$ ...(iii)

From Eq. (ii), $\phi = 0$

$\Rightarrow \quad \phi_1 + \phi_2 + \phi_3 = 0$

$\Rightarrow \quad \phi_3 = -(\phi_1 + \phi_2)$

$\Rightarrow \quad \phi_3 = -\frac{qz\,\pi r^2}{2\pi\varepsilon_0 R^3} \quad$ ...(iv)

As the flux through curved surface is negative, so the field lines should enter the curved surface radially, by symmetry, as shown in Figs. 1 and 2 (side view of Gaussian cylinder).

So, by Eq. (iv), we get

$E_{radial}\cdot 2\pi r(2z)\cos 180° = -\frac{qz\,\pi r^2}{2\pi\varepsilon_0 R^3}$

$\Rightarrow \quad E_{radial} = \frac{qr}{8\pi\varepsilon_0 R^3} \quad$ ...(v)

So, option (b) is correct.

Now, consider motion of positron through ring as shown in Fig. 3.

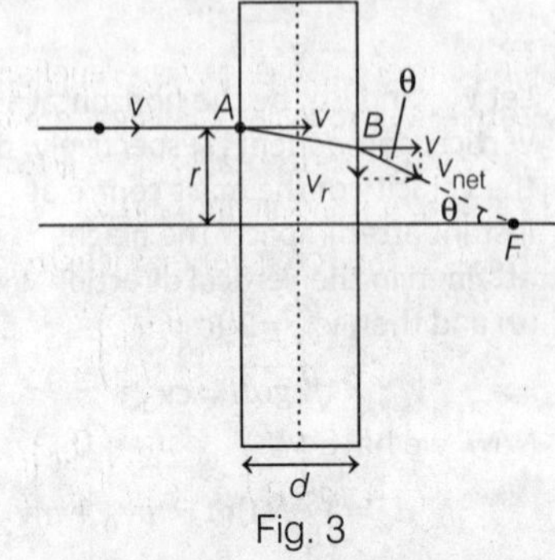

Fig. 3

As the positron moves in active region from A to B, it experiences downward force due to radial field and it acquires a radial velocity v_r as shown.

For motion in axial direction (z-direction), using $t = \frac{s_z}{v_z}$, we get

$t = \frac{d}{v} \quad$ ...(vi)

For motion in radial direction ($-x$-direction),

Using $\; v_x = u_x + a_x t$, we get

$v_r = 0 + \frac{eE_{radial}\,t}{m}$

$\Rightarrow \quad v_r = \frac{eqr}{8\pi\varepsilon_0 R^3 m}\cdot\frac{d}{v} \quad$ ...(vii)

[using Eqs. (v) and (vi)]

So, from velocity triangle in Fig. 3,

$\tan\theta \approx \theta = \frac{v_r}{v}$

$\Rightarrow \quad \theta = \frac{eqrd}{8\pi\varepsilon_0 m R^3 v^2} \quad$ ...(viii)

[using Eq. (vii)]

So, option (c) is correct.

Thus, referring to Figs. 3 and 4, we can see that $f = \frac{r}{\tan\theta} \approx \frac{r}{\theta}$

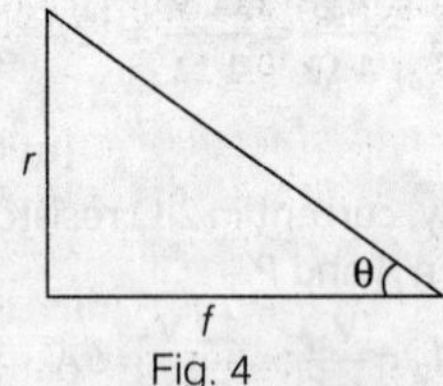

Fig. 4

$\Rightarrow \quad f = \frac{8\pi\varepsilon_0 m v^2 R^3}{qed}$

So, option (d) is correct.

12. Consider various options separately.

(a) and (d) $\rightarrow$ When speed of block is maximum, net force on block is zero. Hence at that instant, spring exerts a force of magnitude mg on both block and ground.

(b) $\rightarrow$ At the instant block is in equilibrium position, its speed is maximum and compression in spring is x given by

$kx = mg \quad$ ...(i)

From conservation of energy,

$mg(L+x) = \frac{1}{2}kx^2 + \frac{1}{2}mv_{max}^2 \quad$ ...(ii)

From Eqs. (i) and (ii), we get

$v_{max} = \frac{3}{2}\sqrt{gL}$

(c) → As, $v_{max} = \frac{3}{2}\sqrt{gL}$

and $\omega = \sqrt{\frac{k}{m}} = 2\sqrt{\frac{g}{L}}$

$\therefore \quad A = \frac{v_{max}}{\omega} = \frac{3}{4}L$

Hence, time taken t, from start of compression till block reaches mean position is given by

$$x = A\sin\omega t_0$$

where, $x = \frac{L}{4}$

$$\therefore \quad t_0 = \sqrt{\frac{L}{4g}}\sin^{-1}\frac{1}{3}$$

Time taken by block to reach from mean position to bottommost position,

$$\frac{T}{4} = \frac{2\pi}{4\omega} = \frac{\pi}{4}\sqrt{\frac{L}{g}}$$

Hence, the required time

$$= \frac{\pi}{4}\sqrt{\frac{L}{g}} + \sqrt{\frac{L}{4g}}\sin^{-1}\left(\frac{1}{3}\right)$$

13. (a) As μ is increased, the focal length decreases. Hence, the object is at a distance larger than focal length. Therefore, final image is real. Also, final image becomes smaller in size in comparison to size of image before the change was made.

(b) If the radius of curvature is doubled, the focal length increases. Hence, the object is at a distance lesser than focal length. Therefore, final image is virtual. Also, final image becomes smaller in size in comparison to size of image before the change was made.

(c) Due to insertion of slab, the effective object for lens shifts rightwards. Hence, final image is virtual. Also, final image becomes smaller in size in comparison to size of image before the change was made.

(d) The object comes to centre of curvature of right spherical surface as a result. Hence, the final image is virtual. Also,final image becomes smaller in size in comparison to size of image before the change was made.

14. Total magnetic flux at any position,

$$\phi = B_z\pi r_0^2 - LI$$

Since, resistance = 0

So, $\phi = B_0(1-\alpha z)\pi r_0^2 - LI$ = constant

From initial condition (z = 0, I =0), the value of constant is $\phi = B_0\pi r_0^2$.

Using the above equation, the current in the ring, $I = \frac{1}{L}B_0\alpha\pi r_0^2 z$

The Lorentz force acting on the ring (which can only be vertical, because of the symmetry of the assembly) can be expressed as $F_z = -B_r\, I(z)\, 2\pi r_0$

$$= -\frac{2B_0^2\alpha\beta\pi^2 r_0^4 z}{L} = -kz$$

Equation of motion of the ring is

$$ma_z = F_z + mg = -kz + mg$$

At equilibrium position,

$$z_0 = -\frac{mg}{k} = -\frac{mgL}{2B_0^2\alpha\beta\pi^2 r_0^4}$$

$$\omega_0 = \sqrt{\frac{k}{m}} = \sqrt{\frac{2B_0^2\alpha\beta\pi^2 r_0^4}{Lm}}$$

$$= B_0\pi r_0^2\sqrt{\frac{2\alpha\beta}{mL}}$$

$$\therefore \quad T = \frac{2\pi}{\omega} = \frac{2\pi}{B_0\pi r_0^2}\sqrt{\frac{mL}{2\alpha\beta}}$$

$$= \frac{1}{B_0 r_0^2}\sqrt{\frac{2mL}{\alpha\beta}}$$

15. Applying Bernoulli's principle for the gas between the nozzle and at the chamber exit, we get

$$\frac{v^2}{2} + \frac{C_pT}{M} = \text{constant}$$

$$\Rightarrow \quad 0 + \frac{C_pT_0}{M} = \frac{v_{exit}^2}{2} + \frac{C_pT_1}{M}$$

$$\Rightarrow \quad v_{exit}^2 = \frac{2C_p(T_0 - T_1)}{M}$$

Now, the thrust applied, $F = -\rho S v_{exit}^2$

and $\rho = \frac{p_1 M}{RT_1}$.

This means that $F = \frac{2C_p(T_0 - T_1)p_1 S}{RT_1}$

Given that, $T_0 >> T_1 \Rightarrow T_0 - T_1 \approx T_0$

and $\quad C_p = C_V + R = \frac{7R}{2}$

$$\therefore \quad F \approx \frac{7T_0 p_1 S}{T_1}$$

16. The current carrying wires repel each other magnetically, causing them to accelerate horizontally. Since gravity is vertical, it plays no initial role.

First get the force per unit length,

$$\frac{F}{L} = \frac{\mu_0}{2\pi}\frac{I^2}{d} = \frac{\mu_0}{2\pi d}\left(\frac{I_0}{\sqrt{2}}\right)^2$$

$$= \frac{\mu_0}{4\pi d}\left(\frac{V}{R}\right)^2 = \frac{\mu_0}{4\pi d}\left(\frac{Q_0}{RC}\right)^2$$

Now apply Newton's second law using the result above,

$$\frac{F}{L} = \frac{m}{L}a = \lambda a = \frac{\mu_0}{4\pi d}\left(\frac{Q_0}{RC}\right)^2$$

Solving for a gives;

$$a = \frac{\mu_0 Q_0^2}{4\pi\lambda R^2C^2 d}$$

From the kinematics equation,

$v_x = u_x + a_x t$, we have

$$v_0 = at = aRC = \frac{\mu_0 Q_0^2}{4\pi\lambda RCd}$$

Conservation of energy of a wire gives,

$$\frac{1}{2}mv_0^2 = mgh$$

$$\Rightarrow \quad h = \frac{v_0^2}{2g}$$

$$= \frac{1}{2g}\left(\frac{\mu_0 Q_0^2}{4\pi\lambda RCd}\right)^2$$

17. For block, by Newton's second law,we get

$$Mg - T = M\frac{dv}{dt} \quad \text{...(i)}$$

For cylindrical tank, by Newton's second law, we get

$$T + \mu v_e - (M - \mu t)g = (M - \mu t)\frac{dv}{dt} \quad \text{...(ii)}$$

From Eqs. (i) and (ii), we get

$$Mg + \mu v_e - (M - \mu t)g = (2M - \mu t)\frac{dv}{dt}$$

$$\Rightarrow \quad (\mu v_e + \mu g t) = (2M - \mu t)\frac{dv}{dt}$$

$$\Rightarrow \quad \frac{dv}{dt} = \frac{\mu(v_e + gt)}{2M - \mu t}$$

18. We find light source images in mirrors. The light incident around O can then be viewed as a superposition of the light emitted from the images.

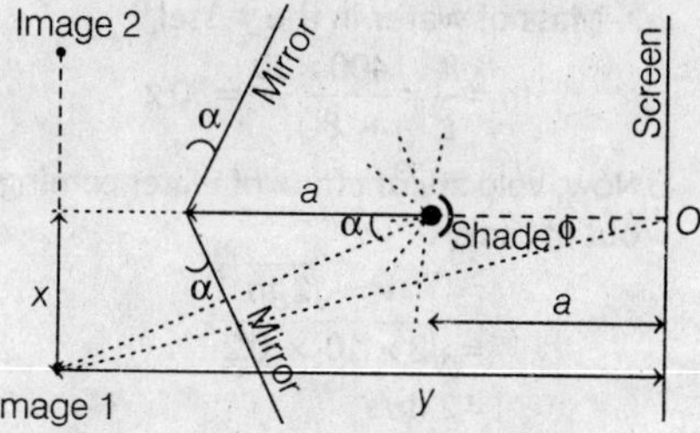

Here, $x = 2a\cos\alpha \cdot \sin\alpha$,

$$y = 2a\cos\alpha \cdot \cos\alpha + a$$

$$\therefore \tan\phi = \frac{x}{y} = \frac{2a\cos\alpha \cdot \sin\alpha}{2a\cos\alpha \cdot \cos\alpha + a},$$

As, $\sin\phi = \dfrac{1}{\sqrt{1+(\cot\phi)^2}}$

$\Rightarrow$

$$\sin\phi = \left[1+\left(\frac{2a\cos\alpha\cdot\cos\alpha + a}{2a\cos\alpha\cdot\sin\alpha}\right)^2\right]^{-1/2}$$

$$= \left[1+\left(\frac{\cos\alpha + 1/2\cos\alpha}{\sin\alpha}\right)^2\right]^{-1/2}$$

$$= \frac{\sin\alpha}{\sqrt{\sin^2\alpha + [\cos\alpha + 1/2\cos\alpha]^2}}$$

$$= \frac{\sin\alpha}{\sqrt{2+1/4\cos^2\alpha}}$$

$$= \frac{\sin 2\alpha}{\sqrt{8\cos^2\alpha + 1}}$$

Let M be the minimum interference at a point near O, so we get a path difference $2d\sin\phi$ compared to M.

This is minimum, if $\lambda = 2d\sin\phi$. So, we get

$$\lambda = \frac{2d\sin 2\alpha}{\sqrt{8\cos^2\alpha + 1}}$$

Knockout 12 (Paper 1)

1. Thermal current in the rod, $I = \dfrac{kA\Delta T}{l}$

where, k is thermal conductivity, A is cross-sectional area, ΔT is temperature difference and l is length of rod.

$$\Rightarrow I = \frac{80\times 10\times 10\times 10^{-4}\times 100}{20\times 10^{-2}}$$

$$= 400 \text{ cal/s}$$

Heat extracted from water in time t is $I\times t$ which can be equated to heat required to freeze m mass of water, i.e. mL, where L is latent heat. So, we get

$$I\times t = m\times L$$

$\therefore$ Mass of water in the vessel,

$$m = \frac{It}{L} = \frac{400\times 10}{80} = 50 \text{ g}$$

Now, velocity of efflux of water coming out of tank,

$$v = \sqrt{2gh}$$

$$= \sqrt{2\times 10\times 0.2}$$

$$= 2 \text{ m/s}$$

Mass flow rate of water coming out of tank,

$$\frac{dm}{dt} = \rho av = 10^3\times 10^{-6}\times 2$$

$$= 2\times 10^{-3} \text{kg/s} = 2 \text{ g/s}$$

Thus, mass of water in the tank after time t will be (as 50 g was already there)

$$m' = (50+2t) \text{ g}$$

If time taken to freeze is t', then we have

$$I\times t' = m'\times L$$

$$\Rightarrow \quad 400\times t' = (50+2t')\times 80$$

$$\Rightarrow \quad t' = \frac{50}{3} \text{s}$$

$\therefore$ Time of delay,

$$= t' - t = \frac{50}{3} - 10$$

$$= 6.67 \text{ s}$$

2. By symmetry all points of octagon's vertex are at same potential. So resistors connecting adjacent vertices with not have any current and so these sixteen resistors can be removed. Now, let vertices of octagon with centre at A be labelled C. So, 8 resistors between A and C will be in parallel. Similarly, if we label vertices of octagon with centre at B be D, 8 resistors between B and D will be in parallel and 8 resistors between C and D will also be in parallel.

So, the equivalent circuit can be drawn as

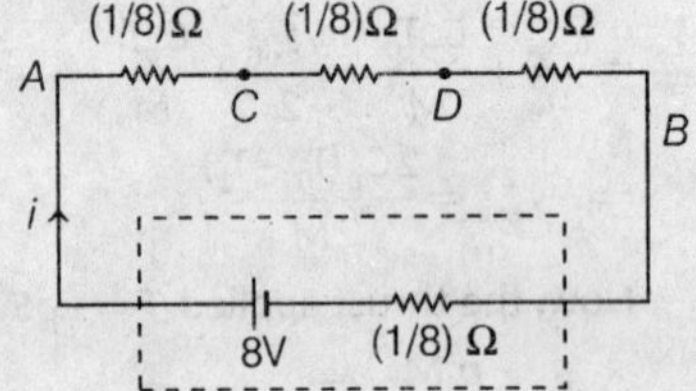

Resistance of external circuit,

$$R = \frac{1}{8} + \frac{1}{8} + \frac{1}{8} = \frac{3}{8}\,\Omega$$

Effective resistance of the circuit,

$$Z = R + \frac{1}{8} = 0.5\,\Omega$$

Therefore, current in the circuit will be

$$i = \frac{V}{Z} = \frac{8}{0.5} = 16 \text{ A}$$

$\therefore$ Power consumed by the circuit will be

$$P = i^2R = (16)^2\times\frac{3}{8} = 96 \text{ W}$$

3. By using formulae of location of CM for straight and quarter circular ring, position of CM is as shown initially and finally.

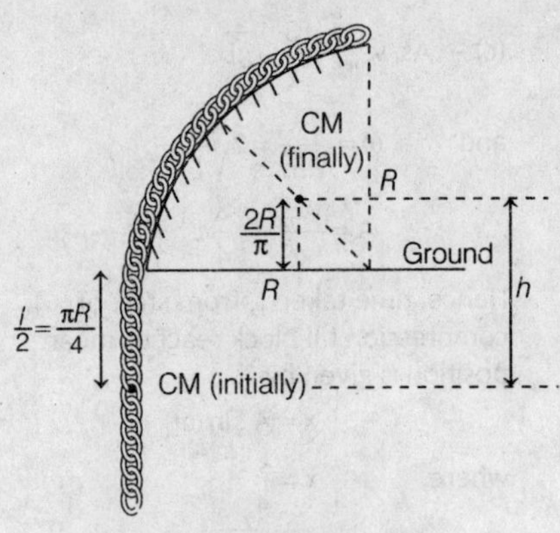

So, gain in the height of CM,

$$h = \left(\frac{2R}{\pi} + \frac{\pi R}{4}\right)$$

Therefore, work done by the man against gravity

$$= \text{Increase in potential energy}$$

$$= mgh = mg\left[\frac{2R}{\pi} + \frac{\pi R}{4}\right]$$

$$= mg\left[\frac{2}{\pi}\cdot 4\pi + \frac{\pi}{4}\cdot 4\pi\right]$$

$$= 18mg = 18\times 0.1\times 9.8$$

$$= 17.64 \text{ J}$$

4. Consider interference of Wave-1 and Wave-2 at any general point of the screen.

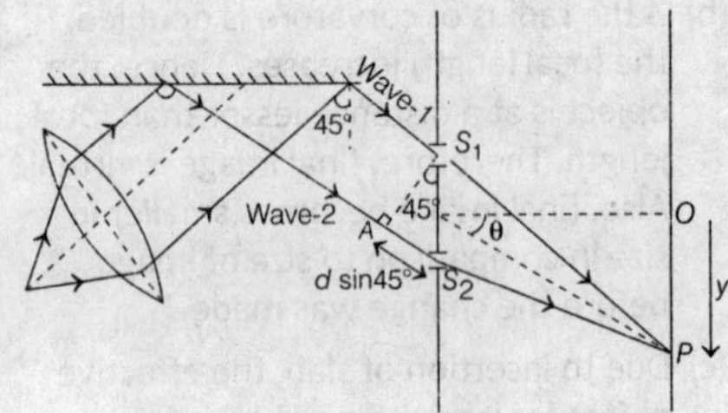

For journey behind the slits, extra path of Wave-2 can be determined by drawing a perpendicular from S_1 at A as shown in figure. Extra path is equal to

$$\Delta x_1 = AS_2 = d\sin 45° \quad \text{...(i)}$$

For journey from slits to screen, at a point at angle θ with respect to line of symmetry, path difference is equal to

$$\Delta x_2 = d\sin\theta \quad \text{...(ii)}$$

For central maxima, net path difference is zero.

$$\Rightarrow \quad \Delta x_1 = \Delta x_2$$

From Eqs. (i) and (ii), we get

$$d\sin 45° = d\sin\theta$$

$\Rightarrow \qquad \theta = 45°$

$\therefore$ Distance of central maxima from O,

$$y = 1.5 \tan 45° = 1.5 \times 1 = 1.5 \text{ m}$$

5. As shown, particle first parabolic path, followed by circular path in magnetic field with radius R and centre of curvature at C.

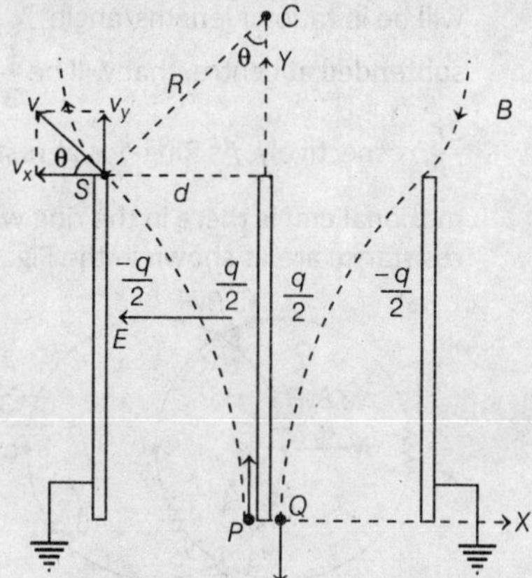

From the figure,

$$d = R \sin \theta = \frac{mv}{qB} \times \frac{v_y}{v} = \frac{mv_y}{qB} = 100 \text{ m}$$

So, for motion from P to S, if electric field is assumed E as shown.

Using $s_x = u_x t + \frac{1}{2} a_x t^2$, we get

$$d = 0 + \frac{1}{2} \frac{qE}{m} t^2$$

$$\Rightarrow \qquad 100 = \frac{1}{2} \times 1 \times E \times t^2 \qquad \text{...(i)}$$

Also, for y-direction motion from P to S, we use

$$s_y = u_y t + \frac{1}{2} a_y t^2$$

$$\Rightarrow \qquad 1 = 100 \times t + 0$$

(as there is no field in y-direction, $a_y = 0$)

$$\Rightarrow \qquad t = \frac{1}{100} \text{ s} \qquad \text{...(ii)}$$

From Eqs. (i) and (ii), we get

$$E = 2 \times 10^6 \text{ V/m} \qquad \text{...(iii)}$$

If we assume charge on middle plate equal to q, it will be distributed symmetrically as shown.

So, charge $\frac{-q}{2}$ will be induced on opposite surface.

As field due to single large surface of area A is $\frac{q}{2A\varepsilon_0}$, so net field between plates will be

$$E = \frac{q}{2A\varepsilon_0} + \frac{q}{2A\varepsilon_0} = \frac{q}{A\varepsilon_0}$$

$$\Rightarrow \quad q = A\varepsilon_0 E$$
$$= 1 \times 8.85 \times 10^{-12} \times 2 \times 10^6 \quad \text{[using Eq. (iii)]}$$
$$= 17.70 \, \mu\text{C}$$

6. As, plate is a variable mass system. Downward force due to striking of dust particles can be calculated using formula.

$$F = v_{\text{rel}} \frac{dm}{dt} = \rho A v_{\text{rel}}^2$$
$$= 10^{-3} \times 10 \times [40 - (-10)]^2$$
$$= 25 \text{ N}$$

So, to move the plate uniformly, tension in string should be equal to F or 25 N.

Also, tension in string connected to pulley of two blocks system,

$$T = \frac{4m_1 m_2 g}{m_1 + m_2}$$

$$\Rightarrow \qquad 25 = \frac{4 \times 3 \times m \times 10}{3 + m}$$

$$\Rightarrow 75 + 25m = 120m$$

$$\Rightarrow \qquad m = 0.79 \text{ kg}$$

7. Velocities of points Q and R of the string w.r.t. ground are as shown in Fig. 1.

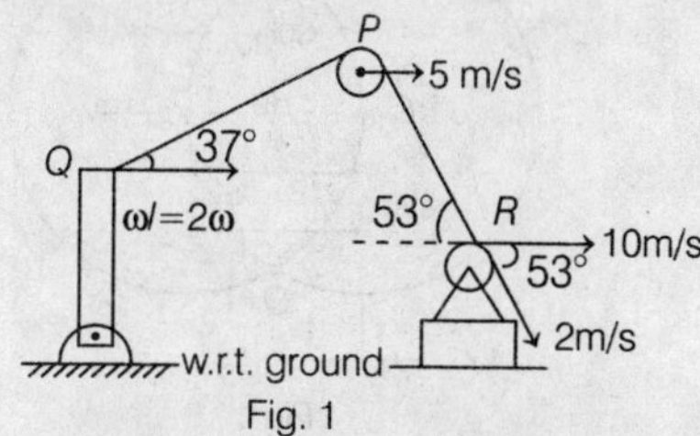

Fig. 1

With respect to pulley P, points Q and R will have an additional negative velocity of 5 m/s as shown in Fig. 2.

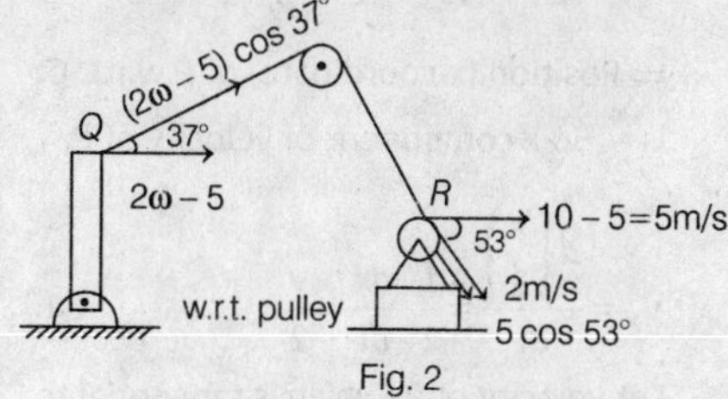

Fig. 2

Thus, velocity components of Q and R along string will be as shown in Fig 2.

As the string is inextensible, these components should be equal.

$$(2\omega - 5) \cos 37° = 5 \cos 53° + 2$$

$$\Rightarrow (2\omega - 5) \frac{4}{5} = 5 \times \frac{3}{5} + 2$$

$$\Rightarrow 2\omega - 5 = \frac{25}{4} \Rightarrow \omega = 5.62 \text{ rad/s}$$

8. As, $I = I_0 \sin^2 \theta$

$$\Rightarrow \qquad \theta = \sin^{-1} \sqrt{\frac{I}{I_0}} \qquad \text{...(i)}$$

$$\Rightarrow \qquad d\theta = \frac{1}{2} \sqrt{\frac{I_0}{I_0 - I}} \frac{dt}{\sqrt{I_0}\sqrt{I}} \qquad \text{...(ii)}$$

Dividing Eq.(ii) by Eq. (i), we get

$$\frac{d\theta}{\theta} = \frac{1}{2} \frac{dt}{\sqrt{I(I_0 - I)} \sin^{-1} \sqrt{\frac{I}{I_0}}}$$

$$= \frac{1}{2} \frac{(0.02)}{\sqrt{5\pi(20\pi - 5\pi)} \frac{\pi}{6}}$$

$$= 4\sqrt{3} \times 10^{-4}$$

Percentage errror will be

$$x = \frac{d\theta}{\theta} \times 100 = 4\sqrt{3} \times 10^{-2}$$

$$\Rightarrow \qquad 100x = 4\sqrt{3} = 6.92$$

9. Degree of freedom of mixture of gases is given by

$$f = \frac{n_1 f_1 + n_2 f_2}{n_1 + n_2}$$

Thus, for equimolar mixture of argon ($f_1 = 3$) and oxygen ($f_2 = 5$), we get

$$f = \frac{f_1 + f_2}{2} = 4$$

Adiabatic exponent, $\gamma = 1 + \frac{2}{f} = 1.5$ ...(i)

As right piston in both vessels is insulating, so compression undergone by rightmost chamber is adiabatic in both vessels. As for adiabatic process, pV^γ = constant.

For gas in rightmost chamber of both vessels,

$$p_f V_f^\gamma = p_i V_i^\gamma$$

$$\Rightarrow \quad p_f \left(\frac{4V_0}{9}\right)^{3/2} = p_0 V_0^{3/2}$$

$$\therefore \qquad p_f = \frac{27 p_0}{8} \qquad \text{...(ii)}$$

Using ideal gas equation, we get

$$\frac{p_f V_f}{T_f} = \frac{p_i V_i}{T_i} \Rightarrow \frac{\frac{27}{8} p_0 \cdot \frac{4V_0}{9}}{T_f} = \frac{p_0 V_0}{T_0}$$

$\therefore$ Final temperature of gas in rightmost chamber,

$$T_f = \frac{3T_0}{2} \qquad \text{...(iii)}$$

Thus, for left vessel, the final situation is as shown in the Fig. 1.

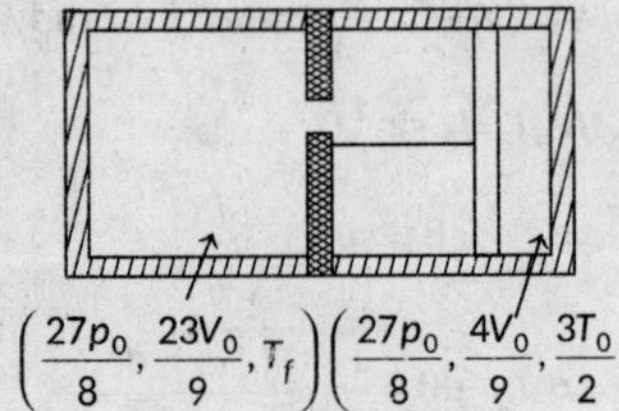

Gases in the left two chambers can be considered as single gas sample as there is a hole in piston. For this sample, using ideal gas equation

$$T_f = \left(\frac{p_f V_f}{p_i V_i}\right) T_i = \frac{69T_0}{16}$$

So, option (a) is incorrect.

Consider final situation in right vessel as shown in Fig. 2. Gases in the three compartments are labelled as *A*, *B*, *C*.

Also for *A*, change in internal energy

$$\Delta U = \frac{1}{\gamma - 1}[p_{\text{final}}V_{\text{final}} - p_{\text{initial}}V_{\text{initial}}]$$

$$= \frac{1}{1.5 - 1}\left[\frac{27}{8}p_0 \frac{14V_0}{9} - p_0V_0\right]$$

$$= \frac{17p_0V_0}{2}$$

For *C* (undergoing adiabatic compression), heat supplied *Q* is zero. Change in internal energy of the gas,

$$\Delta U = \frac{1}{\gamma - 1}[p_{\text{final}}\ V_{\text{final}} - p_{\text{initial}}V_{\text{initial}}]$$

$$\Rightarrow \Delta U_C = \frac{1}{1.5 - 1}\left[\frac{27}{8}p_0 \cdot \frac{4V_0}{9} - p_0V_0\right]$$

$$= p_0V_0$$

So, by first law of thermodynamics, work done on gas *C*,

$$W_C = Q + \Delta U_C = 0 + p_0V_0 = p_0V_0$$

For Gas *A*, by ideal gas equation,

$$T_{\text{final}} = \left(\frac{p_{\text{final}}V_{\text{final}}}{p_{\text{initial}}V_{\text{initial}}}\right)T_{\text{initial}}$$

$$= \left(\frac{27}{8} \times \frac{14}{9}\right)T_0 = \frac{21T_0}{4}$$

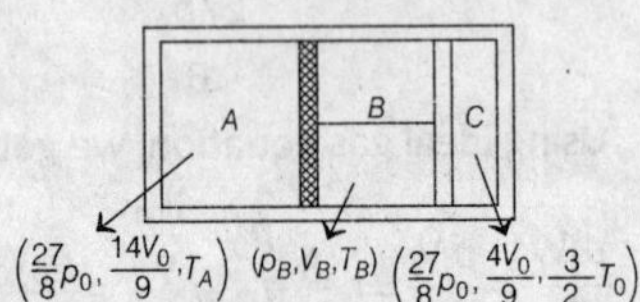

For Gas *B*, temperature is same as that of *A*

$$\Rightarrow \quad T_B = T_A = \frac{21T_0}{4}$$

So, by ideal gas equation, for *B*,

$$p_{\text{final}} = \left(\frac{V_{\text{initial}} \cdot T_{\text{final}}}{V_{\text{final}} \cdot T_{\text{initial}}}\right) p_{\text{initial}}$$

$$\Rightarrow \quad p_B = \frac{21}{4}p_0$$

Thus, ratio of pressure in left vessel to right vessel in the middle compartment

$$= \frac{\frac{27}{8}p_0}{\frac{21}{4}p_0} = \frac{9}{14}$$

As at all instants, pressure of *A* is same as of *C* and displacements of pistons in contact are also same. So, work done by *A* = work done on *C*

$$\Rightarrow \quad W_A = W_C = \Delta U_C = p_0V_0$$

Thus, by first law of thermodynamics, heat supplied by coil-2 to gas *A*,

$$Q_A = \Delta U_A + W_A$$

$$= \frac{17p_0V_0}{2} + p_0V_0 = \frac{19p_0V_0}{2}$$

Similarly, $Q_B = \Delta U_B = \frac{17}{2}p_0V_0$

Heat supplied by coil-2,

$Q = Q_A + Q_B = 18p_0V_0$

10. Consider the figure shown, as distance between C_1 and C_2 is *R*, ΔC_1PC_2 is equilateral.

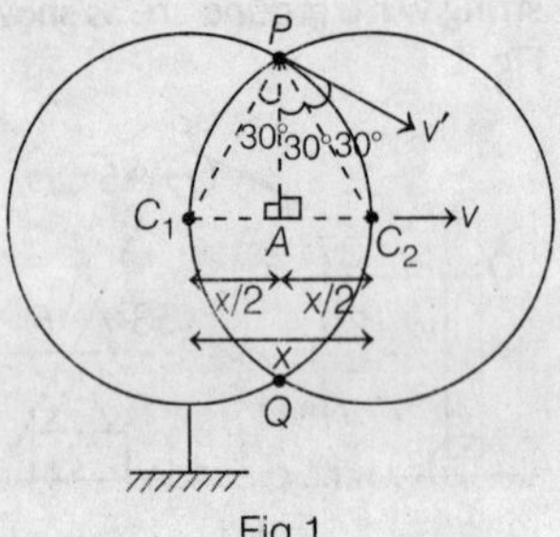

Fig.1

Let *x* be position of C_2 w.r.t. C_1. As $\Delta PC_1A \cong \Delta PC_2A$, we have

$$C_1A = C_2A = \frac{x}{2}$$

⇒ Position (*x*-coordinate) of *P* w.r.t. C_1 is $\frac{x}{2}$, So *x* component of velocity of *P*,

$$v_x = \frac{d\left(\frac{x}{2}\right)}{dt} = \frac{1}{2} \cdot \frac{dx}{dt} = \frac{v}{2} \quad \text{...(i)}$$

Let velocity of *P* (which is tangential to Ring-1) is *v*′. From Fig. 1, *x* component of velocity of *P*,

$$v_x = v' \sin 60° \quad \text{...(ii)}$$

From Eqs. (i) and (ii), we get

$$v' \sin 60° = \frac{v}{2} \Rightarrow v' = \frac{v}{\sqrt{3}}$$

Angular velocity w.r.t. $C_1 = \frac{v'}{R} = \frac{v}{\sqrt{3}R}$

Motional emf between points *P* and *Q* (in both smaller and larger arcs) of Ring-2 will be

$$E = Bv\ (PQ) = Bv\ (\sqrt{3}R)$$

Also, resistance of small and larger arcs will be in ratio of lengths/angle subtended at centre, that will be $\frac{r}{3}$ and $\frac{2r}{3}$, respectively. As Ring-1 is at rest, no motional emf is there in the ring while resistance are as shown in the Fig. 2.

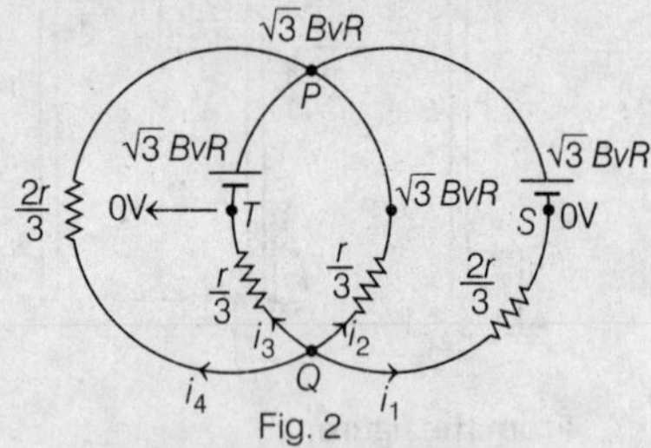

Fig. 2

Assuming potential of *S* equal to zero, potentials of other points are as shown. Potential of *Q* is assumed equal to *x*.

By KCL for junction at *Q*,

$$i_1 + i_2 + i_3 + i_4 = 0$$

$$\Rightarrow \quad \frac{x}{\frac{2r}{3}} + \frac{x}{\frac{r}{3}} + \frac{x - \sqrt{3}BvR}{\frac{r}{3}} + \frac{x - \sqrt{3}BvR}{\frac{2r}{3}} = 0$$

$$\Rightarrow \quad x = \frac{\sqrt{3}BvR}{2}$$

Current in various branches will therefore be as shown in Fig. 3.

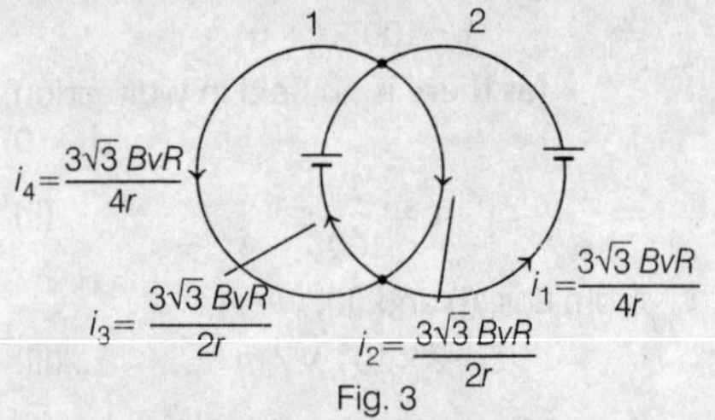

Fig. 3

Force on smaller arc of Ring-2 will be

$$F_1 = Bil = Bi_3\sqrt{3}R \text{(leftwards)}$$

Force on larger arc of Ring-2,

$$F_2 = Bil = Bi_1\sqrt{3}R \text{ (leftwards)}$$

So, net force on Ring-2,

$$F = F_1 + F_2 = B(i_1 + i_3)\sqrt{3}R$$

$$= B\left(\frac{9\sqrt{3}BvR}{4r}\right)\sqrt{3}R = \frac{27B^2R^2v}{4r}$$

Similarly, net force on Ring-1 is non-zero.

11. As λ_{violet} is lesser than λ_{red}, the wavelengths will be marked on axis as shown.

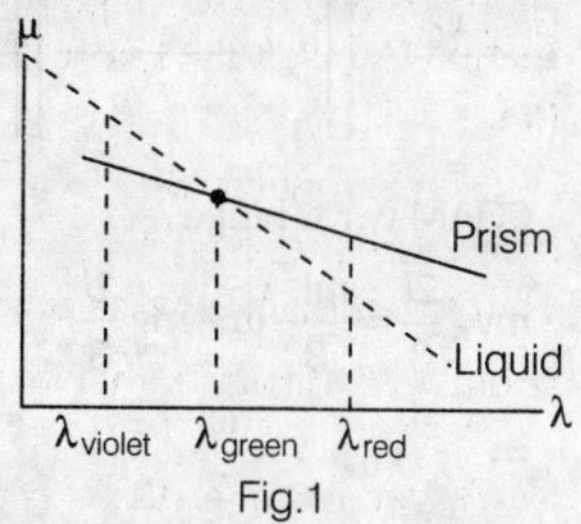

Fig.1

From the graph, μ of liquid is greater for violet or liquid is denser for violet. So, blue ray will deviate clockwise.

As for green, refractive indices of liquid and prism are equal, so the ray does not refract and emerges parallel to base.

Fig.2 shows FBD of prism.

Forces acting on the prism are

(i) Tension (T_A) by string A

(ii) Tension (T_B) by string B

(iii) Weight (mg)

(iv) Buoyant force,

(v) F

$$B = \rho V g = \frac{\sigma}{3} V g = \frac{mg}{3} \quad \text{...(i)}$$

where, ρ is density of liquid given to be one-third of density σ of prism, V is volume and m is mass of prism.

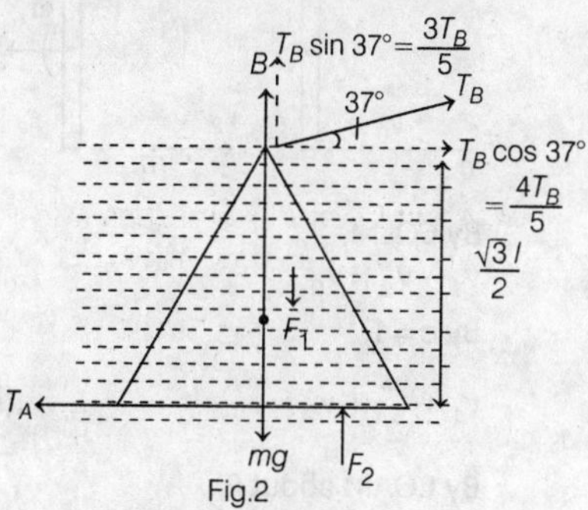

Fig.2

For vertical equilibrium,

$$\frac{3T_B}{5} + B = mg - F$$

$$\Rightarrow \quad \frac{3T_B}{5} + \frac{mg}{3} = mg - F$$

$$\Rightarrow \quad T_B < \frac{10}{9} mg$$

For horizontal equilibrium,

$$T_A = \frac{4T_B}{5} \Rightarrow T_A < \frac{8mg}{9}$$

Force by liquid on the prism is as shown in Fig. 2. Resultant force on inclined surfaces is F_1 downward while force by liquid on base is F_2 upward. Resultant of these forces is buoyancy, i.e. $B = F_2 - F_1$

$$\Rightarrow \quad \frac{mg}{3} = \rho g h \times lb - F_1 \quad \text{[using Eq. (i)]}$$

where, l = side of triangular cross-section, b = width and h = height of triangular cross-section.

$$\Rightarrow \quad F_1 = \frac{\sigma}{3} g \times 2\left(\frac{1}{2} lbh\right) - \frac{mg}{3}$$

$$= \frac{\sigma}{3} g \times 2V - \frac{mg}{3}$$

$$= \frac{2mg}{3} - \frac{mg}{3} = \frac{mg}{3} \quad \text{[using Eq. (i)]}$$

12. Let particle exit the end of the tunnel with velocity v. Speed when it is at maximum distance from earth's centre is v'.

As the path followed is elliptical under gravitational pull F towards centre O of earth the motion can be visualised as shown in Fig. 1

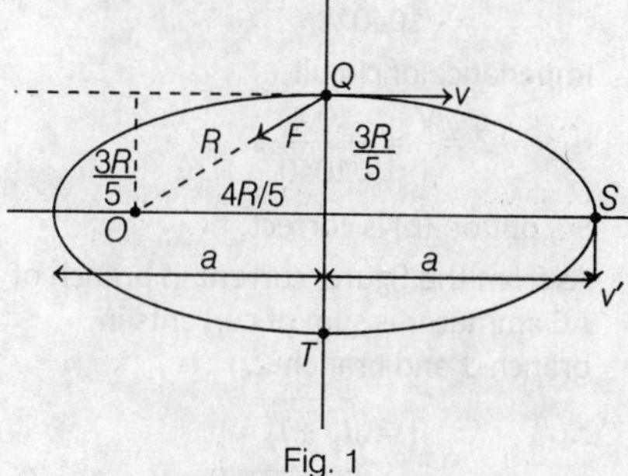

Fig. 1

As distance between focus O of ellipse and point Q where velocity/tangent is parallel to major-axis is equal to semi-major-axis, therefore $a = OQ = R$.

Distance between O and position of maximum height S,

$$OS = \frac{4R}{5} + R = \frac{9R}{5} \quad \text{...(i)}$$

So, option (d) is correct.

As gravitional force is directed towards O, torque of force about O is zero.

So, angular momentum is conserved about O.

Thus, about O, L (at Q) = L (at S)

$$\Rightarrow \quad mv \cdot \frac{3R}{5} = mv' \cdot \frac{9R}{5} \quad \text{[using Eq. (i)]}$$

$$\Rightarrow \quad v' = \frac{v}{3} \quad \text{...(ii)}$$

Also, by energy conservation between Q and S,

$$-\frac{GMm}{R} + \frac{1}{2}mv^2 = -\frac{GMm}{\frac{9R}{5}} + \frac{1}{2}mv'^2$$

$$\Rightarrow \quad -\frac{GMm}{R} + \frac{1}{2}mv^2$$

$$= -\frac{5GMm}{9R} + \frac{1}{2}m\left(\frac{v}{3}\right)^2 \quad \text{[using Eq. (ii)]}$$

$$\Rightarrow \quad v = \sqrt{\frac{GM}{R}}$$

$$\Rightarrow \quad v' = \frac{1}{3}\sqrt{\frac{GM}{R}} \quad \text{[using Eq. (ii)]}$$

So, option (c) is correct.

As tunnel is smooth, so no energy loss occurs for motion from P to Q. Thus, at P, speed is same as that at Q.

Also, as collision is elastic at P, speed before collision will be same. As this speed is equal to orbital speed, so motion would be on circular orbit if it didn't collide with surface at P.

So, option (b) is correct.

also, if we consider collision with surface at P it will be as shown in Fig. 2

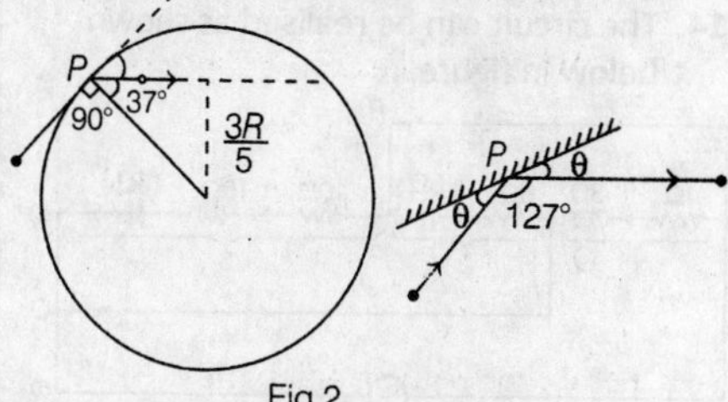

Fig.2

From geometry, deviation on collision is 90° + 37° = 127°. So, if angle between surface of collision and earth's surface is θ, we get

$$\theta + 127° + \theta = 180°$$

$$\Rightarrow \quad \theta = \frac{53°}{2}$$

So, option (a) is incorrect.

13. As the sphere is grounded, potential at any point on its surface will be zero.

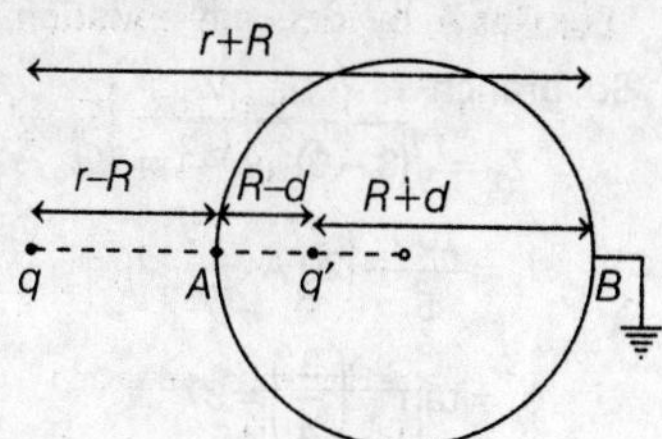

Potential at $A = 0$

$$\Rightarrow \quad \frac{kq}{r-R} + \frac{kq'}{R-d} = 0$$

$$\Rightarrow \quad \frac{q}{q'} = -\left(\frac{r-R}{R-d}\right) \quad \text{...(i)}$$

Also, potential at diametrically opposite point, (point B) = 0

$$\Rightarrow \quad \frac{kq}{r+R}+\frac{kq'}{R+d}=0$$

$$\Rightarrow \quad \frac{q}{q'}=-\left(\frac{r+R}{R+d}\right) \quad \text{...(ii)}$$

From Eqs. (i) and (ii), we get

$$\frac{r-R}{R-d}=\frac{r+R}{R+d}$$

$$\Rightarrow (r-R)(R+d)=(r+R)(R-d)$$

$$\Rightarrow rR+rd-R^2-Rd=rR-rd+R^2-Rd$$

$$\Rightarrow \quad d=\frac{R^2}{r}$$

Putting this value of d in Eq. (i), we get

$$q'=-q\left(\frac{R-d}{r-R}\right)$$

$$=-q\left[\frac{R-\frac{R^2}{r}}{r-R}\right]=-\frac{qR}{r}$$

14. The circuit can be realised as shown below in figure.

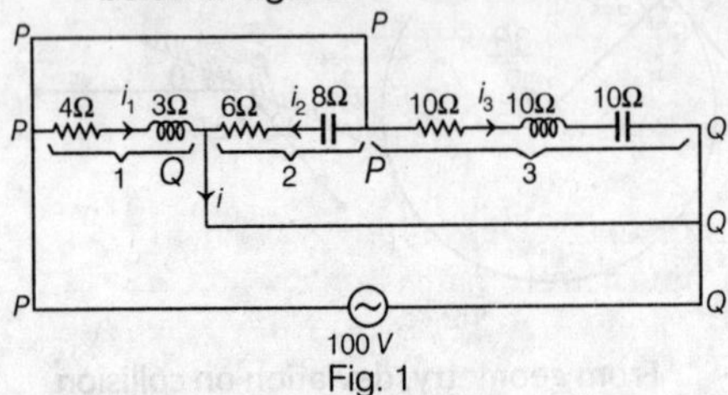

Fig. 1

To find impedance Z of each branch, rms current through them and lead of voltage in terms of phase, we can use the following formulae

$$Z=\sqrt{(X_L-X_C)^2+R^2}$$

$$I=\frac{V}{Z}$$

$$\phi=\tan^{-1}\left(\frac{X_L-X_C}{R}\right)$$

So, branch-1,

$$Z_1=\sqrt{(3-0)^2+4^2}=5\Omega$$

$$I_1=\frac{100}{5}=20\text{ A}$$

$$\phi_1=\tan^{-1}\left(\frac{3}{4}\right)=37°$$

For branch-2,

$$Z_2=\sqrt{(0-8)^2+6^2}=10\,\Omega$$

$$I_2=\frac{100}{10}=10\text{ A}$$

$$\phi_2=\tan^{-1}\frac{-8}{6}=-53°$$

For branch-3,

$$Z_3=\sqrt{(10-10)^2+10^2}=10\,\Omega$$

$$I_3=\frac{100}{10}=10\text{ A}$$

$$\phi_3=\tan^{-1}\left(\frac{10-10}{10}\right)=0$$

Thus, phasor diagram representing various phasors will be as shown.

To find net current, resolve components of current and add as vectors.

10 sin53°=8 I_2=10A
53° 10 cos 53°=6
I_3=10A
37° 20 cos 37°=16
I_1=20A
20 sin37°=12

Fig. 2

Net current will therefore be

$$I=\sqrt{(10+6+16)^2+(12-8)^2}$$

$$=\sqrt{1040}\text{ A}$$

Impedance of circuit,

$$Z=\frac{V}{I}=\frac{100}{\sqrt{1040}}\,\Omega$$

So, option (b) is correct.

As from the figure, current in branch of AC ammeter is sum of currents in branch-1 and branch-2.

$$\therefore \quad I=\sqrt{I_1^2+I_2^2}$$

$$=\sqrt{20^2+10^2}$$

$$=10\sqrt{5}\text{ A}$$

So, option (d) is correct.

As DC ammeter reads average value reading, so DC ammeter reads zero. Also, readings of Voltmeter-1 and Voltmeter-2 both are equal to V_P-V_Q or voltage of AC source, i.e. equal to 100 V.

15. I. Direction of magnetic field is parallel or anti-parallel to velocity, hence magnetic force and acceleration are zero and there is no change in KE.

Also, angular momentum, $L=0$

II. The two infinite line charges will repel q along $-y$-axis.

III. The charge will move on helical path inside solenoid under effect of magnetic force $qvB\sin\theta$ constant in magnitude.

IV. A uniform electric field will provide constant acceleration towards –ve plate only.

So, kinetic energy increases and L increases as well.

16. I.

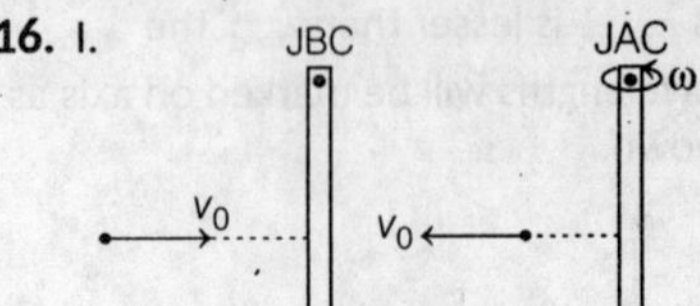

COAM w.r.t. hinge

$$mv_0\frac{2l}{3}=\frac{ml^2}{3}\omega-mv\frac{2l}{3}$$

$$\Rightarrow \quad v_0+v=\frac{\omega l}{2} \quad \text{...(i)}$$

Coefficient of restitution

$$\frac{v+\frac{2\omega l}{3}}{v_0}=1$$

$$v_0\;v=\frac{2\omega l}{3} \quad \text{...(ii)}$$

Adding Eqs. (i) and (ii), we get

$$2v_0=\frac{\omega l}{2}+\frac{2\omega l}{3}=\frac{7\omega l}{6}$$

$$\Rightarrow \quad \omega=\frac{12v_0}{7l}$$

$$v=\frac{\omega l}{2}-v_0$$

$$=\frac{6v_0}{7}-v_0=-\frac{v_0}{7}$$

$$\Rightarrow x+y=12+7=19$$

II.

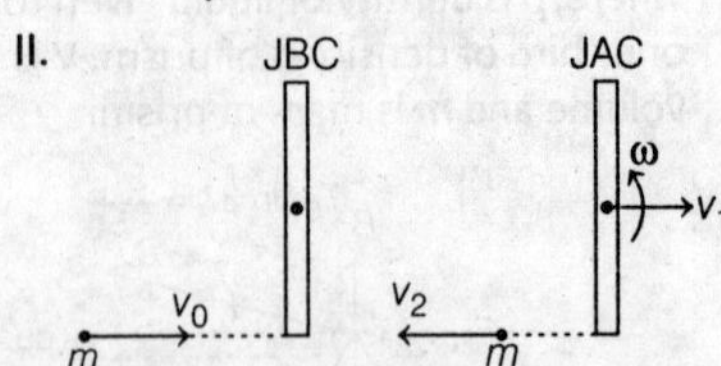

By COLM,

$$v_1-v_2=v_0 \quad \text{...(i)}$$

By $e=1$,

$$v_1+\frac{\omega l}{2}+v_2=v_0 \quad \text{...(ii)}$$

By COAM about P,

$$mv_1\frac{l}{2}=\frac{ml^2}{12}\omega$$

$$\Rightarrow \quad v_1=\frac{\omega l}{6} \quad \text{...(iii)}$$

Solving equations, we get

$$v_1=\frac{2v_0}{5}$$

and $\quad v_2=v_1-v_0$

$$=\frac{2v_0}{5}-v_0$$

$$=-\frac{3v_0}{5}$$

$$\Rightarrow x+y=2+3=5$$

III.

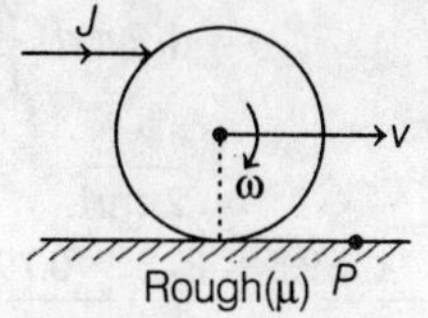

$J = mv \Rightarrow v = J/m$ ...(i)

Also, $Jr = I_{CM}\omega$

$\Rightarrow \frac{JR}{2} = \frac{2}{3}mR^2\omega$

$\Rightarrow \omega = \frac{3J}{4mR}$ ...(ii)

When it starts pure rolling, by COAM about P,

$mvR + \frac{2}{3}mR^2\omega = mv'R + \frac{2}{3}mR^2\left(\frac{v'}{R}\right)$ ...(iii)

Solving Eqs. (i), (ii) and (iii), we get

$\Rightarrow v' = \frac{9J}{10\,m}$

$\Rightarrow \Delta t = \frac{\Delta v}{\mu g} = \frac{J}{10\mu mg}$

$\Rightarrow x + y = 9 + 10 = 19$

IV.

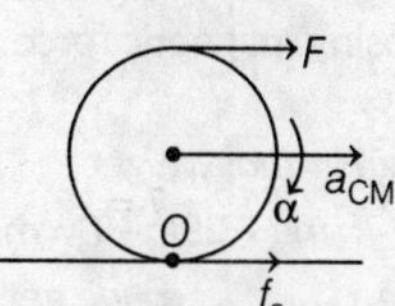

$F(2R) = \frac{5}{3}mR^2\alpha$

$\Rightarrow \alpha R = \frac{6F}{5m} = a_{CM}$

$\Rightarrow F + f_s = ma_{CM} = \frac{6F}{5}$

$\Rightarrow f_s = \frac{F}{5} \le \mu mg$

$\Rightarrow F \le 5\mu mg$

If $F = 10\,\mu mg$

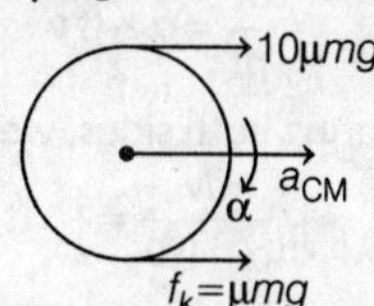

By $\tau_{CM} = I_{CM}\alpha$, we get

$(10\mu mg - \mu mg)R = \frac{2}{3}mR^2\alpha$

$\Rightarrow 9\mu mgR = \frac{2}{3}mR^2\alpha$

$\Rightarrow \alpha = \frac{27\mu g}{2R}$

$\Rightarrow x + y = 5 + 2 = 7$

17. I. Consider the ray diagram shown here.

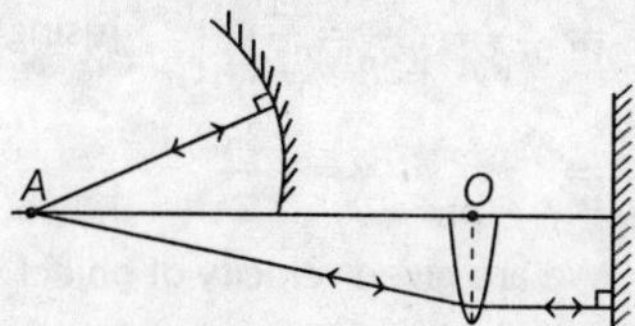

From the diagram, focal length of mirror = 5 cm = x

Focal length of lens = 20 cm = y

II. Consider a point charge placed at centre of shell.

Force due to point charge on considered ring element,

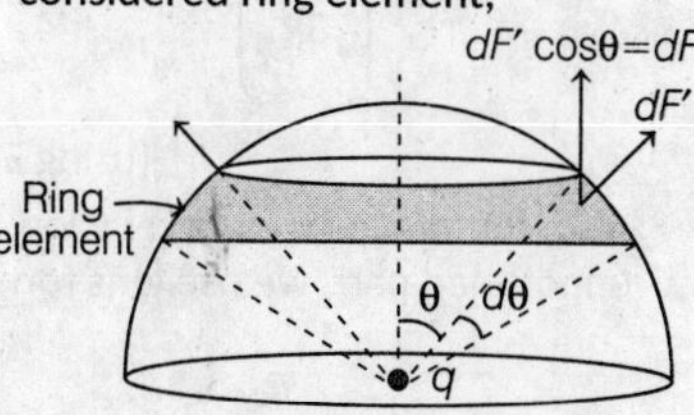

$dF' = \frac{1}{4\pi\varepsilon_0}\frac{q}{R^2}2\pi R\sin\theta\, Rd\theta\sigma$

$= \frac{q}{2\varepsilon_0}\sigma\sin\theta\, d\theta$

$\Rightarrow dF = dF'\cos\theta = \frac{q\sigma}{2\varepsilon_0}\sin\theta\cos\theta\, d\theta$

$= \frac{\sigma q}{4\varepsilon_0}\sin 2\theta\, d\theta$

Case-I

$dF = \frac{\sigma_0 q}{4\varepsilon_0}\sin 2\theta\, d\theta$

$\Rightarrow F = \frac{\sigma_0 q}{4\varepsilon_0}\int_0^{\pi/2}\sin 2\theta\, d\theta = \frac{\sigma_0 q}{4\varepsilon_0}$

$\Rightarrow E = \frac{F}{q} = \frac{\sigma_0}{4\varepsilon_0} \Rightarrow x = 4$

Case-II

$\sigma = \sigma_0\cos\theta$

$\Rightarrow dF = \frac{\sigma_0 q}{2\varepsilon_0}\cos^2\theta\sin\theta\, d\theta$

$\Rightarrow$

$F = \frac{\sigma_0 q}{2\varepsilon_0}\int_0^{\pi/2}\cos^2\theta\sin\theta\, d\theta = \frac{\sigma_0 q}{6\varepsilon_0}$

$\Rightarrow E = \frac{F}{q} = \frac{\sigma_0}{6\varepsilon_0} \Rightarrow y = 6$

III. If a mass $m/4$ was placed at centre of mass of the system and one of the masses was removed, the other mass would experience the same acceleration at any instant. Time m would take to reach centre of mass can be found considering its straight path to be highly eccentric to be equal to half of its time period of revolution around $m/4$ using the expression of time period. Thus,

$\Delta t = \frac{T}{2} = \sqrt{\frac{\pi^2 a^3}{2Gm}} \Rightarrow x = 2$

Also, by conservation of energy,

$\frac{Gm^2}{2a} = \frac{Gm^2}{a} + 2\left(\frac{1}{2}mv^2\right)$

$\Rightarrow mv^2 = \frac{Gm^2}{2a} \Rightarrow v = \sqrt{\frac{Gm}{2a}}$

$\Rightarrow$ Velocity of approach, $2v = \sqrt{\frac{2Gm}{a}}$

$\Rightarrow y = 2$

IV. Field inside cavity is uniform

$= \frac{\rho a}{2\varepsilon_0} = \frac{\rho R}{4\varepsilon_0}$

$\Rightarrow = \frac{\rho R}{4\varepsilon_0} = \frac{x\rho R}{4\varepsilon_0} = \frac{2\rho R}{y\varepsilon_0}$

$x = 1$ and $y = 8$

18. Use ideal gas equation and the facts that for straight line passing through origin y is proportional to x and internal energy is proportional to T. So, the correct match is

I → P, II → R, III → P, IV → Q

Paper 2

1. From FBD of pulleys, tensions at various points will be as shown in figure.

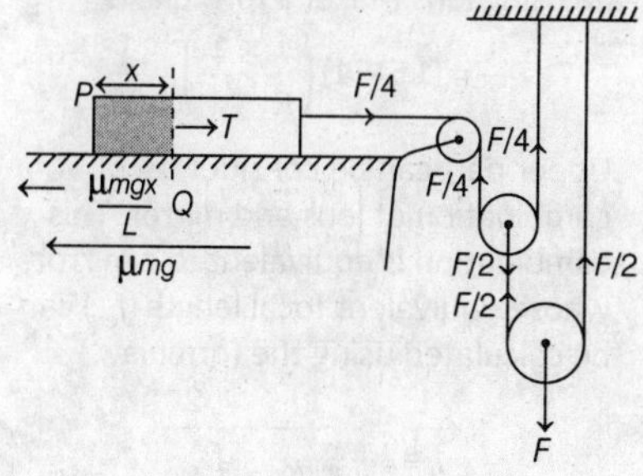

Fig. 1

So, acceleration of the rod,

$a = \frac{\frac{F}{4} - \mu mg}{m} = \frac{F}{4m} - \mu g$ ...(i)

If we now consider portion PQ of the rod having length x, mass of PQ is $\frac{mx}{L}$.

Therefore, friction on it will be $\frac{\mu\, mgx}{L}$.

Using $F = ma$ for PQ, we get

$$T-\frac{\mu mgx}{L}=\frac{mx}{L}a$$

$$\Rightarrow T-\frac{\mu mgx}{L}=\frac{mx}{L}\left(\frac{F}{4m}-\mu g\right)$$

[using Eq. (i)]

$$\Rightarrow \quad T=\frac{F}{4}\cdot\frac{x}{L}$$

So, stress at point Q,

$$\sigma=\frac{T}{A}=\frac{Fx}{4LA} \quad \text{...(ii)}$$

To find elastic potential energy, lets now first consider an element of a thickness dx at a distance x from left end.

As, elastic potential energy in terms of stress σ is given by

$$U=\frac{\sigma^2}{2Y}\times \text{Volume}$$

Potential energy of element,

$$dU=\frac{F^2\cdot x^2\times Adx}{32L^2A^2Y}$$

[using Eq. (ii)]

$\therefore$ Total potential energy of rod,

$$U=\int dU=\frac{F^2L}{96AY}=\frac{(F-0\times mg)^2L}{(10^2-4)AY}$$

$$\Rightarrow \quad a=0, b=10$$

$$\therefore \quad \frac{b}{2+a}=5$$

2. Refractive index of lens,

$$n=\frac{\lambda_{\text{vacuum}}}{\lambda_{\text{lens}}}=\frac{6000}{4000}=1.5$$

Focal length of lower unpolished lens (f_l) using lens Maker's formula, is

$$\frac{1}{f_l}=(1.5-1)\left(\frac{1}{R}-\frac{1}{\infty}\right)=\frac{1}{2R}$$

Upper part can be consider as combination of lens and mirror. This combination is equivalent to a mirror, whose equivalent focal length (f_{eq}) can be calculated using the formula

$$\frac{1}{f_{eq}}=\frac{1}{f_{\text{mirror}}}-\frac{2}{f_{\text{lens}}}$$

As for flat plane mirror, focal length is infinite.

$$\Rightarrow \quad \frac{1}{f_{eq}}=\frac{1}{\infty}-\frac{2}{2R}=-\frac{1}{R}$$

[using Eq. (i)]

$$\Rightarrow \quad f_{eq}=-R \quad \text{...(ii)}$$

Hence, the combination is equivalent to a concave mirror of focal length R.

Thus, for image (I_1) formation by polished part, we use mirror formula

$$\frac{1}{v}+\frac{1}{u}=\frac{1}{f}$$

$$\Rightarrow \quad \frac{1}{v}+\frac{1}{-3R}=\frac{1}{-R} \quad \text{[using Eq. (ii)]}$$

$$\Rightarrow \quad v=-\frac{3R}{2} \quad \text{...(iii)}$$

We are given velocity of object v_0.

As velocity of image v_i for object moving along axis of mirror is given by

$$v_i=-\left(\frac{v}{u}\right)^2 v_0$$

$\therefore$ Velocity of image-1

$$v_1=-\left(\frac{\frac{3R}{2}}{3R}\right)^2 v_0=-\frac{v_0}{4} \quad \text{......(iv)}$$

[using Eq. (iii)]

Also, for image formation by lower unpolished part, we use lens formula

$$\frac{1}{v}-\frac{1}{u}=\frac{1}{f}$$

$$\Rightarrow \quad \frac{1}{v}-\frac{1}{-3R}=\frac{1}{2R} \quad \text{[using Eq. (i)]}$$

$$\Rightarrow \quad v=6R \quad \text{...(v)}$$

As velocity of image v_i for object moving along axis of lens is given by

$$v_i=\left(\frac{v}{u}\right)^2 v_0$$

$$\therefore \text{Velocity of image-2,} \quad v_2=\left(\frac{6R}{-3R}\right)^2 v_0$$

[using Eq. (v)]

$$\Rightarrow \quad v_2=4v_0 \quad \text{...(vi)}$$

Thus, velocity of image-1 w.r.t to image-2 will be

$$v_{\text{relative}}=|v_1-v_2|$$

$$=\left|\frac{-v_0}{4}-4v_0\right|=\frac{17v_0}{4}$$

$$=\frac{17}{4}\times\frac{12}{17}=3 \text{ cm/s}$$

3. As velocity of descent is constant, so net force = 0.

f= viscous force

r, t, l

v=constant

w =weight

$$\Rightarrow \quad w=f$$

$$\Rightarrow \quad w=\eta\cdot 2\pi rl\cdot\frac{v}{t}$$

$$\Rightarrow \quad v=\frac{wt}{2\pi\eta rl}$$

$$=\frac{1\times 9.8\times(0.8-0.796)\times 2}{2\times\pi\times 5\times 10^{-3}\times 0.796\times 0.2\times 2}$$

$$\Rightarrow \quad v\approx 8 \text{ m/s}$$

4. Assuming velocity of CM equal to v at any instant, equivalent circuit diagram showing motional emfs is as shown in figure.

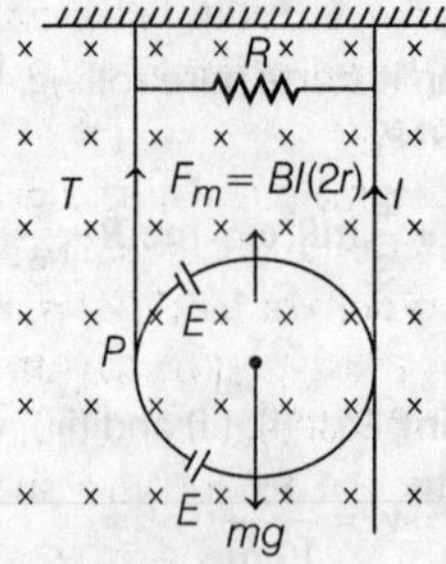

So, induced current flows as given by

$$I=\frac{E}{R}=\frac{2Bvr}{R}$$

Due to this, the ring experiences opposing magnetic force as shown in figure.

Using $F=ma$, we get

$$mg-2BIr-T=ma \quad \text{...(i)}$$

Using $\tau_{CM}=I_{CM}\,\alpha$, we get

$$Tr=mr^2\cdot\frac{a}{r}$$

$$\Rightarrow \quad T=ma \quad \text{...(ii)}$$

From Eqs. (i) and (ii), we get

$$a=\frac{g}{2}-\frac{BIr}{m}$$

$$=\frac{g}{2}-\frac{2B^2r^2}{mR}v$$

Let $\frac{g}{2}=\alpha$ and $\frac{2B^2r^2}{mR}=\beta$, then

$$\Rightarrow \quad \frac{dv}{dt}=\alpha-\beta v$$

Integrating both sides, we get

$$\Rightarrow \quad \int_0^v\frac{dv}{\alpha-\beta v}=\int_0^t dt$$

$$\Rightarrow \quad [\ln(\alpha-\beta v)]_0^v=-\beta t$$

$$\Rightarrow \quad v=\frac{\alpha}{\beta}(1-e^{-\beta t}) \quad \text{...(iii)}$$

At $t=\infty$, $v=\frac{\alpha}{\beta}=\frac{mgR}{4B^2r^2}$

$$=\frac{2\times 10\times 4}{4\times(\sqrt{2})^2\times(\sqrt{5})^2}=2 \text{ m/s}$$

5. For axis to remain stationary, net force on the composite body should be zero.

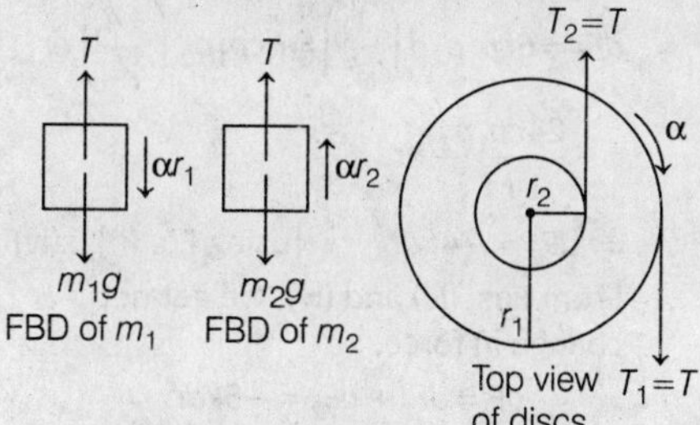

Therefore, tensions in the two strings should be equal. i.e. $T_1 = T_2 = T$ (suppose).

If we assume angular acceleration of the composite disc equal to α, accelerations of blocks of masses m_1 and m_2 are αr_1 and αr_2, respectively as shown in figure.

By using $\tau = I\alpha$, for composite body

$$T r_1 - T r_2 = I\alpha$$

$\Rightarrow$ $T(0.3 - 0.2) = 0.25\alpha$

$\Rightarrow$ $T = 2.5\alpha$ ...(i)

For m_1, using $F = ma$, we get

$$m_1 g - T = m_1 \alpha r_1$$

$\Rightarrow$ $m_1 g - 2.5\alpha = m_1\alpha\,(0.3)$ [using Eq. (i)]

$\Rightarrow$ $m_1 g = (2.5 + 0.3\,m_1)\alpha$ ...(ii)

Similarly, for m_2,

$$T - m_2 g = m_2 \alpha r_2$$

$\Rightarrow$ $2.5\alpha - 2.5g = 2.5\alpha\,(0.2)$

$\Rightarrow$ $\alpha = \frac{5g}{4}$ ...(iii)

Putting value of α from Eq. (iii) into Eq. (ii), we get

$$m_1 g = (2.5 + 0.3\,m_1)\frac{5g}{4}$$

$\Rightarrow$ $4m_1 = 12.5 + 1.5m_1$

$\Rightarrow$ $m_1 = 5\text{ kg}$

$\therefore$ $\frac{m_1}{m_2} = \frac{5}{2.5} = 2$

6. Let a be the side length of square and θ be the position where galvanometer gives zero deflection. To have zero deflection, bridge is to be balanced.

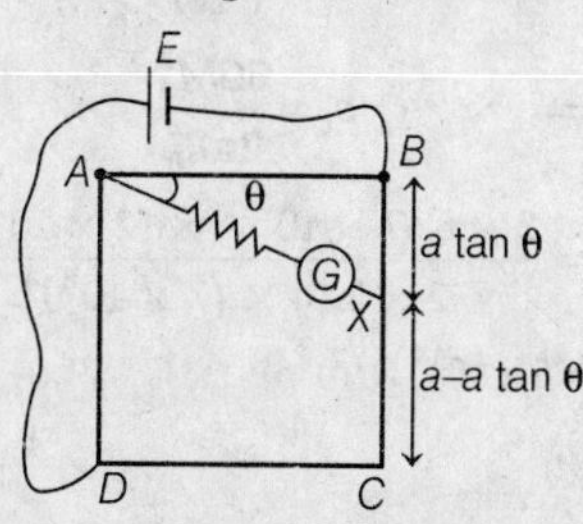

$\Rightarrow$ $\frac{R_{AB}}{R_{AD}} = \frac{R_{BX}}{R_{DC} + R_{CX}}$

[R_{DC} and R_{CX} are in series]

$$\Rightarrow \frac{100}{200} = \frac{\frac{400}{a}\,a\tan\theta}{500 + \frac{400}{a}(a - a\tan\theta)}$$

$$\Rightarrow \frac{1}{2} = \frac{400\tan\theta}{500 + 400(1 - \tan\theta)}$$

Solving this, we get $\tan\theta = 3/4$

$\Rightarrow$ $\theta = 37°$

Let t be the time taken from start, then $\theta = \omega t$ (θ in rad)

$\Rightarrow$ $\frac{\pi}{180} \times 37 = \frac{\pi}{360} \times t$

$\Rightarrow$ $t = 74\text{ s} = n^2 + 10$

$\therefore$ $n = 8$

7. Total increase in length of rods

$$= L\alpha\Delta T + \frac{L}{2}\alpha\Delta T = 3\frac{L}{2}\alpha\Delta T$$

Let the compression in spring A is x_A, B is x_B and C is x_C.

$\Rightarrow$ $k_A x_A = k_B x_B = k_C x_C$

$\Rightarrow$ $kx_A = 2kx_B = kx_C \Rightarrow x_A = 2x_B = x_C$

and $x_A + x_B + x_C = \frac{3}{2}L\alpha\Delta T$

$$2x_B + x_B + 2x_B = 5x_B = \frac{3}{2}L\alpha\Delta T$$

$\Rightarrow$ $x_B = \frac{3}{10}L\alpha\Delta T$ ...(i)

Energy stored,

$$E = \frac{1}{2}kx_A^2 + \frac{1}{2}(2k)x_B^2 + \frac{1}{2}kx_C^2$$

$$= \frac{1}{2}k(2x_B)^2 + kx_B^2 + \frac{1}{2}k(2x_B)^2$$

$$= 2kx_B^2 + kx_B^2 + 2kx_B^2 = 5kx_B^2 \quad \text{...(ii)}$$

Using Eqs. (i) and (ii), we get

$$E = 5k\left(\frac{9}{100}L^2\alpha^2\Delta T^2\right)$$

$$= \frac{9}{20}k\alpha^2L^2\Delta T^2$$

$$= \frac{9}{5\beta}k\alpha^2L^2\Delta T^2$$

$\Rightarrow$ $\beta = 4$

8. Nuclear reaction will be as follows

$$Po^{210} \longrightarrow Pb^{206} + He^4 + Q$$

Mass defect in this equation is

$\Delta m = m_{Po} - m_{Pb} - m_{HO} = 0.00564$ amu

$\therefore$ Energy released by the decay of one polonium nucleus $= (931)\,\Delta m$ MeV

$\Rightarrow$ $Q = 8.4 \times 10^{-13}$ J

693 days of polonium are equivalent to 5 half lives of polonium, because

$$\frac{693}{138.6} = 5$$

So, number of nuclei left after 5 half lives are

$$N = N_0\left(\frac{1}{2}\right)^5 \quad \text{...(i)}$$

Also, $\left(-\frac{dN}{dt}\right) = \lambda N = \frac{\ln(2)}{t_{1/2}} \times N$

So, energy released per day

$$= \left(\frac{\ln 2}{t_{1/2}}\right)N(8.4 \times 10^{-13})\text{ J}$$

But only 10% of this energy is used as electric power, So

$$\left(\frac{10}{100}\right)\left(\frac{\ln(2)}{t_{1/2}}\right)N(8.4 \times 10^{-13}) = 1.2 \times 10^7\text{ J}$$

$$N = \frac{(1.2 \times 10^7)(100)(t_{1/2})}{(10)(\ln 2)(8.4 \times 10^{-13})} = 2.857 \times 10^{22}$$

$\therefore$ Initial number of nuclei required are

$$N_0 = (2^5)N = 9.1424 \times 10^{23} \quad \text{...(ii)}$$

$\therefore$ Mass of polonium required,

$$m = \left(\frac{9.1424 \times 10^{23}}{6 \times 10^{23}}\right) \times 210 = 320\text{ g}$$

$n = 4$

9. Let v_1 and v_2 be velocities of A and B just after collision as shown in Fig. 1.

u → m A u ← $2m$ B — Before collision v_1 → m A v_2 → $2m$ B — After collision

Fig. 1

By conservation of momentum, we get

$$mv_1 + 2mv_2 = mu - 2m(u)$$

$\Rightarrow$ $v_1 + 2v_2 = -u$ ...(i)

By Newton's law of restitution,

$$v_2 - v_1 = u_1 - u_2$$

where, u_1 and u_2 are velocities before collision.

$\Rightarrow$ $v_2 - v_1 = u - (-u)$

$\Rightarrow$ $v_2 - v_1 = 2u$ ...(ii)

From Eqs. (i) and (ii), we get

$$3v_2 = u \Rightarrow v_2 = \frac{u}{3}$$

$\Rightarrow$ $v_1 = \frac{u}{3} - 2u = -\frac{5u}{3}$

[using Eq. (iii)]

So, the blocks move as shown in Fig. 2 just after collision

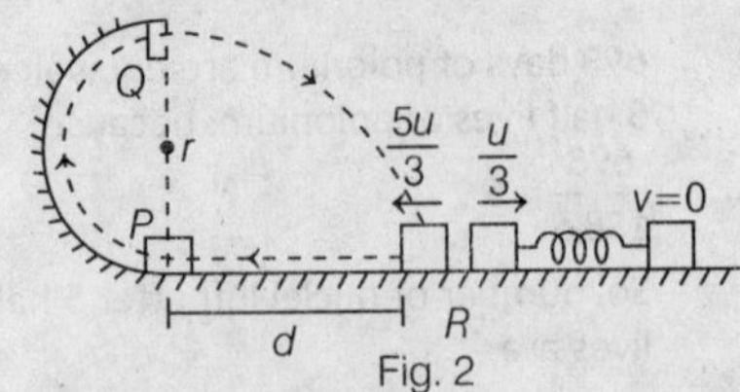

Fig. 2

For vertical looping on a track of radius r, minimum speed required at bottom of track is $\sqrt{5gr}$.

$$\Rightarrow \quad \frac{5u}{3} \geq \sqrt{5gr}$$

$$\Rightarrow \quad u_0 = \frac{3}{5}\sqrt{5gr} = \sqrt{\frac{9}{5}gr}$$

So, for $u = u_0, v_1 = \sqrt{5gr}$.

By conservation of energy for motion of block from P to Q, if v_3 is speed at point Q

$$\frac{1}{2}mv_1^2 = \frac{1}{2}mv_3^2 + mg(2r)$$

$$\Rightarrow \quad v_3 = \sqrt{v_1^2 - 4gr} = \sqrt{gr} \quad \text{...(iii)}$$

Now, time of motion from Q to R (ground) will be

$$T = \sqrt{\frac{2h}{g}} = \sqrt{\frac{2 \times 2r}{g}} \quad \text{...(iv)}$$

$\therefore$ Horizontal displacement of block, $d = v_3 T = 2r$ [using Eqs. (iii) and (iv)]

Now, consider subsequent motion of system of B and C as shown in Fig. 3.

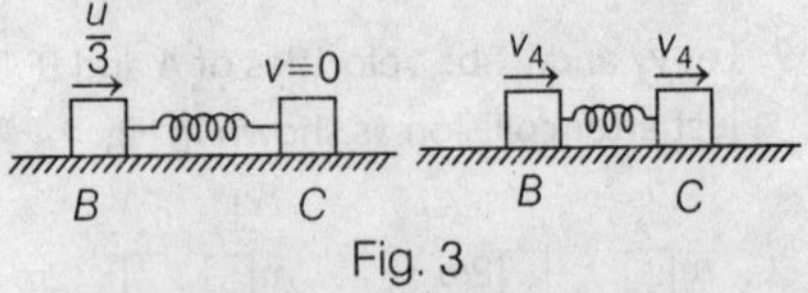

Fig. 3

At the instant of maximum compression, velocities of B and C are equal (suppose v_4). By conservation of momentum,

$$2\,mv + mv = 2m\frac{u}{3}$$

$$\Rightarrow \quad v = \frac{2u}{9}$$

By conservation of energy, we get

$$\frac{1}{2} \cdot 2m \cdot \left(\frac{u}{3}\right)^2 = \frac{1}{2}(m + 2m)\left(\frac{2u}{9}\right)^2 + \frac{1}{2}kx^2$$

$$\Rightarrow \quad x = \frac{u}{3}\sqrt{\frac{2m}{3k}}$$

Velocity of centre of mass of the system of B and C,

$$v_{CM} = \frac{2m \times \frac{u}{3} + m \times 0}{2m + m} = \frac{2u}{9}$$

So, relative initial velocity of $2m$ w.r.t. CM,

$$u_{\text{relative}} = \frac{u}{3} - \frac{2u}{9} = \frac{u}{9}$$

As, block B executes SHM in CM frame, its relative velocity will vary between $\frac{\pm u}{9}$. Therefore, its minimum velocity in ground frame will be

$$v_{\min} = v_{CM} + v_{\min,\,CM}$$

$$= \frac{2u}{9} - \frac{u}{9} = \frac{u}{9}$$

10. Force on a dipole in non-uniform field is given by $p\frac{dE}{dx}$. So, force on dipole-2, due to dipole-1,

$$F = -p_2 \frac{d\left[\frac{2cp_1}{r^3}\right]}{dr} = \frac{6c\,p_1p_2}{r^4}$$

Here, $\quad c = \frac{1}{4\pi\varepsilon_0}$

In equilibrium, F is balanced by spring force kr.

Thus, $\quad kr = \frac{6c\,p_1p_2}{r^4}$

$$\Rightarrow \quad k = \frac{6c\,p_1p_2}{r^5} \quad \text{...(i)}$$

So, option (b) is correct.

Electrostatic potential energy of a dipole is given by

$$U = -pE\cos\theta$$

So, potential energy of dipole-2 in field of dipole-1, $U = -p_2 \cdot \frac{2cp_1}{r^3} \cdot \cos 180°$

$$= \frac{2cp_1p_2}{r^3} \quad \text{...(ii)}$$

Dividing Eq. (ii) by Eq. (i), we get

$$\frac{U}{k} = \frac{r^2}{3} \Rightarrow U = \frac{1}{3}kr^2$$

Also, spring potential energy,

$$U' = \frac{1}{2}kr^2$$

$\therefore$ Total potential energy of system is

$$U + U' = \frac{5}{6}kr^2$$

So, option (a) is incorrect.

If the left ball is held and right ball is slightly displaced, change in spring force,

$$dF_1 = -\,kdr \quad \text{...(iii)}$$

Also, change in electrostatic force,

$$dF_2 = 6cp_1p_2 d\left(\frac{1}{r^4}\right) = 6cp_1p_2\left(\frac{-4}{r^5}\right)dr$$

$$= -\frac{24cp_1p_2}{r^5}dr$$

$$\Rightarrow dF_2 = -\,4kdr \quad \text{[using Eq. (i)] ...(iv)}$$

From Eqs. (iii) and (iv), we get net change in force,

$$dF = dF_1 + dF_2 = -\,5kdr$$

$$\Rightarrow \quad a = \frac{dF}{m} = -\frac{5k}{m}dr$$

As acceleration in SHM is $-\omega^2 x$, so on comparison, we get

$$\omega = \sqrt{\frac{5k}{m}}$$

$$\Rightarrow \quad T = 2\pi\sqrt{\frac{m}{5k}}$$

11. If we assume pressures equal to p and $p + dp$ at distances r and $r + dr$ from the centre as shown in Fig.1, force on shell element due to radiation will be

$$F_1 = p \times 4\pi r^2 - (p + dp) \times 4\pi r^2$$

$$\Rightarrow \quad F_1 = -\,dp \cdot 4\pi r^2 \quad \text{...(i)}$$

Also, mass of shell element,

$$dm = \text{density} \times \text{volume}$$

$$\Rightarrow dm = \rho \times 4\pi r^2 dr \quad \text{...(ii)}$$

$\therefore$ Gravitational pull by mass enclosed by the shell (as shown in Fig. 2) will be

$$F_2 = \frac{GM}{r^2} \cdot dm = \frac{GM}{r^2} \cdot \rho\, 4\pi r^2 dr \quad \text{...(iii)}$$

[using Eq. (ii)]

As according to the problem, radiation pressure is balancing gravity,

$$\Rightarrow \quad F_1 = F_2$$

$$\Rightarrow \quad -dp \cdot 4\pi r^2 = \frac{GM}{r^2}\rho\, 4\pi r^2 dr$$

$$\Rightarrow \quad dp = -\frac{GM}{r^2}\rho\, dr \quad \text{...(iv)}$$

So, in average form,

$$\Rightarrow \quad \Delta p = \frac{-G\frac{M_0}{2}\rho R_0}{\left(\frac{R_0}{2}\right)^2}$$

$$\Rightarrow \quad p_c = \frac{3GM_0^2}{2\pi R_0^4}$$

$$= \frac{3 \times 6.67 \times 10^{-11} \times (2 \times 10^{30})^2}{2 \times 3.14 \times (7 \times 10^8)^4}$$

$$\approx 5 \times 10^{14}\ \text{N/m}^2$$

12. Consider unit length of the double tape line as shown in the figure.

As field due to infinite sheet of current, in terms of current per unit length, is $\frac{\mu_0 \lambda}{2}$, due to upper tape, then magnetic field at any general point O between plates,

$$B_0 = \frac{\mu_0 I}{2b} \quad \text{...(i)}$$

Likewise, magnetic field due to lower tape will also be the same in magnitude. Directions of fields due to the two tapes will be in –ve x-direction, so net field at O will be

$$B = 2B_0 = \frac{\mu_0 I}{b} \quad \text{[using Eq. (i)]}$$

therefore, magnetic flux through cross-section $PQRS$,

$$\phi = Bh = \frac{\mu_0 Ih}{b}$$

$\Rightarrow$ Self-inductance per unit length,

$$L_0 = \frac{\phi}{I} = \frac{\mu_0 h}{b} \quad \text{...(ii)}$$

Also, capacitance of a parallel plate capacitor is given by $C = \frac{\varepsilon_0 A}{d}$

where, A is plate area and d is plate separation.

Therefore, capacitance per unit length,

$$C_0 = \frac{\varepsilon_0 \times b \times 1}{h} = \frac{\varepsilon_0 b}{h} \quad \text{...(iii)}$$

As for an LC circuit, angular frequency of oscillation is given by

$$\omega = \frac{1}{\sqrt{LC}} = \frac{1}{\sqrt{L_0 C_0}}$$

$$= \frac{1}{\sqrt{\mu_0 \varepsilon_0}} = c \quad \text{[using Eqs. (ii) and (iii)]}$$

(As, $\frac{1}{\sqrt{\mu_0 \varepsilon_0}} = c$ as per Maxwell's theory of EM waves)

If k_1 is closed, the circuit will be L-C-E circuit in which charge q varies with time t as given by following equation

$$q = CE(1 - \cos \omega t)$$

$\therefore$ Maximum charge, q_{max}

$$= 2CE = 2C_0 E = \frac{2\varepsilon_0 bE}{h} \quad \text{[using Eq. (iii)]}$$

13. For k_α X-rays, by Moseley's law,

$$(Z-1) \propto \frac{1}{\sqrt{\lambda}}$$

Thus for impurity-1 having Z equal to Z_1

$$\Rightarrow \quad \left(\frac{Z_1 - 1}{Z - 1}\right) = \sqrt{\frac{\lambda_3}{\lambda_1}}$$

$$\Rightarrow \quad \frac{Z_1 - 1}{Z - 1} = 2 \Rightarrow Z_1 = 2Z - 1$$

Similarly, for impurity-2,

$$\frac{Z_2 - 1}{Z - 1} = \sqrt{\frac{\lambda_3}{\lambda_2}} = \frac{1}{2}$$

$$\Rightarrow \quad Z_2 = 0.5(Z + 1)$$

14. For steady state,

$$\left(\frac{dQ}{dt}\right)_{in} = \left(\frac{dQ}{dt}\right)_{out}$$

$$\Rightarrow \quad (V)(i_s) = 45(T - 20)$$

$$\Rightarrow \quad (500)(4.5) = 45(T - 20)$$

$$\Rightarrow \quad T_s = 70°C$$

Resistance at 20°C, $R = \frac{V}{i} = \frac{500}{5}$

$$R_{20} = 100\,\Omega$$

Resistance at 70°C,

$$R = \frac{V}{i} = \frac{500}{4.5} \simeq 111\,\Omega$$

$$\therefore \quad R_f = R_0(1 + \alpha\,\Delta T)$$

$$111 = 100[1 + \alpha(50)]$$

$$\Rightarrow \quad \alpha = \frac{0.11}{50} \cong 2.2 \times 10^{-3}/°C$$

15. As ideal pulley is massless, net force on the pulley is zero. So, tensions can be assumed as depicted in the figure.

Let acceleration of the hanging block (block A) be a and acceleration of block B be a'. As tension force acting on C is half that of tension acting on B, so acceleration will also be half. i.e. $\frac{a'}{2}$.

For subsequent blocks, acceleration will keep on getting halved by same argument.

As per virtual work method, sum of work done by tensions on system is zero.

$$\Rightarrow \quad \Sigma \mathbf{T}_i \cdot \mathbf{x}_i = 0$$

Diferentiating twice w.r.t. time, we get

$$\Sigma \mathbf{T}_i \cdot \mathbf{a}_i = 0$$

$$\Rightarrow Ta \cos 180° + \frac{T}{2} a' \cos 0° + \frac{T}{4}\frac{a'}{2} \cos 0° + \ldots = 0$$

$$\Rightarrow -Ta + \frac{Ta'}{2}\left(1 + \frac{1}{4} + \frac{1}{16} + \ldots\right) = 0$$

$$\Rightarrow \quad -a + \frac{a'}{2}\left(\frac{1}{1 - \frac{1}{4}}\right) = 0$$

(As for infinite GP, summation is $\frac{A}{1-r}$, where A is first term while r is common ratio)

$$\Rightarrow \quad a' = \frac{3}{2}a \quad \text{...(i)}$$

For block A, by $F_{net} = ma$, we get

$$mg - T = ma \quad \text{...(ii)}$$

Similarly, for B, we get.

$$\frac{T}{2} = ma'$$

$$\Rightarrow \quad \frac{T}{2} = m\left(\frac{3a}{2}\right) \quad \text{[using Eq. (i)]}$$

$$\Rightarrow \quad T = 3\,ma \quad \text{...(iii)}$$

From Eqs. (ii) and (iii), we get

$$mg - 3\,ma = ma$$

$$\Rightarrow \quad a = \frac{g}{4} \quad \text{...(iv)}$$

$$\Rightarrow \quad a' = \frac{3a}{2} = \frac{3g}{8} \quad \text{[using Eq. (i)]}$$

Velocity of block B after time t of releasing,

$$v = u + a't = 0 + \frac{3g}{8}t \quad \text{...(v)}$$

Also, tension force on block B,

$$F = \frac{T}{2} = \frac{3ma}{2} = \frac{3mg}{8} \quad \text{...(vi)}$$

[using Eqs. (iii) and (iv)]

Thus, power delivered to B,

$$P = Fv = \frac{9\,mg^2 t}{64}$$

[using Eqs. (v) and (vi)]

16. Angle of incidence i, at general point P, is maximum when the source is at extreme position shown in figure.

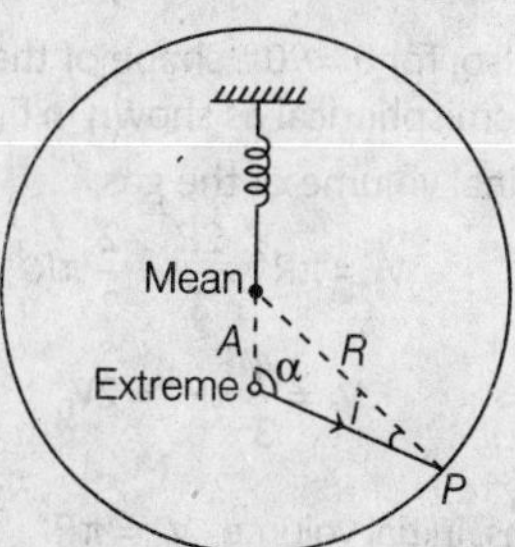

By sine rule in the triangle formed in Fig.1,

$$\frac{\sin i}{A} = \frac{\sin \alpha}{R}$$

$$\Rightarrow \quad \sin i = \frac{A}{R} \sin \alpha$$

So, for given A, i is maximum if point P has $\alpha = 90°$. Also, for TIR, i should be equal to critical angle C.

$\therefore$ For $\quad \alpha = 90°$,

$$A = R \sin C \qquad \text{...(i)}$$

Also, by Snell's law, for refraction at P,

$$n \cdot \sin C = 1 \cdot \sin 90°$$

$$\Rightarrow \quad \sin C = \frac{1}{n} \qquad \text{...(ii)}$$

For an oscillator executing SHM, amplitude A in terms of speed v at mean position is

$$A = v\sqrt{\frac{m}{k}} \qquad \text{...(iii)}$$

Putting values of A and $\sin C$ from Eqs. (ii) and (iii) in Eq. (i), we get

$$v\sqrt{\frac{m}{k}} = \frac{R}{n}$$

$$\Rightarrow \quad v = \frac{R}{n}\sqrt{\frac{k}{m}}$$

17. From FBD of the soap film shown here in figure.

$$p\pi R^2 = p_0 \pi R^2 + T \sin\theta \cdot 4\pi R$$

$$\Rightarrow \quad p = p_0 + \frac{4T \sin\theta}{R}$$

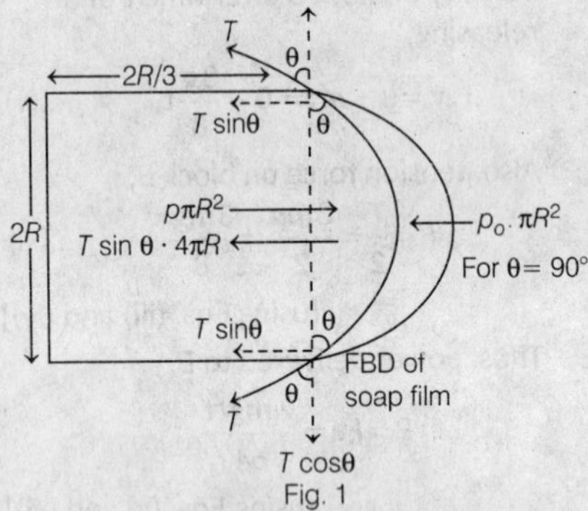

Fig. 1

p is maximum, for $\theta = 90°$

$$\Rightarrow \quad p_{\max} = p_0 + \frac{4T}{R} \qquad \text{...(i)}$$

Also, for $\theta = 90°$, shape of the film is hemispherical as shown in figure.

Final volume of the gas,

$$V_f = \pi R^2 \cdot \frac{2R}{3} + \frac{2}{3}\pi R^3$$

$$\Rightarrow \quad V_f = \frac{4}{3}\pi R^3 = 2V_0 \qquad \text{... (ii)}$$

(as, initial volume, $V_0 = \pi R^2 \cdot \frac{2R}{3} = \frac{2\pi R^3}{3}$)

By conservation of number of moles, if T_f is the final temperature at the instant when pressure is maximum.

$$n_{\text{final}} = n_{\text{initial}}$$

$$\Rightarrow \quad \frac{p_{\max} V_f}{T_f} = \frac{p_0 V_0}{T_0}$$

(using ideal gas equation)

$$\Rightarrow \quad T_f = \left(\frac{p_{\max} V_f}{p_0 V_0}\right) T_0$$

$$= \left(1 + \frac{4T}{p_0 R}\right) 2T_0$$

[using Eqs. (i) and (ii)]

$$= \left(2 + \frac{8T}{p_0 R}\right) T_0$$

18. Let charge on each face of the cube $= q$

Total flux through the cube $= \frac{6q}{\varepsilon_0}$

So, flux through each face $\phi = \frac{q}{\varepsilon_0} \qquad \text{...(i)}$

Also, field due to a sheet of charge, having surface charge density σ, near its surface,

$$E = \frac{\sigma}{2\varepsilon_0}$$

So, flux through each face due to charge on itself,

$$\phi' = \frac{\sigma}{2\varepsilon_0} A = \frac{q}{2\varepsilon_0} \qquad \text{...(ii)}$$

Thus, flux through each face due to remaining five faces,

$$\phi'' = \phi - \phi' = \frac{q}{2\varepsilon_0} \qquad \text{...(iii)}$$

[using Eqs. (i) and (ii)]

Now consider a small element of surface area dA of face, on which we want to find force, as shown in figure. Let its area vector is $d\mathbf{A}$ and electric field at its location is $\mathbf{E}$ as shown.

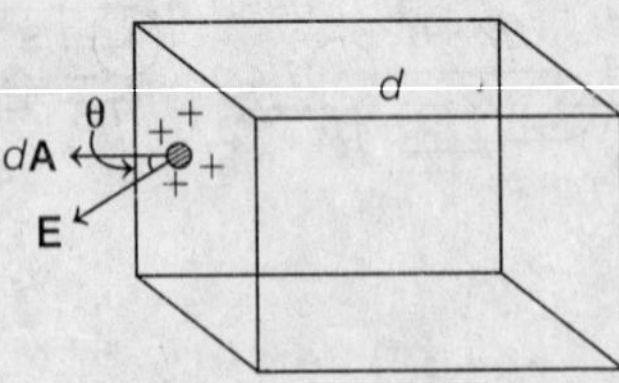

Charge on the element, $dq = \sigma\, dA$

So, force on the element,

$$|d\mathbf{F}| = dq\,|\mathbf{E}|$$

$$= \sigma\, dA\,|\mathbf{E}|$$

$$= \sigma\, dAE \qquad \text{...(iv)}$$

As by symmetry, net force on the face is perpendicular to it. Therefore, net force is summation of components of forces perpendicular to the surface.

$$F = \int dF \cos\theta = \int \sigma E\, dA \cos\theta$$

[using Eq. (iv)]

$$\Rightarrow \quad F = \sigma \int \mathbf{E} \cdot d\mathbf{A} = \sigma\,\phi''$$

$$= \sigma \cdot \frac{q}{2\varepsilon_0} \qquad \text{[using Eq. (iii)]}$$

$$= \frac{\sigma \cdot \sigma d^2}{2\varepsilon_0} = \frac{\sigma^2 d^2}{2\varepsilon_0} \quad [\because q = \sigma d^2]$$

Knockout 13 (Paper 1)

1. FBD of B and C are as shown in the Fig.1.

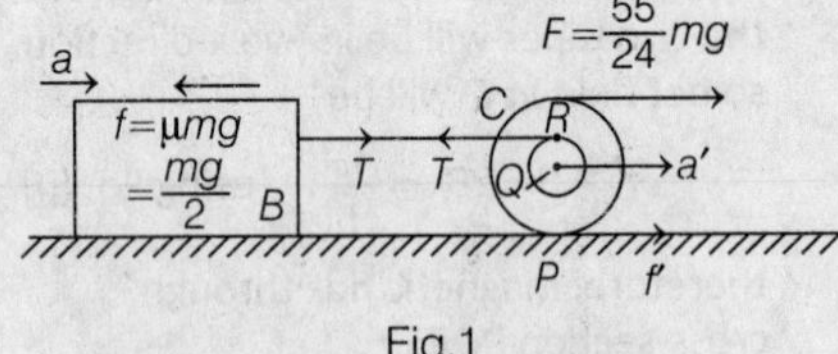

Fig.1

Assuming motion of spool as pure rotation about instantaneous axis of rotation P, accelerations of points Q and R are

$$a_Q = a' = \alpha(2r) \qquad \text{...(i)}$$

$$a_R = a = \alpha(3r) \qquad \text{...(ii)}$$

(as R is connected to B, they have same acceleration)

Dividing Eq. (i) by Eq. (ii), we get

$$a' = \frac{2}{3} a \qquad \text{...(iii)}$$

Using, $\tau = I\alpha$ for spool about instantaneous axis P, we get

$$\frac{55}{24} mg(4r) - T(3r) = [mr^2 + m(2r)^2]\frac{a'}{2r}$$

$$\Rightarrow \frac{55}{6} mgr - 3Tr = 5mr^2 \times \left(\frac{a}{3r}\right)$$

[using Eq. (iii)]

$$\Rightarrow \frac{55}{6} mg - 3T = \frac{5ma}{3} \qquad \text{...(iv)}$$

For block B, using $F_{\text{net}} = ma$, we get

$$T - \frac{mg}{2} = 2ma \qquad \text{...(v)}$$

Dividing Eq. (iv) by Eq. (v), we get

$$2\left(\frac{55}{6} mg - 3T\right) = \frac{5}{3}\left(T - \frac{mg}{2}\right)$$

$$\Rightarrow \quad \frac{23T}{3} = \frac{115mg}{6}$$

$$\Rightarrow \quad T = \frac{5mg}{2} \Rightarrow x = 2.50$$

2. Let us find Q, for all steps.

As, AB is adiabatic,

$$Q_{AB} = 0 \quad \text{...(i)}$$

As, graph of BC is straight line passing through origin,

$$p \propto T$$

$\Rightarrow V =$ Constant (isochoric process)

$$\Rightarrow \quad Q_{BC} = \Delta U + W$$

$$= \frac{f}{2} nR\Delta T + 0$$

$$\Rightarrow \quad Q_{BC} = \frac{f}{2} nR(T_C - T_B) \quad \text{...(ii)}$$

As, CD is adiabatic,

$$Q_{CD} = 0 \quad \text{...(iii)}$$

As, graph of DA is straight line passing through origin,

$$p \propto T$$

$\Rightarrow \quad V =$ constant (isochoric process)

$$\Rightarrow \quad Q_{DA} = \Delta U + W$$

$$= \frac{f}{2} nR\Delta T$$

$$\Rightarrow \quad Q_{DA} = \frac{f}{2} nR(T_A - T_D) \quad \text{...(iv)}$$

For the cycle $ABCDA$, work done by gas,

$$W = Q - \Delta U = Q$$

(As, ΔU is zero for cycle)

$$\Rightarrow \quad W = Q_{AB} + Q_{BC} + Q_{CD} + Q_{DA}$$

$$\Rightarrow \quad W = \frac{f}{2} nR[(T_C - T_B) + (T_A - T_D)] \ldots \text{(v)}$$

[using Eqs. (i), (ii), (iii) and (iv)]

From the given diagram,

$$T_C > T_B$$

While $T_A < T_B$, therefore we get

$Q_{BC} > 0$ [using Eq. (ii)]

$Q_{DA} < 0$ [using Eq. (iv)]

As, heat supplied during cycle is sum of positive values of Q of steps, therefore

$$Q = Q_{BC} = \frac{f}{2} nR(T_C - T_B) \quad \text{...(vi)}$$

Dividing Eq. (v) by Eq. (vi), we get

$$\eta = \frac{W}{Q} = 1 + \frac{T_A - T_D}{T_C - T_B} \quad \text{...(vii)}$$

As, $$T_B = T_A \left(\frac{V_A}{V_B}\right)^{2/5}$$

$$= T_A (32)^{2/5} = 4T_A \quad \text{...(viii)}$$

Similarly for CD, we get

$$T_C = 4T_D \quad \text{...(ix)}$$

Putting values of T_B and T_C, from Eqs. (viii) and (ix) into Eq. (vii), we get

$$\eta = 1 + \frac{T_A - T_D}{4T_D - 4T_A}$$

$$= 1 - \frac{1}{4} = \frac{3}{4} = 0.75$$

3. The image formation is as shown below

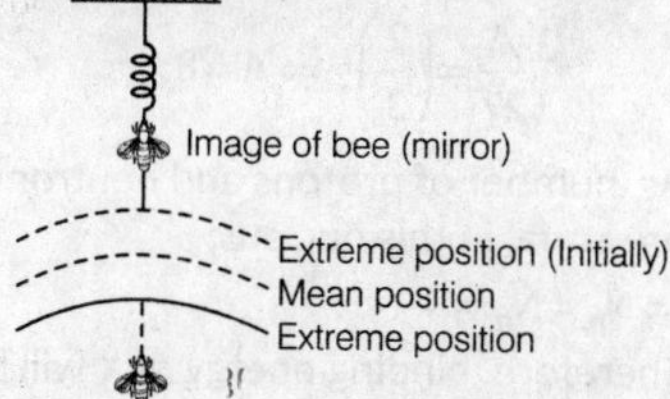

At mean position, $ka = mg$

$\Rightarrow$ Amplitude of oscillation of mirror

$$a = \frac{mg}{k} = \frac{10^{-1} \times 10}{10^3} = 1 \text{ mm} \quad \text{...(i)}$$

Now, for bee, image position is given by

$$\frac{1}{v} + \frac{1}{u} = \frac{1}{f} \Rightarrow \frac{1}{v} + \frac{1}{-50} = \frac{1}{-100}$$

$$\Rightarrow \quad v = 1 \text{ m}$$

Now, to relate small displacement of object (du) and for small displacement of image (dv), lets differentiate mirror formula w.r.t. u

$$\Rightarrow \left(-\frac{1}{v^2}\right)\frac{dv}{du} - \frac{1}{u^2} = 0$$

$$\Rightarrow dv = -\left(\frac{v}{u}\right)^2 du \quad \text{...(ii)}$$

Displacement of bee's image w.r.t. mirror when it moves from upper extreme to mean position,

$$dv = -\left(\frac{1}{-0.5}\right)^2 (1)$$

[as, $du = A$ using Eq. (i)]

Amplitude of oscillation of bee's image,

$$a \text{ mm} = 4 \text{ mm} \Rightarrow a = 4 \quad \text{...(iii)}$$

Time period of oscillation of mirror and bee has to be equal, as they reach mean and extreme simultaneously,

$$\Rightarrow \quad T = 2\pi\sqrt{\frac{m}{k}}$$

$$= 2\pi\sqrt{\frac{0.1}{10^3}} = \frac{\pi}{50} \text{ s}$$

$$= \frac{\pi}{b} \quad \text{(given)}$$

$$b = 50 \quad \text{...(iv)}$$

Using Eqs. (iii) and (iv), we get

$$a + b = 50 + 4 = 54$$

4.

If potential of P is assumed 0 V, after the key is closed, potential of point W will be $E = 10\text{V}$. In branch with inductor and resistor, current i will grow as per the function

$$i = \frac{E}{R}\left(1 - e^{-\frac{Rt}{L}}\right)$$

Potential difference across inductor,

$$V_1 = L\frac{di}{dt} = L \cdot \frac{E}{R} \cdot \frac{R}{L} e^{-\frac{Rt}{L}}$$

$$\Rightarrow \quad V_1 = Ee^{-\frac{Rt}{L}} \quad \text{...(i)}$$

Charge on capacitor grows as per function,

$$q = CE(1 - e^{-t/RC})$$

So, potential difference across capacitor,

$$V_2 = \frac{q}{C} = E(1 - e^{-t/RC}) \quad \text{...(ii)}$$

When voltmeters read the same, $V_1 = V_2$

$$\Rightarrow \quad Ee^{-\frac{Rt}{L}} = E(1 - e^{-t/RC})$$

$$\Rightarrow \quad e^{-t} = 1 - e^{-t}$$

$(\because R = 1\ \Omega, L = 1\text{ H}, C = 1\text{ F})$

$$\Rightarrow \quad e^t = 2$$

$$\Rightarrow \quad t = \ln 2 = 0.69$$

5. Path difference between waves reaching O, as shown in figure, is

$$\Delta x = x_1 - x_2 = \frac{dl}{b} \quad \text{...(i)}$$

For green to be missing, destructive interference occurs for which

$$\Delta x = (2n+1) \times \frac{\lambda}{2} \quad \text{...(ii)}$$

From Eqs. (i) and (ii), we get

$$\frac{dl}{b} = (2n+1) \times \frac{\lambda}{2}$$

$$\Rightarrow \quad l = (2n+1) \times \frac{\lambda b}{2d}$$

For l to be minimum, put $n = 0$

$$\Rightarrow \quad l_1 = \frac{\lambda b}{2d} \quad \text{...(iii)}$$

So, we get $l_1 = \dfrac{5 \times 10^{-7} \times 0.5}{2 \times 10^{-3}}$

$$= 1.25 \times 10^{-4} \text{ m}$$

6. As per Einstein's equation,

$$KE_{max} = E_{photon} - \phi$$

$$\Rightarrow \frac{1}{2} mv^2 = \frac{hc}{\lambda} - \phi$$

For $\lambda = \lambda_1 = 3000$ Å, we get

$$\frac{1}{2} mv^2 = \frac{hc}{\lambda_1} - \phi \quad \text{...(i)}$$

For $\lambda = \lambda_2 = 1650$ Å, as speed of electrons is doubled, so we get

$$\frac{1}{2} m(2v)^2 = \frac{hc}{\lambda_2} - \phi \quad \text{...(ii)}$$

Dividing Eq. (ii) by Eq. (i), we get

$$4\left(\frac{hc}{\lambda_1} - \phi\right) = \frac{hc}{\lambda_2} - \phi$$

$$\Rightarrow \quad 3\phi = \frac{4hc}{\lambda_1} - \frac{hc}{\lambda_2}$$

$$\Rightarrow \quad \frac{hc}{\lambda_0} = \frac{hc}{3}\left[\frac{4}{\lambda_1} - \frac{1}{\lambda_2}\right]$$

$$\Rightarrow \lambda_0 = \frac{3\lambda_1\lambda_2}{4\lambda_2 - \lambda_1}$$

$$= \frac{3 \times 3000 \times 1650}{4(1650) - 3000}$$

$$= 4125 \text{ Å} = 0.41 \ \mu\text{m}$$

7. If the milky-way has N stars each having mass M, mass of milky-way will NM.

Thus, force on revolving star

$$\frac{GNM \cdot M}{R^2} = M\omega^2 R$$

$$\Rightarrow \quad N = \frac{\omega^2 R^3}{GM} = \frac{4\pi^2 R^3}{T^2 GM}$$

$$\Rightarrow N = \frac{4 \times 10 \times (10^{20})^3}{(10^{15})^2 \times \dfrac{20}{3} \times 10^{-11} \times 2 \times 10^{30}}$$

$$N = 3 \times 10^{11}$$

$$\therefore \quad x + y = 14$$

8. For any nucleus of radius R,

A (mass no.) $\propto R^3$

Thus, if A is mass no. of unknown nucleus,

$$\frac{A}{27} = \left(\frac{2}{3}\right)^3 \Rightarrow A = 8$$

As, number of protons and neutrons are equal in this nucleus,

$$\Rightarrow N_p = N_n = 4$$

Therefore, binding energy of X will be

$$BE = (4m_p + 4m_N - m_x) \times 931.5 \text{ MeV}$$

$$= (4 \times 1.007826 + 4 \times 1.008665 - 8.0053) \times 931.5 \text{ MeV}$$

$$= 56.5 \text{ MeV} \approx 56 \text{ MeV}$$

9. Capacitance of a capacitor with dielectric slabs in series is given by

$$C' = \frac{\varepsilon_0 A}{\dfrac{d_1}{K_1} + \dfrac{d_2}{K_2} + \dots}$$

Here, d_1, d_2 etc. are thicknesses of slabs while K_1, K_2 are respective dielectric constants. Therefore, for any of the capacitors with slab, capacitance would be

$$C' = \frac{\varepsilon_0 A}{\dfrac{3d}{4 \times 3} + \dfrac{d}{4}} = \frac{2\varepsilon_0 A}{d}$$

$$= 2C \quad \left(\text{here, } C = \frac{\varepsilon_0 A}{d}\right)$$

Thus, arrangement can be visualised as shown in Fig.1.

Fig.1

As, capacitors in branch-1 are in series, so their equivalent capacitance

$$\frac{1}{C_{eq_1}} = \frac{1}{C_1} + \frac{1}{C_2} = \frac{1}{2C} + \frac{1}{C} = \frac{3}{2C}$$

$$\Rightarrow \quad C_{eq_1} = \frac{2C}{3} \quad \text{...(i)}$$

Similarly, for branch-2 and 3,

$$C_{eq_2} = \frac{C}{3} \quad \text{...(ii)}$$

and $\quad C_{eq_3} = \dfrac{C}{6} \quad$ ...(iii)

As, branches-1, 2 and 3 are in parallel, so final equivalent capacitance,

$$C_{eq} = C_{eq_1} + C_{eq_2} + C_{eq_3}$$

$$= \frac{2C}{3} + \frac{C}{3} + \frac{C}{6}$$

[using, Eqs. (i), (ii) and (iii)]

or $\quad C_{AB} = \dfrac{7C}{6} \quad$ ...(iv)

Before the slabs were inserted, the circuit was as shown in Fig. 2.

Fig.2

By using formula for parallel equivalent, equivalent capacitance between A and B,

$$C'_{AB} = \frac{C}{8} + \frac{C}{4} + \frac{C}{2} = \frac{7C}{8} \quad \text{...(v)}$$

So, charge supplied by cell,

$$Q = (C_{AB} - C'_{AB})E$$

$$= \left(\frac{7C}{6} - \frac{7C}{8}\right)E = \frac{7}{24}CE$$

[using Eqs. (iv) and (v)]

$\therefore$ Work done by cell,

$$W_a = Q \cdot E = \frac{7CE^2}{24} \quad \text{...(vi)}$$

Change in potential energy of the arrangement,

$$\Delta U = \frac{1}{2}(C_{AB} - C'_{AB})E^2$$

$$= \frac{1}{2} \times \frac{7}{24} CE^2 = \frac{7}{48} CE^2 \quad \text{...(vii)}$$

Heat dissipated is given by

$$H = W - \Delta U$$

$$= \frac{7CE^2}{24} - \frac{7CE^2}{48} = \frac{7CE^2}{48}$$

[using Eqs. (vi) and (vii)]

Consider the lowermost branch which can be seen to be a series combination of $\frac{3d}{4}$ thickness of dielectric and $\frac{5d}{4}$ thickness of air cored capacitor.

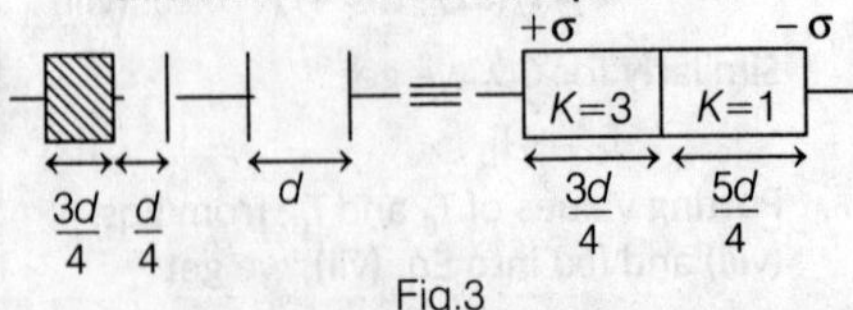

Fig.3

Energy density (energy per unit volume) is given by $\dfrac{\sigma^2}{2K\varepsilon_0}$.

So, if charge density on capacitor is σ, energy stored in volume V of capacitor is given by $U=\dfrac{\sigma^2 V}{2K\varepsilon_0}=\dfrac{\sigma^2 Ad}{2K\varepsilon_0}$

Thus, $U \propto \dfrac{d}{K}$

$$\Rightarrow \frac{U_{\text{dielectric}}}{U_{\text{air}}}=\frac{d_1}{K_1}\times\frac{K_2}{d_2}=\frac{1}{5}$$

10. Net contact force (i.e. resultant of buoyancy and normal contact force by tank's bottom) has to be equal and opposite to weight of hemisphere for equilibrium.

$$\Rightarrow \text{Net contact force} = mg=\sigma\cdot\frac{2}{3}\pi R^3 g$$

$\therefore$ Net contact force is independent of ρ and h.

11. As, cylindrical part of the foil is long and is carrying circumferential current it can be treated as long solenoid. So field at its centre will be field inside ideal solenoid,

$$B=\mu_0 \times \text{Current per unit length}$$

$$\Rightarrow \quad B_1=\mu_0\times\frac{i}{l} \quad \text{...(i)}$$

As, field of one infinite plane sheet of current is given by

$$B=\frac{\mu_0 i}{2l}$$

So, B_2 due to the two planar surfaces,

$$B_2=\frac{\mu_0 i}{l} \quad \text{...(ii)}$$

As, energy stored in magnetic field is given by

$$U=\frac{B^2}{2\mu_0}\times\text{Volume}$$

Ratio of energies in cylindrical volume V_1 to that in volume V_2 between planes,

$$\frac{U_1}{U_2}=\frac{\dfrac{B_1^2}{2\mu_0}\times V_1}{\dfrac{B_2^2}{2\mu_0}\times V_2}=\frac{V_1}{V_2}$$

[$\because B_1=B_2$ as per Eqs. (i) and (ii)]

$$\Rightarrow \quad \frac{U_1}{U_2}=\frac{\pi R^2\cdot i}{\dfrac{R}{k}\cdot kR\cdot l}=\pi$$

If we consider cross-sectional view of the arrangement, magnetic field is in negative z-direction as shown.

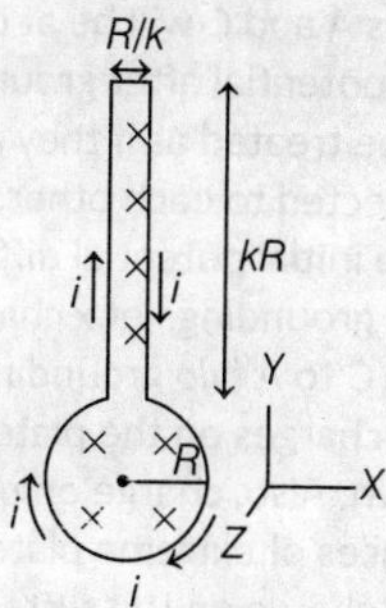

Flux of the field is given by

$$\phi=BA$$

$$\Rightarrow \quad \phi=\frac{\mu_0 i}{l}\left(\pi R^2+kR\cdot\frac{R}{k}\right)$$

$$=\frac{\mu_0 iR^2}{l}(\pi+1)$$

$\therefore$ Self-inductance of arrangement,

$$L=\frac{\phi}{i}=\frac{\mu_0 R^2(\pi+1)}{l}$$

Energy stored in the arrangement can be written as

$$U=\frac{1}{2}Li^2=\frac{1}{2}\frac{\mu_0 R^2}{l}(\pi+1)i^2$$

12. Conveyor belt in this case is a variable mass system. Let F be force on it by rollers to keep it moving with constant speed v.

By Newton's 2nd law,

$$F=\frac{dp}{dt}=\frac{d(mv)}{dt}$$

$$=m\cdot\frac{dv}{dt}+v\cdot\frac{dm}{dt}=0+v\cdot\mu=\mu v$$

(as $v=$ constant)...(i)

Power delivered by this force can be calculated by

$$P=\mathbf{F}\cdot\mathbf{v}=Fv\cos\theta$$

$$\Rightarrow \quad P_F=\mu v\cdot v\cos 0^\circ=\mu v^2$$

[using Eq. (i)]

By work-energy theorem,

$$dW_F+dW_f=dK$$

Here, dW_F, dW_f and dK represent work by F, work by friction and change in kinetic energy, respectively.

$$\Rightarrow \frac{dW_F}{dt}+\frac{dW_f}{dt}=\frac{dK}{dt}$$

$$\Rightarrow P_F\frac{dW_f}{dt}=\frac{d\left(\frac{1}{2}mv^2\right)}{dt}$$

$$\Rightarrow \mu v^2+\frac{dW_f}{dt}=\frac{v^2}{2}\frac{dm}{dt}=\frac{\mu v^2}{2}$$

$$\Rightarrow \frac{dW_f}{dt}=-\mu\frac{v^2}{2}$$

13. From FBD of box shown in Fig.1

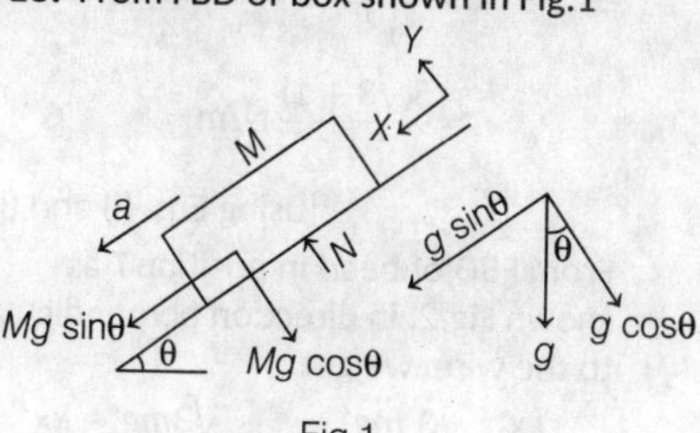

Fig.1

Acceleration of box,

$$a=\frac{Mg\sin\theta}{M}=g\sin\theta$$

$$\Rightarrow \mathbf{a}_{\text{box}}=g\sin\theta\,\hat{\mathbf{i}}$$

$\therefore$ Relative acceleration due to gravity inside box,

$$\mathbf{g}'=\mathbf{g}-\mathbf{a}$$

$$=(g\sin\theta\,\hat{\mathbf{i}}-g\cos\theta\,\hat{\mathbf{j}})-g\sin\theta\,\hat{\mathbf{i}}$$

$$=-g\cos\theta\,\hat{\mathbf{j}}$$

So, relative acceleration due to gravity,

$$g'=g\cos\theta=g\cos 60^\circ=\frac{g}{2}=5\,\text{ms}^{-2}$$

If we rotate the figure of box for simplicity of analysis, we get Fig. 2. Let natural length of spring is l (initially) and spring constant is k.

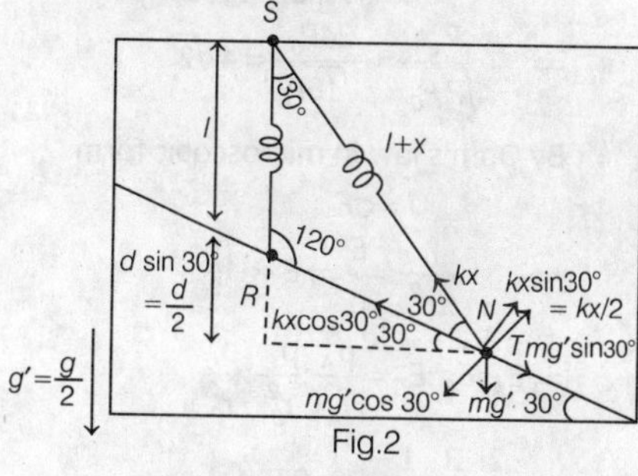

Fig.2

Let extension in spring in final position T be x. By sine rule in ΔRST, we get

$$\frac{l+x}{\sin 120^\circ}=\frac{l}{\sin 30^\circ}$$

$$\Rightarrow \quad l+x=\sqrt{3}\,l$$

$$\Rightarrow \quad x=(\sqrt{3}-1)\,l=(\sqrt{3}-1)(\sqrt{3}+1)$$

$$\Rightarrow x=2\text{ m} \quad \text{...(i)}$$

Maximum displacement of the bead is equal to

$$d=RT=l=(\sqrt{3}+1)\text{ m (given)... (ii)}$$

As, bead comes to rest at T, after release, loss in its potential energy is equal to gain in spring potential energy.

Therefore, $mg'\dfrac{d}{2}=\dfrac{1}{2}kx^2$

$$\Rightarrow \quad k = \frac{mg'd}{x^2} = \frac{1 \times 5 \times (\sqrt{3}+1)}{4}$$

$$= \frac{5(\sqrt{3}+1)}{4} \text{ N/m}$$

[using Eqs. (i) and (ii)]

From FBD of bead in position T as shown Fig.2, in direction perpendicular to the wire, we get

$$N + \frac{kx}{2} = \frac{\sqrt{3}\,mg'}{2} \Rightarrow N = \frac{\sqrt{3}mg' - kx}{2}$$

$$= \frac{\sqrt{3} \times 1 \times 5 - \frac{5(\sqrt{3}+1)}{4} \times 2}{2}$$

$$= \frac{5(\sqrt{3}-1)}{4} \text{ N}$$

14. $P = \text{Power} = i^2R = i^2 \cdot \frac{\rho l}{\pi r^2}$

As, i through all the wires is same.

$$\Rightarrow \quad P \propto \frac{\rho l}{r^2}$$

$$\Rightarrow P_A : P_B : P_C = \frac{\rho_A l_A}{r_A^2} : \frac{\rho_B l_B}{r_B^2} : \frac{\rho_C l_C}{r_C^2}$$

$$= 4 : \frac{3}{2} : \frac{1}{3} = 24 : 9 : 2$$

$$\Rightarrow \quad P_A = 24P_0, P_B = 9P_0, P_C = 2P_0$$

$\therefore \sqrt{P_B P_C}$ = Geometric mean of P_B and P_C

$$= \sqrt{9P_0 2P_0} = \sqrt{18P_0}$$

$$\Rightarrow \quad \frac{P_A}{\sqrt{P_B P_C}} = \frac{24P_0}{\sqrt{18P_0}} = 4\sqrt{2}$$

By Ohm's law in microscopic form.

$$J = \sigma E$$

$$\Rightarrow \quad \frac{i}{\pi r^2} = \frac{E}{\rho} \Rightarrow E \propto \frac{\rho}{r^2}$$

$$\Rightarrow E_A : E_B : E_C = \frac{\rho_A}{r_A^2} : \frac{\rho_P}{r_B^2} : \frac{\rho_C}{r_C^2}$$

$$= \frac{2}{4} : \frac{3}{4} : \frac{1}{9} = 72 : 27 : 4$$

$$\Rightarrow \quad E_A = 72E_0, E_B = 27E_0, E_C = 4E_0$$

$$\Rightarrow \quad \frac{E_B^2}{E_A E_C} = \frac{27^2}{72 \times 4} = \frac{81}{32}$$

$$\Rightarrow \quad 32E_B^2 = 81E_A E_C$$

Drift speed v is related to current i by the relation,

$$v = \frac{i}{NeA} = \frac{i}{Ne\pi r^2} \Rightarrow v \propto \frac{1}{Nr^2}$$

$$\therefore v_A : v_B : v_C = 1 : \frac{1}{8} : \frac{1}{27} = 216 : 27 : 8$$

Also, potential difference,

$$V = IR = \frac{I\rho l}{\pi r^2} \Rightarrow V \propto \frac{\rho l}{r^2}$$

$$\therefore \; V_A : V_B : V_C = 4 : \frac{3}{2} : \frac{1}{3} = 24 : 9 : 2$$

15. I. Plates A and C will be at common zero potential after grounding and so can be treated as if they are connected to each other. Considering some initial potential difference just after grounding, let x charge flows from C to A (*via* grounding). Thus final charges on the plates will be as shown. Also, charge on outer surfaces of extreme plates is half of total charge on the system. So it will be $\frac{10+4+6+8}{2} = 14$. Thus by conservation of charge, charges on various surfaces are as shown.

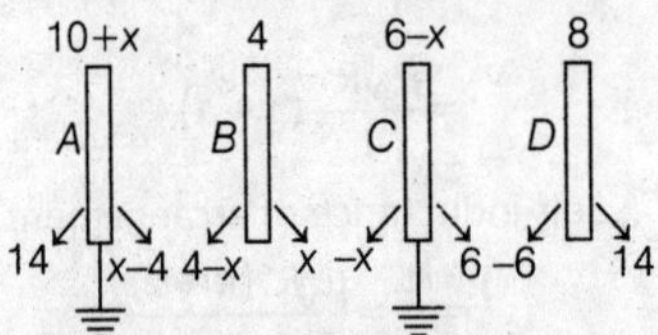

As $V_A = V_C = 0$, finally

$$V_B - V_A = V_B - V_C$$

$$\Rightarrow \quad \frac{4-x}{C_0} = \frac{x}{C_0}$$

Here C_0 is capacitance of any pair of plates

$$\Rightarrow \quad x = 2$$

$\Rightarrow$ Final charge on plate $A = 10 + x = 12$

and final charge on plate $C = 6 - x = 4$

Also, energy of system dissipates as heat due to current flow during charge distribution.

II. Simultaneous grounding of A and C can be seen as connecting of A and C to each other. So, they behave as single sphere. As there is no charge inside A, by Gauss's law, there will be no charge on inner surface of combined system of A and C. Thus, total charge on A and C (30 μC) will move to outer surface of combined system of A and C as shown. Thus net charge on A is zero, which corresponds to flow of electrons from earth to A.

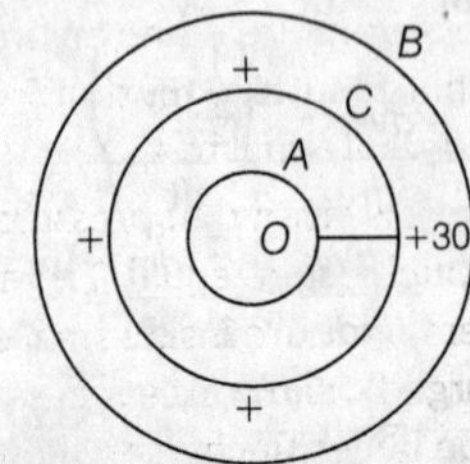

III. Let x charge is supplied by the cell as shown.

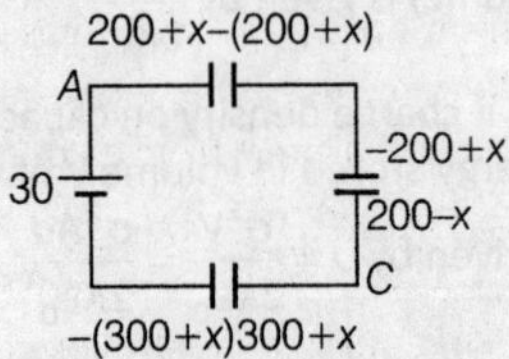

By KVL, moving clockwise, starting from A, we get

$$-\frac{(200+x)}{10} + \frac{200-x}{10} - \frac{(300+x)}{10} + 30 = 0$$

$$\Rightarrow x = 0$$

$\Rightarrow$ No charge flows and so no heat dissipates

$$\Rightarrow V_A - V_C = -\frac{300}{10} + 30 = 0$$

IV. Equal emf (say ε) is induced in all the sides due to symmetry because of change in flux. Thus equivalent circuit diagram is as shown, considering each side has resistance r.

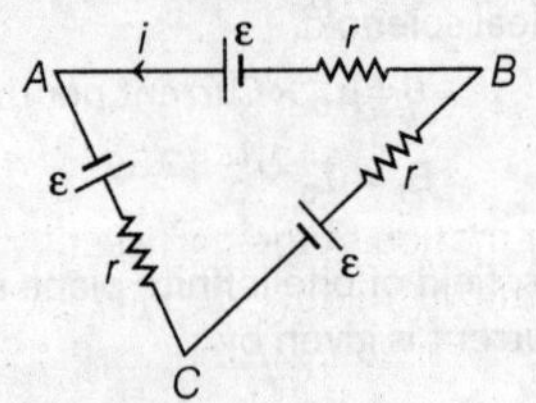

$$\text{So, } i = \frac{3\varepsilon}{3r} = \frac{\varepsilon}{r}$$

$$\Rightarrow \; V_A - V_B = \varepsilon - ir$$

$$= \varepsilon - \left(\frac{\varepsilon}{r}\right) r = 0$$

and $V_B - V_C = \varepsilon - ir = 0$

16. As per standard Bohr's atomic model,

E = Energy of electron (in eV)

$$= -\frac{13.6Z^2}{n^2} = -\frac{54.4}{n^2}$$

U = Potential energy of electron (in eV)

$$= -27.2\frac{Z^2}{n^2} = \frac{-108.8}{n^2}$$

So, for $n = 1$, $E = -54.4$ eV. As per new reference $E = 0$ for $n = 1$ which implies both E and U have been increased by 54.4 eV.

Thus, new values are

$$E' = -\frac{54.4}{n^2} + 54.4 \text{ eV}$$

$$U' = -\frac{108.8}{n^2} + 54.4 \text{ eV}$$

I. $E' = -\frac{54.4}{2^2} + 54.4 = 40.8$ eV

II. Ionisation energy in ground state is difference in total energies between $n=1$ and $n=\infty$ which is equal to

$$IE = \frac{54.4}{1^2} - \frac{54.4}{\infty^2} = 54.4 \text{ eV}$$

which does not depend on reference.

III. Excitation energy

$$= 54.4\left(\frac{1}{1^2} - \frac{1}{2^2}\right)$$
$$= 40.8 \text{ eV}$$
$$= 65.28 \times 10^{-19} \text{ J}$$

IV. $U' = -\frac{108.8}{1^2} + 54.4 = -54.4$ eV

$\Rightarrow -U' = 54.4$ eV

17. Initial velocity of the particle (A) w.r.t. the platform (B) will be

$$\mathbf{v}_{AB} = \mathbf{v}_A - \mathbf{v}_B$$
$$= (v_2\hat{\mathbf{i}} + 25\hat{\mathbf{j}} + v_1\hat{\mathbf{k}}) - 0$$
$$= v_2\hat{\mathbf{i}} + 25\hat{\mathbf{j}} + v_1\hat{\mathbf{k}} \quad \text{...(i)}$$

Relative acceleration,

$$\mathbf{a}_{AB} = \mathbf{a}_A - \mathbf{a}_B$$
$$= -10\hat{\mathbf{j}} - (2\hat{\mathbf{i}} + 2.5\hat{\mathbf{j}})$$
$$= -2\hat{\mathbf{i}} - 12.5\hat{\mathbf{j}} \quad \text{...(ii)}$$

For motion of the particle till it hits the platform, relative displacement is zero in y-direction. So, for y-direction,

$$s_y = u_y t + \frac{1}{2}a_y t^2$$

$$\Rightarrow \quad 0 = 25t + \frac{1}{2}(-12.5)t^2$$

[using Eqs. (i) and (ii)]

$$\Rightarrow \quad t = 4 \text{ s} \quad \text{...(iii)}$$

To hit the platform, relative displacement in x-direction should lie between 8 m to 16 m as per given location and side of the platform.

$$\Rightarrow \quad 8 \le s_x \le 16$$
$$\Rightarrow \quad 8 \le u_x t + \frac{1}{2}a_x t^2 \le 16$$
$$\Rightarrow \quad 8 \le v_2(4) + \frac{1}{2}(-2)(4)^2 \le 16$$

[using Eqs. (i), (ii) and (iii)]

$$\Rightarrow \quad 6 \le v_2 \le 8$$

Similarly, for z-direction

$$16 \le s_z \le 24$$
$$\Rightarrow \quad 16 \le v_1(4) \le 24$$
$$\Rightarrow \quad 4 \le v_1 \le 6$$

Displacement of particle w.r.t. ground at $t = 4$ s,

$$s_y = u_y t + \frac{1}{2}a_y t^2$$
$$= 25(4) + \frac{1}{2}(-10)(4)^2 = 20 \text{ m}$$

18. I. Let the cylinder is displaced as shown in the figure.

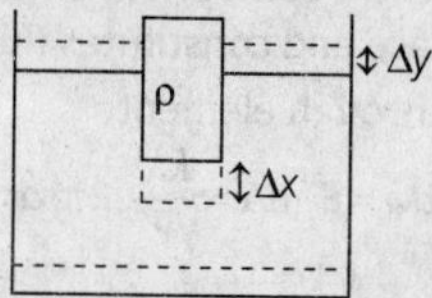

Considering the increase in the level of liquid, by volume conservation, we get

$$A_2\Delta x = (A_1 - A_2)\Delta y$$
$$\Delta y = \frac{A_2\Delta x}{A_1 - A_2}$$

Thus, the restoring force,

$$f_R = 3\rho A_2(\Delta x + \Delta y)g$$
$$= 3\rho A_2\left(\Delta x + \frac{A_2\Delta x}{A_1 - A_2}\right)g$$
$$= 3\rho A_2\left(\frac{A_1\Delta x - A_2\Delta x + A_2\Delta x}{A_1 - A_2}\right)g$$
$$= \frac{3\rho A_1 A_2 g}{A_1 - A_2}\Delta x$$
$$= \rho A_2 h\omega^2 \Delta x$$

From the above equation, we get angular frequency equal to

$$\omega = \sqrt{\frac{3A_1 g}{(A_1 - A_2)h}}$$

$$\Rightarrow T = 2\pi\sqrt{\frac{(A_1 - A_2)h}{3A_1 g}}$$

So, for the two cases, we have

Case-1 $A_1 = 3A_2$

$$T = 2\pi\sqrt{\frac{2A_2 h}{9A_2 g}} = 2\pi\sqrt{\frac{2h}{9g}}$$

Case-2 $A_1 >>>> A_2$

$$T = 2\pi\sqrt{\left(1 - \frac{A_2}{A_1}\right)\frac{h}{3g}} = 2\pi\sqrt{\frac{h}{3g}}$$

Therefore, $x = 9$ and $y = 3$, which means $x = y^2$.

II. Excess pressure inside an uncharged bubble of surface tension S and radius R is equal to $4S/R$.

Now, it is given that pressures in both the bubbles are equal. Therefore, excess pressure inside smaller (charged) bulb = Excess pressure inside larger(uncharged) bubble

$$= 4S/2R = 2S/R$$

So, $x = 2$

Also, as there is no pressure difference between the bubbles, electrostatic pressure is nullifying the excess pressure due to surface tension. So,

$$\frac{\sigma^2}{2\varepsilon_0} = \frac{4(2S)}{\frac{R}{2}}$$

$$\Rightarrow \quad \sigma = 4\sqrt{\frac{2\varepsilon_0 S}{R}} \Rightarrow y = 4$$

So, $\quad y = x^x$

III. Tension at mid-point is average of the pulls at ends. Also, if F_1 and F_2 are forces at ends, as per Hooke's law, extension in rod is given by

$$\frac{F_1\frac{l}{2}}{2A\sigma} + \frac{F_2\frac{l}{2}}{2A\sigma}$$

So, the extensions in the two parts can be calculated as

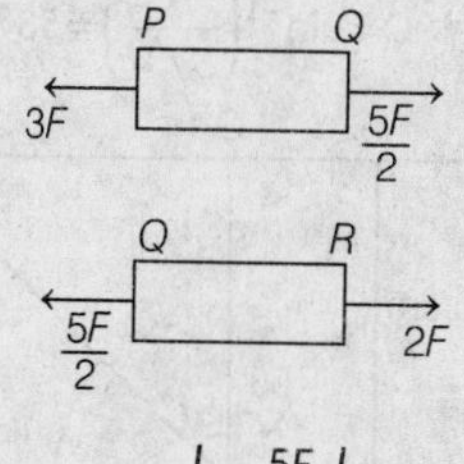

$$\Delta l_{PQ} = \frac{3F\frac{l}{2}}{2A\sigma} + \frac{\frac{5F}{2}\frac{l}{2}}{2A\sigma}$$
$$= \frac{3Fl}{4A\sigma} + \frac{5Fl}{8A\sigma} = \frac{11Fl}{8A\sigma}$$

$$\Delta l_{QR} = \frac{2F\frac{l}{2}}{2A\sigma} + \frac{\frac{5F}{2}\frac{l}{2}}{2A\sigma}$$
$$= \frac{Fl}{2A\sigma} + \frac{5Fl}{8A\sigma} = \frac{9Fl}{8A\sigma}$$

So, $x = 11$ and $y = 8$. Therefore, $x - y = 3$

IV. Force due to surface tension on the sub-hemispherical portion shown due to the remaining part is as shown.

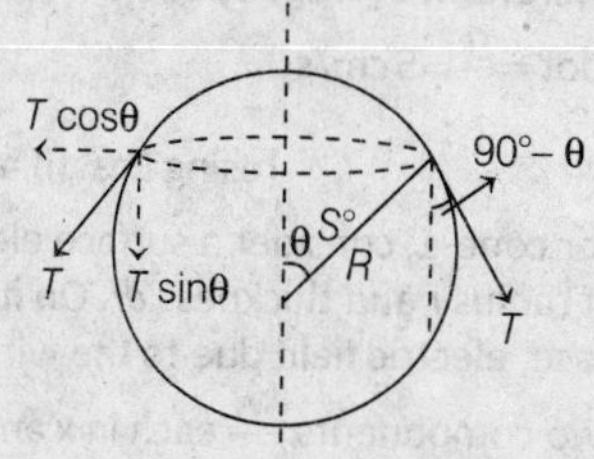

Clearly, the horizontal components cancel, so net force due to the surface tension will be

$$F = \text{Perimeter} \times S \sin\theta$$

$$\Rightarrow \quad F = 4\pi(R\sin\theta)S\sin\theta = 4\pi RS\sin^2\theta$$

Thus, net force on the portion shown can be calculated using the above formula as

$$F_{net} = 4\pi RS[\sin^2 53° - \sin^2 37°] = 4\pi RS\left[\frac{16}{25} - \frac{9}{25}\right] = \frac{28\pi RS}{25}$$

$$\Rightarrow \alpha = 28;\ x = \frac{3\alpha}{14} = 6;\ \beta = 25$$

$$\Rightarrow \quad y = \frac{\beta}{5} = 5$$

(Paper 2)

1. Critical angle for a pair of medium is given by

$$C = \sin^{-1}\left(\frac{n_{rarer}}{n_{denser}}\right)$$

$$\Rightarrow \quad C = \sin^{-1}\left(\frac{1}{5/4}\right) = 53°$$

So, when the ray is incident at 53° as shown, it will emerge grazingly along surface making 37° with line OC striking screen at P. Distance moved by the laser spot,

$$d = OP = 20\tan 37° = 15 \text{ cm} \quad \text{...(i)}$$

Also, time taken for rotation of the cylinder,

$$t = \frac{\theta}{\omega} = \frac{53\pi}{180 \times \dfrac{53\pi}{540}} = 3 \text{ s} \quad \text{...(ii)}$$

Therefore, average speed of the laser spot $= \dfrac{d}{t} = 5$ cm/s

[using Eqs. (i) and (ii)]

2. For cone-1, consider a surface element of radius r and thickness dr. On its base, electric field due to the wire has two components $\dfrac{k\lambda}{r}$ each in x and y-directions as shown.

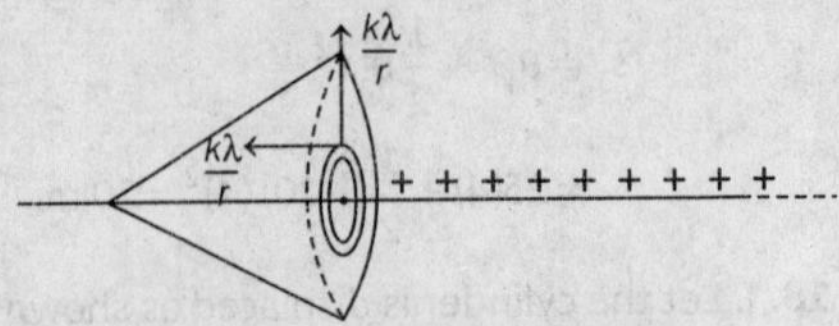

Only the x-component of field crosses the base and constitutes flux.

Flux through element,

$$d\phi = E \cdot dA = \frac{k\lambda}{r} \cdot 2\pi r dr = \frac{\lambda}{2\varepsilon_0} dr$$

$\Rightarrow$ Flux through base,

$$\phi_{base} = \frac{\lambda}{2\varepsilon_0}\int_0^R dr = \frac{\lambda R}{2\varepsilon_0} \quad \text{...(i)}$$

Now, by Gauss' law, for cone-1,

$$\phi = \frac{q_{inside}}{\varepsilon_0}$$

$$\Rightarrow \phi_{lateral} - \phi_{base} = 0 \quad (\text{as, } q_{inside} = 0)$$

$$\Rightarrow \phi_{lateral} = |\phi_{base}| = \frac{\lambda R}{2\varepsilon_0} = \phi_1$$

[using Eq. (i)]

Now, for cone-2, by Gauss' law,

$$\phi = \frac{q_{inside}}{\varepsilon_0} = \frac{\lambda(2R)}{\varepsilon_0}$$

$$\Rightarrow \quad \phi_{base} + \phi_{lateral} = \frac{2\lambda R}{\varepsilon_0}$$

$$\Rightarrow \quad \frac{\lambda R}{2\varepsilon_0} + \phi_{lateral} = \frac{2\lambda R}{\varepsilon_0}$$

[as ϕ_{base} will be same as obtained for cone-1 in Eq. (i)]

$$\Rightarrow \quad \phi_{lateral} = \frac{3\lambda R}{2\varepsilon_0} = \phi_2$$

$$\Rightarrow \quad \frac{\phi_2}{\phi_1} = 3$$

3. de-Broglie wavelength of electron in Bohr's atom is given by

$$\lambda = \frac{2\pi r}{n} \Rightarrow \frac{\lambda}{r} = \frac{2\pi}{n}$$

For 1st excited state, $n = 2$

$$\Rightarrow \quad \frac{\lambda}{r} = \pi = \frac{6\pi}{6}$$

$$\Rightarrow \quad x = 6$$

4. As, the tube is perfectly conducting, temperature of air will remain constant.

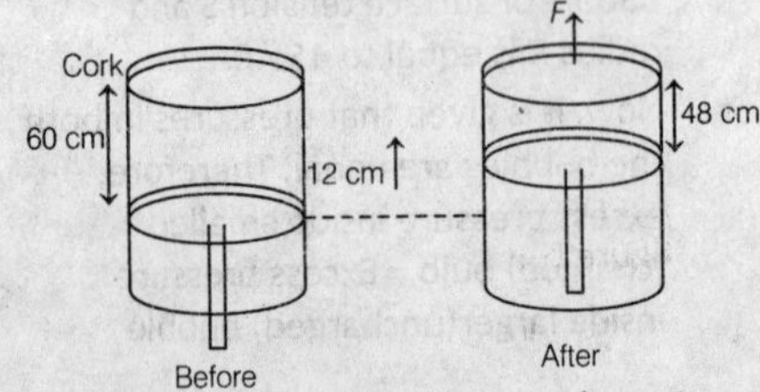

As, $pV = nRT = \text{constant}$

$$\Rightarrow \quad p_{final}V_{final} = p_{initial}V_{initial}$$

$$\Rightarrow p_{final}A(48) = p_0 A(60)$$

$$\Rightarrow p_{final} = p_0 \times \frac{5}{4} = 1.25 \times 10^5 \text{ Pa}$$

$\therefore$ Force = Difference in pressure × Area

$$= (1.25 \times 10^5 - 10^5) \times 1.6 \times 10^{-4} = 4 \text{ N}$$

5. Consider the object as two portions a uniform rod and a frustum with thermal resistances R_1 and R_2 respectively, then

$$R_1 = \frac{l_1}{KA_1} = \frac{l}{K\pi r^2}$$

and

$$R_2 = \frac{l_2}{K_2 A_2} = \frac{l}{(2K)(\pi r_1 r_2)} = \frac{l}{4K\pi r^2}$$

$\therefore$ Equivalent thermal resistance,

$$R_{eq} = R_1 + R_2$$

$$\Rightarrow \quad R_{eq} = \frac{5l}{4K\pi r^2} \quad \text{...(i)}$$

Now, if we consider the same lamina with equivalent thermal conductivity K_{eq}, then

$$R_{eq} = R_1 + R_2 = \frac{l}{K_{eq}\pi r^2} + \frac{l}{K_{eq}(2\pi r^2)} = \frac{3l}{2K_{eq}\pi r^2} \quad \text{...(ii)}$$

By equating the terms of R_{eq} from Eqs. (i) and (ii), we get

$$\frac{5l}{4K\pi r^2} = \frac{3l}{2K_{eq}\pi r^2}$$

$$K_{eq} = \frac{6k}{5}$$

$$\Rightarrow \quad \frac{K_{eq}}{K} = \frac{6}{5} = 1.20$$

$$\Rightarrow \quad 5K_{eq} = 5 \times 1.2 = 6$$

6. The external force on two body systems acts along Y-axis.

The initial momentum of the two body systems is zero. Hence, the CM of two body system always moves along Y-axis.

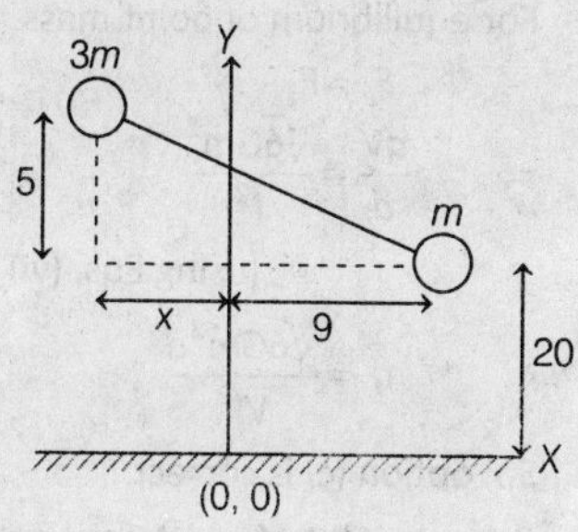

$\because$ CM of two body system lies along Y-axis, the x-coordinate of centre of mass of two body system is $X_{CM} = 0$

$\therefore \quad 3m \times x = m \times 9$

$\Rightarrow \quad x = 3$

$\therefore$ Length of string $= \sqrt{5^2 + (9+3)^2}$

$= 13$ cm

$= x^2 - x + 1$ (given)

$\Rightarrow \quad x = 4$

7. Let v_x and v_y be the horizontal and vertical components of velocity of block C.

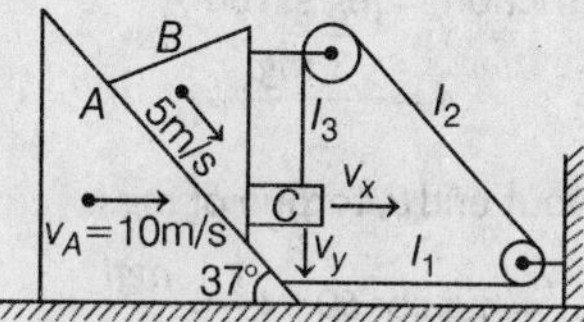

The component of relative velocity of B and C normal to the surface of contact is zero.

$\therefore \quad 10 + 5\cos 37° - v_x = 0$ ...(i)

$v_x = 14$ m/s

From the figure, $l_1 + l_2 + l_3 =$ constant

$\therefore \quad \dfrac{dl_1}{dt} + \dfrac{dl_2}{dt} + \dfrac{dl_3}{dt} = 0$

$(-10) + (-5 - 10\cos 37°)$
$+ (-5\sin 37° + v_y) = 0$

$\therefore \quad v_y = 26$ m/s

So, ratio, $\dfrac{v_x}{v_y} = \dfrac{14}{26} = \dfrac{7}{13}$

$\therefore \quad a = 7$

8. As superconducting loop

$e = \dfrac{d\phi}{dt} = 0$, so

$\phi =$ constant

$\phi = \int \mathbf{B} \cdot d\mathbf{S} + Li$

$= [-\pi x\hat{\mathbf{i}} + (\pi z - B_0)\hat{\mathbf{k}}] \cdot a^2\hat{\mathbf{k}} + Li$

$\phi = (\pi z + B_0)a^2 + Li$

When $z = 0, i = 0$, hence $\phi = B_0 a^2$.

$\therefore \quad B_0 a^2 = (\pi z + B_0)a^2 + Li$

$i = \dfrac{\pi z a^2}{L}$

F_{net} = force acting on sides parallel to Y-axis

$= \dfrac{\pi a}{2} \cdot i \cdot a + \dfrac{\pi a}{2} i \cdot a = \pi a^2 i$, along Z-axis

Equation of motion is $-mg + \pi a^2 i$

$= \dfrac{md^2z}{dt^2}$

$\dfrac{d^2z}{dt^2} = -g - \dfrac{\pi a^2}{m} \cdot \dfrac{\pi z a^2}{L}$

$\Rightarrow \quad \dfrac{d^2z}{dt^2} = \dfrac{\pi^2 a^4 z}{mL} - g$

which is equation of SHM, hence

$\omega = \sqrt{\dfrac{\pi^2 a^4}{mL}} = \dfrac{\pi a^2}{\sqrt{mL}}$

Also, $z = \dfrac{-mgL}{\pi^2 a^4} + A\cos(\omega t + \phi)$ but at

$t = 0, z = 0$ and $\dfrac{dz}{dt} = 0$

Hence, $\phi = 0, A = \dfrac{mgL}{\pi^2 a^4}$, which is extreme value z-coordinate.

As, $\quad z = -\dfrac{A}{2}$

$\Rightarrow \quad \omega t = \dfrac{\pi}{6}$

$\Rightarrow \quad t = 0.1$ s or $\dfrac{1}{10}$ s

$\Rightarrow \quad T = 1$

9. Flux through the ring,

$\phi = \mathbf{B} \cdot \mathbf{A} = B_0(\hat{\mathbf{i}} + t^2\hat{\mathbf{j}}) \cdot \pi r^2 \hat{\mathbf{j}}$

$= B_0 \pi r^2 t^2$

As, per Faraday's law, emf induced in the loop,

$\varepsilon = \left|\dfrac{d\phi}{dt}\right| = 2B_0 \pi r^2 t$

Therefore, induced current in the loop,

$i = \dfrac{\varepsilon}{R} = \dfrac{2B_0 \pi r^2 t}{R}$ ...(i)

(clockwise as observed from top in accordance with Lenz's law)

Thus, magnetic moment of the loop,

$M = iA = \dfrac{2B_0 \pi r^2 t}{R} \cdot \pi r^2 = \dfrac{2B_0 \pi^2 r^4 t}{R}$

(**M** is directed in negative y-direction as per right hand rule as shown in the figure below)

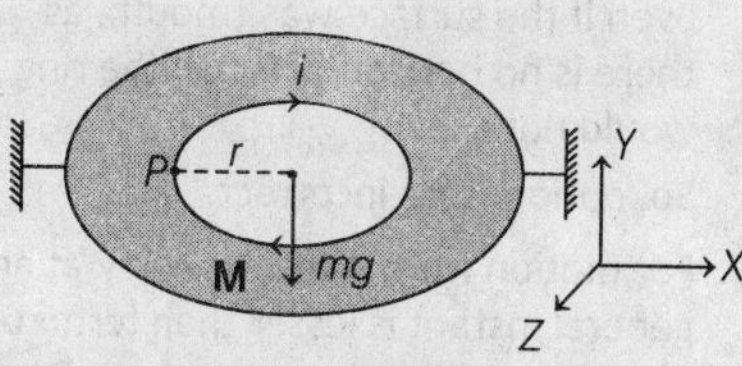

Thus, magnetic torque on the loop,

$\tau = \mathbf{M} \times \mathbf{B} = \left(\dfrac{-2B_0 \pi^2 r^4 t}{R}\hat{\mathbf{j}}\right) \times B_0(\hat{\mathbf{i}} + t^2\hat{\mathbf{j}})$

$\Rightarrow \tau = \dfrac{+2B_0^2 \pi^2 r^4 t}{R}\hat{\mathbf{k}}$ ...(ii)

Direction of τ is $\hat{\mathbf{k}}$ which corresponds to anti-clockwise sense of torque when observed from front.

Thus, the ring has tendency to topple anti-clockwise about P, which is opposed by clockwise torque of mg and given as

$\tau' = -mgr\hat{\mathbf{k}}$ ...(iii)

For toppling to happen, magnetic torque should exceed torque of weight i.e. $\tau > \tau'$

$\Rightarrow \quad \dfrac{2B_0^2 \pi^2 r^4 t}{R} > mgr$

[using Eqs. (ii) and (iii)],

$\Rightarrow \quad t > \dfrac{mgR}{2B_0^2 \pi^2 r^3}$

So, option (b) is correct.

Power dissipated in the loop

$P = i^2 R = \left(\dfrac{2B_0 \pi r^2 t}{R}\right)^2 R$ [using Eq. (i)]

$= \dfrac{4B_0^2 \pi^2 r^4 t^2}{R}$

$\therefore$ Heat dissipated $= \int P\,dt$

$= \dfrac{4B_0^2 \pi^2 r^4}{R} \int_0^t t^2 dt = \dfrac{4B_0^2 \pi^2 r^4 t^3}{3R}$

So, option (c) is correct.

Magnetic force on the ring will be zero as magnetic force on a current carrying loop is zero in uniform magnetic field. Gravitational force on the ring will be mg downward. As, there is no horizontal force, so no tendency of slipping and no friction will act on the ring. The ring will experience normal force only which will be equal but opposite to weight and therefore N will be constant. So, option (a) is incorrect.

Even if the surface was smooth, as there is no horizontal force, the ring would not slip.

So, option (d) is incorrect.

10. For motion from A to B, speed v at any general instant is lesser than terminal speed v_T, while for motion from B to C speed is equal to terminal speed v_T.

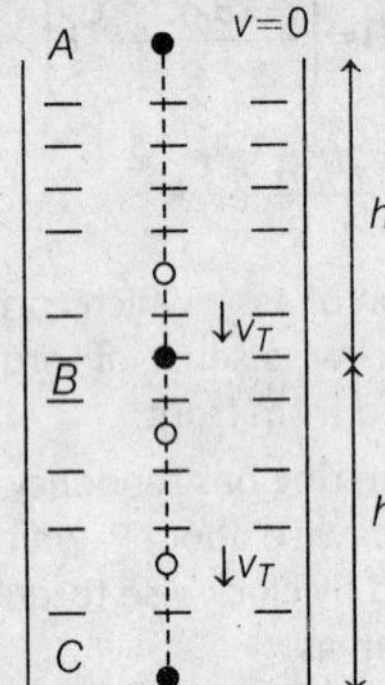

But distances from A to B and B to C are equal. So, time taken for A to B will be greater i.e., $t_1 > t_2$. Also, if instantaneous speed is v, drag force experienced by the ball is $6\pi\eta rv$.

Therefore, work done against friction per unit time,

$P = Fv = 6\pi\eta rv \cdot v \Rightarrow P \propto v^2$

As, for motion from A to B, v at any general instant is lesser compared to speed v_T at any general instant, so P will be lesser and overall work will also be lesser i.e., $W_1 < W_2$.

11. No. of pairs of particles $= {}^4C_2 = \dfrac{4\times 3}{2} = 6$

As, for one pair, potential energy will be $= -\dfrac{Gm\cdot m}{l}$, so for the system, potential energy initially,

$$PE_{\text{initial}} = 6\left(-\frac{Gm^2}{l}\right) = -\frac{6Gm^2}{l} \quad \text{...(i)}$$

During disassembling, if the particles are taken to infinity ($l \to \infty$),

$$PE_{\text{final}} = \frac{-6Gm^2}{\infty} = 0 \quad \text{...(ii)}$$

$\therefore$ Work done to disassemble,

$$W = PE_{\text{final}} - PE_{\text{initial}}$$

$$= 0 - \left(\frac{-6\,Gm^2}{l}\right) = \frac{6\,Gm^2}{l}$$

[using Eqs. (i) and (ii)]

So, option (a) is correct.

As, regular tetrahedron is a regular figure, so its centre is symmetrically located w.r.t. vertices and net field at centre will be zero.

So, option (b) is correct.

If distance between centre and vertex is assumed r, potential due to one mass will be $-\dfrac{Gm}{r}$.

So, net potential,

$$V = -\frac{4Gm}{r} \neq \frac{-4Gm}{l}$$

So, option (d) is incorrect.

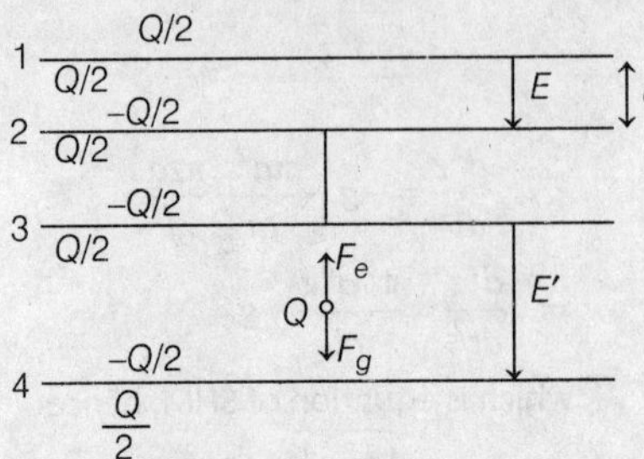

If charge Q is given to top plate, charge distribution will be as shown, as per rule of distribution of charge on plates.

So, electric field between plates-1 and 2 will be

$$E = \frac{Q}{A\varepsilon_0} \quad \text{...(iii)}$$

(here, A is plate area)

and electric field between plates-3 and 4 will be

$$E' = \frac{Q}{A\varepsilon_0} \quad \text{...(iv)}$$

Also, field between plates-1 and 2 can be expressed as $E = \dfrac{V_\varepsilon}{d}$ ...(v)

Using Eqs. (iii), (iv) and (v), we get

$$E' = \frac{Q}{A\varepsilon_0} = \frac{V}{d}$$

If $-q$ charge is given to top particle, electric force on it, will be

$$F_e = qE' = \frac{qV}{d} \text{ (upwards)} \quad \text{...(vi)}$$

If $\mathbf{F}_1, \mathbf{F}_2$ and $\mathbf{F}_3$ are gravitational forces on it, due to three point masses, net force on it,

$$\mathbf{F}_g = \mathbf{F}_1 + \mathbf{F}_2 + \mathbf{F}_3$$

$$\Rightarrow \mathbf{F}_g^2 = \mathbf{F}_1^2 + \mathbf{F}_2^2 + \mathbf{F}_3^2 + 2\mathbf{F}_1\cdot\mathbf{F}_2 + 2\mathbf{F}_2\cdot\mathbf{F}_3 + 2\mathbf{F}_1\cdot\mathbf{F}_3$$

$$= F^2 + F^2 + F^2 + 2FF\cos 60^\circ + 2FF\cos 60^\circ + 2FF\cos 60^\circ$$

(as, angle between any pair of forces is 60° and F is magnitude of force between any two point masses)

$$\Rightarrow F_g = \sqrt{6}\,F = \sqrt{6}\,\frac{Gm^2}{l^2} \quad \text{...(vii)}$$

For equilibrium of point mass,

$$F_e = F_g$$

$$\Rightarrow \frac{qV}{d} = \frac{\sqrt{6}Gm^2}{l^2}$$

[using Eqs. (vi) and (vii)]

$$q = \frac{\sqrt{6}Gm^2 d}{Vl^2}$$

So, option (c) is correct.

12. Consider FBD of rod AB shown, mg has been resolved along and perpendicular to the rod.

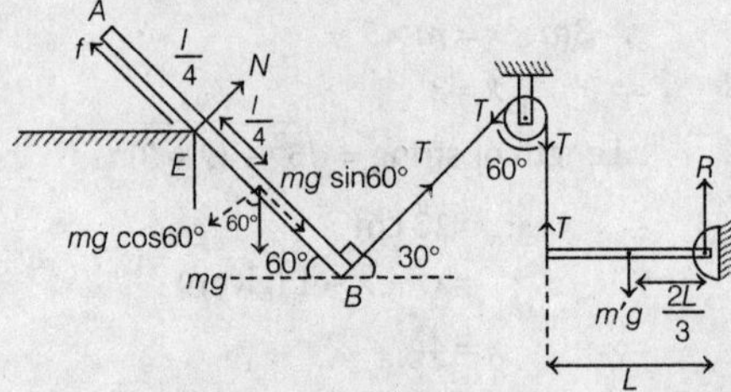

For direction along rod AB, for equilibrium, $F_{\text{net}} = 0$

f (friction) $= mg\sin 60^\circ$

$$\Rightarrow f = \frac{\sqrt{3}\,mg}{2} \quad \text{...(i)}$$

About end B, torque of mg is

$$\tau_{mg} = mg\cos 60^\circ \times \frac{l}{2} = \frac{mgl}{4}$$

(anti-clockwise) ...(ii)

While, torque of N (Normal force) is,

$$\tau_N = N \times \frac{3l}{4} \text{ (clockwise)} \quad \text{...(iii)}$$

For rotational equilibrium, the torques of mg and N should cancel.

i.e. $\tau_{mg} = \tau_N$

$$\Rightarrow mg\frac{l}{4} = N \times \frac{3l}{4}$$

[using Eqs. (ii) and (iii)]

$$\Rightarrow N = \frac{mg}{3} \quad \text{...(iv)}$$

For direction perpendicular to rod, for equilibrium, $F_{\text{net}} = 0$

$\Rightarrow T + N = mg\cos 60^\circ$

$$\Rightarrow T + \frac{mg}{3} = \frac{mg}{2} \quad \text{[using Eq. (iv)]}$$

$$\Rightarrow T = \frac{mg}{6} \quad \text{...(v)}$$

Contact force on rod by the table,

$$F = \sqrt{N^2 + f^2}$$

$$= \sqrt{\left(\frac{mg}{3}\right)^2 + \left(\frac{\sqrt{3}\,mg}{2}\right)^2}$$

[using Eqs. (i) and (iv)]

$$= \frac{\sqrt{31}}{6} mg$$

So, option (a) is incorrect.

Now, centre of mass of non-uniform rod *CD* can be calculated using general formula, i.e.

$$x_{CM} = \frac{\int x\,dx}{\int dm} = \frac{\int x \lambda dx}{\int \lambda dx} = \frac{\int_0^L x \lambda_0 x dx}{\int_0^L \lambda_0 x dx}$$

Here, *L* is assumed length of *CD*.

$$\Rightarrow x_{CM} = \frac{2L}{3}$$

For rotational equilibrium of *CD*, as per FBD of *CD*, for net torque to be zero.

$$\tau_T = \tau_{m'g}$$

$$\Rightarrow \quad T \times L = m' g \cdot \frac{2L}{3}$$

$$\Rightarrow \quad \frac{mg}{6} L = m' g \frac{2L}{3}$$

$$\Rightarrow \quad m = 4m' \quad \text{...(vi)}$$

So, option (b) is correct.

Net force due to tension on pulley, using parallelogram law,

$$F_{net} = \sqrt{T^2 + T^2 + 2T \cdot T \cdot \cos 60°}$$

$$= \sqrt{3}T = \frac{mg}{2\sqrt{3}} \quad \text{[using Eq. (v)]}$$

For pulley to be in equilibrium, the clamp will apply equal but opposite force.

So, option (c) is correct.

From FBD of rod *CD*, for equilibrium,

$$F_{net} = 0 \Rightarrow \frac{mg}{6} + R = m' g$$

$$\Rightarrow \quad R = \frac{mg}{12} \quad \text{[using Eq. (vi)]}$$

So, option (d) is incorrect.

13. As per Wien's displacement law,

$$\lambda_m \propto \frac{1}{T}$$

If *T* is doubled, λ_m will be halved.

Also, as per Stefan's law radiant power,

$$P = e\sigma A T^4$$

$$\Rightarrow \quad P \propto T^4$$

$\therefore$ If temperature is doubled, power will become 16 times.

14. Suppose the ball is moving in left side with angular acceleration α as shown below.

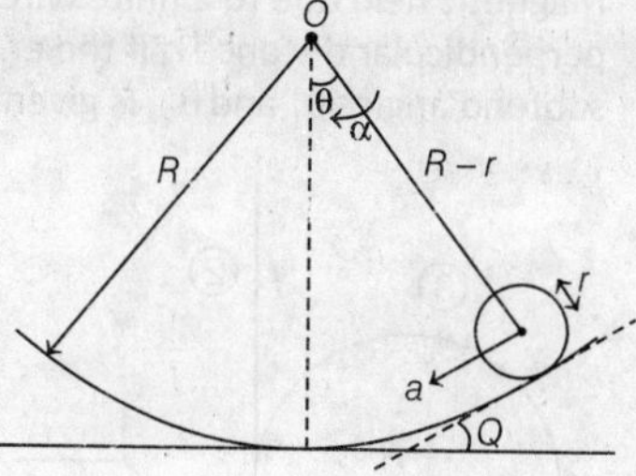

Acceleration of CM in this direction is given by

$$a = \frac{g \sin\theta}{1+\beta} \left(\text{here, } \beta = \frac{I_{CM}}{mr^2}\right)$$

As, for solid ball, $\beta = \frac{\frac{2}{5}mr^2}{mr^2} = \frac{2}{5}$

$$\Rightarrow a = \frac{g \sin\theta}{1+\frac{2}{5}} = \frac{5g \sin\theta}{7} \approx \frac{5g}{7}\theta$$

(as for small θ, $\sin\theta \approx \theta$)

$\therefore$ Angular acceleration about axis of oscillation *O*,

$$\alpha = \frac{a}{R-r} = \frac{5g}{7(R-r)}\theta$$

As in angular SHM, $\alpha = \omega^2\theta$, therefore angular frequency of oscillations,

$$\omega = \sqrt{\frac{5g}{7(R-r)}}$$

$$\Rightarrow \quad T = 2\pi\sqrt{\frac{7(R-r)}{5g}} \quad \text{...(i)}$$

So, option (a) is correct.

% errors in *r*,

$$= \frac{\Delta r}{r} \times 100 = \frac{1}{40} \times 100 = 2.5\%$$

So, option (b) is correct.

% error in *R*,

$$= \frac{\Delta R}{R} \times 100 = \frac{1}{240} \times 100$$

$$= 0.42 \approx 0.4\%$$

So, option (c) is correct.

From Eq. (i), squaring on both sides, we get

$$T^2 = 4\pi^2\left[\frac{7(R-r)}{5g}\right]$$

$$\Rightarrow \quad g = \frac{28\pi^2(R-r)}{5T^2}$$

$$\Rightarrow \left(\frac{\Delta g}{g} \times 100\right)_{max} = \left(\frac{\Delta(R-r)}{R-r} \times 100\right)_{max} + 2\left(\frac{\Delta T}{T} \times 100\right)_{max}$$

$$= \frac{\Delta R + \Delta r}{R-r} \times 100 + \frac{2\Delta T}{T} \times 100$$

$$= \frac{1+1}{240-40} \times 100 + 2 \times \frac{0.01}{1.00} \times 100$$

$$= 1 + 2 = 3\%$$

15. Effective length of the frame,

$$l' = 2x$$

$$= 2\sqrt{y} = 2\sqrt{l}$$

As, current *i* is passed through the inductor, it experiences a magnetic force,

$$F = Bil' = B \cdot i \cdot 2\sqrt{l} \quad \text{...(i)}$$

Due to this leftward force, the frame experiences, change in leftward momentum.

By impulse-momentum theorem,

$$\Delta p = F \cdot t$$

$$\Rightarrow \quad mu = Bi2\sqrt{l}\, t$$

$$\Rightarrow \quad u = \frac{2Bi\sqrt{l}t}{m} \quad \text{...(ii)}$$

Also, the moving frame now has motional emf between ends *P* and *Q* given by

$$V = Bul'$$

This emf will tend to increase current in inductor and as the current increases, it will oppose motion of the frame.

At any later instant, if velocity of frame is *v*, motional emf will be Bvl'.

Magnetic force can be expressed as

$$F = Bil' \quad \text{...(iii)}$$

Also, potential difference across inductor is same as potential difference across frame.

$$\Rightarrow \quad L\frac{di}{dt} = Bvl'$$

$$\Rightarrow \quad L\frac{di}{dt} = B\frac{dx}{dt}l'$$

$$\Rightarrow \quad di = \frac{Bl'}{L}dx$$

$$\Rightarrow \quad \int di = \frac{Bl'}{L}\int dx$$

$$\Rightarrow \quad i = \frac{Bl'}{L}x \quad \text{...(iv)}$$

From Eqs. (iii) and (iv), we get

$$F = \frac{B^2 l'^2}{L}x$$

$$\Rightarrow \quad a = \frac{B^2 l'^2}{mL}x$$

As, in SHM, restoring acceleration, $a = \omega^2 x$, therefore the frame will execute SHM with

$$\omega = \sqrt{\frac{B^2 l'^2}{mL}} = \sqrt{\frac{4B^2 l}{mL}} \quad ...(v)$$

As, in SHM, amplitude is given by

$$A = \frac{u}{\omega} = \frac{2Bi\sqrt{l}\,t}{m} \times \sqrt{\frac{mL}{4B^2 l}}$$

[using Eqs. (ii) and (v)]

$$= it\sqrt{\frac{L}{m}}$$

16. Wavelength of sound in air will be

$$\lambda = \frac{v}{f} = \frac{320}{16 \times 10^3} = 2 \text{ cm} \quad ...(i)$$

For general point P shown in figure, for constructive interference/maxima formation

$$d \sin\theta = n\lambda$$

As, d is 2m (given) and λ is 2 cm as per Eq. (i), we get

$$2 \sin\theta = n(2 \times 10^{-2}) \Rightarrow n = 100 \sin\theta$$

Thus, for $\theta = 0°$, $n = 0$ and for $\theta = 90°$, $n = 100$.

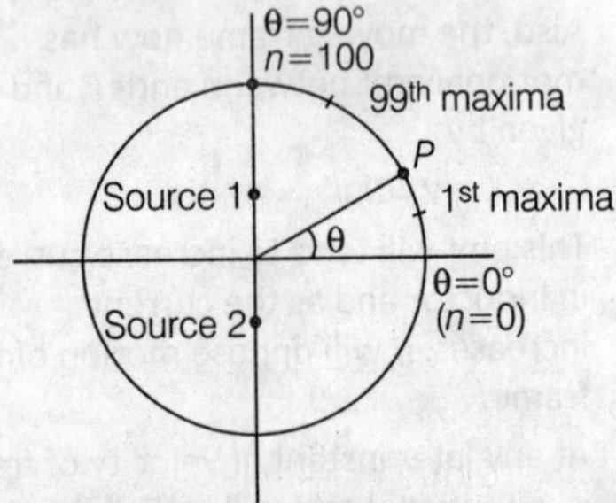

So, for $n = 1$ to $n = 99$, 99 maximas will be formed in 1st quadrant as shown in figure. By symmetry, each quadrant will have 99 maximas. Also, two maximas will be located on axis. So, a total of 400 maximas will be formed on track,

$$\Rightarrow \quad N = 400 \quad ...(ii)$$

Time taken by train to complete one revolution on the track $= \frac{\text{Distance}}{\text{Speed}}$

$$= \frac{2\pi r}{v} = \frac{2\pi \times \frac{1000}{\pi}}{36 \times \frac{5}{18}} = 200 \text{ s} \quad ...(iii)$$

Dividing Eq. (ii) by Eq. (iii), we get number of maximas encountered every second equal to

$$\frac{N}{t} = \frac{400}{200} = 2$$

17. Magnetic field due to infinite wire is given by $\mathbf{B} = \frac{\mu_0 I}{2\pi R}$ ...(i)

Magnetic field due to a finite wire at a perpendicular distance r, if the ends subtend angles θ_1 and θ_2, is given by

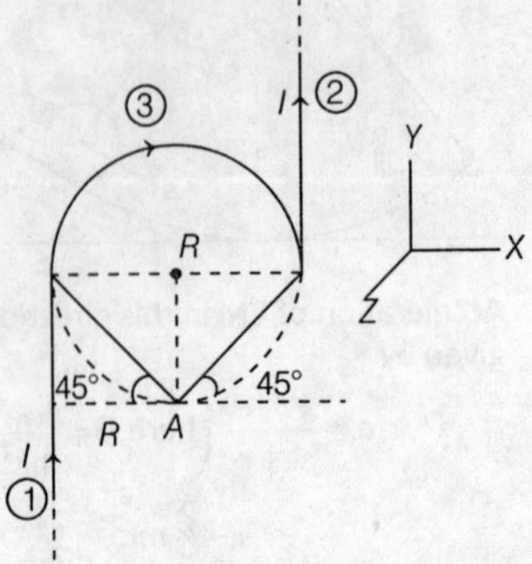

$$B = \frac{\mu_0 I}{4\pi R}(\sin\theta_1 + \sin\theta_2)$$

Therefore, magnetic field due to segment-1 will be

$$B_1 = \frac{\mu_0 I}{4\pi R}(\sin 45° + \sin 90°)$$

(as end at infinity subtends 90°)

Direction of field will be negative z-direction as per right hand rule,

$$\mathbf{B}_1 = \frac{\mu_0 I}{4\pi R}\left(\frac{1+\sqrt{2}}{\sqrt{2}}\right)(-\hat{\mathbf{k}}) \quad ...(ii)$$

Similarly, magnetic field due to segment-2 will be

$$\Rightarrow \quad \mathbf{B}_2 = \frac{\mu_0 I}{4\pi R}(\sin 90° - \sin 45°)\hat{\mathbf{k}}$$

$$\Rightarrow \quad \mathbf{B}_2 = \frac{\mu_0 I}{4\pi R}\left(\frac{\sqrt{2}-1}{\sqrt{2}}\right)\hat{\mathbf{k}} \quad ...(iii)$$

Magnetic field due to semi-circular segment at bottom point is given by formula

$$\mathbf{B}_3 = -\frac{\mu_0 I}{4\pi R}\ln(\sqrt{2}+1)\hat{\mathbf{k}} \quad ...(iv)$$

Thus, total field at A will be

$$\Rightarrow \quad \mathbf{B}' = \mathbf{B}_1 + \mathbf{B}_2 + \mathbf{B}_3$$

$$\Rightarrow \quad \mathbf{B}' = -\frac{\mu_0 I}{4\pi R}[\sqrt{2} + \ln\sqrt{2} + 1)]\hat{\mathbf{k}} \quad ...(v)$$

From Eqs. (i) and (v), we get

$$\mathbf{B}' = \frac{\mathbf{B}}{2}[\sqrt{2} + \ln(\sqrt{2}+1)]$$

$$= \mathbf{B}\left[\frac{1}{\sqrt{2}} + \ln(\sqrt{2}+1)^{\frac{1}{2}}\right]$$

18. Force experienced by cone, as it is perfectly absorbing will be

F = radiation pressure × projected area

As projected area of cone is triangle as shown in Fig. 1, we get

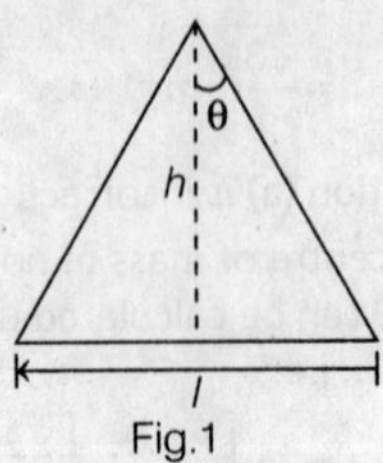

Fig.1

$$F = \frac{I}{c} \times \frac{1}{2} \times b \times h$$

$$\Rightarrow F = \frac{I}{c} \times \frac{1}{2} \times l \times l = \frac{Il^2}{2c} \quad ...(i)$$

$$\left(\text{as } h = \frac{l}{2}\cot\theta = \frac{l}{2} \times 2 = l\right)$$

Let radiation force experienced by square mirror be F'.

As radiation pressure in case of perfectly reflecting surface is given by $\frac{2I\cos^2 i}{c}$ (where, i is angle of incidence)

$\therefore F'$ = Radiation pressure × Area

$$= \frac{2I\cos^2 45°}{c} \times l^2 = \frac{Il^2}{c} \quad ...(ii)$$

This force will acting at centre of the mirror, as force is uniformly distributed as shown in FBD of mirror Fig. 2

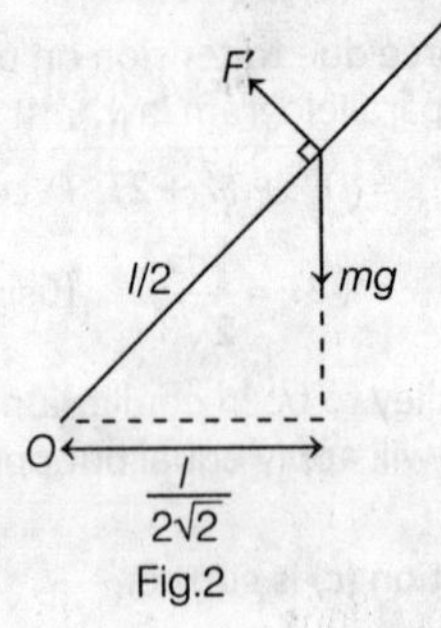

Fig.2

For equilibrium of mirror, net torque is zero.

$\Rightarrow$ Torque of F' = Torque of mg

$$\Rightarrow \quad F'\frac{l}{2} = mg\frac{l}{2\sqrt{2}}$$

$$\Rightarrow \quad F' = \frac{mg}{\sqrt{2}} \quad ...(iii)$$

From Eqs. (ii) and (iii), we get

$$\frac{Il^2}{c} = \frac{mg}{\sqrt{2}} \quad ...(iv)$$

From Eqs. (i) and (iv), we get

$$F = \frac{mg}{2\sqrt{2}}$$

$$\Rightarrow \text{Acceleration of cone} = \frac{F}{m} = \frac{g}{2\sqrt{2}}$$

Knockout 14 (Paper 1)

1. Electric field due to a uniformly charged ring is given by

$$E = \frac{kQx}{(R^2 + x^2)^{3/2}}$$

For E to be maximum, $\frac{dE}{dx} = 0$

$$\Rightarrow kQ\left[\frac{1_{-1}(R^2 + x^2)^{3/2} - \frac{3}{2}(R^2 + x^2)^{\frac{1}{2}} \cdot 2x \cdot x}{(R^2 + x^2)^3}\right] = 0$$

$$\Rightarrow (R^2 + x^2)^{3/2} = 3x^2(R^2 + x^2)^{1/2}$$

$$\Rightarrow \quad R^2 + x^2 = 3x^2$$

$$\Rightarrow \quad x = \frac{R}{\sqrt{2}} = d \quad \text{(given)}$$

$$\Rightarrow \quad R = \sqrt{2}d \quad \text{... (i)}$$

When the ring is rotated, then rotating charge will constitute current in the ring given by

$$i = \frac{Q}{T} = \frac{Q}{2\pi/\omega} = \frac{Q\omega}{2\pi} \quad \text{... (ii)}$$

Magnetic field due to current carrying ring is given by

$$B = \frac{\mu_0 i R^2}{2(R^2 + x^2)^{3/2}} \quad \text{... (iii)}$$

From Eqs. (ii) and (iii), we get

$$B = \frac{\mu_0 Q\omega R^2}{4\pi(R^2 + x^2)^{3/2}} \quad \text{... (iv)}$$

B will constitute flux through the loop given by

$$\phi = BA \Rightarrow \phi = \frac{\mu_0 Q\omega R^2 \pi r^2}{4\pi(R^2 + x^2)^{3/2}}$$

[using Eq. (iv)]

Therefore, by Faraday's law, induced emf will be equal to

$$V = \left|\frac{d\phi}{dt}\right| = \frac{3\mu_0 Q\omega R^2 \pi r^2}{4\pi(R^2 + x^2)^{5/2}} xv \quad \text{...(v)}$$

$$\Rightarrow \quad V \propto \frac{x}{(R^2 + x^2)^{5/2}}$$

For V to be maximum, $\frac{dV}{dx} = 0$

$$\frac{(R^2 + x^2)^{5/2} - \frac{5}{2}(R^2 + x^2)^{3/2} \cdot 2x^2}{(R^2 + x^2)^5} = 0$$

$$\Rightarrow R^2 + x^2 = 5x^2 \Rightarrow x = \frac{R}{2}$$

Putting, $x = \frac{R}{2}$ in Eq. (v), we get

$$V_{max} = \frac{3\mu_0 Q\omega R^2 \pi r^2 \cdot \frac{R}{2} \cdot v}{4\pi\left(R^2 + \frac{R^2}{4}\right)^{5/2}}$$

$$= \frac{12\mu_0 Q\omega r^2 v}{25\sqrt{5}R^2} = \frac{6\mu_0 Q\omega r^2 v}{25\sqrt{5}d^2}$$

[using Eq. (i)]

2. If the wire was not fixed between supports, decrease in its length,

$$\Delta L = L\alpha\left(T_0 - \frac{T_0}{9}\right) = \frac{8L\alpha T_0}{9}$$

But, as the wire is fixed, its length will not be able to decrease, thereby straining it equal to

$$\varepsilon = \text{Thermal strain} = \frac{\Delta L}{L} = \frac{8\alpha T_0}{9}$$

$$\text{Thermal stress, } \sigma = Y\varepsilon = \frac{8Y\alpha T_0}{9}$$

$$\Rightarrow \frac{T}{A} = \frac{8Y\alpha T_0}{9} \text{ (here, } T = \text{tension,}$$

A = cross-sectional area)

$$\Rightarrow \quad T = \frac{8Y\alpha A T_0}{9} \quad \text{... (i)}$$

Frequency of standing wave in nth harmonic is given by $f = \frac{n}{2l}\sqrt{\frac{T}{\mu}}$

As, for 2nd overtone (3rd harmonic),

$$n = 3, \text{ therefore } f = \frac{3}{2l}\sqrt{\frac{T}{\mu}} \quad \text{... (ii)}$$

$$\text{Also, } \mu = \frac{m}{l} = \frac{\rho A l}{l} = \rho A \quad \text{... (iii)}$$

From Eqs. (i), (ii) and (iii), we get

$$f = \frac{3}{2l}\sqrt{\frac{8Y\alpha T_0}{9\rho}} = \sqrt{\frac{2Y\alpha T_0}{\rho l^2}}$$

3. Assuming mass of rod equal to m', FBD of various bodies are as shown in Fig.1.

For block of mass $\frac{3m}{4}$,

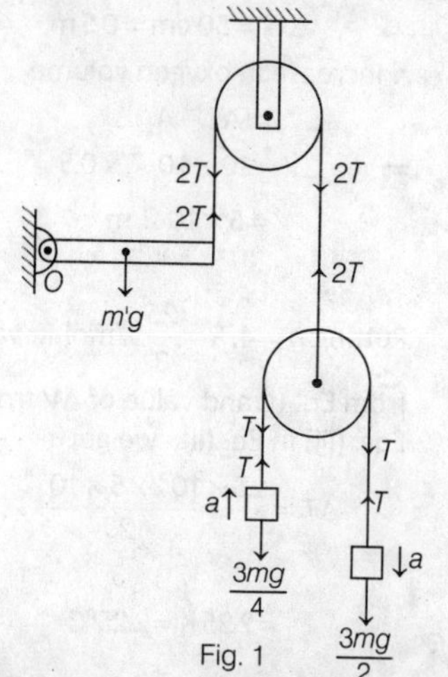

Fig. 1

$$F_{net} = Ma$$

$$\Rightarrow \quad T - \frac{3mg}{4} = \frac{3m}{4}a \quad \text{... (i)}$$

For block of mass $\frac{3m}{2}$,

$$\frac{3mg}{2} - T = \frac{3}{2}ma \quad \text{... (ii)}$$

Solving Eqs. (i) and (ii), we get

$$T = 3ma$$

Putting this value in Eq. (i), we get

$$3ma - \frac{3mg}{4} = \frac{3ma}{4}$$

$$\Rightarrow \quad a = \frac{g}{3}$$

$$\therefore \quad T = \frac{3mg}{3} = mg \quad \text{... (iii)}$$

From FBD of rod, about hinge point O,

τ_1 = torque of $m'g = m'g\frac{l}{2}$ (clockwise)

τ_2 = torque of tension, $2T = 2Tl$ (anti-clockwise)

For equilibrium, $\tau_1 = \tau_2$

$$\Rightarrow \quad m'g\frac{l}{2} = 2Tl$$

$$\Rightarrow \quad m' = \frac{4T}{g} = 4m \quad \text{... (iv)}$$

[using Eq. (iii)]

As, the hoop is initially slipping, so it experiences friction till it begins to execute pure rolling (with assumed speed v') as shown in Fig. 2.

As, angular momentum is conserved about P. Therefore,

$$L_{final} = L_{initial}$$

$$\text{Using,} \quad L = L_{translational} + L_{rotational}$$

$$= mv_{CM}r + I_{CM}\omega$$

We get,

$$m'v'R + m'R^2 \cdot \frac{v'}{R} = m'vR$$

$$\Rightarrow \quad v' = \frac{v}{2} \quad \text{... (v)}$$

Initial kinetic energy of the hoop is

$$K_1 = \frac{1}{2}m'v^2 \text{ (translational only)} \quad \text{...(vi)}$$

And final kinetic energy of the hoop is

$$K_2 = \frac{1}{2}m'v'^2 \text{ (translational)} + \frac{1}{2}I_{CM}\omega^2 \text{ (rotational)}$$

$$= \frac{1}{2}m'v'^2 + \frac{1}{2}m'R^2\left(\frac{v'}{R}\right)^2 = m'v'^2$$

(As, for pure rolling, $v' = \omega R$)

$$= m'\left(\frac{v}{2}\right)^2 \quad \text{[using Eq. (v)]}$$

$$\Rightarrow \quad K_2 = \frac{1}{4} m' v^2 \quad \text{...(vii)}$$

As, by work-energy theorem,

work $= \Delta KE$

$\Rightarrow$ Work by friction on hoop $= K_2 - K_1$

$$= \frac{1}{4} m' v^2 - \frac{1}{2} m' v^2$$

[using Eqs. (vi) and (vii)]

$$= -\frac{1}{4} m' v^2 = -mv^2$$

[using Eq. (iv)]

$\therefore$ Heat dissipated due to friction $= mv^2$

4. Let M and m be masses of each star and particle projected from mid-point, respectively. Gravitational potential at mid-point is

$$V = \left(\frac{-GM}{L/2}\right) + \left(-\frac{GM}{L/2}\right) = -\frac{4GM}{L}$$

Therefore, potential energy (initial) of projectile,

$$U = mV = -\frac{4GMm}{L}$$

By conservation of energy for projectile

$$-\frac{4GMm}{L} + \frac{1}{2} mv^2 = 0$$

$$\Rightarrow \quad v = \sqrt{\frac{8GM}{L}} \quad \text{...(i)}$$

Time period of revolution in twin star system is given by $T = 2\pi \sqrt{\frac{L^3}{G(M_1 + M_2)}}$

(Here, M_1 and M_2 are masses of stars)

$$\Rightarrow \quad T = 2\pi \sqrt{\frac{L^3}{2GM}} \quad \text{... (ii)}$$

Multiplying Eq. (ii) by Eq. (i), we get

$$T = \frac{4\pi L}{v}$$

5. and **6.** 1.5 and 2.25

Let gas (oxygen) pressure is p.

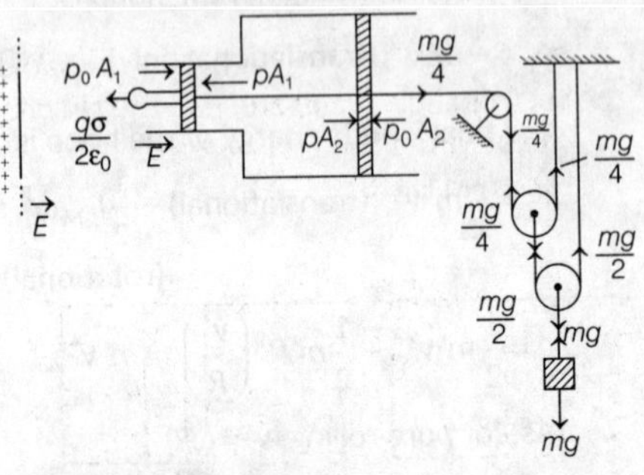

For equilibrium of system of pistons, from the FBD,

$$\frac{q\sigma}{2\varepsilon_0} + pA_1 + p_0 A_2 = p_0 A_1 + pA_2 + \frac{mg}{4}$$

$$\Rightarrow p = p_0 + \frac{q\sigma}{2\varepsilon_0 (A_2 - A_1)} - \frac{mg}{4(A_2 - A_1)}$$

$$= 10^5 + \frac{\frac{1}{400\pi} \times 10^{-6} \times \frac{20}{9}}{2\varepsilon_0 \times 10 \times 10^{-4}} - \frac{20 \times 10}{4 \times 10 \times 10^{-4}}$$

$$= 10^5 + 10^5 - 0.5 \times 10^5$$

$$= 1.5 \times 10^5 \text{ Pa}$$

$$\Rightarrow \quad p = 1.5 \text{ atm} \quad \text{... (i)}$$

As, on slow heating, the system of pistons is moving slowly, so gas pressure remains constant. Thus, the process is isobaric.

By ideal gas equation, $pV = nRT$

$$\Rightarrow \quad p\Delta V = nR\Delta T$$

$$\Rightarrow \quad \Delta T = \frac{p\Delta V}{nR} \quad \text{... (ii)}$$

As, by method of tension, displacement of different components of a system in string pulley arrangement, $\Sigma \mathbf{T}_i \cdot \Delta \mathbf{x}_i = 0$

$\Rightarrow T_1 \Delta x_1 \cos\theta_1 + T_2 \Delta x_2 \cos\theta_2 = 0$

Here, T_1 = tension in string connected to block $= mg$

T_2 = tension in string connected to larger piston $= \frac{mg}{4}$

Δx_1 = displacement of block= 12.5 cm

Δx_2 = displacement of larger piston =?

θ_1 = angle between T_1 and $\Delta x_1 = 180°$

θ_2 = angle between T_2 and $\Delta x_2 = 0°$

$$\Rightarrow mg(12.5)\cos 180° + \frac{mg}{4} (\Delta x_2) \cos 0° = 0$$

$$\Rightarrow \quad \Delta x_2 = 50 \text{ cm} = 0.5 \text{ m}$$

$\therefore$ Increase in oxygen volume

$$= (A_2 - A_1)\Delta x_2$$

$$\Rightarrow \quad \Delta V = 10 \times 10^{-4} \times 0.5$$

$$= 5 \times 10^{-4} \text{ m}^3 \quad \text{... (iii)}$$

Putting $n = 4$, $R = \frac{25}{3}$ J/mol-K, value of p from Eq. (i) and value of ΔV from Eqs. (iii) in Eq. (ii), we get

$$\Delta T = \frac{1.5 \times 10^5 \times 5 \times 10^{-4}}{4 \times \frac{25}{3}}$$

$$= 2.25 \text{ K} = 2.25°\text{C}$$

7. and **8.** 16.6 and 3

Let p_x and p_y be momentum components of He^+ ion after the collision and p_y' be y-component of momentum of neutron, as shown in the figure. Also, $m_n = m$ and $m_{He} = 4m$ masses of neutron and He^+ ion, respectively.

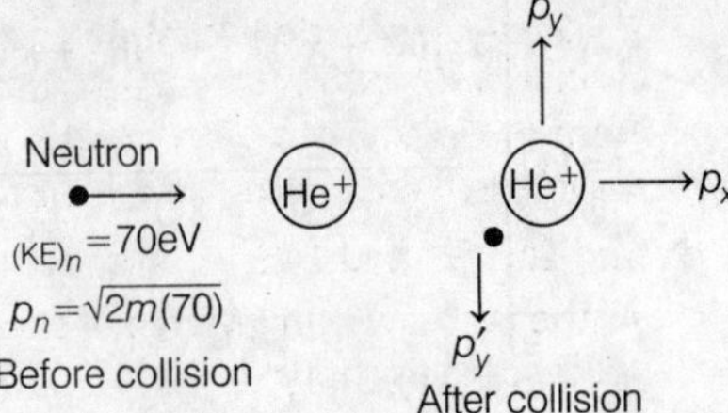

By conservation of momentum in x-direction,

$$p_x = \sqrt{2m(70)} \quad \text{... (i)}$$

By conservation of momentum in y-direction,

$$p_y = p_y' \quad \text{...(ii)}$$

By conservation of energy,

Kinetic energy loss = Energy used to excite He^+.

If KE_n, KE'_{He}, KE_n' are kinetic energies of neutron before collision, He^+ after collision, and neutron after collision respectively, we get

$$KE_n - (KE'_{He} + KE_n') = 13.6\, Z^2 \left(\frac{1}{n_1^2} - \frac{1}{n_2^2}\right)$$

$$\Rightarrow 70 - \left(\frac{p_x^2 + p_y^2}{2(4m)} + \frac{p_y'^2}{2m}\right) = 13.6(2)^2 \left(\frac{1}{1} - \frac{1}{4^2}\right)$$

$$\Rightarrow 70 - \left(\frac{140m + p_y^2}{8m} + \frac{p_y^2}{2m}\right) = 51$$

[using Eqs. (i) and (ii)]

$$\Rightarrow \quad \frac{p_y^2}{m} = 2.4 \text{ eV}$$

$$\Rightarrow \quad p_y = \sqrt{m(2.4)} \quad \text{... (iii)}$$

$\Rightarrow KE_n'$ = KE of neutron after collision

$$= \frac{p_y'^2}{2m} = \frac{p_y^2}{2m} \quad \text{[using Eq. (ii)]}$$

$$= \frac{m(2.4)}{2m} = 1.2 \text{eV} \quad \text{...(iv)}$$

[using Eq. (iii)]

Also, KE'_{He} = KE of He^+ after collision

$$= \frac{p_x^2 + p_y^2}{2(4m)} = \frac{140m + 2.4m}{8m}$$

[using Eqs. (i) and (iii)

$$\Rightarrow \quad KE'_{He} = 17.8 \text{ eV} \quad \text{... (v)}$$

From Eqs. (iv) and (v), we get

$$KE'_{He} - KE'_{n} = 17.8 - 1.2$$
$$= 16.6 \text{ eV}$$

Also, from a single He^+ ion, maximum possible number of photons will be emitted for de-excitation from $n = 4$ to $n = 3$ followed by de-excitation from $n = 3$ to $n = 2$ followed by de-excitation from $n = 2$ and $n = 1$. So, total of 3 wavelength are emitted in the process.

9. and 10. 1.5 and 14.5

As the ray leaves undeviated, it should follow path as shown in Fig. 1.

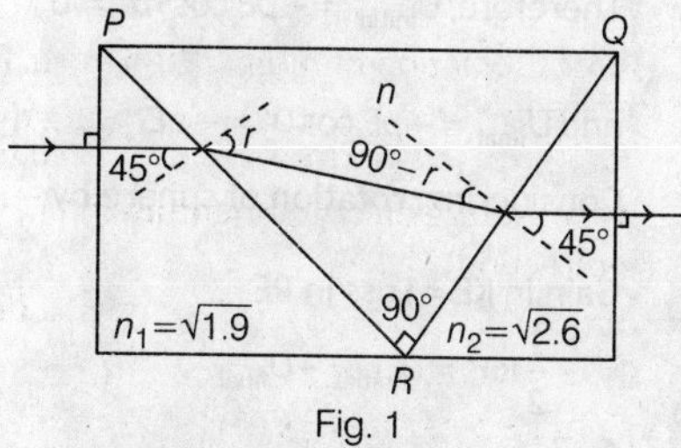

Fig. 1

For refraction at surface *PR*, by Snell's law, $\quad n_1 \sin 45° = n \sin r \quad$ ... (i)

For refraction at surface *RQ*, by geometry, angle of incidence will be $90° - r$. By Snell's law, for the refraction at *RQ*, we get

$$n_2 \sin 45° = n \cdot \sin(90° - r)$$
$$n_2 \sin 45° = n \cos r \quad \text{... (ii)}$$

Squaring and adding Eqs. (i) and (ii), we get

$$(n_1^2 + n_2^2) \sin^2 45° = n^2 (\sin^2 r + \cos^2 r)$$

$$\Rightarrow n = \sqrt{\frac{n_1^2 + n_2^2}{2}} = \sqrt{\frac{1.9 + 2.6}{2}} = 1.5$$

For lens in Fig. 2, using lens Maker's formula, i.e.

$$\frac{1}{f} = (n-1)\left(\frac{1}{R_1} - \frac{1}{R_2}\right)$$

$$\Rightarrow \frac{1}{60} = (1.5 - 1)\left(\frac{1}{R} - \frac{1}{-R}\right)$$

$$\Rightarrow \quad R = 60 \text{ cm} \quad \text{... (iii)}$$

Now, consider rays from O going through the slab. The slab produces a shift given by

$$S = T\left(1 - \frac{1}{n}\right)$$

$$= 3\left(1 - \frac{1}{3/2}\right) = 1 \text{ cm} \quad \text{... (iv)}$$

For next optical event, which is refraction from water surface, O' acts as object. Distance of image O'' from water surface is given by $t' = \dfrac{tn_r}{n_i}$

Here, t = object distance, n_r and n_i are refractive indices of medium of refraction and incidence, respectively.

$$\Rightarrow t' = \frac{t\left(\frac{4}{3}\right)}{1} = \frac{4t}{3}, \text{ as shown in Fig. 2.}$$

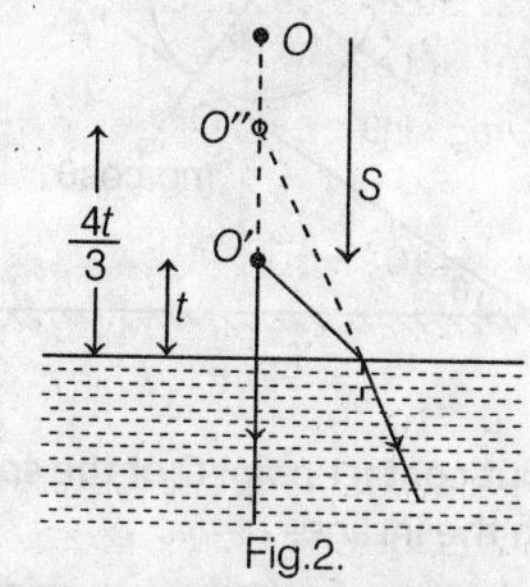

Fig.2.

O'' acts as object for refraction at water lens interface. So, the object distance will be equal to $\dfrac{4t}{3} + 30$ cm as shown.

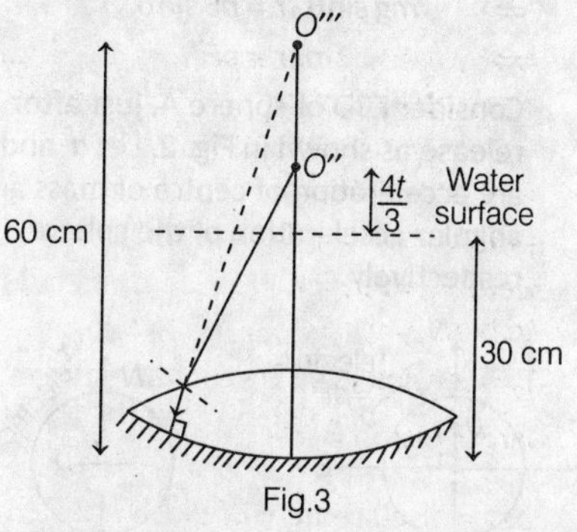

Fig.3

Also, for object image coincidence rays should be incident normally on the silvered surface of the lens.

Therefore, image O''' formed after refraction from water-lens interface will be formed at centre of curvature C of silvered surface, at a distance equal to 60 cm [using Eq. (iii)] as shown in Fig.3. Therefore, for refraction at water-lens interface,

$$\frac{n_2}{v} - \frac{n_1}{u} = \frac{n_2 - n_1}{R}$$

$$\Rightarrow \frac{\frac{3}{2}}{-60} - \frac{\frac{4}{3}}{-\left(\frac{4t}{3} + 30\right)} = \frac{\frac{3}{2} - \frac{4}{3}}{60}$$

∴ Distance of O' from water surface,

$$t = 13.5 \text{ cm} \quad \text{...(v)}$$

∴ Distance of O from water surface,

$$d = t + S = 13.5 + 1$$

[using Eqs. (iv) and (v)]

$$= 14.5 \text{ cm}$$

11. In combination of cells, they are in parallel. To find E_{eq} (equivalent emf) and r_{eq} (equivalent resistance, we can use formula

$$E_{eq} = \frac{\frac{E_1}{r_1} + \frac{E_2}{r_2} + \ldots}{\frac{1}{r_1} + \frac{1}{r_2} + \ldots}$$

and $\quad \dfrac{1}{r_{eq}} = \dfrac{1}{r_1} + \dfrac{1}{r_2} + \ldots$

Using these formula, we get

$$E_{eq} = E \quad \text{...(i)}$$

$$\frac{1}{r_{eq}} = \frac{1}{r} + \frac{1}{2r} + \ldots = \frac{1}{r}\left(1 + \frac{1}{2} + \ldots\right)$$

$$= \frac{1}{r} \times \frac{1}{1 - \frac{1}{2}} = \frac{2}{r} \Rightarrow r_{eq} = \frac{r}{2} \quad \text{...(ii)}$$

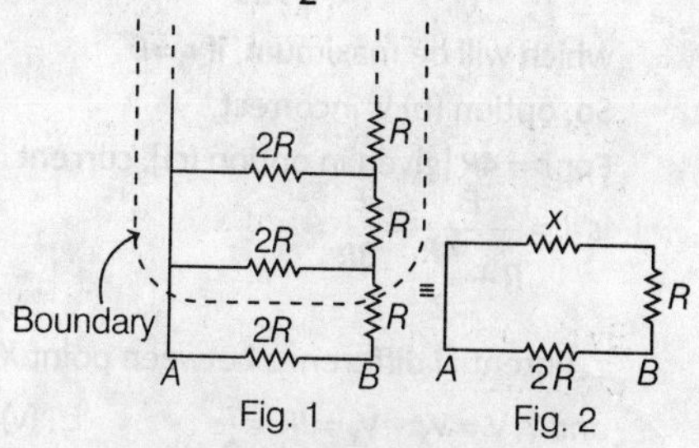

Fig. 1 Fig. 2

Now, consider the network of resistors. Let equivalent resistance of the network is x between ends A and B shown in Fig. 1. If we consider circuit portion in boundary, as it is same as original network, it will also have same equivalent resistance x. So, the circuit can be reduced as shown in Fig. 2.

R and x are in series and their equivalent resistance is in parallel with $2R$. So, effective resistance between A and B is

$$R_{AB} = \frac{(x + R)\,2R}{x + 3R}$$

$$\Rightarrow \quad x = \frac{(x + R)\,2R}{x + 3R}$$

$$\Rightarrow x^2 + Rx - 2R^2 = 0$$

$$\Rightarrow \quad x = R \quad \text{... (iii)}$$

So, from Eqs. (i), (ii) and (iii), the circuit can be simplified and re-drawn as shown in Fig. 3.

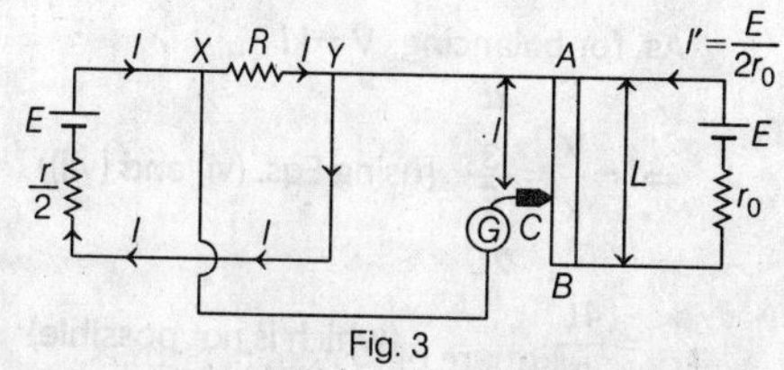

Fig. 3

As per maximum power theorem, to consume maximum power in external circuit its resistance should be equal to internal resistance. So, considering Fig. 3, for maximum power dissipation in R, we should have $R=\frac{r}{2}$

So, option (a) is correct.

But for a given R (i.e. if R is fixed)

Current in the secondary circuit is

$$I=\frac{E}{R+\frac{r}{2}} \quad \text{... (iv)}$$

Therefore, power consumed by R is

$$P=I^2R=\left(\frac{E}{R+\frac{r}{2}}\right)^2 R$$

which will be maximum, if $r=0$

So, option (b) is incorrect.

For $r=4R$ [given in option (c)], current is $I=\frac{E}{R+\frac{4R}{2}}=\frac{E}{3R}$

$\therefore$ Potential difference between point X and Y, $V=V_X-V_Y=IR=\frac{E}{3}$ ... (v)

Now, current in primary potentiometer circuit, $I'=\frac{E}{2r_0}$

$\therefore$ Potential gradient of the circuit

$$k=\frac{V_{AB}}{L}=\frac{\frac{E}{2r_0}\times r_0}{L}=\frac{E}{2L} \quad \text{...(vi)}$$

As for balancing, $V=kl$

$$\Rightarrow \quad l=\frac{V}{k}=\frac{\frac{E}{3}}{E/2L}=\frac{2L}{3}$$

[using Eqs. (v) and (vi)]

For $r=R$, using Eq. (iv), we get

$$I=\frac{E}{R+\frac{R}{2}}=\frac{2E}{3R}$$

$\therefore$ Potential difference between points X and Y

$$V=V_X-Y_Y=IR=\frac{2E}{3} \quad \text{... (vii)}$$

As, for balancing, $V=kl$

$$\Rightarrow l=\frac{V}{k}=\frac{\frac{2E}{3}}{\frac{E}{2L}} \quad \text{[using Eqs. (vi) and (vii)]}$$

$$=\frac{4L}{3} \quad \text{(which is not possible)}$$

12. Consider FBD of sphere B as shown in Fig.1.

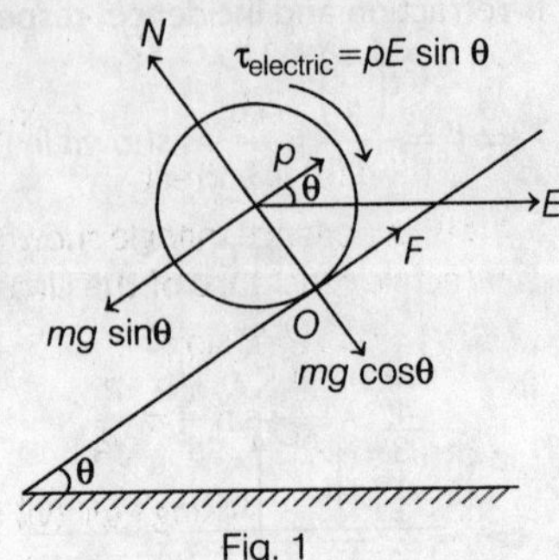

Fig. 1

About contact point O of the sphere with the incline,

$\tau_1=$ torque of $mg\sin\theta=mg\sin\theta\cdot r$ (anti-clockwise)

$\tau_2=$ torque of electric field E due to infinite sheet $=pE\sin\theta$, (clockwise)

For equilibrium of B, $\tau_1=\tau_2$

$$\Rightarrow \quad mg\sin\theta\cdot r=pE\sin\theta$$

$$\Rightarrow \quad mgr=pE \quad \text{... (i)}$$

Consider FBD of sphere A, just after release as shown in Fig. 2. Let a and α are acceleration of centre of mass and angular acceleration of the sphere, respectively.

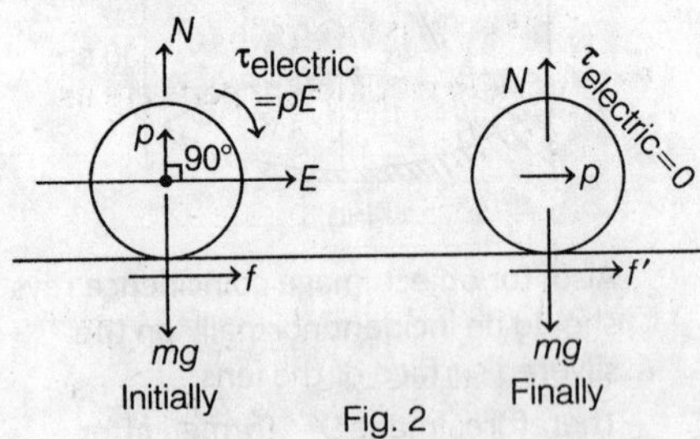

Fig. 2

Moment of inertia of the sphere about O, using parallel axes theorem,

$$I=I_{CM}+md^2=\frac{2}{5}mr^2+mr^2=\frac{7}{5}mr^2 \quad \text{... (ii)}$$

Torque of electric force of sheet on dipole,

$$\tau=pE\sin 90°=pE \quad \text{... (iii)}$$

Using Eqs. (iii) and (ii), we get angular acceleration of the sphere is

$$\alpha=\frac{\tau}{I}=\frac{pE}{\frac{7}{5}mr^2}=\frac{5pE}{7mr^2}$$

By condition of rolling without slipping,

$$a=\alpha r=\frac{5pE}{7mr}=\frac{5mgr}{7mr}$$

[using Eq. (i)]

$$\Rightarrow \quad a=\frac{5g}{7} \quad \text{... (iv)}$$

$\therefore$ Option (a) is correct.

From FBD in Fig. 2, using,

$F=ma$ in horizontal direction, we get

$$f=m\left(\frac{5g}{7}\right)=\frac{5mg}{7}4$$

[using Eq. (iv)]

$\therefore$ Option (b) is incorrect.

Due to electric field torque experienced by sphere A, will rotate the dipole clockwise. Potential energy of a dipole is given by

$$U=-pE\cos\theta$$

Therefore, $U_{initial}=-pE\cos 90°=0$ ... (v)

and $U_{final}=-pE\cos 0°=-pE$ ... (vi)

Considering, rotation of sphere by $\frac{\pi}{2}$,

Gain in KE $=$ Loss in PE

$$\frac{1}{2}I\omega^2=U_{initial}-U_{final}$$

$$\frac{1}{2}\frac{7}{5}mr^2\omega^2=0-(-pE)$$

$$\Rightarrow \omega=\sqrt{\frac{10pE}{7mr^2}}=\sqrt{\frac{10p\left(\frac{\sigma}{2\varepsilon_0}\right)}{7mr^2}}$$

$$=\sqrt{\frac{5p\sigma}{7mr^2\varepsilon_0}}$$

$\Rightarrow$ Option (c) is incorrect.

Finally, when dipole is parallel to horizontal surface, torque due to electric force is equal to

$$\tau=pE\sin 0°=0$$

$$\Rightarrow \quad \alpha_{CM}=\frac{\tau}{I}=0$$

$$\Rightarrow \quad f'=ma_{CM}=0$$

$\therefore$ Option (d) is correct.

13. Effective reactances are as shown in the Fig. 1. Also, maximum currents are shown in various branches.

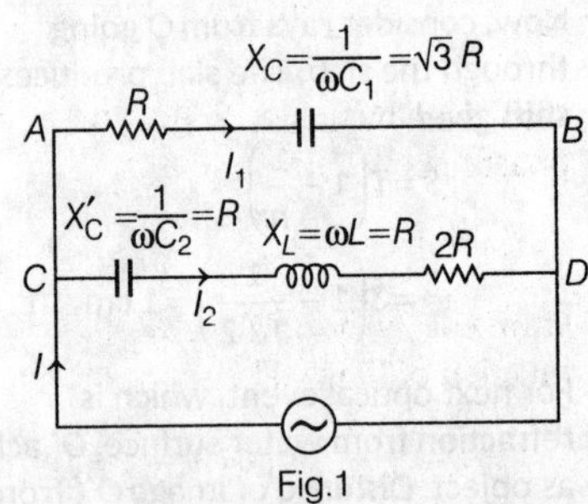

Fig.1

Now, impedance of series combination is given by

$$Z=\sqrt{(X_L-X_C)^2+R^2}$$

While lead of current $=\tan^{-1}\left(\frac{X_L-X_C}{R}\right)$

For branch *AB*

Impedance $=Z_1=\sqrt{R^2+X_C^2}=2R$

$$\Rightarrow \quad I_1=\frac{V_0}{Z_1}=\frac{V_0}{2R} \quad \text{... (i)}$$

Also, lead of current

$$=\tan^{-1}\left(\frac{X_C}{R}\right)=\tan^{-1}\left(\frac{\sqrt{3}R}{R}\right)=\frac{\pi}{3} \quad \text{... (ii)}$$

For branch *CD*

Impedance $=Z_2=\sqrt{(2R)^2+(R-R)^2}$

$$=2R$$

$$\Rightarrow \quad I_2=\frac{V_0}{Z_2}=\frac{V_0}{2R} \quad \text{... (iii)}$$

Also, lead of current $=\tan^{-1}\left(\frac{R-R}{2R}\right)$

$$=0 \quad \text{... (iv)}$$

From calculations in Eqs. (i) to (iv), phasor representation of I_1 and I_2 are as shown in Fig. 2

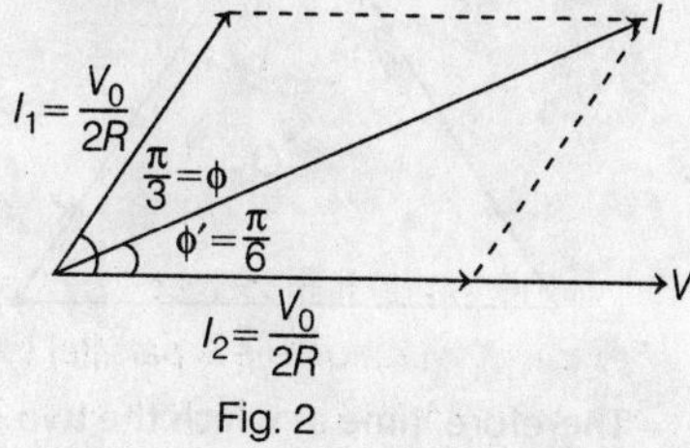

Fig. 2

To find resultant current, i.e. current supplied by AC source, we need to add phasors of I_1 and I_2 as shown in Fig.2. So,

$$I=\sqrt{I_1^2+I_2^2+2I_1I_2\cos\phi}$$

$$=\sqrt{\left(\frac{V_0}{2R}\right)^2+\left(\frac{V_0}{2R}\right)^2+2\frac{V_0}{2R}.\frac{V_0}{2R}.\cos\frac{\pi}{3}}$$

$$\Rightarrow \quad I=\frac{\sqrt{3}V_0}{2R} \quad \text{... (v)}$$

Also, lead of current as shown by phasor, is

$$\phi'=\frac{\pi}{6} \quad \text{...(vi)}$$

From Eqs. (v) and (vi), current as function of time will be

$$i=\frac{\sqrt{3}\,V_0}{2R}\sin\left(\omega t+\frac{\pi}{6}\right)$$

$\therefore$ Option (c) is correct.

Effective impedance of a circuit is given by $Z=\frac{V_0}{I}=\frac{V_0}{\frac{\sqrt{3}\,V_0}{2R}}=\frac{2R}{\sqrt{3}}$ ... (vii)

[using Eq. (v)]

$\therefore$ Option (b) is correct.

From impedance triangle shown in Fig. 3, effective reactance of the circuit is

$$X=Z\sin\phi'$$

$$=\frac{2R}{\sqrt{3}}\sin\frac{\pi}{6}=\frac{R}{\sqrt{3}}$$

[using Eqs. (vi) and (vii)]

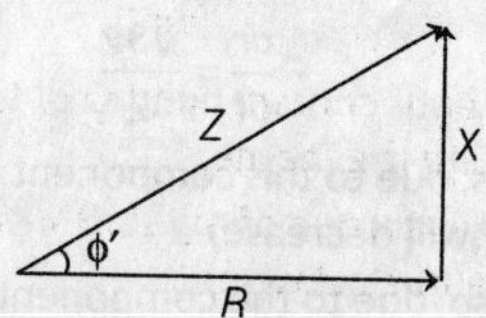

$\therefore$ Option (a) is incorrect.

Also, wattless current is given by component of rms current perpendicular to voltage phasor which will be

$$I_{\text{wattless}}=I_{\text{rms}}\sin\phi'=\frac{I\sin\phi'}{\sqrt{2}}$$

$$=\frac{\sqrt{3}V_0}{4\sqrt{2}R} \quad \text{[using Eq. (v)]}$$

$\therefore$ Option (d) is incorrect.

14. Stresses (σ) in different parts are as shown.

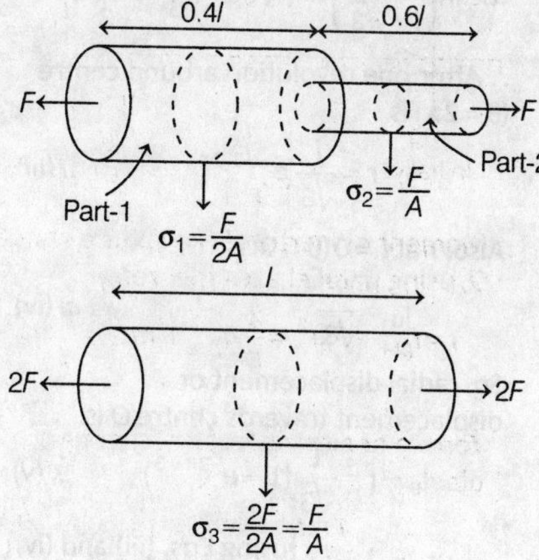

From the figures, clearly,

$$\sigma_2=\sigma_3=\sigma \quad \text{(say)}$$

Therefore σ_1 (as, it is half of σ_2 and σ_3) can be assumed to be $\frac{\sigma}{2}$.

Now, strain energy is given by the formula,

$$U=\frac{\sigma^2}{2Y}\times\text{Volume}$$

Here, $\sigma=$ stress and $Y=$ Young's modulus

Therefore, strain energy of stepped bar is

$$U=U_1+U_2$$

[(Part-1) + (Part-2)]

$$=\frac{\sigma_1^2}{2Y}\times V_1+\frac{\sigma_2^2}{2Y}\times V_2$$

(Here, V_1 and V_2 are respective volumes)

$$=\frac{\left(\frac{\sigma}{2}\right)^2}{2Y}\times 2A\times 0.4l+\frac{\sigma^2}{2Y}\times A\times 0.6l$$

$$=\frac{\sigma^2 Al}{10Y}+\frac{3\sigma^2 Al}{10Y}=\frac{2}{5}\frac{\sigma^2 Al}{Y} \quad \text{...(i)}$$

Strain energy of uniform Bar -2 is,

$$U'=\frac{\sigma^2}{2Y}\times 2A\times l=\frac{\sigma^2 Al}{Y} \quad \text{... (ii)}$$

Dividing Eq. (ii) by Eq. (i), we get

$$U'=\frac{5}{2}U=2.5U$$

$\therefore$ Option (b) is correct.

Also, ratio of strain energies of shorter portion of stepped bar (U_1) to that of longer portion (U_2) is

$$\frac{U_1}{U_2}=\frac{\frac{\sigma^2 Al}{10Y}}{\frac{3\sigma^2 Al}{10Y}}=\frac{1}{3}$$

$\therefore$ Option (c) is incorrect.

Now, Breaking force = Breaking stress × Area

As, breaking stress is the property of material, so breaking force is proportional to area. As, lesser area of the stepped bar (A) is critical area while area of uniform bar is $2A$. So, ratio of breaking force will be in ratio of their areas i.e. 1 : 2.

$\therefore$ Option (d) is correct.

15. As per decay law,

$$N_A=N_0e^{-\lambda t} \quad \text{... (i)}$$

As, B is decaying simultaneously into X and Y, effective decay constant,

$$\lambda_{\text{eff}}=\lambda_X+\lambda_Y=\lambda+2\lambda=3\lambda$$

Therefore, as per decay law,

$$N_B=N_0e^{-3\lambda t} \quad \text{... (ii)}$$

As, decay constants for decay of B into Y and X are 2λ and λ, respectively, so ratio of nuclei of B decayed into Y and X are in the ratio 2 : 1.

Therefore, number of nuclei of Y by decay of B,

$$N_Y = \frac{2}{3}(N_0 - N_0 e^{-3\lambda t}) \quad \text{[using Eq. (ii)]}$$

$$\Rightarrow \quad N_Y = \frac{2N_0}{3}(1 - e^{-3\lambda t}) \quad \text{... (iii)}$$

Also, nuclei of X produced by decay of A is equal to

$$N_1 = N_0(1 - e^{-\lambda t}) \quad \text{[using Eq. (i)] ... (iv)}$$

and nuclei of X produced by decay of B

$$N_2 = \frac{1}{3} \times \text{No. of decayed nuclei of } B$$

$$= \frac{1}{3} \times (N_0 - N_0 e^{-3\lambda t}) \quad \text{...(v)}$$

Therefore, no. of nuclei of X is

$$N_X = N_1 + N_2$$

$$= N_0(1 - e^{-\lambda t}) + \frac{N_0}{3}(1 - e^{-3\lambda t})$$

[Using Eqs. (iv) and (v)]

$$\Rightarrow N_X = N_0\left(\frac{4}{3} - e^{-\lambda t} - \frac{e^{-3\lambda t}}{3}\right) \quad \text{... (vi)}$$

Dividing Eq. (ii) by Eq. (i), we get

$$\frac{N_B}{N_A} = e^{-2\lambda t}$$

∴ Option (a) is correct.

Considering Eq. (vi), option (b) is incorrect.

Also, at the time, when $N_B = N_Y$, Using Eqs. (ii) and (iii), we get

$$N_0 e^{-3\lambda t} = \frac{2N_0}{3}(1 - e^{-3\lambda t})$$

$$\Rightarrow \quad 5e^{-3\lambda t} = 2$$

$$t = \frac{\ln 2.5}{3\lambda}$$

∴ Option (c) is correct.

From Eq. (iii), at $t = \frac{\ln 2}{3\lambda}$, we get

$$N_Y = \frac{2N_0}{3}(1 - e^{-\ln 2}) = \frac{N_0}{3}$$

∴ Option (d) is correct.

16. Let distance of P from centroid of the triangle is r.

Now, by symmetry P, Q and R will always be on an equilateral triangle as shown in Fig. 1.

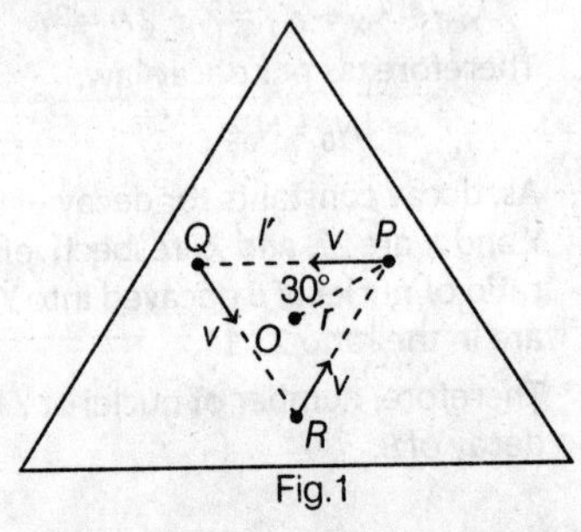

Fig.1

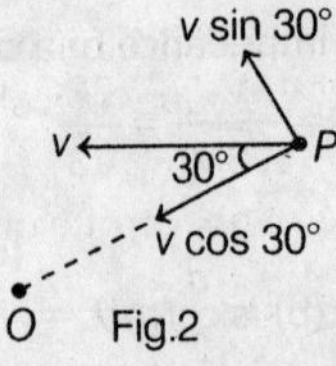

Fig.2

Therefore, line OP will make 30° with velocity of P as shown in Fig. 2. Therefore, components of velocity of P will be as shown.

$$\text{Component along } OP = v\cos 30° = \frac{\sqrt{3}v}{2}$$

$$\Rightarrow \quad -\frac{dr}{dt} = \frac{\sqrt{3}v}{2} \quad \text{... (i)}$$

(As, due to this component length of OP will decrease)

Also, due to the component perpendicular to OP, if angle rotated about O is $d\theta$, then tangential displacement will be $rd\theta$ and so, tangential velocity will be

$$\frac{rd\theta}{dt} = \frac{v}{2} \quad \text{... (ii)}$$

Dividing Eq. (i) by Eq. (ii), we get

$$-\frac{dr}{rd\theta} = \sqrt{3}$$

$$\Rightarrow \quad \int_{l/\sqrt{3}}^{r} \frac{dr}{r} = -\sqrt{3}\int_0^{\theta} d\theta$$

$$\Rightarrow \ln\left(\frac{r}{l/\sqrt{3}}\right) = -\sqrt{3}\theta \Rightarrow r = \frac{l}{\sqrt{3}}e^{-\sqrt{3}\theta}$$

∴ After one revolution around centre $(\theta = 2\pi)$ is

$$r = \frac{l}{\sqrt{3}}e^{-\sqrt{3}.2\pi} \quad \text{... (iii)}$$

Also, r at $t = 0\,(\theta = 0)$ is

$$r_0 = \frac{l}{\sqrt{3}} \quad \text{... (iv)}$$

So, radial displacement or displacement towards centre O is,

$$r_0 - r = \frac{l}{\sqrt{3}}(1 - e^{-2\pi\sqrt{3}}) \quad \text{... (v)}$$

[using Eqs. (iii) and (iv)]

Also, radial velocity, as per Fig. 2,

$$v_r = \frac{\sqrt{3}\,v}{2} \quad \text{...(vi)}$$

Therefore, time of motion to complete one revolution is

$$t = \frac{r_0 - r}{v_r} = \frac{\frac{l}{\sqrt{3}}(1 - e^{-2\sqrt{3}\pi})}{\frac{\sqrt{3}\,v}{2}}$$

[using Eqs. (v) and (vi)]

$$t = \frac{2l}{3v}(1 - e^{-2\sqrt{3}\pi}) \quad \text{... (vii)}$$

As, speed of the particle is constant, therefore, distance travelled will be

$$d = \text{Speed} \times \text{Time}$$

$$= v \times \frac{2l}{3v}(1 - e^{-2\sqrt{3}\pi})$$

[using Eq. (vii)]

$$\Rightarrow \quad d = \frac{2l}{3}(1 - e^{-2\sqrt{3}\pi})$$

∴ Option (c) is correct.

Also, from Eq. (iii), instantaneous separation between P and Q

$$l' = \sqrt{3}\,r = l\,e^{-2\pi\sqrt{3}}$$

(As in Fig. 1)

∴ Option (d) is incorrect.

Now, velocity of approach of P towards Q or relative velocity along the line joining the two particles is

$$v_{\text{app}} = v - \left(-\frac{v}{2}\right) = 3\frac{v}{2}$$

(as shown in Fig. 2)

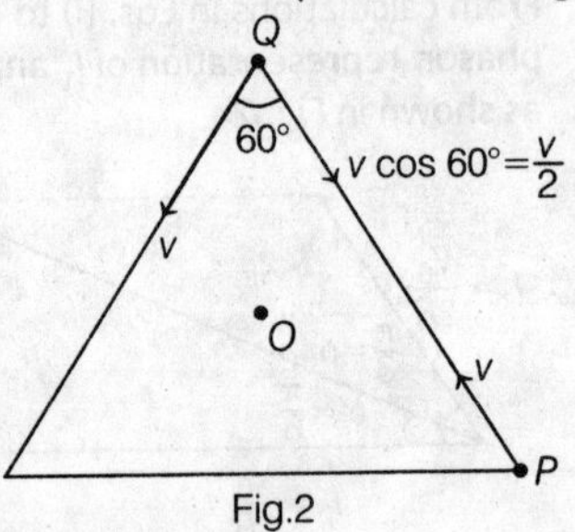

Fig.2

Therefore, time at which the two particles meet will be

$$t = \frac{l}{v_{\text{app}}} = \frac{l}{\frac{3v}{2}} = \frac{2l}{3v} \quad \text{...(viii)}$$

As, the particles meet at centroid O by symmetry, displacement of P

$$s = \frac{l}{\sqrt{3}} \quad \text{...(ix)}$$

Dividing Eq. (ix) by Eq. (viii), we get average velocity,

$$v = \frac{s}{t} = \frac{\sqrt{3}\,v}{2}$$

∴ Option (a) is correct.

As, speed is constant, so in any duration average speed is equal to speed.

17. Assuming σ and ρ be density of cylinder and water respectively, for equilibrium of the cylinder as shown in Fig. 1, we get

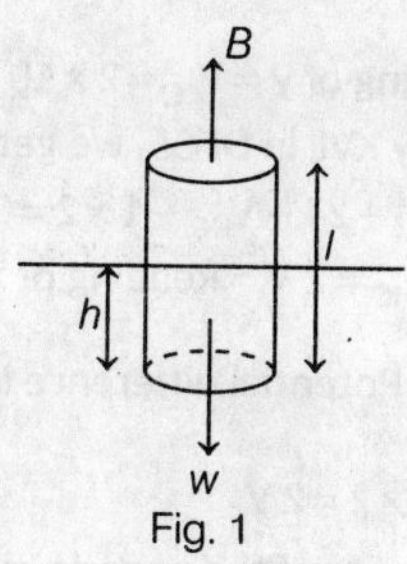

Fig. 1

$$w_{(weight)} = B_{(buoyancy)}$$

$$\Rightarrow \quad mg = B \Rightarrow \sigma Alg = \rho Ahg$$

Here, A is cross-section area of cylinder.

$$\Rightarrow \quad h = \frac{\sigma l}{\rho} \quad \text{... (i)}$$

If the cylinder is displaced slightly by x downwards, restoring (buoyant) force on the cylinder, $F = -\rho \cdot Ax \cdot g$

$\therefore$ Acceleration of cylinder,

$$a = -\frac{\rho Axg}{\sigma Al} = -\frac{\rho g}{\sigma l} x$$

Comparing it with acceleration in SHM or $-\omega^2 x$, we get

$$\omega = \sqrt{\frac{\rho g}{\sigma l}}$$

So, time period of oscillation of cylinder is $T = \frac{2\pi}{\omega} = 2\pi\sqrt{\frac{\sigma l}{\rho g}}$

Substituting given expression of T in LHS, we get

$$\frac{5\pi}{3}\sqrt{\frac{l}{g}} = 2\pi\sqrt{\frac{\sigma l}{\rho g}} \Rightarrow \frac{\sigma}{\rho} = \frac{25}{36} \quad \text{... (ii)}$$

Putting value of $\frac{\sigma}{\rho}$ from Eq. (ii) in Eq. (i), we get

$$h = \frac{25}{36} \times 36 = 25 \text{ cm} \quad \text{... (iii)}$$

Now, consider FBD of the rod as shown in Fig. 2.

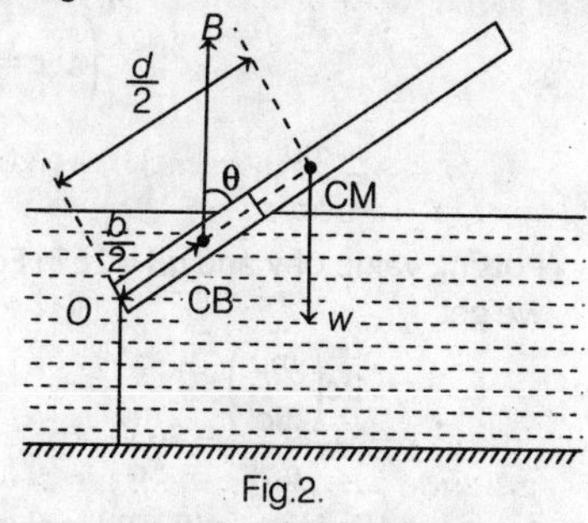

Fig.2.

The rod experiences buoyancy B at centre of buoyancy (CB) which is centre of mass of the displaced fluid at a distance $\frac{b}{2}$ from immersed end O of the rod. Weight w of the rod acts at centre of mass (CM) for equilibrium of the rod, net torque on it should be zero.

$\Rightarrow$ Torque of B = Torque of w

$$\Rightarrow B\frac{b}{2}\sin\theta = w\frac{d}{2}\sin\theta \Rightarrow Bb = wd$$

$$\Rightarrow \rho \cdot a \cdot b \cdot g \cdot b = \sigma \cdot a \cdot d \cdot g \cdot d$$

Here, a = cross-sectional area of the rod.

$$\Rightarrow \quad \frac{b}{d} = \sqrt{\frac{\sigma}{\rho}} = \sqrt{\frac{25}{36}} = \frac{5}{6}$$

[using Eq. (ii)]

$$\Rightarrow \quad b = \frac{5d}{6} = \frac{5}{6} \times 48 = 40\text{cm} \quad \text{... (iv)}$$

From Eqs. (iii) and (iv), we get

$$h + b = 65 \text{ cm}$$

18. The given figure can be drawn as

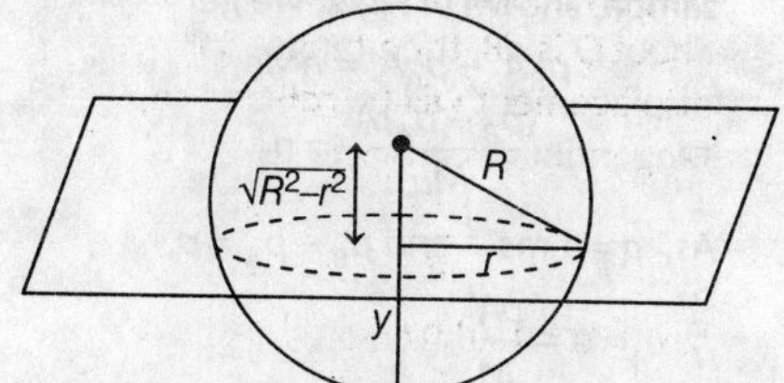

From the figure, $Y = R - \sqrt{R^2 - r^2}$

Differentiating w.r.t. T on both sides, we get

$$\frac{dy}{dT} = \frac{dR}{dT} - \frac{1}{2\sqrt{R^2 - r^2}} \cdot \frac{d(R^2 - r^2)}{dT}$$

$$\Rightarrow 0 = R\alpha' - \frac{1}{2\sqrt{R^2 - r^2}} \cdot \left[2 \cdot R \cdot \frac{dR}{dT} - 2r \cdot \frac{dr}{dT}\right]$$

$$\Rightarrow 0 = R\alpha' - \frac{1}{\sqrt{R^2 - r^2}} \cdot [R \cdot R\alpha' - r \cdot r \cdot \alpha]$$

$$\Rightarrow \quad 0 = 10 \cdot \alpha' - \frac{1}{6}[100\alpha' - 64\alpha]$$

$$\Rightarrow \quad 60\alpha' = 100\alpha' - 64\alpha$$

$$\Rightarrow \quad 64\alpha = 40\alpha' \Rightarrow \frac{8\alpha}{\alpha'} = 5$$

19. For air inside bubble, as the process is isothermal,

$$p_{final} V_{final} = p_{initial} V_{initial}$$

$$\Rightarrow \left(\frac{p_0}{2} + \frac{4T}{r + \frac{25}{100}r}\right)\frac{4}{3}\pi\left(r + \frac{25}{100}r\right)^3 = \left(p_0 + \frac{4T}{r}\right)\frac{4}{3}\pi r^3$$

$$\Rightarrow \left(\frac{p_0}{2} + \frac{16T}{5r}\right)\frac{125}{64} = p_0 + \frac{4T}{r}$$

$$\Rightarrow \frac{125p_0}{128} + \frac{25T}{4r} = p_0 + \frac{4T}{r}$$

$$\Rightarrow \frac{3p_0}{128} = \frac{9T}{4r}$$

$$\therefore \text{Required ratio, } \frac{p_0}{\frac{4T}{r}} = 24$$

(Paper 2)

1. In steady state ($t < 0$) as shown in Fig. 1, capacitor behaves as open circuit while inductor behaves as plain wire.

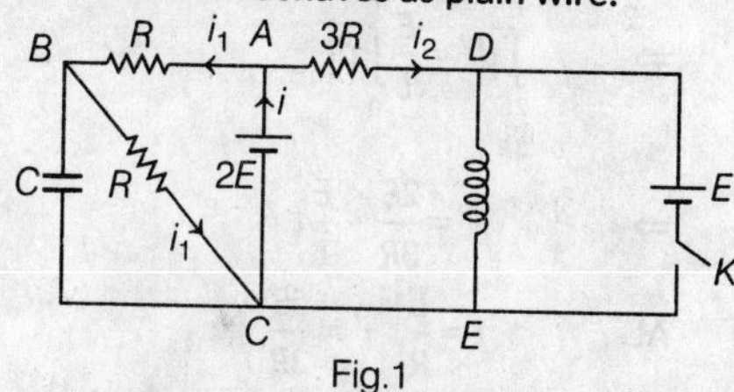

Fig.1

Thus, by KVL in loop $ABCA$, we get

$$2E - i_1 R - i_1 R = 0$$

$$\Rightarrow \quad i_1 = \frac{E}{R} \quad \text{... (i)}$$

By KVL, in $ADECA$, we get

$$2E - i_2(3R) = 0$$

$$\Rightarrow \quad i_2 = \frac{2E}{3R} \quad \text{...(ii)}$$

By KCL, for junction A, we get

$$i = i_1 + i_2 = \frac{E}{R} + \frac{2E}{3R} = \frac{5E}{3R}$$

[using Eqs. (i) and (ii)]

Power supplied by cell of emf, $2E = Vi$

$$= 2E\left(\frac{5E}{3R}\right) = \frac{10E^2}{3R}$$

$\therefore$ Option (a) is correct.

Potential difference across capacitor = Potential difference between points B and C

$$= i_1 R = \frac{E}{R} R = E \quad \text{[using Eq. (i)]}$$

If d is given plate separation, electric field between plates will be $E' = \frac{E}{d}$ (irrespective of K)

Just after closing the key K, circuit will be as shown in the Fig.2

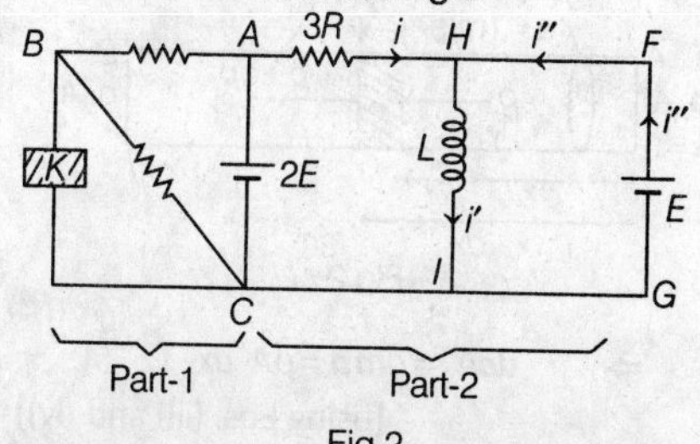

Fig.2

As, cell of emf $2E$ is ideal, so Part-1 and Part-2 of the circuit will behave independently.

So, by KVL in $AFGCA$, we get

$$2E - i(3R) - E = 0$$

$$\Rightarrow \quad i = \frac{E}{3R}$$

$\therefore$ Option (c) is correct.

For inductor, by KVL in $HFGIH$

$$L\frac{di'}{dt} = E \Rightarrow di' = \frac{E}{L}dt$$

$$\Rightarrow \quad \int_{\frac{2E}{3R}}^{i'} di' = \frac{E}{L}\int_0^t dt$$

$$\Rightarrow \quad i' = \frac{2E}{3R} + \frac{E}{L}t$$

At $\quad t = \frac{L}{R}, \; i' = \frac{5E}{3R}$

$\therefore$ Power consumed $= Ei' = E \cdot \frac{5E}{3R} = \frac{5E^2}{3R}$

$\therefore$ Option (d) is incorrect.

2. From FBD of block, using $F = ma$, we get

$$0.8\,mg - T - 0.6mg = ma \quad \text{...(i)}$$

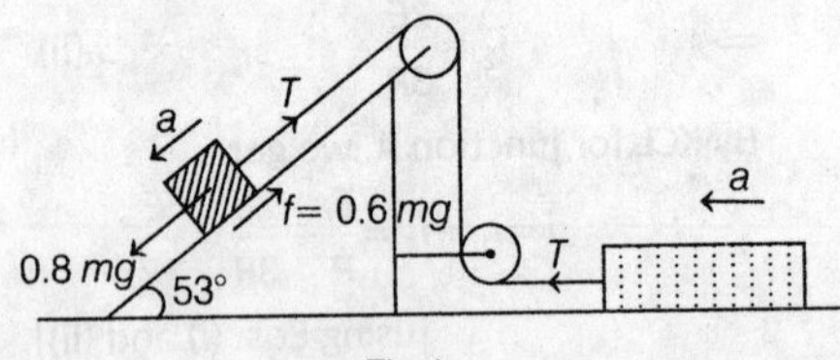

Fig.1

From FBD of box, using $F = ma$, we get

$$T = ma \quad \text{... (ii)}$$

Adding Eqs.(i) and (ii), we get

$$0.2mg = 2ma$$

$$\Rightarrow \quad a = \frac{g}{10} = 1\ \text{m/s}^2 \quad \text{... (iii)}$$

Now, consider FBD of an element of gas sample as shown in Fig. 2.

Mass of the element, $dm = \rho A'\,dx$ ... (iv)

(Here, ρ is density.)

Using $F = ma$ for element, we get

$$(p + dp)\,A' - pA' = dm\,a \quad \text{... (v)}$$

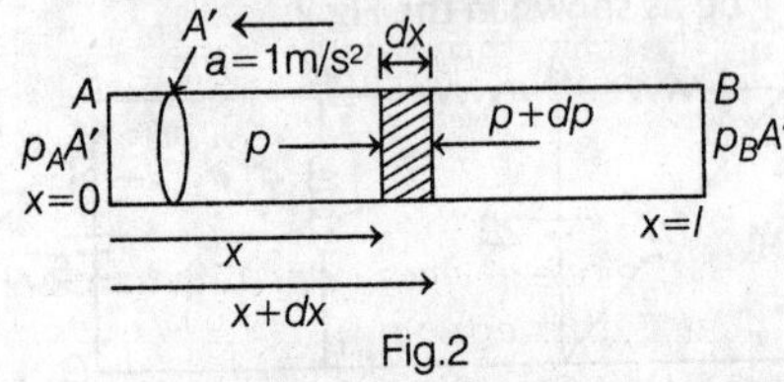

Fig.2

$$\Rightarrow \quad dpA' = dm\,a = \rho A'\,dx$$

[using Eqs. (iii) and (iv)]

$$\Rightarrow \quad dpA' = \frac{pM}{RT}A'\,dx$$

$\left(\because \text{ by ideal gas equation, } \rho = \frac{pM}{RT}\right)$

$$\Rightarrow \quad \frac{dp}{p} = \frac{M}{RT}dx$$

$$\Rightarrow \quad \int_{p_A}^{p_B}\frac{dp}{p} = \frac{M}{RT}\int_0^l dx$$

$$\Rightarrow \quad \ln\frac{p_B}{p_A} = \frac{Ml}{RT}$$

$$\Rightarrow \quad \frac{p_B}{p_A} = e^{\frac{Ml}{RT}}$$

$$\Rightarrow \quad p_B > p_A$$

So, options (b) and (c) are correct.

Also, using $F = ma$, for entire gas sample shown in Fig.2, we get

$$p_BA' - p_AA' = nMa$$

$$\Rightarrow \quad \frac{(p_B - p_A)A'}{Ma} = n$$

As, $a = 1\ \text{ms}^{-2}$ and $p_B - p_A = p$,

$$\therefore \quad n = \frac{pA'}{M}$$

3. As per Faraday's law, emf in the loop CDE,

$$E = \frac{d\phi}{dt} = \frac{d(BA)}{dt} = A\cdot\frac{dB}{dt} = A \times B_0$$

$$= \frac{\pi R^2}{8} \times \frac{192}{\pi R^2} = 24\ \text{V}$$

This emf will not have any component along branches CD and CE, as they are radial. So, entire emf will be in branch DE.

By Faraday's law for $DEGF$, as there is no flux, net emf induced, $E' = \frac{d\phi}{dt} = 0$

So, an emf equal and opposite to that in branch DE is induced in FG as shown in equivalent circuit diagram in figure.

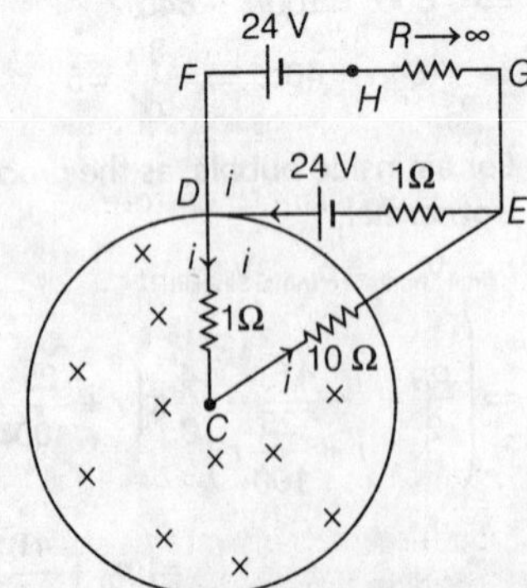

Therefore, current in the circuit will be

$$i = \frac{24}{1 + 10 + 1} = 2\text{A}$$

$\therefore$ Reading of $y = V_{CE} = 2 \times 10 = 20$ V

Now, by KVL in $DFGE$, we get

$$24 - 24 + V_{HG} - 1 \times 2 = 0$$

$$\Rightarrow \quad V_{HG} = 2\ \text{V} = \text{Reading of } x$$

$\int_C^D \mathbf{E}\cdot d\mathbf{l} =$ Potential difference in branch

$CD = 1 \times 2 = 2$ V

4. Let velocity of the particle at any general instant is

$$\mathbf{v} = v_x\hat{\mathbf{i}} + v_y\hat{\mathbf{j}}$$

Force on the particle will therefore be

$$\mathbf{F} = q(\mathbf{v} \times \mathbf{B}) - c\mathbf{v}$$

$$= q(v_x\hat{\mathbf{i}} + v_y\hat{\mathbf{j}}) \times (B\hat{\mathbf{k}}) - c(v_x\hat{\mathbf{i}} + v_y\hat{\mathbf{j}})$$

$$= -qv_xB\hat{\mathbf{j}} + qv_yB\hat{\mathbf{i}} - cv_x\hat{\mathbf{i}} - cv_y\hat{\mathbf{j}}$$

$$= (-cv_x + qv_yB)\hat{\mathbf{i}} + (-cv_y - qv_xB)\hat{\mathbf{j}}$$

$\therefore$ x-component of acceleration,

$$a_x = -\frac{cv_x}{m} + \frac{qv_yB}{m}$$

$$\Rightarrow \quad \frac{dv_x}{dt} = -\frac{c}{m}\cdot\frac{dx}{dt} + \frac{qB}{m}\frac{dy}{dt}$$

$$\Rightarrow \int_0^0 dv_x = -\frac{c}{m}\int_0^x dx + \frac{qB}{m}\int_0^y dy$$

$$\Rightarrow \quad 0 = -cx + qBy$$

$$x = \frac{qBy}{c} \quad \text{... (i)}$$

Similarly, $a_y = -\frac{cv_y}{m} - \frac{qv_xB}{m}$

$$\Rightarrow \quad \int_u^0 dv_y = -\frac{c}{m}\int_0^y dy - \frac{qB}{m}\int_0^x dx$$

$$\Rightarrow \quad mu = cy + qBx \quad \text{... (ii)}$$

From Eqs. (i) and (ii), we get

$$mu = cy + \frac{qB \cdot qBy}{c}$$

$$\Rightarrow \quad y = \frac{c \cdot mu}{c^2 + (qB)^2} = \frac{c \cdot mu}{c^2 + (2c)^2}$$

$$\left(\because c = \frac{qB}{2}\right)$$

$$= \frac{mu}{5c}$$

Putting value of y and $qB = 2c$ in Eq. (i), we get

$$x = \frac{2c\left(\frac{mu}{5c}\right)}{c} = \frac{2mu}{5c}$$

As, magnetic force $[q(\mathbf{v} \times \mathbf{B})]$ is always perpendicular to velocity or instantaneous displacement, work done by magnetic force is zero.

By work-energy theorem,

$$W_{\text{magnetic}} + W_{\text{drag}} = \Delta\,\text{KE}$$

$$\Rightarrow \quad 0 + W_{drag} = 0 - \frac{1}{2}mu^2$$

$$\Rightarrow \quad W_{drag} = -\frac{1}{2}mu^2$$

5. In a cavity inside a uniform sphere, gravitational field is uniform given by

$$\mathbf{E} = -\frac{4\pi G\rho \mathbf{r}}{3}$$

Here, r is distance between centre of sphere and centre of cavity.

$$\Rightarrow \mathbf{E} = -\frac{4\pi G\rho\left(\frac{R}{2}\right)\hat{\mathbf{i}}}{3} = \frac{-2\pi G\rho R\,\hat{\mathbf{i}}}{3} \quad \text{... (i)}$$

So, **E** is uniform and option (a) is incorrect.

$\Rightarrow$ Acceleration of point mass = E

$$= \frac{2\pi G\rho R}{3}$$

To strike surface of the particle, the particle will displace by R.

Using $s = ut + \frac{1}{2}at^2$, we get

$$R = 0 + \frac{1}{2}\cdot\frac{2\pi G\rho R t^2}{3} \Rightarrow t = \sqrt{\frac{3}{\pi G\rho}}$$

So, option (b) is incorrect.

Field outside a solid sphere is given by

$$\mathbf{E}' = -\frac{4\pi\rho G R^3}{3r^2}\mathbf{r}$$

So, field due to removed portion (centred at C_2) at C_1 will be

$$\mathbf{E}' = -\frac{4\pi G\rho\left(\frac{R}{2}\right)^3}{3(R)^2} = \frac{\mathbf{E}}{4} \quad \text{... (ii)}$$

[using Eq. (i)]

Thus, net field at C_2 will be

$$\mathbf{E}_2 = \mathbf{E} - \mathbf{E}' = \frac{3\mathbf{E}_1}{4}$$

[using Eqs. (i) and (ii)]

$$\Rightarrow \quad 4\mathbf{E}_2 = 3\mathbf{E}_1$$

As, potential (V) at C_1 and C_2 will be equal to symmetry, work done,

$$W = m\Delta V = 0$$

6. $[\text{Stress}] = [\text{Pressure}] = \left[\frac{F}{A}\right] = [ML^{-1}T^{-2}]$

$$[\eta] = [ML^{-1}T^{-1}] \text{ and } [R] = [M^0L^0T^0]$$

As, $\frac{L}{R}$ and RC are time constants,

$$\left[\frac{L}{R}\right] = [RC] = [T]$$

As, $\frac{1}{\sqrt{\mu_0\varepsilon_0}} = c$

$$\Rightarrow \left[\frac{1}{\sqrt{\mu_0\varepsilon_0}}\right] = [\text{Terminal speed}]$$

$$= [LT^{-1}]$$

7. and **8.** 4 and 6.75

Consider the situation as shown in the Fig. 1

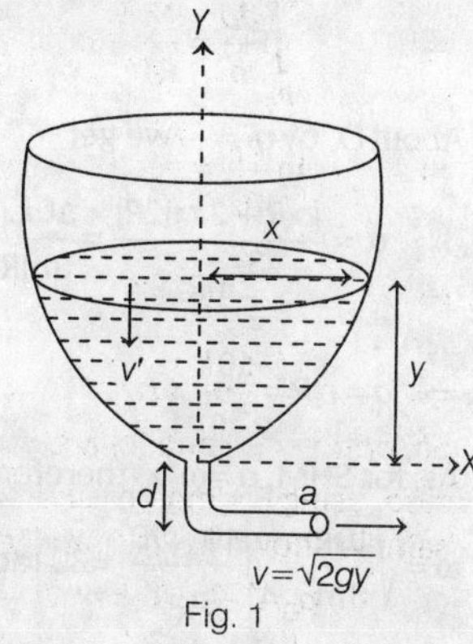

Fig. 1

By Torricelli's equation, velocity of efflux is

$$v = \sqrt{2gy}$$

$\therefore$ Volume flow rate of ejecting fluid,

$$Q_1 = av = a\sqrt{2gy} \quad \text{... (i)}$$

At top surface, radius of cross-section is equal to x. Therefore, cross-sectional area is

$$a' = \pi x^2$$

$\therefore$ Volume flow rate at surface,

$$Q_2 = a'v' = \pi x^2 v' \quad \text{... (ii)}$$

Here, v' is fluid velocity.

By continuity equation,

$$Q_1 = Q_2$$

$$\Rightarrow \quad a\sqrt{2gy} = \pi x^2 v'$$

[using Eqs. (i) and (ii)]

$$\Rightarrow \quad v' = \frac{a\sqrt{2gy}}{\pi x^2}$$

$$\Rightarrow \quad \left|\frac{dh}{dt}\right| = \frac{a\sqrt{2gy}}{\pi x^2}$$

As, $\frac{dh}{dt}$ is given to be independent of y or is constant, therefore,

$$\frac{\sqrt{y}}{x^2} = \text{constant}$$

$$\Rightarrow \quad \frac{y}{x^4} = \text{constant}$$

$$\Rightarrow \quad y \propto x^4 \Rightarrow n = 4$$

Let dm mass of water is striking the block in time dt. Relative velocity with which water strikes the block's surface is

$$v_{rel} = v - u \quad \text{... (iii)}$$

So, change in momentum of dm mass of water is

$$dp = dm\,v_{rel} = dm(v - u)$$

$\therefore$ Force applied by jet on block,

$$F = \frac{dp}{dt} = \frac{dm}{dt}(v - u) \quad \text{... (iv)}$$

Also, relative mass flow rate is

$$\frac{dm}{dt} = \rho a\,v_{rel} = \rho a(v - u) \quad \text{... (v)}$$

[using Eq. (iii)]

Using Eqs. (iv) and (v), we get

$$F = \rho a(v - u)^2$$

Thus, power delivered by jet to the block,

$$P = Fu = \rho a(v - u)^2 u \quad \text{... (vi)}$$

For P to be maximum,

$$\frac{dP}{du} = 0$$

$$\Rightarrow \quad \frac{d[(v - u)^2 u]}{du} = 0$$

$$\Rightarrow \quad -2(v - u)u + (v - u)^2 = 0$$

$$\Rightarrow \quad u = \frac{v}{3}$$

$$\therefore \quad P = \rho a\left(v - \frac{v}{3}\right)^2 \frac{v}{3} = \frac{4\rho a v^3}{27}$$

[using Eq. (vi)]

$$\therefore \quad x = \frac{27}{4} = 6.75$$

9. and **10.** 2.20 and 1.41

Possibility- 1

If the given points having amplitude 2 mm are the anti-nodes, the situation will be as shown in Fig.1.

Fig. 1

As shown in the Fig.1, separation between anti-nodes Q and S, which is also separation between nodes P and R is equal to 20 cm. Therefore, number of loops in the vibrating string,

$$N = \frac{\text{Length of string}}{\text{Separation between nodes}}$$

$$= \frac{240}{20} = 12$$

So, mode of vibration is 12th harmonic or 11th overtone.

$$\Rightarrow \quad n_1 = 11 \text{ and } A_1 = 2 \text{ mm} \quad \text{... (i)}$$

Possibility-2

If adjacent points T, U, V and W separated by 20 cm w.r.t. adjacent points have same amplitude, separation between nodes (X and Y) is 40 cm as shown in Fig.2.

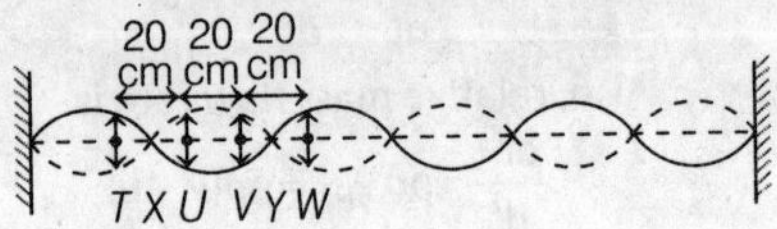

Fig.2

Thus, number of loops in vibrating string,

$$N' = \frac{240}{40} = 6$$

So, mode of vibration is 6th harmonic or 5th overtone,

$$\Rightarrow \quad n_2 = 5 \quad \text{... (ii)}$$

Now, if wavelength of standing wave is λ, separation between nodes,

$$\frac{\lambda}{2} = 40 \text{ cm}$$

$$\Rightarrow \quad \lambda = 80 \text{ cm}$$

If amplitude at anti-node is assumed to be a and amplitude at general position w.r.t. end O is A, they are related as

$$A = a\sin\left(\frac{2\pi}{\lambda}x\right)$$

For point T, $x = 30$ cm as shown in Fig.3 and amplitude is given to be 2 mm.

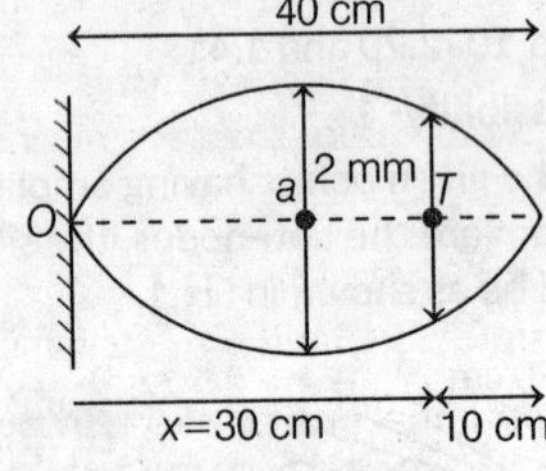

Fig. 3

$$\Rightarrow 2 = a\sin\left(\frac{2\pi}{80}\times 30\right) = a\sin\frac{3\pi}{4}$$

$$\Rightarrow \quad a = A_2 = 2\sqrt{2} \text{ mm} \quad \text{... (iii)}$$

From Eqs. (i) and (ii), we get

$$\frac{n_1}{n_2} = \frac{11}{5} = 2.20$$

From Eqs. (i) and (iii), we get

$$\frac{A_2}{A_1} = \frac{2\sqrt{2}}{2} = \sqrt{2} = 1.41$$

11. and **12.** 4.12 and 1.5

If the disc is displaced by x from the mean position shown, spring connected to centre extends by x while the upper spring extends by $2x$. So, FBD of the disc will be as shown in Fig.1.

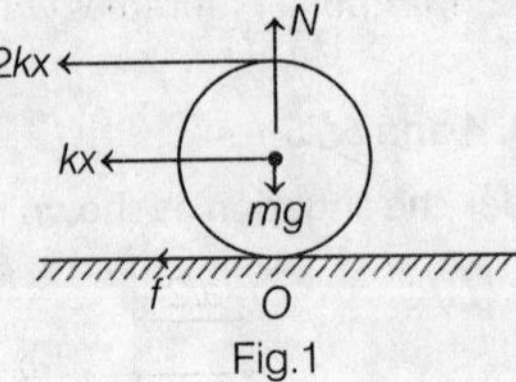

Fig.1

About O, by $\alpha = \frac{\tau}{I}$, we get

$$\alpha = \frac{kxR + 2kx(2R)}{\frac{3}{2}mR^2} = \frac{10kx}{3mR}$$

$$\Rightarrow \quad a = \alpha R = \frac{10k}{3m}x$$

As, for SHM, $a = \omega^2 x$, therefore we get

$$\omega = \sqrt{\frac{10k}{3m}} = \sqrt{\frac{10\times 90}{3\times\frac{1}{3}}} = 30 \text{ rad/s} \quad \text{... (i)}$$

Also, amplitude of SHM is given to be

$$A = 0.2 \text{ mm} \quad \text{... (ii)}$$

As, it is given that, when $\theta = 45°$, the disc is at mean position. Therefore, speed of hinge of B will be

$$v = A\omega = 0.2\times 30 = 6 \text{ mm/s} \quad \text{... (iii)}$$

[using Eqs. (i) and (ii)]

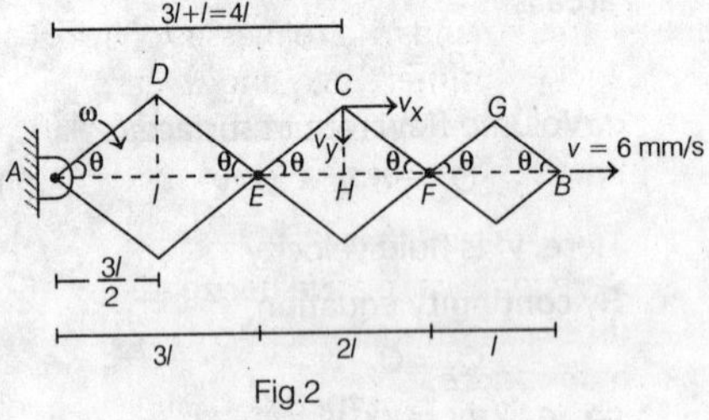

Fig.2

As, $\Delta ADE \sim \Delta ECF \sim \Delta FGB$, so

$$AE : EF : FB = AD : EC : FG = 3:2:1$$

Let us assume lengths AE, EF and FB equal to $3l$, $2l$ and l, respectively.

So, position of C w.r.t. A will be

$$x_C = AE + EH = 3l + l = 4l \quad \text{... (iv)}$$

Also, position of B w.r.t. A will be

$$x_B = AE + EF + FB = 3l + 2l + l$$

$$\Rightarrow \quad x_B = 6l \quad \text{... (v)}$$

Dividing Eq. (iv) by Eq. (v), we get

$$x_C = \frac{2}{3}x_B$$

Differentiating w.r.t. t on both sides, we get

$$\frac{dx_C}{dt} = \frac{2}{3}\frac{d(x_B)}{dt}$$

$$\Rightarrow \quad v_x = \frac{2}{3}v_B = \frac{2}{3}\times v \quad \text{... (vi)}$$

Here, v_x is x component of velocity of C in x-direction.

Similarly, velocity of E will be $\frac{v}{2}$ in x-direction, i.e. $v_E = \frac{v}{2}$ ... (vii)

Velocities of E and C and components of the velocities are as shown in Fig.3. Now, as rod CE is rigid, velocity of C w.r.t. E along the rod is zero. Therefore,

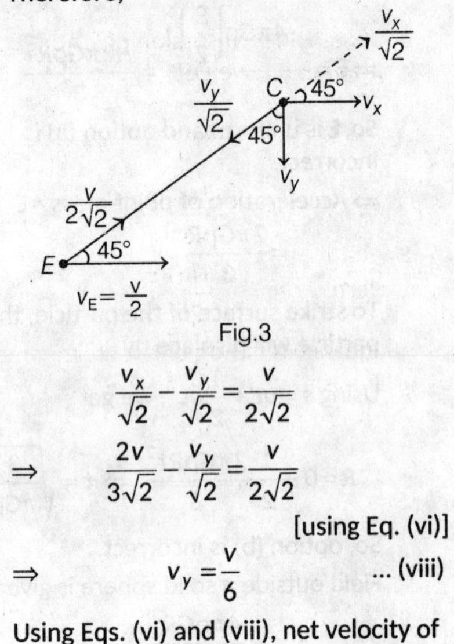

Fig.3

$$\frac{v_x}{\sqrt{2}} - \frac{v_y}{\sqrt{2}} = \frac{v}{2\sqrt{2}}$$

$$\Rightarrow \quad \frac{2v}{3\sqrt{2}} - \frac{v_y}{\sqrt{2}} = \frac{v}{2\sqrt{2}}$$

[using Eq. (vi)]

$$\Rightarrow \quad v_y = \frac{v}{6} \quad \text{... (viii)}$$

Using Eqs. (vi) and (viii), net velocity of C will be

$$v_C = \sqrt{v_x^2 + v_y^2} = \sqrt{\left(\frac{2}{3}v\right)^2 + \left(\frac{v}{6}\right)^2}$$

$$= \frac{\sqrt{17}\,v}{6} = \frac{\sqrt{17}}{6}\times 6 = 4.12 \text{ mm/s}$$

[using Eq. (iii)]

In figure, $\Delta ADI \cong \Delta EDI$, so $AI = IE = \frac{3l}{2}$

Now, from ΔADI,

$$AI = AD\cos\theta$$

$$\Rightarrow \quad \frac{3l}{2} = L\cos\theta$$

$$\Rightarrow \quad \frac{3}{2}\left|\frac{dl}{dt}\right| = L\sin\theta\cdot\left|\frac{d\theta}{dt}\right|$$

$$\Rightarrow \quad \frac{3}{2}\cdot\frac{v}{6} = L\sin 45°\omega$$

$$\left[\because \frac{d(x_B)}{dt} = \frac{d(6l)}{dt} = v\right]$$

$$\Rightarrow \omega = \frac{v}{2\sqrt{2}L} = \frac{6}{2\sqrt{2}\times\sqrt{2}} = 1.5 \text{ rad/s}$$

13-14.

A small magnetic disturbance will induce emf in the disc and so current in the circuit. Due to this current, magnetic field will be produced by the solenoid in turn inducing emf in the disc. If current in the circuit is assumed to be i, magnetic field inside solenoid will be

$$B = \mu_0 \frac{N}{l} i \quad \text{... (i)}$$

Now, motional emf in a rotating disc is given by

$$E = \frac{B\omega a^2}{2} \quad \text{... (ii)}$$

So, putting expression of B from Eq. (i) into Eq. (ii), we get

$$E = \left(\mu_0 \frac{N}{l} i\right) \omega \frac{a^2}{2}$$

$$\Rightarrow \quad E = \frac{\mu_0 N a^2 \omega}{2l} i = ki \quad \text{... (iii)}$$

Here, $k = \dfrac{\mu_0 N a^2 \omega}{2l}$

Equivalent circuit of the arrangement is as shown in the Fig. 1. By KVL, we get

$$L\frac{di}{dt} + iR = E$$

Fig.1

$$\Rightarrow \quad L\frac{di}{dt} + iR = ki \quad \text{[using Eq. (iii)]}$$

$$\Rightarrow \quad L\frac{di}{dt} = i(k - R)$$

$$\Rightarrow \quad \frac{di}{i} = \frac{k - R}{L} dt$$

$$\Rightarrow \quad \int_{i_0}^{i} \frac{di}{i} = \frac{k - R}{L} \int_0^t dt$$

$$\Rightarrow \quad \ln \frac{i}{i_0} = \left(\frac{k - R}{L}\right) t = ct \quad \text{(suppose)}$$

$$\left(\text{Here, } c = \frac{k - R}{L}\right)$$

$$i = i_0 e^{ct} \quad \text{... (iv)}$$

For sustained current $c \geq 0$,

$$\Rightarrow \quad k \geq R$$

$$\Rightarrow \quad \frac{\mu_0 N a^2 \omega}{2l} \geq R$$

$$\Rightarrow \quad \omega \geq \frac{2lR}{\mu_0 N a^2}$$

Now, as current in the disc is radial as shown in Fig.2, magnetic force will be as shown. As, the force is uniformly distributed, so it can be assumed to be acting at mid-point P of radius OA as shown

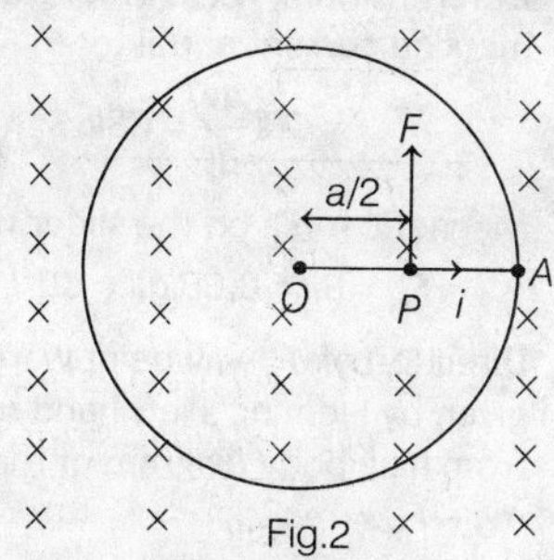

Fig.2

Magnitude of force will be

$$F = Bia = \left(\frac{\mu_0 N i}{l}\right) ia \quad \text{[using Eq. (i)]}$$

$$= \frac{\mu_0 N a}{l} i^2$$

$$\therefore \quad \tau = F \times \frac{a}{2} = \frac{\mu_0 N a^2 i^2}{2l} = \frac{\mu_0 N a^2 i_0^2}{2l} e^{2ct}$$

[using Eq. (iv)]

15-16.

As, there is no external horizontal force, so horizontal displacement of centre of mass of system is zero.

$$\Rightarrow \quad \Delta x_{CM} = 0$$

$$\Rightarrow \quad m_1 \Delta x_1 + m_2 \Delta x_2 = 0$$

Here, m_1 and m_2 are masses of insect and hemisphere, Δx_1 and Δx_2 are horizontal displacements of insect and hemisphere, respectively.

$$\Rightarrow m_1(\Delta x_{1,2} + \Delta x_2) + m_2 \Delta x_2 = 0$$

Here, $\Delta x_{1,2}$ is relative horizontal displacement of insect w.r.t. hemisphere,

$$\Rightarrow \quad \Delta x_2 = \frac{-m_1 \Delta x_{1,2}}{m_1 + m_2} \quad \text{... (i)}$$

As, from the figure shown, relative horizontal displacement of insect is

$$\Delta x_{1,2} = R - R\cos 60° = \frac{R}{2} \quad \text{... (ii)}$$

Also, $m_1 = m$ and $m_2 = 2m$ ... (iii)

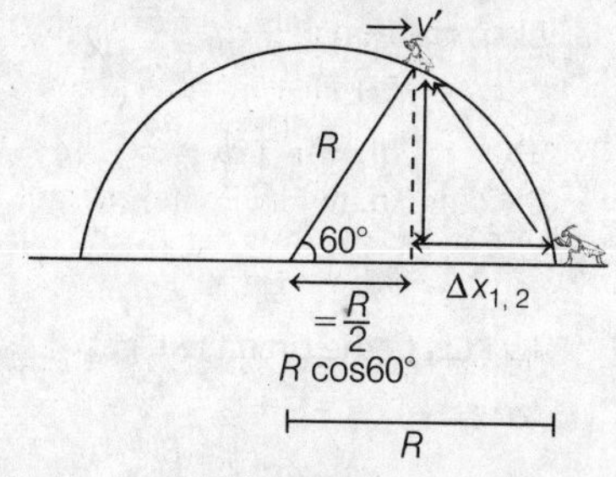

From Eqs. (i), (ii) and (iii), we get

$$\Delta x_2 = \frac{-m\left(\frac{R}{2}\right)}{m + 2m} = -\frac{R}{6}$$

Negative sign signifies that displacement of hemisphere is opposite to that of insect w.r.t. hemisphere or the hemisphere will displace rightwards.

Let v' is a velocity of hemisphere at general instant.

Using momentum conservation,

$$m_2 v' = m_1(v \sin\theta - v')$$

$$\Rightarrow \quad v' = \frac{m_1 v \sin\theta}{m_1 + m_2}$$

$$\Rightarrow \quad a = \frac{dv}{dt} = \frac{mv\cos\theta \times \frac{d\theta}{dt}}{3m}$$

$$= \frac{v^2}{3R} \times \cos 60° = \frac{v^2}{6R}$$

17. If electronic standing wave has n loops, length of the box can be written as

$$l = \frac{n\lambda}{2} \Rightarrow \lambda = \frac{2l}{n}$$

Momentum as per de-Broglie hypothesis,

$$p = \frac{h}{\lambda} = \frac{h}{\frac{2l}{n}} = \frac{nh}{2l}$$

Therefore, kinetic energy will be

$$K = \frac{p^2}{2m} = \frac{\left(\frac{nh}{2l}\right)^2}{2m} = \frac{n^2 h^2}{8ml^2}$$

$$\Rightarrow \quad \frac{2h^2}{ml^2} = \frac{n^2 h^2}{8ml^2} \Rightarrow n = 4 \quad \text{... (i)}$$

Now, potential energy of electron in nth orbit in Bohr's atom is given by

$$E = -\frac{2E_0 Z^2}{n^2}$$

For He^+, $Z = 2$ and $n = 4$ [using Eq. (i)]

So, potential energy of electron will be

$$E = \frac{-2E_0(2)^2}{4^2} = \frac{-E_0}{2}$$

$$\Rightarrow \quad |E| = \frac{E_0}{2} \quad \therefore \quad x = 2$$

18. Magnetic moment of a rotating charged body is given by $M = \dfrac{q}{2m} \times I\omega$

As, charge on a conducting sphere lies on its surface, so using moment of inertia of a hollow sphere, we get

$$M = \frac{q}{2m} \times \frac{2}{3} mR^2 \omega = \frac{q\omega R^2}{3}$$

Magnetic torque on the sphere will, therefore, be

$$\tau = MB\sin\theta = \frac{q\omega R^2}{3} \times B \times \sin 90°$$

$$= \frac{q\omega R^2 B}{3} \quad ...(i)$$

Sense of the torque will be same as $\mathbf{M} \times \mathbf{B}$ or anti-clockwise as shown in the figure.

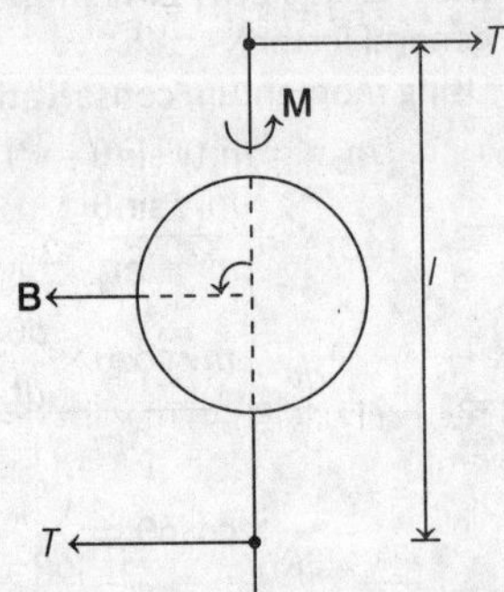

For equilibrium tensions in the strings will be equal but opposite constituting a couple for which torque will be

$$\tau' = \tau l \text{ (clockwise)} \quad ...(ii)$$

As, for equilibrium, net torque is zero,

$$\Rightarrow \quad \tau = \tau'$$

$$\Rightarrow \quad \frac{q\omega R^2 B}{3} = \tau l$$

$$\Rightarrow \quad \tau = \frac{q\omega R^2 B}{3l} = \frac{12 \times 10^{-6} \times 6 \times 2^2 \times 3}{3 \times 8}$$

$$= 36\,\mu\text{N}$$

19. Height of liquid rising in a capillary is independent of shape and so height of liquid in a cylindrical capillary should be 40 mm even if it is inclined.

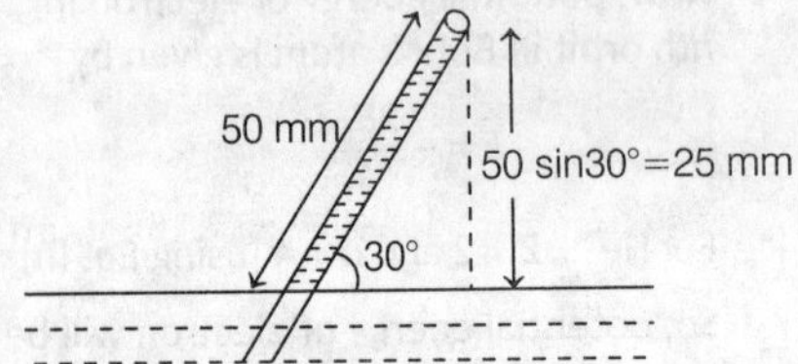

But as height of capillary-2 outside the liquid is 25 mm as shown in figure, it is capillary of insufficient height and so water will rise to the top and therefore, its length would be 50 mm.

Knockout 15 (Paper 1)

1. With k open, let velocity and acceleration of slider at any general instant be v and a, *respectively*.

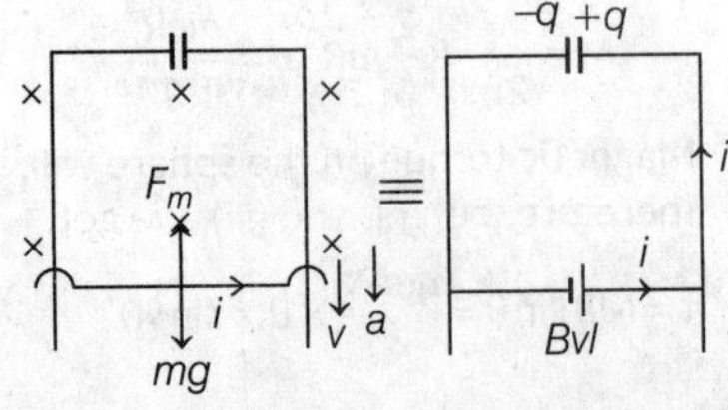

Motional emf in the slider will be Bvl as shown in figure. Charge on the capacitor will be $q = CV = C \cdot Bvl$

Differentiating w.r.t. time, we get induced current equal to

$$i = CBl\frac{dv}{dt} = CBla$$

Magnetic force on the slider will be

$$F_m = Bil = B(CBla)l = CB^2l^2a$$

Direction of F_m will be upwards as given by Fleming's left hand rule. Thus, from free body diagram of the slider

$$mg - F_m = ma$$

$$\Rightarrow mg - CB^2l^2a = ma$$

$$\Rightarrow \quad mg = (m + CB^2l^2)a$$

Putting given value of a equal to $\frac{g}{2}$ in the above equation, we get

$$mg = (m + CB^2l^2)\frac{g}{2}$$

$$\Rightarrow CB^2l^2 = m \quad ...(i)$$

Now, with key closed let velocity and acceleration be v' and a', respectively. Also, the current and charge distribution is as shown in the figure

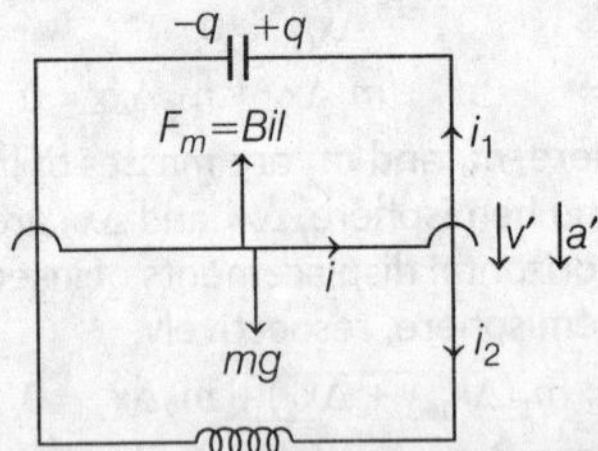

Charge on capacitor, $q = CV = C \cdot Bv'l$

$\therefore$ Current through capacitor is

$$i_1 = \frac{dq}{dt} = CBla' \quad ...(ii)$$

Also, for inductor, motional emf is equal to potential difference across inductor. Thus,

$$L\frac{di_2}{dt} = Bv'l$$

$$\Rightarrow \quad di_2 = \frac{Bl}{L}v'\,dt = \frac{Bl}{L}dx$$

$$\Rightarrow \quad \int di_2 = \frac{Bl}{L}\int dx$$

$$\Rightarrow \quad i_2 = \frac{Blx}{L} \quad ...(iii)$$

By KCL, in the circuit, we get

$$i = i_1 + i_2$$

$$\Rightarrow \quad i = CBla' + \frac{Bl}{L}x$$

[from Eqs. (ii) and (iii)]

Therefore, magnetic force will be equal to

$$F_m = Bil = B\left[CBla' + \frac{Bl}{L}x\right]l$$

$$= CB^2l^2a' + \frac{B^2l^2}{L}x$$

Thus, from free body diagram of the slider

$$mg - \left(CB^2l^2a' + \frac{B^2l^2}{L}x\right) = ma'$$

$$\Rightarrow mg - \frac{B^2l^2}{L}x = a'(m + CB^2l^2)$$

$$\Rightarrow \quad a' = \frac{-\frac{B^2l^2}{L}x + mg}{m + CB^2l^2}$$

$$= \frac{-\frac{m}{CL}x + mg}{2m} \quad \text{[using Eq. (i)]}$$

$$= -\frac{1}{2LC}(x - gLC) \quad ...(iv)$$

The equation is comparable with $a = -\omega^2 \cdot x$.

On comparison, we get

$$\omega = \frac{1}{\sqrt{2LC}} \quad ...(v)$$

and $x_0 = gLC$ as mean position ...(vi)

(because at mean position $x = 0$)

Equation of SHM can thus be assumed as

$$x = x_0 + A\sin(\omega t + \phi) \quad ...(vii)$$

$$\Rightarrow \frac{dx}{dt} = v = A\omega\cos(\omega t + \phi) \quad ...(viii)$$

As at $t = 0$, $v = 0$, therefore from Eq. (viii)

$$0 = \cos\phi$$

$$\Rightarrow \quad \phi = \frac{\pi}{2} \text{ or } -\frac{\pi}{2}$$

Also, at $t = 0$, $x = 0$, therefore from Eq. (vii),

$$0 = x_0 + A\sin\phi$$

$$\Rightarrow \sin\phi = -\frac{x_0}{A}$$

$$\Rightarrow \quad \phi = -\frac{\pi}{2}$$

and $\quad x_0 = A \quad ...(ix)$

From Eqs. (vii) and (ix), we get

$$x = x_0 + x_0\sin\left(\omega t - \frac{\pi}{2}\right)$$

$$= x_0(1 - \cos\omega t)$$

where, x_0 and ω are as given by Eqs. (vi) and (v)

$$\therefore x = gLC\left(1 - \cos\frac{t}{\sqrt{2LC}}\right)$$

2. Let density of the liquid at 0°C be ρ.

Density at t°C will therefore be

$$\rho' = \frac{\rho}{1+\gamma t} \quad ...(i)$$

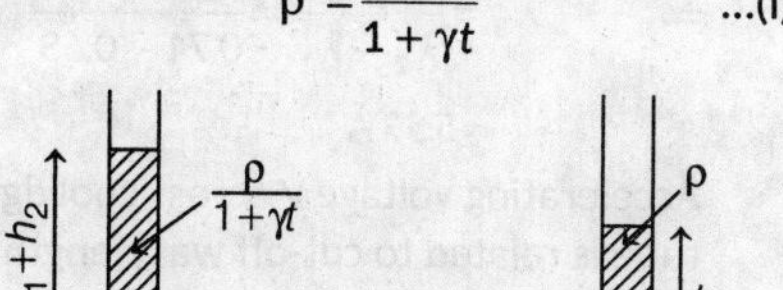
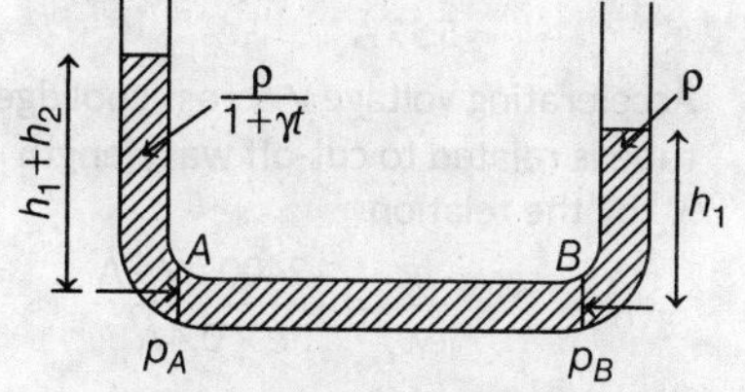

For equilibrium, pressure at points at same horizontal level in liquid are equal. Therefore, $p_A = p_B$

$$\Rightarrow \rho' g h' = \rho g h$$

$$\Rightarrow \frac{\rho}{1+\gamma t} \cdot g \cdot (h_1 + h_2) = \rho \cdot g \cdot h_1$$

[using Eq. (i)]

$$\Rightarrow 1 + \gamma t = \frac{h_2}{h_1} + 1 \Rightarrow \gamma = \frac{h_2}{h_1 t} \quad ...(ii)$$

Now, for floating cylinder, weight is balanced by buoyancy.

So, initially, $w = B$ ...(iii)

After increasing temperature,

$$w = B' \quad ...(iv)$$

From Eq. (iii) and (iv), we get

$$B' = B$$

$$\Rightarrow \rho V g = \rho' V' g$$

$$\Rightarrow \rho A h_3 g = \rho' A' h_3 g$$

$$\Rightarrow \frac{A'}{A} = \frac{\rho'}{\rho}$$

$$\Rightarrow 1 + \beta \Delta t = 1 + \gamma \Delta t$$

(Here, β is coefficient of superficial expansion of cylinder's material)

$$\Rightarrow \beta = \gamma$$

As superficial expansion coefficient is $\frac{2}{3}$ rd of volumetric expansion coefficient, therefore,

$$\frac{2}{3}\gamma_{\text{cylinder}} = \gamma$$

$$\Rightarrow \gamma_{\text{cylinder}} = \frac{3\gamma}{2} = \frac{3h_2}{2h_1 t} \quad \text{[using Eq. (ii)]}$$

3. Let speed of the satellite at P and Q be v and v' respectively.

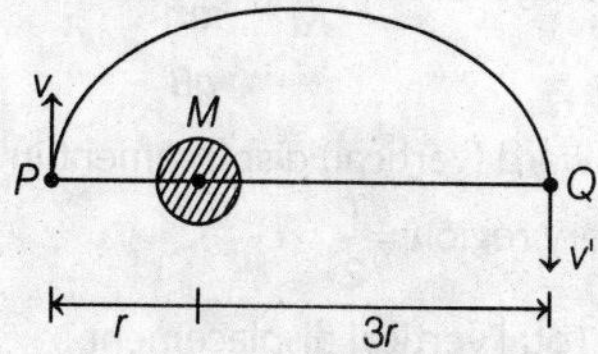

By conservation of angular momentum, between Q and P, we get

$$L_Q = L_P$$

$$\Rightarrow mv'(3r) = mvr$$

$$\Rightarrow v' = \frac{v}{3} \quad ...(i)$$

By conservation of energy, between Q and P, we get

Total energy at Q = Total energy at P

$$\Rightarrow \frac{1}{2}mv'^2 - \frac{GMm}{3r} = \frac{1}{2}mv^2 - \frac{GMm}{r}$$

$$\Rightarrow \frac{1}{2}m(v)^2 - \frac{1}{2}m\left(\frac{v}{3}\right)^2 = \frac{GMm}{r} - \frac{GMm}{3r}$$

$$\Rightarrow v = \sqrt{\frac{3GM}{2r}}$$

So, the speed has to be increased by,

$$\Delta v = \sqrt{\frac{3GM}{2r}} - \sqrt{\frac{GM}{r}} \quad \left(\because \text{At } P,\ v = \sqrt{\frac{GM}{r}}\right)$$

$$= \left(\sqrt{\frac{3}{2}} - 1\right)\sqrt{\frac{GM}{r}}$$

4. Let flux through different surfaces be shown in the figure.

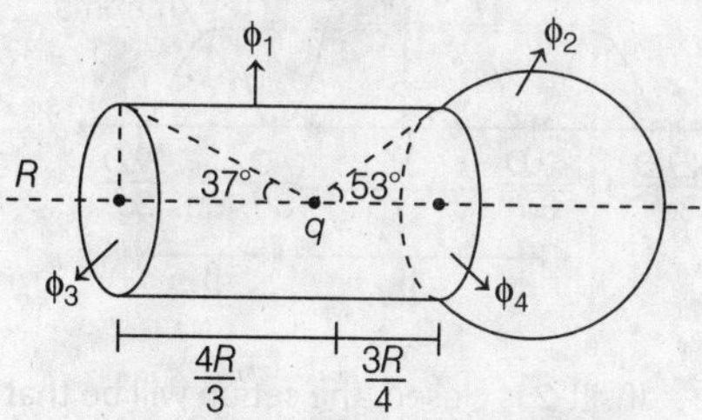

As flux due to a point charge on axis of a disc is $\frac{q}{2\varepsilon_0}(1 - \cos\theta)$

Flux through left flat surface of cylinder,

$$\phi_3 = \frac{q}{2\varepsilon_0}(1 - \cos 37°)$$

$$= \frac{q}{2\varepsilon_0}\left(1 - \frac{4}{5}\right) = \frac{q}{10\varepsilon_0} \quad ...(i)$$

Flux through right surface of cylinder is

$$\phi_4 = \frac{q}{2\varepsilon_0}(1 - \cos 53°)$$

$$= \frac{q}{2\varepsilon_0}\left(1 - \frac{3}{5}\right) = \frac{2q}{10\varepsilon_0} \quad ...(ii)$$

By Gauss law for cylinder,

$$\phi = \phi_1 + \phi_4 + \phi_3 = \frac{q}{\varepsilon_0}$$

$$\Rightarrow \phi_1 = \frac{7q}{10\varepsilon_0} \quad ...(iii)$$

Also by Gauss law for spherical surfaces

$$\phi_4 + \phi_2 = \frac{q_{\text{inside}}}{\varepsilon_0} \Rightarrow \phi_4 + \phi_2 = 0$$

(as charge inside the surface is zero)

$$\Rightarrow |\phi_2| = |\phi_4| = \frac{2q}{10\varepsilon_0} \quad ...(iv)$$

[using Eq. (ii)]

From Eqs. (iii) and (iv), we get

$$\phi_1 - \phi_2 = \frac{7q}{10\varepsilon_0} - \frac{2q}{10\varepsilon_0} = \frac{q}{2\varepsilon_0}$$

5. and **6.** 2.40 and 8.38

Free body diagram of various components of the system is as shown.

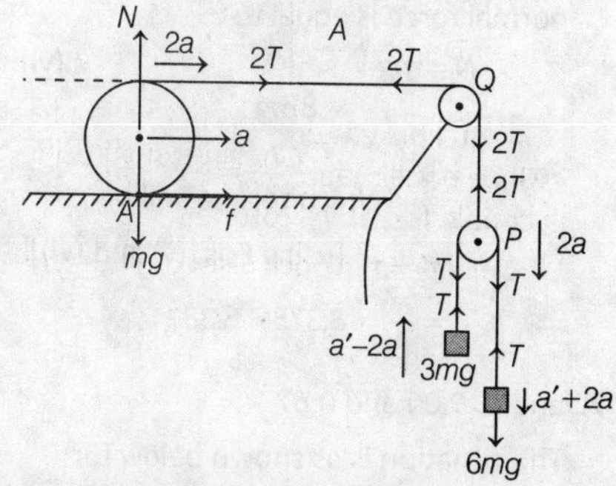

As the cylinder is rolling without slipping, point A is instantly at rest and can be considered instantaneous axis of rotation. Also, acceleration of top points of the cylinder is double that of CM (say a) in pure rolling as shown. So acceleration of pulley, P will also be $2a$. Let a' be relative acceleration of the blocks w.r.t. pulley P.

Moment of inertia of the cylinder about axis through A will be

$I = I_{CM} + md^2$ (parallel axes theorem)

$$= \frac{mR^2}{2} + mR^2 \Rightarrow I = \frac{3}{2}mR^2$$

So, using $\tau = I\alpha$, about A, we get

$$2T(2R) = \frac{3}{2}mR^2\left(\frac{a}{R}\right)$$

(as $\alpha = \frac{a}{R}$ in case of pure rolling on fixed surface)

$$\Rightarrow T = \frac{3}{8}ma \quad ...(i)$$

For $3m$, using $F_{\text{net}} = ma$, we get

$$T - 3mg = 3m(a' - 2a) \quad ...(ii)$$

For $6m$, using $F_{\text{net}} = ma$, we get

$$6mg - T = 6m(a' + 2a) \quad ...(iii)$$

Solving Eqs. (i), (ii) and (iii), we get,

$$T = \frac{12mg}{67} \quad ...(iv)$$

$\therefore$ Tension in thread A

$$=2T=\frac{24mg}{67}=\frac{24\times0.67\times10}{67}=2.40\text{ N}$$

For cylinder, using $F_{NET}=ma$, we get

$$2T+f=ma \Rightarrow f=ma-2T$$

$$=m\left(\frac{8T}{3m}\right)-2T \quad \text{[using Eqs. (i)]}$$

$$=\frac{2T}{3}=\frac{2}{3}\left(\frac{12mg}{67}\right)$$

[using Eqs. (iv)]

$$\Rightarrow f=\frac{8mg}{67} \quad \text{...(v)}$$

For vertical equilibrium of cylinder, normal force is equal to

$$N=mg \quad \text{...(vi)}$$

$$\text{So } \mu_{min}=\mu=\frac{f}{N}=\frac{\frac{8mg}{67}}{mg}=\frac{8}{67}$$

[using Eqs. (v) and (vi)]

$$\Rightarrow \mu^{-1}=\frac{67}{8}=8.375\approx8.38$$

7. and **8.** 9.00 and 0.67

The situation is as shown below for different waves reaching at point P.

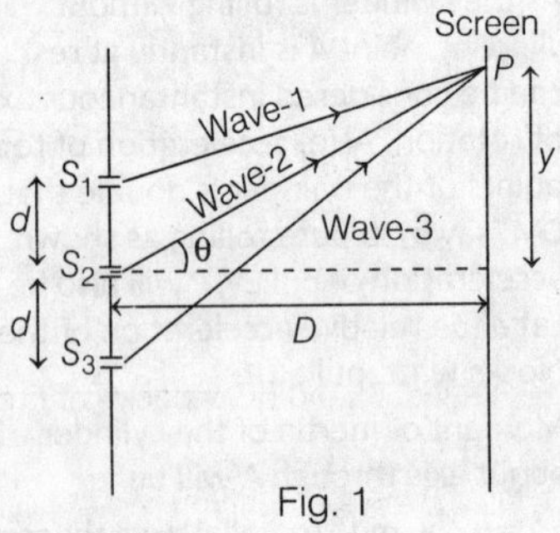

Fig. 1

Path difference between any two adjacent waves reaching a general point P having angular position θ is

$$\Delta x=d\sin\theta\approx\frac{dy}{D}$$

Corresponding phase difference between any two adjacent waves will be

$$\phi=\frac{2\pi}{\lambda}\Delta x=\frac{2\pi}{\lambda}\cdot\frac{dy}{D} \quad \text{...(i)}$$

Thus, phasor diagram for waves is as shown

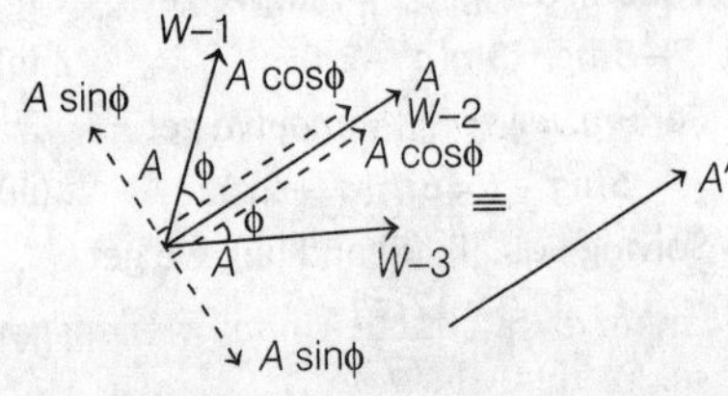

Fig. 2

From figure-2, it can be seen that A sin ϕ components will cancel and resultant will be

$$A'=A\cos\phi+A+A\cos\phi$$

$$A'=A(1+2\cos\phi)$$

As intensity is proportional to square of amplitude. So the resultant intensity is

$$I=kA'^2$$

$$\Rightarrow I=kA^2(1+2\cos\phi)^2$$

$$=kA^2\left[1+2\cos\left(\frac{2\pi\,dy}{\lambda D}\right)\right]^2$$

[Using Eq. (i)]

$$=I_0\left[1+2\cos\left(\frac{2\pi\,dy}{\lambda D}\right)\right]^2$$

$$\Rightarrow I_{max}=9I_0 \text{ and } I_{min}=I_0$$

$$r=\frac{9I_0}{I_0}=9.00$$

The graph of I *versus* y is as shown.

$$\text{Also, } \beta_1-\beta_2=\frac{2\lambda D}{3d}-\frac{\lambda D}{3d}=\frac{\lambda D}{3d} \quad \text{...(ii)}$$

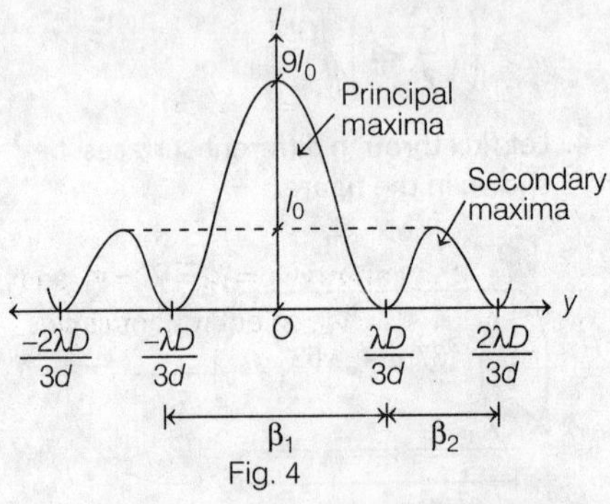

Fig. 4

If slit-2 is closed, the set up will be that of YDSE with slit separation $2d$. So, fringe width will be $\beta_3=\frac{\lambda D}{2d}$ ...(iii)

Dividing Eq. (ii) by Eq. (iii), we get

$$n=\frac{\beta_1-\beta_2}{\beta_3}=\frac{2}{3}=0.67$$

9. and **10.** 5.59 and 31.00

Different X-rays/wavelengths emitted correspond to de-excitation as shown in energy level diagram.

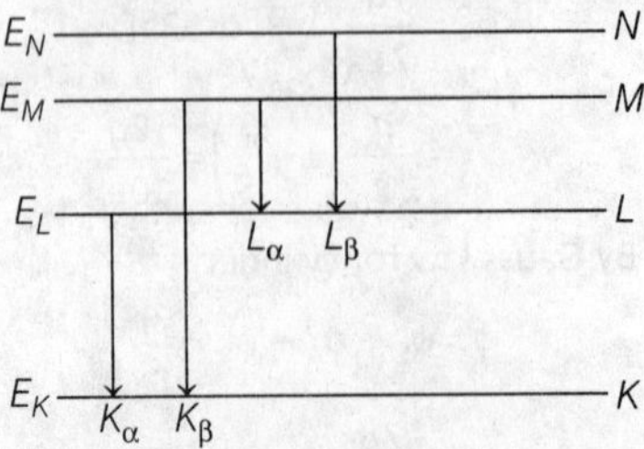

From the diagram,

$$E_{K_\beta}=E_{K_\alpha}+E_{L_\alpha}$$

$$\Rightarrow E_{L_\alpha}=E_{K_\beta}-E_{K_\alpha}$$

$$\Rightarrow \frac{hc}{\lambda_3}=\frac{hc}{\lambda_1}-\frac{hc}{\lambda_2}$$

$$\Rightarrow \lambda_3=\frac{\lambda_1\lambda_2}{\lambda_2-\lambda_1}=\frac{0.63\times0.71}{0.71-0.63}$$

$$=5.59\text{ Å}$$

Accelerating voltage V across coolidge tube is related to cut-off wavelength λ_c by the relation

$$V=\frac{hc}{e\lambda_c}=\frac{12400\text{ eV - Å}}{e\times0.4\text{Å}}$$

$$=31\text{ kV}$$

11. As partition is fixed its displacement is zero, so no work will be done. As the partition is conducting, heat will flow from right to left till temperatures become equal. Let final temperature be T. By conservation of internal energy for the system

$$\frac{f}{2}\cdot2n\cdot RT=\frac{f}{2}nRT_0+\frac{f}{2}nR(2T_0)$$

$$\Rightarrow T=\frac{3T_0}{2}$$

By ideal gas equation,

$$p=\frac{nRT}{V}$$

$$\Rightarrow p\propto T \quad \text{(as } V \text{ is fixed)}$$

When temperature becomes $\frac{3}{2}$ times, p will also become $\frac{3}{2}$ times.

Also, heat flown from right to left is equal to decrease in internal energy

$$=\left|\frac{f}{2}\Delta pV\right|=\frac{3}{2}\left(2p_0V_0-\frac{3p_0}{2}V_0\right)$$

$$=\frac{3}{4}p_0V_0$$

12. The motion of particle in given magnetic field is given as

Region-1 Anticlockwise angular displacement of 60°.

Region-2 Clockwise 60°

Region-3 Anticlockwise 60°

$$\Rightarrow \text{Time of motion}=\frac{T}{6}+\frac{T}{6}+\frac{T}{6}=\frac{T}{2}$$

$$=\frac{2\pi m}{2qB}=\frac{\pi m}{qB}$$

$$\text{Average force}=\frac{\Delta p}{\Delta t}=\frac{mv}{\frac{\pi m}{qB}}=\frac{qvB}{\pi}$$

Upward (vertical) displacement in every region $=\frac{r}{2}$

$\Rightarrow$ Total vertical displacement

$$=\frac{3r}{2}=\frac{3mv}{2qB}$$

13. Using homogeneity principle,

$$[a]=[b][c]$$

$$\Rightarrow \quad [b]=\left[\frac{a}{c}\right]=\left[\frac{LT^{-2}}{LT^{-1}}\right]=[T^{-1}]$$

$$[a]=[d\,e^{fgh}]=[d]$$

$$\Rightarrow \quad [d]=[LT^{-2}]$$

$$\therefore \quad \left[\frac{d}{b}\right]=\left[\frac{LT^{-2}}{T^{-1}}\right]=LT^{-1}$$

As, exponents are dimensionless, so $[fgh]=[M^0L^0T^0]$

$$\Rightarrow \quad [f]=\frac{1}{[g][h]}=\frac{1}{[LT^{-2}][L]}[L^{-2}T^2]$$

$$\left[\frac{k}{l\sin(mn)}\right]=[a]$$

$$\Rightarrow \quad [k]=[l][a]=[L][LT^{-2}]=[L^2T^{-2}]$$

$$\therefore [k][f]=[L^0T^0]$$

As, $[m][n]=[M^0L^0T^0]$

$$\Rightarrow \quad [n]=\frac{1}{[m]}=\frac{1}{[M]}=[M^{-1}]$$

Since, given relation contains unit vectors, so, this can't be established by dimensional analysis.

14. Thermal expansion is photographic in nature.

So, when temperature of ring increases, the area increases in outward direction without changing the gap angle. i.e. t, R and d increase but θ remains constant.

15. Contact force by water on table

$$=\rho gh\times A$$

$$=\rho g\times[3 \text{ times volume of cone}]$$

$$=3mg$$

$\therefore$Contact force by cone on water

$$=2mg, \text{ downwards}$$

$\Rightarrow \quad M(\text{min})=2mg$

Also, normal force on cone by table

$$=3mg-2mg=mg$$

16. Given, $a_0=5\text{ m/s}^2$, $h_0=20$ m

$$v=0 \text{ at } 2h_0$$

$$\therefore \quad h_{max}=2h_0$$

$$=2\times 20=40 \text{ m}$$

As acceleration is proportional to position w.r.t. position of zero acceleration, motion is SHM.

For bottomost position, $a_0=\omega^2 h_0$

$$\Rightarrow \quad \omega=\sqrt{\frac{a_0}{h_0}}=\sqrt{\frac{5}{20}}=\frac{1}{2}$$

$$\Rightarrow \quad T=\frac{2\pi}{\omega}=4\pi \text{ s}$$

$\Rightarrow$Time of motion up to height 10 m

$$=\frac{T}{6}=\frac{2\pi}{3}$$

Also, $v=\omega\sqrt{A^2-x^2}$

$$=\frac{1}{2}\sqrt{20^2-10^2}=5\sqrt{3}\text{ m/s}$$

17. In thermal equilibrium

$$\sigma(4\pi R^2)T^4\frac{\pi R_p^2}{4\pi r^2}=\sigma(4\pi R_p^2)t^4$$

$$\Rightarrow \left(\frac{t}{T}\right)^2=\frac{R}{2r}$$

$$\therefore \quad x+y=2+2=4$$

18. For such a radioactive decay,

$$N=\frac{1}{\lambda}[k-(k-\lambda N_0)e^{-\lambda t}]$$

$$=\frac{1}{\lambda}\left[7\lambda N_0-6\lambda N_0\left(\frac{1}{2}\right)\right]=4N_0$$

$$\therefore \quad x=4$$

19. $\phi=\int_0^l xt\cdot l\,dx+\int_0^l yt\cdot l\,dy=l^3t$

$$i=\frac{\varepsilon}{r}=\frac{d\phi/dt}{r}=\frac{l^3}{r}=3\text{ A}$$

(Paper 2)

1. Due to symmetry $V_A=V_B=V_C=V_D$ and $V_E=V_F=V_G=V_H$, so equivalent circuit can be drawn as

$\frac{R}{4}$ A, B, C, D $\frac{R}{8}$ E, F, G, H

O (Potential $=V$) $I=4I_1$ $I=8I_3$ $I=I_4$

Here $\frac{R}{4}$ is equivalent of four resistors between O and (A, B, C, D).

While $\frac{R}{8}$ is equivalent of eight resistors between O and (E, F, G, H)

Equivalent resistance of the circuit is

$$R_{eq}=\frac{R}{4}+\frac{R}{8}=\frac{3R}{8}$$

So, current flowing in the equivalent circuit

$$I=\frac{V-0}{R_{eq}}=\frac{8V}{3R}$$

From the equivalent circuit,

$$I=4I_1=8I_3=I_4$$

$$\Rightarrow \quad I_1=\frac{I}{4}=\frac{2V}{3R}$$

and $\quad I_3=\frac{I}{8}=\frac{V}{3R}$

and $\quad I_4=I=\frac{8V}{3R}$

Current in plane wires AB, BC, CD, DA is zero by symmetry. i.e. $I_2=0$.

2. **v** of butterfly (object) w.r.t mirror

$$=\mathbf{v}_B-\mathbf{v}_M=6\hat{\mathbf{j}}-(-3\hat{\mathbf{i}})$$

$$=3\hat{\mathbf{i}}+6\hat{\mathbf{j}}$$

$$=(v_0,m)_x\hat{\mathbf{i}}+(v_0,m)_y\hat{\mathbf{j}}$$

Magnification of image of butterfly in mirror, $m=\frac{f}{f-u}=\frac{(-12)}{(-12)-(-6)}=2$

Velocity of image of butterfly w.r.t mirror in x-direction, is given by

$$(v_{i,m})_x=-m^2(v_{0,m})_x$$

$$\Rightarrow (v_{i,m})_x=-2^2(3)=-12\text{ m/s}$$

$$\Rightarrow v_{i,x}-v_{m,x}=-12\text{ m/s}$$

$$\Rightarrow \quad v_{i,x}=-12+v_{m,x}=-12+(-3)$$

$$\Rightarrow \quad v_{i,x}=-15\text{ m/s} \qquad \text{...(i)}$$

For y-direction,

$$h_i=mh_0=\frac{f}{f-u}h_0$$

Differentiating w.r.t. time, we get

$$\frac{dh_i}{dt}=\frac{f}{(f-u)^2}\cdot\frac{du}{dt}h_0+\frac{mdh_0}{dt}$$

$$(v_{i,m})_y=\frac{f}{(f-u)^2}.(v_{0,m})_x h_0+m(v_{0,m})_y$$

$$=\frac{(-12)\times 3}{(-12-(-6))^2}+2\times 6=11\text{ m/s}$$

$$\Rightarrow \quad v_{i,y}=11\text{ m/s} \qquad \text{...(ii)}$$

From Eqs. (i) and (ii), velocity of image in mirror is

$$\mathbf{v}=-15\hat{\mathbf{i}}+11\hat{\mathbf{j}}\text{ m/s} \qquad \text{...(iii)}$$

$\Rightarrow$Relative image velocity w.r.t. butterfly $=\mathbf{v}-\mathbf{v}_B=(-15\hat{\mathbf{i}}+11\hat{\mathbf{j}})-6\hat{\mathbf{j}}$

$$=-15\hat{\mathbf{i}}+5\hat{\mathbf{j}}$$

Thus, relative velocity makes angle $\tan^{-1}\frac{1}{3}$ with vertical as shown in figure

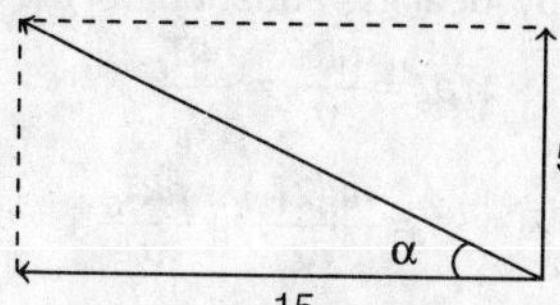

Also, for refraction at plane surface

$$v_{image}=\frac{v_{object}\times n_r}{n_i}.$$

here, n_i = Refractive index of medium of incidence

n_r = refractive index of medium of refraction

On refraction from water surface

$$v_{\text{image}}\text{ (w.r.t. interface)} = \frac{6\times\frac{4}{3}}{1} = 8 \text{ m/s}$$

(in y-direction)

velocity of image of butterfly w.r.t. fish is

$$\mathbf{v}_{B,F} = \mathbf{v}_B - \mathbf{v}_F$$
$$= 8\hat{\mathbf{j}} - (7.5\hat{\mathbf{i}} + 2.5\hat{\mathbf{j}})$$
$$= -7.5\hat{\mathbf{i}} + 5.5\hat{\mathbf{j}} = \frac{-15\hat{\mathbf{i}} + 11\hat{\mathbf{j}}}{2}$$

This is parallel to butterfly's image velocity in mirror.

3. Apparent frequency of sound coming from top side,

$$f_1 = f\left(\frac{v + v/20}{v}\right) = \frac{21f}{20} \quad \text{...(i)}$$

Apparent frequency of sound coming from lower side,

$$f_2 = f\left(\frac{v - \frac{v}{20}}{v}\right) = \frac{19f}{20} \quad \text{... (ii)}$$

$\therefore \quad f_1 : f_2 = 21 : 19$

Beat frequency $= f_1 - f_2 = \frac{f}{10} = 0.1f$

If the detector stops, sounds coming from the two sides will be coherent and as path difference between two sounds is zero, the detector will detect maxima of sound.

4. As process AB is straight line passing through origin

$\Rightarrow \quad T \propto V$

Therefore, while moving from A to B

$$\frac{T_B}{T_A} = \frac{V_B}{V_A} \Rightarrow \frac{KT_0}{T_0} = \frac{2V_0}{V_0}$$

$\Rightarrow \quad K = 2$

$\Rightarrow \quad T_B = 2T_0 = 2T_A$

$\Rightarrow \quad U_B = 2U_A$ [option (d) is correct]

So, by ideal gas equation, for B

$$p_B = \frac{nRT}{V} = \frac{nRT_B}{V_B}$$
$$= \frac{nR(2T_0)}{2V_0} = \frac{nRT_0}{V_0}$$

$\Rightarrow \quad p_B = p_A$ [option (a) is correct]

As BC is an isothermal process,

$$|Q_{BC}| = \left|nRT\ln\frac{V_{\text{final}}}{V_{\text{initial}}}\right|$$
$$= nR(2T_0)\ln\left(\frac{4V_0}{2V_0}\right) = 2nRT_0\ln 2$$

$\Rightarrow \quad |Q_{BC}| = nRT_0 \ln 4$

Also, as DA is also isothermal,

$$|Q_{DA}| = \left|nRT\ln\frac{V_{\text{final}}}{V_{\text{initial}}}\right|$$
$$= \left|nRT_0\ln\frac{V_0}{4V_0}\right|$$

$\Rightarrow |Q_{DA}| = nRT_0 \ln 4 = |Q_{BC}|$

[option (b) is correct]

In process AB, $T \propto V$. Therefore AB is isobaric process. In process BC temperature is constant, so, $p \propto \frac{1}{V}$ so, as the volume increases, the pressure decreases in BC. In process CD, volume is constant, so $p \propto T$.

So, as temperature decreases, pressure decreases. In process DA, temperature is constant. So, as volume decreases, pressure increases. Therefore, pressure is maximum at A while minimum at D,

$$\text{So, } \frac{p_{\max}}{p_{\min}} = \frac{p_A}{p_D} = \frac{\frac{nRT_0}{V_0}}{\frac{nRT_0}{4V_0}} = 4$$

$\Rightarrow p_{\max} = 4p_{\min}$ [option (c) is correct]

5. As per property of electrostatics, charges are induced such that net field inside conductor is zero. Therefore, at C,

$$E_{\text{Net}} = 0$$
$$\Rightarrow \mathbf{E}_{\text{Ring}} + \mathbf{E}_{\text{Induced}} = 0$$
$$\Rightarrow \quad \mathbf{E}_{\text{Induced}} = -\mathbf{E}_{\text{Ring}}$$
$$= -\frac{kQx}{(r^2 + x^2)^{3/2}}(-\hat{\mathbf{j}})$$

and For C, $x = 3R$

$$\Rightarrow \mathbf{E}_{\text{Induced}} = \frac{kQ(3R)}{\{(4R)^2 + (3R)^2\}^{\frac{3}{2}}}\hat{\mathbf{j}}$$
$$= \frac{3kQ}{125R^2}\hat{\mathbf{j}}$$

So, option (a) is incorrect.

Though charge will be locally induced on the sphere's surface but net charge on it will be q equal to zero.

Potential at centre of sphere C due to q will therefore be

$$V_1 = \frac{kq}{r'} = 0 \quad \text{...(i)}$$

Here r' = radius of sphere

Potential at C due to ring will be

$$V_2 = \frac{kQ}{\sqrt{r^2 + x^2}}$$
$$= \frac{kQ}{\sqrt{(4R)^2 + (3R)^2}} = \frac{kQ}{5R} \quad \text{...(ii)}$$

Therefore, net potential at C is

$$V = V_1 + V_2 = 0 + \frac{kQ}{5R} = \frac{kQ}{5R} \quad \text{...(iii)}$$

[using Eqs. (i) and (ii)]

As metal body is equipotential in electrostatic condition, potential at O' will also be the same. So option (b) is correct.

Potential at O due to charge on ring

$$V_3 = \frac{kQ}{\sqrt{r^2 + x^2}} = \frac{kQ}{r} = \frac{kQ}{4R} \quad \text{....(iv)}$$

Therefore, potential at O due to induced charge can be obtained by subtracting V_3 from V.

Thus, potential at O due to induced charge is

$$V_4 = V - V_3 = \frac{kQ}{5R} - \frac{kQ}{4R} = \frac{-kQ}{20R}$$

[using Eqs. (iii) and (iv)]

So, option (c) is correct.

On grounding the sphere, charge (suppose q) flows from or into ground, so that finally potential of the sphere is zero. Therefore, at C,

$$V_{\text{Ring}} + V_{\text{Sphere}} = 0$$
$$\Rightarrow \quad \frac{kQ}{5R} + \frac{kq}{3R} = 0$$
$$\Rightarrow \quad q = -\frac{3Q}{5} = n(-e)$$
$$\Rightarrow \quad n = \frac{3Q}{5e}$$

6. Magnetic field inside a solid cylinder of current is given by,

$$\mathbf{B} = \frac{\mu_0 \mathbf{J} \times \mathbf{r}}{2}$$

Here $\mathbf{r}$ is position vector w.r.t. axis. So magnetic field at a point P inside cavity, as shown in Fig. 1, is

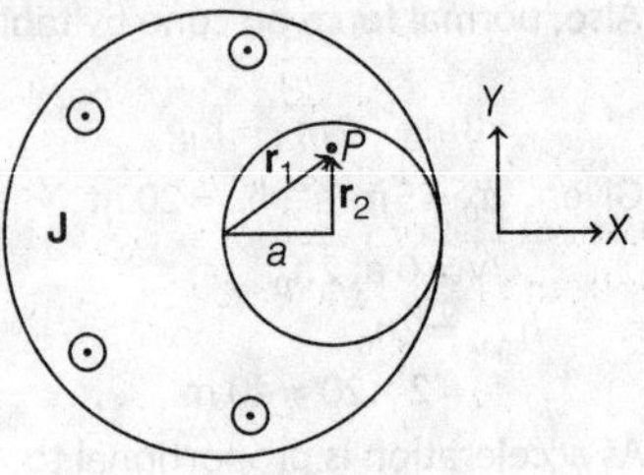

Fig.1

$$\mathbf{B} = \mathbf{B}_{\substack{\text{complete}\\\text{cylinder}}} - \mathbf{B}_{\text{cavity}}$$
$$= \frac{\mu_0 \mathbf{J} \times (\mathbf{r}_1 - \mathbf{r}_2)}{2}$$
$$\Rightarrow \quad \mathbf{B} = \frac{\mu_0 \mathbf{J} \times \mathbf{a}}{2} = \frac{\mu_0 j\hat{\mathbf{k}} \times \frac{R}{2}\hat{\mathbf{i}}}{2}$$

$$\Rightarrow \quad \mathbf{B} = \frac{\mu_0 JR}{4}\hat{\mathbf{j}} \quad ...(i)$$

which is a constant (or uniform) field in y-direction.

So, as $+q$ is projected in x-direction or perpendicular to the field, it will follow circular path in XZ-plane as shown in Fig. 2 while $-q$ experiences no magnetic force (as $F_{magnetic} = qvB\sin 0° = 0$) and moves on straight path in y-direction colliding with the cavity's surface as shown in Fig. 2.

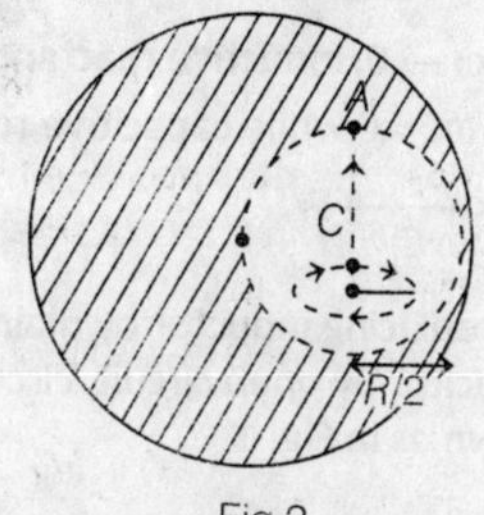

Fig.2

As radius of path of charged particle moving in transverse uniform field is given by

$$r = \frac{mv}{qB}$$

Therefore, radius of path of $+q$ will be

$$r = \frac{mv}{q\dfrac{\mu_0 JR}{4}} = \frac{4mv}{q\mu_0 JR}$$

From the figure-2, for no collision with cylinder, $r < R/2$

$$\Rightarrow \quad \frac{4mv}{q\mu_0 JR} < \frac{R}{2}$$

$$\Rightarrow \quad R > \sqrt{\frac{8mv}{q\mu_0 J}}$$

Also, $-q$ will collide with cylinder at point A. So time of motion of $-q$ from C to A is

$$t_1 = \frac{\text{Distance}}{\text{Speed}} = \frac{R/2}{v} = \frac{R}{2v}$$

As collision is elastic, it bounces without loss of speed and moves to bottom taking time equal to

$$t_2 = \frac{R}{v}$$

It collides again and returns to C taking time equal to $t_3 = \dfrac{R}{2v}$

So, total time of motion

$$= t_1 + t_2 + t_3 = \frac{2R}{v}$$

Now, the motion repeats taking same time. So, time period of the motion is $\dfrac{2R}{v}$.

7. and **8.** 0.16 and 66.67

Due to sudden switching OFF of magnetic field, an electric field E is induced in the region as shown in Fig.1 given by

$$E = \frac{r}{2}\frac{dB}{dt} = \frac{l}{4}\cdot\frac{dB}{dt} \quad ...(i)$$

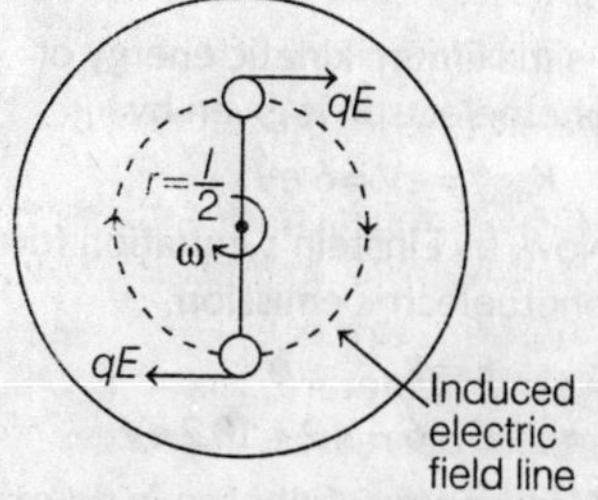

Fig.1

Due to this field, balls A and B experience impulsive torque given by

$$\tau = qEl \quad ...(ii)$$

And due to this impulsive torque, the system acquires angular speed ω, which can be found by equating angular impulse of τ to change in angular momentum. That is

$$\int \tau\, dt = I\omega \quad ...(iii)$$

As moment of inertia of a particle distant r from axis is mr^2. So, I of system will be

$$I = mr^2 + mr^2$$

$$\Rightarrow \quad I = 2mr^2 = 2m\left(\frac{l}{2}\right)^2 = \frac{ml^2}{2} \quad ... (iv)$$

Putting expressions obtained in Eqs. (i), (ii) and (iv) in Eq. (iii), we get

$$\int q\cdot\frac{l}{4}\frac{dB}{dt}\cdot l\, dt = \frac{ml^2}{2}\omega$$

$$\Rightarrow \quad \frac{qB_0 l^2}{4} = \frac{ml^2\omega}{2}$$

$$\Rightarrow \quad \omega = \frac{qB_0}{2m} = \frac{2\times10^{-6}\times10}{2\times1\times10^{-6}}$$

$$\Rightarrow \quad \omega = 10 \text{ rad/s} \quad ...(v)$$

For A to collide with C, the rod has to turn by θ equal to $\dfrac{\pi}{2}$ rad. So, time for turning will be

$$t = \frac{\theta}{\omega} = \frac{\pi}{2\times1\times10} = 0.16 \text{ s} \quad ...(vi)$$

Let angular velocity of system equal to ω' just after collision as shown in Fig.2.

By conservation of angular momentum about O,

$$L_{after} = L_{before}$$

$$\Rightarrow \quad I'\omega' = I\omega$$

$$\Rightarrow \quad 3mr^2\omega' = 2mr^2\omega$$

$$\Rightarrow \quad \omega' = \frac{2}{3}\omega \quad ...(vii)$$

Fig.2

Distance of CM of the system is in inverse ratio of masses i.e. 2 : 1 from m and $2m$ respectively, say $2x$ and x.

So, $\quad 2x + x = l \Rightarrow x = \dfrac{l}{3}$

$\therefore$ Distance of CM from O will be

$$R = \frac{l}{2} - x = \frac{l}{2} - \frac{l}{3} = \frac{l}{6} \quad ...(viii)$$

As CM moves on circle of radius R, acceleration of CM will therefore be

$$a = \omega'^2 R = \left(\frac{2}{3}\omega\right)^2\left(\frac{l}{6}\right) = \frac{2\omega^2 l}{27} \quad ...(ix)$$

[using Eqs. (vii) and (viii)]

Therefore, reaction force on the hinge will be equal to

$$R = \text{Mass} \times \text{acceleration}$$

$$= 3m \times \frac{2\omega^2 l}{27} \text{ [using Eq. (ix)]}$$

$$= \frac{2m\omega^2 l}{9}$$

$$= \frac{2\times1\times10^{-6}\times10^2\times3}{9}$$

$$= 66.67\ \mu\text{N}$$

9. and **10.** 3.75 and 1.00

For refraction by lens

$$\frac{1}{v} - \frac{1}{u} = \frac{1}{f} \Rightarrow \frac{1}{v} - \frac{1}{-30} = \frac{1}{10}$$

$$\Rightarrow \quad v = 15 \text{ cm}$$

Thus, image by lens will be formed at O', a distance 15 cm towards right of the lens as shown in figure

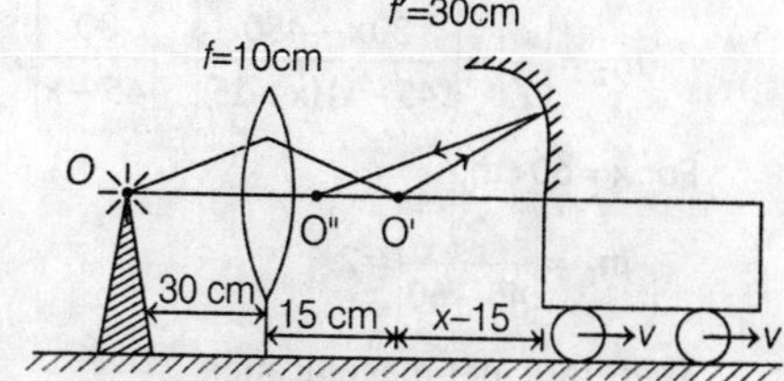

O' will act as object for reflection at mirror. Therefore distant of object O' from mirror will be, as shown in the figure, equal to

$$u = -(x - 15)$$

For reflection of mirror,

$$\frac{1}{v'} + \frac{1}{u'} = \frac{1}{f'}$$

$$\Rightarrow \frac{1}{v'} + \frac{1}{-(x-15)} = \frac{1}{-30}$$

$$\Rightarrow \quad v' = \frac{30x - 450}{45 - x}$$

Differentiating w.r.t. time t, we get

$$\frac{dv'}{dt} = \frac{900}{(45-x)^2} \cdot \frac{dx}{dt}$$

As v' is image distance w.r.t. mirror, $\frac{dv'}{dt}$ will be image velocity w.r.t. mirror ($v_{i,m}$). Also as x is position of cart w.r.t. lens $\frac{dx}{dt}$ is velocity of cart w.r.t. lens, which will be double the velocity of centre of rollers which are in pure rolling. Top point moves with double the velocity of centre. Therefore,

$$v_{i,m} = \frac{900}{(45-x)^2} \cdot 2\, v_{\text{roller}}$$

$$= \frac{900}{(45-x)^2} \cdot 2 \cdot \frac{(45-x)^2}{600}$$

$$= 3 \text{ cm/s}$$

$$\Rightarrow v_i - v_m = 3 \text{ cm/s}$$

$$\Rightarrow \quad v_i = 3 + v_m = 3 + 2 \cdot v_{\text{roller}}$$

$$= 3 + 2 \cdot \frac{(45-x)^2}{600}$$

$$= 3 + \frac{(45-x)^2}{300}$$

For $x = 60$ cm,

$$v_i = 3 + \frac{(45-60)^2}{300}$$

$$= 3.75 \text{ cm/s}$$

Magnification due to lens,

$$m_1 = \left|\frac{v}{u}\right| = \left|\frac{15}{-30}\right| = \frac{1}{2}$$

Magnification due to mirror,

$$m_2 = \left|\frac{v'}{u'}\right| = \left|\frac{30x - 450}{(45-x)(x-15)}\right| = \left|\frac{30}{45-x}\right|$$

For $x = 60$ cm,

$$m_2 = \left|\frac{30}{45-60}\right| = 2$$

Therefore, net magnification

$$m = m_1 \times m_2 = \frac{1}{2} \times 2 = 1$$

11. and **12.** 1.00 and 6.66

As stopping potential is given to be corresponding to electron having de-Broglie wavelength of $\lambda = 5$ Å. Therefore, stopping potential (V) can be calculated by relation between λ and V, which is

$$\lambda \text{(in Å)} = \sqrt{\frac{150}{V\text{(in volt)}}}$$

$$\Rightarrow \quad V = \frac{150}{\lambda^2} = \frac{150}{25} = 6 \text{ V}$$

As maximum kinetic energy of photoelectron is given by

$$K_{\max} = eV = 6 \text{ eV} \quad \text{... (i)}$$

Now, by Einstein's equation for photoelectric emission,

$$E = K_{\max} + \phi$$

$$\Rightarrow \quad E = 6 + 4.2 = 10.2 \text{ eV} \quad \text{...(ii)}$$

Also, energy of photon in de-excitation from n_2th level to n_1th level in hydrogen like atom is given by

$$E = 13.6Z^2 \left(\frac{1}{n_1^2} - \frac{1}{n_2^2}\right)$$

$$\Rightarrow 10.2 = 13.6Z^2 \left(\frac{1}{n^2} - \frac{1}{(n+2)^2}\right)$$

[using Eq. (ii)]

As the above equation is satisfied only for $n = 2$ and $Z = 2$, therefore, $\frac{Z}{n} = 1$

Now, de-Broglie wavelength of electron in Nth orbit is given by

$$\lambda = \frac{2\pi r_0 N}{Z}, \text{ Here } r_0 = \text{Bohr's radius}$$

$$\Rightarrow \quad \lambda = \frac{2(3.14)(0.53)(4)}{2}$$

$$= 6.66 \text{ Å}$$

13. and **14.** As angular velocity of the disc is constant net torque will be zero, i.e.

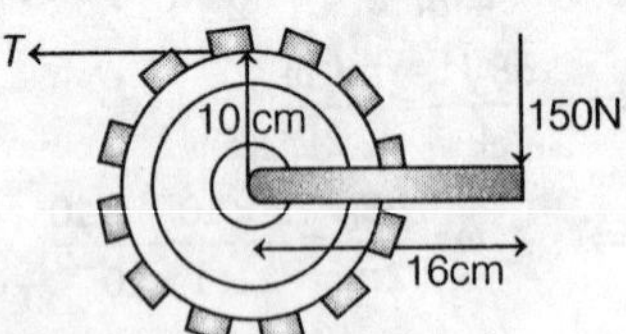

$$\Rightarrow \quad \Sigma\tau = 0$$

$$\Rightarrow 150\text{N} \times 16 \text{ cm} = \text{T} \times 10 \text{ cm}$$

$$\Rightarrow \quad T = 240 \text{ N}$$

Power delivered $= \mathbf{F} \cdot \mathbf{v}$

where, $\mathbf{v}$ is velocity of the point of application of the force.

As $v = R\omega = 16 \text{ cm} \times 2\pi.2$

$$= 0.64\,\pi \text{ m/s}$$

$$\Rightarrow P = 150 \times 0.64\pi = 96\pi \text{ W}$$

15. and **16.** For grazing emergence,

$$\mu = \text{cosec}\, C = \text{cosec}\, 60° = \frac{2}{\sqrt{3}}$$

$$\Rightarrow \quad b = \left(\frac{2}{\sqrt{3}} - 1.105\right)(4000 \text{ Å})^2$$

$$= 0.8 \times 10^6 (\text{Å})^2$$

As per Cauchy's relation,

$$\mu = a + \frac{b}{\lambda^2} = 1.105 + \frac{0.8 \times 10^6}{(6000)^2}$$

$$= 1.127$$

17. For $\omega \to 0$, inductive reactance $X_L = \omega L = 0$ while capacitive reactance $X_C = \frac{1}{\omega C} \to \infty$

So, replacing inductor by plain wire and capacitor by open circuit, circuit can be drawn as in Fig. 1

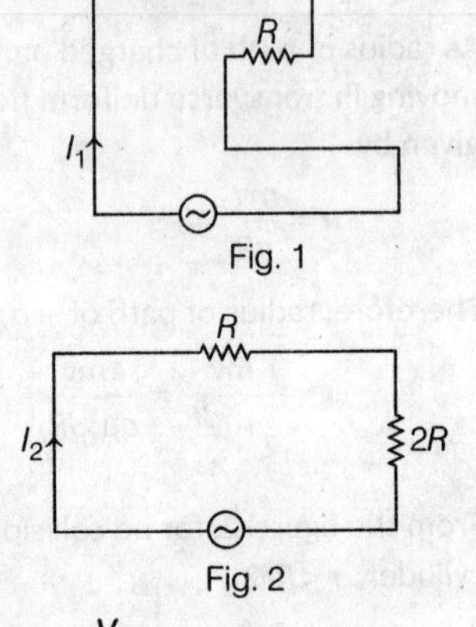

Fig. 1

Fig. 2

So, $I_1 = \frac{V}{R}$ ... (i)

For $\omega \to \infty$, $X_L \to \infty$ while $X_C \to 0$, so circuit can be redrawn as in Fig. 2

So, $I_2 = \frac{V}{3R}$ ... (ii).

Dividing Eq. (i) by Eq. (ii), we get

$$\frac{I_1}{I_2} = 3$$

18. From free body diagram of element shown in figure, tension in string at a distance $x = \frac{l}{2}$ from axis is given by

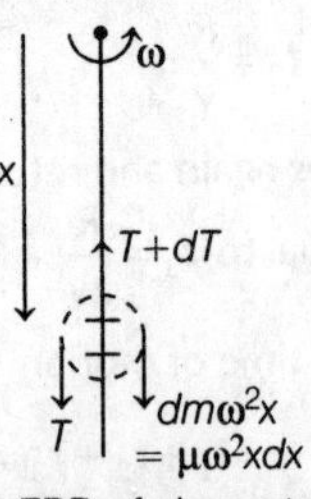

FBD of element

$$T=\int dT=\int_{l/2}^{l}\mu\, dx\,\omega^2 x$$

$$=\frac{\mu\omega^2}{2}\left[l^2-\left(\frac{l}{2}\right)^2\right]=\frac{3\mu\omega^2 l^2}{8}$$

$\Rightarrow$ Speed of string wave

$$=\sqrt{\frac{T}{\mu}}=\sqrt{\frac{3\mu\omega^2 l^2}{8\mu}}=\sqrt{\frac{3}{8}}\,\omega l$$

$$=\sqrt{\frac{3}{8}}\times 10\sqrt{6}\times 1$$

$$=15\text{ m/s}$$

19. The figure can be drawn as

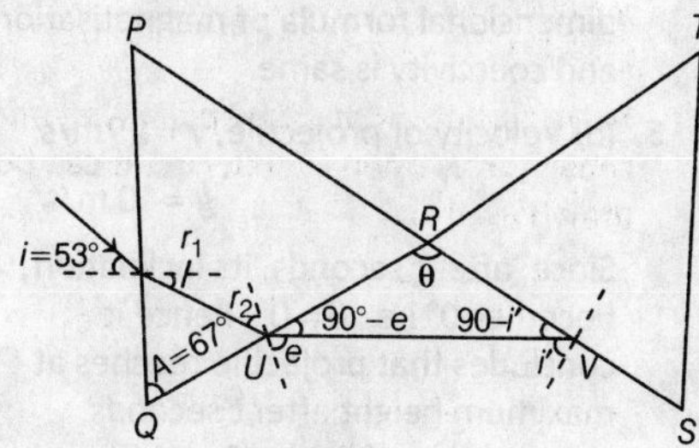

By Snell's law for Prism-1, at surface *PQ*, we get

$$1\cdot\sin 53^\circ=\frac{4}{3}\cdot\sin r_1$$

$$\Rightarrow\quad r_1=37^\circ$$

$$\Rightarrow\quad r_2=A-r_1$$

$$=67^\circ-37^\circ$$

$$=30^\circ$$

By Snell's law, for Prism-1 at surface *QR*, we get

$$\frac{4}{3}\sin 30^\circ=1\cdot\sin e$$

$$\Rightarrow\quad e=\sin^{-1}\frac{2}{3}\qquad\text{...(i)}$$

As it is given that total deviation produced (δ_{total}) is double the deviation by Prism-1 (δ_1), we can write

$$\delta_{total}=2\delta_1\Rightarrow\ \delta_1+\delta_2=2\delta_1$$

$$\Rightarrow\quad \delta_2=\delta_1$$

i.e. deviation by Prism-2 is equal to that by Prism-1. For this to happen angle of incidence i' on Prism-2 should either be i or e.

Also, from ΔRUV,

$$\theta+90^\circ-e+90^\circ-i'=180^\circ$$

$$\Rightarrow\quad \theta=e+i'\qquad\text{...(ii)}$$

Thus, for $i'=i$, we get [using (ii)]

$$\theta=e+i=\theta_1\ \text{(say)}$$

$$\Rightarrow\quad \theta_1=i+e$$

$$=53^\circ+\sin^{-1}\frac{2}{3}\ \text{[using Eq. (i)]}$$

Also, for $i'=e$, we get [using Eq. (ii)]

$$\theta=e+e=2e=\theta_2\quad\text{(say)}$$

$$\Rightarrow\quad \theta_2=2\sin^{-1}\frac{2}{3}\quad\text{[using Eq. (i)]}$$

As $53^\circ=\sin^{-1}\frac{4}{5}>\sin^{-1}\frac{2}{3}$, therefore $\theta_1>\theta_2$.

Therefore, $\theta_1-\frac{\theta_2}{2}=53^\circ$

THE REAL NUTS

Real Nut 1-24 June 2022, Shift-I

1. *(c)* Given, bulk modulus of a liquid,

$$B = 3\times10^{10}\ \text{Nm}^{-2}$$

Percentage decrease in volume of liquid,

$$-\frac{\Delta V}{V} = 2\% = -\frac{2}{100} = -0.02$$

We know that, bulk modulus,

$$B = \frac{\Delta p}{-\frac{\Delta V}{V}}$$

$$\Rightarrow \Delta p = -B\left(\frac{\Delta V}{V}\right)$$

$$= -3\times10^{10}(-0.02)$$

$$= 6\times10^{8}\ \text{N/m}^2$$

2. *(a)* In a uniform magnetic field, moving charged particle experiences magnetic force perpendicular to its direction of motion, which is called Lorentz force and is given as

$$\mathbf{F} = q(\mathbf{v}\times\mathbf{B}) \text{ i.e. } \mathbf{F}\perp\mathbf{v}$$

where, v = velocity, q = charge and B = magnetic field

i.e. force on charged particle always remains perpendicular to its velocity i.e. its displacement.

Hence, work done $= \mathbf{F}\cdot\mathbf{s}$

$$= Fs\cos 90^\circ = 0$$

Hence, according to work-energy theorem,

$$\Delta E_K = W = 0$$

i.e. kinetic energy = constant.

Hence, in uniform magnetic field, speed and energy remains the same for moving charged particle. Therefore, both A and R are correct and R is the correct explanation of A.

3. *(c)* The circuit diagram for the given situation is shown below

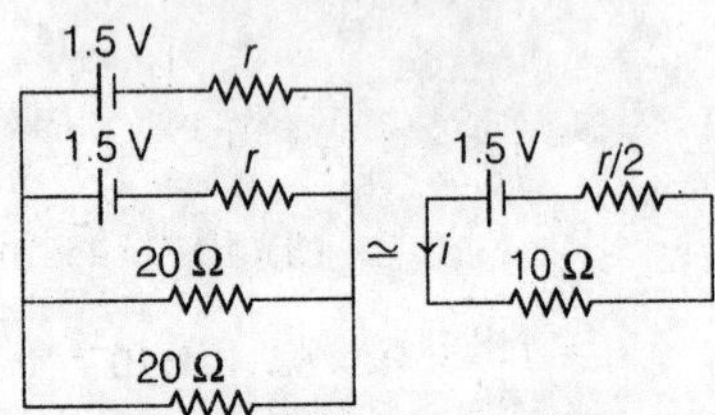

We know that, $V = E - i\dfrac{r}{2}$

$$\Rightarrow 1.2 = 1.5 - i\left(\frac{r}{2}\right)$$

$$\Rightarrow \frac{ir}{2} = 1.5 - 1.2 = 0.3$$

$$\Rightarrow ir = 0.6 \quad \text{... (i)}$$

Again, current flowing through the circuit,

$$i = \frac{\text{total emf}}{\text{total resistance}}$$

$$\Rightarrow \frac{0.6}{r} = \frac{1.5}{10+\frac{r}{2}} \quad \text{[From Eq. (i)]}$$

After solving, we get $r = 5\ \Omega$

4. *(d)* We know that,

$$Q = ms\Delta T$$

$$\Rightarrow s = \frac{Q}{m\cdot\Delta T}$$

∴ where, s = specific heat capacity

$$\therefore [s] = \frac{[Q]}{[m][\Delta T]} = \frac{[\text{ML}^2\text{T}^{-2}]}{[\text{M}]\ [\text{K}]}$$

$$= [\text{L}^2\text{T}^{-2}\text{K}^{-1}]$$

Similarly, latent heat,

$$L = \frac{Q}{M}$$

$$\Rightarrow [L] = \frac{[K]}{[M]} = \frac{\text{ML}^2\text{T}^{-2}]}{[\text{M}]} = [\text{L}^2\text{T}^{-2}]$$

Hence, specific heat capacity and latent heat have different dimensions.

We know, $\dfrac{1}{\lambda} = R\left(\dfrac{1}{n_1^2} - \dfrac{1}{n_2^2}\right)$

Since, n_1 and n_2 are dimensionless, hence dimensions of $\dfrac{1}{\lambda}$ (wave number) and Rydberg constant (R) is same as $[\text{M}^0\text{L}^{-1}\text{T}^0]$.

We know that,

$$\text{Stress} = \frac{\text{Force}}{\text{Area}}$$

$$\therefore [\text{Stress}] = \frac{[\text{Force}]}{[\text{Area}]} = \frac{[\text{MLT}^{-2}]}{[\text{L}^2]}$$

$$= [\text{ML}^{-1}\text{T}^{-2}]$$

Coefficient of elasticity,

$$E = \frac{\text{Stress}}{\text{Strain}}$$

Since, strain is dimensionless, hence dimensions of E is same as dimension of stress.

Magnetisation

$$= \frac{\text{Magnetic dipole moment}}{\text{Volume}}$$

$$[\text{Magnetisation}] = \frac{[\text{A - m}^2]}{[\text{m}^3]} = \frac{[\text{AL}^2]}{[\text{L}^3]}$$

$$= [\text{L}^{-1}\text{M}^0\text{T}^0\text{A}^1]$$

Coercivity is usually measured in oersted or A/m and its dimensional formula is $[\text{L}^{-1}\text{M}^0\text{T}^0\text{A}^1]$, i.e. dimensional formula of magnetisation and coercivity is same.

5. *(d)* Velocity of projectile, $v = 25$ m/s

$$g = 10\ \text{m/s}^2$$

Since, after t seconds, its inclination becomes 0° i.e., $\theta = 0°$, hence it concludes that projectile reaches at maximum height after t seconds.

$$\therefore \quad t = \frac{\text{time of light}}{2} = \frac{2u\sin\theta}{2g}$$

$$t = \frac{u\sin\theta}{g}$$

$$\Rightarrow u = \frac{tg}{\sin\theta} \quad \text{... (i)}$$

Again we know that, horizontal range,

$$R = \frac{u^2\sin 2\theta}{g} = \frac{\frac{t^2g^2}{\sin^2\theta}\times 2\sin\theta\cos\theta}{g}$$

[From Eq. (i)]

$$\Rightarrow R = 2t^2 g\cot\theta$$

$$\Rightarrow \frac{1}{\cot\theta} = \frac{2t^2 g}{R} = \frac{2t^2\times10}{R} = \frac{20t^2}{R}$$

$$\Rightarrow \cot\theta = \frac{R}{20t^2}$$

$$\Rightarrow \theta = \cot^{-1}\left(\frac{R}{20t^2}\right)$$

6. *(b)* Given, mass of block, $m = 10$ kg

Initial velocity, $u = 9.8$ m/s

$$\mu = 0.5$$

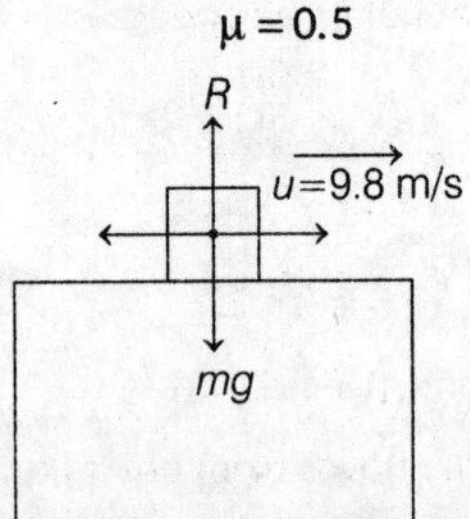

Friction force will act in opposite direction of motion of the block which is given as

$$F = \mu R$$
$$F = \mu mg \quad \text{... (i)}$$

Since, F provides retardation a in the body.

$$\therefore \quad F = ma \quad \text{... (ii)}$$

From Eqs. (i) and (ii), we get

$$\mu mg = ma \Rightarrow a = \mu g$$
$$= 0.5 \times 9.8 = 4.9 \text{ m/s}^2$$

Let s be the distance covered by the block, then using equation of motion,

$$v^2 = u^2 - 2as$$
$$\Rightarrow \quad 0 = u^2 - 2as$$
$$\Rightarrow \quad s = \frac{u^2}{2a} = \frac{(9.8)^2}{2 \times 4.9} = 9.8 \text{ m}$$

7. *(c)* Given, mass of stone, $m = 100$ g $= 0.1$ kg

length of string, $l = 2$ m

maximum tension, $T = 80$ N

Tension in the string provides required centripetal force to the stone to revolve in circular orbit.

i.e. $T = m\omega^2 l$

$$80 = 0.1 \times \omega^2 \times 2$$
$$\Rightarrow \quad \omega^2 = 400$$
$$\Rightarrow \quad \omega = 20 \text{ rad/s}$$
$$\Rightarrow \quad 2\pi f = 20$$
$$\Rightarrow \quad f = \frac{20}{2\pi} = \frac{10}{\pi} \text{ rev/s}$$
$$= \frac{10 \times 60}{\pi} \text{ rev/min}$$
$$= \frac{600}{\pi} \text{ rev/min} = \frac{K}{\pi} \text{ rev/min} \quad \text{(given)}$$
$$\therefore \quad K = 600$$

8. *(b)* Given, mass of water drop, $m = 0.1 \text{ g} = 1 \times 10^{-4}$ kg

Electric field, $E = 4.9 \times 10^5$ N/C

$$g = 9.8 \text{ m/s}^2$$

If q be the charge on water droplet, then at balanced condition,

$$mg = qE$$
$$\Rightarrow \quad q = \frac{mg}{E} = \frac{1 \times 10^{-4} \times 9.8}{4.9 \times 10^5}$$
$$= 2 \times 10^{-9} \text{ C}$$

9. *(c)* Given, $\mathbf{F} = 4x\hat{\mathbf{i}} + 3y^2\hat{\mathbf{j}}$

Particle moves from point (1, 2) to point (2, 3)

According to work-energy theorem,

Work done = change in KE

i.e. $W = \Delta \text{KE}$

$$\Rightarrow \Delta \text{KE} = W = \int\int \mathbf{F} \cdot (dx\hat{\mathbf{i}} + dy\hat{\mathbf{j}})$$
$$= \int\int (4x\hat{\mathbf{i}} + 3y^2\hat{\mathbf{j}}) \cdot (dx\hat{\mathbf{i}} + dy\hat{\mathbf{j}})$$
$$= \int_1^2 4x\, dx + \int_2^3 3y^2 dy$$
$$= [2x^2]_1^2 + [y^3]_2^3$$
$$= (8 - 2) + (27 - 8)$$
$$= 6 + 19 = 25 \text{ J}$$

10. *(b)* Let h be required height,

i.e. weight of body at height h $= \dfrac{\text{weight of body on the surface of earth}}{3}$

$$\Rightarrow \quad mg_h = \frac{mg}{3}$$
$$\Rightarrow \quad g_h = \frac{g}{3}$$
$$\Rightarrow \quad \frac{g}{\left(1 + \frac{h}{R_e}\right)^2} = \frac{g}{3}$$
$$\Rightarrow \quad \left(1 + \frac{h}{R_e}\right)^2 = 3$$
$$1 + \frac{h}{R_e} = \sqrt{3}$$
$$\Rightarrow \quad h = (\sqrt{3} - 1)R_e$$
$$= (1.732 - 1)6400$$
$$= 0.732 \times 6400$$
$$= 4684.8 \text{ km}$$
$$\simeq 4685 \text{ km}$$

11. *(a)* Given, $R = 40\ \Omega$,

$$V_{\text{rms}} = 220 \text{ V}$$
$$f = 50 \text{ Hz}$$

Instantaneous value of alternating current,

$$I = I_0 \sin \omega t$$

For maximum value of alternating current, $I = I_0$

$$\therefore \quad I_0 = I_0 \sin \omega t$$
$$\Rightarrow \quad \sin \omega t = 1$$
$$\Rightarrow \quad \omega t = \frac{\pi}{2}$$
$$\Rightarrow \quad t = \frac{\pi}{2\omega}$$

If t' be the time at rms value, then

$$I_{\text{rms}} = I_0 \sin \omega t'$$
$$\Rightarrow \quad \frac{I_0}{\sqrt{2}} = I_0 \sin \omega t'$$
$$\Rightarrow \quad \frac{1}{\sqrt{2}} = \sin \omega t'$$
$$\Rightarrow \quad \frac{\pi}{4} = \omega t'$$
$$t' = \frac{\pi}{4\omega}$$

$\therefore$ Time taken to change the value of current from maximum value to rms value

$$= t - t' = \frac{\pi}{2\omega} - \frac{\pi}{4\omega}$$
$$= \frac{\pi}{4\omega} = \frac{\pi}{4 \times 2\pi f}$$
$$= \frac{1}{8f} = \frac{1}{8 \times 50} = \frac{1}{400} \text{ s}$$
$$= 2.5 \times 10^{-3} \text{ s}$$
$$= 2.5 \text{ ms}$$

12. *(a)* Equations of the two waves are given as

$y_1 = 5 \sin 2\pi(x - vt)$ cm

$\therefore$ Amplitude, $A_1 = 5$ cm

and $y_2 = 3 \sin 2\pi(x - vt + 1.5)$ cm

$\therefore$ Amplitude, $A_2 = 3$ cm

Phase difference between waves y_1 and y_2 is given as

$$\Delta\phi = 2\pi(1.5) = 3\pi$$

$\therefore$ Amplitude of resultant wave,

$$A = \sqrt{A_1^2 + A_2^2 + 2A_1A_2 \cos(\Delta\phi)}$$
$$= \sqrt{A_1^2 + A_2^2 + 2A_1A_2(-1)}$$
$$[\because \cos 3\pi = \cos \pi = -1]$$
$$= \sqrt{(A_1 - A_2)^2} = A_1 - A_2$$
$$= 5 - 3 = 2 \text{ cm}$$

13. *(c)* Consider the following relations

$$B = \mu_0 \mu_r H \quad \text{...(i)}$$
$$v = \frac{c}{\sqrt{\mu_r \varepsilon_r}} \quad \text{...(ii)}$$
$$E = Bv \quad \text{...(iii)}$$

Here symbols have their usual meaning. Putting B and v from Eqs. (i) and (ii) in Eq. (iii), we get

$$E = \sqrt{\frac{\mu_r}{\varepsilon_r}} \mu_0 Hc$$
$$= \sqrt{\frac{1.61}{6.44}} \times 4\pi \times 10^{-7} \times 4.5 \times 10^{-2} \times 3 \times 10^8$$
$$\approx \sqrt{\frac{16}{64}} \times 4\pi \times 4.5 \times 3 \times 10^{-1}$$
$$= 8.48 \text{ V/m}$$

14. *(c)* According to Rutherford model, electrons revolve around the nucleus in circular orbit i.e. electrons accelerate around the nucleus. The acceleration would cause the electron to radiate energy in the form of electromagnetic waves, which would imply that the electron would continually lose energy. Thus, their velocity would decrease, causing it to spiral and eventually fall into the nucleus. This would imply that atoms are naturally unstable which is not possible because atoms are naturally stable. Therefore, classical atom based on Rutherford's model is doomed to collapse.

15. *(d)* Binding energy per nucleon of nucleus A,

$$E_A = 5.6 \text{ MeV}$$
$$M_B = 105, M_C = 115$$
$$M_A = 220$$

Binding energy per nucleon of nucleus B and C,

$$E_B = E_C = E = 6.4 \text{ MeV}$$

$\therefore$ Released energy per fission

Q = Total binding energy of products nuclei – Total binding energy of reactants nuclei

$$= (M_B + M_C)E - M_A \times E_A$$
$$= (105 + 115)(6.4) - 220 \times 5.6$$
$$= 176 \text{ MeV}$$

16. *(c)* Message or base band signal frequency,

$$f_m = 3.5 \text{ MHz} = 3.5 \times 10^6 \text{ Hz}$$

Carrier signal frequency, $f_c = 3.5$ GHz $= 3.5 \times 10^9$ Hz

Side band frequencies are $f_c - f_m$ or $f_c + f_m$

Since, $f_c >> f_m$

Hence, side band frequency is nearly equal to f_c.

Therefore, minimum length of antenna $= \frac{\lambda}{4} = \frac{c/f_c}{4} = \frac{c}{4f_c}$

$$= \frac{3 \times 10^8}{4 \times 3.5 \times 10^9} = 2.14 \times 10^{-2} \text{ m}$$

$$= 21.4 \times 10^{-3} \text{ m} = 21.4 \text{ mm}$$

17. *(b)* Given, temperature of sink,

$T_2 = 27°\text{C} = (273 + 27)\text{ K} = 300 \text{ K}$

Efficiency, $\eta = 25\% = 0.25$

Let T_1 be the temperature of source, then

$$\eta = 1 - \frac{T_2}{T_1}$$

$$\Rightarrow \quad 0.25 = 1 - \frac{300}{T_1}$$

$$\Rightarrow \quad \frac{300}{T_1} = 0.75$$

$$\Rightarrow \quad T_1 = 400 \text{ K}$$

Now, efficiency is increased by 100% i.e. new efficiency,

$$\eta' = 0.25 + 100\% \text{ of } 0.25$$
$$= 0.25 + \frac{100}{100} \times 0.25 = 0.50$$

Let T' be the new temperature of source, then $\eta' = 1 - \frac{T_2}{T'}$

$$0.5 = 1 - \frac{300}{T'} \Rightarrow T' = 600 \text{ K}$$

$\therefore$ Increase in temperature of source,

$$\Delta T = 600\text{K} - 400\text{K}$$
$$= 200\text{K or } 200°\text{C}$$

18. *(d)* Area of each plate of capacitor,

$$A = 30\pi \text{ cm}^2 = 30\pi \times 10^{-4} \text{ m}^2$$

Separation between the plates,

$$d = 1 \text{ mm} = 10^{-3} \text{ m}$$

Electric field, $E = 3.6 \times 10^7$ V/m

We know that, electric field between the plates of charged capacitor without causing any breakdown,

$$E = \frac{\sigma}{K\varepsilon_0} = \frac{q/A}{K\varepsilon_0} \quad \left[\because \sigma = \frac{q}{A}\right]$$

$$\Rightarrow \quad E = \frac{q}{AK\varepsilon_0}$$

$$\Rightarrow \quad K = \frac{q}{EA\varepsilon_0}$$

$$= \frac{7 \times 10^{-6}}{3.6 \times 10^7 \times 30\pi \times 10^{-4} \times \frac{1}{4\pi \times 9 \times 10^9}} \quad [\because q = 7 \times 10^{-6} \text{C}]$$

$$= 2.33$$

19. *(c)* According to given situation, magnetic field due to current carrying circular loop at the centre,

$$B_c = \frac{\mu_0 I}{2r} \quad \text{... (i)}$$

We know, magnetic field on the axis at a distance x from the centre of circular coil,

$$B = \frac{\mu_0 I r^2}{2(x^2 + r^2)^{3/2}}$$

Here, $x = \frac{r}{2}$,

Hence, $B' = \frac{\mu_0 I r^2}{2\left[\left(\frac{r}{2}\right)^2 + r^2\right]^{3/2}}$

$$= \frac{\mu_0 I r^2}{2\left(\frac{5r^2}{4}\right)^{3/2}} = \frac{\mu_0 I}{2r} \cdot \left(\frac{4}{5}\right)^{3/2}$$

$$= \frac{\mu_0 I}{2r} \cdot \left(\frac{2}{\sqrt{5}}\right)^3 = B_c \left(\frac{2}{\sqrt{5}}\right)^3 \quad \text{[From Eq. (i)]}$$

$$= \left(\frac{2}{\sqrt{5}}\right)^3 B \quad [\because B_c = B]$$

20. *(b)* Since, both blocks M_1 and M_2 are connected in series, hence rate of heat flow through block M_1 = rate of heat flow through block M_2

$$\Rightarrow \quad \frac{K_1 A(\Delta T_1)}{l_1} = \frac{K_2 A(\Delta T_2)}{l_2}$$

$$\Rightarrow \quad \frac{K_1 \Delta T_1}{l_1} = \frac{K_2 \Delta T_2}{l_2}$$

$$\Rightarrow \quad \frac{K_1(100 - 80)}{16 \times 10^{-2}} = \frac{K_2(80 - 0)}{8 \times 10^{-2}}$$

$$\Rightarrow \quad \frac{20K_1}{2} = 80K_2$$

$$\Rightarrow \quad K_1 = 8K_2 = 8K \; [\because K_2 = K \text{ given}]$$

21. *(12)* Given, mass of nitrogen gas, $m = 0.056$ kg

mass of 1 mole of N_2 gas, $m' = 28$ g $= 0.028$ kg

$\therefore$ Number of moles of N_2 gas $= \frac{m}{m'}$

$$= \frac{0.056}{0.028} = 2$$

$$T_1 = 127°\text{C} = (127 + 273)\text{ K} = 400 \text{ K}$$

Since, speed of gas molecule,

$$v_{rms} = \sqrt{\frac{3RT}{M}}$$

i.e. $v_{rms} \propto \sqrt{T}$

$$\frac{T_2}{T_1} = \frac{(v_{rms})_2^2}{(v_{rms})_1^2} = \frac{(2v_{rms})_1^2}{(v_{rms})_1} = 4$$

$$\Rightarrow T_2 = 4T_1 = 4 \times 400 \text{ K} = 1600 \text{ K}$$

$\therefore$ Amount of heat required,

$$Q = \frac{f}{2} nR\Delta T$$

$$= \frac{5}{2} \times 2 \times 2 \times (1600 - 400) \quad [\because f = 5]$$

$$= 12000 \text{ cal}$$
$$= 12 \text{ kcal}$$

22. *(10)* Given, focal length of two thin biconvex lens,

$$f_1 = f_2 = f = 15 \text{ cm}$$

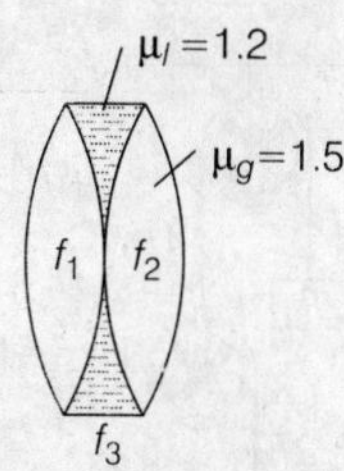

Using lens Maker's formula for first lens,

$$\frac{1}{f_1} = (\mu_g - 1)\left(\frac{1}{R_1} - \frac{1}{R_2}\right)$$

$$\Rightarrow \quad \frac{1}{15} = (1.5 - 1)\left(\frac{1}{R} - \frac{1}{-R}\right)$$

$$\Rightarrow \quad \frac{1}{15} = \frac{1}{R}$$

$$\Rightarrow \quad R = 15 \text{ cm}$$

∴ Focal length of combination is given as

$$\frac{1}{f_{eq}} = \frac{1}{f_1} + \frac{1}{f_2} + \frac{1}{f_3} \quad \text{... (i)}$$

where, $f_1 = f_2 = f = 15$ cm

and $\frac{1}{f_3} = (\mu_l - 1)\left(\frac{1}{-R} - \frac{1}{R}\right)$

$$= (1.2 - 1)\left(\frac{-2}{R}\right) = -\frac{1}{30}$$

$$\Rightarrow \quad f_3 = -30 \text{ cm}$$

Hence, from Eq. (i), we get

$$\frac{1}{f_{eq}} = \frac{1}{15} + \frac{1}{15} - \frac{1}{30} = \frac{3}{30} = \frac{1}{10}$$

$$\Rightarrow \quad f_{eq} = 10 \text{ cm}$$

23. *(750)* Given, load resistance, $R_L = 5 \text{ k}\Omega = 5 \times 10^3 \ \Omega$

Input signal voltage, $\Delta V_i = 10$ mV $= 10 \times 10^{-3}$ V $= 10^{-2}$ V

Change in input current = Change in base current (ΔI_B)

$\Rightarrow \Delta I_B = 10 \ \mu$A

$= 10 \times 10^{-6}$A $= 10^{-5}$ A

∴ Input resistance,

$$r_i = \frac{\Delta V_i}{\Delta I_B} = \frac{10^{-2}}{10^{-5}} = 10^3 \ \Omega$$

∵ Change in collector current, $\Delta I_C = 1.5$ mA $= 1.5 \times 10^{-3}$ A

∴ Current gain, $\beta = \frac{\Delta I_C}{\Delta I_B} = \frac{1.5 \times 10^{-3}}{10^{-5}}$

$= 150$

∴ Voltage gain, $A_V = \frac{r_L}{r_{in}} \times \beta$

$$= \frac{5 \times 10^3}{10^3} \times 150 = 750$$

24. *(242)* Given, $L = 200$ mH $= 0.2$ H

$$V_{rms} = 220 \text{ V}$$

$$f = 50 \text{ Hz}$$

∴ Inductive reactance,

$$X_L = 2\pi f L = 2\pi \times 50 \times 0.2 = 20\pi \ \Omega$$

Peak current, $I_0 = \frac{V_0}{X_L} = \frac{\sqrt{2}\, V_{rms}}{20\,\pi}$

$$= \frac{\sqrt{2} \times 220}{20\,\pi}$$

$$I_0 = \frac{11\sqrt{2}}{\pi}$$

$$\Rightarrow \quad I_0 = \frac{\sqrt{242}}{\pi} \text{ A} \quad \text{... (i)}$$

Since, in inductive circuit, there is a phase difference of $\frac{\pi}{2}$ between alternating current and voltage. Hence, when instantaneous voltage is zero, then current reaches at its peak value, which is given by Eq. (i),

$$I_0 = \frac{\sqrt{242}}{\pi} = \frac{\sqrt{a}}{\pi} \text{ A} \quad \text{(given)}$$

$$\therefore \quad a = 242$$

25. *(3)* Given, $\lambda_1 = 650$ nm $= 650 \times 10^{-9}$ m

$$\lambda_2 = 655 \text{ nm} = 655 \times 10^{-9} \text{ m}$$

Width of aperture, $a = 0.5$ mm $= 5 \times 10^{-4}$ m

Distance between screen and source, $D = 2$ m

We know that, position of first maxima, $a \sin\theta = \frac{3\lambda}{2}$

Since, $\sin\theta \simeq \theta = \frac{Y}{D}$

$$\therefore \quad a.\frac{Y}{D} = \frac{3\lambda}{2}$$

$$\Rightarrow \quad y = \frac{3\lambda D}{2a}$$

$$\therefore \quad y_1 = \frac{3\lambda_1 D}{2a}$$

and $y_2 = \frac{3\lambda_2 D}{2a}$

$$\therefore \quad \Delta y = y_2 - y_1$$

$$= \frac{3\lambda_2 D}{2a} - \frac{3\lambda_1 D}{2a} = \frac{3D}{2a}(\lambda_2 - \lambda_1)$$

$$= \frac{3 \times 2}{2 \times 5 \times 10^{-4}}(655 \times 10^{-9} - 650 \times 10^{-9})$$

$$= 3 \times 10^{-5} \text{ m}$$

26. *(2)* Let ν_0 be the value of threshold frequency.

According to Einstein's photoelectric equation,

$$\frac{1}{2}mv^2 = h\nu - h\nu_0$$

For the first situation, $\nu_1 = 2\nu_0$

i.e. $\frac{1}{2}mv_1^2 = h\nu_1 - h\nu_0$

$$= h \cdot 2\nu_0 - h\nu_0 = h\nu_0$$

$$\Rightarrow \quad \frac{1}{2}mv_1^2 = h\nu_0 \quad \text{... (i)}$$

For the second situation, $\nu_2 = 5\nu_0$,

Then $\frac{1}{2}mv_2^2 = h\nu_2 - h\nu_0$

$$= h.5\nu_0 - h\nu_0$$

$$\Rightarrow \quad \frac{1}{2}mv_2^2 = 4h\nu_0 \quad \text{... (ii)}$$

Dividing Eq. (ii) by Eq. (i), we get

$$\frac{\frac{1}{2}mv_1^2}{\frac{1}{2}mv_2^2} = \frac{h\nu_0}{4h\nu_0} = \frac{1}{4}$$

$$\left(\frac{v_1}{v_2}\right)^2 = \left(\frac{1}{2}\right)^2$$

$$\Rightarrow \quad \frac{v_1}{v_2} = \frac{1}{2}$$

$$\Rightarrow \quad v_2 = 2v_1 = xv_1 \quad \text{(given)}$$

$$\therefore \quad x = 2$$

27. *(3)* Let h be the height of tower.

Situation for the first condition is shown in the figure.

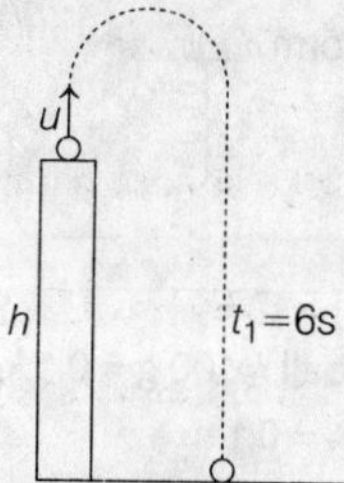

By using equation of motion,

$$h = -ut_1 + \frac{1}{2}gt_1^2$$

$$h = -6u + \frac{1}{2}g(6)^2$$

$$h = -6u + 18g \quad \text{... (i)}$$

Situation for the second condition is shown in the figure.

u

h

$t_2 = 1.5$ s

Now, using equation of motion,

$$h = ut_2 + \frac{1}{2}gt_2^2$$

$$h = 1.5u + \frac{1}{2}g(1.5)^2$$

$$h = 1.5u + \frac{2.25}{2}g \quad \text{... (ii)}$$

Solving Eqs. (i) and (ii), we get

$$h = 4.5g \text{ m}$$

For the third case, when ball is released from rest, i.e. $u = 0$

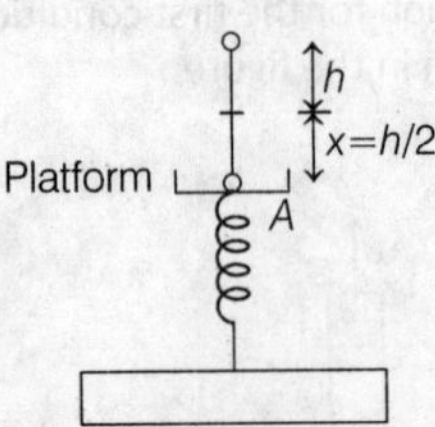

In this case,

$$h = 0 \times t_3 + \frac{1}{2}gt_3^2$$

$$= \frac{1}{2}gt_3^2$$

$$\Rightarrow \quad t_3 = \sqrt{\frac{2h}{g}}$$

$$= \sqrt{\frac{2 \times 4.5g}{g}}$$

$$= \sqrt{9} = 3 \text{ s}$$

28. *(120)* The given situation is shown below

Platform

Mass of ball $= 100 \text{ g} = 0.1 \text{ kg}$

$h = 10 \text{ cm} = 0.1 \text{ m}$

Displacement in the spring,

$$x = \frac{h}{2} = \frac{0.1}{2} = 0.05 \text{ m}$$

By conservation of energy at position A, we get

Total change in potential energy of the ball

= Total potential energy of spring

i.e. $\quad mg(h + x) = \frac{1}{2}kx^2$

$$\Rightarrow 0.1 \times 10(0.1 + 0.05) = \frac{1}{2}k(0.05)^2$$

$$\Rightarrow \quad k = 120 \text{ N/m}$$

29. *(25)* Comparison of emfs of two cells using the experiment of potentiometer is given as

$$\frac{e_1}{e_2} = \frac{l_1}{l_2}$$

where, l_1, and l_2 are their corresponding balancing length.

$$\therefore \quad \frac{3}{2} = \frac{75}{l_2}$$

$$[\because l_1 = 75 \text{ cm given}]$$

$$\Rightarrow \quad l_2 = 50 \text{ cm}$$

$\therefore$ Difference in balancing length

$$= l_1 - l_2$$

$$= 75 - 50$$

$$= 25 \text{ cm}$$

30. *(6)* The given situation is shown below

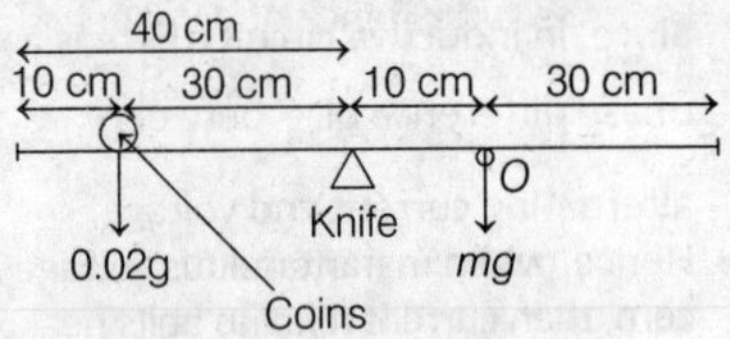

Mass of the two coins $= 2 \times 10$ g $= 0.02$ kg

Let m be the mass of the meter scale which is balanced at point O.

By the principle of moments about knife edge,

$$(0.02\,g) \times (30 \times 10^{-2}) = mg \times 10 \times 10^{-2}$$

$$\Rightarrow \quad m = 6 \times 10^{-2} \text{ kg}$$

$$x = 6$$

Real Nut 2-26 June 2022, Shift-II

1. *(c)* We know that, induced emf across the coil due to change of current flowing through it

i.e. $\quad e = -M\frac{di}{dt}$

$$\Rightarrow \quad M = -\frac{e}{\left[\frac{di}{dt}\right]}$$

$$M = -e \cdot \frac{dt}{di}$$

$$\Rightarrow \quad [M] = [e]\frac{[dt]}{[di]}$$

$$= \left[\frac{W}{q}\right]\frac{[dt]}{[di]}$$

$$= \left[\frac{ML^2T^{-2}}{AT}\right]\frac{[T]}{[A]}$$

$$= [ML^2T^{-2}A^{-2}]$$

2. *(a)* If T be the tension in the lowest block, then the given arrangement can be represented as

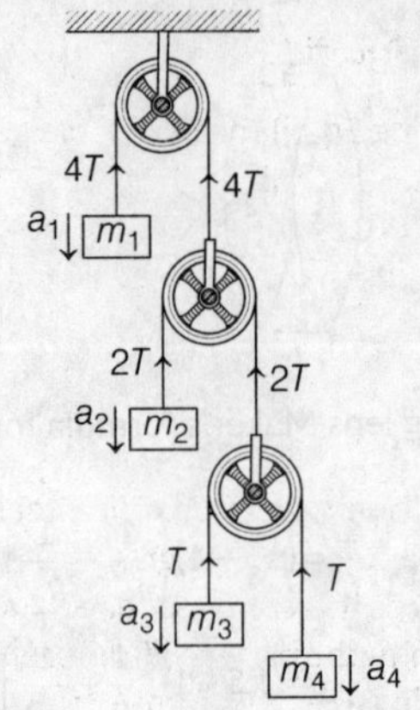

For the given situation of the arrangement of blocks, we have

$$\Sigma \mathbf{T} \cdot \mathbf{a} = 0$$

$$\Rightarrow -4Ta_1 - 2Ta_2 - Ta_3 - Ta_4 = 0$$

$$\Rightarrow \quad -T(4a_1 + 2a_2 + a_3 + a_4) = 0$$

$$\Rightarrow \quad 4a_1 + 2a_2 + a_3 + a_4 = 0$$

3. *(a)* Work done from force-displacement (*F-x*) graph is equal to area enclosed under *F-x* curve.

The area enclosed below the *X*-axis is negative and area above the *X*-axis is taken as positive.

From the given *F-x* graph in Fig. (a), Fig. (b), Fig. (c) and Fig. (d), area under *F-x* curve are arranged as

$$(\text{Area})_{\text{Fig. (c)}} > (\text{Area})_{\text{Fig. (b)}} > (\text{Area})_{\text{Fig. (a)}} > (\text{Area})_{\text{Fig. (d)}}$$

$$\therefore \quad W_3 > W_2 > W_1 > W_4$$

4. *(b)* If R and M are the radius and mass of the sphere, then rotational kinetic energy of spherical ball,

$$K_{\text{rot}} = \frac{1}{2}I\omega^2$$

$$= \frac{1}{2}\left[\frac{2}{5}MR^2\right]\left(\frac{v_{CM}}{R}\right)^2$$

$$\left(\because I_{\text{solid sphere}} = \frac{2}{5}MR^2 \text{ and } \omega = \frac{v_{CM}}{R}\right)$$

$$K_{\text{rot}} = \frac{1}{5}Mv_{CM}^2 \quad \text{...(i)}$$

Translational kinetic energy of spherical ball,

$$K_{\text{trans}} = \frac{1}{2}Mv_{CM}^2$$

Total kinetic energy of spherical ball,

$$K_{\text{tot}} = K_{\text{rot}} + K_{\text{trans}}$$

$$= \frac{1}{5}Mv_{CM}^2 + \frac{1}{2}Mv_{CM}^2$$

$$K_{tot} = \frac{7}{10} M v_{CM}^2 \quad ...(ii)$$

Dividing Eq. (i) by Eq. (ii), we get,

$$\frac{K_{rot}}{K_{tot}} = \frac{\frac{1}{5} M v_{CM}^2}{\frac{7}{10} M v_{CM}^2} = \frac{10}{7} \times \frac{1}{5} = \frac{2}{7}$$

5. *(d)* At every location, the direction of acceleration due to gravity is always towards the centre of earth, but its magnitude changes at different locations i.e. if we move from poles to equator, the direction of acceleration due to gravity of the earth always points towards centre of earth but its magnitude decreases and becomes minimum on reaching at equator. Hence, A is false but R is true.

6. *(c)* Reynold's number is a dimensionless parameter whose value is used to decide the nature of flow of a liquid through a pipe. It is given as

$$R_e = \frac{\rho v d}{\eta}$$

where, ρ = density of liquid,

v = velocity of liquid in pipe,

d = diameter of pipe

and x = coefficient of viscosity.

7. *(*)* Average kinetic energy per molecule for an ideal gas sample having degree of freedom f is given by

$$E = \frac{f}{2} kT$$

Here, k = Bottzmann's constant

T = Thermodynamic temperature

Thus, $E \propto f$

$$\Rightarrow \frac{E_{Argon}}{E_{Oxygen}} = \frac{f_{Argon}}{f_{Oxygen}} = \frac{3}{5}$$

8. *(a)* The given circuit diagram is shown below

10 μF 15 μF 20 μF

C_1 C_2 C_3

+ V −

13 V

Equivalent capacitance is given as

$$\frac{1}{C_{eq}} = \frac{1}{C_1} + \frac{1}{C_2} + \frac{1}{C_3}$$

$$= \frac{1}{10} + \frac{1}{15} + \frac{1}{20}$$

$$= \frac{6+4+3}{60} = \frac{13}{60}$$

$$\Rightarrow \quad C_{eq} = \frac{60}{13} \mu\text{F} = \frac{60}{13} \times 10^{-6} \text{ F}$$

$\therefore$ Charge flow in the circuit,

$$Q = C_{eq} V = \frac{60}{13} \times 10^{-6} \times 13$$

$$= 60 \times 10^{-6} \text{ C} = 60 \ \mu\text{C}$$

Since, in series combination, charge on each capacitor is same, therefore charge on the capacitor of capacitance 15 μF will be 60 μC.

9. *(c)* Initial capacitance of parallel plate capacitor

$$C_1 = \frac{\varepsilon_0 A}{d} \quad ...(i)$$

When dielectric material of dielectric constant ($K = 3$) is filled in half the space i.e. $t = d/2$, then new capacitance

$$C_2 = \frac{\varepsilon_0 A}{(d-t) + \left(\frac{t}{K}\right)}$$

$$= \frac{\varepsilon_0 A}{\left(d - \frac{d}{2}\right) + \left(\frac{d/2}{K}\right)}$$

$$= \frac{\varepsilon_0 A}{\frac{d}{2} + \frac{d}{2K}} = \frac{\varepsilon_0 A}{d\left(\frac{1}{2} + \frac{1}{2K}\right)}$$

$$= \frac{C_1}{\frac{1}{2} + \frac{1}{2K}} \quad \text{[Using Eq. (i)]}$$

$$= \frac{4}{\frac{1}{2} + \frac{1}{2 \times 3}}$$

$$= \frac{4}{4/6} = 6 \ \mu\text{F}$$

10. *(b)* If R be the radius of combined big drop and r be the radius of small drop, then

Volume of big drop = 64 × Volume of small drop

$$\Rightarrow \frac{4}{3}\pi R^3 = 64 \times \frac{4}{3}\pi r^3$$

$$\Rightarrow \quad R^3 = (4r)^3$$

$$\Rightarrow \quad R = 4r$$

$$= 4 \times 0.02 = 0.08 \text{ m}$$

$[\because r = 0.02 \text{ m}]$

Charge on combined drop, $Q = 64 \times$ Charge on one small drop

$= 64\, q = 64 \times 5 \ [\because q = 5 \mu\text{C}]$

$= 320 \ \mu\text{C}$

$$\therefore \frac{\sigma_{bigger}}{\sigma_{smaller}} = \frac{\frac{Q}{4\pi R^2}}{\frac{q}{4\pi r^2}} = \frac{Q}{q} \times \left(\frac{r}{R}\right)^2$$

$$= \frac{320 \times 10^{-6}}{5 \times 10^{-6}} \times \left(\frac{0.02}{0.08}\right)^2$$

$$= 64 \times \left(\frac{1}{4}\right)^2 = \frac{4}{1} \text{ or } 4:1$$

11. *(c)* The given network is shown as

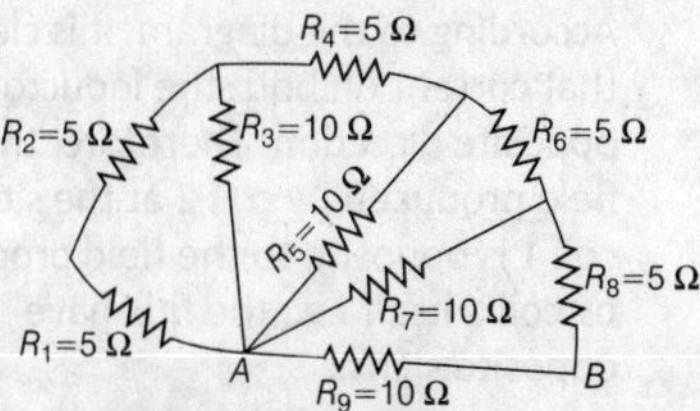

R_1 and R_2 are in series.

$\therefore \quad R_{12} = R_1 + R_2 = 5 + 5 = 10 \ \Omega$

Now, R_{12} and R_3 will be in parallel, hence their equivalent resistance,

$$R_{123} = \frac{R_{12} \times R_3}{R_{12} + R_3} = \frac{10 \times 10}{10 + 10} = 5 \ \Omega$$

Now, R_{123} and R_4 will be in series, hence their equivalent resistance is

$$R_{1234} = 5 + 5 = 10 \ \Omega$$

Again, $R_{1234} || R_5$

$$\therefore R_{12345} = \frac{R_{1234} \times R_5}{R_{1234} + R_5} = \frac{10 \times 10}{10 + 10} = 5 \ \Omega$$

In similar way, we can calculate the equivalent resistance of next levels.

i.e. $R_{123456} = R_{12345} + R_6 = 5 + 5 = 10 \ \Omega$

$$R_{1234567} = \frac{R_{123456} \times R_7}{R_{123456} + R_7} = \frac{10 \times 10}{10 + 10} = 5 \ \Omega$$

$$\therefore \quad R_{12345678} = R_{1234567} + R_8 = 5 + 5 = 10 \ \Omega$$

$$\therefore R_{123456789} = \frac{R_{12345678} \times R_9}{R_{12345678} + R_9} = \frac{10 \times 10}{10 + 10} = 5 \ \Omega$$

12. *(a)* Magnetic dipole moment of bar magnet,

$$M = 2.0 \times 10^5 \text{ J/T}$$

$$B = 14 \times 10^{-5} \text{ T}$$

$$\theta_1 = 0°, \theta_2 = 60°$$

∴Work done in rotating the bar magnet in magnetic field,

$$W = MB(\cos\theta_1 - \cos\theta_2)$$
$$= 2\times10^5 \times 14\times10^{-5}(\cos 0° - \cos 60°)$$
$$= 28\left(1-\frac{1}{2}\right) = 28\times\frac{1}{2} = 14 \text{ J}$$

13. *(d)* The given situation is shown as

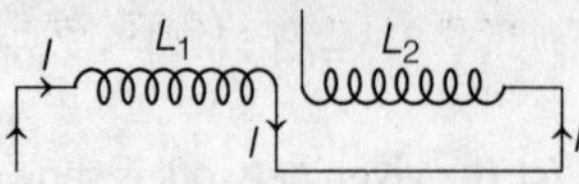

According to the diagram, it is clear that current on both the inductor is in opposite direction. Therefore, the field produced by coil 2 at the site of coil 1 is opposite to the field produced by coil 1 itself i.e., the flux have opposite signs.

An increasing current in coil 1 tends to increase the flux in that coil but an increasing current in coil 2 tends to decrease it. The emf across coil 1 is

$$e_1 = -(L_1 - M)\frac{dI}{dt}$$

Similarly, the emf across coil 2 is

$$e_2 = -(L_2 - M)\frac{dI}{dt}$$

The total emf across both the coils

$$e = e_1 + e_2 = -(L_1 + L_2 - 2M)\frac{dI}{dt}$$

This is same as the emf that would be produced by a single coil with inductance,

$$L_{eq} = L_1 + L_2 - 2M$$

14. *(b)* Given, $l = 1$ m

$$\omega = 5 \text{ rad/s}$$
$$B_H = 0.2\times10^{-4} \text{ T}$$

Induced emf between the two ends of conductor due to its rotation in B_H,

$$e = \frac{B_H \omega l^2}{2}$$
$$= \frac{0.2\times10^{-4}\times5\times1^2}{2}$$
$$= 5\times10^{-5} \text{ V}$$
$$= 50\times10^{-6} \text{ V}$$
$$= 50 \text{ μV}$$

15. *(b)* The increasing order of electromagnetic wave spectrum is given as

$$\lambda_{\text{gamma-ray}} < \lambda_{\text{X-ray}} < \lambda_{\text{visible}} < \lambda_{\text{microwave}}$$

16. *(c)* Given, wavelength coming from galaxy,

$$\lambda_{\text{actual}} = 670 \text{ nm}$$

and $\lambda_{\text{observed}} = 670.7$ nm

Change in wavelength,

$$\Delta\lambda = \lambda_{\text{observed}} - \lambda_{\text{actual}}$$
$$= 670.7 - 670$$
$$= 0.7 \text{ nm} = 7\times10^{-10} \text{ m}$$

According to Doppler's shift, we have

$$\frac{\Delta\lambda}{\lambda_{\text{actual}}} = \frac{V}{C}$$
$$\Rightarrow \frac{7\times10^{-10}}{670\times10^{-9}} = \frac{v}{3\times10^8}$$
$$\Rightarrow \frac{7}{6700} = \frac{v}{3\times10^8}$$
$$\Rightarrow v = \frac{21\times10^8}{6700} = 3.13\times10^5 \text{ m/s}$$

17. *(a)* Given, $\lambda = 4500$ Å $= 4.5\times10^{-7}$ m

Magnetic field, $B = 2$ mT $= 2\times10^{-3}$ T

Radius, $R = 2$ mm $= 2\times10^{-3}$ m

Radius of circular path, $R = \dfrac{mv}{Bq}$

$$\Rightarrow v = \frac{RBq}{m}$$

Kinetic energy of electron,

$$K = \frac{1}{2}mv^2 = \frac{1}{2}m\left(\frac{RBq}{m}\right)^2$$
$$= \frac{1}{2}m\frac{R^2B^2q^2}{m^2} = \frac{R^2B^2q^2}{2m}$$
$$= \frac{(2\times10^{-3})^2\times(2\times10^{-3})^2(1.6\times10^{-19})^2}{2\times9.1\times10^{-31}}$$
$$= 2.25\times10^{-19} \text{ J}$$
$$= \frac{2.25\times10^{-19}}{1.6\times10^{-19}} \text{ eV}$$
$$= 1.4 \text{ eV}$$

Energy of radiation,

$$E = \frac{hc}{\lambda} = \frac{6.62\times10^{-34}\times3\times10^8}{4.5\times10^{-7}} \text{ J}$$
$$= \frac{6.62\times10^{-34}\times3\times10^8}{4.5\times10^{-7}\times1.6\times10^{-19}} \text{ eV}$$
$$= 2.76 \text{ eV}$$

∴Work function,

$$\phi = E - K$$
$$= 2.76 - 1.4 = 1.36 \text{ eV}$$

18. *(d)* Given, half-life for the first process, $(T_{1/2})_1 = 3$ h and half-life for the second process, $(T_{1/2})_2 = 4.5$ h

If λ_1 and λ_2 are the disintegration constants corresponding to process-1 and process -2, then effective disintegration constant is given as

$$\lambda_{\text{eff}} = \lambda_1 + \lambda_2$$
$$\frac{\ln 2}{(T_{1/2})_{\text{eff}}} = \frac{\ln 2}{(T_{1/2})_1} + \frac{\ln 2}{(T_{1/2})_2}$$
$$\Rightarrow \frac{1}{(T_{1/2})_{\text{eff}}} = \frac{1}{(T_{1/2})_1} + \frac{1}{(T_{1/2})_2}$$
$$= \frac{1}{3} + \frac{1}{4.5} = \frac{3+2}{9} = \frac{5}{9}$$
$$\therefore (T_{1/2})_{\text{eff}} = \frac{9}{5} \text{ h} = 1.8 \text{ h}$$

19. *(b)* When positive feedback is given to an amplifier, then it works as an oscillator. Positive feedback means a portion of output voltage is feedback to the input voltage with same phase.

20. *(d)* Given, sinusoidal carrier wave,

$$y(t) = 40\sin(10\times10^6\pi t)$$
$$\therefore \quad \omega_c = 10\times10^6\pi \text{ rad/s}$$
$$= 10^7\pi \text{ rad/s}$$

and $A_c = 40$

Message signal,

$$x(t) = 20\sin(1000\pi t)$$
$$\therefore \quad \omega_m = 1000\pi = 10^3\pi \text{ rad/s}$$

and $A_m = 20$

We know that, equation of amplitude modulated

$$\text{wave} = (A_c + A_m\sin\omega_m t)\sin\omega_c t$$
$$= A_c\left(1 + \frac{A_m}{A_c}\sin\omega_m t\right)\sin\omega_c t$$
$$= A_c(1 + \mu\sin\omega_m t)\sin\omega_c t \quad \left(\because \mu = \frac{A_m}{A_c}\right)$$
$$= A_c\sin\omega_c t + \frac{\mu A_c}{2}[\cos(\omega_c - \omega_m)t - \cos(\omega_c + \omega_m)t]$$

$[\because 2\sin A\sin B = \cos(A-B) - \cos(A+B)]$

∴ Amplitude of minimum frequency component of modulated signal

$$= \frac{\mu A_c}{2} = \frac{A_m}{A_c}\times\frac{A_c}{2} = \frac{A_m}{2} = \frac{20}{2} = 10$$

21. *(6)* Initial velocity of ball, $u = 50$ m/s

Let both balls meet together after t seconds.

For the first ball, height attained by it in t seconds,

$$h_1 = ut - \frac{1}{2}gt^2$$
$$\Rightarrow \quad h_1 = 50t - \frac{1}{2}gt^2 \quad \text{...(i)}$$

After 2 s, second ball is projected vertically upward with $u = 50$ m/s, i.e.

$$t' = t - 2$$

$\therefore$ Height attained by second ball,

$$h_2 = u(t-2) - \frac{1}{2}g(t-2)^2$$

$$\Rightarrow \quad h_2 = 50(t-2) - \frac{1}{2}g(t-2)^2 \quad \text{...(ii)}$$

Both balls will meet, if

$$h_1 = h_2$$

$$50t - \frac{1}{2}gt^2 = 50(t-2) - \frac{1}{2}g(t-2)^2$$

$$\Rightarrow 50t - 50(t-2) = \frac{1}{2}gt^2 - \frac{1}{2}g(t-2)^2$$

$$\Rightarrow \quad 50(t-t+2) = \frac{1}{2}g[t^2 - (t-2)^2]$$

$$\Rightarrow \quad 100 = \frac{g}{2}[(t+t-2)(t-t+2)]$$

$$\Rightarrow 100 = \frac{g}{2}(2t-2)2 = 2g(t-1)$$

$$= 2 \times 10\,(t-1)$$

$$\Rightarrow \quad 100 = 20t - 20$$

$$\Rightarrow \quad 20t = 120$$

$$\Rightarrow \quad t = 6\text{ s}$$

22. ***(12)*** Given, mass of ball, $m = 0.4$ kg

Initial speed, $u = 15$ m/s

Final speed of the ball,

$$v = -u = -15\text{ m/s}$$

$\therefore$ Impulse imparted to the ball,

$$I = \text{Change in momentum}$$

$$= m(v-u)$$

$$= 0.4[15-(-15)]$$

$$= 0.4 \times 30 = 12\text{ N-s}$$

23. ***(36)*** Given, mass of each ball,

$$m = 2\text{ kg}$$

The given situation is shown below.

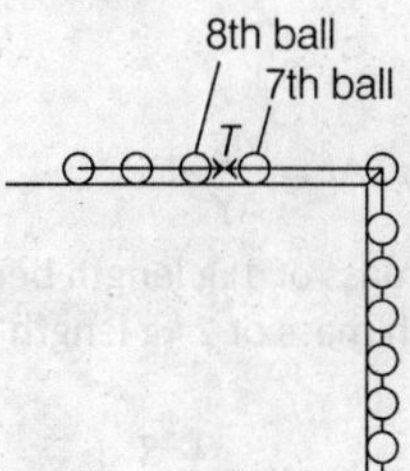

If a be the resultant acceleration, then

$$a = \frac{\text{net force } (F_{\text{net}})}{\text{mass of total ball}} = \frac{6mg}{10\,m}$$

$(\because F_{\text{net}} = $ weight of balls below the 7th ball $= 6\,mg)$

$$\Rightarrow \quad a = \frac{3g}{5}$$

But according to diagram,

$$T = 3ma = 3m \times \frac{3g}{5} = \frac{9}{5}mg$$

$$= \frac{9}{5} \times 2 \times 10 = 36\text{ N}$$

24. ***(42)*** Given, mass of water heated per min,

$$m = 2\text{ kg / min}$$

$$\Delta T = T_2 - T_1$$

$$= 70° - 30° = 40°\text{ C}$$

Heat gained by water per min,

$$= ms\Delta T$$

$$= 2000 \times 4.2 \times 40\text{ J/min}$$

$$= 3.36 \times 10^5\text{ J/min}$$

The rate of combustion of fuel

$$= \frac{dm}{dl} \times L$$

According to given condition,

$$\frac{dm}{dt} \cdot L = 3.36 \times 10^5$$

$$\Rightarrow \quad \frac{dm}{dt} = \frac{3.36 \times 10^5}{L} = \frac{3.36 \times 10^5}{8 \times 10^3}$$

$$\Rightarrow \quad \frac{dm}{dt} = 42\text{ g/min}$$

25. ***(540)*** Given, temperature of cold reservoir,

$$T_2 = 324\text{ K}$$

$$Q_1 = 300\text{ J}, Q_2 = 180\text{ J}$$

Let T_1 be the minimum temperature of hot reservoir, then efficiency of heat engine is given as

$$\eta = \frac{W}{Q_1} = 1 - \frac{T_2}{T_1}$$

$$\Rightarrow \quad \frac{W}{Q_1} = 1 - \frac{T_2}{T_1}$$

$$\Rightarrow \quad \frac{Q_1 - Q_2}{Q_1} = 1 - \frac{T_2}{T_1}$$

$$\Rightarrow \quad 1 - \frac{Q_2}{Q_1} = 1 - \frac{T_2}{T_1}$$

$$\Rightarrow \quad \frac{Q_2}{Q_1} = \frac{T_2}{T_1}$$

$$\Rightarrow \quad T_1 = T_2 \cdot \frac{Q_1}{Q_2}$$

$$= 324 \times \frac{300}{180} = 540\text{ K}$$

26. ***(152)*** Let f be frequency of first tuning fork.

According to given situation,

$$f_1 = f$$

Frequency of second tuning fork,

$$f_2 = f + 4$$

Frequency of third tuning fork,

$$f_3 = f + 2 \times 4$$

$$\vdots$$

$$f_{20} = f + (19 \times 4)$$

Since given that, $f_{20} = 2f_1$

$$\Rightarrow f + (19 \times 4) = 2f$$

$$\Rightarrow \quad f = 76\text{ Hz}$$

$\therefore$ Frequency of last tuning fork $= 2f$ $= 2 \times 76 = 152$ Hz

27. ***(5)*** Given, $l = l_1 = l_2 = 10\text{ cm} = 0.1\text{ m}$

$$i_1 = i_2 = 5\text{A}$$

$$F_1 = F_2 = 10^{-5}\text{ N}$$

If r be the separation between both wires, then force experienced by each wire,

$$F = \frac{\mu_0}{2\pi} \times \frac{i_1 i_2 l}{r}$$

$$\Rightarrow \quad 10^{-5} = \frac{2 \times 10^{-7} \times 5 \times 5 \times 0.1}{r}$$

$$\Rightarrow \quad r = 0.05\text{ m} = 5\text{ cm}$$

28. ***(9)*** The ray diagram for the given situation is shown below.

i.e. $\quad \mu_w = \dfrac{4}{3}$

Depth, $\quad h = \sqrt{7}$ m

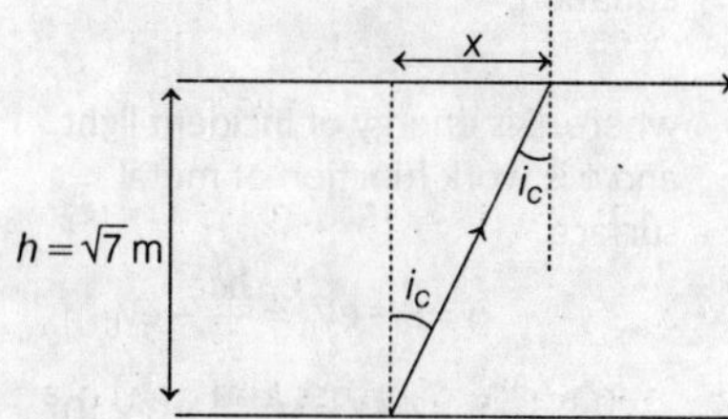

let i_c represents the critical angle, then from the diagram,

$$\tan i_c = \frac{x}{h} = \frac{x}{\sqrt{7}}$$

$$\Rightarrow \quad x = \sqrt{7}\tan i_c \quad \text{...(i)}$$

$$\text{But } \sin i_c = \frac{1}{\mu_w} = \frac{1}{4/3} = \frac{3}{4}$$

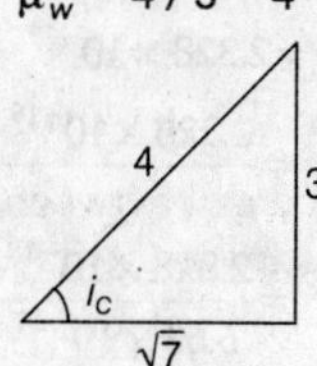

So, from above diagram, $\tan i_c = \dfrac{3}{\sqrt{7}}$

Putting this value in Eq. (i), we get

$$x = \sqrt{7} \times \frac{3}{\sqrt{7}} = 3\text{ m}$$

$\therefore$ Area of surface $= \pi x^2$

$$= \pi \times 3^2 = 9\pi\text{ m}^2$$

$$= x\pi\text{ m}^2 \quad \text{(given)}$$

$$\therefore \quad x = 9$$

29. ***(5)*** Given,

50 Vernier Scale Division (VSD) = 49 Main Scale Division (MSD)

i.e. 50 VSD = 49 MSD

$\Rightarrow \quad 1\text{ VSD} = \frac{49}{50}\text{ MSD}$ ...(i)

$\therefore$ Least count = 1MSD − 1VSD

$= 1\text{MSD} - \frac{49}{50}\text{MSD}$ [From Eq. (i)]

$= \text{MSD}\left(1 - \frac{49}{50}\right)$

$\Rightarrow$ Least count $= \frac{1}{50}$MSD

But, 1 MSD $= \frac{1}{40}$ cm

$\therefore$ Least count $= \frac{1}{50} \times \frac{1}{40}$

$= 5 \times 10^{-6}$ m

30. *(35)* Given, $\lambda = 6630\,\text{Å} = 6.63 \times 10^{-7}$ m

Stopping potential,

$V_0 = 0.42$ V

According to Einstein's photoelectric equation,

$eV_0 = E - \phi$

where, E is energy of incident light and ϕ is work function of metal surface.

$\therefore \quad \phi = E - eV_0 = \frac{hc}{\lambda} - eV_0$

$= \frac{6.63 \times 10^{-34} \times 3 \times 10^{8}}{6.63 \times 10^{-7}} - 1.6 \times 10^{-19} \times 0.42$

$= 3 \times 10^{-19} - 0.672 \times 10^{-19}$

$\phi = 2.328 \times 10^{-19}$ J

But $\phi = h\nu_0$, where ν_0 is threshold frequency.

$\Rightarrow h\nu_0 = 2.328 \times 10^{-19}$

$\Rightarrow \quad \nu_0 = \frac{2.328 \times 10^{-19}}{h}$

$= \frac{2.328 \times 10^{-19}}{6.63 \times 10^{-34}}$

$= 35 \times 10^{13}$/s

$= x \times 10^{13}$/s

$\therefore \quad x = 35$

Real Nut 3-29 June 2022, Shift-I

1. *(d)* Let both balls meet after t seconds.

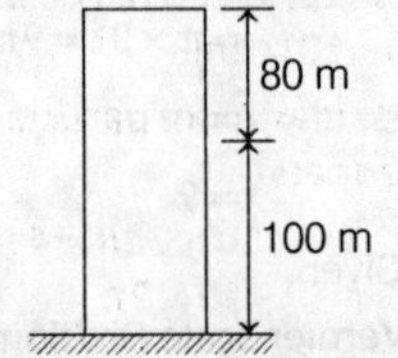

Then, displacement of ball A in t seconds = displacement of ball B in $(t-2)$ seconds

$\Rightarrow \frac{1}{2}gt^2 = x(t-2) + \frac{1}{2}g(t-2)^2$

$\Rightarrow \quad g[t^2 - (t-2)]^2 = 2u(t-2)$

$\Rightarrow \quad g(2)(2t-2) = 2u(t-2)$

$\Rightarrow \quad g(2t-2) = u(t-2)$ ... (i)

Also, displacement of ball A in t seconds = 80 m

$\Rightarrow \quad \frac{1}{2}gt^2 = 80 \Rightarrow t = 4$s .... (ii)

Substituting $t = 4$s in Eq. (i), we get

$g(8-2) = u(4-2)$

$\Rightarrow \quad u = 3 \times g = 30$ m/s

2. *(b)* Masses are in ratio 1:1:2, so masses are $\frac{M}{4}, \frac{M}{4}$ and $\frac{M}{2}$.

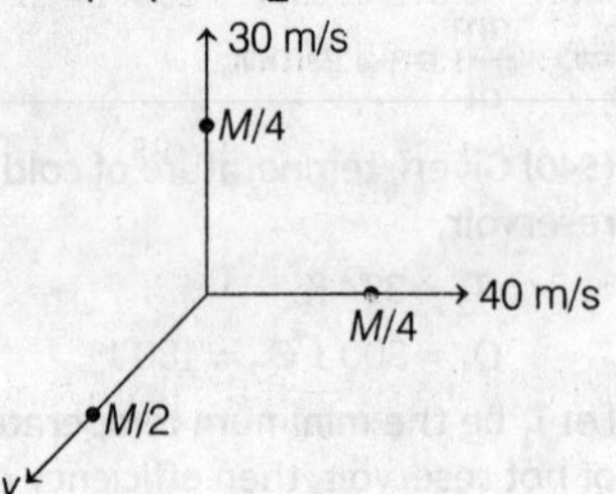

Let velocity of 3rd piece be

$v = v_x\,\hat{\mathbf{i}} + v_y\,\hat{\mathbf{j}}$

As momentum is conserved, $\Delta p_x = 0$ and $\Delta p_y = 0$

$\Rightarrow \quad \frac{M}{4} \times 30 + \frac{M}{2} \times v_y = 0$ ... (i)

and $\quad \frac{M}{4} \times 40 + \frac{M}{2} \times v_x = 0$ ... (ii)

By using Eqs. (i) and (ii), we get

$v_x = -20\,\hat{\mathbf{i}}$ m/s, $v_y = -15\,\hat{\mathbf{j}}$ m/s

Hence, $\quad \mathbf{v} = -20\,\hat{\mathbf{i}} - 15\,\hat{\mathbf{j}}$

or $\quad |\mathbf{v}| = \sqrt{20^2 + 15^2} = 25$ m/s

3. *(b)* Activity after n half-lives is

$R = \frac{R_0}{2^n}$ ... (i)

Here, $\quad R_0 = 2.56 \times 10^{-3}$ Ci

and $\quad R = 2 \times 10^{-5}$Ci

From Eq. (i), we have

$\frac{2 \times 10^{-5}}{2.56 \times 10^{-3}} = \frac{1}{2^n}$

$\Rightarrow \quad \frac{2}{256} = \frac{1}{2^n}$

$\Rightarrow \quad \frac{1}{128} = \frac{1}{2^n}$

or $\quad \frac{1}{2^7} = \frac{1}{2^n}$

or $\quad n = 7$

So, 7 half-lives are elapsed or, time interval $= 7 \times 5 = 35$ days.

4. *(c)* Angular momentum about origin = Angular momentum due to translation + Angular momentum due to rotation

$\Rightarrow \quad L = L_T + L_R$

$= MvR + I\omega$

Now, as $v = R\omega$ and $I = \frac{2}{3}MR^2$

So, $\quad L = MR^2\omega + \frac{2}{3}MR^2\omega$

$= \frac{5}{3}MR^2\omega.$

As $\quad L = \frac{a}{3}MR^2\,\omega$ (given)

So, $\quad a = 5$

5. *(c)* At STP, 1 mole of a gas has a volume of 22.4 L

So, number of moles,

$n = \frac{\text{Gas Volume}}{\text{Molar Volume}} = \frac{44.8}{22.4}$

or $\quad n = 2$

Now, amount of heat required to heat the gas in cylinder of constant volume is

$\Delta Q = n\,C_V \Delta T$

$= 2 \times \frac{3}{2}R \times \Delta T$

(He is monoatomic, $\therefore C_V = \frac{3}{2}R$)

So, $\quad \Delta Q = 2 \times \frac{3}{2} \times 8.3 \times 20$

$= 498$ J

6. *(c)* Using, $\Delta L = \frac{Mg}{AY} \cdot L$

If with mass of 1kg length becomes L_1 and with mass of 2 kg length becomes L_2.

So, $\quad L_1 - L = \frac{1 \cdot g}{AY} \cdot L$ ...(i)

and $\quad L_2 - L = \frac{2 \cdot g}{AY} \cdot L$ ...(ii)

Now, on multiplying Eq. (i) by 2 and then subtracting Eq. (ii) from it, we get

$2(L_1 - L) - (L_2 - L) = \frac{2gL}{AY} - \frac{2gL}{AY}$

or $\quad 2L_1 - 2L - L_2 + L = 0$

or $\quad 2L_1 - L_2 = L$

7. *(b)* By Einstein's photoelectric equation,

$$K_{max} = hf - \phi_0$$

As K_{max} must be positive or zero,

$$hf - \phi_0 \geq 0$$

or $hf \geq \phi_0$ (I statement)

When $hf = \phi_0, K_{max} = 0$ (II statement)

But statement II is not an explanation of statement I because both are different versions of same statement.

8. *(d)* Given velocity, $v = 0.25(x^{5/2})$

So, at $x = 0$, $v = 0$ m/s

and at $x = 4$m, $v = 0.25 \times 4^{5/2}$

$$\Rightarrow \quad v = 0.25 \times (4^{1/2})^5 = 0.25 \times 2^5$$

$$= 0.25 \times 32 = 8 \text{ m/s.}$$

Now by work-energy theorem,

Work done by net force = Change in KE

$$\Rightarrow \text{Work done} = \frac{1}{2} m(v_f^2 - v_i^2)$$

$$= \frac{1}{2} \times \left(\frac{500}{1000}\right) \times 8^2 = 16 \text{ J}$$

9. *(c)* Kinetic energy of a particle rotating in a magnetic field is

$$KE = \frac{1}{2} mv^2 = \frac{B^2q^2r^2}{2m}$$

$$\left[\because r = \frac{mv}{Bq} \Rightarrow v = \frac{rBq}{m}\right]$$

$$\Rightarrow \quad KE \propto r^2$$

$$\Rightarrow \quad \frac{K_f}{K_i} = \left(\frac{r_f}{r_i}\right)^2$$

Given, $K_f = 4K_i$

$$\Rightarrow \quad \left(\frac{r_f}{r_i}\right)^2 = 4$$

$$\Rightarrow \quad r_f = 2r_i$$

or $\quad \frac{r_f}{r_i} = \frac{2}{1}$

10. *(c)* For a series *L-C-R* circuit, *I versus* ω curve is shown below

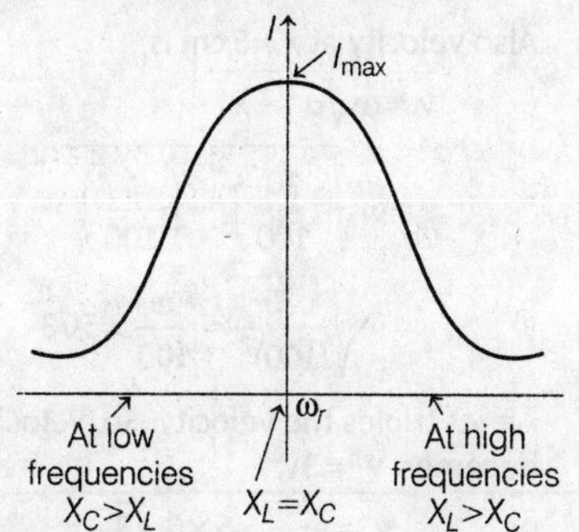

Therefore, to the left of ω_r, $X_C > X_L$ hence circuit is mainly capacitive.

And to the right of ω_r, $X_L > X_C$, hence, circuit is mainly inductive.

As impedance, $Z = \sqrt{(X_L - X_C)^2 + R^2}$

and at resonance $X_L = X_C$.

So, $\quad Z = R$

11. *(c)* Force of jet on block

= rate of change of momentum

or $\quad F = \frac{d}{dt} mv = v \cdot \frac{dm}{dt}$ (as v = constant)

$$\therefore \quad F = v \times \frac{dm}{dt}$$

Here, $v = 10$ m/s and $\frac{dm}{dt} = 1$ kg/s

So, force on block, $F = 10 \times 1 = 10$ N

Acceleration of block,

$$a = \frac{F}{m} = \frac{10}{2} = 5 \text{ ms}^{-2}$$

12. *(c)* As $\frac{a}{V^2}$ is added to pressure, so dimensions of $\frac{a}{V^2}$ must be that of pressure.

Also, dimensions of *b* must be that of volume

$$\Rightarrow \quad \left[\frac{a}{V^2}\right] = [p]$$

$$\Rightarrow \quad \frac{[a]}{[L^6]} = \frac{[MLT^{-2}]}{[L^2]}$$

$$\Rightarrow \quad [a] = [ML^5 T^{-2}]$$

and $\quad [b] = [V] = [L^3]$

So, $\quad \left[\frac{a}{b}\right] = \frac{[ML^5T^{-2}]}{[L^3]} = [ML^2T^{-2}]$

These are dimensions of work or energy and pV = work due to pressure. Hence, $\frac{a}{b} = pV$

13. *(c)* Given, $|\mathbf{A} + \mathbf{B}| = 2|\mathbf{A} - \mathbf{B}|$

or $\quad (\mathbf{A} + \mathbf{B})^2 = 4 \cdot (\mathbf{A} - \mathbf{B})^2$

$$\Rightarrow \quad \mathbf{A}^2 + \mathbf{B}^2 + 2\mathbf{A} \cdot \mathbf{B} = 4 \cdot (\mathbf{A}^2 + \mathbf{B}^2 - 2\mathbf{A} \cdot \mathbf{B})$$

$$\Rightarrow \quad \mathbf{A}^2 + \mathbf{B}^2 + 2\mathbf{AB}\cos\theta = 4(\mathbf{A}^2 + \mathbf{B}^2 - 2\mathbf{AB}\cos\theta)$$

Given, $|\mathbf{A}| = |\mathbf{B}| = x$ (let)

Then, $\quad x^2 + x^2 + 2x^2 \cos\theta = 4(x^2 + x^2 - 2x^2 \cos\theta)$

$$\Rightarrow \quad 2 + 2\cos\theta = 4(2 - 2\cos\theta)$$

$$\Rightarrow \quad 1 + \cos\theta = 4 - 4\cos\theta$$

$$\Rightarrow \quad 5\cos\theta = 3$$

or $\quad \cos\theta = \frac{3}{5} \Rightarrow \theta = \cos^{-1}\left(\frac{3}{5}\right)$

14. *(a)* Escape velocity of a mass over a planet,

$$v_{esc} = \sqrt{\frac{2GM}{R}}, M = \frac{4}{3}\pi R^3 \cdot \rho$$

$$\Rightarrow \quad v_{esc} = \sqrt{\frac{8}{3} G\pi R^2 \cdot \rho} \text{ or } v_{esc} \propto R\sqrt{\rho}$$

$$\Rightarrow \quad \frac{v_B}{v_A} = \frac{R_B}{R_A} \cdot \sqrt{\frac{\rho_B}{\rho_A}}$$

Here, $v_A = 12$ km/s, $\rho_B = 4\rho_A$

and $\quad R_B = \frac{1}{2} R_A$

Hence, $\quad \frac{v_B}{v_A} = \frac{1}{2} \times \sqrt{4}$

$$\Rightarrow \quad v_B = v_A \text{ or } v_B = 12 \text{ km/s}$$

15. *(a)* Given, horizontal component, $B_H = 0.5$ G and angle of dip, $\delta = 30°$

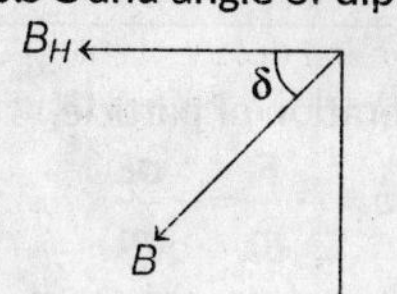

As $\quad B_H = B\cos\delta$

and $\quad B_V = B\sin\delta$

So, $\quad B = \frac{B_H}{\cos\delta}$

And $\quad B_V = \frac{B_H}{\cos\delta} \cdot \sin\delta = B_H \tan\delta$

$$\Rightarrow \quad B_V = 0.5 \times \tan 30° = 0.5/\sqrt{3} \text{ G}$$

Hence, earth's total magnetic field,

$$B = \sqrt{B_H^2 + B_V^2}$$

$$= \sqrt{(0.5)^2 + \frac{(0.5)^2}{3}} = \frac{1}{\sqrt{3}} \text{ G}$$

16. *(b)* Wave equation is given as

$$y = 10\sin\left(2\pi nt - \frac{2\pi}{\lambda} \cdot x\right)$$

$$\text{Wave speed} = \frac{\omega}{k} = \frac{2\pi n}{(2\pi/\lambda)} = n\lambda$$

Maximum speed of oscillating particle $= A\omega = 10(2\pi n)$

Given, maximum particle speed = 4 × wave speed

$$\Rightarrow \quad 10 \times 2\pi n = 4 \times n\lambda$$

$$\Rightarrow \quad \frac{10 \times 2\pi}{4} = \lambda$$

or $\quad \lambda = 5\pi$ units

17. *(a)* Energy of a capacitor charged to potential V,

$$U = \frac{1}{2}CV^2 = \frac{1}{2}\frac{\varepsilon_0 A}{d}\cdot V^2 \cdot K \quad \left[\because C = \frac{\varepsilon_0 KA}{d}\right]$$

$\Rightarrow \frac{U_f}{U_i} = \frac{K_f}{K_i} = \frac{15}{10}$ (as all other parameters remain constant)

Percentage change in energy,

$$\frac{U_f - U_i}{U_i}\times 100 = \frac{K_f - K_i}{K_i}\times 100$$

$$= \left[\frac{K_f}{K_i} - 1\right]\times 100 = \left[\frac{15}{10} - 1\right]\times 100$$

$$= \frac{15-10}{10}\times 100 = 50\%$$

Hence, energy increases by 50%.

18. *(d)* The given situation is shown below

$u = 200$ m/s, a, $q = 40\ \mu$C

Acceleration of particle,

$$a = -\frac{F}{m} = -\frac{qE}{m}$$

$$= -\left(\frac{40\times 10^{-6}\times 1\times 10^5}{100\times 10^{-3}\times 10^{-3}}\right)$$

$$= -\left(\frac{40}{100}\times 10^5\right)$$

$$= -4\times 10^4\ \text{m/s}^2$$

Now, using $v^2 - u^2 = 2as$, we have

$$0 - (200)^2 = 2(-4\times 10^4)\times s$$

$$\Rightarrow \frac{200\times 200}{2\times 4\times 10^4} = s$$

or $s = 0.5$ m

19. *(d)* Fringe width, $\beta = \frac{\lambda D}{d}$

$$\Rightarrow \frac{\beta_2}{\beta_1} = \frac{\lambda_2}{\lambda_1}\times\frac{d_1}{d_2} \quad \text{...(i)}$$

Here, $d_2 = 2\,d_1$ and $\lambda_1 = 5000$ Å

$\lambda_2 = 6000$ Å, and $\beta_1 = 0.5$ mm

Hence, from Eq. (i), we get

$$\beta_2 = 0.5\times\frac{6000}{5000}\times\frac{1}{2}$$

$\Rightarrow \beta_2 = 0.3$ mm

20. *(b)* Wavelength used for optical communicating system

$= 1000$ nm

So, frequency of signal used

$$= f = \frac{v}{\lambda} = \frac{3\times 10^8}{1000\times 10^{-9}}$$

$\Rightarrow f = 3\times 10^{14}$ Hz

Given, channel bandwidth available $= 2\%$ of central frequency

$$= \frac{2}{100}\times 3\times 10^{14}\ \text{Hz}$$

$$= 6\times 10^{12}\ \text{Hz}$$

Number of channels possible

$$= \frac{\text{Total available bandwidth}}{\text{Bandwidth per channel}}$$

$$= \frac{6\times 10^{12}}{8\times 10^3} = 0.75\times 10^9$$

$$= 75\times 10^7\ \text{channels}$$

21. *(15)* Let resistances of coils be R_1 and R_2, V is potential of source and Q is the heat produced.

Then, using $Q = \frac{V^2}{R}t$, we have

For coil-1, $\quad Q = \frac{V^2}{R_1}t_1 \quad$ ... (i)

For coil-2, $\quad Q = \frac{V^2}{R_2}\times t_2 \quad$ ... (ii)

For combination of coils if R is equivalent resistance in parallel, then

$$Q = \frac{V^2}{R}\times t \quad \text{... (iii)}$$

where, t = time required by combination to produce same heat.

n parallel, $\quad \frac{1}{R} = \frac{1}{R_1} + \frac{1}{R_2} \quad$ ... (iv)

Substituting for R, R_1 and R_2 from Eqs. (i), (ii), (iii), in Eq. (iv), we get

$$\frac{Q}{V^2 t} = \frac{Q}{V^2 t_1} + \frac{Q}{V^2 t_2}$$

$$\Rightarrow \frac{1}{t} = \frac{1}{t_1} + \frac{1}{t_2} \quad \text{or} \quad t = \frac{t_1 t_2}{t_1 + t_2}$$

Here, $t_1 = 20$ min and $t_2 = 60$ min

So, $\quad t = \frac{20\times 60}{20+60} = 15$ min

Hence, parallel combination of coil produces same heat in 15 min.

22. *(43)* Intensity, I and magnitude of electric field, E are related as

$$I = \frac{1}{2}\varepsilon_0 E^2\cdot c \Rightarrow E^2 = \frac{2I}{\varepsilon_0\times c}$$

Also, $\quad \frac{E}{B} = c \Rightarrow E = B\cdot c$

So, $\quad B^2 = \frac{2I}{\varepsilon_0\times c^3}$

Substituting values, we get

$$\Rightarrow B^2 = \frac{2\times 0.22}{8.85\times 10^{-12}\times 27\times 10^{24}}$$

$$\Rightarrow B = \sqrt{\left(\frac{2\times 0.22}{8.85\times 27\times 10^{12}}\right)}$$

$$= 0.429\times 10^{-7} = 42.9\times 10^{-9}\ \text{T}$$

or $\quad B \approx 43\times 10^{-9}$ T

23. *(21)* The given figure for two plates A and B is given as

100°C | A: 4.0 cm, K | B: 2.5 cm, $2K$ | 0°C; $A = 120\ \text{cm}^2$

For series combination,

$$R_{\text{series}} = R_1 + R_2 + \ldots$$

$$\Rightarrow \frac{l_1 + l_2 + \ldots}{K_{eq}\,A} = \frac{l_1}{K_1 A} + \frac{l_2}{K_2 A} + \ldots$$

$\Rightarrow$ For two slabs of same area, we have

$$\frac{l_1 + l_2}{K_{eq}} = \frac{l_1}{K_1} + \frac{l_2}{K_2}$$

Here, $l_1 = 4$ cm, $K_1 = K$, $l_2 = 2.5$ cm and $K_2 = 2K$

So, $\quad \frac{4 + 2.5}{K_{eq}} = \frac{4}{K} + \frac{2.5}{2K}$

$$\Rightarrow \frac{6.5}{K_{eq}} = \frac{10.5}{2K}$$

or $\quad K_{eq} = \frac{13K}{10.5} = \frac{26}{21}K = \left(1 + \frac{5}{21}\right)K$

$$= \left(1 + \frac{5}{\alpha}\right)K \quad \text{(given)}$$

$\alpha = 21$

24. *(700)* Initial amplitude of vibration, $a = 10$ cm $= 0.1$ m

Total energy of body = Kinetic energy at mean position

$$\frac{1}{2}m\omega^2 a^2 = \frac{1}{2}m\omega^2 (0.1)^2$$

Potential energy of body (at $x = 5$ cm),

PE ($x = 5$ cm), $\quad U_1 = \frac{1}{2}m\omega^2 x^2$

$$= \frac{1}{2}m\omega^2\left(\frac{5}{100}\right)^2$$

Also velocity at $x = 5$ cm is,

$$v = \omega\sqrt{a^2 - x^2}$$

$$= \omega\sqrt{\left(\frac{10}{100}\right)^2 - \left(\frac{5}{100}\right)^2}$$

$$= \omega\sqrt{\frac{75}{(100)^2}} = \frac{\omega}{100}\times 5\sqrt{3}$$

Air jet triples the velocity. So, velocity becomes, $v' = 3v$

or $\quad v' = \frac{\omega}{100}\times 5\times 3\sqrt{3}$

Now, total energy of body becomes,

$E_{total} = PE + KE$

$$= \frac{1}{2}m\omega^2 \times \left(\frac{5}{100}\right)^2 + \frac{1}{2}m(v')^2$$

$$= \frac{1}{2}m\omega^2 \times \left(\frac{5}{100}\right)^2 + \frac{1}{2}m\omega^2 \times \left(\frac{5}{100}\right)^2 \times (3\sqrt{3})^2$$

$$= \frac{1}{2}m\omega^2 \times \frac{5^2}{100^2}(1+27)$$

$$= \frac{1}{2}m\omega^2 \times \frac{25\times 28}{(100)^2}$$

So, amplitude a' is such that,

$$a'^2 = \frac{25\times 28}{(100)^2}$$

or amplitude, $a' = \sqrt{\frac{25}{100}\times\frac{28}{100}}$

$= \sqrt{\frac{7}{100}}$ m

$= \sqrt{\frac{7}{100}}\times 100$ cm

or $a' = \sqrt{700}$ cm

Hence, $x = 700$

25. *(144)* As, $V = R \cdot I$ (by Ohm's Law)

So, slope of V (on Y-axis) and I (on X-axis) graph is R.

In given graph,

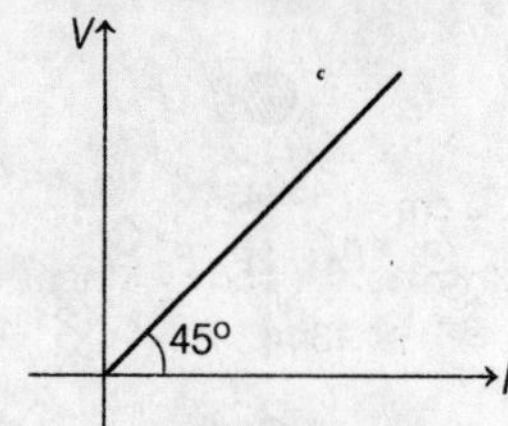

Slope $= \tan\theta = R = 1\,\Omega$

Now, using $R = \rho\frac{l}{A}$

We have resistivity,

$$\rho = \frac{R\times A}{l} = \frac{R\times\pi d^2}{4l}$$

Here diameter, $d = 2.4$ cm,

length, $l = 31.4$ or $\frac{\pi}{10}$ cm

On substituting values, we get

$$\rho = \frac{1\times\pi\times 2.4\times 2.4\times 10^{-4}}{4\times\left(\frac{\pi}{10}\right)\times 10^{-2}}$$

or $\rho = 1.44\times 10^{-3}\ \Omega$-m

$= 144\times 10^{-3}\ \Omega$-cm

So $x = 144$

26. *(102)* For a heat (Carnot) engine,

$$\frac{Q_1}{Q_2} = \frac{T_1}{T_2}$$

Here, $Q_1 = 300$ cal

$Q_2 = 225$ cal

$T_1 = 227\,°C$

$= 500$ K

So, $\frac{300}{225} = \frac{500}{T_2}$

$\Rightarrow T_2 = \frac{500}{300}\times 225$

or $T_2 = 375\text{K} = [375 - 273]\,l$

$= 102\,°C$

So, sink temperature is 102°C.

27. *(3)*

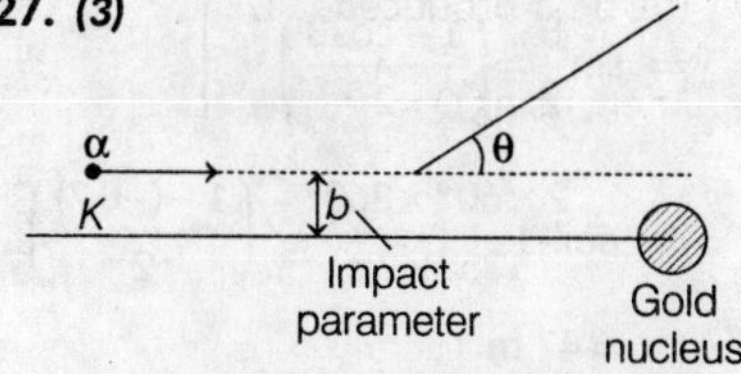

Impact parameter b is given by

$$b = \frac{Ze^2\cdot\cot(\theta/2)}{4\pi\varepsilon_0\cdot(KE_\alpha)}$$

or $b \propto \cot\frac{\theta}{2}$

With given values, we have

$$\therefore \frac{\sqrt{d_1}}{\sqrt{d_2}} = \frac{\cot(60°/2)}{\cot(90°/2)} = \frac{\cot 30°}{\cot 45°}$$

or $\frac{\sqrt{d_1}}{\sqrt{d_2}} = \frac{\sqrt{3}}{1}$

$\Rightarrow d_1 = 3d_2$

Hence, value of x is 3.

28. *(2)* In common emitter configuration,

Power gain,

$$P_{gain} = \frac{\Delta P_{out}}{\Delta P_{in}} = (\beta_{AC})^2 \times \text{Resistance gain}$$

$$= \left(\frac{\Delta i_C}{\Delta i_B}\right)^2 \times \left(\frac{R_o}{R_I}\right)$$

Here, $\Delta i_C = 10\times 10^{-3}$ A

$\Delta i_B = 100\times 10^{-6}$ A

$R_o = 2\times 1000\ \Omega$

$R_I = 1\times 1000\ \Omega$

So, power gain

$$= \left(\frac{10\times 10^{-3}}{100\times 10^{-6}}\right)^2 \times \left(\frac{2\times 1000}{1\times 1000}\right)$$

$= 2\times 10^4$

Hence, $x = 2$

29. *(225)* Given situation is

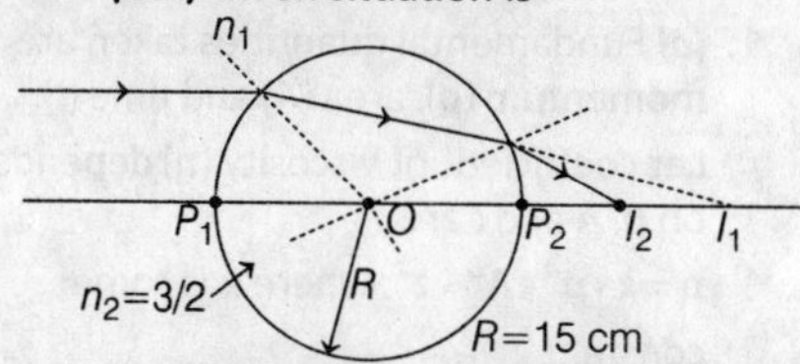

For refraction at first surface,

$u = \infty$, $v = P_1I_1$,

$R = P_1O = +15$ cm

$n_2 = \frac{3}{2}$, $n_1 = 1$

By refraction formula,

$-\frac{n_1}{u} + \frac{n_2}{v} = \frac{n_2 - n_1}{R}$, we get

$$-\frac{1}{\infty} + \frac{3}{2v} = \frac{\frac{3}{2}-1}{15}$$

$\Rightarrow v = 45$ cm.

This image I_1 acts like a virtual object for refraction at second surface.

Fo second surface,

$u = P_2I_1 = 45 - 30 = 15$ cm

$R = -15$ cm, $v = P_2I_2$

And for second surface as light is now going from glass to air, refraction formula will be

$$-\frac{n_2}{u} + \frac{n_1}{v} = \frac{n_1 - n_2}{R_2}$$

So, $-\frac{3}{2\times 15} + \frac{1}{v} = \frac{1-(3/2)}{-15}$

$\Rightarrow v = P_2I_2 = 7.5$ cm

So, distance of image I_2 from centre of the sphere

$= OP_2 + P_2I_2$

$= 15 + 7.5 = 22.5$ cm $= 225$ mm

30. *(10)* The circuit diagram is shown below

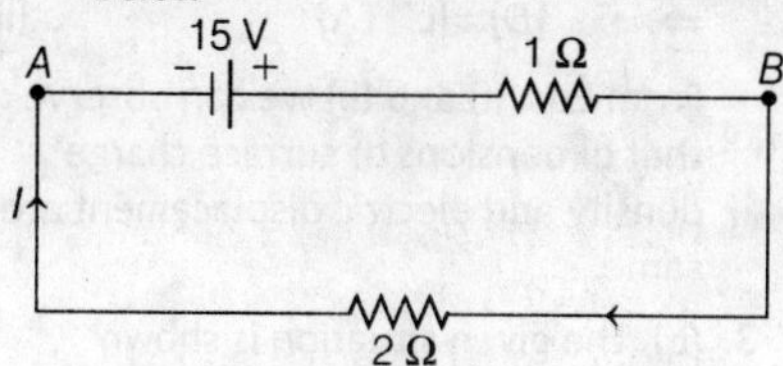

Current in circuit,

$$I = \frac{V}{R_{total}} = \frac{15}{3} = 5\text{ A.}$$

Now potential drop in 2 Ω resistance

$= V_2 = IR$

$= 5\times 2 = 10$ V

Hence, $V_{BA} = V_B - V_A = V_2$

$= 10$ V

Real Nut 4-25 July 2022, Shift-I

1. *(a)* Fundamental quantities taken are momentum (p), area (A) and time (t).

Let coefficient of viscosity (η) depends on p, A and t are

$\eta = k \cdot p^a \cdot A^b \cdot t^c$, where k is some constant

Then writing dimensions of all quantities and comparing, we get

$$[ML^{-1}T^{-1}] = [MLT^{-1}]^a [L^2]^b [T]^c$$

$$\Rightarrow \quad M = M^a \Rightarrow a = 1$$

$$M^{-1} = L^{a+2b}$$

$$\Rightarrow \quad a + 2b = -1$$

$$\text{or} \quad 2b = -2$$

$$\Rightarrow \quad b = -1$$

$$\text{and} \quad T^{-1} = T^{-a+c}$$

$$\Rightarrow \quad -a + c = -1$$

$$\text{or} \quad -1 + c = -1$$

$$c = 0$$

So, coefficient of viscosity has dimension

$$[\eta] = [p^1 A^{-1} t^0] = [pA^{-1} t^0]$$

2. *(a)* Surface charge density,

$$\sigma = \frac{Q}{A} = \frac{I \cdot t}{A}$$

$$\Rightarrow \quad [\sigma] = \frac{[I][t]}{[A]} = \frac{[AT]}{[L^2]}$$

$$\Rightarrow \quad [\sigma] = [L^{-2}TA] \quad \text{...(i)}$$

Electric displacement,

$$\mathbf{D} = \varepsilon_0 faEe\mathbf{E}$$

$$\Rightarrow \quad D = \frac{Q^2}{F \cdot r^2} \cdot \frac{F}{Q} = \frac{Q}{r^2}$$

$$\Rightarrow \quad D = \frac{I \cdot t}{r^2}$$

$$\Rightarrow \quad [D] = \frac{[I][t]}{[r^2]} = \frac{[A][T]}{[L^2]}$$

$$\Rightarrow \quad [D] = [L^{-2}TA] \quad \text{...(ii)}$$

From Eqs. (i) and (ii) we can observe that dimensions of surface charge density and electric displacement are same.

3. *(b)* The given situation is shown below

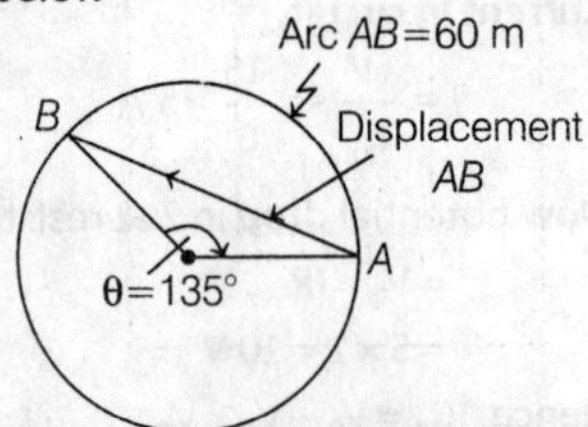

Displacement AB = (chord AB)

$$= 2 \times R \times \sin\left(\frac{\theta}{2}\right)$$

Also, arc $AB = 2\pi R \times \dfrac{\theta}{360°}$

$$\Rightarrow \quad R = \frac{AB \times 360°}{\theta \times 2\pi}$$

So, displacement AB = chord AB

$$= 2 \times \frac{AB \times 360°}{\theta \times 2\pi} \times \sin\left(\frac{\theta}{2}\right)$$

$$= 2 \times \frac{AB \times 360°}{\theta \times 2\pi} \times \left\{\left(\frac{1 - \cos\theta}{2}\right)\right\}^{1/2}$$

$$\left[\because 2\sin^2\frac{\theta}{2} = 1 - \cos\theta\right.$$

$$\left.\Rightarrow \sin\frac{\theta}{2} = \left(\frac{1-\cos\theta}{2}\right)^{1/2}\right]$$

$$= \frac{2 \times 60° \times 360°}{135° \times 2\pi} \times \left(\frac{1 - (-0.7)}{2}\right)^{1/2}$$

$$= 47 \text{ m}$$

4. *(b)* Given, mass of body, $m = 0.5$ kg, velocity of body, $v = (3x^2 + 4)$ m/s

Now velocity at $x = 0$ is,

$$v(x=0) = 3 \times 0^2 + 4 = 4 \text{ m/s}$$

and velocity at $x = 2$ m is,

$$v(x=2) = 3 \times 2^2 + 4 = 16 \text{ m/s}$$

By work-kinetic energy theorem,

Work done by force = change in kinetic energy

$$= \frac{1}{2}m(v^2 - u^2)$$

$$= \frac{1}{2} \times 0.5(16^2 - 4^2)$$

$$= 60 \text{ J}$$

5. *(d)* When a body rolls down an inclined plane,

Potential energy at top of incline = Kinetic energy of rotation + Kinetic energy of translation of CM

$$\Rightarrow \quad Mgh = \frac{1}{2}I\omega^2 + \frac{1}{2}Mv^2$$

$$\Rightarrow \quad Mgh = \frac{1}{2}MK^2\left(\frac{v^2}{r^2}\right) + \frac{1}{2}Mv^2 \quad \left[\because \omega = \frac{v}{r}\right]$$

$$\Rightarrow \quad Mgh = \frac{1}{2}Mv^2\left(1 + \frac{K^2}{R^2}\right) \quad \text{...(i)}$$

Here, I = moment of inertia = MK^2,

K = radius of gyration.

For solid cylinder, $\dfrac{K^2}{R^2} = \dfrac{1}{2}$

For solid sphere, $\dfrac{K^2}{R^2} = \dfrac{2}{5}$

Now, if we take ratio of Eq. (i) for solid cylinder and solid sphere (for both mgh term will be same), we have

$$\frac{(mgh)_{cyl}}{(mgh)_{sphere}} = \frac{\frac{1}{2}Mv_{cyl}^2\left(1 + \frac{K^2}{R}\right)_{cyl}}{\frac{1}{2}Mv_{sphere}^2\left(1 + \frac{K^2}{R^2}\right)_{sphere}}$$

(For both bodies, mass and height are same)

$$\Rightarrow \quad 1 = \frac{v_{cyl}^2}{v_{sphere}^2} \cdot \frac{\left(1 + \frac{1}{2}\right)}{\left(1 + \frac{2}{5}\right)}$$

$$\Rightarrow \quad \frac{v_{cyl}^2}{v_{sphere}^2} = \frac{1 + \frac{2}{5}}{1 + \frac{1}{2}} = \frac{7}{5} \times \frac{2}{3}$$

$$\Rightarrow \quad \frac{v_{cyl}}{v_{sphere}} = \sqrt{\frac{14}{15}}$$

6. *(b)* Given, $m_A = m_B = m_C = m_P = 100$ kg

The given situation is shown below.

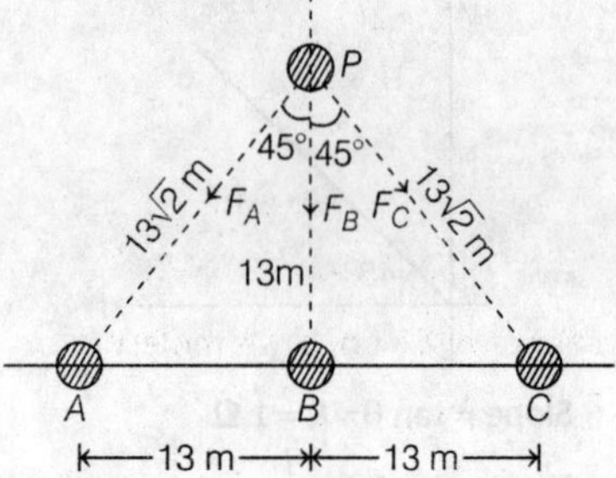

Force F on particle at P is resultant of F_A, F_C and F_B.

$$\therefore \quad F = \sqrt{F_A^2 + F_C^2} + F_B$$

As $F_A = F_C$, we have

$$F = \sqrt{2} \cdot F_A + F_B$$

$$= \sqrt{2} \times \frac{Gm^2}{13^2 \times 2} + \frac{Gm^2}{13^2}$$

$$= \frac{Gm^2}{13^2} \times \left(\frac{1}{\sqrt{2}} + 1\right)$$

$$\approx \frac{G \times 100^2}{13^2} \times \left(\frac{2.4}{1.4}\right) \approx 100\, G$$

7. *(b)*

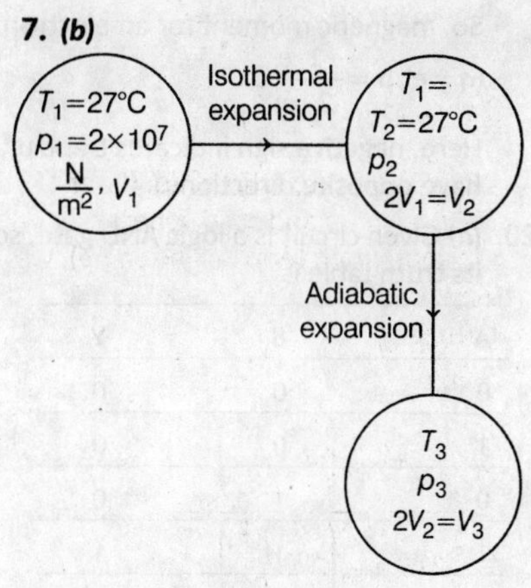

When gas is expanded isothermally,

$$p_1V_1 = p_2V_2$$

Given, $V_2 = 2V_1$

$\Rightarrow \quad p_2 = p_1 \times \frac{V_1}{V_2}$

or $\quad p_2 = p_1 \times \frac{V_1}{2V_1} = \frac{p_1}{2}$

or $\quad p_2 = \frac{2 \times 10^7}{2} = 1 \times 10^7 \text{ Nm}^{-2}$

Now gas is expanded adiabatically,

$\Rightarrow \quad p_2V_2^\gamma = p_3V_3^\gamma$

Given, $V_3 = 2V_2$

So, $p_2 \cdot V_2^\gamma = p_3(2V_2)^\gamma$

$\Rightarrow \quad p_3 = \frac{p_2}{2^\gamma} = \frac{1 \times 10^7}{2^{1.5}}$

$\Rightarrow \quad p_3 = \frac{1 \times 10^7}{(2^{3/2})} = \frac{1 \times 10^7}{2\sqrt{2}}$

$= 0.3536 \times 10^7$

$= 3.536 \times 10^6 \text{ N/m}^2$

8. *(a)* Average KE of a gas molecule is

$E_{avg} = \frac{1}{2}k_BT$

i.e. $E_{avg} \propto T$

So, average energy decrease with decrease of temperature .

$\therefore$Statement (A) is correct.

Average KE of a gas molecule does not depends on pressure volume or nature of gas.

$\therefore$Statement (B) is incorrect.

Average KE does not changes with volume.

$\therefore$Statement (C) is incorrect.

As, $\quad pV = nRT.$

So, $p \propto T$ at constant volume

$\therefore$Statement (D) is correct and statement (E) is incorrect.

9. *(a)* In first case, springs are in parallel so, $k_{eq} = k_1 + k_2 = k + k = 2k$ and mass of oscillating block is $m_{eq} = m + 2m = 3m$,

$\therefore$Time period of oscillation

$$T_1 = 2\pi\sqrt{\frac{m_{eq}}{k_{eq}}}$$

$$\Rightarrow \quad T_1 = 2\pi\sqrt{\frac{3m}{2k}} \quad \text{...(i)}$$

In second case, springs are in parallel,

$$k_{eq} = k + 2k = 3k$$

and mass of oscillating block, $m_{eq} = m$

Time period of oscillation,

$$T_2 = 2\pi\sqrt{\frac{m}{3k}} \quad \text{...(ii)}$$

So, $\quad \frac{T_1}{T_2} = \frac{2\pi\sqrt{\frac{3m}{2k}}}{2\pi\sqrt{\frac{m}{3k}}}$

$\Rightarrow \quad \frac{T_1}{T_2} = \sqrt{\frac{3m}{2k}} \times \sqrt{\frac{3k}{m}}$

$\Rightarrow \quad \frac{T_1}{T_2} = \frac{3}{\sqrt{2}}$

10. *(a)* As, $C = \frac{Q}{V}$; $V = \frac{Q}{C}$

So, when capacitor is fully charged; given

$$Q = 5\,C \text{ and } C = 2 \times 10^{-6} \text{ F}$$

$$V = \frac{5}{2 \times 10^{-6}} = 2.5 \times 10^6 \text{ V}$$

Also, $V = \left(\frac{1}{C}\right) \times Q$

This is equation of a straight line with slope $\frac{1}{C}$.

Hence, correct graph is

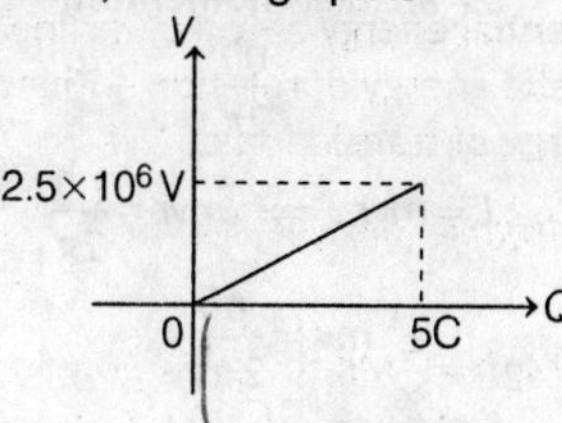

11. *(b)* Given, particles *A* and *B* have same kinetic energies and their mass ratio is $\frac{9}{4}$. Also, ratio of their radii (respectively) is $\frac{6}{5}$.

i.e., $\quad K_A = K_B$

$\Rightarrow \quad \frac{1}{2}m_Av_A^2 = \frac{1}{2}m_Bv_B^2$

and $\quad \frac{m_A}{m_B} = \frac{9}{4}$, also $\frac{r_A}{r_B} = \frac{6}{5}$

Now, $\frac{1}{2}m_Av_A^2 = \frac{1}{2}m_Bv_B^2$

$\Rightarrow \quad \left(\frac{v_A}{v_B}\right)^2 = \frac{m_B}{m_A} = \frac{4}{9}$

or $\quad \frac{v_A}{v_B} = \frac{2}{3}$

As, radius of rotation of a charged particle in magnetic field,

$$r = \frac{mv}{qB}$$

So, $\quad \frac{r_A}{r_B} = \frac{m_Av_A}{q_A \cdot B} \times \frac{q_B \cdot B}{m_Bv_B}$

$\Rightarrow \quad \frac{r_A}{r_B} = \frac{m_A}{m_B} \cdot \frac{v_A}{v_B} \cdot \frac{q_B}{q_A}$

Substituting values $\frac{r_A}{r_B}$, $\frac{m_A}{m_B}$ and $\frac{v_A}{v_B}$, we get

$$\frac{6}{5} = \frac{9}{4} \times \frac{2}{3} \times \frac{q_B}{q_A}$$

$\Rightarrow \quad \frac{q_A}{q_B} = \frac{9}{4} \times \frac{2}{3} \times \frac{5}{6}$

$\Rightarrow \quad \frac{q_A}{q_B} = \frac{5}{4}$

12. *(c)* Resonant frequency of an *L-C-R* circuit is given by

$$\omega_r = \frac{1}{\sqrt{LC}}$$

So, resonance frequency does not depend on resistance of circuit and frequency of supply.

To increase resonance frequency, we have to reduce inductance or capacitance of circuit. As capacitance reduces when capacitors are connected in series (i.e. $\frac{1}{C_{series}} = \frac{1}{C_1} + \frac{1}{C_2}$), we can add another capacitor in series to increase resonant frequency.

13. *(c)*

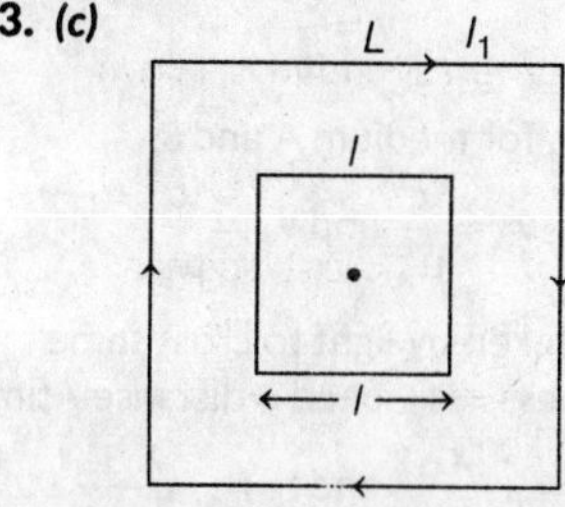

Magnetic field due to one of side at near centre is

$$B_1 = \frac{\mu_0}{4\pi} \cdot \frac{2I_1 \sin 45°}{L/2}$$

Hence, net magnetic field at centre is

$$B = 4B_1 = \frac{\mu_0 I_1 2\sqrt{2}}{4\pi L} \times 4$$

Flux linked with inner coil,

$$\phi_B = B \cdot A = \frac{\mu_0 I_1 \times 2\sqrt{2} \times 4}{4\pi L} \times l^2$$

Mutual inductance of coils is

$$M = \frac{\phi}{I_1} = \frac{\mu_0 \times 2\sqrt{2} \times 4 \times l^2}{4\pi L}$$

$$M = \frac{\mu_0 \times 2\sqrt{2} \times l^2}{\pi L} = \frac{2\sqrt{2}\mu_0 l^2}{\pi L}$$

14. *(b)* For a capacitor with AC supply, current in circuit is

$$i = V/X_L = V\omega C$$

$$C = \frac{i}{V\omega}$$

Here, $i = 6.9 \mu A = 6.9 \times 10^{-6}$ A

$$V = 230 \text{ V}, \omega = 600 \text{ rad/s}$$

Hence, capacity,

$$C = \frac{6.9 \times 10^{-6}}{230 \times 600} = 50 \times 10^{-12} \text{ F}$$

or $\quad C = 50$ pF

15. *(a)* Primary and secondary both rainbows are formed as shown

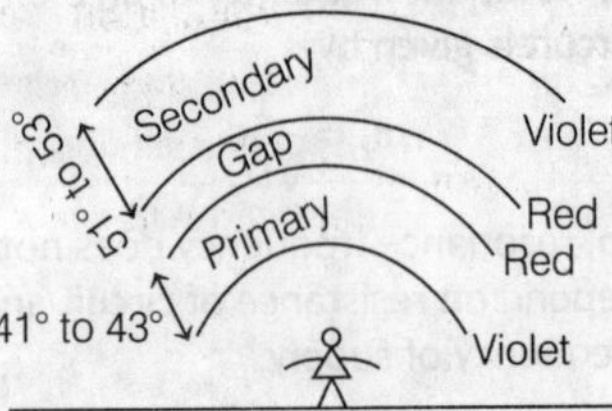

So in primary rainbow, we can be seen violet at the bottom and red colour is at top.

16. *(a)* As, refractive index,

$$\mu = \frac{\text{speed of light in air}}{\text{speed of light in medium}}$$

So, speed of light in a medium,

$$v = \frac{c}{\mu}$$

Hence, for medium A and B,

$$v_A = \frac{c}{\mu_A} \text{ and } v_B = \frac{c}{\mu_B}$$

Time taken by light to cross some thickness x is (speed = distance / time)

$$t_1 = \frac{x}{(c/\mu_A)} \text{ and } t_2 = \frac{x}{(c/\mu_B)}$$

Hence, $t_2 - t_1 = \frac{\mu_B \cdot x}{c} - \frac{\mu_A \cdot x}{c}$

$\Rightarrow \quad t_2 - t_1 = \frac{x}{c}(\mu_B - \mu_A)$

Now given, $\frac{\mu_A}{\mu_B} = \frac{1}{2}$

$\Rightarrow \quad \mu_B = 2\mu_A$

and $\quad t_2 - t_1 = 5 \times 10^{-10}$ s

Substituting these values, we get

$$5 \times 10^{-10} = \frac{x}{c}(2\mu_A - \mu_A)$$

$$\Rightarrow \quad x = 5 \times 10^{-10} \times \frac{c}{\mu_A}$$

But $\frac{c}{\mu_A} = v_A$

$\therefore \quad x = (5 \times 10^{-10} \times v_A)$ m

17. *(c)* Using Einstein's photoelectric equation,

$$\frac{hc}{\lambda} = K_{max} - \phi_0, \text{ we have,}$$

$$\frac{hc}{800} = K - \phi_0 \quad \text{...(i)}$$

and $$\frac{hc}{500} = 2K - \phi_0 \quad \text{...(ii)}$$

Multiplying Eq. (i) by 2 and subtracting from Eq. (ii), we get

$$\frac{hc}{500} - \frac{2 \times hc}{800} = (2K - \phi_0) - 2(K - \phi_0)$$

$$\Rightarrow \quad \frac{hc}{100}\left(\frac{1}{5} - \frac{1}{4}\right) = \phi_0$$

or $$\phi_0 = \frac{1230 \text{ eV - nm}}{100 \text{ nm}}\left(\frac{4-5}{5 \times 4}\right)$$

(we here neglect negative sign which shows absorption of energy)

$$\Rightarrow \quad \phi_0 = 0.615 \text{ eV}$$

18. *(a)* If momentum of electron is $p(= mv)$ then; by Bohr's postulate, we have

$$L = \text{angular momentum}$$

$$= \frac{nh}{2\pi}$$

As, $\quad L = mvr \Rightarrow mvr = \frac{nh}{2\pi}$

$$\Rightarrow \quad mv = \frac{nh}{2\pi r}$$

or $\quad p = mv = \frac{nh}{2\pi r}$

19. *(b)* Ratio of magnetic moment (μ) to angular momentum (L) is known as gyromagnetic ratio and it is equal to half of specific charge.

$$\frac{\mu}{L} = \frac{-1}{2} \cdot \frac{q}{m}$$

So, magnetic moment for an electron $(q = e), \mu = \frac{-1}{2}\frac{e}{m}L$

Here, negative sign indicates L and μ have opposite directions.

20. *(a)* Given circuit is a logic AND gate, so its truth table is

A	B	Y
0	0	0
1	0	0
0	1	0
1	1	1

21. *(3)* Given, $s = 27$ m, $v = 0$

$$u = 150 \text{ km/h} = 150 \times \frac{5}{18} = \frac{125}{3} \text{m/s}$$

Using $v^2 - u^2 = 2as$, we get

$$0 - \frac{125^2}{9} = 2 \times a \times 27$$

$$\Rightarrow \quad a = \frac{-125^2}{2 \times 27 \times 9} \text{ m/s}^2$$

Now, when car is moving with one-third of its initial speed, we have

$$v = 0, u = \frac{1}{3} \times 150 \text{ km/h}$$

or $$u = 50 \times \frac{5}{18} = \frac{125}{9} \text{ m/s}$$

Now again using $v^2 - u^2 = 2as$, we get

$$0 - \frac{125^2}{9^2} = 2 \times \left(\frac{-125^2}{2 \times 27 \times 9}\right) \times s$$

$$\Rightarrow \quad s = \frac{125^2}{9^2} \times \frac{27 \times 9}{125^2} \Rightarrow s = 3 \text{ m}$$

22. *(3)* As forces are in equilibrium, the sum of all horizontal components and vertical components is individually zero.

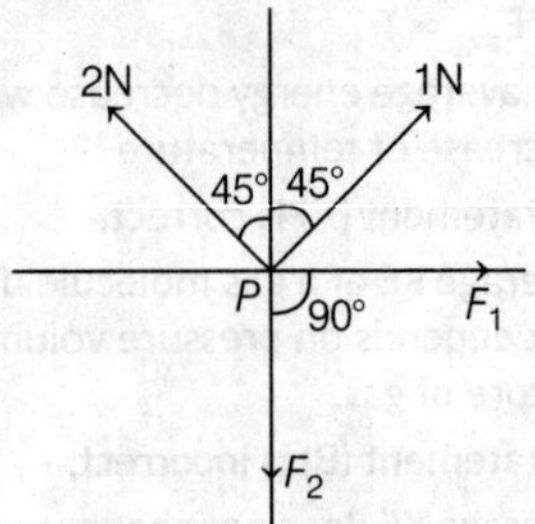

$\Rightarrow \quad \Sigma F_H = 0$ and $\Sigma F_V = 0$

i.e. $\quad F_1 + 1 \times \cos 45° - 2 \cos 45° = 0$

$\Rightarrow \quad F_1 - \frac{1}{\sqrt{2}} = 0$ or $F_1 = \frac{1}{\sqrt{2}}$ N

and $F_2 - 1 \times \cos 45° - 2 \times \cos 45° = 0$

$$F_2 = 3 \times \cos 45^\circ \text{ or } F_2 = \frac{3}{\sqrt{2}} \text{ N}$$

$$\text{Ratio } \frac{F_1}{F_2} = \left(\frac{\frac{1}{\sqrt{2}}}{\frac{3}{\sqrt{2}}} \right) = \frac{1}{3} = \frac{1}{x} \quad \text{(given)}$$

So, $x = 3$

23. *(5)* In first case,

Length of wire $= L$

Radius of wire $= r$

Force on wire $= F$

Change of length, $\Delta L = 5 \times 10^{-2}$ m

$$\therefore \quad Y = \frac{FL}{\pi r^2 \Delta L_1}$$

In second case,

$$Y = \frac{4F \cdot 4L}{\pi (4r)^2 \cdot \Delta L_2}$$

As material and conditions are same, young's modulus value must be same for both wires.

$$\text{So,} \quad \frac{4F \cdot 4L}{\pi (4r)^2 \Delta L_2} = \frac{FL}{\pi r^2 \Delta L_1}$$

$$\Rightarrow \quad \Delta L_2 = \Delta L_1 = 5 \text{ cm}$$

24. *(60)* Given, $L_2 - L_1 = \alpha$ (constant)

$= 20$ cm (Initially)

When temperature increases to ΔT, then

$$L'_2 - L'_1 = L_2(1 + \alpha_{\text{brass}} \Delta T) - L_1(1 + \alpha_{\text{iron}} \Delta T)$$

$$L_2 - L_1 + (L_2 \alpha_{\text{brass}} \Delta T - L_1 \alpha_{\text{iron}} \Delta T)$$

Then, by given condition,

$$L'_2 - L'_1 = L_2 - L_1$$

or $\quad L_2 \alpha_{\text{brass}} \Delta T - L_1 \alpha_{\text{iron}} \Delta T = 0$

or $\quad L_2 \alpha_{\text{brass}} \Delta T = L_1 \alpha_{\text{iron}} \Delta T$

$\Rightarrow \quad L_2 \alpha_{\text{brass}} = L_1 \alpha_{\text{iron}}$

Here, given $L_2 = 40$ cm

$$\alpha_{\text{iron}} = 1.2 \times 10^{-5} \text{ K}^{-1}$$

$$\alpha_{\text{brass}} = 1.8 \times 10^{-5} \text{ K}^{-1}$$

So, we have

$$L_1 = \frac{L_2 \alpha_{\text{brass}}}{\alpha_{\text{iron}}} = \frac{40 \times 1.8 \times 10^{-5}}{1.2 \times 10^{-5}} = \frac{40 \times 18}{12} = 60 \text{ cm}$$

25. *(20)* The given situation is shown below.

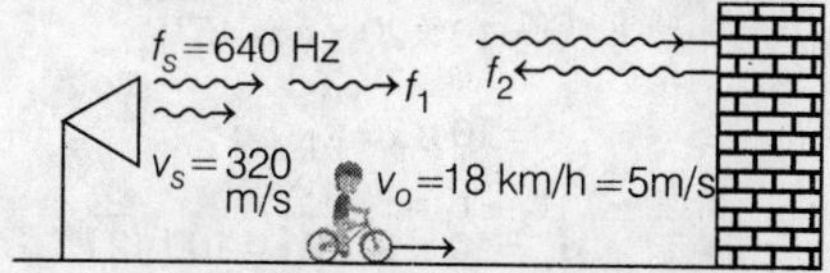

Frequency heard by cyclist from source directly (source stationary observer moving away)

$$f_1 = f_o \left(\frac{v - v_o}{v} \right) = 640 \left(\frac{320 - 5}{320} \right)$$

$$= 315 \times 2 = 630 \text{ Hz}$$

Frequency heard by cyclist of reflected sound from wall (observer moving towards stationary wall)

$$f_2 = f_o \left(\frac{v + v_o}{v} \right) = 640 \left(\frac{320 + 5}{320} \right)$$

$$= 325 \times 2 = 650 \text{ Hz}$$

Beat frequency $= 650 - 630 = 20$ Hz

Note Q is incorrect as we cannot hear beats when $f_{\text{beat}} > 10$

26. *(45)* Number of field lines per unit area $= \dfrac{\text{Flux}}{\text{Area}}$

$$= \frac{Q}{\varepsilon_0 A} = \frac{\rho \times V}{\varepsilon_0 \times A} \quad (\because Q = \rho \times V)$$

$$= \frac{\rho \times \frac{4}{3} \pi R^3}{\varepsilon_0 \times 4 \pi R^2} = \frac{\rho \times R}{3 \varepsilon_0}$$

$$= \frac{2 \times 10^{-6} \times 10^6 \times 6}{8.85 \times 10^{-12} \times 3}$$

$$= \frac{4}{8.85} \times 10^{12} \approx 45 \times 10^{10} \text{ N/C}$$

27. *(4)* The given circuit diagram is shown below

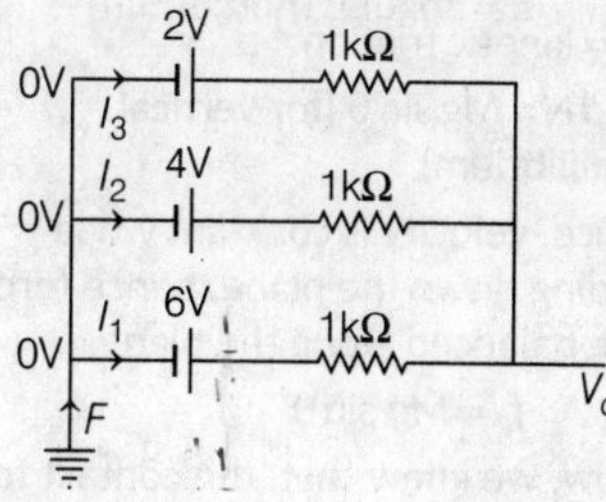

Using Kirchhoff's junction rule,

$$I_1 + I_2 + I_3 = 0$$

$$\frac{6 - V_0}{1 \times 10^3} + \frac{4 - V_0}{1 \times 10^3} + \frac{2 - V_0}{1 \times 10^3} = 0$$

$$\Rightarrow \; 12 - 3V_0 = 0 \;\Rightarrow\; V_0 = 4 \text{ V}$$

28. *(4)* R = resistance of 8 copper wires of length l and diameter d in parallel

$$= \frac{1}{8} \times \frac{\rho l}{\left(\frac{\pi d^2}{4} \right)} = \frac{1}{2} \left(\frac{\rho l}{\pi d^2} \right) \quad \text{...(i)}$$

Also if another copper wire of length $2l$ and diameter x has same resistance, then

$$R = \frac{\rho (2l)}{\pi \left(\frac{x^2}{4} \right)} = 8 \left(\frac{\rho l}{\pi x^2} \right) \quad \text{...(ii)}$$

From Eqs. (i) and (ii), we get

$$\frac{8 \times \rho l}{\pi x^2} = \frac{1}{2} \frac{\rho l}{\pi d^2} \quad \Rightarrow \quad x^2 = 16 d^2$$

or $\quad x = 4d$

29. *(3)* As, $E_g = \dfrac{hc}{\lambda}$

$$\therefore \quad E_g = \frac{1240 \text{ eV-nm}}{4000 \text{ nm}} = 3.1 \text{ eV}$$

$[hc = 1240 \text{ eV-nm}]$

or $\quad E_g \approx 3$ eV

30. *(150)* Population covered

= Area covered × Population density

$$\Rightarrow \text{Area covered} = \frac{\text{Population covered}}{\text{Population density}}$$

$$\Rightarrow \quad 2 \pi R h = \frac{\text{Population covered}}{\text{Population density}}$$

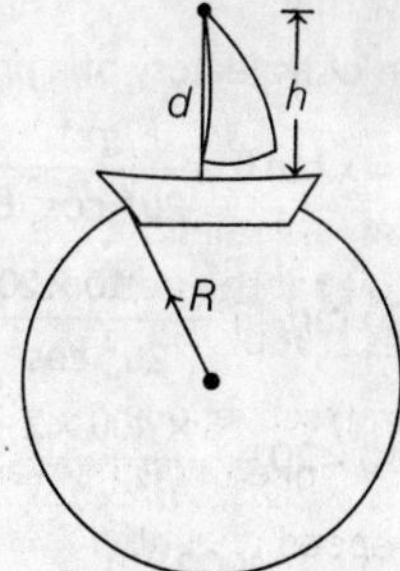

$$\text{So, } 2\pi \times 6400 \times h = \frac{6.03 \times 10^6}{100}$$

$$\Rightarrow \quad h = \frac{6.03 \times 10^6}{2\pi \times 100 \times 6400} \text{ km}$$

$$= \frac{6.03 \times 10^6 \times 1000}{2\pi \times 100 \times 6400} \text{ m}$$

or $\quad h \approx 150$ m

Real Nut 5-27 July 2022, Shift-II

1. *(d)* Energy density, $u = \frac{\alpha}{\beta}\sin\left(\frac{\alpha x}{kt}\right)$

where, α, β = constants, x = displacement

k = Boltzmann constant

We know that, energy density

$= \frac{\text{energy}}{\text{volume}}$

and $\frac{\alpha x}{kt}$ = dimensionless

$\therefore \quad \alpha x = kt$

$\therefore \quad \alpha = \frac{kt}{x} = \frac{[ML^2T^{-2}K^{-1}]\,[K]}{[L]}$

$= [MLT^{-2}]$ ...(i)

Now, $\frac{\alpha}{\beta} = \frac{\text{energy}}{\text{volume}}$

$\Rightarrow \quad \beta = \frac{\alpha \times \text{volume}}{\text{energy}} = \frac{a[L^3]}{[ML^2T^{-2}]}$

$\Rightarrow \quad \beta = \frac{[MLT^{-2}]\,[L^3]}{[ML^2T^{-2}]}$ [From Eq.(i)]

$\Rightarrow \quad \beta = [L^2]$

$\therefore \quad \beta = [M^0L^2T^0]$

2. *(d)* According to the given situation,

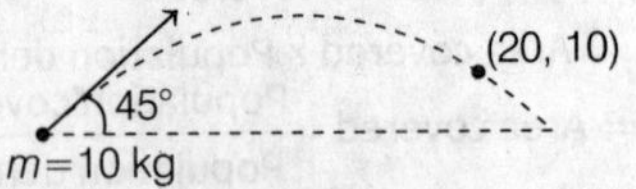

Given, time of flight = T

We know that,

Equation of trajectory of a projectile,

$$y = x\tan\theta - \frac{gx^2}{2u^2\cos^2\theta}$$

$$\Rightarrow 10 = 20\tan 45° - \frac{10 \times 20^2}{2u^2\cos^2 45°}$$

$$\Rightarrow \quad 10 = 20 - \frac{5 \times 400 \times 2}{u^2 \times 1}$$

$$\Rightarrow \quad -10 = -\frac{4000}{u^2}$$

$$\Rightarrow \quad u = 20 \text{ m/s}$$

$$\therefore \quad t = \frac{T}{\sqrt{2}} = \frac{2u\sin\theta}{\sqrt{2}g} \quad \left(\because T = \frac{2u\sin\theta}{g}\right)$$

$$\Rightarrow \quad t = \frac{2 \times 20 \times \sin 45°}{\sqrt{2} \times 10}$$

$$\Rightarrow \quad t = \frac{2 \times 20}{2 \times 10} = 2 \text{ s}$$

$\therefore$ After 2 s, momentum along X-axis $= mv_x$

where $v_x = u\cos\theta \quad (\because a_x = 0 \text{ m/s}^2)$

$$\therefore \quad \mathbf{p}_x = 10 \times u\cos\theta\,\hat{\mathbf{i}}$$

$$= 10 \times 20 \times \cos 45°\,\hat{\mathbf{i}}$$

$$= 10 \times 20 \times \frac{1}{\sqrt{2}}\,\hat{\mathbf{i}}$$

$$\Rightarrow \quad \mathbf{p}_x = 10 \times 10\sqrt{2}\,\hat{\mathbf{i}} = 100\sqrt{2}\,\hat{\mathbf{i}}$$

Also, momentum along Y-axis after 2 s $= mv_y$

where

$v_y = u_y + a_y t = 20\sin 45° - 10 \times 2$

$$\Rightarrow \quad v_y = \frac{20}{\sqrt{2}} - 20 = 20\left(\frac{1-\sqrt{2}}{\sqrt{2}}\right)$$

$$\Rightarrow \quad v_y = -20\left(\frac{\sqrt{2}-1}{\sqrt{2}}\right) \text{ m/s}$$

$$\therefore \quad \mathbf{p}_y = 10x - 20\left(\frac{\sqrt{2}-1}{\sqrt{2}}\right)\hat{\mathbf{j}}$$

$$= -200\left(\frac{\sqrt{2}-1}{\sqrt{2}}\right)\hat{\mathbf{j}}$$

$$\Rightarrow \quad \mathbf{p}_y = -200\left(\frac{\sqrt{2}}{\sqrt{2}} - \frac{1}{\sqrt{2}}\right)\hat{\mathbf{j}}$$

$$\Rightarrow \quad \mathbf{p}_y = \left(-200 + \frac{200}{\sqrt{2}} \times \frac{\sqrt{2}}{\sqrt{2}}\right)\hat{\mathbf{j}}$$

$$\Rightarrow \quad \mathbf{p}_y = (-200 + 100\sqrt{2})\,\hat{\mathbf{j}}$$

$$\therefore \quad \mathbf{p} = \mathbf{p}_x + \mathbf{p}_y$$

$$= 100\sqrt{2}\,\hat{\mathbf{i}} + (100\sqrt{2} - 200)\,\hat{\mathbf{j}}$$

3. *(a)* According to the question,

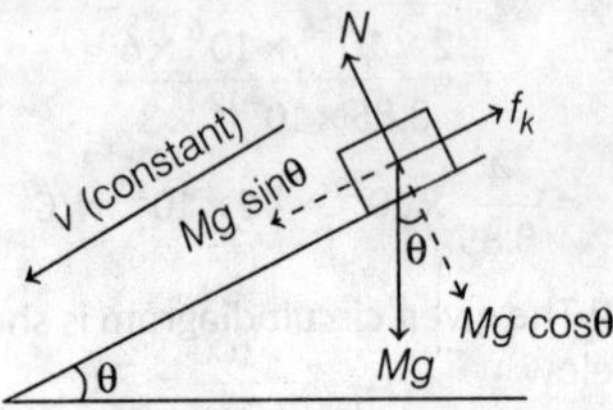

f_k = kinetic friction = $\mu_k N$

and $N = Mg\sin\theta$ (for vertical equilibrium)

Since, velocity is constant while sliding down the plane, hence forces are balanced along the plane.

$\therefore \quad f_k = Mg\sin\theta$

Now, we know that, the contact force,

$$|\mathbf{F}| = \sqrt{(\text{Friction})^2 + (\text{Normal reaction})^2}$$

$$|\mathbf{F}| = \sqrt{(Mg\sin\theta)^2 + (Mg\cos\theta)^2}$$

$$= \sqrt{(Mg)^2[\sin^2\theta + \cos^2\theta]} = Mg \quad [\because \sin^2\theta + \cos^2\theta = 1]$$

$$\therefore \quad |\mathbf{F}| = Mg$$

4. *(c)* Solving the question in the frame of the lift, the lift can be assumed to be at rest.

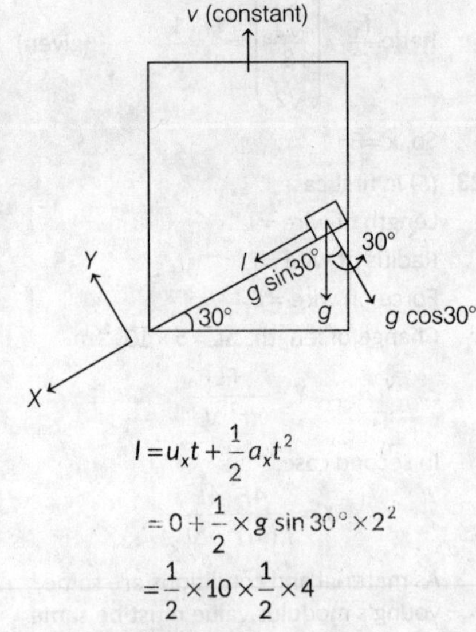

$$l = u_x t + \frac{1}{2}a_x t^2$$

$$= 0 + \frac{1}{2} \times g\sin 30° \times 2^2$$

$$= \frac{1}{2} \times 10 \times \frac{1}{2} \times 4$$

$$l = 10 \text{ m}$$

When the angle of inclined plane is changed to 45°, then

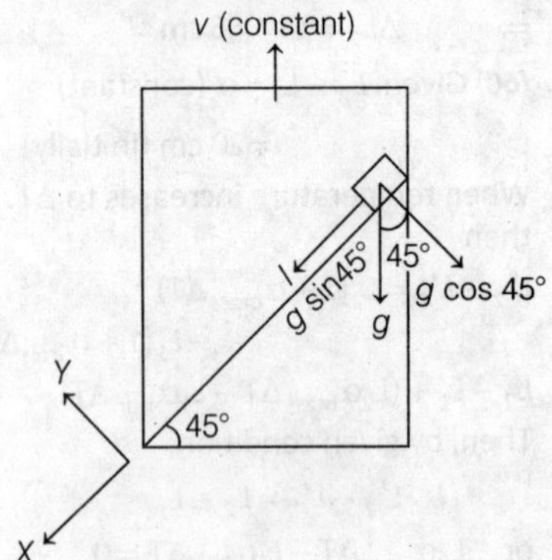

then $l = u_x t + \frac{1}{2}a_x t^2$

$$\Rightarrow \quad 10 = 0 + \frac{1}{2} \times g\sin 45°\, t^2$$

$$\Rightarrow \quad 10 = \frac{1}{2} \times 10 \times \frac{1}{\sqrt{2}}t^2$$

$$\Rightarrow \quad t^2 = 2\sqrt{2}$$

$$\Rightarrow \quad t = \sqrt{2\sqrt{2}} \text{ s}$$

$$\Rightarrow \quad t = \sqrt{2 \times 1.414} \text{ s} \quad (\because \sqrt{2} = 1.414)$$

$$\Rightarrow \quad t = \sqrt{2.828} = 1.68 \text{ s}$$

5. *(c)* According to the situation given in the question,

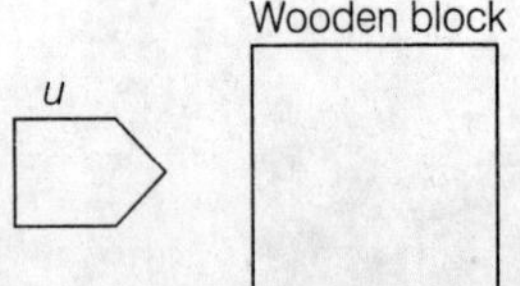

After penetrating 4 cm in the wooden block, its velocity becomes $\left(\frac{u}{3}\right)$ after facing constant resistance.

Therefore,

$$v^2 = u^2 + 2as$$

$$\Rightarrow \left(\frac{u}{3}\right)^2 = u^2 + 2\times a\times\frac{4}{100}$$

$$\Rightarrow a = \left(\frac{u^2}{9} - u^2\right)\times\frac{100}{8}$$

$$\Rightarrow a = -\frac{8u^2}{9}\times\frac{100}{8} = -\frac{100}{9}u^2$$

Now, since the bullet stops completely after travelling further x cm.

$$\therefore \quad v^2 = u^2 + 2ax$$

$$0 = u^2 + 2\times\frac{-100}{9}u^2\frac{(4+x)}{100}$$

$$\Rightarrow \quad -u^2 = \frac{200}{9}\frac{(4+x)}{100}u^2$$

$$\Rightarrow \frac{9}{2} = 4 + x$$

$$\Rightarrow \quad x = \frac{9}{2} - 4 = \frac{9-8}{2} = \frac{1}{2}\text{ m}$$

$$\therefore \quad x = 0.5\text{ m}$$

6. *(b)* The given situation is shown below

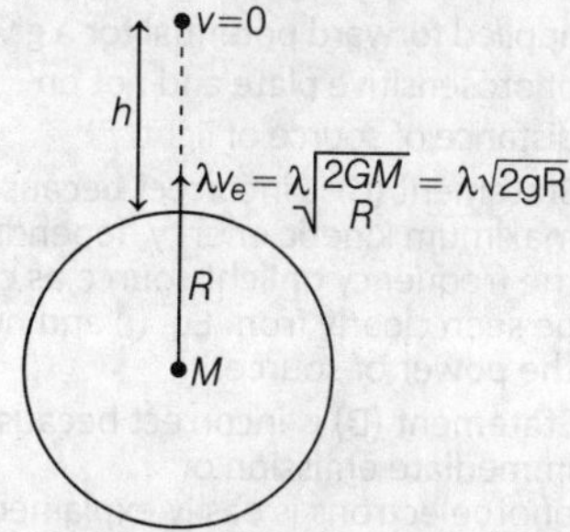

By energy conservation,

Total energy of system, when body is at the surface of earth = Total energy of the system when the body is at height h above the surface of earth

$$-\frac{GMm}{R} + \frac{1}{2}m(\lambda v_e)^2 = -\frac{GMm}{(R+h)} + \frac{1}{2}mv^2$$

$$-\frac{GM}{R} + \frac{1}{2}\lambda^2 v_e^2 = -\frac{GM}{(R+h)} + \frac{1}{2}v^2$$

Since at topmost point, $v = 0$

$$\therefore \quad -\frac{GM}{R} + \frac{1}{2}\lambda^2 v_e^2 = \frac{-GM}{(R+h)} + 0$$

$$\Rightarrow -\frac{GM}{R} + \frac{1}{2}\lambda^2\times\frac{2GM}{R} = -\frac{GM}{(R+h)}$$

$$\left(\because v_e = \sqrt{\frac{2GM}{R}}\right)$$

$$\Rightarrow \quad -\frac{1}{R} + \frac{\lambda^2}{R} = -\frac{1}{R+h}$$

$$\Rightarrow \quad \frac{\lambda^2 - 1}{R} = -\frac{1}{R+h}$$

$$\Rightarrow \quad R + h = \frac{R}{1-\lambda^2} = \text{distance}$$

from centre of earth

7. *(d)* We know that, $Y = \frac{Fl}{A\Delta l}$

$$\Rightarrow \quad \Delta l = \frac{Fl}{AY}$$

Steel	Copper
3.2 m	4.4 m

$\therefore$Net elongation $= \Delta l_{steel} + \Delta l_{copper}$

$$1.4\times10^{-3} = \frac{F\times3.2}{\pi\times(1.4\times10^{-3})^2 Y_{steel}} + \frac{F\times4.4}{\pi\times(1.4\times10^{-3})^2 Y_{copper}}$$

$$\Rightarrow 0.259F\times10^{-5} + 0.6439F\times10^{-5} = 1.4\times10^{-3}$$

$$\Rightarrow F\times0.9\times10^{-5} = 1.4\times10^{-3}$$

$$\Rightarrow \quad F = \frac{1.4\times10^2}{0.9}$$

$$\Rightarrow \quad F = 154\text{ N}$$

8. *(c)* In case I,

Efficiency, $\eta_1 = 1 - \frac{T_{sink}}{T_{source}}$

$$= 1 - \frac{100}{300} = \frac{2}{3}$$

In case II,

300 K → Q_1 → E_1 → W_1; Q_2 → 200 K → Q_1 → E_2 → W_2; Q_2 → 100 K

For E_1,

$$\eta_1' = 1 - \frac{200}{300} = 1 - \frac{Q_2}{Q_1}$$

$$\Rightarrow \quad \frac{Q_2}{Q_1} = 1 - \frac{1}{3}$$

$$\Rightarrow \quad \frac{Q_2}{Q_1} = \frac{2}{3}$$

For E_2,

$$\eta_2' = 1 - \frac{100}{200} = 1 - \frac{Q_2'}{Q_4'}$$

$$\Rightarrow \quad \frac{Q_2'}{Q_1'} = 1 - \frac{1}{2} \Rightarrow \frac{Q_2'}{Q_1'} = \frac{1}{2}$$

$$\therefore \eta_{combination} = 1 - \frac{Q_2'}{Q_1'} = 1 - \left(\frac{Q_2'}{Q_1'}\times\frac{Q_2}{Q_1}\right)$$

$$= 1 - \left(\frac{1}{2}\times\frac{2}{3}\right) = \frac{2}{3} < 1$$

9. *(b)* Statement (A) is incorrect because a molecule with n degrees of freedom have n different ways of storing energy.

- Statement (B) is correct as each degree of freedom is associated with $\frac{1}{2}RT$ average energy per mole.
- Statement (C) is incorrect because a monoatomic gas molecule has no rotational degree of freedom and diatomic gas molecule has 2 rotational degrees of freedom.
- Statement (D) is correct as CH_4 molecule has 3 translational and 3 rotational, i.e. total 6 degrees of freedom.

Hence, option (b) is correct.

10. *(b)* Let the two part of charges are q and $(4-q)\mu$C.

$\therefore$If the distance between the both charges is r, then electrostatic force between the charges is given by

$$F = K\cdot\frac{q(4-q)}{r^2}$$

For maximum value force (F),

$$\frac{dF}{dq} = 0$$

$$\Rightarrow \frac{d}{dq}\cdot Kq\frac{(4-q)}{r^2} = 0$$

$$\Rightarrow \frac{d}{dq}\cdot q(4-q) = 0$$

[$\because k$ and r are constant]

$$\Rightarrow \quad q(0-1) + (4-q) = 0$$

$$\Rightarrow \quad 4 - 2q = 0$$

$$q = 2\mu C$$

$\therefore$second part $= 4 - q$

$$= 4 - 2 = = 2\mu C$$

11. *(a)* We know,

$|$ Drift velocity $| = v_d = \frac{eE\tau}{m}$

where, τ = relaxation time

On increasing temperature, τ decreases

$$\because \quad v_d \propto \tau$$

$\therefore$Since, τ decreases on increasing temperature therefore, v_d decreases with increasing temperature.

$\therefore$(A) is correct.

Now, $v_d = \frac{i}{neA}$

Clearly the drift velocity is inversely proportional to the area of cross-section.

We know $E = \frac{V}{l}$ (where, V = potential difference)

$\therefore \quad v_d = \frac{eV\tau}{ml}$

$v_d \propto V$

$\therefore$(C) is wrong.

Now, drift velocity is dependent on $\frac{V}{l}$ i.e. potential difference per unit length.

$\therefore$it is independent of length of conductor.

Hence, (D) is wrong.

Since, v_d decreases with increase in the temperature of the conductor, therefore (E) is wrong.

$\therefore$Hence option (a) is correct.

12. *(a)* According to the question,

$$f_P = \frac{1}{2\pi}\sqrt{\frac{mB_P\cos 30°}{I}}$$

$$f_Q = \frac{1}{2\pi}\sqrt{\frac{mB_Q\cos 60°}{I}}$$

$$\Rightarrow \quad \frac{f_P}{f_Q} = \sqrt{\frac{B_P}{B_Q} \times \frac{\cos 30°}{\cos 60°}}$$

$$\Rightarrow \quad \frac{20}{10} = \sqrt{\frac{B_P}{B_Q} \times \frac{\sqrt{3} \times 2}{2 \times 1}}$$

$$\Rightarrow \quad 4 = \frac{B_P}{B_Q} \times \sqrt{3}$$

$$\Rightarrow B_Q : B_P = \sqrt{3} : 4$$

13. *(b)* We know in a cyclotron,

$$R = \frac{mv}{qB}$$

$$\Rightarrow \quad v = \frac{qBR}{m}$$

Given, $q = 1.6 \times 10^{-19}$ C,

$m = 1.6 \times 10^{-27}$ kg

$$\therefore \quad KE = \frac{1}{2}mv^2 = \frac{1}{2} \times m \times \frac{q^2B^2R^2}{m^2}$$

$$\Rightarrow \quad KE = \frac{q^2B^2R^2}{2m}$$

$$= \frac{(1.6 \times 10^{-19})^2 \times 1^2 \times (0.6)^2}{2 \times 1.6 \times 10^{-27}} \text{ J}$$

Now,

$$\because \quad 1\text{ J} = \frac{10^{-6}}{1.6 \times 10^{-19}} \text{ MeV}$$

$$\therefore \quad KE = \frac{(1.6 \times 10^{-19})^2 \times (0.6)^2}{2 \times 1.6 \times 10^{-27}} \times \frac{10^{-6}}{1.6 \times 10^{-19}} \text{MeV}$$

$$= \frac{1.6^2 \times 10^{-19} \times 10^{-19} \times 0.36 \times 10^{-6}}{2 \times 1.6^2 \times 10^{-19} \times 10^{-27}} \text{ MeV}$$

$$= \frac{0.36 \times 10^8 \times 10^{-6}}{2} \text{ MeV}$$

$$\therefore \quad KE = \frac{36}{2} \text{ MeV}$$

$$= 18 \text{ MeV}$$

14. *(c)* We know,

$$\text{Resonant Frequency, } \omega_0 = \frac{1}{\sqrt{LC}}$$

$$\omega_0 = \frac{1}{\sqrt{0.01 \times 10^{-6}}} = 10^4 \text{ rad/s}$$

New frequency $= \omega = \omega_0 - 60\%$ of ω_0

$= 40\%$ of ω_0

$\omega = 0.4 \times 10^4$ rad/s

$\Rightarrow \quad \omega = 4000$ rad/s

We have new,

$X_L = \omega L = 4000 \times 0.01 = 40\,\Omega$

and $X_C = \frac{1}{\omega C} = \frac{1}{4000 \times 10^{-6}}$

$= \frac{10^6}{4 \times 10^3} = \frac{10^3}{4} = 250\,\Omega$

$\therefore$New $Z = \sqrt{10^2 + (250 - 40)^2}$

$[\because Z = \sqrt{R^2 + (X_C - X_L)^2}]$

$\Rightarrow Z = \sqrt{100 + 210^2} \Rightarrow Z = 210\,\Omega$

$\therefore$Current amplitude $= \frac{V_m}{Z} = \frac{50}{210}$ A.

$= 0.238$ A $= 238$ mA

15. *(b)* In a plane electromagnetic wave electric field, magnetic field and velocity of wave are all mutually perpendicular to each-other .

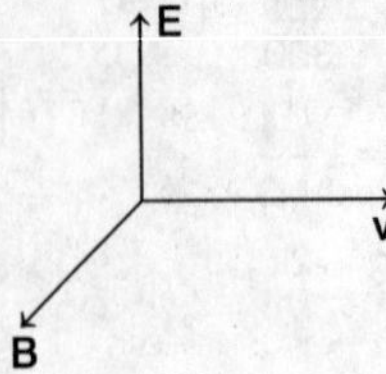

Also, the speed of electromagnetic wave $= \frac{|\mathbf{E}|}{|\mathbf{B}|}$

$\therefore$Only statements B and D satisfy.

16. *(b)* Given, $I_1 : I_2 = 1 : 4$

$\Rightarrow \quad I_1 = k$ and $I_2 = 4k$

$\therefore \quad I_{max} = I_1 + I_2 + 2\sqrt{I_1I_2}$

$\Rightarrow \quad I_{max} = k + 4k + 2\sqrt{k4k}$

$\Rightarrow \quad I_{max} = 5k + 4k = 9k$

Now, $\quad I_{min} = I_1 + I_2 - 2\sqrt{I_1I_2}$

$I_{min} = k + 4k - 4k = k$

$$\therefore \quad \frac{I_{max} + I_{min}}{I_{max} - I_{min}} = \frac{9k + k}{9k - k} = \frac{10k}{8k} = \frac{5}{4}$$

Now, since given that

$$\frac{I_{max} + I_{min}}{I_{max} - I_{min}} = \frac{5}{4} = \frac{2\alpha + 1}{\beta + 3}$$

$\Rightarrow \quad 2\alpha + 1 = 5; \beta + 3 = 4$

$\Rightarrow \quad \alpha = \frac{4}{2} = 2$; and $\beta = 1$

$\therefore \quad \alpha/\beta = 2$

17. *(b)* Statement (A) is correct because according to the photoelectric equation,

$$h\nu = h\nu_0 + (KE)_{max} \quad \text{...(i)}$$

$$\Rightarrow \quad h\nu = h\nu_0 + \frac{1}{2}mv_{max}^2$$

$$\Rightarrow \quad v_{max}^2 = \frac{2h\nu}{m} - \frac{2h\nu_0}{m}$$

$$\Rightarrow v_{max}^2 = \left(\frac{2h}{m}\right)\nu - \left(\frac{2h\nu_0}{m}\right)$$

$$\Rightarrow v_{max}^2 \propto \nu$$

Statement (B) is incorrect because the value of saturation current depends on intensity of light falling and the applied forward potential for a given photosensitive plate and not on distance of source of light.

Statement (C) is incorrect because maximum kinetic energy depends on the frequency of light source as can be seen clearly from Eq. (i) and not on the power of source.

Statement (D) is incorrect because the immediate emission of photoelectrons is easily explained by the particle nature of light.

Statement (E) is correct as threshold wavelength cannot be explained by wave nature of light instead, it is explained by the particle nature of light.

$\therefore$ Hence, option (b) is correct.

18. *(d)* We know,

By the rate equation of radioactivity,

$$R = R_0 e^{-\lambda t}$$

where, R_0 = Initial activity

λ = Rate constant or activity constant

Also, $R_0 = 6.4 \times 10^{-4}$ curie

$R = 5 \times 10^{-6}$ curie

$$\therefore 5 \times 10^{-6} = 6.4 \times 10^{-4}\, e^{-\lambda t} \quad \text{...(i)}$$

We know, $t_{1/2} = \frac{\ln 2}{\lambda}$

$\Rightarrow 5 = \frac{\ln 2}{\lambda} \Rightarrow \lambda = \frac{\ln 2}{5}$

Putting, $\lambda = \left(\frac{\ln 2}{5}\right)$ in Eq. (i),

$$5\times 10^{-6} = 6.4\times 10^{-4}\, e^{-\left(\frac{\ln 2}{5}\right)t}$$

$$\Rightarrow e^{\left(+\frac{\ln 2}{5}\right)t} = \frac{6.4\times 10^{-4}}{5\times 10^{-6}}$$

$$\Rightarrow e^{\left(\frac{\ln 2}{5}\right)^t} = \frac{64}{5\times 10\times 10^{-2}}$$

$$\Rightarrow e^{\left(\frac{\ln 2}{5}\right)^t} = \frac{64\times 100}{50}$$

$$\Rightarrow e^{\left(\frac{\ln 2}{5}\right)^t} = 128$$

$\Rightarrow$ Taking log on both the sides,

$$\Rightarrow \frac{(\ln 2)t}{5}\ln e = \ln 128$$

$$\Rightarrow \frac{(\ln 2)t}{5} = \ln 2^7 \Rightarrow \frac{t}{5}\ln 2 = 7\ln 2$$

$\Rightarrow t/5 = 7 \Rightarrow t = 35$ days

19. *(b)* $V_{CE} = 8$ V, $I_C = 6$ mA from 4 mA

$I_B = 20\,\mu$A to 25 μA

$\therefore$ Current gain,

$$\beta_{av} = \frac{I'_C - I_C}{I'_B - I_B} = \frac{(6-4)\text{ mA}}{(25-20)\,\mu\text{A}} = \frac{2\text{ mA}}{5\,\mu\text{A}}$$

$$\beta_{av} = \frac{2}{5}\times 10^3 = \frac{2000}{5} = 400$$

$\therefore$ Option (b) is correct.

20. *(a)* Modulation index, $\mu = \frac{A_m}{A_c} = \frac{1}{5} = 0.2$

where, A_m = amplitude of modulating signal

A_c = amplitude of carrier wave

21. *(2)* As, we known, $Y = \frac{Fl}{A\Delta l}$ ...(i)

where, F = Load

From the graph,

$$\text{Slope} = \frac{\text{Extension}}{\text{Load}} \times \frac{1}{\text{Wire length}}$$

$$= \frac{\Delta l}{Fl} = \frac{0.25}{10^5} = \frac{1}{4}\times 10^{-5}$$

$$\Rightarrow \frac{\Delta l}{Fl} = \frac{1}{4}\times 10^{-5} \Rightarrow \frac{Fl}{\Delta l} = 4\times 10^5$$

Putting it in Eq. (i), we get

$$Y = \frac{4\times 10^5}{A} = \frac{4\times 10^5}{2\times 10^{-6}}$$

$(\because 2\text{ mm}^2 = 2\times 10^{-6}\text{ m}^2)$

$\Rightarrow Y = 2\times 10^{11}$ Nm^{-2}

$\therefore x = 2$

22. *(40)* We know, in a balanced meter bridge,

$$\frac{R_1}{R_2} = \frac{AC}{CB} \quad \text{...(i)}$$

$$\Rightarrow \frac{R_1}{R_2} = \frac{40}{CB}$$

As we can clearly see from Eq. (i) that the condition for a balanced Wheatstone bridge (balanced meter bridge) is independent of the radius of wire AB, therefore the balancing length will not change and will remain 40 cm only.

23. *(4)* We know that, condition for deviation without dispersion is given by

$$(n_{Y_1} - 1)A_1\omega_1 = (n_{Y_2} - 1)A_2\omega_2$$

$$\Rightarrow (1.5-1)6\omega_1 = (1.55-1)5\omega_2$$

$$\Rightarrow 0.5\times 6\omega_1 = 0.55\times 5\omega_2$$

$$\Rightarrow 3\omega_1 = 2.75\omega_2 \Rightarrow \frac{\omega_1}{\omega_2} = \frac{2.75}{3}$$

Now, net deviation

$$= \delta_{\text{net}} = (n_{Y_1} - 1)A_1\left[1 - \frac{\omega_1}{\omega_2}\right]$$

$$= (1.5-1)6\left[1 - \frac{2.75}{3}\right]$$

$$= 3\times\frac{0.25}{3} = \left(\frac{1}{4}\right)^0$$

$$\therefore \delta_{\text{net}} = \left(\frac{1}{x}\right)^0 = \left(\frac{1}{4}\right)^0$$

$\therefore x = 4$

24. *(12)*

Y, X, Conducting circular loop, 1m = R

Area $= A = \pi R^2 = \pi(1)^2$ or $\mathbf{A} = \pi\,\hat{\mathbf{k}}$

Given, $\mathbf{B} = (3t^3\hat{\mathbf{j}} + 3t^2\hat{\mathbf{k}})$T

$\therefore$ Flux through loop,

$$\phi_B = \mathbf{B}\cdot\mathbf{A} = (3t^3\hat{\mathbf{j}} + 3t^2\hat{\mathbf{k}})\cdot(\pi\hat{\mathbf{k}})$$

$$= 3\pi t^2 \text{ Wb}$$

We know, Induced emf, $\varepsilon = -\frac{N d\phi_B}{dt}$

(where, N = no. of turns)

$$\Rightarrow \varepsilon = -1\frac{d\,3\pi t^2}{dt} = -3\pi\frac{dt^2}{dt} \quad (\because N = 1)$$

$$\Rightarrow \varepsilon = -3\pi\times 2t = -6\pi t \text{ V}$$

Now, at $t = 2$ s

$$\varepsilon = -6\times\pi\times 2 = -12\pi \text{ V}$$

$\therefore n\pi = -12\pi$

$\Rightarrow n = -12$

$\Rightarrow |n| = 12$

25. *(10)*

$E = 10$V, $r = 10\Omega$, $R = 100\Omega$, $C = 1.1\mu$F, K, $R' = 200\Omega$, A, B, P, Q, D, C, i

$$V_A - V_B = E - ir$$

$$\Rightarrow V_A - V_B = 10 - 10i \quad \text{...(i)}$$

Also, $V_P - V_Q = iR$

$$\Rightarrow V_P - V_Q = 100i \quad \text{...(ii)}$$

Since, $V_A - V_B = V_P - V_Q$

$\Rightarrow 10 - 10i = 100i$

[From Eqs. (i) and (ii)]

$\Rightarrow 10 = 110i$

$\Rightarrow i = \frac{1}{11}$ A

$$\therefore V_P - V_Q = 100i = 100\times\frac{1}{11} = \frac{100}{11}\text{ V}$$

Also, $V_P - V_Q = V_D - V_C$

$$\Rightarrow \frac{100}{11} = V_D - V_C$$

$$\Rightarrow V_D - V_C = \frac{100}{11}\text{ V} \quad \text{...(iii)}$$

Since, in steady state there is no current through the capacitor.

$\therefore V_C = V_K$

$\therefore$ From Eq. (iii), $V_D - V_K = \frac{100}{11}$ V

Now, $Q = CV$ (for capacitor)

$$\Rightarrow Q = 1.1\times 10^{-6}\times(V_D - V_K)$$

$$\Rightarrow Q = 1.1\times 10^{-6}\times\frac{100}{11}\text{ C}$$

$$\Rightarrow Q = \frac{10^{-6}\times 100}{10}\text{ C}$$

$$\Rightarrow Q = 10\times 10^{-6}\text{ C}$$

$\therefore$ Answer = 10

26. *(240)* According to the question,

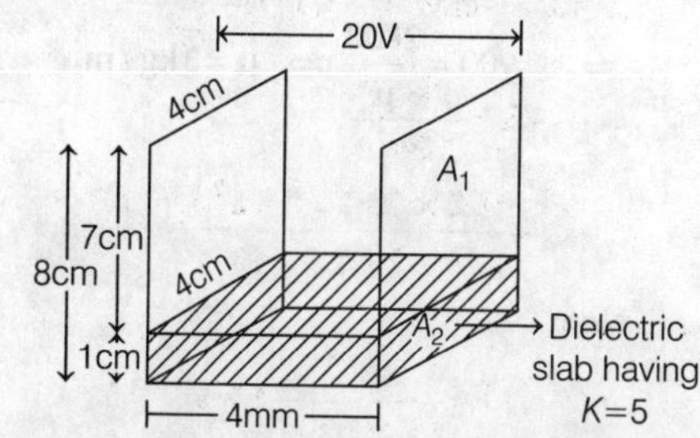

The above situation is a parallel combination of two capacitors,

$\therefore C_{\text{equivalent}} = C_1 + C_2$

$$C_{\text{equivalent}} = \frac{\varepsilon_0 A_1}{d} + \frac{K\varepsilon_0 A_2}{d} \quad ...(i)$$

(Since, on inserting dielectric the capacitance increases K times)

But, $A_1 = (7 \times 4)\ \text{cm}^2 = 28 \times 10^{-4}\ \text{m}^2$

and $A_2 = (1 \times 4)\ \text{cm}^2 = 4 \times 10^{-4}\ \text{m}^2$

$\therefore$ Putting these values in Eq. (i)

$$C_{\text{equivalent}} = \frac{\varepsilon_0}{d}[A_1 + A_2 K]$$

$$= \frac{\varepsilon_0}{4 \times 10^{-3}}[(28 \times 10^{-4}) + (4 \times 10^{-4} \times 5)]$$

$$C_{\text{equivalent}} = \frac{\varepsilon_0}{4 \times 10^{-3}}[48 \times 10^{-4}] = 12 \times 10^{-1}\varepsilon_0$$

$\therefore$ The electrostatic energy of this system,

$$= \frac{1}{2} C_{\text{equivalent}} V^2$$

$$= \frac{1}{2} \times 12 \times 10^{-1} \times 20^2\ \varepsilon_0$$

$$= \frac{1}{2} \times 12 \times 10^{-1} \times 400\ \varepsilon_0$$

$$= 24 \times 10\varepsilon_0 = 240\varepsilon_0$$

27. *(3)* We know, $\frac{nv}{0.6} = f$

where, n = Harmonic number,

v = Speed of waves and

f = Fequency

$\therefore \frac{nv}{0.6} = 400$ and $\frac{(n+1)v}{0.6} = 450$

$\Rightarrow nv = 400 \times 0.6$

and $nv + v = 450 \times 0.6$

$\Rightarrow nv = 240$ and $240 + v = 270$

$\therefore v = 30$

Now, we know that speed of wave in a string $= \sqrt{T/\mu}$

where, T = tension and $\mu = \frac{\text{mass}}{\text{length}}$

$\therefore v = \sqrt{\frac{T}{\mu}} \Rightarrow 30 = \sqrt{\frac{2700}{\mu}}$

$\Rightarrow 900 = \frac{2700}{\mu} \Rightarrow \mu = 3\ \text{kg/m}$

28. *(2)* According to the given situation,

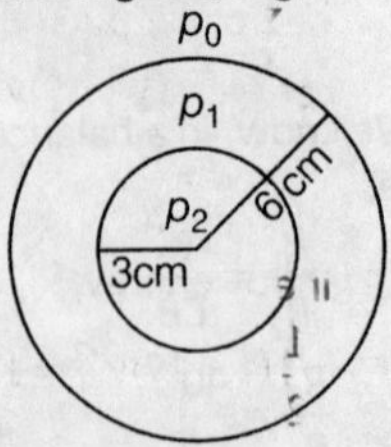

We know, excess pressure inside a soap bubble $= \frac{4T}{r}$

where, T = surface tension of liquid soap solution

$\therefore p_1 - p_0 = \frac{4T}{6}$ and $p_2 - p_1 = \frac{4T}{3}$

Adding both we get,

$$p_2 - p_0 = \frac{4T}{6} + \frac{4T}{3} = \frac{4T + 8T}{6} = \frac{12T}{6}$$

$$\therefore p_2 - p_0 = 2T \quad ...(i)$$

Also, according to the given situation,

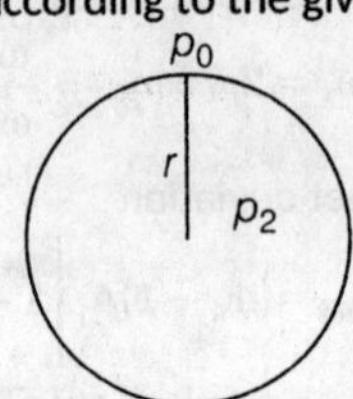

$$p_2 - p_0 = \frac{4T}{r} \quad ...(ii)$$

$\therefore$ From Eqs. (i) and (ii),

$$2T = \frac{4T}{r}$$

$$\Rightarrow r = 2\ \text{cm}$$

29. *(120)* By energy conservation as number of non-conservative forces are acting:

Let it unbinds and falls h height to attain speed of 4 m/s

$$\therefore mgh = \frac{1}{2}mv^2 + \frac{1}{2}I\omega^2$$

($\because$ Decrease in gravitational potential energy = increase in translational kinetic energy + increase in rotational kinetic energy)

$$\Rightarrow mgh = \frac{1}{2}mv^2 + \frac{1}{2}\frac{mR^2}{2}\omega^2$$

$$\Rightarrow gh = \frac{1}{2}v^2 + \frac{1}{4}R^2\omega^2$$

$$\Rightarrow 10h = \frac{4^2}{2} + \frac{1}{4}(v^2) \quad (\because v = R\omega)$$

$$\Rightarrow 10h = \frac{16}{2} + \frac{4^2}{4}$$

$$\Rightarrow 10h = \frac{16}{2} + \frac{16}{4}$$

$$\Rightarrow 10h = 12 \Rightarrow h = \frac{12}{10}\ \text{m} = 1.2\ \text{m}$$

$$= 1.2 \times 100\ \text{cm} = 120\ \text{cm}$$

30. *(2)* The given situation is shown below

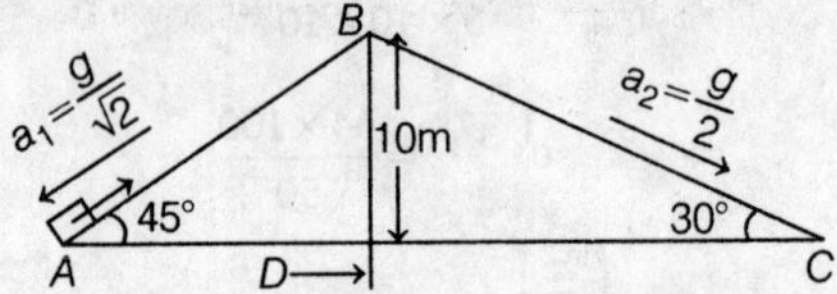

$AB = BD\ \text{cosec}\ 45° = 10\sqrt{2}\ \text{m}$,

$BC = BD\ \text{cosec}30° = 10 \times 2 = 20\ \text{m}$

From energy conservation,

From A to B

$$\frac{1}{2}mv^2 = mgh$$

$$\Rightarrow v = \sqrt{2gh}$$

$$= \sqrt{2 \times 10 \times 10} = 10\sqrt{2}\ \text{m/s}$$

Calculating $t_{A \to B}$

$$\because v = u + at$$

$$0 = 10\sqrt{2} - \frac{g}{\sqrt{2}}t_{A \to B}$$

$$10\sqrt{2} = \frac{10}{\sqrt{2}}t_{A \to B}$$

$$t_{A \to B} = 2\ \text{s}$$

Now, From B to C ($t_{B \to C}$),

$$S = ut + \frac{1}{2}at^2$$

$$BC = 0 + \frac{1}{2} \times \frac{g}{2} \times t_{B \to C}^2$$

$$\Rightarrow 20 = \frac{1}{2} \times \frac{10}{2} \times t_{B \to C}^2$$

$$\Rightarrow 8 = t_{B \to C}^2$$

$$\Rightarrow t_{B \to C} = 2\sqrt{2}\ \text{s}$$

$\therefore$ Total time taken $= t_{A \to B} + t_{B \to C}$

$$= (2 + 2\sqrt{2})\ \text{s} = 2(1 + \sqrt{2})\ \text{s}$$

$\therefore$ The value of $t = 2$ (on comparing).

Real Nut 6 JEE Advanced 2022

Paper 1

1. *(2.30)* v_A : Mass ∝ (Radius)^3

Radius of A is reduced to half. So, mass of A will become $\frac{M_A}{8}$.

$$v_A = \sqrt{\frac{2G\left(\frac{M_A}{8}\right)}{\left(\frac{R}{2}\right)}} = \sqrt{\frac{GM_A}{2R}} \quad ...(i)$$

v_B : $\frac{7M_A}{8}$ mass is deposited over B.

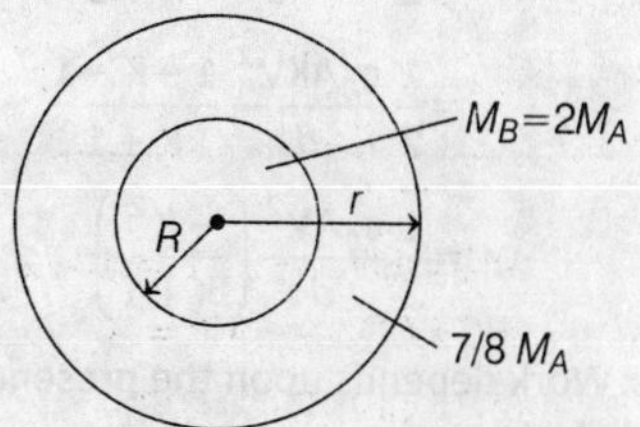

$$\rho_A = \frac{M_A}{\frac{4}{3}\pi R^3} \quad ...(ii)$$

$$\frac{4}{3}\pi(r^3 - R^3)(\rho_A) = \frac{7}{8}M_A \quad ...(iii)$$

Solving Eqs. (ii) and (iii), we get

$$r = \left(\frac{15}{8}\right)^{\frac{1}{3}} R$$

$$\text{Now, } v_B = \sqrt{\frac{2G\left(2M_A + \frac{7}{8}M_A\right)}{\left(\frac{15}{8}\right)^{\frac{1}{3}} R}} \quad ...(iv)$$

From Eqs. (i) and (iv), we get

$$\frac{v_B}{v_A} = \sqrt{\frac{2.30 \times 10}{(15)^{\frac{1}{3}}}}$$

$\therefore \quad n = 2.30$

2. *(2.32 to 2.33)*

$(m_N + m_{He} - m_H - m_O) \times c^2$

$= (16.006 + 4.003 - 1.008 - 19.003) \times 930$

$= -1.86$ MeV

or, 1.86 MeV energy is absorbed in the process.

For minimum kinetic energy needed, loss in kinetic energy should be maximum.

or, the daughter nuclei should move with same velocity. Thus,

$$\Sigma p_i = \Sigma p_f$$

or $4v = (1 + 19)v'$

or $v' = \frac{1}{5}v$

Loss in kinetic energy,

$$\frac{1}{2}(4)v^2 - \frac{1}{2}(1+19)v'^2 = 1.86 \text{ MeV} \quad ...(i)$$

Here, $\frac{1}{2}(4)(v^2)$ = minimum kinetic energy of α-particle = K (say)

Substituting $v' = \frac{v}{5}$ in Eq. (i), we get

$$\frac{4}{5}(K) = 1.86 \text{ MeV}$$

$\therefore \quad K = 2.325$ MeV

$\therefore \quad n = 2.325$

3. *(8.00)* 2 V battery is directly connected with C_3. Therefore, potential difference across C_3 = 2 V

Now, $q_3 = C_3V = (4\mu F)(2 V)$

$= 8\,\mu C$

4. *(6.00)*

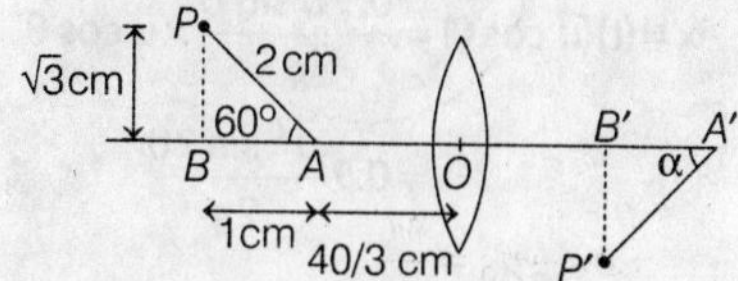

Using lens formula for point A,

$$\frac{1}{v} - \frac{1}{u} = \frac{1}{f}$$

$$\Rightarrow \quad \frac{1}{v} - \frac{1}{\left(-\frac{40}{3}\right)} = \frac{1}{10}$$

$\therefore v = OA' = 40$ cm

For B,

$$\frac{1}{v} - \frac{1}{-\left(\frac{40}{3}+1\right)} = \frac{1}{10}$$

$\therefore \quad v = OB' = \frac{430}{13}$ cm

$\therefore \quad A'B' = OA' - OB'$

$= 40 - \frac{430}{13} = \frac{90}{13}$ cm

Linear magnification for B,

$$m_B = \left(\frac{v}{u}\right)_{\text{For } B} = \frac{\left(\frac{430}{13}\right)}{-\left(\frac{43}{3}\right)} = -\frac{30}{13}$$

$$\therefore P'B' = (PB)(|m_B|) = \frac{30\sqrt{3}}{13}$$

$$\text{Now, } \tan\alpha = \frac{P'B'}{A'B'} = \frac{\left(\frac{30\sqrt{3}}{13}\right)}{\left(\frac{90}{13}\right)}$$

$$= \frac{1}{\sqrt{3}}$$

$\therefore \alpha = 30°$ or $\frac{\pi}{6}$ rad or $n = 6$

5. *(0.52)*

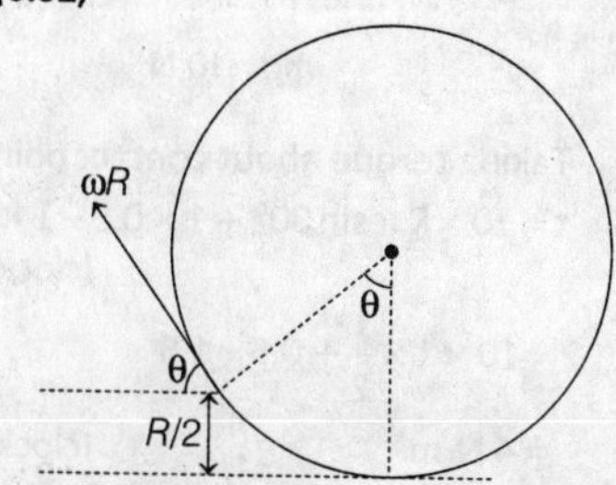

At $t = 0$, $\omega = 0$

At $t = \sqrt{\pi}$, $\omega = \alpha t = \frac{2}{3}\sqrt{\pi}$

$\therefore \quad v = \omega R = \frac{2}{3}\sqrt{\pi}R$

$\Rightarrow \quad v = \frac{2}{3}\sqrt{\pi} \quad [\because R = 1 \text{ m}]$

$\Rightarrow \quad \theta = \frac{1}{2}\alpha t^2$

$\Rightarrow \quad \theta = \frac{1}{2} \times \frac{2}{3} \times \pi = \frac{\pi}{3}$

$\Rightarrow \quad \theta = 60°$

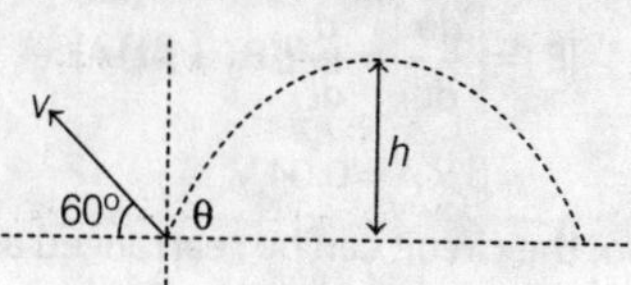

$\because \quad v_y = v\sin 60° = \frac{\sqrt{3}}{2}v$

$\therefore \quad h = \frac{u_y^2}{2g} = \frac{\frac{3}{4}v^2}{2g} \quad [\because v_y = u_y]$

$\Rightarrow \quad h = \frac{\frac{3}{4} \times \frac{4}{9}\pi}{2g}$

$\Rightarrow \quad h = \frac{3\pi}{9 \times 2g} = \frac{\pi}{6g}$

Maximum height from plane,

$$H = \frac{R}{2} + h$$

$$H = \frac{1}{2} + \frac{\pi}{6 \times 10}$$

$$x = \frac{\pi}{6};\ x = 0.52$$

6. *(2.86)*

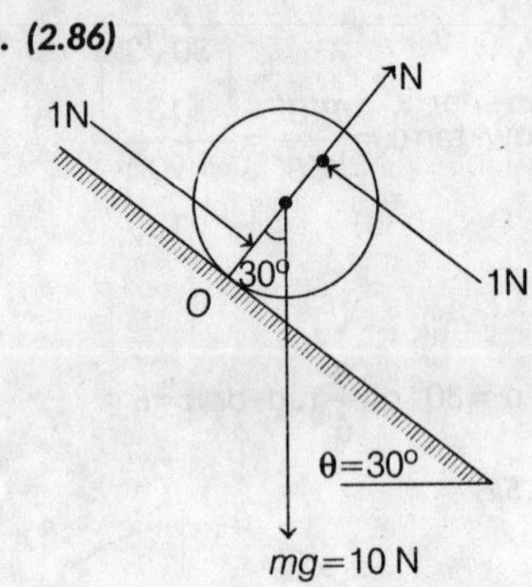

Taking torque about contact point O,

$\tau = 10 \times R \times \sin 30° + 1 \times 0.5 - 1 \times 1.5$ (clockwise)

$= 10 \times 1 \times \frac{1}{2} + 0.5 - 1.5$

$= 4$ N-m (clockwise)

Now, $\tau = I\alpha = \frac{7}{5} mR^2 \alpha$

$= \frac{7}{5} \times (1)(1)^2 \alpha = \frac{7}{5}\alpha$

$\therefore \quad 4 = \frac{7}{5}\alpha$

$\Rightarrow \quad \alpha = \frac{20}{7}$ rad/s^2

So, $a_{CM} = \alpha R = \frac{20}{7}$ m/s^2

$\Rightarrow a_{CM} = 2.86$ m/s^2

7. *(4.00)* Emf induced in the circuit is

$$|E| = \left|\frac{d\phi}{dt}\right| = \frac{d}{dt}[(B_0 + \beta t)A]$$

$$= \beta \times A = 0.04 \text{ V}$$

So, the circuit can be rearranged as

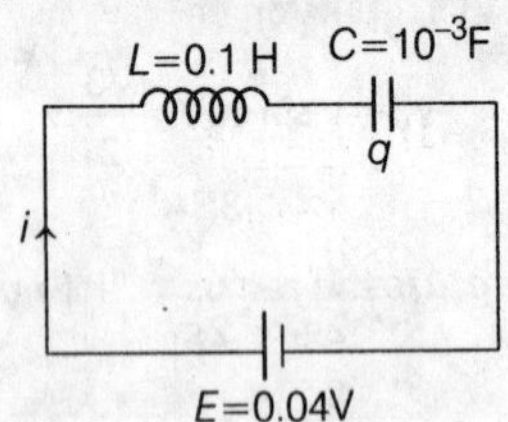

Using Kirchhoff's law we can write

$$E = L\frac{di}{dt} + \frac{q}{C}$$

$$L\frac{di}{dt} = E - \frac{q}{C}$$

or $$\frac{d^2q}{dt^2} = -\frac{1}{LC}(q - CE)$$

Using SHM concept we can write

$$q = CE + A\sin(\omega t + \phi)$$

$$\left(\text{where, } \omega = \frac{1}{\sqrt{LC}}\right)$$

At $t = 0$, $q = 0$ and $i = 0$

So, $A = CE$ and $\phi = -\frac{\pi}{2}$

$$q = CE - CE\cos\omega t$$

So, $i = \frac{dq}{dt} = CE\omega \sin \omega t$

So, $i_{max} = \frac{10^{-3} \times 0.04}{\sqrt{0.1 \times 10^{-3}}} = 4$ mA

8. *(0.95)* $d = \frac{u^2 \sin 2\theta}{g}$

$$H = \frac{u^2 \sin^2\theta}{2g}$$

So, after entering in the new region, time taken by projectile to reach ground,

$$t = \sqrt{\frac{2H}{g'}} = \sqrt{\frac{2u^2 \sin^2\theta \times 0.81}{2g \times g}}$$

$$= \frac{0.94 \sin\theta}{g}$$

So, horizontal displacement of the projectile in new region in reaching from topmost point to ground,

$$x = (t)(u\cos\theta) = \frac{0.9\, u \sin\theta}{g} \times u\cos\theta$$

$$= 0.9\frac{u^2 \sin 2\theta}{2g}$$

So, $d' = \frac{d}{2} + x = 0.95\,d$

$\therefore \quad n = 0.95$

9. *(b)*

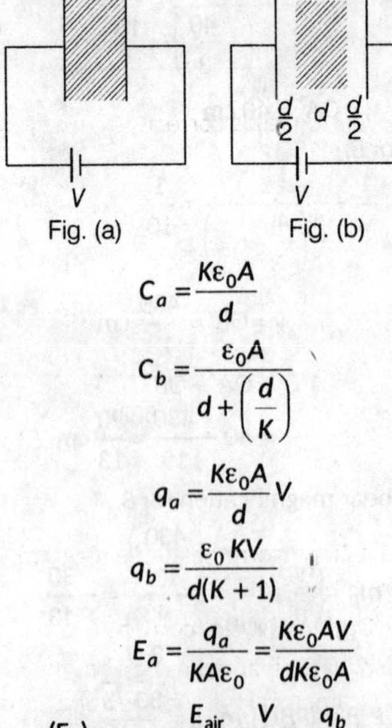

Fig. (a) Fig. (b)

$$C_a = \frac{K\varepsilon_0 A}{d}$$

$$C_b = \frac{\varepsilon_0 A}{d + \left(\frac{d}{K}\right)}$$

$$q_a = \frac{K\varepsilon_0 A}{d}V$$

$$q_b = \frac{\varepsilon_0 KV}{d(K+1)}$$

$$E_a = \frac{q_a}{KA\varepsilon_0} = \frac{K\varepsilon_0 AV}{dK\varepsilon_0 A}$$

$$(E_b)_{\text{dielectric}} = \frac{E_{\text{air}}}{K} = \frac{V}{d} = \frac{q_b}{KA\varepsilon_0}$$

$$= \frac{\varepsilon_0 AKV}{d(K+1)(KA\varepsilon_0)}$$

$$= \frac{V}{d(K+1)}$$

$$C_b = \frac{C_a}{1+K}$$

Work done in the process $= U_f - U_i$

$$= \frac{1}{2}(C_f - C_i)V^2$$

$$= \frac{1}{2}\left(\frac{\varepsilon_0 AK}{d(K+1)} - \frac{K\varepsilon_0 A}{d}\right)V^2$$

$$= \frac{1}{2}V^2\frac{\varepsilon_0 AK}{d}\left(\frac{1}{K+1} - 1\right)$$

$$= \frac{1}{2}\frac{\varepsilon_0 AKV^2}{d}\frac{1-K-1}{K+1}$$

$$= \frac{1}{2}\frac{\varepsilon_0 AV^2}{d}\left(\frac{-K^2}{K+1}\right)$$

$\therefore$ Work depends upon the presence of dielectric.

10. *(a,b,c,d)*

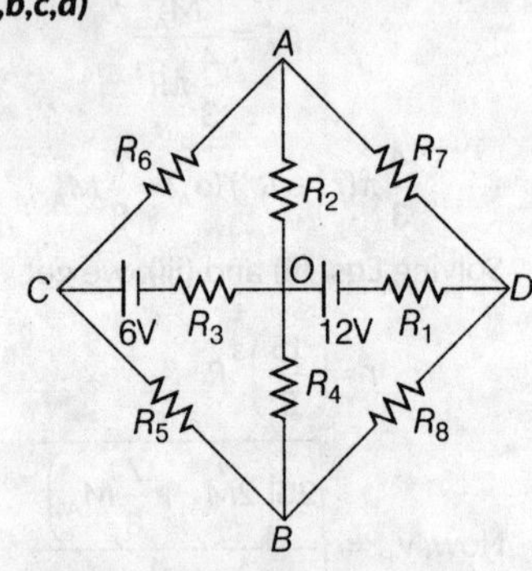

Points A and B are at same potential, so they can be merged/folded.

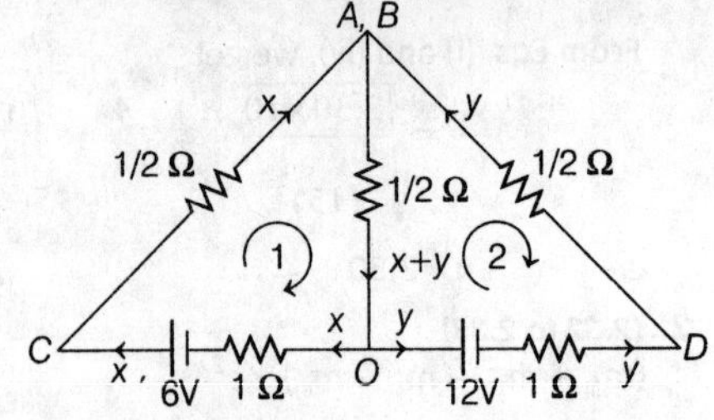

For loop-1,

$$-\frac{1}{2}x - \frac{1}{2}(x+y) - x + 6 = 0$$

$$\Rightarrow \quad -2x - \frac{y}{2} = -6$$

$$\Rightarrow \quad -4x - y = -12$$

$$\Rightarrow \quad 4x + y = 12 \quad \text{...(i)}$$

For loop-2,

$$\frac{1}{2}y + 1y + 12 + \frac{1}{2}(x+y) = 0$$

$\Rightarrow \quad \frac{3}{2}y + \frac{y}{2} + \frac{x}{2} = -12$

$\Rightarrow \quad 2y + \frac{x}{2} = -12$

$\Rightarrow \quad 4y + x = -24 \quad$ ...(ii)

From Eqs. (i) and (ii), we get

$4y + x - 16x - 4y = -24 - 48$

$-15x = -72$

$\Rightarrow \quad x = \frac{72}{15}$

$\Rightarrow \quad 4\left(\frac{72}{15}\right) + y = 12$

$\Rightarrow \quad y = 12 - \frac{288}{15}$

$= \frac{180 - 288}{15} = \frac{-108}{15} = -7.2\text{ A}$

Current in $R_1 = 7.2$ A

Current in $R_2 = \frac{x + y}{2} = \left(\frac{72}{15} - \frac{108}{15}\right)\frac{1}{2}$

$= \frac{1}{2}\left(\frac{36}{15}\right) = \frac{2.4}{2}\text{ A} = 1.2\text{ A}$

Current in $R_3 = x = 4.8$ A

Current in $R_5 = \frac{1}{2}x = 2.4$ A

11. *(b)*

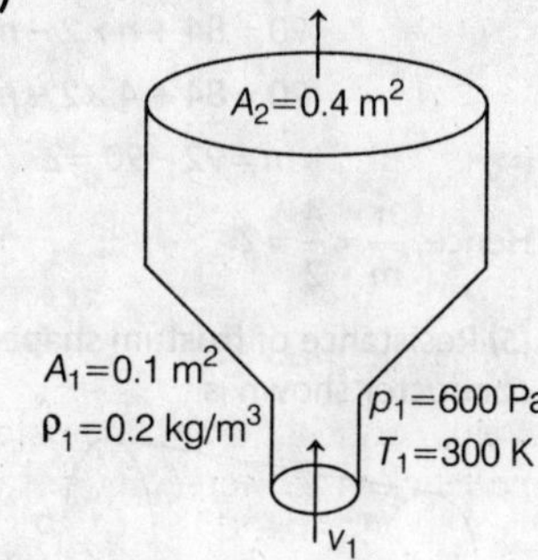

$\frac{dm}{dt} = \rho_1 A_1 v_1 = 0.8$ kg/s A

$\Rightarrow \quad v_1 = \frac{\frac{dm}{dt}}{\rho_1 A_1} = \frac{0.8}{0.2 \times 0.1} = 40$ m/s,

$g = 10\text{ m/s}^2, \; \gamma = 2$

Gas undergoes adiabatic expansion,

$p^{1-\gamma}T^{\gamma} = \text{constant}$

$\frac{p_2}{p_1} = \left(\frac{T_1}{T_2}\right)^{\frac{\gamma}{1-\gamma}}$

$\Rightarrow \quad p_2 = \left(\frac{300}{150}\right)^{\frac{2}{-1}} \times 600$

$\Rightarrow \quad p_2 = \frac{600}{4} = 150$ Pa

Now, $\rho = \frac{pM}{RT} \Rightarrow \rho \propto \frac{p}{T}$

$\because \quad \frac{\rho_1'}{\rho_2} = \left(\frac{p_1}{p_2}\right)\left(\frac{T_1}{T_2}\right)$

$= \left(\frac{150}{600}\right)\left(\frac{300}{150}\right) = \frac{1}{2}$

$\Rightarrow \quad \rho_2 = \frac{\rho_1}{2} = 0.1\text{ kg/m}^3$

Now, $\rho_2 A_2 v_2 = 0.8$

$\Rightarrow \quad v_2 = \frac{0.8}{0.1 \times 0.4}$

$= 20$ m/s

12. *(a, b)*

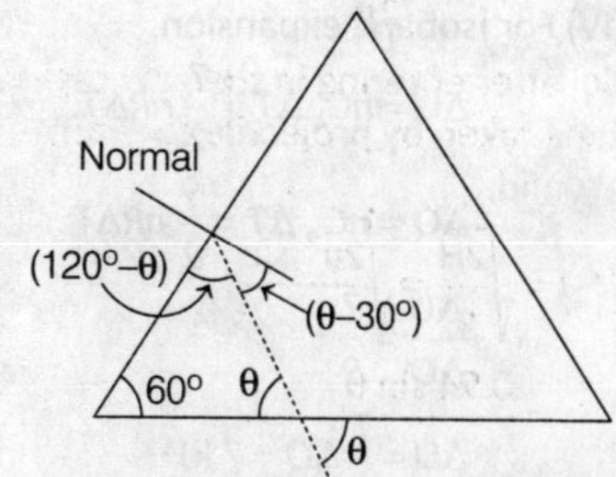

As we can see, for θ=30°, the ray will incident normally and hence, will retrace its path.

$\Rightarrow$ Option (a) is correct.

Considering the symmetry of the situation, we can have

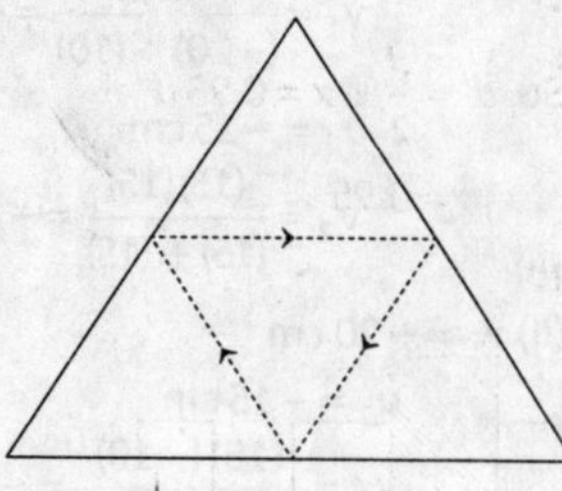

$\Rightarrow$ Option (b) is correct.

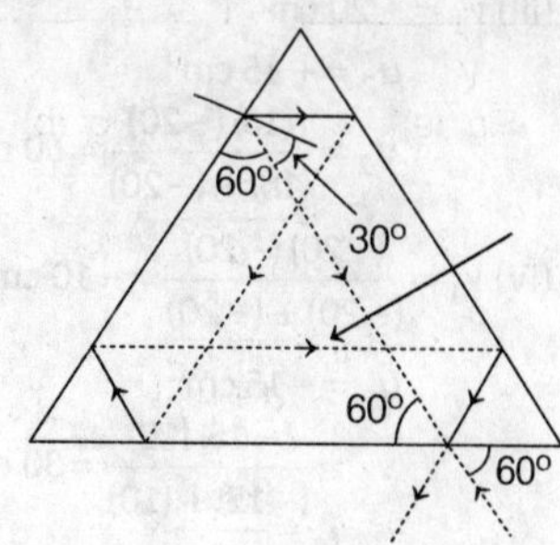

As it clear from the above diagram, ray comes out.

$\Rightarrow$ Option(c) is not correct.

Also, as is clear from the above diagram, total number of reflections = 5

$\Rightarrow$ Option (d) is not correct.

13. *(a,b,c)* When $x = q$, the situation is symmetric

$\Rightarrow$ Electric field at O would be zero.

$\Rightarrow$ Option (a) is correct.

When $x = -q$, we can think of x as $q + (-2q)$

$\Rightarrow$ Magnitude of electric field

At $O = \frac{1}{4\pi\varepsilon_0} \frac{(2q)}{\left(2 \times \frac{\sqrt{3}\,a}{2}\right)^2}$

$= \frac{1}{4\pi\varepsilon_0} \frac{2q}{3a^2} = \frac{q}{6\pi\varepsilon_0 a^2}$

$\Rightarrow$ Option (b) is correct.

For $x = 2q$, potential at O is

$V_0 = 6 \times \frac{1}{4\pi\varepsilon_0} \times \frac{q}{\sqrt{3}a} + \frac{1}{4\pi\varepsilon_0} \frac{q}{\sqrt{3}a}$

$= \frac{7q}{4\sqrt{3}\pi\varepsilon_0 a}$

$\Rightarrow$ Option (c) is correct

For $x = -3q$,

$V_0 = 2 \times \frac{1}{4\pi\varepsilon_0} \times \frac{q}{\sqrt{3}a} = \frac{q}{2\sqrt{3}\pi\varepsilon_0 a}$

$\Rightarrow$ Option(d) is not correct.

14. *(a, b, d)* Total binding energy (without considering repulsions),

$E_b = [Zm_p + (A - Z)m_n - m_x]c^2$

where, ${}^A_Z X$ is the nuclei under consideration.

Now, considering repulsion :

Number of proton pairs = ${}^Z C_2$

$\Rightarrow$ This repulsion energy

$\propto \frac{Z(Z-1)}{2} \times \frac{1}{4\pi\varepsilon_0} \frac{e^2}{R}$

where, R is the radius of the nucleus.

$\Rightarrow \quad E_b^p - E_b^n \propto Z(Z-1)$

$\therefore$ There will be no repulsion term for neutrons.

Also, since $R = R_0 A^{\frac{1}{3}}$

$\Rightarrow \quad E_b^p - E_b^n \propto A^{-\frac{1}{3}}$

Because of repulsion among protons,

$E_b^p < E_b^n$

Since, in β^+ decay, number of protons decrease

$\Rightarrow$ repulsion would decrease

$\Rightarrow E_b^p$ increases

15. *(c)*

16. *(c)* (I) $v_{BA}^2 = v_A^2 + v_B^2 - 2v_{AB}\cos\theta$

As $\omega_A = \omega_B, \theta = 90°$ remains constant

Also, $v_A = v_B = 1$ m/s

So, $v_{BA} = \sqrt{2}$ m/s

(II) $\mathbf{u}_A = \frac{5\pi}{2}\hat{\mathbf{i}} + \frac{5\pi}{2}\hat{\mathbf{j}}$

$$\mathbf{v}_A = \frac{5\pi}{2}\hat{\mathbf{i}} + \left(\frac{5\pi}{2} - 10\cdot\frac{\pi}{3}\right)\hat{\mathbf{j}}$$

$$= \frac{5\pi}{2}\hat{\mathbf{i}} - \frac{5\pi}{6}\hat{\mathbf{j}}$$

$$\mathbf{u}_B = -\frac{5\pi}{2}\hat{\mathbf{i}} + \frac{5\pi}{2}\hat{\mathbf{j}}$$

$$\mathbf{u}_B = -\frac{5\pi}{2}\hat{\mathbf{i}} - \left(\frac{5\pi}{6} + 1\right)\hat{\mathbf{j}}$$

$$\mathbf{v}_{B,A} = -5\pi\,\hat{\mathbf{i}} - \hat{\mathbf{j}}$$

$$v_{BA} = \sqrt{25\pi^2 + 1}$$

(III) $x_A = \sin t$

$$v_A = \cos t = \frac{1}{2}\text{ m/s}$$

$$x_B = \cos$$

$$v_B = -\sin t = -\frac{\sqrt{3}}{2}\text{ m/s}$$

$$v_{BA} = -\frac{\sqrt{3}}{2} - \frac{1}{2} = -\left(\frac{\sqrt{3}+1}{2}\right)$$

(IV) $\mathbf{v}_A$ and $\mathbf{v}_B$ are always perpendicular.

So, $|\mathbf{v}_{BA}| = \sqrt{v_A^2 + v_B^2}$

$$= \sqrt{10}\text{ m/s}$$

17. *(c)* (I) $U = mL - p\Delta V$

$= 10^{-3} \times 2250 - 10^2\text{kP} \times (10^{-3} - 10^{-6})\text{m}^3$

$= 2.25\text{ kJ} - 0.1\text{ kJ}$

$= 2.15\text{ kJ}$

(I) $\rightarrow$ (P)

(II) $C_V = \frac{5R}{2}$ (rigid diatomic)

For isobaric expansion,

$V \propto T$

$$\frac{V_1}{V_2} = \frac{T_1}{T_2} \Rightarrow \frac{V}{3V} = \frac{500}{T_2} \Rightarrow T_2 = 1500\text{ K}$$

$$\Delta U = nC_V\Delta T$$

$$= 0.2 \times \frac{5\times 8}{2} \times (1500 - 500)\text{ J}$$

$$= 4\text{ kJ}$$

(II) $\rightarrow$ (R)

(III) Adiabatic expansion $\left(\gamma = \frac{5}{3}\right)$

$$p_1 \cdot V_1^\gamma = p_2 V_2^\gamma$$

$$\Rightarrow (2\text{kPa}) \times V_0^{\frac{5}{3}} = p_2 \times \left(\frac{V_0}{8}\right)^{\frac{5}{3}}$$

$$p_2 = 64\text{ kPa}$$

$$\Delta U = nC_V\Delta T$$

$$= \frac{3nR\Delta T}{2} = \frac{3}{2}(p_2V_2 - p_1V_1)$$

$$= \frac{3}{2} \times \left(64 \times \frac{1}{3\times 8} - 2 \times \frac{1}{3}\right)$$

$$= \frac{3}{2} \times \left(\frac{8}{3} - \frac{2}{3}\right) = 3\text{ kJ}$$

(III) $\rightarrow$ (T)

(IV) For isobaric expansion,

$$\Delta U = nC_V\Delta T = \frac{7}{2}nR\Delta T$$

$$\Delta Q = nC_p\,\Delta T = \frac{9}{2}nR\Delta T$$

$$\frac{\Delta U}{\Delta Q} = \frac{7}{9}$$

$$\Delta U = \frac{7}{9}\Delta Q = 7\text{ kJ}$$

IV $\rightarrow$ (Q)

18. *(a)* (I) $\frac{1}{v} - \frac{1}{u} = \frac{1}{f}$

$$\Rightarrow \quad v = \frac{uf}{u+f}$$

$$\therefore \quad v_1 = \frac{(-20)(10)}{(-20)+(10)} = +20\text{ cm}$$

$$u_2 = +15\text{ cm}$$

$$v_2 = \frac{(15)(15)}{(15)+(15)} = +7.5\text{ cm}$$

(II) $v_1 = +20$ cm

$$u_2 = +15\text{ cm}$$

$$v_2 = \frac{(15)(-10)}{(15)+(-10)} = -30\text{ cm}$$

(III) $v_1 = +20$ cm

$$u_2 = +15\text{ cm}$$

$$v_2 = \frac{(15)(-20)}{(15)+(-20)} = 60\text{ cm}$$

(IV) $v_1 = \frac{(-20)(-20)}{(-20)+(-20)} = -10$ cm

$$u_2 = -15\text{ cm}$$

$$v_2 = \frac{(-15)(10)}{(-15)+(10)} = 30\text{ cm}$$

Paper_2

1. *(3)* At any general point,

$$\mathbf{r} = x\,\hat{\mathbf{i}} + y\,\hat{\mathbf{j}}$$

We can see that

$$\mathbf{r} \times \mathbf{F} = 0$$

$\therefore$ Torque about origin is always zero.

So, angular momentum about origin remains conserved.

or $m(\mathbf{r}\times\mathbf{v})$ or $(\mathbf{r}\times\mathbf{v})$ = constant

$$\Rightarrow \begin{vmatrix} \hat{\mathbf{i}} & \hat{\mathbf{j}} & \hat{\mathbf{k}} \\ \frac{1}{\sqrt{2}} & \sqrt{2} & 0 \\ -\sqrt{2} & \sqrt{2} & \frac{2}{\pi} \end{vmatrix} = \begin{vmatrix} \hat{\mathbf{i}} & \hat{\mathbf{j}} & \hat{\mathbf{k}} \\ x & y & 0.5 \\ v_x & v_y & \frac{2}{\pi} \end{vmatrix}$$

$$\Rightarrow \hat{\mathbf{i}}\left[\sqrt{2}\times\frac{2}{\pi}\right] - \hat{\mathbf{j}}\left[\frac{\sqrt{2}}{\pi}\right] + \hat{\mathbf{k}}\,[1+2]$$

$$= \hat{\mathbf{i}}\left[\frac{y\times 2}{\pi} - 0.5\,v_y\right] - \hat{\mathbf{j}}\left[\frac{x\times 2}{\pi} - 0.5\,v_x\right] + \hat{\mathbf{k}}[xv_y - yv_x]$$

$$\Rightarrow \quad xv_y - yv_x = 3$$

2. *(2)* Let n = number of α-particles decayed

and m = number of β^--particles decayed

$$\text{Th}_{90}^{230} \rightarrow \text{Po}_{84}^{214} + n\alpha_2^4 + m\beta_{-1}^0$$

$$230 = 214 + 4n$$

$$\Rightarrow \quad n = \frac{16}{4} = 4$$

$$90 = 84 + n\times 2 - m\times 1$$

$$90 = 84 + 4\times 2 - m\times 1$$

$$\Rightarrow \quad m = 92 - 90 = 2$$

Hence, $\frac{n}{m} = \frac{4}{2} = 2$

3. *(5)* Resistance of frustum shaped conductor shown is

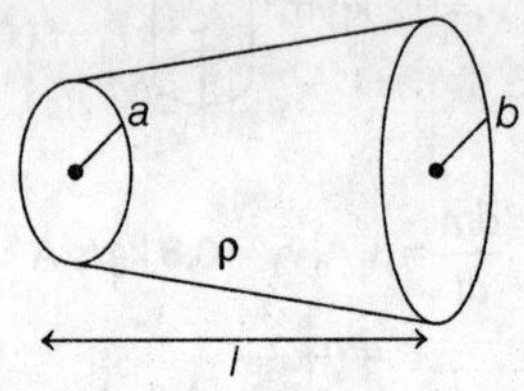

$$R = \rho\frac{l}{\pi ab}$$

For the shown conductor in the diagram,

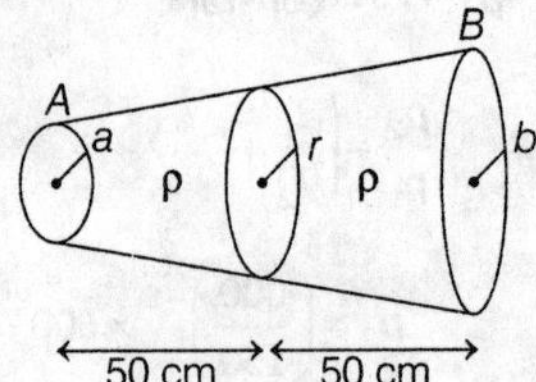

$$r = \frac{a+b}{2} = \frac{0.2+1}{2} = 0.6$$

Thus, the resistance of left half is

$$P = \frac{\rho \times 0.5 \times 10^6}{\pi \times 0.2 \times 0.6}$$

and the resistance of right half is

$$Q = \frac{\rho \times 0.5 \times 10^6}{\pi \times 0.6 \times 1}$$

For Wheatstone to be balanced,

$$\frac{R_1}{P} = \frac{R_2}{Q}$$

$$\Rightarrow \quad \frac{X\pi \times 0.2 \times 0.6}{\rho \times 0.5 \times 10^6} = \frac{1\pi \times 0.6 \times 1}{\rho \times 0.5 \times 10^6}$$

$$\Rightarrow \quad X = 5$$

4. *(4)* $[B] = [e]^{\alpha}[m_e]^{\beta}[h^{\gamma}][k]^{\delta}$

$$[M^1T^{-2}I^{-1}] = [IT]^{\alpha}[M]^{\beta}[ML^2T^{-1}]^{\gamma}[ML^3T^{-4}]^{\delta}$$

So,
$$\beta + \gamma + \delta = 1 \quad \text{...(i)}$$
$$2\gamma + 3\delta = 0 \quad \text{...(ii)}$$
$$\alpha - \gamma - 4\delta = -2 \quad \text{...(iii)}$$
$$\alpha - 2\delta = -1 \quad \text{...(iv)}$$

Solving Eqs. (i) and (iv), we get

So, $\alpha + \beta + \gamma + \delta = 4$

5. *(4)*

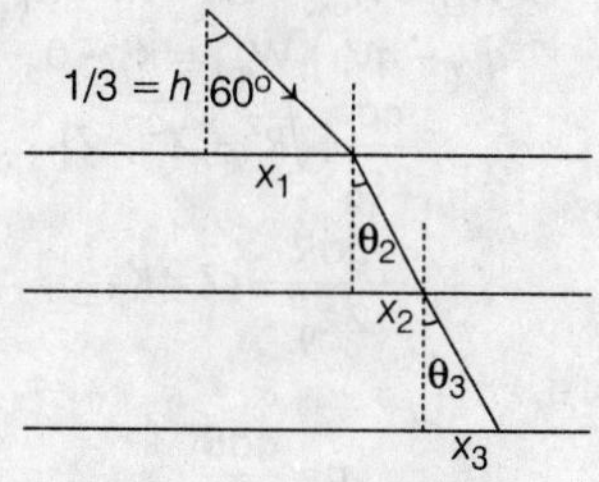

$$x_1 = \frac{1}{3} \times \tan 60° = \frac{1}{\sqrt{3}}\text{ cm}$$

and $1 \times \frac{\sqrt{3}}{2} = \sqrt{\frac{3}{2}} \times \sin\theta_2$

$$\Rightarrow \quad \theta_2 = 45°$$

$$\Rightarrow \quad x_2 = d$$

and $1 \times \frac{\sqrt{3}}{2} = \frac{\sqrt{3}}{2} \times \sin\theta_2$

$$\Rightarrow \quad \theta_3 = 30°$$

$$\Rightarrow \quad x_3 = \frac{d}{\sqrt{3}}$$

$$\therefore \quad x_1 + x_2 + x_3 = \frac{1}{\sqrt{3}} + \frac{(\sqrt{3}-1)}{2}\left(1 + \frac{1}{\sqrt{3}}\right)$$

$$= \frac{2}{\sqrt{3}}\text{ cm}$$

$$\therefore \quad n = \frac{l}{x_1 + x_2 + x_3} = \frac{\frac{8}{\sqrt{3}}}{\frac{2}{\sqrt{3}}} = 4$$

6. *(3)*

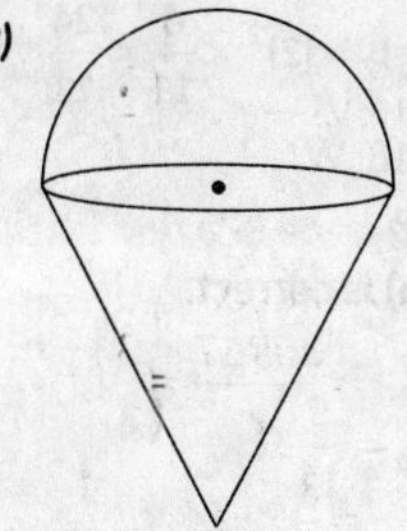

Total flux from complete closed surface $= \frac{q}{\varepsilon_0}$.

Half of the flux will pass through hemisphere.

$$\therefore \text{Flux through cone} = \frac{q}{2\varepsilon_0}$$

or $\quad n = 3$

7. *(6)*

$$l > l_0 \rightarrow k = k_1$$
$$l < l_0 \rightarrow k = k_2$$

Half of the oscillation will be completed with k_1 and the other half with k_2.

Time period of oscillation,

$$T = \frac{T_1}{2} + \frac{T_2}{2}$$

$$T = \pi\sqrt{\frac{m}{k_1}} + \pi\sqrt{\frac{m}{k_2}}$$

$$T = \pi\sqrt{\frac{0.1}{0.009}} + \pi\sqrt{\frac{0.1}{0.016}}$$

$$T = \frac{\pi}{0.3} + \frac{\pi}{0.4} \Rightarrow T = \frac{0.7}{0.12}\pi$$

$$\Rightarrow \quad T = 5.83\,\pi$$

$$\Rightarrow \quad T \approx 6\pi$$

So, $n = 6$

8. *(3)*

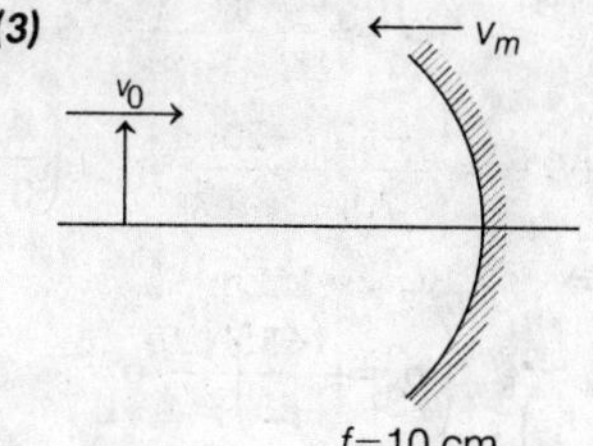

Let

$$u = -30\text{ cm}$$
$$f = -10\text{ cm}$$

$$\therefore \quad \frac{1}{v} + \frac{1}{u} = \frac{1}{f}$$

$$\Rightarrow \quad \frac{1}{v} - \frac{1}{30} = \frac{1}{-10} \quad \text{or } v = -15\text{ cm}$$

Further, $\quad \frac{1}{v} + \frac{1}{u} = \frac{1}{f}$

Differentiating w.r.t. time, we get

$$\frac{du}{dt} = -\frac{v^2}{u^2}\frac{du}{dt}$$

$$\mathbf{v}_{IM} = -\left(\frac{v}{u}\right)^2 \mathbf{v}_{OM}$$

Given, $\mathbf{v}_I = 0$

$$\mathbf{v}_I - \mathbf{v}_M = -\left(\frac{-15}{-30}\right)^2 (\mathbf{v}_{OM})$$

$$\mathbf{v}_I - \mathbf{v}_M = -\frac{1}{4}\mathbf{v}_0 + \frac{1}{4}\mathbf{v}_M$$

$$\mathbf{v}_0 = 15\text{ cm/s }\hat{\mathbf{i}}$$

$$\mathbf{v}_I = 0$$

$$\frac{5}{4}\mathbf{v}_M = \frac{\mathbf{v}_0}{4}$$

$$\mathbf{v}_M = \frac{\mathbf{v}_0}{4} = \frac{15\text{ cm/s }\hat{\mathbf{i}}}{5} = 3\text{ cm/s }\hat{\mathbf{i}}$$

$$|\mathbf{v}_M| = 3\text{ cm s}^{-1}$$

9. *(b)*

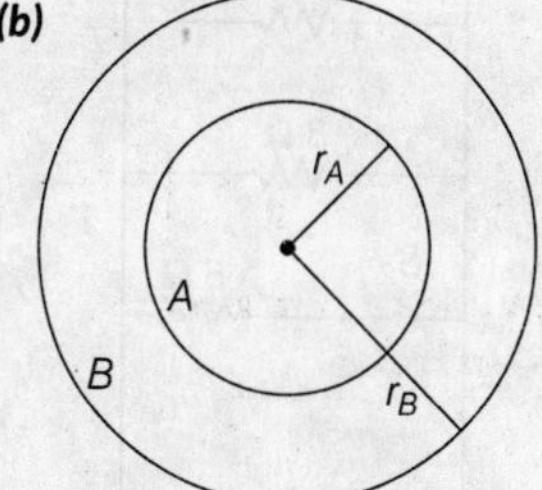

$$Q_{\text{total}} = \int_0^{r_A} kr(4\pi r^2)dr + \int_{r_A}^{r_B} \frac{2k}{r}(4\pi r^2)dr$$

$$= \frac{4\pi k}{4}r_A^4 + \frac{8\pi k}{2}(r_B^2 - r_A^2)$$

$$= \pi k + 4\pi k(r_B^2 - r_A^2)$$

If $r_B = \sqrt{\frac{3}{2}}$,

$$Q_{\text{total}} = \pi k r_A^4 + 4\pi k\left(\frac{3}{2} - r_A^2\right)$$

$$= \pi k + 4\pi k\left(\frac{3}{2} - 1\right)$$

$$= \pi k + 2\pi k = 3\pi k$$

If $r_B = \frac{3}{2}$,

$$Q_{\text{total}} = \pi k + 4\pi k\left(\frac{9}{4} - 1\right)$$

$$= \pi k + 4\pi k\left(\frac{5}{4}\right) = 6\pi k$$

$$V = \frac{1}{4\pi\varepsilon_0}\frac{6\pi k}{r_B} = \frac{3k}{2}\frac{2}{3\varepsilon_0} = \frac{k}{\varepsilon_0}$$

Option (b) is correct.

If $r_B = 2$,

$$Q_{total} = \pi k + 4\pi k(4-1) = 13\pi k$$

Option (c) is incorrect.

If $r_B = \frac{5}{2}$,

$$Q_{total} = \pi k + 4\pi k\left(\frac{25}{4} - 1\right)$$

$$= \pi k + \pi k(21)$$

$$= 22\pi k$$

$$E = \frac{1}{4\pi\varepsilon_0}\frac{22\pi k}{25} \times 4 = \frac{22k}{25\varepsilon_0}$$

10. *(a, b, c)*

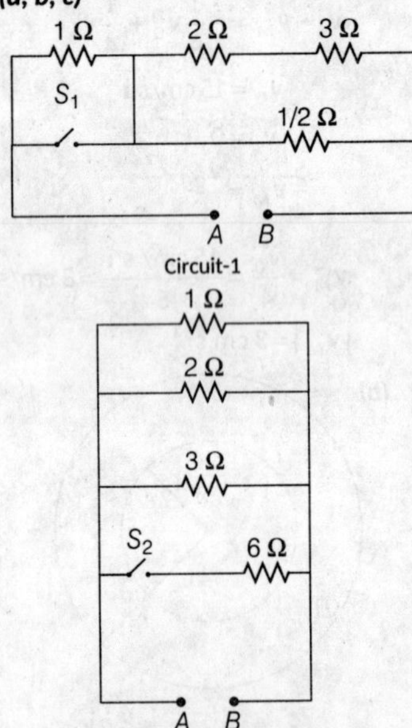

When S_1 and S_2 are open

$$(R_{eq})_1 = 1 + \frac{5 \times \frac{1}{2}}{5 + \frac{1}{2}} = 1 + \frac{5}{11} = \frac{16}{11}\ \Omega$$

$$P_1 = \frac{V^2}{R_{eq}} = \frac{(6)^2}{16} \times 11 = \frac{36 \times 11}{16}$$

$$= 24.75\ \text{W}$$

$$(R_{eq})_2 = \frac{6}{11}\ \Omega$$

$$P_2 = \frac{V^2}{R_{eq}} = \frac{(6)^2}{6} \times 11 = \frac{36 \times 11}{6}$$

$$= 66\ \text{W}$$

$$P_2 > P_1$$

Option (a) is correct.

$\Rightarrow$ If 2 A source is used in both the cases,

$$P_1 = i^2(R_{eq})_1 = (2)^2 \times \frac{16}{11} = \frac{64}{11}$$

$$= 5.818\ \text{W}$$

$$P_2 = i^2(R_{eq})_2 = (2)^2 \times \frac{6}{11} = \frac{24}{11}$$

$$= 2.1818\ \text{W}$$

$$P_1 > P_2$$

Option (b) is correct.

For Q_1,

$$R_{eq} = \frac{5}{11}\ \Omega$$

$$Q_1 = \frac{V^2}{R_{eq}} = \frac{(6)^2}{\frac{5}{11}} = \frac{36 \times 11}{5}$$

$$= 79.2\ \text{W}$$

$$P_1 = 24.75\ \text{W}$$

$$Q_1 > P_1$$

Option (c) is correct.

For option (d),

$$Q_1 = i^2 R_{eq} = (2)^2 \times \frac{5}{11} = \frac{20}{11}$$

$$= 1.81\ \text{W}$$

$$Q_2 = i^2 R_{eq} = (2)^2 \times \frac{1}{2} = \frac{4}{2} = 2\ \text{W}$$

$$Q_2 > Q_1$$

Option (d) is incorrect.

11. *(c, d)* Given, S = surface tension

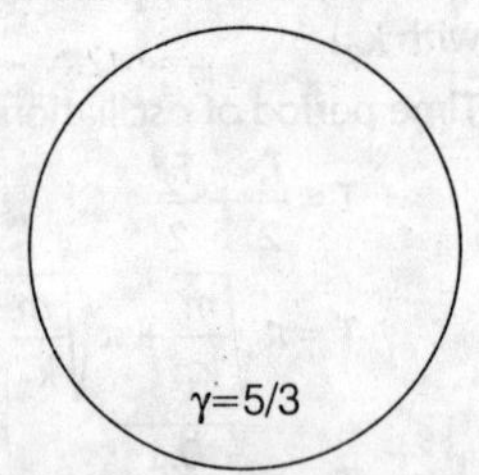

	Pressure	Radius	Temperature
When	p_{a_1}	$\longrightarrow r_1$	$\longrightarrow T_1$
	p_{a_2}	$\longrightarrow r_2$	$\longrightarrow T_2$

For adiabatic process, $p_1 V_1^\gamma = p_2 V_2^\gamma$

$$\left(p_{a_1} + \frac{4T}{r_1}\right)\left(\frac{4}{3}\pi r_1^3\right)^{\frac{5}{3}} = \left(p_{a2} + \frac{4T}{r_2}\right)\left(\frac{4}{3}\pi r_2^3\right)^{\frac{5}{3}}$$

$$\Rightarrow \left(\frac{r_1}{r_2}\right)^5 = \frac{\left(p_{a_2} + \frac{4T}{r_2}\right)}{\left(p_{a_1} + \frac{4T}{r_1}\right)}$$

Further,

$$T_1 V_1^{\gamma-1} = T_2 V_2^{\gamma-1}$$

$$\Rightarrow \frac{T_2}{T_1} = \left(\frac{V_1}{V_2}\right)^{\gamma-1} = \left(\frac{r_1}{r_2}\right)^{3\left(\frac{2}{3}\right)}$$

$$\Rightarrow \left(\frac{T_2}{T_1}\right) = \left(\frac{p_{a_2} + \frac{4T}{r_2}}{p_{a_1} + \frac{4T}{r_1}}\right)^{\frac{2}{5}}$$

For option (b), total internal energy + surface energy will not be same as work done by gas will be there.

Option (b) is incorrect.

For option (c),

$$p_1 V_1 = p_2 V_2$$

$$\left(p_{a_1} + \frac{4T}{r_1}\right)\left(\frac{4}{3}\pi r_1^3\right) = \left(p_{a2} + \frac{4T}{r_2}\right)\left(\frac{4}{3}\pi r_2^3\right)$$

$$\Rightarrow \left(\frac{r_1}{r_2}\right)^3 = \frac{\left(p_{a_2} + \frac{4T}{r_2}\right)}{\left(p_{a_1} + \frac{4T}{r_1}\right)}$$

Option (c) is correct.

12. *(a, c, d)* Applying work-energy theorem,

$$W_{EL} + W_{ext} = \Delta K = K_f - K_i$$

$$qV_f - qV_i + W_{ext} = K_f - 0$$

$$\frac{q\sigma}{2\varepsilon_0}[\sqrt{R^2 + Z^2} - Z]$$

$$-\frac{q\sigma R}{2\varepsilon_0} + cZ = K_f$$

$$c = \frac{q\sigma B}{2\varepsilon_0}$$

Substitute values of β and Z, calculate kinetic energy K_f at $z = 0$.

If kinetic energy is positive, then particle will reach at origin.

If kinetic energy is negative, then particle will not reach at origin.

13. *(a, b)*

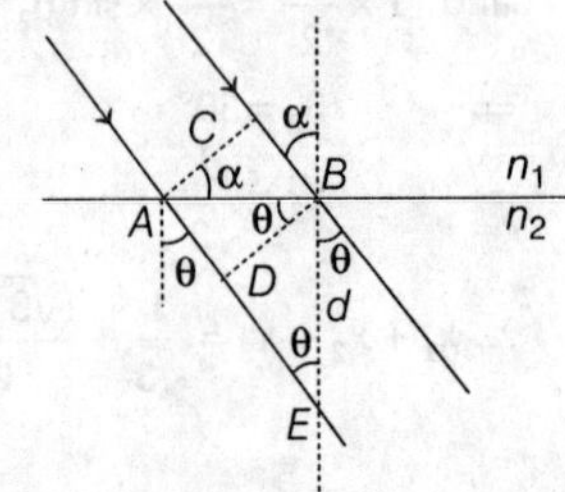

$$AB = (d)(\tan\theta)$$

and $BC = AB \sin\alpha = (d)(\tan\theta)(\sin\alpha)$

Also, $AD = AB \sin\theta$

Path difference (in vacuum) at detector,

$$\Delta x = n_1 BC - n_2 AD$$

$= n_1(AB)\sin\alpha - n_2(AB\sin\theta)$

$= AB(n_1\sin\alpha - n_2\sin\theta)$

From Snell's law, $n_1\sin\alpha = n_2\sin\theta$

$\therefore \quad \Delta x = 0$

or $\quad \Delta\phi = 0$

Therefore, rays interfere constructively at detector.

$\Rightarrow$ (*a*), (*b*) are correct and (*c*), (*d*) are incorrect.

14. ***(b,c,d)*** For adiabatic process ($A \to B$),

$$p_A V_A^{\gamma} = p_B V_B^{\gamma}$$

$$10^5 \times (0.8)^{5/3} = 3 \times 10^5 (V_B)^{5/3}$$

$$\Rightarrow \quad V_B = 0.8 \times \left(\frac{1}{3}\right)^{0.6}$$

$$= 0.4 \text{ m}^3$$

Work done in process $A \to B$,

$$W_{AB} = \frac{p_A V_A - p_B V_B}{\gamma - 1}$$

$$\Rightarrow \quad W_{AB} = \frac{10^5 \times 0.8 - 3 \times 10^5 \times 0.4}{\frac{5}{3} - 1}$$

$$\Rightarrow \quad W_{AB} = -60 \text{ kJ}$$

$$\Rightarrow \quad |W_{AB}| = 60 \text{ kJ}$$

Work done in process $B \to C$ (isothermal process),

$$W_{BC} = nRT\ln\frac{V_C}{V_B} = p_B V_B \ln\frac{V_C}{V_B}$$

$$\Rightarrow \quad W_{BC} = 3 \times 10^5 \times 0.4 \ln\frac{0.8}{0.4}$$

$$\Rightarrow \quad W_{BC} = 84 \text{ kJ}$$

Work done in process $C \to A$,

$$W_{CA} = p\Delta V = 0 \quad (\because \Delta V = 0)$$

So, total work done in the process $A \to B \to C$,

$$W_{ABC} = W_{AB} + W_{BC} + W_{CA}$$

$$= -60 + 84 + 0$$

$$\Rightarrow W_{ABC} = 24 \text{ kJ}$$

So, correct options are (b, c, d).

15. ***(b)*** $v = \omega(2R)$

$v = \omega_0 R$ (For no slipping)

$\therefore \omega_0 = 2\omega$

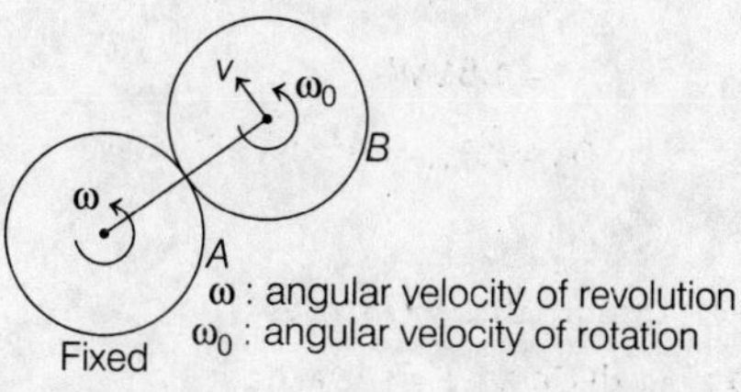

$$\mathbf{L} = m\mathbf{r} \times \mathbf{v}_c + I_c\omega_0 = M2Rv + \frac{1}{2}MR^2\omega_0$$

$$= 4MR^2\omega + \frac{1}{2}MR^2(2\omega) = 5MR^2\omega$$

$\therefore \quad n = 5$

16. ***(a)*** $\frac{hc}{\lambda} = \phi + 6$ (ϕ = work function) ...(i)

$$\frac{hc}{4\lambda} = \phi + 0.6 \quad \text{...(ii)}$$

Subtracting Eq. (i) from Eq. (ii),

$$\frac{3hc}{4\lambda} = 5.4 \text{ eV}$$

$$\therefore \quad \phi = 1.2 \text{ eV}$$

$$\Rightarrow \lambda = \frac{3}{4} \times \frac{6.63 \times 10^{-24} \times 3 \times 10^8}{5.4 \times 1.6 \times 10^{-19}}$$

$$= 1.72 \times 10^{-7} \text{ m}$$

17. ***(c)***

18. ***(c)*** $\mathbf{B}_{net} = \mathbf{B}_{semicircle} + \mathbf{B}_{quarter} + \mathbf{B}_{straight}$

$$= \frac{\mu_0 I}{4\left(\frac{L}{2}\right)}(-\hat{\mathbf{k}}) + \frac{\mu_0 I}{8 \times \left(\frac{L}{4}\right)}(-\hat{\mathbf{k}}) + \frac{\mu_0 I}{4\pi \times L}\left(\frac{1}{\sqrt{2}}\right)(-\hat{\mathbf{k}})$$

$$= \left(\frac{\mu_0 I}{2L} + \frac{\mu_0 I}{2L} + \frac{\mu_0 I}{4\sqrt{2}\pi L}\right)(-\hat{\mathbf{k}})$$

$$= \frac{\mu_0 I}{L}\left(1 + \frac{1}{4\sqrt{2}\pi}\right)(-\hat{\mathbf{k}})$$